Mastering the World of Psychology

Mastering the World of Psychology

Samuel E. Wood

Lindenwood University

Ellen Green Wood

Denise Boyd

Houston Community College System

Boston   New York   San Francisco
Mexico City   Montreal   Toronto   London   Madrid   Munich   Paris
Hong Kong   Singapore   Tokyo   Cape Town   Sydney

Series Editor: *Kelly May*
Editorial Assistant: *Marlana Voerster*
Development Editor: *Kelly Perkins*
Supplements Editor: *Erin Liedel*
Senior Marketing Manager: *Wendy Gordon*
Production Supervisor: *Michael Granger*
Editorial-Production Administrator: *Jane Hoover/Lifland et al., Bookmakers*
Composition and Prepress Buyer: *Linda Cox*
Manufacturing Buyer: *Megan Cochran*
Cover Administrator: *Linda Knowles*
Interior Design: *Carol Somberg*
Electronic Composition: *Monotype Composition Company, Inc.*

For related titles and support materials, visit our online catalog at
www.ablongman.com

Between the time Website information is gathered and then published, it is not unusual for some sites to have closed. Also, the transcription of URLs can result in unintended typographical errors. The publisher would appreciate notification where these errors occur so that they may be corrected in subsequent editions.

Library of Congress Cataloging-in-Publication Data
Wood, Samuel E.
    Mastering the world of psychology / Samuel E. Wood, Ellen Green Wood, Denise Boyd.
      p. cm.
    Includes bibliographical references and indexes.
    ISBN 0-205-35868-3
    1. Psychology.   I. Wood, Ellen R. Green.   II. Boyd, Denise Roberts.   III. Title.

BF121.W656 2003
150—dc21

2003040312

Sam and Evie dedicate this book
with love to their children:
Julie Kalina, Bart Green, Alan Wood,
Susan Benson, and Liane Kelly

Denise dedicates this book to the hundreds
of introductory psychology students she has
taught over the past 15 years. Their
questions, comments, and concerns were
the driving force behind her contributions to
Mastering the World of Psychology.

TABLE OF CONTENTS

1 Introduction to Psychology 2

10 Health and Stress 286

11 Personality Theory and Assessment 312

12 Psychological Disorders   338

13 Therapies   366

14 Social Psychology   392

How to Use This Text: Learn and Remember More

This textbook is organized to help you maximize your learning by following five steps: **Survey, Question, Read, Recite,** and **Review.** Together, these are known as the *SQ3R* method. You will learn and remember more if, instead of simply reading each chapter, you follow these steps. Here's how they work:

Survey

- First, **scan the chapter you are going to read.** The chapter outline helps you preview the content and its organization.
- **Read the section headings and the learning objective questions** (located in the margins), which are designed to focus your attention on key information to learn and remember.
- **Look at the illustrations and tables,** including any *Review and Reflect* tables, which organize, review, and summarize key concepts.
- **Read** *Summarize It!* at the end of the chapter.

This survey process gives you an overview of the chapter.

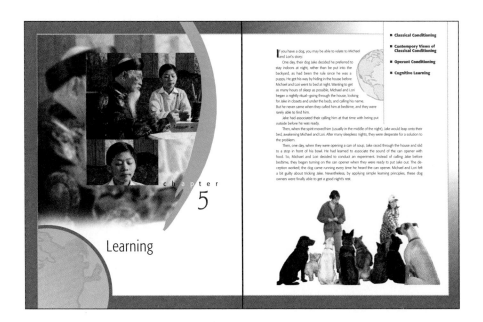

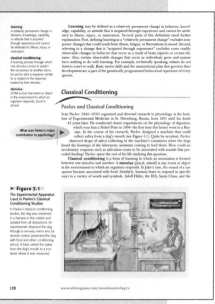

Question

■ Before you actually read each section in a chapter, **turn its heading into one or more questions.** Most sections provide one or more learning objective questions, but you can also jot down additional questions of your own. For example, one heading in Chapter 1 is "The Goals of Psychology." The learning objective question is "What are the four goals of psychology?" You might add this question: "What is meant by *control* as a goal of psychology?" Asking such questions helps focus your reading.

Read

■ **Read the section.** As you read, try to answer the learning objective question(s) and your own question(s).
■ After reading the section, **stop.** If the section is very long or if the material seems especially difficult or complex, you should pause after reading only one or two paragraphs.

Recite

■ After reading part or all of a section, **try to answer the learning objective question(s)** and your own question(s).
■ To better understand each topic, **write a short summary of the material.** If you have trouble summarizing a topic or answering the question(s), scan or read the section once more before trying again.

Review

■ When you have finished a chapter, **turn to the *Summarize It!* and review the Key Terms.** If you don't know the meaning of a term, turn to the page where that term is defined. The *marginal definitions* provide a ready reference for the key terms, which appear in boldface print in the text. All these terms and their definitions also appear in the *Glossary* at the end of the book.
■ **Review each learning objective question in the *Summarize It!* and answer the question in your own words.** The answers provided are only condensed reminders, and you should be able to expand on them.

- Next, **work through the Study Guide material.** Each Study Guide contains five sections. Four of the sections are the same in every chapter: Chapter Review, Fill In the Blank, Comprehensive Practice Test, and Critical Thinking. However, the second section in each Study Guide is different, providing an exercise that is tailored to help you review the material in that particular chapter; examples include Identify the Concept, Important Psychologists, and Complete the Diagrams. An answer key for the Study Guides is provided at the end of the book.

- Finally, **two Practice Tests per chapter can be found at the end of the book.** Consisting of 20 multiple-choice questions, 10 true/false questions and a few short-answer questions, each Practice Test gives you the opportunity to learn whether or not you've truly grasped the material in the chapter. Answers can be found in the Solutions Manual, which can be packaged with your book.

Providing an Unparalleled Level of Support for Today's Psychology Students . . .

Today's college students are vastly different from students who filled classrooms just a few years ago. Indeed, students today are more diverse, more mobile, and more technologically astute than ever before.

A good psychology textbook must communicate clearly to this diverse audience. *Mastering the World of Psychology* appeals to accomplished students, yet is also accessible to students whose academic skills are yet to be fully developed. This book recognizes that different students have different learning preferences, and it addresses that challenge by offering a wide variety of pedagogical support tools that will help students succeed. No book on the market does more to help students get better grades than *Mastering the World of Psychology*.

Joining the Author Team: Denise Boyd, Ed.D.

Denise Boyd of Houston Community College joined with Samuel Wood and Ellen Green Wood to author *Mastering the World of Psychology*. Dr. Boyd has taught introductory psychology courses at Houston Community College–Central for 17 years. The Houston Community College system, with its diverse student body, has given Dr. Boyd extensive experience teaching students of different ages and from varied economic, educational, and cultural backgrounds. Along with her substantial teaching experience, Dr. Boyd brings to the author team a background in learning and development. In addition, she received the Faculty Association Teaching Excellence Award from the HCC Faculty Association in 1995. Dr. Boyd would be delighted to answer questions about *Mastering the World of Psychology*. You can contact her at **denise.boyd@hccs.edu.**

Objectives of This Text

We understand that reading about psychology is not enough. We believe that students should be actively involved in psychology. Highly interactive and engaging, *Mastering the World of Psychology* encourages students to think for themselves as they learn about, relate to, and apply the psychological principles that affect their lives. Various tools in this book guide students to success. To accomplish our goals, we set the following objectives.

Maintain a Clear, Understandable Writing Style First and foremost, a textbook is a teaching instrument. It cannot be a novel; nor should it be an esoteric, academic treatise. A good psychology textbook must communicate clearly to a diverse audience of various ages and levels of academic ability. We seek to achieve this objective by explaining concepts in much the same way as we do in our own psychology classes. This text is filled with everyday examples pertinent to students' lives.

Provide an Accurate and Thoroughly Researched Textbook Featuring Original Sources To introduce the world of psychology accurately and clearly, we have gone back to original sources and have read and reread the basic works of the major figures in psychology and the classic studies in the field. This reading has enabled us to write with greater clarity and assurance, rather than having to hedge or write tentatively when discussing what experts in the field have actually said. This book is one of the most carefully researched, up-to-date, and extensively referenced of all introductory psychology textbooks.

Encourage Students to Become Active Participants in the Learning Process
Reading about psychology is not enough. Students should be able to practice what they have learned, when appropriate. Many of the principles we teach can be demonstrated without elaborate equipment and sometimes as the student reads. Our *Try It!* activities personalize psychology, making it simple for students to actively relate psychology to their everyday lives. See facing page for a complete list of *Try It!* topics.

Show the Practical Applications of Psychology One of our goals is to help students apply psychology to their lives. The *Apply It!* section near the end of every chapter shows a practical application of psychology and demonstrates the role of psychology in daily life. See facing page for a complete list of *Apply It!* topics.

Help Students Understand and Appreciate Human Diversity Diversity has always been woven throughout *The World of Psychology*. In *Mastering the World of Psychology*, we have taken diversity a step further: Every chapter has at least one section that discusses psychological principles as they relate to cultures outside the United States. These sections are highlighted by a Cultures Around the World icon in the margin. See page xxii for a complete list of the locations of Cultures Around the World icons.

Integrated Interactive Learning

One of the primary goals of *Mastering the World of Psychology* is to help students learn better. Each chapter provides multiple ways for students to test their knowledge:

- **Margin Learning Questions.** Learning questions are found in the margins of the text. These questions help students focus on the key concepts of each section.
- **Review and Reflect.** Review and Reflect tables consolidate a wealth of information from the text into at-a-glance charts, for easy student review and comprehension. See page xxii for a list of these tables.
- **Summarize It!** Chapter summaries answer the margin learning questions and list the Key Terms for each section.
- **Surf It!** Following the chapter summary, *Surf It!* reminds students that they can find a wealth of interactive study tools on the text's companion Web site.
- **Chapter-Ending Study Guide.** A comprehensive Study Guide is found at the end of every chapter.
- **Practice Tests.** In addition to the chapter-ending Study Guide, every chapter has two Practice Tests, found at the end of the book. Each Practice Test has 20 multiple-choice questions, 10 true/false questions, and a few short-answer questions, to challenge students' recognition and recall skills. The tests were prepared by Michelle Pilati at Rio Hondo College.

Mastering the World of Psychology also offers additional learning tools to enhance the learning process:

- **Tutor Center.** Every copy of the book is packaged with access to the Tutor Center, which provides free, high-quality, one-on-one tutoring to students. See the student supplements section (page xxv) for more details.
- **MyPsychLab™.** MyPsychLab is an interactive and instructive multimedia resource that provides simulations, animations, controlled assessments, and more. See the student supplements section (page xxv) for more details.
- **Research Navigator™.** Research Navigator quickly and effectively helps students make the most of their research time and write better papers. See the student supplements section (page xxv) for more details.

FEATURES

Try It!

Apply It!

Review and Reflect Tables

Cultures Around the World Icons

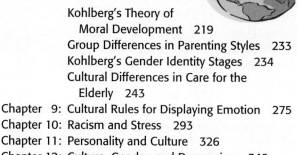

INSTRUCTOR SUPPLEMENTS

Instructor's Manual Written by text author Denise Boyd, this wonderful tool can be used by first-time or experienced teachers. It includes numerous handouts, a sample syllabus, lecture material, chapter outlines, suggested reading and video sources, teaching objectives, and more.

Test Bank Prepared by Dan Houlihan of Minnesota State University, the Test Bank features more than 100 questions per chapter. These include multiple-choice, true/false, short answer, and essay questions. Each question has a difficulty rating, page references, and skill level ranking. This tool is also available in a TestGen 5.0 computerized version, useful for personalizing tests.

PowerPoint Presentation Prepared by Jerry Newell of the Citrus Community College District, this multimedia resource contains textbook images with demonstrations, key points for lectures, and the full Instructor's Manual in digitized form.

Transparencies Approximately 230 newly updated, full-color acetates to enhance classroom lecture and discussion. Includes images from Allyn and Bacon's major introduction to psychology texts.

Insights Into Psychology Video or DVD, Parts I and II These interactive videos illustrate the many theories and concepts surrounding sixteen areas of psychology. The Insights Into Psychology videos contain 2 or 3 video clips per topic, followed by critical thinking questions that challenge students. Also available on DVD.

Allyn and Bacon Digital Media Archive for Psychology, 4.0 This collection of media products–charts, graphs, tables, figures, and audio and video clips–enlivens your classroom with resources that can be easily integrated into your lectures. The video clips include footage on classic psychology experiments.

Course Management Use these preloaded, customizable, content and assessment items to teach your online courses. Available in CourseCompass, Blackboard, and WebCT formats.

In addition to in-text learning tools, several other study aids are available to help students succeed.

Student Solutions Manual This easy-to-reference manual contains the answers to the chapter-by-chapter Practice Tests, with page references. Prepared by Michelle Pilati at Rio Hondo College.

MyPsychLab™ at www.mypsychlab.com . . . Where learning comes to life MyPsychLab is an interactive and instructive multimedia resource that can be used to supplement a traditional lecture course or to administer a course entirely online. Its power lies in its design as an all-inclusive tool, a text-specific e-book plus multimedia tutorials, audio, video, simulations, animations, and controlled assessments to completely engage students and reinforce learning. Fully customizable and easy to use, MyPsychLab meets the individual teaching and learning needs of every instructor and every student. It saves time and increases success.

Tutor Center . . . A support service that's available when you're not Every copy of *Mastering the World of Psychology* is packaged with access to the Tutor Center, which provides free, high-quality, one-on-one tutoring to students. Qualified tutors will answer questions students have about material in the text. The Tutor Center is open when students most often need help–in the late afternoon and evening, 5 to 12 p.m. (EST), Sunday through Thursday during the academic year. For more information, visit **www.aw.com/tutorcenter/psych.**

Research Navigator™ The easiest way for students to start a research assignment or research paper, Research Navigator quickly and efficiently helps them make the most of their time and write better papers. The program provides extensive help with the research process and includes three exclusive databases of credible and reliable source material: EBSCO's ContentSelect Academic Journal Database, The New York Times Search by Subject Archive, and Allyn and Bacon's "Best of the Web" Link Library. For more information, visit **www.researchnavigator.com.**

Research Navigator Guide: Psychology Research Navigator Guide contains an access code to Research Navigator, Allyn and Bacon's online collection of academic and popular journals. This easy-to-read guide helps point students in the right direction as they explore the tremendous array of information on psychology available on the Internet. The guide also provides a wide range of additional annotated Web links for further exploration.

Companion Web Site at www.ablongman.com/woodmastering1e The companion Web site is a unique resource for connecting the textbook to the Internet. Each chapter includes learning objectives, chapter summaries, updated and annotated web links, flash card glossary terms, Introduction to Psychology timeline, online practice tests, and psychology activities.

Mind Matters II CD-ROM The Allyn and Bacon Mind Matters II CD-ROM makes psychology more engaging, interactive, informative and fun! Mind Matters II covers the core concepts of psychology through a combination of text, graphics, simulations, video clips of historic experiments, and activities. Assessments test comprehension at both the topic and the unit levels. New to Mind Matters II are innovative modules on personality, developmental psychology, and social psychology.

ACKNOWLEDGMENTS

We are indebted to an incredible group of people at Allyn and Bacon, who helped bring our plans for *Mastering the World of Psychology* to fruition.

First, thanks to Carolyn Merrill for the idea of expanding the team to include a new author, Denise Boyd, who has many years of experience teaching introductory psychology. Carolyn deserves kudos as well for adding Kelly May to the editorial team. Kelly deserves a great deal of the credit for monitoring the progress of the book and for ensuring that the final product would be a brief introductory text that achieves the goal of being both thorough and concise. We are also grateful for the assistance of development editor Kelly Perkins, whose words of both encouragement and criticism helped immeasurably in the pursuit of this goal. We further express our appreciation to Erin Liedel, supplements editor, who expertly coordinated and oversaw most every ancillary specific to this text, and to editorial assistant Marlana Voerster, who handled many of the finer details of this project with great care.

On the production side, we would like to acknowledge the fine work of Michael Granger, senior editorial-production administrator, who supervised the long and complex process of turning our manuscript into a book. Copyeditors are indispensable to the production of any book, but we feel that the work of Jane Hoover of Lifland et al., Bookmakers, deserves special recognition. Jane and her team painstakingly scrutinized every word of this text. Moreover, thanks to Jane's careful work, each figure, photograph, table, *Try It!*, Review and Reflect table, key term, and learning question is in the right place in the book, is clearly linked to the text, and is understandable to readers. Her suggestions improved our writing and helped us produce a text that is clear, concise, and well organized.

Production is one component of a successful book; marketing is another. And we are indeed fortunate to have a superior, talented marketing team. Wendy Gordon, our marketing manager, has worked tirelessly to promote our book to instructors all across the nation. The sales specialist team of Joyce Nilsen, Brad Parkins, Marcie Mealea, and Kandis Mutter are to be commended for their incredible sales efforts on behalf of the book.

No psychology text is considered complete without an accompanying package of ancillary materials. Thanks to the fine authors of all our supplements.

All the professionals at Allyn and Bacon work hard to maintain a standard of excellence in producing fine books. This certainly includes Bill Barke, Chairman and CEO of Addison-Wesley Higher Education, who has kept in close touch with our books from their inception. We extend our sincere appreciation to Bill for his confidence in us and for his commitment to this project.

To Our Reviewers Numerous reviewers were invaluable to the development of this text. Their help provided a solid foundation for the creation of *Mastering the World of Psychology.*

Kenneth Benson, Hinds Community College
Cari Cannon, Santiago Canyon College
Dennis Cogan, Texas Tech University
Jim Dorman, St. Charles CC
Laura Duvall, Heartland CC
Colleen L. Gift, Highland Community College

Samuel E. Wood received his doctorate from the University of Florida. He has taught at West Virginia University and the University of Missouri–St. Louis and was a member of the doctoral faculty at both universities. From 1984 to 1996, he served as president of the Higher Education Center, a consortium of 14 colleges and universities in the St. Louis area. He was a co-founder of the Higher Education Cable TV channel (HEC-TV) in St. Louis and served as its president and CEO from its founding in 1987 until 1996. Dr. Wood is currently adjunct professor of psychology at Lindenwood University.

Ellen Green Wood received her doctorate in educational psychology from St. Louis University and was an adjunct professor of psychology at St. Louis Community College at Meramec. She has also taught in the clinical experiences program in education at Washington University and at the University of Missouri–St. Louis. In addition to her teaching, Dr. Wood has developed and taught seminars on critical thinking. She received the Telecourse Pioneer Award from 1982 through 1988 for her contributions to the field of distance learning.

Denise Boyd received her Ed.D. in educational psychology from the University of Houston and has been a psychology instructor in the Houston Community College system since 1988. From 1995 until 1998, she chaired the psychology, sociology, and anthropology department at Houston Community College–Central. She has co-authored three other Allyn and Bacon texts: with Helen Bee, *Lifespan Development (Third Edition)* and *The Developing Child (Tenth Edition);* and with Genevieve Stevens, *Current Readings in Lifespan Development.* A licensed psychologist, she has presented a number of papers at professional meetings, reporting research in child, adolescent, and adult development. She has also presented workshops for teachers whose students range from preschool to college.

Together, Sam, Evie, and Denise have more than 45 years of experience teaching introductory psychology to thousands of students of all ages, backgrounds, and abilities. *Mastering the World of Psychology* is the direct result of their teaching experience.

Mastering the World
of Psychology

Introduction to Psychology

Have you ever considered how incredibly well-connected you are? No matter who you are, this is true—because it's true for practically every human being on Planet Earth. You are part of the global community, and never before has there been a world so well-connected, so instantly informed—so globalized—as the one we all share today. In today's Information Age—as you've no doubt discovered—a vast storehouse of information, including the accumulated wisdom of the ages, is literally at your fingertips. Consider some ways globalization and the Information Age may have affected you personally:

- **You can communicate instantly.** Thanks to email and the Internet, a man living in Sydney can view photos of his new Chilean-born granddaughter within hours of her birth.
- **You can "study abroad" without leaving home.** Virtual classrooms and teleconferencing enable students to participate in educational courses based in Moscow, while located in their home cities of Tokyo, Tucson, and Timbuktu.
- **You can conduct e-business.** A fashion designer in New York can collaborate with colleagues in Milan, Paris, and London to construct a new clothing line that will reach across international boundaries.
- **You never have to be out of touch.** Even while backpacking across Europe, college students can stay in touch with their families back home. Internet cafes, cell phones, and text messaging make the students always reachable.
- **You can work from home.** Through the power of telecommuting, the CEO of an international corporation can hold board meetings in her pajamas.

Yes, globalization enables you to interact with people from all over the world, with lightning speed—and thus allows you to better understand and benefit from the perspectives and competencies of various cultures. To remind you of this important fact, this book features a Cultures Around the World icon: As you proceed through the text, whenever you see the globe icon shown below, think about how globalization and cultural issues might affect the psychological principles being discussed.

Psychologists are interested in globalization issues like those mentioned in the chapter opening vignette because of the psychological questions they raise:

- Does the fact that we're always reachable increase or decrease stress?
- How can people of different cultures work together to problem solve?
- How are relationships affected when email communication replaces face-to-face and phone communication?
- What's the best way to ensure that students from different cultures will learn in a combined setting?
- Does a telecommuting parent raise a more well-adjusted child than a parent who works outside the home?

Let's learn how psychologists go about answering these and other exciting questions. We will see how psychology is a science based on research conducted according to the scientific method.

An Introduction

Just what is psychology? Psychology has changed over the years, and so has its definition. **Psychology** is formally defined as the scientific study of behavior and mental processes. Answer true or false for each statement in *Try It! 1.1* to see how much you already know about some of the topics we will explore in *The World of Psychology*. (You'll find the answers in the text that follows.)

psychology
The scientific study of behavior and mental processes.

Try It! 1.1 Science or Common Sense?

Indicate whether each statement is true (T) or false (F).

_____ 1. Once damaged, brain cells never work again.

_____ 2. All people dream during a night of normal sleep.

_____ 3. As the number of bystanders at an emergency increases, the time it takes for the victim to get help decreases.

_____ 4. Humans do not have a maternal instinct.

_____ 5. It's impossible for human beings to hear a watch ticking 20 feet away.

_____ 6. Eyewitness testimony is often unreliable.

_____ 7. Chimpanzees have been taught to speak.

_____ 8. Creativity and high intelligence do not necessarily go together.

_____ 9. When it comes to close personal relationships, opposites attract.

_____ 10. The majority of teenagers have a good relationship with their parents.

Many people believe that the nature of its body of knowledge makes a field of study a science. However, a field of study qualifies as a science if it uses the scientific method to acquire knowledge. For *Try It! 1.1*, relying on common sense rather than on a dependable means of acquiring knowledge may have led you astray; all the odd-numbered items are false, and all the even-numbered items are true.

The Scientific Method

The **scientific method** consists of the orderly, systematic procedures that researchers follow as they identify a research problem, design a study to investigate the problem, collect and analyze data, draw conclusions, and communicate their findings. The scientific method is the most objective method known for acquiring knowledge (Christensen, 2001). The knowledge gained is dependable because of the methods used to obtain it.

What is the scientific method?

Say, for example, a researcher finds that men score higher than women on a test of map reading. If the test and procedures used to obtain the results were reliable and valid, other researchers who use the same test and procedures to collect new data should get the same results.

If the researcher claims that the gender difference in map-reading scores is attributable to the effects of male and female hormones on the brain, she has moved beyond the domain of facts and into that of **theory,** a general principle or set of principles proposed to explain how a number of separate facts are related. Other psychologists might disagree, but they can't simply say that there is no gender difference in map reading if the researcher's results have proven replicable. The term *replicable* means that other researchers have repeated a study and obtained the same results.

You might be thinking: Why bother with theories? Why not just report the facts and let people draw their own conclusions? Theories enable scientists to fit many separate pieces of data into meaningful frameworks. For example, in the hormone theory about the gender difference in map reading, two facts are connected: (1) Men and women differ in hormones; and (2) men and women differ in scores on map-reading tests. Connecting these two facts results in a theory of gender difference from which researchers can make predictions that can be tested.

Theories also stimulate debates that lead to advances in knowledge. A researcher who thinks the gender difference in map reading is due to learning may do a study in which male and female participants are trained in map reading. If women do as well as men after this training, then the researcher has support for his theory and has added a new fact to the knowledge base. Once the adherents of the hormone theory modify it to include the new fact, they are likely to carry out new studies to test the revised theory. As a result of this back-and-forth process, knowledge about a gender difference in map reading increases.

scientific method
The orderly, systematic procedures researchers follow as they identify a research problem, design a study to investigate the problem, collect and analyze data, draw conclusions, and communicate their findings.

theory
A general principle or set of principles proposed to explain how a number of separate facts are related.

The Goals of Psychology

Psychological researchers always seek to accomplish one or more of four basic goals when they plan and conduct their studies. The first goal, *description,* is met when researchers describe the behavior or mental process of interest as accurately and completely as possible. The second goal, *explanation,* requires that the researcher *tell* why a particular behavior or mental process occurred. Reaching this goal involves proposing testable theories. The third goal, *prediction,* is accomplished when researchers can specify the conditions under which a behavior or event is likely to occur. The final goal, *control,* is attained when researchers know how to apply a principle or change a condition to prevent unwanted occurrences or to bring about desired outcomes.

What are the four goals of psychology?

The two types of research that psychologists pursue to accomplish their goals are (1) basic (or pure) research and (2) applied research. The purpose of **basic research** is to seek new knowledge and to explore and advance general scientific understanding. Basic research explores such topics as the nature of memory, brain function, motivation, and emotional expression.

basic research
Research conducted to advance knowledge rather than for its practical application.

To achieve the goal of explaining road rage—and perhaps eventually controlling it—psychological researchers might observe and describe the behavior of motorists under stressful conditions.

applied research
Research conducted to solve practical problems.

critical thinking
The process of objectively evaluating claims, propositions, or conclusions to determine whether they follow logically from the evidence presented.

descriptive research methods
Research methods that yield descriptions of behavior rather than causal explanations.

What is naturalistic observation, and what are its advantages and limitations?

naturalistic observation
A research method in which the researcher observes and records behavior in its natural setting, without attempting to influence or control it.

Applied research is conducted specifically for the purpose of solving practical problems and improving the quality of life. Applied research focuses on such concerns as methods to improve memory or to increase motivation, therapies to treat psychological disorders, ways to decrease stress, and so on. Applied research is primarily concerned with psychology's fourth goal–control–because it specifies ways and means of changing behavior.

Critical Thinking

The scientific method grows out of a kind of thought process we use every day: critical thinking. **Critical thinking** is defined formally as the process of objectively evaluating claims, propositions, or conclusions to determine whether they follow logically from the evidence presented. When we engage in critical thinking, we exhibit the following characteristics:

- *Independent thinking.* When thinking critically, we do not automatically accept and believe what we read or hear.
- *Suspension of judgment.* Critical thinking requires gathering relevant and up-to-date information on all sides of an issue before taking a position.
- *Willingness to modify or abandon prior judgments.* Critical thinking involves evaluating new evidence, even when it contradicts preexisting beliefs.

To think critically about information you encounter in this book and in popular media, it is important that you (1) understand the various research methods psychologists use to achieve their goals, (2) know the advantages and limitations of these methods, and (3) be able to identify the elements that distinguish good research.

Descriptive Research Methods

The goals of psychological research–description, explanation, prediction, and control–are typically accomplished in stages. In the early stages of research, descriptive research methods are usually the most appropriate. **Descriptive research methods** yield descriptions of behavior rather than explanations of its causes. Naturalistic and laboratory observation, the case study, and the survey are examples of descriptive research methods.

Naturalistic and Laboratory Observation

Naturalistic observation is a research method in which researchers observe and record behavior in its natural setting without attempting to influence or control it. Research participants may or may not be aware that they are being observed in studies of this type. The major advantage of naturalistic observation is that it allows the study of behavior in normal settings, where behavior occurs more naturally and spontaneously than it would under artificial and contrived laboratory conditions. Sometimes naturalistic observation is the only feasible way to study behavior. For example, it would otherwise be impossible to study how people typically react during traumatic events such as the terrorist attacks on the World Trade Center and the Pentagon that occurred on September 11, 2001.

Naturalistic observation has its limitations, however. Researchers must wait for events to occur; they cannot speed up or slow down the process. And because they have no control over the situation, researchers cannot reach conclusions about cause-effect relationships. Another potential problem with naturalistic observation is *observer bias,* which often distorts researchers' observations. Observer bias can result when researchers' expectations about a situation cause them to see what they expect to see or to make incorrect inferences about the behavior they observe. The accuracy of observations can be improved substantially when two or more observers view the same behavior. Using videotapes to record behavior can also enhance the accuracy of observations because a tape can be reviewed several times prior to making a decision about how to classify the behavior shown.

Another method of studying behavior involves observation that takes place not in its natural setting, but in the laboratory. With **laboratory observation,** researchers can exert more control and use more precise equipment to measure responses. Much of what is known about sleep or the human sexual response, for example, has been learned through laboratory observation.

The Case Study Method

The **case study,** or case history, is another descriptive research method used by psychologists. In a case study, a single individual or a small number of individuals are studied in great depth, usually over an extended period of time. A case study involves the use of observation, interviews, and sometimes psychological testing. The case study is exploratory in nature, and its purpose is to provide a detailed description of some behavior or disorder. This method is particularly appropriate for studying people who have uncommon psychological or physiological disorders or brain injuries. Case studies often emerge during the course of treatment of these disorders. In some instances, the results of detailed case studies have provided the foundation for psychological theories. Sigmund Freud based his theory primarily on case studies of his own patients.

Although the case study has proven useful in advancing knowledge in several areas of psychology, it has certain limitations. Researchers cannot establish the cause of behaviors observed in a case study, and observer bias is a potential problem. Moreover, because so few individuals are studied, researchers do not know how applicable, or generalizable, their findings may be to larger groups or to different cultures.

Survey Research

The **survey** is a descriptive research method in which researchers use interviews and/or questionnaires to gather information about the attitudes, beliefs, experiences, or behaviors of a group of people.

Selecting a Sample Instead of studying an entire **population** (the group of interest to researchers and to which they wish to apply their findings), researchers who are doing a survey select a sample for study. A **sample** is a part of a population that is studied in order to reach conclusions about the entire population. A **representative sample** is one that mirrors the population of interest–that is, it includes important subgroups in the same proportions as they are found in that population. A *biased sample,* on the other hand, does not adequately reflect the larger population.

The best method for obtaining a representative sample is to select a *random sample* from a list of all members of the population of interest. Participants are selected in such a way that every member of the larger population has an equal chance of being included in the sample. Using random samples, polling organizations can accurately represent the views of the American public with samples as small as 1,000 people (O'Brien, 1996). *Try It! 1.2* illustrates that it is possible to accurately represent a very large population with a very small sample.

The Internet offers psychologists a way of soliciting participants and collecting survey responses that is fast and inexpensive and often generates large numbers of responses (Azar, 2000). However, Internet survey samples are often biased because they represent only the population of Internet users who choose to participate in online research studies. So, the sample represents neither the general population nor the entire population of Internet users. The critical point to remember is that surveys

laboratory observation
A research method in which behavior is studied in a laboratory setting, where researchers can exert more control and take more precise measurements.

case study
An in-depth study of one or a few individuals that consists of information gathered through observation, interviews, and perhaps psychological testing.

 What is a case study, and for what purposes is it particularly well suited?

survey
A method in which researchers use interviews and/or questionnaires to gather information about the attitudes, beliefs, experiences, or behaviors of a group of people.

population
The entire group that is of interest to researchers and to which they wish to generalize their findings; the group from which a sample is selected.

What are the methods and purposes of a survey?

What is a representative sample, and why is it essential for a survey?

sample
A portion of any population that is selected for study and from which generalizations are made about the larger population.

representative sample
A group of participants selected from a larger population in such a way that important subgroups are included in the sample in the same proportions as they are found in the larger population.

Try It! 1.2 Can Small Samples Really Be Representative?

Sometimes students have a hard time believing that 1,000 people or so can represent the entire population of the United States. This activity will help you see that small samples can be representative. You probably know that, when you flip a coin, the chance of getting a head or a tail is 50%. This probability is based on an infinite number of coin tosses. But how well does tossing the coin twice represent that whole population of tosses, that is, an infinite number of tosses? If a sample of 2 tosses—or $n = 2$, as a statistician would express it—doesn't represent the whole population, what about a sample of 5 or 10 or 15 or 20? To answer such a question, you have to take repeated samples of the same size. Toss a coin twice ($n = 2$), and then write the number of heads and tails in the column labeled Sample 1. Repeat the process four more times, recording your results under Sample 2

the second time, under Sample 3 the third time, and so on, until you have a total of five samples, each of which consists of two coin tosses. When the $n = 2$ row is completely filled in, calculate the overall percentages of heads and tails. Next, use the same process to collect data on samples of $n = 5, n = 10, n = 15$, and $n = 20$, until you have filled the table with data.

You can see that, as n gets larger, the overall percentages of heads and tails become more balanced (closer to 50/50). However, notice also that $n = 20$ isn't much better than $n = 15$. And it took a lot longer to collect five samples of 20 coin tosses each. In other words, there wasn't much gain in representativeness for the extra cost in time and energy. So, small samples can be representative, and increasing the size of a sample doesn't always pay off when costs are balanced against benefits.

Sample size	Sample 1		Sample 2		Sample 3		Sample 4		Sample 5		Overall percentages	
	H	T	H	T	H	T	H	T	H	T	H	T
$n = 2$												
$n = 5$												
$n = 10$												
$n = 15$												
$n = 20$												

experimental method
The research method in which researchers randomly assign participants to groups and control all conditions other than one or more independent variables, which are then manipulated to determine their effect on some behavioral measure—the dependent variable in the experiment.

hypothesis
A prediction about the relationship between two or more variables.

in which respondents *choose* whether or not to participate, rather than being selected by the researcher through some kind of random process, are not scientific.

Advantages and Disadvantages of Survey Research If conducted properly, surveys can provide highly accurate information. They can also track changes in attitudes or behavior over time. For example, Johnston and others (2001) have tracked drug use among high school students since 1975. However, surveys also have several disadvantages: (1) They can be costly and time-consuming; (2) respondents may not be truthful; (3) the wording of questions may affect respondents' answers; (4) characteristics of the interviewers (gender, race, etc.) may influence responses; and (5) respondents' desire to please the interviewer (the *social desirability response*) may affect their responses.

The Experimental Method

The descriptive research methods (naturalistic and laboratory observation, the case study, and the survey) are all well suited for satisfying the first goal of psychology—description. But at some point, researchers usually seek to determine the causes of behavior.

What is the main advantage of the experimental method?

The **experimental method,** or the experiment, is the *only* research method that can be used to identify cause-effect relationships. An experiment is designed to test a **hypothesis**—a prediction about a cause-effect relationship between two or more conditions or variables. A *variable* is any factor that can be manipulated, controlled, or measured. One variable of interest to you is the grade you will receive in this psychology course. Another variable that probably interests you is the amount of time you will spend studying for this course. Do you suppose there is a cause-effect relationship between the amount of time students spend studying and the grades they receive?

Consider two other variables that are often thought to be related—alcohol consumption and aggression (e.g., George et al., 2001). Can we assume that alcohol consumption *causes* aggressive behavior?

Alan Lang and his colleagues (1975) conducted an experiment to determine if alcohol consumption increases aggression. The participants in the experiment were 96 male college students who were classified as heavy social drinkers. Half the students were given plain tonic to drink; the other half were given a vodka-and-tonic drink in amounts sufficient to raise their blood alcohol level to .10. Participants were assigned to four groups:

 Under what conditions might the happy, party mood of these young drinkers turn aggressive?

Group 1: Expected alcohol/Received only tonic
Group 2: Expected alcohol/Received alcohol mixed with tonic
Group 3: Expected tonic/Received alcohol mixed with tonic
Group 4: Expected tonic/Received only tonic

After the students had consumed the designated amounts, the researchers had an accomplice, who posed as a participant, purposely provoke half the students by belittling their performance on a difficult task. All the students then participated in a learning experiment in which the same accomplice posed as the learner. The participants were told to administer an electric shock to the accomplice each time he made a mistake on a decoding task. Each participant was allowed to determine the intensity and duration of the "shock." (Although the students thought they were shocking the accomplice, no shocks were actually delivered.) The researchers measured the aggressiveness of the students in terms of the duration and the intensity of the shocks they delivered.

What were the results? The students who had been provoked gave the accomplice stronger shocks than did those who had not been provoked. And, regardless of the actual content of their drinks, the participants who *believed* they were drinking alcohol gave significantly stronger shocks, whether they had been provoked or not, than those who assumed they were drinking only tonic (see Figure 1.1, on page 10). The researchers concluded that it was the expectation of drinking alcohol, not the alcohol itself, that caused the students to be more aggressive.

Independent and Dependent Variables

Every experiment includes one or more **independent variables**—any variable that the researcher manipulates in order to determine the effect on another variable. Sometimes the independent variable is referred to as the *treatment*. In the Lang experiment, there were two independent variables: the alcoholic content of the drink and the expectation of drinking alcohol.

The second type of variable found in all experiments is the **dependent variable.** It is measured at the end of the experiment and is hypothesized to vary (increase or decrease) as a result of the manipulations of the independent variable(s). The dependent variable is presumed to depend on or to be affected by changes in the independent variable. In the Lang study, the dependent variable—aggression—was defined as the intensity and duration of the "shocks" the participants delivered to the accomplice.

Experimental and Control Groups

Most experiments are conducted using two or more groups of participants. There must always be at least one **experimental group**—a group of participants who are exposed to the independent variable, or treatment. The Lang experiment used three experimental groups: groups 1, 2, and 3.

independent variable
In an experiment, any factor or condition that the researcher manipulates in order to determine its effect on another condition or behavior known as the dependent variable.

dependent variable
The variable that is measured at the end of an experiment and is presumed to vary as a result of manipulations of the independent variable.

What is the difference between the independent variable and the dependent variable?

experimental group
In an experiment, the group that is exposed to the independent variable, or the treatment.

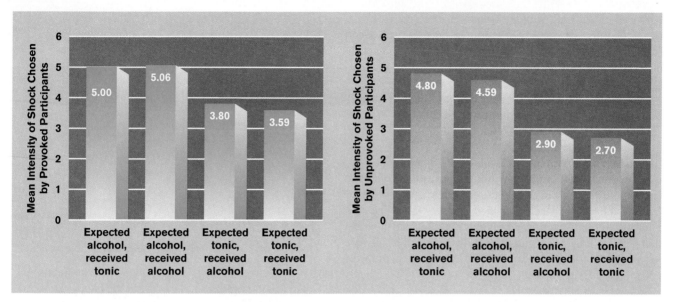

➤ Figure 1.1

The Mean Shock Intensity Chosen by Provoked and Unprovoked Participants

In the Lang experiment, participants who thought they were drinking alcohol chose to give significantly stronger shocks, whether provoked or not, than those who believed they were drinking only tonic. (Data from Lang et al., 1975.)

How do the experimental and control groups differ? ➤

In most experiments, it is desirable to have a **control group**—a group that is similar to the experimental group(s) and is used for purposes of comparison. The control group is exposed to the same experimental environment as the experimental group(s) but is not given the treatment. The fourth group in the Lang study was exposed to neither of the two independent variables; that is, this group did not expect alcohol and did not receive alcohol. Because this group was similar to the experimental groups and was exposed to the same experimental environment, it served as a control group. Control groups are useful because they allow the researcher to compare the effects of the independent variable with "natural" behavior. For example, aggressiveness varies across individuals whether they drink alcohol or not. The control group in the Lang study provided a way of comparing this "natural" variation in aggressiveness to that associated with the expectation of drinking and the actual consumption of alcohol.

control group
In an experiment, a group that is similar to the experimental group and is exposed to the same experimental environment but is not exposed to the independent variable; used for purposes of comparison.

confounding variables
Any factors or conditions other than the independent variable that could cause observed changes in the dependent variable.

selection bias
The assignment of participants to experimental or control groups in such a way that systematic differences among the groups are present at the beginning of the experiment.

Generalizing Experimental Findings

What should be concluded from the Lang experiment? Can we conclude that people in general tend to be more aggressive when they believe they are under the influence of alcohol? Before reaching such a conclusion, we must consider several factors: (1) All participants in this experiment were male college students. We cannot be sure that the same results would have occurred if females or males of other ages had been included. (2) The participants in this experiment were classified as heavy social drinkers. Would the same results have occurred if nondrinkers, moderate social drinkers, or alcoholics had been included? To apply this experiment's findings to other populations, researchers would have to replicate, or repeat, the results of the experiment using different groups from those other populations. (3) The amount of alcohol given to the students was just enough to bring their blood alcohol level to .10. We cannot be sure that the same results would have occurred if they had consumed more or less alcohol.

Potential Problems in Experimental Research

If an experiment is properly designed, the researcher should be able to attribute changes in the dependent variable to the manipulations of the independent variable(s). But some times an experiment is affected by **confounding variables**—factors or conditions other than the independent variable(s) that are not equivalent across groups and that could cause differences among the groups with respect to the dependent variable. By conducting their experiment in a laboratory, Lang and his colleagues were able to control environmental conditions, such as extreme noise or heat, which could have increased aggressive responses. Three additional sources of confounding variables that must be controlled in all experiments are selection bias, the placebo effect, and experimenter bias.

Selection Bias **Selection bias** occurs when participants are assigned to groups in such a way that systematic differences among the groups are present at the beginning of the experiment. If selection bias occurs, then differences at the end of the experiment may not reflect the manipulation of the independent variable but may be due instead to preexisting differences in the groups.

To control for selection bias, researchers must use **random assignment.** This process consists of selecting participants by using a chance procedure (such as drawing the names of participants out of a hat) to guarantee that all participants have an equal probability of being assigned to any of the groups. Random assignment maximizes the likelihood that the groups will be as similar as possible at the beginning of the experiment. If there were preexisting differences in the level of aggressiveness of students in Lang's alcohol experiment, random assignment should have spread those differences across groups.

The Placebo Effect The **placebo effect** occurs when a participant's response to a treatment is due to his or her expectations about the treatment rather than to the treatment itself. Suppose a patient takes a prescription drug and reports improvement. The improvement could be a direct result of the drug, or it could be a result of the patient's expectation that the drug will work. Studies have shown that remarkable improvement in patients can sometimes be attributed solely to the power of suggestion—the placebo effect.

In drug experiments, the control group is usually given a **placebo**—an inert, or harmless, substance such as a sugar pill or an injection of saline solution. To control for the placebo effect, researchers do not let participants know whether they are in the experimental group (receiving the real drug) or in the control group (receiving the placebo). If participants getting the real drug show a significantly greater improvement than those receiving the placebo, then the improvement can be attributed to the drug rather than to the power of suggestion. In the Lang experiment, some students who expected alcohol mixed with tonic were given only tonic. The tonic without alcohol functioned as a placebo. This enabled the researchers to measure the effect of the power of suggestion alone in producing aggression.

Experimenter Bias **Experimenter bias** occurs when researchers' preconceived notions or expectations become a self-fulfilling prophecy and cause the researchers to find what they expect to find. A researcher's expectations can be communicated to participants, perhaps unintentionally, through tone of voice, gestures, or facial expressions. These communications can influence the participants' behavior. Expectations can also influence a researcher's interpretation of the experimental results, even if participants were not influenced during the experiment.

To control for experimenter bias, researchers must not know which participants are assigned to the experimental and control groups until after the research data are collected and recorded. (Obviously, someone assisting the researcher does know.) When neither the participants nor the researchers know which participants are getting the treatment and which are in the control group, the **double-blind technique** is being used.

What is selection bias, and what technique do researchers use to control for it?

What is the placebo effect, and how do researchers control for it?

What is experimenter bias, and how is it controlled?

random assignment
In an experiment, the assignment of participants to experimental and control groups by using a chance procedure, which guarantees that each has an equal probability of being placed in any of the groups; used as a control for selection bias.

placebo effect
The phenomenon that occurs when a person's response to a treatment in an experiment is due to expectations regarding the treatment rather than to the treatment itself.

placebo
(pluh-SEE-bo) Some inert substance, such as a sugar pill or an injection of saline solution, given to the control group in an experiment to avoid the placebo effect.

experimenter bias
A phenomenon that occurs when the researcher's preconceived notions in some way influence the participants' behavior and/or the interpretation of experimental results.

double-blind technique
An experimental procedure in which neither the participants nor the researchers know who is in the experimental and control groups until after the results have been gathered; used as a control for experimenter bias.

Advantages and Limitations of the Experimental Method

The overwhelming advantage of the experimental method is its ability to reveal cause-effect relationships. Because researchers are able to exercise strict control over the experimental setting, they can rule out factors other than the independent variable as possible reasons for differences in the dependent variable. Often, however, the more control a researcher exercises, the more unnatural and contrived the experimental setting becomes and the less generalizable the findings may be to the real world. When participants know they are taking part in an experiment, their behavior may be different from what it would be in a more natural setting.

Another important limitation of the experimental method is that it is either unethical or not possible in many areas of interest to psychologists. Some treatments cannot be given to human participants because their physical or psychological health would be endangered or their constitutional rights would be violated.

The Correlational Method

What is the correlational method, and when is it used?

It is often illegal and always unethical to assign people randomly to experimental conditions that could be harmful. For example, to find out if smoking marijuana causes a decline in academic achievement, no researcher would randomly assign high school students to an experimental study that would require students in the experimental groups to smoke marijuana.

When, for ethical reasons, an experimental study cannot be performed to determine a cause-effect relationship, the **correlational method** is usually used. This research method determines the *correlation*, or degree of relationship, between two characteristics, events, or behaviors. A group is selected for study, and the variables of interest are measured for each participant in the study. For example, the variables might be amount of marijuana previously used and grade point average. Then the researcher applies a statistical formula to obtain a correlation coefficient.

The Correlation Coefficient

A **correlation coefficient** is a numerical value indicating the degree and direction of the relationship between two variables. A correlation coefficient ranges from $+1.00$ (a perfect positive correlation) to .00 (no relationship) to -1.00 (a perfect negative correlation). The number in a correlation coefficient indicates the relative *strength* of the relationship between two variables–the higher the number, the stronger the relationship. Therefore, a correlation of $-.85$ is stronger than a correlation of $+.64$.

What is a correlation coefficient?

The sign of a correlation coefficient ($+$ or $-$) indicates whether the two variables vary in the same or opposite directions. A positive correlation indicates that the two variables vary in the same direction. For example, there is a positive correlation between stress and illness. When stress increases, illness is likely to increase; when stress decreases, illness tends to decrease.

A negative correlation means that an increase in the value of one variable is associated with a decrease in the value of the other variable. There is a negative correlation between the number of cigarettes people smoke and the number of years they can expect to live. As smoking increases, life expectancy decreases. For more information about correlation coefficients, see the Appendix that follows Chapter 14.

Correlation and Prediction

Correlations are useful in making predictions–the stronger the relationship between the variables, the better the prediction. A perfect correlation ($+1.00$ or -1.00) would enable one to make a completely accurate prediction. Many colleges and universities

correlational method
A research method used to establish the degree of relationship (correlation) between two characteristics, events, or behaviors.

correlation coefficient
A numerical value that indicates the strength and direction of the relationship between two variables; ranges from $+1.00$ (a perfect positive correlation) to -1.00 (a perfect negative correlation).

use standardized test scores (SAT or ACT) and high school grades to decide which applicants to admit. They do so because both test scores and high school grades are correlated with success in college. But the fact that there is a correlation between two variables does not necessarily mean that one variable causes the other (see Figure 1.2).

Psychological Tests

Correlational research often involves the use of psychological tests. However, it's important to note that psychological tests are used frequently in other kinds of studies as well. To be useful, psychological tests must have *reliability* and *validity*. A reliable test is one that yields consistent results. In other words, a personality test shouldn't classify you as outgoing one day and shy the next. A valid test is one that measures what it claims to measure. A personality test written in a language you don't understand would be reliable—you would always do poorly on it—but it would not be valid because it would be measuring your knowledge of that language rather than your personality. You will learn more about reliability and validity in the discussion of intelligence testing in Chapter 7.

Review and Reflect 1.1 (on page 14) summarizes the different types of research methods we've discussed.

The relationship between the weather and refreshment-buying behavior illustrates both positive and negative correlations. The hotter it gets, the more likely we are to buy cold treats like ice cream. So, temperature and the sales of cold treats are positively correlated: Temperature goes up; ice cream purchases go up. Conversely, the colder it gets, the more likely we are to buy hot drinks. Thus, temperature and sales of hot drinks are negatively correlated: Temperature goes down; hot drink purchases go up.

Participants in Psychological Research

Ethics in Research

In 2002, the American Psychological Association (APA, 2002) adopted a new set of ethical standards governing research with human participants so as to safeguard their

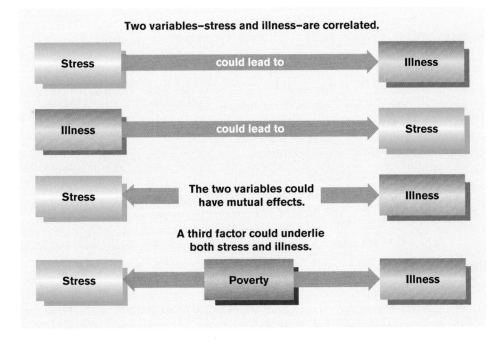

Two variables–stress and illness–are correlated.

Stress ——could lead to—→ Illness

Illness ——could lead to—→ Stress

Stress ←— The two variables could have mutual effects. —→ Illness

A third factor could underlie both stress and illness.

Stress ←— Poverty —→ Illness

➤ **Figure 1.2**

Correlation Does Not Prove Causation

A correlation between two variables does not prove that a cause-effect relationship exists between them. There is a correlation between stress and illness, but that does not mean that stress necessarily causes illness. Both stress and illness may result from another factor, such as poverty or poor general health.

Research Methods in Psychology

METHOD	DESCRIPTION	ADVANTAGES	LIMITATIONS
Naturalistic observation	Observation and recording of behavior in its natural setting. Subjects may or may not know that they are being observed.	Provides descriptive information. Can provide basis for hypotheses to be tested later. Behavior studied in everyday setting is more natural.	Researchers' expectations can distort observations (observer bias). Presence of researcher may influence behavior of subjects. Researcher has little or no control over conditions.
Case study	In-depth study of one or a few individuals using observation, interviews, and/or psychological testing.	Source of information for rare or unusual conditions or events. Can provide basis for hypotheses to be tested later.	May not be representative of condition or event. Time-consuming. Subject to misinterpretation by researcher.
Survey	Interviews and/or questionnaires used to gather information about attitudes, beliefs, experiences, or behaviors of a group of people.	Can provide accurate information about large numbers of people. Can track changes in attitudes and behavior over time.	Responses may be inaccurate. Sample may not be representative. Characteristics of interviewer may influence responses.
Experimental method	Random assignment of participants to groups. Manipulation of the independent variable(s) and measurement of its effect on the dependent variable.	Enables identification of cause-effect relationships.	Laboratory setting may inhibit natural behavior of participants. Findings may not be generalizable to the real world. In some cases, experiment is unethical.
Correlational method	Method used to determine the relationship (correlation) between two events, characteristics, or behaviors.	Can assess strength of relationship between variables. Provides basis for prediction.	Does not demonstrate cause and effect.
Psychological tests	Tests used for measuring intelligence, scholastic achievement, aptitudes, vocational interests, personality traits, or psychiatric problems.	Provide data for educational and vocational decision making, personnel selection, research, and psychological assessment.	Tests may not be reliable or valid.

rights while supporting the goals of scientific inquiry. Following are some of the main provisions of the code:

What are some ethical guidelines governing the use of human participants in research?

- *Legality.* All research must conform to applicable federal, state, and local laws and regulations.
- *Institutional approval.* Researchers must obtain approval from all institutions (e.g., schools) involved in a study.
- *Informed consent.* Participants must be informed of the purpose of the study and its potential for harming them.

- *Deception.* Deception of participants is ethical, but only if absolutely necessary to test the study's hypothesis.
- *Debriefing.* Whenever a researcher deceives participants, including by the use of placebo treatments, he or she must tell participants about the deception as soon as the study is complete.
- *Clients, patients, students, and other subordinates.* When participants are under another's authority (e.g., clients of a therapist, students in a psychology class), researchers must take steps to ensure that participation in a study, and the information obtained during participation, will not damage the participants in any way.
- *Payment for participation.* Participants can be paid, but they must be fully informed about what is expected in return for payment. In addition, researchers must refrain from offering excessive payments that may bias a study's participants in some way.
- *Publication.* Psychological researchers must report their findings in an appropriate forum, such as a scientific journal, and they must make their data available to others who want to verify their findings. Even when a study produces no findings, its results must still be reported. Results must also be made available to participants.

Participant-Related Bias in Psychological Research

The characteristics of participants can be a source of bias in psychological research. For example, projections by the U.S. Bureau of the Census (2000) indicate that the percentage of non-Hispanic Whites in the United States is expected to decrease from 71.5% in the year 2000 to 53% in 2050. Yet, Whites are often overrepresented in psychological studies because the majority of studies with human participants in the last 30 years have used college students (Graham, 1992), and the college student population includes a disproportionately low number of minority students. Moreover, college students, even those of minority ethnicity, are a relatively select group in terms of age, socioeconomic class, and educational level. Thus, they are not representative of the general population.

Gender bias is another type of participant-related bias. For example, Ader and Johnson (1994) found that, when conducting studies in which all of the participants are the same gender, researchers typically specify the gender of the sample clearly when it is female but not when it is male. Such a practice, say Ader and Johnson, reveals a "tendency to consider male participants 'normative,' and results obtained from them generally applicable, whereas female participants are somehow 'different,' and results obtained from them are specific to female participants" (pp. 217–218). On a positive note, however, these researchers report that gender bias in the sampling and selection of research participants has decreased over recent decades.

Another kind of bias is evident when researchers or consumers of research overgeneralize the findings of a study to all members of a particular group. For example, Sandra Graham (1992) reported finding a methodological flaw—failure to include socioeconomic status—in much of the research comparing White Americans and African Americans. Graham points out that African Americans are overrepresented among those who are economically disadvantaged. She maintains that socioeconomic status should be incorporated into research designs "to disentangle race and social class effects" in studies that compare White and African Americans (p. 634).

Ageism is another continuing source of bias, especially apparent in the language used in psychological research (Schaie, 1993). For example, the titles of research on aging tend to focus heavily on loss, deterioration, decline, and dependency. Moreover, researchers are likely to understate the great diversity among the older adults they study. According to Schaie (1993), "most research on adulthood shows that differences between those in their 60s and those in their 80s are far greater than those between 20- and 60-

Researchers should guard against descriptions or conclusions implying that all older adults are defined by deterioration, forgetfulness, and deficits.

year-olds" (p. 50). Researchers should guard against descriptions or conclusions implying that all members of a given age group are defined by deterioration, forgetfulness, and deficits.

The Use of Animals in Research

The APA code of ethics also includes guidelines for using animals in psychological research. Here are a few of the important guidelines:

- *Legality.* Like research with human participants, animal research must follow all relevant federal, state, and local laws.
- *Supervision by experienced personnel.* The use of animals must be supervised by people who are trained in their care.
- *Minimization of discomfort.* Researchers are ethically bound to minimize any discomfort to research animals. And when researchers must terminate the lives of research animals, they must do so in a humane manner.

Even with these safeguards in place, the use of animals in research is controversial. Many animal rights advocates want all animal research stopped immediately. Books on animal rights devote an average of 63.3% of their content to the use of animals in research (Nicholl & Russell, 1990). Yet, of the 6,309 million animals killed each year in the United States, only 0.3% are used in research and education, while 96.5% are used for food, 2.6% are killed by hunters, 0.4% are killed in animal shelters, and 0.2% are used for fur garments (Christensen, 1997).

In a survey of almost 4,000 randomly selected members of the APA, "80% of respondents expressed general support for psychological research on animals" (Plous, 1996, p. 1177). Among the general public, support for animal research is higher when the research is tied to human health and highest when the animals involved in such research are rats and mice rather than dogs, cats, or primates (Plous, 1996). There are at least six reasons why many psychologists use animals in research: (1) They provide a simpler model for studying processes that operate similarly in humans; (2) researchers can exercise far more control over animal subjects and thus be more certain of their conclusions; (3) a wider range of medical and other manipulations can be used with animals; (4) it is easier to study the entire life span and even multiple generations in some animal species; (5) animals are more economical to use and are available at researchers' convenience; and (6) some researchers simply want to learn more about the animals themselves.

> **Why are animals used in research?**

Animal research has yielded much knowledge about the brain and the physiology of vision, hearing, and the other senses (Domjan & Purdy, 1995). It has also increased knowledge in the areas of learning, motivation, stress, memory, and the effects on the unborn of various drugs ingested during pregnancy. Almost half of the research funded by the National Institutes of Health is conducted on animals (Cork et al., 1997). Virtually all of the marvels of modern medicine are due at least in part to experimentation using animals.

Overall, however, the animal rights controversy has had a positive effect on research ethics: It has served to increase concern for the treatment of animals as research subjects and to stimulate a search for alternative research methods that will decrease the numbers of animals needed. "The number of animals used in laboratory experiments is going down" (Mukerjee, 1997, p. 86).

Exploring Psychology's Roots

If you were to trace the development of psychology from the beginning, you would need to stretch far back to the earliest pages of recorded history, even beyond the early Greek philosophers such as Aristotle and Plato. However, it was not until experimental methods were applied to the study of psychological processes that psychology became recognized as a formal academic discipline.

The Founding of Psychology

Historians acknowledge that three German scientists—Ernst Weber, Gustav Fechner, and Hermann von Helmholtz—were the first to systematically study behavior and mental processes. But it is Wilhelm Wundt (1832–1920) who is generally thought of as the "father of psychology." Wundt's vision for the new discipline included studies of social and cultural influences on human thought (Benjafield, 1996). Wundt established a psychological laboratory at the University of Leipzig in Germany in 1879. This event is considered to mark the birth of psychology as a formal academic discipline. Using a method called *introspection,* Wundt and his associates studied the perception of a variety of visual, tactile, and auditory stimuli, including rhythm patterns produced by metronomes set at different speeds. Introspection as a research method involves looking inward to examine one's own conscious experience and then reporting that experience.

Wundt's most famous student, Englishman Edward Bradford Titchener (1867–1927), took the new field to the United States when he set up a psychological laboratory at Cornell University. He gave the name **structuralism** to this first school of thought in psychology, which aimed at analyzing the basic elements, or the structure, of conscious mental experience. Like Wundt before him, Titchener thought that consciousness could be reduced to its basic elements, just as water (H_2O) can be broken down into its constituent elements—hydrogen (H) and oxygen (O). For Wundt, pure sensations—such as sweetness, coldness, or redness—were the basic elements of consciousness. And these pure sensations, he believed, combined to form perceptions.

The work of both Wundt and Titchener was criticized for its primary method, introspection. Introspection was not objective, even though it involved observation, measurement, and experimentation. Nevertheless, the structuralists were responsible for establishing psychology as a science because of their insistence that psychological processes could be measured and studied using methods similar to those employed by scientists in other fields.

Functionalism

As structuralism was losing its influence in the United States in the early 20th century, a new school of psychology called functionalism was taking shape. **Functionalism** was concerned not with the structure of consciousness, but with how mental processes function—that is, how humans and animals use mental processes in adapting to their environment.

The influential work of Charles Darwin (1809–1882), especially his ideas about evolution and the continuity of species, was largely responsible for an increasing use of animals in psychological experiments. Even though Darwin, who was British, contributed important seeds of thought that helped give birth to the new school of psychology, functionalism was primarily American in character and spirit.

The famous American psychologist William James (1842–1910) was an advocate of functionalism. James's best-known work is his highly regarded and frequently quoted textbook *Principles of Psychology,* published more than a century ago (1890). James taught that mental processes are fluid and have continuity, rather than having a rigid or fixed structure as the structuralists suggested. James spoke of the "stream of consciousness," which he said functioned to help humans adapt to their environment.

Functionalism broadened the scope of psychology to include the study of behavior as well as mental processes. It also allowed the study of children, animals, and the mentally impaired; these could not be studied by the structuralists because they could not be trained to use introspection. Functionalism also focused on an applied, more practical use of psychology by encouraging the study of educational psychology, individual differences, and industrial psychology (adaptation in the workplace).

◀ What was Wundt's contribution to psychology?

◀ What were the goals and method of structuralism, the first school of thought in psychology?

◀ What was the goal of the early school of psychology known as functionalism?

structuralism
The first formal school of psychology, aimed at analyzing the basic elements, or structure, of conscious mental experience through the use of introspection.

functionalism
An early school of psychology that was concerned with how mental processes help humans and animals adapt to their environments.

Women and Minorities

For centuries, conventional thought had held that higher education was the exclusive domain of White males, that women should rear the children and be the homemakers, and that minorities were best suited for manual labor. Women and minorities have overcome these prejudices to make notable achievements in and contributions to the study of psychology.

Christine Ladd-Franklin (1847–1930) completed the requirements for a PhD at Johns Hopkins University in the mid-1880s but had to wait over 40 years before receiving her degree in 1926, when the university first agreed to grant it to women. Ladd-Franklin formulated a well-regarded evolutionary theory of color vision.

In 1895, Mary Whiton Calkins (1863–1930) completed the requirements for a doctorate at Harvard. And even though William James described her as one of his most capable students, Harvard refused to grant the degree to a woman (Dewsbury, 2000). Undeterred, Calkins established a psychology laboratory at Wellesley College and developed the paired-associates test, an important research technique for the study of memory. She became the first female president of the American Psychological Association in 1905.

Margaret Floy Washburn (1871–1939) received her PhD in psychology from Cornell University and later taught at Vassar College (Dewsbury, 2000). She wrote several books, among them *The Animal Mind* (1908), an influential book on animal behavior, and *Movement and Mental Imagery* (1916).

Francis Cecil Sumner (1895–1954) was a self-taught scholar. Without having attended high school, he became, in 1920, the first African American to earn a PhD in psychology, from Clark University. This feat was accomplished "in spite of innumerable social and physical factors mitigating against such achievements by black people in America" (Guthrie, 1998, p. 177). Sumner translated more than 3,000 articles from German, French, and Spanish. He chaired the psychology department at Howard University and is known as the "father" of African American psychology.

Albert Sidney Beckham (1897–1964), another African American psychologist, conducted some impressive early studies on intelligence and showed how it is related to success in numerous occupational fields. Beckham also established the first psychological laboratory at an African American institution of higher learning–Howard University.

A more recent African American pioneer, psychologist Kenneth Clark, achieved national recognition for his writings on the harmful effects of racial segregation. His work affected the Supreme Court ruling that declared racial segregation in the schools to be unconstitutional (Benjamin & Crouse, 2002). His wife, Mamie Phipps Clark, also achieved recognition when the couple published their works on racial identification and self-esteem, writings that have become classics in the field (Lal, 2002).

Hispanic American Jorge Sanchez conducted studies on bias in intelligence testing during the 1930s. He pointed out that both cultural differences and language differences work against Hispanic American students when they take IQ tests.

Today, more women than men obtain degrees in psychology. However, even though the proportion of minorities in the U.S. population is about 28%, only 16% of students pursuing graduate degrees in psychology are of minority ethnicity (APA, 2000). Consequently, the American Psychological Association and other organizations have established programs to encourage minority enrollment in graduate programs in psychology.

▼ Today, more women than men obtain degrees in psychology.

Schools of Thought in Psychology

Sparked by the debate between structuralism and functionalism, a veritable explosion of theoretical discussion and research examining psychological processes began in the early 20th century. The foundations of the major schools of thought in the field were established during that period. Each of these schools continues to be influential today.

Behaviorism

Psychologist John B. Watson (1878–1958), who introduced the term *behaviorism*, looked at the study of psychology as defined by the structuralists and functionalists and disliked virtually everything he saw. In his article "Psychology as the Behaviorist Views It" (1913), Watson redefined psychology as the "science of behavior." **Behaviorism** restricted psychological research to examinations of observable and measurable behavior because this approach was believed to be more scientific than such methods as introspection. Behaviorism also emphasized that behavior is determined primarily by factors in the environment.

 How did behaviorism differ from earlier schools of thought in psychology?

Behaviorism is still a major force in modern psychology, in large part because of the profound influence of B. F. Skinner (1904–1990). Skinner agreed with Watson that concepts such as mind, consciousness, and feelings were neither objective nor measurable and, therefore, were not the appropriate subject matter of psychology. Furthermore, Skinner argued that these concepts are not needed in order to explain behavior. One can explain behavior, he claimed, by analyzing the conditions that were present before a behavior occurs and by analyzing the consequences that follow the behavior. You will read more about Skinner's ideas in Chapter 5.

behaviorism
The school of psychology founded by John B. Watson that views observable, measurable behavior as the appropriate subject matter for psychology and emphasizes the key role of environment as a determinant of behavior.

Psychoanalysis

Sigmund Freud (1856–1939), whose life and work you will study in Chapter 11, developed a theory of human behavior based largely on case studies of his patients. Freud's theory, **psychoanalysis,** maintains that human mental life is like an iceberg. The smallest, visible part of the iceberg represents the conscious mental experience of the individual. But underwater, hidden from view, floats a vast store of unconscious impulses, thoughts, wishes, and desires. Freud insisted that individuals do not consciously control their thoughts, feelings, and behavior, which are instead determined by these unconscious forces.

 What is the role of the unconscious in psychoanalysis, Freud's approach to psychology?

The overriding importance that Freud placed on sexual and aggressive impulses caused much controversy both inside and outside the field of psychology. The most notable of Freud's famous students–Carl Jung, Alfred Adler, and Karen Horney–broke away from their mentor and developed their own theories of personality. These three are often collectively referred to as *neo-Freudians*.

The general public has heard of such concepts as the unconscious, repression, rationalization, and the Freudian slip. Such familiarity has made Sigmund Freud a larger-than-life figure rather than an obscure Austrian doctor relevant only to a few historians of psychiatry. Although Freud continues to influence popular culture, the volume of research on psychoanalysis has continued to diminish steadily (Robins et al., 1999). The psychoanalytic approach is still somewhat influential, but mostly in the modified form developed by the neo-Freudians.

psychoanalysis
(SY-ko-ah-NAL-ih-sis) The term Sigmund Freud used for both his theory of personality and his therapy for the treatment of psychological disorders; the unconscious is the primary focus of psychoanalytic theory.

humanistic psychology
The school of psychology that focuses on the uniqueness of human beings and their capacity for choice, growth, and psychological health.

Humanistic Psychology

Humanistic psychology focuses on the uniqueness of human beings and their capacity for choice, growth, and psychological health. Abraham Maslow (1908–1970) and other early humanists, such as Carl Rogers (1902–1987), pointed out that Freud had based his theory primarily on data from his disturbed patients. By contrast, they emphasized a much more positive view of human nature. They maintained that people are innately good and, in contrast to the emphasis on environmental conditioning that is characteristic of behaviorism, that they possess free

 What is the focus of humanistic psychology?

will. The humanists believe that people are capable of making conscious, rational choices, which can lead to growth and psychological health.

As you will learn in Chapter 9, Maslow proposed a theory of motivation that consists of a hierarchy of needs. He considered the need for self-actualization (developing to one's fullest potential) to be the highest need on the hierarchy. Carl Rogers developed his *client-centered therapy*, an approach in which the client, or patient, directs a discussion focused on his or her own view of a problem rather than on the therapist's analysis. Rogers and other humanists also popularized group therapy as part of the human potential movement. Thus, the humanistic perspective continues to be important in research examining human motivation and in the practice of psychotherapy.

Cognitive Psychology

What is the focus of cognitive psychology? ▶

Cognitive psychology grew and developed partly in response to strict behaviorism, especially in the United States (Robins et al., 1999). **Cognitive psychology** sees humans as active participants who use mental processes to transform, remember, and use information. Historically, modern cognitive psychology is derived from two streams of thought: Gestalt psychology and information-processing theory.

Gestalt Psychology **Gestalt psychology** made its appearance in Germany in 1912. The Gestalt psychologists, notably Max Wertheimer, Kurt Koffka, and Wolfgang Köhler, emphasized that individuals perceive objects and patterns as whole units, and that the whole thus perceived is more than the sum of its parts. The German word *Gestalt* roughly means "whole, form, or pattern."

To support the Gestalt theory, Wertheimer, the leader of the Gestalt psychologists, presented his famous experiment demonstrating the *phi phenomenon*. In this experiment, two light bulbs are placed a short distance apart in a dark room. The first light is flashed on and then turned off just as the second light is flashed on. As this pattern of flashing the lights on and off continues, an observer sees what looks like a single light moving back and forth from one position to another. Here, said the Gestaltists, is proof that people perceive wholes or patterns, not collections of separate and independent sensations.

When the Nazis came to power in Germany in the 1930s, the Gestalt school disbanded as its most prominent members emigrated to the United States. Today, the fundamental concept underlying Gestalt psychology, that the mind *interprets* experiences in predictable ways rather than simply reacting to them, is central to cognitive psychologists' ideas about learning, memory, problem solving, and even psychotherapy.

▼ According to information-processing theory, the brain processes information in sequential steps—much the same way as a computer does serial processing, that is, one step at a time.

Information-Processing Theory The advent of the computer provided cognitive psychologists with a new way to conceptualize mental structures and processes, known as **information-processing theory.** According to this view, the brain processes information in sequential steps, much the same way as a computer performs serial processing—that is, one step at a time. But as computers and computer programs became more sophisticated, cognitive psychologists changed their models of brain functioning. "Increasingly, parallel processing models [a process in which several tasks are performed at once] are developed in addition to stage models of processing" (Haberlandt, 1997, p. 22).

A central idea of information-processing theory, one that it shares with Gestalt psychology, is that the brain interprets information rather than just responding to it. For example, consider this statement: *The old woman was sweeping the steps.* If information-processing researchers ask people to recall whether the sentence includes the word *broom*, a majority will say that it does. According to information-processing theorists, there are rules for handling information that lead us to find associations between new input, such as the statement about a woman sweeping, and previously acquired knowledge, such as our understanding that brooms are used for sweeping. As a result, most of us construct a memory of the sentence that leads us to incorrectly recall that it included the word *broom*.

Designing computer programs that can process human language in the same way as the human brain is one of the goals of research in *artificial intelligence*. Today, artificial intelligence represents one of the most important applications of information-processing theory.

Cognitive Psychology Today Over the past 100 years or so, cognitive psychologists have carried out studies that have greatly increased knowledge of how the human memory system works and the mental processes involved in problem solving. Moreover, the principles discovered in these experiments have been used to explain and study all kinds of psychological variables–from gender role development to individual differences in intelligence. As a result, cognitive psychology is currently recognized as the most prominent school of psychological thought (Robins et al., 1999).

Current Trends in Psychology

In addition to the continuing influence of the major schools of thought, there are other important trends in psychology today.

Evolutionary Psychology

Evolutionary psychology focuses on how humans have adapted the behaviors required for survival in the face of environmental pressures over the long course of evolution (Archer, 1996). One of the most influential evolutionary psychologists, David Buss, and his colleagues have conducted a number of fascinating studies examining men's and women's patterns of behavior in romantic relationships (1999, 2000a, 2000b, 2001). For example, one of Buss's consistent findings is that men seem to experience more jealousy when faced with a partner's sexual infidelity than when confronted with her emotional infidelity (Buss, 1999; Buss et al., 1992; Shackelford et al., 2002). By contrast, the women in Buss's research appear to be more concerned about emotional than sexual unfaithfulness in a partner. Figure 1.3 (on page 22) shows that this remains true across cultures.

 What is the focus of evolutionary psychology?

evolutionary psychology
The school of psychology that studies how humans' genetically inherited tendencies and dispositions influence a wide range of behaviors.

Evolutionary psychologists claim that men's jealousy focuses on sexual infidelity because, in the evolutionary past, a man's certainty of his paternity was jeopardized if he learned that his mate had been sexually unfaithful. But the best chance a woman had to pass on her genes to future generations was to be able to rely on material resources, protection, and support from a mate to help her offspring survive and reach sexual maturity. The man's emotional commitment to her, then, was of paramount importance. So, the presumably biological gender difference in reactions to infidelity favors the survival of offspring: Men's insistence on sexual fidelity ensures knowledge of paternity and, therefore, their willingness to commit to an investment in children's upbringing. Women's insistence on emotional commitment promotes family harmony and continuity, even when sexual infidelity occurs. This, in turn, provides a stable environment in which to bring up children.

Biological (Physiological) Psychology

Biological psychology, also called *physiological psychology,* searches for links between behaviors and biological factors. To do this, biological psychologists study the structures of the brain and central nervous system, the functioning of the neurons, the delicate balance of neurotransmitters and hormones, and heredity.

What is the goal of biological psychology?

➤ Figure 1.3

Gender Differences in Jealousy across Cultures

Across all cultures, men experience greater distress in response to sexual infidelity than women do, while women experience greater distress in response to emotional infidelity than men do. (From Buunk et al., 1996.)

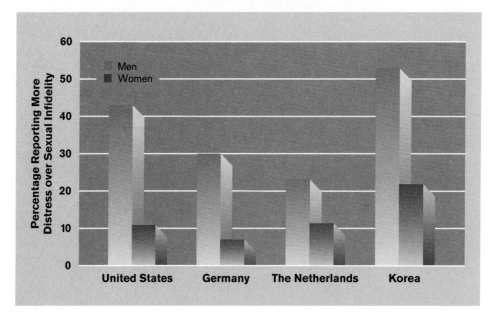

neuroscience
A field that combines the work of psychologists, biologists, biochemists, medical researchers, and others in the study of the structure and function of the nervous system.

For example, one question of interest to biological psychologists is whether too much or too little of a particular chemical in the brain can cause a psychological disorder, such as schizophrenia or depression.

Many biological psychologists work under the umbrella of an interdisciplinary field known as neuroscience. **Neuroscience** combines the work of psychologists, biologists, biochemists, medical researchers, and others in the study of the structure and function of the nervous system. Many important findings in psychology have resulted from this work. For example, researchers have learned that defects in nerve cell membranes interfere with the cells' ability to make use of chemicals in the brain that help control body movement (Kurup & Kurup, 2002). These findings shed light on the physiological processes underlying serious neurological disorders such as Parkinson's disease, thus helping pharmacological researchers in their efforts to create more effective medications for these illnesses.

What kinds of variables interest psychologists who take a sociocultural approach? ➤

Sociocultural Approach

Psychologists using the *sociocultural approach* emphasize social and cultural influences on human behavior and stress the importance of understanding those influences when interpreting the behavior of others. Sociocultural psychologists are interested in how factors such as socioeconomic class, education, ethnicity, religion, and occupation affect people's behavior. For example, several have written about how cultural differences between Asian and Western countries may help explain cross-national achievement differences, as you'll see in Chapter 7 (e.g., Tweed & Lehman, 2002).

Psychological Perspectives

The views of modern psychologists are frequently difficult to categorize into traditional schools of thought. Thus, rather than discussing schools of thought, it is often more useful to refer to **psychological perspectives**–general points of view used for explaining people's behavior and thinking, whether normal or abnormal. So, for example, a psychologist may adopt a behavioral perspective without necessarily agreeing with all of Watson's or Skinner's ideas. What is important is that the psychologist taking such a view would explain behavior in terms of environmental forces.

The following are the major perspectives in psychology today and the kinds of variables each emphasizes in explanations of behavior:

psychological perspectives
General points of view used for explaining people's behavior and thinking, whether normal or abnormal.

Perspectives in Psychology

PERSPECTIVE	EMPHASIS	EXPLANATION OF OLDER ADULTS' PERFORMANCE DEFICIT ON RESEARCHERS' MEMORY TASKS
Behavioral	The role of environment in shaping and controlling behavior	Older adults spend little or no time in environments, such as school, where they would be reinforced for using their memories.
Psychoanalytic	The role of unconscious motivation and early childhood experiences in determining behavior and thought	Older adults' unconscious fear of impending death interferes with memory processes.
Humanistic	The importance of an individual's subjective experience as a key to understanding his or her behavior	Older adults are more concerned with the meaning of life than with performing well on researchers' memory tasks.
Cognitive	The role of mental processes—perception, thinking, and memory—that underlie behavior	Older adults fail to use effective memory strategies.
Evolutionary	The roles of inherited tendencies that have proven adaptive in humans	Declines in memory and in other functions are programmed into human genes so that younger, reproductively healthier individuals will be more attractive as potential mates.
Biological	The role of biological processes and structures, as well as heredity, in explaining behavior	As the brain ages, connections between neurons break down, causing a decline in intellectual functions such as memory.
Sociocultural	The influences of social and cultural factors on behavior	Older people have internalized the ageist expectations of society and, as a result, expect themselves to perform poorly on memory tasks.

- *Behavioral perspective*–environmental factors
- *Psychoanalytic perspective*–emotions, unconscious motivations, early childhood experiences
- *Humanistic perspective*–subjective experiences, intrinsic motivation to achieve self-actualization
- *Cognitive perspective*–mental processes
- *Evolutionary perspective*–inherited traits that enhance adaptability
- *Biological perspective*–biological structures, processes, heredity
- *Sociocultural perspective*–social and cultural variables

 What are the seven major perspectives in psychology today?

Review and Reflect 1.2 lists these perspectives with an illustration of how each might explain the frequent finding that young adults outperform older adults on the kinds of tasks used in memory research.

Many years of research on memory have revealed a number of techniques you can use to help yourself study more efficiently and retain more of what you learn:

- Establish a quiet place, free of distractions, where you do nothing else but study; then, entering that room or area will be your cue to begin work.

- Schedule your study time. Spaced learning is more effective than massed practice (cramming). Instead of studying for 5 hours straight, try five study sessions of 1 hour each.

- To be prepared for each class meeting, set specific goals for each week and for individual study sessions. Your goals should be challenging but not overwhelming. Completing the task you have set for yourself will give you a sense of accomplishment.

- The more active a role you play in the learning process, the more you will remember. Spend some of your study time reciting the material. Write each key term or study question on the front of an index card. On the back, list relevant information from the text and lectures. Use these cards to review for tests.

- *Overlearning* means studying beyond the point at which you can just barely recite the information you are trying to memorize. If you are subject to test anxiety, overlearning will help.

- Forgetting takes place most rapidly within the first 24 hours after you study. No matter how much you have studied for a test, always review shortly before you take it.

- Sleeping immediately after you study will help you retain more of what you have learned. So, it's a good idea to go through your index cards just before going to bed. ■

Psychologists need not limit themselves to only one perspective or approach. Many take an *eclectic perspective,* choosing a combination of approaches to explain a particular behavior. Consequently, a psychologist may explain a behavior in terms of both environmental factors and mental processes. For example, a child's unruly behavior in school may be seen as being maintained by teacher attention (a behavioral explanation) but initially caused by an emotional reaction to a family event such as divorce (a psychoanalytic explanation). This adoption of multiple perspectives allows psychologists' theories and studies to more closely mirror the behavior of real people in real situations.

Psychologists at Work

There are many specialties within the field of psychology. Wherever you find human activity, you are very likely to encounter psychologists.

What are some specialists in the field of psychology?

- *Clinical psychologists* specialize in the diagnosis and treatment of mental and behavioral disorders.
- *Counseling psychologists* help people who have adjustment problems (marital, social, or behavioral) that are less severe than those generally handled by clinical psychologists.

➤ The life and career of *Malcolm in the Middle's* young star Frankie Muniz might interest different types of psychologists for different reasons. For example, developmental psychologists might study how the entertainment industry affects Frankie as he grows into an adult. Social psychologists might study how Frankie interacts with others, in his private and professional life.

- *Physiological psychologists,* also called *neuropsychologists,* study the relationship between physiological processes and behavior.
- *Experimental psychologists* specialize in the use of experimental research methods. They conduct experiments in most fields of specialization in psychology (learning, memory, etc.).
- *Developmental psychologists* study how people grow, develop, and change throughout the life span.
- *Educational psychologists* specialize in the study of teaching and learning. They may help train teachers and other educational professionals or conduct research in teaching and classroom behavior.
- *Social psychologists* investigate how the individual feels, thinks, and behaves in a social setting.
- *Industrial/organizational (I/O) psychologists* study the relationships between people and their work environments.

Figure 1.4 shows the percentages of psychologists who work in the specialties discussed in this section. As you can see, psychology is an enormously broad and diverse field of study.

Professional psychologists have graduate degrees in the field. The American Psychological Association reports that it takes about 5 years of study beyond a bachelor's degree to obtain a doctoral degree in psychology (APA, 2000). However, there are many jobs open to those with bachelor's degrees in psychology. And many men and women who intend to do post-graduate work in other fields—law, for example—major in psychology. In fact, business administration is the only undergraduate major for which more degrees are awarded than psychology (APA, 1995; Horn & Zahn, 2001).

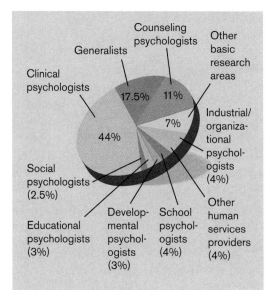

➤ **Figure 1.4**

What Psychologists Do

Clinical psychologists make up the largest percentage of members of the American Psychological Association who work in the field of psychology. (Data provided by the APA, 1995.)

Summarize It !

An Introduction

➤ **What is the scientific method?**

The scientific method consists of the orderly, systematic procedures researchers follow as they identify a research problem, design a study to investigate the problem, collect and analyze data, draw conclusions, and communicate their findings.

➤ **What are the four goals of psychology?**

The four goals of psychology are the description, explanation, prediction, and control of behavior and mental processes.

KEY TERMS

psychology (p. 4)
scientific method (p. 5)
theory (p. 5)
basic research (p. 5)
applied research (p. 6)
critical thinking (p. 6)

Descriptive Research Methods

➤ **What is naturalistic observation, and what are its advantages and limitations?**

In naturalistic observation, researchers observe and record behavior in a natural setting, without attempting to influence or control it. The main advantage of naturalistic observation is that it allows researchers to observe behavior as it naturally occurs. Limitations include researchers' lack of control over the observed situation and the potential for observer bias.

➤ **What is a case study, and for what purposes is it particularly well suited?**

A case study is an in-depth study of one or several individuals through observation, interview, and sometimes psychological testing. It is particularly appropriate for studying people with rare psychological or physiological disorders.

➤ **What are the methods and purposes of a survey?**

In conducting a survey, investigators use interviews and/or questionnaires to gather information about the attitudes, beliefs, experiences, or behaviors of a group of people.

➤ **What is a representative sample, and why is it essential for a survey?**

A representative sample is a group of participants selected from the population of interest in such a way that important subgroups within the whole population are included in the same proportions in the sample. A sample must be representative for the survey findings to be applicable to the larger population.

KEY TERMS

descriptive research methods (p. 6)
naturalistic observation (p. 6)

The Experimental Method

➤ **What is the main advantage of the experimental method?**

The experimental method is the only research method that can be used to identify cause-effect relationships.

➤ **What is the difference between the independent variable and the dependent variable?**

In an experiment, an independent variable is a condition or factor manipulated by the researcher to determine its effect on the dependent variable. The dependent variable, measured at the end of the experiment, is presumed to vary as a result of the manipulations of the independent variable.

➤ **How do the experimental and control groups differ?**

The experimental group is exposed to the independent variable, or treatment. The control group is similar to the experimental group and is exposed to the same experimental environment but is not exposed to the independent variable.

➤ **What is selection bias, and what technique do researchers use to control for it?**

Selection bias occurs when there are systematic differences among the experimental groups before the experiment begins. Random assignment maximizes the probability that the groups are similar at the beginning of the experiment.

➤ **What is the placebo effect, and how do researchers control for it?**

The placebo effect occurs when a person's expectations influence the outcome of a treatment or experiment. To control for the placebo effect, the researcher must ensure that participants do not know if they are members of the experimental group (receiving the treatment) or the control group (receiving the placebo).

➤ **What is experimenter bias, and how is it controlled?**

Experimenter bias occurs when the researcher's expectations affect the outcome of the experiment. It is controlled by using the double-blind technique, in which neither the researcher nor the participants know who is in the experimental group and who is in the control group.

The Correlational Method

➤ **What is the correlational method, and when is it used?**

The correlational method is a research method that determines the correlation, or degree of relationship, between two variables. It is often used when it is either impossible or unethical to conduct an experimental study.

➤ **What is a correlation coefficient?**

A correlation coefficient is a number between -1.00 and $+1.00$ that indicates the strength and direction of the relationship between two variables.

Participants in Psychological Research

➤ **What are some ethical guidelines governing the use of human participants in research?**

Participants in psychological research must give informed consent, and they must be debriefed as soon as possible about any deceptive techniques used by researchers.

➤ **Why are animals used in research?**

Animals provide a simpler model for studying processes similar to those in humans. Researchers can exercise more control over animals and use a wider range of medical and other manipulations. It is easier to study the entire life span and even several generations in some species, and animals are readily available and more economical to study.

Exploring Psychology's Roots

➤ **What was Wundt's contribution to psychology?**

Wundt, considered the father of psychology, established the first psychological laboratory in 1879 and launched the study of psychology as a formal academic discipline.

➤ **What were the goals and method of structuralism, the first school of thought in psychology?**

Structuralism's main goal was to analyze the basic elements, or the structure, of conscious mental experience, which was done through the use of introspection.

➤ **What was the goal of the early school of psychology known as functionalism?**

Functionalism was concerned with how mental processes help humans and animals adapt to their environment.

Schools of Thought in Psychology

➤ **How did behaviorism differ from earlier schools of psychology?**

Behaviorism, the school of psychology founded by John B. Watson, views observable, measurable behavior as the only appropriate subject matter for psychology. Behaviorism also emphasizes the environment as the key determinant of behavior.

➤ **What is the role of the unconscious in psychoanalysis, Freud's approach to psychology?**

According to Freud's theory of psychoanalysis, an individual's thoughts, feelings, and behavior are determined primarily by the unconscious—the part of the mind that one cannot control.

➤ **What is the focus of humanistic psychology?**

Humanistic psychology focuses on the uniqueness of human beings and their capacity for choice, growth, and psychological health.

➤ **What is the focus of cognitive psychology?**

Cognitive psychology is a specialty that focuses on mental processes such as memory, problem solving, concept formation, reasoning and decision making, language, and perception.

KEY TERMS

behaviorism (p. 19)
psychoanalysis (p. 19)
humanistic psychology (p. 19)
cognitive psychology (p. 20)
Gestalt psychology (p. 20)
information-processing theory (p. 20)

Current Trends in Psychology

➤ **What is the focus of evolutionary psychology?**

Evolutionary psychology focuses on how humans have adapted the behaviors necessary for survival in the face of environmental pressures over the course of evolution. This perspective looks at inherited human tendencies and dispositions.

➤ **What is the goal of biological psychology?**

Biological psychologists look for specific connection between biological variables (such as hormone levels) and psychological variables (such as aggression).

➤ **What kinds of variables interest psychologists who take a sociocultural approach?**

Sociocultural approaches focus on how social and cultural factors such as socioeconomic class, education, ethnicity, religion, and occupation affect people's behavior.

➤ **What are the seven major perspectives, or general points of view, in psychology today?**

Seven general points of view taken by today's psychologists are (1) the behavioral perspective, which emphasizes the role of environmental factors in shaping behavior; (2) the psychoanalytic perspective, which focuses on the role of the unconscious and early childhood experiences; (3) the humanistic perspective, which emphasizes the importance of an individual's subjective experience; (4) the cognitive perspective, which stresses the role of the mental processes (perceiving, thinking, remembering, etc.); (5) the evolutionary perspective, which looks at the inherited tendencies that have proved adaptive in humans; (6) the biological perspective, which emphasizes the role of biological processes and heredity as the keys to understanding behavior and thought; and (7) the sociocultural perspective, which emphasizes the influences of social and cultural factors on behavior.

KEY TERMS

evolutionary psychology (p. 21)
neuroscience (p. 22)
psychological perspectives (p. 22)

Psychologists at Work

➤ **What are some specialists in the field of psychology?**

Specialists include clinical and counseling psychologists, physiological psychologists, experimental psychologists, developmental psychologists, educational and school psychologists, social psychologists, and industrial/organizational psychologists.

Surf It!

Want to be sure you've absorbed the material in Chapter 1, "Introduction to Psychology," before the big test? Visiting **www.ablongman.com/woodmastering1e** can put a top grade within your reach. The site is loaded with free practice tests, flashcards, activities, and links to help you review your way to an A.

Companion Website

Study Guide for Chapter 1!

Answers to all the Study Guide questions are provided at the end of the book.

Section One: Chapter Review

1. The orderly, systematic procedures scientists follow in acquiring a body of knowledge is the _____.

2. The four goals of psychology are _____, _____, _____, and _____.

3. Basic research is designed to solve practical problems. (true/false)

4. Which descriptive research method would be best for studying each topic?
   ____ (1) attitudes toward exercise
   ____ (2) gender differences in how people position themselves and their belongings in a library
   ____ (3) physiological changes that occur during sleep
   ____ (4) the physical and emotional effects of a rare brain injury
   a. naturalistic observation
   b. laboratory observation
   c. case study
   d. survey

5. When conducting a survey, a researcher can compensate for a sample that is not representative by using a sample that is very large. (true/false)

6. The experimental method is the *only* research method that can be used to identify cause-effect relationships between variables. (true/false)

7. A researcher investigates the effectiveness of a new anti-depressant drug. She randomly assigns depressed patients to two groups. Group 1 is given the drug, and Group 2 is given a placebo. At the end of the experiment, the level of depression of all participants is measured as a score on a test called a depression inventory. Match the elements of this experiment with the appropriate term.
   ____ (1) score on depression inventory
   ____ (2) the antidepressant drug
   ____ (3) Group 1
   ____ (4) Group 2
   a. experimental group
   b. control group
   c. independent variable
   d. dependent variable

8. Random assignment is used to control for
   a. experimenter bias.   c. selection bias.
   b. the placebo effect.   d. participant bias.

9. The placebo effect occurs when a participant responds according to
   a. the hypothesis.
   b. the actual treatment.
   c. how other participants behave.
   d. his or her expectations.

10. The results of an experiment can be influenced by the expectations of either the participants or the researcher. (true/false)

11. The correlational method is used to demonstrate cause-effect relationships. (true/false)

12. Which of the following correlation coefficients indicates the strongest relationship?
    a. +.65   c. .00
    b. −.78   d. +.25

13. There is a (positive/negative) correlation between the amount of fat people eat and their body weight.

14. Test X has turned out to be a poor predictor of college GPA. Therefore, you can say that Test X is not (reliable/valid) for predicting GPA in college.

15. Psychological tests are sometimes used in case studies, experiments, and correlational studies. (true/false)

16. Psychologists are required to debrief participants thoroughly after a research study when the study
    a. violates participants' rights to privacy.
    b. deceives participants about the true purpose of the research.
    c. exposes participants to unreasonable risk or harm.
    d. wastes taxpayers' money on trivial questions.

17. Which of the following groups has *not* been overrepresented as participants in psychological research?
    a. Whites   c. females
    b. males   d. college students

18. Which of the following was *not* identified in the text as a source of bias in psychological research?
    a. age   c. race
    b. gender   d. religion

19. Investigators use animals in psychological research to learn more about humans. (true/false)

20. The American Psychological Association (APA) has guidelines for ethical treatment of human participants but not of animal subjects. (true/false)

21. Classify each of the following people and concepts as being associated with (a) Wundt, (b) structuralism, or (c) functionalism. (*Hint:* Some items are associated with more than one.)
_____ (1) James
_____ (2) based on Darwin's theory of evolution
_____ (3) stream of consciousness
_____ (4) elements of experience
_____ (5) Titchener
_____ (6) introspection
_____ (7) became known in the 19th century

22. Match each of the following individuals with his or her contribution to psychology:
_____ (1) Francis Cecil Sumner
_____ (2) Mary Whiton Calkins
_____ (3) Kenneth Clark
_____ (4) Christine Ladd-Franklin
_____ (5) Jorge Sanchez
a. first female president of APA
b. published studies on cultural bias in intelligence testing
c. first African American to receive a PhD in psychology
d. studied African American children's self-esteem
e. had to wait 40 years to receive a PhD in psychology after completing the degree requirements

23. Match the school of psychology with its major emphasis:
_____ (1) the scientific study of behavior
_____ (2) the perception of whole units or patterns
_____ (3) the unconscious
_____ (4) the computer as a model for human cognition
_____ (5) the uniqueness of human beings and their capacity for growth
_____ (6) the study of mental processes

a. Gestalt psychology
b. humanistic psychology
c. cognitive psychology
d. behaviorism
e. information-processing theory
f. psychoanalysis

24. Match each of the following variables with the psychological approach that is most likely to be interested in it: (a) evolutionary psychology, (b) biological psychology, or (c) sociocultural psychology.
_____ (1) the effects of drugs and alcohol on reaction time
_____ (2) the relationship between minority status and self-esteem
_____ (3) universal behaviors such as infants' attachment to caregivers
_____ (4) links between hormones and aggression
_____ (5) gender role beliefs that are consistent across cultures
_____ (6) gender role beliefs that vary across cultures

25. Match the psychological perspective with its major emphasis.
_____ (1) the role of biological processes and heredity
_____ (2) the role of environmental factors
_____ (3) the role of mental processes
_____ (4) the role of the unconscious and early childhood experience
_____ (5) the importance of the individual's own subjective experience
_____ (6) the role of social and cultural influences
_____ (7) the role of inherited tendencies that have proved adaptive in humans
a. psychoanalytic
b. biological
c. behavioral
d. cognitive
e. humanistic
f. evolutionary
g. sociocultural

Section Two: Who Said This?

Read each statement below and then, in the blank that follows, identify the person mentioned in Chapter 1 who would be most likely to make the statement.

1. I thought that behavior could be explained by analyzing the conditions that were present before it occurs and the consequences it produces. _____

2. I established the first psychological laboratory in Leipzig, Germany. _____

3. I wrote *Principles of Psychology* and advocated functionalism. _____

4. I introduced the term *behaviorism.* _____

5. I proposed a theory of motivation that consists of a hierarchy of needs. _____

6. I was the first African American to earn a PhD in psychology. _____

7. I became the first female president of the American Psychological Association. _____

8. I invented a popular form of psychotherapy called *client-centered therapy.* _____

9. I demonstrated the phi phenomenon. _____

Section Three: Fill In the Blank

1. A _____ is a general principle or set of principles proposed to explain how a number of separate facts are related.

2. Dr. Smith is interested in using _____ _____ to study cooperative versus competitive play in children in nursery school. To accomplish this, she is going to observe and record children's play behaviors at nursery school without attempting to influence or control the behaviors.

3. Dr. Jones is interested in learning about college students in the United States who begin their education after the age of 30. He knows that there are many such students and that he will not be able to study them all, so he decides to carefully define this _____ _____ (the group to which he hopes to generalize his findings) and then study a _____ _____ of these students. He hopes this approach will allow him to make accurate generalizations.

4. A psychologist believes there is an important relationship between test anxiety and test performance. Her _____ predicts that higher levels of anxiety will interfere with test performance.

5. To test her prediction, the psychologist in question 4 randomly assigns psychology students to two different groups. One group is told that the test they are about to take will determine over half of their semester grade. The other group is told that the test will have no bearing on their grade but will help the psychologist prepare better lectures. The psychologist believes the two groups will have different levels of anxiety and that the first group will perform less well than the second group on a standardized psychology test. In this experiment, the _____ variable is the pretest instructions, and the _____ variable is the test scores.

6. Psychologists who use the _____ approach are interested in how social and cultural variables influence individual behavior.

7. Correlations can be useful in allowing you to make _____ but should not be used to draw conclusions about _____ and _____ .

8. The first formal school of psychology was known as _____, and members of this school were interested in analyzing the basic elements, or structure, of conscious mental experience.

9. Another early school of psychology was _____. Psychologists who used this approach were interested in how mental processes help humans and animals adapt to their environments.

10. The school of psychology that emphasizes the role of unconscious mental forces and conflicts in determining behavior is known as _____.

11. The _____ perspective in psychology studies the role of mental processes–perception, thinking, and memory–in behavior.

12. Sigmund Freud is associated with the _____ perspective in psychology.

13. According to the text, _____ psychologists make up the largest percentage of members of the American Psychological Association.

Section Four: Comprehensive Practice Test

1. Which of the following psychological perspectives likened human mental life to an iceberg?
   a. behaviorism   c. humanistic psychology
   b. psychoanalysis   d. structuralism

2. _____ is the approach to psychology that arose from the belief that the study of the mind and consciousness was not scientific.
   a. Structuralism   c. Humanism
   b. Behaviorism   d. Psychoanalysis

3. The _____ perspective in psychology would explain behavior by referring to the operation of the brain and the central nervous system.
   a. evolutionary   c. behavioral
   b. structuralist   d. biological

4. A _____ psychologist specializes in the diagnosis and treatment of mental and behavioral disorders.
   a. social   c. clinical
   b. developmental   d. cognitive

5. "The whole is perceived as greater than the sum of its parts" is a statement you would be most likely to hear from a _____ psychologist.
   a. behavioral   c. Gestalt
   b. cognitive   d. developmental

6. Description, explanation, prediction, and control of behavior and mental processes are the _____ of psychology.
   a. reasons   c. perspectives
   b. goals   d. methods

7. In an experiment, a researcher would use the double-blind approach to control for _____ .
  a. experimenter bias   **c.** selection bias
  b. placebo bias   **d.** random bias

8. Jack believes that he did not do well on his test because the test had nothing to do with the subject matter of the class. Jack doubts the _____ of the test.
  a. reliability   **c.** standardization
  b. accuracy   **d.** validity

9. If a researcher wants to establish evidence for a cause-effect relationship between variables, he should use _____ .
  a. naturalistic observation
  b. correlation
  c. the experimental method
  d. the survey method

10. Which of the following psychologists is associated with the humanistic perspective?
  a. Maslow   **c.** Watson
  b. Darwin   **d.** Freud

11. Researchers who are interested in the adaptive significance of behavior are known as _____ psychologists.
  a. cognitive
  b. humanistic
  c. evolutionary
  d. psychoanalytic

12. A social psychologist would be most interested in how individuals behave in isolated settings, such as when they are alone at home. (true/false)

13. Basic research is aimed at solving practical problems and improving the quality of life. (true/false)

14. Watson would suggest that Freud's psychological approach is invalid because of Freud's emphasis on unconscious motivation and other mental events. (true/false)

15. In an experiment, the experimental group is exposed to all aspects of the treatment except the independent variable. (true/false)

16. Structuralism used introspection to study the basic elements of conscious mental experience. (true/false)

17. A test gives very different results for the same test taker each time it is administered. This test would be said to have poor reliability. (true/false)

18. The best way to establish a cause-effect relationship between variables is to use the case study method because that method gives a researcher an in-depth knowledge of the subject matter from spending so much time with just a few participants. (true/false)

19. A researcher is studying the relationship between styles of computer keyboards and typing accuracy. In this case, the dependent variable is the different types of computer keyboards included in the study. (true/false)

20. You would probably expect to find a negative correlation between the number of alcoholic drinks consumed and the number of accidents a participant has while being tested on an experimental driving simulator. (true/false)

21. The proportion of minorities in the field of psychology is lower than that in the overall U.S. population. (true/false)

Section Five: Critical Thinking

1. Consider three of the major forces in psychology: behaviorism, psychoanalysis, and humanistic psychology. Which appeals to you most and which least, and why?

2. Suppose you hear on the news that a researcher claims to have "proven" that day care is harmful to infants. How could you use what you've learned in this chapter about research methods to evaluate this statement?

3. If you became a psychologist, in which area (developmental, educational, clinical, counseling, social, etc.) would you specialize? Why?

Biology and Behavior

On September 13, 1848, Phineas Gage, a 25-year-old foreman on a railroad construction crew, was using dynamite to blast away rock and dirt. Suddenly, an unplanned explosion almost took Gage's head off, sending a 3½-foot-long, 13-pound metal rod under his left cheekbone and out through the top of his skull. (The computer-generated image shows the path the rod took through Gage's skull.)

Much of the brain tissue in Gage's frontal lobe was torn away, along with pieces of flesh and fragments of his skull. This should have been the end of Phineas Gage, but it wasn't. He regained consciousness within a few minutes and was loaded onto a cart and wheeled to his hotel nearly a mile away. He got out with a little help, walked up the stairs, entered his room, and walked to his bed. He was still conscious when the doctor arrived nearly 2 hours later.

Gage recovered in about 5 weeks, but he was not the same man. Before the accident, he was described as a hard worker who was polite, dependable, and well-liked. But the new Phineas Gage, without part of his frontal lobe, was found to be loud-mouthed and profane, rude and impulsive, and contemptuous toward others. He no longer planned realistically for the future and was no longer motivated and industrious, as he once had been. Gage lost his job as foreman and joined P. T. Barnum's circus as a sideshow exhibit at carnivals and county fairs. (Adapted from Harlow, 1848.)

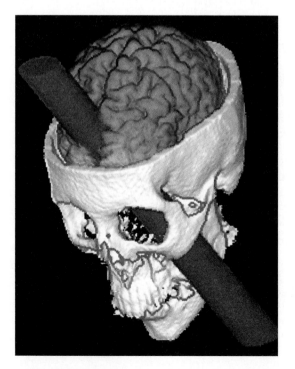

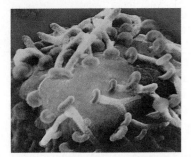

How can the brain sustain such massive damage as in the case of Gage, who survived, while a small bullet fired through the brain in any one of a number of different places can result in instant death? In this chapter, you will learn how this remarkable 3-pound organ can be so tough and resilient and, at the same time, so fragile and vulnerable.

The Neurons and the Neurotransmitters

The Neurons

All our thoughts, feelings, and behavior can ultimately be traced to the activity of **neurons**—the specialized cells that conduct impulses through the nervous system. Most experts estimate that there may be as many as 100 billion neurons in the brain (Swanson, 1995). *Afferent (sensory) neurons* relay messages from the sense organs and receptors—eyes, ears, nose, mouth, and skin—to the brain or spinal cord. *Efferent (motor) neurons* convey signals from the central nervous system to the glands and the muscles, enabling the body to move. *Interneurons,* thousands of times more numerous than motor or sensory neurons, carry information between neurons in the central nervous system.

Although no two neurons are exactly alike, nearly all are made up of three parts. The **cell body** contains the nucleus and carries out the metabolic, or life-sustaining, functions of the neuron. Branching out from the cell body are the **dendrites,** which look much like the leafless branches of a tree. The dendrites are the primary receivers of signals from other neurons, but the cell body can also receive signals directly. The **axon** is the slender, tail-like extension of the neuron that sprouts into many branches, each ending in a bulbous axon terminal. The signals move from the axon terminals to the dendrites or cell bodies of other neurons and to muscles, glands, and other parts of the body. In humans, some axons are short—only thousandths of an inch. Others can be up to a meter (39.37 inches) long—long enough to reach from the brain to the tip of the spinal cord or from the spinal cord to remote parts of the body. Figure 2.1 shows a neuron's structure.

Glial cells are specialized cells that hold the neurons together. They are smaller than neurons and make up more than half of the volume of the human brain. Glial cells remove waste products such as dead neurons from the brain by engulfing and digesting them, and they handle other metabolic and cleanup tasks.

Neurons are not physically connected. The axon terminals are separated from the receiving neurons by tiny, fluid-filled gaps called *synaptic clefts.* The **synapse** is the junction where the axon terminal of a sending (presynaptic) neuron communicates with a receiving (postsynaptic) neuron across the synaptic cleft. There may be as many as 100 trillion synapses in the human nervous system (Swanson, 1995).

And a single neuron may synapse with thousands of other neurons (Kelner, 1997). But if neurons aren't connected, how do they communicate with one another?

Every time you move a muscle, experience a sensation, or have a thought or a feeling, a small but measurable electrical impulse has occurred. How does this biological electricity work? Even though the impulse that travels down the axon is electrical, the axon does not transmit it in the way a wire conducts an electrical current. What actually happens is that the cell membrane of the neuron changes in a way that makes it easier for molecules to move through it and into the cell; the membrane becomes more *permeable*. This process allows ions (electrically charged atoms or molecules) to easily move into and out of the axon.

Body fluids contain ions, some with positive electrical charges and others with negative electrical charges. Inside the axon, there are normally more negative than positive ions. When at rest (not firing), the axon membrane carries a negative electrical potential (or charge) of about -70 millivolts (70 thousandths of a volt) relative to the fluid outside the cell. This slight negative charge is referred to as the neuron's **resting potential.**

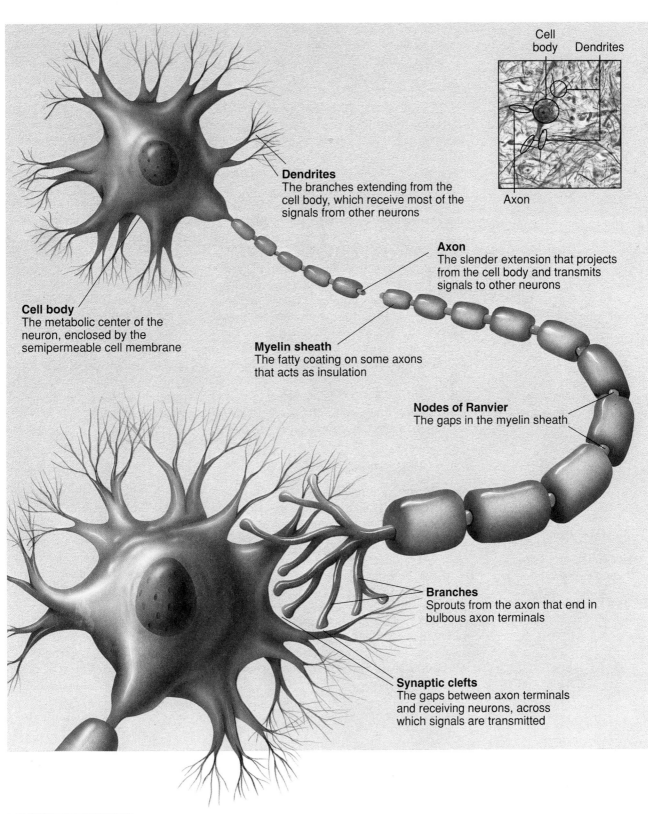

Dendrites
The branches extending from the cell body, which receive most of the signals from other neurons

Cell body   Dendrites

Axon

Axon
The slender extension that projects from the cell body and transmits signals to other neurons

Cell body
The metabolic center of the neuron, enclosed by the semipermeable cell membrane

Myelin sheath
The fatty coating on some axons that acts as insulation

Nodes of Ranvier
The gaps in the myelin sheath

Branches
Sprouts from the axon that end in bulbous axon terminals

Synaptic clefts
The gaps between axon terminals and receiving neurons, across which signals are transmitted

➤ **Figure 2.1**

The Structure of a Typical Neuron

A typical neuron has three major parts: (1) a cell body, which carries out the metabolic functions of the neuron; (2) branched fibers called dendrites, which are the primary receivers of impulses from other neurons; and (3) a slender, tail-like extension called an axon, the transmitting end of the neuron, which ends in many branches, each with an axon terminal. The photograph shows human neurons greatly magnified.

When a neuron is sufficiently stimulated by an incoming signal, ion channels begin to open in the cell membrane on the axon at the point closest to the cell body, allowing positive ions to flow into the axon. This inflow of positive ions causes the membrane potential to change abruptly, to a positive value of about +50 millivolts (Pinel, 2000). This sudden reversal of the resting potential, which lasts for about 1 millisecond (1 thousandth of a second), is the **action potential.** Then, the ion channels admitting positive ions close, and other ion channels open, forcing some positive ions out of the axon. As a result, the original negative charge, or resting potential, is restored. The opening and closing of ion channels continues segment by segment down the length of the axon, causing the action potential to move along the axon (Cardoso et al., 2000).

The action potential operates according to the all-or-none principle—a neuron either fires completely or does not fire at all. Immediately after a neuron fires, it enters a *refractory period,* during which it cannot fire again for 1 to 2 milliseconds. But this rest period is often very short: When stimulated, neurons can fire up to 1,000 times per second. The strength of an impulse is defined in terms of the number of neurons that fire and the rate at which they do so. A weak stimulus, such as feeling mildly anxious about taking a test, stimulates a small number of neurons to fire at a fairly slow rate. By contrast, a strong stimulus, such as encountering a possible mugger on a dark, deserted street, stimulates a large number of neurons to fire at a rapid rate.

The most important factor in speeding an impulse on its way is the **myelin sheath**—a white, fatty coating that is wrapped around some axons and acts as insulation. If you look again at Figure 2.1, you will see that the coating has numerous gaps, called *nodes of Ranvier.* The electrical impulse is retriggered, or regenerated, at each node (or gap) on the axon. This regeneration speeds the impulse along up to 100 times faster than in axons without a myelin sheath.

Neurotransmitters

Messages are transmitted between neurons by one or more of a large group of chemical substances known as **neurotransmitters.** Inside the axon terminal are many small, sphere-shaped containers with thin membranes, called *synaptic vesicles,* which hold the neurotransmitters. (*Vesicle* comes from a Latin word meaning "little bladder.") When an action potential arrives at the axon terminal, synaptic vesicles move toward the cell membrane, fuse with it, and release their neurotransmitter molecules. This process is shown in Figure 2.2.

Each neurotransmitter has a distinctive molecular shape, and **receptors** on the surfaces of dendrites and cell bodies also have distinctive shapes. Neurotransmitters can affect only those neurons that have receptors designed to receive molecules of their particular shape. In other words, each receptor is somewhat like a locked door that only certain neurotransmitter keys can unlock (Cardoso et al., 2000; Restak, 1993).

However, the neurons in the brain that have receptors are living matter; they can expand and contract the volumes of their receptors in response to neurotransmitters. The interaction between the neurotransmitter and the receptor is controlled not by the direct influence of one on the other, but by their *mutual* influence on each other. In such a dynamic interplay, neurotransmitters of slightly different shape may be competing for the same receptor. The receptor will admit only one of the competing neurotransmitters—the one that fits it most perfectly. Thus, a receptor may receive a certain neurotransmitter at one time, but not at other times when other, better-fitting neurotransmitter molecules are present.

When neurotransmitters bind with receptors, their action is either excitatory (influencing the neurons to fire) or inhibitory (influencing them not to fire). Because a single neuron may synapse with thousands of other neurons at the same time, there will always be both excitatory and inhibitory influences on a receiving neuron. For the neuron to fire, the excitatory influences of certain neurotransmitters must exceed the inhibitory influences of other neurotransmitters by a sufficient amount (the threshold).

What is the action potential?

action potential
The sudden reversal of the resting potential, which initiates the firing of a neuron.

myelin sheath
(MY-uh-lin) The white fatty coating wrapped around some axons that acts as insulation and enables impulses to travel much faster than they do in unsheathed axons.

What are neurotransmitters, and what role do they play in the transmission of signals from one neuron to another?

neurotransmitter
(NEW-ro-TRANS-mit-er) A chemical that is released into the synaptic cleft from the axon terminal of a sending neuron, crosses the synapse, and binds to appropriate receptor sites on the dendrites or cell body of a receiving neuron, influencing that cell either to fire or not to fire.

receptors
Sites on the dendrite or cell body of a neuron that will interact only with specific neurotransmitters.

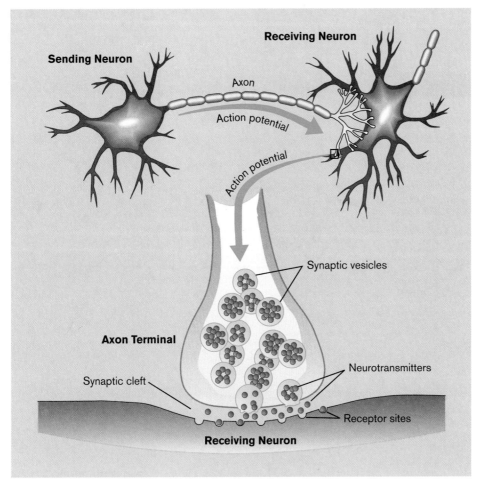

When a neuron fires, the action potential arrives at the axon terminal and triggers the release of neurotransmitters from the synaptic vesicles. Neurotransmitters flow into the synaptic cleft and move toward the receiving neuron, which has numerous receptors. The receptors bind only with neurotransmitters having distinctive molecular shapes that match theirs. Neurotransmitters influence receiving neurons to fire or not to fire.

You may wonder how the synaptic vesicles can continue to pour out neurotransmitters, yet have a ready supply so that the neuron can respond to continuing stimulation. First, the cell body of the neuron is always working to manufacture more of the neurotransmitter molecules. Second, unused neurotransmitter molecules in the synaptic cleft may be broken down into their components and reclaimed by the axon terminal to be recycled and used again. Third, by an important process called **reuptake,** a neurotransmitter can be taken back into the axon terminal, intact and ready for immediate use. This terminates the neurotransmitter's excitatory or inhibitory effect on the receiving neuron.

The Effects of Drugs on Neural Transmission

For any drug to work, it must influence activity at the level of the cell. Like neurotransmitters, drugs are chemicals. Some of them (*agonists*) fit specific receptors on the cell and mimic some of the effects of neurotransmitters; others (*antagonists*) block the cell's receptors so that neurotransmitters are prevented from having their normal effects. Still other drugs increase the effectiveness of neurotransmitters in the synapse by interfering with their reuptake or by slowing their breakdown in the synaptic cleft.

The Variety of Neurotransmitters

Researchers have identified 75 or more chemical substances that are manufactured in the brain, spinal cord, glands, and other parts of the body and may act as neurotransmitters (Greden, 1994). One of the most important is **acetylcholine** (Ach).

reuptake
The process by which neurotransmitter molecules are taken from the synaptic cleft back into the axon terminal for later use, thus terminating their excitatory or inhibitory effect on the receiving neuron.

acetylcholine
(ah-SEET-ul-KOH-leen) A neurotransmitter that plays a role in learning, memory, and rapid eye movement (REM) sleep and causes the skeletal muscle fibers to contract.

What are some of the major neurotransmitters and what are some of the ways in which they affect behavior?

Major Neurotransmitters and Their Functions

NEUROTRANSMITTER	FUNCTIONS
Acetylcholine (Ach)	Affects movement, learning, memory, REM sleep
Dopamine (DA)	Affects movement, attention, learning, reinforcement
Norepinephrine (NE)	Affects eating, alertness, wakefulness
Epinephrine	Affects metabolism of glucose, energy release during exercise
Serotonin	Affects mood, sleep, appetite, impulsivity, aggression
Glutamate	Active in areas of the brain involved in learning, thought, and emotion
GABA	Facilitates neural inhibition in the central nervous system
Endorphins	Provide relief from pain; feelings of pleasure and well-being

dopamine
(DOE-pah-meen) A neurotransmitter that plays a role in learning, attention, and movement.

norepinephrine
(nor-EP-ih-NEF-rin) A neurotransmitter affecting eating and sleep.

epinephrine
(EP-ih-NEF-rin) A neurotransmitter that affects the metabolism of glucose and causes energy stored in muscles to be released during exercise.

serotonin
(ser-oh-TOE-nin) A neurotransmitter that plays an important role in regulating mood, sleep, impulsivity, aggression, and appetite.

This neurotransmitter exerts excitatory effects on cells in the skeletal muscle fibers, causing them to contract so that the body can move. But acetylcholine has an inhibitory effect on the cells in muscle fibers in the heart, which keeps the heart from beating too rapidly. Differences in the receptors on the postsynaptic (receiving) neurons in skeletal and heart muscles cause these opposite effects. Acetylcholine also plays an excitatory role in stimulating the neurons involved in learning new information.

Dopamine (DA), one of four neurotransmitters called *monoamines,* produces both excitatory and inhibitory effects and is involved in several functions, including learning, attention, movement, and reinforcement. Neuroscientists have learned that many of the neurons in the brains of patients with Parkinson's disease and schizophrenia are less sensitive to the effects of dopamine than is typical in those who do not suffer from these disorders (Kurup & Kurup, 2002).

The other three monoamines also serve important functions. **Norepinephrine** (NE) has an effect on eating habits (it stimulates the intake of carbohydrates) and plays a major role in alertness and wakefulness. **Epinephrine** complements norepinephrine by affecting the metabolism of glucose and causing the glucose stored in muscles to be released during strenuous exercise. **Serotonin** plays an important role in regulating mood, sleep, impulsivity, aggression, and appetite.

Two amino acids that serve as neurotransmitters are more common than any other transmitter in the central nervous system. *Glutamate* is the primary excitatory neurotransmitter in the brain (Riedel, 1996). It may be released by about 40% of the brain's neurons and is active in areas of the brain involved in learning, thought, and emotions (Coyle & Draper, 1996). *GABA* is the main inhibitory neurotransmitter in the brain (Miles, 1999). It is thought to facilitate the control of anxiety in humans. Tranquilizers, barbiturates, and alcohol appear to have a calming and relaxing effect because they bind with and stimulate one type of GABA receptor and thus increase GABA's anxiety-controlling effect. An abnormality in the neurons that secrete GABA is believed to be one of the causes of epilepsy, a serious neurological disorder in which neural activity can become so heightened that seizures result.

More than 25 years ago, Candace Pert and her fellow researchers (1974) demonstrated that a localized region of the brain contains neurons with receptors that respond to the opiates—drugs such as opium, morphine, and heroin. Later, it was learned that the brain itself produces its own opiatelike substances, known as **endorphins.** Endorphins provide relief from pain or the stress of vigorous exercise and produce feelings of pleasure and well-being. "Runner's high" is attributed to the release of endorphins. (See Chapter 3 for more information on endorphins.)

Review and Reflect 2.1 summarizes the major neurotransmitters and their functions.

endorphins
(en-DOOR-fins) Chemicals produced naturally by the brain that reduce pain and positively affect mood.

central nervous system (CNS)
The brain and the spinal cord.

spinal cord
An extension of the brain, extending from the base of the brain through the entire spinal column, that transmits messages between the brain and the peripheral nervous system.

The Central Nervous System

The nervous system is divided into two parts: (1) the **central nervous system (CNS),** which is composed of the brain and the spinal cord, and (2) the peripheral nervous system, which connects the central nervous system to all other parts of the body (see Figure 2.3). We will begin by focusing on the CNS.

The Spinal Cord: An Extension of the Brain

The **spinal cord** can best be thought of as an extension of the brain. A cylinder of neural tissue about the diameter of your little finger, the spinal cord extends from the base of the brain down through the hollow center of the spinal column. The spinal cord is protected by bone and also by spinal fluid, which serves as a shock absorber. The spinal cord literally links the body with the

◀ Why is an intact spinal cord important to normal functioning?

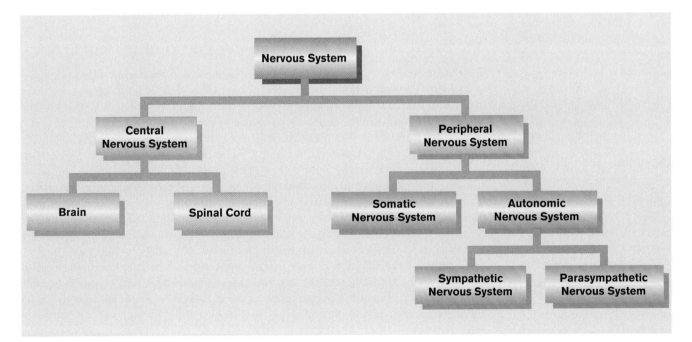

➤ Figure 2.3

Divisions of the Human Nervous System

The human nervous system is divided into two parts: the central nervous system and the peripheral nervous system. The diagram shows the relationships among the parts of the nervous system and provides a brief description of the functions of those parts. The central nervous system is highlighted.

Figure 2.4

Major Structures of the Human Brain

Some of the major structures of the brain are shown in the drawing, and a brief description of the function of each is provided. The brainstem contains the medulla, the reticular formation, and the pons.

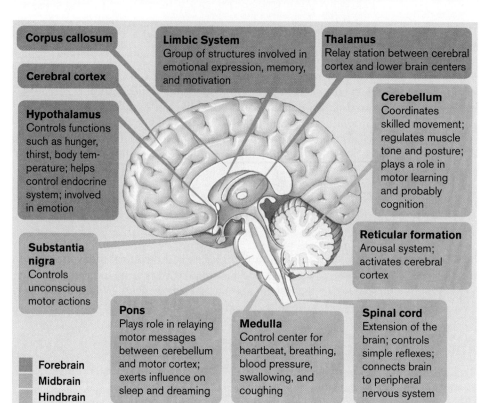

Corpus callosum

Cerebral cortex

Limbic System
Group of structures involved in emotional expression, memory, and motivation

Thalamus
Relay station between cerebral cortex and lower brain centers

Hypothalamus
Controls functions such as hunger, thirst, body temperature; helps control endocrine system; involved in emotion

Cerebellum
Coordinates skilled movement; regulates muscle tone and posture; plays a role in motor learning and probably cognition

Substantia nigra
Controls unconscious motor actions

Reticular formation
Arousal system; activates cerebral cortex

Forebrain
Midbrain
Hindbrain

Pons
Plays role in relaying motor messages between cerebellum and motor cortex; exerts influence on sleep and dreaming

Medulla
Control center for heartbeat, breathing, blood pressure, swallowing, and coughing

Spinal cord
Extension of the brain; controls simple reflexes; connects brain to peripheral nervous system

brainstem
The structure that begins at the point where the spinal cord enlarges as it enters the brain and that includes the medulla, the reticular formation, and the pons.

medulla
(muh-DUL-uh) The part of the brainstem that controls heartbeat, blood pressure, breathing, coughing, and swallowing.

What are the crucial functions handled by the brainstem?

reticular formation
A structure in the brainstem that plays a crucial role in arousal and attention and that screens sensory stimuli entering the brain.

cerebellum
(sehr-uh-BELL-um) The brain structure that executes smooth, skilled body movements and regulates muscle tone and posture

What are the primary functions of the cerebellum?

brain. It transmits messages between the brain and the peripheral nervous system. Thus, sensory information can reach the brain, and messages from the brain can be sent to the muscles, the glands, and other parts of the body.

The Brainstem: The Most Primitive Part of the Brain

Brain structures are often grouped into three areas known as *hindbrain, midbrain,* and *forebrain.* The **brainstem,** a major component of the hindbrain, begins at the point where the spinal cord enlarges as it enters the skull, as shown in Figure 2.4. The brainstem handles functions so critical to physical survival that damage to it is life-threatening. The **medulla** is the part of the brainstem that controls automatic functions such as heartbeat, breathing, blood pressure, coughing, and swallowing.

Extending through the central core of the brainstem is another important structure, the **reticular formation,** sometimes called the *reticular activating system* (RAS). The reticular formation regulates attention and alertness, blocking irrelevant messages and sending relevant ones on for processing in the brain (Kinomura et al., 1996; Steriade, 1996). That is why parents may be able to sleep through a thunderstorm but will awaken to the slightest cry of their baby.

Above the medulla and at the top of the brainstem is a bridgelike structure called the pons that extends across the top front of the brainstem and connects to both halves of the cerebellum. The pons plays a role in body movement and also exerts an influence on sleep and dreaming.

The Cerebellum: A Must for Graceful Movement

The **cerebellum,** another component of the hindbrain, makes up about 10% of the brain's volume. The cerebellum is critically important to the body's ability to execute smooth, skilled movements; it also regulates muscle tone and posture. Furthermore, it has been found to play a role in motor learning and in retaining memories of motor activities and may be involved in more complex learning as well

(Ellis, 2001). The cerebellum guides the graceful movements of ballet dancers and coordinates the series of movements necessary to perform many simple activities—such as walking in a straight line or touching your finger to the tip of your nose—without conscious effort. When people have damage to their cerebellum or are temporarily impaired by too much alcohol, such simple acts may be difficult or impossible to perform.

The Midbrain

As shown in Figure 2.4, the *midbrain* lies between the hindbrain and forebrain. The structures of this brain region act primarily as relay stations through which the basic physiological functions of the hindbrain are linked to the cognitive functions of the forebrain. For example, when you burn your finger on a hot pan, the physical feeling travels through the nerves of your hand and arm, eventually reaching the spinal cord. From there, they are sent through the midbrain to the forebrain where they are interpreted ("Better drop that hot pan because this hurts a lot and may result in serious injury!").

The *substantia nigra* is located in the midbrain. This structure is composed of the darkly colored nuclei of nerve cells that control unconscious motor actions. When you ride a bicycle or walk up stairs without giving your movements any conscious thought, the nuclei of the cells that allow you to do so are found in the substantia nigra. Recent research indicates that deficiencies in the responsiveness of those cells to various neurotransmitters may explain the inability of patients with Parkinson's disease to control their physical movements (Trevitt et al., 2002).

The Thalamus and the Hypothalamus

Above the brainstem lie two extremely important structures: the thalamus and the hypothalamus (refer again to Figure 2.4). The **thalamus,** which consists of two egg-shaped structures, primarily serves as the relay station for virtually all the information that flows into and out of centers of the forebrain, including sensory information for all the senses except smell. (You'll learn more about the sense of smell in Chapter 3.) The thalamus also affects the ability to learn new verbal information and plays a role in the production of language. Another function of the thalamus is the regulation of sleep cycles, which is thought to be accomplished in cooperation with the pons and the reticular formation. The majority of people who have had acute brain injury and remain in an unresponsive "vegetative state" have also suffered significant damage to the thalamus, to the neural tissue connecting it to forebrain centers, or to both (Adams et al., 2000).

The **hypothalamus** lies directly below the thalamus and weighs only about 2 ounces. It regulates hunger, thirst, sexual behavior, and a wide variety of emotional behaviors. The hypothalamus also regulates internal body temperature, starting the process that causes you to perspire when you are too hot and to shiver (conserve body heat) when you are too cold. It also houses the biological clock—the mechanism responsible for the timing of the sleep/wakefulness cycle and the daily fluctuations in more than 100 body functions (Ginty et al., 1993; Salin-Pascual et al., 2001). The physiological changes in the body that accompany strong emotions—sweaty palms, a pounding heart, a hollow feeling in the pit of your stomach—are initiated by neurons concentrated primarily in the hypothalamus.

The Limbic System

The **limbic system,** shown in Figure 2.5 (on page 42), is a group of structures deep within the brain, including the amygdala and the hippocampus, that are collectively involved in emotional expression, memory, and motivation. The **amygdala** plays an important role in emotion, particularly in response to unpleasant or punishing stimuli (LeDoux, 1994, 2000). Damage to the amygdala can impair a person's ability to recognize facial expressions and tones of voice that are associated with fear and anger (LeDoux, 2000; Scott et al., 1997).

thalamus
(THAL-uh-mus) The structure, located above the brainstem, that acts as a relay station for information flowing into or out of the forebrain.

hypothalamus
(HY-po-THAL-uh-mus) A small but influential brain structure that controls the pituitary gland and regulates hunger, thirst, sexual behavior, body temperature, and a wide variety of emotional behaviors.

What is the function of the substantia nigra?

What is the primary role of the thalamus?

limbic system
A group of structures deep within the brain, including the amygdala and hippocampus, that are collectively involved in emotion, memory, and motivation.aversive stimuli.

What are some of the processes regulated by the hypothalamus?

amygdala
(ah-MIG-da-la) A structure in the limbic system that plays an important role in emotion, particularly in response to aversive stimuli.

What is the role of the limbic system?

➤ Figure 2.5

The Principal Structures in the Limbic System

The amygdala plays an important role in emotion; the hippocampus is essential in the formation of conscious memory.

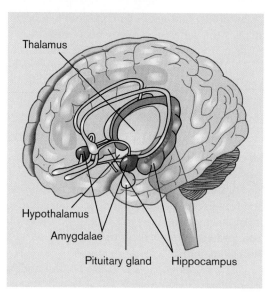

hippocampus

(hip-po-CAM-pus) A structure in the limbic system that plays a central role in the formation of long-term memories.

The **hippocampus** is another important brain structure of the limbic system. The hippocampus plays a central role in the formation of new memories (Eichenbaum, 1997; Gluck & Myers, 1997; McIntyre et al., 2002; Vargha-Khadem et al., 1997), as you will learn in Chapter 6.

The Cerebral Hemispheres

> What are the cerebral hemispheres, the corpus callosum, and the cerebral cortex?

The most essentially human part of the magnificent 3-pound human brain is the cerebrum and its cortex. Like a walnut, which has two matched halves connected to each other, the **cerebrum** is composed of two **cerebral hemispheres**—a left and a right hemisphere resting side by side (see Figure 2.6). The two hemispheres are physically connected at the bottom by a thick band of nerve fibers called the **corpus callosum.** This connection makes possible the transfer of information and the coordination of activity between the hemispheres. In general, the right cerebral hemisphere controls movement and feeling on the left side of the body, and the left hemisphere controls the right side of the body. In over 95% of people, the left hemisphere also controls the language functions.

The cerebral hemispheres have a thin outer covering about $\frac{1}{8}$ inch thick called the **cerebral cortex,** which is primarily responsible for the higher mental processes of language, memory, and thinking. The presence of the cell bodies of billions of neurons in the cortex gives it a grayish appearance. Thus, the cortex is often referred to as *gray matter*. Immediately beneath the cortex are the white myelinated axons (referred to as *white matter*) that connect the neurons of the cortex with those of other brain regions. Research by Andreason and others (1994) indicates that the amount of gray matter is positively correlated with human intelligence.

In humans, the cortex is very large—if it were spread out flat, it would measure about 2 feet by 3 feet. Because the cortex is roughly three times the size of the cerebrum itself, it does not fit smoothly around the cerebrum. Rather, it has numerous folds called *convolutions*. About two-thirds of the cortex is hidden from view in the folds. The cortex of less intelligent animals is much smaller in proportion to total brain size and, therefore, is much less convoluted (folded).

The cerebral cortex can be divided into three types of areas: (1) sensory input areas, where vision, hearing, touch, pressure, and temperature register; (2) motor areas, which control voluntary movement; and (3) **association areas,** which house memories and are involved in thought, perception, and language.

Each of the cerebral hemispheres consists of four lobes—the frontal lobe, the parietal lobe, the occipital lobe, and the temporal lobe. Find them in Figure 2.7.

cerebrum

(seh-REE-brum) The largest structure of the human brain, consisting of the two cerebral hemispheres connected by the corpus callosum and covered by the cerebral cortex.

cerebral hemispheres

(seh-REE-brul) The right and left halves of the cerebrum, covered by the cerebral cortex and connected by the corpus callosum.

corpus callosum

(KOR-pus kah-LO-sum) The thick band of nerve fibers that connects the two cerebral hemispheres and makes possible the transfer of information and the synchronization of activity between them.

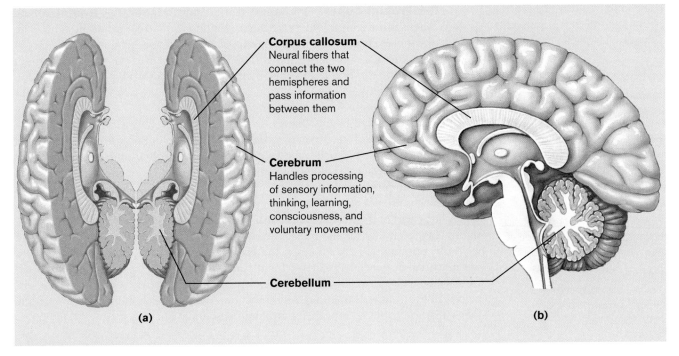

Corpus callosum
Neural fibers that connect the two hemispheres and pass information between them

Cerebrum
Handles processing of sensory information, thinking, learning, consciousness, and voluntary movement

Cerebellum

(a)   (b)

➤ Figure 2.6

Two Views of the Cerebral Hemispheres

(a) The two hemispheres rest side by side like two matched halves, physically connected by the corpus callosum. (b) An inside view of the right hemisphere.

cerebral cortex
(seh-REE-brul KOR-tex) The gray, convoluted covering of the cerebral hemispheres that is responsible for higher mental processes such as language, memory, and thinking.

association areas
Areas of the cerebral cortex that house memories and are involved in thought, perception, learning, and language.

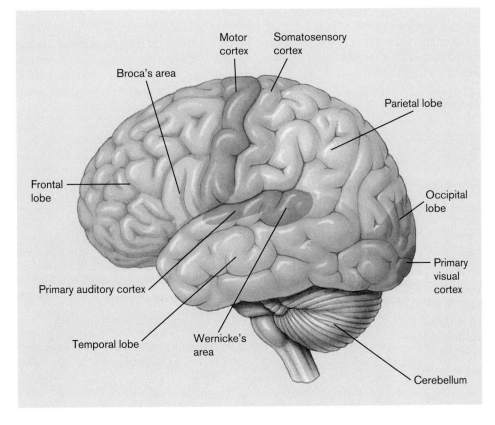

Broca's area

Motor cortex

Somatosensory cortex

Parietal lobe

Frontal lobe

Occipital lobe

Primary visual cortex

Primary auditory cortex

Temporal lobe

Wernicke's area

Cerebellum

➤ Figure 2.7

The Cerebral Cortex of the Left Hemisphere

The left cerebral hemisphere with its four lobes: (1) the frontal lobe, including the motor cortex and Broca's area; (2) the parietal lobe, with the somatosensory cortex; (3) the occipital lobe, with the primary visual cortex; and (4) the temporal lobe, with the primary auditory cortex and Wernicke's area.

What functions are located in the frontal lobes?

frontal lobes
The lobes of the brain that control voluntary body movements, speech production, and such functions as thinking, motivation, planning for the future, impulse control, and emotional responses.

motor cortex
The strip of tissue at the rear of the frontal lobes that controls voluntary body movement.

plasticity
The brain's ability to recover from damage and adapt to new demands.

What are the primary functions of the parietal lobes in general and the somatosensory cortex in particular?

parietal lobes
(puh-RY-uh-tul) The lobes of the brain that contain the somatosensory cortex (where touch, pressure, temperature, and pain register) and other areas that are responsible for body awareness and spatial orientation.

somatosensory cortex
(so-MAT-oh-SENS-or-ee) The strip of tissue at the front of the parietal lobes where touch, pressure, temperature, and pain register in the cerebral cortex.

The Frontal Lobes The largest of the brain's lobes, the **frontal lobes,** begin at the front of the brain and extend to the top center of the skull. The **motor cortex,** at the back edge of the frontal lobes (see Figure 2.7), controls voluntary body movements. The right motor cortex controls movement on the left side of the body, and the left motor cortex controls movement on the right side of the body.

Evidence has come to light showing that the motor cortex also participates in learning and cognitive events (Sanes & Donoghue, 2000). And the **plasticity**—the capacity to adapt and recover from damage—of the motor cortex is maintained throughout life. This plasticity allows synapses to strengthen and reorganize their interconnections when stimulated by experience and practice. Even mental rehearsal, or imaging, can produce changes in the motor cortex (Sanes & Donoghue, 2000), but these changes are not as large as those generated by real rehearsal or performance.

A large part of the frontal lobes consists of association areas involved in thinking, motivation, planning for the future, impulse control, and emotional responses. For example, one frontal lobe structure, the *anterior cingulate cortex,* monitors errors and the information needed to correct them (Luu et al., 2003). Further, damage to the frontal association areas produces changes in emotional responses. Phineas Gage, discussed in this chapter's opening, represents one case in which damage to the frontal lobes drastically altered impulse control and emotional responses.

The Parietal Lobes The **parietal lobes** are involved in the reception and processing of touch stimuli. The front strip of brain tissue in the parietal lobes is the **somatosensory cortex,** the site where touch, pressure, temperature, and pain register in the cortex (refer back to Figure 2.7). The somatosensory cortex also makes you aware of body movements and the positions of your limbs at any given moment.

The two halves of the somatosensory cortex, in the left and the right parietal lobes, are wired to opposite sides of the body. A person with damage to the somatosensory cortex of one hemisphere loses some sensitivity to touch on the opposite side of the body. If the damage is severe enough, the person might not be able to feel the difference between sandpaper and silk, or the affected part of the body might feel numb.

Association areas in the parietal lobes house memories of how objects feel against the human skin, a fact that explains why we can identify objects by touch. A person with damage to these areas could hold a computer mouse, a CD, or a baseball in his or her hand but not be able to identify the object by touch alone. Other parts of the parietal lobes are responsible for spatial orientation and sense of direction.

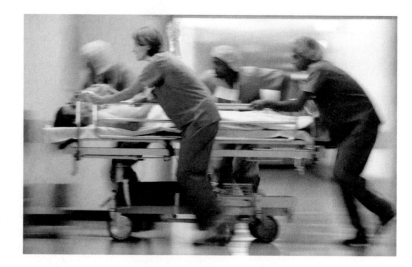

 Treatment of brain damage has come a long way since the days of Phineas Gage. Today, more than a million people are treated for head injuries in U.S. hospitals each year. Firearms and car crashes are the two leading causes of these injuries. Rapid treatment of head injury patients is one reason why more of them survive than in earlier times.

◀ Because the left hand of a professional string player must rapidly and accurately execute fine movements and slight pressure variations, it is not surprising that these musicians have an unusually large area of the somatosensory cortex dedicated to the fingers of that hand.

occipital lobes
(ahk-SIP-uh-tul) The lobes of the brain that contain the primary visual cortex, where vision registers, and association areas involved in the interpretation of visual information.

The Occipital Lobes Behind the parietal lobes, at the rear of the brain, lie the **occipital lobes,** which are involved in the reception and interpretation of visual information (refer back to Figure 2.7). At the very back of the occipital lobes is the **primary visual cortex,** the site where visual stimuli register in the cerebral cortex. Each eye is connected to the primary visual cortex in both the right and left occipital lobe. Look straight ahead and draw an imaginary line down the middle of what you see. Everything to the left of the line is referred to as the left visual field and registers in the right visual cortex. Everything to the right of the line is the right visual field and registers in the left visual cortex. A person who sustains damage to the primary visual cortex in one hemisphere will still have partial vision in both eyes because each eye sends information to both occipital lobes.

◀ What are the primary functions of the occipital lobes in general and the primary visual cortex in particular?

The association areas in the occipital lobes are involved in the interpretation of visual stimuli. The association areas hold memories of past visual experiences and enable us to recognize what is familiar among the things we see. When these areas are damaged, people can lose the ability to identify objects visually, although they are still able to identify the same objects by touch or through some other sense.

primary visual cortex
The area at the rear of the occipital lobes where vision registers in the cerebral cortex.

temporal lobes
The lobes of the brain that contain the primary auditory cortex and association areas for interpreting auditory information.

The Temporal Lobes The **temporal lobes,** located slightly above the ears, are involved in the reception and interpretation of auditory stimuli. The site in the cerebral cortex where hearing registers is known as the **primary auditory cortex.** The primary auditory cortex in each temporal lobe receives sound input from both ears. Injury to the primary auditory cortex in one temporal lobe thus results in reduced hearing in both ears; the destruction of this area in both lobes causes total deafness.

◀ What are the functions of the temporal lobes?

Association areas in the temporal lobes house memories of auditory stimuli and are involved in the interpretation of such stimuli. For example, the association area where your memories of various sounds are stored enables you to recognize your favorite band, a computer booting up, your roommate snoring, and so on. There is also a special association area in the right temporal lobe where familiar melodies are stored.

primary auditory cortex
The part of the temporal lobes where hearing registers in the cerebral cortex.

Specialized Functions of the Left Hemisphere Research has shown that some **lateralization** of the hemispheres exists; that is, each hemisphere is specialized to handle certain functions. For instance, in 95% of right-handers and about 62% of left-handers, the **left hemisphere** handles most of the language functions, includ-

lateralization
The specialization of one of the cerebral hemispheres to handle a particular function.

Try It ! 2.1   Hemispheric Interference

Get a meter stick or yardstick. Try balancing it vertically on the end of your left index finger, as shown in the drawing. Then try balancing it on your right index finger. Most people are better with their dominant hand—the right hand for right-handers, for example. Is this true for you?

Now try this: Begin reciting the ABCs out loud as fast as you can while balancing the stick with your *left hand.* Do you have less trouble this time? Why should that be? The right hemisphere controls the act of balancing with the left hand. However, your left hemisphere, though poor at controlling the left hand, still tries to coordinate your balancing efforts. When you distract the left hemisphere with a steady stream of talk, the right hemisphere can orchestrate more efficient balancing with your left hand without interference.

 What are the specialized functions of the left hemisphere?

left hemisphere
The hemisphere that controls the right side of the body, coordinates complex movements, and, in 95% of right-handers and 62% of left-handers, controls the production of speech and written language.

ing speaking, writing, reading, speech comprehension, and comprehension of the logic of written information (Long & Baynes, 2002). Damage to the left hemisphere often results in *aphasia,* or the loss of ability to produce or understand speech. Math and logic are other left hemisphere specialties.

Two brain regions that are critical to the left hemisphere's control of language functions are **Broca's area,** located in the left frontal lobe, and **Wernicke's area,** found in the left temporal lobe (look back at Figure 2.7). Both are named for the scientists who discovered them. When Broca's area is damaged, patients cannot produce speech or do so with great difficulty (*Broca's aphasia*). By contrast, when Wernicke's area is damaged, patients can speak, but their utterances do not make sense (*Wernicke's aphasia*).

Specialized Functions of the Right Hemisphere   The **right hemisphere** is generally considered to be more adept than the left hemisphere at visual-spatial relations. And the auditory cortex in the right hemisphere appears to be far better able to process music than the left (Zatorre et al., 2002). So, when you arrange your bedroom furniture or notice that your favorite song is being played on the radio, you are calling primarily on your right hemisphere.

To experience an effect of the specialization of the cerebral hemispheres, try your hand at *Try It! 2.1.*

 What are the specialized functions of the right hemisphere?

Broca's area
(BRO-kuz) The area in the left frontal lobe that controls the production of speech sounds.

Wernicke's area
The language area in the left temporal lobe that is involved in comprehension of the spoken word and in formulation of coherent speech and written language.

right hemisphere
The hemisphere that controls the left side of the body and that, in most people, is specialized for visual-spatial perception and for interpreting nonverbal behavior.

Patients with right hemisphere damage have problems with even simple spatial tasks, such as finding their way around in familiar places. And, though the left hemisphere is the "executive" when it comes to control of language, patients with right hemisphere damage may have difficulty understanding metaphors and may be insensitive to the emotional qualities of speech. Nonverbal language is also processed primarily in the right hemisphere (Kucharska-Pietura & Klimkowski, 2002). For example, the subtle clues that tell us someone is lying are processed in the right hemisphere (Etcoff, Ekman, Magee, & Frank, 2000).

Other consequences of right hemisphere damage include attentional deficits and blindness to objects in the left visual field, a condition called *unilateral neglect* (Deovell et al., 2000; Halligan & Marshall, 1994). Patients with this condition may eat only the food on the right side of the plate, read only the words on the right half of a page, groom only the right half of the body, or even deny that the arm on the side opposite the brain damage belongs to them (Bisiach, 1996; Chen-Sea, 2000; Posner, 1996; Tham et al., 2000). Interestingly, too, people who suffer from

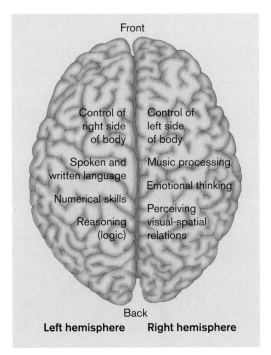

> Figure 2.8

Lateralized Functions of the Brain

Assigning functions to one hemisphere or the other allows the brain to function more efficiently.

right hemisphere damage view their chances for recovery more negatively than do those who have the same degree of impairment to the left hemisphere (Salo et al., 2002). These findings further illustrate the role of the right hemisphere in emotional thinking. Figure 2.8 summarizes the specializations of the left and right hemispheres.

The Split Brain   A few people have been born with no corpus callosum, and some have had their corpus callosum severed in a drastic surgical procedure called the **split-brain operation.** Neurosurgeons Joseph Bogen and Philip Vogel (1963) found that patients with severe epilepsy who suffered frequent and uncontrollable grand mal seizures could be helped by surgery that severed their corpus callosum, making communication between the two hemispheres impossible. The operation usually relieves the seizures and causes no loss of cognitive functioning or change in personality.

Research with split-brain patients by Roger Sperry (1964) revealed some fascinating findings. Look at Figure 2.9 (on page 48). In this illustration, a split-brain patient sits in front of a screen that separates the right and left fields of vision. If an image of an orange is flashed to the right field of vision, it registers in the left (verbal) hemisphere. If asked what he saw, the patient will readily reply, "I saw an orange." Suppose that, instead, an image of an apple is flashed to the left visual field and is relayed to the right (nonverbal) hemisphere. The patient will reply, "I saw nothing."

Why can the patient report that he saw the orange, but not the apple? Sperry maintains that in split-brain patients, only the verbal left hemisphere can report what it sees. In these experiments, the left hemisphere does not see what is flashed to the right hemisphere, and the right hemisphere is unable to report verbally what it has viewed. But did the right hemisphere actually see the apple that was flashed in the left visual field? Yes, because with his left hand (which is controlled by the right hemisphere), the patient can pick out by touch the apple or any other object shown to the right hemisphere. The right hemisphere knows and remembers what it sees just as well as the left, but unlike the left hemisphere, the right cannot name what it has seen. (In these experiments, images must be flashed for no more than $\frac{1}{10}$ or $\frac{1}{20}$ of a second so that the patients do not have time to refixate their eyes and send the information to the opposite hemisphere.)

split-brain operation
An operation, performed in severe cases of epilepsy, in which the corpus callosum is cut, separating the cerebral hemispheres and usually lessening the severity and frequency of grand mal seizures.

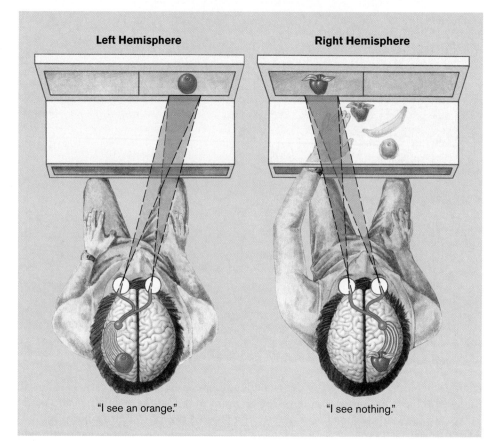

Left Hemisphere

Right Hemisphere

"I see an orange."

"I see nothing."

➤ **Figure 2.9**

Testing a Split-Brain Person

Using special equipment, researchers are able to study the independent functioning of the hemispheres in split-brain persons. In this experiment, when a visual image (an orange) is flashed on the right side of the screen, it is transmitted to the left (talking) hemisphere. When asked what he sees, the split-brain patient replies, "I see an orange." When an image (an apple) is flashed on the left side of the screen, it is transmitted only to the right (nonverbal) hemisphere. Because the split-brain patient's left (language) hemisphere did not receive the image, he replies, "I see nothing." But he can pick out the apple by touch if he uses his left hand, proving that the right hemisphere "saw" the apple. (Based on Gazzaniga, 1983.)

Discovering the Brain's Mysteries

What are some methods that researchers have used to learn about brain function?

Modern researchers need not rely solely on autopsies or wait for injuries to learn more about the human brain. Today, researchers are unlocking the brain's mysteries using the electroencephalograph (EEG), the microelectrode, and modern scanning techniques such as the CT scan, magnetic resonance imaging (MRI), the PET scan, functional MRI, and others.

The EEG and the Microelectrode

What is the electroencephalogram (EEG), and what are three of the brain-wave patterns it reveals?

In 1924, Austrian psychiatrist Hans Berger invented the electroencephalograph, a machine that amplifies a million times the electrical activity occurring in the brain. This electrical activity, detected by electrodes placed at various points on the scalp, provides the power to drive a pen across paper, producing a record of brain-wave activity called an **electroencephalogram (EEG).** The **beta wave** is the brain-wave pattern associated with mental or physical activity. The **alpha wave**

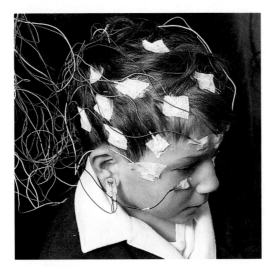

The electroencephalograph (EEG) uses electrodes placed on the scalp to amplify and record electrical activity in the brain.

is associated with deep relaxation, and the **delta wave** with slow-wave (deep) sleep. (You will learn more about these brain-wave patterns in Chapter 4.)

A computerized version of an EEG shows the different levels of electrical activity occurring every millisecond on the surface of the brain (Gevins et al., 1995). It can show an epileptic seizure in progress and can be used to study neural activity in people with learning disabilities, schizophrenia, Alzheimer's disease, sleep disorders, and other neurological problems.

Although the EEG is able to record electrical activity in different areas of the brain, it cannot reveal what is happening in individual neurons. The **microelectrode** can. A microelectrode is a wire so fine that it can be inserted near or into a single neuron without damaging it. Microelectrodes can be used to monitor the electrical activity of a neuron or to stimulate activity within it. Researchers have used microelectrodes to discover the exact functions of single cells within the primary visual cortex and the primary auditory cortex.

The CT Scan and Magnetic Resonance Imaging

The patient undergoing a **CT (computerized tomography) scan** is placed inside a large, doughnut-shaped structure in which an X-ray tube encircles the entire body. The tube rotates in a complete circle and shoots X rays through the brain (or other parts of the body) as it does so. A series of computerized, cross-sectional images reveal the structures within the brain, as well as abnormalities and injuries, including tumors and evidence of past or recent strokes.

Another scanning technique, **MRI (magnetic resonance imaging),** produces clearer and more detailed images than CT without exposing patients to potentially dangerous X rays. MRI can be used to find abnormalities in the central nervous system and in other systems of the body.

Although CT and MRI scans do a remarkable job of showing what the brain looks like both inside and out, they cannot reveal what the brain is doing. But other technological marvels can.

The PET Scan, fMRI, and Other Imaging Techniques

The **PET (positron-emission tomography) scan** is a powerful technique for identifying malfunctions that cause physical and psychological disorders and also for studying normal brain activity. A PET scan can map the patterns of blood flow, oxygen use, and glucose consumption (glucose is the brain's energy source). It can also show the action of drugs and other biochemical substances in the brain and other body organs (Farde, 1996).

A newer technique, **functional MRI (fMRI),** has several important advantages over PET: (1) It can image both brain structure and brain activity; (2) it requires no injections (of radioactive or other material); (3) it can image locations of activity more precisely

electroencephalogram (EEG)
(ee-lek-tro-en-SEFF-uh-lo-gram) A record of brain-wave activity made by a machine called an electroencephalograph.

beta wave
(BAY-tuh) The type of brain wave associated with mental or physical activity.

alpha wave
The type of brain wave associated with deep relaxation.

delta wave
The type of brain wave associated with slow-wave (deep) sleep.

microelectrode
An electrical wire so fine that it can be inserted near or into a single neuron.

CT (computerized tomography) scan
A brain-scanning technique that uses a rotating X-ray tube and high-speed computer analysis to produce slice-by-slice, cross-sectional images of the brain (or other body part).

MRI (magnetic resonance imaging)
A diagnostic scanning technique that produces high-resolution images of the structures of the brain.

PET (positron-emission tomography) scan
A brain-imaging technique that reveals activity in various parts of the brain based on the amounts of oxygen and glucose consumed.

functional MRI (fMRI)
A brain-imaging technique that reveals both brain structure and brain activity.

than PET can; and (4) it can detect changes that take place in less than a second, compared with about a minute for PET ("Brain imaging," 1997).

Still other imaging techniques are now available. SQUID (superconducting quantum interference device) shows brain activity by measuring magnetic changes produced by the electrical discharges of firing neurons. Another technique called MEG (magnetoencephalography) also measures magnetic changes produced by the electrical activity from firing neurons. MEG can image neural activity within the brain as rapidly as it occurs, much faster than PET or fMRI.

Brain-imaging techniques have helped neuroscientists develop an impressive store of knowledge about normal brain function. These techniques have also been used to show abnormal brain patterns that characterize certain psychiatric disorders and to reveal where and how various drugs affect the brain (Tamminga & Conley, 1997). And some neuroscientists are experimenting with combining fMRI and virtual reality to study how the brain responds to situations and environments that would be difficult or impossible to have participants actually experience in a lab (Travis, 1996).

The Peripheral Nervous System

The **peripheral nervous system (PNS)** is made up of all the nerves that connect the central nervous system to the rest of the body. It has two subdivisions: the

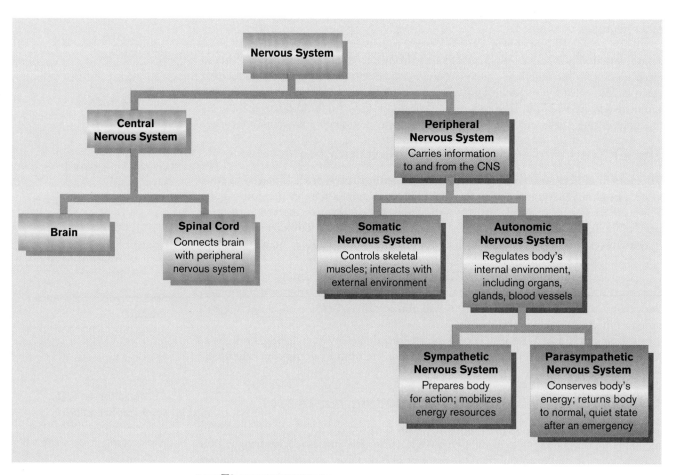

➤ Figure 2.10

Divisions of the Human Nervous System

The nervous system is divided into two parts: the central nervous system and the peripheral nervous system.

somatic nervous system and the autonomic nervous system. Figure 2.10 high-lights the subdivisions within the peripheral nervous system.

The *somatic nervous system* consists of (1) all the sensory nerves, which transmit information from the sensory receptors–eyes, ears, nose, tongue, and skin–to the central nervous system; and (2) all the motor nerves, which relay messages from the central nervous system to all the skeletal muscles of the body. In short, the nerves of the somatic nervous system make it possible for us to sense our environment and to move, and they are primarily under conscious control.

The *autonomic nervous system* operates without any conscious control or awareness on your part. It transmits messages between the central nervous system and the glands, the cardiac (heart) muscle, and the smooth muscles (such as those in the large arteries and the gastrointestinal system), which are not normally under voluntary control. The auto-nomic nervous system is further divided into two parts: the sympathetic and the parasympathetic nervous systems (see Figure 2.11).

Any time you are under stress or faced with an emergency, the **sympathetic nervous system** automatically mobilizes the body's resources, preparing you for action. This physiological arousal produced by the sympathetic nervous sys-

◄ What is the peripheral nervous system?

sympathetic nervous system
The division of the autonomic nervous system that mobilizes the body's resources during stress, emergencies, or heavy exertion, preparing the body for action.

◄ What are the roles of the sympathetic and parasympathetic nervous systems?

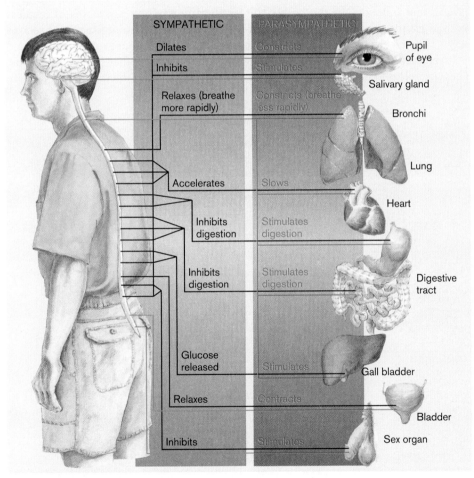

➤ Figure 2.11
The Autonomic Nervous System

The autonomic nervous system consists of (1) the sympathetic nervous system, which mobilizes the body's resources during emergencies or during stress; and (2) the parasympathetic nervous system, which is associated with relaxation and which brings the heightened bodily responses back to normal after an emergency. The diagram shows the opposite effects of the sympathetic and parasympathetic nervous systems on various parts of the body.

parasympathetic nervous system

The division of the autonomic nervous system that is associated with relaxation and the conservation of energy and that brings the heightened bodily responses back to normal following an emergency.

endocrine system

(EN-duh-krin) A number of duct-less glands located in various parts of the body that manufacture and secrete hormones into the bloodstream or lymph fluids, thus affecting cells in other parts of the body.

> What is the endocrine system, and what are some of the glands within it?

hormones

Substances that are manufactured and released in one part of the body but affect other parts of the body.

tem was named the *fight-or-flight response* by Walter Cannon (1929, 1935). If an ominous-looking stranger started following you down a dark, deserted street, your sympathetic nervous system would automatically set to work. Your heart would begin to pound, your pulse rate would increase rapidly, your breathing would quicken, and your digestive system would nearly shut down. The blood flow to your skeletal muscles would be enhanced, and all of your bodily resources would be made ready to handle the emergency—*run!*

But once the emergency is over, the **parasympathetic nervous system** brings these heightened bodily functions back to normal. As shown in Figure 2.11, the sympathetic and parasympathetic branches of the autonomic nervous system act as opposing but complementary forces. Their balanced functioning is essential for health and survival.

The Endocrine System

You have seen how certain chemical substances, the neurotransmitters, exert their influence on the 100 billion or so neurons in the nervous system. There is another system in which chemical substances stimulate and regulate many other important functions in the body. The **endocrine system** is a series of ductless glands, located in various parts of the body, that manufacture and secrete chemical substances known as **hormones.** Hormones are manufactured and released in one part of the body but have an effect on other parts of the body. They are released into the bloodstream and travel throughout the circulatory system,

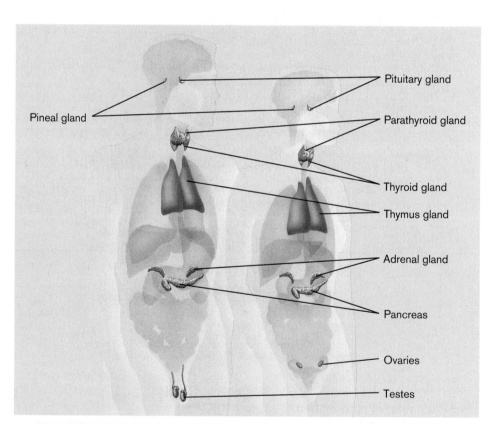

➤ Figure 2.12

The Endocrine System

The endocrine system is a group of glands that manufacture and secrete hormones. The hormones travel through the circulatory system and have important effects on many bodily functions.

www.ablongman.com/woodmastering1e

Apply It !   Handedness: Genes or Culture?

Are you a "righty" or a "lefty"? Have you ever wondered why?

If you are left-handed, you share the hand preference of notable historical figures such as Alexander the Great, Michelangelo, Leonardo da Vinci, Benjamin Franklin, and Albert Einstein, as well as entertainers Whoopi Goldberg and Tom Cruise and former presidents George Bush and Bill Clinton. Still, anthropologists report that left-handedness carries negative connotations across a wide variety of cultures. For example, the French word *gauche* means both "left" and "clumsy." If you examine a deck of Tarot cards, you will see that Justice is right-handed, while Evil is left-handed. Social scientists believe that this universal anti-left bias is the result of the fact that more than 80% of humans are right-handed. Thus, right-handedness is

seen as "normal." But have you ever wondered why there are so few left-handed people?

It used to be believed that cultural forces that shape child-rearing practices were responsible for the large right-handed majority. There is some evidence to support this view. For instance, in cultures where the belief in right-handedness as normal is very strong, there is a great deal of pressure on children to adopt a right-hand preference. As a result, there are lower proportions of left-handers in these cultures than in others, such as the United States, where it is widely believed that forcing children to be right-handed is detrimental to their development (Wilson, 1998). Still, right-handedness continues to predominate, even in cultures that are highly tolerant of left-handedness among children. Why?

Archeological studies of ancient skeletons show that the proportions of left- and right-handers in the human population have been about the same for several thousand years (Steele & Mays, 1995). Furthermore, studies examining ancient artwork and tools in locations all over the world also show that humans have been predominantly right-handed for thousands of years (Wilson, 1998). There is even evidence that prehuman species, such as *Homo erectus*, were predominantly right-handed. These findings tend to support a genetic explanation for handedness.

Animal studies provide further support for the genetic hypothesis. Studies indicate that right-handedness is almost as prevalent among chimpanzees as among humans (Hopkins & Dahl, 2001). By contrast, research involving primate species that are less genetically similar to humans finds a majority of individuals to be left-handed (Westergaard & Lussier, 1999).

Consistent with the genetic hypothesis, handedness appears early in human life. For example, babies almost always point with their right hands (Butterworth et al., 2002). And, when manipulating objects, a large majority of children show a consistent preference for the right hand by the age of 5.

Some neuroscientists believe that the predominance of right-handedness is just one manifestation of a general "rightward bias" in the human nervous system. Even infants, for example, are more likely to attend to an object that appears in the right visual field than one that appears in the left (Butterworth et al., 2002). And more than half of left-handers demonstrate right-side dominance in motor skills that do not involve the hands, such as kicking (Bourassa et al., 1996). These findings suggest that a biologically based and species-wide rightward bias may be a more powerful influence on hand preference than one's own individual heredity. ∎

---

but each hormone performs its assigned job only when it reaches the body cells that have receptors for it. Some of the same chemical substances that are neurotransmitters act as hormones as well—norepinephrine and vasopressin are two examples. Figure 2.12 shows the glands in the endocrine system and their locations in the body.

The **pituitary gland** is located in the brain just below the hypothalamus and is controlled by it (see Figure 2.12). The pituitary is considered to be the master gland of the body because it releases the hormones that turn on, or activate, the other glands in the endocrine system—a big job for a tiny structure about the size of a pea. The pituitary also produces the hormone that is responsible for body growth (Howard et al., 1996). Too little of this powerful substance will make a person a dwarf; too much will produce a giant.

pituitary gland
The endocrine gland located in the brain and often called the "master gland," which releases hormones that control other endocrine glands as well as a growth hormone.

Glands, Hormones, and Their Functions

GLANDS	HORMONES	FUNCTION
Pituitary	Growth hormone Many others	Controls growth rate; regulates functions of other glands
Thyroid	Thyroxine	Regulates metabolism
Pancreas	Insulin Glucagon	Regulates blood sugar level
Adrenals	Epinephrine Norepinephrine Corticoids Sex hormones	Regulate the sympathetic and parasympathetic systems; have a role in puberty and sexual function
Gonads	Sex hormones	Regulate reproductive and sexual function

The *thyroid gland* rests in the front, lower part of the neck, just below the voice box (larynx). The thyroid produces the important hormone thyroxine, which regulates the rate at which food is metabolized, or transformed into energy.

The *pancreas* regulates the body's blood sugar levels by releasing the hormones insulin and glucagon into the bloodstream. In people with diabetes, too little insulin is produced. Without insulin to break down the sugars in food, the blood-sugar levels can get dangerously high.

The two **adrenal glands,** which rest just above the kidneys (as shown in Figure 2.12), produce epinephrine and norepinephrine. By activating the sympathetic nervous system, these two hormones play an important role in the body's response to stress. The adrenal glands also release the corticoids, which control the body's salt balance, and small amounts of the sex hormones.

The *gonads* are the sex glands—the ovaries in females and the testes in males (see Figure 2.12). Activated by the pituitary gland, the gonads release the sex hormones that make reproduction possible and that are responsible for the secondary sex characteristics: pubic and underarm hair in both sexes, breasts in females, and facial hair and a deepened voice in males. Androgens, the male sex hormones, influence sexual motivation. Estrogens and progesterone, the female sex hormones, help regulate the menstrual cycle. Although both males and females have androgens and estrogens, males have considerably more androgens and females have considerably more estrogens. (The sex hormones and their effects are discussed in more detail in Chapter 8.)

Review and Reflect 2.2 summarizes the hormones you have just read about.

adrenal glands
(ah-DREE-nal) A pair of endocrine glands that release hormones that prepare the body for emergencies and stressful situations and also release the corticoids and small amounts of the sex hormones.

Summarize It!

The Neurons and the Neurotransmitters

➤ **What is a neuron, and what are its three parts?**

A neuron is a specialized cell that conducts messages throughout the nervous system. Its three main parts are the cell body, the dendrites, and the axon.

➤ **What is a synapse?**

A synapse is the junction where the axon terminal of a sending neuron communicates with a receiving neuron across the synaptic cleft.

➤ **What is the action potential?**

The action potential is the sudden reversal (from a negative to a positive value) of the resting potential on the cell membrane of a neuron; it initiates the firing of the neuron.

➤ **What are neurotransmitters, and what role do they play in the transmission of signals from one neuron to another?**

Neurotransmitters are chemical substances released into the synaptic cleft from the axon terminal of the sending neuron. They cross the synaptic cleft and bind to receptors on the receiving neuron, influencing that cell to fire or not to fire.

➤ **What are some of the major neurotransmitters, and what are some of the ways in which neurotransmitters affect behavior?**

Neurotransmitters regulate the actions of glands and muscles, affect learning and memory, promote sleep, stimulate mental and physical alertness, and influence moods and emotions ranging from depression to euphoria. Some of the major neurotransmitters are acetylcholine, dopamine, norepinephrine, serotonin, glutamate, GABA, and endorphins.

KEY TERMS

neuron (p. 34)
cell body (p. 34)
dendrites (p. 34)
axon (p. 34)
synapse (p. 34)
resting potential (p. 34)
action potential (p. 36)
myelin sheath (p. 36)
neurotransmitter (p. 36)
receptors (p. 36)
reuptake (p. 37)
acetylcholine (p. 37)
dopamine (p. 38)
norepinephrine (p. 38)
epinephrine (p. 38)
serotonin (p. 38)
endorphins (p. 39)

The Central Nervous System

➤ **Why is an intact spinal cord important to normal functioning?**

The spinal cord is an extension of the brain, connecting it to the peripheral nervous system. The spinal cord must be intact so that sensory information can reach the brain and messages from the brain can reach the muscles and glands.

➤ **What are the crucial functions handled by the brainstem?**

The brainstem contains the medulla, which controls heartbeat, breathing, blood pressure, coughing, and swallowing; the reticular formation, which plays a crucial role in arousal and attention; and the pons, which affects body movement and sleep and dreaming.

➤ **What are the primary functions of the cerebellum?**

The cerebellum allows the body to execute smooth, skilled movements and regulates muscle tone and posture.

➤ **What is the function of the substantia nigra?**

The substantia nigra, located in the midbrain, controls unconscious motor movements.

➤ **What is the primary role of the thalamus?**

The thalamus acts as a relay station for information flowing into and out of centers in the forebrain.

➤ **What are some of the processes regulated by the hypothalamus?**

The hypothalamus regulates hunger, thirst, sexual behavior, body temperature, and a variety of emotional behaviors.

➤ **What is the role of the limbic system?**

The limbic system is a group of structures in the brain, including the amygdala and the hippocampus, which are collectively involved in emotion, memory, and motivation.

➤ **What are the cerebral hemispheres, the corpus callosum, and the cerebral cortex?**

The cerebral hemispheres are the two halves of the cerebrum, connected by the corpus callosum and covered by the cerebral cortex, which is responsible for higher mental processes such as language, memory, and thinking.

➤ **What functions are located in the frontal lobes?**

The frontal lobes contain the motor cortex, which controls voluntary motor activity, and the frontal association areas, which are involved in thinking, motivation, planning for the future, impulse control, and emotional responses.

➤ **What are the primary functions of the parietal lobes in general and the somatosensory cortex in particular?**

The parietal lobes are involved in the reception and processing of touch stimuli. They contain the somatosensory cortex, where touch, pressure, temperature, and pain register.

➤ **What are the primary functions of the occipital lobes in general and the primary visual cortex in particular?**

The occipital lobes are involved in the reception and interpretation of visual information. They contain the primary visual cortex, where vision registers in the cerebral cortex.

➤ **What functions are located in the temporal lobes?**

The temporal lobes contain the primary auditory cortex, where hearing registers in the cortex, and association areas, where memories are stored and auditory stimuli are interpreted.

➤ **What are the specialized functions of the left hemisphere?**

The left hemisphere controls the right side of the body, coordinates complex movements, and handles most of the language functions, including speaking, writing, reading, and understanding the spoken word.

➤ **What are the specialized functions of the right hemisphere?**

The right hemisphere controls the left side of the body; is specialized for visual-spatial perception, singing, and interpreting nonverbal behavior; and is more active in the recognition and expression of emotion.

KEY TERMS

central nervous system (p. 39)
spinal cord (p. 39)
brainstem (p. 40)
medulla (p. 40)
reticular formation (p. 40)
cerebellum (p. 40)
thalamus (p. 41)
hypothalamus (p. 41)
limbic system (p. 41)
amygdala (p. 41)
hippocampus (p. 42)
cerebrum (p. 42)
cerebral hemispheres (p. 42)
corpus callosum (p. 42)
cerebral cortex (p. 42)
association areas (p. 42)
frontal lobes (p. 44)
motor cortex (p. 44)
plasticity (p. 44)
parietal lobes (p. 44)
somatosensory cortex (p. 44)
occipital lobes (p. 45)
primary visual cortex (p. 45)
temporal lobes (p. 45)
primary auditory cortex (p. 45)
lateralization (p. 45)
left hemisphere (p. 46)
Broca's area (p. 46)

Wernicke's area (p. 46)
right hemisphere (p. 46)
split-brain operation (p. 47)

Discovering the Brain's Mysteries

➤ **What are some methods that researchers have used to learn about brain function?**

Researchers have learned about brain function from clinical studies of patients, through electrical stimulation of the brain, and from studies using the EEG, the microelectrode, CT scans, MRI, PET scans, and fMRI.

➤ **What is the electroencephalogram (EEG), and what are three of the brain-wave patterns it reveals?**

The electroencephalogram (EEG) is a record of brain-wave activity. Three normal brain-wave patterns are the beta wave, the alpha wave, and the delta wave.

KEY TERMS

electroencephalogram (EEG) (p. 48)
beta wave (p. 48)
alpha wave (p. 48)
delta wave (p. 49)
microelectrode (p. 49)
CT (computerized tomography) scan (p. 49)
MRI (magnetic resonance imaging) (p. 49)
PET (position emission tomography) scan (p. 49)
functional MRI (fMRI) (p. 49)

The Peripheral Nervous System

➤ **What is the peripheral nervous system?**

The peripheral nervous system connects the central nervous system to the rest of the body. It has two subdivisions: (1) the somatic nervous system, which consists of the nerves that make it possible for the body to sense and move; and (2) the au-

tonomic nervous system, which controls glands and muscles not normally under voluntary control.

➤ **What are the roles of the sympathetic and parasympathetic nervous systems?**

The autonomic nervous system has two parts: (1) the sympathetic nervous system, which mobilizes the body's resources during emergencies or during stress; and (2) the parasympathetic nervous system, which is associated with relaxation and brings the heightened bodily responses back to normal after an emergency.

KEY TERMS

peripheral nervous system (p. 50)
sympathetic nervous system (p. 51)
parasympathetic nervous system (p. 52)

The Endocrine System

➤ **What is the endocrine system, and what are some of the glands within it?**

The endocrine system is a set of glands in various parts of the body that manufacture hormones and secrete them into the bloodstream. The hormones then affect cells in other parts of the body. The pituitary gland releases hormones that control other glands in the endocrine system and also releases a growth hormone. The thyroid gland produces thyroxin, which regulates metabolism. The pancreas produces insulin and regulates blood sugar. The adrenal glands release epinephrine and norepinephrine, which prepare the body for emergencies and stressful situations; they also release small amounts of the male and female sex hormones. The gonads are the sex glands, which produce the sex hormones and make reproduction possible.

KEY TERMS

endocrine system (p. 52)
hormones (p. 52)
pituitary gland (p. 53)
adrenal glands (p. 54)

Surf It!

Want to be sure you've absorbed the material in Chapter 2, "Biology and Behavior," before the big test? Visiting **www.ablongman.com/ woodmastering1e** can put a top grade within your reach. The site is loaded with free practice tests, flashcards, activities, and links to help you review your way to an A.

Companion Website

Answers to all the Study Guide questions are provided at the end of the book.

Section One: Chapter Review

1. The branchlike extensions of neurons that act as receivers of signals from other neurons are the
   a. dendrites.
   c. neurotransmitters.
   b. axons.
   d. cell bodies.

2. The junction where the axon of a sending neuron communicates with a receiving neuron is called the
   a. reuptake site.
   c. synapse.
   b. receptor site.
   d. axon terminal.

3. When a neuron fires, neurotransmitters are released from the synaptic vesicles in the _____ terminal into the synaptic cleft.
   a. dendrite
   c. receptor
   b. cell body's
   d. axon

4. The (resting, action) potential is the firing of a neuron that results when the charge within the neuron becomes more positive than the charge outside the cell membrane.

5. Receptor sites on the receiving neuron
   a. receive any available neurotransmitter molecules.
   b. receive only neurotransmitter molecules of specific shapes.
   c. can only be influenced by neurotransmitters from a single neuron.
   d. are located only on the dendrites.

6. The neurotransmitter called *acetylcholine* is involved in
   a. memory.
   b. motor function.
   c. rapid eye movement during sleep.
   d. all of the above.

7. Endorphins, norepinephrine, dopamine, and serotonin are all examples of
   a. hormones.
   b. neurotransmitters.
   c. neuropeptides.
   d. drugs.

8. The hypothalamus regulates all the following except
   a. internal body temperature.
   b. coordinated movement.
   c. hunger and thirst.
   d. sexual behavior.

9. The part of the limbic system primarily involved in the formation of memories is the (amygdala, hippocampus).

10. Match the brain structure with its description.
    ____ (1) connects the brain with the peripheral nervous system
    ____ (2) controls heart rate, breathing, and blood pressure

    ____ (3) consists of the medulla, the pons, and the reticular formation
    ____ (4) influences attention and arousal
    ____ (5) coordinates complex body movements
    ____ (6) serves as a relay station for sensory information flowing into the brain
    ____ (7) controls unconscious movements
    a. medulla
    b. spinal cord
    c. reticular formation
    d. thalamus
    e. cerebellum
    f. brainstem
    g. substantia nigra

11. What is the thick band of fibers connecting the two cerebral hemispheres?
    a. cortex
    c. cerebrum
    b. corpus callosum
    d. motor cortex

12. The $\frac{1}{8}$-inch outer covering of the cerebrum is the
    a. cerebral cortex.
    c. myelin sheath.
    b. cortex callosum.
    d. white matter.

13. Match the lobes with the brain areas they contain.
    ____ (1) primary auditory cortex
    ____ (2) primary visual cortex
    ____ (3) motor cortex
    ____ (4) somatosensory cortex
    a. frontal lobes
    b. parietal lobes
    c. occipital lobes
    d. temporal lobes

14. Match the specialized area with the appropriate description of function.
    ____ (1) hearing registers
    ____ (2) vision registers
    ____ (3) touch, pressure, and temperature register
    ____ (4) voluntary movement
    ____ (5) thinking, motivation, impulse control
    a. primary visual cortex
    b. motor cortex
    c. frontal association area
    d. primary auditory cortex
    e. somatosensory cortex

15. Match the hemisphere with the specialized abilities usually associated with it.
    ____ (1) visual-spatial skills
    ____ (2) speech
    ____ (3) recognition and expression of emotion

_____ (4) singing

_____ (5) mathematics

a. right hemisphere

b. left hemisphere

16. Which of the following is likely to result in the production of speech that doesn't make sense?

a. damage to Broca's area

b. damage to any area of the temporal lobe

c. lack of dopamine in the temporal association areas

d. damage to Wernicke's area

17. Which of these statements is *not* true of the split-brain operation?

a. It is used on people with severe epilepsy.

b. It provides a means of studying the functions of the individual hemispheres.

c. It causes major changes in intelligence, personality, and behavior.

d. It makes transfer of information between hemispheres impossible.

18. Match the brain-wave pattern with the state associated with it.

_____ (1) slow-wave (deep) sleep

_____ (2) deep relaxation while awake

_____ (3) physical or mental activity

a. beta wave

b. delta wave

c. alpha wave

19. The CT scan and MRI are used to

a. show the amount of activity in various parts of the brain.

b. produce images of the brain's structures.

c. measure electrical activity in the brain.

d. observe neural communication at synapses.

20. Which of the following reveals the electrical activity of the brain by producing a record of brain waves?

a. electroencephalogram   c. PET scan

b. CT scan   d. MRI

21. Which of the following reveals brain activity and function, rather than the structure of the brain?

a. CT scan   c. PET scan

b. EEG   d. MRI

22. Which of the following reveals both brain structure and brain activity?

a. MRI   c. fMRI

b. PET scan   d. CT scan

23. The _____ nervous system connects the brain and spinal cord to the rest of the body.

a. central   c. somatic

b. peripheral   d. autonomic

24. The _____ nervous system mobilizes the body's resources during times of stress; the _____ nervous system brings the heightened bodily responses back to normal when the emergency is over.

a. somatic; autonomic

b. autonomic; somatic

c. sympathetic; parasympathetic

d. parasympathetic; sympathetic

25. The endocrine glands secrete _____ directly into the _____ .

a. hormones; bloodstream

b. enzymes; digestive tract

c. enzymes; bloodstream

d. hormones; digestive tract

26. Match the endocrine gland with the appropriate description.

_____ (1) keeps body's metabolism in balance

_____ (2) acts as a master gland that activates the other glands

_____ (3) regulates the blood sugar

_____ (4) makes reproduction possible

_____ (5) releases hormones that prepare the body for emergencies

a. pituitary gland   d. thyroid gland

b. adrenal glands   e. pancreas

c. gonads

Section Two: Label the Brain

Identify each of the numbered parts in the brain diagram.

1. _____

2. _____

3. _____

4. _____

5. _____

6. _____

7. _____

8. _____

9. _____

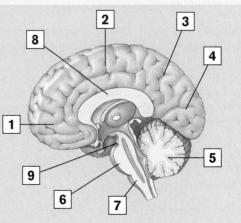

Section Three: Fill in the Blank

1. The _____ is the part of the neuron that receives chemical messages from other neurons.

2. Dopamine, serotonin, and acetylcholine are all examples of _____ .

3. The amygdala and the hippocampus are structures in the _____ system.

4. The _____ _____ _____ is at the back of the occipital lobe.

5. The somatosensory cortex is located in the _____ lobe.

6. Phineas Gage suffered damage to his _____ lobe.

7. Broca's area and Wernicke's area are important for language and are located in the _____ hemisphere.

8. The longest part of a neuron is called the _____ .

9. The central nervous system is composed of the _____ and the _____ .

10. The fight-or-flight response is related to the activity of the _____ nervous system.

11. The _____ monitors and regulates internal body temperature.

12. The _____ _____ occurs when the neuron ion channels open and allow a sudden influx of positive ions into the axon.

13. _____ aphasia is an impairment in the ability to produce speech sounds, or in extreme cases, an inability to speak at all.

14. The limbic system structure thought to play a central role in the formation of memories is the _____ .

15. The primary auditory cortex is located in the _____ lobes.

16. You can write notes in class or execute other smooth, skilled body movements because of the action of the _____ .

17. The somatic and the autonomic nervous systems are the two primary divisions of the _____ nervous system.

18. People who have Parkinson's disease may have damage to neurons whose nuclei are in the _____ .

Section Four: Comprehensive Practice Test

1. Phineas Gage changed from a polite, dependable, well-liked railroad foreman to a rude and impulsive person who could no longer plan realistically for the future after he suffered serious damage to his
   a. occipital lobe.
   b. frontal lobe.
   c. medulla.
   d. cerebellum.

2. Afferent is to efferent as
   a. sensory is to sensation.
   b. sensation is to perception.
   c. motor is to sensory.
   d. sensory is to motor.

3. A deficiency in _____ has been associated with Parkinson's disease, a disease characterized by tremors and rigidity in the limbs.
   a. dopamine
   b. norepinephrine
   c. acetylcholine
   d. GABA

4. Neurons can conduct messages faster if they have
   a. an axon with a myelin sheath.
   b. a positive resting potential.
   c. more than one cell body.
   d. fewer dendrites.

5. The electrical charge inside a neuron is about −70 millivolts and is known as the _____ potential.
   a. action
   b. refractory
   c. resting
   d. impulse

6. The nervous system is divided into the _____ and the _____ systems.
   a. somatic; autonomic
   b. central; peripheral
   c. brain; spinal cord
   d. sympathetic; parasympathetic

7. The structure that is located above the brainstem and serves as a relay station for information to and from the higher brain centers is the
   a. pituitary gland.
   b. hypothalamus.
   c. thalamus.
   d. hippocampus.

8. The structure that is located in the brainstem and is important for basic life functions such as heartbeat and breathing is the
   a. pons.
   b. medulla.
   c. hypothalamus.
   d. amygdala.

9. The _____ is sometimes referred to as the body's thermostat because it controls temperature, hunger, thirst, and emotional behaviors.
   a. corpus callosum
   b. pituitary gland
   c. cerebellum
   d. hypothalamus

10. The lobe that contains the primary visual cortex is the
    a. parietal lobe.   c. temporal lobe.
    b. occipital lobe.   d. frontal lobe.

11. The primary motor cortex is located in the _____ lobe.
    a. frontal   c. temporal
    b. occipital   d. occulovisual

12. The pituitary gland, known as the master gland, is part of the _____ system.
    a. somatic   c. endocrine
    b. peripheral nervous   d. central nervous

13. The adrenal glands control salt balance in the body through the release of
    a. insulin.   c. androgens.
    b. corticoids.   d. endorphins.

14. A researcher interested in getting information about the brain's activity based on the amount of oxygen and glucose consumed should use a(n)
    a. MRI.   c. PET scan.
    b. EEG.   d. CT scan.

15. The _____ nervous system controls skeletal muscles and allows the body to interact with the external environment.
    a. autonomic   c. sympathetic
    b. parasympathetic   d. somatic

16. Damage to Broca's area will result in a type of aphasia in which patients cannot speak. (true/false)

17. Functional MRI (fMRI) reveals both brain structure and brain activity. (true/false)

Section Five: Critical Thinking

1. Much of the brain research you have read about in this chapter was carried out using animals. In many studies, it is necessary to euthanize animals in order to study their brain tissues directly. Many people object to this practice, but others say it is justified because it advances knowledge about the brain. Prepare arguments to support both of the following positions:
   a. The use of animals in brain research projects is ethical and justifiable because of the possible benefits to humankind.
   b. The use of animals in brain research projects is not ethical or justifiable on the grounds of possible benefits to humankind.

2. How would your life change if you had a massive stroke affecting your left hemisphere? How would it change if the stroke damaged your right hemisphere? Which stroke would be more tragic for you, and why?

chapter 3

Sensation and Perception

Meet Helen Keller (1880–1968). When Helen was only 9 months old, she was struck with a serious illness that left her totally blind and deaf. Her sensory world was limited to only three avenues—taste, smell, and touch. The overwhelming reality of her world was permanent darkness and silence. Only the most rudimentary communication with her parents was possible (she could spit out food she disliked). In fact, her ability to give and receive information was far less than that of an ordinary household pet. As Helen grew from infancy into early childhood, her frustration gave way to explosive tantrums. She became a rebellious, unruly "wild child." The Keller family needed a miracle!

Then, when Helen was 6 years old, her father learned that the Perkins Institution had achieved success in teaching the physically handicapped. So, he and the family took Helen to Boston, where they met Anne Sullivan, a talented young teacher, who agreed to tutor Helen. Anne used a manual alphabet to slowly spell out the names of objects with her fingers in the palm of Helen's hand—to teach Helen that everything has a name, a fundamental requirement for communication.

Progress was slow at first. But then one day, as Anne poured water over one of Helen's hands and spelled out w-a-t-e-r in her other hand, a look of surprise and delight lit up Helen's face. That look told Anne that she had gotten through at last. Helen quickly learned to use her fingers to write the names for virtually everything and everyone around—Mama, Papa, Anne, and, of course, Helen. The miracle had happened.

And Helen didn't stop there. She learned to read and write in Braille. She also learned how to understand much of what others were saying by using her thumb to sense the vibrations coming from a speaker's vocal cords and her forefinger to interpret lip movements. With her other three fingers she could "see" facial expressions. And, of course, Helen could recognize and identify anyone she knew by the feel of the person's face. Remarkably, Helen also learned to speak quite well, an amazing achievement for one who had never been able to hear. At 20, Helen enrolled in Radcliffe College and graduated with honors, thanks to the daily help of her tutor and companion, Anne Sullivan.

As the story of Helen Keller illustrates, sensation and perception are intimately related to everyday experience. They are not the same, however. **Sensation** is the process through which the senses detect visual, auditory, and other sensory stimuli and transmit them to the brain. **Perception** is the process by which sensory information is actively organized and interpreted by the brain. Sensation furnishes the raw material of sensory experience, while perception provides the finished product. Young Helen could sense her teacher Anne's fingers tracing letters in her hand, but she could not perceive their symbolic character until her sudden revelation about the spelling of *water*.

In this chapter, we will explore the world of sensation. First, we'll consider the two dominant senses—vision and hearing. Next, we'll turn our attention to the others—smell, taste, touch, pain, and balance. You will learn how the senses detect sensory information and how this sensory information is actively organized and interpreted by the brain.

> What is the difference between sensation and perception?

sensation
The process through which the senses pick up visual, auditory, and other sensory stimuli and transmit them to the brain; sensory information that has registered in the brain but has not been interpreted.

perception
The process by which sensory information is actively organized and interpreted by the brain.

absolute threshold
The minimum amount of sensory stimulation that can be detected 50% of the time.

> What is the difference between the absolute threshold and the difference threshold?

The Process of Sensation

Our senses serve as ports of entry for all information about the world. Yet it is amazing how little of the world around them humans actually sense, compared to animals. Some animals have exceptional hearing (bats and dolphins); others have extremely sharp vision (hawks); still others have an acute sense of smell (bloodhounds); and so on. Nevertheless, humans have remarkable sensory abilities and superior abilities of perception.

The Absolute Threshold

What is the softest sound you can hear, the dimmest light you can see, the most diluted substance you can taste? Researchers in sensory psychology and psychophysics have performed many experiments over the years to answer these questions. Their research has established measures for the senses known as absolute thresholds. Just as the threshold of a doorway is the dividing point between being outside a room and inside, the **absolute threshold** of a sense marks the difference between not being able to perceive a stimulus and being just barely able to perceive it. Psychologists have arbitrarily defined this absolute threshold as the minimum amount of sensory stimulation that can be detected 50% of the time.

> What is the dimmest light this lifeguard could perceive in the darkness? Researchers in sensory psychology have performed many experiments over the years to answer such questions. Their research has established measures known as absolute thresholds. Just as the threshold of a doorway is the dividing point between being outside a room and inside, the absolute threshold of a sense marks the difference between not being able to perceive a stimulus and being just barely able to perceive it.

The Difference Threshold

If you are listening to music, the very fact that you can hear it means that the absolute threshold has been crossed. But how much must the volume be turned up or down for you to notice a difference? The **difference threshold** is a measure of the smallest increase or decrease in a physical stimulus that is required to produce the just noticeable difference. The **just noticeable difference (JND)** is the smallest change in sensation that a person is able to detect 50% of the time. If you were holding a 5-pound weight and 1 pound were added, you could easily notice the difference. But if you were holding 100 pounds and 1 additional pound were added, you could not sense the difference. Why not?

More than 150 years ago, researcher Ernst Weber (1795–1878) observed that the JND for all the senses depends on a proportion or percentage of change rather than a fixed amount of change. This observation became known as **Weber's law.** A weight you are holding must increase or decrease by a ratio of $1/50$, or 2%, for you to notice the difference; in contrast, if you are listening to music, you can notice a difference if a tone becomes higher or lower in pitch by only about 0.33%. According to Weber's law, the greater the original stimulus, the more it must be increased or decreased for the difference to be noticeable.

However, Weber's law applies best to people with average sensitivities and to sensory stimuli that are neither very strong (loud thunder) nor very weak (a faint whisper). For instance, expert wine tasters know if a particular vintage is a little too sweet, even if its sweetness varies by only a fraction of the 20% necessary for changes in taste. Furthermore, people who have lost one sensory ability often gain greater sensitivity in the others. For example, one study found that children with early-onset blindness were more capable of correctly labeling 25 common odors than were sighted children, and another found that congenitally deaf students possessed enhanced motion-perception abilities (Bavelier et al., 2000; Rosenbluth et al., 2000).

Sensory Adaptation

The body's sense organs are equipped with specialized cells called **sensory receptors,** which detect and respond to one type of sensory stimuli–light, sound waves, or odors, for example. Through a process known as *transduction,* the receptors change or convert the sensory stimulation into neural impulses, the electrochemical language of the brain. The neural impulses are then transmitted to precise locations in the brain, such as the primary visual cortex for vision or the primary auditory cortex for hearing.

After a time, the sensory receptors grow accustomed to constant, unchanging levels of stimuli–sights, sounds, or smells–and so we notice them less and less, or not at all. This process is known as **sensory adaptation.** Even though it reduces your sensory awareness, sensory adaptation enables you to shift your attention to what is most important at any given moment. However, sensory adaptation is not likely to occur in the presence of a very strong stimulus–such as the smell of ammonia, an ear-splitting sound, or the taste of rancid food.

How are sensory stimuli in the environment experienced as sensations?

Vision

You cannot see any object unless light is reflected from it or given off by it. Our eyes can respond only to a very narrow band of electromagnetic waves, a band called the **visible spectrum,** shown in Figure 3.1 (on page 66). The shortest light waves we can see appear violet, while the longest visible waves appear red. Still, sight is much more than just response to light.

---

difference threshold
The smallest increase or decrease in a physical stimulus required to produce a difference in sensation that is noticeable 50% of the time.

just noticeable difference (JND)
The smallest change in sensation that a person is able to detect 50% of the time.

Weber's law
The law stating that the just noticeable difference (JND) for all the senses depends on a proportion or percentage of change in a stimulus rather than on a fixed amount of change.

sensory receptors
Specialized cells in the sense organs that detect and respond to sensory stimuli–light, sound, odors, etc.–and transduce (convert) the stimuli into neural impulses.

sensory adaptation
The process of becoming less sensitive to an unchanging sensory stimulus over time.

visible spectrum
The narrow band of electromagnetic waves, 380–760 nanometers in length, that are visible to the human eye.

➤ Figure 3.1

The Electromagnetic Spectrum

Human eyes can perceive only a very thin band of electromagnetic waves, known as the visible spectrum.

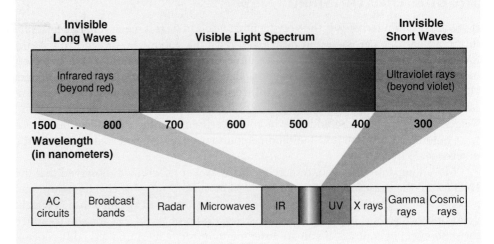

cornea

(KOR-nee-uh) The transparent covering on the front surface of the eyeball that bends light rays inward through the pupil.

lens

The transparent structure behind the iris that changes shape as it focuses images on the retina.

accommodation

The action of the lens in changing shape as it focuses objects on the retina, becoming more spherical for near objects and flatter for far objects.

> How do the cornea, the iris, and the pupil function in vision? ➤

> What are the lens and the retina? ➤

retina

The layer of tissue at the back of the eye that contains the rods and the cones and onto which the incoming image is projected by the lens.

rods

The light-sensitive receptors in the retina that allow humans to see in dim light.

cones

The receptor cells in the retina that enable humans to see color and fine detail in adequate light but that do not function in dim light.

> What roles do the rods and cones play in vision? ➤

The Eye

The globe-shaped human eyeball, shown in Figure 3.2, measures about 1 inch in diameter. Bulging from its front surface is the **cornea**–the tough, transparent, protective layer covering the front of the eye. The cornea performs the first step in vision by bending the light rays inward. It herds the light rays through the *pupil*–the small, dark opening in the center of the *iris,* or colored part of the eye. The iris dilates and contracts the pupil to regulate the amount of light passing through it.

Suspended just behind the iris and the pupil, the **lens** is composed of many thin layers and looks like a transparent disc. The lens performs the task of focusing on objects closer than 20 feet. It flattens as it focuses on objects viewed at a distance, but it becomes more spherical, bulging in the center, as it focuses on close objects. This flattening and bulging action of the lens is known as **accommodation.** With age, the lens loses the ability to change its shape to accommodate for near vision, a condition called *presbyopia* ("old eyes"). This is why many people over age 40 must hold a book or newspaper at arm's length or use reading glasses to magnify the print.

The lens focuses the incoming image onto the **retina**–a layer of tissue, about the size of a small postage stamp and as thin as onion skin, located on the inner surface of the eyeball and containing the sensory receptors for vision. The image projected onto the retina is upside-down and reversed left to right. You can demonstrate this for yourself in *Try It! 3.1.*

In some people, the distance through the eyeball (from the lens to the retina) is either too short or too long for proper focusing. Nearsightedness (*myopia*) occurs when the lens focuses images of distant objects in front of, rather than on, the retina. A person with this condition will be able to see near objects clearly, but distant images will be blurred. Farsightedness (*hyperopia*) occurs when the focal image is longer than the eye can handle, as if the image should focus behind the retina. The individual is able to see far objects clearly, but close objects are blurred. Both conditions are correctable with eyeglasses, contact lenses, or a surgical procedure known as *LASIK.*

At the back of the retina is a layer of light-sensitive receptor cells–the **rods** and the **cones.** Named for their shapes, the rods look like slender cylinders, and the cones appear shorter and more rounded. There are about 120 million rods and 6 million cones in each retina. The cones are the receptor cells that enable us to see color and fine detail in adequate light, but they do not function in very dim light. By contrast, the rods in the human eye are extremely sensitive, allowing the eye to respond to as few as five photons of light (Hecht et al., 1942). Changes in a chemical called *rhodopsin,* found in the rods, enable us to adapt to the darkness of a movie theater or to the brightness of a beach on a sunny day.

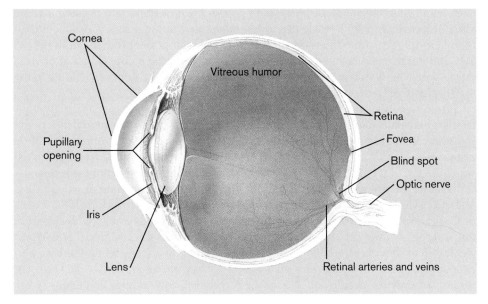

➤ Figure 3.2

The Major Parts of the Human Eye

At the center of the retina is the **fovea,** a small pitlike area about the size of the period at the end of this sentence (refer to Figure 3.2). When you look directly at an object, the image of the object is sharply focused at the center of your fovea. The fovea contains no rods but has about 30,000 cones tightly packed together. The cones are most densely packed at the center of the fovea; their density decreases sharply just a few degrees beyond the fovea's center and levels off more gradually to the periphery of the retina.

Although visual information is processed mostly in the brain, the initial stages of processing take place in the retina's sensory receptors–the rods and cones. They transduce, or change, light waves into neural impulses that are fed to specialized cells called *ganglion cells*. The approximately 1 million axonlike extensions of the ganglion cells are bundled together in a pencil-sized cable that extends through the wall of the retina, leaving the eye and leading to the brain. Where the cable runs through the retinal wall, there can be no rods or cones, and so this point is a blind spot in each eye.

Beyond the retinal wall of the eye, the cable becomes the *optic nerve* (see Figure 3.2). The optic nerves from both eyes come together at the optic chiasm, a point where some of the nerve fibers cross to the opposite side of the brain. The visual fibers from the right half of each retina go to the right hemisphere, and the visual fibers from the left half of

fovea
(FO-vee-uh) A small area of the retina, 1/50 of an inch in diameter, that provides the clearest and sharpest vision because it has the largest concentration of cones.

◄ What path does the neural impulse take from the retina to the primary visual cortex?

Try It / 3.1   Upside-down Image

Take an ordinary teaspoon—one in which you can see your reflection. Looking at the bottom (the convex surface) of the spoon, you will see an image of your face that is right side up—the way the image enters the eye. Turn the spoon over and look at the inside (the concave surface), and you will see your face upside down and reversed left to right—the way the image appears on the retina. The brain, however, perceives images right side up.

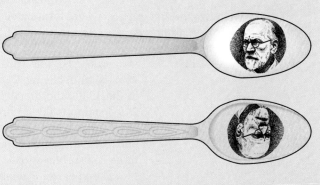

feature detectors
Neurons in the brain that respond to specific features of a sensory stimulus (for example, to lines or angles).

hue
The property of light commonly referred to as color (red, blue, green, etc.), determined primarily by the wavelength of light reflected from a surface.

saturation
The degree to which light waves producing a color are of the same wavelength; the purity of a color.

brightness
The dimension of visual sensation that is dependent on the intensity of light reflected from a surface and that corresponds to the amplitude of the light wave.

each retina go to the left hemisphere. This crossing over is important because it allows visual information from a single eye to be represented in the primary visual cortex of both hemispheres of the brain. Moreover, it plays an important role in depth perception. But if one eye is covered and deprived of vision during a critical period of visual development early in life, the visual cortex almost completely stops responding to that eye (Fagiolini & Hensch, 2000).

From the optic chiasm, the optic nerve travels to the thalamus (specifically, to its lateral geniculate nucleus). There the optic nerve synapses with neural fibers that transmit the impulses to the primary visual cortex. Approximately one-fourth of the primary visual cortex is dedicated exclusively to analyzing input from the fovea, which, as you'll recall, is a very small but extremely important part of the retina.

Thanks to researchers David Hubel and Torsten Wiesel (Hubel, 1963, 1995; Hubel & Wiesel, 1959, 1979), who won a Nobel Prize for their work in 1981, a great deal is known about how specialized the neurons of the visual cortex are. By inserting tiny microelectrodes into single cells in the visual cortices of cats, Hubel and Wiesel were able to determine what was happening in individual cells when the cats were exposed to different kinds of visual stimuli. They discovered that each neuron responded only to specific patterns. Some responded only to lines and angles, while others fired only when the cat saw a vertical or horizontal line. Still others were responsive to nothing but right angles or to lines of specific lengths. Neurons of this type are known as **feature detectors,** and they are already coded at birth to make their unique responses. Yet we see whole images, rather than collections of isolated features, because visual perceptions are complete only when the primary visual cortex transmits millions of pieces of visual information to other areas in the brain, where they are combined and assembled into whole images (Perry & Zeki, 2000).

Color Vision

Some light waves striking an object are absorbed by it, and others are reflected from it. We see only the wavelengths that are reflected, not those that are absorbed. Why does an apple look red? If you hold a red apple in bright light, light waves of all the different wavelengths are striking the apple, but more of the longer red wavelengths of light are reflected from the apple's skin. The shorter wavelengths are absorbed, so you see only the reflected red. Bite into the apple, and it looks white. Why? You see white because, rather than being absorbed, all the wavelengths of the visible spectrum are reflected from the inside part of the apple. The presence of all visible wavelengths gives the sensation of white.

> What are the three dimensions of the colors people perceive?

Our everyday visual experience goes far beyond the colors in the rainbow. We can detect thousands of subtle color shadings. What produces these fine color distinctions? Researchers have identified three dimensions that combine to provide the rich world of color we experience: (1) The chief dimension is **hue,** which refers to the specific color perceived–red or green, for example. (2) **Saturation** refers to the purity of a color. A color becomes less saturated, or less pure, as other wavelengths of light are mixed with it. (3) **Brightness** refers to the intensity of the light energy that is perceived.

> What two major theories attempt to explain color vision?

Two major theories have been offered to explain color vision, and both were formulated before the development of laboratory technology capable of testing them. The *trichromatic theory,* first proposed by Thomas Young in 1802, was modified by Hermann von Helmholtz about 50 years later. This theory states that there are three kinds of cones in the retina and that each kind makes its maximum chemical response to one of three colors: blue, green, or red. Research in the 1950s and the 1960s by Nobel Prize winner George Wald (1964; Wald et al., 1954) supports the trichromatic theory. Wald discovered that even though all cones have basically the same structure, the retina does indeed contain three kinds of cones. Subsequent research demonstrated that each cone is particularly sensitive to one of the three colors–blue, green, or red (Roorda & Williams, 1999).

The other major attempt to explain color vision is the *opponent-process theory,* which was first proposed by physiologist Ewald Hering in 1878 and revised by researchers Leon Hur-

68

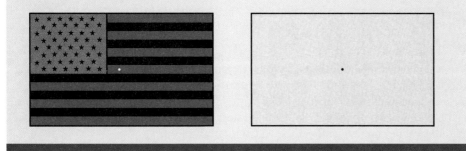

Stare at the dot in the green, black, and yellow flag for approximately 1 minute. Then shift your gaze to the dot in the blank rectangle. You will see the American flag in its true colors—red, white, and blue, which are the opponent-process opposites of green, black, and yellow.

vich and Dorthea Jamison in 1957. According to the opponent-process theory, three classes of cells respond by increasing or decreasing their rate of firing when different colors are present. The red/green cells increase their firing rate when red is present and decrease it when green is present. The yellow/blue cells have an increased response to yellow and a decreased response to blue. Another type of cell increases its response rate for white light and decreases it in the absence of light. Think of the opposing responses as being on a seesaw. As one type of response goes up, the other goes down, and vice versa. The relative firing rates of the three pairs of cells transmit color information to the brain.

If you look long enough at one color in an opponent-process pair (red/green, yellow/blue, black/white) and then look at a white surface, your brain will give you the sensation of the opposite color—a negative **afterimage.** After you have stared at one color in an opponent-process pair, the cell responding to that color tires and the opponent cell begins to fire, producing the afterimage. Demonstrate this for yourself in *Try It! 3.2.*

But which theory of color vision is correct? It turns out that both have merit because each explains a different phase of color processing. It is now generally accepted that the cones, the place where color processing best explained by the trichromatic theory happens, pass on information about wavelengths of light to the ganglion cells, the site of opponent processes. And color perception appears to involve more than just these two phases. Researchers believe that color processing starts at the level of the retina, continues through the ganglion cells, and is completed in the color detectors in the visual cortex (Masland, 1996; Nathans, 1989; Sokolov, 2000).

afterimage
The visual sensation that remains after a stimulus is withdrawn.

▼ On the left a hot air balloon is shown as it would appear to a person with normal color vision; on the right is the same balloon as it would appear to a person with red-green color blindness.

If normal genes for the three color pigments are not present, a person experiences some form of **color blindness**—the inability to distinguish some colors. Very few people are totally color blind. However, about 5% of males and 1% of females in the United States experience some kind of difficulty in distinguishing colors, most commonly red from green (Neitz et al., 1996).

Hearing

Sound

Sound requires a medium through which to move, such as air, water, or a solid object. This fact was first demonstrated by Robert Boyle in 1660 when he suspended a ringing pocket watch by a thread inside a specially designed jar. When Boyle pumped all the air out of the jar, he could no longer hear the watch ring. But when he pumped the air back into the jar, he could again hear the watch ringing.

> What determines the pitch and loudness of a sound, and how is each quality measured?

Frequency is the number of cycles completed by a sound wave in one second. The unit used to measure frequency, or the cycles per second, is known as the hertz (Hz). *Pitch,* how high or low a sound is, is chiefly determined by frequency—the higher the frequency (the more vibrations, or cycles, per second), the higher the sound. The human ear can hear sound frequencies from low bass notes of around 20 Hz up to high-pitched sounds of about 20,000 Hz. The lowest tone on a piano sounds at a frequency of about 28 Hz and the highest tone at about 4,214 Hz. Many mammals—dogs, cats, bats, and rats—can hear tones much higher in frequency than 20,000 Hz. Amazingly, dolphins can respond to sounds up to 100,000 Hz.

The loudness of a sound is determined by the **amplitude**—the magnitude or intensity of a sound wave. The loudness of sounds is measured using a unit called the *bel,* named for Alexander Graham Bell. Because the bel is a rather large unit, sound levels are expressed in tenths of a bel, or **decibels (dB).** The threshold of human hearing is set at 0 dB, which does not mean the absence of sound but rather the softest sound that can be heard in a very quiet setting. Each increase of 10 decibels makes a sound ten times louder. Figure 3.3 shows comparative decibel levels for a variety of sounds.

> **Figure 3.3**
>
> **Decibel Levels of Various Sounds**
>
> The loudness of a sound (its amplitude) is measured in decibels. Each increase of 10 dB makes a sound 10 times louder. A normal conversation at 3 feet measures about 60 dB, which is 10,000 times louder than a soft whisper of 20 dB. Any exposure to sounds of 130 dB or higher puts a person at immediate risk for hearing damage.

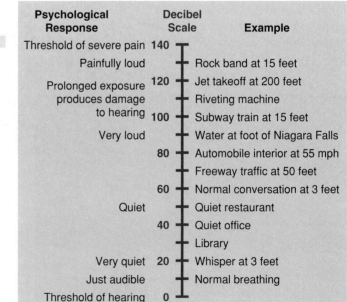

Psychological Response	Decibel Scale	Example
Threshold of severe pain	140	
Painfully loud		Rock band at 15 feet
Prolonged exposure produces damage to hearing	120	Jet takeoff at 200 feet
		Riveting machine
	100	Subway train at 15 feet
Very loud		Water at foot of Niagara Falls
	80	Automobile interior at 55 mph
		Freeway traffic at 50 feet
	60	Normal conversation at 3 feet
Quiet		Quiet restaurant
	40	Quiet office
		Library
Very quiet	20	Whisper at 3 feet
Just audible		Normal breathing
Threshold of hearing	0	

A third characteristic of sound, **timbre**, refers to the distinct quality of a sound that distinguishes it from other sounds of the same pitch and loudness. Unlike the pure sound of a tuning fork, which has only one frequency, most sounds consist of several different frequencies. The frequencies that form the sound pattern above any tone a musical instrument produces are called *overtones*, or harmonics. Overtones give musical instruments their characteristic quality of sound, or timbre. The rich, full sound of a French horn, for example, is due to the large number of overtones it produces.

The Ear

The part of the ear that we see, more accurately labeled the *pinna* (see Figure 3.4), plays only a minor role in **audition**—the sensation of hearing. The **outer ear** consists of the pinna and the *auditory canal*, which is about 1 inch long and lined with hairs at its entrance. At the end of the auditory canal is the *eardrum* (or *tympanic membrane*), a thin, flexible membrane about $\frac{1}{3}$ inch in diameter. The eardrum moves in response to the sound waves that strike it.

The **middle ear** is no larger than an aspirin tablet. Inside its chamber are the *ossicles*, the three smallest bones in your body. Named for their shapes, the three connected ossicles—the hammer, the anvil, and the stirrup—link the eardrum to the oval window (see Figure 3.4). The ossicles amplify the sound by about 22 times (Békésy, 1957).

The **inner ear** begins at the inner side of the oval window on the base of the **cochlea**—a fluid-filled, snail-shaped, bony chamber. When the stirrup pushes against the oval window, it sets up vibrations that move the fluid in the cochlea back and forth in waves. The movement of the fluid sets in motion the thin basilar membrane that runs through the cochlea. Attached to the basilar membrane are about 15,000

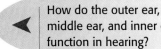

How do the outer ear, middle ear, and inner ear function in hearing?

timbre
(TAM-burr) The distinctive quality of a sound that distinguishes it from other sounds of the same pitch and loudness.

audition
The sensation of hearing; the process of hearing.

outer ear
The visible part of the ear, consisting of the pinna and the auditory canal.

middle ear
The portion of the ear containing the ossicles, which connect the eardrum to the oval window and amplify the sound vibrations as they travel to the inner ear.

inner ear
The innermost portion of the ear, containing the cochlea, the vestibular sacs, and the semicircular canals.

cochlea
(KOK-lee-uh) The snail-shaped, fluid-filled chamber in the inner ear that contains the hair cells (the sound receptors).

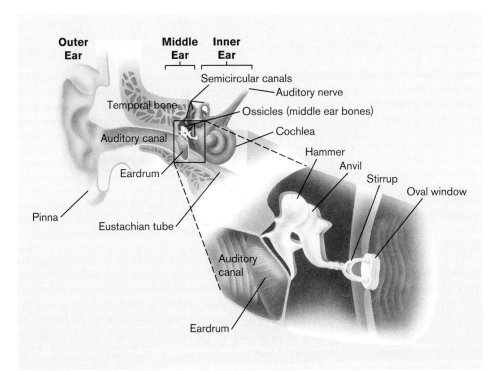

➤ Figure 3.4

Anatomy of the Human Ear

Sound waves pass through the auditory canal to the eardrum, causing it to vibrate and set in motion the ossicles in the middle ear. When the stirrup pushes against the oval window, it sets up vibrations in the inner ear. This moves the fluid in the cochlea back and forth and sets in motion the hair cells, causing a message to be sent to the brain via the auditory nerve.

sensory receptors called **hair cells,** each with a bundle of tiny hairs protruding from it. The tiny hair bundles are pushed and pulled by the motion of the fluid inside the cochlea. If the tip of the hair bundle is moved only as much as the width of an atom, an electrical impulse is generated, which is transmitted to the brain by way of the auditory nerve.

Having two ears, one on each side of the head, enables us to determine the direction from which sounds are coming. In an early study, neuroscientists found that the brain detects differences as small as 0.0001 second in the arrival times of sound impulses from the two ears and interprets them, revealing the direction of the sound (Rosenzweig, 1961). The source of a sound may also be determined by the difference in intensity of the sound reaching each ear (Middlebrooks & Green, 1991). Bats are especially adept at determining the direction and the precise distance to the source of a sound; they use echolocation to find their prey (Covey, 2000).

Theories of Hearing

What two major theories attempt to explain hearing? ▶

In the 1860s, Hermann von Helmholtz helped develop *place theory,* one of the two major theories of hearing. This theory holds that each individual pitch a person hears is determined by the particular spot or place along the basilar membrane of the cochlea that vibrates the most. Observing the living basilar membrane, researchers verified that different locations do indeed vibrate in response to differently pitched sounds (Ruggero, 1992). Even so, place theory cannot explain how humans perceive frequencies below 150 Hz.

Another attempt to explain hearing is *frequency theory.* According to this theory, the hair cell receptors vibrate the same number of times per second as the sounds that reach them. Thus, a tone of 500 Hz would stimulate the hair cells to vibrate 500 times per second as well. However, because individual neurons linked to the hair receptor cells cannot fire more than about 1,000 times per second, frequency theory cannot account for frequencies higher than 1,000 Hz. A receptor might indeed vibrate as rapidly as the sound wave associated with a higher tone, but the information necessary to perceive the pitch wouldn't be faithfully transmitted to the brain. Consequently, frequency theory seems to be a good explanation of how we hear low-frequency (below 500 Hz) tones, but place theory better describes the way in which we hear tones above 1,000 Hz (Matlin & Foley, 1997). Both frequency and location are involved when we hear sounds between 500 and 1,000 Hz.

Smell and Taste

Smell

Olfaction—the sense of smell—is a chemical sense. When odor molecules vaporize, they become airborne and make their way up each nostril to the olfactory epithelium. The **olfactory epithelium** consists of two 1-square-inch patches of tissue, one at the top of each nasal cavity, which together contain about 10 million olfactory neurons—the receptor cells for smell. Each of these neurons contains only one of the 1,000 different types of odor receptors. Differences in the size of the olfactory epithelium explain variations in olfactory sensitivity across species. Dogs, for example, have an olfactory epithelium 20 times the size of that in humans. Figure 3.5 shows a diagram of the human olfactory system.

What path does a smell message take from the nose to the brain? ▶

Olfactory neurons are special types of neurons that both come into direct contact with sensory stimuli and reach directly into the brain. And these neurons have a short life span; after functioning for only about 60 days, they die and are replaced by new cells (Buck, 1996). The axons of the olfactory neurons relay a smell message directly to the **olfactory bulbs**—two brain

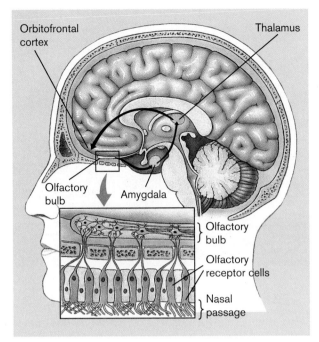

▶ Figure 3.5

The Olfactory System

Odor molecules travel up the nostrils to the olfactory epithelium, which contains the receptor cells for smell. Olfactory receptors are special neurons whose axons form the olfactory nerve. The olfactory nerve relays smell messages to the olfactory bulbs, which pass them on to the thalamus, the orbitofrontal cortex, and other parts of the brain.

structures the size of matchsticks that rest above the nasal cavities (refer to Figure 3.5). From the olfactory bulbs, the message is relayed to the thalamus and orbitofrontal cortex, which distinguish the odor and relay that information to other parts of the brain.

The human olfactory system is capable of sensing and distinguishing 10,000 different odors. But there are large individual differences in sensitivity to smells. For example, perfumers and whiskey blenders can distinguish subtle variations in odors that are indistinguishable to the average person. Women are generally more sensitive to odors than men are, and they are more sensitive still during ovulation. Young people are more sensitive to odors than older people, and nonsmokers are more sensitive than smokers (Matlin & Foley, 1997).

Brain-imaging studies of human olfactory functioning have recently established key connections among the sense of smell, emotion, and memory in the limbic system (Pause & Krauel, 2000; Zald & Pardo, 2000). However, these associations are weaker in older adults than in younger people. The apparent lack of sensitivity of the limbic system to scents that develops in old age may be linked to recent findings demonstrating that measures of olfactory function in the elderly strongly predict the onset of age-related memory problems (Royall et al., 2002; Swan & Carmelli, 2002). Those who show the greatest loss of olfaction are more likely than their peers to develop dementia. Thus, measurement of olfactory function in older adults may be a useful way of identifying those who are at greater risk for the development of dementia–before they exhibit any symptoms.

Many animals excrete chemicals called **pheromones,** which can have a powerful effect on the behavior of other members of the same species. For example, the "queen" of an ant colony emits a pheromone that identifies her to all subordinate colony members (Vander Meer & Alonso, 2002). Pheromones emitted by predators that prey on salamanders serve as cues for the salamanders to adopt predator-foiling behaviors such as hiding (Sullivan et al., 2002). Humans emit and respond to pheromones as well. For example, the human pheromone *androsterone* causes changes in physiological functions such as heart rate and mood states (DeBortoli et al., 2001). An interesting area of research on this pheromone involves *menstrual synchrony,* the tendency of the menstrual cycles of women who live together to synchronize with one another over time. In one study of women living in college dormitories, researchers found that 38% of roommate pairs developed synchronous

olfaction
(ol-FAK-shun) The sensation of smell; the process of smelling.

olfactory epithelium
Two 1-square-inch patches of tissue, one at the top of each nasal cavity, which together contain about 10 million olfactory neurons, the receptors for smell.

olfactory bulbs
Two matchstick-sized structures above the nasal cavities, where smell sensations first register in the brain.

pheromones
Chemicals excreted by humans and other animals that act as signals to and elicit certain patterns of behavior from members of the same species.

Individual differences in sensitivity to pheromones contribute to variations in menstrual synchrony among women who live in college dormitories.

cycles after three months of living together (Morofushi et al., 2000). Roommates who synchronized showed greater olfactory sensitivity to androsterone than did nonsynchronized dormitory residents.

Taste

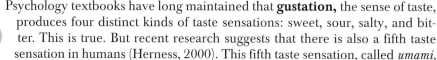

What are the primary taste sensations, and where are they detected?

Psychology textbooks have long maintained that **gustation,** the sense of taste, produces four distinct kinds of taste sensations: sweet, sour, salty, and bitter. This is true. But recent research suggests that there is also a fifth taste sensation in humans (Herness, 2000). This fifth taste sensation, called *umami,* is a response to the chemical *glutamate,* which is widely used in the form monosodium glutamate as a flavoring in Asian foods (Matsunami et al., 2000). Many protein-rich foods, such as meat, milk, aged cheese, and seafood, contain glutamate. All five taste sensations can be detected on all locations of the tongue. Indeed, even a person with no tongue could still taste to some extent, thanks to the taste receptors found in the palate, in the mucus lining of the cheeks and lips, and in parts of the throat, including the tonsils.

If you look at your tongue in a mirror, you will see many small bumps called *papillae.* There are four different types of papillae, and three of them contain **taste buds,** which cluster around the cracks and crevices between the papillae (see Figure 3.6). Each taste bud is composed of between 60 and 100 receptor cells, which resemble the petals of a flower. But the life span of the receptor cells for taste is very short, only about 10 days, and they are continually replaced.

Research indicates that humans can be divided into three groups based on taste sensitivity for certain sweet and bitter substances: nontasters, medium tasters, and supertasters (Yackinous & Guinard, 2002). Nontasters are unable to taste some sweet and bitter compounds, but they do taste most other substances, although with less sensitivity. Supertasters taste certain sweet and bitter compounds with far stronger intensity than do other people. Researchers are currently investigating links between taste sensitivity and eating behaviors and nutritional status. For example, supertasters are particularly sensitive to the chemical that gives fruits and vegetables a bitter taste and thus eat less salad than medium tasters and nontasters do (Yackinous & Guinard, 2002). Still, the supertasters appear no more likely than the medium tasters or nontasters to be overweight. In fact, among individuals who report that they never deliberately restrict their diets to try to lose weight, supertasters have less body fat than medium tasters and nontasters (Tepper & Ullrich, 2002). So, researchers know that taste sensitivity is linked to food preferences, but not how these preferences may be connected to nutritional status.

gustation
The sensation of taste.

taste buds
Structures composed of 60 to 100 sensory receptors for taste.

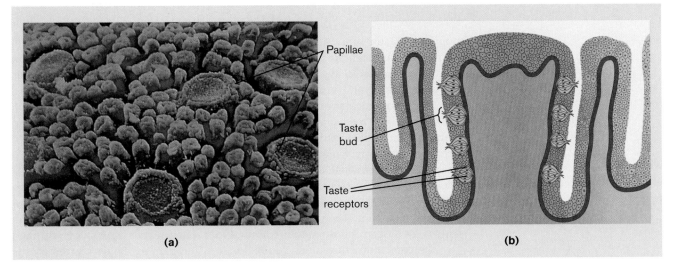

➤ Figure 3.6

The Tongue's Papillae and Taste Buds

(a) A photomicrograph of the surface of the tongue shows several papillae. (b) This vertical cross-section through one of the papillae reveals the location of the taste buds and taste receptors.

The Other Senses

The Skin Senses

Your natural clothing, the skin, is the largest organ of your body. It performs many important biological functions while also providing much of what is known as sensual pleasure. **Tactile** information is conveyed to the brain when an object touches and depresses the skin, stimulating one or more of the several distinct types of receptors found in the nerve endings. These sensitive nerve endings in the skin send the touch message through nerve connections to the spinal cord. The message travels up the spinal cord and through the brainstem and the midbrain, finally reaching the forebrain's somatosensory cortex. (Remember from Chapter 2 that the somatosensory cortex is the strip of brain tissue at the front of the parietal lobes where touch, pressure, temperature, and pain register.) Once the somatosensory cortex has been activated, you become aware of where and how hard you have been touched.

If you could examine the skin from the outermost to the deepest layer, you would find a variety of nerve endings that differ markedly in appearance. Most or all of these nerve endings appear to respond in some degree to all different types of tactile stimulation. The more densely packed a part of the body's surface is with such sensory receptors, the more sensitive it is to tactile stimulation. In the 1890s, one of the most prominent researchers of the tactile sense, Max von Frey, discovered the two-point threshold, which measures how far apart two points must be before they are felt as two separate touches.

Research in the mid-1980s established the importance of touch in human development. Premature infants who were massaged for 15 minutes three times a day gained weight 47% faster than other premature infants who received only regular intensive care treatment (Field et al., 1986). The massaged infants were more responsive and were able to leave the hospital about 6 days earlier, on average, than those who were not massaged. And 8 months later, the massaged infants scored higher on tests of motor and mental ability.

How does the skin provide sensory information?

tactile
Pertaining to the sense of touch.

Pain

What beneficial purpose does pain serve? ▶

Although the tactile sense delivers a great deal of pleasure, it brings us pain as well. Pain motivates us to tend to injuries, to restrict activity, and to seek medical help. Pain also teaches us to avoid pain-producing circumstances in the future. Chronic pain, however, persists long after it serves any useful function and creates a serious medical problem for some 34 million Americans (Brownlee & Schrof, 1997). The three major types of chronic pain are low-back pain, headache, and arthritis pain. For its victims, chronic pain is like a fire alarm that no one can turn off. Yet a course in pain management is required in only a fraction of medical residency programs (Brownlee & Schrof, 1997).

What is the gate-control theory of pain? ▶

Scientists are not certain how pain works, but one major theory seeks to explain it—the *gate-control theory* of Melzack and Wall (1965, 1983). These theorists contend that there is an area in the spinal cord that can act like a gate and either inhibit pain messages or transmit them to the brain. Only so many messages can go through the gate at any one time. You feel pain when pain messages carried by the small, slow-conducting nerve fibers reach the gate and cause it to open. Large, fast-conducting nerve fibers carry other sensory messages from the body, and these can effectively tie up traffic at the gate so that it will close and keep many of the pain messages from getting through. What is the first thing you do when you stub your toe or pound your finger with a hammer? If you rub or apply gentle pressure to the injury, you are stimulating the large, fast-conducting nerve fibers, which get their message to the spinal gate first and block some of the pain messages from the slower nerve fibers. Applying ice, heat, or electrical stimulation to the painful area also stimulates the large nerve fibers and closes the spinal gate.

The gate-control theory also accounts for the fact that psychological factors, both cognitive and emotional, can influence the perception of pain. Melzack and Wall (1965, 1983) contend that messages from the brain to the spinal cord can inhibit the transmission of pain messages at the spinal gate and thereby affect the perception of pain. This explains why some people can undergo surgery under hypnosis and feel little or no pain. It also explains why soldiers injured in battle or athletes injured during games can be so distracted that they do not experience pain until some time after the injury.

Psychological and Cultural Influences on the Experience of Pain

The experience of pain has both a physical and an emotional component, and both components vary from person to person. Pain experts distinguish between pain and suffering: Suffering is the affective, or emotional, response to the physical pain. Sullivan and others (1995) found that people suffered most from pain when they harbored negative thoughts about it, feared its potential threat to their well-being, and expressed feelings of helplessness.

Culture also influences the way pain is experienced and expressed. The most often cited work on pain and culture is that of Zborowski (1952), who compared the responses to pain of Italian, Jewish, Irish, and native-born Anglo-Saxon patients in a large hospital in New York. Among the four groups, Jewish and Italian patients responded more emotionally and showed heightened expressions of pain.

Culture even influences the experience and expression of pain during childbirth. The Chinese value silence, and Chinese women enduring the pain of childbirth typically do not engage in loud and highly emotional responses for fear they will dishonor themselves and their families (Weber, 1996). In stark contrast are some Pakistani women who believe that the greater their suffering and the louder their response to the pain, the more caring their husbands will be during the following weeks (Ahmad, 1994).

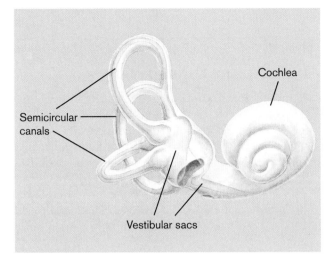

Sensing Balance and Movement

You sense the rotation of your head in any direction because the movement sends fluid coursing through the tubelike semicircular canals in the inner ear. The moving fluid bends the hair cell receptors—which, in turn, send the message to the brain.

The Kinesthetic and Vestibular Senses

The **kinesthetic sense** provides information about (1) the position of body parts in relation to each other and (2) the movement of the entire body and/or its parts. This information is detected by receptors in the joints, ligaments, and muscles. The other senses, especially vision, provide additional information about body position and movement, but the kinesthetic sense works well on its own. Thanks to the kinesthetic sense, we are able to perform smooth and skilled body movements without visual feedback or studied, conscious effort.

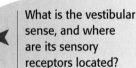

What kind of information does the kinesthetic sense provide, and how is this sensory information detected?

The **vestibular sense** detects movement and provides information about the body's orientation in space. Interestingly, an analysis of the design of the World Trade Center towers following the attack on September 11, 2001 revealed that motion-detection research conducted in 1965 by psychologist Paul Hoffman probably saved many lives (Benson, 2003). Commissioned to find out how sensitive occupants would be to the swaying of the towers in high winds, Hoffman discovered that the human vestibular system is extremely sensitive to such movement. As a result, engineers added considerable reinforcement to the buildings' framework. Analysts now believe this additional reinforcement helped the towers remain standing after the planes crashed into them, allowing time for thousands of people to escape before their ultimate collapse.

What is the vestibular sense, and where are its sensory receptors located?

The vestibular sense organs are located in the semicircular canals and the *vestibular sacs* in the inner ear. The **semicircular canals** sense the rotation of your head, such as when you are turning your head from side to side or when you are spinning around (see Figure 3.7). Because the canals are filled with fluid, rotating movements of the head in any direction send the fluid coursing through the tubelike semicircular canals. In the canals, the moving fluid bends hair cells, which act as receptors and send neural impulses to the brain. Because there are three canals, each positioned on a different plane, the hair cells in one canal will bend more than the hair cells in the other canals, depending on the direction of rotation.

The semicircular canals and the vestibular sacs signal only changes in motion or orientation. If you were blindfolded and had no visual or other external cues, you would not be able to sense motion once your speed reached a constant rate. For example, in an airplane you feel the takeoff and the landing as well as any sudden changes in speed. But once the plane levels off and maintains a fairly constant cruising speed, your vestibular organs do not signal the brain that you are moving, even if you are traveling at a rate of hundreds of miles per hour.

kinesthetic sense
The sense providing information about relative position and movement of body parts.

vestibular sense
(ves-TIB-yu-ler) Sense that provides information about the body's movement and orientation in space through sensory receptors in the semicircular canals and the vestibular sacs, which detect changes in the movement and orientation of the head.

semicircular canals
Three fluid-filled tubular canals in the inner ear that provide information about rotating head movements.

Perception

The Gestalt Principles of Perceptual Organization

Earlier in the chapter, you learned that *perception* is the process by which sensory information is actively organized and interpreted by the brain. The Gestalt psychologists maintained that people cannot understand the perceptual world by breaking down experiences into tiny parts and analyzing them separately. When sensory elements are brought together, something new is formed. The whole is more than just the sum of its parts, insisted the Gestalt psychologists.

The German word **Gestalt** has no exact English equivalent, but it refers roughly to the whole form, pattern, or configuration that a person perceives. The Gestalt psychologists claimed that sensory experience is organized according to certain basic principles of perceptual organization:

- *Figure-ground.* As you view your world, some object (the figure) seems to stand out from the background (the ground) (see Figure 3.8).
- *Similarity.* Objects that have similar characteristics are perceived as a unit. In Figure 3.9(a), dots of a similar color are perceived as belonging together to form horizontal rows on the left and vertical columns on the right.
- *Proximity.* Objects that are close together in space or time are usually perceived as belonging together, as a result of a principle of grouping called *proximity.* Due to their spacing, the lines in Figure 3.9(b) are perceived as four pairs of lines rather than as eight separate lines.
- *Continuity.* We tend to perceive figures or objects as belonging together if they appear to form a continuous pattern, as in Figure 3.9(c).
- *Closure.* We perceive figures with gaps in them to be complete. Even though parts of the figure in Figure 3.9(d) are missing, you use closure and perceive it as a triangle.

Perceptual Constancy

Even though we view objects or other people from different angles and distances and under different lighting conditions, we tend to see them as maintaining the same size, shape, and brightness. Scientists call this phenomenon **perceptual constancy.** For example, when you say good-bye to friends and watch them walk away, the image they cast on your retina grows smaller and smaller until they finally disappear in the distance. But the shrinking-size information that the retina sends to the brain (the sensation) does not fool the perceptual system. As objects or people move farther away, you continue to perceive them as being about the same size. This perceptual phenomenon is known as *size constancy.* We do not make a literal interpretation about the size of objects from the retinal image—the image projected onto the retina of objects in the visual field. If we did, we would believe that objects become larger as they approach and smaller as they move away.

> **What are the Gestalt principles of perceptual organization?**

> **What is perceptual constancy?**

Gestalt
(geh-SHTALT) A German word roughly meaning "form" or "pattern."

perceptual constancy
The tendency to perceive objects as maintaining stable properties, such as size, shape, brightness, and color, despite differences in distance, viewing angle, and lighting.

➤ Figure 3.8

Reversing Figure and Ground

In this illustration, you can see a white vase as figure against a black background, or two black faces in profile on a white background. Exactly the same visual stimulus produces two opposite figure-ground perceptions.

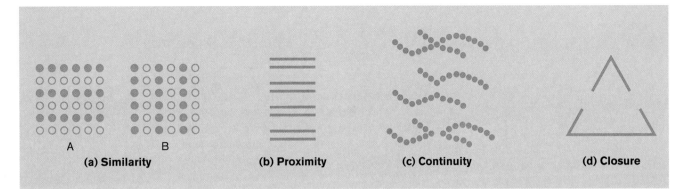

(a) Similarity   (b) Proximity   (c) Continuity   (d) Closure

➤ **Figure 3.9**

Gestalt Principles of Perceptual Grouping

Gestalt psychologists proposed four principles of perceptual grouping: similarity, proximity, continuity, and closure.

The shape or image of an object projected onto the retina changes according to the angle from which it is viewed. But our perceptual ability includes *shape constancy*–the tendency to perceive objects as having a stable or unchanging shape regardless of changes in the retinal image resulting from differences in viewing angle. In other words, you perceive a door as rectangular and a plate as round, no matter what angle you view them from (see Figure 3.10).

People normally see objects as maintaining a constant level of brightness, regardless of differences in lighting conditions–a phenomenon known as *brightness constancy*. Nearly all objects reflect some part of the light that falls on them, and white objects reflect more light than black objects. However, a black asphalt driveway at noon in bright sunlight actually reflects more light than a white shirt does indoors at night in dim lighting. Nevertheless, the driveway still looks black and the shirt still looks white. Why? We learn to infer the brightness of objects by comparing them with the brightness of all other objects viewed at the same time.

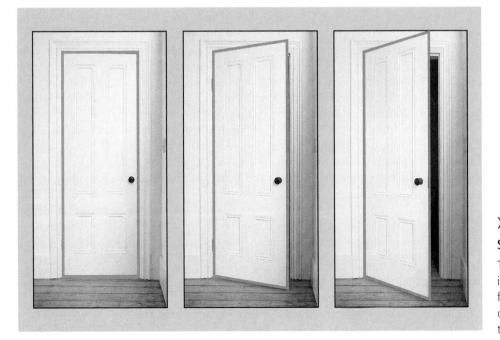

➤ **Figure 3.10**

Shape Constancy

The door projects very different images on the retina when viewed from different angles. But because of shape constancy, you continue to perceive the door as rectangular.

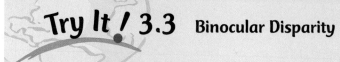

Try It! 3.3 Binocular Disparity

Hold your forefinger or a pencil at arm's length straight in front of you. Close your right eye and focus on the pencil. Now quickly close your left eye at the same time that you open your right eye. Repeat this procedure, closing one eye just as you open the other one. The pencil will appear to move from side to side in front of your face.

Now slowly bring the pencil closer and closer until it almost reaches your nose. The closer you bring the pencil, the more it appears to move from side to side. This is because there is progressively more disparity between the two retinal images as a viewed object gets closer and closer to your eyes.

Depth Perception

depth perception
The ability to see in three dimensions and to estimate distance.

binocular depth cues
Depth cues that depend on two eyes working together; they include convergence and binocular disparity.

> **What are the binocular depth cues?** ▶

> **What are seven monocular depth cues?** ▶

monocular depth cues
(mah-NOK-yu-ler) Depth cues that can be perceived by only one eye.

Depth perception is the ability to perceive the visual world in three dimensions and to judge distances accurately. We judge how far away objects and other people are. We climb and descend stairs without stumbling and perform many other actions that require depth perception. Depth perception is three-dimensional. Yet each eye is able to provide only a two-dimensional view. The images cast on the retina do not contain depth; they are flat, just like a photograph. How, then, do we perceive depth so vividly?

Some cues for depth perception depend on both eyes working together. Called **binocular depth cues,** these are convergence and binocular disparity. *Convergence* occurs when the eyes turn inward to focus on nearby objects–the closer the object, the greater the convergence. Hold the tip of your finger about 12 inches in front of your nose and focus on it. Now slowly begin moving your finger toward your nose. Your eyes will turn inward so much that they virtually cross when the tip of your finger meets the tip of your nose. Many psychologists believe that the tension of the eye muscles as they converge conveys information to the brain that serves as a cue for distance and depth perception. Fortunately, the pupils are just far enough apart, about 2½ inches or so, to give each eye a slightly different view of the objects focused on and, consequently, a slightly different retinal image. The difference between the two retinal images, known as *binocular disparity* (or *retinal disparity*), provides an important cue for depth and distance (see *Try It! 3.3*). The farther away from the eyes the objects being looked at are (up to 20 feet or so), the less the disparity, or difference, between the two retinal images. The brain integrates the two slightly different retinal images and gives the perception of three dimensions.

Close one eye and you will see that you can still perceive depth. The visual depth cues perceived by one eye alone are called **monocular depth cues.** Many of these have been used by artists in Western cultures to give the illusion of depth to their paintings. Seven monocular depth cues are described below. Photos illustrating each type of cue are shown in Figure 3.11.

- *Interposition.* When one object partly blocks your view of another, you perceive the partially blocked object as farther away.
- *Linear perspective.* Parallel lines that are known to be the same distance apart appear to grow closer together, or converge, as they recede into the distance.

Interposition	**Linear Perspective**	**Relative Size**	**Texture Gradient**
When one object partially blocks your view of another, you perceive the partially blocked object as being farther away.	Parallel lines are the same distance apart but appear to grow closer together, or converge, as they recede into the distance.	Larger objects are perceived as being closer to the viewer, and smaller objects as being farther away.	Objects close to you appear to have sharply defined features, and similar objects farther away appear progressively less well defined, or fuzzier in texture.

Atmospheric Perspective	**Shadow or Shading**	**Motion Parallax**
Objects in the distance have a bluish tint and appear more blurred than objects close at hand (sometimes called *aerial perspective*).	When light falls on objects, they cast shadows, which add to the perception of depth.	When you ride in a moving train and look out the window, the objects you see outside appear to be moving in the opposite direction and at different speeds; those closest to you appear to be moving faster than those in the distance.

> **Figure 3.11**
Monocular Depth Cues

- *Relative size.* Larger objects are perceived as being closer to the viewer, and smaller objects as being farther away.
- *Texture gradient.* Near objects appear to have sharply defined textures, but similar objects appear progressively smoother and fuzzier as they recede into the distance.
- *Atmospheric perspective.* Objects in the distance have a bluish tint and appear more blurred than objects close at hand (sometimes called *aerial perspective*).
- *Shadow or shading.* When light falls on objects, they cast shadows. You can distinguish bulges from indentions by the shadows they cast.
- *Motion parallax.* When you ride in a moving vehicle and look out the side window, the objects you see outside appear to be moving in the opposite direction. The objects also seem to be moving at different speeds—those closest to you appear to be moving faster than those in the distance. Objects very far away, such as the moon and the sun, appear to move in the same direction as the viewer.

Extraordinary Perceptions

Before we explore extraordinary perceptions, take a moment to experience them for yourself—answer the questions in *Try It! 3.4* before reading further.

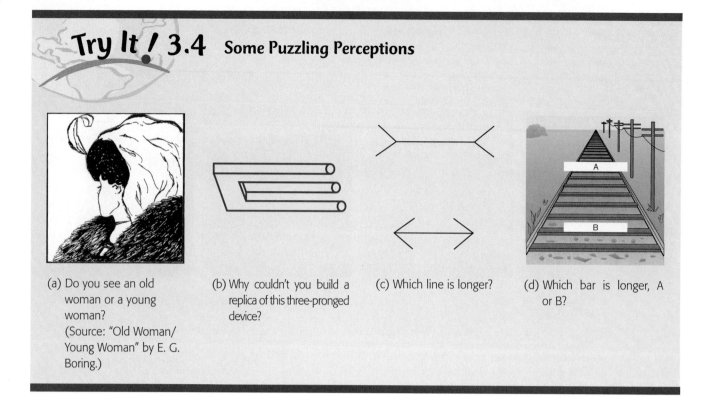

(a) Do you see an old woman or a young woman? (Source: "Old Woman/ Young Woman" by E. G. Boring.)

(b) Why couldn't you build a replica of this three-pronged device?

(c) Which line is longer?

(d) Which bar is longer, A or B?

When you are faced for the first time with an *ambiguous figure,* like the one in part (a) of *Try It! 3.4,* you have no experience to call on. Your perceptual system is puzzled and tries to resolve the dilemma by seeing the ambiguous figure first one way and then another, but not both at once. You never get a lasting impression of ambiguous figures because they seem to jump back and forth beyond your control. In some ambiguous figures, two different objects or figures are seen alternately. The best known of these is the one in the *Try It!*–"Old Woman/Young Woman," by E. G. Boring. If you direct your gaze to the left of the drawing, you are likely to see an attractive young woman, her face turned away. But the young woman disappears when you suddenly perceive the image of the old woman. Such examples of object ambiguity offer striking evidence that perceptions are more than the sum of their sensory parts. It is hard to believe that the same drawing (the same sum of sensory parts) can convey such dramatically different perceptions.

> **What are three types of puzzling perceptions?**

At first glance, many impossible figures do not seem so unusual–not until you examine them more closely. Would you invest your money in a company that manufactured three-pronged devices like the one shown in part (b) of *Try It! 3.4*? Such an object could not actually be made because the middle prong appears to be in two different places at the same time. However, this type of impossible figure is more likely to fool the perception abilities of people from Western cultures. People in some African cultures do not represent three-dimensional visual space in their art, and they do not perceive depth in drawings that contain pictorial depth cues. These people see no ambiguity in drawings similar to the one of the three-pronged device, and they can draw the figure accurately from memory much more easily than people from Western cultures can (Bloomer, 1976).

Illusions, like those in parts (c) and (d) of *Try It! 3.4,* are false perceptions or misperceptions of an actual stimulus in the environment. We can misperceive size, shape, or the relationship of one element to another. We need not pay to see illusions performed by magicians. Illusions occur naturally, and we see them all the time. An oar in the water appears to be bent where it meets the water. The moon looks much larger at the horizon than it does overhead. Why? One explanation of

illusion

A false perception of actual stimuli involving a misperception of size, shape, or the relationship of one element to another.

the moon illusion involves relative size. That is, the moon looks very large on the horizon because it is viewed in comparison to trees, buildings, and other objects. When viewed overhead, the moon cannot be compared with other objects, and it appears smaller. People have been speculating about the moon illusion for 22 centuries and experimenting for 50 years to determine its cause, but there is still no agreement (Hershenson, 1989).

In part (c) of *Try It! 3.4*, the two lines are the same length, but the diagonals extending outward from both ends of the upper line make it look longer than the lower line, which has diagonals pointing inward, a phenomenon known as the *Müller-Lyer illusion*. The *Ponzo illusion* also plays an interesting trick regarding estimation of size. Look at part (d) of *Try It! 3.4*. Contrary to your perception, bars A and B are the same size. Clearly, perceptions of size and distance, which we trust and which are normally accurate in informing us about the real world, can be wrong. If you saw two obstructions like the ones in the illusion on real railroad tracks, the one that looked larger would indeed be larger. So, the Ponzo illusion is not a natural illusion but a contrived one. In fact, all the illusions in the *Try It!* are really misapplications of principles that nearly always work properly in normal everyday experience.

Cultural Differences in the Perception of Visual Illusions

British psychologist R. L. Gregory believed that susceptibility to the Müller-Lyer and other visual illusions is not inborn. Rather, the culture in which people live is responsible to some extent for the illusions they perceive. To test whether susceptibility to the Müller-Lyer and similar illusions is due to experience, Segall and others (1966) tested 1,848 adults and children from 15 different cultures in Africa, the Philippines, and the United States. Included were a group of Zulus from South Africa and a group of Illinois residents. The study revealed that "there were marked differences in illusion susceptibility across the cultural groups included in this study" (Segall, 1994, p. 137). People in all the cultures showed some tendency to see the illusion, indicating a biological component, but experience was clearly a factor. Zulus, who have round houses and see few corners of any kind, were not fooled by the Müller-Lyer illusion, in contrast to the Illinois residents.

Early cross-cultural researchers suggested that race might offer an explanation for the cultural differences observed (Pollack, 1970). But an important study by Stewart (1973), done in response to this claim, provided evidence to indicate that it is fundamentally culture, not race, that drives perceptions of illusions. When two groups of schoolchildren from Illinois (60 African Americans and 60 White Americans) were tested with the Müller-Lyer and other visual illusions, no significant differences were found in susceptibility to them. And in Zambia, researchers tested five different groups of Black African schoolchildren using the same illusions. Children's tendency to see the illusions had

◄ Some visual illusions seem to be culture-dependent. For example, Zulus and people from other cultures in which the houses lack straight sides and corners do not perceive the Müller-Lyer illusion.

Noise and Hearing Loss

Hearing loss is increasing rapidly in the industrialized world, and the main reason for the increase is noise. Explosions, gun blasts, and other extremely loud noises can cause temporary or permanent deafness. Permanent hearing loss is the result when loud noises burst the eardrum or fracture or dislocate the tiny ossicles in the middle ear. Currently, U.S. government regulations protect employees from exposure to sound levels of more than 85 dB in the workplace during an 8-hour day. But there are several sources of noise in our environments that can lead to hearing loss.

Noisy toys In an eye-opening early study, researchers Axelsson and Jerson (1985) tested seven squeaking toys that, at a distance of 10 centimeters, emitted sound levels loud enough to put toddlers at risk for hearing loss at only 2 minutes of daily exposure. And their tests of various toy weapons found that all exceeded the 130-dB peak level that is considered the upper limit for exposure to short-lived explosive sounds if hearing loss is to be avoided.

Firecrackers These popular noise-makers pose a particular hazard if they explode close to the ear. In one study a number of firecrackers were tested at 3 meters, and sound levels were found to range from 130 dB to an unbelievable and highly dangerous 190 dB (Gupta & Vishwakarma, 1989).

Amplified music The decibel levels common at rock concerts can damage

hearing very rapidly. For example, rock musician Kathy Peck lost 40% of her hearing in a single evening after her band opened a stadium concert. Moreover, the rock group The Who entered the *Guinness Book of World Records* in 1986 as the loudest rock band on record, blasting out deafening sound intensities that measured 120 decibels at a distance of 164 feet from the speakers. Unless their ears were protected, audience members within that 164-foot radius probably suffered some irreversible hearing loss. And the band members? Pete Townshend, lead singer of The Who, has severely damaged hearing and, in addition, is plagued by tinnitus, an annoying condition that causes him to experience a continuous ringing in the ears.

Power tools Many types of power tools emit sufficient noise to damage hearing. Experts claim, for example, that exposure to a lawn mower (a noise level of about 90 dB) for more than 8 hours in a 24-hour period can damage hearing. For every increase of 5 dB, maximum exposure time to the tool should be cut in half—4 hours for 95 dB, 2 hours for 100 dB, and 1 hour for 105 dB.

Protecting yourself from hearing loss What can you do to protect yourself from the effects of noise?

- If you must be exposed to loud noise, use earplugs (not the kind used for swimming) or earmuffs.

- If you must engage in an extremely noisy activity, such as cutting wood

with a chain saw, limit periods of exposure.

- Keep the volume down on your Walkman-type radio or CD player. If the volume control is numbered 1 to 10, a volume above 4 probably exceeds the federal standards for noise. If you have a ringing in your ears, if sounds seem muffled, or if you have a tickling sensation in your ears after you remove your headset, you could have sustained some hearing loss.

- Put your fingers in your ears, or leave the scene. ■

nothing to do with race but was strongly influenced by culture. Those children who lived in areas where buildings had angles, edges, corners, and doors were likely to be fooled by the illusions; those who lived in remote villages with primarily round houses were not.

In another classic cross-cultural study of illusions, Pedersen and Wheeler (1983) studied responses to the Müller-Lyer illusion among two groups of Navajos. The Native American group who lived in rectangular houses and had experienced corners, angles, and edges tended to see the illusion. The other Native American group, like the Zulus, tended not to see it because their cultural experience consisted of round houses.

Additional Influences on Perception

Bottom-Up and Top-Down Processing

Psychologists distinguish between two distinct information-processing techniques that people use in recognizing patterns: bottom-up processing and top-down processing. **Bottom-up processing** begins with the individual components of a stimulus that are detected by the sensory receptors. The bits of information are then transmitted to areas in the brain where they are combined and assembled into the whole pattern that a person perceives. In **top-down processing,** on the other hand, past experience and knowledge influence our perceptions in such a way that we are able to find meaningful links between the individual elements taken in by our sensory receptors. If you have ever tried to decipher a prescription written by your doctor (bottom-up processing), you may have been amazed that your pharmacist could fill it. But prior knowledge and experience enabled the pharmacist to use top-down processing. Of course, we use both bottom-up and top-down processing to form perceptions. In unfamiliar situations, we are likely to use bottom-up processing. In familiar situations, where we have some prior knowledge and experience, we tend to use top-down processing.

Perceptual Set

The **perceptual set**—what you *expect* to perceive—determines, to a large extent, what you actually see, hear, feel, taste, and smell. If you were served raspberry sherbet that was colored green, would it still taste like raspberry, or might it taste more like lime? Once their expectations are set, people often bend reality to make it fit them. Thus, perceptual set results from top-down processing. In a classic study of perceptual set, psychologist David Rosenhan (1973) and some of his colleagues were admitted as patients to various mental hospitals with "diagnoses" of schizophrenia. Once admitted, they acted normal in every way. The purpose? They wondered how long it would take the doctors and the hospital staff to realize that they were not mentally ill. But the doctors and the staff members saw only what they expected to see and not what actually occurred. They perceived everything the pseudo-patients said and did, such as note taking, to be symptoms of their illness. But the real patients were not fooled. They were the first to realize that the psychologists were not really mentally ill.

bottom-up processing
Information processing in which individual components or bits of data are combined until a complete perception is formed.

◄ In what types of situations do people rely more on bottom-up processing or top-down processing?

top-down processing
Application of previous experience and conceptual knowledge to recognize the whole of a perception and thus easily identify the simpler elements of that whole.

perceptual set
An expectation of what will be perceived, which can affect what actually is perceived.

◄ How does perceptual set influence perceptions?

Summarize It!

Introduction

➤ What is the difference between sensation and perception?

Sensation is the process through which the senses pick up sensory stimuli and transmit them to the brain. Perception is the process by which this sensory information is actively organized and interpreted by the brain.

KEY TERMS

sensation (p. 64)
perception (p. 64)

The Process of Sensation

➤ What is the difference between the absolute threshold and the difference threshold?

The absolute threshold is the minimum amount of sensory stimulation that can be detected 50% of the time. The difference threshold is a measure of the smallest increase or decrease in a physical stimulus that can be detected 50% of the time.

➤ How are sensory stimuli in the environment experienced as sensations?

For each of the senses, the body has sensory receptors that detect and respond to sensory stimuli. Through the process of transduction, the receptors convert sensory stimuli into neural impulses, which are then transmitted to special locations in the brain.

KEY TERMS

absolute threshold (p. 64)
difference threshold (p. 65)
just noticeable difference (JND) (p. 65)
Weber's law (p. 65)
sensory receptors (p. 65)
sensory adaptation (p. 65)

Vision

➤ **How do the cornea, the iris, and the pupil function in vision?**

The cornea bends light rays inward through the pupil–the small, dark opening in the center of the iris. The iris dilates and contracts the pupil to regulate the amount of light passing through it.

➤ **What are the lens and the retina?**

The lens changes its shape as it focuses images of objects from varying distances on the retina, a thin layer of tissue containing the sensory receptors for vision.

➤ **What roles do the rods and cones play in vision?**

The cones detect color, provide the sharpest vision, and function best in high illumination. The rods enable vision in dim light.

➤ **What path does the neural impulse take from the retina to the primary visual cortex?**

The rods and the cones transduce light waves into neural impulses that pass to the ganglion cells, whose axons form the optic nerve. At the optic chiasm, some of the fibers of the optic nerve cross to the opposite side of the brain, before reaching the thalamus. From the thalamus, the neural impulses travel to the primary visual cortex.

➤ **What are the three dimensions of the colors people perceive?**

The three dimensions of color are hue, saturation, and brightness.

➤ **What two major theories attempt to explain color vision?**

Two major theories that attempt to explain color vision are the trichromatic theory and the opponent-process theory.

KEY TERMS
visible spectrum (p. 65)
cornea (p. 66)
lens (p. 66)
accommodation (p. 66)
retina (p. 66)
rods (p. 66)
cones (p. 66)
fovea (p. 67)
feature detectors (p. 68)

hue (p. 68)
saturation (p. 68)
brightness (p. 68)
afterimage (p. 69)
color blindness (p. 70)

Hearing

➤ **What determines the pitch and loudness of a sound, and how is each quality measured?**

The pitch of a sound is determined by the frequency of the sound waves, which is measured in hertz (Hz). The loudness of a sound is determined largely by the amplitude of the sound waves and is measured in decibels (dB).

➤ **How do the outer ear, middle ear, and inner ear function in hearing?**

Sound waves enter the pinna, the visible part of the outer ear, and travel to the end of the auditory canal, causing the eardrum to vibrate. This sets in motion the ossicles in the middle ear, which amplify the sound waves. The vibration of the oval window causes activity in the inner ear, setting in motion the fluid in the cochlea and moving the hair cells, which transduce the vibrations into neural impulses. The auditory nerve carries the neural impulses to the brain.

➤ **What two major theories attempt to explain hearing?**

Two major theories that attempt to explain hearing are place theory and frequency theory.

KEY TERMS
frequency (p. 70)
amplitude (p. 70)
decibel (p. 70)
timbre (p. 71)
audition (p. 71)
outer ear (p. 71)
middle ear (p. 71)
inner ear (p. 71)
cochlea (p. 71)
hair cells (p. 72)

Smell and Taste

➤ **What path does a smell message take from the nose to the brain?**

The act of smelling begins when odor molecules reach the smell receptors in the olfactory epithelium at the top of the nasal cavity. The axons of these receptors form the olfactory nerve, which relays the smell message to the olfactory bulbs. From there, the smell message travels to the olfactory cortex and on to other parts of the brain.

➤ **What are the primary taste sensations, and where are they detected?**

The primary taste sensations are sweet, salty, sour, and bitter, and a newly discovered one for glutamate. The receptor cells for taste are found in the taste buds on the tongue and in other parts of the mouth and throat.

KEY TERMS
olfaction (p. 72)
olfactory epithelium (p. 72)
olfactory bulbs (p. 72)
pheromones (p. 73)
gustation (p. 74)
taste buds (p. 74)

The Other Senses

➤ **How does the skin provide sensory information?**

Nerve endings in the skin (the sensory receptors) respond to different kinds of stimulation, including heat and cold, pressure, pain, and a vast range of touch sensations. The neural impulses ultimately register in the somatosensory cortex.

➤ **What beneficial purpose does pain serve?**

Pain can be a valuable warning and a protective mechanism, motivating people to tend to an injury, to restrict activity, and to seek medical help if needed.

➤ **What is the gate-control theory of pain?**

Melzack and Wall's gate-control theory of pain holds that pain signals transmitted by slow-conducting nerve fibers can be blocked at the spinal gate (1) if fast-conducting nerve fibers get other sensory messages to the gate first or (2) if the brain sends inhibiting messages to the spinal cord.

➤ **What kind of information does the kinesthetic sense provide, and how is this sensory information detected?**

The kinesthetic sense provides information about the relative position of body parts and movement of those parts. The position or motion is detected by sensory receptors in the joints, ligaments, and muscles.

➤ **What is the vestibular sense, and where are its sensory receptors located?**

The vestibular sense provides information about movement and the body's orientation in space. Sensory receptors in the semicircular canals and in the vestibular sacs detect changes in the movement and orientation of the head.

KEY TERMS

tactile (p. 75)
kinesthetic sense (p. 77)
vestibular sense (p. 77)
semicircular canals (p. 77)

Perception

➤ **What are the Gestalt principles of perceptual organization?**

The Gestalt principles of perceptual organization include figure-ground, similarity, proximity, continuity, and closure.

➤ **What is perceptual constancy?**

Perceptual constancy is the tendency to perceive objects as maintaining the same size, shape, and brightness despite changes in lighting conditions or changes in the retinal image that result when objects are viewed from different angles and distances.

➤ **What are the binocular depth cues?**

The binocular depth cues are convergence and binocular disparity. They help to provide depth perception and depend on both eyes working together.

➤ **What are seven monocular depth cues?**

The monocular depth cues, those that are perceived by one eye, include interposition, linear perspective, relative size, texture gradient, atmospheric perspective, shadow or shading, and motion parallax.

➤ **What are three types of puzzling perceptions?**

Three types of puzzling perceptions are ambiguous figures, impossible figures, and illusions.

KEY TERMS

Gestalt (p. 78)
perceptual constancy (p. 78)
depth perception (p. 80)
binocular depth cues (p. 80)
monocular depth cues (p. 80)
illusion (p. 82)

Additional Influences on Perception

➤ **In what types of situations do people rely more on bottom-up processing or top-down processing?**

People use bottom-up processing more in unfamiliar situations and top-down processing more in situations about which they have some prior knowledge and experience.

➤ **How does perceptual set influence perceptions?**

Expectations generated by perceptual set may predispose people to perceive sensations in a particular way. They may bend reality to make it fit their perceptual set.

KEY TERMS

bottom-up processing (p. 85)
top-down processing (p. 85)
perceptual set (p. 85)

Surf It!

Want to be sure you've absorbed the material in Chapter 3, "Sensation and Perception," before the big test? Visiting **www.ablongman.com/woodmastering1e** can put a top grade within your reach. The site is loaded with free practice tests, flashcards, activities, and links to help you review your way to an A.

Companion Website

Study Guide for Chapter 3 !

Answers to all the Study Guide questions are provided at the end of the book.

Section One: Chapter Review

1. The process through which the senses detect sensory information and transmit it to the brain is called (sensation, perception).

2. The point at which you can barely sense a stimulus 50% of the time is called the (absolute, difference) threshold.

3. The difference threshold is the same for all individuals. (true/false)

4. Which of the following is not true of sensory receptors?
   a. They are specialized to detect certain sensory stimuli.
   b. They transduce sensory stimuli into neural impulses.
   c. They are located in the brain.
   d. They provide the link between the physical sensory world and the brain.

5. The process by which a sensory stimulus is converted into a neural impulse is called _____ .

6. Each morning when Jackie goes to work at a dry cleaner, she smells a strong odor of cleaning fluid. After she is there for a few minutes, she is no longer aware of it. What accounts for this?
   a. signal detection theory
   b. sensory adaptation
   c. transduction
   d. the just noticeable difference

7. Match each part of the eye with its description.
   ____ (1) the colored part of the eye
   ____ (2) the opening in the iris that dilates and constricts
   ____ (3) the transparent covering of the iris
   ____ (4) the transparent structure that focuses an inverted image on the retina
   ____ (5) the thin, photosensitive membrane at the back of the eye on which the lens focuses an inverted image
   a. retina
   b. cornea
   c. pupil
   d. iris
   e. lens

8. The receptor cells in the retina that enable you to see in dim light are the (cones, rods); the cells that enable you to see color and sharp images are (cones, rods).

9. Neural impulses are carried from the retina to the thalamus by the _____ and then relayed to their final destination, the _____ .

   a. optic chiasm; primary visual cortex
   b. rods and cones; optic nerve
   c. optic nerve; primary visual cortex
   d. optic nerve; optic chiasm

10. Pitch is chiefly determined by _____ ; loudness is chiefly determined by _____ .
    a. amplitude; frequency
    b. wavelength; frequency
    c. intensity; amplitude
    d. frequency; amplitude

11. Pitch is measured in (decibels, hertz); loudness is measured in (decibels, hertz).

12. Match the part of the ear with the structures it contains.
    ____ (1) ossicles   a. outer ear
    ____ (2) pinna, auditory canal   b. middle ear
    ____ (3) cochlea, hair cells   c. inner ear

13. The receptors for hearing are found in the
    a. ossicles.   c. auditory membrane.
    b. auditory canal.   d. cochlea.

14. The two major theories that attempt to explain hearing are
    a. conduction theory and place theory.
    b. hair cell theory and frequency theory.
    c. place theory and frequency theory.
    d. conduction theory and hair cell theory.

15. According to the text, which of the following statements about excessive noise is true?
    a. Excessive noise has temporary effects on hearing.
    b. Excessive noise affects hearing only in the elderly.
    c. Excessive noise can have both temporary and permanent effects on hearing.
    d. Excessive noise often leads to total deafness.

16. The technical name for the process or sensation of smell is (gustation, olfaction).

17. The olfactory, or smell, receptors are located in the
    a. olfactory tract.
    b. olfactory nerve.
    c. olfactory epithelium.
    d. olfactory bulbs.

18. The five taste sensations are _____ , _____ , _____ , _____ , and _____ .

19. Each (papilla, taste bud) contains from 60 to 100 receptor cells.

20. Each skin receptor responds only to touch, pressure, warmth, or cold. (true/false)

21. The (kinesthetic, vestibular) sense provides information about the position of body parts in relation to each other and about movement in those body parts.

22. The receptors for the (kinesthetic, vestibular) sense are located in the semicircular canals and vestibular sacs in the (middle ear, inner ear).

23. Match each Gestalt principle with its example:
_____ (1) **** **** **** perceived as three groups of four
_____ (2) - - - - -> perceived as an arrow
_____ (3) ***&&&###@@@ perceived as four groups of three
   a. closure
   b. similarity
   c. proximity

24. Retinal disparity and convergence are two (monocular, binocular) depth cues.

25. Match the appropriate monocular depth cue with each example.

_____ (1) one building partly blocking another
_____ (2) railroad tracks converging in the distance
_____ (3) closer objects appearing to move faster than objects farther away
_____ (4) objects farther away looking smaller than near objects
   a. motion parallax
   b. linear perspective
   c. interposition
   d. relative size

26. An illusion is
   a. an imaginary sensation.
   b. an impossible figure.
   c. a misperception of a real stimulus.
   d. a figure-ground reversal.

27. In situations where you have some prior knowledge and experience, you are likely to rely more on (bottom-up, top-down) processing.

28. Perceptual set is most directly related to a person's
   a. needs.
   b. interests.
   c. expectations.
   d. emotions.

Section Two: Multiple Choice

1. Perception is the process we use to
   a. organize and interpret stimuli.
   b. detect stimuli.
   c. gather information from the environment.
   d. retrieve information from memory.

2. What part of the nose serves the same function as the retina in the eye and the basilar membrane in the ear?
   a. olfactory bulbs
   b. olfactory lining
   c. olfactory neurons
   d. olfactory epithelium

3. The vestibular system is most closely related to
   a. audition.
   b. olfaction.
   c. gustation.
   d. kinesthetics.

4. As you look down a sandy beach, the sand seems to become more fine as it goes into the distance. This depth cue is called
   a. elevation.
   b. convergence.
   c. texture gradient.
   d. linear perspective.

5. The minimum amount of physical stimulation necessary for a person to experience a sensation 50% of the time is called the

   a. figure-to-ground ratio.
   b. blind spot.
   c. difference threshold.
   d. absolute threshold.

6. Which of the following is the correct sequence of structures encountered by light moving toward the retina?
   a. lens, cornea, pupil
   b. pupil, lens, cornea
   c. pupil, cornea, lens
   d. cornea, pupil, lens

7. Which theory suggests that color vision can be explained by the existence of three types of cones, which are maximally sensitive to blue, green, or red?
   a. opponent-process theory
   b. trichromatic theory
   c. signal detection theory
   d. gate-control theory

8. Ms. Scarpaci complains that the street noise in her apartment is much louder than the noise in her upstairs neighbor's apartment. To test her claim, you use a sound meter to check the noise in each apartment. Your meter registers 50 dB in Ms. Scarpaci's apartment and only 30 dB in her neighbor's. From these readings, how much louder is Ms. Scarpaci's apartment than her neighbor's?

a. 20% louder
b. 10 times louder
c. 100 times louder
d. not enough to be noticeable

9. When you hear a tone of 400 Hz, some of the hair cells in your ear are stimulated, but most others are not. This is the basic idea behind the
a. place theory of hearing.
b. volley principle of hearing.
c. frequency theory of hearing.
d. bone conduction theory of hearing.

10. The receptors for odors are located in the
a. olfactory epithelium.
b. projecting septum.
c. turbinate mucosa.
d. vestibular membrane.

11. Nerve endings in the skin send signals to the somatosensory cortex for processing. This area of the brain is found in the
a. frontal lobe.   c. parietal lobe.
b. temporal lobe.   d. occipital lobe.

12. Which of the following sensations would best be explained by the gate-control theory?
a. the pain of a pin prick
b. the smell of dinner cooking
c. the taste of your favorite cookie
d. the sound of paper rustling

13. The receptors for the kinesthetic sense are located in the
a. middle ear.
b. inner ear.
c. joints, ligaments, and muscles.
d. cortex.

14. The depth cue that occurs when your eyes "cross" to see an object that is very near your face is called
a. convergence.   c. aerial perspective.
b. elevation.   d. binocular disparity.

15. Weber's law applies to
a. difference thresholds.
b. absolute thresholds.
c. transduction thresholds.
d. retinal thresholds.

16. Gustation is also known as the sense of
a. taste.   c. smell.
b. hearing.   d. vision.

17. In the Ponzo illusion, two bars of equal length are superimposed over a picture of railroad tracks that recede into the distance and eventually converge at a single point. One reason the bars appear to be of unequal lengths is because the illusion takes advantage of
a. binocular disparity cues.
b. linear perspective cues.
c. apparent motion cues.
d. depth disparity cues.

18. Perceptual set reflects
a. bottom-up processing.
b. top-down processing.
c. subliminal processing.
d. extrasensory processing.

19. The process through which the senses detect sensory stimuli and transmit them to the brain is called
a. consciousness.   c. sensation.
b. perception.   d. reception.

20. If you were listening to music and your friend wanted to know how far he could turn the volume down without your noticing, he would need to know your
a. sensory threshold for sound.
b. absolute threshold for sound.
c. transduction threshold for sound.
d. difference threshold for sound.

21. Margaret is reaching middle age and is having trouble reading fine print. She did not have this problem when she was younger. Her optometrist has concluded that she has presbyopia, or "old eyes." Given this diagnosis, you know that Margaret's difficulty is due to the aging of her
a. corneas.   c. retinas.
b. lenses.   d. rods and cones.

22. The trichromatic theory of color is based on the idea that the retina contains three types of
a. rods.   c. bipolar cells.
b. cones.   d. ganglion cells.

23. Megan watches from the car as her parents drive away from her grandfather's house. Because of _____, Megan knows her grandfather's house remains the same size, even though the image gets smaller as they drive farther away.
a. the law of good continuation
b. the law of proximity
c. size constancy
d. the Müller-Lyer illusion

90

Section Three: Fill In the Blank

1. Sensation is to _____ as perception is to _____.

2. The _____ threshold is a measure of the smallest change in a physical stimulus required to produce a noticeable difference in sensation 50% of the time.

3. Researchers in sensory psychology and _____ study phenomena related to sensation, such as the least amount of a stimulus required for detection.

4. _____ refers to the process by which a sensory stimulus is changed by the sensory receptors into neural impulses.

5. As part of his training in personnel relations, Ted had to spend a whole day in a very noisy factory. Though the sound seemed almost painful at first, he noticed by the end of the day that it didn't seem so loud anymore. This is an example of _____ _____.

6. One of the major parts of the eye, the _____, performs the first step in vision by bending the light rays inward through the pupil.

7. According to the _____ theory of color vision, certain cells in the visual system increase their rate of firing to signal one color and decrease their firing rate to signal the opposing color.

8. An important characteristic of sound, _____ is determined by the number of cycles completed by a sound wave in 1 second.

9. The taste sensation called _____ results from such protein-rich foods as meat, milk, cheese, and seafood.

10. _____ psychologists studied perception and were guided by the principle that "the whole is more than the sum of its parts."

11. That humans seem to perceive the environment in terms of an object standing out against a background is known as the _____ _____ principle.

12. Ted, an artist, creates pictures that force viewers to fill in gaps in the lines, thereby forming a whole pattern. Ted's art takes advantage of the principle of _____.

13. One important contribution to three-dimensional perception is _____ _____, which results when each eye receives a slightly different view of the objects being viewed.

Section Four: Comprehensive Practice Test

1. The process by which humans detect visual, auditory, and other stimuli is known as
   a. perception.   c. sensation.
   b. transduction.   d. threshold.

2. The process of organizing and interpreting the information gathered through vision, hearing, and the other senses is known as
   a. perception.
   b. the absolute threshold.
   c. transduction.
   d. sensory induction.

3. The _____ _____ is the minimum amount of stimulus that can be detected 50% of the time.
   a. difference reaction   c. difference threshold
   b. absolute reaction   d. absolute threshold

4. The _____ _____ is a measure of the smallest change in a stimulus required for a person to detect a change in the stimulus 50% of the time.
   a. difference reaction   c. difference threshold
   b. absolute difference   d. sensory threshold

5. Sense organs have specialized cells called _____ that detect and respond to particular stimuli.
   a. sensory detectors
   b. sensory receptors
   c. perceptual responders
   d. perceptual receptors

6. When you see, hear, taste, smell, or feel a sensory stimulus, the physical energy that caused the stimulus is changed to neural impulses that are processed in your brain. This process is known as
   a. sensory adaptation.
   b. the absolute threshold.
   c. perceptual organization.
   d. transduction.

7. Joe installed an in-ground pool last spring, although his wife thought he was crazy to do that when it was still cool outside. The first day it seemed a little warm Joe jumped in the new pool, but soon he realized just how cold the water really was. As he continued to "enjoy" the water, it seemed to become less cold and even comfortable. This was probably due to a process called
   a. sensory adaptation.
   b. difference threshold.
   c. sensory threshold.
   d. perceptual adaptation.

8. If someone tells you she loves the color of your eyes, she is actually talking about your
   a. pupils.   c. irises.
   b. corneas.   d. retinas.

9. Rods are to cones as _____ is to _____.
   a. dim light; color
   b. color; dim light
   c. bright light; color
   d. color; bright light

10. The blind spot in the back of the eye is where
    a. the rods and cones come together.
    b. the retina converges on the fovea.
    c. the optic nerve leaves the eye.
    d. the blood supply enters the eye.

11. When you read a book, the lenses in your eyes are probably a little more spherical, and when you gaze up at the stars at night, your lenses become flatter. These differences are due to a process known as
    a. retinal disparity.   c. accommodation.
    b. lens reactivity.   d. adaptation.

12. LaShonda tells her roommate that we see color because three kinds of cones react to one of three colors—blue, green, or red. LaShonda has been reading about the _____ theory of color vision.
    a. opponent-process
    b. trichromatic
    c. relative disparity
    d. complementary color

13. The number of cycles completed by a sound wave in 1 second is the wave's
    a. decibel level.   c. amplitude.
    b. timbre.   d. frequency.

14. The job of the _____, also known as the hammer, the anvil, and the stirrup, is to amplify sound as it moves from the eardrum to the oval window.
    a. ossicles   c. hair cells
    b. cochlear bones   d. timbre bones

15. Tomas says that we hear different pitches depending on which spot along the basilar membrane vibrates the most. He is talking about the _____ theory of hearing.
    a. frequency   c. cochlea
    b. position   d. place

16. Olfaction refers to
    a. the sense of taste.
    b. the sense of smell.
    c. the ability to detect skin temperature.
    d. the ability to differentiate sounds.

17. All parts of the tongue can detect sweet, sour, salty, and bitter. (true/false)

18. *Tactile* is used in reference to the sense of
    a. smell.   c. taste.
    b. balance.   d. touch.

19. The gate-control theory of pain suggests that slow-conducting nerve fibers carry pain messages and that these messages can be blocked by messages from fast-conducting nerve fibers. (true/false)

20. An athlete's ability to move gracefully on the parallel bars is due to the _____ sense.
    a. tactile   c. kinesthetic
    b. olfactory   d. eustachian

21. The vestibular sense provides information that allows you to know that a red door is still red even in a dark room. (true/false)

22. The half-time show at a football game involved a hundred people marching on the field—all in different colored uniforms. Then they took on a formation and suddenly all the red uniforms spelled out the initials of the home team. Gestalt psychologists would suggest that the principle of _____ explains why fans could read the initials.
    a. similarity   c. closure
    b. continuity   d. constancy

23. Which of the following is not a Gestalt principle of gouping?
    a. closure   c. constancy
    b. similarity   d. proximity

24. If you move your finger closer and closer to your nose and focus on perceiving only one image of the finger even when it is almost touching the nose, your eyes begin to turn inward. This eye movement is known as
    a. disparity.   c. congruity.
    b. monocular adjustment.   d. convergence.

25. Cues such as interposition, linear perspective, and relative size are known as _____ depth cues.
    a. binocular   c. monocular
    b. divergent   d. bimodal

26. Lines of the same length with diagonals at their ends pointing in or out appear to be of different lengths because of the _____ illusion.
    a. Ponzo   c. trident
    b. Müller-Lyer   d. ambiguous

27. Bottom-up processing is to _____ stimuli as top-down processing is to _____ stimuli.
    a. unfamiliar; familiar   c. familiar; unfamiliar
    b. visual; auditory   d. perceptual; subliminal

Section Five: Critical Thinking

1. Using what you have learned about how noise contributes to hearing loss, prepare a statement indicating what you think the government should do to control noise pollution, even to the extent of banning certain noise hazards. Consider the workplace, the home, automobiles and other vehicles, toys, machinery, rock concerts, and so on.

2. Vision and hearing are generally believed to be the two most highly prized senses. How would your life change if you lost your sight? How would your life change if you lost your hearing? Which sense would you find more traumatic to lose? Why?

3. Explain how perceptual set can lead to errors in witnesses' courtroom testimony.

States of Consciousness

For the most part, British imports have had an extremely positive influence on life in the United States. But this is not so for rave dances. Long popular in Britain, these dances gained quite a following in the 1990s among American adolescents and young adults, and their popularity continues to grow. Typically, rave dances are held in large facilities, where as many as 2,000 tightly packed party-goers dance all night to heavily mixed, electronically generated music accompanied by striking laser light shows. This may sound like fun, but officials at the National Institute on Drug Abuse and others have become alarmed—not because of the dancing, but because of an illegal drug called MDMA, or "Ecstasy," which has become so closely identified with raves that it is virtually synonymous with them.

Users of MDMA describe a wonderfully pleasant state of consciousness, in which even the most shy or self-conscious people shed their inhibitions. Pretenses melt away, and the users become "emotionally synthesized" with other ravers and with the music and the lighting effects. Users feel that the drug allows them to be who they "really are." They report an immediate and deep acceptance and understanding of others; interpersonal barriers disappear, along with emotional and sexual inhibitions. And it is said that the frequent, spontaneous outbursts of mass hugging and kissing make MDMA users feel that they are accepted, even loved. But there is a price to be paid for entering this "joyous" state.

MDMA use can damage brain cells that are essential for memory, sustained attention, analytical thinking, and self-control. More specifically, the drug disables neurons that serve as receptors for the critically important neurotransmitter serotonin (Montoya et al., 2002). And the destructive effects of MDMA may be cumulative or dose-dependent: In one study, 73% of heavy recreational users reported memory problems that were attributed to the drug (Parrott et al., 2002). The largest ongoing study of teenagers and drug use is the "Monitoring the Future" survey conducted at the University of Michigan. The alarming news from this survey is that use of MDMA, or Ecstasy, nearly doubled among American teenagers in only 3 years, from 1998 to 2000. (Johnston et al., 2001).

What Is Consciousness?

consciousness

An awareness of one's own perceptions, thoughts, feelings, sensations, and external environment.

Have you every stopped to think about what we mean when we describe ourselves or someone else as *conscious*? Is *consciousness* nothing more than simply being awake? What about when you arrive home from shopping but have no recollection of the drive from the mall to your home? Certainly, you were awake, so you couldn't say you don't remember because you were unconscious.

What do psychologists mean by the terms *consciousness* and *altered states of consciousness*? ➤

Philosophers and psychologists have produced numerous definitions of consciousness. What most have in common is the notion that **consciousness** includes everything of which we are aware at any given time—our thoughts, feelings, mental processes, and events in the external world.

In recent decades, psychologists have studied consciousness within the context of research that examines physiological rhythms or sleep or other **altered states of consciousness** (changes in awareness produced by meditation, hypnosis, and drugs). Much of this research involves techniques you learned about in Chapter 2, such as CT scans and EEGs. Thus, psychologists are increasingly equating the subjective experience of consciousness with objective observations of what's actually happening in the brain during states such as sleep, hypnosis, and the like (Parvizi & Damasio, 2001).

altered state of consciousness

A mental state other than ordinary waking consciousness, such as sleep, meditation, hypnosis, or a drug-induced state.

Circadian Rhythms

Do you notice changes in the way you feel throughout the day—fluctuations in your energy level, moods, or efficiency? Over 100 bodily functions and behaviors follow **circadian rhythms**—that is, they fluctuate regularly from a high point to a low point over a 24-hour period. Physiological functions such as blood pressure, heart rate, appetite, secretion of hormones and digestive enzymes, sensory acuity, elimination, and even the body's response to medication follow circadian rhythms (Hrushesky, 1994; Morofushi et al., 2001). Many psychological functions, including learning efficiency, ability to perform a wide range of tasks, and moods, also ebb and flow according to these daily rhythms (Boivin et al., 1997; Johnson et al., 1992; Manly et al., 2002).

What is a circadian rhythm? ➤

Neuroscientists have learned that this internal clock is regulated by a structure in the brain known as the *suprachiasmatic nucleus (SCN)* (Ruby et al., 2002). However, environmental cues also play a part. The most significant environmental cue is bright light. Specialized cells (photoreceptors) in the retina at the back of each eye respond to the amount of light reaching the eye and relay this information via the optic nerve to the SCN. The SCN acts on this information by signaling the pineal gland, located in the center of the brain. In response, the pineal gland secretes the hormone *melatonin* from dusk to shortly before dawn and suppresses its secretion during daylight. Melatonin acts to induce sleep; this effect may be a function of its ability to lower the activity of neurons in the SCN (Barinaga, 1997).

circadian rhythm

(sur-KAY-dee-un) The regular fluctuation from high points to low points of certain bodily functions within each 24-hour period.

Jet Lag and Shift Work

Many travelers experience jet lag when they travel across time zones because their internal biological clocks are linked to the zone in which they spend most of their time. Jet lag is associated with a number of problems. For example, travelers whose psychiatric disorders are in remission are at risk of suffering relapses when they cross several time zones (Katz et al., 2002; Oyewumi, 1998). Further, chronic jet lag, such as that experienced by many airline pilots and flight attendants, produces memory deficits that may be permanent (Cho, 2001; Cho et al., 2000). Fortunately, supplemental melatonin has been shown to be an effective treatment for relapses of psychiatric disorders due to jet lag (Katz et al., 1999; Katz et al., 2001). For oth-

What are some problems experienced by people who travel across time zones or who work night shifts? ➤

ers, exposure to bright sunlight during the early morning hours and avoidance of bright light during the evening may be more effective than melatonin for restoring circadian rhythms (Edwards et al., 2000; Zisapel, 2001).

What about the circadian rhythms of shift workers, people who work during the night and sleep all day? During **subjective night**–the time when your biological clock is telling you to go to sleep–energy and efficiency are at their lowest point, reaction time is slowest, productivity is diminished, and industrial accidents are significantly higher. When people must work at night, the rhythms of many of their bodily functions, normally synchronized for efficient daytime functioning, are disrupted. These disruptions in normal rhythms can cause a variety of physical and psychological problems. Shift workers have more gastrointestinal and cardiovascular problems, use more prescription drugs, experience higher levels of personal and family stress and more mood problems, and have higher divorce rates (Campbell, 1995; Garbarino et al., 2002; Moore-Ede, 1993).

What can be done to make shift work less disruptive? Rotating work schedules forward from days to evenings to nights makes adjustment easier because people find it easier to go to bed later and wake up later than to go to bed earlier and wake up earlier. And rotating shifts every 3 weeks instead of every week lessens the effect on sleep even more (Pilcher et al., 2000). Some researchers have even suggested scheduling brief nap periods during each shift to help sleepy workers adjust to rotating shifts (Goh et al., 2000). Others are investigating the use of a new wakefulness drug called *modafinil,* which helps people remain alert without the side effects of stimulants such as caffeine (Wesensten et al., 2002).

Light exposure is another important factor in understanding the effects of shift work. Some researchers have used a device called a *light mask* to reset shift workers' biological clocks. A light mask is a mask that allows researchers to control the amount of light to which the closed eyelids of research participants are exposed. The findings of studies using light masks suggest that exposing participants to bright light during the last 4 hours of sleep is an effective treatment for the kinds of sleep problems experienced by shift workers (Cole et al., 2002).

Research indicates that frequent flyers, such as these airline pilots, are just as likely to suffer from jet lag when crossing several time zones as travelers who are on their first intercontinental journey.

Sleep

Over a lifetime, a person spends about 25 years sleeping. During the 1950s, several universities set up sleep laboratories where people's brain waves, eye movements, chin-muscle tension, heart rate, and respiration rate were monitored while they slept through the night. From analyses of sleep recordings, known as *polysomnograms,* researchers discovered two major categories of sleep, which we consider next.

NREM and REM Sleep

NREM (pronounced NON-rem) **sleep** is sleep in which there are no rapid eye movements. Heart rate and respiration are slow and regular, there is little body movement, and blood pressure and brain activity are at their lowest points of the 24-hour period. There are four stages of NREM sleep: Stages 1, 2, 3, and 4. Stage 1 is the lightest sleep, and Stage 4 is the deepest. Sleepers pass gradually rather than abruptly from one stage to the next. Each stage can be identified by its brain-wave pattern, as shown in Figure 4.1 (on page 98). Growth hormone is secreted primarily in Stage 3 and Stage 4 sleep (Gronfier et al., 1996; Van Cauter, 2000); this timing is significant because older people get little of this slow-wave sleep.

subjective night
The time during a 24-hour period when body temperature is lowest and when the internal clock is telling a person to go to sleep.

NREM sleep
Non–rapid eye movement sleep, consisting of the four sleep stages and characterized by slow, regular respiration and heart rate, an absence of rapid eye movements, and blood pressure and brain activity that are at a 24-hour low point.

 What are the physiological signs of NREM sleep?

➤ Figure 4.1

Brain-Wave Patterns Associated with Different Stages of Sleep

By monitoring brain-wave activity on an EEG throughout a night's sleep, researchers have identified the brain-wave patterns associated with different stages of sleep. As sleepers progress through the four NREM stages, the brain-wave pattern changes from faster, smaller waves in Stages 1 and 2 to the slower, larger delta waves in Stages 3 and 4. Notice that the brain-wave activity during REM sleep is similar to that of wakefulness.

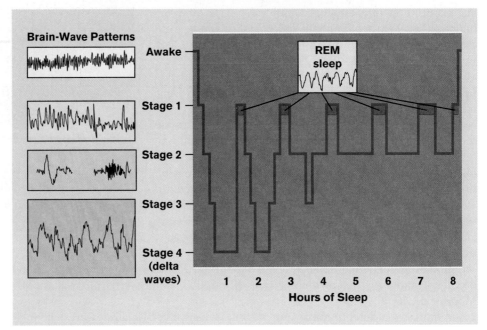

REM sleep, sometimes called *active sleep,* constitutes 20–25% of a normal night's sleep in adults and is characterized by the presence of rapid eye movements. During the REM state, there is intense brain activity. In fact, within 1 to 2 minutes after REM sleep begins, brain metabolism increases and brain temperature rises rapidly (Krueger & Takahashi, 1997). Epinephrine is released into the system, causing blood pressure to rise and heart rate and respiration to become faster and less regular. In contrast to this storm of internal activity, there is an external calm during REM sleep. The large muscles of the body–those in arms, legs, and trunk–become paralyzed (Chase & Morales, 1990). And if you awaken during REM sleep, during which most dreaming occurs, you may not go back into this kind of sleep for at least 30 minutes. This is why most people have experienced the disappointment of waking in the middle of a wonderful dream and then trying to get back to sleep quickly and into the dream again, but being unable to do so.

> **What are the physiological signs of REM sleep?** ➤

Researchers have found that REM sleep is involved in the consolidation of memories. In an important early study of this phenomenon, Karni and others (1994) found that research participants learning a new perceptual skill showed an improvement in performance, with no additional practice, 8 to 10 hours later if they had a normal night's sleep or if the researchers disturbed only their NREM sleep. Performance did not improve, however, in those who were deprived of REM sleep.

> **What function does REM sleep appear to serve, and what happens when people are deprived of it?** ➤

Another indication of the importance of REM sleep is the finding that when people are deprived of REM sleep, they make up for the loss by getting an increased amount of REM sleep after the deprivation. This phenomenon is called **REM rebound.** Because the intensity of REM sleep is increased during a REM rebound, nightmares often occur. Alcohol, amphetamines, cocaine, and LSD suppress REM sleep, and withdrawal from these drugs results in a REM rebound (Porte & Hobson, 1996).

REM sleep
Sleep characterized by rapid eye movements, paralysis of large muscles, fast and irregular heart rate and respiration rate, increased brain-wave activity, and vivid dreams.

Sleep Cycles

> **What is the progression of NREM stages and REM sleep that occurs during a typical night's sleep?** ➤

We all experience **sleep cycles,** each of which lasts about 90 minutes. In each cycle, there are distinct stages. Stage 1 is a transitional period of drowsiness between waking and sleeping. In Stage 2, sleepers are somewhat more deeply asleep and harder to awaken. About 50% of a total night's sleep is spent in Stage 2 sleep. As sleep gradually becomes deeper, brain activity slows, and more **delta**

waves (slow waves) appear on the EEG. When the EEG registers 20% delta waves, sleepers enter Stage 3 sleep, the beginning of **slow-wave sleep** (or deep sleep). Delta waves continue to increase during Stage 3. When they exceed 50% of the waves registered on the EEG, people enter Stage 4 sleep—the deepest sleep, from which they are hardest to awaken.

In Stage 4 sleep, delta waves may comprise nearly 100% of the waves on the EEG, but after about 40 minutes in this stage, brain activity increases and the delta waves begin to disappear. Sleepers ascend back through Stage 3 and Stage 2 sleep, then enter their first REM period, which lasts 10 or 15 minutes. At the end of this REM period, the first sleep cycle is complete and the second sleep cycle begins. Unless sleepers awaken after the first sleep cycle, they go directly from REM into Stage 2 sleep. They then follow the same progression as in the first sleep cycle, through Stages 3 and 4 and back again into REM sleep.

After the first two sleep cycles (which together take about 3 hours), the sleep pattern changes and sleepers usually get no more Stage 4 sleep. From this point on, during each 90-minute sleep cycle, people alternate mainly between Stage 2 and REM sleep for the remainder of the night. With each sleep cycle, the REM period (and, therefore, dreaming time) gets progressively longer. At the end of the night, the REM period may last 30 to 40 minutes. Most people have about five sleep cycles ($7\frac{1}{2}$ to 8 hours of sleep) and average about $1\frac{1}{2}$ hours of slow-wave sleep and $1\frac{1}{2}$ hours of REM sleep.

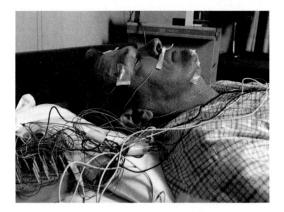

In a sleep laboratory or sleep clinic, researchers attach electrodes to a person's head to monitor brain-wave activity, eye movements, and muscle tension.

Variations in Sleep

There are significant age variations in patterns of sleep. Infants and young children have the longest sleep time and the highest percentages of REM and slow-wave sleep. Children from age 6 to puberty fall asleep easily and sleep soundly for 8 or 9 hours a night. Teenagers average 7.2 hours of sleep each night (Wolfson & Carskadon, 1998). The duration of sleep gradually declines in the first decade of adulthood. Then, the quantity of sleep remains stable until late adulthood, but the proportion of time spent in slow-wave sleep decreases. By contrast, the percentage of REM sleep stays about the same (Moran & Stoudemire, 1992; Mourtazaev et al., 1995; Van Cauter, 2000). After age 60 or so, the average amount of sleep per night drops to just over 6 hours, and a large proportion of people, more than 80% in some studies, report difficulty falling and remaining asleep (Foley et al., 1995; Prinz et al., 1990).

There are individual differences in sleep patterns as well, and these differences may have important health consequences. In a longitudinal study begun in 1982, more than 1 million Americans were asked about their sleep habits. Twenty years later, people who reported sleeping 6 or fewer hours per night, along with those who slept more than 8, were far more likely to have died than adults who slept about 7 hours each night (Kripke et al., 2002).

Does this mean that we should all strive to sleep exactly 7 hours each night? Not at all, because such studies deal with averages. There is considerable individual variation in the amount of sleep people need, and, for each individual, a certain amount of sleep may be sufficient at one point in life but insufficient at another. What accounts for the large variation in the need for sleep? Genetics appears to play a part. Identical twins, for example, have more strikingly similar sleep patterns than do fraternal twins (Webb & Campbell, 1983). Laboratory animals have even been bred to be short or long sleepers. Still, there is no doubt that, whatever the optimal amount of sleep for each of us individually, we don't perform as well when we are deprived of it.

The Functions of Sleep

Two complementary theories have been advanced to explain the function of sleep, and, taken together, they provide a useful explanation. One, the **restorative theory,** holds that being awake produces wear and tear on the body and the brain, and sleep serves the

REM rebound
The increased amount of REM sleep that occurs after REM deprivation; often associated with unpleasant dreams or nightmares.

sleep cycle
A period of sleep lasting about 90 minutes and including one or more stages of NREM sleep followed by REM sleep.

delta waves
The slowest brain-wave pattern, associated with Stage 3 and Stage 4 sleep.

slow-wave sleep
Stage 3 and Stage 4 sleep; deep sleep.

restorative theory
The theory that the function of sleep is to restore body and mind.

What are the two main theories that attempt to explain the function of sleep?

function of restoring body and mind (Gökcebay et al., 1994). There is convincing evidence for this theory: The functions of sleep do include the restoration of brain energy and the consolidation of memory (Kunz & Herrmann, 2000). The second explanation of sleep, the **circadian theory,** is based on the premise that sleep evolved to keep humans out of harm's way during the dark of night and possibly from becoming prey for some nocturnal predator.

Alexander Borbely (1984; Borbely et al., 1989) has explained how a synthesis of the circadian and restorative theories can be used to explain the function of sleep. That people feel sleepy at certain times of day is consistent with the circadian theory. And that sleepiness increases the longer a person is awake is consistent with the restorative theory. In other words, the urge to sleep is partly a function of how long a person has been awake and partly a function of the time of day (Webb, 1995).

Sleep Deprivation

You probably already know from personal experience that sleep deprivation affects your mood, making you "cranky" and irritable (Bonnet & Arand, 1995; Landis et al., 1998). But research also indicates that even small amounts of sleep deprivation, such as delaying your bedtime on weekends, can interfere with your intellectual performance (Harrison & Horne, 2000; Raz et al., 2001; Yang & Spielman, 2001). And studies consistently show that longer periods of sleep deprivation lead to significant declines in cognitive functioning (See Figure 4.2).

The effects of sleep deprivation on the brain appear to be responsible for these declines. Drummond and others (2000) used brain-imaging techniques to map the patterns of brain activity during a verbal learning task in two groups of participants: Those in an experimental group were deprived of sleep for about 35 hours, while those in a control group had slept normally. In the control group, the prefrontal cortex was highly active, as were the temporal lobes. As expected, on average, these rested participants scored significantly higher on the learning task than did their sleep-deprived counterparts. Surprisingly, however, areas of the prefrontal cortex were even more active in the sleep-deprived participants than in those who slept normally. Moreover, the temporal lobes that were so active in the rested group were almost totally inactive in the sleep-deprived group. The parietal lobes of the latter group became highly active, however, as if to compensate for their sleep-deprived condition. And the more active the parietal lobes, the higher a sleep-deprived participant scored on the learning task.

Dreaming

How do REM and NREM dreams differ?

Humans have always been fascinated by dreams and have experimented with many techniques for controlling them (see *Try It! 4.1*). The vivid dreams people remember and talk about are usually **REM dreams**—the type that occur almost continuously during each REM period. But people also have **NREM dreams;** these occur during NREM sleep and are typically less frequent, less memorable, and more thoughtlike than REM dreams (Foulkes, 1996). REM dreams have a story-like quality and are more visual, vivid, and emotional than NREM dreams (Hobson, 1989).

Because dreams are notoriously hard to remember, the features that stand out tend to be those that are bizarre or emotional. Individuals who suffer from delusional psychological disorders, such as

circadian theory
The theory that sleep evolved to keep humans out of harm's way during the night and that sleepiness ebbs and flows according to a circadian rhythm.

REM dreams
A type of dream having a storylike quality and occuring almost continuously during each REM period; more vivid, visual, and emotional than NREM dreams.

NREM dreams
Mental activity occurring during NREM sleep that is more thoughtlike in quality than REM dreams are.

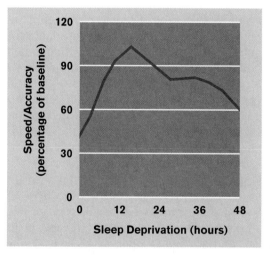

▶ **Figure 4.2**

Effect of Sleep Deprivation on Cognitive Performance

Sleep deprivation lasting for 48 hours had a negative effect on performance of a cognitive task (serial addition and subtraction exercises). The initial upward slope of the performance curve is a learning curve for the task. (Department of Behavior Biology, Walter Reed Army Institute of Research, 1997.)

100

schizophrenia, report more bizarre dreams than do nonsufferers (Watson, 2001). But researchers don't know whether their dreams really are more bizarre or whether their mental problems cause them to focus on the bizarre qualities of the dreams to a greater extent than do people who are mentally healthy.

Brain-imaging studies suggest that the general perception that events in REM dreams are stranger and more emotion-provoking than waking experiences is probably true. The areas of the brain associated with emotions, as well as the primary visual cortex, are active during REM dreams (Braun et al., 1998). By contrast, the prefrontal cortex, the more rational part of the brain, is inactive, suggesting that the bizarre events that happen in dreams result from the inability of the brain to structure perceptions logically during REM sleep. Areas associated with memory are also suppressed, which may explain why REM dreams are difficult to remember.

Different neurotransmitters are dominant in the cortex during wakefulness and during REM sleep (Gottesmann, 2000). When we are awake, powerful inhibiting influences exert control over the functioning of the cortex, keeping us anchored to reality, less subject to impulsive thoughts and acts, and more or less "sane." These inhibiting influences are maintained principally by neurons in the cortex that respond to serotonin and noradrenalin (norepinephrine). These neurotransmitters are far less plentiful during REM sleep, when a higher level of dopamine causes other neurons in the cortex to show intense activity. This uninhibited and dopamine-stimulated activity of the dreaming brain has been likened to a psychotic mental state (Gottesmann, 2000).

▲ You may think you're learning a lot during an "all-nighter" cram session. However, the effects of sleep deprivation on your memory may cancel out the benefits.

Interpreting Dreams

Sigmund Freud believed that dreams function to satisfy unconscious sexual and aggressive wishes. Because such wishes are unacceptable to the dreamer, they have to be disguised and therefore appear in a dream in symbolic form. Freud (1900/1953a) claimed that objects such as sticks, umbrellas, tree trunks, and guns symbolize the male sex organ; objects such as chests, cupboards, and boxes represent the female sex organ. Freud differentiated between the *manifest content* of the dream—the dream as recalled by the dreamer—and the underlying meaning of the dream, called the *latent content,* which he considered more significant.

Try It ! 4.1 Dream Control

Try following these steps when you go to bed to see whether you can control your dreams.

1. Relax.

2. Close your eyes and focus on an imaginary spot in your field of vision.

3. Focus your attention on the intention to control your dreams.

4. Tell yourself that you're going to dream about whatever you want.

5. Imagine yourself in a dream of the type you want to have.

6. Repeat the steps until you fall asleep.

In recent years, there has been a major shift away from the Freudian interpretation of dreams. Now there is a greater focus on the manifest content, the actual dream itself, which is seen more as an expression of a broad range of the dreamer's concerns than primarily as an expression of sexual impulses (Webb, 1975). And from an evolutionary viewpoint, dreams are viewed as a mechanism for simulating threatening and dangerous events so that the dreamer can "rehearse" and thus enhance her or his chances for survival (Revensuo, 2000).

Well-known sleep researcher J. Allan Hobson (1988) rejects the notion that nature would equip humans with a capability and a need to dream dreams that require a specialist to interpret. Hobson and McCarley (1977) advanced the *activation-synthesis hypothesis of dreaming*. This hypothesis suggests that dreams are simply the brain's attempt to make sense of the random firing of neurons during REM sleep. Just as people try to make sense of input from the environment during their waking hours, they try to find meaning in the conglomeration of sensations and memories that are generated internally by this random firing of brain cells. Hobson (1989) believes that dreams also have psychological significance, because the meaning a person imposes reflects that person's experiences, memories, associations, drives, and fears.

Parasomnias

Parasomnias are sleep disturbances in which behaviors and physiological states that normally occur only in the waking state take place during sleep or the transition from sleep to wakefulness (Schenck & Mahowald, 2000). For example, sleepwalking (*somnambulism*) occurs during a partial arousal from Stage 4 sleep in which the sleeper does not come to full consciousness. Sleepwalkers may get up and roam through the house or simply stand for a short time and then get back into bed. Occasionally, they get dressed, eat a snack, or go to the bathroom. Some sleepwalkers have even been known to drive during an episode (Schenck & Mahowald, 1995). Typically, though, there is no memory of the episode the following day (Moldofsky et al., 1995).

What are the characteristics common to sleepwalking and sleep terrors? ▶

Sleep terrors also happen during partial arousal from Stage 4 sleep and usually begin with a piercing scream. The sleeper springs up in a state of panic—eyes open, perspiring, breathing rapidly, with the heart pounding at two or more times the normal rate (Karacan, 1988). Episodes usually last from 5 to 15 minutes, and then the person falls back to sleep. Up to 5% of children have sleep terrors (Keefauver & Guilleminault, 1994), but only about 1% of adults experience them (Partinen, 1994). Parents should not be unduly alarmed by sleep terrors in young children, but episodes that continue through adolescence into adulthood are more serious (Horne, 1992). Sleep terrors in adults often indicate extreme anxiety or other psychological problems.

What is a sleep terror? ▶

Unlike sleep terrors, *nightmares* are very frightening dreams that occur during REM sleep and are likely to be remembered in vivid detail. The most common themes are falling and being chased, threatened, or attacked. Nightmares can be a reaction to traumatic life experiences, and they are more frequent at times of high fevers, anxiety, and emotional upheaval. REM rebound during drug withdrawal or following long periods without sleep can also produce nightmares. Sleep terrors occur early in the night, during Stage 4 sleep, while anxiety nightmares occur toward morning, when the REM periods are longest. Frequent nightmares may be associated with psychological maladjustment (Berquier & Aston, 1992).

How do nightmares differ from sleep terrors? ▶

Sleeptalking (*somniloquy*) can occur during any sleep stage and is more frequent in children than in adults. There is no evidence at all that sleeptalking is related to a physical or psychological disturbance—not even to a guilty conscience. Sleeptalkers rarely reply to questions, and they usually mumble words or phrases that make no sense to the listener.

Major Sleep Disorders

What are the major symptoms of narcolepsy? ▶

Some sleep disorders can be so debilitating that they affect a person's entire life. For instance, *narcolepsy* is an incurable sleep disorder characterized by excessive daytime sleepiness and uncontrollable attacks of REM sleep, usually lasting 10–20 min-

102

utes (American Psychiatric Association, 1994). People with narcolepsy, who number from 250,000 to 350,000 in the United States, are more likely to be involved in accidents virtually everywhere–driving automobiles, at work, and at home (Broughton & Broughton, 1994). Narcolepsy is caused by an abnormality in the part of the brain that regulates sleep, and it appears to have a strong genetic component (Billiard et al., 1994; Partinen et al., 1994). Some dogs are subject to narcolepsy, and much has been learned about the genetics of this disorder from research on canine subjects (Lamberg, 1996). Although there is no cure for narcolepsy, stimulant medications improve daytime alertness in most patients (Guilleminault, 1993; Mitler et al., 1994). Experts also recommend scheduled naps to relieve sleepiness (Garma & Marchand, 1994).

Over 1 million Americans–mostly obese men–suffer from another sleep disorder, called *sleep apnea*. Sleep apnea consists of periods during sleep when breathing stops, and the individual must awaken briefly in order to breathe (White, 1989). The major symptoms of sleep apnea are excessive daytime sleepiness and extremely loud snoring (as loud as a jackhammer), often accompanied by snorts, gasps, and choking noises. A person with sleep apnea will drop off to sleep, stop breathing altogether, and then awaken struggling for breath. After gasping several breaths in a semi-awakened state, the person falls back to sleep and stops breathing again. People with severe sleep apnea may partially awaken as many as 800 times a night to gasp for air. Alcohol and sedatives aggravate the condition (Langevin et al., 1992).

Severe sleep apnea can lead to chronic high blood pressure, heart problems, and even death (Lavie et al., 1995). Physicians sometimes treat sleep apnea by surgically modifying the upper airway (Sher et al., 1996). When the surgery is effective, patients not only sleep better, they also exhibit higher levels of performance on tests of verbal learning and memory (Dahloef et al., 2002). These findings suggest that the interrupted sleep experienced by individuals with this disorder affects cognitive, as well as physiological, functioning.

Approximately one-third of adults in the United States suffer from *insomnia*–a sleep disorder characterized by difficulty falling or staying asleep, by waking too early, or by sleep that is light, restless, or of poor quality. Any of these symptoms can lead to distress and impairment in daytime functioning (Costa E Silva et al., 1996; Roth, 1996b; Sateia et al., 2000). Transient (temporary) insomnia, lasting 3 weeks or less, can result from jet lag, emotional highs (an upcoming wedding) or lows (losing a loved one or a job), or a brief illness or injury that interferes with sleep (Reite et al., 1995). Much more serious is chronic insomnia, which lasts for months or even years and plagues about 10% of the adult population (Roth, 1996b). The percentages are even higher for women, the elderly, and people suffering from psychological and medical disorders (Costa E Silva et al., 1996). Chronic insomnia may begin as a reaction to a psychological or medical problem but persist long after the problem is resolved. Individuals with chronic insomnia experience "higher psychological distress [and] greater impairments of daytime functioning, are involved in more fatigue-related accidents, take more sick leave, and utilize health care resources more often than good sleepers" (Morin & Wooten, 1996, p. 522).

Altering Consciousness through Concentration and Suggestion

Meditation

Meditation (the concentrative form) is a group of techniques that involve focusing attention on an object, a word, one's breathing, or one's body movement in order to block out all distractions, to enhance well-being, and to achieve an altered state of consciousness. Some forms of concentrative meditation–yoga, Zen, and transcendental meditation (TM)–have their roots in Eastern religions and are practiced by followers of those religions to attain a higher spiritual state. In the United

Sleep researcher William Dement holds a dog that is experiencing a narcoleptic sleep attack. Much has been learned about narcolepsy through research with dogs.

◀ What is sleep apnea?

◀ What is insomnia?

meditation
In the concentrative form, a group of techniques that involve focusing attention on an object, a word, one's breathing, or one's body movement in order to block out all distractions, to enhance well-being, and to achieve an altered state of consciousness.

 ◀ For what purposes is meditation used?

Many people engage in some form of meditation to achieve an enhanced state of well-being. Here "material girl" Madonna is practicing yoga, perhaps seeking a more spiritual state.

What is hypnosis, and when is it most useful? ▶

hypnosis
A procedure through which one person, the hypnotist, uses the power of suggestion to induce changes in thoughts, feelings, sensations, perceptions, or behavior of another person, the subject.

States, concentrative meditation is widely used to increase relaxation, reduce arousal, or expand consciousness. Brain-imaging studies show that blood flow increases in the cerebral cortex during meditation, indicating that it is a complex cognitive task (Newberg et al., 2001). Moreover, prayer can induce psychological and physiological states very much like those associated with meditation (Bernardi et al., 2001).

Herbert Benson (1975) suggests the contemplation of any word or sound can be used for meditation, although some would disagree with him. Moreover, he claims that the beneficial effects of meditation can be achieved through simple relaxation techniques. Do *Try It! 4.2* to experience Benson's relaxation response.

Hypnosis

Hypnosis may be defined as a procedure through which one person, the hypnotist, uses the power of suggestion to induce changes in thoughts, feelings, sensations, perceptions, or behavior of another person, the subject. Under hypnosis, people suspend their usual rational and logical ways of thinking and perceiving and allow themselves to experience distortions in perceptions, memories, and thinking. They may experience positive hallucinations, in which they see, hear, touch, smell, or taste things that are not present in the environment. Or they may have negative hallucinations in which they fail to perceive things that are actually present.

About 80–95% of people are hypnotizable to some degree, but only 5% can reach the deepest levels of the hypnotic state (Nash & Baker, 1984). The ability to become completely absorbed in imaginative activities is characteristic of highly hypnotizable people (Nadon et al., 1991). Silva and Kirsch (1992) found that proneness to fantasizing and the expectation that one will respond to hypnotic suggestions were predictors of individuals' hypnotizability.

Despite what many people believe, and what is often portrayed in the media, people who are hypnotized retain the ability to refuse to comply with the hypnotist's suggestions, and they will not do anything that is contrary to their moral beliefs. Moreover, although it is true that hypnotized subjects supply more information and are more confident of their recollections, the information is often inaccurate (Dywan & Bowers, 1983; Kihlstrom & Barnhardt, 1993; Nogrady et al., 1985; Weekes et al., 1992). In fact, in the process of trying to help people recall certain events, hypnotists may instead create in them false memories, or *pseudomemories* (Lynn & Nash, 1994;

Try It ! 4.2 The Relaxation Response

Find a quiet place and sit in a comfortable position.

1. Close your eyes.
2. Relax all your muscles deeply. Beginning with your feet and moving slowly upward, relax the muscles in your legs, buttocks, abdomen, chest, shoulders, neck, and finally your face. Allow your whole body to remain in this deeply relaxed state.
3. Now concentrate on your breathing, and breathe in and out through your nose. Each time you breathe out, silently say the word *one* to yourself.
4. Repeat this process for 20 minutes. (You can open your eyes to look at your watch periodically but don't use an alarm.) When you are finished, remain seated for a few minutes—first with your eyes closed, then with them open.

Benson recommends that you maintain a passive attitude. Don't try to force yourself to relax. Just let it happen. If a distracting thought comes to mind, ignore it. It is best to practice this exercise one or two times a day, but not within 2 hours of your last meal. Digestion interferes with the relaxation response.

Yapko, 1994). Thus, hypnosis is not like a truth serum; people can keep secrets or lie under hypnosis.

Still, hypnosis is recognized as a viable technique for use in medicine, dentistry, and psychotherapy (Lynn et al., 2000). For example, experimental studies have shown that patients who are hypnotized and exposed to suggestions designed to induce relaxation prior to surgery experience less postsurgical pain than do nonhypnotized controls (Montgomery et al., 2002). Hypnosis has also been used successfully to treat posttraumatic stress disorder (Cardena, 2000). However, hypnosis has been only moderately effective in weight control and virtually useless in overcoming drug and alcohol abuse or nicotine addiction (Abbot et al., 2000; Green & Lynn, 2000; Orne, 1983).

What accounts for people's behavior under hypnosis? According to the *sociocognitive theory of hypnosis,* the behavior of a hypnotized person is a function of that person's expectations about how subjects behave under hypnosis. People are motivated to be good subjects, to follow the suggestions of the hypnotist, and to fulfill the social role of the hypnotized person as they perceive it (Spanos, 1986, 1991, 1994).

However, Ernest Hilgard (1986, 1992) has proposed a *neodissociation theory of hypnosis,* suggesting that hypnosis induces a split, or dissociation, between two aspects of the control of consciousness that are ordinarily linked—the planning and the monitoring functions. During hypnosis, it is the planning function that carries out the suggestions of the hypnotist and remains a part of the subject's conscious awareness. The monitoring function monitors or observes everything that happens to the subject, but without his or her conscious awareness. Hilgard called the monitoring function, when separated from conscious awareness, "the hidden observer."

Bowers and his colleagues (Bowers, 1992; Woody & Bowers, 1994) have proposed an explanation called the *theory of dissociated control,* maintaining that hypnosis weakens the control of the executive function over other parts (subsystems) of consciousness. In their view, the hypnotist's suggestions not only affect the executive function, but influence the other subsystems directly. Bowers further believes that the hypnotized person's responses are automatic and involuntary, not mediated by normal cognitive functions (Kirsch & Lynn, 1995). And, indeed, some research supports this belief (Bowers & Woody, 1996; Hargadon et al., 1995).

Although the majority of hypnosis researchers seem to support the sociocognitive theory of hypnosis, most clinicians apparently believe that hypnosis is a unique altered state of consciousness (Kirsch & Lynn, 1995). Kihlstrom (1986) has suggested that a more complete picture of hypnosis would emerge from some combination of the sociocognitive approach and the neodissociation theory. But even though psychologists have some serious theoretical differences, hypnosis is increasingly used in clinical practice, as well as in selected areas of medicine and dentistry.

A hypnotized person is in a state of heightened suggestibility. This hypnotherapist suggested to the subject that a balloon was tied to his right hand and his arm raised accordingly.

What are the three main theories that have been proposed to explain hypnosis?

Culture and Altered States of Consciousness

In every culture around the world, and throughout recorded history, human beings have found ways to induce altered states of consciousness. Some methods of inducing altered states that are used in other cultures may seem strange and exotic to most Westerners. Entering a ritual trance and experiencing spirit possession are forms of altered states of consciousness that occur in many cultures in the course of religious rites and tribal ceremonies. Typically, people induce a ritual trance by flooding the senses with repetitive chanting, clapping, or singing; by whirling in circles until they achieve a dizzying speed; or by burning strong, pungent incense.

The ritualized spinning dance of the whirling dervishes produces an altered state of consciousness that is recognized as part of their religious practice.

The fact that so many different means of altering consciousness are practiced by members of so many cultures around the world has led some experts to ask whether "there may be a universal human need to produce and maintain varieties of conscious experiences" (Ward, 1994, p. 60). And like the methods used to induce it, the experience of an altered state of consciousness can vary greatly from one culture to another.

Altered States of Consciousness and Psychoactive Drugs

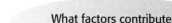

psychoactive drug
A drug that alters normal mental functioning—mood, perception, or thought—and thus may be abused.

A **psychoactive drug** is a substance that has psychological effects; it alters mood, perception, or thought. Because of their ability to alter psychological states, such substances are abused by many people. Unfortunately, after several years of decline, the proportion of young people who use drugs for recreational purposes in the United States began to rise again in the late 1990s (see Figure 4.3).

Substance Abuse

What factors contribute to substance abuse?

When people intentionally use drugs to induce an altered state of consciousness, they risk developing a substance abuse problem. Psychologists usually define *substance abuse* as continued use of a substance after several episodes in which use of the substance has negatively affected the individual's work, education, and social relationships (American Psychiatric Association, 1994). For example, a person who has missed work several times because of alcohol intoxication, but who continues to drink, has a substance abuse problem.

What causes people to progress from substance use to substance abuse? The physical pleasure associated with drug-induced altered states of consciousness is one reason. Physical pleasure—whether derived from sex, a psychoactive chemical, or any other source—is often associated with an increase in the availability of the neurotransmitter dopamine in a part of the brain's limbic system known as the *nucleus accumbens* (Gerrits et al., 2002; Robinson et al., 2001). There is ample evidence that a surge of dopamine is involved in the rewarding and motivational effects produced by a long list of psy-

▶ Figure 4.3

Results of a Survey of 8th, 10th, and 12th Graders about Their Use of Any Illicit Drug during the Previous 12 Months

The graph shows the percentage of high school seniors for 1976 through 2000 and the percentages of 8th and 10th graders for 1991 through 2000 who reported using any illicit (illegal) drug during the previous 12 months. After declining steeply from 1982 to 1992, the use of illicit drugs began to increase dramatically in 1992 and continued to climb until 1997. Then drug use decreased slightly in 1997 and 1998 but was beginning to creep upward again in 1999. (Data from Johnston et al., 2001.)

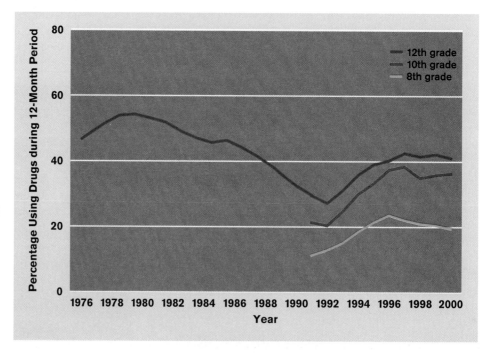

choactive drugs (Carlson, 1998; Landry, 1997; Pich et al., 1997; Pontieri et al., 1996; Tanda et al., 1997; Volkow et al., 1997, 1999).

Genetically based individual differences in the way people respond physiologically to drugs also contribute to substance abuse. For example, some people feel intoxicated after drinking very small amounts of alcohol; others require a much larger "dose." People who have to drink more to experience intoxication are more likely to become alcoholics, and genetic researchers are currently searching for the gene or genes that contribute to a low physiological response to alcohol (Schuckit et al., 2001). However, personality and social factors contribute to substance abuse as well. Impulsivity, for instance, is associated with experimentation with drugs (Simons & Carey, 2002), and stress-related variables, such as having been a victim of child abuse or domestic violence, are reliable predictors of substance abuse (Gordon, 2002; Sussman & Dent, 2000).

 Some people feel intoxicated after drinking very small amounts of alcohol, while others require a much larger "dose." People who have to drink more to experience intoxication are more likely to become alcoholics.

Drug Dependence

Some people progress from substance abuse to full-blown *substance dependence*, commonly called *addiction*. **Physical drug dependence** comes about as a result of the body's natural ability to protect itself against harmful substances by developing a **drug tolerance.** This means that the user becomes progressively less affected by the drug and must take larger and larger doses to get the same effect, or "high" (Ramsay & Woods, 1997). Tolerance occurs because the brain adapts to the presence of the drug by responding less intensely to it. In addition, the liver produces more enzymes to break down the drug. Thus, various bodily processes adjust in order to continue to function with the drug in the system.

Once drug tolerance is established, a person cannot function normally without the drug. If the drug is taken away, the user begins to suffer withdrawal symptoms. The **withdrawal symptoms,** both physical and psychological, are usually the exact opposite of the effects produced by the drug. For example, withdrawal from stimulants leaves a person exhausted and depressed; withdrawal from tranquilizers leaves a person nervous and agitated. Since taking the drug is the only way to escape the unpleasant withdrawal symptoms, they support continued addiction. Moreover, the lasting behavioral and cognitive effects of abused substances on the brain also often interfere with attempts to stop using them. Among other effects, researchers have learned that addiction is associated with attention and memory deficits, loss of the ability to accurately sense the passage of time, and declines in the capacity to plan and control behavior (Bates et al., 2002; Buhusi & Meck, 2002; Lyvers, 2000). Abusers need all of these skills to overcome addiction and rebuild their lives, but regaining them once drug abuse is stopped, if they *can* be regained, takes time.

Psychological drug dependence is a craving or irresistible urge for a drug's pleasurable effects, and it is more difficult to combat than physical dependence (O'Brien, 1996). Continued use of drugs to which an individual is physically addicted is influenced by the psychological component of the habit. There are also drugs (e.g., marijuana) that are probably not physically addictive but may create psychological dependence.

Learning processes are important in the development and maintenance of psychological dependence. For example, because of classical conditioning, drug-taking cues–the people, places, and things associated with using–can produce a strong craving for the substance of abuse (Hillebrand, 2000). In fact, some researchers have found that people addicted to opiates selectively pay attention to drug-related cues, ignoring virtually all other cues any time those drug-related cues are present (Lubman et al., 2000). However, "selective attention" probably isn't the most descriptive term for what is happening in a drug addict's brain. PET scans of cocaine addicts' brains indi-

> What is the difference between physical and psychological drug dependence?

physical drug dependence
A compulsive pattern of drug use in which the user develops a drug tolerance coupled with unpleasant withdrawal symptoms when the drug use is discontinued.

drug tolerance
A condition in which the user becomes progressively less affected by the drug so that larger and larger doses are necessary to achieve the same effect.

withdrawal symptoms
The physical and psychological symptoms (usually the opposite of those produced by the drug) that occur when a regularly used drug is discontinued and that terminate when the drug is taken again.

psychological drug dependence
A craving or irresistible urge for a drug's pleasurable effects.

Amphetamines affect the nucleus accumbens as well as the parts of the brain that control attention and concentration. This helps explain why these drugs are useful in the treatment of attention problems in school children.

How do stimulants affect the user? ▶

stimulants
A category of drugs that speed up activity in the central nervous system, suppress appetite, and cause a person to feel more awake, alert, and energetic; also called *uppers.*

What effects do amphetamines have on the user? ▶

How does cocaine affect the user? ▶

depressants
A category of drugs that decrease activity in the central nervous system, slow down bodily functions, and reduce sensitivity to outside stimulation; also called *downers.*

What are some of the effects of depressants, and what drugs make up this category? ▶

cate that the drug-related cues arouse a cue-specific neural network, which may explain why it is difficult for addicts to divert their attention from them (Bonson et al., 2002). Further, research with animals indicates that drug-related cues elicit the same responses in the brain as the drugs themselves (Kiyatkin & Wise, 2002). These findings underscore the necessity of changes in addicts' physical and social environments in the treatment of both physical and psychological drug dependence.

Types of Psychoactive Drugs and Their Effects

Psychoactive drugs alter consciousness in a variety of ways. **Stimulants,** often called *uppers,* speed up the central nervous system, suppress appetite, and can make a person feel more awake, alert, and energetic. One familiar stimulant, *caffeine,* makes people more mentally alert and can help them stay awake (Wesensten et al., 2002). Like caffeine, nicotine increases alertness. However, caffeine may have undesirable side effects (see the *Apply It!* at the end of the chapter), and nicotine use is associated with lung cancer and a host of other diseases. We will discuss the health effects of nicotine use in Chapter 10.

Amphetamines are powerful stimulants that increase arousal, relieve fatigue, improve alertness, suppress the appetite, and give a rush of energy. Animal research suggests that amphetamines stimulate the release of dopamine in the frontal cortex as well as in the nucleus accumbens, which may account for some of their desirable cognitive effects such as increases in attention span and concentration (Frantz et al., 2002). But amphetamines are addictive and can be quite dangerous. In high doses (100 milligrams or more), they can cause confused and disorganized behavior, extreme fear and suspiciousness, delusions and hallucinations, aggressiveness and antisocial behavior, even manic behavior and paranoia.

Cocaine, a stimulant derived from coca leaves, can be sniffed as a white powder, injected intravenously, or smoked in the form of "crack." The effects of snorting cocaine are felt within 2 to 3 minutes, and the high lasts 30 to 45 minutes. The euphoria from cocaine is followed by an equally intense crash, marked by depression, anxiety, agitation, and a powerful craving for more of the drug. Cocaine appears to stimulate the reward circuits, or "pleasure" pathways, in the brain, which use the neurotransmitter dopamine (Kimmel et al., 2003; Landry, 1997). With continued use, the reward circuits fail to function normally, and the user becomes incapable of feeling any pleasure except from the drug. Further, over time, or even quickly with high doses, cocaine can cause heart palpitations, an irregular heartbeat, and heart attacks, and high doses can cause strokes in healthy young individuals.

Animals become addicted more readily to cocaine, especially in its crack form, than to any other drug, and those that are addicted to multiple substances prefer cocaine when offered a choice of drugs (Manzardo et al., 2002). Given unlimited access to cocaine, animals will lose interest in everything else—food, water, sex—and will rapidly and continually self-administer cocaine. They die within 14 days, usually from cardiopulmonary collapse (Gawin, 1991). Cocaine-addicted monkeys will press a lever as many as 12,800 times to get one cocaine injection (Yanagita, 1973).

Another class of drugs, the **depressants** (sometimes called *downers*) decrease activity in the central nervous system, slow down body functions, and reduce sensitivity to outside stimulation. Within this category are alcohol, barbiturates, and tranquilizers. When different depressants are taken together, their sedative effects are additive and thus potentially dangerous. In addition, abuse or addiction to any of these substances can have serious consequences for both physical and mental health. For example, excessive use of tranquilizers is associated with both temporary and permanent impairment of memory (Paraherakis et al., 2001). We will discuss alcohol in more depth in Chapter 10 and tranquilizers in Chapter 13.

Narcotics are derived from the opium poppy and produce both a pain-relieving and a calming effect. Opium affects mainly the brain and the bowel. It paralyzes the intestinal muscles, which is why it is used medically to treat diarrhea. Both morphine and codeine, two drugs prescribed for pain, are natural components of opium.

A highly addictive narcotic derived from morphine is *heroin*. Heroin addicts describe a sudden "rush" of euphoria, followed by drowsiness, inactivity, and impaired concentration. Withdrawal symptoms begin about 6 to 24 hours after use, and the addict becomes physically sick. Nausea, diarrhea, depression, stomach cramps, insomnia, and pain grow worse and worse until they become intolerable—unless the person gets another fix.

The **hallucinogens,** or psychedelics, are drugs that can alter and distort perceptions of time and space, alter mood, and produce feelings of unreality. Hallucinogens have been used in religious and recreational rituals and ceremonies in diverse cultures since ancient times (Millman & Beeder, 1994). Rather than producing a relatively predictable effect, like most other drugs do, hallucinogens usually magnify the mood of the user at the time the drug is taken. And, contrary to the belief of some, hallucinogens hamper rather than enhance creative thinking (Bourassa & Vaugeois, 2001).

Marijuana is perhaps the most popular drug among the hallucinogens. The ingredient in marijuana that produces the high is THC (tetrahydrocannabinol), which remains in the body "for days or even weeks" (Julien, 1995). Marijuana impairs attention and coordination and slows reaction time, and these effects make operating complex machinery such as an automobile dangerous, even after the feeling of intoxication has passed. Marijuana can interfere with concentration, logical thinking, and the ability to form new memories. It can produce fragmentation in thought and confusion in remembering recent occurrences (Herkenham, 1992). A 17-year longitudinal study of Costa Rican men supports the claim that long-term use has a negative impact on short-term memory and the ability to focus sustained attention (Fletcher et al., 1996).

Chronic use of marijuana has been associated with loss of motivation, general apathy, and decline in school performance—referred to as *amotivational syndrome* (Andreasen & Black, 1991). Studies comparing marijuana users who began before age 17 with those who started later show that early marijuana use is associated with a somewhat smaller brain volume and a lower percentage of the all-important gray matter in the brain's cortex. Marijuana users who started younger were also shorter and weighed less than users who started when older (Wilson et al., 2000). Further, marijuana smoke contains many of the same carcinogenic chemicals as cigarette smoke.

However, an advisory panel of the National Institute of Drug Abuse, after reviewing the scientific evidence, concluded that marijuana shows promise as a treatment for certain medical conditions. It has been found effective for treating the eye disease glaucoma, for controlling nausea and vomiting in cancer patients receiving chemotherapy, and for improving appetite and curtailing weight loss in some AIDS patients (Fackelmann, 1997). But there is a continuing controversy over whether marijuana should be legalized for medical purposes.

Another hallucinogen, *LSD (lysergic acid diethylamide)*, is sometimes referred to simply as "acid." The average LSD "trip" lasts for 10 to 12 hours and usually produces extreme perceptual and emotional changes, including visual hallucinations and feelings of panic (Miller & Gold, 1994). On occasion, bad LSD trips have ended tragically, in accidents, death, or suicide. Former LSD users sometimes experience flashbacks, or brief recurrences of previous trips that occur suddenly and without warning. Some develop a syndrome called *hallucinogen persisting perception disorder (HPPD)*, in which the visual cortex becomes highly stimulated whenever the eyes are closed, causing chronic visual hallucinations whenever the person tries to sleep (Abraham & Duffy, 2001).

As the chapter opening vignette noted, *MDMA,* or Ecstasy, produces a distinctive form of altered consciousness involving both stimulant and psychedelic effects. The drug's main appeal is its psychological effect—a feeling of relatedness and connectedness with others (Taylor, 1996). But MDMA is more toxic than most other hallucinogens and should be considered a dangerous drug. Brain

What are the general effects of narcotics, and what are several drugs in this category?

narcotics
A class of depressant drugs derived from the opium poppy and producing pain-relieving and calming effects.

hallucinogens
(hal-LU-sin-o-jenz) A category of drugs, sometimes called *psychedelics,* that alter perception and mood and can cause hallucinations.

What are the main effects of hallucinogens, and what are three psychoactive drugs classified as hallucinogens?

What are some harmful effects of chronic marijuana use?

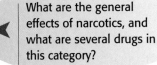
Farm workers in developing countries may not know that the sales of narcotics derived from the poppies they harvest sometimes help finance international terrorism.

The Effects and Withdrawal Symptoms of Some Psychoactive Drugs

PSYCHOACTIVE DRUG	EFFECTS	WITHDRAWAL SYMPTOMS
Stimulants		
Caffeine	Produces wakefulness and alertness; increases metabolism but slows reaction time	Headache, depression, fatigue
Tobacco (nicotine)	Effects range from alertness to calmness; lowers appetite for carbohydrates; increases pulse rate and other metabolic processes	Irritability, anxiety, restlessness, increased appetite
Amphetamines	Increase metabolism and alertness; elevate mood; cause wakefulness; suppress appetite	Fatigue, increased appetite, depression, long periods of sleep, irritability, anxiety
Cocaine	Brings on euphoric mood, energy boost, feeling of excitement; suppresses appetite	Depression, fatigue, increased appetite, long periods of sleep, irritability
Depressants		
Alcohol	First few drinks stimulate and enliven while lowering anxiety and inhibitions; higher doses have a sedative effect, slowing reaction time, impairing motor control and perceptual ability	Tremors, nausea, sweating, depression, weakness, irritability, and, in some cases, hallucinations
Barbiturates (e.g., phenobarbital)	Promote sleep; have calming and sedative effect; decrease muscular tension; impair coordination and reflexes	Sleeplessness, anxiety; sudden withdrawal can cause seizures, cardiovascular collapse, and death
Tranquilizers (e.g., Valium, Xanax)	Lower anxiety; have calming and sedative effect; decrease muscular tension	Restlessness, anxiety, irritability, muscle tension, difficulty sleeping
Hallucinogens		
Marijuana	Generally produces euphoria, relaxation; affects ability to store new memories	Anxiety, difficulty sleeping, decreased appetite, hyperactivity
LSD	Produces excited exhilaration, hallucinations; experiences perceived as insightful and profound	
MDMA (Ecstasy)	Typically produces euphoria and feelings of understanding others and accepting them; lowers inhibitions; often causes overheating, dehydration, nausea; can cause jaw clenching, eye twitching, and dizziness	Depression, fatigue, and in some cases a "crash," during which the person may be sad, scared, or annoyed

damage—resulting in impairments in memory and verbal reasoning (Morgan, 1999; Reneman et al., 2000) and in tasks that require sustained attention (McCann et al., 1999)—has been linked to chronic, moderate to heavy use of MDMA. The neurotransmitter serotonin has been implicated in these cognitive impairments. Serotonin, as you learned in Chapter 2, influences cognitive performance (including memory), as well as moods, sleep cycles, and the ability to control impulses (Reneman et al., 2000; Volkow & Fowler, 2000).

Review and Reflect 4.1 summarizes the effects of various drugs on the nervous system and on behavior.

Apply It! Should You Kick Your Caffeine Habit?

The most popular caffeine-containing beverage in the United States is coffee. Americans drink more than a half-billion cups of coffee daily, with most drinkers consuming at least two cups. In addition to appreciating coffee's flavor and aroma, drinkers say that it makes them feel more energetic and alert. The caffeine in coffee improves muscular coordination, thus facilitating work activities such as typing, and it may improve memory and reasoning. For people with tight airways, it opens breathing passages. It is also a mild diuretic. Caffeine, in short, is a natural stimulant.

Does caffeine cause health problems? During the past two decades, extensive research has been conducted on possible links between caffeine use and various health problems. The results have been mixed: For every study that implicates caffeine as a possible health risk, another finds no connection. For example, coffee consumption had been linked to increased risk of coronary artery disease and heart attack, but a 1996 study found that when researchers adjusted for cigarette smoking among coffee drinkers, the link disappeared (Mayo Clinic, 1997).

This is not to say that caffeine is entirely harmless. Even a couple of cups of coffee can make you nervous, anxious, and irritable. It can produce heartburn and irritate existing ulcers, and it causes bladder irritation in some people. It can also cause a temporary rise in blood pressure.

Who is most likely to be affected by caffeine? Any health problems related to caffeine consumption are usually found only in people who drink large quantities of coffee—eight or more cups a day (Mayo Clinic, 1997). Thus, the effects of caffeine on an individual depend on the amount consumed, the frequency of consumption, the individual's metabolism, and the individual's sensitivity to caffeine.

Is caffeine addictive? Some people say that they are "addicted" to coffee because they feel unable to start the day without it. What they really mean is that they depend on caffeine's stimulant effects to get them going. It has been suggested that dependence on caffeine is similar to dependence on alcohol or tobacco. The major evidence for this is that halting caffeine consumption abruptly can cause withdrawal symptoms such as headaches, fatigue, and depression. It is also true that regular consumption leads to a tolerance for many of the effects of caffeine. However, caffeine consumption patterns differ

from those associated with serious drug dependence: Caffeine use does not result in a craving for ever-higher doses, and it is not very difficult to stop consuming it. And most consumers of caffeine do not exhibit the compulsive behavior characteristics of those dependent on illicit drugs. As one expert points out, "Addiction means a dysfunctional use of a drug . . . that a drug has taken control of a person's life" (O'Brien, quoted in International Food Information Council [IFIC], 2000). This is certainly not true in the case of caffeine. According to the World Health Organization, "There is no evidence whatsoever that caffeine use has even remotely comparable physical and social consequences [to those] associated with serious drugs of abuse" (quoted in IFIC, 1998).

Should you try to kick your caffeine habit? If you are particularly sensitive to caffeine or have been consuming it in large quantities, you may be experiencing side effects such as excessive nervousness ("coffee nerves") and insomnia. If so, you may wish to cut back on or eliminate caffeine. This does not mean that you have to suffer withdrawal symptoms. Experts agree that these can be avoided by tapering off your consumption gradually—the slower the tapering, the easier the withdrawal. While you're cutting back, decaffeinated coffee, tea, or soft drinks can provide the flavor you're used to without the stimulant effects. Finally, if you're not trying to eliminate caffeine altogether, consider avoiding it for 3 days every 2 or 3 weeks to give your body a rest from the continual stimulation. ■

Summarize It!

What Is Consciousness?

➤ What do psychologists mean by the terms *consciousness* and *altered states of consciousness*?

The term *consciousness* refers to awareness of one's own perceptions, thoughts, feelings, sensations, and the outside environment. An altered state of consciousness is one in which this awareness has been changed in some way. Altered states occur when we sleep, meditate, are hypnotized, or use drugs.

KEY TERMS

consciousness (p. 96)
altered state of consciousness (p. 96)

Circadian Rhythms

➤ What is a circadian rhythm?

A circadian rhythm is the regular fluctuation in any of a number of body functions from a high point to a low point within a 24-hour period.

➤ What are some problems experienced by people who travel across time zones or who work night shifts?

People who travel across time zones experience jet lag, a condition in which circadian rhythms are disrupted. Night shift workers are subject to such disruptions as well, resulting in sleep difficulties, lowered alertness, efficiency, productivity, and safety during their subjective night; and a variety of psychological and physical problems.

KEY TERMS

circadian rhythm (p. 96)
subjective night (p. 97)

Sleep

➤ What are the physiological signs of NREM sleep?

During NREM sleep, heart rate and respiration are slow and regular, blood pressure and brain activity are at a 24-hour low point, and there is little body movement and no rapid eye movements.

➤ What are the physiological signs of REM sleep?

During REM sleep, the large muscles of the body are paralyzed, respiration and heart rate are fast and irregular, brain activity increases, and rapid eye movements and vivid dreams occur.

➤ What function does REM sleep appear to serve, and what happens when people are deprived of it?

REM sleep appears to aid in learning and memory. Following REM deprivation, people experience a REM rebound—a temporary increase in the percentage of REM sleep.

➤ What is the progression of NREM stages and REM sleep that occurs during a typical night's sleep?

During a typical night, a sleeper goes through about five sleep cycles, each lasting about 90 minutes. The first sleep cycle consists of Stages 1, 2, 3, and 4 and REM sleep; the second has Stages 2, 3, and 4 and REM sleep. In the remaining sleep cycles, the sleeper alternates mainly between Stage 2 and REM sleep, with each sleep cycle having progressively longer REM periods.

➤ What are the two main theories that attempt to explain the function of sleep?

The two main theories about the function of sleep are the restorative theory and the circadian theory.

➤ How do REM and NREM dreams differ?

REM dreams have a storylike quality and are more vivid, visual, emotional, frequent, and memorable than the more thoughtlike NREM dreams.

➤ What are the characteristics common to sleepwalking and sleep terrors?

Sleepwalking and sleep terrors occur during a partial arousal from Stage 4 sleep, and the person does not come to full consciousness. Episodes are rarely recalled. These two sleep disorders are typically found in children, who outgrow them by adolescence.

➤ What is a sleep terror?

A sleep terror is a parasomnia in which the sleeper awakens from Stage 4 sleep with a scream, dazed and groggy, in a panic state, and with a racing heart.

➤ How do nightmares differ from sleep terrors?

Nightmares are frightening dreams that occur during REM sleep and are remembered in vivid detail. Sleep terrors occur during Stage 4 sleep and are rarely remembered.

➤ What are the major symptoms of narcolepsy?

The symptoms of narcolepsy include excessive daytime sleepiness and sudden attacks of REM sleep.

➤ What is sleep apnea?

Sleep apnea is a serious sleep disorder in which a sleeper's breathing stops and the person must awaken briefly to breathe. Its major symptoms are excessive daytime sleepiness and loud snoring.

➤ What is insomnia?

Insomnia is a sleep disorder that involves difficulty in falling or staying asleep, waking too early, or sleep that is light, restless, or of poor quality.

KEY TERMS

NREM sleep (p. 97)
REM sleep (p. 98)
REM rebound (p. 98)
sleep cycle (p. 98)
delta waves (p. 98)
slow-wave sleep (p. 99)
restorative theory (p. 99)
circadian theory (p. 100)
REM dreams (p. 100)
NREM dreams (p. 100)
parasomnias (p. 102)

Altering Consciousness through Concentration and Suggestion

➤ For what purposes is meditation used?

Meditation is used by some to promote relaxation and reduce arousal and by others to expand consciousness or attain a higher spiritual level.

➤ **What is hypnosis, and when is it most useful?**

Hypnosis is a procedure through which a hypnotist uses the power of suggestion to induce changes in the thoughts, feelings, sensations, perceptions, or behavior of a subject. It has been used most successfully for the control of pain.

➤ **What are the three main theories that have been proposed to explain hypnosis?**

The three main theories proposed to explain hypnosis are the sociocognitive theory, the neodissociation theory, and the theory of dissociated control.

KEY TERMS

meditation (p. 103)
hypnosis (p. 104)

Altered States of Consciousness and Psychoactive Drugs

➤ **What factors contribute to substance abuse?**

All addictive drugs increase the availability of dopamine in the nucleus accumbens, causing pleasurable sensations that contribute to drug abuse. Individual differences in physiological responses to drugs also play a role. Personality and social variables also contribute to abuse.

➤ **What is the difference between physical and psychological drug dependence?**

With physical drug dependence, the user develops a drug tolerance and so larger and larger doses are needed to get the same effect. Withdrawal symptoms appear when the drug is discontinued and disappear when the drug is taken again. Psychological drug dependence involves an intense craving for the drug.

➤ **How do stimulants affect the user?**

Stimulants speed up activity in the central nervous system, suppress appetite, and make a person feel more awake, alert, and energetic.

➤ **What effects do amphetamines have on the user?**

Use of amphetamines energizes, increases arousal, and suppresses the appetite. In high doses, however, these stimulants can have negative effects: confused behavior, delusions and hallucinations, and aggressiveness, for example.

➤ **How does cocaine affect the user?**

Cocaine energizes, causes a feeling of euphoria, and is highly addictive. Heavy use can cause heart damage, seizures, and even heart attacks.

➤ **What are some of the effects of depressants, and what drugs make up this category?**

Depressants decrease activity in the central nervous system, slow down body functions, and reduce sensitivity to outside stimulation. Depressants include alcohol, barbiturates, and tranquilizers.

➤ **What are the general effects of narcotics, and what are several drugs in this category?**

Narcotics, which include opium, codeine, morphine, and heroin, have both pain-relieving and calming effects.

➤ **What are the main effects of hallucinogens, and what are three psychoactive drugs classified as hallucinogens?**

Hallucinogens—including marijuana, LSD, and MDMA—can alter perception and mood and cause hallucinations.

➤ **What are some harmful effects of chronic marijuana use?**

Chronic marijuana use can cause memory problems, loss of motivation, general apathy, and a decline in school performance.

KEY TERMS

psychoactive drug (p. 106)
physical drug dependence (p. 107)
drug tolerance (p. 107)
withdrawal symptoms (p. 107)
psychological drug dependence (p. 107)
stimulants (p. 108)
depressants (p. 108)
narcotics (p. 108)
hallucinogens (p. 109)

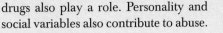

Surf It!

Want to be sure you've absorbed the material in Chapter 4, "States of Consciousness," before the big test? Visiting **www.ablongman.com/ woodmastering1e** can put a top grade within your reach. The site is loaded with free practice tests, flashcards, activities, and links to help you review your way to an A.

Companion Website

Study Guide for Chapter 4 !

Answers to all the Study Guide questions are provided at the end of the book.

Section One: Chapter Review

1. Which of the following best defines consciousness?
   a. awareness
   b. wakefulness
   c. receptiveness
   d. rationality

2. The structure that regulates the body's internal clock is the _____ .

3. People who are suffering from jet lag or the effects of working rotating shifts or night shifts are experiencing
   a. a deficiency in melatonin production.
   b. an excess of melatonin production.
   c. a defect in their suprachiasmatic nucleus.
   d. a disturbance in their circadian rhythms.

4. The performance of shift workers is enhanced during their subjective night. (true/false)

5. State the type of sleep–NREM or REM–that corresponds to each characteristic.
   ____ **(1)** paralysis of large muscles
   ____ **(2)** slow, regular respiration and heart rate
   ____ **(3)** rapid eye movements
   ____ **(4)** intense brain activity
   ____ **(5)** vivid dreams

   a. REM
   b. NREM

6. The average length of a sleep cycle in adults is
   a. 30 minutes.
   b. 60 minutes.
   c. 90 minutes.
   d. 120 minutes.

7. After the first two sleep cycles, most people get equal amounts of deep sleep and REM sleep. (true/false)

8. Which type of sleep seems to aid learning and memory?
   a. Stage 1
   b. Stage 2
   c. Stages 3 and 4
   d. REM sleep

9. Following REM deprivation, there is usually
   a. an absence of REM sleep.
   b. an increase in REM sleep.
   c. a decrease in REM sleep.
   d. no change in the amount of REM sleep.

10. Match the age group with the appropriate description of sleep.
   ____ **(1)** have most difficulty sleeping
   ____ **(2)** sleep 8 to 9 hours
   ____ **(3)** have highest percentage of REM and deep sleep
   a. infants
   b. children aged 6 to puberty
   c. elderly adults

11. The two main theories that attempt to explain the function of sleep are the _____ and the _____ .

12. Compared to REM dreams, NREM dreams are
   a. more emotional.
   b. more visual.
   c. more thoughtlike.
   d. more vivid.

13. Dreams are difficult to remember because most of them occur during Stage 4 sleep. (true/false)

14. According to researchers,
   a. most dreams are bizarre in nature.
   b. dreams involving bizarre content are more likely to be remembered than other kinds of dreams.
   c. people who have delusional disorders rarely have bizarre dreams.
   d. only children have bizarre dreams.

15. Experts tend to agree on how dreams should be interpreted. (true/false)

16. Sleepwalking and sleep terrors occur during a partial arousal from
   a. Stage 1 sleep.
   b. Stage 2 sleep.
   c. Stage 4 sleep.
   d. REM sleep.

17. Sleepwalking episodes and sleep terrors are rarely recalled. (true/false)

18. Match each sleep problem with the description or associated symptom.
   ____ **(1)** uncontrollable sleep attacks during the day
   ____ **(2)** cessation of breathing during sleep
   ____ **(3)** difficulty falling or staying asleep
   ____ **(4)** very frightening REM dream
   a. sleep apnea
   b. nightmare
   c. insomnia
   d. narcolepsy

19. Which is not a proposed use of meditation?
   a. to promote relaxation
   b. to substitute for anesthesia during surgery
   c. to bring a person to a higher level of spirituality
   d. to alter consciousness

20. Many people who meditate are motivated by a desire to attain a higher spiritual state of consciousness. (true/false)

21. According to Herbert Benson, the beneficial effects of meditation cannot be duplicated with simple relaxation techniques. (true/false)

22. Which of the following statements is true of people under hypnosis?
    a. They will often violate their moral code.
    b. They are much stronger than they are in the normal waking state.
    c. They can be made to experience distortions in their perceptions.
    d. Their memory is more accurate than it is during the normal waking state.

23. For a fairly hypnotizable person, which use of hypnosis would probably be most successful?
    a. for relief from pain
    b. instead of a general anesthetic during surgery
    c. for treating drug addiction
    d. for improving memory

24. The three main theories proposed to explain hypnosis are the _____, _____, and _____ theories.

25. Drug use among adolescents has been steadily declining since the early 1990s. (true/false)

26. Which of the following does not necessarily occur with drug tolerance?
    a. The body adjusts to functioning with the drug in the system.
    b. The user needs larger and larger doses of the drug to get the desired effect.
    c. The user becomes progressively less affected by the drug.
    d. The user develops a craving for the pleasurable effects of the drug.

27. During withdrawal from a drug, the user experiences symptoms that are the opposite of the effects produced by the drug. (true/false)

28. Psychological dependence on a drug is more difficult to combat than physical dependence. (true/false)

29. Match the stimulant with the appropriate description.
    ____ (1) used to increase arousal, relieve fatigue, and suppress appetite
    ____ (2) found in coffee
    ____ (3) snorted or injected
    ____ (4) smokable form of cocaine
    a. caffeine
    b. amphetamines
    c. crack
    d. cocaine

30. Decreased activity in the central nervous system is the chief effect of
    a. stimulants.   c. hallucinogens.
    b. depressants.   d. narcotics.

31. Which of the following is a narcotic?
    a. cocaine   c. LSD
    b. heroin   d. Valium

32. Narcotics have
    a. pain-relieving effects.
    b. stimulating effects.
    c. energizing effects.
    d. perception-altering effects.

33. Which category of drugs alters perception and mood and can cause hallucinations?
    a. stimulants   c. hallucinogens
    b. depressants   d. narcotics

34. Which of the following is *not* associated with chronic use of marijuana?
    a. decline in school performance
    b. loss of motivation
    c. general apathy
    d. increased risk of heart attack and stroke

35. Addictive drugs increase the effect of the neurotransmitter _____ in the nucleus accumbens.
    a. acetylcholine   c. dopamine
    b. GABA   d. serotonin

Section Two: Identify the Drug

Match the description of drug effects with the drug.

____ (1) Produces excited exhilaration and hallucinations

____ (2) Produces wakefulness and alertness with increased metabolism but slowed reaction time

____ (3) Increase metabolism and alertness, elevate mood and wakefulness, and decrease appetite

____ (4) Produce euphoria and relaxation but also affect ability to store new memories

____ (5) Produces an energy boost and feeling of excitement while suppressing appetite

____ (6) Initial doses stimulate and enliven while lowering anxiety, but higher doses have a sedative effect

____ (7) Produces euphoria and feelings of social acceptance; stimulates appetite; leads to depression and fatigue

a. alcohol
b. hallucinogens
c. LSD
d. caffeine
e. cocaine
f. amphetamines
g. MDMA (Ecstasy)

Section Three: Fill In the Blank

1. The text defined _____ as an awareness of one's own perceptions, thoughts, feelings, sensations, and external environment.

2. The _____ wave is the slowest brain wave and occurs during Stages 3 and 4 sleep.

3. After a person loses REM sleep because of illness or drug use, he or she might experience _____ .

4. Luis awoke in the middle of a strange dream in which he flew across a river. This dream probably occurred during _____ sleep.

5. A person who experiences sleepwalking or sleeptalking is suffering from one of a class of sleep disturbances collectively known as _____ .

6. Sleep _____ is a condition in which breathing stops during sleep.

7. _____ is characterized by daytime sleepiness and sudden REM sleep.

8. Psychoactive drugs are a group of substances that alter _____ , _____ , or _____ .

9. _____ is a group of techniques designed to block out all distractions so as to achieve an altered state of consciousness.

10. A compulsive pattern of drug use in which the user develops a tolerance coupled with unpleasant withdrawal symptoms when drug use is discontinued is referred to as physical drug _____ .

11. The euphoric high from cocaine lasts only a short time and is followed by an equally intense _____ , which is marked by depression, anxiety, agitation, and a powerful craving for more cocaine.

12. Cocaine's action in the human brain includes blocking the reuptake of the neurotransmitter _____ , thereby leading to the continual excitatory stimulation of the reward pathways in the brain.

13. The most highly addictive drug is _____ .

Section Four: Comprehensive Practice Test

1. Psychologists use brain-imaging techniques such as CT scanning to study consciousness. (true/false)

2. People who work during their _____ , when their biological clock is telling them it is time to sleep, can suffer lowered efficiency and productivity.
   a. REM rebound
   b. subjective night
   c. circadian rebound
   d. episodes of narcolepsy

3. REM sleep is the _____ stage of sleep in a typical sleep cycle.
   a. first
   b. second
   c. last
   d. middle

4. Delta waves appear primarily in Stages _____ sleep.
   a. 1 and 2
   b. 2 and 3
   c. 3 and 4
   d. 1 and 4

5. Another name for slow-wave sleep is
   a. light sleep.
   b. deep sleep.
   c. REM sleep.
   d. dream sleep.

6. Researchers have found that REM sleep
   a. is increased in the elderly.
   b. is associated with memory consolidation.
   c. occurs only in some sleep cycles.
   d. is rarely associated with dreaming.

7. As we grow older we sleep more than when we were younger; we also sleep more deeply, with more REM sleep. (true/false)

8. Freud believed dreams functioned to satisfy unconscious _____ and _____ urges.
   a. parental; childhood
   b. sexual; superego
   c. aggressive; violent
   d. sexual; aggressive

9. J. Allan Hobson believes dreams are merely the brain's attempt to make sense of the random firing of brain cells. This view is known as the
   a. Hobson dream hypothesis.
   b. somniloquy hypothesis.
   c. activation-synthesis hypothesis.
   d. physiological activation hypothesis.

10. The technical term for sleepwalking is
    a. somniloquy.
    b. mobile insomnia.
    c. narcolepsy.
    d. somnambulism.

11. People who talk in their sleep often reveal secrets or strong negative opinions. (true/false)

12. Some people suffer from a sleep disorder known as _____ , which causes them to stop breathing and then to wake for a brief time in order to start breathing again.
    a. narcolepsy
    b. sleep apnea
    c. somniloquy
    d. somnambulism

13. The sleep disorder characterized by either difficulty falling asleep or frequently waking is known as
   a. sleep apnea.
   b. insomnia.
   c. somnambulism.
   d. REM rebound.

14. Jack pleaded not guilty to his public indecency charges. He claimed he would never do such a thing if he were in his right mind and that he was the victim of the effects of hypnosis. A psychologist would probably support this claim. (true/false)

15. Personality has little impact on substance abuse. (true/false)

16. LSD, MDMA, and marijuana are classified as
   a. narcotics.
   b. stimulants.
   c. hallucinogens.
   d. depressants.

17. Animals addicted to several drugs prefer _____ when offered a choice of drugs.
   a. marijuana
   b. heroin
   c. cocaine
   d. alcohol

18. While caffeine is considered a relatively harmless stimulant in most cases, evidence suggests that some people can experience anxiety, depression, or hostility after using it. (true/false)

Section Five: Thinking Critically

1. Suppose you have been hired by a sleep clinic to formulate a questionnaire for evaluating patients' sleep habits. List 10 questions you would include in your questionnaire.

2. Luanne is a full-time student who wants to find a way to keep up her class schedule while working full-time. She decides to work the 11:00 PM to 7:00 AM shift at a hospital, then attend morning classes. After her classes end at noon, she intends to sleep from 1:00 PM until 7:00 PM, at which time she will get up and study until time to leave for work. Based on what you have learned about circadian rhythms in this chapter, what kinds of problems do you think Luanne will encounter in trying to carry out her plan?

3. You have been asked to make a presentation to 7th and 8th graders about the dangers of drugs. What are the most persuasive general arguments you can give to convince them not to start using drugs? What are some convincing, specific arguments against using each of these drugs: alcohol, marijuana, cocaine, and MDMA (Ecstasy)?

Learning

If you have a dog, you may be able to relate to Michael and Lori's story:

One day, their dog Jake decided he preferred to stay indoors at night, rather than be put into the backyard, as had been the rule since he was a puppy. He got his way by hiding in the house before Michael and Lori went to bed at night. Wanting to get as many hours of sleep as possible, Michael and Lori began a nightly ritual—going through the house, looking for Jake in closets and under the beds, and calling his name. But he never came when they called him at bedtime, and they were rarely able to find him.

Jake had associated their calling him at that time with being put outside before he was ready.

Then, when the spirit moved him (usually in the middle of the night), Jake would leap onto their bed, awakening Michael and Lori. After many sleepless nights, they were desperate for a solution to the problem.

Then, one day, when they were opening a can of soup, Jake raced through the house and slid to a stop in front of his bowl. He had learned to associate the sound of the can opener with food. So, Michael and Lori decided to conduct an experiment. Instead of calling Jake before bedtime, they began turning on the can opener when they were ready to put Jake out. The deception worked; the dog came running every time he heard the can opener. Michael and Lori felt a bit guilty about tricking Jake. Nevertheless, by applying simple learning principles, these dog owners were finally able to get a good night's rest.

learning
A relatively permanent change in behavior, knowledge, capability, or attitude that is acquired through experience and cannot be attributed to illness, injury, or maturation.

classical conditioning
A learning process through which one stimulus comes to predict the occurrence of another stimulus and to elicit a response similar to or related to the response evoked by that stimulus.

stimulus
(STIM-yu-lus) Any event or object in the environment to which an organism responds; plural is *stimuli*.

Learning may be defined as a relatively permanent change in behavior, knowledge, capability, or attitude that is acquired through experience and cannot be attributed to illness, injury, or maturation. Several parts of this definition need further explanation. First, defining learning as a "relatively permanent change" excludes temporary changes that could result from illness, fatigue, or fluctuations in mood. Second, referring to a change that is "acquired through experience" excludes some readily observable changes in behavior that occur as a result of brain injuries or certain diseases. Also, certain observable changes that occur as individuals grow and mature have nothing to do with learning. For example, technically speaking, infants do not *learn* to crawl or walk. Basic motor skills and the maturational plan that governs their development are a part of the genetically programmed behavioral repertoire of every species.

Classical Conditioning

Pavlov and Classical Conditioning

Ivan Pavlov (1849–1936) organized and directed research in physiology at the Institute of Experimental Medicine in St. Petersburg, Russia, from 1891 until his death 45 years later. He conducted classic experiments on the physiology of digestion, which won him a Nobel Prize in 1904—the first time this honor went to a Russian. In the course of his research, Pavlov designed a machine that could collect saliva from a dog's mouth (see Figure 5.1). Quite by accident, Pavlov observed drops of saliva collecting in the machine's containers when the dogs heard the footsteps of the laboratory assistants coming to feed them. How could an involuntary response such as salivation come to be associated with sounds that preceded feeding? Pavlov spent the rest of his life studying this question.

> What was Pavlov's major contribution to psychology?

Classical conditioning is a form of learning in which an association is formed between one stimulus and another. A **stimulus** (plural, *stimuli*) is any event or object in the environment to which an organism responds. In Jake's case, the sound of a can opener became associated with food. Similarly, humans learn to respond in specific ways to a variety of words and symbols. Adolf Hitler, the IRS, Santa Claus, and the

➤ Figure 5.1

The Experimental Apparatus Used in Pavlov's Classical Conditioning Studies

In Pavlov's classical conditioning studies, the dog was restrained in a harness in the cubicle and isolated from all distractions. An experimenter observed the dog through a one-way mirror and, by remote control, presented the dog with food and other conditioning stimuli. A tube carried the saliva from the dog's mouth to a container where it was measured.

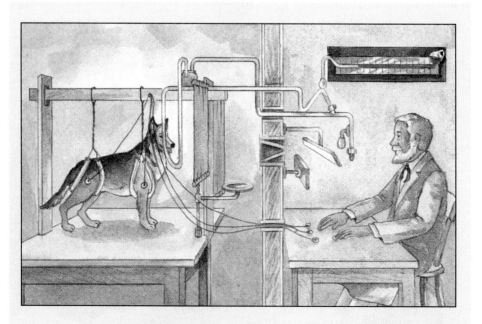

120

Ivan Pavlov (1849–1936) earned fame by studying a conditioned reflex in dogs.

American flag are just names and symbols, but they tend to evoke strong emotional responses because of their associations. People's lives are profoundly influenced by the associations learned through classical conditioning, sometimes referred to as *respondent conditioning,* or *Pavlovian conditioning.*

Pavlov (1927/1960) used tones, bells, buzzers, lights, geometric shapes, electric shocks, and metronomes in his conditioning experiments. In a typical experiment, food powder was placed in the dog's mouth, causing salivation. Because dogs do not need to be conditioned to salivate to food, the salivation is an unlearned response, or **unconditioned response (UR).** Any stimulus, such as food, that without learning will automatically elicit, or bring forth, an unconditioned response is called an **unconditioned stimulus (US).**

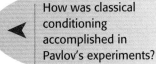

How was classical conditioning accomplished in Pavlov's experiments?

Unconditioned Stimulus (US)		*Unconditioned Response (UR)*
food	→	salivation
loud noise	→	startle
light in eye	→	contraction of pupil
puff of air in eye	→	eyeblink response

Pavlov demonstrated that dogs could be conditioned to salivate to a variety of stimuli never before associated with food. During the conditioning process, the researcher would present a neutral stimulus such as a musical tone shortly before placing food powder in the dog's mouth. The food powder would cause the dog to salivate. Pavlov found that after the tone and food were paired many times, usually 20 or more, the tone alone would elicit salivation (Pavlov, 1927/1960, p. 385). Pavlov called the tone the learned stimulus, or **conditioned stimulus (CS),** and he called salivation after the tone the learned response, or **conditioned response (CR).** (See Figure 5.2, on page 122.)

In a modern view of classical conditioning, the conditioned stimulus can be thought of as a signal that the unconditioned stimulus will follow (Schreurs, 1989). In Pavlov's experiment, the tone became a signal that food would follow shortly. So, the signal (conditioned stimulus) gives advance warning, and the organism (animal or person) is prepared with the proper response (conditioned response), even before the unconditioned stimulus arrives (Gallistel & Gibbon, 2000).

Because the conditioned stimulus serves as a signal for the unconditioned stimulus, conditioning takes place fastest if the conditioned stimulus occurs shortly before the unconditioned stimulus. It takes place more slowly or not at all when the two stimuli occur at the same time. The ideal time between the presentations of the conditioned and the unconditioned stimuli is about $\frac{1}{2}$ second, but this time varies according to the type of response being conditioned and the nature and intensity of the conditioned stimulus and the unconditioned stimulus (see Wasserman & Miller, 1997).

unconditioned response (UR)
A response that is invariably elicited by the unconditioned stimulus without prior learning.

unconditioned stimulus (US)
A stimulus that elicits a specific response without prior learning.

conditioned stimulus (CS)
A neutral stimulus that, after repeated pairing with an unconditioned stimulus, becomes associated with it and elicits a conditioned response.

conditioned response (CR)
A response that comes to be elicited by a conditioned stimulus as a result of its repeated pairing with an unconditioned stimulus.

➤ Figure 5.2

Classically Conditioning a Salivation Response

A neutral stimulus (a tone) elicits no salivation until it is repeatedly paired with the unconditioned stimulus (food). After many pairings, the neutral stimulus (now called the conditioned stimulus) alone produces salivation. Classical conditioning has occurred.

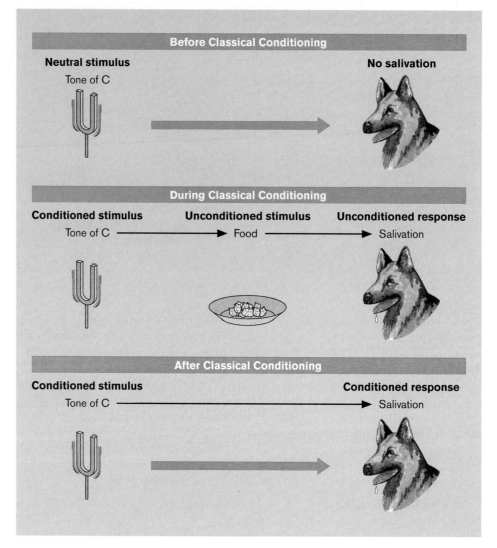

higher-order conditioning
Conditioning that occurs when a neutral stimulus is paired with an existing conditioned stimulus, becomes associated with it, and gains the power to elicit the same conditioned response.

extinction
In classical conditioning, the weakening and often eventual disappearance of the conditioned response, caused by repeated presentation of the conditioned stimulus without the unconditioned stimulus.

What is higher-order conditioning? ➤

spontaneous recovery
The reappearance of an extinguished response (in a weaker form) when an organism is exposed to the original conditioned stimulus after a rest period.

Further, conditioned stimuli may be linked together to form a series of signals, a process called **higher-order conditioning.** For example, think about what happens when you have to have some kind of blood test. Typically, you sit in a chair next to a table on which the nurse prepares materials such as needles, syringes, and such. Next, some kind of constricting device is tied around your arm, and the nurse pats on the surface of your skin until a vein becomes visible. Each step in the sequence tells you that the unavoidable needle "stick" and the pain (largely the result of reflexive muscle tension) that follows is coming. The stick itself is the unconditioned stimulus to which you reflexively respond. But all the steps that precede it are conditioned stimuli that cause you to anticipate the pain of the stick itself. And with each successive step, your muscles respond to your anxiety by contracting a bit more in anticipation of the stick, a conditioned response.

After conditioning an animal to salivate to a tone, what would happen if you continued to sound the tone but no longer paired it with food? Pavlov found that without the food, salivation to the tone became weaker and weaker and then finally disappeared altogether–a process known as **extinction.** After the response had been extinguished, Pavlov allowed the dog to rest and then brought it back to the laboratory. He found that the dog would again salivate to the tone. Pavlov called this recurrence **spontaneous recovery.** But the spontaneously recovered response was weaker and shorter in duration than the original conditioned response. Figure 5.3 shows the rate of responses during the processes of extinction and spontaneous recovery.

122

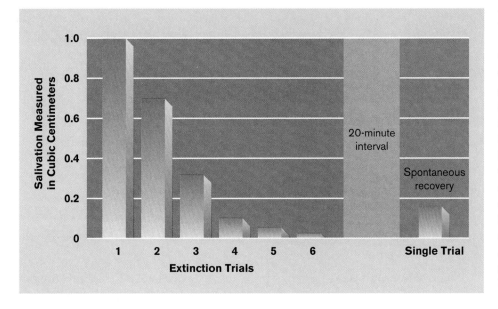

➤ **Figure 5.3**
Extinction of a Classically Conditioned Response

When a classically conditioned stimulus (the tone) was presented in a series of trials without the unconditioned stimulus (the food), Pavlov's dogs salivated less and less until there was virtually no salivation. But after a 20-minute rest, one sound of the tone caused the conditioned response to reappear in a weakened form (producing only a small amount of salivation), a phenomenon Pavlov called spontaneous recovery. (Data from Pavlov, 1927/1960, p. 58.)

Pavlov also found that a tone similar to the original conditioned stimulus would produce the conditioned response (salivation), a phenomenon called **generalization.** But the salivation decreased as the tone became less similar to the original conditioned stimulus, until the tone became so different that the dog would not salivate at all. Once the tone became sufficiently different, the dog exhibited **discrimination;** that is, it had learned to respond only to tones within a certain range.

> How do extinction, generalization, and discrimination develop in classical conditioning?

It is easy to see the value of generalization and discrimination in daily life. For instance, if you enjoyed being in school as a child, you probably feel more positive about your college experiences than your classmates who enjoyed school less. Because of generalization, we do not need to learn a conditioned response to every stimulus that may differ only slightly from an original one. Further, discriminating between the odors of fresh and spoiled milk will spare you an upset stomach. Discriminating between a rattlesnake and a garter snake could save your life.

John Watson, Little Albert, and Peter

In 1919, John Watson (1878–1958) and his assistant, Rosalie Rayner, conducted a now-infamous study to prove that fear could be classically conditioned. In the laboratory, Rayner presented an 11-month-old infant, known as Little Albert, with a white rat. As Albert reached for the rat, Watson struck a steel bar with a hammer just behind Albert's head. This procedure was repeated, and Albert "jumped violently, fell forward and began to whimper" (Watson & Rayner, 1920, p. 4). A week later, Watson continued the experiment, pairing the rat with the loud noise five more times. Then, at the sight of the white rat alone, Albert began to cry (see Figure 5.4, on page 124). Moreover, when Albert returned to the laboratory 5 days later, the fear had generalized to a rabbit, a dog, a fur coat, Watson's hair, and a Santa Claus mask. After 30 days Albert made his final visit to the laboratory. His fears were still evident, although they were somewhat less intense. Watson concluded that conditioned fears "persist and modify personality throughout life" (Watson & Rayner, 1920, p. 12).

> How did Watson demonstrate that fear could be classically conditioned?

Although Watson had formulated techniques for removing conditioned fears, Albert and his family moved away before they could be tried on him. Since Watson apparently knew that Albert would be leaving the area before these fear-removal techniques could be applied, he clearly showed a disregard for the child's welfare. Fortunately, the American Psychological Association now has strict ethical standards for the use of human and animal participants in research experiments and would not sanction an experiment such as Watson's.

generalization
In classical conditioning, the tendency to make a conditioned response to a stimulus similar to the original conditioned stimulus.

discrimination
The learned ability to distinguish between similar stimuli so that the conditioned response occurs only with the original conditioned stimulus, not similar stimuli.

➤ **Figure 5.4**

The Conditioned Fear Response

Little Albert's fear of a white rat was a conditioned response that was generalized to other stimuli, including a rabbit and, to a lesser extent, a Santa Claus mask.

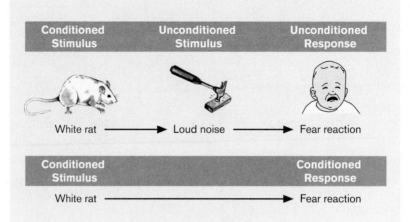

Some of Watson's ideas for removing fears were excellent and laid the groundwork for some behavior therapies used today. Three years after his experiment with Little Albert, Watson and a colleague, Mary Cover Jones (1924), found 3-year-old Peter, who, like Albert, was afraid of white rats. He was also afraid of rabbits, a fur coat, feathers, cotton, and a fur rug. Peter's fear of the rabbit was his strongest fear, and this became the target of Watson's fear-removal techniques.

Peter was brought into the laboratory, seated in a high chair, and given candy to eat. A white rabbit in a wire cage was brought into the room but kept far enough away from Peter that it would not upset him. Over the course of 38 therapy sessions, the rabbit was brought closer and closer to Peter, who continued to enjoy his candy. Occasionally, some of Peter's friends were brought in to play with the rabbit at a safe distance from Peter so that he could see firsthand that the rabbit did no harm. Toward the end of Peter's therapy, the rabbit was taken out of the cage and eventually put in Peter's lap. By the final session, Peter had grown fond of the rabbit. What is more, he had lost all fear of the fur coat, cotton, and feathers, and he could tolerate the white rats and the fur rug.

So far, we have considered classical conditioning primarily in relation to Pavlov's dogs and Watson's human research participants. How is classical conditioning viewed today?

Contemporary Views of Classical Conditioning

Pavlov viewed classical conditioning as a mechanical process that resulted in a conditioned reflex more or less automatically. Beginning in the late 1960s, though, researchers began to discover exceptions to some of the general principles Pavlov identified.

The Cognitive Perspective

Psychologist Robert Rescorla (1967, 1968, 1988; Rescorla & Wagner, 1972) was able to demonstrate that the critical element in classical conditioning is not the repeated pairing of the conditioned stimulus and the unconditioned stimulus. Rather, the important factor is whether the conditioned stimulus provides information that enables the organism to reliably predict the occurrence of the unconditioned stimulus. Using rats as his subjects, Rescorla used a tone as the conditioned stimulus and a shock as the unconditioned stimulus. For one group of rats, the tone and shock were paired 20 times—the shock always occurred during the tone. The other group of rats likewise received a shock 20 times while the tone was

> According to Rescorla, what is the critical element in classical conditioning? ➤

sounding, but this group also received 20 shocks that were not paired with the tone. Only the first group, for which the tone was a reliable predictor of the shock, developed the conditioned fear response to the tone. The second group showed little evidence of conditioning, because the shock was just as likely to occur without the tone as with it. In other words, for this group, the tone provided no additional information about the shock.

Biological Predispositions

According to Martin Seligman (1972), most common fears "are related to the survival of the human species through the long course of evolution" (p. 455). Seligman (1970) has suggested that humans and other animals are prepared to associate only certain stimuli with particular consequences. One example of this preparedness is the tendency to develop a **taste aversion**—the intense dislike and/or avoidance of a particular food that has been associated with nausea or discomfort. For example, experiencing nausea and vomiting after eating, say, a hotdog can be enough to condition a long-lasting taste aversion to hotdogs.

In a classic study of the role played by classical conditioning in the development of a taste aversion, Garcia and Koelling (1966) exposed rats to a three-way conditioned stimulus: a bright light, a clicking noise, and flavored water. For one group of rats, the unconditioned stimulus was being exposed to either X rays or lithium chloride, either of which produces nausea and vomiting several hours after exposure; for the other group, the unconditioned stimulus was an electric shock to the feet. The rats that were made ill associated the flavored water with the nausea and avoided it at all times, but they would still drink unflavored water when the bright light and the clicking sound were present. The rats receiving the electric shock continued to prefer the flavored water over unflavored water, but they would not drink at all in the presence of the bright light or the clicking sound. The rats in one group associated nausea only with the flavored water; those in the other group associated electric shock only with the light and the sound.

Garcia and Koelling's research established two exceptions to traditional ideas of classical conditioning. First, the finding that rats formed an association between nausea and flavored water ingested several hours earlier contradicted the principle that the conditioned stimulus must be presented shortly before the unconditioned stimulus. The finding that rats associated electric shock only with noise and light and nausea only with flavored water revealed that animals are apparently biologically predisposed to make certain associations and that associations between any two stimuli cannot be readily conditioned.

Other research on conditioned taste aversions has led to the solution of practical problems such as helping cancer patients. Bernstein and colleagues (Bernstein, 1985; Bernstein et al., 1982) devised a technique to help cancer patients avoid developing aversions to desirable foods. A group of cancer patients were given a novel-tasting, maple-flavored ice cream before chemotherapy. The nausea caused by the treatment resulted in a taste aversion to the ice cream. The researchers found that when an unusual or unfamiliar food becomes the "scapegoat," or target, for taste aversion, other foods in the patient's diet may be protected, and the patient will continue to eat them regularly. So, cancer patients should refrain from eating preferred or nutritious foods prior to chemotherapy. Instead, they should be given an unusual-tasting or unfavored food shortly before treatment. As a result, they are less likely to develop aversions to foods they normally eat and, in turn, more likely to maintain their body weight during treatment.

Classical Conditioning in Everyday Life

Many of our emotional responses—positive and negative—result from classical conditioning. You may have a fear, or phobia, that was learned

taste aversion
The dislike and/or avoidance of a particular food that has been associated with nausea or discomfort.

What two exceptions to traditional ideas about classical conditioning did Garcia and Koelling discover?

Chemotherapy treatments can result in conditioned taste aversions, but providing patients with a "scapegoat" target for the taste aversion can help them maintain a proper diet.

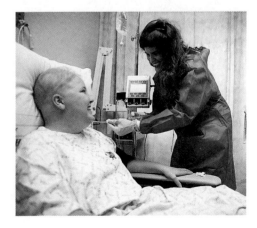

through classical conditioning. For example, many people who have had painful dental work develop a dental phobia. Not only do they come to fear the dentist's drill, but they develop anxiety in response to a wide range of stimuli associated with it—the dentist's chair, the waiting room, or even the building where the dentist's office is located. Neuroscientists have learned that this kind of fear conditioning is associated with both the amygdala and the hippocampus (Anagnostaras et al., 2000).

Through classical conditioning, environmental cues associated with drug use can become conditioned stimuli and later produce the conditioned responses of drug craving (Field & Duka, 2002; London et al., 2000). Consequently, drug counselors strongly urge recovering addicts to avoid any cues (people, places, and things) associated with their past drug use. Relapse is far more common in those who do not avoid such associated environmental cues. This observation helps explain why the American soldiers who used heroin heavily in Vietnam had only a 7% addiction rate when they returned to the United States, where they no longer encountered many of the environmental cues associated with use of the drug (Basic Behavioral Science Task Force, 1996).

Businesspeople wine and dine customers, hoping that they and their product or service will elicit the same positive response as the pleasant setting and fine food. Advertisers seek to classically condition consumers when they show products along with great-looking models or celebrities or in situations where people are enjoying themselves. Advertisers reason that if the "neutral" product is associated with people, objects, or situations consumers particularly like, then in time the product will elicit a similarly positive response. Pavlov found that presenting the tone just before the food was the most efficient way to condition salivation in dogs. Television advertisements, too, are most effective when the products are presented before the beautiful people or situations are shown (van den Hout & Merckelbach, 1991). You might want to get an idea of just how the principles of classical conditioning are applied in TV advertising by doing *Try It! 5.1*.

Research indicates that even the immune system is subject to classical conditioning (Ader, 1985; Ader & Cohen, 1982, 1993; Exton et al., 2000). In a classic study of this kind, Robert Ader was conducting an experiment with rats, conditioning them to avoid saccharin-sweetened water. Immediately after drinking the sweet water (which rats consider a treat), the rats were injected with a tasteless drug (cyclophosphamide) that causes severe nausea. The conditioning worked, and from that time on, the rats would not drink the sweet water, whether or not they had received the drug. Attempting to reverse the conditioned response, Ader force-fed the sweet water to the rats for many days; later, unexpectedly, many of them died. Ader was puzzled, because the sweet water was in no way lethal. Checking further into the properties of the tasteless drug, Ader learned that it suppresses the immune system. A few doses of an immune-suppressing drug paired with sweetened water had produced a conditioned response. As a result, the sweet water alone continued to suppress the immune system, causing the rats to die. Ader and Cohen successfully repeated the experiment with strict controls to rule out other explanations. How far-reaching the power of classical conditioning must be if a neutral stimulus such as sweetened water can produce effects similar to those of a powerful drug! And not only can classically conditioned stimuli suppress the immune system, they can be used to boost it as well (Exton et al., 2000; Markovic et al., 1993).

Recent research (Stanton, 2000) suggests that three basic components of learning are involved in classical conditioning: sensorimotor, affective (emotional), and cognitive components. Even the simplest of conditioned responses, such as the eyeblink reflex, involves all three of these learning components. The sensorimotor component of learning results in the eyeblink itself and is handled by neural circuits in the

▼ Classical conditioning has proved to be a highly effective tool for advertisers—and for the milk industry. In a series of ads, a neutral product (milk) is paired with images of famous people, and the result is more milk moustaches on movie stars and moviegoers alike.

brain's cerebellum. The affective component of learning encodes the conditioned "fear" and depends on the neural circuitry of the amygdala. The cognitive component of learning consists of all higher-order learning and memory processes. It forms a representation of the entire conditioning episode, including the relationship between the conditioned stimulus and the unconditioned stimulus and the context (environment) in which conditioning occurs. The neural circuitry handling this cognitive component of learning is in the hippocampus (Stanton, 2000; Green & Woodruff-Pak, 2000).

Research indicates that the amygdala is involved in the conditioning of emotions such as fear. However, memories of such conditioning are stored in other areas of the brain, even though the neural circuits in the amygdala produce the intense emotions that occur with fear conditioning (Lehmann et al., 2000; Vazdarjanova, 2000). An intact hippocampus is also essential to the conditioning of emotions (Anagnostaras et al., 2000). The cerebellum is the essential brain structure for motor (movement) conditioning and also the storage site for the memory traces formed during such conditioning (Steinmetz, 2000; Thompson et al., 2000).

Operant Conditioning

Thorndike and the Law of Effect

Based on his studies of *trial-and-error learning* in cats, dogs, chicks, and monkeys, American psychologist Edward Thorndike (1874–1949) formulated several laws of learning, the most important being the law of effect (Thorndike, 1911/1970). The **law of effect** states that the consequence, or effect, of a response determines whether the tendency to respond in the same way in the future will be strengthened or weakened. Responses closely followed by satisfying consequences are more likely to be repeated. Thorndike (1898) insisted that it was "unnecessary to invoke reasoning" to explain how the learning took place.

In Thorndike's best-known experiments, a hungry cat was placed in a wooden box with slats, which was called a *puzzle box*. It was designed so that the animal had to manipulate a simple mechanism—pressing a pedal or pulling down a loop—to escape and claim a food reward just outside the box. The cat would first try to squeeze through the slats; when these attempts failed, it would scratch, bite, and claw inside the box. In time, the cat would accidentally trip the mechanism, which

> **What was Thorndike's major contribution to psychology?**

law of effect
Thorndike's law of learning, which states that the connection between a stimulus and a response will be strengthened if the response is followed by a satisfying consequence and weakened if the response is followed by discomfort.

operant conditioning
A type of learning in which the consequences of behavior are manipulated in order to increase or decrease that behavior in the future.

would open the door and release it. Each time, after winning freedom and claiming the food reward, the cat was returned to the box. After many trials, the cat learned to open the door almost immediately after being placed in the box. Thorndike's law of effect formed the conceptual starting point for B. F. Skinner's work in operant conditioning.

B. F. Skinner and Operant Conditioning

Burrhus Frederic Skinner (1904–1990) became fascinated at an early age by the complex tricks he saw trained pigeons perform at country fairs. He was also interested in constructing mechanical devices and in collecting an assortment of animals, which he kept as pets. These interests were destined to play a major role in his later scientific achievements (Bjork, 1993). Following a failed attempt at becoming a writer after graduating from college, Skinner began reading the books of Pavlov and Watson. He became so intrigued that he entered graduate school at Harvard and completed his PhD in psychology in 1931. Like Watson, Skinner believed that the causes of behavior are in the environment and do not result from inner mental events such as thoughts, feelings, or perceptions. Rather, Skinner claimed that these inner mental events are themselves behaviors, and like any other behaviors, are shaped and determined by environmental forces. Although Skinner's social theories generated controversy, little controversy exists about the significance of his research on operant conditioning.

> *What was Skinner's major contribution to psychology?*

In **operant conditioning,** the consequences of behavior are manipulated in order to increase or decrease the frequency of a response or to shape an entirely new response. Behavior that is reinforced–followed by rewarding consequences–tends to be repeated. A **reinforcer** is anything that strengthens or increases the probability of the response it follows.

reinforcer
Anything that strengthens a response or increases the probability that it will occur.

Operant conditioning permits the learning of a broad range of new responses. For example, humans can learn to modify their brain-wave patterns through operant conditioning if they are given immediate positive reinforcement for the brain-wave changes that show the desired direction of change. Such operantly conditioned changes can result in better performance on motor tasks and faster responses on a variety of cognitive tasks (Pulvermüller et al., 2000).

> *How are responses acquired through operant conditioning?*

Shaping, a technique Skinner used, is particularly effective in conditioning complex behaviors. With shaping, rather than waiting for the desired response to occur and then reinforcing it, a researcher (or parent or animal trainer) reinforces any movement in the direction of the desired response, gradually guiding the responses closer and closer to the ultimate goal. The series of more closely matching responses are known as **successive approximations.**

> *How is shaping used to condition a response?*

Skinner designed a soundproof apparatus, commonly called a **Skinner box,** with which he conducted his experiments in operant conditioning. One version of the box is equipped with a lever or bar that a rat presses to gain a reward of food pellets or water from a dispenser. A record of the animal's bar pressing is registered on a device called a *cumulative recorder,* also invented by Skinner. Through the use of shaping, a rat in a Skinner box is conditioned to press a bar for rewards. It may be rewarded first for simply turning toward the bar. The next reward comes only when the rat moves closer to the bar; each step closer to the bar is rewarded. Next, the rat must touch the bar to receive a reward. Finally, it is rewarded only when it presses the bar.

shaping
An operant conditioning technique that consists of gradually molding a desired behavior (response) by reinforcing responses that become progressively closer to it.

successive approximations
A series of gradual steps, each of which is more like the final desired response.

Skinner box
A soundproof chamber with a device for delivering food and either a bar for rats to press or a disk for pigeons to peck; used in operant conditioning experiments.

extinction
In operant conditioning, the weakening and often eventual disappearance of the conditioned response when reinforcement is withheld.

Shaping–rewarding successive approximations of the desired response–has been used effectively to condition complex behaviors in people as well as other animals. Parents may use shaping to help their children develop good table manners, praising them each time they show an improvement. Teachers often use shaping with disruptive children, reinforcing them at first for very short periods of good behavior and then gradually expecting them to work productively for longer and longer periods. Through shaping, circus animals have learned to perform a wide range of amazing feats (see Figure 5.5) and pigeons have learned to bowl and play Ping-Pong.

www.ablongman.com/woodmastering1e

You have seen that responses followed by reinforcers tend to be repeated and that responses no longer followed by reinforcers will occur less and less frequently and eventually die out. In operant conditioning, **extinction** occurs when reinforcers are withheld. A rat in a Skinner box will eventually stop pressing a bar when it is no longer rewarded with food pellets. The process of spontaneous recovery, which we discussed in relation to classical conditioning, also occurs in operant conditioning. A rat whose bar pressing has been extinguished may again press the bar a few times when it is returned to the Skinner box after a period of rest.

How does extinction develop in operant conditioning?

Skinner conducted many of his experiments with pigeons placed in a specially designed Skinner box. The box contained small illuminated disks that the pigeons could peck to receive bits of grain from a food tray. Using this technique, Skinner found that **generalization** occurs in operant conditioning. A pigeon reinforced for pecking at a yellow disk is likely to peck at another disk similar in color. The less similar a disk is to the original color, the lower the rate of pecking will be.

Discrimination in operant conditioning involves learning to distinguish between a stimulus that has been reinforced and other stimuli that may be very similar. Discrimination develops when the response to the original stimulus is reinforced but responses to similar stimuli are not reinforced. For example, to encourage discrimination, a researcher would reinforce the pigeon for pecking at the yellow disk but not for pecking at the orange or red disk. Pigeons have even been conditioned to discriminate between a cubist-style Picasso painting and a Monet with 90% accuracy. However, they weren't able to tell a Renoir from a Cezanne ("Psychologists' pigeons . . . ," 1995).

Certain cues come to be associated with reinforcement or punishment. For example, children are more likely to ask their parents for a treat when the parents are smiling than when they are frowning. A stimulus that signals whether a certain response or behavior is likely to be rewarded, ignored, or punished is called a **discriminative stimulus.** If a pigeon's pecking at a lighted disk results in a reward but pecking at an unlighted disk does not, the pigeon will soon be pecking at the lighted disk but not at the unlighted one. The presence or absence of the discriminative stimulus—in this case, the lighting of a disk—will control whether the pecking takes place.

Why do children sometimes misbehave with a grandparent but not with a parent, or make one teacher's life miserable yet behave like model students for another? The

B. F. Skinner designed the Skinner box to shape rats' bar-pressing behavior.

generalization
In operant conditioning, the tendency to make a learned response to a stimulus that is similar to one which was originally reinforced.

discriminative stimulus
A stimulus that signals whether a certain response or behavior is likely to be followed by reward or punishment.

➤ **Figure 5.5**

Shaping and Successive Approximations

If you were an animal trainer, what successive approximations would you use to train an elephant to stand on her hind legs, on command?

reinforcement
An event that follows a response and increases the strength of the response and/or the likelihood that it will be repeated.

What is the difference between positive reinforcement and negative reinforcement?

positive reinforcement
A reward or pleasant consequence that follows a response and increases the probability that the response will be repeated.

negative reinforcement
The termination of an unpleasant condition after a response in order to increase the probability that the response will be repeated.

primary reinforcer
A reinforcer that fulfills a basic physical need for survival and does not depend on learning.

secondary reinforcer
A neutral stimulus that becomes reinforcing after repeated pairings with other reinforcers.

continuous reinforcement
Reinforcement that is administered after every desired or correct response; the most effective method of conditioning a new response.

partial reinforcement
A pattern of reinforcement in which some portion, rather than 100%, of the correct responses are reinforced.

What is the partial-reinforcement effect?

children may have learned that in the presence of some people (the discriminative stimuli), their misbehavior will almost certainly lead to punishment, but in the presence of certain other people, it may be overlooked, or even rewarded.

Reinforcement

Reinforcement is a key concept in operant conditioning and may be defined as any event that strengthens or increases the probability of the response that it follows. There are two types of reinforcement: positive and negative. **Positive reinforcement,** roughly the same thing as a reward, refers to any pleasant or desirable consequence that, if applied after a response, increases the probability of that response. Many employees will work hard for a raise or a promotion, salespeople will increase their efforts to get awards and bonuses, students will study to get good grades, and children will throw temper tantrums to get candy or ice cream. In these examples, the raises, promotions, awards, bonuses, good grades, candy, and ice cream are positive reinforcers.

Just as people engage in behaviors to get positive reinforcers, they also engage in behaviors to avoid or escape aversive, or unpleasant, stimuli. With **negative reinforcement,** a person's or animal's behavior is reinforced by the termination or avoidance of an aversive stimulus. If you find that a response successfully ends an aversive stimulus, you are likely to repeat it. You will turn on the air conditioner to terminate the heat and will get out of bed to turn off a faucet and end the annoying "drip, drip, drip." Heroin addicts will do almost anything to obtain heroin to terminate their painful withdrawal symptoms. In these instances, negative reinforcement involves putting an end to the heat, the dripping faucet, and the withdrawal symptoms.

Responses that end discomfort and those that are followed by rewards are likely to be strengthened or repeated because both lead to a more desirable outcome. Some behaviors are influenced by a combination of positive and negative reinforcement. If you eat a plateful of rather disgusting leftovers to relieve intense hunger, you are eating solely to remove hunger, a negative reinforcer. But if your hunger is relieved by a delicious dinner at a fine restaurant, both positive and negative reinforcement have played a role: Your hunger has been removed, and the dinner has been a reward in itself.

A **primary reinforcer** is one that fulfills a basic physical need for survival and does not depend on learning. Food, water, sleep, and termination of pain are examples of primary reinforcers. And sex is a powerful reinforcer that fulfills a basic physical need for survival of the species. Fortunately, learning does not depend solely on primary reinforcers. If that were the case, people would need to be hungry, thirsty, or sex-starved before they would respond at all. Much observed human behavior occurs in response to secondary reinforcers. A **secondary reinforcer** is acquired or learned by association with other reinforcers. Some secondary reinforcers (money, for example) can be exchanged at a later time for other reinforcers. Praise, good grades, awards, applause, attention, and signals of approval such as a smile or a kind word are all examples of secondary reinforcers.

Initially, Skinner conditioned rats by reinforcing each bar-pressing response with a food pellet. Reinforcing every correct response, known as **continuous reinforcement,** is the most efficient way to condition a new response. However, after a response has been conditioned, partial or intermittent reinforcement is more effective in maintaining or increasing the rate of response. **Partial reinforcement** is operating when some but not all responses are reinforced.

Partial reinforcement results in a greater resistance to extinction than does continuous reinforcement (Lerman et al., 1996). This result is known as the *partial-reinforcement effect.* There is an inverse relationship between the percentage of responses that have been reinforced and resistance to extinction. That is, the lower the percentage of responses that are reinforced, the longer extinction will take when reinforcement is withheld. The strongest resistance to extinction ever observed occurred in one experiment in which pigeons were conditioned to peck

www.ablongman.com/woodmastering1e

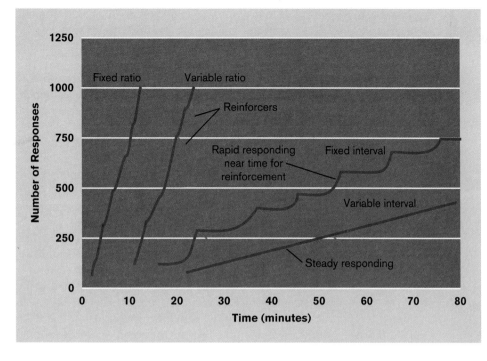

Four Types of Reinforcement Schedules

Skinner's research revealed distinctive response patterns for four partial-reinforcement schedules (the reinforcers are indicated by the diagonal marks). The ratio schedules, based on the number of responses, yielded a higher response rate than the interval schedules, which are based on the amount of time elapsed between reinforcers.

at a disk. Holland and Skinner (1961) report that "after the response had been maintained on a fixed ratio of 900 and reinforcement was then discontinued, the pigeon emitted 73,000 responses during the first $4\frac{1}{2}$ hours of extinction" (p. 124).

Schedules of Reinforcement

Partial reinforcement may be administered according to different **schedules of reinforcement.** Different schedules produce distinct rates and patterns of responses, as well as varying degrees of resistance to extinction when reinforcement is discontinued (see Figure 5.6). The two basic types of schedules are ratio and interval schedules. *Ratio schedules* require that a certain number of responses be made before one of the responses is reinforced. With *interval schedules,* a given amount of time must pass before a reinforcer is administered. These types of schedules are further subdivided into fixed and variable categories.

On a **fixed-ratio schedule,** a reinforcer is given after a fixed number of nonreinforced responses. If the fixed ratio is set at 30 responses (FR-30), a reinforcer is given after 30 correct responses. Examples are payments to factory workers according to the number of units produced and to migrant farm workers for each bushel of fruit they pick. A fixed-ratio schedule is a very effective way to maintain a high response rate, because the number of reinforcers received depends directly on the response rate. The faster people or animals respond, the more reinforcers they earn and the sooner they earn them. When large ratios are used, people and animals tend to pause after each reinforcement but then return to the characteristic high rate of responding.

The pauses after reinforcement that occur with a high fixed-ratio schedule normally do not occur with the **variable-ratio schedule.** On a variable-ratio schedule, a reinforcer is given after a varying number of nonreinforced responses based on an average ratio. With a variable ratio of 30 responses (VR-30), people might be reinforced first after 10 responses, then after 50, then again after 30 responses, and so on. They cannot predict exactly what number of responses will be reinforced, but, in this example, reinforcement is averaging 1 in 30. Variable-ratio schedules result in higher, more stable rates of responding than fixed-ratio schedules. Skinner (1953) reports that on this schedule "a pigeon may respond as rapidly as five times per second and maintain this rate for many hours" (p. 104). The best example of the power of the variable-

> What are the four types of schedules of reinforcement, and which type yields the highest response rate and the greatest resistance to extinction?

schedule of reinforcement
A systematic program for administering reinforcements that has a predictable effect on behavior.

fixed-ratio schedule
A schedule in which a reinforcer is given after a fixed number of correct responses.

variable-ratio schedule
A schedule in which a reinforcer is given after a varying number of nonreinforced responses based on an average ratio.

Many computer solitaire players find themselves in this predicament, knowing they should stop playing the game and get to work, but they just can't seem to tear themselves away. Why? The power of a variable-ratio schedule of reinforcement motivates them to stick with the game until the next win, and the next, and the next . . . .

fixed-interval schedule
A schedule in which a reinforcer is given following the first correct response after a fixed period of time has elapsed.

variable-interval schedule
A schedule in which a reinforcer is given after the first correct response following a varying time of nonreinforcement based on an average time.

How does punishment differ from negative reinforcement?

ratio schedule is found in the gambling casino. Slot machines, roulette wheels, and most other games of chance pay on this type of schedule. In general, the variable-ratio schedule produces the highest response rate and the most resistance to extinction.

On a **fixed-interval schedule,** a specific time interval must pass before a response is reinforced. For example, on a 60-second fixed-interval schedule (FI-60), a reinforcer is given for the first correct response that occurs 60 seconds after the last reinforced response. People working on salary are reinforced on the fixed-interval schedule. Unlike ratio schedules, reinforcement on interval schedules does not depend on the number of responses made, only on the one correct response made after the time interval has passed. Characteristic of the fixed-interval schedule is a pause or a sharp decline in responding immediately after each reinforcement and a rapid acceleration in responding just before the next reinforcer is due.

Variable-interval schedules eliminate the pause after reinforcement that is typical with fixed-interval schedules. On a **variable-interval schedule,** a reinforcer is given after the first correct response following a varying time of nonreinforced responses based on an average time. Rather than being given every 60 seconds, for example, a reinforcer might be given after a 30-second interval, with successive reinforcers following after 90-, 45-, and 75-second intervals. But the average time elapsing between reinforcers would be 60 seconds (VI-60). This schedule maintains remarkably stable and uniform rates of responding, but the response rate is typically lower than that with ratio schedules, because reinforcement is not tied directly to the number of responses made. Random drug testing in the workplace is an excellent example of application of the variable-interval schedule and appears to be quite effective. *Review and Reflect 5.1* summarizes the characteristics of the four types of schedules of reinforcement.

Factors other than the schedule of reinforcement influence the operant conditioning process. For example, as the magnitude of reinforcement increases, acquisition of a response is faster, the rate of responding is higher, and resistance to extinction is greater (Clayton, 1964; Dallery et al., 2001; Katz et al., 2002). In addition, the longer the delay in reinforcement, the more slowly a response is acquired (Church, 1989; Mazur, 1993). The motivation of the learner contributes as well. Skinner found that when food is the reinforcer, a hungry animal will learn faster than a full animal. To maximize motivation, he used rats that had been deprived of food for 24 hours and pigeons that were maintained at 75–80% of their normal body weight.

Punishment

Punishment is the opposite of reinforcement. Punishment lowers the probability of a response by following it with an aversive, or unpleasant, consequence. However, punishment can be accomplished by either adding an unpleasant stimulus or removing a pleasant stimulus. The added unpleasant stimulus might take the form of criticism, a scolding, a disapproving look, a fine, or a prison sentence. The removal of a pleasant stimulus might consist of withholding affection and attention, suspending a driver's license, or taking away a privilege such as watching television.

It is common to confuse punishment and negative reinforcement because both involve an unpleasant stimulus, but there is a big difference between the two. Punishment may involve adding an aversive stimulus, but with negative reinforcement, an aversive stimulus is terminated or avoided. Moreover, the two have opposite effects: Unlike punishment, negative reinforcement increases the probability of a desired response by removing an unpleasant stimulus when the correct response is made. "Grounding" can be used as either punishment or negative reinforcement. If a teenager fails to clean her room after many requests to do so, her parents could ground her for the weekend—a punishment. An alternative approach

Reinforcement Schedules Compared

SCHEDULE OF REINFORCEMENT	RESPONSE RATE	PATTERN OF RESPONSES	RESISTANCE TO EXTINCTION
Fixed-ratio schedule	Very high	Steady response with low ratio. Brief pause after each reinforcement with very high ratio.	The higher the ratio, the more resistance to extinction.
Variable-ratio schedule	Highest response rate	Constant response pattern, no pauses.	Most resistance to extinction.
Fixed-interval schedule	Lowest response rate	Long pause after reinforcement, followed by gradual acceleration.	The longer the interval the more resistance to extinction.
Variable-interval schedule	Moderate	Stable, uniform response.	More resistance to extinction than fixed-interval schedule with same average interval.

would be to use negative reinforcement–to tell her she is grounded until the room is clean. Which approach is more likely to be effective?

A number of potential problems are associated with the use of punishment:

1. According to Skinner, *punishment does not extinguish an undesirable behavior; rather, it suppresses that behavior when the punishing agent is present.* But the behavior is apt to continue when the threat of punishment is removed and in settings where punishment is unlikely. If punishment (imprisonment, fines, and so on) reliably extinguished unlawful behavior, there would be fewer repeat offenders in the criminal justice system.

2. *Punishment indicates that a behavior is unacceptable but does not help people develop more appropriate behaviors.* If punishment is used, it should be administered in conjunction with reinforcement or rewards for appropriate behavior.

3. *The person who is severely punished often becomes fearful and feels angry and hostile toward the punisher.* These reactions may be accompanied by a desire to retaliate or to avoid or escape from the punisher and the punishing situation. Many runaway teenagers leave home to escape physical abuse. Punishment that involves a loss of privileges is more effective than physical punishment and engenders less fear and hostility (Walters & Grusec, 1977).

4. *Punishment frequently leads to aggression.* Those who administer physical punishment may become models of aggressive behavior–people who demonstrate aggression as a way of solving problems and discharging anger. Children of abusive, punishing parents are at greater risk than other children of becoming aggressive and abusive themselves (Widom, 1989).

If punishment can lead to such problems, what can be done to discourage undesirable behavior? Many psychologists believe that removing the rewarding conse-

What are some disadvantages of punishment?

punishment
The removal of a pleasant stimulus or the application of an unpleasant stimulus, which tends to suppress a response.

quences of the behavior is the best way to extinguish an undesirable or problem behavior. According to this view, parents should extinguish a child's temper tantrums not by punishment, but by never giving in to the child's demands during a tantrum. A parent might best extinguish problem behavior performed merely to get attention by ignoring it and giving attention to more appropriate behavior. Sometimes, simply explaining why a certain behavior is not appropriate is all that is required to extinguish it. Using positive reinforcement such as praise will make good behavior more rewarding for children. This approach brings with it the attention that children want and need—attention that often comes only when they misbehave. *Review and Reflect 5.2* summarizes the differences between reinforcement and punishment.

Making Punishment More Effective

It is probably unrealistic to believe that punishment can be dispensed with entirely. If a young child runs into the street, puts a finger near an electrical outlet, or reaches for a hot pan on the stove, a swift punishment may save the child from a potentially disastrous situation. Research has revealed several factors that influence the effectiveness of punishment: its timing, its intensity, and the consistency of its application (Parke, 1977).

> **What three factors increase the effectiveness of punishment?**

1. *Punishment is most effective when it is applied during the misbehavior or as soon afterward as possible.* Interrupting the problem behavior is most effective because doing so abruptly halts its rewarding aspects. The longer the delay between the response and the punishment, the less effective the punishment is in suppressing the response (Camp et al., 1967). When there is a delay, most animals do not make the connection between the misbehavior and the punishment. With humans, however, if the punishment must be delayed, the punisher should remind the perpetrator of the incident and explain why the behavior was inappropriate.

2. *Ideally, punishment should be of the minimal severity necessary to suppress the problem behavior.* Animal studies reveal that the more intense the punishment, the greater the suppression of the undesirable behavior (Church, 1963). But the intensity of the punishment should match the seriousness of the misdeed. Unnecessarily severe punishment is likely to produce the negative side effects mentioned earlier. Yet, if the initial punishment is too mild, it will have no effect. Similarly, gradually increasing the intensity of the punishment is not effective; the perpetrator will gradually adapt to it, and the unwanted behavior will persist (Azrin & Holz, 1966). At a minimum, if a behavior is to be suppressed, the punishment must be more punishing than the misbehavior is rewarding. In human terms, a $200 ticket is more likely to suppress the urge to speed than a $2 ticket.

   A person who wishes to apply punishment must understand that the purpose of punishment is not to vent anger but rather to modify behavior. Punishment meted out in anger is likely to be more intense than necessary to bring about the desired result.

3. *To be effective, punishment must be applied consistently.* A parent cannot ignore misbehavior one day and punish the same act the next. And both parents should react to the same misbehavior in the same way. An undesired response will be suppressed more effectively when the probability of punishment is high. Would you be tempted to speed if you saw a police car in your rear-view mirror?

Culture and Punishment

Punishment has been used throughout recorded history to control and suppress people's behavior. It is administered when important values, rules, regulations, and laws are violated. But not all cultures share the same values or have the same laws regulating behavior. U.S. citizens traveling in other countries need to be aware of how different cultures view and administer punishment. A memorable incident—widely publicized when it occurred a decade ago and still relevant today—revealed sharp differences in concepts of crime and punishment between the United States and Singapore.

The Effects of Reinforcement and Punishment

REINFORCEMENT (INCREASES OR STRENGTHENS A BEHAVIOR)	PUNISHMENT (DECREASES OR SUPRESSES A BEHAVIOR)
Adding a pleasant stimulus (positive reinforcement) Presenting food, money, praise, attention, or other rewards.	**Adding an aversive stimulus** Delivering a pain-producing or otherwise aversive stimulus, such as a spanking or an electric shock.
Subtracting an aversive stimulus (negative reinforcement) Removing or terminating some pain-producing or otherwise aversive stimulus, such as an electric shock.	**Subtracting a pleasant stimulus** Removing some pleasant stimulus or taking away privileges, such as TV watching, use of automobile.

In 1994, Michael Fay, an 18-year-old American living in Singapore, was arrested and charged with 53 counts of vandalism, including the spray painting of dozens of cars. He was fined approximately $2,000, sentenced to 4 months in jail, and received four lashes with a rattan cane, an agonizingly painful experience. In justifying their system of punishment, the officials in Singapore were quick to point out that their city, about the same size as Los Angeles, is virtually free of crime—few murders, rapes, beatings, or robberies. Among Americans, sentiment about the caning was mixed. Some, including Michael's parents, viewed it as barbarous and cruel. But many Americans (51% in a CNN poll) expressed the view that caning might be an effective punishment under certain circumstances.

Escape and Avoidance Learning

Learning to perform a behavior because it terminates an aversive event is called *escape learning*, and it reflects the power of negative reinforcement. Taking aspirin to relieve a pounding headache is an example of an escape behavior. *Avoidance learning*, in contrast, depends on two types of conditioning: classical and operant. Through classical conditioning, an event or condition comes to signal an aversive state. For example, a child may associate an increase in the volume of his parent's voice with an impending punishment. Because of such associations, people may engage in behaviors to avoid the anticipated aversive consequences. So, the child stops an unacceptable behavior when his parent, in a louder-than-usual voice, tells him to do so, in order to avoid the punishment that is sure to follow.

Many avoidance behaviors occur in response to phobias. Students who have had a bad experience speaking in front of a class may begin to fear any situation that involves speaking before a group. Such students may avoid taking courses that require class presentations or taking leadership roles that necessitate public speaking. Avoiding such situations prevents them from suffering the perceived dreaded consequences. But the avoidance behavior is negatively reinforced and thus is strengthened through operant conditioning. Maladaptive avoidance behaviors are very difficult to extinguish, because people never give

▼ Culture shapes ideas about punishment. Because ideas about humane punishment have changed in Western society, public humiliation is no longer considered to be an appropriate punishment, regardless of its potential for reducing crime.

learned helplessness
The learned response of resigning oneself passively to aversive conditions, rather than taking action to escape or avoid them; learned through repeated exposure to inescapable or unavoidable aversive events.

biofeedback
The use of sensitive equipment to give people precise feedback about internal physiological processes so that they can learn, with practice, to control them.

behavior modification
The systematic application of the learning principles of operant or classical conditioning or observational learning to individuals or groups in order to eliminate undesirable behavior and/or encourage desirable behavior.

token economy
A program that motivates and reinforces socially acceptable behaviors with tokens that can be exchanged for desired items or privileges.

What are some applications of operant conditioning? ➤

With biofeedback devices, people can see or hear evidence of internal physiological states and learn how to control them through various mental strategies.

themselves a chance to learn that the dreaded consequences probably will not occur or that they are greatly exaggerated.

There is an important exception to the ability of humans and other animals to learn to escape or avoid aversive situations: **Learned helplessness** is a passive resignation to aversive conditions learned by repeated exposure to aversive events that are inescapable and unavoidable. The initial experiment on learned helplessness was conducted by Overmeier and Seligman (1967). Dogs in the experimental group were strapped into harnesses from which they could not escape and were exposed to electric shocks. Later, these same dogs were placed in a box with two compartments separated by a low barrier. The dogs then experienced a series of trials in which a warning signal was followed by an electric shock administered through the box's floor. However, the floor was electrified only on one side, and the dogs could have escaped the electric shocks simply by jumping the barrier. Surprisingly, the dogs did not do so. Dogs in the control group had not previously experienced the inescapable shock and behaved in an entirely different manner; they quickly learned to jump the barrier when the warning signal sounded, thus escaping the shock. Seligman (1975) later reasoned that humans who have suffered painful experiences they could neither avoid nor escape may also experience learned helplessness. Then, having experienced this helplessness, they may simply give up and react to disappointment in life by becoming inactive, withdrawn, and depressed (Seligman, 1991).

Applications of Operant Conditioning

Operant conditioning has numerous applications. For example, the principles of operant conditioning are used effectively to train animals that help physically challenged people lead more independent lives. Dogs and monkeys have been trained to help people who are paralyzed or confined to wheelchairs, and, of course, for years, seeing-eye dogs have been trained to assist the blind.

Biofeedback, a procedure in which people learn to consciously control autonomic functions such as heart rate, is another important application of operant conditioning principles. Biofeedback devices have sensors that monitor slight changes in these physiological responses and then amplify and convert the changes into visual or auditory signals. Thus, people can see or hear evidence of internal processes, and by trying out various strategies (thoughts, feelings, or images), they can learn which ones routinely increase, decrease, or maintain a particular level of activity. Biofeedback has been used to regulate heart rate and to alleviate migraine and tension headaches, gastrointestinal disorders, asthma attacks, anxiety tension states, epileptic seizures, sexual dysfunctions, and neuromuscular disorders due to cerebral palsy, spinal-cord injuries, and stroke (Kalish, 1981; L. Miller, 1989; N. E. Miller, 1985)

Behavior modification is a method of changing behavior through a systematic program based on the principles of operant conditioning. Many institutions—schools, mental hospitals, homes for youthful offenders, and prisons—have used behavior modification programs with varying degrees of success. One type of behavior modification program is a **token economy**—a program that motivates socially desirable behavior by reinforcing it with tokens. The tokens (poker chips or coupons) may later be exchanged for desired goods such as candy or cigarettes and privileges such as weekend passes, free time, or participation in desired activities. Token economies have been used effectively in mental hospitals to encourage patients to attend to grooming, to interact with other patients, and to carry out housekeeping tasks (Ayllon & Azrin, 1965, 1968). They have also been used in schools in an effort to encourage students to increase desirable behaviors such as reading books. However, the results of more than 100 studies suggest that the overuse of tangible rewards may have certain long-term negative effects, such as undermining people's intrinsic motivation to regulate their own behavior (Deci et al., 1999). *Try It! 5.2* challenges you to come up with your own behavior modification plan.

Before moving on to cognitive learning, review the basic components of classical and operant conditioning in *Review and Reflect 5.3* (on page 138).

Try It ! 5.2 Behavior Modification

You can develop a behavior modification plan to address one of your own behaviors you would like to change. Say, for example, you want to increase the time you spend studying. Follow these steps:

1. State the desired behavior change in measurable terms: "I would like to study at least an hour and a half a day" lends itself more easily to measurement than a goal such as "I would like to study more."

2. Find out the current frequency of the behavior, known as the *baseline* in behavior modification terms. Make a chart showing how many minutes you study each day for a week and calculate the average number of minutes per day you are studying now.

3. Identify a reinforcer. You might decide to reinforce yourself for studying by "allowing" yourself to spend some time watching television after completing a certain amount of studying.

4. Decide on a *reinforcement contingency*—that is, how much studying will be required to earn TV-watching time. It's best if both the time allotted to television and the amount of studying required to earn it are fixed. For example, you might choose to allow yourself 15 minutes of TV time for every 30 minutes of studying.

5. Implement your plan, and chart the number of minutes you spend studying each day for 2 weeks. This is the *behavior modification phase* of the plan.

6. After 2 weeks, stop reinforcing yourself for studying and keep a *maintenance chart* showing how many minutes per day you study when not using reinforcement. Did the study habits you developed during the behavior modification phase continue after reinforcement was stopped? If not, put yourself through another behavior modification phase, perhaps for a longer time or with a more powerful reinforcer.

Cognitive Learning

According to cognitive theorists, **cognitive processes**–thinking, knowing, problem solving, remembering, and forming mental representations–are critically important to a more complete, more comprehensive view of learning than that provided by the conditioning theories.

Insight and Latent Learning

In his book *The Mentality of Apes* (1925), Wolfgang Köhler (1887–1967) describes an experiment in which he hung a bunch of bananas inside a cage containing chimps but overhead, out of reach of the apes; boxes and sticks were left in the cage. Köhler observed the chimps' unsuccessful attempts to reach the bananas by jumping up or swinging sticks at them. Eventually the chimps solved the problem by piling the boxes one on top of the other until they could reach the bananas, as if it had come to them in a flash of **insight.** They seemed to have suddenly discovered the relationship between the sticks or boxes and the bananas. Köhler insisted that insight, rather than trial-and-error learning, accounted for the chimps' successes, because they could easily repeat the solution and transfer this learning to similar problems. Humans often learn through insight, as you may have experienced if you have had a sudden "Aha! Now I understand!" moment when trying to solve some type of problem.

Edward Tolman (1886–1959) maintained that **latent learning,** like insight, could occur without reinforcement (Tolman, 1932). A classic experimental study by Tolman and Honzik (1930) supports this position. Three groups of rats were placed in a maze daily for 17 days. The first group always received a food reward at the end of the maze.

cognitive processes
(COG-nuh-tiv) Mental processes such as thinking, knowing, problem solving, and remembering.

insight
The sudden realization of the relationship between elements in a problem situation, which makes the solution apparent.

► What is insight, and how does it affect learning?

latent learning
Learning that occurs without apparent reinforcement but that is not demonstrated until sufficient reinforcement is provided.

Classical and Operant Conditioning Compared

CHARACTERISTICS	CLASSICAL CONDITIONING	OPERANT CONDITIONING
Type of association	Between two stimuli	Between a response and its consequence
State of subject	Passive	Active
Focus of attention	On what precedes response	On what follows response
Type of response typically involved	Involuntary or reflexive response	Voluntary response
Bodily response typically involved	Internal responses; emotional and glandular reactions	External responses; muscular and skeletal movement and verbal responses
Range of responses	Relatively simple	Simple to highly complex
Responses learned	Emotional reactions; fears, likes, dislikes	Goal-oriented responses

What is latent learning? ▶

The second group never received a reward, and the third group did not receive a food reward until the 11th day. The first group showed a steady improvement in performance over the 17-day period. The second group showed slight, gradual improvement. The third group, after being rewarded on the 11th day, showed a marked improvement the next day and from then on, outperformed the rats that had been rewarded daily. The rapid improvement of the third group indicated to Tolman that latent learning had occurred—that the rats had actually learned the maze during the first 11 days.

cognitive map
A mental representation of a spatial arrangement such as a maze.

The rats in Tolman's experiment did learn something before reinforcement and without exhibiting any evidence of learning by overt, observable behavior. But what did they learn? Tolman concluded that the rats had learned to form a **cognitive map,** a mental representation or picture, of the maze but had not demonstrated their learning until they were reinforced. In later studies, Tolman showed how rats quickly learn to rearrange learned cognitive maps and find their way through increasingly complex mazes with ease.

Observational Learning

What is observational learning? ▶

The earlier discussion of operant conditioning described how people and other animals learn by directly experiencing the consequences, positive or negative, of their behavior. But must people experience rewards and punishment firsthand in order to learn? Not according to Albert Bandura (1986), who contends that many behaviors or responses are acquired through observational learning, or, as he now calls it, *social-cognitive learning.* **Observational learning,** sometimes called **modeling,** results when people observe the behavior of others and note the consequences of that behavior. And observational learning is not restricted to humans. Monkeys, for example, learn specific fears by observing other monkeys (Cook et al., 1985).

The person who demonstrates the behavior or whose behavior is imitated is called the **model.** Parents, movie stars, and sports personalities can be powerful models. The effectiveness of a model is related to his or her status, competence, and power. Other important factors are the age, sex, attractiveness, and ethnicity of the model. Whether learned behavior is actually performed depends largely on whether the observed model is rewarded or punished for the behavior and whether the observer expects to be rewarded for the behavior (Bandura, 1969, 1977a). Research has also shown that observational learning is improved when several sessions of observation (watching the behavior) precede attempts to perform the behavior and are then repeated in the early stages of practicing it (Weeks & Anderson, 2000).

But repetition alone isn't enough to cause an observer to learn from a model: An observer must be physically and cognitively capable of performing the behavior in order to learn it. In other words, no matter how much time you devote to watching Jennifer Capriati play tennis or Tiger Woods play golf, you won't be able to acquire skills like theirs unless you possess physical talents equal to theirs. Similarly, it is doubtful that a kindergartener will learn geometry from watching her 10th-grade brother do his homework.

Emotional responses are often acquired through observational learning. For instance, Gerull and Rappe (2002) found that toddlers whose mothers expressed fear at the sight of rubber snakes and spiders displayed significantly higher levels of fear of these objects when tested later than did toddlers in a control group whose mothers had not expressed such fears. Conversely, children who see "a parent or peer behaving nonfearfully in a potentially fear-producing situation may be 'immunized' " to feeling fear when confronted with a similar frightening situation later (Basic Behavioral Science Task Force, 1996, p. 139).

Bandura suspected that aggressive behavior is particularly likely to be copied as a result of observational learning and that aggression and violence on TV programs, including cartoons, tend to increase aggression in children. One of his classic studies involved three groups of preschool children. Children in one group individually observed an adult model punching, kicking, and using a mallet to hit a 5-foot, inflated plastic "Bobo Doll," while uttering aggressive phrases, as shown in Figure 5.7 (Bandura et al., 1961, p. 576). Children in the second group observed a nonaggressive model who ignored the Bobo Doll and sat quietly assembling Tinker Toys. Children in the third group (the control group) were placed in the same setting with no adult present. Later, each child was observed through a one-way mirror. Children exposed to the aggressive model imitated much of the aggression and also engaged in significantly more nonimitative aggression than did children in either of the other two groups. Children who had observed the nonaggressive model showed less aggressive behavior than did children in the control group.

observational learning
Learning by observing the behavior of others and the consequences of that behavior; learning by imitation.

modeling
Another name for observational learning.

model
The individual who demonstrates a behavior or serves as an example in observational learning.

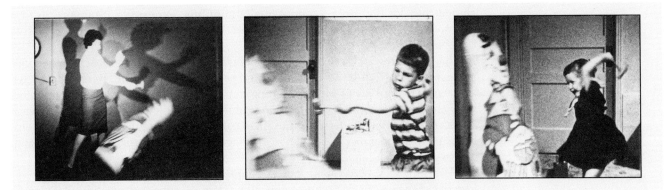

➤ Figure 5.7

Bandura's Famous "Bobo Doll" Research

In Bandura's observational learning research, children learned to copy aggression by observing adult models act aggressively toward a Bobo doll.

How often have you thought that you could accomplish a great deal more if only you had more time? Instead of wishing for the impossible, you can learn how to overcome the greatest time waster of all—procrastination. You can use behavior modification techniques, such as those in the *Try It!* on page 137, to systematically apply the following suggestions for keeping procrastination from interfering with your studying.

- *Identify the environmental cues that habitually interfere with your studying.* Television, computer or video games, and even food can be powerful distractors that consume hours of valuable study time. However, these distractors can be useful positive reinforcers to enjoy *after* you've finished studying.

- *Schedule your study time and reinforce yourself for adhering to your schedule.* Once you've set a study schedule, be just as faithful to it as you are to a work schedule set by an employer. And be sure to schedule something you enjoy to immediately follow the study time.

- *Get started.* The most difficult part is getting started. Give yourself an extra reward for starting on time and, perhaps, a penalty for not starting on time.

- *Use visualization.* Procrastination often results from the failure to consider its negative consequences. Visualizing the consequences of not studying, such as trying to get through an exam you haven't prepared adequately for, can be an effective tool for combating procrastination.

- *Beware of jumping to another task when you reach a difficult part of an assignment.* This is a procrastination tactic designed to give you the feeling that you are busy and accomplishing something, but it is, nevertheless, an avoidance tactic.

- *Beware of preparation overkill.* Procrastinators may spend hours preparing for the task rather than actually working on the task itself. They may gather enough materials in the library to write a book rather than a five-page term paper. This enables them to postpone writing the paper.

- *Keep a record of the reasons you give yourself for postponing studying or completing important assignments.* If a favorite rationalization is "I'll wait until I'm in the mood to do this," count the number of times in a week you are seized with the desire to study. The mood for studying typically arrives after you begin, not before.

Don't procrastinate! Begin now! Apply the steps outlined here to gain more control over your behavior and win the battle against procrastination. ■

A further study compared the degree of aggression in children following exposure to (1) a live aggressive model, (2) a filmed version of the episode, and (3) a film depicting an aggressive cartoon character using the same aggressive behaviors in a fantasylike setting (Bandura et al., 1963). A control group was not exposed to any of the three aggressive models. The groups exposed to the aggressive models used significantly more aggression than the control group. The researchers concluded that "of the three experimental conditions, exposure to humans on film portraying aggression was the most influential in eliciting and shaping aggressive behavior" (p. 7).

Bandura's research provided the impetus for studying the effects of televised violence and aggression in both cartoons and regular programming. Researchers have also shown in a variety of ways—including carefully controlled laboratory experiments with children, adolescents, and young adults—that violent video games increase aggressive behavior (Anderson & Bushman, 2001). Moreover, the effects of media violence are evident across a wide range of categories: music, music videos, advertising, and the Internet (Villani, 2001).

Watching excessive violence gives people an exaggerated view of the pervasiveness of violence in society, while making them less sensitive to the victims of violence. Media violence also encourages aggressive behavior in children by portraying aggression as an acceptable and effective way to solve problems and by teaching new forms of aggression (Wood et al., 1991).

Some have argued that when televised violence is followed by appropriate consequences, such as arrest, children may learn not to engage in aggression. However,

Portrayals on television of violence as an acceptable way to solve problems tend to encourage aggressive behavior in children.

experimental research has demonstrated that children do not process information about consequences in the same way adults do (Krcmar & Cooke, 2001). Children appear to judge the rightness or wrongness of an act of violence in terms of provocation; that is, they believe that violence as retaliation is morally acceptable, even if it is punished by an authority figure.

However, just as children imitate the aggressive behavior they observe on television, they also imitate the prosocial, or helping, behavior they observe. Programs such as *Mister Rogers' Neighborhood* and *Sesame Street* have been found to have a positive influence on children.

Summarize It!

Classical Conditioning

➤ **What was Pavlov's major contribution to psychology?**

Pavlov's study of a conditioned reflex provided a model of learning called classical conditioning.

➤ **How was classical conditioning accomplished in Pavlov's experiments?**

In Pavlov's experiments, a neutral stimulus (a tone) was presented shortly before the unconditioned stimulus (food), which naturally elicited, or brought forth, an unconditioned response (salivation). After repeated pairings, the conditioned stimulus (the tone) alone elicited the conditioned response (salivation).

➤ **What is higher-order conditioning?**

Higher-order conditioning is a form of conditioning that results when a series of conditioned stimuli become associated.

➤ **How do extinction, generalization, and discrimination develop in classical conditioning?**

Extinction has occurred when the conditioned stimulus can be presented repeatedly without the unconditioned stimulus and the conditioned response no longer appears. Generalization has occurred when an organism makes a conditioned response to a stimulus similar to the original conditioned stimulus. Discrimination is the ability to distin-

guish between similar stimuli, so that the organism makes the conditioned response only to the original conditioned stimulus.

➤ **How did Watson demonstrate that fear could be classically conditioned?**

Watson showed that fear could be classically conditioned by presenting Little Albert with a white rat along with a loud, frightening noise, thereby conditioning the infant to fear the white rat.

KEY TERMS

learning (p. 120)
classical conditioning (p. 120)
stimulus (p. 120)

unconditioned response (UR) (p. 121)
unconditioned stimulus (US) (p. 121)
conditioned stimulus (CS) (p. 121)
conditioned response (CR) (p. 121)
higher-order conditioning (p. 122)
extinction (p. 122)
spontaneous recovery (p. 122)
generalization (p. 123)
discrimination (p. 123)

Contemporary Views of Classical Conditioning

➤ **According to Rescorla, what is the critical element in classical conditioning?**

The critical element in classical conditioning is whether the conditioned stimulus provides information that enables the organism to reliably predict the occurrence of the unconditioned stimulus.

➤ **What two exceptions to traditional ideas about classical conditioning did Garcia and Koelling discover?**

The fact that rats formed an association between nausea and the flavored water ingested several hours earlier was an exception to the principle that the conditioned stimulus must be presented shortly before the unconditioned stimulus. The finding that rats associated electric shock only with noise and light and nausea only with flavored water proved that associations cannot be readily conditioned between any two stimuli.

➤ **What types of responses can be acquired through classical conditioning?**

Types of responses that can be acquired through classical conditioning include taste aversions, positive and negative emotional responses (including likes, dislikes, fears, and phobias), drug cravings in former drug users, and conditioned immune responses.

KEY TERMS

taste aversion (p. 125)

Operant Conditioning

➤ **What was Thorndike's major contribution to psychology?**

Thorndike formulated the law of effect, which was the conceptual starting point for Skinner's work on operant conditioning.

➤ **What was Skinner's major contribution to psychology?**

Skinner's major contribution to psychology was his extensive and significant research on operant conditioning.

➤ **How are responses acquired through operant conditioning?**

In operant conditioning, the consequences of a behavior are manipulated to shape a new response or to increase or decrease the frequency of an existing response.

➤ **How is shaping used to condition a response?**

In shaping, rather than waiting for the desired response to be emitted, a researcher selectively reinforces successive approximations toward the desired response until that response is achieved.

➤ **How does extinction develop in operant conditioning?**

In operant conditioning, extinction occurs when reinforcement is withheld.

➤ **What is the difference between positive reinforcement and negative reinforcement?**

Both positive reinforcement and negative reinforcement strengthen or increase the probability of a response. With positive reinforcement, the response is followed by a pleasant consequence; with negative reinforcement, it is followed by the termination of an aversive condition.

➤ **What is the partial-reinforcement effect?**

The partial-reinforcement effect is the greater resistance to extinction that occurs when responses are maintained under partial reinforcement rather than under continuous reinforcement.

➤ **What are the four types of schedules of reinforcement, and which type yields the highest response rate and the greatest resistance to extinction?**

The four types of schedules of reinforcement are fixed-ratio, variable-ratio, fixed-interval, and variable-interval schedules. A variable-ratio schedule provides the highest response rate and the greatest resistance to extinction.

➤ **How does punishment differ from negative reinforcement?**

Punishment is used to decrease the frequency of a response; negative reinforcement is used to increase the frequency of a response.

➤ **What are some disadvantages of punishment?**

Punishment generally suppresses rather than extinguishes behavior. It does not help people develop more appropriate behaviors. And it can cause fear, anger, hostility, and aggression in the punished person.

➤ **What three factors increase the effectiveness of punishment?**

Punishment is most effective when it is given immediately after undesirable behavior, when it is consistently applied, and when it is just intense enough to suppress the unwanted behavior.

➤ **What are some applications of operant conditioning?**

Applications of operant conditioning include training animals to provide entertainment or to help physically challenged people, the use of biofeedback to gain control over internal physiological processes, and the use of behavior modification techniques to eliminate undesirable behavior and/or encourage desirable behavior in individuals or groups.

KEY TERMS

law of effect (p. 127)
operant conditioning (p. 128)
reinforcer (p. 128)
shaping (p. 128)
successive approximations (p. 128)
Skinner box (p. 128)
extinction (p. 129)
generalization (p. 129)
discriminative stimulus (p. 129)
reinforcement (p. 130)
positive reinforcement (p. 130)
negative reinforcement (p. 130)
primary reinforcer (p. 130)
secondary reinforcer (p. 130)
continuous reinforcement (p. 130)
partial reinforcement (p. 130)
schedule of reinforcement (p. 131)
fixed-ratio schedule (p. 131)
variable-ratio schedule (p. 131)

fixed-interval schedule (p. 132)
variable-interval schedule (p. 132)
punishment (p. 132)
learned helplessness (p. 136)
biofeedback (p. 136)
behavior modification (p. 136)
token economy (p. 136)

Cognitive Learning

➤ **What is insight, and how does it affect learning?**

Insight is the sudden realization of the relationship of the elements in a problem situation that makes the solution apparent; this solution is easily learned and transferred to new problems.

➤ **What is latent learning?**

Latent learning occurs without apparent reinforcement, but it is not demonstrated in the organism's performance until the organism receives sufficient reinforcement to do so.

➤ **What is observational learning?**

Observational learning is learning by observing the behavior of others (called models) and the consequences of that behavior.

Surf It !

Want to be sure you've absorbed the material in Chapter 5, "Learning," before the big test? Visiting **www.ablongman.com/woodmastering1e** can put a top grade within your reach. The site is loaded with free practice tests, flashcards, activities, and links to help you review your way to an A.

Companion Website

Study Guide for Chapter 5!

Answers to all the Study Guide questions are provided at the end of the book.

Section One: Chapter Review

1. Classical conditioning was originally researched most extensively by _____.

2. A dog's salivation in response to a musical tone is a(n) (conditioned, unconditioned) response.

3. The weakening of a conditioned response that occurs when a conditioned stimulus is presented without the unconditioned stimulus is called _____.

4. For higher-order conditioning to occur, a neutral stimulus is typically paired repeatedly with an (existing conditioned stimulus, unconditioned stimulus).

5. Five-year-old Jesse was bitten by his neighbor's collie. He won't go near that dog but seems to have no fear of other dogs, even other collies. Which learning process accounts for his behavior?
   a. generalization
   b. discrimination
   c. extinction
   d. spontaneous recovery

6. In Watson's experiment with Little Albert, the white rat was the (conditioned, unconditioned) stimulus, and Albert's crying when the hammer struck the steel bar was the (conditioned, unconditioned) response.

7. Albert's fear of the white rat transferred to a rabbit, a dog, a fur coat, and a mask. What learning process did this demonstrate?
   a. generalization
   b. discrimination
   c. extinction
   d. spontaneous recovery

8. Garcia and Koelling's research supports Pavlov's contention that almost any neutral stimulus can serve as a conditioned stimulus. (true/false)

9. Which of the following responses contradicts the general principle of classical conditioning that the unconditioned stimulus should occur immediately after the conditioned stimulus andμ the two should be paired repeatedly?
   a. salivation response
   b. immune response
   c. taste aversion
   d. conditioned drug cravings

10. Counselors usually advise recovering drug addicts to avoid cues (people, places, and things) that are associated with their past drug use because the environmental cues may serve as conditioned stimuli for drug cravings. (true/false)

11. Classical conditioning can be used to suppress or to boost the immune system. (true/false)

12. Who researched trial-and-error learning using cats in puzzle boxes and formulated the law of effect?
    a. Watson
    b. Thorndike
    c. Skinner
    d. Pavlov

13. Operant conditioning was researched most extensively by
    a. Watson.
    b. Thorndike.
    c. Skinner.
    d. Pavlov.

14. Operant conditioning can be used effectively for all of the following except
    a. learning new responses.
    b. learning to make an existing response to a new stimulus.
    c. increasing the frequency of an existing response.
    d. decreasing the frequency of an existing response.

15. Which of the following processes occurs in operant conditioning when reinforcers are withheld?
    a. generalization
    b. discrimination
    c. spontaneous recovery
    d. extinction

16. Many people take aspirin to relieve painful headaches. Taking aspirin is a behavior that is likely to continue because of the effect of (positive, negative) reinforcement.

17. (Partial, Continuous) reinforcement is most effective in conditioning a new response.

18. Jennifer and Ashley are both employed raking leaves. Jennifer is paid $1 for each bag of leaves she rakes; Ashley is paid $4 per hour. Jennifer is paid according to the _____ schedule; Ashley is paid according to the _____ schedule.
    a. fixed-interval; fixed-ratio
    b. variable-ratio; fixed-interval
    c. variable-ratio; variable-interval
    d. fixed-ratio; fixed-interval

19. Which schedule of reinforcement yields the highest response rate and the greatest resistance to extinction?
    a. variable-ratio schedule
    b. fixed-ratio schedule
    c. variable-interval schedule
    d. fixed-interval schedule

20. Danielle's parents have noticed that she has been making her bed every day, and they would like this to continue. Because they understand the partial-reinforcement effect, they will want to reward her *every* time she makes the bed. (true/false)

21. Recall what you have learned about classical and operant conditioning. Which of the following is descriptive of operant conditioning?

   a. An association is formed between a response and its consequence.
   b. The responses acquired are usually emotional reactions.
   c. The subject is usually passive.
   d. The response acquired is usually an involuntary or reflexive response.

22. Punishment is roughly the same as negative reinforcement. (true/false)

23. Punishment usually does not extinguish undesirable behavior. (true/false)

24. Depending on the circumstances, avoidance learning can be either adaptive or maladaptive. (true/false)

25. Victims of spousal abuse who have repeatedly failed to escape or avoid the abuse may eventually passively resign themselves to it, a condition known as _____ _____.

26. Using sensitive electronic equipment to monitor physiological processes in order to bring them under conscious control is called _____.

27. Applying learning principles to eliminate undesirable behavior and/or encourage desirable behavior is called _____ _____.

28. The sudden realization of the relationship between the elements in a problem situation that results in the solution to the problem is called (latent learning, insight).

29. Learning that is not demonstrated until one is reinforced to perform the behavior is called

   a. learning by insight.
   b. observational learning.
   c. classical conditioning.
   d. latent learning.

30. Hayley has been afraid of snakes for as long as she can remember, and her mother has the same paralyzing fear. Hayley most likely acquired her fear through

   a. learning by insight.
   b. observational learning.
   c. classical conditioning.
   d. latent learning.

31. You are most likely to learn a modeled behavior if you

   a. repeat the behavior many times after watching the model perform it.
   b. are physically capable of performing the behavior.
   c. have never seen the behavior before.
   d. are personally acquainted with the model.

32. Match the researcher with the subject(s) researched.

   ____ (1) Edward Tolman
   ____ (2) Albert Bandura
   ____ (3) Wolfgang Köhler
   a. observational learning
   b. cognitive maps
   c. learning by insight
   d. latent learning

Section Two: Identify the Concept

In the blank following each statement below, list the learning principle illustrated by the statement.

1. Ben continues to play a slot machine even though he never knows when it will pay off. _____

2. Alice watched a movie about tornadoes and is now afraid of bad storms. _____

3. Joey is crying and asking for a candy bar. His mother gives in because doing so will make him stop crying for now—but Joey will most likely behave this way again. _____

4. Jan got sick eating lasagna and now never eats food containing tomato sauce. _____

5. Helen washed the dinner dishes, and her mother allowed her to watch television for 30 extra minutes that evening. _____

6. Sarah's parents are advised to stop paying attention to her crying when it is time for bed and instead ignore it. _____

7. Frank is paid for his factory job once every two weeks. _____

8. Marty is scolded for running into the road and never does it again. _____

9. Ellen watches her lab partner mix the chemicals and set up the experiment. She then repeats the same procedure and completes her assignment. _____

10. Through associations with such things as food and shelter, pieces of green paper with pictures of past U.S. presidents on them become very powerful reinforcers. _____

11. Although he studied the problem, Jack did not seem to be able to figure out the correct way to reconnect the pipes under the sink. He took a break before he became too frustrated. Later he returned and immediately saw how to do it. _____

Section Three: Fill In the Blank

1. Classical conditioning is based on the association between _____ , and operant conditioning is based on the association between a _____ and its _____ .

2. _____ is a relatively permanent change in behavior, knowledge, capability, or attitude that is acquired through experience and cannot be attributed to illness, injury, or maturation.

3. Ed feeds the horses on his ranch every day at the same time. He notices that the horses now run to their feed troughs and whinny as if they know dinner is on its way as soon as they hear his truck coming up the drive. In this example, the conditioned stimulus is _____ .

4. In question 3, the unconditioned stimulus is _____ .

5. The unconditioned response of Pavlov's dogs was _____ .

6. In Pavlov's classic experiment, the bell was originally a(n) _____ stimulus.

7. To get coyotes to stop eating sheep, ranchers poison sheep carcasses in the hope that coyotes that eat the carcasses will get sick enough to avoid eating sheep from that point on. The ranchers hope that the coyotes will avoid all types and sizes of sheep–which is an example of _____ in classical conditioning.

8. The ranchers in question 7 also hope that the coyotes will be able to distinguish between sheep and other more appropriate sources of food. This is an example of _____ in classical conditioning.

9. Eduardo loved eating at a certain fast-food restaurant. After a while even the giant logo sign in front of the restaurant would make him hungry every time he saw it. The restaurant ran a TV ad showing a clown standing by the logo sign. Pretty soon, every time Eduardo saw a clown, he became hungry. Eduardo's responses are examples of _____ conditioning.

10. If Watson had wanted to extinguish Little Albert's conditioned fear of white furry things, he would have presented the _____ stimulus without presenting the _____ stimulus.

11. The law of _____, developed by _____, states that a response that is followed by a satisfying consequence will tend to be repeated, while a response followed by discomfort will tend to be weakened.

12. Since researchers cannot tell rats to press the bar in a Skinner box for food or have them read "The Skinner Box Owner's Manual," they must initiate the bar-pressing response by rewarding _____ _____, an approach known as *shaping*.

13. Reinforcement is any event that follows a response and increases the probability of the response. _____ reinforcement involves the removal of a stimulus and _____ reinforcement involves the presentation of a stimulus.

14. You're driving on an interstate highway and suddenly notice that you've been going 80 miles per hour without realizing it. Immediately after you slow down, you see the flashing light of a state police car, and you know you're about to be pulled over. In this case the flashing light is a _____ stimulus.

15. Food is considered a _____ reinforcer; money is considered a _____ reinforcer.

16. If you were going to train a rat to press a bar for food, you would probably use _____ reinforcement for the initial training period and a _____-reinforcement schedule to strengthen the learned bar-pressing behavior.

17. In his experiments, Skinner used animals that had been deprived of food for 24 hours because _____ influences the rate at which operant conditioning occurs.

18. Bandura's research demonstrated that children may learn _____ behaviors from watching models perform them on television.

Section Four: Comprehensive Practice Test

1. Pavlov is associated with
   a. classical conditioning.
   b. operant conditioning.
   c. cognitive conditioning.
   d. Watsonian conditioning.

2. This theorist believed that the causes of behavior are in the environment and that inner mental events are themselves shaped by environmental forces.
   a. Bandura   c. Skinner
   b. Pavlov   d. Tolman

3. Which of the following theorists developed the concepts of latent learning and cognitive mapping?
   a. Pavlov   c. Tolman
   b. Köhler   d. Skinner

4. This theorist researched observational learning and the effects of modeling on behavior.
   a. Köhler
   b. Thorndike
   c. Skinner
   d. Bandura

5. Which of the following theorists is associated with research on reinforcement theory?

   a. Pavlov   **c.** Tolman
   b. Skinner   **d.** Bandura

6. The concept that is associated with cognitive learning is

   a. negative reinforcement.
   b. positive reinforcement.
   c. latent learning.
   d. the discriminative stimulus.

7. Jim has been sober since he completed a treatment program for alcoholics. He was told to stay away from his old drinking places. The danger is that he may start drinking again as a result of the conditioned stimuli in those environments. If he did, it would be a practical example of _____ in classical conditioning.

   a. extinction
   b. spontaneous recovery
   c. stimulus generalization
   d. observational response sets

8. The seductive nature of a slot machine in a gambling casino is based on its _____ schedule of reinforcement.

   a. continuous   **c.** variable-ratio
   b. fixed-interval   **d.** variable-interval

9. For Little Albert, the conditioned stimulus was

   a. the white rat.
   b. a loud noise.
   c. Watson.
   d. based on negative reinforcement.

10. Positive reinforcement increases behavior; negative reinforcement

   a. decreases behavior.
   b. has no effect on behavior.
   c. removes a behavior.
   d. also increases behavior.

11. A good example of a fixed-interval schedule of reinforcement is

   a. factory piece work.
   b. a child's weekly allowance.
   c. a slot machine.
   d. turning on a light switch.

12. The nice thing about continuous reinforcement is that it creates a behavior that is very resistant to extinction. (true/false)

13. Drug tolerance and taste aversion are real-world examples of

   a. operant conditioning.
   b. classical conditioning.
   c. observational learning.
   d. cognitive mapping.

14. In _____ learning, a person or animal learns a response that _____ a negative reinforcer.

   a. escape; prevents the occurrence of
   b. escape; terminates
   c. avoidance; terminates
   d. avoidance; initiates

15. Ms. Doe, a new teacher, is having a difficult time with her misbehaving second graders. When the principal enters the room, the children behave like perfect angels. In this case, the principal may be thought of as a(n)

   a. positive reinforcer.
   b. unconditioned stimulus.
   c. shaping reinforcer.
   d. discriminative stimulus.

16. According to Tolman, _____ _____ is defined as learning that occurs without apparent reinforcement but is not demonstrated until the organism is sufficiently reinforced to do so.

   a. classical conditioning   **c.** latent learning
   b. modeling behavior   **d.** cognitive mapping

17. Skinner asserted that classical conditioning is based on unconscious motivation, while operant conditioning is based on conscious control of emotions. (true/false)

Section Five: Critical Thinking

1. Outline the strengths and limitations of classical conditioning, operant conditioning, and observational learning in explaining how behaviors are acquired and maintained.

2. The use of behavior modification has been a source of controversy among psychologists and others. Prepare arguments supporting each of these positions:

   a. Behavior modification should be used in society to shape the behavior of others.

   b. Behavior modification should not be used in society to shape the behavior of others.

3. Think of a behavior of a friend, family member, or professor that you would like to change. Using what you know about classical conditioning, operant conditioning, and observational learning, formulate a detailed plan for changing the targeted behavior.

chapter

6

Memory

"Shut up, or I'll cut you," Jennifer's attacker warned her as he held the knife against her throat. Just moments before, Jennifer had screamed as the man grabbed her, threw her down on the bed, and pinned her hands behind her. Now, feeling the pain of the knife's sharp point on her throat, she knew he meant what he said. But she steeled herself to study the rapist—his facial features, scars, tattoos, voice, mannerisms—vowing to herself that she would remember the man well enough to send him to prison.

Hours after her ordeal, Jennifer Thompson viewed police photos of potential suspects, searching for that of her rapist—his pencil-thin moustache, eyebrows, nose, and other features. She then selected a composite photo that looked like the rapist. A week later, she viewed six suspects holding cards numbered 1 to 6. Jennifer looked at suspect number 5 and announced with total confidence, "That's the man who raped me."

The man was Ronald Cotton, who had already served a year and a half in prison for attempted sexual assault. In court, Thompson was unshakably confident, so sure that this man had raped her. Cotton was nervous and frightened. His alibis didn't check out, and a piece missing from one of his shoes resembled a piece found at the crime scene. But it was the confident, unwavering testimony of the only eyewitness, Jennifer Thompson, that sealed his fate. The jury found him guilty and sentenced him to life in prison, just as Thompson had hoped.

"God knows I'm innocent," said Cotton, and he vowed to prove it somehow.

Remarkably, after Cotton had been in prison for more than a year, a new inmate, Bobby Poole, convicted of a series of brutal rapes, joined him at his work assignment in the kitchen. When Cotton told Poole that he had been convicted of raping Jennifer Thompson, Poole laughed and bragged that Cotton was doing some of his time.

Finally, after Cotton had served 11 years, law professor Richard Rosen heard his story and agreed to help him. Rosen knew that DNA tests could be performed that were far more sophisticated than those that had been available 11 years earlier. It was Cotton's DNA samples that cleared him of the crime. Poole's DNA samples, however, proved that he had raped Thompson.

After being proved innocent and released from prison, Ronald Cotton talked with and forgave Jennifer Thompson, who had falsely accused him. Cotton is now married with a beautiful daughter, Raven. With Thompson's help, he got a six-figure settlement from the state government. (Adapted from O'Neil, 2000.)

- Remembering
- The Nature of Remembering
- Factors Influencing Retrieval
- Biology and Memory
- Forgetting
- Improving Memory

What three processes are involved in the act of remembering? ▶

What is sensory memory? ▶

Does this case simply reflect the rare and unusual in human memory, or are memory errors common occurrences? This and many other questions you may have about memory will be answered in this chapter.

Remembering

The Three Processes in Memory

The act of remembering requires three processes: encoding, storage, and retrieval (see Figure 6.1). The first process, **encoding,** involves transforming information into a form that can be stored in memory. For example, if you met someone named Will at a party, you might associate his name with that of the actor Will Smith. The second memory process, **storage,** involves keeping or maintaining information in memory. The final process, **retrieval,** occurs when information stored in memory is brought to mind. Calling Will by name the next time you meet him shows that you have retrieved his name from memory.

Physiological changes must occur during a process called **consolidation,** which allows new information to be stored in memory for later retrieval. These physiological changes require the synthesis of protein molecules (Lopez, 2000). Until recently, conventional wisdom held that the process of consolidation had to occur only once for each item memorized. But as we will see later in the chapter, in the section on the causes of forgetting, some seemingly consolidated memories can be induced to disappear (Nader et al., 2000).

The Three Memory Systems

How are memories stored? According to one widely accepted view, the *Atkinson-Shiffrin model,* there are three different, interacting memory systems, known as sensory, short-term, and long-term memory (Atkinson & Shiffrin, 1968; Broadbent, 1958). We will examine each of these three memory systems, which are shown in Figure 6.2.

As information comes in through the senses, virtually everything you see, hear, or otherwise sense is held in **sensory memory,** but only for the briefest period of time. Exactly how long does visual sensory memory last? For a fraction of a second, glance at the three rows of letters shown below and then close your eyes. How many of the items can you recall?

X B D F
M P Z G
L C N H

Most people can recall correctly only four or five of the items when they are briefly presented. Does this indicate that visual sensory memory can hold only four or five items at a time? To find out, researcher George Sperling (1960) briefly flashed 12 items, as shown above, to participants. Immediately upon turning off the display, he sounded a high, medium, or low tone that signaled the participants to report only

▶ **Figure 6.1**

The Processes Required in Remembering

The act of remembering requires successful completion of all three of these processes: encoding, storage, and retrieval.

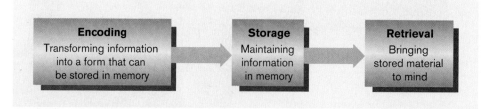

Encoding	Storage	Retrieval
Transforming information into a form that can be stored in memory	Maintaining information in memory	Bringing stored material to mind

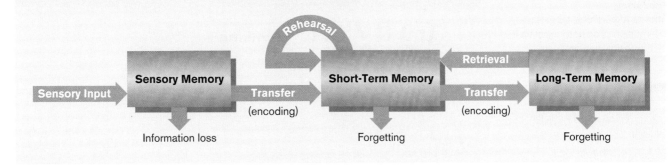

Figure 6.2

The Three Memory Systems

According to the Atkinson-Shiffrin model, there are three separate memory systems: sensory memory, short-term memory, and long-term memory.

the top, middle, or bottom row of items. Before they heard the tone, the participants had no way of knowing which row they would have to report. Yet Sperling found that, when the participants could view the letters for $\frac{15}{1000}$ to $\frac{1}{2}$ second, they could report correctly all the items in any row nearly 100% of the time. But the items fade from sensory memory so quickly that during the time it takes to report three or four of the items, the other eight or nine have already disappeared.

Auditory sensory memory lasts about 2 seconds (Klatzky, 1980). You may have the sense that words are echoing in your mind after someone stops speaking to you. This phenomenon is the result of the relatively long time that auditory information remains in sensory memory, compared to visual information. Thus, your brain has much more time to attend to sounds and to move information about them to the next phase of processing.

From sensory memory, information moves to **short-term memory.** Whatever you are thinking about right now is in your short-term memory. Unlike sensory memory, which holds virtually the exact sensory stimulus, short-term memory usually codes information according to sound (Conrad, 1964). The letter T is coded as the sound "tee," not as the shape T. In addition, short-term memory has a very limited capacity—about seven (plus or minus two) different items or bits of information at one time. When short-term memory is filled to capacity, displacement can occur (just as you start to lose things when the top of your desk becomes overcrowded!). In **displacement,** each new incoming item pushes out an existing item, which is then forgotten.

One way to overcome the limitation on the capacity of short-term memory to seven or so bits of information is to use a technique that George A. Miller (1956), a pioneer in memory research, calls *chunking*—organizing or grouping separate bits of information into larger units, or chunks. A *chunk* is an easily identifiable unit such as a syllable, a word, an acronym, or a number (Cowan, 1988). For example, the numbers 5 2 9 7 3 1 2 5 can be chunked as 52 97 31 25, giving short-term memory the easier task of dealing with four chunks of information rather than eight separate bits. Complete *Try It! 6.1* (on page 152) to get a feeling for the superiority of chunking over trying to memorize individual items one at a time.

Anytime you chunk information on the basis of knowledge stored in long-term memory—in other words, by associating it with some kind of meaning—you increase the effective capacity of short-term memory (Lustig & Hasher, 2002). And when you increase the effective capacity of short-term memory, you are more likely to transfer information to long-term memory. (*Hint:* The headings and subheadings in textbook chapters are labels for manageable chunks of information. You will remember more of a chapter if you use them as organizers for your notes and as cues to recall chapter information when you are reviewing for an exam.)

displacement
The phenomenon that occurs when short-term memory is holding its maximum amount of information and each new item entering short-term memory pushes out an existing item.

What are the characteristics of short-term memory?

Sensory memory holds a visual image, such as a lightning bolt, for a fraction of a second—just long enough for you to perceive a flow of movement.

rehearsal
The act of purposely repeating information in order to maintain it in short-term memory or to transfer it to long-term memory.

long-term memory
The relatively permanent memory system with a virtually unlimited capacity.

elaborative rehearsal
A technique used to encode information into long-term memory by considering its meaning and associating it with other information already stored in long-term memory.

declarative memory
The subsystem within long-term memory that stores facts, information, and personal life experiences; also called *explicit memory*.

episodic memory
(ep-ih-SOD-ik) The part of declarative memory that contains memories of personally experienced events.

semantic memory
The part of declarative memory that holds general knowledge; a mental encyclopedia or dictionary.

What is long-term memory, and what are its subsystems? ➤

nondeclarative memory
The subsystem within long-term memory that consists of skills acquired through repetitive practice, habits, and simple classically conditioned responses; also called *implicit memory*.

levels-of-processing model
A model of memory as a single system in which retention depends on how deeply information is processed.

Try It! 6.1 Chunking

Read the following letters individually at the rate of about one per second and then see if you can repeat them.

N-F   L-C-B   S-U-S   A-V-C   R-F-B   I

Did you have difficulty? Probably so, because there are 15 different letters.
Now try this:

NFL   CBS   USA   VCR   FBI

Did you find that five chunks are easier to remember than 15 separate items?

Items in short-term memory are lost in less than 30 seconds unless you repeat them over and over to yourself. This process is known as **rehearsal.** But rehearsal is easily disrupted. Distractions that are stressful are especially likely to disrupt short-term memory. And a threat to survival certainly does so, as researchers showed when they pumped the odor of a feared predator, a fox, into a laboratory where rats were performing a task requiring short-term memory (Morrison et al., 2002; Morrow et al., 2000).

How long does short-term memory last if rehearsal is prevented? In a series of early studies, participants were briefly shown three consonants (such as H, G, and L) and then asked to count backward by threes from a given number (for example, 738, 735, 732, . . .) (Peterson & Peterson, 1959). After intervals lasting from 3 to 18 seconds, participants were instructed to stop counting backward and recall the three letters. Following a delay of 9 seconds, the participants could recall an average of only one of the three letters. After 18 seconds, there was practically no recall whatsoever. An 18-second distraction had completely erased the three letters from short-term memory.

Allan Baddeley (1990, 1992, 1995) has suggested that *working memory* is a more fitting term than short-term memory. In other words, this memory system is where you *work on* information to understand it, remember it, use it to solve a problem, or to communicate with someone. Research shows that the prefrontal cortex is the primary area of the brain responsible for working memory (Courtney et al., 1997; Rao et al., 1997).

Some of the information in short-term memory makes its way into long-term memory. **Long-term memory,** the type of memory most people are referring to when they use the word "memory," is each individual's vast storehouse of permanent or relatively permanent memories. There are no known limits to the storage capacity of long-term memory, and long-term memories can last for years, some of them for a lifetime. Long-term memory holds all the knowledge you have accumulated, the skills you have acquired, and the memories of your past experiences. Information in long-term memory is usually stored in verbal form, although visual images, sounds, and odors can be stored there, as well.

But how did this vast store of information make its way from short-term memory into long-term memory? Sometimes, through mere repetition or rehearsal, a person is able to transfer information into long-term memory. Your teachers may have used a drilling technique to try to cement the multiplication tables and other material in your long-term memory. Another approach is **elaborative rehearsal.** The goal of this strategy is to relate new information to information already in your long-term memory (Symons & Johnson, 1997). For example, you might remember the French word *maison* (house) by relating it to the English word *mansion* (a type of house). Forming such associations, especially if they are personally relevant, increases your chances of retrieving new information later. Figure 6.3 summarizes the three memory systems.

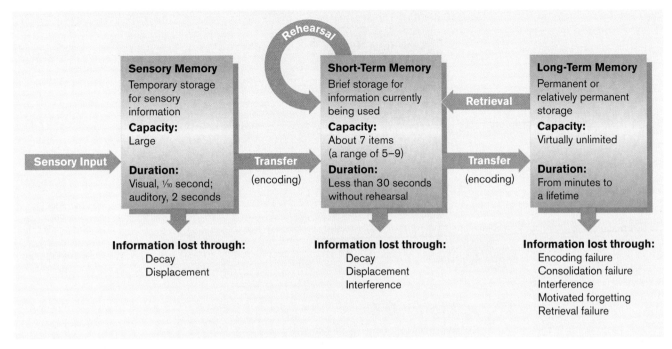

> ## Figure 6.3
Characteristics of and Processes Involved in the Three Memory Systems
The three memory systems differ in what and how much they hold and for how long they store it. (From Peterson & Peterson, 1959.)

There are two main subsystems within long-term memory. The first, **declarative memory** (also called *explicit memory*), stores information that can be brought to mind in the form of words or images and then stated, or declared. **Episodic memory** is the part of declarative memory that holds memories of events as they have been subjectively experienced (Wheeler et al., 1997). It is somewhat like a mental diary, recording the episodes of your life—the people you have known, the places you have seen, and the experiences you have had. **Semantic memory,** the second part of declarative memory, is memory for general knowledge, or objective facts and information. In other words, semantic memory is a mental dictionary or encyclopedia of stored knowledge.

The second subsystem of long-term memory, **nondeclarative memory** (also called *implicit memory*), consists of motor skills, habits, and simple classically conditioned responses (Squire et al., 1993). Acquired through repetitive practice, motor skills include such things as eating with a fork, riding a bicycle, and driving a car. Although acquired slowly, once learned, these skills become habit, are quite reliable, and can be carried out with little or no conscious effort. Figure 6.4 (on page 154) shows the subsystems of long-term memory.

Declarative memory stores facts, information, and personal life events, such as a trip to a foreign country. Nondeclarative memory encompasses motor skills, such as the expert swing of professional golfer Tiger Woods. Once learned, such movements can be carried out with little or no conscious effort.

The Levels-of-Processing Model

Not all psychologists support the notion of three memory systems. Craik and Lockhart (1972) propose instead a **levels-of-processing model.** They suggest that whether people remember an item for a few seconds or a lifetime depends on how deeply they process the information. With the shallowest levels of processing, a person is merely aware of the incoming sensory information. Deeper processing takes place only when the person does something more with the information, such as forming relationships, making associations, attaching meaning to a sensory impression, or engaging in active elaborations on new material. However, the deeper levels of processing that establish a memory also require background knowledge, so that lasting connections can be formed between the person's existing store of knowledge and the new information (Willoughby et al., 2000).

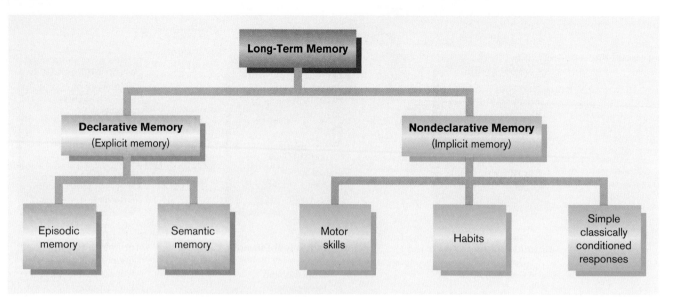

➤ Figure 6.4

Subsystems of Long-Term Memory

Declarative memory can be divided into two parts: episodic memory, which stores memories of personally experienced events, and semantic memory, which stores facts and information. Nondeclarative memory consists of motor skills acquired through repetitive practice, habits, and simple classically conditioned responses.

Three Kinds of Memory Tasks

> What are three kinds of tasks used by psychologists to measure memory retention?

Psychologists have used three main types of tasks to measure memory retention: recall, recognition, and the relearning method. In **recall,** a person must produce required information by searching memory without the help of **retrieval cues**–the stimuli or bits of information that aid in the retrieval of particular information from long-term memory. Trying to remember someone's name, recalling items on a shopping list, and answering fill-in-the-blank and essay items on exams are all recall tasks. Often, serial recall (recalling items in a certain order) is easier than free recall (recalling items in any order) because in serial recall, each letter, word, or number may serve as a cue for the one that follows. Indeed, research suggests that, in free-recall tasks, order associations are more resistant to distractions than meaningful associations (Howard, 2002).

Recognition is exactly what the word implies. A person simply recognizes something as familiar–a face, a name, a taste, a melody. Recent brain-imaging studies have discovered that the hippocampus plays an extensive role in memory tasks involving recognition, but the degree of hippocampal activity varies for different tasks. When the task is recognizing famous faces, widespread brain activity takes place in both hemispheres, involving the prefrontal and temporal lobes and including the hippocampus and surrounding hippocampal region. Less widespread brain activity is observed during the recognition of recently encoded faces or the encoding of faces seen for the first time (Henson et al., 2002). Studies with monkeys having brain damage limited to the hippocampal region also show that this region is essential for normal recognition tasks (Teng et al., 2000; Zola et al., 2000).

There is yet another way to measure memory retention that is even more sensitive than recognition. With the **relearning method,** or the *savings method,* retention is expressed as the percentage of time saved when material is relearned, compared with the time required to learn the material originally. Suppose it took you 40 minutes to memorize a list of words, and 1 month later you were tested, using recall or recognition. If you could not recall or recognize a single word, would this mean that you had absolutely no

recall
A measure of retention that requires a person to remember material with few or no retrieval cues, as in an essay test.

retrieval cue
Any stimulus or bit of information that aids in the retrieval of a particular memory from long-term memory.

recognition
A measure of retention that requires a person to identify material as familiar, or as having been encountered before.

relearning method
A way of measuring memory retention in terms of the percentage of time saved in relearning material compared with the time required to learn it originally; also called the *savings method.*

memory of anything on the test? Or could it mean that the recall and recognition methods were not sensitive enough to pick up what little information you may have stored? How could a researcher measure a remnant of this former learning? Using the relearning method, a researcher could time how long it took you to relearn the list of words. If it took 20 minutes to relearn the list, this would represent a 50% savings compared to the original learning time of 40 minutes. College students demonstrate the relearning method each semester when they study for comprehensive final exams. Relearning material for a final exam takes less time than it took to learn the material originally.

The Nature of Remembering

Memory as a Reconstruction

Wilder Penfield (1969), a Canadian neurosurgeon, claimed that experiences leave a "permanent imprint on the brain . . . as though a tape recorder had been receiving it all" (p. 165). Penfield (1975) based this conclusion on observations made while performing more than 1,100 operations on patients with epilepsy. He found that when parts of the temporal lobes were stimulated with an electrical probe, 3.5% of patients reported flashback experiences, as though they were actually reliving parts of their past.

After reviewing Penfield's findings, Ulrich Neisser and other memory researchers (Neisser, 1967) suggested that the experiences the patients reported were "comparable to the content of dreams," rather than the recall of actual experiences (p. 169). Thus, today's memory researchers recognize that memory seldom works like a video cassette recorder, capturing every part of an experience exactly as it happens. Rather a memory is a **reconstruction**–an account pieced together from a few highlights, using information that may or may not be accurate (Loftus & Loftus, 1980). Put another way, remembering "is not so much like reading a book as it is like writing one from fragmentary notes" (Kihlstrom, 1995, p. 341). As a result, memory is quite often inaccurate, and recall is, even for people with the most accurate memories, partly truth and partly fiction.

An early memory researcher, Englishman Sir Frederick Bartlett (1886–1969), suggested that memory is influenced by **schemas**–integrated frameworks of knowledge stored in long-term memory. Schemas aid in processing large amounts of material because they provide frameworks into which people can incorporate new information and experience. For example, if you have taken a course in the past that included discussion of psychoanalytic theory, the information about Freud and other psychoanalysts in Chapter 11 of this book will be easier for you to learn than it will be for students who have no prior knowledge of psychoanalytic theory. Your prior knowledge is organized into schemas that provide "shelves" on which to store the new information.

Schemas can also distort memory, though. When you witness an event, your schemas may cause you to omit some facts about what actually occurred or to add nonfactual details. Schema-based distortion can also occur when people alter the memory of an event or an experience in order to fit their beliefs, expectations, logic, or prejudices. The tendency to distort often causes gross inaccuracies in what people remember. For instance, people often distort memories of their own lives in the positive direction. Bahrick and others (1996) found that 89% of college students accurately remembered the A's they earned in high school, but only 29% accurately recalled the D's. *Try It! 6.2* (on page 156) demonstrates schema-based memory distortion.

Try It! 6.2 shows that we are very likely to alter or distort what we see or hear to make it fit with what we believe should be true. All the words on the *Try It!* list are related to sleep, so it seems logical that *sleep* should be one of the words. In experiments using word lists similar to that one, between 40% and 55% of the participants "remembered" the key related word that was not on the list (Roediger & McDermott,

 Are you better at remembering faces than names? Have you ever wondered why? It's because the task involves recognition rather than recall. You must recall the name but merely recognize the face.

What is meant by the statement "Memory is reconstructive in nature"?

What are schemas, and how do they affect memory?

reconstruction
An account that is not an exact replica of a remembered event but has been pieced together from a few highlights, using information that may or may not be accurate.

schemas
The integrated frameworks of knowledge about people, objects, and events, which are stored in long-term memory and affect the encoding and recall of information.

1995). If you "remembered" the word *sleep,* you created a false memory, which probably seemed as real to you as a true memory (Dodson et al., 2000).

Eyewitness Testimony

What conditions reduce the reliability of eyewitness testimony?

As the story at the beginning of this chapter suggests, eyewitness testimony is highly subject to error. In fact, most memory experts say that it should always be viewed with caution (Loftus, 1979). Nevertheless, it does play a vital role in the U.S. justice system. Says Loftus (1984), "We can't afford to exclude it legally or ignore it as jurors. Sometimes, as in cases of rape, it is the only evidence available, and it is often correct" (p. 24).

Fortunately, eyewitness mistakes can be minimized. Eyewitnesses to crimes often identify suspects from a lineup. If shown photographs of a suspect before viewing the lineup, eyewitnesses may mistakenly identify that suspect in the lineup because the person looks familiar. Research suggests that it is better to have an eyewitness first describe the perpetrator and then search for photos matching that description than to have the eyewitness start by looking through photos and making judgments as to their similarity to the perpetrator (Pryke et al., 2000).

The composition of the lineup is also important. Other individuals in a lineup must resemble the suspect in age and body build and must certainly be of the same race. Even then, if the lineup does not contain the perpetrator, eyewitnesses may identify the person who most closely resembles him or her (Gonzalez et al., 1993). Eyewitnesses are less likely to make errors if a sequential lineup is used, that is, if the participants in the lineup are viewed one after the other, rather than simultaneously (Loftus, 1993a). Some police officers and researchers prefer a "showup"–a procedure that involves presenting only one suspect and having the witness indicate whether that person is the perpetrator. There are fewer misidentifications with a showup, but also more failures in making positive identifications (Wells, 1993).

When people recall an event, such as a car accident, they are actually reconstructing it from memory by piecing together bits of information that may or may not be totally accurate.

Eyewitnesses are more likely to identify the wrong person if the person's race is different from their own. According to Egeth (1993), misidentifications are approximately 15% higher in cross-race than in same-race identifications. Misidentification is also somewhat more likely to occur when a weapon is used in a crime. The witnesses may pay more attention to the weapon than to the physical characteristics of the criminal (Steblay, 1992).

Even questioning witnesses after a crime can influence what they later remember. Because leading questions can substantially change a witness's memory of an event, it is critical that the interviewers ask neutral questions (Leichtman & Ceci, 1995). Misleading information supplied to the witness after the event can result in erroneous recollections of the actual event, a phenomenon known as the *misinformation effect* (Kroll et al., 1988; Loftus & Hoffman, 1989). Loftus (1997) and her students have conducted "more than 20 experiments involving over 20,000 participants that document how exposure to misinformation induces memory distortion" (p. 71). Furthermore, after eyewitnesses have repeatedly recalled information, whether accurate or inaccurate, they become even more confident when they testify in court because the information is so easily retrieved (Shaw, 1996). And the confidence eyewitnesses have in their testimony is not necessarily an indication of its accuracy (Loftus, 1993a; Sporer et al., 1995). In fact, eyewitnesses who perceive themselves to be more objective have more confidence in their testimony, regardless of its accuracy, and they are more likely to include incorrect information in their verbal descriptions (Geiselman et al., 2000).

The composition of this police lineup is consistent with research findings that suggest that all individuals in a lineup should be similar to the suspect in age, race, body build, and other physical characteristics.

Recovering Repressed Memories

Perhaps because of the frequency of such cases in novels, on television, and in movies, recent studies have found that many people in the United States believe that unconscious memories of abuse can lead to serious psychological disorders (Stafford & Lynn, 2002). Such beliefs have also been fostered by self-help books such as *The Courage to Heal*, published in 1988, by Ellen Bass and Laura Davis. This best-selling book became the "bible" for sex abuse victims and the leading "textbook" for some therapists who specialized in treating them. Bass and Davis not only sought to help survivors who remembered having suffered sexual abuse, but also reached out to people who had no memory of any sexual abuse and tried to help them determine whether they might have been abused. These authors suggested that "if you are unable to remember any specific instances . . . but still have a feeling that something abusive happened to you, it probably did" (p. 21). They offered a definite conclusion: "If you think you were abused and your life shows the symptoms, then you were" (p. 22). And they freed potential victims of sexual abuse from the responsibility of establishing any proof: "You are not responsible for proving that you were abused" (p. 37).

> What is the controversy regarding the therapy used to recover repressed memories of childhood sexual abuse?

However, many psychologists are skeptical, claiming that the "recovered" memories are actually false memories created by the suggestions of therapists. Critics point out that numerous studies have shown that traumatic memories are rarely, if ever, repressed (e.g., Bowers & Farvolden, 1996; Merckelbach et al., 2003). Moreover, they maintain that "when it comes to a serious trauma, intrusive thoughts and memories of it are the most characteristic reaction" (p. 359). According to Loftus (1993b), "the therapist convinces the patient with no memories that abuse is likely, and the patient obligingly uses reconstructive strategies to generate memories that would support that conviction" (p. 528). Repressed-memory therapists believe, however, that healing hinges on their patients' being able to recover the repressed memories.

Critics further charge that recovered memories of sexual abuse are suspect because of the techniques therapists usually use to uncover them: hypnosis and guided imagery. As you have learned, hypnosis does not improve the accuracy of memory, only the confidence that what one remembers is accurate.

> Does hypnosis improve the memory of eyewitnesses?

Can merely imagining experiences lead people to believe that those experiences actually happened to them? Yes, according to some studies. Many research participants who are instructed to imagine that a fictitious event happened do, in fact, develop a false memory of the imagined event (Hyman & Pentland, 1996; Hyman et al., 1995; Loftus & Pickrell, 1995; Worthen & Wood, 2001).

False childhood memories can also be experimentally induced. Garry and Loftus (1994) were able to implant a false memory of being lost in a shopping mall at 5 years of age in 25% of participants aged 18 to 53, after verification of the fictitious experience by a relative. Repeated exposure to suggestions of false memories can create those memories (Zaragoza & Mitchell, 1996).

Critics are especially skeptical of recovered memories of events that occurred in the first few years of life. The hippocampus, which is vital in the formation of episodic memories, is not fully developed then, and neither are the areas of the cortex where memories

These eyewitnesses to the aftermath of the terrorist attacks on the World Trade Center almost certainly formed flashbulb memories of the horrific events they witnessed. Do you remember where you were and what you were doing when you heard the news on September 11, 2001?

are stored (Squire et al., 1993). Furthermore, young children, who are still limited in language ability, do not store memories in categories that are accessible to adults. Accordingly, Widom and Morris (1997) found that memories of abuse are better when the victimization took place between the ages of 7 and 17 than when it occurred in the first 6 years of life.

The American Psychological Association (1994), the American Psychiatric Association (1993c), and the American Medical Association (1994) have issued status reports on memories of childhood abuse. The position of all three groups is that current evidence supports the possibilities that repressed memories exist *and* that false memories can be constructed in response to suggestions of abuse. This position suggests that recovered memories of abuse should be verified independently before they are accepted as facts. Taking such a position is critically important. As you saw in *Try It! 6.2,* false memories are easily formed. And, once formed, they are often relied on with great confidence (Dodson et al., 2000; Henkel et al., 2000).

Flashbulb Memories

We probably all remember where we were and what we were doing when we heard about the tragic events of September 11, 2001. This type of extremely vivid memory is called a **flashbulb memory** (Bohannon, 1988). Brown and Kulik (1977) suggest that a flashbulb memory is formed when a person learns of an event that is very surprising, shocking, and highly emotional. You might have a flashbulb memory of receiving the news of the death or serious injury of a close family member or a friend.

Several studies suggest that flashbulb memories are not as accurate as people believe them to be. Neisser and Harsch (1992) questioned university freshmen about the Challenger disaster the morning after the space shuttle exploded in 1986. When the same students were questioned again 3 years later, one-third gave accounts that differed markedly from those given initially, even though they were extremely confident of their recollections. Further, flashbulb memories appear to be forgotten at about the same rate and in the same ways as other kinds of memories (Curci et al., 2001).

Memory and Culture

Sir Frederick Bartlett (1932) believed that some impressive memory abilities operate within a social or cultural context and cannot be understood as a pure process. He stated that "both the manner and matter of recall are often predominantly determined by social influences" (p. 244). Studying memory in a cultural context, Bartlett (1932) described the amazing ability of the Swazi people of Africa to remember the slight differences in individual characteristics of their cows. One Swazi herdsman, Bartlett claimed, could remember details of every cow he had tended the year before. Such a feat is less surprising when you consider that the key component of traditional Swazi culture is the herds of cattle the people tend and depend on for their living. Do the Swazi people have superior memory powers? Bartlett asked young Swazi men and young European men to recall a message consisting of 25 words. The Swazi had no better recall ability than the Europeans.

Among many of the tribal peoples in Africa, the history of the tribe is preserved orally. Thus, an oracle, or specialist, must be able to encode, store, and retrieve huge volumes of historical data (D'Azevedo, 1982). Elders of the Iatmul people of New Guinea are also said to have committed to memory the lines of descent for the various clans of their people stretching back for many generations (Bateson, 1982). The unerring memories of the elders for these kinship patterns are used to resolve disputed property claims (Mistry & Rogoff, 1994).

Barbara Rogoff, an expert in cultural psychology, maintains that such phenomenal, prodigious memory feats are best explained and understood in their cultural con-

flashbulb memory
An extremely vivid memory of the conditions surrounding one's first hearing the news of a surprising, shocking, or highly emotional event.

text (Rogoff & Mistry, 1985). The tribal elders perform their impressive memory feats because it is an integral and critically important part of the culture in which they live. Most likely, their ability to remember lists of nonsense syllables would be no better than your own.

Studies examining memory for locations among a tribal group in India, the Asur, who do not use artificial lighting of any kind, provide further information about the influence of culture on memory (Mishra & Singh, 1992). Researchers hypothesized that members of this group would perform better on tests of memory for locations than on conventional tasks used by memory researchers. This is because, lacking artificial lights, the Asur have to remember locations so that they can move around in the dark without bumping into things. When the Asur people were tested, they did indeed remember locations better than word pairs.

In classic research, cognitive psychologists have also found that people more easily remember stories set in their own culture than those set in others. In one of the first of these studies, researchers told a story about a sick child to women in the United States and to Aboriginal women in Australia (Steffensen & Calker, 1982). Participants were randomly assigned to groups for whom story outcomes were varied. In one version, the girl got well after being treated by a physician. In the other, a traditional native healer was called in to help the girl. Aboriginal participants better recalled the story with the native healer, and American participants were more accurate in their recall of the story in which a physician treated the girl.

In many traditional cultures, some elders are oral historians, remembering and passing on the details of tribal traditions and myths as well as genealogical data.

Factors Influencing Retrieval

The Serial Position Effect

If you were introduced to a dozen people at a party, you would most likely recall the names of the first few individuals you met and the last one or two, but forget many of the names of those in between. The reason is the **serial position effect**—the finding that, for information learned in sequence, recall is better for items at the beginning and the end than for items in the middle of the sequence.

Information at the beginning of a sequence is subject to the **primacy effect**—it is likely to be recalled because it already has been placed in long-term memory. Information at the end of a sequence is subject to the **recency effect**—it has an even higher probability of being recalled because it is still in short-term memory. The poorer recall of information in the middle of a sequence occurs because that information is no longer in short-term memory and has not yet been placed in long-term memory. The serial position effect lends strong support to the notion of separate systems for short-term and long-term memory (Postman & Phillips, 1965).

Environmental Context and Memory

Have you ever stood in your living room and thought of something you needed from your bedroom, only to forget what it was when you got there? Did the item come to mind when you returned to the living room? Tulving and Thompson (1973) suggest that many elements of the physical setting in which a person learns information are encoded along with the information and become part of the memory. If part or all of the original context is reinstated, it may serve as a retrieval cue. That is why returning to the living room elicits the memory of the object you intended to get from the bedroom. In fact, just visualizing yourself

serial position effect
The tendency to remember the beginning and ending items of a sequence or list better than the middle items.

> What is the serial position effect?

primacy effect
The tendency to recall the first items on a list more readily than the middle items.

recency effect
The tendency to recall the last items on a list more readily than those in the middle of the list.

> How does environmental context affect memory?

in the living room might do the trick (Smith, 1979). (Next time you're taking a test and having difficulty recalling something, try visualizing yourself in the room where you studied!)

Godden and Baddeley (1975) conducted one of the early studies of context and memory with members of a university scuba diving club. Participants memorized a list of words when they were either 10 feet underwater or on land. They were later tested for recall of the words in the same or in a different environment. Words learned underwater were best recalled underwater, and words learned on land were best recalled on land. In fact, when the scuba divers learned and recalled the words in the same context, their scores were 47% higher than when the two contexts were different (see Figure 6.5). More recent studies have found similar context effects (e.g., Bjorklund et al., 2000).

Odors can also supply powerful and enduring retrieval cues for memory. In a study by Morgan (1996), participants were placed in isolated cubicles and exposed to a list of 40 words. They were instructed to perform a cognitive task using the words but were not asked to remember them. Then, back in the cubicle 5 days later, participants were unexpectedly tested for recall of the 40 words. Experimental participants who experienced a pleasant odor during the initial task and again when tested 5 days later had significantly higher recall than control participants who did not experience the odor at either time.

The State-Dependent Memory Effect

People tend to recall information better if they are in the same internal emotional state as they were when the information was encoded; psychologists call this the **state-dependent memory effect.** Anxiety appears to affect memory more than other emotions. For example, when researchers exposed college students to spiders and/or snakes while they were learning lists of words, the students recalled more words when the creatures were also present during tests of recall (Lang et al., 2001).

What is the state-dependent memory effect?

Adults who are clinically depressed tend to recall more of their negative life experiences (Clark & Teasdale, 1982) and are likely to remember their parents being unloving and rejecting (Lewinsohn & Rosenbaum, 1987). Moreover, a review of 48 studies revealed a significant relationship between depression and memory impairment. Recognition and recall were more impaired in younger depressed patients than in older ones (Burt et al., 1995). But as depression lifts, the tendency toward negative recall and the memory impairment reverse themselves.

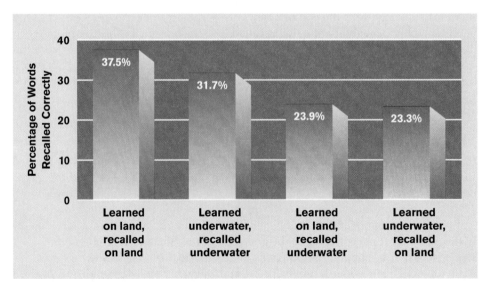

> ## Figure 6.5

Context-Dependent Memory

Godden and Baddeley showed the strong influence of environmental context on recall. Scuba divers who memorized a list of words, either on land or underwater, had significantly better recall in the same physical context in which the learning had taken place. (Data from Godden & Baddeley, 1975.)

Biology and Memory

Brain Damage

Researchers are finding specific locations in the brain that house and mediate functions and processes in memory. One important source of information comes from people who have suffered memory loss resulting from damage to specific brain areas. One especially important case is that of H.M., a man who suffered from such severe epilepsy that, out of desperation, he agreed to a radical surgical procedure. The surgeon removed the part of H.M.'s brain believed to be causing his seizures, the medial portions of both temporal lobes–the amygdala and the **hippocampal region,** which includes the hippocampus itself and the underlying cortical areas. It was 1953, and H.M. was 27 years old.

> After his surgery, H.M. remained intelligent and psychologically stable, and his seizures were drastically reduced. But unfortunately, the tissue cut from H.M.'s brain housed more than the site of his seizures. It also contained his ability to use working memory to store new information in long-term memory. Though the capacity of his short-term memory remained the same, and he remembers the events of his life stored well before the operation, H.M. suffers from **anterograde amnesia.** He has not been able to remember a single event that has occurred since the surgery. And though H.M. turned 75 in 2001, as far as his conscious long-term memory is concerned, it was still 1953 and he was still 27 years old.
>
> Surgery affected only H.M.'s declarative, long-term memory–his ability to store facts, personal experiences, names, faces, telephone numbers, and the like. But researchers were surprised to discover that he could still form nondeclarative memories; that is, he could still acquire skills through repetitive practice although he could not remember having done so. For example, since the surgery, H.M. has learned to play tennis and improve his game, but he has no memory of ever having played. (Adapted from Milner, 1966, 1970; Milner et al., 1968.)

Animal studies support the conclusion that the parts of H.M.'s brain that were removed are critical to the functioning of short-term memory (Ragozzino et al., 2002). Moreover, other patients who have suffered similar brain damage show the same types of memory loss (Squire, 1992). Recent research supports the hypothesis that the hippocampus is especially important in forming episodic memories (Eichenbaum, 1997; Gluck & Myers, 1997; Spiers et al., 2001). Semantic memory, however, depends not only on the hippocampus, but also on other parts of the hippocampal region underlying it (Vargha-Khadem et al., 1997). Consequently, many researchers argue that neurological bases for episodic and semantic memory are entirely separate (e.g., Tulving, 2002).

One interesting study (Maguire et al., 2000) suggests that the hippocampus may also support navigational skills by helping to create intricate neural spatial maps. MRI scans revealed that the rear (posterior) region of the hippocampus of London taxi drivers was significantly larger than that of participants in a matched control group whose living did not depend on navigational skills (see Figure 6.6 on page 162). In addition, the longer the time spent as a taxi driver, the greater the volume of the posterior hippocampus. Similarly, in many birds and small mammals, the volume of the hippocampus increases seasonally, as navigational skills for migration and spatial maps showing where food is hidden become critical for survival (Clayton, 1998; Colombo & Broadbent, 2000). Moreover, animal studies show that the hippocampus also plays an important role in the reorganization of previously learned spatial information (Lee & Kesner, 2002).

Neuronal Changes in Memory

The first close look at the nature of memory in single neurons was provided by Eric Kandel and his colleagues, who traced the effects of learning and memory in the sea snail *Aplysia* (Dale & Kandel, 1990). Using tiny

hippocampal region
A part of the brain's limbic system, which includes the hippocampus itself (primarily involved in the formation of episodic memories) and its underlying cortical areas (involved in the formation of semantic memories).

> What role do the hippocampus and the rest of the hippocampal region play in episodic and semantic memory?

anterograde amnesia
The inability to form long-term memories of events occurring after a brain injury or brain surgery (although memories formed before the trauma are usually intact).

▼ Mood and memory are correlated: When depressed, people more easily recall negative than positive life events. Memories of negative life events increase feelings of sadness, which, in turn, lead to more memories of negative events. As a result, depression deepens. But deliberate efforts to "think positive" or therapy that helps a person alter negative thoughts can break the mood-memory cycle.

➤ Figure 6.6

MRI Scans Showing the Larger Size of the Posterior Hippocampus in the Brain of an Experienced Taxi Driver

The posterior (rear) hippocampus of an experienced London taxi driver, shown in red in MRI scan (a), is significantly larger than the posterior hippocampus of a research participant who was not a taxi driver, shown in red in scan (b). (Adapted from Maguire et al., 2000.)

(a) (b)

electrodes implanted in several single neurons in the sea snail, the researchers mapped the neural circuits that are formed and maintained as the animal learns and remembers. They also discovered the different types of protein synthesis that facilitate short-term and long-term memory (Sweatt & Kandel, 1989). Kandel won a Nobel Prize in 2000 for his work. But the studies of learning and memory in *Aplysia* reflect only simple classical conditioning, which forms a type of nondeclarative memory. Other researchers studying mammals report that physical changes occur in the neurons and synapses in regions of the brain involved in declarative memory (Lee & Kesner, 2002).

> **What is long-term potentiation, and why is it important?** ➤

Most neuroscientists believe that **long-term potentiation (LTP)**—an increase in the efficiency of neural transmission at the synapses that lasts for hours or longer—is the physiological process that underlies the formation of memories (Bliss & Lomo, 2000; Martinez & Derrick, 1996; Nguyen et al., 1994). (To potentiate means "to make potent or to strengthen.") Research demonstrating that blocking LTP interferes with learning supports their hypothesis. For instance, Davis and colleagues (1992) gave rats enough of a drug that blocks certain receptors to interfere with their performance in a maze-running task and discovered that LTP in the hippocampus of the rats was also disrupted. In contrast, Riedel (1996) found that LTP is enhanced and memory is improved when a drug that excites those same receptors is administered to rats shortly after maze training.

Hormones and Memory

The strongest and most lasting memories are usually those fueled by emotion. Research by Cahill and McGaugh (1995) suggests that there may be two pathways for forming memories—one for ordinary information and another for memories that are fired by emotion. When a person is emotionally aroused, the adrenal glands release the hormones adrenalin (epinephrine) and noradrenaline (norepinephrine) into the bloodstream. Long known to be involved in the "fight or flight" response, these hormones enable humans to survive, and they also help to establish powerful and enduring memories of the circumstances surrounding threatening situations. Such emotionally laden memories activate the amygdala (known to play a central role in emotion) and other parts of the memory system. Emotional memories are lasting memories, and this may be the most important factor in explaining the intensity and durability of flashbulb memories.

> **How do memories of threatening situations that elicit the "fight or flight" response compare with ordinary memories?** ➤

Other hormones may have important effects on memory. Excessive levels of the stress hormone *cortisol,* for example, have been shown to interfere with memory in patients who suffer from diseases of the adrenal glands, the site of cortisol production (Jelicic & Bonke, 2001). Furthermore, people whose bodies react to experimenter-induced stressors, such as forced public speaking, by releasing higher-than-average levels of cortisol perform less well on memory tests than those whose bodies release lower-than-average levels in the same situations (Al'absi et al., 2002).

long-term potentiation (LTP)
A long-lasting increase in the efficiency of neural transmission at the synapses.

Forgetting

Ebbinghaus and the First Experimental Studies on Forgetting

Hermann Ebbinghaus (1850–1909) conducted the first experimental studies on learning and memory. He (1885/1964) conducted his studies on memory using 2,300 *nonsense syllables*–combinations of letters that can be pronounced but have no meaning, such as LEJ, XIZ, LUK, and ZOH–as his material and himself as the only participant. He carried out all of his experiments at about the same time of day in the same surroundings, eliminating all possible distractions. Ebbinghaus memorized lists of nonsense syllables by repeating them over and over at a constant rate of 2.5 syllables per second, marking time with a metronome or a ticking watch. He repeated a list until he could recall it twice without error, a point that he called *mastery*.

Ebbinghaus recorded the amount of time or the number of trials it took to memorize his lists to mastery. Then, after different periods of time had passed and forgetting had occurred to some extent, he recorded the amount of time or number of trials needed to relearn the same list to mastery. Ebbinghaus compared the time or trials required for relearning with those of the original learning and then computed the percentage of time saved–the *savings score*. The percentage of savings represented the percentage of the original learning that remained in memory.

Ebbinghaus learned and relearned more than 1,200 lists of nonsense syllables to discover how rapidly forgetting occurs. Figure 6.7 shows his famous *curve of forgetting*, which consists of savings scores at various time intervals after the original learning. The curve of forgetting shows that the largest amount of forgetting occurs very quickly, but after that forgetting tapers off. If Ebbinghaus retained information as long as a day or two, very little more of it would be forgotten even a month later. When researchers measured psychology students' retention of names and concepts, they found that the pattern of forgetting was similar to Ebbinghaus's curve. Forgetting of names and concepts was rapid over the first several months, leveled off in approximately 36 months, and remained about the same for the next 7 years (Conway et al., 1991).

The Causes of Forgetting

There are many reasons why people fail to remember. Often, however, when people say they cannot remember, they have not actually forgotten. Instead, the inability to remember may be a result of **encoding failure**–the fact that the infor-

> What was Ebbinghaus's major contribution to psychology?

encoding failure
A breakdown in the process by which information enters long-term memory, which results in an inability to recall the information.

> What are six causes of forgetting?

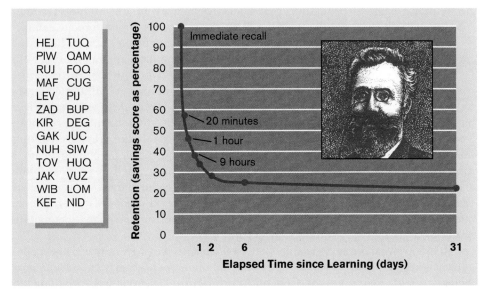

➤ Figure 6.7

Ebbinghaus's Curve of Forgetting

After memorizing lists of nonsense syllables similar to those on the left, Ebbinghaus measured his retention after varying intervals of time using the relearning method. Forgetting was most rapid at first, as shown by his retention of only 58% after 20 minutes and 44% after 1 hour. Then the rate of forgetting tapered off, with a retention of 34% after 1 day, 25% after 6 days, and 21% after 31 days. (Data from Ebbinghaus, 1885/1964.)

decay theory
A theory of forgetting that holds that the neural trace, if not used, disappears with the passage of time.

interference
Memory loss that occurs because information or associations stored either before or after a given memory hinder the ability to recall it.

consolidation failure
Any disruption in the consolidation process that prevents a permanent memory from forming.

mation never entered long-term memory in the first place. For example, when you do *Try It! 6.3*, you might think you have "forgotten" what a penny looks like.

In your lifetime you have seen thousands of pennies, but unless you are a coin collector, you probably have not encoded the details of a penny's appearance. If you did poorly on the *Try It!*, you have plenty of company. After studying a large group of participants, Nickerson and Adams (1979) reported that few people could reproduce a penny from recall. In fact, only a handful of participants could even recognize a drawing of a real penny when it was presented along with incorrect drawings. (The correct penny is the one labeled A in the *Try It!*)

Decay theory, probably the oldest theory of forgetting, assumes that memories, if not used, fade with time and ultimately disappear entirely. The term *decay* implies a change in the "neural trace" or physiological record, of the experience. According to this theory, the neural trace may decay or fade within seconds, days, or much longer periods of time. Most psychologists now accept the notion of decay, or fading of the neural trace, as a cause of forgetting in sensory and short-term memory but not in long-term memory. There does not appear to be a gradual, inevitable decay of the long-term memory trace. In one study, Harry Bahrick and others (1975) found that after 35 years, participants could recognize 90% of their high school classmates' names and photographs—the same percentage as for recent graduates.

A major cause of forgetting that affects people every day is **interference.** Whenever you try to recall any given memory, two types of interference can hinder the effort, as shown in Figure 6.8. *Proactive interference* occurs when information or experiences already stored in long-term memory hinder the ability to remember newer information (Underwood, 1957). For example, Isabel's romance with her new boyfriend, José, got off to a bad start when she accidentally called him Dave, her former boyfriend's name. *Retroactive interference* happens when new learning interferes with the ability to remember previously learned information. The more similar the new learning is to the previous learning, the more interference there is. For example, when you take a psychology class, it may interfere with your ability to remember what you learned in your sociology class, especially with regard to theories (for example, psychoanalytic theory) that are shared by the two disciplines but applied and interpreted differently. To minimize interference, you can follow a learning activity with sleep and arrange learning time so that you do not study similar subjects back to back.

Recall from earlier in the chapter that *consolidation* is the process by which encoded information is stored in memory. When a disruption in this process occurs, a long-term memory usually does not form. **Consolidation failure** can result from anything that

> What is interference, and how can it be minimized? ▶

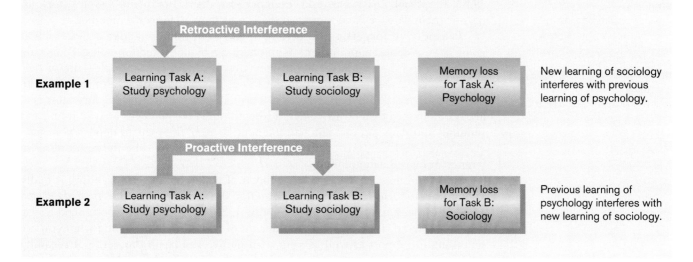

Retroactive Interference

| Example 1 | Learning Task A: Study psychology | Learning Task B: Study sociology | Memory loss for Task A: Psychology | New learning of sociology interferes with previous learning of psychology. |

Proactive Interference

| Example 2 | Learning Task A: Study psychology | Learning Task B: Study sociology | Memory loss for Task B: Sociology | Previous learning of psychology interferes with new learning of sociology. |

➤ **Figure 6.8**

Retroactive and Proactive Interference

As shown in Example 1, retroactive interference occurs when new learning hinders the ability to recall information learned previously. As shown in Example 2, proactive interference occurs when prior learning hinders new learning.

causes a person to lose consciousness—a car accident, intoxication, a blow to the head, a grand mal seizure, or an electroconvulsive shock treatment given for severe depression. Memory loss of the experiences that occurred shortly before the loss of consciousness is called **retrograde amnesia.**

Nader and a team of researchers (Nader et al., 2000) demonstrated that conditioned fears in rats can be erased by infusing into the rats' brains a drug that prevents protein synthesis (such synthesis is necessary for memory consolidation). Rats experienced a single pairing of a tone (the conditioned stimulus) and a foot shock (the unconditioned stimulus). Later, the rats were exposed to the sound of the tone alone (the conditioned stimulus) and showed a fear response of "freezing" (becoming totally immobile as if paralyzed by fright). Clearly, the rats remembered the feared stimulus. Twenty-four hours later, the rats were again exposed to the tone alone, and it elicited fear, causing them to freeze. Immediately, the drug anisomycin, which prevents protein synthesis in the brain, was infused into the rats' amygdala (the part of the brain that processes fear responses). After the drug was infused, the rats were shocked again, but they showed no fear response (freezing) when the tone was sounded. The rats in the study had already consolidated the memory of the fear, but it was completely wiped out after the drug prevented protein synthesis from occurring. This means that fear memories, once activated, must be "reconsolidated," or they may disappear. This finding has positive implications. If fear memories can be activated and then wiped out with drugs that prevent protein synthesis, a new therapy may be on the horizon for people who suffer from debilitating fears (Nader et al., 2000).

Of course, there are occasions when people may prefer to avoid remembering—times when they want to forget. Earlier in the chapter, we discussed the possibility that people may repress memories of traumatic events. But even people who have not suffered severe trauma use **motivated forgetting** to protect themselves from experiences that are painful, frightening, or otherwise unpleasant. With one form of motivated forgetting, known as *suppression,* a person makes a conscious, active attempt to put a painful, disturbing, or anxiety- or guilt-provoking memory out of mind, but the person is still aware that the event occurred. With another type of motivated forgetting—**repression**—unpleasant memories are literally removed from consciousness, and the person is no longer aware that the unpleasant event ever occurred (Freud,

retrograde amnesia
(RET-ro-grade) A loss of memory affecting experiences that occurred shortly before a loss of consciousness.

motivated forgetting
Forgetting through repression in order to protect oneself from a memory that is too painful, anxiety- or guilt-producing, or otherwise unpleasant.

repression
Removing from one's consciousness disturbing, guilt-provoking, or otherwise unpleasant memories so that one is no longer aware that a painful event occurred.

amnesia

A partial or complete loss of memory resulting from brain trauma or psychological trauma.

prospective forgetting

Forgetting to carry out some action, such as mailing a letter.

1922). People who have **amnesia** (memory loss) that is not due to loss of consciousness or brain damage have repressed the events they no longer remember.

Prospective forgetting, forgetting to carry out some intended action—such as going to your dentist appointment—is another type of motivated forgetting. People are most likely to forget to do the things they view as unimportant, unpleasant, or burdensome. They are less likely to forget things that are pleasurable or important to them (Winograd, 1988). However, as you probably know, prospective forgetting isn't always motivated by a desire to avoid something. Have you ever arrived home and suddenly remembered that you had intended to go to the bank to deposit your paycheck? In such cases, prospective forgetting is more likely to be the result of interference or consolidation failure.

Endel Tulving (1974) claims that much of what people call forgetting is really an inability to locate the needed information in memory—as in the *tip-of-the-tongue (TOT) phenomenon* (Brown & McNeil, 1966). Surely you have experienced trying to recall a name, a word, or some other bit of information, knowing what you are searching for almost as well as your own name. You're on the verge of recalling the word or name, perhaps aware of the number of syllables and the beginning or ending letter of the word. It's on the tip of your tongue, but it just won't quite come out.

Improving Memory

Organizing material to be learned is a tremendous aid to memory. One way of organizing a textbook chapter is to make an outline; another is to associate important concepts with the psychologists who proposed or discovered them. You can prove the value of organization as a memory strategy by completing *Try It! 6.4.*

What are four study habits that can aid memory?

Do you still remember the words to songs that were popular when you were in high school? Can you recite many of the nursery rhymes you learned as a child even though you haven't heard them in years? You probably can because of **overlearning.** Research suggests that people remember material better and longer if they overlearn it—that is, if they practice or study beyond the minimum needed to barely learn it (Ebbinghaus, 1885/1964). A pioneering study in overlearning by Krueger (1929) showed substantial long-term gains for participants who engaged in 50% and 100% overlearning (see Figure 6.9). Furthermore, overlearning makes material more resistant to interference and is perhaps the best insurance against stress-related forgetting. So, the next time you study for a test, don't stop studying as soon as you think you know the material. Spend another hour or so going over it, and you will be surprised at how much more you will remember.

What is overlearning, and why is it important?

Most students have tried cramming for examinations, but spacing study over several different sessions is generally more effective than **massed practice**—learning in one long practice session without rest periods (Glover & Corkill, 1987). You will remember more from less total study time if you space your study over several sessions. Long periods of memorizing make material particularly subject to interference and often result in fatigue and lowered concentration. Also, when you space your practice, you probably create a new memory that may be stored in a different place, thus increasing your chance for recall. The spacing effect applies to learning motor skills as well as to learning facts and information. Music students can tell you that it is better to practice for half an hour each day, every day, than to practice many hours in a row once a week.

overlearning

Practicing or studying material beyond the point where it can be repeated once without error.

massed practice

Learning in one long practice session, as opposed to spacing the learning in shorter practice sessions over an extended period.

Many students simply read and reread their textbook and notes when they study for an exam. Research over many years shows that you will recall more if you increase the amount of recitation you use as you study. For example, it is better to read a page or a few paragraphs and then recite what you have just read. Then con-

Try It! 6.4 Organizing for Memory Improvement

Have a pencil and a sheet of paper handy. Read the following list of items out loud and then write down as many as you can remember.

peas	shaving cream	cookies
toilet paper	fish	grapes
carrots	apples	bananas
ice cream	pie	ham
onions	perfume	chicken

If you organize this list, the items are much easier to remember. Now read each category heading and the items listed beneath it. Write down as many items as you can remember.

Desserts	Fruits	Vegetables	Meat	Toilet Articles
pie	bananas	carrots	chicken	perfume
ice cream	apples	onions	fish	shaving cream
cookies	grapes	peas	ham	toilet paper

tinue reading, stop and recite again, and so on. In a classic study, A. I. Gates (1917) tested groups of students who spent the same amount of time in study, but who spent different percentages of that time in recitation and rereading. Participants recalled two to three times more if they increased their recitation time up to 80% and spent only 20% of their study time rereading.

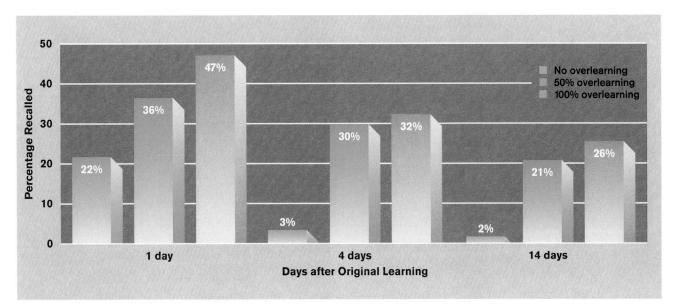

➤ Figure 6.9

Overlearning

When a person learns material only to the point of one correct repetition, forgetting is very rapid. Just 22% is retained after 1 day, 3% after 4 days, and 2% after 14 days. When participants spend 50% more time going over the material, the retention increases to 36% after 1 day, 30% after 4 days, and 21% after 14 days. (Data from Krueger, 1929.)

Writing notes, making lists, writing on a calendar, or keeping an appointment book is often more reliable and accurate than trusting your memory. But what if you need information at some unpredictable time, when you do not have external aids handy? Several *mnemonics,* or memory devices, have been developed over the years to aid memory.

Rhyme Rhymes are a common aid to remembering material that otherwise might be difficult to recall. Perhaps as a child you learned to recite "i before e except after c" when you were trying to spell a word.

The method of loci The *method of loci* is a mnemonic device that can be used when you want to remember a list of items such as a grocery list or when you give a speech and need to make your points in order without using notes. The word *loci* (pronounced LOH-sye) is the plural form of *locus,* which means "location" or "place."

Figure 6.10 shows how to use the method of loci. Select any familiar location—your home, for example—and simply associate the items to be remembered with places there. Begin by picturing the first locus, for example, your driveway; the second locus, your

garage; the third locus, front door step; and the fourth locus, perhaps the front hall closet. Progress through your house from room to room in an orderly fashion. Visualize the first item or idea you want to remember in its place on the driveway, the second item in your garage, the third at your front door, and so on, until you have associated each item you want to remember with a specific place. You may find it helpful to conjure up oversized images of the items that you place at each location. When you want to recall the items, take an imaginary walk starting at the first place—the first item will pop into your

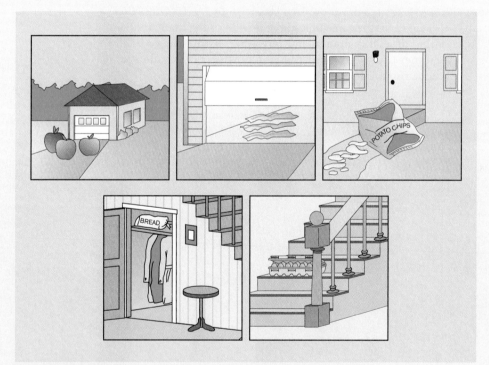

➤ **Figure 6.10**
The Method of Loci
Begin by thinking of locations, perhaps in your home, that are in a sequence. Then visualize one of the items to be remembered in each location.

mind. When you think of the second place, the second item will come to mind, and so on.

The first-letter technique Another useful technique is to take the first letter of each item to be remembered and form a word, a phrase, or a sentence with those letters (Matlin, 1989). For example, suppose you had to memorize the seven colors of the visible spectrum in their proper order:

Red

Orange

Yellow

Green

Blue

Indigo

Violet

You could make this task easier by using the first letter of each color to form the name Roy G. Biv. Three chunks are easier to remember than seven different items.

The pegword system Another mnemonic that has been proven effective is the pegword system (Harris & Blaiser, 1997). Developed in England around 1879, it uses rhyming words: one = bun; two = shoe; three = tree; four = door; five = hive; six = sticks; seven = heaven; eight = gate; nine = wine; ten = hen. The rhyming words are memorized in sequence and then linked through vivid associations with any items you wish to remember in order, as shown in Figure 6.11.

For example, suppose you want to remember to buy five items at the store: milk, bread, grapefruit, laundry

detergent, and eggs. Begin by associating the milk with the bun (your first pegword) by picturing milk pouring over a bun. Next picture the shoe, the second pegword, kicking a loaf of bread. Then continue by associating each item on your list with a pegword. To recall the items, simply go through your list of pegwords and the associated word will immediately come to mind.

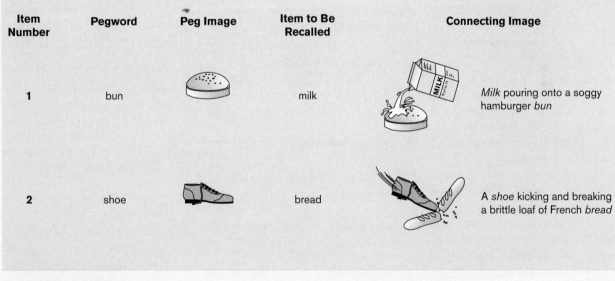

Item Number	Pegword	Peg Image	Item to Be Recalled	Connecting Image
1	bun		milk	*Milk* pouring onto a soggy hamburger *bun*
2	shoe		bread	A *shoe* kicking and breaking a brittle loaf of French *bread*

➤ **Figure 6.11**

The Pegword System

Items to be recalled are each associated with a pegword using a mental image. (Adapted from Bower, 1973.)

Summarize It !

Remembering

➤ **What three processes are involved in the act of remembering?**

Three processes involved in remembering are (1) encoding, or transforming information into a form that can be stored in memory; (2) storage, or maintaining information in memory; and (3) retrieval, or bringing stored material to mind.

➤ **What is sensory memory?**

Sensory memory holds information coming in through the senses for up to several seconds. This is just long enough for the nervous system to begin to process the information and send some of it on to short-term memory.

➤ **What are the characteristics of short-term memory?**

Short-term (or working) memory holds about seven unrelated items of information for less than 30 seconds without rehearsal. Short-term memory also acts as a mental workspace while the person carries out any mental activity.

➤ **What is long-term memory, and what are its subsystems?**

Long-term memory is the permanent or relatively permanent memory system with a virtually unlimited capacity. Its subsystems are (1) declarative memory, which holds facts and information (semantic memory) along with personal life experiences (episodic memory); and (2) nondeclarative memory, which consists of motor skills acquired through repetitive practice, habits, and simple classically conditioned responses.

➤ **What are three kinds of tasks used by psychologists to measure memory retention?**

Three tasks used to measure memory retention are (1) recall, in which information must be supplied with few or no retrieval cues; (2) recognition, in which information must simply be recognized as having been encountered before; and (3) the relearning method, which measures retention in terms of the time saved when relearning material compared with the time required to learn it originally.

KEY TERMS

encoding (p. 150)
storage (p. 150)
retrieval (p. 150)
consolidation (p. 150)
sensory memory (p. 150)
short-term memory (p. 151)
displacement (p. 151)
rehearsal (p. 152)
long-term memory (p. 152)
elaborative rehearsal (p. 152)
declarative memory (p. 153)
episodic memory (p. 153)
semantic memory (p. 153)
nondeclarative memory (p. 153)
levels-of-processing model (p. 153)
recall (p. 154)
retrieval cue (p. 154)
recognition (p. 154)
relearning method (p. 154)

The Nature of Remembering

➤ **What is meant by the statement "Memory is reconstructive in nature"?**

Memory does not work like a video cassette recorder. People reconstruct memories, piecing them together from a few highlights and using information that may or may not be accurate.

➤ **What are schemas, and how do they affect memory?**

Schemas are the integrated frameworks of knowledge that people have about other people, objects, and events. Schemas affect how people encode and recall information.

➤ **What conditions reduce the reliability of eyewitness testimony?**

The reliability of eyewitness testimony is reduced when witnesses view a photograph of the suspect before viewing the lineup, when participants in a lineup are viewed at the same time rather than one by one, when the perpetrator's race is different from that of the eyewitness, when a weapon has been used in the crime, and when leading questions are asked to elicit information.

➤ **What is the controversy regarding the therapy used to recover repressed memories of childhood sexual abuse?**

Critics argue that therapists using hypnosis and guided imagery to help their patients recover repressed memories of childhood sexual abuse are actually implanting false memories in those patients. Therapists who use these techniques believe that a number of psychological problems can be treated successfully by helping patients recover repressed memories of sexual abuse.

➤ **Does hypnosis improve the memory of eyewitnesses?**

Hypnotized subjects supply more information and are more confident of their recollections, but they also supply more inaccurate information.

KEY TERMS

reconstruction (p. 155)
schemas (p. 155)
flashbulb memory (p. 158)

Factors Influencing Retrieval

➤ **What is the serial position effect?**

The serial position effect is the tendency, when recalling a list of items, to remember the items at the beginning of the list (primacy effect) and the items at the end of the list (recency effect) better than items in the middle.

➤ **How does environmental context affect memory?**

People tend to recall material more easily if they are in the same physical location during recall as they were during the original learning.

➤ **What is the state-dependent memory effect?**

The state-dependent memory effect is the tendency to recall information better if one is in the same psychological state as when the information was learned.

KEY TERMS

serial position effect (p. 159)
primacy effect (p. 159)

recency effect (p. 159)
state-dependent memory effect (p. 160)

Biology and Memory

➤ **What role do the hippocampus and the rest of the hippocampal region play in episodic and semantic memory?**

The hippocampus itself is involved primarily in the formation of episodic memories; the rest of the hippocampal region is involved primarily in forming semantic memories.

➤ **What is long-term potentiation, and why is it important?**

Long-term potentiation (LTP) is a long-lasting increase in the efficiency of neural transmission at the synapses in the brain. It may be the physiological basis for learning and memory.

➤ **How do memories of threatening situations that elicit the "fight or flight" response compare with ordinary memories?**

Memories of threatening situations tend to be more powerful and enduring than ordinary memories.

KEY TERMS

hippocampal region (p. 161)
anterograde amnesia (p. 161)
long-term potentiation (LTP) (p. 162)

Forgetting

➤ **What was Ebbinghaus's major contribution to psychology?**

Hermann Ebbinghaus conducted the first experimental studies of learning and memory. He invented the nonsense syllable, conceived the relearning method as a test of memory, and plotted the curve of forgetting.

➤ **What are six causes of forgetting?**

Six causes of forgetting are encoding failure, consolidation failure, decay, interference, motivated forgetting, and retrieval failure.

➤ **What is interference, and how can it be minimized?**

Interference is a memory loss that occurs when information or associations stored either before or after a given memory hinder the ability to recall it. To minimize interference, follow a learning activity with sleep and arrange learning time so that you do not study similar subjects back to back.

KEY TERMS

encoding failure (p. 163)
decay theory (p. 164)
interference (p. 164)
consolidation failure (p. 164)
retrograde amnesia (p. 165)

motivated forgetting (p. 165)
repression (p. 165)
amnesia (p. 166)
prospective forgetting (p. 166)

Improving Memory

➤ **What are four study habits that can aid memory?**

Four study habits that can aid memory are organization, overlearning, spaced practice (rather than massed practice), and recitation (in addition to rereading material).

➤ **What is overlearning, and why is it important?**

Overlearning means practicing or studying material beyond the point where it can be repeated once without error. You remember overlearned material better and longer, and it is more resistant to interference and stress-related forgetting.

KEY TERMS

overlearning (p. 166)
massed practice (p. 166)

Surf It !

Want to be sure you've absorbed the material in Chapter 6, "Memory," before the big test? Visiting **www.ablongman.com/woodmastering1e** can put a top grade within your reach. The site is loaded with free practice tests, flashcards, activities, and links to help you review your way to an A.

Companion Website

Study Guide for Chapter 6 !

Answers to all the Study Guide questions are provided at the end of the book.

Section One: Chapter Review

1. Transforming information into a form that can be stored in memory is called _____; bringing to mind the material that has been stored is called _____ .
   a. encoding; decoding
   b. consolidation; retrieval
   c. consolidation; decoding
   d. encoding; retrieval

2. Match the memory system with the best description of its capacity and the duration of time it holds information:
   ____ (1) sensory memory
   ____ (2) short-term memory
   ____ (3) long-term memory
   a. virtually unlimited capacity; long duration
   b. large capacity; short duration
   c. very limited capacity; short duration

3. Match each example with the appropriate memory system:
   ____ (1) semantic memory
   ____ (2) episodic memory
   ____ (3) nondeclarative memory
   ____ (4) working memory
   a. playing tennis
   b. remembering your high school graduation
   c. deciding what you will do tomorrow
   d. naming the presidents of the United States

4. In which subsystem of long-term memory are responses that make up motor skills stored?
   a. episodic memory
   b. semantic memory
   c. nondeclarative memory
   d. declarative memory

5. Which of the following methods can detect learning when other methods cannot?
   a. recall
   b. recognition
   c. relearning
   d. retrieval

6. Match the example with the corresponding method of measuring retention:
   ____ (1) identifying a suspect in a lineup
   ____ (2) answering a fill-in-the-blank question on a test
   ____ (3) having to study less for a comprehensive final exam than for all of the previous exams put together
   ____ (4) answering questions in this Study Guide
   ____ (5) reciting one's lines in a play
   a. recognition
   b. relearning
   c. recall

7. What early memory researcher proposed the concept of the schema?
   a. Freud
   b. Ebbinghaus
   c. Bartlett
   d. Skinner

8. Which of the following is *not* true of schemas?
   a. Schemas are the integrated frameworks of knowledge and assumptions a person has about people objects, and events.
   b. Schemas affect the way a person encodes information.
   c. Schemas affect the way a person retrieves information.
   d. When a person uses schemas, memories are accurate.

9. There are few errors in eyewitness testimony if
   a. eyewitnesses are identifying a person of their own race.
   b. eyewitnesses view suspects' photos prior to a lineup.
   c. a weapon has been used in the crime.
   d. questions are phrased to provide retrieval cues for the eyewitness.

10. As a rule, people's memories are more accurate under hypnosis. (true/false)

11. When you remember where you were and what you were doing when you received a shocking piece of news, you are experiencing
    a. flashbulb memory.   c. semantic imagery.
    b. sensory memory.   d. interference.

12. When children learn the alphabet, they often learn "A, B, C, D" and "W, X, Y, Z" before learning the letters in between. This is due to the
    a. primacy effect.   c. serial position effect.
    b. recency effect.   d. state-dependent memory.

13. Recall is about as good when people visualize the context in which learning occurred as it is when recall and learning occur in the same context. (true/false)

14. Scores on recognition tests (either multiple-choice or true/false) will be higher if testing and learning take place in the same physical environment. (true/false)

15. Which best explains why information learned when one is feeling anxious is best recalled when experiencing feelings of anxiety?
    a. consistency effect
    b. state-dependent memory effect
    c. context-dependent effect
    d. consolidation failure

16. Compared to nondepressed people, depressed people tend to have more sad memories. (true/false)

17. H.M. retained his ability to add to his nondeclarative memory. (true/false)

18. The hippocampus itself is involved primarily in the formation of _____ memories; the rest of the hippocampal region is involved primarily in the formation of _____ memories.

19. What is the term for the long-lasting increase in the efficiency of neural transmission at the synapses that may be the basis for learning and memory at the level of the neurons?
  a. long-term potentiation
  b. synaptic facilitation
  c. synaptic potentiation
  d. presynaptic potentiation

20. Memories of circumstances surrounding threatening situations that elicit the "fight or flight" response tend to be more powerful and enduring than ordinary memories. (true/false)

21. Who invented the nonsense syllable and plotted the curve of forgetting?
  a. George Sperling   **c.** Frederick Bartlett
  b. H. E. Burtt   **d.** Hermann Ebbinghaus

22. The curve of forgetting shows that memory loss
  a. occurs most rapidly at first and then levels off to a slow decline.
  b. begins to occur about 3 to 4 hours after learning.
  c. occurs at a fairly steady rate over a month's time.
  d. occurs slowly at first and increases steadily over a month's time.

23. Match the example with the appropriate cause of forgetting:
  _____ (1) encoding failure
  _____ (2) consolidation failure
  _____ (3) retrieval failure
  _____ (4) repression
  _____ (5) interference
  a. failing to remember the answer on a test until after you turn in the test
  b. forgetting a humiliating childhood experience
  c. not being able to describe the back of a dollar bill
  d. calling a friend by someone else's name
  e. waking up in the hospital and not remembering you had an automobile accident

24. To minimize interference, it is best to follow learning with
  a. rest.   **c.** sleep.
  b. recreation.   **d.** unrelated study.

25. Most psychologists accept decay theory as a good explanation for the loss of information from long-term memory. (true/false)

26. According to the text, the major cause of forgetting is interference. (true/false)

27. When studying for an exam, it is best to spend
  a. more time reciting than rereading.
  b. more time rereading than reciting.
  c. equal time rereading and reciting.
  d. all of the time reciting rather than rereading.

28. The ability to recite a number of nursery rhymes from childhood is probably due mainly to
  a. spaced practice.   **c.** mnemonics.
  b. organization.   **d.** overlearning.

Section Two: Complete the Diagrams

Fill in the blanks in each diagram with the missing words.

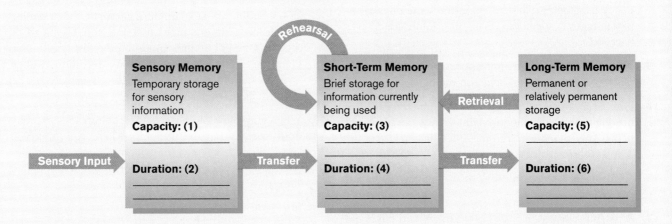

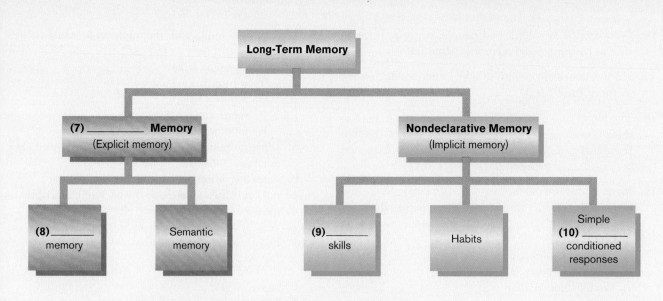

Section Three: Fill In the Blank

1. The first step in the memory process is _____.

2. Short-term memory seems to have a limited life span—less than 30 seconds. If you want to keep a phone number in short-term memory, you will need to use some form of _____, such as repeating the number several times.

3. Another name for short-term memory is _____ memory.

4. When people talk about memory, they are usually talking about _____-term memory.

5. When you take a test in your psychology class, you may be asked to list the names of famous psychologists and their major contributions to psychology. For this task you would use _____ memory.

6. A fill-in-the-blank question requires you to _____ the correct answers.

7. In a list of items, those in the _____ position are the items least easily remembered.

8. The _____ _____ memory effect is the tendency to remember best when in the same physical or psychological state as when the information was encoded.

9. The _____ of the brain appears to be very important in the formation of long-term memory.

10. One theory of memory suggests that neural transmission becomes more efficient at certain synapses along neural paths. This increase in transmission efficiency is known as long-term _____.

11. Strategies or devices used to help memory are called _____.

12. A patient survived delicate brain surgery and displayed no signs of personality change or loss of intelligence.

Days after the surgery, however, the doctor realized that the patient was unable to form long-term memories. He was, however, able to remember everything from before the surgery. The patient was diagnosed as having _____ _____.

13. When Raquel moved to a new town, she had trouble remembering her new zip code. Every time she tried to think of her new zip code, her old zip code seemed to interfere with her recall. This is probably an example of _____ interference.

14. A patient cannot remember the period of his life ranging from age 5 through 7. A doctor can find no physical cause for this amnesia. The patient also has no history of injury or other trauma at any age. This is very likely a case of _____.

15. Serge found himself in trouble during his physics test—he could not remember the formulas from class. He realized that he should have been paying more attention during the lectures. His current memory problem is probably due to _____ failure.

16. Pete started studying for his psychology test six nights ago, spending about 45 minutes per night. Fiona studied for her test all in one night, in a non-stop, 6-hour study session. Pete got a better grade on the test than Fiona. Fiona unfortunately used a study technique called _____ practice, a strategy that is usually not as effective as spacing sessions.

17. When you study for your next psychology test, you may want to study beyond the point where you think you know the material. If you repeat or rehearse the material over and over, you will probably remember it better. This study technique is known as _____.

Section Four: Comprehensive Practice Exam

1. The first step in the memory process is known as _____, when information is transformed into a form that can be stored in short-term memory.
   a. retrieval
   b. storage
   c. encoding
   d. rehearsal

2. The process in which information is stored in permanent memory involves a change in the brain's physiology. This change is known as
   a. consolidation.
   b. transformation.
   c. hippocampal transformation.
   d. recalcitration.

3. You are at a party and meet someone you are really interested in. You get that person's phone number but have no way to write it down, so you use the process of _____ in order to get it into memory.
   a. encoding
   b. latent retrieval
   c. rehearsal
   d. recalcitration

4. The kind of memory that has a large capacity but a very short duration is _____ memory.
   a. short-term
   b. sensory
   c. long-term
   d. temporary

5. Alice's ability to remember all the actions required to ride her motorcycle is due to her repetitive practice, to the point where riding it is almost reflexive. Any set of skills acquired this way is part of _____ memory.

6. Implicit memory is to explicit memory as _____ are to _____.
   a. motor skills; facts and information
   b. episodic memories; semantic memories
   c. semantic memories; episodic memories
   d. facts and information; motor skills

7. Cristina and her friends were talking about some great times they had in high school. Recounting those stories as if they had happened yesterday, the friends were relying on _____ memory.
   a. semantic
   b. implicit
   c. personal
   d. episodic

8. You use _____ memory when you answer questions such as "What is the capital of California?"
   a. episodic
   b. semantic
   c. geographic
   d. flashbulb

9. An example of good recall is doing well on an essay test. (true/false)

10. An example of good recognition ability is doing well on a fill-in-the-blank test. (true/false)

11. Freud did extensive research on memory. He used nonsense syllables to determine forgetting curves. (true/false)

12. When she was 16 years old, Sarah was severely injured in a car accident and was unconscious for 14 days. She can remember nothing immediately preceding the accident. This is known as _____ amnesia.
    a. trauma
    b. retroactive
    c. proactive
    d. retrograde

13. With retroactive interference, _____ information interferes with _____ information.
    a. new; old
    b. old; new
    c. unpleasant; pleasant
    d. factual; emotional

14. Using _____, a person removes an unpleasant memory from consciousness.
    a. regression
    b. traumatic amnesia
    c. repression
    d. degeneration

15. Penfield believed that what patients whose temporal lobes were stimulated experienced were vivid memories; Neisser suggested that these experiences were more like the contents of _____.
    a. flashbulb memories.
    b. repression recall.
    c. dreams.
    d. desires.

16. Psychologists doubt the validity of people's recovered memories of having been abused in infancy because the hippocampal region of the infant brain is not sufficiently developed to form such memories. (true/false)

17. Experts say that overlearning is basically a waste of time–that is, after you have gone over material once, you will not benefit from further study. (true/false)

18. It appears that the _____ is important in the formation of episodic memory.
    a. hippocampus
    b. cerebellum
    c. amygdala
    d. temporal lobe

19. Pablo's vivid memory of the day Princess Diana was killed is known as a _____ memory.
    a. histrionic
    b. flashbulb
    c. semantic
    d. retroactive

20. Eyewitnesses are more likely to identify the wrong person if the person is of a different race. (true/false)

Section Five: Critical Thinking

1. Some studies cited in this chapter involved only one or a few participants.
   a. Select two of these studies and discuss the possible problems in drawing conclusions based on results from so few participants.
   b. Suggest several possible explanations for the findings other than those proposed by the researchers.

2. Drawing on your knowledge, formulate a plan that you can put into operation to help improve your memory and avoid the pitfalls that cause forgetting.

Cognition, Language, and Creativity

Can you imagine a person being able to control an artificial limb almost as precisely as a real limb by using brain power alone? Researcher John Chapin and colleagues (Taylor et al., 2002; Whitehouse, 2000) have accomplished just that. First, researchers used computer-controlled equipment to "record" on a microchip the electrical activity in a motor neuron in the brain of a rat when one of the rat's limbs was moved. Then, duplicate microchips were implanted in the brains of rats in early experiments and in those of humans in later studies. The microchips enabled both rat and human amputees to control robotic limbs, using their own brains, with the same speed and accuracy as they could natural limbs. Moreover, their movement skills improved with practice, just as with natural limbs (König & Verschure, 2002).

- **Imagery and Concepts**
- **Decision Making**
- **Problem Solving**
- **Language**
- **The Nature of Intelligence**
- **Measuring Intelligence**
- **The IQ Controversy**
- **Emotional Intelligence**
- **Creativity**

What is meant by cognition, and what specific processes does it include? ➤

cognition
The mental processes that are involved in acquiring, storing, retrieving, and using information and that include sensation, perception, imagery, concept formation, reasoning, decision making, problem solving, and language.

What is imagery? ➤

imagery
The representation in the mind of a sensory experience—visual, auditory, gustatory, motor, olfactory, or tactile.

concept
A mental category used to represent a class or group of objects, people, organizations, events, situations, or relations that share common characteristics or attributes.

What is a concept? ➤

▼ Many professional athletes use visualization to improve performance.

Clearly, many of the achievements of computer technology are impressive, but can computers really think? The answer hinges, of course, on how *thinking* is defined. Today's supercomputers far outclass any human in mathematical computation and search-and-match activity. But some experts point out that even supercomputers do not really think on their own. After all, computers can do only what human programmers instruct them to do. So the real question is not whether computers think, but what is it about human thinking and intelligence that has allowed us to develop machines that can mimic the mental processes that enable us to acquire, store, and use information—collectively referred to by psychologists as **cognition?**

Imagery and Concepts

Can you imagine hearing a recording of your favorite song or someone calling your name? In doing such a thing, you take advantage of your own ability to use mental **imagery**—that is, to represent or picture a sensory experience. In an early survey of 500 adults conducted by McKellar (1972), 97% said they had visual images; 93% reported auditory images (imagine your psychology professor's voice); 74% claimed to have motor imagery (imagine raising your hand); 70%, tactile or touch images (imagine rubbing sandpaper); 67%, gustatory images (imagine the taste of a dill pickle); and 66%, olfactory images (imagine smelling a rose). Not only can we form a mental image of an object, but we can manipulate and move it around mentally, much as we would if we were actually holding and looking at the object (Cooper & Shepard, 1984; Farah, 1995; Kosslyn & Sussman, 1995).

Studies measuring participants' regional cerebral blood flow (rCBF) while they are engaged in imaging have shown that verbal descriptions of objects activate regions of the brain known to be involved in higher-level visual processing (Mellet et al., 2000). And research examining the brain's responses to stimuli indicate that the same areas are activated when we hear a sound as when we imagine hearing a sound (Cho & Lee, 2001). Brain-imaging studies also show that the same regions in the motor cortex and related areas that are involved in the physical movements required for rotation of objects are very active during mental imaging of such activity, although the cerebellum is more active during actual performance than during visualization (Lotze et al., 1999; Richter et al., 2000).

Fortunately, human thinking is not limited to conjuring up images of sights, sounds, touches, tastes, and smells. We are capable of conceptualizing as well. A **concept** is a mental category used to represent a class or group of objects, people, organizations, events, situations, or relations that share common characteristics or attributes. *Furniture, tree, student, college,* and *wedding* are all examples of concepts. As fundamental units of thought, concepts are useful tools that help us to order our world and to think and communicate with speed and efficiency.

Thanks to our ability to use concepts, we are not forced to consider and describe everything in great detail before we make an identification. If you see a hairy, brown-and-white, four-legged animal with its mouth open, tongue hanging out, and tail wagging, you recognize it immediately as a representative of the concept *dog. Dog* is a concept that stands for a class of animals that share similar characteristics or attributes, even though they may differ in significant ways. Great Danes, dachshunds, collies, Chihuahuas, and other breeds—you recognize all these varied creatures as fitting into the concept *dog.* Moreover, the concepts we form do not exist in isolation, but rather in hierarchies. For example, dogs represent one subset of the concept *animal;* at a higher level, animals are a subset of the concept *living things.* Thus, concept formation has a certain logic to it.

Psychologists identify two basic types of concepts: formal (also known as artificial) concepts and natural (also known as fuzzy) concepts. A **formal concept** is one that is clearly defined by a set of rules, a formal definition, or a classification system. Most of the concepts we form and use are **natural concepts,** acquired not from definitions but

A prototype is an example that embodies the most typical features of a concept. Which of the animals shown here best fits your prototype for the concept *bird*?

through everyday perceptions and experiences. A leading cognition researcher, Eleanor Rosch, and her colleagues studied concept formation in its natural setting and concluded that in real life, natural concepts (such as *fruit, vegetable,* and *bird*) are somewhat fuzzy, not clear-cut and systematic (Rosch, 1973, 1978).

Many formal concepts are acquired in school. For example, we learn that an equilateral triangle is one in which all three sides are the same size. We acquire many natural concepts through experiences with examples, or positive instances of the concept. When children are young, parents may point out examples of a car—the family car, the neighbor's car, cars on the street, and pictures of cars in books. But if a child points to some other type of moving vehicle and says "car," the parent will say, "No, that's a truck," or "This is a bus." *Truck* and *bus* are negative instances, or nonexamples, of the concept *car*. After experience with positive and negative instances of the concept, a child begins to grasp some of the properties of a car that distinguish it from other wheeled vehicles.

How do we use concepts in our everyday thinking? One view suggests that, in using natural concepts, we are likely to picture a **prototype** of the concept—an example that embodies its most common and typical features. Your *bird* prototype is more likely to be robin or a sparrow than either a penguin or a turkey: Those birds can fly, while penguins and turkeys can't. Nevertheless, both penguins and turkeys are birds. So not all examples of a natural concept fit it equally well. This is why natural concepts often seem less clear-cut than formal ones. Nevertheless, the prototype most closely fits a given natural concept, and other examples of the concept most often share more attributes with that prototype than with the prototype of any other concept.

A more recent theory of concept formation suggests that concepts are represented by their **exemplars**—individual instances, or examples, of a concept that are stored in memory from personal experience (Estes, 1994). So, if you work with penguins or turkeys every day, your exemplar of *bird* might indeed be a penguin or a turkey. By contrast, most people encounter robins or sparrows far more often than penguins or turkeys (except the roasted variety!). Thus, for the majority of people, robins or sparrows are exemplars of the *bird* concept.

Decision Making

Decision making is the process of considering alternatives and choosing among them. Decisions are influenced by many factors, including values, interests, life goals, experiences, and knowledge. There are several strategies we use when making decisions.

The Additive Strategy

Suppose you wanted to rent an apartment starting next semester. How would you go about deciding among different apartments? You could use the **additive strategy**—a decision-making approach in which each alternative is rated on each of the

What is the difference between a formal concept and a natural concept?

formal concept
A concept that is clearly defined by a set of rules, a formal definition, or a classification system; also known as an *artificial concept*.

natural concept
A concept acquired not from a definition but through everyday perceptions and experiences; also known as a *fuzzy concept*.

prototype
An example that embodies the most common and typical features of a concept.

exemplars
The individual instances, or examples, of a concept that are stored in memory from personal experience.

decision making
The process of considering alternatives and choosing among them.

additive strategy
A decision-making approach in which each alternative is rated on each important factor affecting the decision and then the alternative rated highest overall is chosen.

How are the additive and elimination strategies used in problem solving?

How do you choose a fast-food restaurant when you want a quick bite? Chances are you use a representativeness heuristic—a prototype that guides your expectations about how long it will take to get your food and what it will taste like. Restaurant chains use the same ingredients and methods at every location to help establish customers' representativeness heuristics for fast-food buying decisions.

heuristic
(yur-RIS-tik) A rule of thumb that is derived from experience and used in decision making and problem solving, even though there is no guarantee of its accuracy or usefulness.

availability heuristic
A cognitive rule of thumb that says that the probability of an event or the importance assigned to it is based on its availability in memory.

representativeness heuristic
A thinking strategy based on how closely a new object or situation is judged to resemble or match an existing prototype of that object or situation.

important factors affecting the decision and the alternative with the highest overall rating is chosen. Two important factors in choosing where to live are location and price. So, your goal would be to find an apartment in a safe location near where you work or attend school that is within your price range.

A variation on the additive strategy is *elimination by aspects* (Tversky, 1972). With this approach, the factors on which the alternatives are to be evaluated are ordered from most important to least important. Any alternative that does not satisfy the most important factor is automatically eliminated. The process of elimination continues as each factor is considered in order. The alternative that survives is the one chosen. For example, if the most important factor for your apartment search was that the maximum rent you could afford was $800 per month, then you would automatically eliminate all the apartments that rented for more than that. Then, if the second most important factor was availability of parking, you would look at the list of apartments that cost $800 or less per month and weed out those without appropriate parking. You would then continue with your third most important factor and so on, until you had trimmed the list down.

Heuristics

Sometimes we make decisions based on **heuristics**—rules of thumb that are derived from experience and used in decision making and problem solving, although there is no guarantee of their accuracy or usefulness. For instance, decision making is quite likely to be influenced by how quickly and easily information affecting or related to the decision comes to mind—that is, how readily available that information is in memory. The cognitive rule of thumb that the probability of an event or the importance assigned to it is based on its availability in memory is known as the **availability heuristic.** Any information affecting a decision, whether it is accurate or not, is more likely to be considered if it is readily available. In 1998, Oprah Winfrey was sued by a group of cattle ranchers for comments made on her show about "mad cow disease" and the possibility that it made eating hamburgers too risky. In other words, the cattle ranchers were blaming Oprah for establishing an availability heuristic that led viewers to decide not to eat their product.

Another common heuristic used in decision making, in judging people, or in predicting the probability of certain events is the representativeness heuristic. The **representativeness heuristic** is a thinking strategy based on how closely a new object or situation is judged to resemble or match an existing prototype of that object or situation (Pitz & Sachs, 1984). The representativeness heuristic is an effective decision-making strategy that can lead to good decisions if the instance selected truly matches the appropriate prototype.

What is the availability heuristic?

What is the representativeness heuristic?

However, the representativeness heuristic can mislead as well. Suppose you were playing a coin-tossing game in which you had to predict whether the outcome of each toss would be heads or tails. Let's say the first five coin tosses came up heads. What would you predict the next toss to be? Many people would predict tails to be more likely on the next toss, because a sample of coin tosses should be approximately 50% heads. Thus, a tail is long overdue, they reason. Nevertheless, the next toss is just as likely to be a head as a tail. After 100 coin tosses, the proportions of heads and tails should be about equal, but for each individual coin toss, the probability still remains 50–50.

Framing

Framing refers to the way information is presented so as to emphasize either a potential gain or a potential loss as the outcome. To study the effects of framing on decision making, Kahneman and Tversky (1984) presented the following options to a group of participants. Which program would you choose?

◄ What is framing?

> The United States is preparing for the outbreak of a dangerous disease, which is expected to kill 600 people. There have been designed two alternative programs to combat the disease. If program A is adopted, 200 people will be saved. If program B is adopted, there is a one-third probability that all 600 will be saved and a two-thirds probability that no people will be saved.

The researchers found that 72% of the participants selected the "sure thing" of program A over the "risky gamble" of program B. Now consider the options as they were reframed:

framing
The way information is presented so as to emphasize either a potential gain or a potential loss as the outcome.

> If program C is adopted, 400 people will die. If program D is adopted, there is a one-third probability that nobody will die and a two-thirds probability that all 600 people will die.

Which program did you choose? Of research participants given this version of the problem, 78% chose program D. A careful reading will reveal that program D has exactly the same consequences as program B in the earlier version. How can this result be explained? The first version of the problem was framed to focus attention on the number of lives that could be saved. And when people are primarily motivated to achieve gains (save lives), they are more likely to choose a safe option over a risky one, as 72% of the participants did. The second version was framed to focus attention on the 400 lives that would be lost. When trying to avoid losses, people appear much more willing to choose a risky option, as 78% of the participants were.

Framing has numerous practical applications to decision making. Customers are more readily motivated to buy products if they are on sale than if they are simply priced lower than similar products to begin with. As a result, customers focus on what they save (a gain) rather than on what they spend (a loss). People seem more willing to purchase an $18,000 car and receive a $1,000 rebate (a gain) than to simply pay $17,000 for the same car. Heuristics can be effective and efficient cognitive techniques, but they can also lead to errors in perceptions and decisions.

Problem Solving

We all face problems–great and small–that we must solve. **Problem solving** refers to thoughts and actions required to achieve a desired goal that is not readily attainable. How would you go about solving the problem described in *Try It!* 7.1 (on page 182)?

How did you choose to solve the *Try It!* problem? Some people examine the problem carefully and devise a strategy–such as placing the 1 or the 7 in the middle box because each has only one forbidden consecutive number (2 or 6) to avoid. Many people, however, simply start placing the numbers in the boxes and then change them around when a combination doesn't work. This approach, called **trial and error,** involves trying one solution after another, in no particular order, until hitting

problem solving
Thoughts and actions required to achieve a desired goal that is not readily attainable.

trial and error
An approach to problem solving in which one solution after another is tried in no particular order until an answer is found.

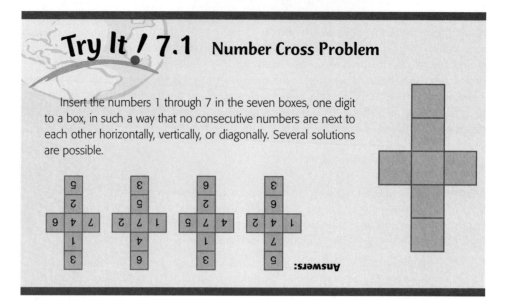

Try It! 7.1 Number Cross Problem

Insert the numbers 1 through 7 in the seven boxes, one digit to a box, in such a way that no consecutive numbers are next to each other horizontally, vertically, or diagonally. Several solutions are possible.

Answers:

on the answer by chance. Even nonhuman animals use trial and error. However, other techniques are far more effective and less time-consuming.

Another major problem-solving method is the algorithm (Newell & Simon, 1972). An **algorithm** is a systematic, step-by-step procedure that guarantees a solution to a problem of a certain type if the algorithm is appropriate and is executed properly. Formulas used in mathematics and sciences are algorithms. Another type of algorithm is a systematic strategy for exploring every possible solution to a problem until the correct one is reached. In some cases, millions or even billions or more possibilities may have to be considered before the solution is found. Computers are programmed to solve many problems using algorithms because, with a computer, an accurate solution is guaranteed and millions of possible solutions can be tried in a few seconds.

Many problems do not lend themselves to solution by algorithms, however. Suppose you were a contestant on *Wheel of Fortune,* trying to solve this missing-letter puzzle:

P _ Y _ _ _ L _ _ Y.

An exhaustive search algorithm would be out of the question—even Vanna White's smile would fade long before the nearly 9 billion possibilities could be considered. An easier way to solve such problems is by using a heuristic. Using a heuristic does not guarantee success but offers a promising way to attack a problem and arrive at a solution. The missing-letter puzzle is easily solved through a simple heuristic that makes use of your existing knowledge of words (prefixes, roots, suffixes). You can supply the missing letters and spell out PSYCHOLOGY.

One heuristic that is effective for solving some problems is **working backwards,** sometimes called the *backward search.* This approach starts with the solution, a known condition, and works back through the problem. Once the backward search has revealed the steps to be taken and their order, the problem can be solved. Try working backwards to solve the water lily problem in *Try It! 7.2.*

Another popular heuristic strategy is **means–end analysis,** in which the current position is compared with a desired goal, and a series of steps is formulated and then taken to close the gap between the two (Sweller & Levine, 1982). Many problems are large and complex and must be broken down into smaller steps or subproblems before a solution can be reached. If your professor assigns a term paper, for example, you probably do not simply sit down and write it. You must first determine how you will approach the topic, research the topic, make an outline, and then write the sections over a period of time. At last, you will be ready to assemble the complete term paper, write several drafts, and put the finished product in final form before handing it in and receiving your A.

What is an algorithm? ▶

algorithm
A systematic, step-by-step procedure, such as a mathematical formula, that guarantees a solution to a problem of a certain type if applied appropriately and executed properly.

working backwards
A heuristic strategy in which a person discovers the steps needed to solve a problem by defining the desired goal and working backwards to the current condition; also called *backward search.*

What are three heuristics used in problem solving? ▶

means–end analysis
A heuristic strategy in which the current position is compared with the desired goal and a series of steps are formulated and taken to close the gap between them.

182

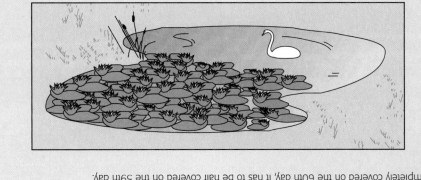

Try It! 7.2 Water Lily Problem

Water lilies double the area they cover every 24 hours. At the beginning of the summer there is one water lily on a pond. It takes 60 days for the pond to become covered with water lilies. On what day is the pond half covered? (From Fixx, 1978.)

Answer: The most important fact is that the lilies double in number every 24 hours. If the pond is to be completely covered on the 60th day, it has to be half covered on the 59th day.

The **analogy heuristic**–applying a solution used for a past problem to a current problem that has many similar features–is another problem-solving strategy. Situations with many features in common are said to be *analogous*. When faced with a new problem to solve, you can look for commonalities between the new problem and problems you have solved before and then apply a strategy similar to one that has worked in the past. For example, if your car is making strange sounds and you take it to an auto mechanic, the mechanic may be able to diagnose the problem by analogy–the sounds your car is making are comparable to sounds heard before and associated with a particular problem.

analogy heuristic
A rule of thumb that applies a solution that solved a problem in the past to a current problem that shares many features with the past problem.

Impediments to Problem Solving

Sometimes we face problems that seem to defy solution despite our best efforts. We lack the relevant knowledge or experience to solve some problems and have insufficient material resources to solve others. In some cases, though, we are hampered in our efforts to solve problems in daily life because of **functional fixedness**–the failure to use familiar objects in novel ways to solve problems. We tend to see objects only in terms of their customary functions. Just think of all the items you use daily–tools, utensils, and other equipment–that help you perform certain functions. Often, the normal functions of such objects become fixed in your thinking so that you do not consider using them in new and creative ways.

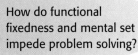
How do functional fixedness and mental set impede problem solving?

Suppose you wanted a cup of coffee, but the glass carafe for your coffeemaker was broken. If you suffered from functional fixedness, you might come to the conclusion that there was nothing you could do to solve your problem at that moment. But, rather than thinking about the object or utensil that you don't have, think about the function that it needs to perform. What you need is something to catch the coffee, not necessarily the specific type of glass carafe that came with the coffeemaker. Could you catch the coffee in a bowl or cooking utensil, or even in coffee mugs?

Another impediment to problem solving, similar to functional fixedness but much broader, is mental set. **Mental set** is a mental rut in one's approach to solving problems, the tendency to continue to use the same old method even though another approach might be better. Perhaps you hit on a way to solve a problem once in the

functional fixedness
The failure to use familiar objects in novel ways to solve problems because of a tendency to view objects only in terms of their customary functions.

mental set
The tendency to apply a familiar strategy to the solution of a problem without carefully considering the special requirements of that problem.

> Many of us are hampered in our efforts to solve problems in daily life because of functional fixedness—the failure to use familiar objects in novel ways to solve problems.

artificial intelligence
The programming of computer systems to simulate human thinking in solving problems and in making judgments and decisions.

past and continue to use the same technique in similar situations, even though it is not highly effective or efficient. People are much more susceptible to mental set when they fail to consider the special requirements of a problem. Not surprisingly, the same people who are subject to mental set are also more likely to have trouble with functional fixedness when they attempt to solve problems (McKelvie, 1984).

Artificial Intelligence and Robotics

Artificial intelligence, or AI, refers to the programming of computer systems to simulate human thinking in solving problems and in making judgments and decisions. However, computers cannot, as humans can, take exceptions into account, consider the context, or make countless other interpretations as they "think." They cannot execute many of the tasks that humans perform with ease, such as recognizing a particular face or interpreting a slurred, indistinct word in a conversation (Lenat, 1995).

What is artificial intelligence?

Researchers hope to make artificial intelligence programs that will more closely approximate human thinking by devising computer systems based on an understanding of how neurons in certain parts of the brain are connected and how the connections develop (Buonomano & Merzenich, 1995; Hinton et al., 1995). Computer systems that are intended to mimic the human brain are called **neural networks.** Like those in the brain, connections in a computer neural network can be strengthened or weakened as a result of experience. Computer-based voice recognition systems used in a variety of commercial settings are supported by such neural networks. But unlike humans, such computer systems cannot understand the subtleties of language—tone of voice, quality of nonverbal behavior, or even level of politeness (Peterson, 1993).

▼ Chess champion Garry Kasparov contemplates a move against Deep Blue, an IBM computer that exhibits artificial intelligence in the area of top-level chess play.

One area in which human cognition has been applied to develop technological marvels is **robotics**—the science of automating human and animal functions. In some cases, robotics have made it possible to manipulate variables in experiments that previously could be investigated only in correlational studies. Scientists studying the mating behavior of bowerbirds, for example, observed the females of the species repeatedly crouching during the attraction phase of mating (Patricelli et al., 2002). To examine the crouching variable in an experiment, they built a robotic version of a female bowerbird whose crouching actions could be remotely controlled. By systematically exposing male bowerbirds to crouching and noncrouching behavior and by varying the amount and frequency of crouching, they

were able to learn that males use females' crouching behavior as cues to initiate displays of their colorful plumage.

Experiments involving robotic birds may seem far removed from any kind of practical application. However, projects such as this one help scientists and engineers learn more about how to build and program robots to behave much like their living counterparts. Consequently, the technology needed to use robotics to improve human life is expanded. Indeed, the potential for robotics to improve life is tremendous—the robotic limbs described at the beginning of the chapter are just one example.

Language

Language is a means of communicating thoughts and feelings, using a system of socially shared but arbitrary symbols (sounds, signs, or written symbols) arranged according to rules of grammar. Language expands our ability to think because it allows us to consider abstract concepts—such as justice—that are not represented by physical objects. Further, thanks to language, we can share our knowledge and thoughts with one another in an extremely efficient way. Thus, whether spoken, written, or signed, language is our most important cognitive tool. In Chapter 8, we will discuss how language is acquired by infants. Here, we explore the components and the structure of this amazing form of human communication.

The Structure of Language

Psycholinguistics is the study of how language is acquired, produced, and used and how the sounds and symbols of language are translated into meaning. Psycholinguists use specific terms for each of the five basic components of language.

The smallest units of sound in a spoken language—such as *b* or *s* in English—are known as **phonemes.** Three phonemes together form the sound of the word *cat: c* (which sounds like *k*), *a*, and *t*. Combinations of letters that form particular sounds are also phonemes, such as the *th* in *the* and the *ch* in *child.* The same phoneme may be represented by different letters in different words; this occurs with the *a* in *stay* and the *ei* in *sleigh.* And the same letter can serve as different phonemes. The letter *a*, for example, is sounded as four different phonemes in *day, cap, watch,* and *law.*

Morphemes are the smallest units of meaning in a language. A few single phonemes serve as morphemes, such as the article *a* and the personal pronoun *I.* The ending *-s* gives a plural meaning to a word and is thus a morpheme in English. Many words in English are single morphemes—*book, word, learn, reason,* and so on. In addition to root words, morphemes may also be prefixes (such as *re-* in *relearn*) or suffixes (such as *-ed* to show past tense, as in *learned*). The single morpheme *reason* becomes a dual morpheme in *reasonable.* The morpheme *book* (singular) becomes two morphemes in *books* (plural).

Syntax is the aspect of grammar that specifies the rules for arranging and combining words to form phrases and sentences. The rules of word order, or syntax, differ from one language to another. For example, an important rule of syntax in English is that adjectives usually come before nouns. So English speakers refer to the residence of the U.S. President as "the White House." In Spanish, in contrast, the noun usually comes before the adjective, and Spanish speakers say *"la Casa Blanca,"* or "the House White."

Semantics refers to the meaning derived from morphemes, words, and sentences. The same word can have different meanings depending on how it is used in sentences: "I don't mind." "Mind your manners." "He has lost his mind." Or consider another example: "Loving to read, the young girl read three books last week." Here, the word *read* is pronounced two different ways and, in one case, is the past tense.

Finally, **pragmatics** is the term psycholinguists use to refer to aspects of language such as *intonation,* the rising and falling patterns that are used to express meaning. For

neural networks
Computer systems that are intended to mimic the human brain.

robotics
The science of automating human and animal functions.

language
A means of communicating thoughts and feelings, using a system of socially shared but arbitrary symbols (sounds, signs, or written symbols) arranged according to rules of grammar.

What are the five basic components of language?

psycholinguistics
The study of how language is acquired, produced, and used and how the sounds and symbols of language are translated into meaning.

phonemes
The smallest units of sound in a spoken language.

morphemes
The smallest units of meaning in a language.

syntax
The aspect of grammar that specifies the rules for arranging and combining words to form phrases and sentences.

semantics
The meaning or the study of meaning derived from morphemes, words, and sentences.

pragmatics
The patterns of intonation and social roles associated with a language.

example, think about how you would say the single word *cookie* to express each of the following meanings: "Do you want a cookie?" or "What a delicious looking cookie!" or "That's a cookie." The subtle differences reflect your knowledge of the pragmatic rules of English; for example, questions end with a rising intonation, while statements end with a falling intonation. Pragmatic rules also come into play when you speak in one way to your friend and another to your professor. That is, the social rules associated with language use are also included in pragmatics.

Animal Language

How does language in trained chimpanzees differ from human language?

Ask people what capability most reliably sets humans apart from all other animal species, and most will answer language. And for good reason. As far as scientists know, humans are the only species to have developed this rich, varied, and complex system of communication. As early as 1933 and 1951, researchers attempted to teach chimpanzees to speak by raising the chimps in their homes. These experiments failed because the vocal tract in chimpanzees and the other apes is not adapted to human speech, so researchers turned to sign language. Psychologists Allen and Beatrix Gardner (1969) took in a 1-year-old chimp named Washoe and taught her sign language. Washoe learned signs for objects and certain commands, such as *flower, give me, come, open,* and *more.* By the end of her fifth year, she had mastered about 160 signs (Fleming, 1974).

Psychologist David Premack (1971) taught another chimp, Sarah, to use an artificial language he developed. Its symbols consisted of magnetized chips of various shapes, sizes, and colors, as shown in Figure 7.1. Premack used operant conditioning techniques to teach Sarah to select the magnetic chip representing a fruit and place it on a magnetic language board. The trainer would then reward Sarah with the fruit she had requested. Sarah mastered the concepts of similarities and differences, and eventually she could signal whether two objects were the same or different with nearly perfect accuracy (Premack & Premack, 1983). Even more remarkable, Sarah could view a whole apple and a cut apple and, even though she had not seen the apple being cut, could match the apple with the utensil needed to cut it—a knife.

At the Yerkes Primate Research Center at Emory University, a chimp named Lana participated in a computer-controlled language training program. She learned to press keys imprinted with geometric symbols that represented words in an artificial language called Yerkish. Researcher Sue Savage-Rumbaugh and a colleague (1986; Rumbaugh, 1977) varied the location, color, and brightness of the keys, so Lana had to learn which symbols to use no matter where they were located. One day, her trainer Tim had an orange that she wanted. Lana had available symbols for many fruits—apple, banana, and so on—but none for an orange. Yet there was a symbol for the color orange. So Lana improvised and signaled, "Tim give apple which is orange." Impressive!

But was humanlike language being displayed in these studies with primates? Not according to Herbert Terrace (1979, 1981), who examined the research of others and conducted his own. Terrace and coworkers taught sign language to a chimp they called Nim Chimpsky (after the famed linguist Noam Chomsky) and reported Nim's progress from the age of 2 weeks to 4 years. Nim learned 125 symbols, which is respectable, but does not amount to language, according to Terrace (1985, 1986). Terrace believed that chimps like Nim and Washoe were simply imitating their trainers

➤ Figure 7.1

Sarah's Symbols

A chimpanzee named Sarah learned to communicate using plastic chips of various shapes, sizes, and colors to represent words in an artificial language developed by her trainer, David Premack. (From Premack, 1971.)

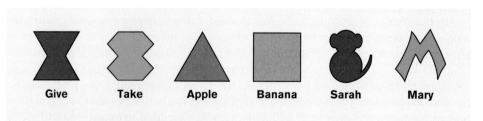

Give   Take   Apple   Banana   Sarah   Mary

and making responses to get reinforcers, according to the laws of operant conditioning, not the laws of language. Finally, Terrace suggested that the studies with primates were probably influenced by experimenter bias; trainers might unconsciously tend to interpret the behavior of the chimps as more indicative of progress toward developing language than it really was. However, Terrace had not heard of Kanzi when he expressed his skepticism.

From their studies of communication among chimps and other animals, researchers have gained useful insights into the nature of language. The pygmy chimp Kanzi became skilled at using a special symbol board to communicate.

The most impressive performance in language training so far is that of a pygmy chimpanzee, Kanzi, who developed an amazing ability to communicate with his trainers without any formal training. During the mid-1980s, researchers had taught Kanzi's mother to press symbols representing words. Her progress was not remarkable; but her infant son Kanzi, who stood by and observed her during training, was learning rapidly (thanks to observational learning, discussed in Chapter 5). When Kanzi had a chance at the symbol board, his performance quickly surpassed that of his mother and of every other chimp the researchers had tested.

Kanzi demonstrated an advanced understanding (for chimps) of spoken English and could respond correctly even to new commands, such as "Throw your ball to the river," or "Go to the refrigerator and get out a tomato" (Savage-Rumbaugh, 1990; Savage-Rumbaugh et al., 1992). By the time Kanzi was 6 years old, a team of researchers who worked with him had recorded more than 13,000 "utterances" and reported that Kanzi could communicate using some 200 different geometric symbols (Gibbons, 1991). Kanzi could press symbols to ask someone to play chase with him and even ask two others to play chase while he watched. And if Kanzi signaled someone to "chase" and "hide," he was insistent that his first command, "chase," be done first (Gibbons, 1991). Kanzi was not merely responding to nearby trainers whose actions or gestures he might have copied. He responded just as well when requests were made over earphones so that no one else in the room could signal to him purposely or inadvertently.

Do such seemingly remarkable feats indicate that chimps are capable of using anything close to human language? Impressive as Kanzi's accomplishments seem to be, Premack firmly maintains that it is unlikely that animals are capable of language. They can be taught to signal, to choose, and to solve some problems, but mere strings of words spoken, written, or signed do not amount to language unless they are structured grammatically.

Most animal species studied by language researchers are limited to motor responses such as sign language, gestures, using magnetic symbols, or pressing keys on symbol boards. But these limitations do not extend to some bird species such as parrots, which are capable of making humanlike speech sounds. One remarkable case is Alex, an African gray parrot that not only mimics human speech but seems to do so intelligently. Able to recognize and name various colors, objects, and shapes, Alex answers questions about them in English. Asked "Which object is green?" Alex easily names the green object (Pepperberg, 1991, 1994b). And he can count as well. When asked such questions as "How many red blocks?" Alex answers correctly about 80% of the time (Pepperberg, 1994a).

Research with sea mammals such as whales and dolphins has established that they apparently use complicated systems of grunts, whistles, clicks, and other sounds to communicate within their species (Herman, 1981; Savage-Rumbaugh, 1993). Researchers at the University of Hawaii have trained dolphins to respond to fairly complex commands requiring an understanding of directional and relational concepts. Dolphins can learn to pick out an object and put it on the right or left of a basket, for example, and comprehend such commands as "in the basket" and "under the basket" (Chollar, 1989).

Language and Thinking

If language is unique to humans, then does it drive human thinking? Does the fact that you speak English mean that you reason, think, and perceive your world differently than does someone who speaks Spanish, or Chinese, or Swahili? According to one hypothesis pre-

In general, does thought influence language more, or does language influence thought more?

linguistic relativity hypothesis
The notion that the language a person speaks largely determines the nature of that person's thoughts.

sented about 50 years ago, it does. Benjamin Whorf (1956) put forth his **linguistic relativity hypothesis,** suggesting that the language a person speaks largely determines the nature of that person's thoughts. According to this hypothesis, people's worldview is constructed primarily by the words in their language. As proof, Whorf offered his classic example. The languages used by the Eskimo people have a number of different words for snow–"*apikak,* first snow falling; *aniv,* snow spread out; *pukak,* snow for drinking water"–while the English-speaking world has but one word, *snow* (Restak, 1988, p. 222). Whorf claimed that such a rich and varied selection of words for various snow types and conditions enabled Eskimos to think differently about snow than do people whose languages lack such a range of words.

Eleanor Rosch (1973) tested whether people whose language contains many names for colors would be better at thinking about and discriminating among colors than people whose language has only a few color names. Her participants were English-speaking Americans and the Dani, members of a remote tribe in New Guinea whose language has only two names for colors–*mili* for dark, cool colors and *mola* for bright, warm colors. Rosch showed members of both groups single-color chips of 11 colors–black, white, red, yellow, green, blue, brown, purple, pink, orange, and gray–for 5 seconds each. Then, after 30 seconds, she had the participants select the 11 colors they had viewed from an assortment of 40 color chips. Did the Americans outperform the Dani participants, for whom brown, black, purple, and blue are all *mili,* or dark? No. Rosch found no significant differences between the Dani and the Americans in discriminating, remembering, or thinking about those 11 basic colors. Rosch's study did not support the linguistic relativity hypothesis.

Clearly, however, it would be a mistake to go too far in the opposite direction and assume that language has no influence on how people think. Thought both influences and is influenced by language, and language appears to reflect cultural differences more than it determines them (Pinker, 1994; Rosch, 1987). For example, consider the generic use of the pronoun *he* to refer to people in general. If your professor says, "I expect each student in this class to do the best he can," does this announcement mean the same to males and females? Not according to research conducted by Gastil (1990), in which participants read sentences worded in three different forms. Perform Gastil's experiment yourself by completing *Try It! 7.3.*

Whether you are male or female, the odds are high that you imaged a male after reading the first sentence in the *Try It!* Other studies confirm that the generic *he* is not interpreted very generically. It is interpreted heavily in favor of males (Hamilton, 1988; Henley, 1989; Ng, 1990). If this were not the case, the following sentence would not seem unusual at all: Like other mammals, man bears his offspring live.

Bilingualism

Most native-born Americans speak only one language, English. But a sizeable minority are *bilingual,* that is, they speak both English and another language. Indeed, in the United States today, there are between 30 and 35 million people aged 5 and older for

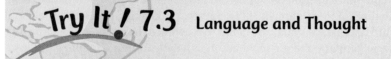

Try It! 7.3 Language and Thought

After reading each of these three sentences, pause and jot down any image that comes to mind.

1. The average American believes he watches too much television.

2. The average American believes he/she watches too much television.

3. Average Americans believe they watch too much television.

whom English is a second language. Among the languages spoken at home by these people, Spanish is by far the leader (used by 17–18 million people). Following Spanish, other languages spoken in many U.S. homes are French (by under 2 million people), German (a little over 1.5 million), Italian (1.4 million), and Chinese (1.3 million) (U.S. Bureau of the Census, 2001).

Most linguists are convinced that being bilingual has many advantages (Genesee, 1994). For example, in Canada, where most students study both French and English, bilingual students are said to score higher on aptitude and math tests than their counterparts who speak only one language (Lambert et al., 1993). But what about the effect of learning two languages on the process of language development itself? (You'll learn more about the basic process in Chapter 8.) Research suggests that there are both advantages and disadvantages to learning two languages early in life.

◄ What are the advantages and disadvantages of bilingualism in childhood?

One of the benefits is that, among preschool and school-age children, bilingualism is associated with better *metalinguistic skills,* the capacity to think about language (Bialystok et al., 2000; Mohanty & Perregaux, 1997). In addition, most bilingual children display greater ability than monolingual children in focusing attention on language tasks (Bialystok & Majumder, 1998). And bilingual children seem to more easily grasp the connection between sounds and symbols than do their monolingual peers (Bialystok, 1997; Oller et al., 1998).

On the downside, infants in bilingual homes reach some milestones later than those learning a single language. For example, bilingual infants' vocabularies are as large as those of monolingual infants, but the words they know are divided between two languages (Patterson, 1998). Consequently, they are behind monolingual infants in word knowledge, no matter which language is considered, a difference that persists into the school years. And even in adulthood, bilingualism is sometimes associated with decreased efficiency in memory tasks involving words (Gollan & Silverberg, 2001; McElree et al., 2000). However, bilinguals appear to develop compensatory strategies that allow them to make up for these inefficiencies. Consequently, bilinguals often perform such memory tasks just as accurately as monolinguals do, though they may respond more slowly.

Research further indicates that bilingual children who are equally fluent in both of their languages encounter few, if any, learning problems in school (Vuorenkoski et al., 2000). Similarly, teens and adults who are equally fluent in two languages demonstrate few, if any, differences in efficiency of verbal memory (McElree et al., 2000). However, most children do not attain equal fluency in both languages. As a result, they tend to think more slowly in the language in which they have lower fluency (Chincotta & Underwood, 1997). When the language in which they are less fluent is the language in which they are schooled, they are at risk for learning problems (Thorn & Gathercole, 1999). Further, in adulthood, these "unbalanced" bilinguals are more likely than monolinguals or bilinguals with equal fluency in both languages to display reduced speed and accuracy on verbal memory tasks (McElree et al., 2000).

The one clear advantage to learning two languages earlier in life is that people who are younger when they learn a second language are far more likely to be able to speak it with an appropriate accent (McDonald, 1997). One reason for this difference between early and late language learners may have to do with slight variations in neural processing in Broca's area, the area of the brain that controls speech production. Research by Kim and others (1997) suggests that bilinguals who learned their second language early (younger than age 10 or 11)

▼ Growing up in a bilingual home provides distinct advantages in adolescence and adulthood. Spanish and English are the languages spoken by the majority of bilinguals in the United States.

rely on the same patch of tissue in Broca's area for both of the languages they speak. But in bilinguals who were older when they learned their second language, two different sections of Broca's area are active while language tasks are being performed—one section for the first language learned and another for the second. Yet the two sections are very close, only ⅓ inch apart.

Language and the Brain

What parts of the brain are key in processing language? Paulesu and colleagues (2000) used PET (positron emission tomography) scans to view activity in areas of the brains of Italian and English speakers while they read aloud a list of words and nonwords. The PET scans of all participants in this study revealed heightened activity in a widespread area of the brain known to be associated with reading, as was expected. But the new information that the researchers uncovered is that the brain activity in three regions varied according to the speaker's native language. Compared with the English speakers, the Italian speakers showed greater brain activity in an upper area of the left temporal lobe when reading words and nonwords. English speakers showed increased brain activity in the left frontal lobe and in an upper region of the left temporal lobe when reading nonwords. The researchers explained the cross-linguistic difference in terms of characteristics of the two languages. Italian has few spelling inconsistencies; a particular combination of letters almost always represents the same sound. By contrast, English includes many combinations of letters—such as *ough*—that can have several different pronunciations (*cough, bough, though,* and so on). Consequently, processing written language requires the involvement of different brain areas in the two languages.

But what about semantics and syntax? Two brain areas that are important for processing these aspects of language are Broca's area and Wernicke's area (which you learned about in Chapter 2). The role of Broca's area was long believed to be largely restricted to the physical production of speech. But a recent brain-imaging study (Ni et al., 2000) revealed that Broca's area was highly activated when participants were processing errors in syntax, such as the wrong usage in the sentence "Trees can grew." Other research has confirmed the role of Broca's area in syntactic processing (Dogil et al., 2002). Further, both Wernicke's area and part of the cerebellum are activated when people make judgments about the grammatical characteristics of language.

The Nature of Intelligence

The Search for a Useful Definition of Intelligence

First, let's ask the most obvious question: What is intelligence? A task force of experts from the American Psychological Association (APA) defined **intelligence** as an individual's "ability to understand complex ideas, to adapt effectively to the environment, to learn from experience, to engage in various forms of reasoning, and to overcome obstacles by taking thought" (Neisser et al., 1996, p. 77). Nevertheless, no concept in psychology has been at the center of more public policy debates and more scientific disagreement than intelligence (Moffitt et al., 1993). Is intelligence a single, general capability, or are there multiple types of intelligence? Is intelligence influenced more by heredity or by environment? Is it fixed or changeable, culture-free or culture-bound? The nature of intelligence continues to be hotly debated.

English psychologist Charles Spearman (1863–1945) observed that people who are bright in one area are usually bright in other areas as well. In other words, they tend to be generally intelligent. Spearman (1927) came to believe that intelligence is composed of a general ability that underlies all intellectual functions. Spearman concluded that intelligence tests tap this ***g* factor,** or general intelligence, and a number of *s* factors, or specific intellectual abilities. Spearman's influ-

intelligence
An individual's ability to understand complex ideas, to adapt effectively to the environment, to learn from experience, to engage in various forms of reasoning, and to overcome obstacles through mental effort.

***g* factor**
Spearman's term for a general intellectual ability that underlies all mental operations to some degree.

ence can be seen in those intelligence tests, such as the Stanford–Binet, that yield one IQ score to indicate the level of general intelligence.

Another early researcher in testing, Louis L. Thurstone (1938), rejected Spearman's notion of general intellectual ability, or *g* factor. After analyzing the scores of many participants on some 56 separate ability tests, Thurstone identified seven **primary mental abilities:** verbal comprehension, numerical ability, spatial relations, perceptual speed, word fluency, memory, and reasoning. He maintained that all intellectual activities involve one or more of these primary mental abilities. Thurstone and his wife, Thelma G. Thurstone, developed their Primary Mental Abilities Tests to measure these seven abilities. Thurstone believed that a single IQ score obscured more than it revealed. He suggested that a profile showing relative strengths and weaknesses on the seven primary mental abilities would provide a more accurate picture of a person's intelligence.

Some theorists, instead of searching for the factors that underlie intelligence, propose that there are different types of intelligence. For example, Harvard psychologist Howard Gardner (1983) denies the existence of a *g* factor. Instead he proposes eight independent and equally important forms of intelligence, as shown in Figure 7.2. Gardner's theory "has enjoyed wide popularity, especially among educators, but [his] ideas are based more on reasoning and intuition than on the results of empirical research studies" (Aiken, 1997, p. 196). Still, Gardner's theory has provided psychologists, educators, and others who are interested in intelligence with a helpful way of describing and discussing the varying kinds of abilities people have.

Psychologist Robert Sternberg (1985a, 1986a) has formulated a **triarchic theory of intelligence,** which, as the term *triarchic* implies, proposes that there are three types of intelligence, as shown in Figure 7.3 (on page 192). Sternberg claims that traditional IQ tests measure only one type–*componential intelligence*–which is

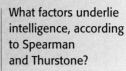

What factors underlie intelligence, according to Spearman and Thurstone?

primary mental abilities
According to Thurstone, seven relatively distinct capabilities that singly or in combination are involved in all intellectual activities.

What types of intelligence have Gardner and Sternberg identified?

triarchic theory of intelligence
Sternberg's theory that there are three types of intelligence: componential (analytical), experiential (creative), and contextual (practical).

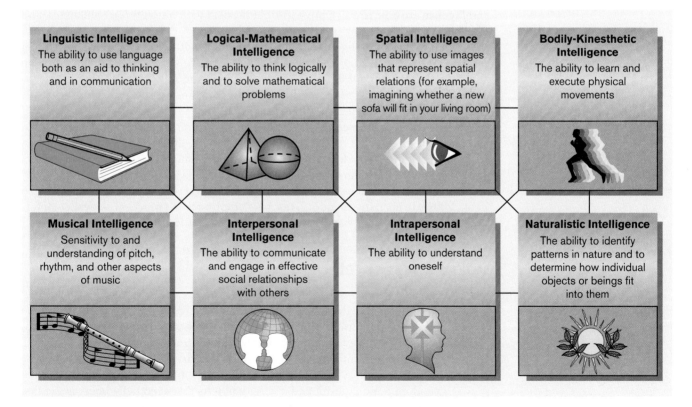

➤ **Figure 7.2**
Gardner's Eight Frames of Mind

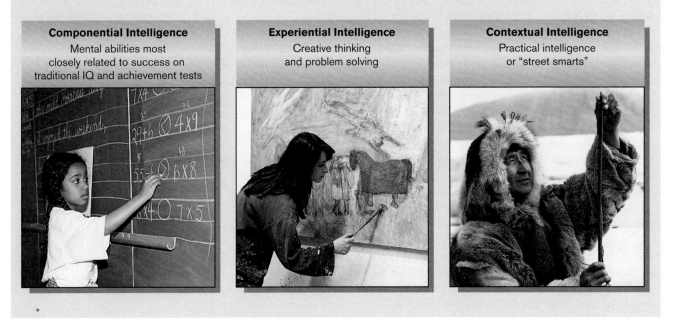

Componental Intelligence Mental abilities most closely related to success on traditional IQ and achievement tests	**Experiential Intelligence** Creative thinking and problem solving	**Contextual Intelligence** Practical intelligence or "street smarts"

➤ Figure 7.3

Sternberg's Triarchic Theory of Intelligence

According to Sternberg, there are three types of intelligence: componental, experiential, and contextual.

strongly correlated with success in school. A second type—*experiential intelligence*—is reflected in creative thinking and problem solving. People with high experiential intelligence are able to solve novel problems, deal with unexpected challenges, and find creative ways to perform common daily tasks. A third type—*contextual intelligence*, or practical intelligence—might be equated with common sense or "street smarts." People with high contextual intelligence are survivors who capitalize on their strengths, compensate for their weaknesses, and adapt well to their environment. People who have succeeded in spite of hardships and adverse circumstances probably have a great deal of contextual intelligence.

Sternberg and his associates are developing a promising new intelligence test that measures all three types of abilities (Sternberg et al., 2001). Moreover, Sternberg's ideas have become popular among educators. Several studies have shown that instruction based on the idea that traditional tests and curricula tap into only one of the three types of intelligence can be effective with students who are low achievers (Grogorenko et al., 2002). In such interventions, teachers emphasize the practical relevance of formal academic knowledge and help students apply it to real-world problems.

Measuring Intelligence

What is Binet's major contribution to psychology? ➤

The first successful effort to measure intelligence resulted not from a theoretical approach, but as a practical means of solving a problem. In 1903, the French government formed a special commission to look for a way of assessing the intellectual potential of individual school children. One of the commission members, Alfred Binet (1857–1911), with the help of his colleague, psychiatrist Theodore Simon, developed a variety of tests that eventually became the first intelligence test, the *Binet–Simon Intelligence Scale*, first published in 1905.

The Binet–Simon Scale used a type of score called *mental* age. A child's mental age was based on the number of items she or he got right as compared with the average number right for children of various ages. In other words, if a child's score equaled the average for 8-year-olds, the child was assigned a mental age of 8, regardless of her or his chronological age (age in years). To determine whether children were bright, average, or retarded, Binet compared the children's mental and chronological ages. A child who was mentally 2 years ahead of his or her chronological age was considered bright; one who was 2 years behind was considered retarded. But there was a flaw in Binet's scoring system. A 4-year-old with a mental age of 2 is far more retarded than a 12-year-old with a mental age of 10. How could a similar degree of retardation at different ages be expressed?

German psychologist William Stern (1914) provided an answer. In 1912, he devised a simple formula for calculating an index of intelligence—*the intelligence quotient.* But it was American psychologist Lewis M. Terman, a professor at Stanford University, who perfected this new way of scoring intelligence tests. In 1916, Terman published a thorough revision of the Binet–Simon scale, consisting of items adapted for use with American children. Terman also established new **norms,** or age-based averages, based on the scores of large numbers of children. Within 3 years, 4 million American children had taken Terman's revision, known as the *Stanford–Binet Intelligence Scale.* It was the first test to make use of Stern's concept of the **intelligence quotient (IQ).** (Terman also introduced the abbreviation *IQ.*) Terman's formula for calculating an IQ score was

$$\frac{\text{Mental Age}}{\text{Chronological Age}} \times 100 = \text{IQ}$$

For example,

$$\frac{14}{10} \times 100 = 140 \text{ (superior IQ)}$$

The highly regarded Stanford–Binet is an individually administered IQ test for those aged 2 to 23. It contains four subscales: verbal reasoning, quantitative reasoning, abstract visual reasoning, and short-term memory. An overall IQ score is derived from scores on the four subscales, and the test scores correlate well with achievement test scores (Laurent et al., 1992). Intelligence testing became increasingly popular in the United States in the 1920s and 1930s, but it quickly became obvious that the Stanford–Binet was not useful for testing adults. The original IQ formula could not be applied to adults, because at a certain age people achieve maturity in intelligence. According to the original IQ formula, a 40-year-old with the same IQ test score as the average 20-year-old would be considered mentally retarded, with an IQ of only 50. Obviously, something was wrong with the formula when applied to populations of all ages.

In 1939, psychologist David Wechsler developed the first successful individual intelligence test for adults, designed for those aged 16 and older. Scores are based on how much an individual deviates from the average score for adults rather than on mental and chronological ages. The original test has been revised, restandardized, and renamed the *Wechsler Adult Intelligence Scale (WAIS-R)* and is one of the most widely used psychological tests. The test contains both verbal and performance (nonverbal) subtests, which yield separate verbal and performance IQ scores as well as an overall IQ score. This is a key difference from the Stanford–Binet, which yields a single IQ score. Wechsler also published the *Wechsler Intelligence Scale for Children (WISC-R)* and the *Wechsler Preschool and Primary Scale of Intelligence (WPPSI),* which is normed for children aged 4 to 6½. One advantage of the Wechsler scales is their ability to identify intellectual strengths in nonverbal areas as well as verbal ones. Wechsler also believed that differences in a person's scores on the various verbal and performance subtests could be used for diagnostic purposes.

What is the Stanford–Binet Intelligence Scale?

norms
Standards based on the range of test scores of a large group of people who are selected to provide the bases of comparison for those who take the test later.

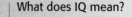
What does IQ mean?

intelligence quotient (IQ)
An index of intelligence, originally derived by dividing mental age by chronological age and then multiplying by 100, but now derived by comparing an individual's score with the scores of others of the same age.

What did Wechsler's tests provide that the Stanford–Binet did not?

Working with psychiatrist Theodore Simon to develop a test for evaluating children's intelligence, Alfred Binet (shown here) began testing Parisian students in 1904.

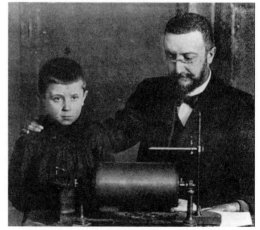

Individual intelligence tests such as the Stanford–Binet and the Wechsler scales must be given to one person at a time by a qualified professional. For testing large numbers of people in a short period of time (often necessary due to budget limitations), group intelligence tests are the answer. Group intelligence tests such as the *California Test of Mental Maturity,* the *Cognitive Abilities Test,* and the *Otis–Lennon Mental Ability Test* are widely used.

Requirements of Good Tests

If your watch gains 6 minutes one day and loses 3 or 4 minutes the next day, it is not reliable. You want a watch you can rely on to give the correct time day after day.

Like a watch, an intelligence test must have **reliability;** the test must consistently yield nearly the same score when the same person is tested and then retested on the same test or an alternative form of the test. The higher the correlation between the two scores, the more reliable the test.

Tests can be highly reliable but worthless if they are not valid. **Validity** is the ability or power of a test to measure what it is intended to measure. For example, a thermometer is a valid instrument for measuring temperature; a bathroom scale is valid for measuring weight. But no matter how reliable your bathroom scale is, it will not take your temperature. It is valid only for weighing.

Aptitude tests are designed to predict a person's probable achievement or performance at some future time. Selecting students for admission to college or graduate schools is based partly on the predictive validity of aptitude tests such as the Scholastic Assessment Test (SAT), the American College Testing Program (ACT), and the Graduate Record Examination (GRE). How well do SAT scores predict success in college? Moderately, at best. The correlation between SAT scores and the grades of first year college students is about .40 (Linn, 1982).

Once a test is proven to be valid and reliable, the next requirement is **standardization.** There must be standard procedures for administering and scoring the test. Exactly the same directions must be given, whether written or oral, and the same amount of time must be allowed for every test taker. But even more important, standardization means establishing norms by which all scores are interpreted. A test is standardized by administering it to a large sample of people representative of those who will be taking the test in the future. The group's scores are analyzed, and then the average score, standard deviation, percentile rankings, and other measures are computed. These comparative scores become the norms used as the standard against which all other scores on that test are measured.

The Range of Intelligence

You may have heard the term *bell curve* and wondered just exactly what it is. When large populations are measured on intelligence or physical characteristics such as height and weight, the frequencies of the various scores or measurements usually conform to a *bell-shaped* distribution known as the *normal curve*–hence the term *bell curve.* The majority of the scores cluster around the mean (average). The more scores deviate from the mean (that is, the farther away from it they fall), either above or below, the fewer there are. And the normal curve is perfectly symmetrical; that is, there are just as many cases above as below the mean. The average IQ test score for all people in the same age group is arbitrarily assigned an IQ score of 100. On the Wechsler intelligence tests, approximately 50% of the scores are in the average range, between 90 and 110. About 68% of the scores fall between 85 and 115, and about 95% fall between 70 and 130. Some 2% of the scores are above 130, which is considered superior, and about 2% fall below 70, in the range of mental retardation (see Figure 7.4).

But what does it mean to have a "superior" IQ? In 1921, to try to answer this question, Lewis Terman (1925) launched a longitudinal study, now a classic, in which 1,528 gifted students were selected and measured at different ages throughout their lives. Tested on the Stanford–Binet, the participants–857 males and 671 females–had unusu-

---

What do the terms *reliability, validity,* **and** *standardization* **mean?**

reliability
The ability of a test to yield nearly the same score when the same people are tested and then retested on the same test or an alternative form of the test.

validity
The ability of a test to measure what it is intended to measure.

aptitude test
A test designed to predict a person's achievement or performance at some future time.

standardization
Establishing norms for comparing the scores of people who will take a test in the future; administering tests using a prescribed procedure.

What are the ranges of IQ scores considered average, superior, and in the range of mental retardation?

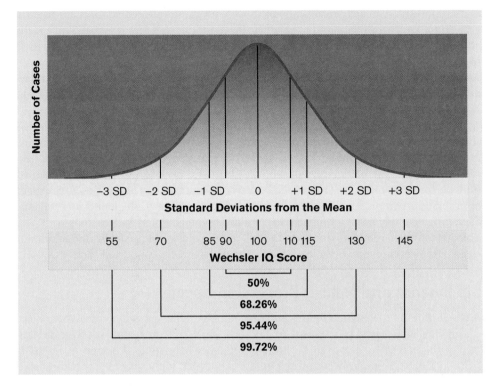

When a large number of test scores are compiled, they are typically distributed in a normal (bell-shaped) curve. On the Wechsler scales, the average, or mean, IQ score is set at 100. As the figure shows, about 68% of the scores fall between 15 IQ points (1 standard deviation) above and below 100 (from 85 to 115), and about 95.5% of the scores fall between 30 points (2 standard deviations) above and below 100 (from 70 to 130).

ally high IQs, ranging from 135 to 200, with an average of 151. Terman's early findings put an end to the myth that mentally superior people are more likely to be physically inferior. In fact, Terman's gifted participants excelled in almost all the abilities he studied–intellectual, physical, emotional, moral, and social. Terman also exploded many other myths about the mentally gifted (Terman & Oden, 1947). For example, you may have heard the saying that there is a thin line between genius and madness. Actually, Terman's gifted group enjoyed better mental health than the general population. And Terman's participants earned more academic degrees, achieved higher occupational status and higher salaries, were better adjusted both personally and socially, and were healthier than their less mentally gifted peers. However, most women at that time did not pursue careers outside of the home, so the findings related to occupational success applied primarily to the men. Terman (1925) concluded that "there is no law of compensation whereby the intellectual superiority of the gifted is offset by inferiorities along nonintellectual lines" (p. 16). The Terman study continues today, with the surviving participants in their 80s or 90s. In a report on Terman's study, Shneidman (1989) states its basic findings–that "an unusual mind, a vigorous body, and a relatively well-adjusted personality are not at all incompatible" (p. 687).

At the opposite end of the continuum from Terman's sample are the 2% of the U.S. population whose IQ scores are in the range of **mental retardation.** There are many causes of mental retardation, including brain injuries, chromosomal abnormalities such as Down syndrome, chemical deficiencies, and hazards present during fetal development. And studies continue to document the enduring mental deficits produced by early exposure to lead (Garavan et al., 2000; Morgan et al., 2000). Individuals are not classified as mentally retarded unless (1) their IQ score is below 70 and (2) they have a severe deficiency in everyday adaptive functioning–the ability to care for themselves and relate to others (Grossman, 1983). There are degrees of retardation from mild to profound. Individuals with IQs ranging from 55 to 70 are considered mildly retarded; from 40 to 54, moderately retarded; from 25 to 39, severely retarded; and below 25, profoundly retarded. Mildly retarded individuals are able to acquire academic skills such as reading up to about a sixth-grade level and may be able to become economically

> According to the Terman study, how do the gifted differ from the general population?

mental retardation
Subnormal intelligence reflected by an IQ below 70 and by adaptive functioning severely deficient for one's age.

> What two criteria must a person meet to be classified as mentally retarded?

inclusion
Educating mentally retarded students in regular rather than special schools by placing them in regular classes for part of the day or having special classrooms in regular schools; also called *mainstreaming*.

self-supporting. The academic skills of those with moderate retardation are usually limited to the first- or second-grade level; these individuals can learn self-care skills and often function well in sheltered work environments. People with severe levels of retardation typically are unable to acquire academic skills but can communicate verbally and learn habits such as brushing their teeth. At the profound level of retardation, individuals usually learn only rudimentary motor skills and limited self-help skills such as feeding themselves.

Before the late 1960s, mentally retarded children in the United States were educated almost exclusively in special schools. Since then, there has been a movement toward **inclusion**—or educating mentally retarded students in regular schools. Inclusion, also called *mainstreaming*, may involve placing these students in classes with nonhandicapped students for part of the day or in special classrooms in regular schools. Resources spent on training programs for the mentally retarded are proving to be sound investments. Such programs rely heavily on behavior modification techniques and are making it possible for some retarded individuals to become employed workers earning the minimum wage or better. Everyone benefits—the individual, his or her family, and society as well.

Intelligence and Neural Processing Speed

> What is the relationship between intelligence and the speed of neural processing?

A growing number of neuroscientists and psychologists believe that individual differences in intelligence may be the result of differences in neural processing speed, a variable that has been shown to be strongly influenced by genes (Luciano et al., 2001, 2003). Presumably, according to this hypothesis, higher IQ test scores are associated with faster neural processing. To test the hypothesis, researchers are using PET scans and other brain-imaging techniques to compare the efficiency and speed of neural processing in people with a range of intelligence levels. Other researchers, using reaction-time tasks such as measuring the amount of time required for a participant to identify or classify objects, have also found that processing speed is related to intelligence (Fry & Hale, 1996; Neisser et al., 1996). But researchers find it challenging to distinguish neural processing time from physical reaction time (Brody, 1992). For example, a participant must decide whether two objects flashed on a screen are the same or different and then respond physically by pushing one of two buttons, labeled "S" and "D." Consequently, the time taken for the mental task (processing speed) may be affected by the time needed for the physical task (reaction time), and that physical factor may have nothing to do with intelligence.

A research technique that measures inspection time is a better way to gauge processing speed (Deary & Stough, 1996; Scheuffgen et al., 2000). A typical inspection-time task is shown in Figure 7.5. An image of the incomplete stimulus, part (a), is flashed to the participant very briefly and then immediately masked by a stimulus that covers it, part (b). The participant then is asked whether the longer side of the original stimulus appeared on the left or the right. Of course, the experiment is very simple, but the relevant factor is how much inspection time (from a few hundred milliseconds to 10 milliseconds or less) is needed for a participant to consistently achieve a given level of accuracy—say, 75% or 85%. The shorter the inspection time, the greater the "speed of intake of information" (Deary & Stough, 1996). Is inspection time (perceptual speed) related to intelligence? Apparently so. Deary and Stough claim that "inspection time is, to date, the only single information-processing index that accounts for approximately 20% of intelligence-test variance" (p. 599). Even so, experts in intelligence still lack a sufficient understanding of the relationship between inspection time and intelligence (Brody, 1992).

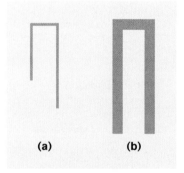

(a)   **(b)**

➤ **Figure 7.5**

A Typical Inspection-Time Task

(From Deary & Stough, 1996.)

The IQ Controversy

Intelligence testing has become a major growth industry. And many Americans have come to believe that a "magical" number—an IQ score, a percentile rank, or some other derived score—unfailingly portrays a person's intellectual capacity, ability, or potential. It is true that studies indicate that intelligence test scores are related to a wide range of social outcomes, including achievement test scores, job performance, income, social status, and years of education completed (Neisser et al., 1996), and they are fairly good predictors of academic performance (grades). However, abuses occur when a score on an intelligence or aptitude test is the only, or even the major, criterion for admitting individuals to various educational programs. Intelligence tests do not measure attitude and motivation, critical ingredients of success. Many people are admitted to educational programs who probably should not be, while others are denied admission who could profit from the programs and possibly make significant contributions to society.

◄ What do intelligence tests predict fairly well?

Early categorization based solely on IQ scores can doom children to slow-track educational programs that are not appropriate for them. Many poor and minority children (particularly those for whom English is a second language) and visually or hearing impaired children have been erroneously placed in special education programs. IQ tests predicted that they were not mentally able to profit from regular classroom instruction. There would be no problem if IQ test results were consistently accurate, but in fact they are not.

◄ What are some abuses of intelligence tests?

One criticism that continues to plague advocates of IQ testing is the suggestion that minority children and those for whom English is a second language are at a disadvantage when they are assessed on conventional tests because their cultural backgrounds differ from that assumed by the tests' authors. In response, attempts have been made to develop **culture-fair intelligence tests** designed to minimize cultural bias. The questions do not penalize individuals whose cultural experience or language differs from that of the mainstream or dominant culture. See Figure 7.6 for an example of the type of test item found on a culture-fair test.

A new testing technique called *dynamic assessment* represents a different approach to moderating the effects of cultural bias on IQ scores. In dynamic assessment, examinees are taught the goal and format of each IQ subtest before actually being tested. The rationale behind the technique is that children from middle-class backgrounds have more experience with testing procedures than do children from low-income homes, and they better understand that the goal of testing is to demonstrate competency. Thus, the goal of dynamic assessment is to provide children from disadvantaged backgrounds with the same skills middle-class children bring to the testing situation, thereby improving their scores. And the assumptions of this technique appear to be valid: Studies of dynamic assessment show that it significantly increases the number of minority children who achieve above-average IQ scores (Lidz & Macrine, 2001)

culture-fair intelligence test
An intelligence test that uses questions that will not penalize those whose culture differs from the mainstream or dominant culture.

nature–nurture controversy
The debate over whether intelligence and other traits are primarily the result of heredity or environment.

The Heritability of IQ Scores

The most vocal area of disagreement concerning intelligence has been the **nature–nurture controversy,** the debate over whether intelligence is primarily the result of heredity or environment. Englishman Sir Francis Galton (1874) initiated this debate, which

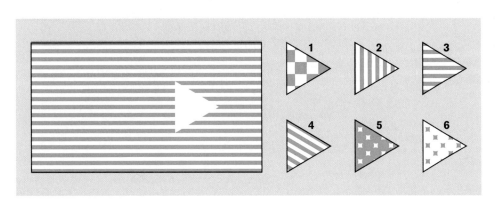

➤ Figure 7.6

An Example of an Item on a Culture-Fair Test

This culture-fair test item does not penalize test takers whose language or cultural experiences differ from those of the urban middle or upper classes. Test takers select, from the six samples on the right, the patch that completes the pattern. Patch number 3 is the correct answer. (Adapted from the Raven Standard Progressive Matrices Test.)

behavioral genetics
A field of research that investigates the relative effects of heredity and environment on behavior and ability.

What is behavioral genetics, and what are the primary methods used in the field today? ➤

How do twin studies support the view that intelligence is inherited? ➤

twin study method
A method researchers use to study the relative effects of heredity and environment on a variety of characteristics by comparing pairs of identical and fraternal twins.

heritability
An index of the degree to which a characteristic is estimated to be influenced by heredity.

adoption study method
A method researchers use to study the relative effects of heredity and environment on behavior and ability in children adopted shortly after birth, by comparing them with their biological and adoptive parents.

➤ **Figure 7.7**

Correlations between the IQ Scores of Persons with Various Relationships

The more closely related two individuals are, the more similar their IQ scores tend to be. Thus, there is a strong genetic contribution to intelligence. (Based on data from Bouchard & McGue, 1981; Erlenmeyer-Kimling & Jarvik, 1963.)

has raged for more than 100 years, and coined the term. After studying a number of prominent families in England, Galton concluded that intelligence was inherited. Hereditarians agree with Galton, claiming that intelligence is largely inherited—the result of nature. Environmentalists, on the other hand, insist that it is influenced primarily by one's environment—the result of nurture. Most psychologists now agree that both nature and nurture contribute to intelligence, but they continue to debate the proportions contributed by each.

Behavioral genetics is a field of research that investigates the relative effects of heredity and environment on behavior and ability (Plomin et al., 1997). One of the primary methods used by behavioral geneticists is the **twin study method,** in which researchers study *identical twins* (monozygotic twins, who have exactly the same genes) and *fraternal twins* (dizygotic twins, who are no more alike genetically than other siblings) to determine how much they resemble each other on a variety of characteristics. If identical twins raised apart (that is, in different environments) are more alike than fraternal twins raised together (that is, in the same environment), then genes are assumed to contribute more strongly than environment to the particular trait being studied. **Heritability** is an index of the degree to which a characteristic is estimated to be influenced by heredity. Figure 7.7 shows estimates of the proportional contributions of genetic and environmental factors to intelligence. Some research using the **adoption study method,** comparing children to both their adoptive and biological parents, also supports the assertion that genes strongly influence IQ scores.

Minnesota is the site of the most extensive U.S. study of identical and fraternal twins. The Minnesota Center for Twin and Adoption Research has assembled the *Minnesota Twin Registry,* which in 1998 included over 10,000 twin pairs (Bouchard, 1998). Since 1979, researchers at the center, headed by Thomas Bouchard, have studied about 60 pairs of fraternal twins and 80 pairs of identical twins who were reared apart. Of all the traits Bouchard and his colleagues studied, the most heritable trait turned out to be intelligence. Bouchard (1997) reports that various types of twin studies have consistently yielded heritability estimates of .60 to .70 for intelligence. (The heritability of some personality traits is discussed in Chapter 11.)

Not all researchers agree with Bouchard's heritability estimate for intelligence. Combining data from a number of twin studies, Plomin and others (1994) found the heritabil-

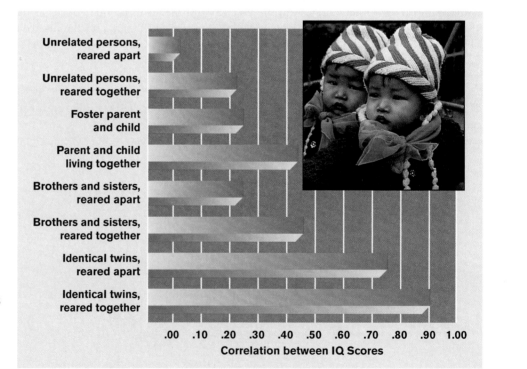

198

ity estimate for general intelligence to be .52. Similar findings emerged from analyses of dozens of adoption studies and twin studies involving over 10,000 pairs of twins. These analyses concluded that the heritability of general cognitive ability is about .50 (McClearn et al., 1997; Plomin, 2003). Psychologists who consider environmental factors to be the chief contributors to differences in intelligence also take issue with Bouchard's findings. They claim that most separated identical twins are raised by adoptive parents who have been matched as closely as possible to the biological parents. This fact, the critics say, could account for the similarity in IQ. In response to his critics, Bouchard (1997) has pointed out that children who are not related biologically but are raised in the same home are no more similar in intelligence once they reach adulthood than complete strangers.

Adding support to the nature side of the debate, adoption studies reveal that children adopted shortly after birth have IQs more closely resembling those of their biological parents than those of their adoptive parents. The family environment has an influence on IQ early in life, but that influence seems to diminish. Twin and adoption studies indicate that for people in adulthood, genes are most closely correlated with IQ (Loehlin et al., 1988, 1989; McCartney et al., 1990; Plomin & Rende, 1991). In fact, the influence of genes seems to increase predictably as people age: There is a heritability of .30 in infancy, .40 in childhood, .50 in adolescence, and about .60 in adulthood (McGue et al., 1993). But does this mean that intelligence is immune to the effects of environment?

Environmental Effects on IQ

Clearly, the high degree of similarity in the intelligence scores of identical twins who have been reared apart makes a strong case for the powerful influence of genes. But even Bouchard and his colleagues (1990) caution against trying to generalize their findings to people raised in disadvantaged environments. Bouchard (1997) states: "A child raised in crushing poverty by illiterate parents is unlikely to score well on IQ tests, no matter what his mental inheritance. . . . Twin studies tend to attract few subjects in such dire straits, so their findings may not always apply to people exposed to extremes of deprivation or privilege" (p. 56).

Several studies indicate that IQ test scores are not fixed but can be modified with an enriched environment. Several decades ago, Sandra Scarr and Richard Weinberg (1976) studied 130 African American and interracial children who had been adopted by highly educated, upper-middle-class White American families; 99 of the children had been adopted in the first year of life. The adoptees were fully exposed to middle-class cultural experiences and vocabulary, the "culture of the tests and the school" (p. 737). How did the children perform on IQ and achievement tests? For these children, the 15-point IQ gap between Blacks and Whites that had been observed by some researchers was bridged by an enriched environment. Compared to an average IQ score of 90, which would be expected had these children been reared by their biological parents, the average IQ score of the 130 adoptees was 106.3. And their achievement test scores were slightly above the national average, not below. On the average, the earlier the children were adopted, the higher their IQs. The mean IQ score of the 99 early adoptees was 110.4, about 10 IQ points above the average for White Americans. Similarly, studies in France also show that IQ scores and achievement are substantially higher when children from lower-class environments are adopted by middle- and upper-middle-class families (Duyme, 1988; Schiff and Lewontin, 1986).

In addition to these encouraging adoption studies, research examining the effects of early childhood interventions on the IQ scores of children from poor families clearly indicates that early educational experiences can affect IQ scores. Some of the best known of these interventions have been carried out by developmental psychologist Craig Ramey of the University of North Carolina (Burchinal et al., 1997; Campbell & Ramey, 1994; Campbell et al., 2001; Ramey, 1993; Ramey & Campbell, 1987). And unlike many studies of early interventions, Ramey's research involves true experiments—so it is clear that the outcomes are caused by the interventions.

In one of Ramey's programs (Campbell and Ramey, 1994), 6- to 12-month-old infants of low-IQ, low-income mothers were randomly assigned to either an intensive 40-

What kinds of evidence suggest that IQ is affected by environmental factors?

hour-per-week day-care program that continued throughout the preschool years or a control group that received only medical care and nutritional supplements. When the children reached school age, half in each group (again based on random assignment) were enrolled in a special after-school program that helped their families learn how to support school learning with educational activities at home. Ramey followed the progress of the children in all four groups through age 12, giving them IQ tests at various ages. Figure 7.8 shows that those who participated in the infant and preschool program scored higher on IQ tests than peers who received either no intervention or only the school-aged intervention. Perhaps more important, during the elementary school years, about 40% of the control group participants had IQ scores classified as borderline or retarded (scores below 85), compared with only 12.8% of those who were in the infant program. Further, more recent research shows that the cognitive advantage enjoyed by the infant intervention groups has persisted into adulthood (Campbell et al., 2001). Ramey's work clearly shows that the environment has great potential to influence IQ scores.

Historical evidence also suggests that environmental factors have a strong influence on IQ scores. Americans and similarly advantaged populations all over the world have gained about 3 IQ points per decade since 1940. James Flynn (1987, 1999; Dickens & Flynn, 2001) analyzed 73 studies involving some 7,500 participants ranging in age from 12 to 48 and found that "every Binet and Wechsler [standardization group] from 1932 to 1978 has performed better than its predecessor" (Flynn, 1987, p. 225). This consistent improvement in IQ scores over time is known as the *Flynn effect* (Holloway, 1999). The average IQ in Western industrialized nations is currently about 15 IQ points higher than it was 50 years ago. Regarding the Black–White IQ gap among U.S. adults, Flynn (1987) asserts that "the environmental advantage Whites enjoy over Blacks is similar to what Whites (adults) of today enjoy over their own parents or grandparents of 50 years ago" (p. 226).

It should not be surprising that enriched environments alter traits that are highly heritable. Consider the fact that American and British adolescents are 6 inches taller on average than their counterparts a century and a half ago (Tanner, 1990). Height has the same heritability (.90) today as it did in the mid–19th century. So this tremendous average gain in height of 6 inches is entirely attributable to environmental influences: better health, better nutrition, and so on. The highest heritability estimates for intelligence are far lower than those for height. It seems clear, then, that environmental influences have the power to affect intelligence and achievement. For example, poverty affects nutrition, and research clearly shows that malnutrition, especially early in life, can harm intellectual development (Brown & Pollitt, 1996; Grogorenko, 2003).

➤ **Figure 7.8**

Ramey's Infant Intervention

In the Ramey study, children were randomly assigned in infancy to an experimental group with special day care (the "full intervention" group) or to a control group. From kindergarten through third grade, half of each group received supplementary family support, and the other half did not. The difference in IQ between the intervention and control groups remained statistically significant even at age 12. (From Campbell & Ramey, 1994.)

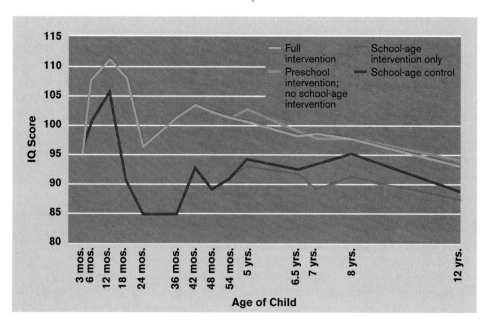

Gender Differences in Cognitive Abilities

Concerning gender differences in cognitive abilities, there are two important points to keep in mind: First, the differences within each gender are greater than the differences between the genders. Second, even though gender differences in cognitive abilities have been generally small on average, there tends to be more variation in such abilities among males than among females—that is, the range of test scores is typically greater for males.

Researchers Janet Hyde and Marcia Linn (1988) examined 165 studies reporting test results on verbal ability for approximately 1.5 million males and females. But they found no significant gender differences in verbal ability. Hedges and Nowell (1995) analyzed the results of the National Assessment of Educational Progress, which has tested a representative sample of 70,000 to 100,000 American schoolchildren, aged 9, 13, and 17, annually in reading comprehension, writing, math, and science. The researchers compared the achievement of the 17-year-olds from 1971 through 1992 and reported that females outperformed males in reading and writing, while males did better in science and math. Although average gender differences were small, there was one prominent exception: "Females performed substantially better than males in writing every year" (p. 44). Furthermore, Hedges and Nowell reported that more males than females were near the bottom of the distribution, not only in writing, but in reading comprehension as well. Finally, in high school, girls are generally more fluent verbally than boys are (Halpern, 1992) and do considerably better in spelling (Lubinsky & Benbow, 1992).

> For what cognitive abilities have gender differences been proven?

But do males have the edge in math? In one of the largest studies conducted to date on gender differences in mathematics, Hyde and others (1990) analyzed 100 studies, which together represented test results for more than 3 million participants. They found no significant gender difference in the understanding of mathematical concepts among the various age groups. Although females did slightly better in mathematical problem solving in elementary and middle school, males scored moderately higher in high school and college. Benbow and Stanley (1980, 1983) found a significant male superiority in a select segment of the population—the brightest of the bright in mathematics ability. On the math portion of the SAT, twice as many boys as girls scored above 500, and 13 times as many scored above 700. Hedges and Nowell (1995) reported that twice as many boys as girls were in the top 3% of the Project Talent Mathematics total scale, and seven times as many boys were in the top 1%.

Parents often expect boys to do better than girls in math (Lummis & Stevenson, 1990). Such expectations may become a *self-fulfilling prophecy,* leading girls to lack confidence in their math ability and to decide not to pursue advanced math courses (Eccles & Jacobs, 1986). A report by the American Association of University Women Education Foundation provided evidence that many science teachers and some math teachers, as well, tend to pay noticeably more attention to boys than to girls (Chira, 1992). Such treatment may discourage girls with math or science aptitude from choosing careers in these areas.

Some psychologists think that males' higher math achievement test scores are the result of superior spatial abilities. Researchers have found that, in general, males tend to perform somewhat better than females on tests of spatial skills (Kimura, 1992; Linn & Hyde, 1989; Linn & Peterson, 1985). This gender difference has been found on some but not all of the various spatial tasks (Geary, 1996; Kimura, 1992). Some research has shown that spatial abilities appear to be enhanced by prenatal exposure to high levels of androgens (Berenbaum et al., 1995). However, this finding does not minimize the role of social experiences and expectations in shaping children's abilities and interests.

Cultural Beliefs, Expectations, Effort, and Academic Achievement

In a classic study of cross-cultural differences in achievement, Stevenson and others (1986) compared the math ability of randomly selected elementary school children from three comparable cities—Taipei in Taiwan, Sendai in Japan, and Minneapolis in

Asian students consistently score higher on math achievement tests than their American counterparts. It appears that the reasons for this difference are cultural and relate to parental expectations.

the United States. By the fifth grade, the Asian students were outscoring the Americans by about 15 points in math ability. And the Asian superiority held firmly from the highest to the lowest achievement levels. Of the lowest 100 students in math achievement, 67 were Americans; of the top 100, only 1 was. The Japanese children scored the highest of the three groups in fifth grade, and even the lowest-scoring Japanese classes did better than the top-scoring classes in the United States.

How can such differences in achievement for children from different cultures be explained? Research carried out by Stevenson and others (1990) suggests that cultural beliefs and practices may be a major factor in explaining the gap in math ability. Their research was conducted with first and fifth graders from the same three cities as in the math comparison study, a total of 1,440 students (480 from each of the three countries). The children were tested in reading and mathematics and interviewed along with their mothers. In a follow-up study 4 years later, the first graders (now fifth graders) were tested again, and they and their mothers were interviewed once more.

Stevenson and his colleagues (1990) reported that the Chinese and Japanese mothers considered academic achievement to be the *most important pursuit of their children,* whereas American parents did not value it as a central concern. The Asian, but not the American, families structured their home activities to promote academic achievement as soon as their first child started elementary school.

More importantly, perhaps, the Asian parents downplayed the role of innate ability in school achievement. Instead, they emphasized the value of hard work and persistence (Stevenson, 1992). American parents, in contrast, believed more firmly in genetic limitations on ability and achievement. Such a belief has devastating effects, according to Stevenson, who states, "When parents believe success in school depends for the most part on ability rather than effort, they are less likely to foster participation in activities related to academic achievement" (p. 73). Also, American mothers tended to overestimate the cognitive abilities of their children, but the Chinese and Japanese mothers did not. Asian mothers held higher standards for their children and also gave more realistic assessments of their children's abilities (see Figure 7.9).

In follow-up studies, Stevenson and others (1993) found that the achievement gap between Asian and American students persisted over a 10-year period. Differences in high school achievement were explained in part by the fact that the American students spent more time working at part-time jobs and socializing than their Asian counter-

> ## Figure 7.9

Mothers' Satisfaction with Their Children's Academic Performance

Even though American students had by far the poorest achievement record of the children studied in the United States, Taiwan, and Japan, American mothers expressed much higher satisfaction with their children's academic performance than did mothers from the two Asian countries. (From Stevenson, 1992.)

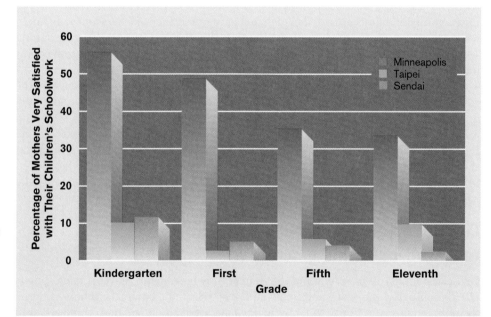

parts did, a finding confirmed by several other cross-cultural researchers (Fuligni & Stevenson, 1995; Larson & Verma, 1999).

But are Asian students more likely than students in the United States to be depressed, nervous, stressed, and heavily burdened by pressures to maintain academic excellence? One large cross-cultural study comparing 11th-grade students from Japan, Taiwan, and the United States did find a correlation between achievement in mathematics and psychological distress—but, surprisingly, for the American students, not the Asian students (Crystal et al., 1994). Moreover, contrary to popular belief, adolescent suicide rates are lower in Japan than in the United States.

Why should high-achieving American students, but not Asian students, pay a price in terms of psychological distress? The researchers found that Asian teenagers typically enjoy support and encouragement for their academic achievement from family and peers alike. In contrast, high-achieving teenagers in the United States are torn between studying hard to excel academically and pursuing nonacademic social interests. Such interests may be strongly encouraged by their peers and often by parents who want their children to be "well-rounded." Which of these two cultural tendencies is more likely to maximize the development of one's intellectual potential? Perhaps the answer to the stunning record of academic achievement of Asian students lies not in their genes, but in the cultural values that nurture them.

Emotional Intelligence

Daniel Goleman (1995) claims that success in life is more markedly influenced by emotional intelligence than by IQ. **Emotional intelligence** refers to a set of capabilities that are separate from IQ but necessary for success in life—in the workplace, in intimate personal relations, and in social interactions. Research supports this view, showing that emotional intelligence is unrelated to IQ scores (Lam & Kirby, 2002; Van der Zee et al., 2002). Moreover, scores on tests of emotional intelligence predict both academic and social success (Rozell et al., 2002). For these reasons, emotional intelligence has become an important concept in psychology.

The foundation of emotional intelligence is *self-knowledge*. It involves an awareness of emotions, an ability to manage those emotions, and self-motivation. Awareness of one's own emotions—recognizing and acknowledging feelings as they happen—is at the very heart of emotional intelligence. It means being aware not only of moods, but of thoughts about those moods as well. Those who are able to monitor their feelings as they arise are more likely to be able to manage them rather than being ruled by them.

> What are the personal components of emotional intelligence?

Managing emotions does not mean suppressing them, any more than it means giving free rein to every feeling and impulse. As Goleman (1995) puts it, "The goal is balance, not emotional suppression: every feeling has its value and significance. A life without passion would be a dull wasteland of neutrality, cut off and isolated from the richness of life itself" (p. 56). Thus, to manage emotions is to express them in an appropriate manner and not let them get out of control. For example, if not tempered with reason, uncontrolled anger can lead to rage and violence. People high in emotional intelligence have learned how to regulate their moods and not let anger, boredom, or depression ruin their day (or their lives). You manage your emotions when you do something to cheer yourself up, soothe your own hurts, reassure yourself, or otherwise temper an inappropriate or out-of-control emotion.

Self-motivation refers to an aspect of self-control that enables a person to get moving and pursue worthy goals, persist at tasks even when frustrated, and resist the temptation to act on impulse. Resisting impulsive behavior is, according to Goleman (1995), "the root of all emotional self-control" (p. 81). Indeed, of all the attributes of emotional intelligence, the ability to postpone immediate gratification and to persist in working toward some greater future gain is most closely related to success—whether one is trying to get a college degree, build a business, or even stay on a diet. One researcher has found that

emotional intelligence
A type of intelligence that includes an awareness of and an ability to manage one's own emotions, the ability to motivate oneself, empathy, and the ability to handle relationships successfully.

4-year-old children who mastered the art of delaying instant gratification in order to advance toward some greater future goal are "far superior as students" later, when they graduate from high school, than are four-year-olds who were not able to resist the impulse to satisfy their immediate wishes (Shoda et al., 1990).

What are the interpersonal components of emotional intelligence?

The interpersonal aspects of emotional intelligence are sensitivity to and understanding of others' emotions and the ability to handle relationships. Two components of emotional intelligence that are prerequisites for handling relationships are (1) the ability to manage one's own emotions and (2) *empathy,* or the ability to perceive, understand, and relate to the emotions of others. These two components combine to produce the ability to respond appropriately to emotions in others. And this, Goleman (1995) maintains, is the very center of the art of handling relationships. But he does not mean "handling" in an autocratic, dominating sense. People who handle relationships well, says Goleman, are able to shape encounters, "to mobilize and inspire others to thrive in intimate relationships, to persuade and influence, to put others at ease" (p. 113).

Although it is not one of the five main domains of emotional intelligence identified by Salovey and Mayer (1990), *optimism* appears to be a component of emotional intelligence. People who are optimistic have a "strong expectation in general [that] things will turn out all right in life" (p. 88). The most significant aspect of optimism in the context of emotional intelligence is the way in which optimists explain their successes and failures. When optimists fail, they attribute their failure to something in the situation that can be changed. Thus, they believe that by trying harder, they can succeed the next time. But when pessimists fail, they blame themselves and attribute their failure to some personal characteristic or flaw that cannot be changed.

creativity
The ability to produce original, appropriate, and valuable ideas and/or solutions to problems.

Creativity

Creativity can be thought of as the ability to produce original, appropriate, and valuable ideas and/or solutions to problems. Some psychologists go beyond this basic definition and suggest that creative people have the ability to see connections between objects or ideas that are rarely noticed by the noncreative. In fact one of the first tests of creativity, the *Remote Associates Test,* tapped into this aspect of creativity (Mednick & Mednick, 1967). *Try It! 7.4* can help you find out how much of this kind of creativity you possess.

What is creativity, and how is it related to intelligence?

Try It! 7.4   Word Associations

One indication of creativity may be the ability to make associations among several elements that seem only remotely related or unrelated. Test your ability to find associations for these 10 sets of words, which are similar to those on the Remote Associates Test. Think of a fourth word that is related in some way to all three of the words in each row. For example, the words *keeper, text,* and *worm* are related to the word *book* and become *bookkeeper, textbook,* and *bookworm.*

1. sales, collector, income
2. flower, room, water
3. red, shot, dog
4. ball, hot, stool
5. rock, man, classical
6. story, true, sick
7. news, plate, waste
8. stuffed, sleeve, sweat
9. class, temperature, bath
10. wrist, man, stop

Answers: 1. tax 2. bed 3. hot 4. foot 5. music 6. love 7. paper 8. shirt 9. room 10. watch

Research indicates that there is a modest correlation between creativity and IQ. Highly creative people tend to be well above average in intelligence, but in the upper IQ ranges (over 120) there seems to be little correlation between IQ and creativity (Barron & Harrington, 1981). Moreover, genuine creativity rarely appears in the form of sudden flashes (Haberlandt, 1997). For the most part, creative ideas that come to conscious awareness have been incubating for some time. One theorist has suggested that there are four basic stages in the creative problem-solving process (Goleman et al., 1992):

1. *Preparation*—searching for information that may help solve the problem
2. *Incubation*—letting the problem "sit" while the relevant information is digested; perhaps the most important part of the process; takes place below the level of awareness
3. *Illumination*—being suddenly struck by the right solution
4. *Translation*—transforming the new insight into useful action

◀ **What are the four stages in the creative process?**

Psychologists studying exceptionally creative individuals (e.g., Bloom et al., 1985) have learned that they share a number of characteristics that distinguish them from less creative individuals. For one, they have a great deal of expertise in a specific area that has been built up over years of disciplined study and practice. Creative individuals are also open to new experiences and ideas, even those that may seem quite odd

Apply It! How to Build a Powerful Vocabulary

Of all the cognitive skills humans possess, none is more important for clarity of thinking and academic success than vocabulary. How, then, can you build a more powerful vocabulary? The best way is to realize that almost all words belong to larger networks of meaning and to understand that your mind is already geared toward organizing information in terms of meaning. Thus, with a little effort, you can greatly increase your vocabulary by supporting the kind of learning your brain is already inclined to do. Here are a few techniques for following this advice.

Learn to think analytically about words you already know and relate new words to them. What do the words *antiseptic* and *septic tank* have in common? You use an *antiseptic* to prevent bacterial infection of a wound; a *septic tank* is used for removing harmful bacteria from water containing human waste. A logical conclusion would be that *septic* has something to do with bacteria. Knowing this, what do you think a doctor means when she says that a patient is suffering from *sepsis*? By linking *sepsis* to *septic tank* and *antisep-*

tic, you can guess that she is referring to some kind of bacterial infection.

Be aware of word connections that may be hidden by spelling differences. You may know that both *Caesar* and *Czar* refer to some kind of ruler or leader. But you may not know that they are exactly the same word spoken and spelled somewhat differently in Ancient Rome (*Caesar*) and in Russia (*Czar*). Now, if you learn in a history class about *Kaiser Wilhelm* who led Germany during World War I, thinking analytically about his title may help you realize that it is exactly the same word as *Caesar* and *Czar*, but with a German spelling. Here's another example: Can you guess something about the location and climate of the nation of *Ecuador* by relating its name to a word that differs only slightly in spelling?

Use your knowledge of word parts to actively seek out new words. Don't learn new words one at a time. Instead, be on the lookout for "word families"—root words and prefixes and suffixes. Here is one important root

word, *spect.* You've seen it in many words. *Spect* means "look," "look at," "watch," "see." And *spect* appears in dozens of different words, such as *inspect.* What do you do when you *inspect* something? You *look* closely at it. Once you are equipped with this knowledge, other *spect* words may start to come to mind along with an entirely new way of thinking about their meanings: *spectacular, spectator, spectacle, spectacles, perspective, prospect, respect, disrespect, retrospect, suspect,* and so on. The word *circumspect* may be new to you. Look it up in a dictionary, and think about how the literal meaning of the word ("look around") relates to the way this word is frequently used. And, when you read Chapter 1, might it have been easier to understand and remember the meaning of Wundt's research method, *introspection,* if you had thought about the *spect* part of the word? Probably so.

A strong vocabulary based on root words, prefixes, and suffixes will yield the word power that will profit you in many ways. ■

to others; moreover, they seem to be inherently curious and inquisitive (Sternberg, 1985a). Creative people also tend to be independent thinkers who are less influenced by the opinions of others than their less creative counterparts are. Perhaps because of their independence, creative individuals are more likely to be motivated by the anticipation, excitement, and enjoyment of their work than by a desire to please others. Finally, creative endeavor requires hard work and persistence in the face of failure. For instance, Albert Einstein published 248 papers on his theory of relativity before it was finished, and Mozart, when he died at age 35, had created 609 musical compositions (Haberlandt, 1997).

> **What are some characteristics of creative people?**

Summarize It !

> **What is meant by cognition, and what specific processes does it include?**

Cognition refers collectively to all the mental processes involved in acquiring, storing, retrieving, and using knowledge. These mental processes include sensation, perception, imagery, concept formation, reasoning, decision making, problem solving, and language.

KEY TERM

cognition (p. 178)

Imagery and Concepts

> **What is imagery?**

Imagery is the mental representation of a sensory experience–visual, auditory, gustatory, motor, olfactory, or tactile.

> **What is a concept?**

A concept is a mental category that represents a class or group of objects, people, organizations, events, or relations that share common characteristics or attributes.

> **What is the difference between a formal concept and a natural concept?**

A formal concept is one that is clearly defined by a set of rules, a formal definition, or a characteristic. A natural concept is formed on the basis of everyday perceptions and experiences and is somewhat fuzzy. In using a natural concept, a person is likely to picture a prototype of the concept–an example that embodies its most common and typical features.

KEY TERMS

imagery (p. 178)
concept (p. 178)

formal concept (p. 178)
natural concept (p. 178)
prototype (p. 179)
exemplars (p. 179)

Decision Making

> **How are the additive and elimination strategies used in decision making?**

The additive strategy is a decision-making approach in which each alternative is rated on each important factor affecting the decision and then the alternative rated highest overall is chosen.

> **What is the availability heuristic?**

The availability heuristic is a rule of thumb that says that the probability of an event or the importance assigned to it is based on its availability in memory–that is, the ease with which the information comes to mind.

> **What is the representativeness heuristic?**

The representativeness heuristic is a thinking strategy that is used in decision making and that assesses how closely a new object or situation matches an existing prototype of that object or situation.

> **What is framing?**

Framing is the way information is presented so as to focus on either a potential gain or a potential loss.

KEY TERMS

decision making (p. 179)
additive strategy (p. 179)
heuristic (p. 180)
availability heuristic (p. 180)

representativeness heuristic (p. 180)
framing (p. 181)

Problem Solving

> **What is an algorithm?**

An algorithm is a systematic, step-by-step procedure or formula that guarantees a solution to a certain type of problem if applied appropriately and executed properly.

> **What are three heuristics used in problem solving?**

Three heuristics used in problem solving are working backwards, means–end analysis, and the analogy heuristic.

> **How do functional fixedness and mental set impede problem solving?**

Functional fixedness, or the tendency to view objects only in terms of their customary functions, results in a failure to use the objects in novel ways to solve problems. Mental set is the tendency to apply a strategy that was successful in the past to solve new problems, even though the strategy may not be appropriate for the requirements of the new problem.

> **What is artificial intelligence?**

Artificial intelligence refers to the programming of computer systems to simulate human thinking in solving problems and in making judgments and decisions.

KEY TERMS

problem solving (p. 181)
trial and error (p. 181)
algorithm (p. 182)
working backwards (p. 182)
means–end analysis (p. 182)
analogy heuristic (p. 183)

functional fixedness (p. 183)
mental set (p. 183)
artificial intelligence (p. 184)
neural networks (p. 184)
robotics (p. 184)

Language

➤ **What are the five basic components of language?**

The five components of language are (1) phonemes, the smallest units of sound in a spoken language; (2) morphemes, the smallest units of meaning; (3) syntax, the grammatical rules for arranging and combining words to form phrases and sentences; (4) semantics, the meaning derived from phonemes, morphemes, and sentences; and (5) pragmatics, the intonation patterns and social rules associated with language use.

➤ **How does language in trained chimpanzees differ from human language?**

Chimpanzees do not have a vocal tract adapted to speech, and their communication using sign language or symbols consists of constructions strung together rather than actual sentences.

➤ **In general, does thought influence language more, or does language influence thought more?**

In general, thought has a greater influence on language than vice versa. Whorf's linguistic relativity hypothesis has not been supported by research.

➤ **What are the advantages and disadvantages of bilingualism in childhood?**

Bilingual children exhibit better metalinguistic skills and more rapid understanding of sound–symbol connections than monolingual children. However, they acquire vocabulary more slowly and may be schooled in the language in which they are least fluent.

KEY TERMS

language (p. 185)
psycholinguistics (p. 185)
phonemes (p. 185)
morphemes (p.185)
syntax (p. 185)
semantics (p. 185)
pragmatics (p. 185)
linguistic relativity hypothesis (p. 188)

The Nature of Intelligence

➤ **What factors underlie intelligence, according to Spearman and Thurstone?**

Spearman believed that intelligence is composed of a general ability (*g* factor), which underlies all intellectual functions, and a number of specific abilities (*s* factors). Thurstone points to seven primary mental abilities, which singly or in combination are involved in all intellectual activities.

➤ **What types of intelligence have Gardner and Sternberg identified?**

Gardner claims that there are eight independent and equally important types of intelligence: linguistic, logical-mathematical, spatial, bodily-kinesthetic, musical, interpersonal, intrapersonal, and naturalist. Sternberg's triarchic theory of intelligence identifies three types: componential (conventional intelligence), experiential (creative intelligence), and contextual (practical intelligence).

KEY TERMS

intelligence (p. 190)
g factor (p. 190)
primary mental abilities (p. 191)
triarchic theory of intelligence (p. 191)

Measuring Intelligence

➤ **What is Binet's major contribution to psychology?**

Binet's major contribution to psychology is the concept of mental age and a method for measuring it–the intelligence test.

➤ **What is the Stanford–Binet Intelligence Scale?**

The Stanford–Binet Intelligence Scale is a highly regarded individual intelligence test for those aged 2 to 23. It yields one overall IQ score.

➤ **What does IQ mean?**

IQ stands for intelligence quotient, an index of intelligence originally derived by dividing a person's mental age by his or her chronological age and then multiplying by 100.

➤ **What did Wechsler's tests provide that the Stanford–Binet did not?**

Wechsler developed the first successful individual intelligence test for adults, the Wechsler Adult Intelligence Scale (WAIS-R). His tests for adults, for children, and for preschoolers yield separate verbal and performance (nonverbal) IQ scores, as well as an overall IQ score.

➤ **What do the terms *reliability, validity,* and *standardization* mean?**

Reliability is the ability of a test to yield nearly the same score each time a person takes the test or an alternative form of the test. Validity is the power of a test to measure what it is intended to measure. Standardization refers to prescribed procedures for administering a test and to established norms that provide a means of evaluating test scores.

➤ **What are the ranges of IQ scores considered average, superior, and in the range of mental retardation?**

Fifty percent of the U.S. population have IQ scores ranging from 90 to 110, considered average; 2% have scores above 130, considered superior; and 2% have scores below 70, in the range of mental retardation.

➤ **According to the Terman study, how do the gifted differ from the general population?**

Terman's longitudinal study revealed that, in general, the gifted enjoy better physical and mental health and are more successful than members of the general population.

➤ **What two criteria must a person meet to be classified as mentally retarded?**

To be classified as mentally retarded, an individual must have an IQ score below 70 and show severe deficiencies in everyday adaptive functioning.

➤ **What is the relationship between intelligence and the speed of neural processing?**

People who are more intelligent generally have a faster neural processing speed.

KEY TERMS

norms (p. 193)
intelligence quotient (IQ) (p. 193)
reliability (p. 194)
validity (p. 194)
aptitude test (p. 194)
standardization (p. 194)

mental retardation (p. 195)
inclusion (p. 196)

The IQ Controversy

➤ **What do intelligence tests predict fairly well?**

IQ tests are good predictors of academic performance (grades).

➤ **What are some abuses of intelligence tests?**

Abuses occur when an IQ test score is the only criterion for admitting individuals to educational programs, for tracking children, or for placing them in classes for the mentally retarded. Many people claim that IQ tests are biased in favor of those from mainstream culture.

➤ **What is behavioral genetics, and what are the primary methods used in the field today?**

Behavioral genetics is the study of the relative effects of heredity and environment on behavior and ability. The twin study method and the adoption study method are the primary methods used.

➤ **How do twin studies support the view that intelligence is inherited?**

Twin studies provide evidence that intelligence is primarily inherited because identical twins are more alike in intelligence than fraternal twins, even if they have been reared apart.

➤ **What kinds of evidence suggest that IQ is affected by environmental factors?**

Several adoption studies have revealed that the IQ scores of children from disadvantaged environments adopted as infants by middle- and upper-middle-class parents are higher on average than would otherwise be expected. Research also shows that infant intervention programs can increase IQ scores. Also, IQ scores have been rising steadily over the past 50 years in Western industrialized nations, presumably because of increases in the standard of living and educational opportunities.

➤ **For what cognitive abilities have gender differences been proven?**

Females outperform males in reading and writing; males seem to do better in science, math, and some spatial tasks. More males than females show the very highest levels of mathematics ability.

KEY TERMS

culture-fair intelligence test (p. 197)
nature–nurture controversy (p. 197)
behavioral genetics (p. 198)
twin study method (p. 198)
heritability (p. 198)
adoption study method (p. 198)

Emotional Intelligence

➤ **What are the personal components of emotional intelligence?**

The personal components of emotional intelligence are an awareness of and an ability to control one's own emotions and the ability to motivate oneself.

➤ **What are the interpersonal components of emotional intelligence?**

The interpersonal components of emotional intelligence are empathy and the ability to handle relationships.

KEY TERM

emotional intelligence (p. 203)

Creativity

➤ **What is creativity, and how is it related to intelligence?**

Creativity is the ability to produce original, appropriate, and valuable ideas and/or solutions to problems. Highly creative people tend to have well above average intelligence, but there seems to be little correlation between very high IQ (above 120) and creativity.

➤ **What are the four stages in the creative process?**

The four stages in the creative process are preparation, incubation, illumination, and translation.

➤ **What are some characteristics of creative people?**

Creative people share some distinctive characteristics: expertise, openness to experience, independence of mind, intrinsic motivation, and perseverance.

KEY TERM

creativity (p. 204)

Surf It!

Want to be sure you've absorbed the material in Chapter 7, "Cognition, Language, and Creativity," before the big test? Visiting **www.ablongman.com/ woodmastering1e** can put a top grade within your reach. The site is loaded with free practice tests, flashcards, activities, and links to help you review your way to an A.

Companion Website

Study Guide for Chapter 7 !

Answers to all the Study Guide questions are provided at the end of the book.

Section One: Chapter Review

1. The two most common forms of imagery are
  a. visual and motor.
  c. visual and auditory.
  b. auditory and tactile.
  d. visual and gustatory.

2. A mental category that represents a class or group of items that share common characteristics or attributes is called a(n)
  a. image.
  c. positive instance.
  b. concept.
  d. prototype.

3. A prototype is the most _____ example of a concept.
  a. abstract
  c. recent
  b. unusual
  d. typical

4. The (additive strategy, elimination by aspects strategy) allows the more desirable aspects of a situation to compensate for other less desirable aspects.

5. _____ refers to the way information is presented so as to focus on a potential gain or loss.

6. Which of the following is guaranteed, if properly applied, to result in the correct answer to a problem?
  a. an algorithm
  c. trial and error
  b. a heuristic
  d. applying prior knowledge

7. Working backwards and means–end analysis are examples of
  a. algorithms.
  c. mental sets.
  b. heuristics.
  d. functional fixedness.

8. John uses a wastebasket to keep a door from closing. In solving his problem, he was not hindered by
  a. a heuristic.
  c. functional fixedness.
  b. an algorithm.
  d. mental set.

9. One characteristic of good problem solvers is mental set. (true/false)

10. Artificial intelligence systems surpass the problem solving ability of experts in a number of fields. (true/false)

11. Match the component of language with the appropriate description.
  ____ (1) the smallest units of meaning
  ____ (2) the meaning derived from phonemes, morphemes, and sentences
  ____ (3) grammatical rules for arranging and combining words to form phrases and sentences
  ____ (4) the smallest units of sound in a spoken language
  ____ (5) intonation patterns
  a. pragmatics
  b. syntax
  c. morphemes
  d. semantics
  e. phonemes

12. Communication in trained chimpanzees approaches human language in form and complexity. (true/false)

13. The linguistic relativity hypothesis is not supported by research. (true/false)

14. In general, thought influences language more than language influences thought. (true/false)

15. Match the theorist with the theory of intelligence.
  ____ (1) seven primary abilities   **a.** Spearman
  ____ (2) multiple intelligences   **b.** Thurstone
  ____ (3) the *g* factor   **c.** Gardner

16. The first successful effort to measure intelligence was made by
  a. Binet and Simon.
  c. Wechsler.
  b. Spearman.
  d. Terman.

17. According to Terman's formula, what is the IQ of a child with a mental age of 12 and a chronological age of 8?
  a. 75
  c. 125
  b. 150
  d. 100

18. In which range will the scores of the largest percentage of people taking an IQ test fall?
  a. 85 to 115
  c. 100 to 130
  b. 85 to 100
  d. 70 to 85

19. What field of research investigates the relative effects of heredity and environment on behavior and ability?
  a. genetics
  c. biology
  b. behavioral genetics
  d. physiology

20. Twin studies suggest that environment is stronger than heredity as a factor in shaping IQ differences. (true/false)

21. In general, differences in cognitive abilities are greater within each gender than between the genders. (true/false)

22. For each cognitive ability, indicate whether males or females, in general, tend to score higher on tests of that ability.
  ____ (1) writing   **a.** males
  ____ (2) science   **b.** females
  ____ (3) spatial ability
  ____ (4) reading comprehension
  ____ (5) mathematics

23. Emotional intelligence means controlling and suppressing one's emotions. (true/false)

24. Which of the following does *not* demonstrate emotional intelligence?
  a. Feeling depressed and distracted, Kyra takes a break and goes to the movies.

b. When he fails a test, Alan thinks to himself, "It was my girlfriend's fault for being so needy and demanding so much of my time."

c. Mike notices that his boss is in a particularly bad mood and stays out of her way for the afternoon.

d. Gisela really knows how to get her team moving to solve a problem.

25. (Pessimism, Optimism) is an important component of emotional intelligence.

26. People with high IQ scores are typically highly creative. (true/false)

27. The stages in the creative problem-solving process occur in the following sequence:
  a. illumination, incubation, preparation, translation
  b. incubation, illumination, preparation, translation
  c. preparation, incubation, illumination, translation
  d. translation, preparation, incubation, illumination

Section Two: Important Concepts and Psychologists

On the line opposite each term, write the name of the theorist or researcher who is most closely associated with it.

1. formal concepts

2. elimination by aspects

3. algorithm

4. linguistic relativity hypothesis

5. *g* factor

6. triarchic theory of intelligence

7. Stanford–Binet Intelligence Scale

8. WAIS-R

9. nature–nurture controversy

10. emotional intelligence

Section Three: Fill in the Blank

1. The mental processes involved in the acquisition, storage, retrieval, and use of knowledge are known as _____ .

2. _____ is defined as the representation of sensory experience in the mind.

3. If you are a member of a Western culture, your concept of food probably includes meat. Beef, pork, and chicken most likely are _____ of the concept, but whale blubber probably is not.

4. Duane decides to list the four most important features of a new car. He then rates the cars he sees based on color, price, gas mileage, and safety and selects the car that ranks highest on these factors. He is using the _____ strategy for decision making.

5. Jordan must consider many alternatives and factors in making a particular decision. She decides to rank the factors from most important to least important. She then starts to eliminate alternatives as they fail to meet the highest ranked factors. This is an example of the _____ strategy for decision making.

6. The study of how language is acquired, produced, and used and how sounds and symbols of language are translated into meaning is known as _____ .

7. When we speak of the rules of language use, we are talking about _____ .

8. Kwoon asserts that the language you use determines the nature of your thoughts. Kwoon is a proponent of the _____ _____ hypothesis.

9. The theory proposing eight different kinds of intelligence, including linguistic intelligence and intrapersonal intelligence, was developed by _____ .

10. If Taylor scores very low on an IQ test and then is found to be at the top of her class in academic performance, we can assume that the IQ test does not have very good _____ .

11. Research using brain-imaging techniques has indicated that people of higher intelligence tend to exhibit higher rates of _____ _____ _____ when performing mental tasks than those who are less gifted.

12. Jack is the kind of person who seems to be able to make the world work for him. He knows how to fit into a situation or change the situation to his needs, and he is very successful in business because of this talent. Sternberg would say that Jack has a high level of _____ intelligence.

13. James takes the same IQ test on two different days. His score on the second day is much higher than his score on the first day. We can assume that the test does not have good _____ .

14. The ability to produce original, appropriate, and valuable ideas and/or solutions to problems is known as _____ .

Section Four: Comprehensive Practice Test

1. The mental processes involved in acquiring, storing, retrieving, and using knowledge are known collectively as
   a. conceptualization.
   b. cognition.
   c. imagery.
   d. thinking.

2. *Dog, car, honesty,* and *trees* are all examples of
   a. images.
   b. concepts.
   c. verbal images.
   d. typographs.

3. A gun would be identified by many people as a _____ of the concept *weapon.*

4. Artificial concepts are also known as fuzzy concepts. (true/false)

5. A good example of a formal concept is
   a. the periodic table of the elements.
   b. social display rules.
   c. ethical guidelines.
   d. established table manners.

6. If, while working at your computer, you forgot a command, and you then tried all the commands you could remember until you found the one that worked, this would be an example of using
   a. a syllogism.
   b. the additive heuristic.
   c. inductive reasoning.
   d. trial and error.

7. Students who learn systematic, step-by-step procedures to solve their statistics problems are learning
   a. algorithms.
   b. trial and error.
   c. elimination by aspects.
   d. means–end analysis.

8. A neural network is a computer system that is designed to mimic
   a. artificial intelligence.
   b. animal intelligence.
   c. human heuristics.
   d. the human brain.

9. _____ are the smallest units of sound in a spoken language.
   a. Phonemes
   b. Semantics
   c. Morphemes
   d. Consonants

10. It is obvious that other animals have no real language or communication abilities at all. Any apparent display of such abilities has been shown to be simply a matter of operant conditioning. (true/false)

11. Research suggests that gender-specific pronouns such as "he" influence interpretation of sentences in favor of males. (true/false)

12. Thurstone believed that the single IQ score method of measuring and describing intelligence was the most effective manner of measuring intelligence. (true/false)

13. Sternberg's experiential intelligence includes
   a. the ability to learn from past events.
   b. the ability to manipulate people's opinions.
   c. creative problem solving.
   d. basic academic skills.

14. The WAIS-R intelligence test provides two different sub-test scores, in addition to an overall IQ score. The two subtests are
   a. verbal and mathematics.
   b. contextual and componential.
   c. performance and musical.
   d. verbal and performance.

15. Mike has just taken a test that is designed to predict future achievement or performance. Mike took a(n)
   a. aptitude test.
   b. projective test.
   c. intelligence test.
   d. creativity test.

16. About what percentage of IQ test scores fall between -1 and $+1$ standard deviation from the mean of 100 on a normal curve?
   a. 34%   b. 68%   c. 50%   d. 13%

17. Culture-fair intelligence tests were designed to represent different cultural values equally on the same test. (true/false)

18. Behavioral genetics is a field of inquiry that investigates
   a. how our behavior affects our genes.
   b. how our genes affect our behavior and ability.
   c. how our genes affect our biology.
   d. how our behavior affects our ability.

19. Intelligence is not fixed at birth; rather, evidence suggests that improved environmental factors can increase IQ scores. (true/false)

20. Although intelligence may be necessary for creativity, it is not sufficient. (true/false)

Section Five: Critical Thinking

1. Review the three basic approaches to problem solving discussed in this chapter. Which approach do you think is most practical and efficient for solving everyday problems?

2. Which of the theories of intelligence best fits your notion of intelligence? Why?

3. Prepare an argument supporting each of the following positions:
   a. Intelligence tests should be used in the schools.
   b. Intelligence tests should not be used in the schools.

4. Give several examples of how you might bring more creativity into your educational and personal life.

chapter 8

Human
Development

On July 3, 1945, in a small East Texas town, a daughter was born to a sharecropper and his wife, a domestic who did housework for White families in town. The daughter, Ruth Simmons, shared the sharecropper's shack with her 11 brothers and sisters. Schools were segregated in this separate and unequal society, and it was rare for young African Americans to go to college, but Simmons was an exception. She won a scholarship to Dillard University, and her high school teachers took up a collection to buy her a coat and some suitable clothes for college. She went on to earn her PhD in Romance languages at Harvard University.

During her career, Dr. Ruth Simmons became a professor and later a college president at prestigious Smith College. But, the crowning success of her career—at least so far—came in 2001, when she became president of Brown University, the first African American to head an Ivy League college or university. Although Dr. Simmons is near 60, don't be surprised if her "next first" is even more impressive.

What in her environment could have helped form Ruth Simmons and prepare her for her outstanding achievements? Simmons credits her mother, her "hero," whose life was built on hard work, civility, kindness, and high standards. Like Ruth Simmons, all of us experience a variety of influences across our lives. This chapter explains how many of these factors affect our development.

Issues in Developmental Psychology

What are three important issues in developmental psychology?

Developmental psychology is the study of how humans grow, develop, and change throughout the life span. Developmental psychologists must consider several controversial issues as they pursue their work. First, as you learned in Chapter 7, the nature–nurture controversy is among the oldest debates in psychology: How much of a child's development is due to genes and how much to environment? It is not always easy to separate these two sets of influences.

Developmental psychologists also differ as to whether personal traits, such as shyness, are stable over time. The learning theories you studied in Chapter 5 claim that traits can change as a result of external influences and can even vary from situation to situation. Other theories disagree, suggesting that personal traits appear early in life and remain stable throughout the life span. In this chapter, you will read about one such group of traits—temperament. And we will return to this topic in Chapter 11.

Finally, perhaps the most important debate in developmental psychology revolves around the question of whether development is continuous or occurs in stages. The learning theories assume that development happens in a continuous fashion as a result of environmental influence. Stage theories, by contrast, assert that development occurs in phases that are distinct from one another. Since these theories have been very influential in developmental psychology, we explore three of the most important of them in the next section.

developmental psychology
The study of how humans grow, develop, and change throughout the life span.

scheme
Piaget's term for a cognitive structure or concept used to identify and interpret information.

Stage Theories of Development

Piaget's Theory of Cognitive Development

What did Piaget claim regarding stages of cognitive development?

Thanks to the work of Swiss psychologist Jean Piaget (PEE-ah-ZHAY) (1896–1980), psychologists have gained insights into the cognitive processes of children. According to Piaget, cognitive development begins with a few basic **schemes**—cognitive structures or concepts used to identify and interpret objects, events, and other information in the environment. Confronted with new objects, events, experiences, and information, children try to fit them into their existing schemes, a process known as **assimilation.** But not everything can be assimilated into children's existing schemes. If children call a stranger "Daddy" or the neighbor's cat "doggie," assimilation has led them to make an error. When parents or others correct them or when they discover for themselves that something cannot be assimilated into an existing scheme, children will use a process known as **accommodation.** In accommodation, existing schemes are modified or new schemes are created to process new information.

According to Piaget (1963, 1964; Piaget & Inhelder, 1969), changes in schemes underlie four stages of cognitive development, each of which reflects a qualitatively different way of reasoning and understanding the world. The stages occur in a fixed sequence in which the accomplishments of one stage provide the foundation for the next stage. Although children throughout the world seem to progress through the stages in the same order, they show individual differences in the rate at which they pass through them. And each child's rate is influenced by her or his level of maturation and experiences, such as going to school. The transition from one stage to another

assimilation
The process by which new objects, events, experiences, or information are incorporated into existing schemes.

accommodation
The process by which existing schemes are modified and new schemes are created to incorporate new objects, events, experiences, or information.

is gradual, not abrupt, and children often show aspects of two stages while going through these transitions.

In Piaget's first stage, the *sensorimotor stage* (age birth to 2 years), infants gain an understanding of the world through their senses and their motor activities (actions or body movements). An infant's behavior, which is mostly reflexive at birth, becomes increasingly complex and gradually evolves into intelligent behavior. At this stage, intelligence is about action rather than thought, and it is confined to objects that are present and events that are directly perceived. The child learns to respond to and manipulate objects and to use them in goal-directed activity.

The major achievement of the sensorimotor period is the development of **object permanence**—the realization that objects (including people) continue to exist, even when they are out of sight. This concept develops gradually and is complete when the child is able to represent objects mentally in their absence. The attainment of this ability marks the end of the sensorimotor period.

Children acquire what Piaget called the **symbolic function**—the understanding that one thing can stand for another—during the *preoperational stage* (age 2 to 7 years). Two ways in which children display the symbolic function are through the use of words to represent objects and through *pretend play*, such as imagining that a block is a car or a doll is a real baby. As children practice using symbols, they become increasingly able to represent objects and events mentally with words and images.

During the preoperational stage, children exhibit a tendency Piaget called *egocentrism:* They believe that everyone sees what they see, thinks as they think, and feels as they feel. As a result, their thinking is often illogical. In addition, their thinking about objects is dominated by appearances. For example, a 3-year-old may believe that a cookie is ruined when it breaks. Adults' attempts to convince her otherwise usually fail because adult thinking is based on the assumption that the identity of an object does not change when its appearance changes, a concept that is not yet understood by children in this stage.

In the third stage, the *concrete operations stage* (age 7 to 11 or 12 years), new schemes allow children to understand that a given quantity of matter remains the same despite rearrangement or change in its appearance, as long as nothing is added or taken away—a concept Piaget called **conservation.** Conservation develops because new schemes enable children in this stage to understand the concept of **reversibility**—the understanding that any change in the shape, position, or order of matter can be reversed mentally. As a result, they can think about a broken cookie before and after it broke, realizing that the change in appearance did not change the substance that makes up the cookie. You can see how younger and older children differ in their reasoning about such problems by doing *Try It! 8.1* (on page 216).

The concepts of conservation of number, substance (liquid or mass), length, area, weight, and volume are not all acquired at once. They come in a certain sequence and usually at specific ages (see Figure 8.1, on page 217). Moreover, children in the concrete operations stage are unable to apply logic to hypothetical situations. For instance, they find it difficult to think logically about careers they might pursue as adults. They also have difficulty with problems that involve systematically coordinating several variables. For example, they usually cannot solve reasoning problems like these: If Mary is taller than Bill, and Bill is taller than Harry, is Harry shorter than Mary? or How many different two-letter, three-letter, and four-letter combinations of the letters A, B, C, and D are possible? This kind of reasoning isn't possible until children enter the next stage.

The *formal operations stage* (age 11 or 12 years and beyond) is Piaget's fourth and final stage of cognitive development. At this stage, preadolescents and adolescents can apply logical thought to abstract, verbal, and hypothetical situations and to problems in the past, present, or future—a capacity Piaget called **hypothetico-deductive thinking.** Teenagers can comprehend abstract subjects such as philosophy and politics, and they become interested in the world of ideas as they begin

object permanence
The realization that objects continue to exist, even when they can no longer be perceived.

 What occurs during Piaget's sensorimotor stage?

symbolic function
The understanding that one thing—an object, a word, a drawing—can stand for another.

What cognitive limitations characterize children's thinking during the preoperational stage?

conservation
The concept that a given quantity of matter remains the same despite being rearranged or changed in appearance, as long as nothing is added or taken away.

What cognitive abilities do children acquire during the concrete operations stage?

reversibility
The realization that any change in the shape, position, or order of matter can be reversed mentally.

hypothetico-deductive thinking
The ability to base logical reasoning on a hypothetical premise.

 What cognitive abilities develop during the formal operations stage?

Show a preschooler two glasses of the same size and then fill them with the same amount of juice. After the child agrees they are the same, pour the juice from one glass into a taller, narrower glass and place that glass beside the other original one. Now ask the child if the two glasses have the same amount of juice, or if one glass has more than the other. Children at this stage will insist that the taller, narrower glass has more juice, although they will quickly agree that you neither added juice nor took any away.

Now, repeat the procedure with a school-aged child. The older child will be able to explain that even though there appears to be more liquid in the taller glass, pouring liquid into a different container doesn't change its quantity.

to formulate their own theories. However, not all people attain full formal operational thinking (Kuhn, 1984; Neimark, 1981). High school math and science experience seems to facilitate it (Sharp et al., 1979). Failure to achieve formal operational thinking has been associated with below-average scores on intelligence tests (Inhelder, 1966). *Review and Reflect 8.1* (on page 218) provides a summary of Piaget's four stages.

Cross-cultural studies have affirmed the universality of the types of reasoning and the sequence of stages formulated by Piaget. But cross-cultural research has also revealed differences in the rates of cognitive development in various domains. Whereas the children Piaget observed began to acquire the concept of conservation between ages 5 and 7, Australian Aboriginal children show this change between the ages of 10 and 13 (Dasen, 1994). Yet the Aboriginal children function at the concrete operations level earlier on spatial tasks than on quantification (counting) tasks, while the reverse is true for Western children. This difference makes sense in light of the high value Aborigines place on spatial skills and the low premium they place on quantification. In the Australian desert, moving from place to place, hunting, gathering, and searching for water, Aborigines have few possessions and rarely count things. Their language has words for numbers up to five, and their word for "many" applies to anything above five.

One important cultural variable that contributes to cognitive development is formal education. Developmental psychologists know that children who live in cultures in which they have access to formal education progress more rapidly through Piaget's stages than peers whose societies do not require them to attend school or do not provide them with educational opportunities (Mishra, 1997). Moreover, formal operational thinking is so strongly correlated with formal education that some psychologists have suggested that it may be more a product of specific learning experiences than of a universal developmental process, as Piaget hypothesized.

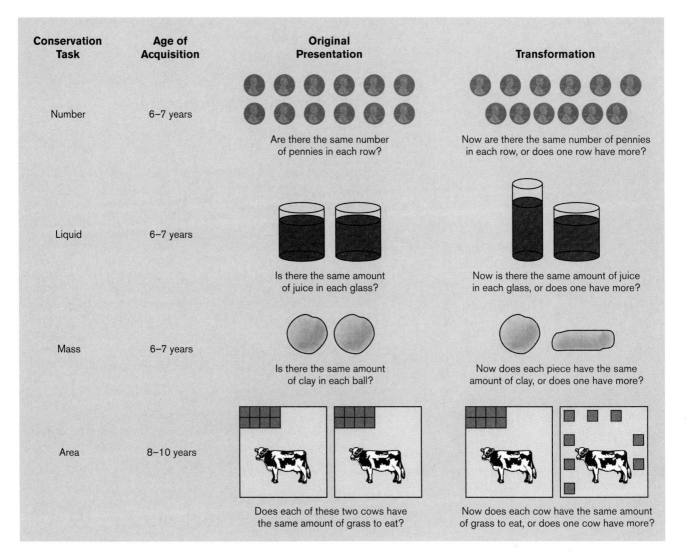

Conservation Task	Age of Acquisition	Original Presentation	Transformation
Number	6–7 years	Are there the same number of pennies in each row?	Now are there the same number of pennies in each row, or does one row have more?
Liquid	6–7 years	Is there the same amount of juice in each glass?	Now is there the same amount of juice in each glass, or does one have more?
Mass	6–7 years	Is there the same amount of clay in each ball?	Now does each piece have the same amount of clay, or does one have more?
Area	8–10 years	Does each of these two cows have the same amount of grass to eat?	Now does each cow have the same amount of grass to eat, or does one cow have more?

➤ Figure 8.1

Piaget's Conservation Tasks

Pictured here are several of Piaget's conservation tasks. The ability to answer each task correctly develops at approximately the age indicated. (From Berk, 1994.)

Although Piaget's genius and his monumental contribution to scientists' knowledge of mental development are rarely disputed, his methods and some of his findings and conclusions have been criticized (Halford, 1989). It now seems clear that children are more advanced cognitively and adults less competent cognitively than Piaget believed (Flavell, 1985, 1992; Mandler, 1990; Siegler, 1991). According to Flavell (1996), "Piaget's greatest contribution was to found the field of cognitive development as we currently know it" (p. 200). Today, few developmental psychologists believe that cognitive development takes place in the general stagelike fashion proposed by Piaget.

Kohlberg's Theory of Moral Development

Lawrence Kohlberg (1927–1987) believed (Kohlberg, 1981, 1984, 1985) that moral reasoning is closely related to cognitive development and that it, too, evolves in stages. Kohlberg (1969) studied moral development by presenting a series of moral dilemmas to male participants from the United States and other countries. Read one of his best-known dilemmas in *Try It! 8.2* (on page 219).

> What did Kohlberg believe about moral development?

Piaget's Stages of Cognitive Development

STAGE		DESCRIPTION
Sensorimotor (0 to 2 years)		Infants experience the world through their senses, actions, and body movements. At the end of this stage, toddlers develop the concept of object permanence and can mentally represent objects in their absence.
Preoperational (2 to 7 years)		Children are able to represent objects and events mentally with words and images. They can engage in imaginary play (pretend), using one object to represent another. Their thinking is dominated by their perceptions, and they are unable to consider more than one dimension of an object at the same time (centration). Their thinking is egocentric; that is, they fail to consider the perspective of others.
Concrete operational (7 to 11 or 12 years)		Children at this stage become able to think logically in concrete situations. They acquire the concepts of conservation and reversibility, can order objects in a series, and can classify them according to multiple dimensions.
Formal operational (11 or 12 years and beyond)		At this stage, adolescents learn to think logically in abstract situations, learn to test hypotheses systematically, and become interested in the world of ideas. Not all people attain full formal operational thinking.

Kohlberg was less interested in whether the participants judged Heinz's behavior (as described in the *Try It!*) right or wrong than in the reasons for their responses. He found that moral reasoning could be classified into three levels, with each level having two stages.

> **What are Kohlberg's three levels of moral reasoning?** ▶

At Kohlberg's first level of moral development, the **preconventional level,** moral reasoning is governed by the standards of others rather than one's own internalized standards of right and wrong. An act is judged good or bad based on its physical consequences. In Stage 1, "right" is whatever avoids punishment; in Stage 2, "right" is whatever is rewarded, benefits the individual, or results in a favor being returned. "You scratch my back and I'll scratch yours" is the type of thinking common at this stage. Children usually function at the preconventional level through age 10.

At Kohlberg's second level of moral development, the **conventional level,** the individual has internalized the standards of others and judges right and wrong in terms of those standards. At Stage 3, sometimes called the *good boy–nice girl orientation,* "good behavior is that which pleases or helps others and is approved by them"

preconventional level
Kohlberg's lowest level of moral development, in which moral reasoning is based on the physical consequences of an act; "right" is whatever avoids punishment or gains a reward.

Try It ! 8.2 A Moral Dilemma

In Europe, a woman was near death from a special kind of cancer. There was one drug the doctors thought might save her. It was a form of radium that a druggist in the same town had recently discovered. The drug was expensive to make, and the druggist was charging ten times what it cost him. He paid $200 for the radium and charged $2,000 for a small dose of the drug. The sick woman's husband, Heinz, went to everyone he knew to borrow the money, but he could only get together $1,000, which was half of what the drug cost. He told the druggist that his wife was dying and asked him to sell it cheaper or let him pay later. But the druggist said, "No, I discovered the drug, and I am going to make money from it." So Heinz got desperate and broke into the man's store to steal the drug for his wife (Colby et al., 1983, p. 77).

What moral judgment would you make about the dilemma? Should Heinz have stolen the drug? Why or why not?

(Kohlberg, 1968, p. 26). At Stage 4, the orientation is toward "authority, fixed rules, and the maintenance of the social order. Right behavior consists of doing one's duty, showing respect for authority, and maintaining the given social order for its own sake" (p. 26). Kohlberg believed that a person must function at Piaget's concrete operations stage to reason morally at the conventional level.

Kohlberg's highest level of moral development is the **postconventional level,** which requires the ability to think at Piaget's stage of formal operations. Postconventional reasoning is most often found among middle-class, college-educated people. At this level, people do not simply internalize the standards of others. Instead, they weigh moral alternatives, realizing that the law may sometimes conflict with basic human rights. At Stage 5, the person believes that laws are formulated to protect both society and the individual and should be changed if they fail to do so. At Stage 6, ethical decisions are based on universal ethical principles, which emphasize respect for human life, justice, equality, and dignity for all people. People who reason morally at Stage 6 believe that they must follow their conscience even if it results in a violation of the law.

Review and Reflect 8.2 (on page 220) summarizes Kohlberg's six stages of moral development. Kohlberg claimed that people progress through these stages one at a time in a fixed order, without skipping any stage; if movement occurs, it is to the next higher stage. Postconventional reasoning is not possible, Kohlberg said, until people fully attain Piaget's level of formal operations. They must be able to think abstractly and to apply ethical principles in hypothetical situations (Kohlberg & Gilligan, 1971; Kuhn et al., 1977). As Kohlberg came to realize, discussion of moral dilemmas does not reliably improve moral behavior. He eventually agreed that direct teaching of moral values is necessary and compatible with his theory (Higgins, 1995; Power et al., 1989).

In a classic review of 45 studies of Kohlberg's theory conducted in 27 countries, Snarey (1985) found support for the universality of Stages 1 through 4 and for the invariant sequence of these stages in all groups studied. Although extremely rare, Stage 5 was found in almost all samples from urban or middle-class populations and absent in all of the tribal or village folk societies studied. And Snarey's more recent research (1995) supports the conclusions of his earlier work.

One controversy concerning Kohlberg's theory involves the possibility of gender bias. Kohlberg indicated that the majority of women remain at Stage 3, while most men attain Stage 4. Do men typically attain a higher level of moral reasoning than women? Carol Gilligan (1982) asserts that Kohlberg's theory is sex-biased. Not only did Kohlberg fail to include females in his original research, Gilligan points out, but he limited morality to abstract reasoning about moral dilemmas. And, at his high-

conventional level
Kohlberg's second level of moral development, in which right and wrong are based on the internalized standards of others; "right" is whatever helps or is approved of by others, or whatever is consistent with the laws of society.

postconventional level
Kohlberg's highest level of moral development, in which moral reasoning involves weighing moral alternatives; "right" is whatever furthers basic human rights.

◄ What do cross-cultural studies reveal about the universality of Kohlberg's theory?

Kohlberg's Stages of Moral Development

LEVEL	STAGE
Level I: Preconventional level (Ages 4–10) Moral reasoning is governed by the standards of others; an act is good or bad depending on its physical consequences—whether it is punished or rewarded.	**Stage 1** The stage in which behavior that avoids punishment is right. Children obey out of fear of punishment. **Stage 2** The stage of self-interest. What is right is what benefits the individual or gains a favor in return. "You scratch my back and I'll scratch yours."
Level II: Conventional level (Ages 10–13) The child internalizes the standards of others and judges right and wrong according to those standards.	**Stage 3** The morality of mutual relationships. The "good boy–nice girl" orientation. Child acts to please and help others. **Stage 4** The morality of the social system and conscience. Orientation toward authority. Morality is doing one's duty, respecting authority, and maintaining the social order.
Level III: Postconventional level (After age 13, at young adulthood, or never) Moral conduct is under internal control; this is the highest level and the mark of true morality.	**Stage 5** The morality of contract; respect for individual rights and laws that are democratically agreed on. Rational valuing of the wishes of the majority and the general welfare. Belief that society is best served if citizens obey the law. **Stage 6** The highest stage of the highest social level. The morality of universal ethical principles. The person acts according to internal standards independent of legal restrictions or opinions of others.

est level, Stage 6, Kohlberg emphasized justice and equality but not mercy, compassion, love, or concern for others. Gilligan suggests that females, more than males, tend to view moral behavior in terms of compassion, caring, and concern for others. Thus, she agrees that the content of moral reasoning differs between the sexes, but she contends that males and females do not differ in the complexity of their moral reasoning. More recent evidence suggests that females do tend to emphasize care and compassion in resolving moral dilemmas, while males tend to stress justice or at least to give it equal standing with caring (Garmon et al., 1996; Wark & Krebs, 1996). Although Kohlberg's theory does emphasize rights and justice over concern for others, researchers, nevertheless, have found that females score as high as males in moral reasoning (Walker, 1989).

Other critics claim that Kohlberg's theory has a built-in liberal bias and is culture-bound, favoring Western middle-class values (Simpson, 1974; Sullivan, 1977). Yet Snarey (1985), in his review of 45 studies, found that samples from India, kibbutzim in Israel, Taiwan, and Turkey "ranked higher than parallel groups from the United States at one or more points in the life cycle" (p. 228).

Finally, some critics point out that moral reasoning and moral behavior are not one and the same. Kohlberg readily acknowledged that people can be capable of making mature moral judgments yet fail to live morally. But, said Kohlberg (1968), "The man who understands justice is more likely to practice it" (p. 30). Regardless of whether we agree with Kohlberg's theory, most of us would agree that moral reasoning and moral behavior are critically important aspects of human development. Moral individuals make moral societies.

Erikson's Theory of Psychosocial Development

Erik Erikson (1902–1994) proposed the only major theory of development to include the entire life span. According to Erikson, individuals progress through eight **psychosocial stages,** each of which is defined by a conflict involving the individual's relationship with the social environment, which must be resolved satisfactorily in order for healthy development to occur. The stages are named for a "series of alternative basic attitudes," one of which will result, depending on how the conflict is resolved (Erikson, 1980).

◄ What is Erikson's theory of psychosocial development?

According to Erikson's view, the foundations of adult personality are laid in four childhood stages. During the first stage, *basic trust versus basic mistrust,* infants (birth to 1 year) develop a sense of trust or mistrust depending on the degree and regularity of care, love, and affection they receive from the mother or primary caregiver. Erikson (1980) considered "basic trust as the cornerstone of a healthy personality" (p. 58). During the second stage, *autonomy versus shame and doubt,* children aged 1 to 3 begin to express their independence (often by saying "No!") and develop their physical and mental abilities. In the third stage, *initiative versus guilt,* 3- to 6-year-old children go beyond merely expressing their autonomy and begin to develop initiative. During the fourth stage, *industry versus inferiority,* school-aged children (age 6 years to puberty) begin to enjoy and take pride in making things and doing things.

◄ What are Erikson's four stages of psychosocial development in childhood?

Erikson's later stages begin with puberty, but they are not as strongly tied to chronological age as those that occur during childhood. Instead, the adolescent and adult stages represent important themes of adult life. These themes occur in a fixed sequence, Erikson claimed, because the resolution of each depends on how well prior stages were resolved.

The first of these stages is *identity versus role confusion,* during which adolescents experience a phenomenon Erikson called the *identity crisis.* During the identity crisis, teens must develop an idea of how they will fit into the adult world. A healthy identity, Erikson claimed, is essential to the next stage, *intimacy versus isolation,* which begins around age 18. During this stage, young adults must find a life partner or come to a healthy acceptance of living in a single state. The next major theme of adult life, *generativity versus stagnation,* is at its peak during the years of middle age. Generativity, according to Erikson, is the desire to guide the next generation, through parenting, teaching, or mentoring. Finally, in later years, adults experience *ego integrity versus despair.* The goal of this stage is an acceptance of one's life in preparation for facing death. *Review and Reflect 8.3* (on page 222) summarizes Erikson's psychosocial stages.

◄ What are Erikson's four stages of psychosocial development in adolescence and adulthood?

Most research on Erikson's theory has focused on trust in infants, identity formation in adolescents, and generativity in middle-aged adults. Specific predictions derived from Erikson's descriptions of these three stages have received mixed research support. On the positive side, there is a great deal of evidence that a relationship with a trusted caregiver in infancy is critical to later development.

In contrast, most research examining the development of identity has shown that the process does begin in adolescence, but it is not complete until well into the early adult years (Waterman, 1985). Many college students, for example, have not yet settled on a major or future career when they begin taking classes, and they use experiences in their first few semesters to make these important decisions. One reason for the apparent delay may be that advances in logical reasoning, such as those associated with Piaget's formal operational stage, are strongly related to identity formation (Klaczynski et al., 1998). Formal operational thinking evolves slowly across

psychosocial stages
Erikson's eight developmental stages for the entire life span; each is defined by a conflict that must be resolved satisfactorily in order for healthy personality development to occur.

Erikson's Psychosocial Stages of Development

STAGE	AGES	DESCRIPTION
Trust vs. mistrust	Birth to 1 year	Infants learn to trust or mistrust depending on the degree and regularity of care, love, and affection provided by parents or caregivers.
Autonomy vs. shame and doubt	1 to 3 years	Children learn to express their will and independence, to exercise some control, and to make choices. If not, they experience shame and doubt.
Initiative vs. guilt	3 to 6 years	Children begin to initiate activities, to plan and undertake tasks, and to enjoy developing motor and other abilities. If not allowed to initiate or if made to feel stupid and considered a nuisance, they may develop a sense of guilt.
Industry vs. inferiority	6 years to puberty	Children develop industriousness and feel pride in accomplishing tasks, making things, and doing things. If not encouraged or if rebuffed by parents and teachers, they may develop a sense of inferiority.
Identity vs. role confusion	Adolescence	Adolescents must make the transition from childhood to adulthood, establish an identity, develop a sense of self, and consider a future occupational identity. Otherwise, role confusion can result.
Intimacy vs. isolation	Young adulthood	Young adults must develop intimacy—the ability to share with, care for, and commit themselves to another person. Avoiding intimacy brings a sense of isolation and loneliness.
Generativity vs. stagnation	Middle adulthood	Middle-aged people must find some way of contributing to the development of the next generation. Failing this, they may become self-absorbed and emotionally impoverished and reach a point of stagnation.
Ego integrity vs. despair	Late adulthood	Individuals review their lives, and if they are satisfied and feel a sense of accomplishment, they will experience ego integrity. If dissatisfied, they may sink into despair.

the adolescent years. Consequently, people may not have the cognitive ability to engage in the kind of thinking necessary for the development of identity until the early adult years.

With regard to generativity, in one study of young, midlife, and older women, researchers found that generativity did increase in middle age as Erikson's theory predicts (Zucker et al., 2002). However, it did not decline in old age. The oldest group of participants (with an average age of 66) cited generative concerns as important to them just as frequently as the middle-aged group did. So, generativity may be more a characteristic of middle than of early adulthood, as Erikson predicted, but it appears to continue to be important in old age.

Now that you have had an introduction to three important stage theories, let's turn our attention to the major milestones of each phase of development.

genes
The segments of DNA that are located on the chromosomes and are the basic units for the transmission of all hereditary traits.

chromosomes
Rod-shaped structures in the nuclei of body cells, which contain all the genes.

Heredity and Prenatal Development

The Mechanism of Heredity: Genes and Chromosomes

Genes, the biological blueprints that determine and direct the transmission of all hereditary traits, are segments of DNA located on the rod-shaped structures called **chromosomes** found in the nuclei of body cells. Normal human cells, with two exceptions, have 23 pairs of chromosomes (46 chromosomes in all). The two exceptions are the sperm cells and the mature egg cells, each of which has 23 single chromosomes. At conception, the sperm adds its 23 single chromosomes to the 23 of the egg. From this union, a single cell called a *zygote* is formed. The zygote has the full complement of 46 chromosomes (23 pairs), which contain about 30,000 genes–all the genetic information needed to make a human being.

The chromosomes of the 23rd pair are called **sex chromosomes** because they carry the genes that determine a person's sex, primary and secondary sex characteristics, and other sex-linked traits such as red-green color blindness, male pattern baldness, and hemophilia. The sex chromosomes of females consist of two X chromosomes (XX); males have an X chromosome and a Y chromosome (XY). The egg cell always contains an X chromosome. Half of a man's sperm cells carry an X chromosome and half carry a Y. Therefore, the sex of a child depends on whether the egg (X) is fertilized by a sperm carrying an X chromosome, which produces a female (XX), or a sperm carrying a Y chromosome, which produces a male (XY).

When two different genes are transmitted for the same trait, one is usually a **dominant gene,** causing the dominant trait to be expressed in the individual. The gene for brown hair, for example, is dominant over the gene for blond hair. A person having one gene for brown hair and one gene for blond hair will have brown hair (see Figure 8.2). The gene for blond hair is recessive. A **recessive gene** will be expressed if it is paired with another recessive gene. Therefore, blond people have two recessive genes for blond hair.

sex chromosomes
The 23rd pair of human chromosomes, which carry the genes that determine one's sex, primary and secondary sex characteristics, and other sex-linked traits.

How are hereditary traits transmitted?

dominant gene
The gene of any pair that is expressed in the individual.

recessive gene
A gene that will not be expressed if paired with a dominant gene but will be expressed if paired with another recessive gene.

When are dominant or recessive genes expressed in an individual's traits?

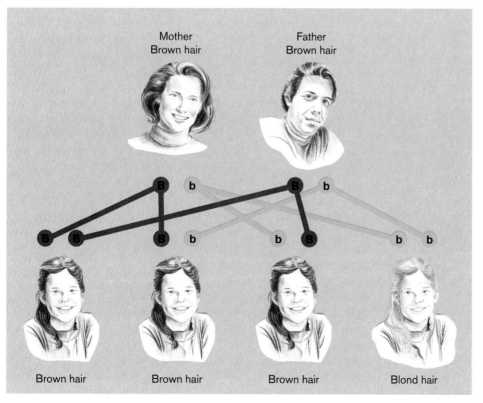

▶ Figure 8.2

Gene Transmission for Hair Color

This figure shows all the possible combinations in children when both parents carry a gene for brown hair (B) and a gene for blond hair (b). The chance of their having a blond-haired child (bb) or a brown-haired child (BB) is 25% in each case. There is a 50% chance of having a brown-haired child who carries both the dominant gene (B) and the recessive gene (b).

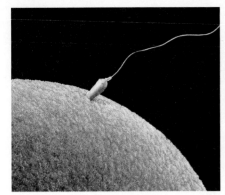
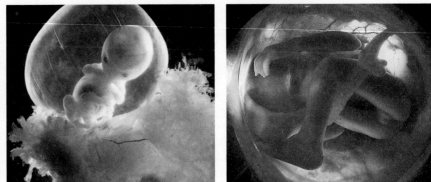

 These photos show the fertilization of an egg by a sperm (left), an embryo at 7 weeks (center), and a fetus at 22 weeks (right).

period of the zygote
The approximately 2-week-long period between conception and the attachment of the zygote to the uterine wall.

> What are the three stages of prenatal development?

prenatal
Occurring between conception and birth.

embryo
The developing human organism during the period (week 3 through week 8) when the major systems, organs, and structures of the body develop.

fetus
The developing human organism during the period (week 9 until birth) when rapid growth and further development of the structures, organs, and systems of the body occur.

> What are some negative influences on prenatal development, and during what time is their impact greatest?

Many traits, such as height, involve several genes and are referred to as *polygenic*. Most polygenic traits do not involve dominant and recessive genes. Instead, several genes work together to produce such a trait. Many polygenic traits are also *multifactorial;* that is, they are influenced by both heredity and environment. For example, an individual's adult height is influenced by several genes, but environmental factors present during childhood are also influential. Thus, people who are poorly nourished during childhood may not reach their potential genetic height. Some psychological traits, such as intelligence, are also polygenic and multifactorial.

The Stages of Prenatal Development

Conception usually takes place in one of the fallopian tubes, and within the next 2 weeks the zygote travels to the uterus and attaches itself to the uterine wall. During this 2-week period, called the **period of the zygote,** rapid cell division occurs. At the end of this first stage of **prenatal** development, the zygote is only the size of the period at the end of this sentence. The second stage is the *period of the embryo,* when the major systems, organs, and structures of the body develop. Lasting from week 3 through week 8, this period ends when the first bone cells form. Only 1 inch long and weighing $^1/_7$ of an ounce, the **embryo** already resembles a human being, with limbs, fingers, toes, and many internal organs that have begun to function. The final stage of prenatal development, called the *period of the fetus,* lasts from the end of the second month until birth. The **fetus** undergoes rapid growth and further development of the structures, organs, and systems of the body. Table 8.1 describes the characteristics of each stage of prenatal development.

In the case of **identical (monozygotic) twins,** one egg is fertilized by one sperm, but the zygote splits and develops into two embryos with identical genes. Thus, identical twins are always of the same sex. This splitting of the zygote seems to be a chance occurrence accounting for about 4 in 1,000 births. **Fraternal (dizygotic) twins** develop when two eggs are released during ovulation and are fertilized by two different sperm. The two zygotes develop into two siblings who are no more alike genetically than other brothers and sisters. The likelihood of fraternal twins increases if there is a family history of multiple births, if the mother is between ages 35 and 40, or if the mother has recently stopped taking birth control pills. Also, fertility drugs often cause the release of more than one egg.

Negative Influences on Prenatal Development

Most of the time, prenatal development results in a healthy baby. However, there are several factors that can negatively affect the process. One is lack of prenatal care, so pregnant women would do well to follow the advice in the *Apply It!* at the end of the chapter. Another is maternal health. The babies of women who suffer from chronic conditions such as diabetes may experience retardation or acceleration of fetal growth (Levy-Shiff et al., 2002). And when the

Table 8.1 Stages of Prenatal Development

Stage	Time after Conception	Major Activities of the Stage
Period of the zygote	1 to 2 weeks	Zygote attaches to the uterine lining. At 2 weeks, zygote is the size of the period at the end of this sentence.
Period of the embryo	3 to 8 weeks	Major systems, organs, and structures of the body develop. Period ends when first bone cells appear. At 8 weeks, embryo is about 1 inch long and weighs $1/7$ of an ounce.
Period of the fetus	9 weeks to birth (38 weeks)	Rapid growth and further development of the body structures, organs, and systems.

mother suffers from a viral disease such as *rubella, chicken pox,* or *HIV,* she may deliver an infant with physical and behavioral abnormalities (Amato, 1998; Kliegman, 1998).

Teratogens are substances that can have a negative impact on prenatal development, causing birth defects and other problems. A teratogen's impact depends on both its intensity and the time during prenatal development when it is present. Teratogens generally have their most devastating consequences during the period of the embryo. During this time, there are **critical periods** when certain body structures develop. If drugs or other harmful substances interfere with development during a critical period, the body structure will not form properly; nor will it develop later (Kopp & Kaler, 1989).

The use of heroin, cocaine, and crack during pregnancy has been linked to miscarriage, prematurity, low birthweight, breathing difficulties, physical defects, and fetal death. Alcohol also crosses the placental barrier, and alcohol levels in the fetus almost match the levels in the mother's blood (Little et al., 1989). Women who drink heavily during pregnancy risk having babies with **fetal alcohol syndrome.** Babies with this syndrome are mentally retarded and have abnormally small heads with wide-set eyes and a short nose. They also have behavioral problems such as hyperactivity (Julien, 1995). Some children prenatally exposed to alcohol have *fetal alcohol effects*–they show some of the characteristics of fetal alcohol syndrome but in less severe form. The Surgeon General warns women to abstain from drinking alcohol altogether during pregnancy, but about 20% ignore the warnings (Braun, 1996).

Smoking decreases the amount of oxygen and increases the amount of carbon monoxide crossing the placental barrier. The embryo or fetus is exposed to nicotine and several thousand other chemicals as well. Smoking while pregnant increases the probability that the baby will be premature or of low birthweight (McDonald et al., 1992; Nordentoft et al., 1996). Further, because researchers disagree as to whether heavy caffeine consumption has an adverse effect on the fetus, the wisest course of action is to restrict caffeine consumption to less than 300 milligrams (3 cups) daily.

Most teratogens are associated with an increased risk of delivering either a low-birthweight or preterm infant. **Low-birthweight babies** are those weighing less than 5.5 pounds. Infants of this weight born at or before the 37th week are considered **preterm infants.** The smaller and more premature the baby, the greater the risk of problems that range from subtle learning and behavior problems in babies closer to normal birthweight to "severe retardation, blindness, hearing loss, and even death" in the smallest newborns (Apgar & Beck, 1982, p. 69).

identical (monozygotic) twins
Twins with exactly the same genes, who develop after one egg is fertilized by one sperm and then the zygote splits into two parts.

fraternal (dizygotic) twins
Twins, no more alike genetically than ordinary siblings, who develop after two eggs are released during ovulation and fertilized by two different sperm.

teratogens
Harmful agents in the prenatal environment, which can have a negative impact on prenatal development or even cause birth defects.

critical period
A period so important to development that a harmful environmental influence at that time can keep a bodily structure from developing normally or can impair later intellectual or social development.

fetal alcohol syndrome
A condition, caused by maternal alcohol intake during pregnancy, in which the baby is born mentally retarded, with a small head and facial, organ, and behavioral abnormalities.

low-birthweight baby
A baby weighing less than 5.5 pounds.

preterm infant
An infant born before the 37th week and weighing less than 5.5 pounds; a premature infant.

Infancy

Neonates (newborn babies) come equipped with an impressive range of **reflexes**—built-in responses to certain stimuli that are needed to ensure survival in their new world. Sucking, swallowing, coughing, and blinking are some necessary behaviors that newborns can perform right away. Newborns will move an arm, a leg, or other body part away from a painful stimulus and will try to remove a blanket or cloth placed over the face. Stroke a baby on the cheek and you will trigger the rooting reflex—the baby opens his or her mouth and actively searches for a nipple. Moreover, all five senses are working at birth, although a number of refinements are still to come.

Perceptual Development

> **What are the perceptual abilities of the newborn?**

The newborn already has preferences for certain odors, tastes, sounds, and visual configurations. Hearing is much better developed than vision in the neonate and is functional even before birth (Busnel et al., 1992). A newborn is able to turn his or her head in the direction of a sound and shows a general preference for female voices. Newborns are able to discriminate among and show preferences for certain odors and tastes (Bartoshuk & Beauchamp, 1994; Leon, 1992). They favor sweet tastes and are able to differentiate between salty, bitter, and sour solutions. Newborns are also sensitive to pain (Porter et al., 1988) and are particularly responsive to touch, reacting positively to stroking and fondling.

Robert Fantz (1961) made a major breakthrough when he realized that a baby's interest in an object can be gauged by the length of time it fixates on it. Fantz demonstrated that infants prefer the image of a human face to other images such as a black-and-white abstract pattern (see Figure 8.3). Fantz's study and others have shown that newborns have clear preferences and powers of discrimination—and even memory recognition and learning ability.

At birth, an infant's vision is about 20/600, and it typically does not reach 20/20 until the child is about 2 years old (Courage & Adams, 1990; Held, 1993). Newborns

neonate
A newborn infant up to 1 month old.

reflexes
Built-in responses to certain stimuli that neonates need to ensure survival in their new world.

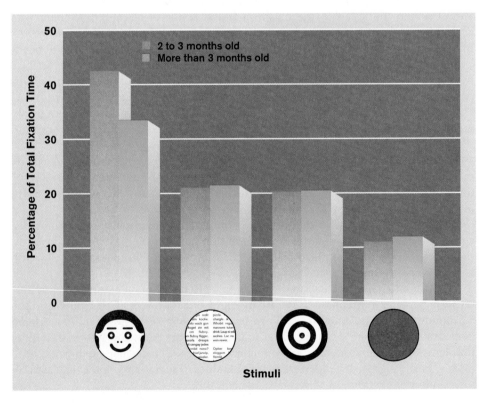

➤ Figure 8.3

Results of Fantz's Study

Using a device called a *viewing box* to observe and record infants' eye movements, Fantz (1961) found that they preferred faces to black-and-white abstract patterns.

focus best on objects about 9 inches away, and they can follow a slowly moving object. Infants from 22 to 93 hours old already indicate a preference for their own mother's face over that of an unfamiliar female (Field et al., 1984). Although newborns prefer colored stimuli to gray ones, babies can't distinguish all of the colors adults normally can until they are about 2 months old (Brown, 1990).

One famous experiment was devised to study depth perception in infants and other animals. Gibson and Walk (1960) designed an apparatus called the **visual cliff,** which is "a board laid across a sheet of heavy glass, with a patterned material directly beneath the glass on one side and several feet below it on the other" (p. 65). This arrangement made it appear that there was a sudden drop-off, or "visual cliff," on one side. Most babies aged 6 to 14 months could be coaxed by their mothers to crawl to the shallow side, but only three would crawl onto the deep side. Gibson and Walk concluded that most babies "can discriminate depth as soon as they can crawl" (p. 64).

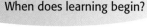 When placed on the visual cliff, most infants older than 6 months will not crawl out over the deep side, indicating that they can perceive depth.

Learning and Motor Development

In a classic study of prenatal learning, DeCasper and Spence (1986) had 16 pregnant women read *The Cat in the Hat* to their developing fetuses twice a day during the final 6 weeks of pregnancy. A few days after birth, the infants could adjust their sucking on specially designed, pressure-sensitive nipples to hear their mother reading either *The Cat in the Hat* or *The King, the Mice, and the Cheese,* a story they had never heard before. By their sucking behavior, the infants showed a definite preference for the familiar story. Clearly, this study and others like it show that babies come into the world ready to learn.

 When does learning begin?

The ability to recognize the sound of a particular story results from the experience of hearing the story read repeatedly. In contrast, the rapid changes in motor skills babies undergo during the first few years of life arise primarily because of maturation. **Maturation** occurs naturally according to the infant's own genetically determined biological timetable of development. Many motor milestones, such as sitting, standing, and walking (shown in Figure 8.4, on page 228), depend on the growth and development of the central nervous system.

What is the primary factor influencing attainment of the major motor milestones?

Still, experience does have some influence on the development of motor skills. For instance, the rate at which milestones are achieved is slowed when an infant is subjected to extremely unfavorable environmental conditions, such as severe malnutrition or maternal or sensory deprivation. Further, cross-cultural research reveals that in some African cultures in Uganda and Kenya, mothers use special motor-training techniques that enable their infants to attain some of the major motor milestones earlier than most infants in the United States (Kilbride & Kilbride, 1975; Super, 1981). But speeding up the attainment of motor skills has no lasting impact on development. Babies will walk, talk, and be toilet-trained according to their own developmental schedules.

visual cliff
An apparatus used to test depth perception in infants and young animals.

maturation
Changes that occur according to one's genetically determined biological timetable of development.

temperament
A person's behavioral style or characteristic way of responding to the environment.

Temperament

Is each baby born with an individual behavior style or characteristic way of responding to the environment—a particular **temperament**? The New York Longitudinal Study was undertaken in 1956 to investigate temperament and its effect on development. Thomas, Chess, and Birch (1970) studied 2- to 3-month-old infants and followed them into adolescence and adulthood using observation, interviews with parents and teachers, and psychological tests. They found that "children do show distinct individuality in temperament in the first weeks of life independently of their parents' handling or personality style" (p. 104). Three general types of temperament emerged from the study.

What is temperament, and what are the three types of temperament identified by Thomas, Chess, and Birch?

➤ Figure 8.4

The Progression of Motor Development

Most infants develop motor skills in the sequence shown in the figure. The ages indicated are only averages, so normal, healthy infants may develop any of these milestones a few months earlier or several months later than the average. (From Frankenburg et al., 1992.)

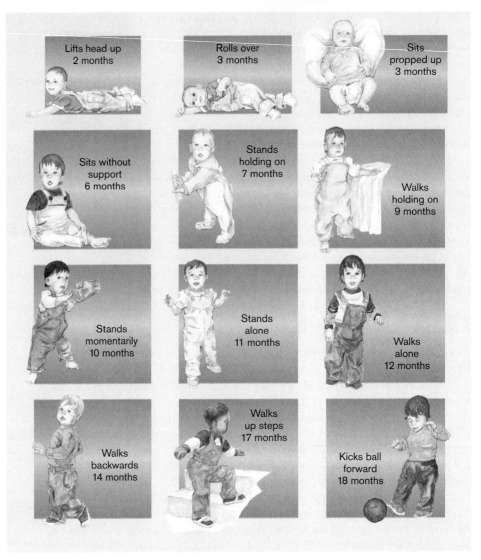

"Easy" children—40% of the group studied—had generally pleasant moods, were adaptable, approached new situations and people positively, and established regular sleeping, eating, and elimination patterns. "Difficult" children—10% of the group—had generally unpleasant moods, reacted negatively to new situations and people, were intense in their emotional reactions, and showed irregularity of bodily functions. "Slow-to-warm-up" children—15% of the group—tended to withdraw, were slow to adapt, and were "somewhat negative in mood." The remaining 35% of the children studied were too inconsistent to categorize.

Thomas and others (1970) believe that personality is molded by the continuous interaction of temperament and environment. Although the environment can intensify, diminish, or modify these inborn behavioral tendencies, "the original characteristics of temperament tend to persist in most children over the years" (p. 104). Adjustment in children seems to rest in part on the fit between individual temperament and the accommodation of family and environment to behavioral style. A difficult child may stimulate hostility and resentment in parents and others, which, in turn, may perpetuate the child's negative behavior. On the other hand, an easy child usually elicits a positive response from parents and others, which reinforces the child's behavior and increases the likelihood that the behavioral style will continue.

Several studies have revealed that children who were undercontrolled or impulsive at a young age tended to become aggressive, danger-seeking, impulsive adolescents (Hart et al., 1997) with strong negative emotions (Caspi & Silva, 1995).

Overcontrolled children were found to be "more prone to social withdrawal" (Hart et al., 1997) and lacking in social potency as adolescents; that is, "they were submissive, not fond of leadership roles, and had little desire to influence others" (Caspi & Silva, 1995, p. 495).

Attachment

Almost all infants form a strong **attachment** to their mothers or primary caregivers. But what precisely is the glue that binds caregiver (usually the mother) and infant?

A series of classic studies conducted by Harry Harlow on attachment in rhesus monkeys was critical to developmentalists' understanding of infant–caregiver attachment. Harlow constructed two surrogate (artificial) monkey "mothers." One was a plain wire-mesh cylinder with a blocky wooden head; the other was a wire-mesh cylinder that was padded, covered with soft terry cloth, and fitted with a somewhat more monkeylike head. A baby bottle could be attached to either surrogate mother for feeding. Newborn monkeys were placed in individual cages where they had equal access to a cloth surrogate and a wire surrogate. The source of their nourishment (cloth or wire surrogate) was unimportant. "The infants developed a strong attachment to the cloth mothers and little or none to the wire mothers" (Harlow & Harlow, 1962, p. 141). Harlow found that it was *contact comfort*–the comfort supplied by bodily contact–rather than nourishment that formed the basis of the infant monkey's attachment to its mother. If the cloth mother was not present when unfamiliar objects were placed in the cage, the monkey would huddle in the corner, clutching its head, rocking, sucking its thumb or toes, and crying in distress. But when the cloth mother was present, it would first cling to her and then explore and play with the unfamiliar objects.

Numerous studies have shown that the attachment process is similar in human infants (Posada et al., 2002). The mother holds, strokes, and talks to the baby and responds to the baby's needs, and the baby gazes at and listens to the mother and even moves in synchrony with her voice (Condon & Sander, 1974; Lester et al., 1985). Once the attachment has formed, infants show **separation anxiety**–fear and distress when the parent leaves them. Occurring from about 8 months to 24 months, separation anxiety peaks between 12 and 18 months of age (Fox & Bell, 1990). At about 6 or 7 months of age, infants develop a fear of strangers called **stranger anxiety,** which increases in intensity until the first birthday and then declines in the second year (Marks, 1987). Stranger anxiety is greater in an unfamiliar setting, when the parent is not close at hand, and when a stranger abruptly approaches or touches the child.

There are important differences in the quality of attachment. In a classic study of mother-child attachment, Mary Ainsworth (1973, 1979) observed mother–child interactions in the home during the infants' first year and then again at age 12 months in a laboratory. Based on infants' reactions to their mothers after brief periods of separation, Ainsworth and others (1978; Main & Solomon, 1990) identified four patterns of attachment.

The first pattern is *secure attachment* (observed in about 65% of American infants). Although usually distressed when separated from their mother, securely attached infants eagerly seek to re-establish the connection and then show an interest in play. They use the mother as a safe base of operation from which to explore and are typically more responsive, obedient, cooperative, and content than other infants. In addition, secure attachment seems to protect infants from the potentially adverse effects of risk factors such as poverty (Belsky & Fearon, 2002). And parents who were securely attached as infants are more responsive to their own babies (van IJzendoorn, 1995).

Infants with a pattern called *avoidant attachment* (approximately 20% of American infants) are usually not responsive to their mother when she is present and not troubled when she leaves. When the parent returns, the infant may actively avoid contact with her or, at least, not be quick to greet her. In short, these infants do not act much more attached

Harlow found that infant monkeys developed a strong attachment to a cloth-covered surrogate mother and little or no attachment to a wire surrogate mother—even when the wire mother provided nourishment.

 What did Harlow's studies reveal about attachment in infant monkeys?

 When does separation anxiety, a sign of attachment, reach its peak?

 What are the four attachment patterns identified in infants?

attachment
The strong affectionate bond a child forms with the mother or primary caregiver.

separation anxiety
The fear and distress shown by a toddler when the parent leaves, occurring from 8 to 24 months and reaching a peak between 12 and 18 months.

stranger anxiety
A fear of strangers common in infants at about 6 months and increasing in intensity until about 12 months, and then declining in the second year.

to the parent than to a stranger. Mothers of avoidant infants tend to show little affection and to be generally unresponsive to their infants' needs and cries.

Prior to a period of separation, infants who show *resistant attachment* (10–15% of American infants) seek and prefer close contact with their mother. Yet, in contrast to securely attached infants, they do not tend to branch out and explore. And when the mother returns to the room after a period of separation, the resistant infant displays anger and may push the mother away or hit her. When picked up, the infant is hard to comfort and may continue crying.

The pattern of *disorganized/disoriented attachment* (seen in 5–10% of American infants) is the most puzzling and apparently the least secure pattern. When reunited with the mother, the infant with this pattern of attachment exhibits contradictory and disoriented responses. Rather than looking at the mother while being held, the child may purposely look away or approach the mother with an expressionless or depressed demeanor. Also characteristic are a dazed and vacant facial expression and a peculiar, frozen posture after being calmed by the mother.

Although mother–child, rather than father–child, attachment relationships have been the traditional focus of research, fathers can be as responsive and competent as mothers (Roberts & Moseley, 1996), and their attachments can be just as strong. Indeed, father–child interactions have many enduring positive influences on children. Children who experience regular interaction with their fathers tend to have higher IQs and to do better in social situations and at coping with frustration than children lacking such interaction. They also persist longer in solving problems and are less impulsive and less likely to become violent (Adler, 1997; Bishop & Lane, 2000; Roberts & Moseley, 1996). Positive father–son relationships are also associated with higher-quality parenting behavior by sons when they have children of their own (Shears et al., 2002).

Interactions with fathers may be important for development because mothers and fathers interact differently with infants and children. Fathers engage in more exciting and arousing physical play with children (McCormick & Kennedy, 2000). Mothers are more likely to cushion their children against overstimulation and potential injury. Consequently, some developmentalists believe that fathers are more supportive than mothers of children's confidence and identity development (Moradi, cited in Adler, 1997). For example, fathers allow infants to crawl farther away, up to twice as far as mothers usually allow. And fathers remain farther away as the infant explores novel stimuli and situations. Ideally, of course, children need both kinds of influences.

Fathers tend to engage in more physical play with their children than do mothers. However, many fathers today also share basic child-care responsibilities, such as feeding and diaper changing, with mothers.

What are the typical differences in the ways mothers and fathers interact with infants and children? ▶

Early and Middle Childhood

Language Development

What are the stages of language development, from cooing through the acquisition of grammatical rules? ▶

During their first few months, infants communicate distress or displeasure through crying. But then they begin rapidly to acquire language.

During the second or third month, infants begin *cooing*–repeatedly uttering vowel sounds such as "ah" and "oo." At about 6 months, infants begin **babbling.** They utter *phonemes*–the basic speech sounds of any language, which form words when combined. During the first part of the babbling stage, infants babble all the basic speech sounds that occur in all the languages of the world. Language up to this point seems to be biologically determined, because all babies throughout the world, even deaf children, vocalize this same range of speech sounds.

At about 8 months, babies begin to focus attention on those speech sounds (phonemes) common to the language spoken around them and on the rhythm and intonation of that language. And by 1 year, the babbling stage gives way to the one-word stage. The first words usually represent objects that move or those that infants can act on

babbling
Vocalization of the basic speech sounds (phonemes), which begins between 4 and 6 months.

www.ablongman.com/woodmastering1e

or interact with. From 13 to 18 months of age, children markedly increase their vocabulary (Woodward et al., 1994), and 2-year-olds know about 270 words (Brown, 1973).

Initially a child's understanding of words differs from that of an adult. When they lack the correct word, children may act on the basis of shared features and apply a word to a broader range of objects than is appropriate. This is known as **overextension.** For example, any man may be called "dada" and any four-legged animal, "doggie." **Underextension** occurs, too; this is when children fail to apply a word to other members of the class. The family's poodle is a "doggie," but the German shepherd next door is not.

Between 18 and 20 months of age, when their vocabulary is about 50 words, children begin to put nouns, verbs, and adjectives together in two-word phrases and sentences. At this stage, children depend to a great extent on gesture, tone, and context to convey their meaning (Slobin, 1972). Depending on intonation, their sentences may indicate questions, statements, or possession. Children adhere to a rigid word order. You might hear "mama drink," "drink milk," or "mama milk," but not "drink mama," "milk drink," or "milk mama."

Between 2 and 3 years of age, children begin to use short sentences, which may contain three or more words. Labeled **telegraphic speech** by Roger Brown (1973), these short sentences follow a rigid word order and contain only essential content words, leaving out all plurals, possessives, conjunctions, articles, and prepositions. Telegraphic speech reflects the child's understanding of *syntax*–the rules governing how words are ordered in a sentence. When a third word is added to a sentence, it usually fills in the word missing from the two-word sentence (for example, "mama drink milk"). After using telegraphic speech for a time, children gradually begin to add modifiers to make their sentences more precise.

Children pick up grammatical rules intuitively and apply them rigidly. **Overregularization** is the kind of error that results when a grammatical rule is misapplied to a word that has an irregular plural or past tense (Marcus, 1996). Thus, children who have correctly used the words "went," "came," and "did" incorrectly apply the rule for past tenses and begin to say "goed," "comed," and "doed." What the parents see as a regression in speech actually means that the child has acquired a grammatical rule.

Learning theorists have long maintained that language is acquired in the same way as other behaviors–as a result of learning through reinforcement and imitation. B. F. Skinner (1957) asserted that parents selectively criticize incorrect speech and reinforce correct speech through praise, approval, and attention. Thus, the child's utterances are progressively shaped in the direction of grammatically correct speech. Others believe that children acquire vocabulary and sentence construction mainly through imitation (Bandura, 1977a). However, imitation cannot account for patterns of speech such as telegraphic speech or for systematic errors such as overregularization. And parents seem to reinforce children more for the content of the utterance than for the correctness of the grammar (Brown et al., 1968).

Noam Chomsky (1957) believes that language ability is largely innate, and he has proposed a very different theory. Chomsky (1968) maintains that the brain contains a *language acquisition device (LAD),* which enables children to acquire language and discover the rules of grammar easily and naturally. Language develops in stages that occur in a fixed order and appear at about the same times in most normal children. Lenneberg (1967) claims that biological maturation underlies language development in much the same way as it underlies physical and motor development. These claims are known as the *nativist position.*

The nativist position is better able than learning theory to account for the fact that children throughout the world go through the same basic stages in language development. It also accounts for the similar errors all children make when they are first learning to form plurals, past tenses, and negatives–errors not acquired through imitation or reinforcement.

Nevertheless, some environmental factors do contribute to language development. For example, babies whose parents are responsive to their babbling vocalize more than infants whose parents are not responsive to them (Whitehurst et al., 1989). Moreover,

overextension
The act of using a word, on the basis of some shared feature, to apply to a broader range of objects than is appropriate.

underextension
Restricting the use of a word to only a few, rather than to all, members of a class of objects.

telegraphic speech
Short sentences that follow a strict word order and contain only essential content words.

overregularization
The act of inappropriately applying the grammatical rules for forming plurals and past tenses to irregular nouns and verbs.

How do learning theory and the nativist position explain the acquisition of language?

Deaf mothers use sign language to communicate with their young children, but they do so in "motherese," signing slowly and with frequent repetitions.

parents can facilitate language acquisition by adjusting their speech to their infant's level of development. Parents often use *motherese*–highly simplified speech with shorter phrases and sentences and simpler vocabulary, which is uttered slowly, at a high pitch, and with exaggerated intonation and much repetition (Fernald, 1993). Deaf mothers communicate with their infants in a similar way, signing more slowly and with exaggerated hand and arm movements and frequent repetition (Masataka, 1996).

Throughout the industrialized world, children must master written as well as spoken language. As you might expect, many aspects of the development of spoken language are critical to the process of learning to read. *Phonological awareness,* or sensitivity to the sound patterns of a language and how they are represented as letters, is particularly important. Children who can correctly answer questions such as "What would *bat* be if you took away the [b]?" by the age of 4 or so learn to read more rapidly than their peers who cannot (de Jong & van der Leij, 2002). Moreover, children who have good phonological awareness skills in their first language learn to read more easily even when reading instruction is conducted in a second language (Mumtaz & Humphreys, 2002; Quiroga et al., 2002).

Children seem to learn phonological awareness skills through word play. Among English-speaking children, learning nursery rhymes facilitates the development of these skills (Layton et al., 1996). Japanese parents foster phonological awareness in their children by playing a game with them called *shiritori,* in which one person says a word and another must supply a word that begins with its ending sound (Serpell & Hatano, 1997). Activities in which parents and children work together to read or write a story also foster the development of phonological awareness (Aram & Levitt, 2002).

Socialization

The process of learning socially acceptable behaviors, attitudes, and values is called **socialization.** Although parents have the major role in their children's socialization, peers affect the process as well.

A longitudinal study that followed individuals from age 5 to age 41 revealed that "children of warm, affectionate parents were more likely to be socially accomplished adults who, at age 41, were mentally healthy, coping adequately, and psychosocially mature in work, relationships, and generativity" (Franz et al., 1991, p. 593). The methods parents use to control children's behavior contribute to socialization as well. Diane Baumrind (1971, 1980, 1991) studied the continuum of parental control and identified three parenting styles–authoritarian, authoritative, and permissive.

Authoritarian parents make the rules, expect unquestioned obedience from their children, punish misbehavior (often physically), and value obedience to authority. Rather than giving a rationale for a rule, authoritarian parents consider "because I said so" a sufficient reason for obedience. Parents using this parenting style tend to be uncommunicative, unresponsive, and somewhat distant, and Baumrind (1967) found preschool children disciplined in this manner to be withdrawn, anxious, and unhappy. The authoritarian style has been associated with low intellectual performance and lack of social skills, especially in boys (Maccoby & Martin, 1983).

Authoritative parents set high but realistic and reasonable standards, enforce limits, and at the same time encourage open communication and independence. They are willing to discuss rules and supply rationales for them. Knowing why the rules are necessary makes it easier for children to internalize them and to follow them, whether in the presence of their parents or not. Authoritative parents are generally warm, nurturant, supportive, and responsive, and they show respect for their children and their opinions. Their children are more mature, happy, self-reliant, self-controlled, assertive, socially competent, and responsible than their peers. The authoritative par-

What are the three parenting styles identified by Baumrind, and which did she find most effective?

What outcomes are often associated with authoritative, authoritarian, and permissive parenting styles?

socialization
The process of learning socially acceptable behaviors, attitudes, and values.

www.ablongman.com/woodmastering1e

enting style is associated with higher academic performance, independence, higher self-esteem, and internalized moral standards in middle childhood and adolescence (Lamborn et al., 1991; Steinberg et al., 1989).

Although they are rather warm and supportive, **permissive parents** make few rules or demands and usually do not enforce those that are made. They allow children to make their own decisions and control their own behavior. Children raised in this manner are the most immature, impulsive, and dependent, and they seem to be the least self-controlled and self-reliant.

Permissive parents also come in the indifferent, unconcerned, uninvolved variety (Maccoby & Martin, 1983). This parenting style is associated with drinking problems, promiscuous sex, delinquent behavior, and poor academic performance in adolescents.

The positive effects of authoritative parenting have been found across all ethnic groups in the United States (Querido et al., 2002; Steinberg & Dornbusch, 1991). The one exception is among first-generation Asian immigrants, where the authoritarian style is more strongly associated with academic achievement (Chao, 2001). Developmental psychologist Ruth Chao suggests that this finding may be explained by the traditional idea in Asian culture that making a child obey is an act of affection. Moreover, strict parenting tends to be tempered by emotional warmth in Asian families, so children probably get the idea that their parents expect unquestioning obedience because they love them.

Friendships begin to develop by the age of 3 or 4, and relationships with peers become increasingly important. These early relationships are usually based on shared activities; two children think of themselves as friends while they are playing together. During the elementary school years, friendships tend to be based on mutual trust (Dunn et al., 2002). By middle childhood, membership in a peer group is central to a child's happiness. Peer groups are usually composed of children of the same race, sex, and social class (Schofield & Francis, 1982). The peer group serves a socializing function by providing models of behavior, dress, and language. Peer groups provide objective measures against which children can evaluate their own traits. They are also a continuing source of both reinforcement for appropriate behavior and punishment for deviant behavior. In fact, peer rejection often results in excessive aggression (Wood et al., 2002).

Gender Role Development

Traditionally, males have been expected to be independent and competitive; females have been expected to be warm and nurturant. Psychologists use the term **gender roles** to refer to such expectations. Children display play behavior that is consistent with gender roles fairly early in life, by age 2 or so. Psychologists differ in how they explain gender role development.

According to the biological view, genes and prenatal sex hormones have an important influence on gender role development. In a review of studies on the effects of prenatal androgens (male sex hormones) Collaer and Hines (1995) found that these hormones have a reasonably strong influence on children's play behavior. Girls exposed to prenatal androgens are more likely than girls not exposed to these hormones to prefer to play with toys favored by boys, such as trucks, cars, and fire engines (Berenbaum & Snyder, 1995). Prenatal androgens are also known to affect brain development and functioning in humans and many other animal species (Beyenburg et al., 2000).

Of course, biological influences on gender role development don't operate in an environmental vacuum. For example, from infancy on, most of the presents children receive are gender-consistent: Girls are given dolls and tea sets, while boys get trucks and sports equipment. And while a girl may feel complimented if someone calls her

▲ Parenthood can cause stress and conflict in a marriage, but it is also immensely satisfying for most couples.

◀ How do peers contribute to the socialization process?

authoritarian parents
Parents who make arbitrary rules, expect unquestioned obedience from their children, punish transgressions, and value obedience to authority.

authoritative parents
Parents who set high but realistic standards, reason with the child, enforce limits, and encourage open communication and independence.

permissive parents
Parents who make few rules or demands and allow children to make their own decisions and control their own behavior.

gender roles
Cultural expectations about the behavior appropriate for each gender.

a "tomboy," almost every boy considers it an insult to be called a "sissy" (Doyle & Paludi, 1995).

What are three psychological theories that attempt to explain gender role development?

As you might expect, for social learning theorists, environmental influences are considered more important than biological forces in explaining gender role development (Mischel, 1966). These theorists point out that children are usually reinforced for imitating behaviors considered appropriate for their gender. When behaviors are not appropriate (a boy puts on lipstick, or a girl pretends to shave her face), children are quickly informed, often in a reprimanding tone, that boys or girls do not do that. However, there is little evidence that parents reinforce gender role–appropriate behavior in girls and boys often enough to account for the early age at which children begin to show gender-typed behavior (Fagot, 1995). Thus, imitation and reinforcement probably play some part in gender role development, but they do not provide a full explanation of this phenomenon.

Cognitive developmental theory, proposed by Lawrence Kohlberg (1966; Kohlberg & Ullian, 1974), suggests that an understanding of gender is a prerequisite to gender role development. According to Kohlberg, children go through a series of stages in acquiring the concept of gender. Between ages 2 and 3, children acquire *gender identity*–their sense of being a male or a female. Between ages 4 and 5, children acquire the concept of *gender stability*–awareness that boys are boys and girls are girls for a lifetime. Finally, between ages 6 and 8, children understand *gender constancy*–that gender does not change regardless of the activities people engage in or the clothes they wear. Moreover, according to Kohlberg, when children realize their gender is permanent, they are motivated to seek out same-sex models and learn to act in ways considered appropriate for their gender.

Cross-cultural studies reveal that Kohlberg's stages of gender identity, gender stability, and gender constancy occur in the same order in cultures as different as those in Samoa, Kenya, Nepal, and Belize (Munroe et al., 1984). However, this theory fails to explain why many gender-appropriate behaviors and preferences are observed in children as young as age 2 or 3, long before gender constancy is acquired (Bussey & Bandura, 1999; Jacklin, 1989; Martin & Little, 1990).

Gender-schema theory, proposed by Sandra Bem (1981), provides a more complete explanation of gender role development. Like social learning theory, gender-schema theory suggests that young children are motivated to pay attention to and behave in a way consistent with gender-based standards and stereotypes of the culture. Like cognitive developmental theory, gender-schema theory stresses that children begin to use gender as a way to organize and process information (Bussey & Bandura, 1999). But gender-schema theory holds that this process occurs earlier, when gender identity rather than gender constancy is attained (Bem, 1985). According to Martin and Little (1990), "Once children can accurately label the sexes, they begin to form gender stereotypes and their behavior is influenced by these gender-associated expectations" (p. 1438). They develop strong preferences for sex-appropriate toys and clothing, and they favor same-sex peers over those of the other sex (Powlishta, 1995). To a large extent, children's self-concepts and self-esteem depend on the match between their abilities and behaviors and the cultural definition of what is desirable for their gender. Consequently, the desire to maintain self-esteem, according to gender-schema theory, motivates children to align their behavior with culturally defined gender roles.

The Influence of Television

Many parents, teachers, and psychologists have expressed concerns about how repeated viewing of the horrific events of September 11, 2001 will affect children. Because these events were so bizarre and shocking, developmental psychologists have little research on which to make predictions about their long-term effects (Atwood & Donnelly, 2002). However, they do know a lot about how the more typical stimuli on television influence children.

Literally thousands of studies suggest that TV violence leads to aggressive behavior in children and teenagers (Slaby et al., 1995). Other studies show that excessive TV viewing is linked to childhood obesity (Tuncer & Yalcin, 2000). Television, however, can be an effective educational medium. *Mister Rogers' Neighborhood* has been found to increase prosocial behavior, imaginative play, and task persistency in preschoolers (Stein & Friedrich, 1975). Children viewing *Sesame Street* at ages 3 and 4 had larger vocabularies and better prereading skills at age 5 (Rice et al., 1990). Jerome and Judith Singer (cited in Leland, 1997) found that *Barney & Friends* encouraged creative play among 2- to 3-year-olds.

Adolescence

The concept of **adolescence**—a period of transition from childhood to adulthood— did not exist until psychologist G. Stanley Hall first wrote about it in his book by that name in 1904. He portrayed this stage in life as one of "storm and stress," the inevitable result of biological changes occurring during the period. Anna Freud (1958), daughter of Sigmund Freud, even considered a stormy adolescence a necessary part of normal development. However, for at least half of all adolescents, the period is marked by healthy development (Takanishi, 1993). And researchers continue to find that the majority of adolescents say that they are happy and self-confident (Diener & Diener, 1996).

How difficult is adolescence for most teenagers?

adolescence
The developmental stage that begins at puberty and encompasses the period from the end of childhood to the beginning of adulthood.

Puberty

Adolescence begins with the onset of **puberty**—a period of rapid physical growth and change that culminates in sexual maturity. Although the average onset of puberty is age 10 for girls and age 12 for boys, the normal range extends from age 7 to age 14 for girls and from 9 to 16 for boys (Tanner, 1990). Puberty begins with a surge in hormone production followed by a marked acceleration in growth known as the *adolescent growth spurt*. On average, the growth spurt occurs from age 10 to 13 in girls and about 2 years later in boys, from age 12 to 15 (Tanner, 1990). Because various parts of the body grow at different rates, the adolescent often has a lanky, awkward appearance. Girls attain their full height between ages 16 and 17, and boys, between ages 18 and 20 (Tanner, 1990).

What physical changes occur during puberty?

puberty
A period of rapid physical growth and change that culminates in sexual maturity.

During puberty, the reproductive organs in both sexes mature and **secondary sex characteristics** appear—those physical characteristics not directly involved in reproduction that distinguish the mature male from the mature female. In girls, the breasts develop, and the hips round; in boys, the voice deepens, and facial and chest hair appears; and in both sexes, there is growth of pubic and underarm (axillary) hair. The major landmark of puberty for males is the first ejaculation, which occurs, on average, at age 13 (Jorgensen & Keiding, 1991). And for females, it is **menarche**—the onset of menstruation—which occurs at an average age of 12, although from 10 to 15 is considered the normal range (Tanner, 1990).

secondary sex characteristics
Those physical characteristics that are not directly involved in reproduction but distinguish the mature male from the mature female.

The timing of puberty can have important psychological consequences, coming as it does at a time when a sense of security is gained from being like other members of the peer group. Many studies show that early-maturing boys, taller and stronger than their classmates, have an advantage in sports and are likely to have a positive body image, to feel confident, secure, independent, and happy, and to be more successful academically as well (Alsaker, 1995; Blyth et al., 1981; Peterson, 1987). However, early-maturing boys may also be more hostile and aggressive than later-maturing peers (Ge et al., 2001). In addition, among boys from poor families, earlier-than-average puberty is correlated with affiliation with deviant peers (Ge et al., 2002).

What are the psychological effects of early and late maturation for boys and girls?

Early-maturing girls, who may tower over their peers, feel more self-conscious about their developing bodies and their size. Consequently, they are more likely than late-maturing girls to develop eating disorders (Kaltiala-Heino et al., 2001). In addi-

menarche
(men-AR-kee) The onset of menstruation.

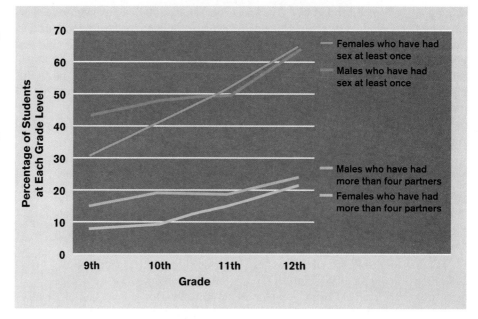

➤ Figure 8.5

Incidence of Sexual Activity in U.S. High School Students

This graph, based on a survey of several thousand high school students in 1999, shows that the proportions of sexually active boys and girls increase dramatically from grade 9 to 12. (Data from CDC, 2000.)

tion to having earlier sexual experiences and more unwanted pregnancies than late-maturing girls, early-maturing girls are more likely to be exposed to alcohol and drug use (Caspi et al., 1993). And, having had such experiences, early-maturing girls, not surprisingly, tend to perform less well academically than their age mates (Stattin & Magnusson, 1990). Late-maturing girls often experience considerable stress when they fail to develop physically along with their peers, but they are likely to be taller and slimmer than their early-maturing age mates.

Sexuality and Adolescence

As Figure 8.5 indicates, the incidence of sexual activity among teenagers in the United States increases dramatically across grades 9 to 12 (Centers for Disease Control [CDC], 2000). Public health officials point out that one particularly alarming statistic is the proportion of teens who have had multiple sex partners before leaving high school, because the more partners an individual has (whether teen or adult), the more likely he or she is to contract a sexually transmitted disease.

Teens who tend to be less experienced sexually attend religious services frequently and live with both biological parents, who are neither too permissive nor too strict in their discipline and rules (Miller et al., 1998; White & DeBlassie, 1992). Early intercourse is also less prevalent among adolescents whose academic achievement is above average and who are involved in sports (Brooks-Gunn & Furstenberg, 1989; Savage & Holcomb, 1999).

Teenage Pregnancy

The rate of teenage pregnancy is higher in the United States than in any other developed country. For example, there are about 50 births per year for every 1,000 teenage girls in the United States, while the rate is only 4 per 1,000 in Japan (Singh & Darroch, 2000). It's important to keep in mind, though, that most teen pregnancies occur after the age of 16 and that the incidence of teen pregnancy has actually declined in the United States since the 1960s. What has increased is the number of births to *unmarried* adolescent mothers. In the 1960s, about 80% of teen mothers were married, compared with only 20% in the late 1990s (Singh & Darroch, 2000).

Early pregnancy can have serious physical consequences. Pregnant teens are more likely to come from poor backgrounds and less likely to receive early prenatal

What are some of the consequences of teenage pregnancy?

medical care and adequate nutrition. As a result, they are at higher risk for miscarriage, stillbirth, and complications during delivery. They are also more likely to deliver premature or low-birthweight babies, who have a higher infant mortality rate (Fraser et al., 1995; Goldenberg & Klerman, 1995; Scholl et al., 1996).

Among young women who give birth before age 18 and choose to keep their babies, half never complete high school. As a group, their earning power is about half that of their counterparts who did not have babies at this early age (National Research Council, 1993), and many of these very young mothers eventually depend on welfare (Grogger & Bronars, 1993). As a result, children of teen mothers are more likely to grow up in poverty than those of older mothers (Bee & Boyd, 2004).

Adolescent Thought

Formal operational thinking enables adolescents to think of what might be. Thus, they begin to conceive of "perfect" solutions to the world's and their own problems. For example, a teen whose parents are divorced may idealize her noncustodial parent and believe that her life would be wonderful if only she could live with that parent. Piaget used the term **naive idealism** to refer to this kind of thinking.

Psychologist David Elkind (1967, 1974) claims that the early teenage years are marked by another kind of unrealistic thought, *adolescent egocentrism,* which takes two forms: the imaginary audience and the personal fable. The **imaginary audience** consists of admirers and critics that adolescents conjure up and that exist only in their imagination. In their minds, they are always on stage. Teens may spend hours in front of the mirror trying to please this audience. Teenagers also have an exaggerated sense of personal uniqueness and indestructibility that Elkind calls the **personal fable.** Many believe they are somehow indestructible and protected from the misfortunes that befall others, such as unwanted pregnancies or drug overdoses.

Social Relationships in Adolescence

Most adolescents have good relationships with their parents (Steinberg, 1990). And of the three parenting styles discussed earlier in the chapter–authoritative, authoritarian, and permissive–the authoritative style is most effective and the permissive least effective for adolescents (Baumrind, 1991; Steinberg et al., 1994). In a study of about 2,300 adolescents, those with permissive parents were more likely to use alcohol and drugs and to have conduct problems and less likely to be interested in academic success than were those with authoritative or authoritarian parents (Lamborn et al., 1991). The authoritarian style was related to more psychological distress and less self-reliance and self-confidence in adolescents.

Even adolescents who have good relationships with their parents usually feel the need to separate from them to some degree. As a result, friends become a vital source of emotional support and approval for most of them. Adolescents usually choose friends of the same sex and race (Clark & Ayers, 1992), who have similar values, interests, and backgrounds (Duck, 1983; Epstein, 1983). Interactions with peers are critical while young people are forming their identities. Adolescents can try out different roles and observe the reactions of their friends to their behavior and their appearance. The peer group provides teenagers with a standard of comparison for evaluating their personal assets, as well as a vehicle for developing social skills (Berndt, 1992).

What are some of the functions of the adolescent peer group?

Early and Middle Adulthood

The long period of 50 or more years known as adulthood is generally divided into three parts: young or early adulthood (ages 20 to 40 or 45), middle adulthood (ages 40 or 45 to 65), and late adulthood (after age 65 or 70). These ages are only approxi-

naive idealism
A type of thought in which adolescents construct ideal solutions for problems.

imaginary audience
A belief of adolescents that they are or will be the focus of attention in social situations and that others will be as critical or approving as they are of themselves.

personal fable
An exaggerated sense of personal uniqueness and indestructibility, which may be the basis for adolescent risk taking.

mate because there are no biological or psychological events that neatly define the beginning or ending of a period. Obviously, some things change; but, in many ways, adults remain much the same as they were in their earlier years. The most obvious changes are usually physical ones.

Physical Changes

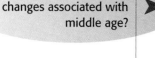

What are the physical changes associated with middle age?

Most people enjoy good general health and vitality in their 20s and 30s, but the first of these decades is the period of top physical condition, when physical strength, reaction time, reproductive capacity, and manual dexterity all peak. After age 30, there is a slight decline in these physical capacities, which is barely perceptible to most people other than professional athletes. Middle-aged people often complain about a loss of physical vigor and endurance. But such losses have to do less with aging than with exercise, diet, and health habits. One unavoidable change in the mid- to late 40s, though, is **presbyopia,** a condition in which the lenses of the eyes no longer accommodate adequately for near vision, and reading glasses or bifocals are required for reading.

The major biological event for women during middle age is **menopause**—the cessation of menstruation, which usually occurs between ages 45 and 55 and signifies the end of reproductive capacity. The most common symptom associated with menopause and the sharp decrease in the level of estrogen is *hot flashes*—sudden feelings of being uncomfortably hot. Some women also experience symptoms such as anxiety, irritability, and/or mood swings, and about 10% become depressed. However, most women do not experience psychological problems in connection with menopause (Busch et al., 1994; Matthews, 1992).

Although men do not have a physical event equivalent to menopause, they do experience a gradual decline in testosterone from age 20 until about age 60. During late middle age, many men also experience a reduction in the functioning of the prostate gland that affects the production of semen. Usually coupled with these reductions in testosterone and semen production is a reduction in the sex drive. However, though women are not able to conceive after menopause, many men can and do father children during late adulthood.

presbyopia

(prez-bee-O-pee-uh) A condition, occurring in the mid- to late 40s, in which the lenses of the eyes no longer accommodate adequately for near vision, and reading glasses or bifocals are required for reading.

menopause

The cessation of menstruation, occurring between ages 45 and 55 and signifying the end of reproductive capacity.

Intellectual Capacity

In general, do adults show an increase or a decrease in intellectual performance from their 20s to their 60s?

Young adults outperform middle-aged and older adults on tests requiring speed or rote memory. But on tests measuring general information, vocabulary, reasoning ability, and social judgment, older participants usually do better than younger ones because of their greater experience and education (Horn, 1982). Adults actually continue to gain knowledge and skills over the years, particularly when they lead intellectually challenging lives.

Schaie (1994, 1995) analyzed data from the Seattle Longitudinal Study, which assessed the intellectual abilities of some 5,000 participants. Many of the participants were tested six times over the course of 35 years. Schaie found that in five areas—verbal meaning, spatial orientation, inductive reasoning, number, and word fluency—participants showed modest gains from young adulthood to the mid-40s. Decline did not occur, on average, until after age 60, and even then the decline was modest until the 80s. Half of the participants, even at age 81, showed no decline compared to their earlier performance. The study also revealed several gender differences: Females performed better on tests of verbal meaning and inductive reasoning; males tended to do better on tests of number and spatial orientation. The only ability found to show a continuous decline from the mid-20s to the 80s was perceptual speed.

Careers

A career can define your lifestyle—the friends you choose, the neighborhood you live in, your habits, and even your ideas and opinions. And satisfying work also seems to be an important component of overall life satisfaction for most adults (Meeus et al., 1997). As you might expect, pursuing a career that is suited to one's personality is one ingredient of a satisfying work life. Moreover, working in an environment where supervisors are encouraging and most employees are optimistic and satisfied with their jobs also contributes to satisfaction (Blustein et al., 1997).

One of the most profound changes in employment patterns has been the tremendous increase of women in the workplace. In the 1960s, for example, only 18% of mothers with children younger than 6 years of age worked outside the home; by 1999, the proportion had increased to 61% (United States Census Bureau, 2001). However, women's career patterns are different from those of men. Many women follow an "in-and-out" pattern in which they work for several years, then take time off to have children, then return to the workforce a few months or years later. As a result, women, on average, do not advance as rapidly in the workplace as their male coworkers do. The combination of slower advancement and sex discrimination results in lower average salaries for women.

Personality and Social Development

Many people consider middle age the prime of life. Researcher Bernice Neugarten (1968) states that society "may be oriented towards youth," but it is "controlled by the middle-aged" (p. 93). People aged 40 to 60 are the decision makers in industry, government, and society. Neugarten found that very few at this age "express a wish to be young again" (p. 97). As a participant in one of her studies said, "There is a difference between wanting to feel young and wanting to be young" (p. 97).

> Why is middle age often considered the prime of life?

Reaching middle age, many men and women begin to express personality characteristics they had formerly suppressed. Men generally become more nurturant, and women more assertive. For many women, middle age is a time of increased freedom. Wink and Helson (1993) found that after children leave home, most women work at least part-time and tend to experience an increase in self-confidence and a heightened sense of competence and independence. Contrary to the conventional notion of the *empty nest syndrome,* most parents seem to be happier when their children are on their own (Norris & Tindale, 1994). Parents have more time and money to pursue their own goals and interests. For most people, an empty nest is a happy nest!

Later Adulthood

In the early years of the 20th century, life expectancy in the United States was only 49 years. By the century's end, the expected life span of someone born in the United States was about 76 years. As a result, older adults (those over 65) now constitute a larger proportion of the U.S. population than ever before—more than 15% (United States Census Bureau, 2001). Other industrialized nations have experienced similar increases in the proportion of elderly adults. And, amazingly, adults over the age of 100 belong to one of the most rapidly growing age groups worldwide. One result of this trend has been increased interest in and concerns about the quality of life in old age. What are your perceptions of life after 65? Before reading further, complete *Try It! 8.3* (on page 240) by answering true or false to the statements about older adults.

Physical Changes

It was long assumed that the number of neurons in the brain declined sharply in later adulthood, but this assumption appears to be false (Gallagher & Rapp, 1997). Research has shown that the shrinking volume of the aging cortex is due more to breakdown of the myelin that covers the axons in the white matter than to loss of the neurons that make up the gray matter (Peters et al., 1994; Wickelgren, 1996).

> What are some physical changes associated with later adulthood?

Try It ! 8.3   Is There Life after 65?

Are the following statements true (T) or false (F)?

_____ 1. Older adults tend to express less satisfaction with life in general than younger adults do.

_____ 2. A lack of money is a serious problem for most people over age 65.

_____ 3. Marital satisfaction declines in old age.

_____ 4. Mandatory retirement forces most workers out of jobs before they are ready to leave.

_____ 5. The majority of retirees do not adjust well to retirement.

_____ 6. A large percentage of individuals over age 85 end up in nursing homes or institutions.

Answers: All of the statements are false!

As you learned in Chapter 2, the myelin sheath facilitates the rapid conduction of neural impulses. The breakdown of myelin thus explains one of the most predictable characteristics of aging–the slowing of behavior (Birren & Fisher, 1995). With degeneration of the myelin, the brain takes longer to process information, and reaction time is slower.

With advancing age, the elderly typically become more farsighted, have increasingly impaired night vision, and suffer hearing loss in the higher frequencies (Long & Crambert, 1990; Slawinski et al., 1993). Joints become stiffer, and bones lose calcium and become more brittle, increasing the risk of fractures from falls.

About 80% of Americans over age 65 have one or more chronic conditions such as arthritis, heart problems, or high blood pressure. For both males and females, the three leading causes of death are heart disease, cancer, and stroke. But the good news is that, in spite of all of these changes, the majority of people over age 65 consider their health good. One-half of those aged 75 to 84 and more than one-third of those over 85 do not have to curb their activities because of health problems (Toufexis, 1988). In short, the majority of older adults are active, healthy, and self-sufficient (Schaie & Willis, 1996). An interesting study of the "oldest old"–those over 95–revealed that they are often in better mental and physical condition than those 20 years younger (Perls, 1995). They often remain employed and sexually active through their 90s and carry on "as if age were not an issue" (p. 70). How do they do it? They appear to have a genetic advantage that makes them particularly resistant to the diseases that kill or disable most people at younger ages.

Men and women in their 60s and 70s who exercise properly and regularly can have the energy and fitness of someone 20 to 30 years younger (deVries, 1986). Research suggests that physical exercise even enhances the performance of older adults on tests of reaction time, working memory, and reasoning (Clarkson-Smith & Hartley, 1990). "People rust out faster from disuse than they wear out from overuse" (Horn & Meer, 1987, p. 83). In one study, 100 frail nursing-home residents, average age 87, exercised their thigh and hip muscles vigorously on exercise machines for 45 minutes three times a week. At the end of 10 weeks, participants had increased their stair-climbing power by 28.4% and their walking speed by 12%, and four of them were able to exchange their walkers for canes (Fiatarone et al., 1994). For most of us, remaining fit and vigorous as we age lies within our power.

Masters and Johnson (1966) studied the sexual response in older men and women and found that regular sexual relations are necessary to maintain effective sexual performance. In a survey of adults aged 80 to 102 who were not taking medication, 70% of the men and 50% of the women admitted fantasizing about intimate sexual relations often or very often. But 63% of these older men and 30% of the women were doing more than fantasizing–they were still having sex (McCarthy, 1989).

Cognitive Changes

Intellectual decline in late adulthood is not inevitable. Older adults who keep mentally and physically active tend to retain their mental skills as long as their health is good (Meer, 1986). They do well on tests of vocabulary, comprehension, and general information, and their ability to solve practical problems is generally higher than that of young adults. And they are just as capable as younger adults at learning new cognitive strategies (Saczynski et al., 2002).

Researchers often distinguish between two types of intelligence (Horn, 1982): **Crystallized intelligence**–one's verbal ability and accumulated knowledge–tends to increase over the life span. **Fluid intelligence**–abstract reasoning and mental flexibility–peaks in the early 20s and declines slowly as people age. The rate at which people process information also slows gradually with age (Hertzog, 1991; Lindenberger et al., 1993; Salthouse, 1996). This explains, in part, why older adults perform more poorly on tests requiring speed.

Is it accurate to equate old age with forgetfulness? In laboratory memory tasks, older people do as well or almost as well as younger people on recognition tasks (Hultsch & Dixon, 1990) and on recall of information in their areas of expertise (Charness, 1989). But on tasks requiring speed of processing in short-term memory or recall of items that hold no particular meaning for them, younger participants do significantly better than older ones (Verhaeghen et al., 1993).

Several factors are positively correlated with good cognitive functioning in the elderly: a higher education level (Anstey et al., 1993; Lyketsos et al., 1999), a complex work environment, a long marriage to an intelligent spouse, and a higher income (Schaie, 1990). And gender is a factor as well. Women not only outlive men, they generally show less cognitive decline during old age. But intellectual functioning can be hampered by physical problems (Manton et al., 1986) or by psychological problems such as depression. A study by Shimamura and others (1995) revealed that people who continue to lead intellectually stimulating and mentally active lives are far less likely to suffer mental decline as they age. So, "use it or lose it" is good advice if you want to remain mentally sharp as you age.

◄ What happens to mental ability in later adulthood?

crystallized intelligence
Aspects of intelligence, including verbal ability and accumulated knowledge, that tend to increase over the life span.

fluid intelligence
Aspects of intelligence involving abstract reasoning and mental flexibility, which peak in the early 20s and decline slowly as people age.

◄ Older adults take more time to learn new skills, but they apply newly learned skills as accurately as younger adults do.

Alzheimer's Disease and Other Types of Dementia

Senile dementia, or *senility,* is a state of severe mental deterioration marked by impaired memory and intellect, as well as by altered personality and behavior. It afflicts about 5–8% of those over age 65, 15–20% of those over 75, and 25–50% of those over 85 (American Psychiatric Association, 1997). Senility is caused by physical deterioration of the brain. It can result from such conditions as cerebral arteriosclerosis (hardening of the arteries in the brain), chronic alcoholism, and irreversible damage by a series of small strokes.

What is Alzheimer's disease?

About 50–60% of all cases of senility result from Alzheimer's disease. In **Alzheimer's disease,** there is a progressive deterioration of intellect and personality that results from widespread degeneration of brain cells. Just over 4 million people in the United States suffer from this incurable disorder (National Institute on Aging, 2001). At first, victims show a gradual impairment in memory and reasoning and in efficiency in carrying out everyday tasks. Many have difficulty finding their way around in familiar locations. As the disorder progresses, Alzheimer's patients become confused and irritable, tend to wander away from home, and become increasingly unable to take care of themselves. Eventually, their speech becomes unintelligible, and they become unable to control bladder and bowel functions. If they live long enough, they reach a stage where they do not respond when spoken to and no longer recognize even spouse or children.

Age and a family history of Alzheimer's disease are the two risk factors that have been consistently associated with the disorder (Farrer & Cupples, 1994; Payami et al., 1994; Williams, 2003). Can Alzheimer's disease be delayed? According to Alexander and others (1997), a high IQ coupled with lifelong intellectual activity may delay or lessen the symptoms of Alzheimer's in those who are at risk for the disease. Tang and others (1996) reported that postmenopausal women who had taken estrogen supplements for 10 years reduced their risk of developing Alzheimer's by almost 40%. And certain antiinflammatory drugs (such as ibuprofen) and the antioxidant vitamin E may provide a measure of protection (Nash, 1997; Sano et al., 1997). Other substances and drugs currently being studied for use in the prevention of Alzheimer's include folic acid (Reynolds, 2002), antioxidants such as vitamin C (Brown et al., 2002), and nicotine (Murray & Abeles, 2002).

Social Adjustment

Would you say that people are more satisfied with their marriages and with life in general when they are young adults or when they are over 65? It may surprise you to learn that in several major national surveys, life satisfaction and feelings of well-being were about as high in older adults as in younger ones (Inglehart, 1990) (see Figure 8.6). Life satisfaction appears to be most strongly related to good health, as well as to a feeling of control over one's life (Schulz & Heckhausen, 1996). Levenson and others (1993) found that older couples tended to be happier in their marriages than middle-aged couples, experiencing less conflict and more sources of pleasure than their younger counterparts.

Most retirees are happy to leave the world of work; less than 12.5% of people over age 65 remain in the workforce. Generally, those most reluctant to retire are better educated, hold high-status jobs with a good income, and find fulfillment in their work. Life satisfaction after retirement also appears to be related to participation in community service and in social activities (Harlow & Cantor, 1996). Bosse and others (1991) found that only 30% of retirees reported finding retirement stressful, and of those who did, most were likely to be in poor health and to have financial problems.

Poverty is a stress factor for many elders. About 10.5% of Americans over age 65 live below the poverty line, and among them are disproportionately high numbers of African Americans (26.4%) and Hispanic Americans (21%) (U.S. Bureau of the Census, 2001). But many adults in the 65-plus group live comfortably. With homes that are paid for and no children to support, people over 65 tend to view their financial situation more positively than do younger adults.

senile dementia
A state of mental deterioration caused by physical deterioration of the brain and characterized by impaired memory and intellect and by altered personality and behavior; also referred to as *senility.*

Alzheimer's disease
(ALZ-hye-merz) An incurable form of dementia characterized by progressive deterioration of intellect and personality, resulting from widespread degeneration of brain cells.

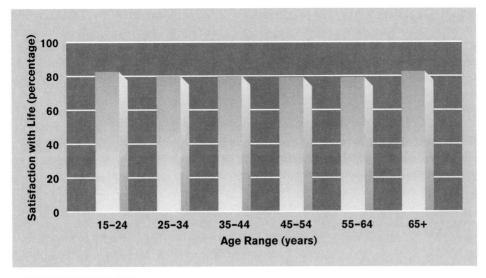

➤ Figure 8.6

Age and Life Satisfaction

Surveys including participants from many nationalities reveal that levels of life satisfaction and happiness remain much the same and relatively high (approximately 80%) throughout life. (Data from Inglehart, 1990.)

Yet old age undoubtedly involves many losses. Health declines, friends die, and some who do not wish to retire must do so because of company policies or for health reasons. One spouse eventually dies, and if the other lives long enough, he or she will be increasingly dependent on others. When life becomes more burdensome than enjoyable, an older person can fall victim to depression, a serious problem affecting about 15% of the elderly. This depression can even be deadly. White males over age 75 have the highest suicide rate of any age group in this society (U.S. Bureau of the Census, 1997).

For most people, losing a spouse is the most stressful event in a lifetime, and more women than men experience this loss. In 1999, 46% of women over age 65 had lost a spouse, compared with only 15% of men. There were only about 69.5 males for every 100 females aged 65 and older (U.S. Bureau of the Census, 2001). Both widows and widowers are at a greater risk for health problems due to suppression of the immune functions, and both have a higher mortality rate, particularly within the first 6 months, than their age mates who are not bereaved (Martikainen & Valkonen, 1996).

Cultural Differences in Care for the Elderly

Are there cultural differences in the ways older family members are viewed, treated, and cared for? Only about 18% of older parents live in the same household with one of their adult children (Crimmins & Ingegneri, 1990). Older African Americans as well as older Asian and Hispanic Americans are more likely to live with and be cared for by their adult children than are other elderly Americans. African Americans are more likely than Whites to regard elderly persons with respect and to feel that children should help their older parents (Mui, 1992).

Economic and social necessity often dictate living arrangements. In many Latin American countries, the majority of elderly people live in the same household with younger generations in an extended family setting (De Vos, 1990). In Korea, 80% of the elderly are cared for by family members (Sung, 1992). And three-generation households have long been the rule rather than the exception among the Japanese.

How do attitudes toward providing care for aged relatives differ between the United States and Japan? Researchers examining this question studied women's attitudes, because the care of aged relatives is typically provided by female family members in both countries (Brody et al., 1984; Campbell & Brody, 1985). The studies yielded some surprising findings. The American women expressed a stronger sense of obligation toward elderly members of their family, such as helping them with household chores, than the Japanese women did. The American women also expressed stronger agreement that their aged parents should be able to look to them for help.

How can these differences be explained? Campbell and Brody (1985) point out that daughters typically care for their elderly parents in the United States. In Japan, daughters-in-law most often care for elderly family members, who are more likely to live in the home of their oldest son. Relations between daughters and parents are likely to be more positive than relations between daughters-in-law and parents-in-law.

Brody and others (1992) found that married daughters experienced less strain and less depression resulting from parent care than those who were single, divorced, or widowed. Also, African Americans caring for elderly relatives suffering from Alzheimer's report less stress and depression than do their White counterparts (Hayley et al., 1996).

Death and Dying

One of the developmental tasks for every elderly person is to accept the inevitability of death and to prepare for it. At no time, however, does this task become more critical than when an individual—no matter what age—faces a terminal illness. Elisabeth Kübler-Ross (1969) interviewed some 200 terminally ill people and found they shared common reactions to their impending death. In her book *On Death and Dying,* she identifies five stages people go through in coming to terms with death.

According to Kübler-Ross, what stages do terminally ill patients experience as they come to terms with death?

In the first stage, *denial,* most patients react to the diagnosis of their terminal illness with shock and disbelief (surely, the doctors must be wrong). The second stage, *anger,* is marked by feelings of anger, resentment, and envy of those who are young and healthy. In the third stage, *bargaining,* the person attempts to postpone death in return for a promise of "good behavior." An individual may offer God some special service or a promise to live a certain kind of life in exchange for an opportunity to attend a child's wedding or a grandchild's graduation. The fourth stage, *depression,* brings a great sense of loss and may take two forms—depression over past losses and depression over impending losses. Given enough time, patients may reach the final stage, *acceptance,* in which they stop struggling against death and contemplate its coming without fear or despair. Kübler-Ross claims that the family also goes through stages similar to those experienced by the patient.

Critics deny the universality of Kübler-Ross's proposed stages and their invariant sequence (Butler & Lewis, 1982; Kastenbaum, 1992). Each person is unique. The reactions of all the terminally ill cannot be expected to conform to some rigid sequence of stages.

Death comes too soon for most people, but not soon enough for others. Some who are terminally ill and subject to intractable pain would welcome an end to their suffering. Should dying patients be left with no choice but to suffer to the end? In answer to this highly controversial question, Dr. Jack Kevorkian has said, "No!" Known as "Dr. Death" to those who oppose his "assisted suicides," Kevorkian has defied both laws and criticism and helped many terminally ill patients end their lives. Although Dr. Kevorkian was convicted of murder in 1999 and remains in prison, he brought to the nation's attention the plight of many hopelessly, terminally ill individuals who wish to end their lives.

What are some benefits of hospice care?

A rapidly growing alternative to hospitals and nursing homes is *hospice care.* Hospices are agencies that care for the needs of the dying more humanely and affordably than hospitals can and that use special facilities or, in some cases, the patient's own home. A hospice follows a set of guidelines that make it more attuned to the patient's personal needs and preferences than a hospital or nursing home typically can be.

Finally, many of us have experienced the *grieving process*—the period of bereavement that follows the death of a loved one and sometimes lingers long after the person has gone.

Apply It ! The Importance of Prenatal Care

Are you pregnant or planning to become pregnant? If so, the first thing you should do is see your doctor. Good prenatal care is essential to your health and your baby's, both during pregnancy and after the baby is born. Prenatal medical care usually begins with an initial visit that includes a complete physical examination, followed by monthly checkups early in the pregnancy and weekly ones toward the end. These regular exams, which include blood and urine tests, are critical to the early detection and treatment of complications that may arise during pregnancy. In addition to medical care, prenatal care also involves a variety of maternal health practices. These include good nutrition, exercise, and avoidance of cigarettes, alcohol, and any drugs that might harm the fetus. It is also important to reduce stress during pregnancy.

Nutrition Although it is common-place to say that a pregnant woman is "eating for two," a woman's nutritional needs actually increase by only 300 calories a day during pregnancy. Those extra calories should come from the major food groups and be supplemented with an extra serving of milk or other dairy product (to provide calcium for bone formation) and about 10 more grams of protein (for cell formation). Fats should not be increased beyond the recommended 30% or less of total calories.

Exercise Pregnancy is a normal condition, not an illness, and there is no reason for pregnant women to stop exercising. Moderate aerobic exercise increases the flow of oxygen and nutrients to the fetus and reduces fluid retention, hemorrhoids, and varicose veins in the mother. It's important to exercise safely, though—by walking, cycling, or swimming, for example. Activities that might lead to falls—such as skiing, rollerblading, and horseback riding—should be avoided.

Smoking If you are a smoker and planning to become a mother, there couldn't be a better time to stop. Smoking has a variety of effects on the reproductive system, including lowering a woman's ability to conceive and making a man's sperm less viable. It is also hazardous to the health of a fetus. A woman who smokes is almost twice as likely as one who doesn't to have a low-birthweight baby. Smoking can also cause a miscarriage, stillbirth, or premature birth. Children born to mothers who smoke tend to have respiratory problems such as chronic coughing and are twice as likely to develop asthma. They may also be retarded in their physical and intellectual development. In short, the evidence is overwhelming: A pregnant woman should not smoke or be exposed to second-hand smoke.

Alcohol As you learned earlier in this chapter, fetal alcohol syndrome is a serious condition that results from prenatal exposure to excessive alcohol. However, experts disagree on what constitutes an "excessive" amount of drinking for pregnant women. The American Academy of Pediatrics therefore recommends that women avoid alcohol altogether during pregnancy (McAnulty & Burnette, 2001).

Drugs Every drug a woman takes during pregnancy reaches the fetus. This means that before taking any drug, even a common one like aspirin, a pregnant woman should consult a physician about the potential effects. Some prescription drugs can have devastating effects on a fetus; an example is Accutane, a drug used to treat acne, which has been found to cause birth defects in many cases. Also harmful to the fetus are illegal drugs such as cocaine and heroin. Use of these drugs can lead to several dangerous conditions, including premature birth, cerebral hemorrhage, and sudden infant death syndrome.

Stress Stressors in a pregnant woman's life—relationship problems, job difficulties, financial woes—can also affect prenatal development. Such sources of stress are linked to high blood pressure in the mother, and premature birth and low birthweight in the newborn. Consequently, physicians suggest that pregnant women find effective ways to relax.

In sum, having regular medical checkups, watching your diet, exercising, avoiding harmful substances, and finding time to relax will put you on track for a healthy pregnancy, a trouble-free delivery, and a healthy baby. ■

Contrary to what many believe, research (Bonanno et al., 1995) has shown that bereaved individuals who suffer the most intense grief initially, who weep inconsolably and feel the deepest pain, do not get through their bereavement more quickly than others. And other research (Folkman et al., 1996) has found that the grieving process for male caregivers whose partners have died of AIDS is very similar to that experienced by spouses.

Death and dying are not pleasant subjects, but remember that life itself is a terminal condition, and each day of life should be treasured like a precious gift.

Summarize It !

Issues in Developmental Psychology

➤ **What are three important issues in developmental psychology?**

Three important issues are the nature–nurture controversy, the debate over the existence of stages in development, and the issue of trait stability.

KEY TERM

developmental psychology (p. 214)

Stage Theories of Development

➤ **What did Piaget claim regarding stages of cognitive development?**

Piaget claimed that cognitive ability develops in four stages, each involving a qualitatively different form of reasoning and understanding. He believed the stages to be universal and sequential, although children may progress through them at different rates.

➤ **What occurs during Piaget's sensorimotor stage?**

During the sensorimotor stage (age birth to 2 years), infants gain knowledge and understanding of the world through their senses and motor activities. The major accomplishment of this stage is object permanence.

➤ **What cognitive limitations characterize children's thinking during the preoperational stage?**

Children at the preoperational stage (age 2 to 7 years) are increasingly able to represent objects and events mentally, but they exhibit egocentrism and have not developed the concepts of reversibility and conservation.

➤ **What cognitive abilities do children acquire during the concrete operations stage?**

When working on concrete problems, children at the concrete operations stage (age 7 to 11 or 12 years) become able to decenter their thinking and to understand the concepts of reversibility and conservation.

➤ **What cognitive abilities develop during the formal operations stage?**

During the formal operations stage, adolescents develop the ability to think abstractly, to attack problems by systematically testing hypotheses, to draw conclusions through deductive reasoning, and to think hypothetically.

➤ **What did Kohlberg believe about moral development?**

Kohlberg believed that moral development was linked to cognitive development and happened in stages.

➤ **What are Kohlberg's three levels of moral reasoning?**

At the preconventional level (Stages 1 and 2), moral reasoning is based on the physical consequences of an act–"right" is whatever averts punishment or brings a reward. At the conventional level (Stages 3 and 4), right and wrong are based on the internalized standards of others–"right" is whatever helps or is approved of by others, or whatever is consistent with the laws of society. Postconventional moral reasoning (Stages 5 and 6) involves weighing moral alternatives–"right" is whatever furthers basic human rights.

➤ **What do cross-cultural studies reveal about the universality of Kohlberg's theory?**

Cross-cultural studies support the universality of Stages 1 through 4 of Kohlberg's moral development as well as their invariant sequence. Stage 5 was found in almost all of the urban or middle-class samples but was absent in tribal and village folk societies.

➤ **What is Erikson's theory of psychosocial development?**

Erikson believed that all individuals progress through eight psychosocial stages during the life span, and each stage is defined by a conflict with the social environment, which must be resolved.

➤ **What are Erikson's four stages of psychosocial development in childhood?**

The four stages in childhood are basic trust versus basic mistrust (age birth to 2 years), autonomy versus shame and doubt (age 1 year to 3 years), initiative versus guilt (age 3 to 6 years), and industry versus inferiority (age 6 years to puberty).

➤ **What are Erikson's four stages of psychosocial development in adolescence and adulthood?**

In the identity versus role confusion stage, adolescents seek to establish their identity and to find values to guide their lives. In Erikson's sixth stage, intimacy versus isolation, young adults must establish intimacy in a relationship to avoid a sense of isolation and loneliness. Erikson's seventh stage, generativity versus stagnation, occurs during middle age. To avoid stagnation, individuals must develop generativity–an interest in establishing and guiding the next generation. Erikson's psychosocial stage for old age, ego integrity versus despair, is a time for reflection. People look back on their lives with satisfaction and a sense of accomplishment, or they have major regrets about mistakes and missed opportunities.

KEY TERMS

scheme (p. 214)
assimilation (p. 214)
accommodation (p. 214)
object permanence (p. 215)
symbolic function (p. 215)
conservation (p. 215)
reversibility (p. 215)
hypothetico-deductive thinking (p. 215)
preconventional level (p. 218)
conventional level (p. 218)
postconventional level (p. 219)
psychosocial stages (p. 221)

Heredity and Prenatal Development

➤ **How are hereditary traits transmitted?**

Hereditary traits are transmitted by the genes, which are located on the 23 pairs of chromosomes.

➤ **When are dominant or recessive genes expressed in an individual's traits?**

When there is more than one gene for a specific trait, the dominant gene will be expressed. A recessive gene is expressed when it is paired with another recessive gene.

➤ **What are the three stages of prenatal development?**

The three stages of prenatal development are the period of the zygote, the period of the embryo, and the period of the fetus.

➤ **What are some negative influences on prenatal development, and during what time is their impact greatest?**

Some common negative influences on prenatal development include certain prescription and nonprescription drugs, psychoactive drugs, poor maternal nutrition, and maternal infections and illnesses. The impact of such influences is greatest during the period of the embryo.

KEY TERMS

genes (p. 223)
chromosomes (p. 223)
sex chromosomes (p. 223)
dominant gene (p. 223)
recessive gene (p. 223)
period of the zygote (p. 224)
prenatal (p. 224)
embryo (p. 224)
fetus (p. 224)
identical (monozygotic) twins (p. 224)
fraternal (dizygotic) twins (p. 224)
teratogens (p. 225)
critical period (p. 225)
fetal alcohol syndrome (p. 225)
low-birthweight baby (p. 225)
preterm infant (p. 225)

Infancy

➤ **What are the perceptual abilities of the newborn?**

All of the newborn's senses are functional at birth, and he or she already shows preferences for certain odors, tastes, sounds, and visual patterns.

➤ **When does learning begin?**

Learning begins prior to birth.

➤ **What is the primary factor influencing attainment of the major motor milestones?**

Maturation is the primary factor influencing attainment of the major motor milestones.

➤ **What is temperament, and what are the three types of temperament identified by Thomas, Chess, and Birch?**

Temperament refers to an individual's characteristic way of responding to the environment. The three types of temperament are easy, difficult, and slow-to-warm-up.

➤ **What did Harlow's studies reveal about attachment in infant monkeys?**

Harlow found that the basis of attachment in infant monkeys is contact comfort, whether with the real mother or with a cloth surrogate mother.

➤ **When does separation anxiety, a sign of attachment, reach its peak?**

Separation anxiety reaches its peak between 8 and 12 months of age.

➤ **What are the four attachment patterns identified in infants?**

The four attachment patterns identified in infants are secure, avoidant, resistant, and disorganized/disoriented.

➤ **What are the typical differences in the ways mothers and fathers interact with infants and children?**

Mothers tend to spend more time caretaking, and fathers spend more time playing with their children.

KEY TERMS

neonate (p. 226)
reflexes (p. 226)
visual cliff (p. 227)
maturation (p. 227)
temperament (p. 227)

attachment (p. 229)
separation anxiety (p. 229)
stranger anxiety (p. 229)

Early and Middle Childhood

➤ **What are the stages of language development, from cooing through the acquisition of grammatical rules?**

The stages of language development are cooing (age 2 to 3 months), babbling (beginning at 6 months), single words (about 1 year), two-word sentences (18 to 20 months), and telegraphic speech (2½ years), followed by the acquisition of grammatical rules.

➤ **How do learning theory and the nativist position explain the acquisition of language?**

Learning theory suggests that language is acquired through imitation and reinforcement. The nativist position is that language ability is largely innate, because it is acquired in stages that occur in a fixed order at the same ages in most normal children throughout the world.

➤ **What are the three parenting styles identified by Baumrind, and which did she find most effective?**

The three parenting styles identified by Baumrind are authoritarian, permissive, and authoritative. She found the authoritative parenting style to be the most effective.

➤ **What outcomes are often associated with authoritative, authoritarian, and permissive parenting styles?**

Authoritative parenting is most effective and is associated with psychosocial competence in children. Children with authoritarian parents are typically the most anxious and the least academically and socially competent. Permissive parenting is least effective and is often associated with adolescent drug use and behavior problems.

➤ **How do peers contribute to the socialization process?**

The peer group serves a socializing function by modeling and reinforcing behaviors it considers appropriate, by punishing inappropriate behavior, and by providing an objective measure children can use to evaluate their own traits and abilities.

➤ What are three psychological theories that attempt to explain gender role development?

Three psychological theories that explain gender role development are social learning theory, cognitive developmental theory, and gender schema theory.

babbling (p. 230)
overextension (p. 231)
underextension (p. 231)
telegraphic speech (p. 231)
overregularization (p. 231)
socialization (p. 232)
authoritarian parents (p. 232)
authoritative parents (p. 232)
permissive parents (p. 233)
gender roles (p. 233)

Adolescence

➤ How difficult is adolescence for most teenagers?

At least half of teenagers enjoy a period of healthy development and good relationships with family and friends; the majority say they are happy and confident.

➤ What physical changes occur during puberty?

Puberty is characterized by the adolescent growth spurt, further development of the reproductive organs, and the appearance of the secondary sex characteristics.

➤ What are the psychological effects of early and late maturation for boys and girls?

Early maturation provides enhanced status for boys because it brings an early advantage in sports and greater attractiveness to girls. Late maturation puts boys at a disadvantage in these areas, resulting in a lack of confidence that can persist into adulthood. Early maturation makes girls more likely to be exposed prematurely to alcohol and drug use and to have early sexual experiences and unwanted pregnancies.

➤ What are some of the consequences of teenage pregnancy?

Teens are at higher risk for delivering premature or low-birthweight babies. Half of teenage mothers never finish high school, and many eventually depend on welfare. Their children are more likely to receive inadequate parenting, nutrition, and health care and to have behavior and academic problems in school.

➤ What are some of the functions of the adolescent peer group?

The adolescent peer group (usually composed of teens of the same sex and race and similar social background) provides a vehicle for developing social skills and a standard of comparison against which teens' attributes can be evaluated.

adolescence (p. 235)
puberty (p. 235)
secondary sex characteristics (p. 235)
menarche (p. 235)
naive idealism (p. 237)
imaginary audience (p. 237)
personal fable (p. 237)

Early and Middle Adulthood

➤ What are the physical changes associated with middle age?

Physical changes associated with middle age are a need for reading glasses, the end of reproductive capacity (menopause) in women, and a decline in testosterone level and often sex drive in men.

➤ In general, do adults show an increase or a decrease in intellectual performance from their 20s to their 60s?

Although younger people tend to do better on tests requiring speed or rote memory, the intellectual performance of adults shows modest gains until the mid-40s. Some decline occurs from the 60s to the 80s.

➤ Why is middle age often considered the prime of life?

The decision makers in society are usually aged 40 to 60. When children grow up and leave home, parents have more time and money to pursue their own goals and interests.

presbyopia (p. 238)
menopause (p. 238)

Later Adulthood

➤ What are some physical changes associated with later adulthood?

Physical changes associated with later adulthood include a general slowing, a decline in sensory capacity, and the development of chronic conditions such as arthritis, heart problems, and high blood pressure.

➤ What happens to mental ability in later adulthood?

Crystallized intelligence shows no significant age-related decline; fluid intelligence does decline. Although older adults perform tasks more slowly, if they keep mentally and physically active, they can usually maintain their mental skills as long as their health holds out.

➤ What is Alzheimer's disease?

Alzheimer's disease is an incurable form of dementia characterized by a progressive deterioration of intellect and personality, resulting from widespread degeneration of brain cells.

➤ According to Kübler-Ross, what stages do terminally ill patients experience as they come to terms with death?

Kübler-Ross maintains that terminally ill patients go through five stages in coming to terms with death: denial, anger, bargaining, depression, and acceptance.

➤ What are some benefits of hospice care?

Hospice agencies care for the needs of the dying more humanely and affordably than hospitals do, and they also provide support for family members.

crystallized intelligence (p. 241)
fluid intelligence (p. 241)
senile dementia (p. 242)
Alzheimer's disease (p. 242)

Surf It!

Want to be sure you've absorbed the material in Chapter 8, "Human Development," before the big test? Visiting **www.ablongman.com/ woodmastering1e** can put a top grade within your reach. The site is loaded with free practice tests, flashcards, activities, and links to help you review your way to an A.

Companion
Website

Study Guide for Chapter 8 !

Answers to all the Study Guide questions are provided at the end of the book.

Section One: Chapter Review

1. Which statement reflects Piaget's thinking about the stages of cognitive development?
   a. All people pass through the same stages but not necessarily in the same manner.
   b. All people progress through the stages in the same order but not at the same rate.
   c. All people progress through the stages in the same order and at the same rate.
   d. Very bright children sometimes skip stages.

2. Match Kohlberg's level of moral reasoning with the rationale for engaging in a behavior.
   ____ (1) to avoid punishment or gain a reward
   ____ (2) to ensure that human rights are protected
   ____ (3) to gain approval or follow the law
   a. conventional
   b. preconventional
   c. postconventional

3. According to Erikson, satisfactory resolution of the conflict associated with each stage of his psychosocial stages is required for healthy development in future stages. (true/false)

4. A dominant gene cannot be expressed if the individual carries
   a. two dominant genes for the trait.
   b. one dominant gene and one recessive gene for the trait.
   c. two recessive genes for the trait.
   d. either one or two dominant genes for the trait.

5. Fraternal twins are no more alike genetically than ordinary brothers and sisters. (true/false)

6. Match the stage of prenatal development with its description.
   ____ (1) first 2 weeks of life
   ____ (2) rapid growth and further development of body structures and systems
   ____ (3) formation of major systems, organs, and structures
   a. period of the fetus
   b. period of the embryo
   c. period of the zygote

7. Which of the following statements about infant sensory development is *not* true?
   a. Vision, hearing, taste, and smell are all fully developed at birth.
   b. Vision, hearing, taste, and smell are all functional at birth.
   c. Infants can show preferences in what they want to look at, hear, and smell shortly after birth.
   d. Hearing is better developed at birth than vision.

8. The primary factor influencing the attainment of the major motor milestones is
   a. experience.   c. learning.
   b. maturation.   d. habituation.

9. Which statement best describes Thomas, Chess, and Birch's thinking about temperament?
   a. Temperament develops gradually as a result of parental handling and personality.
   b. Temperament is inborn and is not influenced by the environment.
   c. Temperament is inborn but can be modified by the family and the environment.
   d. Temperament is set at birth and is unchangeable.

10. Ainsworth found that most infants had secure attachment. (true/false)

11. Match the linguistic stage with the example.
    ____ (1) "ba-ba-ba"
    ____ (2) "He eated the cookies"
    ____ (3) "Mama see ball"
    ____ (4) "oo," "ah"
    ____ (5) "kitty," meaning a lion
    a. telegraphic speech
    b. overregularization
    c. babbling
    d. overextension
    e. cooing

12. Learning theory is better able than the nativist position to account for how language development can be encouraged. (true/false)

13. Match the parenting style with the approach to discipline.
    ____ (1) expecting unquestioned obedience
    ____ (2) setting high standards, giving rationale for rules
    ____ (3) setting few rules or limits
    a. permissive
    b. authoritative
    c. authoritarian

14. The peer group usually has a negative influence on social development. (true/false)

15. Which theory of gender role development does *not* require that children understand the concept of gender?

a. Kohlberg's theory
b. social learning theory
c. gender schema theory
d. none of the above

16. Adolescence is a stormy time for most teenagers. (true/false)

17. The secondary sex characteristics
a. are directly involved in reproduction.
b. appear at the same time in all adolescents.
c. distinguish mature males from mature females.
d. include the testes and ovaries.

18. Although teen pregnancy has many negative consequences for the mother, it has relatively few for the child. (true/false).

19. The teenager's personal fable includes all of the following except
a. a sense of personal uniqueness.
b. a belief that he or she is indestructible and protected from misfortunes.
c. a belief that no one has ever felt so deeply before.
d. a feeling that he or she is always on stage.

20. Most teenagers have good relationships with their parents. (true/false).

21. During which decade do people reach their peak physically?
a. teens   b. 30s   c. 20s   d. 40s

22. Research on Erikson's stage of identity versus role confusion has shown that identity development is completed (earlier; later) than he proposed.

23. Which of the following statements is true of adults over 65?
a. They are considerably less satisfied with life than young adults are.
b. Their financial situation is considerably worse than that of younger adults.
c. Most retirees are happy to be retired.
d. A large percentage of adults over 85 end up in nursing homes.

24. Compared to older adults who are mentally and physically active, younger adults do better on
a. tests requiring speed.
b. comprehension tests.
c. general information tests.
d. practical problem solving.

25. According to Kübler-Ross, the first stage experienced by terminally ill patients in coming to terms with death is _____ ; the last stage is _____ .
a. anger; depression
b. denial; depression
c. bargaining; acceptance
d. denial; acceptance

Section Two: Important Psychologists and Concepts

On the line opposite each name, list the major concept or theory associated with that name.

Name   **Major Concept or Theory**

1. Piaget   _____

2. Erikson   _____

3. Thomas, Chess, and Birch   _____

4. Ainsworth   _____

5. Chomsky   _____

6. Kohlberg   _____

7. Kübler-Ross   _____

8. Bem   _____

Section Three: Fill In the Blank

1. Piaget's term for an individual's cognitive structure or concept that is used to make sense of information is a _____ .

2. Tamara believes that pleasing others defines a good person. She is at the _____ level of moral development.

3. Charles is at a point in his life when he is wrestling with a sense of who he is and where he will go from here. He would be considered to be in Erikson's _____ stage of psychosocial development.

4. The period of the _____ is the first stage of prenatal development.

5. Substances in the prenatal environment that may cause birth defects are called _____ .

6. The pediatrician said that Sandra began to crawl when she did because she had achieved a sufficient degree of _____ in her genetically programmed biological timetable of development.

7. The chapter identified four different patterns of attachment. Ainsworth would say that a child who does not seem to be responsive to his or her mother and does not seem to be troubled when she is gone demonstrates _____ attachment.

8. Watching one of the family dogs sleeping on the couch right next to her, 2-year-old Peg says, "Doggie sleep." This is an example of _____ .

9. One day, her mother asked Peg where the dog was. Peg responded, "Doggie goed outside." This is an example of _____ .

10. According to _____ , children label themselves as boys or girls before they understand that all boys grow up to be men and all girls grow up to be women.

11. According to the concept of the _____ , adolescents may take risks such as driving fast, smoking cigarettes, or having unprotected sex because they believe they are indestructible.

12. _____ intelligence is to verbal ability as _____ intelligence is to abstract reasoning.

13. _____ is the third stage of grieving, according to Kübler-Ross's theory.

Section Four: Comprehensive Practice Test

1. From the evidence presented in this book, it appears that the nature–nurture controversy has been solved: Human development is based primarily on biology. (true/false)

2. Except for sperm cells and egg cells, how many chromosomes does each body cell contain?
a. 23
b. 23 pairs
c. 46 pairs
d. different cells can have different numbers

3. The period of time from conception to birth is called the period of _____ development.
a. neonatal
b. prenatal
c. post-zygotic
d. post-fertilization

4. The second stage of prenatal development is known as the period of
a. germination.
b. the embryo.
c. the fetus.
d. the zygote.

5. Monozygotic is to dizygotic as _____ is to _____ .
a. identical; fraternal
b. female; male
c. male; female
d. fraternal; identical

6. Researchers have found that resolution of Erikson's stage of identity versus isolation typically occurs in adulthood rather than in adolescence. One reason for this finding is that identity development is correlated with
a. work experience.
b. cognitive development.
c. physical maturation.
d. finding a life partner.

7. A baby is considered preterm if she or he is born
a. some place other than a hospital.
b. prior to the parents paying the doctor's bill.
c. before the 45th week of pregnancy.
d. before the 37th week of pregnancy.

8. Jorge is just a few days old. He can see, but not as well as he will later. If he is a typical baby, he probably has _____ vision.
a. 20/40
c. 40/20
b. 20/600
d. 10/40

9. Maturation is
a. genetically determined biological changes that follow a timetable of development.
b. behavioral changes based on the child's interaction with the environment.
c. behavioral changes that take place when the child enters high school.
d. applicable only to physiology and not to cognition or psychomotor development.

10. Cindy says that her new baby's responses to things that happen in the environment are generally happy and positive. Cindy is talking about her baby's
a. response system.
c. latent personality.
b. temperament.
d. infant personification.

11. Assimilation is a process used with _____ ; accommodation is a process used with _____ .
a. new schemas; existing schemas
b. existing schemas; new schemas
c. positive responses; negative responses
d. negative responses; positive responses

12. The nativist position on speech development is that language ability is basically innate. (true/false)

13. Which of the following is *not* an example of a secondary sex characteristic?
a. development of breasts in females
b. differentiation of internal reproductive organs
c. deepening of the voice in males
d. rounding of the hips in females

14. Piaget's final stage of cognitive development is known as the _____ stage.
  a. concrete operations **c.** generativity
  b. cognitive integrity **d.** formal operations

15. A child in Kohlberg's _____ level of moral reasoning is governed by the standards of others rather than by internalized ideas of right and wrong.
  a. postconventional **c.** preconventional
  b. conventional **d.** preadolescent

16. A person must be at Piaget's stage of formal operations in order to attain Kohlberg's _____ level of moral reasoning.
  a. conventional **c.** postconventional
  b. formal conventional **d.** ego integrity

17. Evidence suggests that females tend to stress care and compassion in resolving moral dilemmas, whereas males tend to stress _____ (or to give it and caring equal weight).
  a. romance **c.** justice
  b. aggression **d.** morality

18. The children of teenage mothers tend to display academic and/or behavioral difficulties. (true/false)

19. The most obvious changes as an individual gets older are usually
  a. cognitive.
  b. physical.
  c. social.
  d. sexual.

20. The average wages of working women are lower than those of working men. One reason for this difference is
  a. the "in-and-out" career pattern displayed by many women.
  b. very few women qualify for high-paying jobs.
  c. men demonstrate higher levels of competence on the job and are rewarded accordingly.
  d. women work primarily for personal fulfillment rather than to make money.

21. The results of current research seem to indicate that older adults are _____ younger adults.
  a. less happy and satisfied with life than
  b. as satisfied with life as
  c. as dissatisfied with life as
  d. less satisfied but more secure than

22. For the majority of those who stop working, retirement is not as stressful as popularly believed. (true/false)

23. The most stressful event faced by people in their lifetimes is
  a. retirement.
  b. losing a spouse.
  c. children leaving home.
  d. restricted physical ability due to age.

Section Five: Critical Thinking

1. Evaluate Erikson's stages of psychosocial development, explaining what aspects of his theory seem most convincing. Support your answer.

2. Using Baumrind's categories, classify the parenting style your mother and/or father used in rearing you.
  a. Cite examples of techniques they used that support your classification.
  b. Do you agree with Baumrind's conclusions about the effects of that parenting style on children? Why or why not?

3. Think back to your junior high school and high school years. To what degree did early or late maturation seem to affect how boys and girls were treated by their peers, their parents, or their teachers? Did early or late maturation affect their adjustment? Explain your answer.

Motivation and Emotion

On the fateful morning of September 11, 2001, Orio Palmer, a 20-year veteran of the Fire Department of New York and chief of Manhattan's Ladder 12 Engine 3 Battalion 7, went to work just as he had done hundreds of times before. Taped to his refrigerator was a motto "Live while you're alive." And on that particular day, living, for Chief Palmer, meant responding to the call that took him and the rest of his battalion to the World Trade Center.

Recordings of walkie-talkie communications reveal that Chief Palmer was the first firefighter to reach the 78th floor of the south tower, the lowest of that building's seven floors directly hit by the plane. When he arrived, Chief Palmer reported that there were numerous people on the floor who had survived the plane's impact but were too badly injured to descend on their own. He devised an evacuation plan for them and radioed emergency medical personnel, describing the various injuries so that survivors could be transported to the most appropriate treatment facilities. Chief Palmer also quickly put together a plan for extinguishing the active fires he was able to see from his vantage point in the floor's express elevator lobby. People who have heard the tapes say that there was no panic or fear in his voice, just focused determination to get the survivors out of the building as quickly as possible and put out the fires. Sadly, only ten of the injured on the 78th floor, those who were able to walk with little or no assistance, got out of the building. Chief Palmer lost his life in the building's collapse, along with 15 other firefighters from Battalion 7. He left a wife and three children. In September 2002, a street in the Bronx, where Chief Palmer grew up, was named after him.

A New York City firefigher in the ashes of the World Trade Center on September 11, 2001.

The stock reaction to heroics like Chief Palmer's is that emergency personnel are trained to respond in just this way. Does this mean that only special training can motivate human beings to put aside their own interests for the sake of others? If so, then what about the many ordinary citizens who bravely risked their own safety to assist others to get out of the Pentagon or the World Trade Center, or those who gave their lives to prevent Flight 93 from reaching its hijackers' intended target?

You may remember from Chapter 1 that, to be useful, a psychological theory has to account for most, or preferably all, of the relevant data. Thus, a full explanation of human motivation must be able to explain the motives that drove both the heroes and the villains of September 11th. Because of the complexities involved, today's motivation researchers are typically not searching for a general theory that explains all types of motivation. Instead, they study particular kinds of motivated behavior and the biological, behavioral, cultural, and emotional variables that influence them (Petri, 1996).

What Is Motivation?

Defining Motivation

When you say "I need to study for an exam, but I'm just not *motivated* to do it right now," you probably mean that there is nothing pushing you toward the goal of studying for the exam. For psychologists, **motivation** is a very broad term that encompasses all the processes that initiate, direct, and sustain behavior. Generally, psychologists break motivation down into three subprocesses: activation, persistence, and intensity. *Activation* is the initiation of motivated behavior; it involves taking the first steps required to achieve a goal or complete a project. So, when you say that you're not motivated to study for an exam, you're most likely talking about the activation component of motivation. *Persistence* is the faithful and continued effort put forth in order to achieve a goal or finish a project. Once you take that first step of opening your textbook or notebook, the persistence component is whatever pushes you to keep studying. *Intensity* refers to the focused energy and attention applied in order to achieve a goal or complete a project. For instance, you may persist in studying because you get caught up in the subject matter or are interested in getting a good grade.

At any given time, your behavior might be explained by one or a combination of **motives**—needs or desires that energize and direct behavior toward a goal. Motives can arise from something inside yourself, such as when you keep studying because you find the subject matter interesting. Such activities are pursued as ends in themselves, simply because they are enjoyable, not because any external reward is attached. This type of motivation is known as **intrinsic motivation.**

Other motives originate from outside, as when some external stimulus, or **incentive,** pulls or entices you to act. When the desire to get a good grade—or to avoid a bad grade—causes you to study, the grade is serving as this kind of external incentive. When we act in order to gain some external reward or to avoid some undesirable consequence, we are pulled by **extrinsic motivation.**

Another important way of classifying motives has to do with whether they are learned or unlearned. *Biological motives* are programmed into our nature; they are unlearned. For instance, no one had to teach you to be interested in eating or sex. By contrast, *social motives* are learned as a result of living in human society. From your social environment, you have acquired ideas about physical attractiveness. So, discriminating between two potential partners on the basis of their physical attractiveness involves a social motive, or one that has been learned.

In real life, the motives for many activities are both intrinsic and extrinsic. You may love your job, but you would probably be motivated to leave if your salary, an important extrinsic motivator, were taken away. Table 9.1 gives examples of intrinsic and extrinsic motivation. Next, we'll consider four theories of motivation.

What is the difference between intrinsic and extrinsic motivation?

motivation
The process that initiates, directs, and sustains behavior to satisfy physiological or psychological needs or wants.

motives
Needs or desires that energize and direct behavior toward a goal.

intrinsic motivation
The desire to perform an act because it is satisfying or pleasurable in and of itself.

incentive
An external stimulus that motivates behavior (examples: money, fame).

extrinsic motivation
The desire to perform an act to gain a reward or to avoid an undesirable consequence.

256

Table 9.1 Intrinsic and Extrinsic Motivation

	Description	Examples
Intrinsic motivation	An activity is pursued as an end in itself because it is enjoyable and rewarding.	A person anonymously donates a large sum of money to a university to fund scholarships for deserving students. A child reads several books each week because reading is fun.
Extrinsic motivation	An activity is pursued to gain an external reward or to avoid an undesirable consequence.	A person agrees to donate a large sum of money to a university for the construction of a building, provided it will bear the family name. A child reads two books each week to avoid losing TV privileges.

Instinct Theory

By observing animal behavior, scientists have learned much about *instincts*–inborn, unlearned, fixed patterns of behavior characteristic of an entire species. Spiders spin their intricate webs without being taught the technique by other spiders. An instinct does not improve with practice, and an animal will behave in that particular way even if it has never seen another member of its species. Even when their web-spinning glands are removed, spiders still perform the complex spinning movements and then lay their eggs in the imaginary webs they have spun. So instincts explain much of animal behavior.

But can human motivation be explained by **instinct theory**–the notion that human behavior is motivated by certain innate, unlearned tendencies or instincts that are shared by all individuals? Instinct theory was widely accepted by many early psychologists, and thousands of instincts (e.g., the "maternal" instinct) were proposed to explain human behavior. However, most psychologists today reject instinct theory, as observation alone suggests that human behavior is too richly diverse–and often too unpredictable–to be considered fixed and invariant across the entire species.

Drive-Reduction Theory

Another major attempt to explain motivation is **drive-reduction theory,** which was popularized by Clark Hull (1943). According to Hull, all living organisms have certain biological needs that must be met if they are to survive. A need gives rise to an internal state of tension called a **drive,** and the person or organism is motivated to reduce it. For example, when you are deprived of food or go too long without water, your biological need causes a state of tension–in this case, the hunger or thirst drive. You become motivated to seek food or water to reduce the drive and satisfy your biological need.

Drive-reduction theory is derived largely from the biological concept of **homeostasis**–the tendency of the body to maintain a balanced, internal state in order to ensure physical survival. Body temperature, blood sugar level, water balance, blood oxygen level–in short, everything required for physical existence–must be maintained in a state of equilibrium, or balance. When such a state is disturbed, a drive is created to restore the balance, as shown in Figure 9.1 (on page 258). But drive-reduction theory cannot fully account for the broad range of human motivation. Drive-reduction theory cannot explain why some people, often called *sensation seekers* by

instinct theory
The notion that human behavior is motivated by certain innate tendencies, or instincts, shared by all individuals.

◀ How does instinct theory explain motivation?

drive-reduction theory
A theory of motivation suggesting that a need creates an unpleasant state of arousal or tension, that is, a drive, which impels the organism to engage in behavior that will satisfy the need and reduce the tension.

drive
A state of tension or arousal brought about by an underlying need, which motivates an organism to engage in behavior that will satisfy the need and reduce the tension.

◀ How does drive-reduction theory explain motivation?

homeostasis
The tendency of the body to maintain a balanced internal state with regard to oxygen level, body temperature, blood sugar, water balance, and so forth.

Drive-Reduction Theory

Drive-reduction theory is based on the biological concept of homeostasis—the natural tendency of a living organism to maintain a state of internal balance, or equilibrium. When the equilibrium becomes disturbed (by a biological need such as thirst), a drive (internal state of arousal) emerges. Then the organism is motivated to take action to satisfy the need, thus reducing the drive and restoring equilibrium.

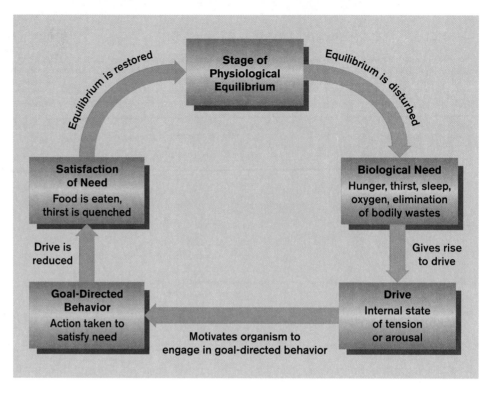

arousal
A state of alertness and mental and physical activation.

arousal theory
A theory suggesting that the aim of motivation is to maintain an optimal level of arousal.

> How does arousal theory explain motivation? ▶

stimulus motives
Motives that cause humans and other animals to increase stimulation and that appear to be unlearned (examples: curiosity and the need to explore, manipulate objects, and play).

Yerkes-Dodson law
The principle that performance on tasks is best when the arousal level is appropriate to the difficulty of the task—higher arousal for simple tasks, moderate arousal for tasks of moderate difficulty, and lower arousal for complex tasks.

psychologists, love the thrill they experience when engaging in activities that produce states of tension—like skydiving or bungee-jumping.

Arousal Theory

Arousal refers to a person's state of alertness and mental and physical activation. Arousal levels can range from no arousal (when a person is comatose), to moderate arousal (when pursuing normal day-to-day activities), to high arousal (when excited and highly stimulated). Unlike drive-reduction theory, arousal theory does not suggest that people are always motivated to reduce arousal or tension. **Arousal theory** states that people are motivated to maintain an optimal level of arousal. If arousal is less than the optimal level, we do something to stimulate it; if arousal exceeds the optimal level, we seek to reduce the stimulation.

When arousal is too low, **stimulus motives**—such as curiosity and the motives to explore, to manipulate objects, and to play—cause humans and other animals to increase stimulation. Young monkeys will play with mechanical puzzles for long periods just for the stimulus of doing so (Harlow, 1950). A very early study found that rats will explore intricate mazes when they are neither thirsty nor hungry and when no reinforcement is provided (Dashiell, 1925). According to Berlyne (1960), rats will spend more time exploring novel objects than familiar objects. So will humans.

There is often a close link between arousal and performance. According to the **Yerkes-Dodson law,** performance on tasks is best when arousal level is appropriate to the difficulty of the task. Performance on simple tasks is better when arousal is relatively high. Tasks of moderate difficulty are best accomplished when arousal is moderate; complex or difficult tasks, when arousal is lower (see Figure 9.2). But performance suffers when arousal level is either too high or too low for the task. For instance, how often have you heard great athletes who "choke" in critical situations compared to those who "come through" under pressure? Perhaps high-pressure situations push the athletes who choke past the optimal point of arousal but have just the opposite effect on the reliable athletes.

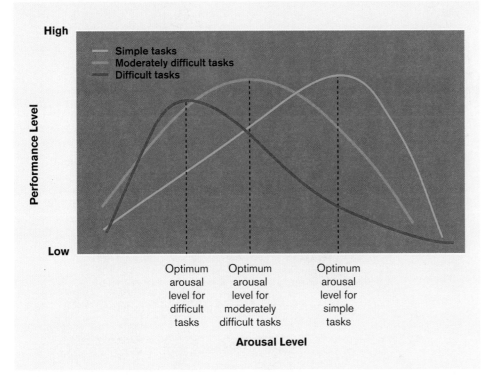

Figure 9.2
The Yerkes-Dodson Law

The optimal level of arousal varies according to the difficulty of the task. Arousal levels should be relatively high for simple tasks, moderate for moderately difficult tasks, and lower for difficult tasks.

Maslow's Hierarchy of Needs

The motivational theories you've learned about so far emphasize physiological processes such as homeostasis and arousal. Another view of motivation, that associated with the humanistic personality theory of Abraham Maslow, suggests that such motivations are the foundation for so-called higher-level motives (Maslow, 1970). As shown in Figure 9.3 (on page 260), Maslow proposed that our need for self-fulfillment depends on how well our needs for physical well-being, safety, belonging, and esteem have been met. His theory claims that we are motivated by the lowest unmet need. Thus, we don't worry about safety when we are in need of food. Similarly, love and esteem are of little concern when we are in danger.

Maslow studied people he believed were using their talents and abilities to their fullest—in other words, those who exemplified *self-actualization*. He studied some historical figures, such as Abraham Lincoln and Thomas Jefferson, and some individuals who made significant contributions during his own lifetime, including Albert Einstein, Eleanor Roosevelt, and Albert Schweitzer. Maslow found these self-actualizers to be accurate in perceiving reality—able to judge honestly and to spot quickly the fake and the dishonest. Self-actualizers are comfortable with life; they accept themselves and others, and nature as well, with good humor and tolerance. Most of them believe that they have a mission to accomplish or need to devote their life to some larger good. Self-actualizers tend not to depend on external authority or other people but seem to be inner-driven, autonomous, and independent. They feel a strong fellowship with all of humanity, and their relationships with others are characterized by deep and loving bonds. They can laugh at themselves, and their sense of humor—though well developed—never involves hostility or criticism of others. Finally, the hallmark of self-actualizers is frequently occurring *peak experiences*—experiences of deep meaning, insight, and harmony within and with the universe.

Review and Reflect 9.1 (on page 260) summarizes the theoretical approaches to motivation we have discussed.

People vary greatly in the amount of arousal they can tolerate. For some people, the heightened level of arousal experienced when hanging off a precipice is enjoyable. Others prefer less arousing activities.

Maslow's Hierarchy of Needs

According to humanistic psychologist Abraham Maslow, "higher" motives, such as the need for love, go unheeded when "lower" motives, such as the need for safety, are not met.

Need for Self-Actualization
Need to realize one's fullest potential

Esteem Needs
Needs to achieve, to gain competence, to gain respect and recognition from others

Belonging and Love Needs
Need to love and be loved; need to affiliate with others and be accepted

Safety Needs
Need for safety and security

Physiological Needs
Need to satisfy the basic biological needs for food, water, oxygen, sleep, and elimination of bodily wastes

Review and Reflect **9.1**

Theories of Motivation

THEORY	VIEW	EXAMPLE
Instinct theory	Behavior is the result of innate, unlearned tendencies. (This view has been rejected by most modern psychologists.)	Two people fighting because of their aggressive instinct
Drive-reduction theory	Behavior results from the need to reduce an internal state of tension or arousal.	Eating to reduce hunger
Arousal theory	Behavior results from the need to maintain an optimal level of arousal.	Climbing a mountain for excitement; listening to classical music for relaxation
Maslow's hierarchy of needs	Lower needs must be met before higher needs will motivate behavior.	Schoolchildren unable to focus on achievement because they are hungry or don't feel safe

Hunger

Primary drives are unlearned motives that serve to satisfy biological needs. For instance, thirst is a basic biological drive. The motivation to drink is largely governed by physiological variables, such as the amount of salt in the body's cells. But what about hunger?

Internal and External Cues

Like thirst, hunger is influenced by physiological processes. Researchers have found two areas of the hypothalamus that are of central importance in regulating eating behavior and thus affect the hunger drive (Steffens et al., 1988). As researchers discovered long ago, the **lateral hypothalamus (LH)** acts as a *feeding center* to excite eating. Stimulating the feeding center causes animals to eat even when they are full (Delgado & Anand, 1953). And when the feeding center is destroyed, animals initially refuse to eat (Anand & Brobeck, 1951). The **ventromedial hypothalamus (VMH)** apparently acts as a *satiety* (or *fullness*) *center* that inhibits eating (Hernandez & Hoebel, 1989). If the VMH is surgically removed, animals soon eat their way to gross obesity (Hetherington & Ranson, 1940; Parkinson & Weingarten, 1990). Moreover, some of the substances secreted by the gastrointestinal tract during digestion, such as the hormone cholecystokinin (CCK), act as satiety signals (Bray, 1991; Flood et al., 1990; Woods & Gibbs, 1989).

Changes in blood sugar level and the hormones that regulate it also contribute to sensations of hunger. Blood levels of the sugar called *glucose* are monitored by nutrient detectors in the liver that send this information to the brain (Friedman et al., 1986). Hunger is stimulated when the brain receives the message that blood levels of glucose are low. Similarly, insulin, a hormone produced by the pancreas, chemically converts glucose into energy that is usable by the cells. Elevations in insulin cause an increase in hunger, in food intake, and in a desire for sweets (Rodin et al., 1985). In fact, chronic oversecretion of insulin stimulates hunger and often leads to obesity.

As you may have learned from everyday experience, hunger can also be stimulated by external cues. What happens when you smell a steak on the grill or chocolate chip cookies in the oven? For many, the hands of the clock alone, signaling mealtime, are enough to prompt a quest for food. Table 9.2 summarizes the factors that

primary drive
A state of tension or arousal arising from a biological need; one not based on learning.

lateral hypothalamus (LH)
The part of the hypothalamus that acts as a feeding center and, when activated, signals an animal to eat; when the LH is destroyed, the animal refuses to eat.

◀ What are the roles of the lateral hypothalamus and the ventromedial hypothalamus in the regulation of eating behavior?

ventromedial hypothalamus (VMH)
The part of the hypothalamus that acts as a satiety center and, when activated, signals an animal to stop eating; when the VMH is destroyed, the animal overeats, becoming obese.

◀ What are some of the body's hunger and satiety signals?

Table 9.2 Biological and Environmental Factors That Inhibit and Stimulate Eating

	Biological	Environmental
Factors that inhibit eating	Activity in ventromedial hypothalamus	Unappetizing smell, taste, or appearance of food
	Raised blood glucose levels	Acquired taste aversions
	Distended (full) stomach	Learned eating habits
	CCK (hormone that acts as satiety signal)	Desire to be thin
	Sensory-specific satiety	Reaction to stress, unpleasant emotional state
Factors that stimulate eating	Activity in lateral hypothalamus	Appetizing smell, taste, or appearance of food
	Low blood levels of glucose	Acquired food preferences
	Increase in insulin	Being around others who are eating
	Stomach contractions	Foods high in fat and sugar
	Empty stomach	Learned eating habits
		Reaction to boredom, stress, unpleasant emotional state

> **What are some nonbiological factors that influence what and how much people eat?**

stimulate and inhibit eating. And to find out more about how internal and external signals influence what you eat, do *Try It! 9.1*.

Explaining Variations in Body Weight

Why are there such wide variations in human body weight? Heredity is one reason. Across all weight classes, from very thin to very obese, children adopted from birth tend to resemble their biological parents more than their adoptive parents in body size. And a review of studies encompassing more than 100,000 participants found that 74% of identical twin pairs had similar body weights. Only 32% of fraternal twins, however, had comparable body weights. The researchers reported an estimated heritability for body weight between .50 and .90 (Barsh et al., 2000). More than 40 genes appear to be related to obesity and body weight regulation (Barsh et al., 2000).

> **What are some factors that account for variations in body weight?**

But what exactly do people inherit that affects body weight? Researchers Friedman and colleagues identified the hormone *leptin*, which directly affects the feeding and satiety centers in the brain's hypothalamus and is known to be a key element in the regulation of body weight (Friedman, 1997, 2000; Kochavi et al., 2001). Leptin is produced by the body's fat tissues, and the amount produced is a direct measure of body fat: The more leptin produced, the higher the level of body fat. Decreases in body fat cause lower levels of leptin in the body, and lower levels of leptin stimulate food intake. When leptin levels increase sufficiently, energy expenditure exceeds food intake, and people lose weight. Obese mice injected with leptin lost 30% of their body weight within 2 weeks (Halaas et al., 1995). In humans, a mutation of the gene that controls leptin receptors can cause obesity as well as pituitary abnormalities (Clément et al., 1998). Changes in the body's leptin levels can affect the immune and reproductive systems as well as the processes involved in bone formation. Thus, leptin plays a key role in linking nutrition to overall human physiology (Friedman, 2000).

The rate at which the body burns calories to produce energy is called the **metabolic rate,** and it is also influenced by genes. Further, *set-point theory* suggests that each person is genetically programmed to carry a certain amount of body weight (Keesey, 1988). **Set point**—the weight the body maintains when one is trying neither to gain

metabolic rate
(meh-tuh-BALL-ik) The rate at which the body burns calories to produce energy.

set point
The weight the body normally maintains when one is trying neither to gain nor to lose weight; if weight falls below the normal level, appetite increases and metabolic rate decreases; if weight is gained, appetite decreases and metabolic rate increases to its original level.

nor to lose weight—is affected by the number of fat cells in the body and by metabolic rate, both of which are influenced by the genes (Gurin, 1989).

Dieting

Manipulating the diet in order to lose weight, or *dieting,* is a common behavior in the industrialized world. Most diets produce an initial weight loss—but not a permanent one (Serdula et al., 1993; Wadden, 1993). The complexities of the processes involved in appetite regulation and energy metabolism explain why diets often do not work (Campbell & Dhand, 2000). To be effective, any weight-loss program must help people decrease energy intake (eat less), increase energy expenditure (exercise more), or both (Bray & Tartaglia, 2000). Unfortunately, most people who are trying to lose weight focus only on cutting calories. At first, when overweight people begin to diet and cut their calories, they do lose weight. But after a few pounds are shed initially, the dieter's metabolic rate slows down as if to conserve the remaining fat store because fewer calories are being consumed (Hirsch, 1997). Moreover, starvation diets are self-defeating in the long run. When a person restricts calories too severely, even exercise cannot reverse the body's drastic lowering of metabolism and its natural tendency to conserve remaining fat (Ballor et al., 1990).

Understanding the complexities of the hunger regulation system can help an overweight person realize that successful weight loss involves more than simply counting calories. For instance, calories eaten in the form of fat are more likely to be stored as body fat than calories eaten as carbohydrates. Miller and colleagues (1990b) found that even when obese and thin people have the same caloric intake, thin people derive about 29% of their calories from fats, while obese people average 35% from fat. So, the composition of the diet may have as much to do with weight gain as the amount of food eaten and the lack of exercise. Counting and limiting the grams of fat may be more beneficial than counting calories to help a person achieve and maintain a desirable body weight.

> ◀ Why is it almost impossible to maintain weight loss by cutting calories alone?

Eating Disorders

Eating disorders are a category of mental disorder in which eating and dieting behaviors go far beyond the everyday extremes of overeating and dieting many people experience. Sadly, there has been an increase in the incidence of these disorders in recent years (Halmi, 1996).

Anorexia nervosa is characterized by an overwhelming, irrational fear of gaining weight or becoming fat, compulsive dieting to the point of self-starvation, and excessive weight loss. Some anorexics lose as much as 20–25% of their original body weight. The disorder typically begins in adolescence, and most of those afflicted are females. About 1% of females between ages 12 and 40 suffer from this disorder (Johnson et al., 1996). The greater prevalence of eating disorders among females appears to be a general phenomenon, rather than a culturally specific one. In a large sample of Norwegian adults, for example, women were twice as likely as men to have an eating disorder (Augestad, 2000).

> ◀ What are the symptoms of anorexia nervosa?

There are important differences between dieting (even obsessive dieting) and anorexia nervosa. For one, anorexics' perception of their body size is grossly distorted. No matter how emaciated they become, they continue to perceive themselves as fat. Researchers have learned that anorexics' unrealistic perceptions of their own bodies may result from a general tendency toward distorted thinking (Tchanturia et al., 2001). Moreover, an unusually high rate of *obsessive-compulsive disorder*—a psychiatric disorder characterized by an obsessive need for control—has been found among anorexics (Milos et al., 2002). These findings suggest that, for some sufferers, anorexia may be only one component of a larger psychiatric problem.

Frequently, anorexics not only starve themselves but also exercise relentlessly in an effort to accelerate the weight loss. Further, anorexics don't necessarily avoid food or the ritual of eating. Indeed, most anorexics are fascinated with food and the process of preparing it (Faunce, 2002). Many become skilled in giving the appearance of eat-

anorexia nervosa
An eating disorder characterized by an overwhelming, irrational fear of being fat, compulsive dieting to the point of self-starvation, and excessive weight loss.

ing while not actually swallowing food. To accomplish this, some anorexics habitually chew and spit out their food, often with such dexterity that others with whom they eat don't notice (Kovacs et al., 2002).

Among young female anorexics, progressive and significant weight loss eventually results in amenorrhea (cessation of menstruation). Anorexics may also develop low blood pressure, impaired heart function, dehydration, electrolyte disturbances, and sterility (American Psychiatric Association, 1993a), as well as decreases in the gray matter volume in the brain, which are thought to be irreversible (Lambe et al., 1997). Unfortunately, up to 20% of those suffering from anorexia nervosa eventually die of starvation or complications from organ damage (Brotman, 1994).

It is difficult to pinpoint the cause of this disorder. Most anorexic individuals are well-behaved and academically successful (Vitousek & Manke, 1994). Psychological risk factors for eating disorders include being overly concerned about physical appearance, worrying about perceived attractiveness, and feeling social pressure in favor of thinness (Whisenhunt et al., 2000). Some investigators believe that young women who refuse to eat are attempting to control a portion of their lives, which they may feel unable to control in other respects.

Anorexia is very difficult to treat. Most anorexics are steadfast in their refusal to eat, while insisting that nothing is wrong with them. The main thrust of treatment, therefore, is to get the anorexic individual to gain weight. The patient may be admitted to a hospital, fed a controlled diet, and given rewards for small weight gains and increases in food intake. The treatment usually includes some type of psychotherapy and/or a self-help group.

Up to 50% of anorexics also develop **bulimia nervosa,** a chronic disorder characterized by repeated and uncontrolled (and often secretive) episodes of binge eating (American Psychiatric Association, 1993a). And individuals who are not anorexic can develop bulimia alone. Many bulimics come from families in which family members make frequent negative comments about others' physical appearances (Crowther et al., 2002).

An episode of binge eating has two main features: (1) the consumption of much larger amounts of food than most people would eat during the same period of time, and (2) a feeling that one cannot stop eating or control the amount eaten. Binges—which generally involve foods that are rich in carbohydrates, such as cookies, cake, and candy—are frequently followed by purging. Purging consists of self-induced vomiting and/or the use of large quantities of laxatives and diuretics. Bulimics may also engage in excessive dieting and exercise. Athletes are especially susceptible to this disorder. But many bulimics are of average size and purge after an eating binge simply to maintain their weight.

Bulimia nervosa can cause a number of physical problems. The stomach acid in vomit eats away at the teeth and may cause them to rot, and the delicate balance of body chemistry is destroyed by excessive use of laxatives and diuretics. The bulimic may have a chronic sore throat as well as a variety of other symptoms, including dehydration, swelling of the salivary glands, kidney damage, and hair loss. The disorder also has a strong emotional component; the bulimic person is aware that the eating pattern is abnormal and feels unable to control it. Depression, guilt, and shame accompany both binging and purging. Some evidence suggests that decreased function of the neurotransmitter serotonin appears to contribute to this disorder (Jimerson et al., 1997).

Bulimia nervosa tends to appear in the late teens and affects about 1 in 25 women (Kendler et al., 1991). Like anorexics, bulimics have high rates of obsessive-compulsive disorder (Milos et al., 2002). Further, perhaps as many as a third of bulimics have engaged in other kinds of self-injurious behavior, such as cutting themselves intentionally (Paul et al., 2002).

About 10–15% of all bulimics are males, and homosexuality or bisexuality seems to increase males' risk for bulimia (Carlat et al., 1997). In addition, researchers are finding more evidence of a cultural component to bulimia. Westernized attitudes in Turkey, for example, are clashing with the country's traditional values and, according to researchers, creating an increase in cases of bulimia (Elal et al., 2000). Apparently, some Turkish citizens are succumbing to Western media pressure to have an ultrathin body.

▲ Jamie-Lynn Sigler, who plays the daughter of James Gandolfini on the hit TV series *The Sopranos,* suffered from anorexia: "I would hide from mirrors because I didn't want to see what I had become." She is currently recovering from the disease while pursuing her acting and musical careers.

What are the symptoms of bulimia nervosa? ▶

bulimia nervosa
An eating disorder characterized by repeated and uncontrolled episodes of binge eating, usually followed by purging—that is, self-induced vomiting and/or the use of large quantities of laxatives and diuretics.

264

Bulimia, like anorexia, is difficult to treat. Sometimes treatment is complicated by the fact that a person with an eating disorder is likely to have a personality disorder as well or to be too shy to interact effectively with therapists (Goodwin & Fitzgibbon, 2002; Rosenvinge et al., 2000). Some behavior modification programs have helped extinguish bulimic behavior (Traverso et al., 2000), and cognitive-behavioral therapy has been used successfully to help bulimics modify their eating habits and their abnormal attitudes about body shape and weight (Halmi, 1996; Johnson et al., 1996). Certain antidepressant drugs have been found to reduce the frequency of binge eating and purging and to result in significant attitudinal change (Agras et al., 1994; "Eating disorders," 1997).

Sexual Motives

Sexual Attitudes and Behavior

The research of Alfred Kinsey and his associates brought the subject of sex out into the open in the 1940s. They interviewed thousands of American men and women about their sexual behaviors and attitudes. Their results—published in a two-volume report, *Sexual Behavior in the Human Male* (1948) and *Sexual Behavior in the Human Female* (1953)—shocked the public. Despite the fact that society frowned on sex outside marriage in those days, Kinsey found that 50% of the females and nearly 90% of the males reported having *coitus* (sexual intercourse) before marriage. He also reported that about 26% of the married women and half of the married men admitted to having had extramarital affairs. Unfortunately, though, Kinsey's sample was not representative: He reported no information on African Americans; elderly people, rural residents, and those with only grade school educations were underrepresented; Protestants, the college-educated, the middle class, and urban residents were overrepresented. Above all, you need to keep in mind that Kinsey's studies were not direct studies of behavior.

The most comprehensive survey of sexual behavior in the United States since Kinsey was published in 1994. The *Social Organization of Sexuality* by Laumann and others (1994) is believed to be the most valid and reliable survey of its kind to date. The findings were based on interviews of a nationwide representative sample composed of 3,432 males and females aged 18 to 59. The major findings are summarized in Figure 9.4.

Throughout all age groups in the United States, men report having had more sex partners and express a more permissive attitude toward casual premarital sex than women do (Oliver & Hyde, 1993). According to Sprecher and Hatfield (1996), African American college students tend to have more permissive premarital sexual standards than White American students, and Mexican American students have more conserv-

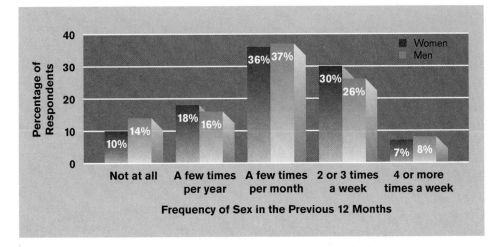

> ➤ **Figure 9.4**
> **Some Results of a 1994 U.S. Sex Survey**
>
> Contrary to what is generally portrayed in the media, most Americans are having sex a few times a month or less. Of the respondents to the survey, 83% reported having either one or no sex partner during the past 12 months.

ative sexual standards than White American students do. In general, males are likely to be more interested in purely physical sex, and "females tend to be more interested . . . in love, nurturant relationships, and lasting social bonds" (Baldwin & Baldwin, 1997, p. 182). Males tend to be less inhibited than females of the same age about masturbation—and to do it far more often. Perhaps this explains, in part, why males, more than females, can think of sex as a quick, easy, casual release without any emotional commitment (Baldwin & Baldwin, 1997).

In a study of first-year college students, Cohen and Shotland (1996) found that the men expected sexual intercourse to become part of a dating relationship far sooner than the women did. Nearly all of the men in the study expressed a willingness to have sex on the basis of physical attraction alone, with no emotional involvement; fewer than two-thirds of the women were willing to do so. And approximately one-third of the men, but only 5% of the women, admitted to having had sex with someone they were neither attracted to nor emotionally involved with. Another interesting finding was that most research participants reported believing that "the average person of their gender was considerably more permissive" in sexual matters than they were (p. 291).

From 1990 to 1995, researchers Sprecher and Regan (1996) surveyed college students who were virgins to determine their reasons for and feelings about their virginity. For both men and women, it was not lack of sexual desire that prompted their decision to remain virgins. The main reason given was not having found the "right" person, followed by fear of pregnancy or other potential negative consequences of sexual activity, including AIDs and other sexually transmitted diseases. Moral and religious beliefs were also cited by some of the students.

Sexual Desire and Arousal

What are the four phases of the sexual response cycle?

Dr. William Masters and Dr. Virginia Johnson conducted the first laboratory investigations of the human sexual response in 1954. They monitored their volunteer participants, who engaged in sex while connected to electronic sensing devices. Masters and Johnson (1966) concluded that both males and females experience a **sexual response cycle** with four phases, as shown in Figure 9.5.

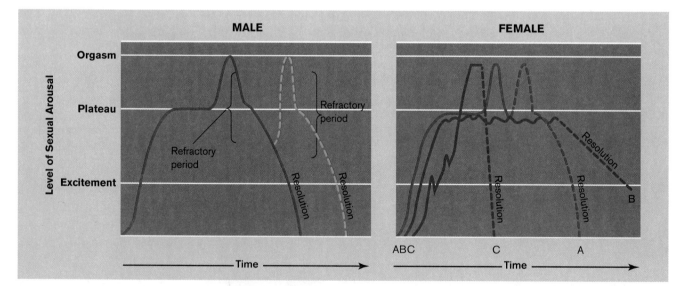

➤ Figure 9.5

The Sexual Response Cycle

Masters and Johnson identified four phases in the sexual response patterns of men and women. However, progression through the phases differs for males and females.

The *excitement phase* is the beginning of the sexual response. Visual cues such as watching a partner undress are more likely to initiate the excitement phase in men than in women. Tender, loving touches coupled with verbal expressions of love arouse women more readily than visual stimulation. And men can become aroused almost instantly, while arousal for women is often a more gradual, building process. For both partners, muscular tension increases, heart rate quickens, and blood pressure rises. As additional blood is pumped into the genitals, the male's penis becomes erect and the female feels a swelling of the clitoris. Vaginal lubrication occurs as the inner two-thirds of the vagina expands and the inner lips of the vagina enlarge. In women especially, the nipples harden and stand erect.

After the excitement phase, the individual enters the *plateau phase,* when excitement continues to mount. Blood pressure and muscle tension increase still more, and breathing becomes heavy and more rapid. The man's testes swell, and drops of liquid, which can contain live sperm cells, may drip from the penis. The outer part of the woman's vagina swells as the increased blood further engorges the area. The clitoris withdraws under the clitoral hood (its skin covering), and the breasts become engorged with blood. Excitement builds steadily during the plateau phase.

The *orgasm,* the shortest of the phases, is the highest point of sexual pleasure, marked by a sudden discharge of accumulated sexual tension. Involuntary muscle contractions may seize the entire body during orgasm, and the genitals contract rhythmically. Orgasm is a two-stage experience for the male. First is his awareness that ejaculation is near and that he can do nothing to stop it; second is the ejaculation itself, when semen is released from the penis in forceful spurts.

The experience of orgasm in women builds in much the same way as for men. Marked by powerful, rhythmic contractions, the female's orgasm usually lasts longer than that of the male. About 40–50% of women regularly experience orgasm during intercourse (Wilcox & Hager, 1980). Although vaginal orgasms and clitoral orgasms may feel different, according to the research conducted by Masters and Johnson (1966), the actual physiological response in the female is the same.

The orgasm gives way to the *resolution phase,* a tapering-off period, when the body returns to its unaroused state. Men experience a *refractory period* in the resolution phase, during which they cannot have another orgasm. The refractory period may last from only a few minutes for some men to as long as several hours for others. Women do not have a refractory period and may, if restimulated, experience another orgasm right away.

The sexual response cycle is strongly influenced by hormones. The sex glands manufacture hormones—*estrogen* and *progesterone* in the ovaries, and androgens in the testes. The adrenal glands in both sexes also produce small amounts of these hormones. Females have considerably more estrogen and progesterone than males do, so these are known as the female sex hormones. Males have considerably more androgens, the male sex hormones.

Testosterone, the most important androgen, influences the development and maintenance of male sex characteristics, as well as sexual motivation. Males must have a sufficient level of testosterone in order to maintain sexual interest and have an erection. Females, too, need small amounts of testosterone in the bloodstream to maintain sexual interest and responsiveness (Andersen & Cyranowski, 1995). Deficiencies in sexual interest and activity can sometimes be reversed in both men and women with the use of testosterone patches or ointments (Meyer, 1997).

Psychological factors play a large role in sexual arousal. Part of the psychological nature of sexual behavior stems from preferences and practices that people learn from their culture. And cultural norms about sexual behavior vary widely, covering everything from the age at which initiation of sexual behavior is proper to the partners, conditions, settings, positions, and specific sexual acts that are

sexual response cycle
The four phases—excitement, plateau, orgasm, and resolution—that make up the human sexual response in both males and females, according to Masters and Johnson.

▼ Psychological factors play an important role in sexual attraction and arousal. Such factors include preferences and attitudes we learn from our culture.

considered acceptable. Moreover, what is perceived as sexually attractive in a male and a female may differ dramatically from culture to culture.

Sexual fantasies also influence sexual arousal. Both men and women are likely to fantasize during intercourse. Most sexual fantasies involve conventional imagery about one's current or past partner or an imaginary lover. There are consistent gender differences in fantasies: "Men more than women imagine doing something sexual to their partner, whereas women more than men imagine something sexual being done to them" (Leitenberg and Henning, 1995, p. 491). Men's fantasies generally involve more specific visual imagery, and women's fantasies have more emotional and romantic content. Although 95% of males and females admit to having sexual fantasies, about 25% experience strong guilt about them (Leitenberg & Henning, 1995). But research seems to suggest an association between a higher incidence of sexual fantasies and a more satisfactory sex life and fewer sexual problems.

External stimuli, such as images in magazines or movies, can also influence arousal. Men are more likely to seek out such sources of stimulation. Some studies reveal that people may come to value their partner and relationship less after exposure to erotic sexual material. Male college students who agreed to view sexually explicit films featuring highly attractive females reported being less pleased with their wives or girlfriends than were control groups of college men who did not view such materials (Kenrick & Gutierres, 1980; Weaver et al., 1984). Also, people may feel disappointed with their own sexual performance after comparing it to the performances of actors in sexually explicit films.

Of course, there is much more to sex than the physical response. Many people view sex as a casual recreational activity that has little to do with love. Masters and Johnson have been accused of reducing the sex act to its clinical, physical components, but their book *The Pleasure Bond* (1975) argues strongly against separating the physical act of sex from the context of love and commitment. They are critical of those who "consider the physical act of intercourse as something in and of itself, a skill to be practiced and improved . . . an activity to exercise the body, or a game to be played." "To reduce sex to a physical exchange," they say, "is to strip it of richness and subtlety and, even more important, ultimately means robbing it of all emotional value." In Masters and Johnson's view, it is "total commitment, in which all sense of obligation is linked to mutual feelings of loving concern, [that] sustains a couple sexually over the years" (1975, p. 268).

Sexual Orientation

Now we turn our attention to **sexual orientation**—the direction of an individual's sexual preference, erotic feelings, and sexual activity. In heterosexuals, the human sexual response is oriented toward members of the opposite sex; in homosexuals, toward those of the same sex; and in bisexuals, toward members of both sexes. Homosexuality has been reported in all societies throughout recorded history (Carrier, 1980; Ford & Beach, 1951). Kinsey and his associates (1948, 1953) estimated that 4% of the male participants had nothing but homosexual relations throughout life, and about 2–3% of the female participants had been in mostly or exclusively lesbian relationships. Gay and lesbian rights groups, however, claim that about 10% of the U.S. population is predominantly homosexual. In what is said to be the most definitive and reliable sex survey to date, Laumann and others (1994) reported that the percentages of Americans who identified themselves as homosexual or bisexual were 2.8% of men and 1.4% of women. But 5.3% of men and 3.5% of women said that they had had a sexual experience with a person of the same sex at least once since puberty. And even larger percentages of those surveyed—10% of males and 8–9% of females—said that they had felt some same-sex desires. Notably, all estimates suggest that homosexuality is twice as prevalent in males as in females.

sexual orientation
The direction of one's sexual preference—toward members of the opposite sex (heterosexuality), toward one's own sex (homosexuality), or toward both sexes (bisexuality).

Determinants of Sexual Orientation

Psychologists continue to debate whether sexual orientation is biologically fixed or acquired through learning and experience. Some researchers have suggested that abnormal levels of androgens during prenatal development might influence sexual orientation (Collaer & Hines, 1995). Too much or too little androgen at critical periods of brain development might masculinize or feminize the brain of the developing fetus, making a homosexual orientation more likely (Berenbaum & Snyder, 1995). A few studies have revealed an increase in the incidence of lesbianism among females who had been exposed prenatally to synthetic estrogen (Meyer-Bahlburg et al., 1995) or to an excess of androgens (Ehrhardt et al., 1968; Money & Schwartz, 1977).

What are the various biological factors that have been suggested as possible determinants of a gay or lesbian sexual orientation?

Neuroscientist Simon LeVay (1991) reported that an area in the hypothalamus governing sexual behavior is about twice as large in heterosexual men as in homosexual men. Critics were quick to point out that all of the gay men included in LeVay's sample died of AIDS. Many researchers questioned whether the brain differences LeVay observed might have resulted from AIDS, rather than being associated with sexual orientation (Byne, 1993).

Researchers looking for a genetic contribution to sexual orientation suggest that a number of "feminizing" genes work together to shift male brain development in the female direction (Miller, 2000). If only a few of these feminizing genes are acting, males who inherit them are more tender-minded and sensitive. But if many such genes are active during development, their effect probably contributes to homosexuality. Moreover, a similar effect may occur with other genes, resulting in lesbianism in females (Miller, 2000). In earlier research on the influence of heredity on sexual orientation, Bailey and Pillard (1991) studied gay males who had twin brothers. They found that 52% of the gay identical twins and 22% of the gay fraternal twins had a gay twin. Among adoptive brothers of gay twins, however, only 11% shared a homosexual orientation. In a similar study, Whitam and others (1993) found that 66% of the identical twins and 30% of the fraternal twins of gay males studied were also gay. Such studies indicate a substantial genetic influence on sexual orientation, but they suggest that environmental influences are at work as well.

Bailey and Benishay (1993) found that 12.1% of lesbian participants had a sister who was also lesbian, compared with 2.3% of heterosexual female participants. Bailey and others (1993) report that for a sample of lesbians, 48% of their identical twins, 16% of their fraternal twins, 14% of their nontwin biological sisters, and 6% of their adopted sisters were also lesbian. Bailey and Pillard (1994) claim that, according to their statistical analysis, the heritability of sexual orientation is about 50%.

Hamer and colleagues (1993) found that brothers of gay participants had a 13.5% chance of also being gay. Furthermore, with respect to the participants' male relatives, those on the mother's side of the family, but not on the father's side, had a significantly higher rate of homosexuality. This led the researchers to suspect that a gene influencing sexual orientation might be located on the X chromosome, the sex chromosome contributed by the mother. After studying the DNA on the X chromosomes of 40 pairs of gay brothers, the researchers found that 33 of the pairs carried matching genetic information at one end tip of the X chromosome. But an exact gene has not been identified from among the several hundred genes carried on that end. And precisely how the gene might influence sexual orientation is not known (LeVay & Hamer, 1994). Some researchers have questioned the validity of Hamer's findings, and a colleague has charged that Hamer excluded from the study some pairs of brothers whose sexual orientations contradicted his findings (Horgan, 1995).

Some researchers (Byne, 1993; Byne & Parsons, 1993, 1994) maintain that, in the absence of studies of identical twins reared apart, the influence of environment cannot be

In the United States, social attitudes concerning homosexuality appear to be moving slowly toward acceptance. However, men continue to hold more negative attitudes about homosexuality than women do.

social motives

Motives acquired through experience and interaction with others.

need for achievement (*n* Ach)

The need to accomplish something difficult and to perform at a high standard of excellence.

emotion

A feeling state involving physiological arousal, a cognitive appraisal of the situation arousing the state, and an outward expression of the state.

James-Lange theory

The theory that emotional feelings result when an individual becomes aware of a physiological response to an emotion-provoking stimulus (for example, feeling fear because of trembling).

ruled out as the cause of a higher incidence of homosexuality in certain families. Furthermore, they suggest that if one or more genes are involved, they may not be genes directly influencing sexual orientation. Rather, they could be genes affecting personality or temperament, which might influence how people react to environmental stimuli (Byne, 1994).

The Developmental Experiences of Gay Men and Lesbians

Many psychologists, such as Charlotte Patterson (1995), suggest that sexual orientation should be studied as a complex interaction of nature and nurture, using theoretical models similar to those used by developmental psychologists to explain other phenomena. For instance, developmentalists often study the ways in which family characteristics contribute to the development of children's traits and behavior. In one early study that examined homosexuality from this perspective, Bell, Weinberg, and Hammersmith (1981) conducted extensive face-to-face interviews with 979 homosexual participants (293 women, 686 men) and 477 heterosexual controls. The researchers found no single condition of family life that in and of itself appeared to be a factor in either homosexual or heterosexual development.

Other researchers have examined whether homosexuality in adulthood is related in some consistent way to childhood behavior. Some researchers (e.g., Zuger, 1990) believe that effeminate behavior in boys is an early stage of homosexuality. Such effeminate behavior might include a boy's cross-dressing, expressing the desire to be a girl or insisting that he is in fact a girl, and/or preferring girls as playmates and girls' games over boys' games and sports. In one study, Bailey and others (1995) found a strong association between sexual orientation and effeminate behavior in childhood as recalled by both gay men and their mothers. And a recent German study suggests that homosexual men who exhibited effeminate behavior as boys find it easier to accept their sexual orientation than peers who were more masculine (Grossman, 2002).

In another study of recalled childhood experiences and sexual orientation, Phillips and Over (1995) found that lesbian women were more likely than heterosexual peers to recall imagining themselves as males, preferring boy's games, and being called "tomboys." Yet, some heterosexual women recalled childhood experiences similar to those of the majority of lesbians, and some lesbians recalled experiences more like those of the majority of heterosexual women. Thus, it is probably true that homosexual men and women are more likely than their heterosexual peers to have exhibited cross-gender behavior as children. However, the link between childhood behaviors such as play preferences and adult sexual orientation is clearly not strong enough to make it possible to predict which children will be homosexual and which will be heterosexual in adulthood.

Social Motives

Do you have a strong need to be with other people (affiliation) or a need for power or achievement? These needs are examples of **social motives,** which we learn or acquire through social and cultural experiences.

In early research examining social motives, Henry Murray (1938) developed the *Thematic Apperception Test (TAT),* which consists of a series of pictures of ambiguous situations. The person taking the test is asked to write a story about each picture—to describe what is going on in the picture, what the person or persons pictured are thinking about, what they may be feeling, and what is likely to be the outcome of the situation. The stories are presumed to reveal the test taker's needs and the strength of those needs. One of the social motives identified by Murray was the **need for achievement** (abbreviated *n* **Ach**), or the motive "to accomplish something difficult. . . . To overcome obstacles and attain a high standard.

What is Murray's contribution to the study of motivation and what is the need for achievement?

To excel one's self. To rival and surpass others. To increase self-regard by the successful exercise of talent" (p. 164). The need for achievement, rather than being satisfied with accomplishment, seems to grow as it is fed.

Researchers David McClelland and John Atkinson have conducted many studies of the need for achievement (McClelland, 1958, 1961, 1985; McClelland et al., 1953). People with a high *n* Ach pursue goals that are challenging, yet attainable through hard work, ability, determination, and persistence. Goals that are too easy, those anyone can reach, offer no challenge and hold no interest because success would not be rewarding (McClelland, 1985). Impossibly high goals and high risks are not pursued because they offer little chance of success and are considered a waste of time. The goals of those with high *n* Ach are self-determined and linked to perceived abilities; thus, these goals tend to be realistic (Conroy et al., 2001).

By contrast, people with low *n* Ach, the researchers claim, are not willing to take chances when it comes to testing their own skills and abilities. They are motivated more by their fear of failure than by their hope and expectation of success. This is why they set either ridiculously low goals, which anyone can attain, or impossibly high goals (Geen, 1984). After all, who can fault a person for failing to reach a goal that is impossible for almost anyone?

Some experts believe that child-rearing practices and values in the home are important factors in developing achievement motivation (McClelland & Pilon, 1983). Parents can foster higher *n* Ach if they give their children responsibilities, teach them to think and act independently from the time they are very young, stress excellence, persistence, and independence, and praise them sincerely for their accomplishments (Ginsberg & Bronstein, 1993; Gottfried et al., 1994). Birth order appears to be related to achievement motivation, with first-born and only children showing higher *n* Ach than younger siblings (Falbo & Polit, 1986). Younger siblings, however, tend to be more sociable and likable than first-born or only children, and this has its rewards, too.

People with a high need for achievement relish opportunities to take on new challenges. For example, after a successful career in professional basketball, Michael Jordan played minor league baseball.

> What are some characteristics shared by people who are high in achievement motivation?

The What and Why of Emotions

Much of our motivation to act is fueled by emotional states. In fact, the root of the word **emotion** means "to move," indicating the close relationship between motivation and emotion. But what, precisely, are emotions?

Explaining the Components of Emotions

Typically, psychologists have studied emotions in terms of three components—the physical, the cognitive, and the behavioral (Wilken et al., 2000). The three components appear to be interdependent. For instance, in one study, participants who were better at detecting heartbeat variations (the physical component) rated their subjective experiences of emotion (the cognitive component) as being more intense than did participants who were less able to detect physical changes (Wilken et al., 2000). However, neither the physical nor cognitive components completely determine how emotion is expressed (the behavioral component). Moreover, there is a long-standing debate among psychologists about which component comes first in the overall experience of emotion.

> What are the three components of emotions?

American psychologist William James (1884) argued that an event causes physiological arousal and a physical response, after which the individual perceives the physical response as an emotion. At about the same time James proposed his theory, a Danish physiologist and psychologist, Carl Lange, independently formulated nearly the same theory. The **James-Lange theory** of emotion (Lange & James, 1922) suggests that different patterns of arousal in the autonomic nervous system produce the different emotions people feel, and that the physiological arousal appears before the emotion is perceived. See Figure 9.6 (on page 272).

> What are the James-Lange, Cannon-Bard, and Schachter-Singer theories of emotion?

➤ Figure 9.6

The James-Lange Theory of Emotion

The James-Lange theory of emotion is the exact opposite of what subjective experience tells us. If a dog growls at you, the James-Lange interpretation is that the dog growls, your heart begins to pound, and only after perceiving that your heart is pounding do you conclude that you must be afraid.

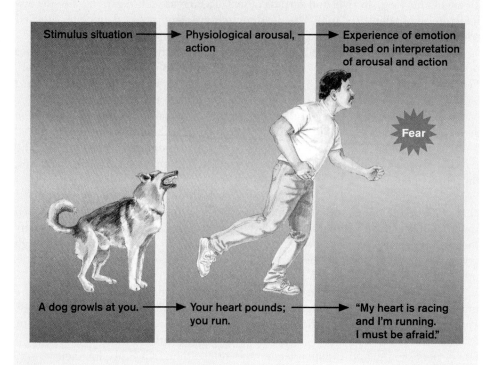

Cannon-Bard theory
The theory that an emotion-provoking stimulus is transmitted simultaneously to the cortex, providing the feeling of an emotion, and the sympathetic nervous system, causing the physiological arousal.

Schachter-Singer theory
A two-stage theory of emotion stating that for an emotion to occur, there must be (1) physiological arousal and (2) a cognitive explanation for the arousal.

Lazarus theory
The theory of emotion stating that an emotion-provoking stimulus triggers a cognitive appraisal, which is followed by the emotion and the physiological arousal.

According to Lazarus, what sequence of events occurs when an individual feels an emotion? ➤

Another early theory of emotion that challenged the James-Lange theory was proposed by Walter Cannon (1927), who did pioneering work on the fight-or-flight response and the concept of homeostasis. Cannon claimed that the bodily changes caused by the various emotions are not sufficiently distinct to allow people to distinguish one emotion from another. Cannon's original theory was later expanded by physiologist Philip Bard (1934). The **Cannon-Bard theory** suggests that the following chain of events occurs when a person feels an emotion: Emotion-provoking stimuli are received by the senses and are then relayed simultaneously to the cerebral cortex, which provides the conscious mental experience of the emotion, and to the sympathetic nervous system, which produces the physiological state of arousal. In other words, the feeling of an emotion (fear, for example) occurs at about the same time as the experience of physiological arousal (a pounding heart). One does not cause the other.

Stanley Schachter believed that the early theories of emotion left out a critical component—the subjective cognitive interpretation of why a state of arousal has occurred. Schachter and Singer (1962) proposed a two-factor theory. According to the **Schachter-Singer theory,** two things must happen in order for a person to feel an emotion: (1) The person must first experience physiological arousal; (2) there must then be a cognitive interpretation, or explanation, of the physiological arousal so that the person can label it as a specific emotion. Thus, Schachter concluded, a true emotion can occur only if a person is physically aroused and can find some reason for it. When people are in a state of physiological arousal but do not know why they are aroused, they tend to label the state as an emotion that is appropriate to their situation at the time. Some attempts to replicate the findings of Schachter and Singer have been unsuccessful (Marshall & Zimbardo, 1979). Also, the notion that arousal is general rather than specific has been questioned by later researchers who have identified some distinctive patterns of arousal for some of the basic emotions (Ekman et al., 1983; Levenson, 1992; Scherer & Wallbott, 1994).

The theory of emotion that most heavily emphasizes the cognitive aspect has been proposed by Richard Lazarus (1991a, 1991b, 1995). According to the **Lazarus theory,** a cognitive appraisal is the first step in an emotional response; all other aspects of an emotion, including physiological arousal, depend

Theories of Emotion

THEORY	VIEW	EXAMPLE
James-Lange theory	An event causes physiological arousal. You experience an emotion only *after* you interpret the physical response.	You are walking home late at night and hear footsteps behind you. Your heart pounds and you begin to tremble. You interpret these physical responses as *fear*.
Cannon-Bard theory	An event causes a physiological *and* an emotional response simultaneously. One does not cause the other.	You are walking home late at night and hear footsteps behind you. Your heart pounds, you begin to tremble, *and* you feel afraid.
Schachter-Singer theory	An event causes physiological arousal. You must then be able to identify a reason for the arousal in order to label the emotion.	You are walking home late at night and hear footsteps behind you. Your heart pounds and you begin to tremble. You know that walking alone at night can be dangerous, and so you feel afraid.
Lazarus theory	An event occurs, a cognitive appraisal is made, and then the emotion and physiological arousal follow.	You are walking home late at night and hear footsteps behind you. You think it could be a mugger. So you feel afraid, and your heart starts to pound and you begin to tremble.

on the cognitive appraisal. This theory is most compatible with the subjective experience of an emotion's sequence of events—the sequence that William James reversed long ago. Faced with a stimulus—an event—a person first appraises it. This cognitive appraisal determines whether the person will have an emotional response and, if so, what type of response. The physiological arousal and all other aspects of the emotion flow from the appraisal. In short, Lazarus contends that emotions are provoked when cognitive appraisals of events or circumstances are positive or negative—but not neutral.

Critics of the Lazarus theory point out that some emotional reactions are instantaneous—occurring too rapidly to pass through a cognitive appraisal (Zajonc, 1980, 1984). Lazarus (1984, 1991a) responds that some mental processing occurs without conscious awareness. And there must be some form of cognitive realization, however brief, or else a person would not know what he or she is responding to or what emotion to feel—fear, happiness, embarrassment, and so on. Further, researchers have found that reappraisal, or changing one's thinking about an emotional stimulus, is related to a reduction in physiological response (Gross, 2002). By contrast, suppression of emotional behavior without cognitive reappraisal is not.

Review and Reflect 9.2 summarizes the four major theories of emotion: James-Lange, Cannon-Bard, Schachter-Singer, and Lazarus.

Emotion and the Brain

What brain structure processes the emotion of fear?

Fear has stimulated more research by neuroscientists than any other emotion (LeDoux, 1996, 2000). And the brain structure most closely associated with fear is

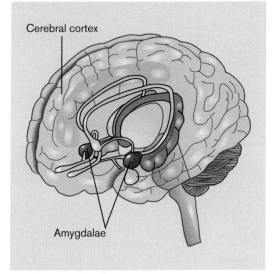

➤ Figure 9.7

Emotion and the Amygdala

The amygdala plays an important role in emotion. It is activated by fear before any direct involvement of the cerebral cortex occurs.

the amygdala (see Figure 9.7). Information comes to the amygdala directly from all five of the senses and is acted on immediately, without initial involvement of the primary "thinking" area of the brain, the cortex. But, as with reflex actions, the cortex does become involved as soon as it "catches up" with the amygdala (LeDoux, 2000). Thus, emotions can be stirred up even before the cortex knows what is going on.

When the emotion of fear first materializes, much of the brain's processing is nonconscious. The person becomes conscious of it later, of course, but the amygdala is activated before she or he is aware that a threat is present (Damasio, 1994, 1999). Interestingly, the amygdala becomes more highly activated when a person looks at photos of angry- or fearful-looking faces than it does when the person views photos of happy faces (LeDoux, 2000).

Emotions may also be lateralized. Sad feelings, for example, are associated with greater activity in the left cerebral hemisphere (Papousek & Schoulter, 2002). Perception of others' emotions appears to be lateralized to the right side of the brain. However, this pattern of lateralization may be more pronounced in females than in males. In one study, participants listened to emotional expressions alternately with the left and right ears. (Recall that the left ear feeds the right side of the brain, while the right ear sends information to the left side.) A left-ear advantage for accurate identification of a speaker's emotional state was evident only for women (Voyer & Rodgers, 2002).

The Expression of Emotion

Expressing emotions comes as naturally to humans as breathing. No one has to be taught how to smile or frown or how to express fear, sadness, surprise, or disgust. And the facial expressions of the basic emotions are similar in all cultures.

The Range of Emotion

Two leading researchers on emotion, Paul Ekman (1993) and Carroll Izard (1992), insist that there are a limited number of basic emotions. **Basic emotions** are unlearned and universal; that is, they are found in all cultures, are reflected in the same facial expressions, and emerge in children according to their own biological timetable of development. Fear, anger, disgust, surprise, joy or happiness, and sadness or distress are usually considered basic emotions. Izard (1992, 1993) suggests that there are distinct neural circuits that underlie each of the basic emotions, and Levenson and others (1990) point to specific autonomic nervous system activity associated with the basic emotions.

> What are basic emotions? ➤

In studying the range of emotion, Ekman (1993) has suggested considering emotions as comprising families. The anger family would range from annoyed to irritated, angry, livid, and, finally, enraged. Furthermore, the anger family, if it exists, also includes various forms in which the emotion is expressed, according to Ekman (1993). Resentment, for example, is a form of anger "in which there is a sense of grievance" (p. 386). Just as there are many words in the English language to describe the variations in the range of any emotion, Ekman and Friesen claim that subtle distinctions in the facial expression of a single emotion convey its intensity (Ekman, 1993).

How do we learn to express emotions? There is considerable evidence that the basic emotions (fear, anger, disgust, surprise, joy or happiness, and sadness or distress), or at least the facial expressions we make when we feel them, are biologically rather than culturally determined.

basic emotions
Emotions that are found in all cultures, that are reflected in the same facial expressions across cultures, and that emerge in children according to their biological timetable; fear, anger, disgust, surprise, joy or happiness, and sadness or distress are usually considered basic emotions.

274

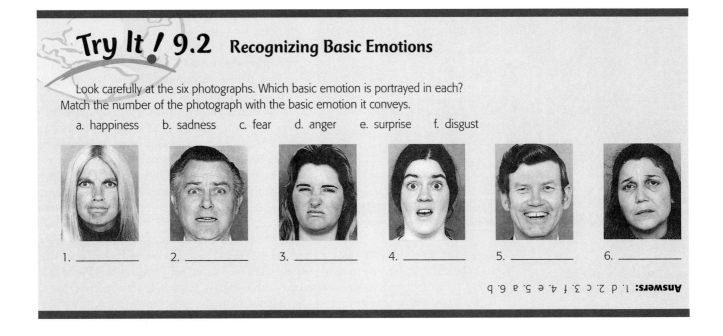

Try It! 9.2 Recognizing Basic Emotions

Look carefully at the six photographs. Which basic emotion is portrayed in each?
Match the number of the photograph with the basic emotion it conveys.

a. happiness   b. sadness   c. fear   d. anger   e. surprise   f. disgust

1. _____   2. _____   3. _____   4. _____   5. _____   6. _____

Answers: 1. d 2. c 3. f 4. e 5. a 6. b

Facial Expressions

Charles Darwin (1872/1965) maintained that most emotions and the facial expressions that convey them are genetically inherited and characteristic of the entire human species. If Darwin was right, then everyone should label the expressions in *Try It! 9.2* the same way. Do your labels agree with those of others?

To test his belief, Darwin asked missionaries and people of different cultures around the world to record the facial expressions that accompany the basic emotions. Based on those data, he concluded that facial expressions were similar across cultures. Later researchers (Scherer & Wallbott, 1994) have found a great deal of overlap in the patterns of emotional expressions reported from cultures in 37 different countries on five continents. However, they have also found important cultural differences in the ways emotions are elicited and regulated and in how they are shared socially.

> ◀ How do facial expressions develop, and are they universal?

Strong support for the notion that facial expressions are universal comes from the way in which they develop in infants. Like the motor skills of crawling and walking, facial expressions of emotions develop according to a biological timetable of maturation and are influenced very little by experience. In fact, blind babies develop them in exactly the same sequence and at the same times as infants who can see.

Within hours of birth, infants are capable of expressing certain emotions—specifically, distress, pleasure, and interest in the environment. By 3 months, babies can express happiness and sadness (Lewis, 1995), and laughter appears somewhere around 3½ to 4 months (Provine, 1996). Between the ages of 4 and 6 months, the emotions of anger and surprise appear, and by about 7 months, infants show fear. The self-conscious emotions do not emerge until later. Between 18 months and 3 years, children begin to show first empathy, envy, and embarrassment, followed by shame, guilt, and pride (Lewis, 1995). Of course, a great deal of experience is required before children know how to control their emotions.

display rules
Cultural rules that dictate how emotions should be expressed, and when and where their expression is appropriate.

Cultural Rules for Displaying Emotion

While the facial expressions of the basic emotions are much the same in cultures around the world, each culture can have very different **display rules**—cultural rules that dictate how emotions should generally be expressed and where and when their expression is appropriate (Ekman, 1993; Ekman & Friesen, 1975; Scherer & Wallbott, 1994).

There are many situations in which people must disguise their emotions to comply with the display rules of their culture, which dictate when and how feelings should be expressed. For example, these soccer players—both winners and losers—are expected to be good sports, even if it means hiding their true feelings.

One significant cultural difference concerns the tendency to have an independent, disengaged Western emotional style (as in the United States) as opposed to an interdependent, socially engaged Eastern emotional style (as in Japan) (Kitayama et al., 2000).

Often a society's display rules require people to give evidence of certain emotions that they may not actually feel or to disguise their true feelings. For example, Americans are expected to look sad at funerals, to hide disappointment at not winning, and to refrain from making facial expressions of disgust when served food that tastes bad. In one study, Cole (1986) found that 3-year-old American girls, when given an unattractive gift, smiled nevertheless. They had already learned a display rule and signaled an emotion they very likely did not feel. Davis (1995) found that among 1st to 3rd graders, girls were better able than boys to hide disappointment.

Different cultures, neighborhoods, and even families may have very different display rules. Display rules in Japanese culture dictate that negative emotions must be disguised when other people are present (Ekman, 1972; Triandis, 1994). In many societies in the West, women are expected to smile often, whether they feel happy or not. And in East Africa, young males from traditional Masai society are expected to appear stern and stony-faced and to "produce long, unbroken stares" (Keating, 1994). So it appears that much emotion that is displayed is not authentic, not truly felt, but merely reflects compliance with display rules.

Not only can emotions be displayed but not felt, they can also be felt but not displayed (Russell, 1995). Consider Olympic medalists waiting to receive their gold, silver, or bronze. Though obviously flooded with happiness, the athletes display few smiles until their medals have been presented and they are interacting with the authorities and responding to the crowd (Fernández-Dols & Ruiz-Belda, 1995). Further, researchers have learned that, in the United States, teens conform to unspoken display rules acquired from peers that discourage public displays of emotion. The resulting subdued emotional expressions can cause them to appear to be aloof, uncaring, and even rude to parents and other adults (Salisch, 2001). Psychologists speculate that conformity to these peer-based display rules may be the basis of much miscommunication between teens and their parents and teachers.

Most of us learn display rules very early and abide by them most of the time. Yet you may not be fully aware that such rules dictate where, when, how, and even how long certain emotions should be expressed.

The Facial-Feedback Hypothesis

Researcher Sylvan Tomkins (1962, 1963) claimed that the facial expression itself—that is, the movement of the facial muscles producing the expression—triggers both the physiological arousal and the conscious feeling associated with the emotion. The notion that the muscular movements involved in certain facial expressions produce the corresponding emotion is called the **facial-feedback hypothesis** (Izard, 1971, 1977, 1990; Strack et al., 1988). Do you think making particular facial expressions can affect your emotions? A simple experiment you can try alone or with friends or classmates is described in *Try It! 9.3.*

Ekman and colleagues (1983) documented the effects of facial expressions on physiological indicators of emotion using 16 participants (12 professional actors and 4 scientists). The participants were guided to contract specific muscles in the face so that they could assume the facial expressions of six basic emotions: surprise, disgust, sadness, anger, fear, and happiness. They were never actually told to smile, frown, or put on an angry face, however.

What is the facial-feedback hypothesis?

facial-feedback hypothesis
The idea that the muscular movements involved in certain facial expressions trigger the corresponding emotions (for example, smiling makes one feel happy).

Try It ! 9.3　Does Facial Feedback Occur?

Hold a pencil between your lips with your mouth closed, as shown in the left-hand drawing, for about 15 seconds. Pay attention to your feelings. Now hold the pencil between your teeth, letting your teeth show, as shown in the right-hand drawing, for about 15 seconds.

Did you have more pleasant feelings with the pencil between your lips or between your teeth? Why do you think that was so? (Adapted from Strack et al., 1988.)

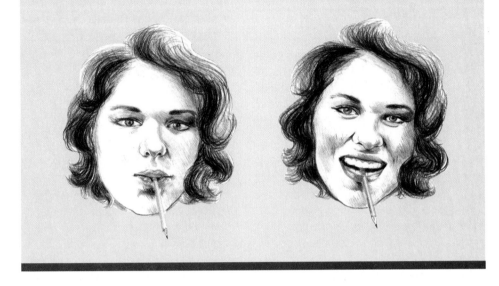

As each participant produced each facial expression, electronic instruments recorded physiological changes in heart rate, galvanic skin response (to measure perspiring), muscle tension, and hand temperature. The same measurements were recorded when researchers asked participants to relive experiences that had produced each of the six basic emotions. A distinctive physiological response pattern emerged for the emotions of fear, sadness, anger, and disgust, whether the participants relived one of their emotional experiences or simply made the corresponding facial expression. In fact, in some cases, the physiological measures of emotion were greater when the actors and scientists made the facial expression than when they imagined an emotional experience (Ekman et al., 1983).

If facial expressions can activate emotions, is it possible that intensifying or weakening a facial expression might intensify or weaken the corresponding feeling state? Izard (1990) believes that learning to self-regulate emotional expression can help in controlling emotions. You might learn to change the intensity of an emotion by inhibiting, weakening, or amplifying its expression. Or you might change the emotion itself by simulating the expression of another emotion. Izard proposes that this approach to the regulation of emotion might be a useful adjunct to psychotherapy. Regulating or modifying an emotion by simulating an expression of its opposite may be effective if the emotion is not unusually intense.

Why, you may be wondering, does it matter whether we control our emotions? For one thing, better control of emotions is associated with a lower incidence of drug problems (Simons & Carey, 2002). Furthermore, expressing feelings such as anger may make you feel better, but will it help or hinder you in accomplishing your goals? If you are good at managing your emotions, you can express them when they are helpful and suppress them when they are not (Salovey & Pizarro, 2003).

"Life, Liberty and the pursuit of Happiness"—these ringing words from the Declaration of Independence are familiar to most of us, and most of us would agree that happiness is a desirable goal. But what exactly is happiness, and how can one attain it? These questions are not as easily answered as you might expect.

Psychologists usually equate happiness with the feeling of well-being, the pervasive sense that life is good. As David G. Myers, a leader in the field of happiness research, puts it, well-being "is an ongoing perception that this time of one's life, or even life as a whole, is fulfilling, meaningful, and pleasant" (1992, p. 23). Happiness is closely related to life satisfaction—people who feel happy also tend to believe that their lives are satisfying. Of course, there are factors in everyone's life that can't be changed, some of which can result in unhappiness. However, people can use several strategies to exercise greater control over the way they respond emotionally to their life situations:

■ *Count your blessings.* One important factor affecting happiness is the tendency to compare one's situation with that of other people. If you feel that you are struggling to make ends meet while everyone around you appears to be living in comfort and security, you will feel less joy and more stress. Indeed, surveys have shown that perceived wealth matters more than absolute wealth.

■ *Smile.* Smiling really does induce feelings of happiness. Smile at other people—even people you don't like a lot. As the song goes, "Put on a happy face." Don't worry if it feels like pretending; after a while, it will come naturally.

■ *Stay connected to people.* Another way to make your life happier is to make the most of social occasions—phone calls, visits, meals with friends. Such occasions often require you to behave as if you were happy, which can actually serve to free you from unhappiness.

■ *Keep busy.* You will also feel happier if you get so caught up in an activity that you become oblivious to your surroundings. Psychologists refer to this feeling as *flow*. To be experiencing flow is to be unselfconsciously absorbed (Csikszentmihalyi, 1990). People who are engaged in some activity that fully utilizes their skills—whether it is work, play, or simply driving a car—report more positive feelings.

You may not be able to control every aspect of your life situation, but you do have some control over how you respond to it. ■

Gender Differences in Experiencing Emotion

How do males and females differ in the experience of emotions?

According to the evolutionary perspective, your answer to the following question is likely to be gender-specific: What emotion would you feel first if you were betrayed or harshly criticized by another person? When asked to respond to this question, male research participants were more likely to report that they would feel angry, while female participants were more likely to say that they would feel hurt, sad, or disappointed (Brody, 1985). Of course, both males and females express anger, but typically not in the same ways. Women are just as likely

Some studies indicate that females are more attuned than males are to verbal and nonverbal expressions of emotion. Do these findings fit with your experiences?

as men to express anger in private (at home) but much less likely than men to express it publicly (Cupach & Canary, 1995).

Research by evolutionary psychologists also suggests clear and consistent differences between the sexes concerning feelings of jealousy. Men, more than women, experience jealousy over evidence or suspicions of sexual infidelity. A woman, however, is more likely than a man to be jealous of her partner's emotional attachment and commitment to another, and over the attention, time, and resources diverted from the relationship (Buss, 1999, 2000a; Pietrzak et al., 2002; White & Mullen, 1989). In married couples, women appear to be more finely tuned to the relationship's overall emotional climate and are more likely to be its "emotional manager" (Gottman, 1994).

Researchers have also found that women appear to be more attuned than men are to verbal and nonverbal expressions of emotions by other people and less reluctant than men are to discuss their personal experiences and reveal their emotions (Dindia & Allen, 1992). Some evidence suggests that these differences arise from females' tendency to be people-oriented and males' tendency to be object-oriented. Further, the gender difference in orientation toward people versus objects appears to hold across the life span (McGuinness, 1993).

Summarize It !

What Is Motivation?

➤ What is the difference between intrinsic and extrinsic motivation?

With intrinsic motivation, an act is performed because it is satisfying or pleasurable in and of itself; with extrinsic motivation, an act is performed in order to bring a reward or to avert an undesirable consequence.

➤ How does instinct theory explain motivation?

Instinct theory suggests that human behavior is motivated by certain innate, unlearned tendencies, or instincts, which are shared by all people.

➤ How does drive-reduction theory explain motivation?

Drive-reduction theory suggests that a biological need creates an unpleasant state of arousal or tension, that is, a drive, which impels the organism to engage in behavior that will satisfy the need and reduce the tension.

➤ How does arousal theory explain motivation?

Arousal theory suggests that the aim of motivation is to maintain an optimal level of arousal. If arousal is less than optimal, a person engages in activities that stimulate arousal; if arousal exceeds the optimal level, the person seeks to reduce stimulation.

KEY TERMS

motivation (p. 256)
motives (p. 256)
intrinsic motivation (p. 256)
incentive (p. 256)
extrinsic motivation (p. 256)
instinct theory (p. 257)
drive-reduction theory (p. 257)
drive (p. 257)
homeostasis (p. 257)
arousal (p. 258)
arousal theory (p. 258)
stimulus motives (p. 258)
Yerkes-Dodson law (p. 258)

Hunger

➤ What are the roles of the lateral hypothalamus and the ventromedial hypothalamus in the regulation of eating behavior?

The lateral hypothalamus (LH) apparently acts as a feeding center—when it is activated, it signals the animal to eat; when it is destroyed, the animal refuses to eat. The ventromedial hypothalamus (VMH) evidently acts as a satiety center—when it is activated, it signals the animal to stop eating; when it is destroyed, the animal overeats, becoming obese.

➤ What are some of the body's hunger and satiety signals?

Some of the body's hunger signals are stomach contractions, low blood glucose levels, and high insulin levels. Some satiety signals are a full stomach, high blood glucose levels, and the presence in the blood of other substances that signal satiety (such as CCK) and are secreted by the gastrointestinal tract during digestion.

➤ What are some nonbiological factors that influence what and how much people eat?

External eating cues, such as the smell of food and the time of day, can cause people to eat more food than they actually need.

➤ What are some factors that account for variations in body weight?

Variations in body weight are influenced by genes, metabolic rate, set point, activity level, and eating habits.

➤ Why is it almost impossible to maintain weight loss by cutting calories alone?

It is almost impossible to maintain weight loss by cutting calories alone, because a dieter's metabolic rate slows down to compensate for the lower intake of calories. Exercise both prevents the lowering of metabolic rate and burns up additional calories.

> **What are the symptoms of anorexia nervosa?**

The symptoms of anorexia nervosa are an overwhelming, irrational fear of being fat, compulsive dieting to the point of self-starvation, and excessive weight loss.

> **What are the symptoms of bulimia nervosa?**

The symptoms of bulimia nervosa are repeated and uncontrolled episodes of binge eating, usually followed by purging—that is, self-induced vomiting and/or the use of large quantities of laxatives and diuretics.

KEY TERMS

primary drive (p. 261)
lateral hypothalamus (LH) (p. 261)
ventromedial hypothalamus (p. 261)
metabolic rate (p. 262)
set point (p. 262)
anorexia nervosa (p. 263)
bulimia nervosa (p. 264)

Sexual Motives

> **What are the four phases of the sexual response cycle?**

According to Masters and Johnson, the sexual response cycle consists of four phases: excitement phase, plateau phase, orgasm, and resolution phase.

KEY TERM

sexual response cycle (p. 266)

Sexual Orientation

> **What are the various biological factors that have been suggested as possible determinants of a gay or lesbian sexual orientation?**

The biological factors suggested as possible causes of a gay or lesbian sexual orientation are (1) abnormal levels of androgens during prenatal development, which could masculinize or feminize the brain of the developing fetus; (2) structural differ-ences in an area of the hypothalamus of gay men; and (3) genetic factors.

KEY TERM

sexual orientation (p. 268)

Social Motives

> **What is Murray's contribution to the study of motivation and what is the need for achievement?**

Murray defined a list of social motives, or needs, and developed the Thematic Apperception Test (TAT) to assess a person's level of these needs. One of the social motives identified by Murray was the need for achievement (n Ach), or the need to accomplish something difficult and to perform at a high standard of excellence.

> **What are some characteristics shared by people who are high in achievement motivation?**

People high in achievement motivation enjoy challenges and like to compete. They tend to set goals of moderate difficulty and attribute their success to their ability and hard work.

KEY TERMS

social motives (p. 270)
need for achievement (n Ach) (p. 270)

The What and Why of Emotions

> **What are the three components of emotions?**

An emotion is a feeling state that involves physiological arousal, cognitive appraisal of the situation, and outward expression of the emotion.

> **What are the James-Lange, Cannon-Bard, and Schachter-Singer theories of emotion?**

According to the James-Lange theory, environmental stimuli produce a physiological response, and then awareness of this response causes the emotion to be experienced. The Cannon-Bard theory suggests that emotion-provoking stimuli received by the senses are relayed simultaneously to the cortex, pro-viding the mental experience of the emotion, and to the sympathetic nervous system, producing the physiological arousal. The Schachter-Singer theory states that for an emotion to occur (1) there must be physiological arousal and (2) the person must perceive some reason for the arousal in order to label the emotion.

> **According to Lazarus, what sequence of events occurs when an individual feels an emotion?**

An emotion-provoking stimulus triggers a cognitive appraisal, which is followed by the emotion and the physiological arousal.

> **What brain structure processes the emotion of fear?**

The emotion of fear is processed by the amygdala, without initial involvement of the brain's cortex.

KEY TERMS

emotion (p. 271)
James-Lange theory (p. 271)
Cannon-Bard theory (p. 272)
Schachter-Singer theory (p. 272)
Lazarus theory (p. 272)

The Expression of Emotion

> **What are basic emotions?**

The basic emotions (happiness, sadness, disgust, and so on) are those that are unlearned and that are reflected in the same facial expressions in all cultures.

> **How do facial expressions develop, and are they universal?**

The facial expressions of different emotions develop in a particular sequence in infants and seem to be the result of maturation rather than learning. There is a great deal of consistency in emotional expression across cultures. However, display rules differ from one society to another.

> **What is the facial-feedback hypothesis?**

The facial-feedback hypothesis suggests that the muscular movements involved in certain facial expressions trigger the corresponding emotions (for example, smiling triggers happiness).

➤ **How do males and females differ in the experience of emotions?**
When betrayed, men are more likely to feel anger than other emotions. Women are more likely to feel sadness. Women are also less likely than men to express anger in public. For men, jealousy arises from suspicions or fear of a partner's sexual infidelity. For women, jealousy is more likely to occur in relation to emotional infidelity.

KEY TERMS

basic emotions (p. 274)
display rules (p. 275)
facial-feedback hypothesis (p. 276)

Surf It!

Want to be sure you've absorbed the material in Chapter 9, "Motivation and Emotion," before the big test? Visiting **www.ablongman.com/woodmastering1e** can put a top grade within your reach. The site is loaded with free practice tests, flashcards, activities, and links to help you review your way to an A.

Companion Website

Answers to all the Study Guide questions are provided at the end of the book.

Section One: Chapter Review

1. When you engage in an activity in order to gain a reward or to avoid an unpleasant consequence, your motivation is (intrinsic, extrinsic).

2. Drive-reduction theory states that people are motivated to
   a. reduce tension created by biological drives.
   b. seek emotional highs such as the feelings you have on a roller coaster.
   c. obey genetically programmed instincts.
   d. maintain appropriate levels of arousal.

3. Which theory suggests that human behavior is motivated by certain innate, unlearned tendencies that are shared by all individuals?
   a. arousal theory
   b. instinct theory
   c. Maslow's theory
   d. drive-reduction theory

4. According to arousal theory, people seek _____ arousal.
   a. minimized
   b. increased
   c. decreased
   d. optimal

5. According to Maslow's hierarchy of needs, which needs must be satisfied before a person will try to satisfy the belonging and love needs?
   a. safety and self-actualization needs
   b. self-actualization needs and esteem needs
   c. physiological and safety needs
   d. physiological and esteem needs

6. The lateral hypothalamus (LH) acts as a (feeding, satiety) center; the ventromedial hypothalamus (VMH) acts as a (feeding, satiety) center.

7. All of the following are hunger signals except
   a. activity of the lateral hypothalamus.
   b. low levels of glucose in the blood.
   c. the hormone CCK.
   d. a high insulin level.

8. The smell of food
   a. has little effect on hunger.
   b. can substitute for food itself when you are dieting.
   c. may make you feel hungry even when you are not.
   d. motivates you to eat only when you are very hungry.

9. Which factor is most responsible for how fast your body burns calories to produce energy?
   a. calories consumed
   b. fat cells
   c. eating habits
   d. metabolic rate

10. According to set-point theory, the body works to (increase, decrease, maintain) body weight.

11. Which of the following might indicate a tendency for obesity to be inherited?
    a. metabolic rate
    b. set point
    c. hormones
    d. all of the above

12. Adopted children are more likely to be very thin or obese if their (biological, adoptive) parents are very thin or obese.

13. Increased exercise during dieting is important to counteract the body's tendency to
    a. increase the fat in the fat cells.
    b. increase the number of fat cells.
    c. lower its metabolic rate.
    d. raise its metabolic rate.

14. Self-starvation is the defining symptom of _____ ; binge eating followed by purging is the main symptom of _____ .

15. Who conducted the first major surveys of sexual attitudes and behaviors of American males and females?
    a. Alfred Kinsey
    b. Masters and Johnson
    c. George Gallup
    d. Laumann and others

16. Men and women have equally permissive attitudes toward premarital sex. (true/false)

17. Which of the following statements about the human sexual response is false?
    a. It consists of four phases.
    b. It occurs in sexual intercourse and can occur in other types of sexual activity.
    c. It is quite different in males and females.
    d. It was researched by Masters and Johnson.

18. Androgens, estrogen, and progesterone are present in both males and females. (true/false)

19. Testosterone plays a role in maintaining sexual interest in males and females. (true/false)

20. The direction of one's sexual preference—toward members of the opposite sex or members of one's own sex—is termed one's
    a. sexual role.
    b. sexual orientation.
    c. sexual desire.
    d. sexual motive.

21. Statistics suggest that homosexuality is twice as common in males as in females. (true/false)

22. Which of the following did Bell, Weinberg, and Hammersmith's study reveal about the childhood experiences of their gay and lesbian participants?
    a. Abuse was more common in their families than in those of heterosexuals.
    b. No single characteristic of family life distinguished their families from those of heterosexuals.
    c. Most were raised in single-parent homes.
    d. Most were from middle-class backgrounds.

23. Social motives are mostly unlearned. (true/false)

24. Goals that are too easy are not interesting to people who are high in *n* Ach. (true/false)

25. People who are high in *n* Ach usually attribute success to luck or other factors beyond their control. (true/false)

26. According to the text, emotions have all of the following *except* a _____ component.
    a. physical   c. sensory
    b. cognitive   d. behavioral

27. Which theory of emotion holds that you feel a true emotion only when you become physically aroused and can identify some cause for the arousal?
    a. Schachter-Singer theory
    b. James-Lange theory
    c. Cannon-Bard theory
    d. Lazarus theory

28. Which theory of emotion suggests that you would feel fearful because you were trembling?
    a. Schachter-Singer theory
    b. James-Lange theory
    c. Cannon-Bard theory
    d. Lazarus theory

29. Which theory suggests that the feeling of emotion and the physiological response to an emotional situation occur at about the same time?
    a. Schachter-Singer theory
    b. James-Lange theory

    c. Cannon-Bard theory
    d. Lazarus theory

30. Which theory suggests that the physiological arousal and the emotion flow from a cognitive appraisal of an emotion-provoking event?
    a. Schachter-Singer theory
    b. James-Lange theory
    c. Cannon-Bard theory
    d. Lazarus theory

31. Which of the following is *not* true of the basic emotions?
    a. They are reflected in distinctive facial expressions.
    b. They are found in all cultures.
    c. There are several hundred known to date.
    d. They are unlearned.

32. Which of the following is not one of the emotions represented by a distinctive facial expression?
    a. happiness   c. surprise
    b. hostility   d. sadness

33. Facial expressions associated with the basic emotions develop naturally according to a child's own biological timetable of maturation. (true/false)

34. All of the following are true of display rules *except* that they
    a. are the same in all cultures.
    b. dictate when and where emotions should be expressed.
    c. dictate what emotions should not be expressed.
    d. often cause people to display emotions they do not feel.

35. The idea that making a happy, sad, or angry face can actually trigger the psychological response and feeling associated with the emotion is called the
    a. emotion production theory.
    b. emotion and control theory.
    c. facial-feedback hypothesis.
    d. facial expression theory.

Section Two: Important Psychologists and Concepts

On the line opposite each name, list the major concept or theory discussed in this chapter.

Name	Major Concept or Theory
1. Hull	_____
2. Maslow	_____
3. Murray	_____
4. James and Lange	_____
5. Cannon and Bard	_____
6. Lazarus	_____
7. Tomkins	_____

Section Three: Fill In the Blank

1. _____ are needs or desires that energize and direct behavior toward a goal.

2. Anthony mows his parents' lawn and, in the winter, shovels his own and his elderly neighbor's sidewalk. He does this because he enjoys helping others. Anthony is responding to _____ motivation.

3. Cleo will help around the house only if she receives a financial reward or special privilege. Cleo responds to _____ motivation.

4. Your dog walks around her bed three times before she lies down, and other dog owners tell you similar stories about their pets. This behavior seems to be inborn, unlearned, and fixed, and is thus an example of an _____ .

5. Jack always wants to ride the wildest rides at the amusement park. He also seems to get bored very easily and then finds a way to create action in his environment. His behavior would probably best be explained by the _____ theory of motivation.

6. The _____ hypothalamus acts as the feeding center, and the _____ hypothalamus acts as the satiety center.

7. The most important factor in successful long-term weight loss is _____ .

8. _____ nervosa involves rigid restriction of calorie intake; _____ nervosa involves a cycle of bingeing and purging.

9. Needs for affiliation, power, or achievement are _____ motives.

10. The _____ theory of emotion says that we experience emotion as a result of becoming aware of our physical response to a situation.

11. The _____ theory of emotion says that our physical response to a stimulus and our emotional response occur at the same time.

12. The _____ theory of emotion says that we experience a physical response to a stimulus and then give it meaning; from this comes our emotional response.

13. Feelings of fear, anger, disgust, surprise, joy, or happiness have been identified as _____ emotions.

14. Facial expressions are first observed in children at _____ .

15. The _____ phase is the beginning of the human sexual response cycle.

16. Males must have a sufficient level of _____ in order to maintain sexual interest and have an erection.

17. The tendency of the body to maintain a balanced internal state with regard to oxygen level, body temperature, blood sugar, water balance, and so forth is called _____ .

18. Simon LeVay, a neuroscientist, reported that an area in the hypothalamus governing sexual behavior is about twice as large in _____ men as in _____ men.

Section Four: Comprehensive Practice Test

1. If James is responding to an incentive, he is responding to an _____ stimulus.
   a. external
   b. internal
   c. explicit
   d. intrinsic

2. Courtney reads books on research and statistics because these subjects fascinate her; she really enjoys learning about new approaches to research and the results of major research projects. Courtney is being driven by _____ motivation.
   a. intrinsic
   b. intellectual
   c. academic
   d. extrinsic

3. Keisha studies chemistry every night because she wants to excel in this field; she believes she will make a great deal of money as a chemist. Keisha is being driven mainly by _____ motivation.
   a. career
   b. intrinsic
   c. extrinsic
   d. academic

4. The primary characteristics of motivation are
   a. activation, persistence, and goal.
   b. activation, persistence, and reward.
   c. activation, persistence, and focus.
   d. activation, persistence, and intensity.

5. A _____ is a state of tension or arousal brought about by an underlying need, which motivates one to engage in behavior that will satisfy the need and reduce the tension.
   a. drive
   b. balance stimulus
   c. tension stimulus
   d. homeostatic condition

6. Angel's behavior sometimes scares his friends. He drives his motorcycle fast, he loves bungee jumping, and he can't wait for his first parachute jump. These interests could be explained by the _____ theory of motivation.
   a. instinct
   b. risky shift
   c. arousal
   d. homeostasis

7. According to Maslow, the need for love and affiliation is satisfied _____ basic biological needs and the need for safety.
   a. instead of
   b. before
   c. at the same time as
   d. after

8. Cody realizes that the goals he has set for himself are going to take too much time and effort so he decides to compromise and go for what he considers less difficult but more rational goals. Cody is a good example of a high achiever. (true/false)

9. When you are hungry, you experience the effects of the _____ hypothalamus; when you have eaten and feel full, you experience the effects of the _____ hypothalamus.
   a. proximal; distal
   b. distal; proximal
   c. ventromedial; lateral
   d. lateral; ventromedial

10. The orgasm is the shortest phase in the sexual response cycle. (true/false)

11. Murray developed the Thematic Apperception Test as a way to measure
   a. anger.
   b. personal perceptions of success.
   c. personal needs.
   d. social needs.

12. A person with a _____ *n* Ach is likely to set either very low goals or impossibly high goals.
   a. high   **c.** low
   b. moderate   **d.** borderline

13. Masters and Johnson concluded that the sexual response cycle is _____ for males and females.
   a. quite similar
   b. different
   c. variable
   d. instinctive

14. Boys who display early effeminate behavior usually are homosexual in adulthood. (true/false)

15. Which of the following theories asserts that, when presented with an emotion-producing stimulus, we feel the physiological effects and the subjective experience of emotion at about the same time?
   a. James-Lange
   b. Lazarus
   c. Cannon-Bard
   d. Schachter-Singer

16. All researchers who are doing work in the physiology of emotions agree that humans experience both basic emotions and instinctual responses such as fear, rage, and joy. (true/false)

17. Children need to be at least _____ months old before they show emotions such as empathy, envy, or embarrassment.
   a. 6   **c.** 12
   b. 9   **d.** 18

18. Trina smiled and thanked her friend for a birthday gift that she really did not like. Trina has learned the _____ of her culture.
   a. social rules   **c.** display rules
   b. interpersonal rules **d.** expressive rules

19. The facial-feedback hypothesis states that the muscular movements that cause facial expressions trigger the corresponding emotions. (true/false)

Section Five: Critical Thinking

1. In your view, which theory or combination of theories best explains motivation: drive-reduction theory, arousal theory, or Maslow's hierarchy of needs? Which theory do you find least convincing? Support your answers.

2. Using what you have learned about body weight and dieting, select any well-known weight-loss plan (for example,

Weight Watchers, Jenny Craig, Slim Fast) and evaluate it, explaining why it is or is not an effective way to lose weight and keep it off.

3. Which level of Maslow's hierarchy provides the strongest motivation for your behavior in general? Give specific examples to support your answer.

chapter

10

Health and
Stress

Some of us first knew Michael J. Fox in the 1980s as Alex P. Keaton, a sarcastic yet endearing teenager on the hit TV series *Family Ties*. Others were introduced to him as Marty McFly, who raced back and forth in time in the *Back to the Future* trilogy. Still others came to know him when he returned to prime time television as Michael Flaherty, New York's deputy mayor on *Spin City*. Then, in 1998, many were stunned when they learned that this much-loved star is a victim of Parkinson's disease, an affliction Fox had been battling in secret for 7 years.

Parkinson's is a debilitating degenerative disease that strikes the circuits and inner workings of the neurons in the brain that control movement. Symptoms of Parkinson's include slow or jerky movements, mild to uncontrollable shaking, and garbled speech. Clearly, this is an especially devastating disease for an actor. Can you imagine the heavy load of stress Fox had to endure in keeping his illness a secret? In wondering how long he could continue his profession as an actor?

Fox was deeply stressed, but not devastated. In fact, he didn't even slow down. Choosing to retire from *Spin City* in 2000, he shifted his focus away from the demanding world of producing and performing in a TV series and toward spending more time with his family and helping to find a cure for Parkinson's. In fact, Fox recently authored a book about his life titled *Lucky Man: A Memoir* (Fox, 2002). How could a person who is struggling with an ever-worsening, debilitating terminal disease consider himself lucky? Fox knows that his treasures far outweigh his troubles. Not only has he had a successful career in a most competitive field, but—more important to him—he has the love and full support of his wife, actress Tracy Pollan, and their children. This man is more than a successful actor. He is a man who has turned tragedy into triumph and who now spends his time, his financial resources, and his talents serving others. He chairs the Michael J. Fox Foundation for Parkinson's Disease Research to raise awareness about the disease and secure funds to help find a cure.

Michael J. Fox knows, first hand, that one's health is far more important than fame and fortune.

stress
The physiological and psychological response to a condition that threatens or challenges a person and requires some form of adaptation or adjustment.

In this chapter, we discuss many issues related to health and stress, and we begin by looking at stress. Stress is necessary for survival, but, if it is chronic and excessive, it can disable or kill.

Sources of Stress

What is stress?

Most psychologists define **stress** as the physiological and psychological response to a condition that threatens or challenges an individual and requires some form of adaptation or adjustment. Stress is usually associated with the **fight-or-flight response** in which the body's parasympathetic nervous system triggers the release of hormones that prepare the body to fight or escape from a threat (see Chapter 2). Let's look at some of the different kinds of **stressors,** or stimuli that elicit the fight-or-flight response.

fight-or-flight response
A response to stress in which the sympathetic nervous system and the endocrine glands prepare the body to fight or flee.

Holmes and Rahe's Social Readjustment Rating Scale

What was the Social Readjustment Rating Scale designed to reveal?

Researchers Holmes and Rahe (1967) developed the **Social Readjustment Rating Scale (SRRS)** to measure stress by ranking different life events from most to least stressful and assigning a point value to each event. Life events that produce the greatest life changes and require the greatest adaptation are considered the most stressful, regardless of whether the events are positive or negative. The 43 life events range from death of a spouse (assigned 100 stress points) to minor law violations such as getting a traffic ticket (11 points). Add up the number of stress points in your life—complete *Try It! 10.1.*

stressor
Any stimulus or event capable of producing physical or emotional stress.

Holmes and Rahe claim that there is a connection between the degree of life stress and major health problems. People who score 300 or more on the SRRS, the researchers say, run about an 80% risk of suffering a major health problem within the next 2 years. And those who score between 150 and 300 have a 50% chance of becoming ill within a 2-year period (Rahe et al., 1964). Most researchers, however, do not consider a high score on the SRRS a reliable predictor of future health problems (Krantz et al., 1985; McCrae, 1984). One of the main shortcomings of the SRRS is that it assigns a point value to each life change without taking into account whether the change is for better or worse. For example, life changes such as divorce, pregnancy, retirement from work, and changing jobs or residences may be either welcome or unwelcome.

Social Readjustment Rating Scale (SRRS)
Holmes and Rahe's stress scale, which ranks 43 life events from most to least stressful and assigns a point value to each.

Daily Hassles

Richard Lazarus believes that the little stressors, which he calls **hassles,** add up to bring more stress than major life events. Daily hassles are the "irritating, frustrating, distressing demands and troubled relationships that plague us day in and day out" (Lazarus & DeLongis, 1983, p. 247). Kanner and others (1981) developed the Hassles Scale to assess various categories of hassles. Unlike the Holmes and Rahe scale, the Hassles Scale takes into account that items may or may not represent stressors and that the amount of stress produced by an item varies from person to person. People completing the scale indicate the items that have been a hassle for them and rate the items for severity on a 3-point scale. Table 10.1 (on page 290) shows the ten hassles most frequently reported by college students.

What roles do hassles and uplifts play in the stress of life, according to Lazarus?

DeLongis and others (1988) studied 75 American couples over a 6-month period and found that daily stress (as measured on the Hassles Scale) related significantly to present and future "health problems such as flu, sore throat, headaches, and backaches" (p. 486). Research also indicates that minor hassles that accompany stressful major life events such as those measured by the SRRS are better predictors of the level of psychological distress than the major life events themselves (Pillow et al., 1996).

hassles
Little stressors, which include the irritating demands and troubled relationships that can occur daily and, according to Lazarus, can cause more stress than do major life changes.

According to Lazarus, **uplifts,** or positive experiences in life, may neutralize or cancel out the effect of many of the hassles. Lazarus and his colleagues constructed an Uplifts Scale similar to the Hassles Scale. People completing the Uplifts Scale make a

uplifts
The positive experiences in life, which can neutralize the effects of many of the hassles.

288

Try It! 10.1 Finding a Life Stress Score

To assess your life in terms of life changes, check all of the events listed that have happened to you in the past year. Add up the points to derive your life stress score. (Based on data from Holmes & Masuda, 1974.)

Rank	Life Event	Life Change Unit Value	Your Points
1	Death of spouse	100	____
2	Divorce	73	____
3	Marital separation	65	____
4	Jail term	63	____
5	Death of close family member	63	____
6	Personal injury or illness	53	____
7	Marriage	50	____
8	Getting fired at work	47	____
9	Marital reconciliation	45	____
10	Retirement	45	____
11	Change in health of family member	44	____
12	Pregnancy	40	____
13	Sex difficulties	39	____
14	Gain of new family member	39	____
15	Business readjustment	39	____
16	Change in financial state	38	____
17	Death of close friend	37	____
18	Change to different line of work	36	____
19	Change in number of arguments with spouse	35	____
20	Taking out loan for major purchase (e.g., home)	31	____
21	Foreclosure of mortgage or loan	30	____
22	Change in responsibilities at work	29	____
23	Son or daughter leaving home	29	____
24	Trouble with in-laws	29	____
25	Outstanding personal achievement	28	____
26	Spouse beginning or stopping work	26	____
27	Beginning or ending school	26	____
28	Change in living conditions	25	____
29	Revision of personal habits	24	____
30	Trouble with boss	23	____
31	Change in work hours or conditions	20	____
32	Change in residence	20	____
33	Change in schools	20	____
34	Change in recreation	19	____
35	Change in church activities	19	____
36	Change in social activities	18	____
37	Taking out loan for lesser purchase (e.g., car or TV)	17	____
38	Change in sleeping habits	16	____
39	Change in number of family get-togethers	15	____
40	Change in eating habits	15	____
41	Vacation	13	____
42	Christmas	12	____
43	Minor violation of the law	11	____
		Life stress score:	____

cognitive appraisal of what they consider a positive experience. Items viewed as uplifts by some people may actually be stressors for other people. Kanner and others (1981) found that for middle-aged people, uplifts were often health- or family-related, whereas for college students, uplifts often came in the form of having a good time.

Making Choices

Sometimes conflicting motives can be sources of stress. When a person must make a choice between two desirable alternatives, a situation known as an **approach–approach conflict,** stress may be the result. Some approach–approach conflicts are minor, such as deciding which movie to see. Others can have major consequences, such as the conflict between building a promising career or interrupting a career to raise a child. In approach–approach conflicts, both choices are desirable. In an **avoidance–avoidance conflict,** a person must choose between two undesirable alternatives. You may want to avoid studying for an exam, but at the same time you want to avoid failing the test. **Approach–avoidance conflicts** include both desirable and undesirable features in the same choice. The person facing this type of conflict is simultaneously drawn to and repelled by a choice—for example, wanting to take a wonderful vacation but having to empty a savings account to do so.

Even positive life events, such as getting married, can cause stress.

> How do approach–approach, avoidance–avoidance, and approach–avoidance conflicts differ?

Unpredictability and Lack of Control

> How do unpredictability and lack of control over a stressor affect its impact?

Unpredictable stressors are more difficult to cope with than predictable stressors. Laboratory tests have shown that rats receiving electric shocks without warning develop more ulcers than rats given shocks just as often but only after a warning (Weiss, 1972). Likewise, humans who are warned of a stressor before it occurs and have a chance to prepare themselves for it experience less stress than those who must cope with an unexpected stressor.

Our physical and psychological well-being is profoundly influenced by the degree to which we feel a sense of control over our lives (Rodin & Salovey, 1989). Langer and

Table 10.1 The Ten Most Common Hassles for College Students

Hassle	Percentage of Times Checked
1. Troubling thoughts about future	76.6
2. Not getting enough sleep	72.5
3. Wasting time	71.1
4. Inconsiderate smokers	70.7
5. Physical appearance	69.9
6. Too many things to do	69.2
7. Misplacing or losing things	67.0
8. Not enough time to do the things you need to do	66.3
9. Concerns about meeting high standards	64.0
10. Being lonely	60.8

Source: From Kanner et al., 1981.

www.ablongman.com/woodmastering1e

Rodin (1976) studied the effects of control on nursing-home residents. Residents in one group were given some measure of control over their lives, such as choices about how to arrange their rooms and when they could see movies. These residents showed improved health and well-being and had a lower death rate than residents in another group who were not given control. Within 18 months, 30% of the residents given no choices had died, compared with only 15% of those who had been given some control over their lives. Control is important for cancer patients, too. Some researchers suggest that a sense of control over their daily physical symptoms and emotional reactions may be even more important for cancer patients than control over the course of the disease itself (Thompson et al., 1993).

Several studies suggest that we are less subject to stress when we have the power to do something about it, whether we exercise that power or not. Glass and Singer (1972) subjected two groups of participants to the same loud noise. Only one group was told that they could, if necessary, terminate the noise by pressing a switch. This group (which had the control) suffered less stress, even though they never did exercise the control they were given. Friedland and others (1992) suggest that when people experience a loss of control because of a stressor, they are motivated to try to reestablish control in the stressful situation. Failing this, they often attempt to increase their sense of control in other areas of their lives.

approach–approach conflict
A conflict arising from having to choose between desirable alternatives.

avoidance–avoidance conflict
A conflict arising from having to choose between undesirable alternatives.

approach–avoidance conflict
A conflict arising when the same choice has both desirable and undesirable features.

Stress in the Workplace

Everyone who works is subject to a certain amount of job-related stress, but the amount and sources of the stress differ, depending on the type of job and the kind of organization. Albrecht (1979) suggests that if people are to function effectively and find satisfaction on the job, the following nine variables (also summarized in Figure 10.1) must fall within their comfort zone:

◀ For people to function effectively and find satisfaction on the job, what nine variables should fall within their comfort zone?

- ■ *Workload.* Too much or too little work to do can cause people to feel anxious, frustrated, and unrewarded.
- ■ *Clarity of job description and evaluation criteria.* Anxiety arises from confusion about job responsibilities and performance criteria or a job description that is too rigidly defined to leave room for individual initiative.

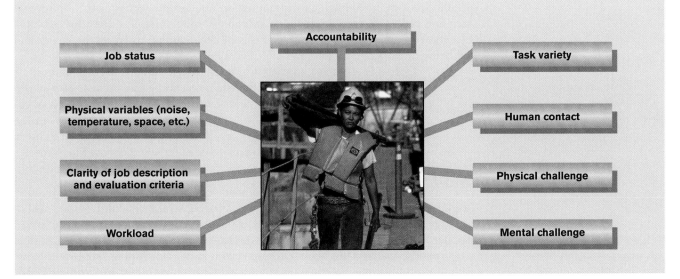

➤ Figure 10.1

Variables in Work Stress

For a person to function effectively and find satisfaction on the job, these nine variables should fall within his or her comfort zone. (Based on Albrecht, 1979.)

➤ Air-traffic controllers have an extremely high-stress job. The on-the-job stress they experience increases the risk of coronary disease and stroke.

- *Physical variables.* Temperature, noise, humidity, pollution, amount of work space, and physical positions (e.g., prolonged standing or sitting) required to carry out job duties can contribute to job stress.
- *Job status.* People with very low status–garbage collectors or janitors, for example–may feel psychological discomfort; those with celebrity status often cannot handle the stress that fame brings.
- *Accountability.* Accountability underload occurs when workers perceive their jobs as meaningless; overload occurs when people have responsibility for the physical or psychological well-being of others but only a limited degree of control, such as air-traffic controllers and emergency-room nurses and doctors.
- *Task variety.* To function well, people need a comfortable amount of variety.
- *Human contact.* Some workers have virtually no human contact on the job (forest-fire lookouts); others have almost continuous contact with others (welfare and employment-office workers). People vary greatly in how much interaction they enjoy or even tolerate.
- *Physical challenge.* Jobs range from physically demanding (construction work, professional sports) to those requiring no physical activity. Some jobs (fire fighting, police work) involve physical risk as well.
- *Mental challenge.* Jobs that tax people beyond their mental capability, as well as those that require too little mental challenge, can be frustrating.

Workplace stress can be especially problematic for women because of gender-specific stressors, including sex discrimination and sexual harassment in the workplace and problems combining work and family roles. These added stressors have been shown to increase the negative effects of occupational stress on the health and well-being of working women (Swanson, 2000).

What are some of the psychological and health consequences of job stress? ➤ Job stress can have a variety of consequences. Perhaps the most frequent is reduced effectiveness on the job. But stress can also lead to absenteeism, tardiness, accidents, substance abuse, and lower morale. However, as you might predict, unemployment is far more stressful for most people than any of the variables associated with on-the-job stress (Price et al., 2002). So, given a choice between a high-stress job and no job at all, most of us would choose the former.

Catastrophic Events

Catastrophic events such as the terrorist attacks of September 11, 2001 or the crash of the space shuttle Columbia in early 2003 are stressful not only for people who experience them directly but also for those who learn of the events via news media. Most people manage the stress associated with such catastrophes quite well. However, for some, these events lead to **posttraumatic stress disorder (PTSD)**, a prolonged and severe stress reaction to a catastrophic event (such as a plane crash or an earthquake) or to chronic intense stress (such as occurs in combat or during imprisonment as a hostage or POW).

What is posttraumatic stress disorder? ➤

To illustrate the potential impact of catastrophic events on the incidence of PTSD, consider results of surveys from before and after September 11, 2001. Prior to Sep-

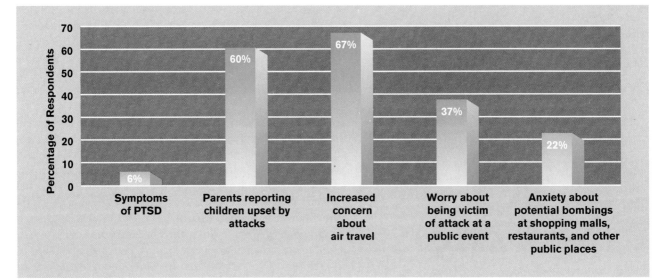

> **Figure 10.2**

Americans' Stress Levels after September 11, 2001

Researchers have found that Americans were continuing to experience increased levels of stress and anxiety several months after the terrorist attacks of September 11, 2001. (Sources: Clay, 2002; Clay et al., 2002; Schlenger et al., 2002; Silver et al., 2002)

tember 11, most surveys found that between 1% and 2% of Americans met the diagnostic criteria for PTSD (Foa & Meadows, 1997). Two months after the attacks, about 17% of Americans surveyed by researchers at the University of California–Irvine reported symptoms of PTSD. When the researchers conducted follow-up interviews with survey participants 6 months after the attacks, 6% of participants were still experiencing distress. Other researchers have found additional lingering effects associated with September 11 (see Figure 10.2).

People with posttraumatic stress disorder often have flashbacks, nightmares, or intrusive memories that make them feel as though they are actually reexperiencing the traumatic event. They suffer increased anxiety and startle easily, particularly in response to anything that reminds them of the trauma (Green et al., 1985). Many survivors of war or catastrophic events experience survivor guilt because they lived while others died. Some feel that perhaps they could have done more to save others. Extreme combat-related guilt in Vietnam veterans is a risk factor for suicide or preoccupation with suicide (Hendin & Haas, 1991). And a study of women with PTSD revealed that they were twice as likely as women without PTSD to experience first-onset depression and three times as likely to develop alcohol use disorder (Breslau et al., 1997). PTSD sufferers also experience cognitive difficulties such as poor concentration (Vasterling et al., 2002).

posttraumatic stress disorder (PTSD)
A prolonged and severe stress reaction to a catastrophic event or to chronic intense stress.

Racism and Stress

A significant source of chronic stress is being a member of a minority group in a majority culture. A study of White and Black participants' responses to a questionnaire about ways of managing stress revealed that a person may experience racial stress from simply being one of a few or the only member of a particular race in any of a variety of settings, such as a classroom, a workplace, or a social situation. The feeling of stress experienced in such situations can be intense, even in the absence of racist attitudes, discrimination, or any other overt evidence of racism (Plummer & Slane, 1996).

Some theorists have proposed that a phenomenon called *historical racism*–experienced by members of groups that have a history of repression–can also be a source

What evidence is there for an association between perceived racism and health in African Americans?

Partly because of their lower average socioeconomic level, Hispanic Americans and other minorities are less likely than White Americans to have access to adequate health care.

of stress. African Americans have received the most attention from researchers interested in the effects of historical racism. Many of these researchers claim that the higher incidence of high blood pressure among African Americans is attributable to stress associated with historical racism. Surveys have shown that African Americans experience more race-related stress than members of other minority groups (Utsey et al., 2002). Research shows that African Americans who express the highest levels of concern about racism display higher levels of cardiovascular reactivity to experimentally induced stressors, such as sudden loud noises, than do African Americans who express less concern about racism (Bowen-Reid & Harrell, 2002). Thus, there may indeed be a link between perceptions of historical racism and high blood pressure.

However, African Americans are also more likely than members of other minority groups to have a strong sense of ethnic identity, a variable that helps moderate the effects of racial stress (Utsey et al., 2002). And some studies show that personal variables such as hostility may increase the effects of racial stress (Fang & Myers, 2001). So, the relationship between historical racism and cardiovascular health is probably fairly complex, with considerable variation across individuals. Moreover, some researchers believe that the association must be studied more thoroughly in other historically repressed groups, such as Native Americans, before firm conclusions can be drawn (Belcourt-Dittloff & Stewart, 2000).

general adaptation syndrome (GAS)
The predictable sequence of reactions (alarm, resistance, and exhaustion stages) that organisms show in response to stressors.

Responding to Stress

Selye and the General Adaptation Syndrome

What is the general adaptation syndrome? ▶

Hans Selye (1907–1982), the researcher most prominently associated with the effects of stress on health, established the field of stress research. The heart of Selye's concept of stress is the **general adaptation syndrome (GAS),** consisting of three stages: the alarm stage, the resistance stage, and the exhaustion stage (Selye, 1956). (See Figure 10.3.)

▶ Figure 10.3

The General Adaptation Syndrome

The three stages in Selye's general adaptation syndrome are (1) the alarm stage, during which there is emotional arousal and the defensive forces of the body are mobilized for fight or flight; (2) the resistance stage, in which intense physiological efforts are exerted to resist or adapt to the stressor; and (3) the exhaustion stage, when the organism fails in its efforts to resist the stressor. (Based on Selye, 1956.)

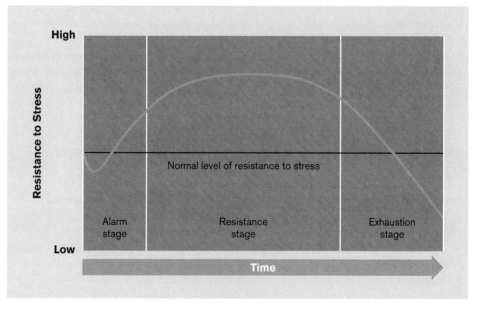

The body's first response to a stressor is the **alarm stage,** in which the adrenal cortex releases hormones called *glucocorticoids* that increase heart rate, blood pressure, and blood-sugar levels, supplying a burst of energy that helps the person deal with the stressful situation (Pennisi, 1997). Next, the organism enters the **resistance stage,** during which the adrenal cortex continues to release the glucocorticoids to help the body resist stressors. The length of the resistance stage depends both on the strength or intensity of the stressor and on the body's power to adapt. If the organism finally fails in its efforts to resist, it reaches the **exhaustion stage,** at which point all the stores of deep energy are depleted, and disintegration and death follow.

Selye found that the most harmful effects of stress are due to the prolonged secretion of glucocorticoids. Such prolonged secretion can lead to a permanent increase in blood pressure, suppression of the immune system, and weakening of muscles and can even cause damage to the hippocampus (Stein-Behrens et al., 1994). Thanks to Selye, the connection between extreme, prolonged stress and certain diseases is now widely accepted by medical experts.

Lazarus's Cognitive Theory of Stress

Richard Lazarus (1966; Lazarus & Folkman, 1984) contends that it is not the stressor itself that causes stress, but a person's perception of the stressor. According to Lazarus, when people are confronted with a potentially stressful event, they engage in a cognitive process that involves a primary and a secondary appraisal. A **primary appraisal** is an evaluation of the meaning and significance of the situation–whether its effect on one's well-being is positive, irrelevant, or negative. An event that is appraised as stressful may involve: (1) harm or loss (damage that has already occurred); (2) threat (the potential for harm or loss); or (3) challenge (the opportunity to grow or gain). An appraisal of threat, harm, or loss can occur in relation to anything important to you–a friendship, a part of your body, your property, your finances, or your self-esteem. When people appraise a situation as involving harm, loss, or threat, they experience negative emotions such as anxiety, fear, anger, or resentment (Folkman, 1984). An appraisal of a situation as involving challenge, on the other hand, is usually accompanied by positive emotions such as excitement, hopefulness, and eagerness.

During **secondary appraisal,** if people judge the situation to be within their control, they evaluate available resources: physical (health, energy, stamina), social (support network), psychological (skills, morale, self-esteem), material (money, tools, equipment), and time. Then, they consider the options and decide how to deal with the stressor. The level of stress they feel is largely a function of whether their resources are adequate to cope with the stressor, and how severely those resources will be taxed in the process. Figure 10.4 (on page 296) summarizes the Lazarus and Folkman psychological model of stress. There is research support for Lazarus and Folkman's claim that physiological, emotional, and behavioral reactions to stressors depend partly on whether the stressors are appraised as challenging or threatening.

Coping Strategies

Coping refers to a person's efforts, both action and thought, to deal with demands perceived as taxing or overwhelming. **Problem-focused coping** is direct; it consists of reducing, modifying, or eliminating the source of stress itself. If you are getting a poor grade in history and appraise this as a threat, you may study harder, talk over your problem with your professor, form a study group with other class members, get a tutor, or drop the course.

Emotion-focused coping may involve reappraising a stressor. If you lose your job, you may decide that it isn't a major tragedy and instead view it as a challenge– an opportunity to find a better job with a higher salary. Despite what you may have heard, ignoring a stressor, one form of emotion-focused coping, can be an effective way of managing stress. Researchers studied 116 people who had experienced heart

alarm stage
The first stage of the general adaptation syndrome, when there is emotional arousal and the defensive forces of the body are prepared to fight or flee.

resistance stage
The second stage of the general adaptation syndrome, when there are intense physiological efforts to either resist or adapt to the stressor.

exhaustion stage
The final stage of the general adaptation syndrome, occurring if the organism fails in its efforts to resist the stressor.

primary appraisal
An evaluation of the meaning and significance of a potentially stressful event according to how it will affect one's well-being—whether it is perceived as irrelevant or as involving harm or loss, threat, or challenge.

What are the roles of primary and secondary appraisal when a person is confronted with a potentially stressful event?

secondary appraisal
An evaluation of one's coping resources prior to deciding how to deal with a stressful event.

coping
Efforts, through action and thought, to deal with demands that are perceived as taxing or overwhelming.

What is the difference between problem-focused and emotion-focused coping?

problem-focused coping
A response aimed at reducing, modifying, or eliminating a source of stress.

emotion-focused coping
A response aimed at reducing the emotional impact of the stressor.

Lazarus and Folkman's Psychological Model of Stress

Lazarus and Folkman emphasize the importance of a person's perceptions and appraisal of stressors. The stress response depends on the outcome of the primary and secondary appraisals, whether the person's coping resources are adequate to cope with the threat, and how severely the resources are taxed in the process. (From Folkman, 1984.)

Potentially Stressful Event

Primary Appraisal
Person evaluates event as positive, neutral, or negative.
Negative appraisal can involve:
- **Harm or loss** (damage has already occurred)
- **Threat** (the potential for harm or loss)
- **Challenge** (the opportunity to grow or gain)

Secondary Appraisal
If the situation is judged to be within the person's control:
1. Person evaluates coping resources (physical, social, psychological, material) to determine if they are adequate to deal with stressor.
2. Person considers options in dealing with stressor.

Stress Response
- **Physiological:** Autonomic arousal, fluctuations in hormones
- **Emotional:** Anxiety, fear, grief, resentment, excitement
- **Behavioral:** Coping behaviors (including problem-focused and emotion-focused coping strategies)

proactive coping
Efforts or actions taken in advance of a potentially stressful situation to prevent its occurrence or to minimize its consequences.

attacks (Ginzburg et al., 2002). All of the participants reported being worried about suffering another attack. However, those who tried to ignore their worries were less likely to exhibit anxiety-related symptoms such as nightmares and flashbacks. But a combination of problem-focused and emotion-focused coping is probably the best stress-management strategy (Folkman & Lazarus, 1980). So, a heart patient may try to ignore her anxiety (emotion-focused coping) while conscientiously adopting recommended lifestyle changes, such as increasing exercise (problem-focused coping).

Some stressful situations can be anticipated in advance, allowing active measures to be taken to avoid or minimize them. Such active measures are known as **proactive coping** (Aspinwall & Taylor, 1997). Proactive coping consists of actions taken in advance of a potentially stressful situation to prevent its occurrence or to minimize its consequences. Proactive copers anticipate and then prepare for upcoming stressful events and situations, including those that are certain and those that are only likely.

Health and Illness

Two Approaches to Health and Illness

How do the biomedical and biopsychosocial models differ in their approaches to health and illness?

For many decades, the predominant view in medicine was the **biomedical model,** which explains illness in terms of biological factors. Today, both physicians and psychologists recognize that the **biopsychosocial model** more fully explains both health and illness than the biomedical model (Engel, 1977, 1980; Schwartz, 1982). The biopsychosocial model is depicted in Figure 10.5.

Growing acceptance of the biopsychosocial approach gave rise to a subfield, **health psychology,** which is "the field within psychology devoted to under-

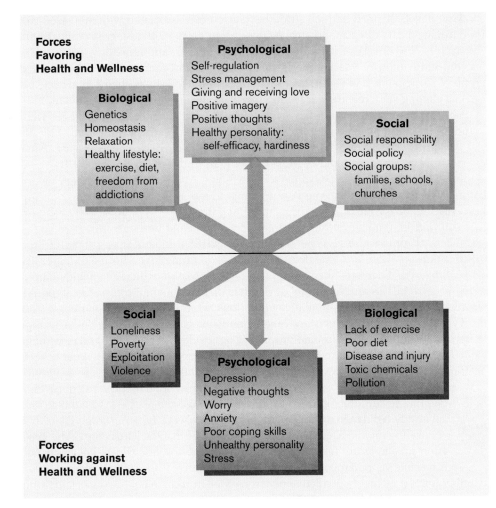

➤ Figure 10.5

The Biopsychosocial Model of Health and Wellness

The biopsychosocial model focuses on health and illness and holds that both are determined by a combination of biological, psychological, and social factors. Most health psychologists endorse the biopsychosocial model. (From Green & Shellenberger, 1990.)

standing psychological influences on how people stay healthy, why they become ill, and how they respond when they do get ill" (Taylor, 1991, p. 6). Health psychology has become particularly important because many of today's health menaces are diseases related to unhealthy lifestyle and stress (Taylor & Repetti, 1997).

Coronary Heart Disease

In order to survive, the heart muscle requires a steady, sufficient supply of oxygen and nutrients carried by the blood. Coronary heart disease is caused by the narrowing or blockage of the coronary arteries—the arteries that supply blood to the heart muscle. Although coronary heart disease remains the leading cause of death in the United States, responsible for 31% of all deaths, the death rate due to this cause has declined 50% during the past 30 years (National Center for Health Statistics, 2000).

A health problem of modern times, coronary heart disease is largely attributable to lifestyle and is therefore an important field of study for health psychologists. A *sedentary lifestyle*—one that includes less than 20 minutes of exercise three times per week— is the primary modifiable risk factor contributing to death from coronary heart disease. Other risk factors are high serum cholesterol levels, cigarette smoking, obesity, high blood pressure, and diabetes. Though not modifiable, another important risk factor is a family history. The association between family history and coronary heart disease is both genetic and behavioral. For instance, individuals whose parents have high blood pressure, but who have not yet developed the disorder themselves, exhibit the same kinds of emotional reactivity and poor coping strategies as their parents (Frazer et al., 2002).

biomedical model
A perspective that focuses on illness rather than on health, explaining illness in terms of biological factors without regard to psychological and social factors.

biopsychosocial model
A perspective that focuses on health as well as illness and holds that both are determined by a combination of biological, psychological, and social factors.

health psychology
The field concerned with the psychological factors that contribute to health, illness, and recovery.

Hostility is a key component of the Type A behavior pattern.

What are the Type A and Type B behavior patterns?

What aspect of the Type A behavior pattern is most clearly linked to coronary heart disease?

High levels of stress and job strain have also been associated with increased risk for coronary heart disease and stroke (Rosengren et al., 1991; Siegrist et al., 1990). Apparently, the effects of stress can enter the bloodstream almost as if they were injected intravenously. Malkoff and others (1993) report that after an experimental group of participants had experienced laboratory-induced stress, their blood platelets (special clotting cells) released large amounts of a substance that promotes the buildup of plaque in blood vessels and may lead to heart attack and stroke. No changes were found in the blood platelets of unstressed control-group participants.

Personality type is also associated with an individual's risk of heart disease. After extensive research, cardiologists Meyer Friedman and Ray Rosenman (1974) concluded that there are two types of personality: Type A, associated with a high rate of coronary heart disease, and Type B, commonly found in persons unlikely to develop heart disease. Are your characteristics more like those of a Type A or a Type B person? Before reading further, complete *Try It! 10.2* and find out.

People with the **Type A behavior pattern** have a strong sense of time urgency and are impatient, excessively competitive, hostile, and easily angered. They are "involved in a chronic, incessant struggle to achieve more and more in less and less time" (Friedman & Rosenman, 1974, p. 84). Type A's would answer "true" to most or all of the questions in the *Try It!* In contrast, people with the **Type B behavior pattern** are relaxed and easygoing and do not suffer from a sense of time urgency. They are not impatient or hostile and are able to relax without guilt. They play for fun and relaxation rather than to exhibit superiority over others. Yet the Type B individual may be as bright and ambitious as the Type A, and more successful as well. Type B's would answer "false" to most or all of the *Try It!* questions.

In a review of a number of studies, Miller and others (1991) found that 70% of middle-aged men with coronary heart disease were Type A, compared to 46% of healthy middle-aged men. Research indicates that the lethal core of the Type A personality is not time urgency but anger and hostility, which fuel an aggressive, reactive temperament (Miller et al., 1996; Smith & Ruiz, 2002; Williams, 1993). Hostility is not only highly predictive of coronary heart disease but also associated with ill health in general (Miller et al., 1996).

Cancer

Cancer is the second leading cause of death in the United States, accounting for 23% of all deaths (National Center for Health Statistics, 2000). Cancer strikes frequently in the adult population, and about 30% of Americans—over 75 million people—will develop cancer at some time in their lives. The young are not spared the scourge of cancer, for it takes the lives of more children aged 3 to 14 than any other disease.

Cancer, a collection of diseases rather than a single illness, can invade cells in any part of a living organism—whether a human, another animal, or even a plant. Normal cells in all parts of the body divide, but fortunately they have built-in instructions about when to stop dividing. Unlike normal cells, cancer cells do not stop dividing. And unless caught in time and destroyed, they continue to grow and spread, eventually killing the organism. Health psychologists point out that an unhealthy diet, smoking, excessive alcohol consumption, promiscuous sexual behavior, and becoming sexually active in the early teens (especially for females) are all behaviors that increase the risk of cancer.

The 1 million people in the United States who are diagnosed with cancer each year have the difficult task of adjusting to a potentially life-threatening disease and the chronic stressors associated with it. Thus, cancer patients need more than medical treatment, say researchers. Their therapy should include help with the psychological and behavioral factors that can influence their quality of life. Researchers Carver and others (1993) found that 3 months and 6 months after surgery, breast-cancer patients who maintained an optimistic outlook, accepted the reality of their situation, and maintained a sense of humor experienced less distress. Patients who used denial—refusal to accept the reality of their situation—and had thoughts of giving up experi-

Type A behavior pattern
A behavior pattern marked by a sense of time urgency, impatience, excessive competitiveness, hostility, and anger; considered a risk factor in coronary heart disease.

Type B behavior pattern
A behavior pattern marked by a relaxed, easygoing approach to life; not associated with coronary heart disease.

298

enced much higher levels of distress. Dunkel-Schetter and others (1992) found that the most effective elements of a strategy for coping with cancer were social support (such as through self-help groups), a focus on the positive, and distraction. Avoidant coping strategies such as fantasizing, denial, and social withdrawal were associated with higher levels of emotional distress.

The Immune System

An army of highly specialized cells and organs, the immune system works to identify and search out and destroy bacteria, viruses, fungi, parasites, and any other foreign matter that may enter the body. The key components of the immune system are white blood cells known as **lymphocytes,** which include B cells and T cells. B cells are so named because they are produced in the bone marrow; T cells derive their name from the thymus gland, where they are produced. All cells foreign to the body (bacteria, viruses, and so on) are known as *antigens*. B cells produce proteins called *antibodies,* which are highly effective in destroying antigens that live in the bloodstream and in the fluid surrounding body tissues (Paul, 1993). But for defeating harmful foreign invaders that have taken up residence inside the body's cells, T cells are critically important.

The immune system may, however, turn on healthy cells or specific organs and attack them, as happens in autoimmune diseases such as juvenile diabetes, multiple sclerosis, rheumatoid arthritis, and lupus. Moreover, the system itself may be the target of a disease-causing organism. The most feared disease related to the immune system is **acquired immune deficiency syndrome (AIDS),** caused by the **human immunodeficiency virus (HIV).** The virus attacks the T cells, gradually but relentlessly weakening the immune system until it is essentially nonfunctional.

Although the first case was diagnosed in this country in 1981, there is still no cure for AIDS. However, efforts to develop a way to immunize people against HIV have yielded several potential vaccines, at least one of which is currently being tested on humans (Beyrer, 2003). By the end of 2001, 816,249 cases of AIDS and

lymphocytes
The white blood cells, including B cells and T cells, that are key components of the immune system.

acquired immune deficiency syndrome (AIDS)
A devastating and incurable illness that is caused by the human immunodeficiency virus (HIV) and progressively weakens the body's immune system, leaving the person vulnerable to opportunistic infections that usually cause death.

human immunodeficiency virus (HIV)
The virus that causes AIDS.

Answer true or false for each statement.

1. AIDS is a single disease. (true/false)

2. AIDS symptoms vary widely from country to country, and even from risk group to risk group. (true/false)

3. Those at greatest risk for getting AIDS are people who have sex without using condoms, drug users who share needles, and infants born to AIDS-infected mothers. (true/false)

4. AIDS is one of the most highly contagious diseases. (true/false)

5. One way to avoid contracting AIDS is to use an oil-based lubricant with a condom. (true/false)

Answers:

1. False: AIDS is not a single disease. Rather, a severely impaired immune system leaves a person with AIDS highly susceptible to a whole host of infections and diseases.

2. True: In the United States and Europe, AIDS sufferers may develop Kaposi's sarcoma (a rare form of skin cancer), pneumonia, and tuberculosis. In Africa, people with AIDS usually waste away with fever, diarrhea, and symptoms caused by tuberculosis.

3. True: Those groups are at greatest risk. Screening of blood donors and testing of donated blood have greatly reduced the risk of contracting AIDS through blood transfusions. Today, women make up the fastest-growing group of infected people worldwide, as AIDS spreads among heterosexuals, especially in Africa.

4. False: AIDS is not among the most highly infectious diseases. You cannot get AIDS from kissing, shaking hands, or using objects handled by people who have AIDS.

5. False: Do not use oil-based lubricants, which can eat through condoms. Latex condoms with an effective spermicide are safer. Learn the sexual history of any potential partner, including HIV test results. Don't have sex with prostitutes.

467,910 deaths from AIDS had been reported to the Centers for Disease Control (2002). Worldwide, in 2001, 3 million people died from AIDS and 40 million people were living with HIV infection (CDC, 2002). Test your knowledge about AIDS in *Try It! 10.3*.

HIV attacks the immune system, leaving it severely impaired and virtually unable to function. The diagnosis of AIDS is made when the immune system is so damaged that victims develop rare forms of cancer or pneumonia or other so-called opportunistic infections. The average time from infection with HIV to advanced AIDS is about 10 years, but the time may range from 2 years to as long as 15 years or more (Nowak & McMichael, 1995). The disease progresses faster in smokers, in the very young, in people over 50, and, apparently, in women. AIDS also progresses faster in those who are repeatedly exposed to the virus and in those who were infected by someone in an advanced stage of the disease.

Researchers believe that HIV is transmitted primarily through the exchange of blood, semen, or vaginal secretions during sexual contact or when IV (intravenous) drug users share contaminated needles or syringes. Figure 10.6 illustrates the proportion of AIDS cases attributable to each means of transmitting the disease. The rate of AIDS among gay men is higher than in other groups because gay men are likely to have anal intercourse. Anal intercourse is more dangerous than coitus because rectal tissue often tears during penetration, allowing HIV ready entry into the bloodstream.

It is a mistake to view AIDS as a disease confined to gay men, however. About twenty-five percent of the AIDS cases reported in the United States in 2001 were females, forty percent of whom contracted it through heterosexual contact and twenty percent through IV drug abuse (CDC, 2002). In Africa, where AIDS is currently epidemic and is believed to have originated, it strikes men and women about equally, and heterosexual activity is believed to be the primary means of transmission (Quinn,

▼ The producers of *Sesame Street* introduced an HIV-positive Muppet to the show's cast to help educate young viewers about the plight of children living with the infection.

2002). AIDS is transmitted 12 times more easily from infected men to women than vice versa (Padian et al., 1991). AIDS may also be transmitted from mother to child during pregnancy or breast-feeding (Prince, 1998).

The reaction to the news that one is HIV-positive is frequently a state of shock, bewilderment, confusion, or disbelief. To cope with the stress of living with HIV, patients need education and information about the disease. They can be helped by psychotherapy, self-help groups, and medications such as antidepressants and antianxiety drugs. Self-help groups and group therapy may serve as a substitute family for some patients.

Stress and the Immune System

Psychoneuroimmunology is a field of study in which psychologists, biologists, and medical researchers combine their expertise to learn the effects of psychological factors–emotions, thinking, and behavior–on the immune system (Cohen, 1996). Researchers know that the immune system is not merely a separate system to fight off foreign invaders. Rather, it is an incredibly complex, interconnected defense system, working with the brain to keep the body healthy (Ader, 2000).

Psychological factors, emotions, and stress are all related to immune system functioning (Kiecolt-Glaser et al., 2002). The immune system exchanges information with the brain, and what goes on in the brain can apparently influence the immune system for good or ill. In one study, researchers gave volunteers nasal drops containing a cold virus. Within the next few days, symptoms of the viral infection rose sharply in some of the 151 women and 125 men who participated in the study, but less so or not at all in others. Participants with a rich social life in the form of frequent interactions with others–spouses, children, parents, coworkers, friends, and volunteer and religious groups–seemed to enjoy a powerful shield of protection against the virus infection. And this pattern of protection held across age and racial groups, for both sexes, at all educational levels, and at every season of the year (Ader, 2000; Cohen et al., 1997).

Close social ties–to family, friends, and others–apparently have good effects on the immune system. Ill effects often come from stress. High periods of stress are correlated with increased symptoms of many infectious diseases, including oral and genital herpes, mononucleosis, colds, and flu. And stress has caused decreased levels of the immune system's B and T cells. Kiecolt-Glaser and others (1996) found that elderly men and women experiencing chronic stress due to years of caring for a spouse with Alzheimer's disease showed an impaired immune response to flu shots. Physicians have long observed that stress and anxiety can worsen autoimmune diseases. And "if fear can produce relapses [in autoimmune diseases], then even the fear of a relapse may become a self-fulfilling prophecy" (Steinman, 1993, p. 112). Reviews of studies also show that stress is associated with an increase in illness behaviors–reporting physical symptoms and seeking medical care (Cohen & Herbert, 1996; Cohen & Williamson, 1991).

Stress has the power to suppress the immune system long after the stressful experience is over. An experimental group of medical students who were enduring the stress of major exams was compared with a control group of medical students who were on vacation from classes and exams. When tested for the presence of disease-fighting antibodies, participants in the exam group, but not those in the control group, had a significant reduction in their antibody count because of the stress. The lowered antibody count was still present 14 days after the exams were over. At that point, the students were not even aware that they were still stressed and reported feeling no stress (Deinzer et al., 2000).

In addition to academic pressures, poor marital relationships and sleep deprivation have been linked to lowered immune response (Kiecolt-Glaser et al., 1987; Maier & Laudenslager, 1985). Several researchers have reported that severe, inca-

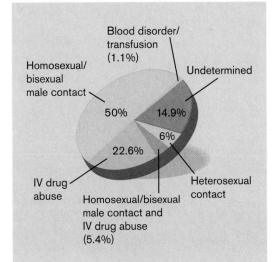

> ## Figure 10.6

How HIV Was Transmitted in Adult/Adolescent AIDS Cases Reported in the United States

The primary means of transmission of HIV is through homosexual/bisexual male contact (50%). Intravenous drug use (sharing needles) accounts for 22.6% of the AIDS cases in the United States. (From U.S. Bureau of the Census, 1997.)

What are the effects of stress and depression on the immune system?

psychoneuroimmunology (sye-ko-NEW-ro-IM-you-NOLL-oh-gee) A field in which psychologists, biologists, and medical researchers study the effects of psychological factors on the immune system.

pacitating depression is also related to lowered immune activity (Herbert & Cohen, 1993). For several months after the death of a spouse, the widow or widower suffers weakened immune system function and is at a higher risk of mortality. Severe bereavement weakens the immune system, increasing a person's chance of suffering from a long list of physical and mental ailments for up to 2 years following a partner's death (Prigerson et al., 1997).

Personal Factors Reducing the Impact of Stress and Illness

There are several personal factors that seem to insulate people from the effects of stress and illness. For one, people who are generally optimistic tend to cope more effectively with stress, and this in turn may reduce their risk of illness (Seligman, 1990). An important characteristic optimists share is that they generally expect good outcomes. And such positive expectations help make them more stress-resistant than pessimists, who tend to expect bad outcomes. An especially lethal form of pessimism is hopelessness. A longitudinal study of a large number of Finnish men revealed that participants who reported feeling moderate to high hopelessness died from all causes at two to three times the rates of those reporting low or no hopelessness (Everson et al., 1996).

What four personal factors are associated with health and resistance to stress?

Studying male executives with high levels of stress, psychologist Suzanne Kobasa (1979; Kobasa et al., 1982) found three psychological characteristics that distinguished those who remained healthy from those who had a high incidence of illness. The three qualities, which she referred to collectively as **hardiness,** were *commitment, control,* and *challenge.* Hardy individuals feel a strong sense of commitment to both their work and their personal life. They see themselves not as victims of whatever life brings, but as agents who have control over consequences and outcomes. They act to solve their own problems. And they welcome challenges in life, viewing them not as threats but as opportunities for growth and improvement.

Florian and others (1995) found that commitment and control alone are apparently sufficient to produce hardiness. In stressful situations, commitment and control are compatible, complementary attributes. Commitment ensures a continuing involvement in the situation and provides the staying power to see it through. A person who is committed does not give up. Control provides the confidence that the person is in charge of the situation and capable of finding the right solution to solve the problem at hand.

Another personal factor that contributes to resistance to stress and illness is religious faith. One longitudinal study (conducted over a period of 28 years) revealed that frequent attendance at religious services is correlated with better health habits (Strawbridge et al., 1997). A review of 42 separate studies combined data on some 126,000 individuals and revealed that religious involvement is positively associated with measures of physical health and lower rates of cancer, heart disease, and stroke (McCullough et al., 2000). Also, measures of religious involvement were reliable predictors of greater longevity when all causes of mortality were considered. The specific measures of religious involvement most closely related to a lower mortality rate were regular attendance at worship services, religious orthodoxy, and a personal sense of comfort and strength from one's religion (McCullough et al., 2000). This study and others have found the association between religious involvement and lower mortality to be stronger for women than for men (Hummer et al., 1999; Strawbridge et al., 1997).

Another factor contributing to better health is **social support** (Cohen, 1988; Kaplan et al., 1994). Social support is support provided, usually in time of need, by a spouse or other family members or by friends, neighbors, colleagues, support groups, or others. It can involve tangible aid, information, and advice, as well as emotional support. It can also be viewed as the feeling of being loved, valued, and cared for by others for whom the person feels a mutual obligation.

Social support appears to have positive effects on the body's immune system, as well as on the cardiovascular and endocrine systems (Miller et al., 2002; Uchino et al., 1996). Social support may help encourage health-promoting behaviors and reduce the

hardiness
A combination of three psychological qualities shared by people who can undergo high levels of stress yet remain healthy: a sense of control over one's life, commitment to one's personal goals, and a tendency to view change as a challenge rather than as a threat.

social support
Tangible support, information, advice, and/or emotional support provided in time of need by family, friends, and others; the feeling of being loved, valued, and cared for.

impact of stress so that people will be less likely to resort to unhealthy methods of coping, such as smoking or drinking. Social support has been shown to reduce the impact of stress from unemployment, long-term illness, retirement, and bereavement. And a large study of soldiers who had enlisted in the U.S. Army showed that a high level of social support from peers was an essential ingredient in reducing stress (Bliese & Castro, 2000). People with social support recover more quickly from illnesses and lower their risk of death from specific diseases. Social support may even increase the probability of surviving a heart attack, because it buffers the impact of stress on cardiovascular function (Steptoe, 2000). A longitudinal study of 4,775 people over a 9-year period found that those low in social support died at twice the rate of those high in social support (Berkman & Syme, 1979).

A strong social support network can help speed a person's recovery from illness or accident.

Research on natural disasters reveals that initial social support is common but that the support tends to deteriorate, because the needs of victims overwhelm the tangible and emotional resources of friends and family. Similarly, chronic physical or mental illness may deplete resources and lead to burnout in those supplying care and social support.

Social support researchers have begun to distinguish between *perceived support,* the degree to which a person believes help is available when needed, and *received support,* the actual help a person receives from others. Interestingly, many have found that perceived support is more important than received support (Norris & Kaniasty, 1996). Other research has shown that high levels of perceived social support are associated with lower levels of depression and even with recovery from depression (Lara et al., 1997). And perceived support may be more a function of individual personality than of the actual availability of family and friends who can offer help. One longitudinal study found that college-aged participants who had sociable, outgoing personalities were more likely to report having high levels of perceived social support later in adulthood (Von Dras & Siegler, 1997). These results underscore the importance of psychological variables in health.

Lifestyle and Health

For most Americans, health enemy number one is their own habits—lack of exercise, too little sleep, alcohol or drug abuse, an unhealthy diet, and overeating. A longitudinal study on the health consequences of certain lifestyle factors tracked nearly 117,000 female nurses from 1976 through 1992. The study showed that the overweight nurses were from 2 to 2.5 times more likely to suffer a stroke than were their leaner counterparts. But the most dangerous unhealthy behavior of all is smoking.

What are the major unhealthy lifestyle factors?

Smoking and Health

The Surgeon General continues to warn that smoking remains the number one cause of preventable disease and death in the United States (U.S. Department of Health and Human Services, 2000). That message appears to be taking root, because the prevalence of smoking among American adults has been decreasing and is now under 25% (National Center for Health Statistics, 2000). There are, however, wide variations in smoking habits according to gender and ethnic group. The highest rates of smoking are found among Native American men (41%) and women (29%), while the lowest rates are reported

Why is smoking considered the single most preventable cause of death?

for Asian American men (18%) and women (11%) (U.S. Department of Health and Human Services, 2000).

Even though the prevalence of smoking is decreasing, every year more than 1 million young Americans become regular smokers, and more than 400,000 American adults die from diseases related to tobacco use (U.S. Department of Health and Human Services, 2000). Smoking increases the risk for heart disease, lung cancer, other cancers that are smoking-related, and emphysema. Furthermore, smoking suppresses the action of pulmonary (lung) T cells, increasing susceptibility to respiratory tract infections and tumors (McCue et al., 2000).

Millions of nonsmokers who must breathe smoke-filled air suffer the ill effects of this *passive,* or *secondhand, smoke.* Research indicates that nonsmokers who are regularly exposed to passive smoke have twice the risk of heart attack of those who are not exposed (Kawachi et al., 1997). And think of the suffering of millions from chronic bronchitis, emphysema, and other respiratory diseases; the deaths and injuries from fires caused by smoking; and the low birthweights and retarded fetal development of babies of smoking mothers. Furthermore, mothers who smoke during pregnancy tend to have babies who are at greater risk for anxiety and depression and are five times more likely to become smokers themselves (Cornelius et al., 2000).

Because smoking is so addictive, smokers have great difficulty breaking the habit. Even so, 90% of ex-smokers quit smoking on their own (Novello, 1990). The average smoker makes five or six attempts to quit before finally succeeding (Sherman, 1994). Some aids, such as nicotine gum and the nicotine patch, help many people kick the habit. A review of 17 studies involving over 5,000 participants revealed that 22% of people who used the nicotine patch were smoke-free, compared with only 9% of those who received a placebo. And 27% of those receiving the nicotine patch plus antismoking counseling or support remained smoke-free (Fiore, cited in Sherman, 1994). But even with the patch, quitting is difficult, because the patch only lessens withdrawal symptoms, which typically last 2 to 4 weeks (Hughes, 1992). Half of all relapses occur within the first 2 weeks after people quit, and relapses are most likely when people are experiencing negative emotions or are using alcohol. It takes just one cigarette, sometimes only one puff, to cause a relapse.

Researchers have found smoking rates to be high in people suffering from drug and alcohol abuse and schizophrenia. Furthermore, a link has been found between smoking and a history of major depression, both of which are thought to be influenced by genetic factors (Breslau et al., 1993; Kendler, Neale, MacLean, et al., 1993). Some smokers who try to quit are at higher risk for major depression. Withdrawal brings on depression in more than 85% of those with a history of depression, compared with only 20% of those with no such history (Glassman, 1993). Consequently, depressed smokers are much less likely to succeed at quitting (Borrelli et al., 1996; Stage et al., 1996).

Alcohol Abuse

Recall from Chapter 4 that *substance abuse* is defined as continued use of a substance after several episodes in which use of the substance has negatively affected an individual's work, education, and social relationships (American Psychiatric Association, 1994). Alcohol is perhaps the most frequently abused substance of all, and the health costs of alcohol abuse are staggering—fatalities, medical bills, lost work, family problems.

What are some health risks of alcohol abuse? ▶

Approximately 10 million Americans are alcoholics (Neimark et al., 1994). Alcohol abuse and dependence are three times more prevalent in males than in females (Grant et al., 1991). And people who begin drinking before age 15 are four times more likely than those who begin later to become alcoholics (Grant & Dawson, 1998). For many, alcohol provides a method of coping with life stresses that they feel powerless to control (Seeman & Seeman, 1992). As many as 80% of men and women who are alcoholics complain of episodes of depression. A large study of almost 3,000 alcoholics concluded that some depressive episodes are independent of alcohol, whereas others are substance-induced (Schuckit et al., 1997).

Alcohol can damage virtually every organ in the body, but it is especially harmful to the liver and is the major cause of cirrhosis, which kills 26,000 people each year (Neimark et al., 1994). Other causes of death are also more common in alcoholics than in nonalcoholics. One Norwegian longitudinal study involving more than 40,000 male participants found that the rate of death prior to age 60 was significantly higher among alcoholics than nonalcoholics (Rossow & Amundsen, 1997). Alcoholics were 3 times as likely to die in automobile accidents as nonalcoholics, but they were also almost 3 times as likely to die of heart disease and had twice the rate of deaths from cancer.

Shrinkage in the cerebral cortex of alcoholics has been found by researchers using MRI (Jernigan et al., 1991). CT scans also show brain shrinkage in a high percentage of alcoholics, even in young subjects and in those who appear to be intact mentally (Lishman, 1990). Moreover, heavy drinking can cause cognitive impairment that continues for several months after the alcoholic quits drinking (Sullivan et al., 2002). The only good news in recent studies is that some of the effects of alcohol on the brain seem to be partially reversible with prolonged abstinence.

▲ Regular aerobic exercise improves cardiovascular fitness in people of all ages.

Alcoholism's toll goes beyond the physical damage to the alcoholic. In 1999, alcohol was involved in 30% of the traffic fatalities in the United States (National Institute on Alcohol Abuse and Alcoholism [NIAAA], 2001). Alcohol has been implicated in 40% of violent crimes and 75% of domestic abuse cases (U.S. Department of Justice, 1998).

The American Medical Association maintains that alcoholism is a disease and that it is incurable. According to this view, even a small amount of alcohol can cause an irresistible craving for more, leading alcoholics to lose control of their drinking (Jellinek, 1960). Thus, total abstinence is seen as the only acceptable and effective method of treatment. The medical establishment and Alcoholics Anonymous endorse both the disease concept and the total abstinence approach to treatment. But there is a drug that may make abstinence somewhat easier. German researchers report that the drug acamprosate helps prevent relapse in recovering alcoholics (Sass et al., 1996).

Some studies suggest a genetic factor in alcoholism and lend support to the disease model. For example, neuroscientist Henri Begleiter and his colleagues have accumulated a large body of evidence suggesting that the brains of alcoholics respond differently to visual and auditory stimuli than those of nonalcoholics (Hada et al., 2001). Further, many relatives of alcoholics, even children and adults who have never consumed any alcohol in their lives, display the same types of response patterns (Zhang et al., 2001). And relatives of alcoholics who display these patterns are more likely to become alcoholics themselves or to suffer from other types of addictions (Anokhim et al., 2000; Beirut et al., 1998). Begleiter has suggested that the kinds of brain-imaging techniques he uses in his research may someday be used to determine which relatives of alcoholics are genetically predisposed to addiction and which are not (Porjesz et al., 1998) .

◄ What are some benefits of regular aerobic exercise?

Exercise

Many studies show that regular aerobic exercise pays rich dividends in the form of physical and mental fitness. **Aerobic exercise** (such as running, swimming, brisk walking, bicycling, rowing, and jumping rope) is exercise that uses the large muscle groups in continuous, repetitive action and increases oxygen intake and breathing and heart rates. To improve cardiovascular fitness and endurance and to lessen the risk of heart attack, aerobic exercise should be performed regularly. This means three or four times a week for 20–30 minutes, with additional 5–10 minute warm-up and cool-down periods (Alpert et al., 1990; Shepard, 1986). Less than 20 minutes of aerobic exercise

aerobic exercise
(ah-RO-bik) Exercise that uses the large muscle groups in continuous, repetitive action and increases oxygen intake and breathing and heart rates.

3 times a week has "no measurable effect on the heart," and more than 3 hours per week "is not known to reduce cardiovascular risk any further" (Simon, 1988, p. 3).

In case you are not yet convinced, consider the following benefits of exercise:

- Increases the efficiency of the heart, enabling it to pump more blood with each beat and reduces the resting pulse rate and improves circulation
- Raises levels of HDL (the good blood cholesterol), which helps rid the body of LDL (the bad blood cholesterol) and removes plaque buildup on artery walls
- Burns extra calories, helping to lose or maintain weight
- Makes bones denser and stronger, helping to prevent osteoporosis in women
- Moderates the effects of stress
- Increases energy level and resistance to fatigue
- Benefits the immune system by increasing natural killer cell activity (Fiatarone et al., 1988)

Apply It! Should You Turn to the Internet for Health Advice?

What if you found out a close friend had multiple sclerosis, but you knew nothing about the disease? Or what if you started experiencing dryness in your eyes, just often enough to make you wonder if you should see a doctor? Where would you turn? An increasing number of people all over the world are turning to the Internet for information about their health.

One study of 188 women with breast cancer found that about half of them used the Internet to find out more about the disease (Fogel et al., 2002). Surveys of older adults have shown that Internet use helped them gain a sense of control over their health care decisions (Kalichman et al., 2003: McMellon & Schiffman, 2002). Chat rooms devoted to specific diseases may represent an important source of social support for patients, especially those suffering from rare disorders (Kummervold et al., 2002). And using email to coach and encourage patients in the management of chronic diseases such as diabetes has proven to be effective both for patients' health and for efficient management of health care professionals' time (McKay et al., 2002).

But how good is the information patients are getting on the Internet? In a large-scale study of health-related Web sites sponsored by the American Medical Association, researchers found that the

quality of information varied widely from one site to another (Eysenbach et al., 2002). A study of Internet-based advice for managing children's fever sponsored by the British Medical Association found that most Web sites contained erroneous information (Impicciatore et al., 1997). Moreover, in a follow-up study 4 years later, the researchers found that about half the sites were no longer available; those that remained showed little improvement in the quality of information (Pandolfini & Bonati, 2002).

Despite these difficulties, physicians' organizations acknowledge the potential value of the Internet for helping patients learn about and manage their own health. And because so many older adults are using the Internet to learn about health issues, the American Association of Retired Persons (2002) has published a list of points to keep in mind when surfing the Web for health information and advice:

- *There are no rules governing what is published on the Internet.* Unlike articles published in scientific journals, which are usually reviewed by experts in the field, articles can be posted on the Web by anyone, without review of any kind. Without expert knowledge, it is extremely difficult to tell whether the information and advice these articles contain is valid or not.

- *Consider the source.* Generally, Web sites sponsored by medical schools, government agencies, and public health organizations are reliable. Others, especially those promoting a health-related product, should be considered suspect.

- *Get a second opinion.* Ask your health care provider about Internet-based information, or read what's available from several different sources on the topic.

- *Examine references.* Sites referring to sources (e.g., books, other Web sites) that are credible and that you can find yourself on the Web or in a library or bookstore are probably more reliable than sites that offer no references to support their advice.

- *How current is the information?* Health-related information changes frequently. Be certain that you are reading the most current findings and recommendations about the topic.

- *Is it too good to be true?* As in all areas of life, if something sounds too good to be true (e.g., a vitamin that cures cancer), it probably is. Try to find experimental, placebo-controlled studies that support any claims.

Using these guidelines, you can become a better consumer of Internet-based health information. ■

Summarize It!

Sources of Stress

➤ What is stress?

Stress is the physiological and psychological response to a condition that threatens or challenges an individual and requires some form of adaptation or adjustment.

➤ What was the Social Readjustment Rating Scale designed to reveal?

The SRRS assesses stress in terms of life events that produce change and require adaptation. Holmes and Rahe found a relationship between degree of life stress (as measured on the scale) and major health problems.

➤ What roles do hassles and uplifts play in the stress of life, according to Lazarus?

According to Lazarus, daily hassles typically cause more stress than major life changes. Positive life experiences–or uplifts–can neutralize the effects of many of the hassles.

➤ How do approach–approach, avoidance–avoidance, and approach–avoidance conflicts differ?

In an approach–approach conflict, a person must decide between equally desirable alternatives; in an avoidance–avoidance conflict, between two undesirable alternatives. In an approach–avoidance conflict, a person is both drawn to and repelled by a choice.

➤ How do unpredictability and lack of control over a stressor affect its impact?

Stressors that are unpredictable and uncontrollable are more difficult to cope with than those that are predictable and controllable.

➤ For people to function effectively and find satisfaction on the job, what nine variables should fall within their comfort zone?

Nine variables that should fall within a worker's comfort zone are workload, clarity of job description and evaluation criteria, physical variables, job status, accountability, task variety, human contact, physical challenge, and mental challenge.

➤ What are some of the psychological and health consequences of job stress?

Job stress can cause serious illnesses such as depression, high blood pressure, and cardiovascular disease; it can also cause headaches, exhaustion, absenteeism, and reduced productivity. However, unemployment is also a significant source of stress for most people.

➤ What is posttraumatic stress disorder?

Posttraumatic stress disorder (PTSD) is a prolonged, severe stress reaction to a catastrophic event or to chronic intense stress.

➤ What evidence exists for an association between perceived racism and health in African Americans?

Some researchers believe that African Americans have higher levels of high blood pressure than members of other groups because of historical racism. African Americans who express high levels of concern about racism display larger cardiovascular responses to experimentally induced stressors than do African Americans who have lower levels of such concern.

KEY TERMS

stress (p. 288)
fight-or-flight response (p. 288)
stressor (p. 288)
Social Readjustment Rating Scale (SRRS) (p. 288)
hassles (p. 288)
uplifts (p. 288)
approach-approach conflict (p. 290)
avoidance-avoidance conflict (p. 290)
approach-avoidance conflict (p. 290)
posttraumatic stress disorder (PTSD) (p. 292)

Responding to Stress

➤ What is the general adaptation syndrome?

The general adaptation syndrome (GAS) is the predictable sequence of reactions that organisms show in response to stressors. It consists of the alarm stage, the resistance stage, and the exhaustion stage.

➤ What are the roles of primary and secondary appraisal when a person is confronted with a potentially stressful event?

According to Lazarus, when confronted with a potentially stressful event, a person engages in a cognitive appraisal process consisting of (1) a primary appraisal, to evaluate the effect of the event on one's well-being (whether positive, irrelevant, negative) and whether it involves harm or loss, threat, or challenge, and (2) a secondary appraisal to determine how to cope with the stressor.

➤ What is the difference between problem-focused and emotion-focused coping?

Problem-focused coping is a response aimed at reducing, modifying, or eliminating the source of stress; emotion-focused coping is aimed at reducing the emotional impact of the stressor.

KEY TERMS

general adaptation syndrome (GAS) (p. 294)
alarm stage (p. 295)
resistance stage (p. 295)
exhaustion stage (p. 295)
primary appraisal (p. 295)
secondary appraisal (p. 295)
coping (p. 295)
problem-focused coping (p. 295)
emotion-focused coping (p. 295)
proactive coping (p. 296)

Health and Illness

➤ How do the biomedical and biopsychosocial models differ in their approaches to health and illness?

The biomedical model focuses on illness rather than on health and explains illness in terms of biological factors. The biopsychosocial model focuses on both health and illness and holds that both are determined by a combination of biological, psychological, and social factors.

➤ What are the Type A and Type B behavior patterns?

The Type A behavior pattern, often cited as a risk factor for coronary heart disease, is characterized by a sense of time urgency, impatience, excessive competitive drive, hostility, and easily aroused anger. The Type B behavior pattern is characterized by a relaxed, easygoing approach to life.

➤ What aspect of the Type A behavior pattern is most clearly linked to coronary heart disease?

Hostility is the aspect of the Type A pattern most clearly linked to coronary heart disease.

➤ What are the effects of stress and depression on the immune system?

Both stress and depression have been associated with lowered immune response, and stress has been linked with increased symptoms of various infectious diseases.

➤ What four personal factors are associated with good health and resistance to stress?

Personal factors related to good health and resistance to stress are optimism, psychological hardiness, religious involvement, and social support.

KEY TERMS

biomedical model (p. 296)
biopsychosocial model (p. 296)
health psychology (p. 296)
Type A behavior pattern (p. 298)
Type B behavior pattern (p. 298)
lymphocytes (p. 299)
acquired immune deficiency syndrome (AIDS) (p. 299)
human immunodeficiency virus (HIV) (p. 299)
psychoneuroimmunology (p. 301)
hardiness (p. 302)
social support (p. 302)

Lifestyle and Health

➤ What are the major unhealthy lifestyle factors?

Unhealthy lifestyle factors include smoking, overeating, an unhealthy diet, too much alcohol, drug abuse, and/or too little exercise and rest.

➤ Why is smoking considered the single most preventable cause of death?

Smoking is considered the single most preventable cause of death because it is directly related to over 400,000 deaths each year, including deaths from heart disease, cancer, and lung disease.

➤ What are some health risks of alcohol abuse?

Alcohol abuse damages virtually every organ in the body, especially the liver and the brain; and it is involved in over 40% of motor vehicle fatalities.

➤ What are some benefits of regular aerobic exercise?

Regular aerobic exercise reduces the risk of cardiovascular disease, increases muscular strength, moderates the effects of stress, makes bones denser and stronger, and helps with weight loss or maintenance.

KEY TERM

aerobic exercise (p. 305)

Surf It !

Want to be sure you've absorbed the material in Chapter 10, "Health and Stress," before the big test? Visiting **www.ablongman.com/ woodmastering1e** can put a top grade within your reach. The site is loaded with free practice tests, flashcards, activities, and links to help you review your way to an A.

Companion Website

Study Guide for Chapter 10 !

Answers to all the Study Guide questions are provided at the end of the book.

Section One: Chapter Review

1. On the Social Readjustment Rating Scale, only negative life changes are considered stressful. (true/false)

2. The Social Readjustment Rating Scale takes account of the individual's perceptions of the stressfulness of the life change in assigning stress points. (true/false)

3. According to Lazarus, hassles typically account for more life stress than major life changes. (true/false)

4. Lazarus's approach to measuring hassles and uplifts considers individual perceptions of stressful events. (true/false)

5. Travis cannot decide whether to go out or stay home and study for his test. What kind of conflict does he have?
   a. approach–approach
   b. avoidance–avoidance
   c. approach–avoidance
   d. ambivalence–ambivalence

6. What factor or factors increase stress, according to research on the topic?
   a. predictability of the stressor
   b. unpredictability of the stressor
   c. predictability of and control over the stressor
   d. unpredictability of and lack of control over the stressor

7. Sources of workplace stress for women include
   a. sexual harassment.
   b. discrimination.
   c. balancing family and work demands.
   d. all of the above.

8. Victims of catastrophic events usually panic. (true/false)

9. Posttraumatic stress disorder is a prolonged and severe stress reaction that results when a number of common sources of stress occur simultaneously. (true/false)

10. The group that has received the most attention from researchers interested in the association between stress and racism is
    a. Native Americans.
    b. Hispanic Americans.
    c. Asian Americans.
    d. African Americans.

11. The stage of the general adaptation syndrome marked by intense physiological efforts to adapt to the stressor is the (alarm, resistance) stage.

12. Susceptibility to illness increases during the (alarm, exhaustion) stage of the general adaptation syndrome.

13. Selye focused on the (psychological, physiological) aspects of stress; Lazarus focused on the (psychological, physiological) aspects of stress.

14. During secondary appraisal, a person
    a. evaluates his or her coping resources and considers options for dealing with the stressor.
    b. determines whether an event is positive, neutral, or negative.
    c. determines whether an event involves loss, threat, or challenge.
    d. determines whether an event causes physiological or psychological stress.

15. Coping aimed at reducing, modifying, or eliminating a source of stress is called (emotion-focused, problem-focused) coping; that aimed at reducing an emotional reaction to stress is called (emotion-focused, problem-focused) coping.

16. People typically use a combination of problem-focused and emotion-focused coping when dealing with a stressful situation. (true/false)

17. Proactive coping involves taking action (before, after) a stressor occurs.

18. The biomedical model focuses on _____ ; the biopsychosocial model focuses on _____ .
    a. illness; illness
    b. health and illness; illness
    c. illness; health and illness
    d. health and illness; health and illness

19. Most research has pursued the connection between the Type A behavior pattern and
    a. cancer.   c. stroke.
    b. coronary heart disease.   d. ulcers.

20. Recent research suggests that the most toxic component of the Type A behavior pattern is
    a. hostility.   c. a sense of time urgency.
    b. impatience.   d. perfectionism.

21. HIV eventually causes a breakdown in the _____ system.
    a. circulatory   c. immune
    b. vascular   d. respiratory

22. The incidence of AIDS in the United States is highest among
   a. homosexuals and IV drug users.
   b. homosexuals and hemophiliacs.
   c. homosexuals and bisexuals.
   d. heterosexuals, IV drug users, and hemophiliacs.

23. Lowered immune response has been associated with
   a. stress.
   b. depression.
   c. stress and depression.
   d. neither stress nor depression.

24. Some research suggests that optimists are more stress-resistant than pessimists. (true/false)

25. Which of the following is not a dimension of psychological hardiness?
   a. a feeling that adverse circumstances can be controlled and changed
   b. a sense of commitment and deep involvement in personal goals
   c. a tendency to look on change as a challenge rather than a threat
   d. close, supportive relationships with family and friends

26. Social support tends to reduce stress but is unrelated to health outcomes. (true/false)

27. Which is the most important factor leading to disease and death?
   a. unhealthy lifestyle
   b. a poor health care system
   c. environmental hazards
   d. genetic disorders

28. Which health-compromising behavior is responsible for the most deaths?
   a. overeating
   c. lack of exercise
   b. smoking
   d. excessive alcohol use

29. (Alcohol, Smoking) damages virtually every organ in the body.

30. To improve cardiovascular fitness, aerobic exercise should be done
   a. 15 minutes daily.
   b. 1 hour daily.
   c. 20 to 30 minutes daily.
   d. 20 to 30 minutes three or four times a week.

Section Two:
The Biopsychosocial Model of Health and Illness

List at least two forces for each of the following:
1. Biological forces favoring health and wellness
2. Biological forces working against health and wellness
3. Psychological forces favoring health and wellness
4. Psychological forces working against health and wellness
5. Social forces favoring health and wellness
6. Social forces working against health and wellness

Section Three: Fill In the Blank

1. Medicine has been dominated by the _____ model, which focuses on illness rather than on health, whereas the _____ model asserts that both health and illness are determined by a combination of biological, psychological, and social factors.

2. The field of psychology that is concerned with the psychological factors that contribute to health, illness, and recovery is known as _____ _____ .

3. The fight-or-flight response is controlled by the _____ and the endocrine glands.

4. The first stage of the general adaptation syndrome is the _____ stage.

5. The stage of the general adaptation syndrome during which the adrenal glands release hormones to help the body resist stressors is called the _____ stage.

6. Lazarus's theory is considered a _____ theory of stress and coping.

7. Noelle knew that her upcoming job interview would be difficult, so she tried to anticipate the kinds of questions she would be asked and practiced the best possible responses. Noelle was practicing _____ coping.

8. The most feared disease related to the immune system is _____ .

9. The primary means of transmission of HIV is through sexual contact between _____ .

10. Daily _____ are the "irritating, frustrating, distressing demands and troubled relationships that plague us day in and day out."

11. Tiffany is a psychologist who works with biologists and medical researchers to determine the effects of psychological factors on the immune system. Tiffany works in the field of _____ .

12. People with the Type _____ behavior pattern have a strong sense of time urgency and are impatient, excessively competitive, hostile, and easily angered.

13. The effects of alcohol on _____ may continue for several months after an alcoholic stops drinking.

14. _____ appraisal is an evaluation of the significance of a potentially stressful event according to how it will affect one's well-being–whether it is perceived as irrelevant or as involving harm, loss, threat, or challenge.

15. African Americans may have a greater incidence of _____ _____ _____ than White Americans because of the stress associated with historical racism.

16. A _____ is any event capable of producing physical or emotional stress.

17. Cole wants to get a flu shot, but he is also very afraid of needles. He is faced with an _____ – _____ conflict.

Section Four: Comprehensive Practice Test

1. Stress consists of the threats and problems we encounter in life. (true/false)

2. Hans Selye developed the
   a. diathesis stress model.
   b. general adaptation syndrome model.
   c. cognitive stress model.
   d. conversion reaction model.

3. The fight-or-flight response is seen in the _____ stage of the general adaptation syndrome.
   a. alarm   c. resistance
   b. exhaustion   d. arousal

4. Lack of exercise, poor diet, and disease and injury are considered to be _____ forces that work against health and wellness.
   a. environmental c. biological
   b. psychological d. social

5. Charlotte has been looking for new bedroom furniture and has found two styles that she really likes. She is trying to decide which one she will purchase. Charlotte is experiencing an _____ conflict.
   a. approach–approach
   b. approach–avoidance
   c. avoidance–avoidance
   d. avoidance–approach

6. People's sense of control over a situation can have an important beneficial influence on how a stressor affects them even if they do not exercise that control. (true/false)

7. Posttraumatic stress leaves some people more vulnerable for future mental health problems. (true/false)

8. Which of the following is not a variable in work stress?
   a. workload
   b. clarity of job description
   c. perceived equity of pay for work
   d. task variety

9. Research indicates that African Americans who are highly concerned about _____ are more sensitive to stressors than their peers who are less concerned.

10. Religious faith helps people cope with negative life events. (true/false)

11. Lazarus's term for the positive experiences that can serve to cancel out the effects of day-to-day hassles is
    a. stress assets.   c. uplifts.
    b. coping mechanisms.   d. appraisals.

12. Type B behavior patterns seem to be more correlated with heart disease than do Type A behavior patterns. (true/false)

13. B cells produce antibodies that are effective in destroying antigens that live _____ the body cells; T cells are important in the destruction of antigens that live _____ the body cells.
    a. outside; inside
    b. inside; outside

14. AIDS is caused by HIV, often called the AIDS virus. (true/false)

15. HIV weakens the immune system by attacking T cells. (true/false)

Section Five: Critical Thinking

1. In your view, which is more effective for evaluating stress– the Social Readjustment Rating Scale or the Hassle Scale? Explain the advantages and disadvantages of each.

2. Prepare two arguments–one supporting the position that alcoholism is a genetically inherited disease, and the other supporting the position that alcoholism is not a medical disease but results from learning.

3. Choose several stress-producing incidents from your life and explain what problem-focused and emotion-focused coping strategies you used. From the knowledge you have gained in this chapter, list other coping strategies that might have been more effective.

chapter 11

Personality Theory
and Assessment

In 1924, two young Chicago men, 18-year-old Nathan Leopold and 19-year-old Richard Loeb, brutally killed a 13-year-old boy in an effort to prove their intellectual superiority. They believed that their superior cognitive abilities exempted them from society's rules. Moreover, they thought that their intelligence would enable them to murder at will, without risk of detection by the presumably intellectually inferior authorities. However, the police were able to trace a pair of glasses Leopold carelessly left at the murder scene and arrested the pair a few days after the crime.

Leopold and Loeb confessed, and their wealthy families hired well-known attorney Clarence Darrow to try to save them from the death penalty. Arguing from several books and articles authored by Sigmund Freud, Darrow tried to convince the judge who would pass sentence that Leopold and Loeb's parents were at least partially responsible for the crime because they had deprived the young men of emotional warmth when they were children (Higdon, 1975). Darrow hired psychologists to testify that the two murderers were emotionally equivalent to young children and should not be put to death for their crime. At the end of the trial, the judge sided with Darrow and sentenced the two young men to life in prison.

Publicity surrounding the Leopold and Loeb trial was how Freud's theory first became widely known among the general public in the United States (Torrey, 1992). The claim that two murderers' parents might be morally responsible for their heinous crime caused many people to see Freud's theory as repugnant. But it was Darrow, not Freud, who turned the theory into a "blame your parents" legal defense. Indeed, Freud's assertion that early childhood experiences contribute to adult behavior is accepted by both psychologists and nonpsychologists and may be his most enduring contribution. But can early childhood experiences alone account for variations among adults?

Richard Loeb (left) and Nathan Leopold (right) in prison, 1924, for the murder of Robert Franks.

To what two aspects of Freud's work does the term *psychoanalysis* apply?

What are Freud's three levels of awareness in consciousness?

Psychologists use the term *personality* to capture what we mean when we talk about the ways in which one person is different from another. **Personality** is formally defined as an individual's characteristic patterns of behaving, thinking, and feeling (Carver & Scheier, 1996). This chapter explores some of the theories, including Freud's, that have been proposed to explain personality.

Sigmund Freud and Psychoanalysis

When you hear the term *psychoanalysis*, you may picture a psychiatrist treating a troubled patient on a couch. But **psychoanalysis** refers not only to a therapy for treating psychological disorders devised by Sigmund Freud, but also to the influential personality theory he proposed. The central idea of psychoanalytic theory is that unconscious forces shape human thought and behavior.

The Conscious, the Preconscious, and the Unconscious

Freud believed that there are three levels of awareness in consciousness: the conscious, the preconscious, and the unconscious. The **conscious** consists of whatever a person is aware of at any given moment—a thought, a feeling, a sensation, or a memory. Freud's **preconscious** is very much like long-term memory. It contains all the memories, feelings, experiences, and perceptions that an individual is not consciously thinking about at the moment, but that may be easily brought to consciousness.

The most important of the three levels is the **unconscious,** which Freud believed to be the primary motivating force of human behavior. The unconscious holds memories that once were conscious but were so unpleasant or anxiety-provoking that they were repressed (involuntarily removed from consciousness). The unconscious also contains all of the instincts (sexual and aggressive), wishes, and desires that have never been allowed into consciousness. Freud traced the roots of psychological disorders to these impulses and repressed memories.

The Id, the Ego, and the Superego

Freud proposed three systems of personality. Figure 11.1 shows these three systems and how they relate to the conscious, preconscious, and unconscious levels. These systems do not exist physically; they are only concepts, or ways of looking at personality.

➤ **Figure 11.1**

Freud's Conception of Personality

According to Freud, personality, which may be conceptualized as a giant iceberg, is composed of three structures: the id, the ego, and the superego. The id, completely unconscious, is wholly submerged, floating beneath the surface. The ego is largely conscious and visible, but partly unconscious. The superego also operates at both the conscious and unconscious levels.

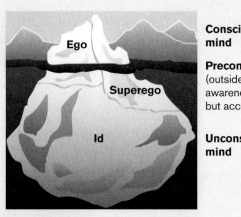

Conscious mind

Preconscious (outside awareness but accessible)

Unconscious mind

According to Freud, the **id** is the only part of the personality that is present at birth. It is inherited, primitive, inaccessible, and completely unconscious. The id contains (1) the life instincts, which are the sexual instincts and the biological urges such as hunger and thirst; and (2) the death instinct, which accounts for aggressive and destructive impulses (Freud, 1933/1965). The id operates according to the *pleasure principle;* that is, it tries to seek pleasure, avoid pain, and gain immediate gratification of its wishes. The id is the source of the *libido,* the psychic energy that fuels the entire personality; yet the id can only wish, imagine, fantasize, or demand.

The **ego** is the logical, rational, realistic part of the personality. The ego evolves from and draws its energy from the id. One of the ego's functions is to satisfy the id's urges. But the ego, which is mostly conscious, acts according to the *reality principle.* It must consider the constraints of the real world in determining appropriate times, places, and objects for gratification of the id's wishes. The art of the possible is its guide, and sometimes compromises must be made—for example, when you settle for a McDonald's hamburger instead of steak or lobster.

When a child is 5 or 6 years old, the **superego**—the moral component of the personality—is formed. The superego has two parts: (1) behaviors for which the child has been punished and about which he or she feels guilty constitute the *conscience;* (2) behaviors for which the child has been praised and rewarded and about which he or she feels pride and satisfaction make up the *ego ideal.* At first, the superego reflects only the parents' expectations of what is good and right, but it expands over time to incorporate broader social and cultural values. In its quest for moral perfection, the superego sets guidelines that define and limit the ego's flexibility. A harsher judge than any external authority, including one's parents, the superego governs not only behavior, but also thoughts, feelings, and wishes.

Defense Mechanisms

All would be well if the id, the ego, and the superego had compatible aims. But the id's demands for pleasure are often in direct conflict with the superego's desire for moral perfection. At times, the ego needs some way to defend itself against the anxiety created by the excessive demands of the id and the harsh judgments of the superego. When it cannot solve problems directly, the ego may use a **defense mechanism,** a means of fighting anxiety and maintaining self-esteem. All people use defense mechanisms to some degree, but research supports Freud's view that the overuse of defense mechanisms can adversely affect mental health (Watson, 2002). *Review and Reflect 11.1* (on page 316) summarizes the defense mechanisms.

According to Freud, *repression* is the most frequently used defense mechanism. Repression can remove painful or threatening memories, thoughts, ideas, or perceptions from consciousness and keep them in the unconscious. It may also prevent unconscious sexual and aggressive impulses from breaking into consciousness. Several studies have shown that people do indeed try to repress unpleasant thoughts (Koehler et al., 2002). Freud believed that repressed thoughts lurk in the unconscious and can cause psychological disorders in adults. He thought that the way to cure such disorders was to bring the repressed material back to consciousness. This was what he tried to accomplish through his system of therapy, psychoanalysis.

The Psychosexual Stages of Development

The sex instinct, Freud said, is the most important factor influencing personality. It is present at birth and then develops through a series of **psychosexual stages.** Each stage centers on a particular part of the body that provides pleasurable sensations and around which a conflict arises (1905/1953b, 1920/1963b). If the conflict is not resolved relatively easily, the child may develop a **fixation.** This means that a portion of the libido (psychic energy) remains invested at that stage, leaving less psychic energy to meet the challenges of

What are the roles of the id, the ego, and the superego?

ego
(EE-go) In Freudian theory, the rational, largely conscious system of personality, which operates according to the reality principle.

superego
(sue-per-EE-go) The moral system of the personality, which consists of the conscience and the ego ideal.

defense mechanism
An unconscious, irrational means used by the ego to defend against anxiety; involves self-deception and the distortion of reality.

psychosexual stages
A series of stages through which the sexual instinct develops; for each stage, a part of the body becomes the center of new pleasures and conflicts.

fixation
Arrested development at a psychosexual stage occurring because of excessive gratification or frustration at that stage.

What is a defense mechanism?

What are two ways in which repression operates?

What are the psychosexual stages, and why did Freud consider them so important in personality development?

Defense Mechanisms

DEFENSE MECHANISM	DESCRIPTION	EXAMPLE
Repression	Involuntarily removing an unpleasant memory from consciousness or barring disturbing sexual and aggressive impulses from consciousness	Jill forgets a traumatic incident from childhood.
Projection	Attributing one's own undesirable traits or impulses to another	A very lonely divorced woman accuses all men of having only one thing on their minds.
Denial	Refusing to acknowledge consciously the existence of danger or a threatening situation	Amy fails to take a tornado warning seriously and is severely injured.
Rationalization	Supplying a logical, rational reason rather than the real reason for an action or event	Fred tells his friend that he didn't get the job because he didn't have connections.
Regression	Reverting to a behavior characteristic of an earlier stage of development	Susan bursts into tears whenever she is criticized.
Reaction formation	Expressing exaggerated ideas and emotions that are the opposite of disturbing, unconscious impulses and desires	A former purchaser of pornography, Bob is now a tireless crusader against it.
Displacement	Substituting a less threatening object for the original object of an impulse	After being spanked by his father, Bill hits his baby brother.
Sublimation	Rechanneling sexual and aggressive energy into pursuits that society considers acceptable or even admirable	Tim goes to a gym to work out when he feels hostile and frustrated.

Oedipus complex
(ED-uh-pus) Occurring in the phallic stage, a conflict in which the child is sexually attracted to the opposite-sex parent and feels hostility toward the same-sex parent.

What is the Oedipus complex?

later stages. Overindulgence at a stage may leave a person psychologically unwilling to move on to the next stage. But too little gratification may leave the person trying to make up for previously unmet needs. Freud believed that certain personality characteristics develop as a result of difficulty at one or another of the stages. *Review and Reflect 11.2* provides a summary of Freud's psychosexual stages.

One of the most controversial features of Freud's theory is called the **Oedipus complex** (after the central character in the Greek tragedy *Oedipus Rex,* by Sophocles). Freud claimed that, during the phallic stage (age 3 to 6), "boys concentrate their sexual wishes upon their mother and develop hostile impulses against their father as being a rival" (1925/1963a, p. 61). The boy usually resolves the Oedipus complex by identifying with his father and repressing his sexual feelings for his mother. Through identification, the child takes on his father's behaviors, mannerisms, and superego standards, thus developing a superego (Freud, 1930/1962).

Freud's Psychosexual Stages of Development

STAGE	PART OF THE BODY	CONFLICTS/EXPERIENCES	ADULT TRAITS ASSOCIATED WITH PROBLEMS AT THIS STAGE
Oral (birth to 12–18 months)	Mouth	Weaning Oral gratification from sucking, eating, biting	Optimism, gullibility, dependency, pessimism, passivity, hostility, sarcasm, aggression
Anal (12–18 months to 3 years)	Anus	Toilet training Gratification from expelling and withholding feces	Excessive cleanliness, orderliness, stinginess, messiness, rebelliousness, destructiveness
Phallic (3 to 5-6 years)	Genitals	Oedipal conflict Sexual curiosity Masturbation	Flirtatiousness, vanity, promiscuity, pride, chastity
Latency (5–6 years to puberty)	None	Period of sexual calm Interest in school, hobbies, same-sex friends	
Genital (puberty onward)	Genitals	Revival of sexual interests Establishment of mature sexual relationships	

Sigmund Freud (1856–1939), with his daughter Anna

personal unconscious

In Jung's theory, the layer of the unconscious containing all of the thoughts and experiences that are accessible to the conscious, as well as repressed memories and impulses.

collective unconscious

In Jung's theory, the most inaccessible layer of the unconscious, which contains the universal experiences of humankind transmitted to each individual.

archetype

(AR-kea-type) Existing in the collective unconscious, an inherited tendency to respond in particular ways to universal human situations.

According to Jung, what are the three components of personality?

Carl Jung (1875–1961)

When girls in the phallic stage discover they have no penis, they develop "penis envy," Freud claimed, and they turn to their father because he has the desired organ (1933/1965). They feel sexual desires for him and develop jealousy and rivalry toward their mother. But eventually, girls, too, experience anxiety as a result of their hostile feelings. They repress their sexual feelings toward the father and identify with the mother, leading to the formation of their superego (Freud, 1930/1962).

According to Freud, failure to resolve these conflicts can have serious consequences for both boys and girls. Freud thought that tremendous guilt and anxiety could be carried over into adulthood and cause sexual problems, great difficulty relating to members of the opposite sex, and even homosexuality.

Evaluating Freud's Contribution

Psychology is indebted to Freud for introducing the idea that unconscious forces may motivate behavior and for emphasizing the influence of early childhood experiences on later development. Moreover, psychoanalysis is still viewed as a useful therapeutic technique (Bartlett, 2002). And Freud's concept of defense mechanisms provides a useful way of categorizing the cognitive strategies people use to manage stress (Fauerbach et al., 2002; Tori & Bilmes, 2002). Critics charge, however, that much of Freud's theory defies scientific testing. In too many cases, any behavior or even a lack of behavior can be interpreted as supporting Freud's theory. How, for instance, can psychologists ever test the idea that little boys are in love with their mothers and want to get rid of their fathers? How can researchers verify or falsify the idea that one component of personality is motivated entirely by the pursuit of pleasure? Chiefly because of the difficulty involved in finding scientific answers to such questions, there are very few strict Freudians left today.

The Neo-Feudians

Several personality theorists, referred to as *neo-Freudians,* started their careers as followers of Freud but began to disagree on certain basic principles of psychoanalytic theory. One of the most important of the neo-Freudians, Carl Jung (1875–1961), did not consider the sexual instinct to be the main factor in personality; nor did he believe that the personality is almost completely formed in early childhood. For Jung (1933), middle age was an even more important period for personality development. Jung conceived of the personality as consisting of three parts: the ego, the personal unconscious, and the collective unconscious, as shown in Figure 11.2. He saw the ego as the conscious component of personality, which carries out normal daily activities. Like Freud, he believed the ego to be less important than the unconscious.

The **personal unconscious** develops as a result of individual experience and is therefore unique to each person. It contains all the experiences, thoughts, and perceptions accessible to the conscious, as well as repressed memories, wishes, and impulses. The **collective unconscious** contains the universal experiences of humankind throughout evolution. Jung believed that this part of the personality accounts for the similarity of certain myths, dreams, symbols, and religious beliefs in cultures widely separated by distance and time. Moreover, the collective unconscious contains what Jung called **archetypes**–inherited tendencies to respond to universal human situations in particular ways. Jung would say that the tendencies of people to believe in a god, a devil, evil spirits, and heroes all result from inherited archetypes that reflect the shared experience of humankind.

Another neo-Freudian, Alfred Adler (1870–1937), emphasized the unity of the personality rather than separate warring components of id, ego, and superego. Adler (1927, 1956) also maintained that the drive to overcome feelings of inferiority acquired in childhood motivates most adult behavior. He (1956) claimed that people develop

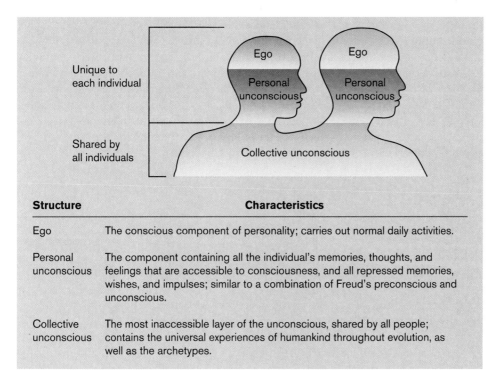

Jung's Conception of Personality

Like Freud, Carl Jung saw three components in personality. The ego and the personal unconscious are unique to each individual. The collective unconscious accounts for the similarity of myths and beliefs in diverse cultures.

Structure	Characteristics
Ego	The conscious component of personality; carries out normal daily activities.
Personal unconscious	The component containing all the individual's memories, thoughts, and feelings that are accessible to consciousness, and all repressed memories, wishes, and impulses; similar to a combination of Freud's preconscious and unconscious.
Collective unconscious	The most inaccessible layer of the unconscious, shared by all people; contains the universal experiences of humankind throughout evolution, as well as the archetypes.

a "style of life" at an early age—a unique way in which the child and later the adult will go about the struggle to achieve superiority. Sometimes inferiority feelings are so strong that they prevent personal development, and Adler originated a term to describe this condition—the "inferiority complex" (Dreikurs, 1953). Because Adler's theory stressed the uniqueness of each individual's struggle to achieve superiority and referred to the "creative self," a conscious, self-aware component of the individual's personality, it is known as *individual psychology*.

◄ What did Adler consider to be the driving force of the personality?

The work of neo-Freudian Karen Horney (1885–1952) centered on two main themes: the neurotic personality (Horney, 1937, 1945, 1950) and feminine psychology (Horney, 1967). Horney did not accept Freud's division of personality into id, ego, and superego, and she flatly rejected his psychosexual stages and the concepts of the Oedipus complex and penis envy. Furthermore, Horney thought that Freud overemphasized the role of the sexual instinct and neglected cultural and environmental influences on personality. Although she did stress the

◄ Why is Horney considered a pioneer in psychology?

◄ More than half a century ago, psychologist Karen Horney insisted that, rather than envying the penis, as Freud believed, women really want the same opportunities and privileges as men—for example, to pursue whatever careers they choose.

reciprocal determinism
Bandura's concept that behavior, cognitive factors, and environment all influence and are influenced by one another.

self-efficacy
A person's belief in his or her ability to perform competently in whatever is attempted.

importance of early childhood experiences, Horney (1939) believed that personality could continue to develop and change throughout life.

Horney argued forcefully against Freud's notion that a woman's desire to have a child and a man is nothing more than a conversion of the unfulfilled wish for a penis. Horney (1945) believed that many of women's psychological difficulties arise from failure to live up to an idealized version of themselves. To be psychologically healthy, she claimed, women—and men, for that matter—must learn to overcome irrational beliefs about the need for perfection. Her influence may be seen in modern cognitive-behavioral therapies, which we will explore in Chapter 13.

Learning Theories and Personality

Using principles such as those associated with B. F. Skinner's operant conditioning, learning theories explain personality as a function of environmental influences rather than unconscious thoughts and feelings. For this reason, many psychologists regard these theories as more scientific and easily tested than Freud's psychoanalysis. However, learning theories are often criticized for paying too little attention to emotions and other internal processes.

One learning theory that does take internal factors into account is the social-cognitive approach of Albert Bandura (1977a, 1986). He maintains that cognitive factors (such as a child's or adult's stage of cognitive development), behavior, and the external environment all influence and are influenced by one another (Bandura, 1989). Bandura calls this mutual relationship **reciprocal determinism** (see Figure 11.3).

One of the cognitive factors Bandura (1997a, 1997b) considers especially important is **self-efficacy**—the perception people hold of their ability to perform competently in whatever they attempt. According to Bandura, people high in self-efficacy approach new situations confidently, set high goals, and persist in their efforts because they believe success is likely. People low in self-efficacy, on the other hand, expect failure; consequently, they avoid challenges and typically give up on tasks they find difficult. Bandura's research has shown that people with high self-efficacy are less likely than those with low self-efficacy to experience depression (Bandura, 1997a, 1997b).

Julian Rotter proposes a similar cognitive factor called **locus of control.** Some people see themselves as primarily in control of their behavior and its consequences. This perception Rotter (1966, 1971, 1990) defines as an *internal* locus of control. Others perceive that whatever happens to them is in the hands of fate, luck, or chance. They exhibit an *external* locus of control and may claim that it does not matter what they do, because "whatever will be, will be." Rot-

> **What are the components of Bandura's concept of reciprocal determinism, and how do they interact?**

> **What does Rotter mean by an internal or external locus of control?**

➤ Figure 11.3

Albert Bandura's Reciprocal Determinism

Albert Bandura takes a social-cognitive view of personality. He suggests that three components— the environment, behavior, and personal/cognitive factors such as beliefs, expectancies, and personal dispositions—play reciprocal roles in determining personality and behavior.

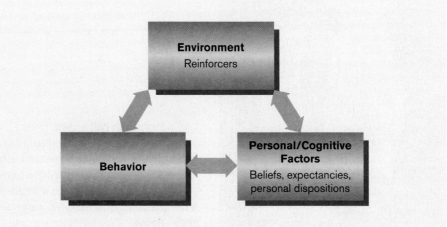

320

Try It! 11.1 Where Is Your Locus of Control?

For each statement, indicate which choice best expresses your view.

1. Heredity determines most of a person's personality.
   a. strongly disagree   c. neutral   e. strongly agree
   b. disagree   d. agree

2. Chance has a lot to do with being successful.
   a. strongly disagree   c. neutral   e. strongly agree
   b. disagree   d. agree

3. Whatever plans you make, something will always interfere.
   a. strongly disagree   c. neutral   e. strongly agree
   b. disagree   d. agree

4. Being at the right place at the right time is essential for getting what you want in life.
   a. almost never   c. sometimes   e. most of the time
   b. rarely   d. quite often

5. Intelligence is a given, and it cannot be improved.
   a. strongly disagree   c. neutral   e. strongly agree
   b. disagree   d. agree

6. If I successfully accomplish a task, it's because it was an easy one.
   a. strongly disagree   c. neutral   e. strongly agree
   b. disagree   d. agree

7. You cannot change your destiny.
   a. strongly disagree   c. neutral   e. strongly agree
   b. disagree   d. agree

8. School success is mostly a result of one's socioeconomic background.
   a. strongly disagree   c. neutral   e. strongly agree
   b. disagree   d. agree

9. People are lonely because they are not given the chance to meet new people.
   a. strongly disagree   c. neutral   e. strongly agree
   b. disagree   d. agree

10. If you set realistic goals, you can succeed at almost anything.
   a. strongly disagree   c. neutral   e. strongly agree
   b. disagree   d. agree

Score your responses as follows: a = 10 points, b = 7.5, c = 5, d = 2.5, e = 0. A perfect score is 100 points, and the higher your total score, the more internal your locus of control is. The more internal your locus of control, the more likely you are to succeed in life!

---

ter contends that people with an external locus of control are less likely to change their behavior as a result of reinforcement, because they do not see reinforcers as being tied to their own actions. Students who have an external locus of control tend to be procrastinators and, thus, are less likely to be academically successful than those with an internal locus of control (Janssen & Carton, 1999). Where is your locus of control? To find out, complete *Try It! 11.1*.

Humanistic Personality Theories

In *humanistic psychology*, people are assumed to have a natural tendency toward growth and the realization of their fullest potential. As a result, humanistic personality theories are more optimistic than Freud's psychoanalysis and give greater weight to emotional experiences than the learning theories do. However, like Freud's theory, these perspectives are often criticized as being difficult to test scientifically.

For humanistic psychologist Abraham Maslow (1908–1970), motivational factors were at the root of personality. You may remember from Chapter 9 that Maslow constructed a hierarchy of needs, ranging from physiological needs at the bottom up through safety needs, belonging and love needs, esteem needs, and finally to the highest need–the need for self-actualization (Figure 9.3 on page 260). **Self-actualization** means developing to one's fullest potential. A healthy person is ever growing and becoming all that he or she can be. In his research, Maslow found self-actualizers to be accurate in perceiving reality–able to judge honestly and to spot quickly the fake and the dishonest. Most of them believe they have a mission to accomplish or feel the need to devote their life to some larger good. Self-

locus of control
A concept used to explain how people account for what happens in their lives—people with an internal locus of control see themselves as primarily in control of their behavior and its consequences; those with an external locus of control perceive what happens to be in the hands of fate, luck, or chance.

self-actualization
Developing to one's fullest potential.

What is self-actualization?

> Abrabam Maslow (1908–1970)

actualizers tend not to depend on external authority or other people but seem to be inner-driven, autonomous, and independent. Finally, the hallmark of self-actualizers is frequently occurring *peak experiences*–experiences of deep meaning, insight, and harmony within and with the universe. Current researchers have modified Maslow's definition of self-actualization to include effectiveness in personal relationships, as well as peak experiences (Hanley & Abell, 2002).

According to another humanistic psychologist, Carl Rogers (1902–1987), our parents set up **conditions of worth**–conditions on which their positive regard hinges. Conditions of worth force us to live and act according to someone else's values rather than our own. In our efforts to gain positive regard, we deny our true self by inhibiting some of our behavior, denying and distorting some of our perceptions, and closing ourselves to parts of our experience. In so doing, we experience stress and anxiety, and our whole sense of self may be threatened.

> According to Rogers, why don't all people become fully functioning persons?

For Rogers, a major goal of psychotherapy is to enable people to open themselves up to experiences and begin to live according to their own values rather than according to the values of others in order to gain positive regard. He called his therapy *person-centered therapy,* preferring not to use the term *patient* (Rogers's therapy will be discussed in Chapter 13). Rogers believed that the therapist must give the client **unconditional positive regard**–that is, show positive regard no matter what the client says, does, has done, or is thinking of doing. Unconditional positive regard is designed to reduce threat, eliminate conditions of worth, and bring the person back in tune with his or her true self. If successful, the therapy helps the client become what Rogers called a *fully functioning person*–one who is functioning at an optimal level and living fully and spontaneously according to his or her inner value system.

conditions of worth
Conditions on which the positive regard of others rests.

unconditional positive regard
Unqualified caring and nonjudgmental acceptance of another.

Trait Theories

Traits are the qualities or characteristics that make it possible for us to face a wide variety of situational demands and deal with unforeseen circumstances (De Raad & Kokkonen, 2000). *Trait theories* attempt to explain personality and differences between people in terms of personal characteristics that are stable across situations.

> What are trait theories of personality?

Early Trait Theories

traits
Personal characteristics used to describe or explain personality.

Gordon Allport (1897–1967) claimed that each person inherits a unique set of raw materials for given traits, which are then shaped by experiences (Allport & Odbert, 1936). A *cardinal trait* is "so pervasive and so outstanding in a life that . . . almost every

This hypothetical personality profile is based on Cattell's Sixteen Personality Factor Questionnaire. Along each of the 16 dimensions of bipolar traits, circle the point you think would apply to you if you took the 16 PF. (From Cattell, 1993.)

Reserved	Warm
Concrete	Abstract
Reactive	Emotionally stable
Avoids conflict	Dominant
Serious	Lively
Expedient	Rule-conscious
Shy	Socially bold
Utilitarian	Sensitive
Trusting	Suspicious
Practical	Imaginative
Forthright	Private
Self-assured	Apprehensive
Traditional	Open to change
Group-oriented	Self-reliant
Tolerates disorder	Perfectionistic
Relaxed	Tense

act seems traceable to its influence" (Allport, 1961, p. 365). It is so strong a part of a person's personality that he or she may become identified with or known for that trait. *Central traits* are those, said Allport (1961), that one would "mention in writing a careful letter of recommendation" (p. 365), such as being decisive or industrious.

> How did Allport differentiate between cardinal and central traits?

Raymond Cattell (1950) referred to observable qualities of personality as *surface traits*. Using observations and questionnaires, Cattell studied thousands of people and found certain clusters of surface traits that appeared together time after time. He thought these were evidence of deeper, more general, underlying personality factors, which he called *source traits*. People differ in the degree to which they possess each source trait. For example, Cattell claimed that intelligence is a source trait: Everyone has it, but the amount varies from person to person.

> How did Cattell differentiate between surface and source traits?

Cattell found 23 source traits in normal individuals, 16 of which he studied in great detail. Cattell's Sixteen Personality Factor Questionnaire, commonly called the *16 PF*, yields a personality profile (Cattell et al., 1950, 1977). This test continues to be widely used in research (e.g., Brody et al., 2000) and for personality assessment in career counseling, schools, and employment settings. You can chart your own source traits in *Try It! 11.2.*

Factor Models of Personality

The early trait theories represented the beginning of a movement that continues to be important in personality research. Cattell's notion of personality "factors" has been especially influential. One factor model that has shaped much personality research is that of British psychologist Hans Eysenck (1990). Eysenck places particular emphasis on two dimensions: Extraversion (extraversion versus introversion) and Neuroticism (emotional stability versus instability). Extraverts are sociable, outgoing, and active, whereas introverts are withdrawn, quiet, and introspective. Emotionally stable people are calm, even-tempered, and often easygoing; emotionally unstable people are anxious, excitable, and easily distressed.

> What does Eysenck consider to be the two most important dimensions of personality?

Extraversion and Neuroticism are also important in today's most talked-about personality theory—the **five-factor theory,** also known as the *Big Five* (Wiggins, 1996).

five-factor theory
A trait theory that attempts to explain personality using the Big Five, broad dimensions that are composed of a constellation of personality traits.

According to the five-factor theory of personality, extraverts are sociable, outgoing, and active—both Britney Spears and Jay Leno could be considered extraverts, even though their personalities differ. What are some characteristics of introverts?

What are the Big Five personality dimensions in the five-factor theory as described by McCrae and Costa?

According to Robert McCrae and Paul Costa (1987; McCrae, 1996), the most influential proponents of the five-factor theory, the Big Five dimensions are as follows:

1. *Extraversion.* This dimension contrasts such traits as sociable, outgoing, talkative, assertive, persuasive, decisive, and active with more introverted traits such as withdrawn, quiet, passive, retiring, and reserved.

2. *Neuroticism.* People high on Neuroticism are prone to emotional instability. They tend to experience negative emotions and to be moody, irritable, nervous, and inclined to worry. Neuroticism differentiates people who are anxious, excitable, and easily distressed from those who are emotionally stable and thus calm, even-tempered, easygoing, and relaxed.

3. *Conscientiousness.* This factor differentiates individuals who are dependable, organized, reliable, responsible, thorough, hard-working, and persevering from those who are undependable, disorganized, impulsive, unreliable, irresponsible, careless, negligent, and lazy.

4. *Agreeableness.* This factor is composed of a collection of traits that range from compassion to antagonism toward others. A person high on Agreeableness would be pleasant, good-natured, warm, sympathetic, and cooperative; one low on Agreeableness would tend to be unfriendly, unpleasant, aggressive, argumentative, cold, and even hostile and vindictive.

5. *Openness to Experience.* This factor contrasts individuals who seek out varied experiences and who are imaginative, intellectually curious, and broad-minded with those who are concrete-minded and practical and whose interests are narrow. Researchers have found that being high on Openness to Experience is a requirement for creative accomplishment (King et al., 1996).

To measure the Big Five dimensions of personality, Costa and McCrae (1985, 1992, 1997) developed the NEO Personality Inventory (NEO-PI) and, more recently, the Revised NEO Personality Inventory (NEO-PI-R). Their test is currently being used in a wide variety of personality research studies. For example, psychologists in the Australian army have used the test to measure personality differences between effective and ineffective leaders (McCormack & Mellor, 2002). And all five factors have been found in cross-cultural studies involving participants from Canada, Finland, Poland, Germany, Russia, Hong Kong, Croatia, Italy, South Korea, and Portugal (McCrae et al., 2000; Paunonen et al., 1996).

But how important are the Big Five in everyday behavior? A 3-year longitudinal study among university students revealed that Neuroticism, Extraversion, and Conscientiousness were correlated with reported high levels of frustration due to daily hassles. There was only a small correlation of hassled feelings with Openness to Experience and none at all with Agreeableness (Vollrath, 2000). The Big Five have also proved useful in predicting job performance in the United States (Costa, 1996) and Europe (Salgado, 1997).

The Situation-versus-Trait Debate

One of the severest critics of trait theories, Walter Mischel (1968), initiated the situation-versus-trait debate over the relative importance of factors within the situation and factors within the person that account for behavior (Rowe, 1987). For instance, you probably wouldn't steal money from a store, but what if you see a stranger unknowingly drop a five-dollar bill? Mischel and those who agree with him say that characteristics of the two situations dictate your behavior, not a trait such as honesty. Stealing from a store might require devising and carrying out a complicated plan, and it would carry a heavy penalty if you were caught, so you opt for honesty. Picking up a five-dollar bill is easy and may only result in embarrassment if you get caught, so you are likely to do it. Mischel (1973, 1977) later modified his original position and admitted that behavior is influenced by both the person and the situation. Mischel views a *trait* as a conditional probability that a particular action will occur in response to a particular situation (Wright & Mischel, 1987).

Advocates of the trait side of the debate point out that support for trait theories has come from many longitudinal studies (McCrae, 2002). McCrae and Costa (1990) studied people's personality traits over time and found them to be stable for periods of 3 to 30 years. Typically, personality changes very little with age. As McCrae (1993) puts it, "stable individual differences in basic dimensions are a universal feature of adult personality" (p. 577). An extensive recent review found that the consistency of personality traits increased from .31 in childhood to .54 for college students, rose to .64 by age 30, and peaked at .74 between the ages of 50 and 70 (Roberts & DelVecchio, 2000).

Research on personality suggests that some traits, such as agreeableness, tend to change very little with age.

The weight of evidence supports the view that internal traits strongly influence behavior across situations (Carson, 1989; McAdams, 1992). However, many situations in life call forth similar behavior from most people, even though their internal traits differ drastically. Even the most talkative and boisterous among us tend to be quiet during a religious service, a funeral, or another solemn occasion. Characteristic traits, say the trait theorists, determine how we behave most of the time, not all of the time. Even the most optimistic, happy, and outgoing people have "down" days, fall ill, and frown occasionally.

Nature, Nurture, and Personality

Recall from the discussion of behavioral genetics in Chapter 7 that twin studies are often used to assess the degree to which psychological traits may be inherited. You may also remember that one of the best known of these studies, the Minnesota twin study, revealed that the IQ scores of identical twins are strongly correlated regardless of whether they are raised in the same or in different environments. Using data from the same participants, Tellegen and others (1988) found that identical twins are also quite similar on several personality factors, again regardless of whether they are raised together or apart.

> What has research in behavioral genetics revealed about the influence of genes and the environment on personality?

In another twin study, Rushton and colleagues (1986) found that nurturance, empathy, and assertiveness are substantially influenced by heredity. Even altruism and aggressiveness, traits one would expect to be strongly influenced by parental upbringing, were more heavily influenced by heredity. A review by Miles and Carey (1997) revealed that the heritability of aggressiveness may be as high as .50 (50%). Moreover, a number of longitudinal studies indicate that heredity makes a substantial contribution to individual differences in the Big Five personality factors, as shown in Figure 11.4 (on page 326) (Bouchard, 1994; Caspi, 2000; Loehlin, 1992; Pesonen et al., 2003).

Adoption studies have also shown that heredity strongly influences personality. Loehlin and others (1987) assessed the personalities of 17-year-olds who had been adopted at birth. When the adopted children were compared with other children in their adoptive families, the researchers found that the shared family environment had virtually no influence on their personalities. In another study, Loehlin and colleagues (1990) measured change in personality of adoptees over a 10-year period and found that children tended "to change on the average in the direction of their genetic parents' personalities" (p. 221). The prevailing thinking in behavioral genetics, then, is that the shared environment plays a negligible role in the for-

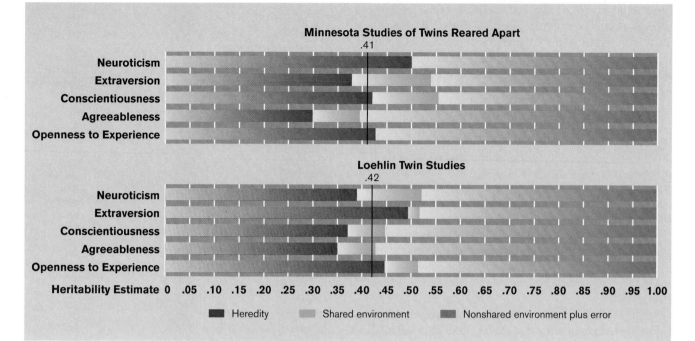

> **Figure 11.4**

Estimated Influence of Heredity and Environment on the Big Five Personality Dimensions

The Minnesota studies of twins reared apart yield an average heritability estimate of .41 (41%) for the Big Five personality dimensions; the Loehlin twin studies, a heritability estimate of .42 (42%). Both studies found the influence of the shared environment to be only about .07 (7%). The remaining percentage represents a combination of nonshared environmental influences and measurement error. (Adapted from Bouchard, 1994.)

individualism/collectivism dimension

The term used to signify a culture's emphasis either on individuals or on group relationships.

mation of personality (Loehlin et al., 1988), although there have been a few dissenting voices (Rose et al., 1988).

Despite the evidence supporting the role of heredity, most psychologists agree that heredity and environment interact in personality development. For example, a child who has a genetic tendency towards shyness may be gently encouraged by parents to be more sociable. But in another family, parents may reject and ridicule a shy child. In either case, how parents respond to a child's inborn tendencies will influence how those characteristics are manifested later in life.

Personality and Culture

How does personality differ across cultures?

Important among environmental influences on personality are the diverse cultures in which humans live and work. Hofstede (1980, 1983) analyzed responses to a questionnaire measuring the work-related values of more than 100,000 IBM employees in 53 countries around the world. Factor analysis revealed four separate dimensions related to culture and personality, but one factor, the **individualism/collectivism dimension,** is of particular interest.

"Individualist cultures emphasize independence, self-reliance, [and] creativity" (Triandis et al., 1993, p. 368). Individualists "see themselves as more differentiated and separate from others, and place more importance on asserting their individuality" (Bochner, 1994, p. 274). More emphasis is placed on individual achievement than on group achievement. High-achieving individuals are accorded honor and prestige in individualist cultures. People in collectivist cultures, on the other hand, tend to be more interdependent and to define themselves and their personal interests in terms of their group membership. Asians, for example, have highly collectivist cultures, and collectivism is compatible with Confucianism, the predominant religion of these Eastern cultures. In fact, according to the Confucian values, the individual finds his or her identity in interrelatedness—as a part of, not apart from, the larger group. Moreover, this interrelatedness is an important ingredient of happiness for Asians (Kitayama & Markus, 2000).

Hofstede rank-ordered the 53 countries on each of the four dimensions. It should not be surprising that the United States ranked as the most individualist culture in the sample, followed by Australia, Great Britain, Canada, and the Netherlands. At the other end of the continuum were the most collectivist, or least individualist, cultures—Guatemala, Ecuador, Panama, Venezuela, and Colombia, all Latin American countries.

Although, according to Hofstede, the United States ranks first in individualism, there are many distinct minority cultural groups in the United States that may be decidedly less individualistic. Native Americans number close to 2 million, but even within this relatively small cultural group, there are over 200 different tribes and no single language, religion, or culture (Bennett, 1994). Yet Native Americans have many shared values—collectivist values—such as the importance of family, community, cooperation, and generosity. Native Americans value a generous nature as evidenced by gift giving and helpfulness. Such behaviors bring more honor and prestige than accumulating property and building individual wealth.

For these native Alaskans, participating in the traditional blanket toss ceremony is one manifestation of their culture's values related to community and cooperation.

Hispanic Americans, who number almost 28.3 million (U.S. Bureau of the Census, 1997), also tend to be more collectivist than individualist. Although there are significant cultural differences among various Hispanic American groups, there are striking similarities as well. The clearest shared cultural value is a strong identification with and attachment to the extended family. Another important value is *simpatía*—the desire for smooth and harmonious social relationships, which includes respect for the dignity of others, avoidance of confrontation, and avoidance of words or actions that might hurt the feelings of another (Marín, 1994).

But to observe that Native American and Hispanic American cultures are more collectivist than individualist does not mean that any one member of these cultures is necessarily less individualistic than any given member of the majority American culture. Moreover, many people could value both orientations, being individualistic at work, for example, and collectivistic in the home and community (Kagitcibasi, 1992).

Job interviews today are likely to include personality tests. Many companies ask each job candidate to complete an interest inventory, to determine the type of position a candidate is best suited for, or a vocational preference inventory, to assess how well the person's traits and interests relate to specific jobs.

Personality Assessment

Various ways of measuring personality are used by clinical and counseling psychologists, psychiatrists, and counselors in the diagnosis of patients and in the assessment of progress in therapy. Personality assessment is also used by personnel managers to aid in hiring decisions and by counselors to give vocational and educational assessments.

Observation, Interviews, and Rating Scales

Psychologists use observation in personality assessment in a variety of settings—hospitals, clinics, schools, and workplaces. Behaviorists, in particular, prefer observation to other methods of personality assessment. Using an observational technique known as *behavioral assessment,* psychologists can count and record the frequency of particular behaviors. This method is

often used in behavior modification programs in settings such as mental hospitals, where psychologists may chart the patients' progress in reducing aggressive acts or other undesirable or abnormal behaviors. However, behavioral assessment is time-consuming, and behavior may be misinterpreted. Probably the most serious limitation is that the very presence of the observer can alter the behavior being observed.

Clinical psychologists and psychiatrists use interviews to help in the diagnosis and treatment of patients. Counselors use interviews to screen applicants for admission to colleges or other special programs, and employers use them to evaluate job applicants and employees for job promotions. Interviewers consider not only a person's answers to questions, but also the person's tone of voice, speech, mannerisms, gestures, and general appearance. Interviewers often use a *structured interview,* in which the content of the questions and the order and manner in which they are asked are preset. The interviewer tries not to deviate in any way from the structured format so that more reliable comparisons can be made between different people being interviewed.

Sometimes examiners use *rating scales* to record data from interviews or observations. Rating scales are useful because they provide a standardized format, including a list of traits or behaviors to evaluate. A rating scale helps to focus the rater's attention on the relevant traits to be considered so that none is overlooked or weighed too heavily. The major limitation of rating scales is that the ratings are often subjective. Another problem in evaluation is the *halo effect*–the tendency of raters to be excessively influenced in their overall evaluation of a person by one or a few favorable or unfavorable traits. Often traits or attributes that are not even on the rating scale, such as physical attractiveness or similarity to the rater, heavily influence a rater's perception of an individual. To overcome these limitations, it is often necessary to have individuals rated by more than one interviewer.

Personality Inventories

One objective method for measuring personality, in which the personal opinions and ratings of observers or interviewers do not unduly influence the results, is the **personality inventory,** a paper-and-pencil test with questions about an individual's thoughts, feelings, and behaviors, which measures several dimensions of personality and is scored according to a standard procedure. Psychologists favoring the trait approach prefer to use a personality inventory because it reveals where people fall on various dimensions of personality and yields a personality profile.

What is a personality inventory, and what are the MMPI-2 and the CPI designed to reveal?

The most widely used personality inventory is the *Minnesota Multiphasic Personality Inventory (MMPI)* and its revision, the MMPI-2. The MMPI is the most heavily researched personality test for diagnosing psychiatric problems and disorders and for use in psychological research (Butcher & Rouse, 1996). There have been more than 115 authorized translations of the MMPI, and it is used in more than 65 countries (Butcher & Graham, 1989).

Published in 1943 by J. C. McKinley and Starke Hathaway, the MMPI was originally intended to identify tendencies toward various types of psychiatric disorders. The researchers administered over 1,000 questions about attitudes, feelings, and specific psychiatric symptoms to selected groups of psychiatric patients who had been clearly diagnosed with various specific disorders and to a control group of normal men and women. They retained the 550 items that differentiated the specific groups of psychiatric patients from the group of participants considered to be normal.

Because the original MMPI had become outdated, the MMPI-2 was published in 1989 (Butcher et al., 1989). Most of the original test items were retained, but new items were added to more adequately cover areas such as alcoholism, drug abuse, suicidal tendencies, eating disorders, and Type A behavior. New norms were established to reflect national census data and thus achieve a better geographical, racial, and cultural balance (Ben-Porath & Butcher, 1989).

Table 11.1 shows the 10 clinical scales of the MMPI-2. Following are examples of items on the test, which are to be answered "true," "false," or "cannot say."

personality inventory
A paper-and-pencil test with questions about a person's thoughts, feelings, and behaviors, which is scored according to a standard procedure.

Table 11.1 The Clinical Scales of the MMPI-2

Scale Name	Interpretation
1. Hypochondriasis (Hs)	High scorers exhibit an exaggerated concern about their physical health.
2. Depression (D)	High scorers are usually depressed, despondent, and distressed.
3. Hysteria (Hy)	High scorers complain often about physical symptoms that have no apparent organic cause.
4. Psychopathic deviate (Pd)	High scorers show a disregard for social and moral standards.
5. Masculinity/femininity (Mf)	High scorers show "traditional" masculine or feminine attitudes and values.
6. Paranoia (Pa)	High scorers demonstrate extreme suspiciousness and feelings of persecution.
7. Psychasthenia (Pt)	High scorers tend to be highly anxious, rigid, tense, and worrying.
8. Schizophrenia (Sc)	High scorers tend to be socially withdrawn and to engage in bizarre and unusual thinking.
9. Hypomania (Ma)	High scorers are usually emotional, excitable, energetic, and impulsive.
10. Social introversion (S)	High scorers tend to be modest, self-effacing, and shy.

- I wish I were not bothered by thoughts about sex.
- When I get bored I like to stir up some excitement.
- In walking I am very careful to step over sidewalk cracks.
- If people had not had it in for me, I would have been much more successful.

A high score on any of the scales does not necessarily mean that a person has a problem or symptoms of a psychiatric disorder. Rather, the psychologist looks at the individual's MMPI profile—the pattern of scores on all the scales—and then compares it to the profiles of normal individuals and those with various psychiatric disorders.

But what if someone lies on the test in order to appear mentally healthy? Embedded in the test to provide a check against lying are items such as these:

- Once in a while I put off until tomorrow what I ought to do today.
- I gossip a little at times.
- Once in a while, I laugh at a dirty joke.

Most people would almost certainly have to answer "true" in response to such items—unless, of course, they were lying. Another scale controls for people who are faking psychiatric problems, such as someone who is hoping to be judged not guilty of a crime by reason of insanity. Research seems to indicate that the validity scales in the MMPI-2 are effective in detecting test takers who were instructed to fake psychological disturbance or to lie to make themselves appear more psychologically healthy (Bagby et al., 1994; Butcher et al., 1995). Even when given specific information about various psychological disorders, test takers could not produce profiles similar to those of people who actually suffered from the disorders (Wetter et al., 1993).

The MMPI-2 is reliable, easy to administer and score, and inexpensive to use. It is useful in the screening, diagnosis, and clinical description of abnormal behavior, but does not reveal differences among normal personalities very well. The MMPI had been somewhat unreliable for African Americans, women, and adolescents (Levitt &

Duckworth, 1984). But this problem has been addressed by establishing norms for the MMPI-2 that are more representative of the national population. A special form of the test, the MMPI-A, was developed for adolescents in 1992. The MMPI-A has some items that are especially relevant to adolescents, referring to eating disorders, substance abuse, and problems with school and family.

The MMPI-2 has been translated for use in Belgium, Chile, China, France, Hong Kong, Israel, Italy, Japan, Korea, Norway, Russia, Spain, and Thailand (Butcher, 1992). Lucio and others (1994) administered the Mexican (Spanish) version of MMPI-2 to more than 2,100 Mexican college students. They found the profiles of these students "remarkably similar" to those of U.S. college students.

An important limitation of the MMPI-2, though, is that it is designed to assess abnormality. By contrast, the *California Psychological Inventory (CPI)* is a highly regarded personality test developed especially for normal individuals aged 13 and older. The CPI has many of the same questions as the MMPI, but it does not include any questions designed to reveal psychiatric illness (Gough, 1987). The CPI is valuable for predicting behavior, and it has been "praised for its technical competency, careful development, cross-validation and follow-up, use of sizable samples and separate sex norms" (Domino, 1984, p. 156). The CPI was revised in 1987, to make it provide "a picture of the subject's life-style and the degree to which his or her potential is being realized" (McReynolds, 1989, p. 101). The CPI is particularly useful in predicting school achievement in high school and beyond; leadership and executive success; and effectiveness of police, military personnel, and student teachers (Gregory, 1996).

The *Myers-Briggs Type Indicator (MBTI)* is another personality inventory that is useful for measuring normal individual differences. This test is based on Jung's theory. The MBTI is a forced-choice, self-report inventory that is scored on four bipolar dimensions:

Extraversion (E) ———————— Introversion (I)
Sensing (S) ———————— Intuition (N)
Thinking (T) ———————— Feeling (F)
Judging (J) ———————— Perceptive (P)

A person can score anywhere along each continuum, and the four individual scores are usually summarized according to a typology. Sixteen types of personality profile can be derived from the possible combinations of the four bipolar dimensions. For example, a person whose scores were more toward Extraversion, Intuition, Feeling, and Perceptive would be labeled an ENFP personality type, which is described as follows:

> Relates more readily to the outer world of people and things than to the inner world of ideas (E); prefers to search for new possibilities over working with known facts and conventional ways of doing things (N); makes decisions and solves problems on the basis of personal values and feelings rather than relying on logical thinking and analysis (F); and prefers a flexible, spontaneous life to a planned and orderly existence (P). (Gregory, 1996)

The MBTI is growing in popularity, especially in business and industry and in schools. Critics point to the absence of rigorous, controlled validity studies of this test (Pittenger, 1993). And it has been criticized for being interpreted too often by unskilled examiners, who may make overly simplistic interpretations (Gregory, 1996). Sufficiently sophisticated methods for interpreting the MBTI do exist, however, as revealed by almost 500 research studies to date. And interest in this tool continues to be strong (Allen, 1997).

projective test
A personality test in which people respond to inkblots, drawings of ambiguous human situations, incomplete sentences, and the like by projecting their own inner thoughts, feelings, fears, or conflicts onto the test materials.

How do projective tests provide insight into personality, and what are some of the most commonly used projective tests?

Projective Tests

Responses on interviews and questionnaires are conscious responses and, for this reason, are less useful to therapists who wish to probe the unconscious. Such therapists may choose a completely different technique called a projective test. A **projective test** is a personality test consisting of inkblots, drawings of ambiguous human situations, or incomplete sentences for which there are no obvious correct or incorrect responses. People respond by projecting their own inner thoughts, feelings, fears, or conflicts into the test materials.

One of the oldest and most popular projective tests is the *Rorschach Inkblot Method,* developed by Swiss psychiatrist Hermann Rorschach (ROR-shok) in 1921. It consists of ten inkblots, which the test taker is asked to describe (see Figure 11.5 for an example). To develop his test, Rorschach put ink on paper and then folded the paper so that symmetrical patterns would result. Earlier, psychologists had used standardized series of inkblots to study imagination and other variables, but Rorschach was the first to use inkblots to investigate personality. He experimented with thousands of inkblots on different groups of people and found that ten of the inkblots could be used to discriminate among different diagnostic groups, such as manic depressives, paranoid schizophrenics, and so on. These ten inkblots—five black-and-white, and five with color—were standardized and are still widely used.

➤ **Figure 11.5**

An Inkblot Similar to One Used for the Rorschach Inkblot Method

The Rorschach can be used to describe personality, make differential diagnoses, plan and evaluate treatment, and predict behavior (Ganellen, 1996; Weiner, 1997). For the last 20 years, it has been second in popularity to the MMPI for use in research and clinical assessment (Butcher & Rouse, 1996). The test taker is shown the ten inkblots and asked to tell everything he or she thinks about what each inkblot looks like or resembles. The examiner writes down the test taker's responses and then goes through the cards again, asking questions to clarify what the test taker has reported. In scoring the Rorschach, the examiner considers whether the test taker uses the whole inkblot in the description or only parts of it. The test taker is asked whether the shape of the inkblot, its color, or something else prompted the response. The examiner also considers whether the test taker sees movement, human figures or parts, animal figures or parts, or other objects in the inkblots.

Until the 1990s, the main problem with the Rorschach was that the results were too dependent on the interpretation and judgment of the examiner. In response to such criticisms, Exner (1993) developed the Comprehensive System—a more reliable system for scoring the Rorschach. It provides some normative data so that the responses of a person taking the test can be compared to those of others with known personality characteristics. Using this system, some researchers have found high agreement among different raters interpreting the same responses (interrater agreement) (McDowell & Acklin, 1996). Others believe that more research is necessary before it can be concluded that the Comprehensive System yields reliable and valid results (Wood et al., 1996). However, a number of research reviews indicate that the Rorschach Inkblot Method has "psychometric soundness and practical utility" (Weiner, 1996).

Another projective test is the *Thematic Apperception Test (TAT)* developed by Henry Murray and his colleagues in 1935 (Morgan & Murray, 1935; Murray, 1938). You may remember from Chapter 9 that researchers have used the TAT to study the need for achievement, but it is also useful for assessing other aspects of personality. The TAT consists of 1 blank card and 19 other cards showing vague or ambiguous black-and-white drawings of human figures in various situations. If you were tested on the TAT, this is what you would be told:

> This is a test of your creative imagination. I shall show you a picture, and I want you to make up a plot or story for which it might be used as an illustration. What is the relation of the individuals in the picture? What has happened to them? What are their present thoughts and feelings? What will be the outcome? (Morgan & Murray, 1962, p. 532)

What does the story you write have to do with your personality or your problems or motives? Murray (1965) stresses the importance of "an element or theme that recurs three or more times in the series of stories" (p. 432). For example, if many of a person's story themes are about illness, sex, fear of failure, aggression, power, or interpersonal conflict, such a recurring theme is thought to reveal a problem in the person's life. Murray (1965) also claims that the strength of the TAT is "its capacity to reveal

Why, in a given situation, do some people—typically called *optimists*—expect good things to happen, while their opposites—*pessimists*—believe that bad outcomes are more likely? According to psychologist Martin Seligman, who has studied optimists and pessimists for many years, pessimists tend to believe that bad events are their own fault and are an inescapable part of their lives. Pessimism can thus stand in the way of achievement and a happy and productive life. Optimists, on the other hand, tend to believe that a bad event is just a temporary setback, that its causes are unique, and that it is due to circumstances, bad luck, or other people. In the face of illness, failure, or other difficulties, optimists will keep trying to overcome obstacles. As a result, they feel more in control of their lives.

The ABCs of pessimism Seligman believes that an individual can learn to be more optimistic and thereby improve his or her general health and sense of well-being. First, though, the person must learn to identify pessimistic thoughts. Seligman has developed a method for identifying a sequence of thoughts associated with pessimism that he calls the *ABC method,* for adversity, beliefs, and consequences. Here is how this method might work (Seligman, 1990, pp. 214–215):

- *Adversity* (anything that causes you to feel discouraged): I decided to join a gym, and when I walked into the place I saw nothing but firm, toned bodies all around me.

- *Belief* (how you explain the adversity): What am I doing here? I look like a beached whale compared to these people! I should get out of here while I still have my dignity.

- *Consequences* (the way you feel about the adverse event): I felt totally self-conscious and ended up leaving after 15 minutes.

The method can also identify a series of thoughts that will produce optimism:

- *Adversity* (anything that causes you to feel discouraged): I decided to join a gym, and when I walked into the place I saw nothing but firm, toned bodies all around me.

- *Belief* (how you explain the adversity): I look like a beached whale compared to these people! I can't wait until my new exercise regime gives me a body like theirs.

- *Consequences* (the way you feel about the adverse event): I felt totally self-conscious, but I focused on how my body was going to look in the future instead of how embarrassed I felt about looking out-of-shape in my workout clothes.

What you can do If your reactions to adversity consistently follow a pessimistic pattern, you can do several specific things to change your thought patterns. Seligman has identified three useful techniques: distraction, disputation, and distancing.

- *Distraction.* Start by attempting to distract yourself—slap your hand against the wall and shout "Stop!" Then try to think about something else.

- *Disputation.* Argue with yourself about the adverse event. Take a close look at the facts. "The most convincing way of disputing a negative belief is to show that it is factually incorrect" (Seligman, 1990, p. 221). An advantage of this technique is that it is realistic. Learned optimism is based on accuracy, not merely on making positive statements. For example, a student whose grades are somewhat below expectations might say, "I'm blowing things out of proportion. I hoped to get all As, but I got a B, a B+, and a B−. Those aren't awful grades. I may not have done the best in the class, but I didn't do the worst in the class either" (Seligman, 1990, p. 219).

- *Distancing.* Still another way of dealing with pessimistic beliefs is distancing. Try to dissociate yourself from your pessimistic thoughts, at least long enough to judge their accuracy objectively. Recognize that simply believing something doesn't make it so.

Once you have challenged your pessimistic beliefs and convinced yourself that bad events are temporary and will not affect everything you do for the rest of your life, you will be able to look forward to better times in the future. ■

things that the patient is unwilling to tell or is unable to tell because he [or she] is unconscious of them" (p. 427).

The TAT is time-consuming and difficult to administer and score. Although it has been used extensively in research, it suffers from the same weaknesses as other projective techniques: (1) It relies heavily on the interpretation skills of the examiner, and (2) it may reflect too strongly a person's temporary motivational and emotional state and not reveal the more permanent aspects of personality.

Summarize It!

Sigmund Freud and Psychoanalysis

➤ **To what two aspects of Freud's work does the term _psychoanalysis_ apply?**

Psychoanalysis is the term Freud used for both his theory of personality and his therapy for the treatment of psychological disorders.

➤ **What are Freud's three levels of awareness in consciousness?**

According to Freud, the three levels of awareness in consciousness are the conscious, the preconscious, and the unconscious.

➤ **What are the roles of the id, the ego, and the superego?**

The id is the primitive, unconscious part of the personality, which contains the instincts and operates on the pleasure principle. The ego is the rational, largely conscious system, which operates according to the reality principle. The superego is the moral system of the personality, consisting of the conscience and the ego ideal.

➤ **What is a defense mechanism?**

A defense mechanism is an unconscious, irrational means that the ego uses to defend against anxiety and to maintain self-esteem; it involves self-deception and the distortion of reality.

➤ **What are two ways in which repression operates?**

Through repression, (1) painful memories, thoughts, ideas, or perceptions are involuntarily removed from consciousness, and (2) disturbing sexual or aggressive impulses are prevented from breaking into consciousness.

➤ **What are the psychosexual stages, and why did Freud consider them important in personality development?**

Freud believed that the sexual instinct is present at birth and develops through a series of psychosexual stages, providing the driving force for all feelings and behaviors. The stages are the oral stage, the anal stage, the phallic stage (followed by the latency period), and the genital stage.

➤ **What is the Oedipus complex?**

The Oedipus complex, occurring in the phallic stage, is a conflict in which the child is sexually attracted to the opposite-sex parent and feels hostility toward the same-sex parent.

KEY TERMS

personality (p. 314)
psychoanalysis (p. 314)
conscious (p. 314)
preconscious (p. 314)
unconscious (p. 314)
id (p. 315)
ego (p. 315)
superego (p. 315)
defense mechanism (p. 315)
psychosexual stages (p. 315)
fixation (p. 315)
Oedipus complex (p. 316)

The Neo-Freudians

➤ **According to Jung, what are the three components of personality?**

Jung conceived of the personality as having three parts: the ego, the personal unconscious, and the collective unconscious.

➤ **What did Adler consider to be the driving force of the personality?**

Adler claimed that the predominant force of the personality is the drive to overcome and compensate for feelings of weakness and inferiority and to strive for superiority or significance.

➤ **Why is Horney considered a pioneer in psychology?**

Horney took issue with Freud's sexist view of women and added the feminine dimension to the world of psychology.

KEY TERMS

personal unconscious (p. 318)
collective unconscious (p. 318)
archetype (p. 318)

Learning Theories and Personality

➤ **What are the components of Bandura's concept of reciprocal determinism, and how do they interact?**

The external environment, behavior, and personal/cognitive factors are the three components of reciprocal determinism, each influencing and being influenced by the others.

➤ **What does Rotter mean by an internal or external locus of control?**

According to Rotter, people with an internal locus of control see themselves as primarily in control of their behavior and its consequences; those with an external locus of control believe their destiny is in the hands of fate, luck, or chance.

KEY TERMS

reciprocal determinism (p. 320)
self-efficacy (p. 320)
locus of control (p. 321)

Humanistic Personality Theories

➤ **What is self-actualization?**

Self-actualization means developing to one's fullest potential.

➤ **According to Rogers, why don't all people become fully functioning persons?**

Individuals often do not become fully functioning persons because in childhood they did not receive unconditional positive regard from their parents. To gain positive regard, they had to meet their parents' conditions of worth.

KEY TERMS

self-actualization (p. 321)
conditions of worth (p. 322)
unconditional positive regard (p. 322)

Trait Theories

➤ **What are trait theories of personality?**

Trait theories of personality are attempts to explain personality and differences between people in terms of their personal characteristics.

➤ **How did Allport differentiate between cardinal and central traits?**

Allport defined a cardinal trait as a personal quality that is so strong a part of a person's personality that he or she may become identified with that trait or known for it. A central trait is the type one might mention when writing a letter of recommendation.

➤ **How did Cattell differentiate between surface and source traits?**

Cattell viewed surface traits as observable qualities of personality. Source traits underlie the surface traits, make up the most basic personality structure, and cause behavior.

➤ **What does Eysenck consider to be the two most important dimensions of personality?**

Eysenck considers the two most important dimensions of personality to be Extraversion (extraversion versus introversion) and Neuroticism (emotional stability versus instability).

➤ **What are the Big Five personality dimensions in the five-factor theory as described by McCrae and Costa?**

According to McCrae and Costa, the Big Five are Extraversion, Neuroticism, Conscientiousness, Agreeableness, and Openness to Experience.

KEY TERMS

traits (p. 322)
five-factor theory (p. 323)

Nature, Nurture, and Personality

➤ **What has research in behavioral genetics revealed about the influence of genes and the environment on personality?**

Research in behavioral genetics has revealed that heredity (genes) strongly influences personality.

➤ **How does personality differ across cultures?**

The cultural dimension known as individualism/collectivism is associated with personality. Individualist cultures encourage people to view themselves as separate from others and to value independence and assertiveness. Collectivist cultures emphasize social connectedness among people and encourage individuals to define themselves in terms of their group membership.

KEY TERM

individualism/collectivism dimension (p. 326)

Personality Assessment

➤ **What is a personality inventory, and what are the MMPI-2 and the CPI designed to reveal?**

A personality inventory is a paper-and-pencil test with questions about a person's thoughts, feelings, and behaviors, which is scored according to a standard procedure. The MMPI-2 is designed to screen and diagnose psychiatric problems, and the CPI is designed to assess the normal personality.

➤ **How do projective tests provide insight into personality, and what are some of the most commonly used projective tests?**

In a projective test, people respond to inkblots, drawings of ambiguous human situations, incomplete sentences, or other items by projecting their own inner thoughts, feelings, fears, or conflicts into the test materials. Examples of widely used projective tests are the Rorschach Inkblot Method and the Thematic Apperception Test (TAT).

KEY TERMS

personality inventory (p. 328)
projective test (p. 330)

Surf It !

Want to be sure you've absorbed the material in Chapter 11, "Personality Theory and Assessement," before the big test? Visiting **www.ablongman. com/woodmastering1e** can put a top grade within your reach. The site is loaded with free practice tests, flashcards, activities, and links to help you review your way to an A.

Companion Website

Study Guide for Chapter 11 !

Answers to all the Study Guide questions are provided at the end of the book.

Section One: Chapter Review

1. Psychoanalysis is both a theory of personality and a therapy for the treatment of psychological disorders. (true/false)

2. Freud considered the (conscious, unconscious) to be the primary motivating force of human behavior.

3. The part of the personality that would make you want to eat, drink, and be merry is your
   a. id.
   b. ego.
   c. superego.
   d. ego ideal.

4. You just found a gold watch in a darkened movie theater. Which part of your personality would urge you to turn it in to the lost and found?
   a. id
   b. ego
   c. superego
   d. ego ideal

5. The part of the personality that determines appropriate ways to satisfy biological urges is the
   a. id.
   b. ego.
   c. superego.
   d. ego ideal.

6. Defense mechanisms are used only by psychologically unhealthy individuals. (true/false)

7. Repression is used to avoid unpleasant thoughts. (true/false)

8. According to Freud, the sex instinct arises at (birth, puberty).

9. Which of the following lists presents Freud's stages in the order in which they occur?
   a. anal, oral, genital, phallic
   b. genital, anal, oral, phallic
   c. oral, phallic, anal, genital
   d. oral, anal, phallic, genital

10. Rich's excessive concern with cleanliness and order could indicate a fixation at the _____ stage.
    a. oral   b. anal   c. phallic   d. genital

11. When a young boy develops sexual feelings toward his mother and hostility toward his father, he is said to have a conflict called the _____ _____ .

12. According to Freud, which of the following represents a primary source of influence on personality?
    a. heredity
    b. life experiences after beginning school
    c. the relative strengths of the id, ego, and superego
    d. the problems experienced during adolescence

13. In Jung's theory, the inherited part of the personality that stores the experiences of humankind is the (collective, personal) unconscious.

14. Which personality theorist believed that the basic human drive is to overcome and compensate for inferiority and strive for superiority and significance?
    a. Sigmund Freud
    b. Carl Jung
    c. Alfred Adler
    d. Karen Horney

15. On which of the following did Horney focus?
    a. psychoanalysis
    b. trait theory
    c. feminine psychology
    d. humanistic psychology

16. Bandura's concept of reciprocal determinism refers to the mutual effects of
    a. a person's behavior, personality, and thinking.
    b. a person's feelings, attitudes, and thoughts.
    c. a person's behavior, personal/cognitive factors, and the environment.
    d. classical and operant conditioning and observational learning.

17. Which statement is *not* true of people low in self-efficacy?
    a. They persist in their efforts.
    b. They lack confidence.
    c. They expect failure.
    d. They avoid challenge.

18. Who proposed the concept of locus of control?
    a. B. F. Skinner
    b. Albert Bandura
    c. Hans Eysenck
    d. Julian Rotter

19. Humanistic psychologists would *not* say that
    a. human nature is innately good.
    b. human beings have a natural tendency toward self-actualization.
    c. human beings have free will.
    d. researchers should focus primarily on observable behavior.

20. Which psychologist identified characteristics that he believed self-actualized persons share?
    a. Carl Rogers
    b. Gordon Allport
    c. Abraham Maslow
    d. Hans Eysenck

21. Which psychologist believed that individuals often do not become fully functioning persons because, in childhood, they fail to receive unconditional positive regard from their parents?
    a. Carl Rogers
    b. Gordon Allport
    c. Abraham Maslow
    d. Hans Eysenck

22. According to Allport, the kind of trait that is a defining characteristic of one's personality is a _____ trait.
    a. common
    b. source
    c. secondary
    d. cardinal

23. According to Cattell, the differences between people are explained by the number of source traits they possess. (true/false)

24. Who claimed that psychologists can best understand personality by assessing people on two major dimensions, Extraversion and Neuroticism?
   a. Hans Eysenck
   b. Gordon Allport
   c. Raymond Cattell
   d. Carl Jung

25. This chapter suggests that, according to a growing consensus among trait theorists, there are _____ major dimensions of personality.
   a. 3   c. 7
   b. 5   d. 16

26. Behavioral geneticists have found that the shared family environment has a (strong, negligible) effect on personality development.

27. Children adopted at birth are more similar in personality to their adoptive parents than to their biological parents. (true/false)

28. Match each personality test with its description.
   ____ (1) MMPI-2
   ____ (2) Rorschach
   ____ (3) TAT
   ____ (4) CPI
   ____ (5) MBTI
   a. inventory used to diagnose psychopathology
   b. inventory used to assess normal personality
   c. projective test using inkblots
   d. projective test using drawings of ambiguous human situations
   e. inventory used to assess personality types

29. Clay has an unconscious resentment toward his father. Which test might best detect this?
   a. MMPI-2   c. Rorschach
   b. CPI   d. TAT

30. Which of the following items might appear on the MMPI-2?
   a. What is happening in the picture?
   b. Hand is to glove as foot is to _____ .
   c. My mother was a good person.
   d. What is your favorite food?

Section Two: Complete the Table

Approach	Key Theorist(s)	Major Assumption about Behavior
1. Psychoanalytic	_____	_____
2. Social-cognitive	_____	_____
3. Humanistic	_____	_____
4. Trait	_____	_____

Section Three: Fill In the Blank

1. According to Freud, the _____ is the personality structure that is completely unconscious and operates on the pleasure principle.

2. According to Freud, the _____ is the logical and rational part of the personality.

3. Freud's _____ is very much like long-term memory.

4. The stages of psychosexual development, in the proper order, are _____, _____, _____, _____, and _____ .

5. Mother Teresa would be said to have possessed the _____ trait of altruism.

6. According to Cattell, _____ traits are the observable qualities of personality.

7. Bandura asserted that personal/cognitive factors, one's behavior, and the external environment all influence each other and are influenced by each other. He called this relationship _____ _____ .

8. According to Jung, the _____ _____ accounts for the similarity of certain myths, dreams, symbols, and religious beliefs in different cultures.

9. According to Eysenck, _____ are more important in determining personality than is the _____ .

10. Psychologists who adopt a behavioral perspective on personality usually prefer the _____ method to other methods of personality assessment.

11. The Myers-Briggs Type Indicator is a personality inventory that is based on _____ theory of personality.

12. The Rorschach Inkblot Method is an example of a _____ test.

13. The _____ is the most widely used of the many different personality inventories.

14. _____ refers to a person's belief that he or she can perform competently in what is attempted.

15. Cattell defined _____ traits as those traits that make up the most basic personality structure and cause behavior.

16. In Jung's view, an _____ exists in the collective unconscious and is an inherited tendency to respond in particular ways to universal human situations.

17. Cultures that encourage people to define themselves in terms of social relationships represent the _____ side of the _____/_____ dimension.

Section Four: Comprehensive Practice Test

1. A person's unique pattern of behaving, thinking, and feeling is his or her
   a. motivation.
   c. personality.
   b. emotion.
   d. cognition.

2. Freud's theory of personality and his therapy for the treatment of psychological disorders are both known as
   a. behaviorism.
   c. psychoanalysis.
   b. psychosocialism.
   d. humanism.

3. Of Freud's three conceptual systems of personality, the _____ is mainly in the conscious, the _____ is split between the conscious and the unconscious, and the _____ is completely unconscious.
   a. id; ego; superego
   c. superego; ego; id
   b. ego; superego; id
   d. ego; id; superego

4. The libido is Freud's name for the psychic or sexual energy that comes from the superego and provides the energy for the entire personality. (true/false)

5. Ava is 13 months old, and whatever she can pick up is likely to go into her mouth. Ava is in Freud's _____ stage of psychosexual development.
   a. anal
   c. phallic
   b. oral
   d. genital

6. Clint is 5 years old, and he thinks his mother is as beautiful as a princess; he would rather spend time with her than with his father. Clint is in Freud's _____ stage of psychosexual development.
   a. anal
   c. phallic
   b. oral
   d. genital

7. A central theme in Adler's theory is the individual's quest for feelings of
   a. superiority.
   c. adequacy.
   b. the collective unconscious.
   d. ego integrity.

8. According to Horney, maladjustment is often caused by
   a. guilt related to failing to live up to an ideal self.
   b. observation of maladjusted role models.
   c. inherited traits.
   d. repressed memories.

9. Allport and Cattell were proponents of the _____ theory of personality.
   a. stage
   c. biological
   b. trait
   d. humanistic

10. Which of the following Big Five personality factors has been found to be a requirement for creative accomplishment?
   a. extroversion
   c. neuroticism
   b. conscientiousness
   d. openness to experience

11. Bandura's theory includes the concept of _____, the belief a person has regarding his or her ability to perform competently whatever is attempted.
   a. reciprocal determinism
   b. self-efficacy
   c. extroversion
   d. conditions of worth

12. Trey believes that what happens to him is based on fate, luck, or chance, and his philosophy of life is "whatever will be will be." Rotter would say that Trey has a(n) _____ locus of control.
   a. internal
   c. external
   b. explicit
   d. regressed

13. Rogers's theory included the concept of conditions of worth—the idea that our parents teach us important values in life and that we as individuals will be motivated to seek out those values. (true/false)

14. The MMPI-2 is a good example of a projective personality test. (true/false)

15. The California Psychological Inventory was developed to evaluate the personalities of
   a. the mentally ill.
   c. normal people.
   b. males.
   d. females.

16. You are shown a black-and-white scene and asked to tell a story about it. You are probably responding to
   a. the Rorschach Inkblot Method.
   b. the CPI.
   c. the Myers-Briggs Type Indicator.
   d. the TAT.

Section Five: Critical Thinking

1. In your opinion, which of the major personality theories discussed in this chapter is the most accurate, reasonable, and realistic? Which is the least accurate, reasonable, and realistic? Give reasons to support your answers.

2. Most social scientists say that American culture is individualist. What aspects of culture in the United States exemplify individualism? Are there some features of American culture that are collectivist in nature? If so, what are they?

3. How do you think the Big Five dimensions of personality affect your behavior?

chapter 12

Psychological
Disorders

By the fall of 1985, 60-year-old William Styron had gained wide recognition as one of the finest writers of his time. His novels had brought him financial and critical success, and he had won many awards, including the Pulitzer Prize for his 1968 novel *The Confessions of Nat Turner.* When he received word that he had won a prestigious European prize, Styron was looking forward to the trip to Paris to accept the award. But as the time approached, he began to fall into a deep, debilitating depression. He struggled with intense anxiety, had difficulty sleeping, and could not concentrate sufficiently to write. While in Paris, he suddenly realized that he had to get psychiatric help immediately or he would succumb to the suicidal thoughts that were growing in frequency and intensity every day. In his 1990 memoir of the depression, *Darkness Visible: A Memoir of Madness,* Styron wrote of the afternoon he received the award:

> It was past four o'clock, and my brain had begun to endure its familiar siege: panic and dislocation and a sense that my thought processes were being engulfed by a toxic and unnamable tide that obliterated any enjoyable response to the living world. . . . I was feeling in my mind a sensation close to, but indescribably different from, actual pain. (p. 16).

Styron returned home and entered treatment, but the relief he had hoped to get from antidepressant medications didn't come. Instead, his depression became worse. Plagued by feelings of self-hatred, he could no longer engage in normal conversation. He couldn't sleep for more than an hour or so at a time, yet he could not force himself to get out of bed. His concentration was so poor that he did not trust himself to drive a car. Finally, on a December evening, in the midst of a dinner party at his home, he decided to end his life.

In the early morning hours the next day, however, he sat thinking about the home in Roxbury, Connecticut, that he and his wife had shared for many years. Memories of his children's early years, and even of the many pets the family had owned, flooded his mind. He suddenly realized that he was not yet ready to leave his family behind. The next day, he committed himself to a mental hospital in the hope of saving his life.

William Styron was fortunate. After months of intense treatment, he recovered from his depression and continues to write even today, in his late seventies. As he explained in *Darkness Visible,* many other artists have not been so lucky. As a group, artistic individuals appear to suffer higher rates of mental illness, especially emotional disorders like depression, than others. And the ranks of those who have died from suicide include many well-known names: Vincent Van Gogh, Ernest Hemingway, Sylvia Plath, and Kurt Cobain, to name a few.

psychological disorders
Mental processes and/or behavior patterns that cause emotional distress and/or substantial impairment in functioning.

What causes people, even those who are enormously successful in life and appear to have so much to live for, to become so despondent that they no longer want to live? Psychologists don't yet have a definitive answer to this question, but they have learned a great deal about psychological disorders in recent years. **Psychological disorders** are mental processes and/or behavior patterns that cause emotional distress and/or substantial impairment in functioning. This chapter explores their symptoms and their possible causes. But first, let's ask the obvious question: What is abnormal?

What Is Abnormal?

Defining Mental Disorders

> What criteria can be used to differentiate normal from abnormal behavior?

Human behavior lies along a continuum, and most of us are fairly well adjusted and experience only occasional maladaptive thoughts or behavior. Where along the continuum does behavior become abnormal? Several questions can help determine whether behavior is abnormal:

■ *Is the behavior considered strange within the person's own culture?* What is considered normal and abnormal in one culture is not necessarily considered so in another. In some cultures, it is normal for women to appear in public bare-breasted, but it would be abnormal for a female executive in New York to go to work that way.

■ *Does the behavior cause personal distress?* When people experience considerable emotional distress without any life experience that warrants it, they may be diagnosed as having a psychological disorder. Some people may be sad and depressed, some anxious; others may be agitated or excited, and still others frightened, or even terrified by delusions and hallucinations.

■ *Is the behavior maladaptive?* Some experts believe that the best way to differentiate between normal and abnormal behavior is to consider whether it leads to healthy or impaired functioning. Washing your hands before you eat is adaptive; washing them 100 times a day is not.

■ *Is the person a danger to self or others?* To be committed to a mental hospital, a person must be judged both mentally ill and a danger to self or others.

■ *Is the person legally responsible for his or her acts?* The term *insanity* is often used to label those who behave abnormally, but mental health professionals do not use this term. It is properly used only in court proceedings to declare people not

Abnormal behavior is defined by each culture. For example, homelessness is considered abnormal in some cultures and completely normal in others.

www.ablongman.com/woodmastering1e

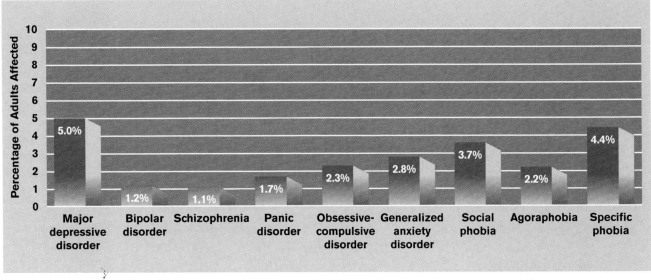

Annual Prevalence Rates of Selected Psychological Disorders among Adults in the United States
(Data from NIMH, 2001.)

legally responsible for their acts. Mass murderer Jeffrey Dahmer was ruled legally responsible for his acts, yet his behavior was clearly abnormal.

Prevalence of Psychological Disorders

Psychological disorders are more common than many physical ailments. For instance, each year in the United States, less than 1% of adults–about 1.3 million people–are diagnosed with cancer (American Cancer Society, 2002). By contrast, 22%–or more than 44 million adults–are diagnosed with a mental disorder of some kind (National Institute of Mental Health [NIMH], 2001). The annual prevalence rates of a few of the more common mental disorders are shown in Figure 12.1.

Another way of thinking about the frequency of an illness or disorder is to examine how likely an individual is to be diagnosed with it in his or her lifetime. The lifetime prevalence rate of cancer in the United States is about 30%; in other words, about 30% of Americans will be diagnosed with cancer sometime in their lives (National Center for Health Statistics [NCHS], 2000). Again, mental disorders are more common, with a lifetime prevalence rate of nearly 50% (Kessler et al., 1994). Lifetime rates of a few mental disorders are illustrated in Figure 12.2 (on page 342). Clearly, such disorders represent a significant source of personal misery for individuals and a great deal of lost productivity for society. Thus, research aimed at identifying their causes and treatments is just as important as research examining causes and treatments of physical diseases.

Perspectives on the Causes, Treatment, and Diagnosis of Psychological Disorders

Review and Reflect 12.1 (on page 343) summarizes current perspectives on psychological disorders. Each approach has its place in the description, analysis, and treatment of these disorders.

The *biological perspective* views abnormal behavior as arising from a physical cause, such as genetic inheritance, biochemical abnormalities or imbalances, structural abnormalities within the brain, and/or infection. Thus, proponents of this perspective favor biological treatments such as drug therapy. The *biopsychosocial perspective* agrees that physical causes are of central importance but also recognizes the influence of biological, psychological, and social factors in the study, identification, and treatment of psychological disorders. Consequently, biopsychosocial psychologists often advocate treatment strategies that include both drugs and psychotherapy.

◀ What are various perspectives that attempt to explain the causes of psychological disorders?

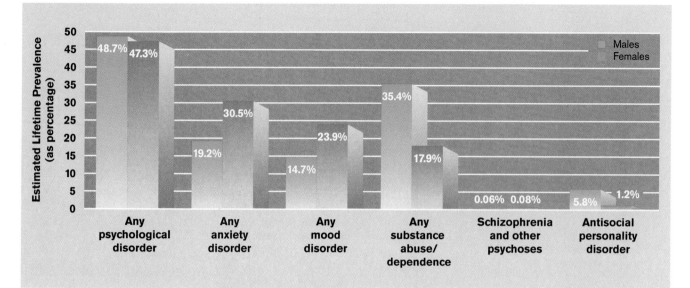

➤ Figure 12.2

Lifetime Prevalence Rates of Psychological Disorders for Males and Females in the United States

The percentages of males and females in the United States who will suffer from various psychological disorders at some time in their lives are based on the findings of the National Comorbidity Survey. Almost 50% of the respondents interviewed in this large national survey suffered from at least one psychological disorder in their lifetime. Males and females had about the same rate for experiencing some type of disorder. Males had higher rates for substance abuse and dependence and antisocial personality disorder. Females had higher rates for anxiety disorders and mood disorders. (Data from Kessler et al., 1994.)

DSM-IV
The *Diagnostic and Statistical Manual of Mental Disorders,* Fourth Edition, a manual published by the American Psychiatric Association, which describes about 290 mental disorders and their symptoms.

Originally proposed by Freud, the *psychodynamic perspective* maintains that psychological disorders stem from early childhood experiences and unresolved, unconscious conflicts, usually of a sexual or aggressive nature. The cause assumed by the psychodynamic approach also suggests the cure—psychoanalysis—which Freud developed to uncover and resolve such unconscious conflicts (see Chapter 11).

According to the *learning perspective,* psychological disorders are learned and sustained in the same way as any other behavior. According to this view, people who exhibit abnormal behavior either are victims of faulty learning or have failed to learn appropriate patterns of thinking and acting. Behavior therapists use learning principles to eliminate distressing behavior and to establish new, more appropriate behavior in its place.

The *cognitive perspective* suggests that faulty thinking or distorted perceptions can contribute to some types of psychological disorders. Treatment consistent with this perspective is aimed at changing thinking, which presumably will lead to a change in behavior. Moreover, the cognitive perspective offers advice that may prevent psychological disorders. For example, one step toward healthy thinking is to recognize and avoid five cognitive traps: (1) setting unrealistic standards for yourself; (2) negative "what if" thinking (such as "What if I lose my job?"); (3) turning a single negative event, such as a poor grade, into a catastrophe ("I'll never pass this course"); (4) judging anything short of perfection to be a failure; and (5) demanding perfection in yourself and others. If any of these are conditions on which your happiness depends, you are setting the stage for disappointment or even depression.

Regardless of their theoretical perspective, all clinicians and researchers use the same set of criteria to classify psychological disorders. The American Psychiatric Association publishes a manual listing these criteria. The most recent edition, the *Diagnostic and Statistical Manual of Mental Disorders* (Fourth Edition), commonly known

What is the *DSM-IV?* ➤

Perspectives on Psychological Disorders

PERSPECTIVE	CAUSES OF PSYCHOLOGICAL DISORDERS	TREATMENT
Biological perspective	A psychological disorder is a symptom of an underlying physical disorder caused by a structural or biochemical abnormality in the brain, by genetic inheritance, or by infection.	Diagnose and treat like any other physical disorder Drugs, electroconvulsive therapy, or psychosurgery
Biopsychosocial perspective	Psychological disorders result from a combination of biological, psychological, and social causes.	An eclectic approach employing treatments from one or more of the other perspectives.
Psychodynamic perspective	Psychological disorders stem from early childhood experiences; unresolved, unconscious sexual or aggressive conflicts; and/or imbalance among id, ego, and superego.	Bring disturbing repressed material to consciousness and help patient work through unconscious conflicts Psychoanalysis
Learning perspective	Abnormal thoughts, feelings, and behaviors are learned and sustained like any other behaviors, or there is a failure to learn appropriate behaviors.	Use classical and operant conditioning and modeling to extinguish abnormal behavior and to increase adaptive behavior Behavior therapy Behavior modification
Cognitive perspective	Faulty and negative thinking can cause psychological disorders.	Change faulty, irrational, and/or negative thinking Beck's cognitive therapy Rational-emotive therapy

as the **DSM-IV,** appeared in 1994. An updated version, the *DSM-IV-TR* (Text Revision), was published in 2000. Table 12.1 (on page 344) summarizes the major *DSM-IV* categories of disorders.

Schizophrenia

Schizophrenia is a serious psychological disorder characterized by loss of contact with reality, a condition often referred to as **psychosis.**

schizophrenia
(SKIT-soh-FREE-nee-ah) A severe psychological disorder characterized by loss of contact with reality, hallucinations, delusions, inappropriate or flat affect, some disturbance in thinking, social withdrawal, and/or other bizarre behavior.

psychosis
(sy-CO-sis) A psychological disorder marked by loss of contact with reality and a seriously impaired ability to function.

Table 12.1 Major *DSM-IV* Categories of Mental Disorders

Disorder	Symptoms	Examples
Schizophrenia and other psychotic disorders	Disorders characterized by the presence of psychotic symptoms, including hallucinations, delusions, disorganized speech, bizarre behavior, and loss of contact with reality	Schizophrenia, paranoid type Schizophrenia, disorganized type Schizophrenia, catatonic type Delusional disorder, jealous type
Mood disorders	Disorders characterized by periods of extreme or prolonged depression or mania or both	Major depressive disorder Bipolar disorder
Anxiety disorders	Disorders characterized by anxiety and avoidance behavior	Panic disorder Social phobia Obsessive-compulsive disorder Posttraumatic stress disorder
Somatoform disorders	Disorders in which physical symptoms are present that are psychological in origin rather than due to a medical condition	Hypochondriasis Conversion disorder
Dissociative disorders	Disorders in which one handles stress or conflict by forgetting important personal information or one's whole identity, or by compartmentalizing the trauma or conflict into a split-off alter personality	Dissociative amnesia Dissociative fugue Dissociative identity disorder
Personality disorders	Disorders characterized by long-standing, inflexible, maladaptive patterns of behavior beginning early in life and causing personal distress or problems in social and occupational functioning	Antisocial personality disorder Histrionic personality disorder Narcissistic personality disorder Borderline personality disorder
Substance-related disorders	Disorders in which undesirable behavioral changes result from substance abuse, dependence, or intoxication	Alcohol abuse Cocaine abuse Cannabis dependence
Disorders usually first diagnosed in infancy, childhood, or adolescence	Disorders that include mental retardation, learning disorders, communication disorders, pervasive developmental disorders, attention-deficit and disruptive behavior disorders, tic disorders, and elimination disorders	Conduct disorder Autistic disorder Tourette's syndrome Stuttering
Eating disorders	Disorders characterized by severe disturbances in eating behavior	Anorexia nervosa Bulimia nervosa

Source: Based on the *DSM-IV* (American Psychiatric Association, 1994).

Positive Symptoms of Schizophrenia

> What are some of the major positive and negative symptoms of schizophrenia?

Positive symptoms are the abnormal behaviors that are present in people with schizophrenia. One of the clearest positive symptoms of schizophrenia is the presence of **hallucinations**—imaginary sensations. Schizophrenic patients may see, hear, feel, taste, or smell strange things in the absence of any stimulus in the environment, but hearing voices is the most common type of hallucination. These voices typically accuse or curse the patients or engage in a running commentary on their behavior. Visual hallucinations, less common than auditory hallucinations, are usually in black-and-white and commonly take the form of friends, relatives, God, Jesus, or the devil. People with schizophrenia may also experience exceedingly frightening and painful bodily sensations; they may feel that they are being beaten, burned, or sexually violated.

Delusions, false beliefs not generally shared by others in the culture, is another type of positive symptom. A schizophrenic patient with **delusions of grandeur** may believe that he or she is a famous person (the president or Jesus Christ, for example) or a powerful or important person who possesses some great knowledge, ability, or

hallucination
A sensory perception in the absence of any external sensory stimulus; an imaginary sensation.

www.ablongman.com/woodmastering1e

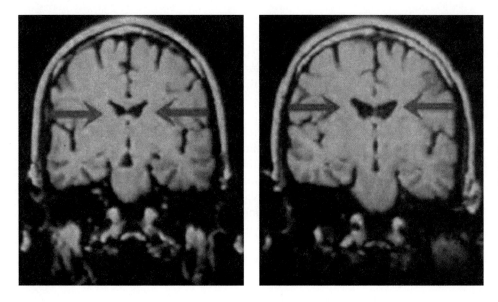

The MRI scan on the left is that of an individual who is not schizophrenic. The scan on the right is that of the individual's twin, who has schizophrenia. Note the enlarged ventricles (at the tips of the red arrows) in the brain of the twin with schizophrenia. (From Clinical Brain Disorders Branch, National Institute of Mental Health.)

authority. Those with **delusions of persecution** have the false notion that some person or agency is trying to harass, cheat, spy on, conspire against, injure, kill, or in some other way harm them.

Another positive symptom of schizophrenia is loosening of associations, or *derailment,* which occurs when a patient does not follow one line of thought to completion but, on the basis of vague connections, shifts from one subject to another in conversation or writing. *Grossly disorganized behavior,* another positive symptom of schizophrenia, can include such things as childlike silliness, inappropriate sexual behavior (masturbating in public), disheveled appearance, and peculiar dress. There may also be unpredictable agitation, including shouting and swearing, and unusual or inappropriate motor behavior, including strange gestures, facial expressions, or postures. People with schizophrenia may also display *inappropriate affect;* that is, their facial expressions, tone of voice, and gestures may not reflect the emotion that would be expected under the circumstances. A person might cry when watching a TV comedy and laugh when watching a news story showing bloody bodies at the scene of a fatal automobile accident.

Negative Symptoms of Schizophrenia

A *negative symptom* of schizophrenia is a loss of or deficiency in thoughts and behaviors that are characteristic of normal functioning. Negative symptoms include social withdrawal, apathy, loss of motivation, lack of goal-directed activity, very limited speech, slowed movements, poor hygiene and grooming, poor problem-solving abilities, and a distorted sense of time (Davalos et al., 2002; Hatashita-Wong et al., 2002; Skrabalo, 2000). Some schizophrenic patients have *flat affect,* showing practically no emotional response at all, even though they often report feeling the emotion. These patients may speak in a monotone, have blank and emotionless facial expressions, and act and move more like robots than humans.

Not all people who suffer from schizophrenia have negative symptoms. Those who do, though, seem to have the poorest outcomes (Fenton & McGlashan, 1994). Negative symptoms are predictors of impaired overall social and vocational functioning. Patients who exhibit them tend to withdraw from normal social contacts and retreat into their own world. They have difficulty relating to people, and often their functioning is too impaired for them to hold a job or even to care for themselves.

Brain Abnormalities in Schizophrenics

Several abnormalities in brain structure and function have been found in schizophrenic patients, including low levels of neural activity in the frontal lobes (Glantz &

delusion
A false belief, not generally shared by others in the culture, that cannot be changed despite strong evidence to the contrary.

delusions of grandeur
False beliefs that one is a famous person or a person who has some great knowledge, ability, or authority.

delusions of persecution
False beliefs that a person or group is trying in some way to harm one.

What are the four types of schizophrenia?

A person with catatonic schizophrenia may become frozen in an unusual position, like a statue, for hours at a time.

Lewis, 2000; Kim et al., 2000). Many schizophrenic patients have defects in the neural circuitry of the cerebral cortex and limbic system (Benes, 2000; McGlashan & Hoffman, 2000). There is also evidence of reduced volume in the hippocampus, amygdala, thalamus, and frontal lobe gray matter (Gur et al., 2000; Sanfilippo et al., 2000; Staal et al., 2000). Further, individuals with schizophrenia display abnormal lateralization of brain functions and slow communication between left and right hemispheres (Florio et al., 2002).

Abnormal dopamine activity has been found in the brains of many schizophrenics. Such altered dopamine activity sometimes results from cocaine abuse, which can pose an increased risk for schizophrenia (Benes, 2000; Tzschentke, 2001). Much of the brain's dopamine activity occurs in the limbic system, which is involved in human emotions. Drugs that are effective in reducing the symptoms of schizophrenia block the action of dopamine, although about one-third of the patients who are given such drugs do not show improvement with them.

Types of Schizophrenia

Certain symptoms and features distinguish one type of schizophrenia from another. For example, people with **paranoid schizophrenia** usually suffer from delusions of grandeur or persecution. They may be convinced that they have an identity other than their own—that they are the president, the Virgin Mary, or God—or that they possess great ability or talent. They may feel that they are in charge of the hospital or on a secret assignment for the government. And they often show exaggerated anger and suspiciousness. If they have delusions of persecution and feel that they are being harassed or threatened, patients with paranoid schizophrenia may become violent in an attempt to defend themselves against their imagined persecutors. The behavior that characterizes paranoid schizophrenia is usually not as obviously disturbed as that of the catatonic or disorganized type, and the chance for recovery is better.

Disorganized schizophrenia, the most serious type, tends to occur at an earlier age than the other types do, and is marked by extreme social withdrawal, hallucinations, delusions, silliness, inappropriate laughter, grimaces, grotesque mannerisms, and other bizarre behavior. These patients show flat or inappropriate affect and are frequently incoherent. They often exhibit obscene behavior, may masturbate openly, and swallow almost any kind of object or material. Disorganized schizophrenia results in the most severe disintegration of the personality, and its victims have the poorest chance of recovery (Fenton & McGlashan, 1991).

Persons with **catatonic schizophrenia** may display complete stillness and stupor, or great excitement and agitation. Frequently they alternate rapidly between the two. They may become frozen in a strange posture or position, and remain there for hours without moving. **Undifferentiated schizophrenia** is the general or catchall category used when schizophrenic symptoms either do not conform to the criteria of any single type of schizophrenia or conform to more than one type.

The Causes of Schizophrenia

Genetic factors appear to play a major role in the development of schizophrenia (Cannon et al., 1998; Gottesman, 1991; Kendler & Diehl, 1993; Plomin et al., 2003). Figure 12.3 shows how the chance of developing schizophrenia varies with the degree of relationship to a schizophrenic person. However, genes are not destiny; schizophrenia develops when there is both a genetic predisposition toward the disorder and more stress than a person can handle. Any environmental factor—birth trauma, a virus, malnutrition, head injury, and so on—that can interfere with nor-

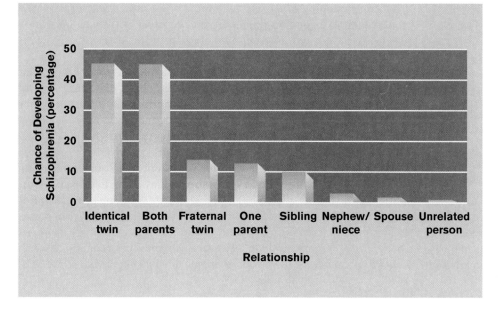

➤ **Figure 12.3**
Genetic Similarity and Probability of Developing Schizophrenia

Research strongly indicates that a genetic factor operates in many cases of schizophrenia. Identical twins have identical genes, and if one twin develops schizophrenia, the other twin has a 46% chance of developing it also. For fraternal twins, the chance is only 14%. A person with one parent who has schizophrenia has a 13% chance of developing schizophrenia, but a 46% chance if both parents have the disorder. (Data from Nicol & Gottesman, 1983.)

mal brain development brings an increased risk for schizophrenia (McDonald & Murray, 2000; McNeil et al., 2000).

What are some suggested causes of schizophrenia?

Gender and Schizophrenia

Schizophrenia is more likely to strike men than women. Men also tend to develop the disorder at an earlier age (Takahashi et al., 2000), they typically do not respond as well to treatment, they spend more time in mental hospitals, and they are more likely to relapse. The earlier age of onset of the disorder among males appears to be independent of culture and socioeconomic variables. Studies of male and female schizophrenics conducted in Japan more than 40 years apart (in the 1950s and the 1990s) revealed that Japanese males with the disorder had an earlier onset than Japanese females and that the average age of onset did not change over the 40-year period. Thus, the age of onset was not influenced by the dramatic cultural and socioeconomic changes in Japan during the postwar period (Takahashi et al., 2000).

Mood Disorders

Mood disorders involve moods or emotions that are extreme and unwarranted. In the most serious of these disorders, mood ranges from the depth of severe depression to the height of extreme elation.

mood disorders
Disorders characterized by extreme and unwarranted disturbances in feeling or mood.

Depressive Disorders

People with **major depressive disorder** feel an overwhelming sadness, despair, and hopelessness, and they usually lose their ability to experience pleasure. They may experience changes in appetite, weight, and sleep patterns, loss of energy, and difficulty in thinking or concentrating. Key symptoms of major depressive disorder are psychomotor disturbances (Sobin & Sackeim, 1997). For example, body movements, reaction time, and speech may be so slowed that the depressed person seems to be doing everything in slow motion. Others experience the opposite extreme and are constantly moving and fidgeting, wringing their hands, and pacing. Depression can be so severe that its victims suffer from delusions

major depressive disorder
A mood disorder marked by feelings of great sadness, despair, guilt, worthlessness, and hopelessness.

What are the symptoms of major depressive disorder?

Although depression is more common among women, it also affects men. Comedian Jim Carrey is among many adults who have this disorder.

or hallucinations, which are symptoms of *psychotic depression*. And the more deeply a person descends into depression over an extended period, the less and less she or he engages in social activities (Judd et al., 2000).

According to the American Psychiatric Association (1994), 1 year after their initial diagnosis of major depressive disorder, 40% of patients are without symptoms; 40% are still suffering from major depression; and 20% are depressed, but not enough to warrant a diagnosis of major depression. Slightly fewer than one-half of those hospitalized for major depressive disorder are fully recovered after 1 year (Keitner et al., 1992). For many, recovery from depression is aided by antidepressant drugs. However, some studies show that psychotherapy can be just as effective (Hollon et al., 2002). Some victims suffer only one major depressive episode, but 50–60% will have a recurrence. Risk of recurrence is greatest for females (Winokur et al., 1993) and for individuals with an onset of depression before age 15 (Brown, 1996). Recurrences may be frequent or infrequent, and for 20–35% of patients, the episodes are chronic, lasting 2 years or longer.

Culture, Gender, and Depression

A large study involving participants from ten countries revealed that the lifetime risk for developing depression varied greatly around the world, as shown in Figure 12.4. Asian countries (Taiwan and Korea) showed significantly lower rates of the disorder (Weissman et al., 1996). Still, major depressive disorder is the number one cause of disability throughout the world (NIMH, 1999c).

In most countries, the rate of depression for females is about twice that of males (Culbertson, 1997). Before boys reach puberty, they are more likely than girls to be depressed; then, in adolescence, a dramatic reversal in the gender-related depression rate takes place (Cyranowski et al., 2000). Not only are women more likely to suffer from depression, they are also more likely to be affected by negative consequences as a result. Early-onset depressive disorder adversely affects the educational attainment and earning power of women, but not men (Berndt et al., 2000). The National Task Force on Women and Depression suggests that the higher rate of depression in women is largely

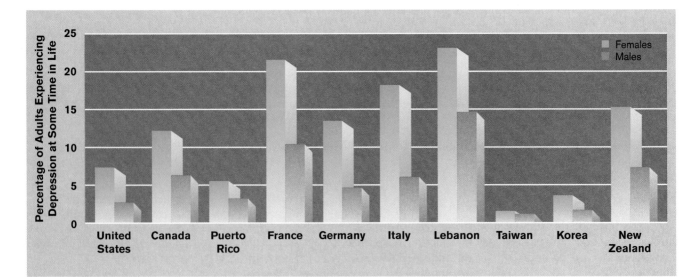

> ## Figure 12.4
Lifetime Risk for Developing Depression in Ten Countries

The lifetime prevalence of depression for 38,000 men and women in ten different countries reveals that women are more susceptible to depression worldwide. (Data from Weissman et al., 1996.)

due to social and cultural factors. In fulfilling her many roles—mother, wife, lover, friend, daughter, neighbor—a woman is likely to put the needs of others ahead of her own.

Bipolar Disorder

Another type of mood disorder is **bipolar disorder,** in which patients exhibit two radically different moods—extreme highs, called *manic episodes* (or *mania*), and the extreme lows of major depression—usually with relatively normal periods in between. A **manic episode** is marked by excessive euphoria, inflated self-esteem, wild optimism, and hyperactivity. People in a manic state have temporarily lost touch with reality and frequently have delusions of grandeur along with their euphoric highs. They may waste large sums of money on grand, get-rich-quick schemes. If family members try to stop them, they are likely to become irritable, hostile, enraged, or even dangerous. Quite often, patients must be hospitalized during manic episodes to protect them and others from the disastrous consequences of their poor judgment.

> What are the extremes of mood suffered by those with bipolar disorder?

Bipolar disorder is much less common than major depressive disorder; it affects about 1.2% of the U.S. population in any given year, and the lifetime prevalence rates are about the same for males and females (NIMH, 2001). Bipolar disorder tends to appear in late adolescence or early childhood. Unfortunately, about 90% of those with the disorder have recurrences, and half experience another episode within a year of recovering from a previous one. The good news is that 70–80% of patients return to normal after an episode (American Psychiatric Association, 1994). In many cases, individuals with bipolar disorder can manage their symptoms, and live a normal life, with the help of drugs such as lithium and divalproex. Moreover, psychotherapy can help them cope with the stress of facing life with a potentially disabling mental illness (Hollon et al., 2002).

Causes of Mood Disorders

Biological factors such as genetic inheritance and abnormal brain chemistry play a major role in bipolar disorder and major depressive disorder. PET scans have revealed abnormal patterns of brain activity in both of these disorders (George et al., 1993). Drevets and others (1997) located a brain area that may trigger both the sadness of major depression and the mania of bipolar disorder. A small, thimble-size patch of brain tissue in the lower prefrontal cortex (about 2–3 inches behind the bridge of the nose) is 40–50% smaller in people with hereditary depression. Earlier research established that this area of the brain plays a key role in the control of emotions.

> What are some suggested causes of major depressive disorder and bipolar disorder?

People who have relatives with mood disorders are at higher risk of developing such problems (Kendler, Walters, et al., 1994). Based on a study of 1,721 identical and fraternal female twins, Kendler, Neale, Kessler, and others (1993) estimated the heritability of major depression to be 70% and the contribution of environment to be 30%. Adoption studies have also shown that among adult adoptees who had developed depression, there was 8 times as much major depression and 15 times more suicides in biological than in adoptive family members (Wender et al., 1986). The genetic link is even stronger for bipolar disorder than for depression (Kalidini & McGuffin, 2003).

Norepinephrine and serotonin are two neurotransmitters that play important roles in mood disorders (Lambert et al., 2000). Both are localized in the limbic system and the hypothalamus, parts of the brain that help regulate emotional behavior. Too little norepinephrine is associated with depression, and too much is related to mania.

Cognitive factors contribute to depression as well (Haaga et al., 1991). Depressed individuals view themselves, their world, and their future in negative ways (Beck, 1967, 1991). They see their interactions with the world as a series of burdens and obstacles that usually end in failure. Depressed persons believe they are deficient, unworthy, and inadequate, and they attribute their perceived failures to their own physical, mental, or moral inadequacies. Depressed patients may reason in self-defeating ways: "Everything always turns out wrong," "I never win," "Things will never get better," and "It's no use."

The vast majority of first episodes of depression strike after *major life stress* (Brown et al., 1994; Frank et al., 1994). Cui and Vaillant (1996), in a longitudinal study of Har-

bipolar disorder
A mood disorder in which manic episodes alternate with periods of depression, usually with relatively normal periods in between.

manic episode
(MAN-ik) A period of extreme elation, euphoria, and hyperactivity, often accompanied by delusions of grandeur and by hostility if activity is blocked.

vard graduates that continued for over 40 years, found that negative life events, as well as family history, played significant roles in the development of mood disorders. This seems particularly true of women, who are more likely to have experienced a severe negative life event just prior to the onset of depression (Spangler et al., 1996). Yet recurrences of depression, at least in people who are biologically predisposed, often occur without significant life stress (Brown et al., 1994).

Suicide and Race, Gender, and Age

Some depressed people commit the ultimate act of desperation—suicide. Mood disorders and schizophrenia, along with substance abuse, are major risk factors for suicide in all age groups (Mościcki, 1995; Shaffer et al., 1996). There is also evidence that suicidal behavior runs in families (Brent et al., 1996, 2002). Even among people who have severe mood disturbances, such as bipolar disorder, those with a family history of suicide attempts are far more likely to kill themselves than those without such a family history (Tsai et al., 2002).

Between 30,000 and 31,000 suicides are reported annually in the United States. Figure 12.5 shows the differences in U.S. suicide rates according to race, gender, and age (NCHS, 2001a, 2002a). As you can see, White Americans are more likely to commit suicide than African Americans. Native American suicide rates are almost equal to those of Whites; rates for Hispanic Americans are similar to those for African Americans (NCHS, 2001b). Asian Americans have the lowest suicide rates of all racial or ethnic groups in the United States (NCHS, 2002a).

You will also note in the figure that suicide rates are far lower for women—White and African American—than for men. However, studies show that women are 2 to 3 times more likely than men to *attempt* suicide (Garland & Zigler, 1993). Most observers believe that the higher rate of completed suicides in males is due to the methods men and women use: Men tend to use guns, while women prefer pills or other slower methods of inducing death.

Although suicide rates among teens and young adults have increased over past decades, older Americans are at far greater risk for suicide than younger people. White males aged 85 and over have the highest recorded suicide rate, with over 75

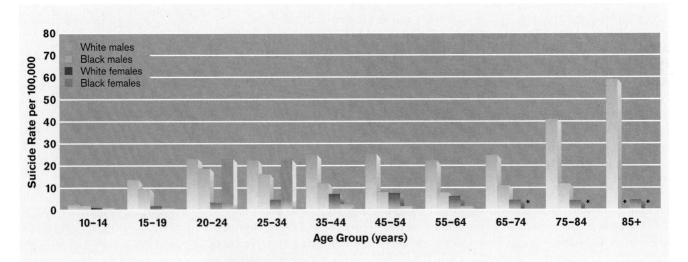

➤ Figure 12.5

Differences in Suicide Rate According to Race, Gender, and Age

In every age group, the suicide rate is highest for White American males and second highest for African American males. The general conclusion is that males are more likely to commit suicide than females, and Whites are more likely to do so than African Americans. Suicide rates indicated by asterisks (*) are too low to be statistically reliable. (Data from NCHS, 2001a, 2002a.)

www.ablongman.com/woodmastering1e

suicides for every 100,000 people in that age group, more than six times the average national suicide rate of 12.2 per 100,000 (U.S. Bureau of the Census, 2001). Poor general health, serious illness, loneliness (often due to the death of a spouse), and decline in social and economic status are conditions that may push many older Americans, especially those aged 75 and over, to commit suicide.

About 90% of individuals who commit suicide give clues (Shneidman, 1994). They may communicate verbally: "You won't be seeing me again." They may show behavioral clues, such as giving away their most valued possessions, withdrawing from friends, family, and associates, taking unnecessary risks, showing personality changes, acting and looking depressed, and losing interest in favorite activities. These warning signs should always be taken seriously. If you are faced with a suicidal person, the best service you can render is to encourage the person to get professional help. There are 24-hour suicide hotlines all over the country. A call might save a life.

Anxiety Disorders

Anxiety disorders account for more than 4 million visits to doctors' offices each year in the United States (NCHS, 2002b). Figure 12.6 shows the percentages of males and females who have suffered from various anxiety disorders during their lifetime. **Anxiety disorders** are characterized by severe *anxiety,* a vague, general uneasiness or an ominous feeling that something bad is about to happen. This feeling may be associated with a particular situation—a big exam, a job interview, or a first date, for example. Sometimes, however, anxiety is free-floating, not associated with anything specific. Take a minute right now to complete the anxiety disorder checklist in *Try It! 12.1* (on page 352).

Generalized Anxiety Disorder

Generalized anxiety disorder is the diagnosis given to people who are plagued by chronic, excessive worry for 6 months or longer. These unfortunate people expect the worst; their worrying is either unfounded or greatly exaggerated

> What is generalized anxiety disorder?

anxiety disorders
Psychological disorders characterized by severe anxiety (e.g., panic disorder, phobias, general anxiety disorder, obsessive-compulsive disorder).

generalized anxiety disorder
An anxiety disorder in which people experience excessive anxiety or worry that they find difficult to control.

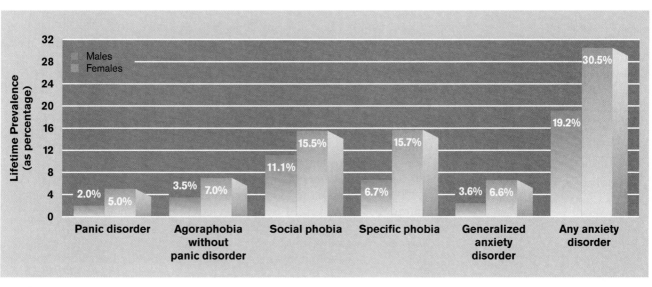

➤ Figure 12.6

Lifetime Prevalence Rates of Anxiety Disorders for Males and Females in the United States

The percentages of males and females in the United States who have suffered from various anxiety disorders during their lifetimes are based on the findings of the National Comorbidity Survey. (Data from Kessler et al., 1994.)

Try It! 12.1 Identifying Anxiety Disorders

Read each of the four descriptions below and place a checkmark beside each description that sounds like you or someone you know.

_____ 1. You are always worried about things, even when there are no signs of trouble. You have frequent aches and pains that can't be traced to physical illness or injury. You tire easily, and yet you have trouble sleeping. Your body is constantly tense.

_____ 2. Out of the blue, your heart starts pounding. You feel dizzy. You can't breathe. You feel like you are about to die. You've had these symptoms over and over again.

_____ 3. Every day you fear you will do something embarrassing. You've stopped going to parties because you're afraid to meet new people. When other people look at you, you break out in a sweat and shake uncontrollably. You stay home from work because you're terrified of being called on in a staff meeting.

_____ 4. You are so afraid of germs that you wash your hands repeatedly until they are raw and sore. You can't leave the house until you check the locks on every window and door over and over again. You are terrified that you will harm someone you care about. You just can't get those thoughts out of your head.

As you continue through this section of the chapter, you'll learn which anxiety disorders these symptoms represent. (From NIMH, 1999.)

and, thus, difficult to control. They may be unduly worried about their finances, their own health or that of family members, their performance at work, or their ability to function socially. Their excessive anxiety may cause them to feel tense, tired, and irritable and to have difficulty concentrating and sleeping. Other symptoms include trembling, palpitations, sweating, dizziness, nausea, diarrhea, and frequent urination. This disorder affects twice as many women as men and leads to considerable distress and impairment in functioning (Brawman-Mintzer & Lydiard, 1996, 1997; Kranzler, 1996). The heritability of generalized anxiety disorder is estimated to be about 30% (Kendler et al., 1992). But, as troubling as this disorder is, it is less severe than panic disorder.

Panic Disorder

During **panic attacks**–attacks of overwhelming anxiety, fear, or terror–people commonly report a pounding heart, uncontrollable trembling or shaking, and sensations of choking or smothering. Some say that they believe they are going to die or are "going crazy." Recent studies have revealed that the more catastrophic such beliefs are, the more intense the panic attack is likely to be (Hedley et al., 2000). People who suffer from recurring panic attacks may be diagnosed with **panic disorder.** Panic disorder sufferers must cope not only with repeated attacks but with anxiety about the occurrence and consequences of further attacks. This apprehension can lead them to avoid situations that have been associated with previous panic attacks. About 2% of men and 5% of women in the United States suffer from panic disorder (Kessler et al., 1994).

Panic disorder can have significant social and health consequences (Sherbourne et al., 1996). Patients with this disorder tend to overuse the health care system (Katon, 1996) and are at increased risk for abuse of alcohol and other drugs (Marshall, 1997). In a study of panic disorder involving 40,000 patients in ten countries (the United States, Canada, Puerto Rico, France, Germany, Italy, Lebanon, Korea, New Zealand, and Taiwan), Weissman and others (1997) found a similar incidence, age of onset, and male/female ratio in all countries except Taiwan, where the incidence was considerably lower.

> **What are the symptoms of panic disorder?** ➤

panic attack
An attack of overwhelming anxiety, fear, or terror.

panic disorder
An anxiety disorder in which a person experiences recurrent unpredictable attacks of overwhelming anxiety, fear, or terror.

Phobias

A person suffering from a **phobia** experiences a persistent, irrational fear of some specific object, situation, or activity that poses no real danger (or whose danger is blown all out of proportion). Phobics realize that their fears are irrational, but they nevertheless feel compelled to avoid the feared objects or situations.

The phobia most likely to drive people to seek professional help is **agoraphobia.** A person with agoraphobia has an intense fear of being in a situation from which immediate escape is not possible or in which help would not be available if the person should become overwhelmed by anxiety or experience a panic attack or paniclike symptoms. In some cases, a person's entire life must be planned around avoiding feared situations such as busy streets, crowded stores, restaurants, and/or public transportation. Some individuals with agoraphobia will not leave home unless accompanied by a friend or family member and, in severe cases, not even then. Women are four times more likely than men to be diagnosed with agoraphobia (Bekker, 1996).

Although agoraphobia can occur without panic attacks, it typically begins during the early adult years with repeated panic attacks (Horwath et al., 1993). The intense fear of having another attack causes the person to avoid any place or situation where previous attacks have occurred. Some researchers believe that agoraphobia is actually an extreme form of panic disorder (Sheehan, 1983). *Panic disorder with agoraphobia (PDA)* is one of the most debilitating of psychological disorders, and it is more common in women than in men. It can affect most areas of life–physical, psychological, social, occupational, interpersonal, and economic.

People who suffer from **social phobia** are intensely afraid of any social or performance situation in which they might embarrass or humiliate themselves in front of others–where they might shake, blush, sweat, or in some other way appear clumsy, foolish, or incompetent. Social phobia may take the form of specific performance anxiety. Surprisingly, many professional entertainers experience this kind of specific social phobia; Barbra Streisand's extreme performance anxiety kept her from appearing live in concert for many years. About one-third of those with social phobias fear only speaking in public (Kessler et al., 1998); in a survey of 449 individuals who had not been formally diagnosed with social phobia, one-third said they would experience excessive anxiety if they had to speak in front of a large audience (Stein et al., 1996). If you are one of the millions who are afraid of public speaking, see the *Apply It!* at the end of this chapter for advice on overcoming your fear.

Although less debilitating than agoraphobia, social phobia can be a disabling disorder (Stein & Kean, 2000). In its extreme form, it can seriously affect people's performance at work, prevent them from advancing in their careers or pursuing an education, and severely restrict their social lives (Greist, 1995; Stein & Kean, 2000). And often those with social phobia turn to alcohol and tranquilizers to lessen their anxiety in social situations. Mickey Mantle, for example, used alcohol to calm himself when making public appearances (Jefferson, 1996).

Specific phobia–a marked fear of a specific object or situation–is a catchall category for any phobia other than agoraphobia and social phobia. Faced with the feared object or situation, a person with a phobia experiences intense anxiety, even to the point of shaking or screaming; he or she will go to great lengths to avoid the feared object or situation. The categories of specific phobias, in order of frequency of occurrence, are (1) *situational phobias* (e.g., fear of elevators, airplanes, enclosed places, heights, tunnels, or bridges), (2) fear of the natural environment (e.g., storms or water), (3) animal phobias (e.g., fear of dogs, snakes, insects, or mice), and (4) *blood-injection-injury phobia* (e.g., fear of seeing blood or an injury, or of receiving an injection) (Fredrikson et al., 1996). Two types of situational phobias–*claustrophobia* (fear of closed spaces) and *acrophobia* (fear of heights)–are the specific phobias treated most often by therapists.

The causes of phobias vary, depending on which type of phobia is involved. However, heredity is an important predictor of who will or will not develop a phobia. A person has three times the risk of developing a phobia if a close relative suffers from one (Fyer, 1993). Heredity appears to be especially important in the development of agora-

phobia
(FO-bee-ah) A persistent, irrational fear of an object, situation, or activity that the person feels compelled to avoid.

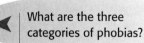
What are the three categories of phobias?

agoraphobia
(AG-or-uh-FO-bee-uh) An intense fear of being in a situation from which immediate escape is not possible or in which help is not immediately available in case of incapacitating anxiety.

social phobia
An irrational fear and avoidance of social situations in which one might embarrass or humiliate oneself by appearing clumsy, foolish, or incompetent.

specific phobia
A marked fear of a specific object or situation; any phobia other than agoraphobia and social phobia.

The talented singer Barbra Streisand suffers from extreme performance anxiety, which kept her from appearing live in concerts for many years.

phobia. Frightening experiences also appear to set the stage for the acquisition of phobias. Many specific and social phobias are acquired in childhood or adolescence through direct conditioning, modeling (observational learning), or the transmission of information (Rachman, 1997). For instance, a person may be able to trace the beginning of a specific phobia to a traumatic childhood experience with the feared object or situation (Hirschfeld, 1995; Jefferson, 1996; Stemberger et al., 1995), and children who hear their parents talk about a frightening encounter with a dog may develop a fear of dogs.

Principles of learning are often used to treat phobias. A therapist may use classical conditioning to teach patients to associate pleasant emotions with feared objects or situations. For example, a child who fears dogs might be given ice cream while in a room where a dog is present. Behavior modification, in which patients are reinforced for exposing themselves to fearful stimuli, may also be useful. Observation of models who do not exhibit fear in response to the feared object or situation has also been used successfully to treat phobias. Finally, antidepressant drugs have been shown to help people overcome agoraphobia (Kampman et al., 2002; Marshall et al., 1997).

Obsessive-Compulsive Disorder

What is obsessive-compulsive disorder?

Obsessive-compulsive disorder (OCD) is an anxiety disorder in which people suffer from recurrent obsessions or compulsions, or both. **Obsessions** are persistent, recurring, involuntary thoughts, images, or impulses that invade consciousness and cause a person great distress. People with obsessions might worry about contamination or about whether they performed a certain act, such as turning off the stove or locking the door (Insel, 1990). Other types of obsessions center on aggression, religion, or sex. One minister reported obsessive thoughts of running naked down the church aisle and shouting obscenities at his congregation.

A person with a **compulsion** feels literally compelled to repeat certain acts or perform specific rituals over and over. The individual knows that such acts are irrational and senseless but not performing them leads to an intolerable buildup of anxiety—anxiety that can be relieved only by yielding to the compulsion. Many of us have engaged in compulsive behavior like stepping over cracks on the sidewalk, counting stairsteps, or performing little rituals from time to time. The behavior becomes a psychological problem only if the person cannot resist performing it, if it is very time-consuming, and if it interferes with the person's normal activities and relationships with others.

Compulsions exhibited by people with obsessive-compulsive disorder often involve cleaning and washing behaviors, counting, checking, touching objects, hoarding, and excessive organizing. These cleaning and checking compulsions affect 75% of OCD patients receiving treatment (Ball et al., 1996). Sometimes compulsive acts or rituals resemble magical thinking and must be performed faithfully to ward off some danger. People with OCD do not enjoy these time-consuming rituals—the endless counting, checking, or cleaning. They realize that their behavior is not normal; but they simply cannot help themselves, as shown in the following example.

> Mike, a 32-year-old patient, performed checking rituals that were preceded by a fear of harming other people. When driving, he had to stop the car often and return to check whether he had run over people, particularly babies. Before flushing the toilet, he had to check to be sure that a live insect had not fallen into the toilet, because he did not want to be responsible for killing a living thing. At home he repeatedly checked to see that the doors, stoves, lights, and windows were shut or turned off. . . . Mike performed these and many other checking rituals for an average of 4 hours a day. (Kozak et al., 1988, p. 88)

Mike's checking compulsion is extreme, but it has been estimated that 2–3% of the U.S. population may suffer from OCD. Fairly similar rates have been reported in studies in Canada, Puerto Rico, Germany, Korea, and New Zealand (Weissman et al., 1994).

Studies have shown that early autoimmune system diseases, early strep infections, and changes in the brain caused by infection may predispose a person to develop OCD (Giedd et al., 2000; Hamilton & Swedo, 2001). Several twin and family studies suggest that a genetic factor is also involved in the development of OCD (Nestadt

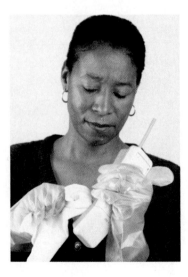

Like this woman, many people with obsessive-compulsive disorder take great pains to avoid contamination from germs and dirt.

et al., 2000; Rasmussen & Eisen, 1990). Genes affecting serotonin action are suspected of causing OCD in some people, many of whom are helped by antidepressant drugs that are believed to increase serotonin levels in the brain (Pigott, 1996).

Somatoform and Dissociative Disorders

Somatoform Disorders

The **somatoform disorders** involve bodily symptoms that cannot be identified as any known medical condition. Although the symptoms are psychological in origin, patients are sincerely convinced that they spring from real physical disorders. People with somatoform disorders are not consciously faking illness to avoid work or other activities.

People with **hypochondriasis** are overly concerned about their health and fear that their bodily symptoms are a sign of some serious disease. A person with this disorder "might notice a mole and think of skin cancer or read about Lyme disease and decide it might be the cause of that tired feeling" (Barsky, 1993, p. 8). Yet their symptoms are not usually consistent with known physical disorders, and even when a medical examination reveals no physical problem, they are not convinced. Hypochondriacs may "doctor shop," going from one physician to another, seeking confirmation of their worst fears. Unfortunately, hypochondriasis is not easily treated, and there is usually a poor chance for recovery.

A person is diagnosed with a **conversion disorder** when there is a loss of motor or sensory functioning in some part of the body that is not due to a physical cause but that solves a psychological problem. The person may become blind, deaf, or unable to speak or may develop a paralysis in some part of the body. Many of Freud's patients suffered from conversion disorder, and he believed that they unconsciously developed a physical disability to help resolve an unconscious sexual or aggressive conflict. Psychologists now believe that conversion disorder can act as an unconscious defense against any situation that brings intolerable anxiety and that the person cannot otherwise escape. For example, a soldier who desperately fears going into battle might escape the anxiety by developing a paralysis or some other physically disabling symptom. One reason for this hypothesis is that sufferers exhibit a calm and cool indifference to their symptoms, called "la belle indifference." Furthermore, many seem to enjoy the attention, sympathy, and concern their disability brings them.

Dissociative Disorders

In response to unbearable stress, some people develop a **dissociative disorder** and lose the ability to consciously integrate their identities and personal memories. Their consciousness becomes dissociated from their identity or their memories of important personal events, or both. For example, **dissociative amnesia** is a complete or partial loss of the ability to recall personal information or identify past experiences that cannot be attributed to ordinary forgetfulness or substance use. It is often caused by a traumatic experience—a psychological blow, so to speak—or a situation that creates unbearable anxiety and causes the person to escape by "forgetting."

Several people previously thought to have been killed in the terrorist attacks on the World Trade Center on September 11, 2001, were discovered in mental hospitals many months later with diagnoses of dissociative amnesia ("Two missing," 2002). They were brought to hospitals on the day of the tragedy with no identification on their persons and were unable to remember their names or other identifying information. Tedious investigative work, including DNA testing in some cases, was required before they were identified. The fact that some were homeless people with schizophrenia who lived on the streets or in the subway stations near the World Trade Center made the task of identifying them all the more difficult. Such cases illustrate one of the strange quirks of dissociative amnesia: Sufferers forget items of personal reference such as their name, age, and

What are two somatoform disorders, and what symptoms do they share?

somatoform disorders (so-MAT-uh-form) Disorders in which physical symptoms are present but are due to psychological rather than physical causes.

hypochondriasis (HI-poh-kahn-DRY-uh-sis) A somatoform disorder in which persons are preoccupied with their health and convinced that they have some serious disorder even though there is no evidence of any medical problem.

conversion disorder A somatoform disorder in which a person suffers a loss of motor or sensory functioning in some part of the body; the loss has no physical cause but solves some psychological problem.

dissociative disorders Disorders in which, under stress, one loses the ability to integrate one's consciousness, identity, and memories of important personal events.

What are dissociative amnesia and dissociative fugue?

dissociative amnesia A dissociative disorder in which there is a loss of memory of limited periods in one's life or of one's entire identity.

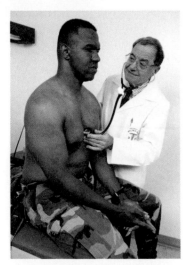

A soldier who continually complains of various symptoms and seeks medical treatment for them, even though doctors can discover nothing physically wrong, may be suffering from conversion disorder due to intense fear of battle.

What are some of the identifying symptoms of dissociative identity disorder?

dissociative fugue
(FEWG) A dissociative disorder in which one has a complete loss of memory of one's entire identity, travels away from home, and may assume a new identity.

dissociative identity disorder (DID)
A dissociative disorder in which two or more distinct personalities occur in the same person, each taking over at different times.

address and may fail to recognize their parents, other relatives, and friends, but they do not forget how to carry out routine tasks, how to read and write or solve problems, and their basic personality structure remains intact.

Even more puzzling than dissociative amnesia is **dissociative fugue.** In a fugue state, people not only forget their identity, they also travel away from home. Some take on a new identity that is usually more outgoing and uninhibited than their former identity. The fugue state may last for hours, days, or even months. It is usually a reaction to some severe psychological stress, such as a natural disaster, a serious family quarrel, a deep personal rejection, or military service in wartime. Fortunately, for most sufferers, recovery from dissociative fugue is rapid, although they may have no memory of the initial stressor that brought on the episode. And when people recover from the fugue state, they often have no memory of events that occurred during its duration.

In **dissociative identity disorder (DID),** two or more distinct, unique personalities exist in the same individual, and there is severe memory disruption concerning personal information about the other personalities. In 50% of the cases, there are more than ten different personalities. The change from one personality to another often occurs suddenly and usually during stress. The personality in control of the body the largest percentage of the time is known as the *host personality* (Kluft, 1984). The alternate personalities, or *alter personalities,* may differ radically in intelligence, speech, accent, vocabulary, posture, body language, hairstyle, taste in clothes, manners, and even handwriting and sexual orientation. In 80% of cases of dissociative identity disorder, the host personality does not know of the alter personalities, but the alters have varying levels of awareness of each other (Putnam, 1989, p. 114). The host and alter personalities commonly show amnesia for certain periods of time or for important life events such as a graduation or wedding. A common complaint concerns "lost time"–periods for which a given personality has no memory because he or she was not in control of the body.

Dissociative identity disorder usually begins in early childhood but is rarely diagnosed before adolescence (Vincent & Pickering, 1988). About 90% of the treated cases have been women (Ross et al., 1989), and more than 95% of the patients reveal early histories of severe physical and/or sexual abuse (Coons, 1994; Putnam, 1992). The splitting off of separate personalities is apparently a way of coping with the intolerable abuse. Research has found corroborating evidence to confirm the severe trauma and abuse suffered by many patients with this disorder (Gleaves, 1996).

Some clinicians believe that dissociative identity disorder is extremely rare or nonexistent and may be a device used by some patients to escape the consequences of their deviant behavior (Chodoff, 1987; Thigpen & Cleckley, 1984). Other clinicians believe that the disorder is even more common than reported and claim that it is widely misdiagnosed and underdiagnosed (Bliss & Jeppsen, 1985; Kluft, 1993). During the 1980s, there was a dramatic increase in the number of cases reported in the United States (Putnam & Loewenstein, 1993). And more cases were also reported in Puerto Rico (Martinez-Taboas, 1991) and in a number of other countries–Canada (Ross et al., 1991), Switzerland (Modestin, 1992), the Netherlands, Turkey (Sar et al., 1996), and 11 other countries outside of North America (Coons et al., 1991). Experts believe that these increases were due to improvements in diagnostic techniques rather than representing an actual jump in the incidence of the disorder (Kluft, 1999). Dissociative identity disorder is believed to have an incidence of 3–4% of psychiatric patients. It can be treated by psychotherapy, and empirical evidence indicates that DID patients respond well to treatment (Ellason & Ross, 1997).

Other Psychological Disorders

Gender Identity and Sexual Disorders

DSM-IV includes several psychological disorders that are associated with sexual identity or behavior (see Table 12.2). *Gender identity disorders* involve a problem in accept-

Table 12.2 Other Psychological Disorders

Type of Disorder	Symptoms
Gender identity disorders	Problems accepting one's identity as a male or female
Paraphilias	Recurrent sexual urges, fantasies, and behavior involving objects, chldren, other non-consenting persons, or the suffering or humiliation of the individual or his/her partner
Fetishism	Sexual urges, fantasies, and behavior involving an inanimate object, such as women's undergarments or shoes
Pedophilia	Sexual urges, fantasies, and behavior involving sexual activity with a prepubescent child or children
Exhibitionism	Sexual urges, fantasies, and behavior involving exposing one's genitals to an unsuspecting stranger
Voyeurism	Sexual urges, fantasies, and behavior involving watching unsuspecting people naked, undressing, or engaging in sexual activity
Sexual masochism	Sexual urges, fantasies, and behavior involving being beaten, humiliated, bound, or otherwise made to suffer
Sexual sadism	Sexual urges, fantasies, and behavior involving inflicting physical or psychological pain and suffering on another
Other paraphilias	Sexual urges, fantasies, and behavior involving, among other things, animals, feces, urine, corpses, filth, or enemas
Sexual dysfunctions	Low sexual desire; the inability to attain or maintain sexual arousal; a delay or absence of orgasm; premature ejaculation; or genital pain associated with sexual activity
Personality disorders	Inflexible maladaptive behavior and impaired functioning
Antisocial personality disorder	Callous disregard for the rights and feelings of others; behavior that is manipulative, impulsive, selfish, aggressive, irresponsible, reckless; willingness to break the law, lie, cheat, or exploit others for personal gain, without remorse; failure to hold a job
Paranoid personality disorder	Behavior characterized as suspicious, untrusting, guarded, hypersensitive, easily slighted, lacking in emotion; holding grudges
Histrionic personality disorder	Seeking for attention and approval; overly dramatic, self-centered, shallow personality; demanding, manipulative, easily bored, suggestible behavior; craving for excitement; often an attractive and sexually seductive person
Narcissistic personality disorder	Exaggerated sense of self-importance and entitlement; behavior that is self-centered and arrogant, demanding, exploitive, envious; craving for admiration and attention; lack of empathy
Borderline personality disorder	Unstable in mood, behavior, self-image, and social relationships; intense fear of abandonment; impulsive and reckless behavior, inappropriate anger; suicidal gestures and self-mutilating acts

Source: Based on the *DSM-IV* (American Psychiatric Association, 1994),

ing one's identity as male or female. Children either express a desire to be or insist that they are of the other gender. They show a preference for the clothes, games, pastimes, and playmates of the opposite sex. These disorders are fairly rare.

Far more common are *sexual disorders*–sexual problems that are destructive, guilt- or anxiety-producing, compulsive, or a cause of discomfort or harm to one or both parties. One group of sexual disorders diagnosed only rarely by clinical psychologists are the *paraphilias*–recurrent sexual urges, fantasies, or behaviors involving children, other non-consenting partners, nonhuman objects, or the suffering or humiliation of the individual or a partner. However, *DSM-IV* notes that the quantity of sexual material of a paraphiliac nature available for purchase, such as child pornography, suggests that paraphilias

What is a sexual dysfunction? ➤

may be far more common than clinical reports suggest. By contrast, clinical psychologists frequently work with individuals suffering from sexual dysfunctions. **Sexual dysfunctions** are persistent, recurrent, and distressing problems involving sexual desire, sexual arousal, or the pleasure associated with sex or orgasm.

A common sexual dysfunction in men is *male erectile disorder*–the repeated inability to have or sustain an erection firm enough for coitus. The term does not apply to the failures all males have on occasion as a result of physical fatigue, illness, or drinking too much alcohol. Male erectile disorder may be physical or psychological in origin, but most cases involve some combination of the two (Ackerman & Carey, 1995; Rosen, 1996). Physical causes may include diabetes, alcoholism, and drugs such as cocaine, amphetamines, barbiturates, tranquilizers, and blood pressure medication. The most common psychological cause of erectile disorder is performance anxiety. When a man fails repeatedly to achieve an erection, his worst psychological enemy is the fear that he will not be able to have an erection when he most wants one. A number of medical treatments have been found to be effective in treating this problem (Rosen, 1996).

The most common sexual dysfunction in women is *female orgasmic disorder*–a persistent inability to reach orgasm or a delay in reaching orgasm despite adequate sexual stimulation. Some women have never been able to reach orgasm; others who were formerly orgasmic no longer can achieve orgasm. Some women are able to have orgasms only under certain circumstances or during certain types of sexual activity; others have orgasms only from time to time. Women with this disorder may be uninterested in sex, or they may still find it exciting, satisfying, and enjoyable, despite the lack of orgasms.

Drug treatments for sexual dysfunctions in both men and women have proved successful. For men, the drug *sildenafil citrate (Viagra)* has proven effective in restoring erectile function. And orgasmic disorders and other sexual dysfunctions in women are increasingly being treated with hormones such as *dehydroepiandrosterone (DHEA)* (Munarriz et al., 2002). However, experts in sexual dysfunction point out that biochemical treatments may restore or enhance physiological functions, but other interventions, including individual and couples therapy, are required to improve sufferers' intimate relationships (Besharat, 2001; Heiman, 2002; Lieblum, 2002).

Another important aspect of treatment for sexual dysfunction concerns the link between depression and sexual dysfunction in both men and women (Seidman, 2002). Depression is both a cause and an effect of sexual dysfunctions. Consequently, sexual dysfunction researchers often advise health professionals to question patients who complain of sexual difficulties about factors that may indicate the presence of depression. Antidepressant drugs, however, often increase the incidence of sexual difficulties (Coleman et al., 2001). Thus, experts advocate combined biochemical and psychological interventions that address both mood and sexual functioning for depressed patients (Montejo et al., 2001).

sexual dysfunction
A persistent or recurrent problem that causes marked distress and interpersonal difficulty and that may involve any or some combination of the following: sexual desire, sexual arousal, the pleasure associated with sex or orgasm.

personality disorder
A continuing, inflexible, maladaptive pattern of behaving and relating to others that causes great distress or impaired functioning and differs significantly from the patterns expected in the person's culture.

Personality Disorders

Do you know someone who is impossible to get along with and who always blames others for problems? Such a person may have a **personality disorder**–a long-standing, inflexible, maladaptive pattern of behaving and relating to others, which usually begins early in childhood or adolescence (Widiger et al., 1988). People with personality disorders tend to have problems in their social relationships and at work and may experience personal distress as well. Some of these people know that their behavior causes problems in their lives, yet they seem unable to change. Most of them, however, are self-centered and do not see themselves as responsible for their difficulties. Instead, they tend to blame other people or situations for their problems.

What characteristics are shared by most people with personality disorders? ➤

There are several different types of personality disorders, but one of particular interest is antisocial personality disorder. People with **antisocial personality disorder** have a "pervasive pattern of disregard for, and violation of, the rights of others that begins in childhood or early adolescence and continues into adulthood" (American Psychiatric Association, 1994, p. 645). As children they lie, steal, vandalize, initiate

antisocial personality disorder
A disorder marked by lack of feeling for others; selfish, aggressive, irresponsible behavior; and willingness to break the law, lie, cheat, or exploit others for personal gain.

Apply It! Overcoming the Fear of Public Speaking

Do you break out in a cold sweat and start trembling when you have to speak in public? If so, you're in good company: Fear of public speaking is the number one fear reported by American adults in surveys. More people fear public speaking than flying, sickness, or even death!

What causes it? Fear of public speaking is a form of performance anxiety, a common type of social phobia. Much of the fear of public speaking stems from fear of being embarrassed or being judged negatively by others. Some people cope with this fear by trying to avoid situations in which they may be required to speak in public. This can adversely affect their professional lives and close off opportunities to advance in their careers. A more practical approach is to examine the incorrect beliefs that can cause fear of public speaking and then take specific steps to overcome it. Here are some incorrect beliefs associated with public speaking (Orman, 1996):

- To succeed, you need to be perfect. (Not true; no audience expects perfection.)

- A good speaker presents as many facts and details about the subject as possible. (Not true; all you need is two or three main points.)

- If some members of the audience aren't paying attention, you need to do something about it. (Not true; you can't please everyone, and it's a waste of time to try to do so.)

What can you do? Some of the steps you can take to manage fear of public speaking deal with how you present yourself to your audience; others focus on what's going on inside you. Here are some of the many suggestions offered by experts (Toastmasters International, 2003):

- *Know your material well.* Practice aloud and revise your speech if necessary.

- *Visualize your speech.* Imagine yourself giving your speech in a confident, clear manner.

- *Relax.* Reduce your tension by doing deep breathing or relaxation exercises.

- *Be familiar with the place where you will speak.* Arrive early and practice using the microphone and any other equipment you plan to use.

- *Connect with the audience.* Greet some members of the audience as they arrive; then speak to them as if they were a group of friends.

- *Project confidence through your posture.* Stand or sit in a self-assured manner, smile, and make eye contact with the audience.

- *Focus on your message, not on yourself.* Turn your attention away from your nervousness and focus on the purpose of your speech, which is to transmit information to your audience.

- *Remember that the audience doesn't expect you to be perfect.* Don't apologize for any problems you think you have with your speech. Just be yourself.

Applying these few simple tips, you can overcome nervousness and speak confidently on any topic—even on the spur of the moment. ■

---

fights, skip school, run away from home, and may be physically cruel to others and to animals (Arehart-Treichel, 2002). By early adolescence they usually drink excessively, use drugs, and engage in promiscuous sex. As adults, they cannot keep a job, act as a responsible parent, honor financial commitments, or obey the law.

Many individuals with antisocial personality disorder are intelligent and may seem charming and very likable at first. They are good con men, and they are more often men–5.8% of the U.S. male population but less than 1.3% of the U.S. female population has this disorder (Kessler et al., 1994). Checkley (1941), one of the first to study antisocial personality, revealed that persons with the disorder seem to lack the ability to love or feel loyalty and compassion toward others. They do not appear to have a conscience and feel little or no guilt or remorse no matter how cruel or despicable their actions might be. As Hare (1995) puts it, they "use charm, manipulation, intimidation, and violence to control others and satisfy their own selfish needs" (p. 4).

Brain-imaging studies suggest that people with antisocial personality disorder do not comprehend the emotional significance of words and images (Hare, 1995). They show the same level of arousal, measured by EEG recordings of brain activity, whether confronting neutral stimuli (words such as *chair, table,* and *stone*) or emotionally charged stimuli (words such as *cancer, rape,* and *murder*). Such findings suggest a neurophysiological basis for the lack of normal empathic responses in most individuals with antisocial personality disorder (Habel et al., 2002). Some experts estimate that as many as 20% of people who are in prisons in the United States may have this disorder.

Summarize It !

What Is Abnormal?

➤ **What criteria can be used to differentiate normal from abnormal behavior?**

Behavior may be considered abnormal if it deviates radically from what is considered normal in one's own culture, if it leads to personal distress or impaired functioning, or if it results in one's being a danger to self and/or others.

➤ **What are various perspectives that attempt to explain the causes of psychological disorders?**

Five perspectives on the causes of psychological disorders are the biological perspective, the biopsychosocial perspective, the psychodynamic perspective, the learning perspective, and the cognitive perspective.

➤ **What is the *DSM-IV*?**

The *DSM-IV*, published by the American Psychiatric Association, is the manual that lists the criteria used in the United States to classify psychological disorders.

KEY TERMS

psychological disorder (p. 340)
DSM-IV (p. 343)

Schizophrenia

➤ **What are some of the major positive and negative symptoms of schizophrenia?**

The positive symptoms of schizophrenia are abnormal behaviors and charac-teristics including hallucinations, delusions, disorganized thinking and speech, bizarre behavior, and inappropriate affect. The negative symptoms are deficiencies in thoughts and behaviors and include social withdrawal, apathy, loss of motivation, very limited speech, slowed movements, flat affect, and poor hygiene and grooming.

➤ **What are the four types of schizophrenia?**

The four types of schizophrenia are paranoid, disorganized, catatonic, and undifferentiated schizophrenia.

➤ **What are some suggested causes of schizophrenia?**

Some suggested causes of schizophrenia are a genetic predisposition, sufficient stress in people who are predisposed to the disorder, and excessive dopamine activity in the brain.

KEY TERMS

schizophrenia (p. 343)
psychosis (p. 343)
hallucination (p. 344)
delusion (p. 344)
delusions of grandeur (p. 344)
delusions of persecution (p. 345)
paranoid schizophrenia (p. 346)
disorganized schizophrenia (p. 346)
catatonic schizophrenia (p. 346)
undifferentiated schizophrenia (p. 346)

Mood Disorders

➤ **What are the symptoms of major depressive disorder?**

Major depressive disorder is characterized by feelings of great sadness, despair, guilt, worthlessness, hopelessness, and, in extreme cases, suicidal intentions.

➤ **What are the extremes of mood suffered by those with bipolar disorder?**

Bipolar disorder is a mood disorder in which a person suffers from manic episodes (periods of extreme elation, euphoria, and hyperactivity) alternating with major depression.

➤ **What are some suggested causes of major depressive disorder and bipolar disorder?**

Some of the proposed causes of major depressive disorder and bipolar disorder are (1) a genetic predisposition, (2) an imbalance in the neurotransmitters norepinephrine and serotonin, (3) distorted and negative views of oneself, the world, and the future, and (4) stress.

KEY TERMS

mood disorders (p. 347)
major depressive disorder (p. 347)
bipolar disorder (p. 349)
manic episode (p. 349)

Anxiety Disorders

➤ **What is generalized anxiety disorder?**

Generalized anxiety disorder is characterized by chronic worry that is so severe that it interferes with the person's daily functioning.

➤ **What are the symptoms of panic disorder?**

Panic disorder is marked by recurrent, unpredictable panic attacks—attacks of overwhelming anxiety, fear, or terror, during which people experience palpitations, trembling or shaking, choking or smothering sensations, and the feeling that they are going to die or lose their sanity.

➤ **What are the three categories of phobias?**

The three categories of phobias are (1) agoraphobia, fear of being in situations where escape is impossible or help is not available in case of incapacitating anxiety; (2) social phobia, fear of social situations where one might be embarrassed or humiliated by appearing clumsy or incompetent; and (3) specific phobia, a marked fear of a specific object or situation—that is, any phobia other than agoraphobia or social phobia.

➤ **What is obsessive-compulsive disorder?**

Obsessive-compulsive disorder is characterized by obsessions (persistent, recurring, involuntary thoughts, images, or impulses that cause great distress) and/or compulsions (persistent, irresistible, irrational urges to perform an act or ritual repeatedly).

KEY TERMS

anxiety disorders (p. 351)
generalized anxiety disorder (p. 351)
panic attack (p. 352)

panic disorder (p. 352)
phobia (p. 353)
agoraphobia (p. 353)
social phobia (p. 353)
specific phobia (p. 353)
obsessive-compulsive disorder (OCD) (p. 354)
obsession (p. 354)
compulsion (p. 354)

Somatoform and Dissociative Disorders

➤ **What are two somatoform disorders, and what symptoms do they share?**

Somatoform disorders involve bodily symptoms that cannot be identified as any of the known medical conditions. Hypochondriasis involves a persistent fear that bodily symptoms are the sign of some serious disease, and conversion disorder involves a loss of motor or sensory functioning in some part of the body, as in paralysis or blindness.

➤ **What are dissociative amnesia and dissociative fugue?**

People with dissociative amnesia have a loss of memory for limited periods of their life or for their entire personal identity. In dissociative fugue, people forget their entire identity, travel away from home, and may assume a new identity somewhere else.

➤ **What are some of the identifying symptoms of dissociative identity disorder?**

Dissociative identity disorder is a disorder in which two or more distinct, unique personalities occur in the same person, each taking over at different times. Most patients are females who have been victims of early, severe physical and/or sexual abuse.

KEY TERMS

somatoform disorders (p. 355)
hypochondriasis (p. 355)
conversion disorder (p. 355)
dissociative disorders (p. 355)
dissociative amnesia (p. 355)
dissociative fugue (p. 356)
dissociative identity disorder (DID) (p. 356)

Other Psychological Disorders

➤ **What is a sexual dysfunction?**

A sexual dysfunction is a persistent, recurrent, and distressing problem involving sexual desire, sexual arousal, or orgasm.

➤ **What characteristics are shared by most people with personality disorders?**

People with personality disorders have long-standing, inflexible, maladaptive patterns of behavior that cause problems in their social relationships and at work and often cause personal distress. Such people seem unable to change, and they blame others for their problems.

KEY TERMS

sexual dysfunction (p. 358)
personality disorder (p. 358)
antisocial personality disorder (p. 358)

Surf It !

Want to be sure you've absorbed the material in Chapter 12, "Psychological Disorders," before the big test? Visiting **www.ablongman.com/ woodmastering1e** can put a top grade within your reach. The site is loaded with free practice tests, flashcards, activities, and links to help you review your way to an A.

Companion Website

Study Guide for Chapter 12 !

Answers to all the Study Guide questions are provided at the end of the book.

Section One: Chapter Review

1. It is relatively easy to differentiate normal behavior from abnormal behavior. (true/false)

2. The *DSM-IV* is a manual that is published by the American Psychiatric Association and is used to
   a. diagnose psychological disorders.
   b. explain the causes of psychological disorders.
   c. outline the treatments for various psychological disorders.
   d. assess the effectiveness of treatment programs.

3. Match the perspective with its suggested cause of abnormal behavior.
   ____ (1) faulty learning
   ____ (2) unconscious, unresolved conflicts
   ____ (3) genetic inheritance or biochemical or structural abnormalities in the brain
   ____ (4) faulty thinking
   a. psychodynamic
   b. biological
   c. learning
   d. cognitive

4. Match the symptom of schizophrenia with the example.
   ____ (1) Brendon believes he is Moses.
   ____ (2) Dina thinks her family is spreading rumors about her.
   ____ (3) Avi hears voices cursing him.
   ____ (4) Dean laughs at tragedies and cries when he hears a joke.
   a. delusions of grandeur
   b. hallucinations
   c. inappropriate affect
   d. delusions of persecution

5. There is substantial research evidence that all of the following have roles as causes of schizophrenia *except*
   a. genetic factors.
   b. stress in people predisposed to the disorder.
   c. excessive dopamine activity.
   d. unhealthy family interaction patterns.

6. Match the subtype of schizophrenia with the example.
   ____ (1) Amy stands for hours in the same strange position.
   ____ (2) Trevin believes the CIA is plotting to kill him.
   ____ (3) Matt makes silly faces, laughs a lot, and masturbates openly.
   ____ (4) Francesca has the symptoms of schizophrenia but does not fit any one type.

   a. paranoid schizophrenia
   b. disorganized schizophrenia
   c. catatonic schizophrenia
   d. undifferentiated schizophrenia

7. Monteil has periods in which he is so depressed that he becomes suicidal. At other times he is energetic and euphoric. He would probably receive the diagnosis of
   a. antisocial personality disorder.
   b. dissociative fugue.
   c. bipolar disorder.
   d. major depressive disorder.

8. Match the type of factor with the proposed cause of depression:
   ____ (1) negative thoughts about oneself, the world, and one's future
   ____ (2) hereditary predisposition or biochemical imbalance
   ____ (3) negative life events
   a. stress
   b. cognitive factor
   c. biological factor

9. Drugs are seldom used in the treatment of mood disorders. (true/false)

10. The suicide rate is lower for
   a. males than for females.
   b. African American males than for White males.
   c. the elderly than for teenagers.
   d. people who suffer psychological disorders than for those who do not.

11. Anxiety disorders are the least common of all psychological disorders. (true/false)

12. Phobias may result from frightening experiences and observational learning. (true/false)

13. Obsessive-compulsive disorder appears to be caused primarily by psychological rather than biological factors. (true/false)

14. Match the psychological disorder with the example.
   ____ (1) Lana refuses to eat in front of others for fear her hand will shake.
   ____ (2) Ronin is excessively anxious about his health and his job, even though there is no concrete reason to be.
   ____ (3) Kyla has been housebound for 4 years.
   ____ (4) Jackson gets hysterical when a dog approaches him.

_____ (5) Lauren has incapacitating attacks of anxiety that come on her suddenly.

_____ (6) Michael repeatedly checks his doors, windows, and appliances before he goes to bed.

a. panic disorder
b. agoraphobia
c. specific phobia
d. generalized anxiety disorder
e. social phobia
f. obsessive-compulsive disorder

15. Somatoform disorders have physiological rather than psychological causes. (true/false)

16. Dissociative disorders are often associated with trauma. (true/false)

17. Match the psychological disorder with the example.

_____ (1) Jan is convinced he has some serious disease, although his doctors can find nothing physically wrong.

_____ (2) Lonnie is found far away from his home town, calling himself by another name and having no memory of his past.

_____ (3) Natalia suddenly loses her sight, but doctors can find no physical reason for the problem.

_____ (4) Colane has no memory of being in the boat with other family members the day her older brother drowned.

_____ (5) Cassandra has no memory for blocks of time in her life and often finds clothing in her closet that she cannot remember buying.

a. dissociative identity disorder
b. dissociative fugue
c. dissociative amnesia
d. hypochondriasis
e. conversion disorder

18. (Sexual dysfunctions, Paraphilias) are disorders in which sexual urges, fantasies, and behaviors involve children, other nonconsenting partners, or objects.

19. Which statement is true of personality disorders?
a. Personality disorders usually begin in adulthood.
b. Persons with these disorders usually realize that they have a problem.
c. Personality disorders typically cause problems in social relationships and at work.
d. Persons with these disorders typically seek professional help.

20. Bruce lies, cheats, and exploits others without feeling guilty. His behavior best fits the diagnosis of _____ personality disorder.
a. avoidant
b. histrionic
c. antisocial
d. narcissistic

Section Two: Identify the Disorder

Name the disorder characterized by each set of symptoms.

Symptoms   **Disorder**

1. Markedly diminished interest or pleasure in all or most activities, combined with psychomotor disturbances, fatigue, insomnia, feelings of worthlessness, and recurrent thoughts of death   _____

2. Grossly disorganized behavior combined with inappropriate affect, disturbed speech and loose associations, and delusions of grandeur—for example, a belief that one is working for a secret government agency and is being followed by foreign spies   _____

3. Intense mood swings, ranging from euphoric and hyperactive highs marked by delusions of grandeur to extreme depression   _____

4. Intense fear of being in a situation from which immediate escape is not possible or help is not available in the case of panic   _____

5. Complete loss of the ability to recall personal information or past experiences, with no physical explanation for the problem   _____

6. A pattern of unstable and intense interpersonal relationships combined with impulsivity, inappropriate and intense anger, a poor self-image, and recurrent thoughts of suicide

_____

7. Problems involving sexual desire, sexual arousal, or the pleasure associated with sex or orgasm

_____

8. Spending excessive amounts of time engaged in daily rituals such as counting and cleaning, accompanied by obsessions

_____

Section Three: Fill In the Blank

1. The _____ perspective views abnormal behavior as a symptom of an underlying physical disorder.

2. The most serious psychological disorder is _____ .

3. Hallucinations, delusions, and disorganized speech are considered to be _____ symptoms of schizophrenia.

4. Ricardo believes that there are three men who follow him around and whisper messages in his ear, telling him to do bad things. Ricardo's false belief is called a _____ .

5. Symptoms such as social withdrawal, apathy, slowed movements, and limited speech are examples of the _____ symptoms of schizophrenia.

6. Alice has been unable to make herself go to work for several weeks. She lies in bed for hours wishing for death. Alice may be suffering from _____ _____ _____ .

7. Yolanda called her best friend one night at 2 a.m., extremely excited about her great idea: She was going to have Creed perform in her backyard for her birthday. She planned to call the band members as soon as she got off the phone with her friend. Yolanda was probably having a _____ episode.

8. Hypochondriasis is an example of a _____ disorder.

9. Taryn experiences sudden and unexplained waves of fear that seem to come out of nowhere. She is suffering from _____ disorder.

10. An obsession is characterized by _____ _____ ; a compulsion involves an _____ _____ _____ _____ _____ .

11. There seems to be no physical reason for Jason's paralysis. It is likely that he is suffering from a _____ disorder.

12. Dissociative identity disorder is the new term for what used to be called _____ _____ disorder.

13. Histrionic, borderline, antisocial, and narcissistic disorders are collectively known as _____ disorders.

14. Kim has never felt comfortable with her gender and believes she should have been a male. According to the _DSM-IV_ she has _____ _____ disorder.

15. _____ are sensory perceptions in the absence of any external stimulation, for example, seeing things that are not really there.

16. A _____ is a persistent, irrational fear of an object, situation, or activity that a person feels compelled to avoid.

17. The _____ personality disorder is marked by a lack of feeling for others, selfishness, aggressive and irresponsible behavior, and a willingness to break the law or exploit others for personal gain.

Section Four: Comprehensive Practice Test

1. Which perspective sees abnormal behavior as a symptom of an underlying physical disorder?
   a. cognitive   **c.** biological
   b. psychoanalytic   **d.** behavioral

2. Which perspective sees abnormal behavior as the result of faulty and negative thinking?
   a. psychoanalytic   **c.** behavioral
   b. cognitive   **d.** biological

3. Which perspective sees abnormal behavior as the result of early childhood experiences and unconscious sexual and aggressive conflicts?

   a. cognitive   **c.** humanistic
   b. biological   **d.** psychoanalytic

4. Which perspective sees psychological disorders as resulting from both physical and psychological causes?
   a. cognitive   **c.** biological
   b. biopsychosocial   **d.** behavioral

5. Psychosis is a loss of contact with reality. (true/false)

6. Panic disorder, phobia, and obsessive-compulsive disorder are all examples of _____ disorders.
   a. neurotic   **c.** personality
   b. anxiety   **d.** somatoform

7. Dawn is convinced that she has a disease and goes from one doctor to another searching for a diagnosis; however, every doctor she consults says there is nothing physically wrong with her. Dawn is suffering from
   a. hypochondriasis.
   b. dissociative identity disorder.
   c. a conversion disorder.
   d. body dysmorphic disorder.

8. Dissociative amnesia, characterized by loss of memory of one's identity, is generally brought on by physical trauma. (true/false)

9. A common early experience of patients with dissociative identity disorder is
   a. drug use by their mother while pregnant.
   b. measles or mumps when young.
   c. parental divorce.
   d. early physical and/or sexual abuse.

10. Hallucinations, delusions, and disorganized thinking and speech are _____ symptoms of schizophrenia.
    a. negative   c. dissociative
    b. positive   d. psychotic

11. Thao's belief that he is a secret agent for the devil is a good example of a delusion. (true/false)

12. A patient who sits completely still for hours as if he were in a stupor and sometimes experiences periods of great agitation and excitement is suffering from _____ schizophrenia.
    a. disorganized   c. paranoid
    b. undifferentiated   d. catatonic

13. Major depression and bipolar disorder are examples of _____ disorders.
    a. personality   c. mood
    b. psychotic   d. emotional

14. Depression is diagnosed more often in women than in men. (true/false)

15. _____ is characterized by periods of inflated self-esteem, wild optimism, and hyperactivity known as manic episodes.
    a. Schizophrenia
    b. Major depression
    c. Borderline personality disorder
    d. Bipolar disorder

16. The risk of suicide is especially high in patients who suffer from
    a. catatonic schizophrenia.   c. depression.
    b. paraphilia.   d. simple phobia.

17. The psychoanalytic perspective asserts that depression stems from faulty thinking and distorted perceptions. (true/false)

18. Depression seems to be the result of
    a. biological factors only.
    b. both biological and environmental factors.
    c. environmental factors only.
    d. poor parenting in early childhood.

19. Sexual masochism, sexual sadism, and exhibitionism are all examples of
    a. paraphilias.
    b. gender identity disorders.
    c. sexual dysfunctions.
    d. pedophilias.

Section Five: Critical Thinking

1. Formulate a specific plan that will help you recognize and avoid the five cognitive traps that contribute to unhealthy thinking. You might enlist the help of a friend to monitor your negative statements.

2. Some psychological disorders are more common in women (depression, agoraphobia, and simple phobia), and some are more common in men (antisocial personality disorder and substance abuse). Give some possible reasons for such gender differences in the prevalence of these disorders. Support your answer.

3. There is continuing controversy over whether specific psychological disorders are chiefly biological in origin (nature) or result primarily from learning and experience (nurture). Select any two disorders from this chapter, and prepare arguments for both the nature and nurture positions for both disorders.

chapter

13

Therapies

Bill, a 21-year-old college student, suffered from a debilitating phobia—an intense fear of any kind of sudden loud noise. He had become so anxious about possible exposure to noises that he had almost no social life. Balloons were especially frightening (they might pop!), so he avoided birthday parties, weddings, and other events where balloons might be present. Bill's girlfriend insisted that he get help.

On the first day of his therapy, two people led Bill—with his permission—into a small room filled with 100 large balloons. One person stood close to Bill, while the other person explained that he was going to begin popping the balloons. While some 50 balloons were popped with a pin, Bill shook uncontrollably, tears streaming down his face. Bill had to endure the popping of another 50 balloons before he was allowed to leave. And he returned for the next 2 days for still more balloon popping.

During the course of the 3 days, Bill became progressively less fearful and was eventually able to join in, stepping on hundreds of balloons and popping them. A year later, in a follow-up interview, Bill reported that he experienced no distress in the presence of balloons and no longer avoided situations where he might encounter them. Neither was he ill at ease when he sat relatively near a fireworks display on the Fourth of July. (Adapted from Houlihan et al., 1993.)

psychotherapy
The treatment for psychological disorders that uses psychological rather than biological means and primarily involves conversations between patient and therapist.

insight therapy
Any type of psychotherapy based on the notion that psychological well-being depends on self-understanding.

psychodynamic therapies
Therapies that attempt to uncover childhood experiences that explain a patient's current difficulties.

psychoanalysis
(SY-ko-uh-NAL-ul-sis) Freud's method of psychotherapy; uses free association, dream analysis, and transference.

free association
A psychoanalytic technique used to explore the unconscious by having patients reveal whatever thoughts or images come to mind.

> What are the basic techniques of psychoanalysis, and how are they used to help patients?

transference
An intense emotional reaction by a patient during psychoanalysis involving the display of feelings and attitudes toward the analyst that were present in a significant past relationship of the patient.

Freud's famous couch was used by his patients during psychoanalysis.

Bill's therapists were using a rapid treatment technique known as *flooding,* a form of behavior therapy in which the patient agrees to be instantly and totally immersed in the feared situation or surrounded by the feared object. Flooding is known to be effective in treating various types of phobias (Coles & Heinberg, 2000). But flooding is only one of the many effective therapies you will learn about in this chapter.

Psychotherapy uses psychological, rather than biological, means to treat emotional and behavioral disorders. The practice of psychotherapy has grown and changed enormously in the more than 100 years that have passed since Freud and his colleagues began using it.

Insight Therapies

Some forms of psychotherapy are collectively referred to as **insight therapies** because their assumption is that psychological well-being depends on self-understanding—understanding of one's own thoughts, emotions, motives, behavior, and coping mechanisms.

Psychodynamic Therapies

Psychodynamic therapies attempt to uncover childhood experiences that explain a patient's current difficulties. The techniques associated with the first such therapy, Freud's **psychoanalysis,** are still used by psychodynamic therapists today (Epstein et al., 2001). One such technique is **free association,** in which the patient is asked to reveal whatever thoughts, feelings, or images come to mind, no matter how trivial, embarrassing, or terrible they might seem. The analyst then pieces together the free-flowing associations, explains their meaning, and helps the patient gain insight into the thoughts and behavior that are troubling him or her. But some patients avoid revealing certain painful or embarrassing thoughts while engaging in free association, a phenomenon Freud called *resistance.* Resistance may take the form of halting speech during free association, "forgetting" appointments with the analyst, or even arriving late.

Dream analysis is another technique used by psychoanalysts. Freud believed that areas of emotional concern repressed in waking life are sometimes expressed in symbolic form in dreams. And Freud claimed that patient behavior may have a symbolic quality as well. At some point during psychoanalysis, Freud said, the patient reacts to the analyst with the same feelings that were present in another significant relationship—usually that with the patient's mother or father. This reaction he called **transference.** Freud believed that encouraging patients to achieve transference was an essential part of psychotherapy. He claimed that transference allows the patient to relive troubling experiences from the past with the analyst as parent substitute, thereby resolving any hidden conflicts.

Many therapists today practice *brief psychodynamic therapy* in which the therapist and patient decide on the issues to explore at the outset rather than waiting for them to emerge in the course of treatment. The therapist assumes a more active role and places more emphasis on the present than in traditional psychoanalysis. Brief psychodynamic therapy may require only one or two visits per week for as few as 12 to 20 weeks. In a review of 11 well-controlled studies, Crits-Christoph (1992) found brief psychodynamic therapy to be as effective as other psychotherapies. And more recent research has also supported this evaluation (Hager et al., 2000).

Carl Rogers (at far right) facilitates discussion in a therapy group.

Humanistic Therapies

Humanistic therapies assume that people have the ability and freedom to lead rational lives and make rational choices. **Person-centered therapy,** developed by Carl Rogers (1951), is one of the most frequently used humanistic therapies. According to this view, people are innately good and, if allowed to develop naturally, will grow toward *self-actualization*–the realization of their inner potential. The humanistic perspective suggests that psychological disorders result when a person's natural tendency toward self-actualization is blocked either by the person or by others. In the 1940s and 1950s, person-centered therapy enjoyed a strong following among psychologists.

 What are the role and the goal of the therapist in person-centered therapy?

The person-centered therapist attempts to create an accepting climate–based on unconditional positive regard for the client. The therapist also empathizes with the client's concerns and emotions. When the client speaks, the therapist follows by restating or reflecting back the client's ideas and feelings. Using these techniques, the therapist allows the direction of the therapy sessions to be controlled by the client. Rogers rejected all forms of therapy that cast the therapist in the role of expert and the client in the role of a patient who expects the therapist to prescribe something that "cures" his or her problem. Thus, person-centered therapy is called **nondirective therapy.**

person-centered therapy
A nondirective humanistic therapy in which the therapist creates a warm, accepting climate, freeing clients to be themselves and releasing their natural tendency toward positive growth.

nondirective therapy
An approach in which the therapist acts to facilitate growth, giving understanding and support rather than proposing solutions, answering questions, or actively directing the course of therapy.

Gestalt Therapy

Gestalt therapy, developed by Fritz Perls (1969), emphasizes the importance of clients' fully experiencing, in the present moment, their feelings, thoughts, and actions and then taking responsibility for them. The goal of Gestalt therapy is to help clients achieve a more integrated self and become more authentic and self-accepting. In addition, they must learn to assume personal responsibility for their behavior, rather than blaming society, past experiences, parents, or others.

 What is the major emphasis of Gestalt therapy?

Gestalt therapy is a **directive therapy,** one in which the therapist takes an active role in determining the course of therapy sessions. The well-known phrase "getting in touch with your feelings" is an ever-present objective of the Gestalt therapist. Perls suggested that individuals who are in need of therapy carry around a heavy load of unfinished business, which may be in the form of resentment toward or conflicts with parents, siblings, lovers, employers, or others. If not resolved, these conflicts are carried forward into the person's present relationships. One method for dealing with unfinished business is the "empty chair" technique (Paivio & Greenberg, 1995). The client sits facing an empty chair and imagines, for example, that a wife, husband, father, or mother sits there, and then proceeds to tell the chair what he or she truly feels about that person. Next, the client trades places and sits in the empty chair and role-plays what the imagined person's response would be to what the client has said.

Gestalt therapy
A therapy that was originated by Fritz Perls and that emphasizes the importance of clients' fully experiencing, in the present moment, their feelings, thoughts, and actions and taking personal responsibility for their behavior.

directive therapy
An approach in which the therapist takes an active role in determining the course of therapy sessions and provides answers and suggestions to the patient.

Relationship Therapies

Relationship therapies look not only at the individual's internal struggles but also at his or her interpersonal relationships. Some deliberately create new relationships for people, relationships that can support them in their efforts to address psychological problems.

Interpersonal Therapy

Interpersonal therapy (IPT) is a brief psychotherapy that has proven very effective in the treatment of depression (Elkin et al., 1989, 1995; Klerman et al., 1984). This type of therapy is designed specifically to help patients cope with four types of problems commonly associated with major depression:

What four problems commonly associated with major depression is interpersonal therapy designed to treat?

1. *Unusual or severe responses to the death of a loved one.* The therapist and patient discuss the patient's relationship with the deceased person and feelings (such as guilt) that may be associated with the death.
2. *Interpersonal role disputes.* The therapist helps the patient understand others' points of view and explore options for bringing about change.
3. *Difficulty in adjusting to a role transition such as divorce, a career change, or retirement.* The patient is helped to see the change not as a threat but rather as a challenge and an opportunity for growth that can be mastered.
4. *Deficits in interpersonal skills.* Through role-playing and analysis of the patient's communication style, the therapist tries to help the patient develop the interpersonal skills necessary to initiate and sustain relationships.

Interpersonal therapy is relatively brief, consisting of 12 to 16 weekly sessions. A large study conducted by the National Institute of Mental Health found this type of psychotherapy to be an effective treatment, even for severe depression, and one with a low dropout rate (Elkin et al., 1989, 1995). Research also indicates that patients who recover from major depression can enjoy a longer period without relapse when they continue with monthly sessions of interpersonal therapy (Frank et al., 1991).

Couple and Family Therapy

There are therapists who specialize in treating the troubled family. Some therapists work with couples in *couple therapy* to help them resolve their difficulties. In **family therapy,** parents and children enter therapy as a group. The therapist pays attention to the dynamics of the family unit—how family members communicate, how they act toward one another, and how they view each other. The goal of the therapist is to help the family members reach agreement on certain changes that will help heal the wounds of the family unit, improve communication patterns, and create more understanding and harmony within the group.

What is the goal of couple therapy and family therapy?

Couple or family therapy appears to have positive effects in treating a number of disorders and clinical problems (Lebow & Gurman, 1995). When used along with medication, family therapy can be beneficial in the treatment of schizophrenia and can reduce relapse rates (Carpenter, 1996). Patients with schizophrenia are more likely to relapse if their family members express emotions, attitudes, and behaviors that involve criticism, hostility, or emotional overinvolvement (Linszen et al., 1997). This pattern is labeled *high in expressed emotion,* or *high EE* (Falloon, 1988; Jenkins & Karno, 1992). Family therapy can help other family members modify their behavior toward the patient. Family therapy also seems to be the most favorable setting for treating adolescent drug abuse (Lebow & Gurman, 1995).

Group Therapy

Group therapy is a form of therapy in which several clients (usually seven to ten) meet regularly with one or more therapists to resolve personal problems. Besides

Group therapy can give individuals a sense of belonging and an opportunity to give and receive emotional support.

being less expensive than individual therapy, group therapy gives the individual a sense of belonging, an opportunity to express feelings, to get feedback from others in the group, and to give and receive help and emotional support. Learning that others share their problems leaves people feeling less alone and ashamed. A review of studies comparing prisoners who participated in group therapy to those who did not found that group participation was helpful for a variety of problems, including anxiety, depression, and low self-esteem (Morgan & Flora, 2002).

A variant of group therapy is the *self-help group*. About 12 million people in the United States participate in roughly 500,000 self-help groups, most of which focus on a single problem such as substance abuse or depression. Self-help groups usually are not led by professional therapists. They are simply groups of people who share a common problem and meet to give and receive support. One of the oldest and best-known self-help groups is Alcoholics Anonymous (AA), which claims 1.5 million members worldwide. Self-help groups patterned after Alcoholics Anonymous have been formed to help individuals overcome many other addictive behaviors, from overeating (Overeaters Anonymous) to gambling (Gamblers Anonymous). One study indicated that people suffering from anxiety-based problems were helped by a commercial multimedia self-help program called "Attacking Anxiety." Of the 176 individuals who participated in the study, 62 were reported to have achieved clinically significant improvement, and another 40 reported some improvement (Finch et al., 2000).

What are some advantages of group therapy?

Behavior Therapies

A **behavior therapy** is a treatment approach consistent with the learning perspective on psychological disorders—that abnormal behavior is learned. Instead of viewing the maladaptive behavior as a symptom of some underlying disorder, the behavior therapist sees the behavior itself as the disorder. If a person comes to a therapist with a fear of flying, that fear of flying is seen as the problem. Behavior therapies use learning principles to eliminate inappropriate or maladaptive behaviors and replace them with more adaptive ones, an approach referred to as **behavior modification.** The goal is to change the troublesome behavior, not to change the individual's personality structure or to search for the origin of the problem behavior.

What is a behavior therapy?

Behavior Modification Techniques Based on Operant Conditioning

Behavior modification techniques based on operant conditioning seek to control the consequences of behavior. *Extinction* of an undesirable behavior is accomplished by

behavior therapy
A treatment approach employing the principles of operant conditioning, classical conditioning, and/or observational learning theory to eliminate inappropriate or maladaptive behaviors and replace them with more adaptive ones.

behavior modification
The systematic application of learning principles to help a person eliminate undesirable behaviors and/or acquire more adaptive behaviors; also called *behavior therapy.*

> Time out is a behavior modification technique that is based on the idea of removing reinforcers.

What operant conditioning techniques do behavior therapists use to modify behavior?

terminating, or withholding, the reinforcement that is maintaining that behavior (Lerman & Iwata, 1996). Behavior therapists also seek to reinforce any desirable behavior in order to increase its frequency. Institutional settings such as hospitals, prisons, and school classrooms are well suited to these techniques, because they provide a restricted environment in which the consequences of behavior can be more strictly controlled.

Some institutions use **token economies,** which reward appropriate behavior with tokens (such as poker chips, play money, or gold stars). These tokens can later be exchanged for desired goods (such as candy, gum, or cigarettes) and/or privileges (such as weekend passes, free time, or participation in desirable activities). Sometimes individuals are fined a given number of tokens for undesirable behavior. For decades, mental hospitals have successfully used token economies with chronic schizophrenics to improve their self-care skills and social interaction (Ayllon & Azrin, 1965, 1968).

Another effective method used to eliminate undesirable behavior, especially in children and adolescents, is **time out** (Brantner & Doherty, 1983). Children are told in advance that if they engage in certain undesirable behaviors, they will be removed from the situation and will have to pass a period of time (usually no more than 15 minutes) in a place containing no reinforcers (no television, books, toys, friends, and so on). Theoretically, the undesirable behavior will stop if it is no longer followed by attention or any other positive reinforcers.

Behavior therapies based on operant conditioning have been particularly effective in modifying some behaviors of seriously disturbed people. Although these techniques do not cure schizophrenia, autism, or mental retardation, they can increase the frequency of desirable behaviors and decrease the frequency of undesirable behaviors in individuals who suffer from these conditions. For example, a large proportion of people who suffer from schizophrenia smoke cigarettes. Monetary reinforcement has been found to be as effective as nicotine patches for the reduction of smoking among them (Tidey et al., 2002). Sometimes, modifying such behaviors enables the family members of people with schizophrenia to accept and care for them more easily.

Behavior modification techniques can also be used by people who want to break bad habits such as smoking and overeating or to develop good habits such as a regular exercise regime. If you want to modify any of your behaviors, devise a reward system for desirable behaviors, and remember the principles of shaping. Reward gradual changes in the direction of your ultimate goal. If you are trying to develop better eating habits, don't try to change a lifetime of bad habits all at once. Begin with a small step such as substituting frozen yogurt for ice cream. Set realistic weekly goals that you are likely to be able to achieve.

token economy
A behavior modification technique that reinforces appropriate behaviors with tokens that can be exchanged later for desired objects, activities, and/or privileges.

time out
A behavior modification technique used to decrease the frequency of undesirable behavior by withdrawing an individual from all reinforcement for a period of time.

 Flooding can be a useful treatment for phobias, such as fear of heights.

Therapies Based on Classical Conditioning

Therapies based on classical conditioning can be used to rid people of fears and other undesirable behaviors. One of the pioneers of this approach, psychiatrist Joseph Wolpe (1958, 1973), reasoned that if he could get people to relax and stay relaxed while they thought about a feared object, person, place, or situation, they could conquer their fear or phobia. In Wolpe's therapy, **systematic desensitization,** clients are trained in deep muscle relaxation. Then they confront a hierarchy of fears—a graduated series of anxiety-producing situations—either *in vivo* (in real life) or in imagination, until they can remain relaxed even in the presence of the most feared situation. The technique can be used for everything from fear of animals to claustrophobia, test anxiety, and social and other situational fears. Try creating such a hierarchy in *Try It! 13.1* (on page 374).

What behavior therapies are based on classical conditioning?

Many experiments, demonstrations, and case reports confirm that systematic desensitization is a highly successful treatment for eliminating fears and phobias in a relatively short time (Kalish, 1981; Rachman & Wilson, 1980). This technique has proved effective for specific problems such as test anxiety, stage fright, and anxiety related to sexual disorders.

How do therapists use systematic desensitization to rid people of fears?

Flooding, a behavior therapy used in the treatment of phobias, was the type of therapy used to help Bill, who was featured in this chapter's opening story. It involves exposing clients to the feared object or event (or asking them to vividly imagine it) for an extended period until their anxiety decreases. Clients are exposed to the fear all at once, not gradually as in systematic desensitization. An individual with a fear of heights, for example, might have to go onto the roof of a tall building and remain there until the fear subsided.

 What is flooding?

Flooding sessions typically last from 30 minutes to 2 hours and should not be terminated until patients are markedly less afraid than they were at the beginning of the session. Additional sessions are required until the fear response is extinguished or reduced to an acceptable level. It is rare for a patient to need more than six treatment sessions (Marshall & Segal, 1988). *In vivo* flooding, the real-life experience, works faster and is more effective than simply imagining the feared object or event (Chambless & Goldstein, 1979; Marks, 1972). For example, a person who fears flying would be better off taking an actual plane trip than just thinking about one.

Exposure and Response Prevention

Exposure and response prevention has been successful in treating obsessive-compulsive disorder (Baer, 1996; Foa, 1995; Rhéaume & Ladouceur, 2000). The first component of this therapy involves *exposure*—confronting patients with objects or situations they have

Try It! 13.1   A Possible Hierarchy of Fears

Use what you have learned about systematic desensitization to create a step-by-step approach to help someone overcome a fear of taking tests. The person's hierarchy of fears begins with reading in the syllabus that a test will be given and culminates in actually taking the test. Fill in successive steps, according to a possible hierarchy of fears, that will lead to the final step. One set of possible steps is given below.

Suggested Answers: (1) Preparing for each class session by reading the assigned material and/or completing any homework assignments. (2) Attending each class session and taking notes on the material the test will cover. (3) Reviewing the new notes after each class period. (4) Reviewing all class materials beginning one week before the test. (5) Reciting key information from memory the day before the test. (6) Arriving early to take the test, having gotten a good night's sleep.

Taking the test in class

6. _____
5. _____
4. _____
3. _____
2. _____
1. _____

Reading in the syllabus that a test will be given on a certain day

---

How does exposure and response prevention help people with obsessive-compulsive disorder? ▶

been avoiding because those things trigger obsessions and compulsive rituals. The second component is *response prevention,* in which patients agree to resist performing their compulsive rituals for progressively longer periods of time.

Initially, the therapist identifies the thoughts, objects, or situations that trigger the compulsive ritual. For example, touching a doorknob, a piece of unwashed fruit, or garbage might ordinarily send people with a fear of contamination to the nearest bathroom to wash their hands. Patients are gradually exposed to stimuli they find more and more distasteful and anxiety-provoking. They must agree not to perform the normal ritual (hand washing, bathing, or the like) for a specified period of time after exposure. A typical treatment course—about ten sessions over a period of 3 to 7 weeks—can bring about considerable improvement in 60–70% of patients (Jenike, 1990). And patients treated with exposure and response prevention are less likely to relapse after treatment than those treated with drugs alone (Greist, 1992). This therapy has also proved useful in the treatment of posttraumatic stress disorder (Cloitre et al., 2002).

aversion therapy
A behavior therapy in which an aversive stimulus is paired with an undesirable behavior until the behavior becomes associated with pain and discomfort.

Aversion Therapy

How does aversion therapy rid people of a harmful or undesirable behavior? ▶

Aversion therapy is used to rid clients of a harmful or socially undesirable behavior by pairing it with a painful, sickening, or otherwise aversive stimulus. Electric shock, emetics (substances that cause nausea and vomiting), or other unpleasant stimuli are paired with the undesirable behavior time after time until a strong negative association is formed and the person comes to avoid that behavior, habit, or substance. Treatment continues until the bad habit loses its appeal and becomes associated with pain or discomfort.

374

Alcoholics are sometimes given a nausea-producing substance such as Antabuse, which reacts violently with alcohol in a person's stomach, causing retching and vomiting. But for most problems, aversion therapy need not be so intense as to make a person physically ill. A controlled comparison of treatments for chronic nail biting revealed that mild aversion therapy–painting a bitter-tasting substance on the fingernails–yielded significant improvement (Allen, 1996).

Participant Modeling

Therapies derived from Albert Bandura's work on observational learning are based on the belief that people can overcome fears and acquire social skills through modeling. The most effective type of therapy based on observational learning theory is called **participant modeling** (Bandura, 1977a; Bandura et al., 1975, 1977). In this therapy, a model demonstrates the appropriate response in graduated steps, and the client attempts to imitate the model step by step, while the therapist gives encouragement and support. Most specific phobias can be extinguished in only 3 or 4 hours with participant modeling.

Cognitive Therapies

Cognitive therapies, based on the cognitive perspective toward psychological disorders, assume that maladaptive behavior can result from irrational thoughts, beliefs, and ideas, which the therapist tries to change.

Rational-Emotive Therapy

Clinical psychologist Albert Ellis (1961, 1977, 1993) developed **rational-emotive therapy** in the 1950s. Rational-emotive therapy is based on Ellis's *ABC theory*. The A refers to the activating event; the B, to the person's belief about the event; and the C, to the emotional consequence that follows. Ellis claims that it is not the event itself that causes the emotional consequence, but rather the person's belief about the event. In other words, A does not cause C; B causes C. If the belief is irrational, then the emotional consequence can be extreme distress, as illustrated in Figure 13.1 (on page 376).

Rational-emotive therapy is a directive, confrontational form of psychotherapy designed to challenge clients' irrational beliefs about themselves and others. With this form of therapy, most clients see a therapist individually, once a week, for 5 to 50 sessions. In Ellis's view, as clients begin to replace irrational beliefs with rational ones, their emotional reactions become more appropriate, less distressing, and more likely to lead to constructive behavior. One review of 28 studies showed that patients receiving rational-emotive therapy did better than those receiving no treatment or a placebo and about the same as those undergoing systematic desensitization (Engles et al., 1993).

Cognitive Therapy

Psychiatrist Aaron T. Beck (1976) claims that much of the misery endured by a depressed and anxious person can be traced to *automatic thoughts*–unreasonable but unquestioned ideas that rule the person's life ("To be happy, I must be liked by everyone"; "If people disagree with me, it means they don't like me"). Beck (1991) believes that depressed persons hold "a negative view of the present, past, and future experiences" (p. 369). These persons notice only negative, unpleasant things and jump to upsetting conclusions.

The goal of **cognitive therapy** is to help patients stop their negative thoughts as they occur and replace them with more objective thoughts. After identifying and chal-

How does participant modeling help people overcome fears?

participant modeling
A behavior therapy in which an appropriate response is modeled in graduated steps and the client attempts each step, encouraged and supported by the therapist.

cognitive therapies
Therapies that assume that maladaptive behavior can result from irrational thoughts, beliefs, and ideas, which the therapist tries to change.

What is the aim of rational-emotive therapy?

rational-emotive therapy
A directive, confrontational therapy developed by Albert Ellis and designed to challenge and modify the irrational beliefs thought to cause personal distress.

How does cognitive therapy help people overcome depression and anxiety disorders?

cognitive therapy
A therapy designed to change maladaptive behavior by changing the person's irrational thoughts, beliefs, and ideas.

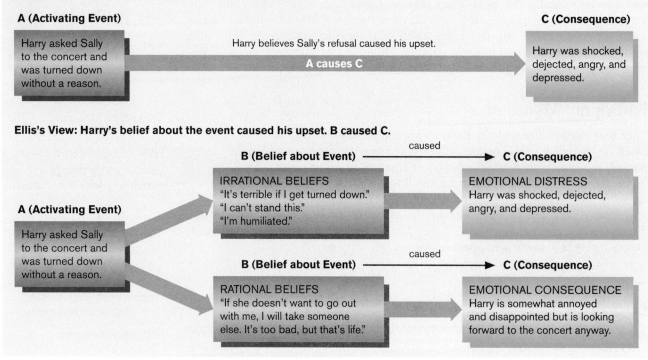

Harry's View: Sally's refusal caused his upset. A caused C.

A (Activating Event)

Harry asked Sally to the concert and was turned down without a reason.

Harry believes Sally's refusal caused his upset.
A causes C

C (Consequence)

Harry was shocked, dejected, angry, and depressed.

Ellis's View: Harry's belief about the event caused his upset. B caused C.

B (Belief about Event) —— caused —→ **C (Consequence)**

IRRATIONAL BELIEFS
"It's terrible if I get turned down."
"I can't stand this."
"I'm humiliated."

EMOTIONAL DISTRESS
Harry was shocked, dejected, angry, and depressed.

A (Activating Event)

Harry asked Sally to the concert and was turned down without a reason.

B (Belief about Event) —— caused —→ **C (Consequence)**

RATIONAL BELIEFS
"If she doesn't want to go out with me, I will take someone else. It's too bad, but that's life."

EMOTIONAL CONSEQUENCE
Harry is somewhat annoyed and disappointed but is looking forward to the concert anyway.

➤ **Figure 13.1**

The ABCs of Rational-Emotive Therapy

Rational-emotive therapy teaches clients that it is not the activating event (A) that causes the upsetting consequences (C). Rather, it is the client's beliefs (B) about the activating event. Irrational beliefs cause emotional distress, according to Albert Ellis. Rational-emotive therapists help clients identify their irrational beliefs and replace them with rational ones.

Aaron T. Beck, an early proponent of cognitive therapy.

lenging patients' irrational thoughts, the therapist sets up a plan and guides patients so that their own experience can provide actual evidence from the real world to refute their false beliefs. Patients are given homework assignments, such as keeping track of automatic thoughts and the feelings evoked by them and substituting more rational thoughts. When cognitive therapy is combined with behavioral techniques such as relaxation training or exposure, it is called *cognitive-behavioral therapy*.

Cognitive therapy is brief, usually lasting only 10 to 20 sessions (Beck, 1976). This therapy has been researched extensively and is reported to be highly successful in the treatment of mild to moderately depressed patients (Holloa et al., 2002; Thase et al., 1991). There is some evidence that depressed people who have received cognitive therapy are less likely to relapse than those who have been treated with antidepressant drugs (Evans et al., 1992; Scott, 1996).

Cognitive therapy has also been shown to be effective for treating panic disorder (Barlow, 1997; Power et al., 2000). Cognitive therapy teaches patients to change the catastrophic interpretations of their symptoms and thereby prevent the symptoms from escalating into panic. Studies have shown that about 90% of patients with panic disorder are panic-free after 3 months of cognitive therapy (Robins & Hayes, 1993). Not only does cognitive therapy have a low dropout rate and a low relapse rate, but patients often continue to improve even after the treatment is completed (Öst & Westling, 1995). Also, cognitive therapy has proved effective as a treatment for generalized anxiety disorder (Beck, 1993; Wetherell et al., 2003), obsessive-compulsive disorder (OCD) (Abramowitz, 1997), cocaine addiction (Carroll et al., 1994), and bulimia (Agras et al., 2000). Some research even indicates that cognitive therapy is effective in treating both negative and positive symptoms of schizophrenia (Bach & Hayes, 2002; Lecomte & Lecomte, 2002; Sensky et al., 2000).

Biological Therapies

Professionals who favor the biological perspective–the view that psychological disorders are symptoms of underlying physical disorders–usually favor a **biological therapy.** The three main biological therapies are drug therapy, electroconvulsive therapy, and psychosurgery.

 What are the three main biological therapies?

Drug Therapy

The most frequently used biological treatment is drug therapy. Breakthroughs in drug therapy, coupled with the federal government's effort to reduce involuntary hospitalization of mental patients, reduced the mental hospital patient population from about 559,000 in 1955, when the drugs were introduced, to about 100,000 by 1990. And that population continued to drop throughout the 1990s. (See Figure 13.2.) Furthermore, the average stay of patients who do require hospitalization is now usually a matter of days.

Antipsychotic drugs, also known as *neuroleptics,* are prescribed primarily for schizophrenia. You may have heard of these drugs by their brand names–Thorazine, Stelazine, Compazine, and Mellaril. Their purpose is to control hallucinations, delusions, disorganized speech, and disorganized behavior (Andreasen et al., 1995). The neuroleptics work primarily by inhibiting the activity of the neurotransmitter dopamine. About 50% of patients have a good response to the standard antipsychotic drugs (Kane, 1996). But many patients, particularly those with an early onset of schizophrenia, are not helped by them (Meltzer et al., 1997), and others show only slight or modest improvement in symptoms. The long-term use of these antipsychotic drugs carries a high risk of a severe side effect, *tardive dyskinesia*–almost continual twitching and jerking movements of the face and tongue and squirming movements of the hands and trunk (Glazer et al., 1993).

Newer antipsychotic drugs, called *atypical neuroleptics* (clozapine, risperidone, olanzipine), can treat both the positive symptoms and the negative symptoms of schizophrenia, leading to marked improvement in patients' quality of life (Worrel et al.,

How do antipsychotic drugs help schizophrenic patients?

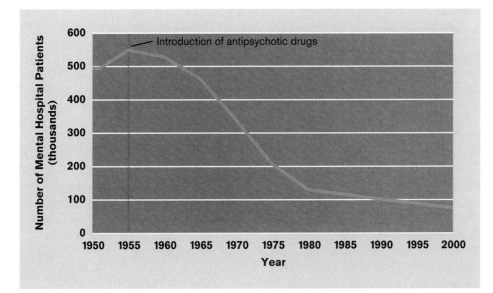

> ## Figure 13.2

Decrease in Patient Populations in State and County Mental Hospitals (1950–2000)

State and county mental hospital patient populations peaked at approximately 560,000 in 1955. In the same year, the antipsychotic drugs were introduced. The drugs, coupled with the federal government's efforts to reduce involuntary hospitalization of mental patients, resulted in a dramatic decrease in the patient population–down to about 100,000 in 1990 and lower than that in 2000. (Data from Manderscheid & Henderson, 2000.)

antidepressants
Drugs that are prescribed to treat depression and some anxiety disorders.

For what conditions are antidepressants prescribed?

lithium
A drug used in bipolar disorder to control the symptoms in a manic episode and to even out the mood swings and reduce recurrence of future manic or depressive states.

How does lithium help patients with bipolar disorder?

2000). Atypical neuroleptics target both dopamine receptors and seratonin receptors in the brain (Kawanishi et al., 2000). About 10% of patients who take clozapine find the results so dramatic that they almost feel as though they have been reborn. Clozapine produces fewer side effects than typical neuroleptics, and patients taking it are less likely to develop tardive dyskinesia (Casey, 1996). However, clozapine is extremely expensive, and without careful monitoring, it can cause a fatal blood defect in 1–2% of patients who take it. Risperidone appears to be effective and safe and has fewer side effects than typical neuroleptics (Marder, 1996; Tamminga, 1996). Yet another advantage is that risperidone is much more effective than other neuroleptics in treating the negative symptoms of schizophrenia (Marder, 1996).

Antidepressants act as mood elevators for people who are severely depressed (Elkin et al., 1995), and they are also helpful in treating certain anxiety disorders. About 65–75% of patients who take antidepressants find themselves significantly improved, and 40–50% of those essentially recover completely (Frazer, 1997). The first generation of antidepressants are known as the *tricyclics* (amitriptyline, imipramine) (Nutt, 2000). The tricyclics work against depression by blocking the reuptake of norepinephrine and serotonin into the axon terminals, thus enhancing the action of these neurotransmitters in the synapses. But tricyclics can have some unpleasant side effects—sedation, dizziness, nervousness, fatigue, dry mouth, forgetfulness, and weight gain (Frazer, 1997). Progressive weight gain (an average of more than 20 pounds) is the main reason people stop taking tricyclics, in spite of the relief these drugs provide from distressing psychological symptoms.

The second-generation antidepressants, the *selective serotonin reuptake inhibitors (SSRIs),* block the reuptake of the neurotransmitter serotonin, increasing its availability at the synapses in the brain (Nutt, 2000; Vetulani & Nalepa, 2000). SSRIs (fluoxetine, clomipramine) have fewer side effects (Nelson, 1997) and are safer in overdose than tricyclics (Thase & Kupfer, 1996). SSRIs have been found to be promising in treating obsessive-compulsive disorder (Goodwin, 1996), social phobia (Jefferson, 1995), panic disorder (Coplan et al., 1997; Jefferson, 1997), and binge eating (Hudson et al., 1996). However, SSRIs can cause sexual dysfunction, although normal sexual functioning returns when the drug is discontinued. Early publicity that SSRIs, especially fluoxetine (Prozac), increase the risk of suicide has not been substantiated (Warshaw & Keller, 1996).

Another drug treatment for depression involves the *monoamine oxidase (MAO) inhibitors* (sold under the names Marplan, Nardil, and Parnate). By blocking the action of an enzyme that breaks down norepinephrine and serotonin in the synapses, MAO inhibitors increase the availability of norepinephrine and serotonin. MAO inhibitors are usually prescribed for depressed patients who do not respond to other antidepressants (Thase et al., 1992). They are also effective in treating panic disorder (Sheehan & Raj, 1988) and social phobia (Marshall et al., 1994). But MAO inhibitors have many of the same unpleasant side effects as tricyclic antidepressants, and patients taking MAO inhibitors must avoid certain foods or run the risk of stroke.

Lithium, in the form of a naturally occurring salt, is considered a wonder drug for 40–50% of patients suffering from bipolar disorder (Thase & Kupfer, 1996). It is said to begin to quiet the manic state within 5 to 10 days. This is an amazing accomplishment, because the average episode, if untreated, lasts about

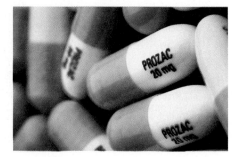

 Prozac, which has milder side effects than the other SSRIs, is widely prescribed as an antidepressant and is also used to treat obsessive-compulsive disorder and posttraumatic stress disorder.

3 to 4 months. A proper maintenance dose of lithium yields reductions in depressive episodes as well as manic ones. Published reports over a period of three decades show that the clinical effectiveness of lithium for treating depression and bipolar disorder is unmatched (Ross et al., 2000). But 40–60% of those who take a maintenance dose will experience a recurrence (Thase & Kupfer, 1996). Also, careful measurement of the lithium level in the patient's system is necessary every 2 to 6 months to guard against lithium poisoning and permanent damage to the nervous system (Schou, 1997). Recent research suggests that *anticonvulsant drugs,* such as divalproex, may be just as effective as lithium for managing bipolar symptoms (Bowden et al., 2000; Kowatch et al., 2000). Moreover, the best treatment outcomes occur when a mood stabilizer (lithium or divalproex) is combined with an antipsychotic drug (Sachs et al., 2002).

The family of minor tranquilizers, called *benzodiazepines,* includes, among others, the well-known drugs sold as Valium and Librium and the newer high-potency drug Xanax (pronounced ZAN-ax). Used primarily to treat anxiety, benzodiazepines are prescribed more often than any other class of psychiatric drugs (Medina et al., 1993). They have been found to be an effective treatment for panic disorder (Davidson, 1997; Noyes et al., 1996) and generalized anxiety disorder (Lydiard et al., 1996).

Xanax, the largest-selling psychiatric drug (Famighetti, 1997), appears to be particularly effective in relieving anxiety and depression. Xanax is effective in the treatment of panic disorder (Noyes et al., 1996), and it works faster and has fewer side effects than antidepressants (Ballenger et al., 1993; Jonas & Cohon, 1993). However, if patients discontinue treatment, relapse is likely (Rickels et al., 1993). And there is a downside to Xanax: Many patients, once they are panic-free, find themselves unable to discontinue the drug because they experience moderate to intense withdrawal symptoms, including intense anxiety (Otto et al., 1993). Valium seems to be just as effective as Xanax for treating panic disorder, and withdrawal is easier. Although withdrawal is a problem with benzodiazepines, the abuse and addiction potential of these drugs is fairly low (Romach et al., 1995).

It's important to note that antipsychotics, antidepressants, and lithium do not cure psychological disorders, so patients usually experience a relapse if they stop taking the drugs when their symptoms fade. Maintenance doses of antidepressants following a major depression reduce the probability of recurrence (Prien & Kocsis, 1995). Maintenance doses are usually required with anxiety disorders as well, or symptoms are likely to return (Rasmussen et al., 1993).

> ◄ What are some of the problems with drug therapy?

Electroconvulsive Therapy

Antidepressant drugs are relatively slow-acting: A severely depressed patient needs at least 2 to 6 weeks to obtain relief, and 30% don't respond at all. This can be too risky for suicidal patients. **Electroconvulsive therapy (ECT),** in which an electric current is passed through the brain, causing a seizure, is sometimes used with such patients. ECT has a bad reputation because it was misused and overused in the 1940s and 1950s. Nevertheless, when used appropriately,

> ◄ For what purpose is electroconvulsive therapy (ECT) used?

electroconvulsive therapy (ECT)
A treatment in which an electric current is passed through the brain, causing a seizure; usually reserved for severely depressed patients who are either suicidal or unresponsive to other treatment.

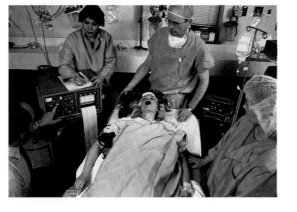

◄ In electroconvulsive therapy, a mild electric current is passed through the brain for 1–2 seconds, causing a brief seizure.

Summary and Comparison of the Therapies

TYPE OF THERAPY	PERCEIVED CAUSE OF DISORDER	GOALS OF THERAPY	METHODS USED	PRIMARY DISORDERS TREATED
Psycho-analysis	Unconscious sexual and aggressive urges or conflicts; fixations; weak ego	Help patient bring disturbing, repressed material to consciousness and work through unconscious conflicts; strengthen ego functions	Psychoanalyst analyzes and interprets dreams, free associations, resistances, and transference.	General feelings of unhappiness; unresolved problems from childhood
Person-centered therapy	Blocking of normal tendency toward self-actualization; incongruence between real and desired self; overdependence on positive regard of others	Increase self-acceptance and self-understanding; help patient become more inner-directed; increase congruence between real and desired self; enhance personal growth	Therapist shows empathy, unconditional positive regard, and genuineness, and reflects client's expressed feelings back to client.	General feelings of unhappiness; interpersonal problems
Inter-personal therapy	Difficulty with relationships and/or life transitions, as well as possible biological causes	Adjust to bereavement; overcome interpersonal role disputes; improve interpersonal skills; adjust to role transitions such as divorce, career change, and retirement	Therapist helps patient (1) release the past and become actively interested in the present, (2) explore options for changing excessive role expectations (often involving other family members), (3) view change as a challenge rather than a threat, and/or (4) improve interpersonal skills, using techniques such as role-playing.	Depression

ECT is a highly effective treatment for major depression (Folkerts, 2000). And depressed patients who are 75 and older tolerate the procedure as well as younger patients do and reap comparable therapeutic benefits (Tew et al., 1999).

For many years, ECT involved passing an electric current through both cerebral hemispheres, a procedure known as *bilateral ECT*. Today, electric current is administered to the right hemisphere only, and the procedure is called *unilateral ECT*. Research suggests that unilateral ECT is as effective as the more intense bilateral ECT while producing milder cognitive effects (Sackeim et al., 2000). Also, a patient undergoing ECT today is given anesthesia, controlled oxygenation, and a muscle relaxant.

Experts think that ECT changes the biochemical balance in the brain, which in turn results in a lifting of depression. When ECT is effective, cerebral blood flow in the prefrontal cortex is reduced, and delta waves (usually associated with slow-wave sleep) appear (Sackeim et al., 1996). Some psychiatrists and neurologists have spoken

Summary and Comparison of the Therapies

TYPE OF THERAPY	PERCEIVED CAUSE OF DISORDER	GOALS OF THERAPY	METHODS USED	PRIMARY DISORDERS TREATED
Family and couple therapy	Problems caused by faulty communication patterns, unreasonable role expectations, drug and/or alcohol abuse, and so on	Create more understanding and harmony within the relationships; improve communication patterns; adjust to the emotional turmoil of divorce	Therapist sees clients individually or several family members at a time and explores such things as communication patterns, power struggles, and unreasonable demands and expectations.	Family problems such as marriage or relationship problems, troubled or troublesome teenagers, abusive relationships, drug or alcohol problems, schizophrenic family member
Behavior therapy	Learning of maladaptive behaviors or failure to learn appropriate behaviors	Extinguish maladaptive behaviors and replace with more adaptive ones; help patient acquire needed social skills	Therapist uses methods based on classical and operant conditioning and modeling, which include systematic desensitization, flooding, exposure and response prevention, and aversion therapy.	Fears, phobias, panic disorder, obsessive-compulsive disorder, bad habits
Cognitive therapy	Irrational and negative assumptions and ideas about self and others	Change faulty, irrational, and/or negative thinking	Therapist helps client identify irrational and negative thinking and substitute rational thinking.	Depression, anxiety, panic disorder, general feelings of unhappiness
Biological therapies	Underlying physical disorder caused by structural or biochemical abnormality in the brain; genetic inheritance	Eliminate or control biological cause of abnormal behavior; restore balance of neurotransmitters	Physician prescribes drugs such as antipsychotics, antidepressants, lithium, or tranquilizers; ECT; or psychosurgery.	Schizophrenia, depression, bipolar disorder, anxiety disorders

out against the use of ECT, claiming that it causes pervasive brain damage and memory loss. But advocates of ECT say that claims of brain damage are based on animal studies in which dosages of ECT were much higher than those now used in human patients. No structural brain damage from ECT has been revealed in studies comparing MRI or CT scans of human patients before and after a series of treatments (Devanand et al., 1994).

There are other methods of physically stimulating the brain. Toward the end of the 20th century, a new therapy known as *rapid transcranial magnetic stimulation (rTMS)* appeared. This magnetic therapy is not invasive in any way. It is performed on patients who are not sedated; it causes no seizures or memory loss and has no known side effects. Its therapeutic value is similar to that of ECT, and it is much more accepted by the public (Vetulani & Nalepa, 2000). This therapy has also been used effectively in conjunction with SSRIs in treating depressed patients (Conca et al., 2000).

Psychosurgery

What is psychosurgery, and for what problems is it used?

An even more drastic treatment than ECT is **psychosurgery**–brain surgery performed strictly to alleviate serious psychological disorders, such as severe depression, severe anxiety, and obsessions, or to provide relief from unbearable chronic pain. The first experimental brain surgery for human patients was developed by Portuguese neurologist Egas Moniz in 1935 to treat severe phobias, anxiety, and obsessions. In his technique, the *lobotomy,* surgeons severed the neural connections between the frontal lobes and the deeper brain centers involved in emotion. But no brain tissue was removed. At first the procedure was considered a tremendous contribution, and Moniz won the Nobel Prize in Medicine in 1949 for developing it. Eventually, it became apparent, however, that this treatment left patients in a severely deteriorated condition.

Modern psychosurgery procedures result in less intellectual impairment because, rather than using conventional surgery, surgeons deliver electric currents through electrodes to destroy a much smaller, more localized area of brain tissue. In one procedure, called a *cingulotomy,* electrodes are used to destroy the cingulum, a small bundle of nerves connecting the cortex to the emotional centers of the brain. Several procedures, including cingulotomy, have been helpful for some extreme cases of obsessive-compulsive disorder (Baer et al., 1995; Trivedi, 1996). But the results of psychosurgery are still not predictable, and the consequences–whether good or bad–are irreversible. For this reason, the treatment is considered experimental and absolutely a last resort.

psychosurgery
Brain surgery to treat some severe, persistent, and debilitating psychological disorder or severe chronic pain.

Evaluating the Therapies

How effective are the various therapies summarized in *Review and Reflect 13.1?* Research results are mixed. In a classic study of therapeutic effectiveness, researchers Smith and others (1980) reanalyzed the results of 475 studies, which involved 25,000 patients. Their review revealed that psychotherapy was better than no treatment, but no one type of therapy was more effective than another. A subsequent reanalysis of the same data by Hans Eysenck (1994), however, showed a slight advantage for behavioral therapies over other types. And a study by Holloa and others (2002) found that cognitive and interpersonal therapies have an advantage over psychodynamic approaches for depressed patients.

What therapy, if any, has proved to be the most effective in treating psychological disorders?

But how do the patients themselves rate the therapies? To answer this question, *Consumer Reports* (1995) conducted the largest survey to date on patient attitudes toward psychotherapy. Martin Seligman (1995, 1996), a consultant for the study, summarized its findings:

- Overall, patients believed that they benefited substantially from psychotherapy.
- Patients seemed equally satisfied with their therapy, whether it was provided by a psychologist, a psychiatrist, or a social worker.
- Patients who were in therapy for more than 6 months did considerably better; generally, the longer patients stayed in therapy, the more they improved.
- Patients who took a drug such as Prozac or Xanax believed that it helped, but overall, psychotherapy alone seemed to work about as well as psychotherapy plus drugs.

Choosing a therapist with the type of training best suited to your problem can be a key factor in how helpful the therapy turns out to be. Table 13.1 lists the various types of mental health professionals.

One important difference among professionals that confuses many people is that a **psychologist** has an advanced degree, usually at the doctoral level, in psychology, while a **psychiatrist** is a medical doctor. Historically, drug therapy has been available only from psychiatrists. At present, however, there is a movement in the United States to allow psychologists with special training in psychopharmacology to prescribe drugs. To date, only the U.S. military and a couple of states have authorized prescribing privileges for psychologists. But the movement is gaining momentum.

psychologist
A mental health professional who possesses a doctoral degree in psychology.

psychiatrist
A mental health professional who is a medical doctor.

Table 13.1 Mental Health Professionals

Professional Title	Training	Services Provided
Psychiatrist	Medical degree (M.D. or O.D.); residency in psychiatry	Psychotherapy; drug therapy; hospitalization for serious psychological disorders
Psychoanalyst	M.D., Ph.D., or Psy.D.; additional training in psychoanalysis	Psychodynamic therapy
Clinical psychologist	Ph.D. or Psy.D.; internship in clinical psychology	Diagnosis and treatment of psychological disorders; can prescribe drugs in some settings after additional training; psychological testing
Counseling psychologist	Ph.D. or Ed.D.; internship in counseling psychology	Assessment and therapy for normal problems of life (e.g., divorce); psychological testing
School psychologist	Ph.D., Ed.D., or master's degree; internship in school psychology	Assessment and treatment of school problems in children and adolescents; psychological testing
Clinical or psychiatric social worker (M.S.W.)	Master's degree; internship in psychiatric social work	Diagnosis and treatment of psychological disorders; identification of supportive community services
Licensed professional counselor (L.P.C.)	Master's degree; internship in counseling	Assessment and therapy for normal problems of life; some psychological testing
Licensed marriage and family therapist (L.M.F.T.)	Master's degree; internship in couple and family therapy	Assessment and therapy for relationship problems
Licensed chemical dependency counsleor (L.C.D.C.)	Educational requirements vary from one state to another; often former addicts	Treatment and education for substance abuse problems

Culturally Sensitive and Gender-Sensitive Therapy

Among many psychotherapists, there is a growing awareness of the need to consider cultural variables in diagnosing and treating psychological disorders (Bernal & Castro, 1994). According to Kleinman and Cohen (1997), people experience and suffer from psychological disorders within a cultural context that may dramatically affect the meaning of symptoms, outcomes, and responses to therapy. Consequently, cultural differences between therapist and client may undermine the *therapeutic alliance,* the bond between therapist and client that is known to be a factor in the effectiveness of psychotherapy (Blatt et al., 1996). Thus, many experts advocate an approach called **culturally sensitive psychotherapy** in which knowledge of a client's cultural background guides the choice of therapeutic intervention (Kumpfer et al., 2002).

Culturally sensitive therapists recognize that language differences between therapists and patients can pose problems (Santiago-Rivera & Altarriba, 2002). For example, a patient who speaks both Spanish and English but is more fluent in Spanish may exhibit hesitations, back-tracking, and delayed responses to questions when being interviewed in English. Consequently, he or she may be thought to be suffering from the kind of disordered thinking that is often displayed by people with schizophrenia (Martinez, 1986). Such language differences may also affect patients' results on standardized tests used by clinicians. In one frequently cited study, researchers found that when a group of Puerto Rican patients took the Thematic Apperception Test (TAT) in English, their pauses and their choices of

Cultures Around the World

Why is it important to consider cultural variables and gender in the therapeutic setting?

culturally sensitive psychotherapy
An approach to therapy that considers cultural variables in the diagnosis and treatment of psychological disorders.

Martha Ainsworth was experiencing a major life problem while on an extended business trip. She found a therapist on the Internet and ended up communicating with him daily for about 2 years. "It was probably one of the most significant and powerful relationships I have ever had," she comments (Walker, 2000).

Ainsworth is among the thousands who are turning to e-therapy—ongoing online interaction with a trained therapist, also called *life coaching, psychoeducation,* or *e-mail counseling.* This therapy typically involves the exchange of e-mail messages over a period of hours or days, but it can also involve video-conferencing and telephone sessions (Day & Schneider, 2002). One important limitation of e-therapy is that it is not appropriate for diagnosing and treating serious psychological disorders such as schizophrenia or bipolar disorder (Manhal-Baugus, 2001). However, e-therapy can be therapeutic for many people.

Advantages and disadvantages
Besides being convenient, e-therapy enables clients to be much less inhibited than they might be in a face-to-face situation. It is also less expensive than traditional therapy (Roan, 2000). Another advantage is that the therapist and the client do not have to be in the same place at the same time.

On the other hand, because of the anonymity of the Internet, it is easy for imposters to pose as therapists. So far, there is no system for regulating or licensing e-therapists. In addition, e-therapy poses some potential ethical

problems, such as the possibility of breaches of confidentiality. Like all reputable therapists, however, the best e-therapists do everything they can to protect clients' privacy and confidentiality—except when disclosure may be necessary to protect them or someone else from immediate harm (Ainsworth, 2000). Perhaps the most serious drawback of e-therapy is the fact that the therapist cannot see the client and therefore cannot use visual and auditory cues to determine when the person is becoming anxious or upset (Roan, 2000; Walker, 2000).

Should you choose e-therapy over face-to-face therapy? E-therapy is not for everyone. Most important, it is not appropriate for someone who is in the midst of a serious crisis. There are better ways to get immediate help, such as suicide hotlines. E-therapy is also not effective for people with extremely complex problems. Some researchers (Ainsworth, 2000; Walker, 2000), however, claim that e-therapy can be a valuable alternative to psychotherapy for individuals who (1) are often away from home or have full schedules, (2) cannot afford traditional therapy, (3) live in rural areas where they do not have ready access to mental health care, (4) have disabilities, or (5) are too timid or embarrassed to make an appointment with a therapist.

Finding an e-therapist A reputable therapist will provide his or her name, credentials, location, and telephone number. In return, the therapist will probably ask you to provide your name,

address, and phone number so that he or she can help you if you experience a crisis (Ainsworth, 2000). If you wish to locate an e-therapist, the best place to start is http://www.metanoia.org. The site lists online therapists whose credentials have been checked by Mental Health Net. It provides information about the location of the therapist, the services offered, payment method, and so forth (Roan, 2000). When choosing an e-therapist, be sure to do the following (Ainsworth, 2000):

- Make sure that the person's credentials have been verified by a third party.

- Get real-world contact information.

- Verify that you'll receive a personal reply to your messages.

- Find out in advance how much the therapist charges.

If you decide to contact an e-therapist, bear this in mind: While e-therapy may be a good way to get started, if you have persistent problems, it would be wise in the long run to obtain traditional psychotherapy (Roan, 2000). ■

words were incorrectly interpreted as indications of psychological problems (Suarez, 1983). Thus, culturally sensitive therapists become familiar with patients' general fluency in the language in which they will be assessed prior to interviewing and testing them.

When working with recent immigrants to the United States, culturally sensitive therapists take into account the impact of the immigration experience on patients' thoughts and emotions (Lijtmaer, 2001; Smolar, 1999). Some researchers who have studied the responses of recent Asian immigrants to psychotherapy recommend that, prior to initiating diagnosis and treatment, therapists encourage patients who are immigrants to talk about feelings of sadness they have experienced as a result of leaving their native culture. Discussions of the patients' anxieties about adapting to life in a new society may also be helpful. Using this strategy, therapists may be able to separate depression and anxiety related to the immigration experience from true psychopathology.

Some advocates of culturally sensitive therapy point out that there are culture-specific practices that can be used as models for therapeutic interventions. Traditional Native American *healing circles,* for example, are being used by many mental health practitioners who serve Native Americans (Garrett et al., 2001). Members of a healing circle are committed to promoting the physical, mental, emotional, and spiritual well-being of one another. The members engage in group activities such as discussion, meditation, and prayer. Sometimes, a recognized Native healer leads the group in traditional healing ceremonies.

Culturally sensitive therapists also attempt to address group differences that can affect the results of therapy. For example, many studies have found that African Americans with mental disorders show less compliance with instructions about medication than do White Americans with the same diagnoses (Fleck et al., 2002; Hazlett-Stevens et al., 2002). A culturally sensitive approach to this problem might be based on a therapist's understanding of the importance of kinship networks and community relationships among African Americans. A therapist might increase an African American patient's medication compliance by having the patient participate in a support group with other African Americans suffering from the same illness and taking the same medications (Muller, 2002). In addition, researchers and experienced therapists recommend that non–African American therapists and African American patients openly discuss their differing racial perspectives prior to beginning therapy (Bean et al., 2002).

Many psychotherapists also note the need for **gender-sensitive therapy**– therapeutic techniques that take into the account the effects of gender on both the therapist's and the client's behavior (Gehart & Lyle, 2001). First, therapists must examine their own gender-based prejudices. They may assume men to be more analytical and women to be more emotional, for example. Or they may place too much emphasis on gender issues and misinterpret clients' problems. In one study, researchers found that therapists expect people who are working in nontraditional fields–female engineers and male nurses, for instance–to have more psychological problems (Rubinstein, 2001). Thus, therapists working with clients pursuing careers in nontraditional fields may assume that the clients' difficulties arise from conflicts about gender roles when, in reality, their problems may have an altogether different origin.

gender-sensitive therapy
An approach to therapy that takes into account the effects of gender on both the therapist's and the patient's behavior.

Summarize It!

Insight Therapies

➤ **What are the basic techniques of psychoanalysis, and how are they used to help patients?**

The basic techniques of psychoanalysis are free association, dream analysis, and transference. They are used to uncover the repressed memories, impulses, and conflicts presumed to be causing patients' problems.

➤ **What are the role and the goal of the therapist in person-centered therapy?**

Person-centered therapy is a nondirective therapy in which the therapist provides a climate of unconditional positive regard. Thus, clients are free to be themselves, and their natural tendency toward positive growth is released.

➤ **What is the major emphasis of Gestalt therapy?**

Gestalt therapy emphasizes the importance of clients' fully experiencing, in the present moment, their feelings, thoughts, and actions, and taking personal responsibility for their behavior.

KEY TERMS

psychotherapy (p. 368)
insight therapy (p. 368)

psychodynamic therapies (p. 368)
psychoanalysis (p. 368)
free association (p. 368)
transference (p. 368)
humanistic therapies (p. 369)
person-centered therapy (p. 369)
nondirective therapy (p. 369)
Gestalt therapy (p. 369)
directive therapy (p. 369)

Relationship Therapies

➤ **What four problems commonly associated with major depression is interpersonal therapy designed to treat?**

Interpersonal therapy (IPT) is designed to help depressed patients cope with severe responses to the death of a loved one, interpersonal role disputes, difficulties in adjusting to role transitions, and deficits in interpersonal skills.

➤ **What is the goal of couple therapy and family therapy?**

The purpose of these two therapies is to help couples or families improve communication and create more interpersonal understanding and harmony.

➤ **What are some advantages of group therapy?**

Group therapy is less expensive than individual therapy and gives people a sense of belonging and an opportunity to express feelings to other group members, to get feedback from them, and to give and receive help and emotional support.

KEY TERMS
relationship therapies (p. 370)
interpersonal therapy (IPT) (p. 370)
family therapy (p. 370)
group therapy (p. 370)

Behavior Therapies

➤ **What is a behavior therapy?**

A behavior therapy is a treatment approach that employs the principles of operant conditioning, classical conditioning, and/or observational learning theory to replace inappropriate or maladaptive behaviors with more adaptive ones.

➤ **What operant conditioning techniques do behavior therapists use to modify behavior?**

The operant conditioning techniques used by behavior therapists involve the withholding of reinforcement to eliminate undesirable behaviors (as in time out) or the use of reinforcement to shape or increase the frequency of desirable behaviors (as in token economies).

➤ **What behavior therapies are based on classical conditioning?**

Behavior therapies that are based on classical conditioning are systematic desensitization, flooding, exposure and response prevention, and aversion therapy.

➤ **How do therapists use systematic desensitization to rid people of fears?**

Therapists using systematic desensitization train clients in deep muscle relaxation and then have them confront a series of graduated anxiety-producing situations, either real or imagined, until they can remain relaxed even in the presence of the most feared situation.

➤ **What is flooding?**

Flooding is a behavior therapy used in the treatment of phobias. Clients are exposed to the feared object or event or asked to imagine it vividly for an extended period until their anxiety decreases and they realize that none of the dreaded consequences come to pass.

➤ **How does exposure and response prevention help people with obsessive-compulsive disorder?**

In exposure and response prevention, people with obsessive-compulsive disorder are exposed to the anxiety-generating stimulus but gradually increase the time before they begin their compulsive rituals and thus learn to tolerate their anxiety.

➤ **How does aversion therapy rid people of a harmful or undesirable behavior?**

Aversion therapy pairs the unwanted behavior with an aversive stimulus until the bad habit becomes associated with pain or discomfort.

➤ **How does participant modeling help people overcome fears?**

In participant modeling, an appropriate response is modeled in graduated steps, and the client is asked to imitate each step, with the encouragement and support of the therapist.

KEY TERMS
behavior therapy (p. 371)
behavior modification (p. 371)
token economy (p. 372)
time out (p. 372)
systematic desensitization (p. 373)
flooding (p. 373)
exposure and response prevention (p. 373)
aversion therapy (p. 374)
participant modeling (p. 375)

Cognitive Therapies

➤ **What is the aim of rational-emotive therapy?**

Rational-emotive therapy is a directive form of therapy designed to challenge and modify the client's irrational beliefs, which are believed to be the cause of his or her distress.

➤ **How does cognitive therapy help people overcome depression and anxiety disorders?**

Cognitive therapy helps people overcome depression and anxiety disorders by pointing out the irrational thoughts that are causing them misery and by helping them learn other, more realistic ways of looking at themselves and their experiences.

KEY TERMS
cognitive therapies (p. 375)
rational-emotive therapy (p. 375)
cognitive therapy (p. 375)

Biological Therapies

➤ **What are the three main biological therapies?**

The three main biological therapies are drug therapy, ECT, and psychosurgery.

➤ **How do antipsychotic drugs help schizophrenic patients?**

Antipsychotic drugs control the major symptoms of schizophrenia by inhibiting the activity of the neurotransmitter dopamine.

➤ **For what conditions are antidepressants prescribed?**

Antidepressants are prescribed for depression, generalized anxiety disorder, panic disorder, agoraphobia, and obsessive-compulsive disorder.

➤ **How does lithium help patients with bipolar disorder?**

Lithium is used to control the symptoms of manic episodes and to even out the mood swings in bipolar disorder.

➤ **What are some of the problems with drug therapy?**

Common problems are the unpleasant or dangerous side effects associated with many drugs and the fact that relapse is likely if the drug therapy is discontinued.

➤ **For what purpose is electroconvulsive therapy (ECT) used?**

ECT is a treatment of last resort for people with severe depression, and it is most often reserved for those who are in imminent danger of committing suicide.

➤ What is psychosurgery, and for what problems is it used?

Psychosurgery is brain surgery performed strictly to relieve some severe, persistent, and debilitating psychological disorder; it is considered experimental and absolutely a last resort.

KEY TERMS

biological therapy (p. 377)
antipsychotic drugs (p. 377)
antidepressants (p. 378)

lithium (p. 378)
electroconvulsive therapy (ECT) (p. 379)
psychosurgery (p. 380)

Evaluating the Therapies

➤ What therapy, if any, has proved to be the most effective in treating psychological disorders?

Although, overall, no one therapeutic approach has proved generally superior, specific therapies have proven effective in treating particular disorders.

KEY TERMS

psychologist (p. 382)
psychiatrist (p. 382)

Culturally Sensitive and Gender-Sensitive Therapy

➤ Why is it important to consider cultural variables and gender in the therapeutic setting?

Cultural background and gender influence both patients' responses to the therapy and the therapist and therapists' responses to patients.

KEY TERMS

culturally sensitive psychotherapy (p. 383)
gender-sensitive therapy (p. 385)

Surf It!

Companion Website

Want to be sure you've absorbed the material in Chapter 13, "Therapies," before the big test? Visiting **www.ablongman.com/woodmastering1e** can put a top grade within your reach. The site is loaded with free practice tests, flashcards, activities, and links to help you review your way to an A.

Study Guide for Chapter 13 !

Answers to all the Study Guide questions are provided at the end of the book.

Section One: Chapter Review

1. In psychoanalysis, the technique whereby a patient reveals every thought, idea, or image that comes to mind is called _____; the patient's attempt to avoid revealing certain thoughts is called _____ .
   a. transference; resistance
   b. free association; transference
   c. revelation; transference
   d. free association; resistance

2. (Person-centered, Gestalt) therapy is the directive therapy that emphasizes the importance of the client's fully experiencing, in the present moment, his or her thoughts, feelings, and actions.

3. (Person-centered, Gestalt) therapy is the nondirective therapy developed by Carl Rogers in which the therapist creates a warm, accepting climate so that the client's natural tendency toward positive change can be released.

4. (Psychodynamic, Humanistic) therapy presumes that the cause of the patient's problems are repressed memories, impulses, and conflicts.

5. Which depressed person would be *least* likely to be helped by interpersonal therapy (IPT)?
   a. Tyrone, who is unable to accept the death of his wife
   b. Beth, who has been depressed since she was forced to retire
   c. Jen, who was sexually abused by her father
   d. Tony, who feels isolated and alone because he has difficulty making friends

6. Which of the following is *not* true of group therapy?
   a. It allows people to get feedback from other members.
   b. It allows individuals to receive help and support from other members.
   c. It is not conducted by trained therapists.
   d. It is less expensive than individual therapy.

7. Self-help groups are generally ineffective because they are not led by professionals. (true/false)

8. Techniques based on (classical, operant) conditioning are used to change behavior by reinforcing desirable behavior and removing reinforcers for undesirable behavior.

9. Behavior therapies based on classical conditioning are used mainly to
   a. shape new, more appropriate behaviors.
   b. rid people of fears and undesirable behaviors or habits.

   c. promote development of social skills.
   d. demonstrate appropriate behaviors.

10. Exposure and response prevention is a treatment for people with
    a. panic disorder.
    b. phobias.
    c. generalized anxiety disorder.
    d. obsessive-compulsive disorder.

11. Match the description with the therapy.
    ____ (1) flooding
    ____ (2) aversion therapy
    ____ (3) systematic desensitization
    ____ (4) participant modeling
    a. practicing deep muscle relaxation during gradual exposure to feared object
    b. pairing painful or sickening stimuli with undesirable behavior
    c. being exposed directly to a feared object without relaxation
    d. imitating a model responding appropriately in a feared situation

12. Cognitive therapists believe that, for the most part, emotional disorders
    a. have physical causes.
    b. result from unconscious conflict and motives.
    c. result from faulty and irrational thinking.
    d. result from environmental stimuli.

13. Rational-emotive therapy is a nondirective therapy that requires a warm, accepting therapist. (true/false)

14. The goal of cognitive therapy is best described as helping people
    a. develop effective coping strategies.
    b. replace automatic thoughts with more objective thoughts.
    c. develop an external locus of control.
    d. develop realistic goals and aspirations.

15. Cognitive therapy has proved very successful in the treatment of
    a. depression and mania.
    b. schizophrenia.
    c. fears and phobias.
    d. anxiety disorders and depression.

16. For the most part, advocates of biological therapies assume that psychological disorders have a physical cause. (true/false)

17. Match the disorder with the drug most often used for its treatment.

____ (**1**) panic disorder
____ (**2**) schizophrenia
____ (**3**) bipolar disorder
____ (**4**) depression
____ (**5**) obsessive-compulsive disorder

  a. lithium
  b. antipsychotics
  c. antidepressants

18. Medication that relieves the symptoms of schizophrenia is thought to work by blocking the action of

  a. serotinin.   **c.** norepinephrine.
  b. dopamine.   **d.** epinephrine.

19. Which of the following is *not* true of drug therapy for psychological disorders?

  a. Some patients must take more than one psychiatric drug to relieve their symptoms.
  b. Drugs sometimes have unpleasant side effects.
  c. Patients often relapse if they stop taking the drugs.
  d. Drugs are usually not very effective.

20. For which disorder is ECT typically used?

  a. severe depression   **c.** anxiety disorders
  b. schizophrenia   **d.** panic disorder

21. The major side effect of ECT is tardive dyskinesia. (true/false)

22. Psychosurgery techniques are now so precise that the exact effects of the surgery can be predicted in advance. (true/false)

23. What is true regarding the effectiveness of therapies?

  a. All are equally effective for any disorder.
  b. Specific therapies have proved effective in treating particular disorders.
  c. Insight therapies are consistently best.
  d. Therapy is no more effective than no treatment for emotional and behavioral disorders.

24. Match the problem with the most appropriate therapy.

____ (**1**) fears, bad habits
____ (**2**) schizophrenia
____ (**3**) general unhappiness, interpersonal problems
____ (**4**) severe depression

  a. behavior therapy
  b. insight therapy
  c. drug therapy

25. One must have a medical degree to become a

  a. clinical psychologist.
  b. sociologist.
  c. psychiatrist.
  d. clinical psychologist, psychiatrist, or psychoanalyst.

26. The responses and outcomes of patients in therapy (are, are not) influenced by cultural factors.

Section Two: Identify the Therapy

Indicate which type of therapy each sentence is describing: (a) psychoanalytic, (b) behavioral, (c) humanistic, (d) cognitive, (e) Gestalt, (f) interpersonal, or (g) biological.

____ **1.** This is a directive therapy that has as an important objective "getting in touch with your feelings"; clients are encouraged to fully experience the present moment.

____ **2.** This approach emphasizes early childhood experience and the conflicts one encounters in different stages of development; important concepts include free association and transference.

____ **3.** Practitioners of this approach believe that faulty and irrational thinking results in emotional distress; a popular application of this approach is rational-emotive therapy.

____ **4.** This therapy is considered a brief psychotherapy and is used in cases of depression due to problems such as the death of a loved one or deficits in interpersonal skills.

____ **5.** This approach is based on the principles of learning theory and includes treatment strategies that use operant conditioning, classical conditioning, and observational learning.

____ **6.** This approach sees psychological problems as symptoms of underlying physical disorders and uses medical treatments such as drug therapy and electroconvulsive therapy.

____ **7.** This approach, often seen as being in direct opposition to psychoanalytic theory, views people as having free choice; clients are encouraged to seek personal growth and fulfill their potential.

Section Three: Fill in the Blank

1. Psychotherapy uses _____ rather than _____ means to treat emotional and behavioral disorders.

2. Helene begins to behave toward her therapist the same way she behaved toward a significant person in her past. Helene is experiencing _____ .

3. A therapy approach in which the therapist takes an active role in determining the course of therapy sessions and provides answers and suggestions to the client is known as _____ therapy.

4. One approach to treating depression is _____ therapy, which has been shown to be especially helpful for people dealing with problems such as severe bereavement and difficulty in adjusting to role transitions.

5. An approach that has been shown to be helpful for problems such as troubled or troublesome teenagers, alcoholic parents, and abusive family situations is _____ therapy.

6. Alcoholics Anonymous is the prototypical example of a _____ _____ _____ .

7. The techniques of token economy and time out are based on _____ conditioning.

8. Marco acts out in class by throwing spitballs, making funny noises, and passing notes to classmates. The teacher decides to ignore Marco when he behaves this way, in the hope that withholding attention will reduce the behavior. The teacher is using a _____ _____ technique.

9. Rational-emotive therapy is a type of _____ therapy.

10. The class of drugs known as neuroleptics is mainly used to treat _____ .

11. SSRIs and MAO inhibitors are drugs that are used mainly to treat _____ .

12. Lithium is used to treat _____ _____ .

13. Electroconvulsive therapy, although an extremely controversial method of therapy, may be the treatment of choice for patients suffering from _____ _____ .

14. A _____ psychologist specializes in the assessment, treatment, and/or researching of psychological problems and behavioral disturbances.

15. The psychoanalytic technique that involves having patients reveal whatever thoughts or images come to mind is known as _____ _____ .

16. Emily sends her son to his room for 20 minutes each time he misbehaves. Emily is using the behavior modification technique known as _____ _____ .

17. A surgical technique known as _____ involves severing the nerve fibers connecting the frontal lobes and the deeper brain.

18. A _____ is usually a psychiatrist, with special training in psychoanalysis.

Section Four: Comprehensive Practice Test

1. Your therapist asks you to reveal whatever thoughts, feelings, or images come to mind, no matter how trivial, embarrassing, or terrible they might seem. Your therapist is using a technique known as
a. analysis of resistance.
b. psychodrama.
c. free association.
d. stimulus satiation.

2. Which of the following is *not* considered an insight therapy?
a. psychoanalysis
c. rational-emotive therapy
b. Gestalt therapy
d. person-centered therapy

3. Which of the following is important in humanistic therapy?
a. challenging irrational beliefs
b. dream analysis
c. empathy
d. behavior modification

4. Person-centered therapy is most effective when the therapist proposes valuable solutions and offers solid advice while directing the therapeutic process. (true/false)

5. In this directive form of therapy, the therapist helps, prods, or badgers clients to experience their feelings as deeply and genuinely as possible, and then to admit responsibility for them.
a. behavioral modification
b. psychodynamic therapy
c. rational-emotive therapy
d. Gestalt therapy

6. Which type of therapy seems to offer the most effective setting for treating adolescent drug abuse?
a. family therapy
c. person-centered therapy
b. Gestalt therapy
d. behavioral therapy

7. This therapy involves the application of principles of classical and operant conditioning.
a. Gestalt therapy
c. psychoanalysis
b. behavior modification
d. humanistic therapy

8. A therapist treating you for fear of heights takes you to the top floor of a tall building and asks you to look out the window toward the ground until she can see that your fear is significantly diminished. What technique is she using?
a. flooding
c. systematic desensitization
b. psychodrama
d. stimulus satiation

9. Which therapy emphasizes acceptance and unconditional positive regard?
a. person-centered therapy
b. cognitive therapy
c. rational-emotive therapy
d. psychoanalysis

10. A technique based on Albert Bandura's observational learning theory is
a. flooding.
b. participant modeling.
c. systematic desensitization.
d. implosive therapy.

11. A type of therapy that is used to treat phobias and employs relaxation training techniques is called
    a. cognitive-behavioral therapy.
    b. systematic desensitization.
    c. psychoanalysis.
    d. client-centered therapy.

12. Which insight therapy was developed by Fritz Perls?
    a. Gestalt therapy
    b. rational-emotive therapy
    c. client-centered therapy
    d. psychoanalysis

13. This type of biological therapy helps reduce symptoms of severe depression by producing a seizure in the patient.
    a. psychosurgery
    b. lobotomy
    c. electroconvulsive therapy
    d. chemotherapy

14. This biological therapy uses an electrical current to destroy a localized section of brain cells.
    a. psychosurgery
    b. prefrontal lobotomy
    c. electroconvulsive therapy
    d. chemotherapy

15. This group of drugs includes tricyclics, MOA inhibitors, and SSRIs.
    a. antimania drugs
    b. antidepressant drugs
    c. antianxiety drugs
    d. antipsychotic drugs

16. This group of drugs is used to treat symptoms including hallucinations and delusions.
    a. antimania drugs
    b. antidepressant drugs
    c. antianxiety drugs
    d. antipsychotic drugs

17. The most severe side effect of typical antipsychotic drugs is
    a. cramps.   c. tardive dyskinesia.
    b. muscle spasms.   d. mania.

18. In a major review of 475 studies, researchers concluded that people who received therapy were better off than those who did not. (true/false)

19. The main problem with interpersonal therapy is the fact that it is so time-consuming. (true/false)

20. The B in Albert Ellis's ABC theory of rational-emotive therapy stands for *behavior*. (true/false)

Section Five: Critical Thinking

1. What are the major strengths and weaknesses of the following approaches to therapy: psychoanalysis, person-centered therapy, behavior therapy, cognitive therapy, and drug therapy?

2. From what you have learned in this chapter, prepare a strong argument to support each of these positions:
    a. Psychotherapy is generally superior to drug therapy in the treatment of psychological disorders.
    b. Drug therapy is generally superior to psychotherapy in the treatment of psychological disorders.

3. In selecting a therapist for yourself or advising a friend or family member, what are some important questions you would ask a therapist in order to determine whether he or she would be a good choice?

chapter

14

Social
Psychology

In the 1960s, an advertisement appeared in newspapers in New Haven, Connecticut, and other communities near Yale University. It read, "Wanted: Volunteers to serve as subjects in a study of memory and learning at Yale University." Many people responded to the ad, and 40 male participants between the ages of 20 and 50 were selected. Yet, instead of a memory experiment, a staged drama was planned. The cast of characters consisted of the experimenter, a 31-year-old high school biology teacher dressed in a gray laboratory coat, who assumed a stern and serious manner; the learner, a middle-aged man (an actor and accomplice of the experimenter); and, the teacher, one of the volunteers.

The experimenter led the teacher and the learner into one room, where the learner was strapped into a chair wired to deliver shocks. The teacher was given a sample shock of 45 volts, supposedly for the purpose of testing the equipment and showing the teacher what the learner would feel. Next, the script called for the learner to complain of a heart condition and say that he hoped the electric shocks would not be too painful. The experimenter admitted that the stronger shocks would hurt but added, "Although the shocks can be extremely painful, they cause no permanent tissue damage" (Milgram, 1963, p. 373).

The experimenter took the teacher to an adjoining room and seated him in front of an instrument panel with 30 lever switches arranged horizontally across the front. The first switch on the left, he was told, delivered only 15 volts, but each successive switch was 15 volts stronger than the last, up to the final switch, which carried 450 volts. The switches on the instrument panel were labeled with designations ranging from "Slight Shock" to "Danger: Severe Shock." The experimenter instructed the teacher to read a list of word pairs to the learner and then test his memory. When the learner made the right choice, the teacher was supposed to go on to the next pair. If the learner missed a question, the teacher was told to flip a switch and shock him, moving one switch to the right—delivering 15 additional volts—each time the learner missed a question.

The learner performed well at first but then began missing about three out of every four questions. The teacher began flipping the switches. When he hesitated, the experimenter urged him to continue. If he still hesitated, the experimenter ordered him, "The experiment requires that you continue," or, more strongly, "You have no other choice, you must go on" (Milgram, 1963, p. 374). At the 20th switch, 300 volts, the

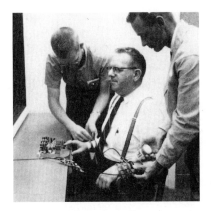

script required the learner to pound on the wall and scream, "Let me out of here, let me out, my heart's bothering me, let me out!" (Meyer, 1972, p. 461). From this point on, the learner answered no more questions. If the teacher expressed concern or a desire to discontinue the experiment, the experimenter answered, "Whether the learner likes it or not, you must go on" (Milgram, 1963, p. 374). At the flip of the next switch—315 volts—the teacher heard only groans from the learner. Again, if the teacher expressed reluctance to go on, the experimenter told him, "You have no other choice, you must go on" (p. 374). But if the teacher insisted on stopping at this point, the experimenter allowed him to do so.

➤ Figure 14.1

The Results of Milgram's Classic Experiment on Obedience

In his classic study, Stanley Milgram showed that a large majority of participants would obey authority, even if obedience caused great pain or was life-threatening to another. Milgram reported that 87.5% of the participants continued to administer what they thought were painful electric shocks of 300 volts to a victim who complained of a heart condition. Amazingly, 65% of the participants obeyed authority to the bitter end and continued to deliver what they thought were dangerous, severe shocks to the maximum of 450 volts. (Data from Milgram, 1963.)

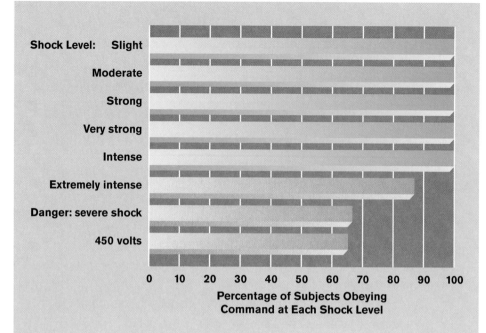

social psychology
The study of how the actual, imagined, or implied presence of others influences the thoughts, feelings, and behavior of individuals.

confederate
Someone who is posing as a participant in an experiment but is actually assisting the experimenter.

naive subject
A person who has agreed to participate in an experiment but is not aware that deception is being used to conceal its real purpose.

primacy effect
The tendency for an overall impression of another to be influenced more by the first information that is received about that person than by information that comes later.

attribution
An inference about the cause of one's own or another's behavior.

situational attribution
Attributing a behavior to some external cause or factor operating in the situation; an external attribution.

dispositional attribution
Attributing a behavior to some internal cause, such as a personal trait, motive, or attitude; an internal attribution.

How many of the 40 participants in the Milgram study do you think obeyed the experimenter to the end–450 volts? Not a single participant stopped before the 20th switch, supposedly 300 volts, when the learner began pounding the wall. Amazingly, 26 participants–65% of the sample–obeyed the experimenter to the bitter end, as shown in Figure 14.1. But this experiment took a terrible toll on the participants. They "were observed to sweat, tremble, stutter, bite their lips, groan, and dig their fingernails into their flesh. These were characteristic rather than exceptional responses to the experiment" (Milgram, 1963, p. 375).

You have just read a description of a classic experiment in **social psychology,** the area of study that attempts to explain how the actual, imagined, or implied presence of others influences the thoughts, feelings, and behaviors of individuals. A study like Milgram's could not be performed today because it would violate the American Psychological Association's code of conduct governing ethics in research. Still, deception has traditionally played a prominent part in social psychologists' research. To accomplish this deception, the researcher often must use one or more **confederates**–people who pose as participants in a psychology experiment but who are actually assisting the experimenter, such as the learner in the Milgram experiment. A **naive subject**–like the teacher in Milgram's study–is an actual participant who has agreed to participate but is not aware that deception is being used to conceal the real purpose of the experiment. You will continue to see why it is often necessary to conceal the purpose of an experiment as you read about other classic studies in social psychology.

Social Perception

Other people can be puzzling, but our ability to understand others is important because we live in a social world. The process we use to obtain critically important social information about others is known as *social perception* (Allison et al., 2000).

Impression Formation

When we meet people for the first time, we begin forming impressions about them right away, and, of course, they are busily forming impressions of us. Naturally, we notice the obvious attributes first—gender, race, age, dress, and how physically attractive or unattractive someone appears (Shaw & Steers, 2001). We may wonder: What's her occupation? Is he married? Answers to such questions, combined with people's verbal and nonverbal behavior, play a part in forming first impressions. Research shows that a firm handshake still makes a positive first impression (Chaplin et al., 2000). It conveys that a person is confident and outgoing, not shy or weak-willed. Moods also play a part—when we are happy, our impressions of others are usually more positive than when we are unhappy.

A number of studies reveal that an overall impression or judgment of another person is influenced more by the first information received about the person than by information that comes later (Luchins, 1957). This phenomenon is called the **primacy effect.** It seems that we attend to initial information more carefully, and once an impression is formed, it provides the framework through which we interpret later information (Gawronski et al., 2002). Any information that is consistent with the first impression is likely to be accepted, thus strengthening the impression. Information that does not fit with the earlier information is more likely to be disregarded. Remember, any time you list your personal traits or qualities, always list your most positive qualities first. It pays to put your best foot forward—first.

Attribution

Why do people do the things they do? To answer this question, we all make **attributions**—that is, we assign, or attribute, causes to explain the behavior of others and to explain our own behavior as well. One kind of attribution is called a **situational attribution** (an external attribution), in which we attribute a person's behavior to some external cause or factor operating within the situation. After failing an exam, you might say, "The test was unfair" or "The professor didn't give us enough time." Another kind of attribution is a **dispositional attribution** (an internal attribution)—attributing a person's behavior to some internal cause such as a personal trait, motive, or attitude. You might attribute failing the exam to lack of ability or to a poor memory.

We tend to use situational attributions to explain our own failures, because we are aware of factors in the situation that influenced us to act as we did (Jones, 1976, 1990; Jones & Nisbett, 1971). When we explain others' failures, we focus more on personal factors than on the factors operating within the situation (Gilbert & Malone, 1995; Leyens et al., 1996). For example, in the United States, the plight of individuals who are homeless or receiving welfare payments is often attributed to laziness, an internal attribution, rather than to factors in their situation that might explain their condition.

The tendency to attribute our own shortcomings primarily to situational factors and those of others to internal or dispositional factors is known as the **actor-observer effect.** Members of both Catholic and Protestant activist groups in Northern Ireland are subject to the actor-observer effect. Each group attributes the violence of the other group to internal or dispositional characteristics (they are murderers, they have evil intentions, etc.). And each group attempts to justify its own violence by attributing it to external or situational causes (we were protecting ourselves, we were retaliating for their actions, etc.) (Hunter et al., 2000).

There is one striking inconsistency in the way we view our own behavior: the self-serving bias. We use the **self-serving bias** when we attribute our successes to internal, or dispositional, causes and blame our failures on external, or situational, causes (Baumgardner et al., 1986; Brown & Rogers, 1991; Pansu & Gilibert, 2002). If you interview for a job and get it, it is probably because you have the right qualifications. If someone else gets the job, it is probably because he or she knew the right people. The self-serving bias allows us to take credit for our successes and shift the blame for our failures to the situation. Research examining the attributions of professional athletes,

 Why are first impressions so important and enduring?

actor-observer effect
The tendency to attribute one's own behavior primarily to situational factors and the behavior of others primarily to internal or dispositional factors.

self-serving bias
The tendency to attribute personal successes to dispositional causes and failures to situational causes.

What is the difference between a situational attribution and a dispositional attribution for a specific behavior?

How do the kinds of attributions people tend to make about themselves differ from those they make about other people?

What first impression have you formed of this person?

for example, has shown that they attribute victories to internal traits, such as ability and effort, and losses to situational factors, such as poor officiating and the like (Roesch & Amirkhan, 1997). Interestingly, too, managers prefer job applicants who make dispositional attributions during their interview, especially when the attributions focus on effort rather than natural ability (Pansu & Gilibert, 2002).

Attraction

Think for a moment about your friends. What makes you like, or even fall in love with, one person and ignore or react negatively to someone else?

Factors Influencing Attraction

There are several factors that influence attraction. One is physical **proximity,** or geographic closeness. Obviously, it is much easier to make friends with people who are close at hand. One reason proximity matters is the **mere-exposure effect,** the tendency to feel more positively toward stimuli with repeated exposure. People, food, songs, and styles become more acceptable the more we are exposed to them. Advertisers rely on the positive effects of repeated exposure to increase people's liking for products and even for political candidates.

> *Why is proximity an important factor in attraction?*

Our own moods and emotions, whether positive or negative, can influence how much we are attracted to people we meet. We may develop positive or negative feelings toward others simply because they are present when very good or very bad things happen to us. And we tend to like the people who also like us–or who we *believe* like us–a phenomenon called *reciprocity* or *reciprocal liking.*

Beginning in elementary school and continuing through life, people are also more likely to pick friends of the same age, gender, race, and socioeconomic class. We are likely to choose friends and lovers who hold similar views on most things that are important to us. Having similar interests and attitudes toward leisure-time activities makes it more likely that time spent together is rewarding.

proximity
Geographic closeness; a major factor in attraction.

mere-exposure effect
The tendency of people to develop a more positive evaluation of some person, object, or other stimulus with repeated exposure to it.

Physical Attractiveness

Perhaps no other factor influences attraction more than physical attractiveness. People of all ages have a strong tendency to prefer physically attractive people (Langlois et al., 2000). Even 6-month-old infants, when given the chance to look at a photograph of an attractive or an unattractive woman, man, or infant, will spend more time looking at the attractive face. How people behave, especially the simple act of smiling, influences our perceptions of their attractiveness (Reis et al., 1990). But physical appearance matters as well.

> *How important is physical attractiveness in attraction?*

Based on studies involving computer-generated faces, researchers Langlois and Roggman (1990) reported that perceptions of attractiveness are based on features that approximate the mathematical average of the features in a given general population. But Perrett and others (1994) found that simply averaging facial features only partially accounted for facial beauty. These researchers generated two composite images, one of 60 Caucasian female faces and another of the most attractive 15 of the 60 faces. Then, by exaggerating the differences between the two composite images, they derived the most attractive image, with larger eyes, higher cheekbones, and a thinner jaw. Averaging faces tends to make them more symmetrical. And symmetrical faces and bodies are seen as more attractive and sexually appealing (Singh, 1995; Thornhill & Gangestad, 1994).

Cross-cultural research shows that males and females in many cultures have similar ideas about the physical attractiveness of members of the opposite sex (Langlois et al., 2000). For example, when native Asian, Hispanic, and Caucasian American male students rated photographs of Asian, Hispanic, African American, and Caucasian females on attractiveness, Cunningham and others (1995) reported a very high mean

correlation (.93) among the groups in attractiveness ratings. When African American and Caucasian American men rated photos of African American women, their agreement on facial features was also very high—the correlation was .94. Evolutionary psychologists suggest that this cross-cultural similarity is because of a tendency, shaped by natural selection, to look for indicators of health in potential mates (Fink & Penton-Voak, 2002).

Why does physical attractiveness matter? When people have one trait or quality that we either admire or dislike very much, we often assume that they also have other admirable or negative traits—a phenomenon known as the **halo effect** (Nisbett & Wilson, 1977). Dion and others (1972) found that people generally attribute other favorable qualities to those who are attractive. Attractive people are seen as more exciting, personable, interesting, and socially desirable than unattractive people. As a result, job interviewers are more likely to recommend highly attractive people (Dipboye et al., 1975).

Does this mean that unattractive people don't have a chance? Fortunately not. Eagly and her colleagues (1991) suggest that the impact of physical attractiveness is strongest in the perception of strangers. Once we get to know people, other qualities assume more importance. In fact, as we come to like people, they begin to look more attractive to us, and people with undesirable personal qualities begin to look less attractive.

The halo effect—the attribution of other favorable qualities to those who are attractive—helps explain why physical attractiveness is so important.

Romantic Attraction and Mating

Even though most of us may be attracted to handsome or beautiful people, the **matching hypothesis** suggests that we are likely to end up with someone similar to ourselves in attractiveness and other assets (Berscheid et al., 1971; Feingold, 1988; Walster & Walster, 1969). Furthermore, couples mismatched in attractiveness are more likely to end the relationship (Cash & Janda, 1984). It has been suggested that most people estimate their social assets and realistically expect to attract someone with approximately equal assets. In terms of physical attractiveness, some people might consider a movie star or supermodel to be the ideal man or woman, but they do not seriously consider the ideal to be a realistic, attainable possibility. Fear of rejection keeps many people from pursuing those who are much more attractive than they are. But instead of marrying an extremely handsome man, a very beautiful woman may base her choice not on physical attractiveness but on money and social status. Extremely handsome men have been known to make similar "sacrifices." The matching hypothesis is generally applicable to friendships as well as romantic relationships (Cash & Derlega, 1978), although it is more true of males than of females (Feingold, 1988).

But is a virtual "clone" of oneself the most desirable life partner? Not necessarily. Robert Winch (1958) proposes that men and women tend to choose mates with needs and personalities that are complementary rather than similar to their own. Winch sees complementary needs as not necessarily opposite, but as supplying what the partner lacks. A talkative person may seek a quiet mate who prefers to listen. There is some support for this view (Dryer & Horowitz, 1997).

Most research, however, indicates that similarity in needs is mainly what attracts (Buss, 1984; Phillips et al., 1988). Similarity in personality, physical traits, intellectual ability, education, religion, ethnicity, socioeconomic status, and attitudes are all related to partner choice (O'Leary & Smith, 1991). And similarity in needs and in personality appears to be related to marital success as well as to marital choice (O'Leary & Smith, 1991). Similarities wear well.

If you were to select a marriage partner, what qualities would attract you? Complete *Try It! 14.1* (on page 398) to evaluate your preferences.

halo effect
The tendency to infer generally positive or negative traits in a person as a result of observing one major positive or negative trait.

matching hypothesis
The notion that people tend to have spouses, lovers, or friends who are approximately equivalent in social assets such as physical attractiveness.

You are more likely to be attracted to someone who is like you than to someone who is your opposite.

In your choice of a mate, which qualities are most and least important to you? Rank these 18 qualities of a potential mate from most important (1) to least important (18) to you.

_____ Ambition and industriousness

_____ Chastity (no previous sexual intercourse)

_____ Desire for home and children

_____ Education and intelligence

_____ Emotional stability and maturity

_____ Favorable social status or rating

_____ Good cooking and housekeeping skills

_____ Similar political background

_____ Similar religious background

_____ Good health

_____ Good looks

_____ Similar education

_____ Pleasing disposition

_____ Refinement/neatness

_____ Sociability

_____ Good financial prospects

_____ Dependable character

_____ Mutual attraction/love

Compare your selections in the *Try It!* to those of men and women from over 33 countries. Generally, men and women across cultures rate these four qualities as most important in mate selection: (1) mutual attraction/love, (2) dependable character, (3) emotional stability and maturity, and (4) pleasing disposition (Buss et al., 1990). Aside from these four first choices, however, women and men differ somewhat in the attributes they prefer. According to Buss (1994), "Men prefer to mate with beautiful young women, whereas women prefer to mate with men who have resources and social status" (p. 239). These preferences, he claims, have been adaptive in human evolutionary history. To a male, beauty and youth suggest health and fertility—the best chance to pass his genes onto the next generation. To a female, resources and social status provide security for her and her children (Buss, 2000b).

Sternberg's Theory of Love

In Western culture, affection is an important part of most relationships, including friendships, and being "in love" is the most important factor in the formation of a long-term romantic relationship. But what is love? Robert Sternberg (1986b, 1987), whose triarchic theory of intelligence was discussed in Chapter 7, proposes a **triangular theory of love.** Its three components are *intimacy, passion,* and *commitment.* Sternberg explains intimacy as "those feelings in a relationship that promote closeness, bondedness, and connectedness" (1987, p. 339). Passion refers to those drives in a loving relationship "that lead to romance, physical attraction, [and] sexual consummation" (1986b, p. 119). The commitment, or decision/commitment, component consists of (1) a short-term aspect (the decision that one loves another person) and (2) a long-term aspect (a commitment to maintaining that love over time).

> How does Sternberg's triangular theory of love explain love?

Sternberg proposes that these three components, singly and in various combinations, produce seven different kinds of love (see Figure 14.2):

- *Liking* has only one of the love components—intimacy. In this case, liking is not used in a trivial sense. Sternberg says that liking characterizes true friendships.
- *Infatuated love* consists solely of passion and is often what is felt as "love at first sight."
- *Empty love* consists of the decision/commitment component without intimacy or passion. Sometimes a stronger love deteriorates into empty love. In cultures in which arranged marriages are common, relationships often begin as empty love.
- *Romantic love* is a combination of intimacy and passion. Romantic lovers are bonded emotionally (as in liking) and physically through passionate arousal.

triangular theory of love
Sternberg's theory that three components—intimacy, passion, and decision/commitment—singly and in various combinations, produce seven different kinds of love.

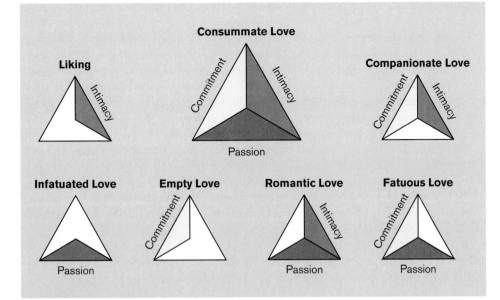

> ## Figure 14.2
Sternberg's Triangular Theory of Love
Sternberg identifies three components of love—passion, intimacy, and commitment—and shows how the three, singly and in various combinations, produce seven different kinds of love. Consummate love, the most complete form of love, has all three components. (Based on Sternberg, 1986b.)

- *Fatuous love* has the components of passion and decision/commitment but not intimacy. This type of love can be exemplified by a whirlwind courtship and marriage in which a commitment is motivated largely by passion without the stabilizing influence of intimacy.
- *Companionate love* consists of intimacy and commitment. This type of love is often found in marriages in which the passion has gone out of the relationship, but a deep affection and commitment remain.
- *Consummate love* is the only type that has all three components—intimacy, decision/commitment, and passion. It represents the ideal love relationship for which many people strive.

Social Influence

Conformity

Conformity is changing or adopting a behavior or an attitude in order to be consistent with the social norms of a group or the expectations of other people. **Social norms** are the standards of behavior and the attitudes that are expected of members of a group. Some conformity is necessary if there is to be any social order at all. We cannot drive on either side of the street at whim, for example. And we conform to other people's expectations in order to have their esteem, their love, or even their company. Moreover, there are times when conformity is beneficial to us. Researchers have found that teenagers who attend schools where the majority of students are opposed to smoking, drinking, and drug use are less likely to use these substances than peers who attend schools where the majority approves of these behaviors (Kumar et al., 2002).

The best-known experiment on conformity was conducted by Solomon Asch (1951, 1955), who designed the simple test shown in Figure 14.3 (on page 400). Eight male participants were seated around a large table and were asked, one by

conformity
Changing or adopting an attitude or behavior to be consistent with the social norms of a group or the expectations of other people.

social norms
The attitudes and standards of behavior expected of members of a particular group.

What did Asch find in his famous experiment on conformity?

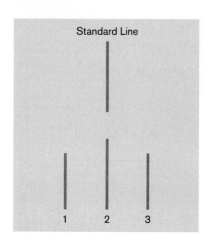

Standard Line

1 2 3

➤ Figure 14.3

Asch's Classic Study of Conformity

If you were one of eight participants in the Asch experiment who were asked to pick the line (1, 2, or 3) that matched the standard line shown at the top, which line would you choose? If the other participants all chose line 3, would you conform and answer line 3? (Based on Asch, 1955.)

What did researchers find when the circumstances of Milgram's classic study of obedience were varied?

➤ In Asch's experiment on conformity, all but one of the "participants" were really confederates of the experimenter. They deliberately chose the wrong line to try to influence the naive participant (second from right here) to go along with the majority.

one, to tell the experimenter which of the three lines matched the standard line (see Figure 14.3). But only one of the eight was an actual participant; the others were confederates assisting the experimenter. There were 18 trials—18 different lines to be matched. During 12 of these trials, the confederates all gave the same wrong answer, which of course puzzled the naive participant. Remarkably, Asch found that 5% of the subjects conformed to the incorrect, unanimous majority all of the time, 70% conformed some of the time, and 25% remained completely independent and were never swayed by the group.

Varying the experiment with groups of 2, 3, 4, 8, and 10–15, Asch found that the tendency to "go along" with the majority opinion was operating, even when there was a unanimous majority of only 3 confederates. Surprisingly, unanimous majorities of 15 produced no higher conformity rate than did those of 3. Asch also discovered that if just one other person voiced a dissenting opinion, the tendency to conform was not as strong. When just one confederate in the group disagreed with the incorrect majority, the naive participants' errors dropped drastically, from 32% to 10.4%.

Other research on conformity reveals further interesting aspects. For instance, people who are high in three of the Big Five personality dimensions—emotional stability, Agreeableness, and Conscientiousness (discussed in Chapter 11)—are more likely to conform than those who are low in these factors (DeYoung et al., 2002). Contrary to conventional wisdom, women are no more likely to conform than men (Eagly & Carli, 1981). But conformity is greater for everyone if the sources of influence are perceived as belonging to one's own group (Abrams et al., 1990). And with respect to nonconformity, those who hold minority opinions on an issue have more influence in changing a majority view if they present a well-organized, clearly stated argument and if they are especially consistent in advocating their views (Wood et al., 1994).

Obedience

Some obedience is necessary if civilized society is to function, but unquestioned obedience can cause humans to commit unbelievably horrible acts. One of the darkest chapters in human history was due to the obedience of officials in Nazi Germany in carrying out Adolph Hitler's orders to exterminate Jews and other "undesirables."

The study you read about at the beginning of this chapter demonstrated how far ordinary citizens would go to obey orders; remember, more than 60% of Milgram's participants went all the way to 450 volts despite the pleading and eventual collapse of the "learner." Another researcher repeated the experiment in a three-room office suite in a run-down building rather than at prestigious Yale University. Even there, 48% of the participants administered the maximum shock (Meyer, 1972).

Milgram (1965) conducted a variation of the original experiment in which each trial involved three teachers, two of whom were confederates and the other, a naive participant. One confederate was instructed to refuse to continue after 150 volts, and the other confederate after 210 volts. In this situation, 36 out of 40 naive participants (90%) defied the experimenter before the maximum shock could be given, compared with only 14 participants in the original experiment (Milgram, 1965). In Milgram's experiment, as in Asch's conformity study, the presence of another person who refused to go along gave many of the participants the courage to defy the authority.

Compliance

There are many times when people act not out of conformity or obedience, but in accordance with the wishes, suggestions, or direct requests of another person. This type of action is called **compliance.**

400

One strategy people use to gain the compliance of others, the **foot-in-the-door technique,** is designed to gain a favorable response to a small request first. The intent is to make the person more likely to agree later to a larger request (the result desired from the beginning).

In a classic study of the foot-in-the-door technique, a researcher claiming to represent a consumers' group called a number of homes and asked whether the people answering the phone would mind answering a few questions about the soap products they used. Then, a few days later, the same person called those who had agreed to the first request and asked if he could send five or six of his assistants to conduct an inventory of the products in their home. The researcher told the people that the inventory would take about 2 hours, and that the inventory team would have to search all drawers, cabinets, and closets in the house. Nearly 53% of those who had earlier answered the questions agreed to the second request, compared with 22% of a control group who were contacted only once, with that request (Freedman & Fraser, 1966).

With the **door-in-the-face technique,** a large, unreasonable request is made first. The expectation is that the person will refuse but will then be more likely to respond favorably to a later, smaller request (the result desired from the beginning). In one of the best-known studies on the door-in-the-face technique, college students were approached on campus. They were asked to agree to serve without pay as counselors to juvenile delinquents for 2 hours each week for a minimum of 2 years. As you would imagine, not a single person agreed (Cialdini et al., 1975). Then, the experimenters countered with a much smaller request, asking if the students would agree to take a group of juveniles on a 2-hour trip to the zoo. Half the students agreed, a fairly high compliance rate. The researchers used another group of college students as controls, asking them to respond only to the smaller request, the zoo trip. Only 17% agreed when the smaller request was presented alone.

Another method used to gain compliance is the **low-ball technique.** A very attractive initial offer is made to get people to commit themselves to an action, and then the terms are made less favorable. In a frequently cited study of this technique, college students were asked to enroll in an experimental course for which they would receive credit. Only after the students had agreed to participate were they informed that the class would meet at 7:00 a.m. Control group participants were told of the time when first asked to enroll. More than 50% of the low-balled group agreed to participate, but only 25% of control participants agreed to take the class (Cialdini et al., 1978).

Group Influence

It is obvious that being in a group influences our behavior and our performance. We behave differently in a variety of ways when we are alone and when we are part of a group, small or large.

Social Facilitation

In certain cases, individual performance can be either helped or hindered by the mere physical presence of others. The term **social facilitation** refers to any effect on performance, whether positive or negative, that can be attributed to the presence of others. Research on this phenomenon has focused on two types of effects: (1) **audience effects,** or the impact of passive spectators on performance; and (2) **co-action effects,** or the impact on performance caused by the presence of other people engaged in the same task.

In one of the first studies in social psychology, Norman Triplett (1898) looked at co-action effects. He had observed in official bicycle records that bicycle racers ped-

What are three techniques used to gain compliance?

compliance
Acting in accordance with the wishes, suggestions, or direct requests of another person.

foot-in-the-door technique
A strategy designed to secure a favorable response to a small request at first, with the aim of making the person more likely to agree later to a larger request.

door-in-the-face technique
A strategy in which someone makes a large, unreasonable request with the expectation that the person will refuse but will then be more likely to respond favorably to a smaller request at a later time.

low-ball technique
A strategy to gain compliance by making a very attractive initial offer to get a person to agree to an action and then making the terms less favorable.

social facilitation
Any positive or negative effect on performance due to the presence of others, either as an audience or as co-actors.

audience effects
The impact of passive spectators on performance.

co-action effects
The impact on performance of the presence of others engaged in the same task.

Under what conditions does social facilitation have either a positive or a negative effect on performance?

Social Facilitation: Performing in the Presence of Others

The presence of others (either as an audience or as co-actors engaged in the same task) may have opposite effects, either helping or hindering an individual's performance. Why? Robert Zajonc explained that (1) the presence of others heightens arousal and (2) heightened arousal leads to better performance on easier tasks and worse performance on more difficult tasks. (Based on Zajonc & Sales, 1966.)

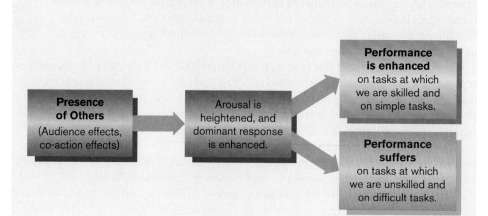

Presence of Others (Audience effects, co-action effects) → Arousal is heightened, and dominant response is enhanced. →

Performance is enhanced on tasks at which we are skilled and on simple tasks.

Performance suffers on tasks at which we are unskilled and on difficult tasks.

social loafing
The tendency to put forth less effort when working with others on a common task than when working alone.

group polarization
The tendency of members of a group, after group discussion, to shift toward a more extreme position in whatever direction they were leaning initially—either more risky or more cautious.

What is social loafing, and what factors lessen or eliminate it? ➤

groupthink
The tendency for members of a very cohesive group to feel such pressure to maintain group solidarity and to reach agreement on an issue that they fail to weigh available evidence adequately or to consider objections and alternatives.

aled faster when they were pedaling against other racers than when they were racing against the clock. Was this pattern of performance peculiar to competitive bicycling? Or was it part of a more general phenomenon in which people worked faster and harder in the presence of others than when performing alone? Triplett set up a study in which he told 40 children to wind fishing reels as quickly as possible under two conditions: (1) alone and (2) in the presence of other children performing the same task. He found that the children worked faster when other reel turners were present than when they performed alone. But later studies on social facilitation found that, in the presence of others, performance improves on tasks that can be done easily, but suffers on difficult tasks (Michaels et al., 1982). See Figure 14.4.

Social Loafing

Researcher Bibb Latané used the term **social loafing** to refer to people's tendency to exert less effort when working with others on a common task than when working alone. Social loafing occurs in situations where no one person's contribution to the group can be identified and individuals are neither praised for a good performance nor blamed for a poor one (Williams et al., 1981). Social loafing is a problem in many workplaces, especially where employees have unlimited access to the Internet (Lim, 2002). Employees tend to justify "cyberloafing" in terms of perceived injustices committed by their supervisors.

In one experiment, Latané and others (1979) asked male students to shout and clap as loudly as possible, first alone and then in groups. In groups of two, individuals made only 71% of the noise they had made alone; in groups of four, each person put forth 51% of his solo effort; and with six persons each made only a 40% effort. But Harkins and Jackson (1985) found that social loafing disappeared when participants in a group were led to believe that each person's output could be monitored and his or her performance evaluated. Even the possibility that the group performance may be evaluated against some standard can be sufficient to eliminate the loafing effect (Harkins & Szymanski, 1989).

Some 80 experimental studies have been conducted on social loafing in diverse cultures, including those of Taiwan, Japan, Thailand, India, China, and the United States. Social loafing on a variety of tasks was evident to some degree in all of the cultures studied. But it appears to be more common in individualistic Western cultures such as the United States (Karau & Williams, 1993).

Group Polarization and Groupthink

It is commonly believed that groups tend to make more moderate decisions than individuals. However, research shows that group discussion often causes members of a group to shift to a more extreme position in whatever direction the group was leaning initially—a phenomenon known as **group polarization** (Isenberg, 1986; Lamm, 1988). Group members, it seems, will decide to take a greater risk if they were leaning in a risky direction to begin with, but they will shift toward a more cautious position if they were, on average, somewhat cautious at the beginning of the discussion (Myers & Lamm, 1975). Myers and Bishop (1970) found that as a result of group polarization, group discussions of racial issues can either increase or decrease prejudice. However, group members do not always all lean in the same direction at the beginning of a discussion. When evidence both for and against a particular stand on a given topic is presented, group polarization occurs infrequently (Kuhn & Lao, 1996). Moreover, when subgroups within a larger group hold opposing views, compromise rather than polarization is the likely outcome (Vinokur & Burnstein, 1978).

Groupthink is the term social psychologist Irving Janis (1982) applies to the decisions often reached by tightly knit groups. When a tightly knit group is more concerned with preserving group solidarity and uniformity than with evaluating all possible alternatives objectively, individual members may hesitate to voice any dissent. The group may also discredit opposing views from outsiders and begin to believe it is incapable of making mistakes. To guard against groupthink, Janis suggests that the group encourage an open discussion of alternative views and encourage the expression of any objections and doubts. He further recommends that outside experts sit in and challenge the views of the group. At least one group member should take the role of devil's advocate whenever a policy alternative is evaluated. Finally, to avoid groupthink in the workplace, managers should withhold their own opinions when problem-solving and decision-making strategies are being considered (Bazan, 1998).

Social Roles

Social roles are socially defined behaviors that are considered appropriate for individuals occupying certain positions within a given group. Roles can shape people's behavior, sometimes quickly and dramatically. Consider a classic experiment in which psychologist Philip Zimbardo (1972) simulated a prison experience. College student volunteers were randomly assigned to be either guards or prisoners. The guards, wearing uniforms and carrying small clubs, strictly enforced harsh rules. The prisoners were stripped naked, searched, and deloused. Then they were given prison uniforms, assigned numbers, and locked away in small, bare cells. The guards quickly adopted their role, some even to the point of becoming heartless and sadistic. One guard remembered forcing prisoners to clean toilets with their bare hands. Prisoners began to behave like real prisoners, acting debased and subservient. The role playing became all too real—so much so that the experiment had to be ended in only 6 days.

Of course, social roles can have positive effects on behavior as well. In classic research involving adolescents with learning disabilities, Palinscar and Brown (1984) reported that students' learning behaviors were powerfully affected by their being assigned to play either the "teacher" or "student" role in group study sessions. Participants summarized reading assignments more effectively and, as a result, learned more from them when functioning as teachers than when functioning as students.

Studying in a group could lead to social loafing through a diffusion of responsibility effect.

How are the initial attitudes of group members likely to affect group decision making?

social roles
Socially defined behaviors considered appropriate for individuals occupying certain positions within a group.

Zimbardo's experiment simulated the prison environment by randomly assigning participants to the social roles of prison guards or inmates. The social roles influenced the individuals' behavior: The prisoners began acting like real prisoners, and the prison guards, like real prison guards.

Attitudes and Attitude Change

Attitudes

Essentially, **attitudes** are relatively stable evaluations of persons, objects, situations, or issues along a continuum ranging from positive to negative (Petty et al., 1997). Most attitudes have three components: (1) a cognitive component consisting of thoughts and beliefs about the attitudinal object, (2) an emotional component composed of feelings toward the attitudinal object, and (3) a behavioral component made up of predispositions concerning actions toward the object (Breckler, 1984). Figure 14.5 shows these three components of an attitude. Attitudes enable us to appraise people, objects, and situations and provide structure and consistency in the social environment (Fazio, 1989). Attitudes also help us process social information (Pratkanis, 1989), guide our behavior (Sanbonmatsu & Fazio, 1990), and influence our social judgments and decisions (Jamieson & Zanna, 1989).

Some attitudes are acquired through firsthand experience with people, objects, situations, and issues. Others are acquired when children hear parents, other family members, friends, and teachers express positive or negative attitudes toward certain issues or people. The mass media, including advertising, influence people's attitudes and reap billions of dollars annually for their efforts. As you might expect, however, the attitudes that people form through their own direct experience are stronger than those they acquire vicariously and are also more resistant to change (Wu & Shaffer, 1987). And, despite ageist stereotypes, many studies have found that older adults are more likely than middle-aged adults to change their attitudes (Visser & Krosnick, 1998).

We often hear that attitude change is the key to behavior change. However, a number of early studies showed that attitudes predict behavior only about 10% of the time (e.g., Wicker, 1969). People, for example, may express strong attitudes in favor of protecting the environment and conservation of resources, yet not take their aluminum cans to a recycling center or join carpools. However, attitudes are better pre-

> What are the three components of an attitude?

attitude
A relatively stable evaluation of a person, object, situation, or issue.

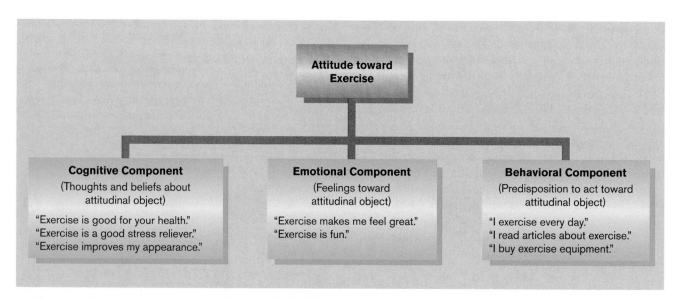

➤ Figure 14.5

The Three Components of an Attitude

An attitude is a relatively stable evaluation of a person, object, situation, or issue. Most of our attitudes have (1) a cognitive component, (2) an emotional component, and (3) a behavioral component.

dictors of behavior if they are strongly held, are readily accessible in memory (Bassili, 1995; Fazio & Williams, 1986; Kraus, 1995), and vitally affect the holder's interests (Sivacek & Crano, 1982).

If people discover that some of their attitudes are in conflict with others or that their attitudes are not consistent with their behavior, they are likely to experience an unpleasant state. Leon Festinger (1957) called this state **cognitive dissonance.** People usually try to reduce this dissonance by changing the behavior or the attitude or by somehow explaining away the inconsistency or reducing its importance (Aronson, 1976; Festinger, 1957). A change in attitude does seem to reduce the discomfort caused by cognitive dissonance (Elliot & Devine, 1994).

Smoking is a perfect behavior for illustrating cognitive dissonance. Faced with a mountain of evidence linking smoking to a number of diseases, what are smokers to do? The healthiest, but perhaps not the easiest, way to reduce the cognitive dissonance is to change the behavior–quit smoking. Another way is to change the attitude–to convince themselves that smoking is not as dangerous as it is said to be. Smokers might also tell themselves that they will stop smoking long before any permanent damage is done, or that medical science is advancing so rapidly that a cure for cancer or emphysema is just around the corner. Figure 14.6 illustrates the methods a smoker might use to reduce cognitive dissonance.

Expanding the applicability of the concept of cognitive dissonance, Aronson and Mills (1959) argued that the more people have to sacrifice, give up, or suffer to become a member of an organization–say, a fraternity or sorority–the more positive their attitudes are likely to become toward the group, in order to justify their sacrifice. Members of cults are often required to endure hardships and make great sacrifices, such as severing ties with their families and friends and turning over their property and possessions to the group. Such extreme sacrifice can then be justified only by a strong and radical defense of the cult, its goals, and its leaders.

Persuasion

Persuasion is a deliberate attempt to influence the attitudes and/or the behavior of another person. Attempts at persuasion are pervasive parts of work experience, social experience, and even family life. Researchers have identified four elements of persuasion: (1) the source of the communication (who is doing the per-

> What is cognitive dissonance, and how can it be resolved?

> What are the four elements of persuasion?

cognitive dissonance
The unpleasant state that can occur when people become aware of inconsistencies among their attitudes or between their attitudes and their behavior.

persuasion
A deliberate attempt to influence the attitudes and/or behavior of another.

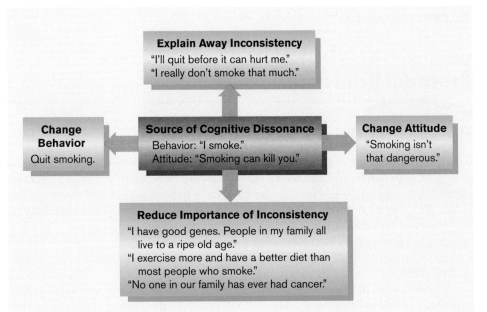

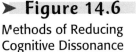

> **Figure 14.6**
Methods of Reducing Cognitive Dissonance

Cognitive dissonance can occur when people become aware of inconsistencies in their attitudes or between their attitudes and their behavior. People try to reduce dissonance by (1) changing their behavior, (2) changing their attitude, (3) explaining away the inconsistency, or (4) reducing its importance. Here are examples of how a smoker might use these methods to reduce the cognitive dissonance created by his or her habit.

Celebrity status can make someone more persuasive than she would otherwise be—a key factor in political campaigning.

suading), (2) the audience (who is being persuaded), (3) the message (what is being said), and (4) the medium (the means by which the message is transmitted).

Some factors that make the source (the communicator) more persuasive are credibility, attractiveness, and likability. A credible communicator is one who has expertise (knowledge of the topic at hand) and trustworthiness (truthfulness and integrity). Other characteristics of the source—such as physical attractiveness, celebrity status, and similarity to the audience—also contribute to audience responses to the sources of persuasive messages.

Audience characteristics influence responses to persuasion as well. In general, people with low intelligence are easier to persuade than those who are highly intelligent (Rhodes & Wood, 1992). Evidence suggests that a one-sided message is usually most persuasive if the audience is not well informed on the issue, is not overly intelligent, or already agrees with the point of view. A two-sided message (where both sides of an issue are mentioned) works best when the audience is well informed on the issue, is fairly intelligent, or is initially opposed to the point of view. A two-sided appeal will usually sway more people than a one-sided appeal (Hovland et al., 1949; McGuire, 1985). And people tend to scrutinize arguments that are contrary to their existing beliefs more carefully and exert more effort refuting them; they are also more likely to judge such arguments as weaker than those that support their beliefs (Edwards & Smith, 1996).

> What qualities make a source most persuasive?

A message can be well reasoned, logical, and unemotional ("just the facts"); a message can be strictly emotional ("scare the hell out of them"); or it can be a combination of the two. Arousing fear seems to be an effective method for persuading people to quit smoking and wear seat belts. Appeals based on fear are most effective when the presentation outlines definite actions the audience can take to avoid the feared outcomes (Buller et al., 2000; Stephenson & Witte, 1998). By contrast, nutritional messages are more effective when framed in terms of the benefits of dietary change than in terms of the harmful effects of a poor diet (van Assema et al., 2001).

Another important factor in persuasion is repetition. The more often a product or a point of view is presented, the more people will be persuaded to buy it or embrace it. Advertisers apparently believe in this *mere-exposure effect*, for they repeat their messages over and over (Bornstein, 1989). But messages are likely to be less persuasive if they include vivid elements (colorful language, striking examples) that hinder the reception of the content (Frey & Eagly, 1993).

Prosocial Behavior

Reasons for Helping

There are many kinds of **prosocial behavior**—behavior that benefits others, such as helping, cooperation, and sympathy. Such impulses arise early in life. Researchers agree that young children respond sympathetically to companions in distress, usually before their second birthday (Hay, 1994; Kochanska, 1993). The term **altruism** is usually reserved for behavior that is aimed at helping others and requires some self-sacrifice but is not performed for personal gain. Batson and colleagues (1989) believe that we help out of *empathy*—the ability to take the perspective of others, to put oneself in their place.

Cultures vary in their norms for helping others—that is, their *social responsibility norms.* According to Miller and others (1990), people in the United States tend to feel an obligation to help family, friends, and even strangers in life-threatening circum-

prosocial behavior
Behavior that benefits others, such as helping, cooperation, and sympathy.

altruism
Behavior aimed at helping another, requiring some self-sacrifice and not designed for personal gain.

stances, but only family in moderately serious situations. In contrast, in India, the social responsibility norm extends to strangers whose needs are only moderately serious or even minor.

The Bystander Effect

There are a variety of social circumstances that contribute to the decision to help another person. One such circumstance involves the **bystander effect:** As the number of bystanders at an emergency increases, the probability that the victim will receive help from them decreases, and the help, if given, is likely to be delayed. In now-classic research, Darley and Latané (1968a) placed research participants one at a time in a small room and told them that they would be participating in a discussion group by means of an intercom system. Some participants were told that they would be communicating with only one other participant, some believed that two other participants would be involved, and some were told that five other people would participate. There really were no other participants in the study—only the prerecorded voices of confederates assisting the experimenter.

Shortly after the discussion began, the voice of one confederate was heard over the intercom calling for help, indicating that he was having an epileptic seizure. Of the participants who believed that they alone were hearing the victim, 85% went for help before the end of the seizure. When participants believed that one other person heard the seizure, 62% sought help. But when they believed that four other people were aware of the emergency, only 31% tried to get help before the end of the seizure. Figure 14.7 shows how the number of bystanders affects both the number of people who try to help and the speed of response.

Latané and Darley suggest that, when bystanders are present in an emergency, they generally feel that the responsibility for helping is shared by the group, a phenomenon known as **diffusion of responsibility.** Consequently, each person feels less compelled to act than if she or he were alone and felt the total responsibility. Each thinks that "somebody else must be doing something" (Darley & Latané, 1968a). Another reason for the bystander effect, according to Darley & Latané, is the influence of other calm-appearing bystanders. When others appear calm, people may conclude that nothing is really wrong and no intervention is necessary (Darley & Latané, 1968b).

Interestingly, during catastrophes such as those on September 11, 2001, the bystander effect is greatly reduced. In fact, people are likely to put forth extraordinary effort to help others in such situations. This phenomenon was evidenced by the countless individual acts of altruism that occurred in both Washington, DC, and New York City immediately after the terrorist attacks. And those who couldn't help directly contributed millions of dollars to the families of 9/11 victims within hours after the events.

Why do people often ignore someone who is unconscious on the sidewalk? Diffusion of responsibility is one possible explanation.

What is the bystander effect, and what factors have been suggested to explain why it occurs?

bystander effect
The fact that as the number of bystanders at an emergency increases, the probability that the victim will receive help decreases, and help, if given, is likely to be delayed.

diffusion of responsibility
The feeling among bystanders at an emergency that the responsibility for helping is shared by the group, so each person feels less compelled to act than if he or she alone bore the total responsibility.

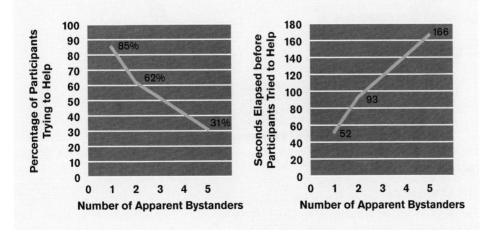

> **Figure 14.7**
The Bystander Effect

In their intercom experiment, Darley and Latané showed that the more people a participant believed were present during an emergency, the longer it took the participant to respond and help a person in distress. (Data from Darley & Latané, 1968a.)

Research examining public responses to large-scale disasters would predict just such a level of response (Shepperd, 2001).

Aggression

Aggression is the intentional infliction of physical or psychological harm on others. Aggression may form and take place in a variety of locations—at home, at work, or even among drivers on the road. Acts of aggression against others' person or property take place frequently in the United States, as shown in Figure 14.8. But why does one person intentionally harm another?

Biological Factors in Aggression

Sigmund Freud believed that humans have an aggressive instinct that can be turned inward as self-destruction or outward as aggression or violence toward others. While rejecting this view, many psychologists do concede that biological factors are involved. A review of 24 twin and adoption studies of several personality measures of aggression revealed a heritability estimate of about .50 for aggression (Miles & Carey, 1997). Twin and adoption studies have also revealed a genetic link for criminal behavior (DiLalla & Gottesman, 1991). Cloninger and others (1982) found that adoptees with a criminal biological parent were four times as likely as members of the general population to commit a crime, adoptees with a criminal adoptive parent were at twice the risk of committing a crime, but adoptees with both a biological and an adoptive parent who had a criminal record were fourteen times as likely to commit a crime. This finding indicates the power of the combined influences of nature and nurture.

What biological factors are thought to be related to aggression?

aggression
The intentional infliction of physical or psychological harm on another.

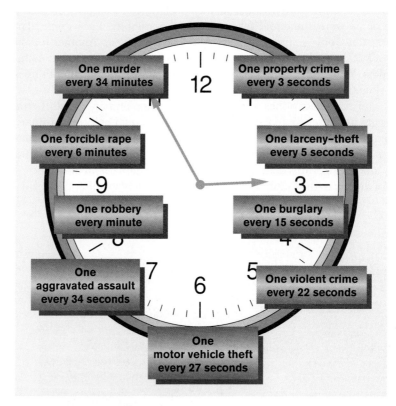

➤ Figure 14.8

The Crime Clock

This clock shows the frequency at which certain crimes occur in the United States. (Federal Bureau of Investigation, 1999.)

One biological factor that seems closely related to aggression is a low arousal level of the autonomic nervous system (Raine, 1996). Low arousal level (low heart rate and lower reactivity) has been linked to antisocial and violent behavior (Brennan et al., 1997). People with low arousal levels tend to seek stimulation and excitement and often exhibit fearlessness, even in the face of danger.

Men are more physically aggressive than women (Green et al., 1996), and the male hormone testosterone is partly the cause. In fact, the primary biological variable related to domestic violence (both verbal and physical abuse) appears to be high testosterone levels, which are highly heritable (Soler et al., 2000). A correlation between high testosterone level and aggressive behavior has been found in males (Archer, 1991; Dabbs & Morris, 1990), and Harris and others (1996) found testosterone levels in both male *and* female college students to be positively correlated with aggression and negatively correlated with prosocial behavior. And violent behavior has been associated with low levels of the neurotransmitter serotonin (Gartner & Whitaker-Azimitia, 1996; Mitsis et al., 2000).

Brain damage, brain tumors, and temporal lobe epilepsy have all been related to aggressive and violent behavior (Mednick et al., 1988; van Elst et al., 2000). A study of 15 death row inmates revealed that all had histories of severe head injuries (Lewis et al., 1986). According to Eronen and others (1996), homicide rates are eight times higher in men with schizophrenia and ten times higher in men with antisocial personality disorder. The risk of violence is even greater when individuals with these disorders abuse alcohol (Hodgins et al., 1996; Tiihonen et al., 1997). In children, high levels of lead exposure (Needleman et al., 1996) and low IQ and problems paying attention (Loeber & Hay, 1997) are related to aggressive behavior and delinquency.

Alcohol and aggression are also frequent partners. A review of 30 experimental studies indicated that alcohol is related to aggression (Bushman & Cooper, 1990). Alcohol and other drugs that affect the brain's prefrontal cortex lead to aggressive behavior in humans and other animals by disrupting normal emotional and behavioral control functions (Lyvers, 2000). Ito and others (1996) found that alcohol intoxication is particularly likely to lead to aggression in response to frustration. People who are intoxicated commit the majority of murders, spouse beatings, stabbings, and acts of physical child abuse.

▲ Crowding may or may not be stressful depending on the situation—waiting in a crowded airport terminal is more likely to be perceived as stressful than being part of a large crowd at a rally on Martin Luther King Jr. Day.

frustration-aggression hypothesis
The hypothesis that frustration produces aggression.

scapegoating
Displacing aggression onto minority groups or other innocent targets not responsible for the frustrating situation.

Aggression in Response to Frustration and Aversive Events

The **frustration-aggression hypothesis** suggests that frustration produces aggression (Dollard et al., 1939; Miller, 1941). If a traffic jam delayed you and you were frustrated, would you lean on your horn, shout obscenities out of your window, or just sit patiently and wait? Frustration doesn't always cause aggression, but it is especially likely to if it is intense and seems to be unjustified (Doob & Sears, 1939; Pastore, 1950). Berkowitz (1988) points out that even if frustration is justified and not aimed specifically at an individual, it can cause aggression if it arouses negative emotions.

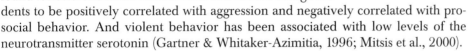
What is the frustration-aggression hypothesis?

Aggression in response to frustration is not always aimed at the people causing it. If the preferred target is too threatening or not available, the aggression may be displaced. For example, children who are angry with their parents may take out their frustrations on younger siblings. Sometimes members of minority groups or others who have not been responsible for a frustrating situation become targets of displaced aggression, a practice known as **scapegoating** (Koltz, 1983).

People often become aggressive when they are in pain (Berkowitz, 1983) or are exposed to loud noise or foul odors (Rotton et al., 1979). Extreme heat has also been linked to aggression in several studies (Anderson & Anderson,

What kinds of aversive events and unpleasant emotions have been related to aggression?

1996; Rotton & Cohn, 2000). These and other studies lend support to the *cognitive-neoassociationistic model* proposed by Berkowitz (1990). He has suggested that anger and aggression result from aversive events and from unpleasant emotional states such as sadness, grief, and depression. The cognitive component of Berkowitz's model involves the angered person's appraising the aversive situation and making attributions about the motives of the people involved. As a result of the cognitive appraisal, the initial reaction of anger can be intensified or reduced or suppressed. This process makes the person either more or less likely to act on the aggressive tendency.

Personal space is an area surrounding each individual, much like an invisible bubble, that the person considers part of himself or herself and uses to regulate the closeness of interactions with others. Personal space serves to protect personal privacy and to regulate the level of intimacy with others. The size of personal space varies according to the person or persons with whom an individual is interacting and the nature of the interaction. And when personal space is reduced, aggression can result.

Crowding—the subjective judgment that there are too many people in a confined space—often leads to higher physiological arousal. Males typically experience the effects of crowding more negatively than females do, and those effects also vary across cultures and situations. Researchers have studied the effects of crowding on such diverse populations as male heads of households in India and middle-class male and female college students in the United States (Evans & Lepore, 1993). In both of these studies, psychological distress was linked to household crowding. And studies in prisons have shown that the more inmates per cell, the greater the number of violent incidents (Paulus et al., 1988). However, keep in mind that a prison is an atypical environment with a population whose members have been confined precisely because they tend to be aggressive.

The Social Learning Theory of Aggression

The *social learning theory of aggression* holds that people learn to behave aggressively by observing aggressive models and by having their aggressive responses reinforced (Bandura, 1973). It is well known that aggression is higher in groups and subcultures that condone violent behavior and accord high status to aggressive members. A leading advocate of the social learning theory of aggression, Albert Bandura (1976), claims that aggressive models in the subculture, the family, and the media all play a part in increasing the level of aggression in society.

> According to social learning theory, what causes aggressive behavior?

Abused children certainly experience aggression and see it modeled day after day. And the rate of physical abuse is seven times greater in families in which there is a stepparent (Daly & Wilson, 1996). "One of the most commonly held beliefs in both the scholarly and popular literature is that adults who were abused as children are more likely to abuse their own children" (Widom, 1989, p. 6). There is some truth to this belief. On the basis of original research and an analysis of 60 other studies, Oliver (1993) concludes that one-third of people who are abused go on to become abusers, one-third do not, and the final third may become abusers if their lives are highly stressful.

Most abusive parents, however, were not abused as children (Widom, 1989). Although abused and neglected children are at higher risk of becoming delinquent, criminal, or violent, the majority do not (Widom & Maxfield, 1996). Several researchers suggest that the higher risk for aggression may not be due solely to an abusive family environment but may be partly influenced by the genes (DiLalla & Gottesman, 1991). Some abused children become withdrawn and isolated rather than aggressive and abusive (Dodge et al., 1990).

The research evidence overwhelmingly supports a relationship between TV violence and viewer aggression (Huesmann & Moise, 1996; Singer et al., 1999). And the negative effects of TV violence are even worse for individuals who are, by nature, highly aggressive (Bushman, 1995). According to Eron (1987, p. 438), "One of the best predictors of how aggressive a young man would be at age 19 was the violence of the TV programs he preferred when he was 8 years old." A longitudinal study conducted in Finland also found that the viewing of TV violence was related to criminality in young adulthood (Viemerö, 1996). And a review of 28 studies of the effects of media violence on children and adolescents revealed that "media violence enhances children's and adolescents' aggression in interactions with strangers, classmates, and friends" (Wood et al., 1991, p. 380). It may stimulate physiological arousal, lower inhibitions, cause unpleasant feelings, and decrease sensitivity to violence and make it more acceptable to people.

Researchers have also found a correlation between playing violent video games and aggression (Anderson & Dill, 2000). Moreover, aggressiveness increases as more time is spent playing such games (Colwell & Payne, 2000). However, researchers in the Netherlands found that boys who chose aggressive video games tended to be more aggressive, less intelligent, and less prosocial in their behavior (Weigman & van Schie, 1998). So the link between aggression and video games may reflect the tendency of individuals who are more aggressive to prefer entertainment media that feature aggression.

Prejudice and Discrimination

Prejudice consists of (usually negative) attitudes toward others based on their gender, religion, race, or membership in a particular group. Prejudice involves beliefs and emotions (not actions) that can escalate into hatred. **Discrimination** consists of behavior—actions (usually negative) toward members of a group. Many Americans have experienced prejudice and discrimination—minority racial groups (racism), women (sexism), the elderly (ageism), the handicapped, homosexuals, religious groups, and others. What are the roots of prejudice and discrimination?

> What is the difference between prejudice and discrimination?

prejudice
Negative attitudes toward others based on their gender, religion, race, or membership in a particular group.

discrimination
Behavior, usually negative, directed toward others based on their gender, religion, race, or membership in a particular group.

The Roots of Prejudice and Discrimination

One of the oldest explanations of how prejudice arises is that it comes from competition among various social groups who must struggle against one another for scarce resources—good jobs, homes, schools, and so on. Commonly called the **realistic conflict theory,** this view suggests that as competition increases, so do prejudice, discrimination, and hatred among the competing groups. Some historical evidence supports the realistic conflict theory. Prejudice and hatred were high between the early settlers and the Native Americans who struggled over land during the westward expansion. The multitudes of Irish and German immigrants who came to the United States in the 1830s and 1840s felt the sting of prejudice and hatred from other Americans who were facing economic scarcity. But prejudice and discrimination are attitudes and actions too complex to be explained solely by economic conflict and competition.

Prejudice can also spring from the distinct social categories into which people divide the world—us versus them (Turner et al., 1987). An **in-group** is a social group in which there is a strong feeling of togetherness and from which others are excluded. Members of college fraternities and sororities often exhibit strong in-group feelings. An **out-group** consists of individuals or groups specifically identified by an in-group as not belonging. Us-versus-them thinking can lead to excessive competition, hostility, prejudice, discrimination, and even war. Prejudiced individuals who most strongly identify with their racial in-group are most reluctant to admit others to the group if there is the slightest doubt about their racial purity (Blascovich et al., 1997).

A famous study by Sherif and Sherif (1967) shows how in-group/out-group conflict can escalate into prejudice and hostility rather quickly, even between groups that are very much alike. The researchers set up their experiment at the Robber's Cave summer camp. Their subjects were 22 bright, well-adjusted, 11- and 12-year-old Cau-

realistic conflict theory
The notion that prejudices arise when social groups must compete for scarce resources and opportunities.

> What are in-groups and out-groups?

in-group
A social group in which there is a strong sense of togetherness and from which others are excluded.

out-group
A social group specifically identified by an in-group as not belonging.

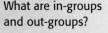

casian middle-class boys from Oklahoma City. Divided into two groups and housed in separate cabins, the boys were kept apart for all their daily activities and games. During the first week, in-group solidarity, friendship, and cooperation developed within each of the groups.

During the second week of the study, competitive events were purposely scheduled so that the goals of one group could be achieved "only at the expense of the other group" (Sherif, 1958, p. 353). The groups were happy to battle each other, and intergroup conflict quickly emerged. Name-calling began, fights broke out, and accusations were hurled back and forth. During the third week of the experiment, the researchers tried to put an end to the hostility and to turn rivalry into cooperation. They simply brought the groups together for pleasant activities such as eating meals and watching movies. "But far from reducing conflict, these situations only served as opportunities for the rival groups to berate and attack each other. . . . They threw paper, food and vile names at each other at the tables" (Sherif, 1956, pp. 57–58).

Finally, the researchers manufactured a series of crises that could be solved only if all the boys combined their efforts and resources and cooperated. The water supply, sabotaged by the researchers, could be restored only if all the boys worked together. After a week of several activities requiring cooperation, cut-throat competition gave way to cooperative exchanges. Friendships developed between groups, and before the end of the experiment, peace was declared. Working together toward shared goals had turned hostility into friendship.

> **How does prejudice develop, according to the social learning theory?**

According to social learning theory, people learn attitudes of prejudice and hatred the same way they learn other attitudes. If children hear their parents, teachers, peers, and others openly express prejudices toward different racial, ethnic, religious, or cultural groups, they may be quick to learn such attitudes. And if parents, peers, and others reward children with smiles and approval for parroting their own prejudices (operant conditioning), children may learn these prejudices even more quickly. Phillips and Ziller (1997) suggest that people learn to be nonprejudiced in the same way.

Emotion- and learning-based views help explain how prejudice develops. But a more recent view suggests that social cognition plays a role in giving birth to prejudice. **Social cognition** refers to the ways in which people typically process social information—the natural thinking processes used to notice, interpret, and remember information about the social world. The very processes we use to simplify, categorize, and order the social world are the same processes that distort our views of it. So prejudice may arise not only from heated negative emotions and hatred toward other social groups, but also from cooler cognitive processes that govern how we think and process social information (Kunda & Oleson, 1995).

> **What are stereotypes?**

One way people simplify, categorize, and order the world is by using stereotypes. **Stereotypes** are widely shared beliefs about the characteristics of members of various social groups (racial, ethnic, religious), which include the assumption that "they" are usually all alike. Macrae and colleagues (1994) suggest that people apply stereotypes in their interactions with others because doing so requires less mental energy than trying to understand others as individuals. Stereotyping allows people to make quick, automatic (thoughtless) judgments about others and apply their mental resources to other activities (Forgas & Fiedler, 1996). Research by Anderson and others (1990) showed that participants could process information more efficiently and answer questions faster when they were using stereotypes.

Some research has revealed that people tend to perceive more diversity—more variability—within the groups to which they belong (in-groups), but they see more similarity among members of other groups (out-groups) (Ostrom et al., 1993). Caucasian Americans see more diversity among themselves but more sameness within groups of African or Asian Americans. This tendency in stereotypical thinking can be based on race, gender, age, or any other characteristic. Another study showed that young college students believed that there was much more variability in 100 of them than in a group of 100 elderly Americans, whom the students perceived to be

social cognition
Mental processes that people use to notice, interpret, understand, remember, and apply information about the social world and that enable them to simplify, categorize, and order that world.

stereotypes
Widely shared beliefs about the characteristic traits, attitudes, and behaviors of members of various social groups (racial, ethnic, religious), including the assumption that the members of such groups are usually all alike.

much the same (Linville et al., 1989). And a study involving elderly adults showed that they perceived more variability within their own age group than among college students. Age stereotypes can be even more pronounced and negative than gender stereotypes (Kite et al., 1991).

Some research indicates that prejudice and stereotyping (whether conscious or not) may be means of bolstering one's self-image by disparaging others (Fein & Spencer, 1997). Moreover, some minority group members may protect their self-esteem by attempting to minimize discrimination or by denying its significance (Ruggiero & Taylor, 1997).

Can you perceive differences among the young girls shown here? Research shows that people typically perceive more variability among members of groups to which they belong and more similarity among members of groups with which they are unfamiliar.

Discrimination in the Workplace

Research conducted at Princeton University by Word and others (1974) indicates that stereotypic thinking can govern people's expectancies. And often what we expect is what we get, regardless of whether our expectancies are high or low. Participants in one study were Caucasian American undergraduates who were to interview Caucasian and African American job applicants (actually confederates of the researchers). The researchers secretly videotaped the interviews and studied the tapes to see if the student interviewers had treated the African American and Caucasian American applicants differently. The researchers found substantial differences in the interviews based on the race of the applicants. The interviewers spent less time with the African American applicants, maintained a greater physical distance from them, and generally were less friendly and outgoing. During interviews with these applicants, the interviewers' speech deteriorated–they made more errors in grammar and pronunciation.

In a followup study, the same researchers trained Caucasian American confederates to copy the two different interview styles used in the first study (Word et al., 1974). The confederates then used the different styles to interview a group of Caucasian American job applicants. These interviews were videotaped as well, and later a panel of judges evaluated the tapes. The judges agreed that applicants who were subjected to the interview style for African Americans were more nervous and performed more poorly than applicants interviewed according to the "Caucasian" style. The experimenters concluded that, as a result of the interview style they experienced, the African American job applicants from the first study were not given the opportunity to demonstrate their skills and qualifications to the best of their ability. Thus, they were subjected to a subtle form of discrimination in which their performance was hampered by the expectancies of their interviewers.

Even though federal legislation forbids hiring, promoting, laying off, or awarding benefits to workers on the basis of sex, race, color, national origin, or religion, studies continue to show that workplace discrimination exists (Renzetti & Curran, 1992). A considerable body of research refutes the notion that deficiencies due to gender or race explain why so few women and minorities are in upper management (Morrison & Von Glinow, 1990). Nevertheless, the mere perception of deficiencies, if held by the dominant corporate leaders, is sufficient to produce bias and discrimination.

Morrison and Von Glinow (1990) claim that "discrimination occurs in part because of the belief by Caucasian men that women and people of color are less suited for management than white men" (p. 202). The dominant group's belief that customers, employees, and others are more comfortable dealing with or working for Caucasian male managers may lead to discrimination. In such cases, these managers may be less willing to promote women and minorities to sensitive, responsible management positions.

Tokenism is a subtle form of discrimination in which people are hired or promoted primarily because they represent a specific group or category rather than strictly on the basis of their qualifications. Female and minority employees may be perceived by the White male majority as "tokens," especially as they move up in the ranks of man-

One form of discrimination that African Americans may face as job applicants is a tendency for White interviewers to use an interviewing style based on stereotypical thinking.

agement. But "tokens" are interchangeable. If placed in a position solely to meet a company's affirmative action goals, one token is as good as another, as long as he or she represents the right category. No matter how eminently qualified an employee may be, if the employee perceives that he or she is a token, the individual suffers and so does the organization.

Is Prejudice Increasing or Decreasing?

Few people would readily admit to being prejudiced. Gordon Allport (1954), a pioneer in research on prejudice, said, "Defeated intellectually, prejudice lingers emotionally" (p. 328). Even those who are sincerely intellectually opposed to prejudice may still harbor some prejudiced feelings (Devine, 1989). However, most people feel guilty when they catch themselves having prejudiced thoughts or engaging in discriminatory behavior (Volis et al., 2002).

Is there any evidence that prejudice is decreasing in U.S. society? Gallup polls revealed that Caucasian Americans became more racially tolerant over the final decades of the 20th century (Gallup & Hugick, 1990). When Caucasian Americans were asked in 1990 whether they would move if African Americans were to move next door to them, 93% said no, compared with 65% in 1965. Even if African Americans were to move into their neighborhood in great numbers, 68% of Caucasians still said they would not move. Moreover, both Caucasian and African Americans overwhelmingly agree that conditions have improved for minorities in the United States over the past several decades (Public Agenda Online, 2002). However, there are still marked differences of opinion among ethnic and racial groups as to whether racism continues to be a problem in the United States, as you can see in Figure 14.9.

Recall, too, that attitudes do not always predict behavior. In a recent study, researchers asked participants to judge whether a fictitious woman was qualified to be the president of a parent-teacher organization (Lott & Saxon, 2002). Participants were provided with information about the woman's occupation and education. In addition, they were told, based on random assignment, that the woman's ethnic background was Hispanic, Anglo-Saxon, or Jewish. The experimenters found that participants who believed the woman to be Hispanic were more likely than those who thought her

> ## Figure 14.9
Perceptions of Racism in the United States

African Americans and Hispanic Americans are more likely than White Americans to say that racism is a major problem in various areas of U.S. society. (Data from Princeton Survey Research/Kaiser 9/99.)

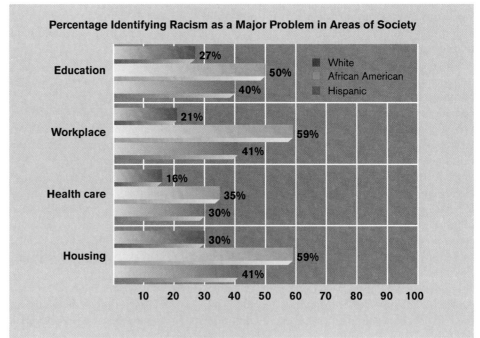

Percentage Identifying Racism as a Major Problem in Areas of Society

Education — White 27%, African American 50%, Hispanic 40%

Workplace — White 21%, African American 59%, Hispanic 41%

Health care — White 16%, African American 35%, Hispanic 30%

Housing — White 30%, African American 59%, Hispanic 41%

www.ablongman.com/woodmastering1e

Apply It !   "Unlearning" Prejudice

Today's U.S. college population is more diverse than ever before. Minorities are attending college in higher numbers, and people from all over the world come to the United States to further their educations. Consequently, for many people, campus life represents a unique opportunity to interact with others of different racial, ethnic, or cultural groups. How can students make the most of this chance to "unlearn" the prejudices they may bring with them to the college experience? Here are some opportunities you may find on your campus (and if you don't, step up and create them yourself!).

Intergroup contact As you learned from Sherif's Robber's Cave experiment, intergroup contact can sometimes lead to more stereotyping (Sherif & Sherif, 1967). Under the right conditions, though, intergroup contact can reduce prejudice. Sherif outlined the conditions under which intergroup contact reduces prejudice, and his findings have been confirmed and extended by others (Aronson, 1990; Finchilescu, 1988).

- Interacting groups should be approximately equal in social and economic status and in their ability to do the tasks to be performed.
- The intergroup contact must be cooperative (not competitive) in nature, and work should be confined to shared goals.
- The contact should be informal, so that friendly interactions develop more easily and group members get to know each other individually.

- The contact situation should be one in which conditions favor group equality.
- The individuals involved should perceive each other as typical members of the groups to which they belong.

There are few, if any, campuses on which equal representation of all groups has been achieved. Still, college can provide a context in which students from diverse backgrounds study together, endure the same trials (midterms and finals), develop a shared sense of school spirit, join clubs in which members from different backgrounds share common goals, and so on. So campus life offers some potential for reducing prejudice merely through intergroup contact.

The jigsaw technique Methods such as the *jigsaw technique*—a strategy that works well in college classrooms and, as a game, in less formal interactions—represent a more direct approach. First, participants are divided into "jigsaw" groups in which genders and races are equally represented. Then each participant is given a small amount of information and asked to teach it to other participants. The group must use all the individual pieces of information to solve a problem. This approach increases interaction among participants and helps them develop empathy for members of other ethnic and racial groups (Aronson, 1988; Aronson et al., 1998; Singh, 1991; Walker & Crogan, 1998). A side benefit is that it is an effective way of learning a new solution to a problem.

Diversity education Many colleges offer students and faculty opportunities to participate in seminars and workshops designed to combat racism, which can also help to reduce prejudice and discrimination. In such settings, participants learn about racial and cultural perspectives that may differ from their own. They also learn to identify behaviors of their own that may be construed as racist by others, even though that may not be what they intend. Researchers have found that such programs help to reduce automatic stereotyping among participants (Hill & Augoustinos, 2001; Rudman et al., 2001).

Open discussions of prejudice and discrimination Perhaps the greatest potential of the college campus for reducing prejudice and discrimination lies in the nature of its intellectual climate. Traditionally, college classes, as well as club meetings, gatherings at restaurants, all-night study sessions in coffee shops, and late-night debates in dorm rooms, often feature lively discussions of a variety of topics. And hearing others speak passionately about racism, sexism, and other types of injustice can encourage people to adopt more tolerant attitudes themselves.

So, the next time you hear someone make a statement you feel is racist or sexist or that may promote discrimination, speak up! You never know how influential your voice might be. ■

---

to be Anglo-Saxon or Jewish to say that she was not qualified for the position. Moreover, researchers have learned that teachers are more likely to attribute Caucasian children's behavior problems to situational variables and those of minority children to dispositional factors (Jackson, 2002).

Such studies suggest that racial stereotyping is still evident in the United States. But there are many things we can do to combat prejudice and discrimination, as you will learn from reading the *Apply It!*

Summarize It!

Social Perception

➤ **Why are first impressions so important and enduring?**

First impressions are important because people attend more carefully to the first information they receive about another person and because, once formed, an impression acts as a framework through which later information is interpreted.

➤ **What is the difference between a situational attribution and a dispositional attribution for a specific behavior?**

An attribution is an inference about the cause of one's own or another's behavior. In making situational attributions, people attribute the cause of behavior to some factor in the environment. With dispositional attributions, the inferred cause is internal—some personal trait, motive, or attitude.

➤ **How do the kinds of attributions people tend to make about themselves differ from those they make about other people?**

People tend to attribute their own behavior primarily to situational factors and the behavior of others primarily to internal or dispositional factors, a tendency known as the actor-observer effect.

KEY TERMS

social psychology (p. 394)
confederate (p. 394)
naive subject (p. 394)
primacy effect (p. 395)
attribution (p. 395)
situational attribution (p. 395)
dispositional attribution (p. 395)
actor-observer effect (p. 395)
self-serving bias (p. 395)

Attraction

➤ **Why is proximity an important factor in attraction?**

Proximity influences attraction because people find it easier to develop relationships with others who are close at hand. Also, proximity increases the likelihood that there will be repeated contacts, and mere exposure tends to increase attraction (the mere-exposure effect).

➤ **How important is physical attractiveness in attraction?**

Physical attractiveness plays a major role in attraction for people of all ages. People attribute positive qualities to those who are physically attractive—a phenomenon called the halo effect.

➤ **How does Sternberg's triangular theory of love explain love?**

In his triangular theory of love, Sternberg proposes that three components—intimacy, passion, and decision/commitment—singly and in various combinations, produce seven different kinds of love: infatuated, empty, romantic, fatuous, companionate, and consummate love, as well as liking.

KEY TERMS

proximity (p. 396)
mere-exposure effect (p. 396)
halo effect (p. 397)
matching hypothesis (p. 397)
triangular theory of love (p. 398)

Social Influence

➤ **What did Asch find in his famous experiment on conformity?**

In Asch's classic experiment on conformity, 5% of the participants went along with the incorrect, unanimous majority all the time; 70% went along some of the time; and 25% remained completely independent.

➤ **What did researchers find when the circumstances of Milgram's classic study of obedience were varied?**

Participants were almost as likely to obey experimenters when the study was repeated at a shabby office building rather than at Yale University. However, Milgram also found that when participants were paired with confederates who refused to obey the experimenter, they were more likely to disobey themselves.

➤ **What are three techniques used to gain compliance?**

Three techniques used to gain compliance are the foot-in-the-door technique, the door-in-the-face technique, and the low-ball technique.

KEY TERMS

conformity (p. 399)
social norms (p. 399)
compliance (p. 400)
foot-in-the-door technique (p. 401)
door-in-the-face technique (p. 401)
low-ball technique (p. 401)

Group Influence

➤ **Under what conditions does social facilitation have either a positive or a negative effect on performance?**

When others are present, either as an audience or as co-actors, a person's performance on easy tasks is usually improved, but performance on difficult tasks is usually impaired.

➤ **What is social loafing, and what factors lessen or eliminate it?**

Social loafing is people's tendency to put forth less effort when they are working with others on a common task than when working alone. It is less likely to occur when individual output can be monitored or when people have a personal stake in the outcome.

➤ **How are the initial attitudes of group members likely to affect group decision making?**

Following group discussions, group decisions usually shift to a more extreme position in whatever direction the members were leaning toward initially—a phenomenon known as group polarization.

KEY TERMS

social facilitation (p. 401)
audience effects (p. 401)
co-action effects (p. 401)
social loafing (p. 402)
group polarization (p. 403)
groupthink (p. 403)
social roles (p. 403)

Attitudes and Attitude Change

➤ **What are the three components of an attitude?**

An attitude usually has a cognitive, an emotional, and a behavioral component.

➤ **What is cognitive dissonance, and how can it be resolved?**

Cognitive dissonance is an unpleasant state that can occur when people become aware of inconsistencies among their attitudes or between their attitudes and their behavior. People can resolve cognitive dissonance by rationalizing away the inconsistency or by changing the attitude or the behavior.

➤ **What are the four elements of persuasion?**

The four elements of persuasion are the source, the audience, the message, and the medium.

➤ **What qualities make a source most persuasive?**

Persuasive attempts are most successful when the source is credible (expert and trustworthy), attractive, and likable.

KEY TERMS

attitude (p. 404)
cognitive dissonance (p. 405)
persuasion (p. 405)

Prosocial Behavior

➤ **What is the bystander effect, and what factors have been suggested to explain why it occurs?**

The bystander effect is the fact that, as the number of bystanders at an emergency increases, the probability that the victim will receive help decreases, and help, if given, is likely to be delayed. The bystander effect may be due in part to diffusion of responsibility or, in ambiguous situations, to the assumption that no emergency exists.

KEY TERMS

prosocial behavior (p. 406)
altruism (p. 406)

bystander effect (p. 407)
diffusion of responsibility (p. 407)

Aggression

➤ **What biological factors are thought to be related to aggression?**

Biological factors thought to be related to aggression are genes, high testosterone levels, low levels of serotonin, and brain damage.

➤ **What is the frustration-aggression hypothesis?**

The frustration-aggression hypothesis holds that frustration produces aggression and that this aggression may be directed at the source of the frustration or displaced onto another target, as in scapegoating.

➤ **What kinds of aversive events and unpleasant emotions have been related to aggression?**

Aggression has been associated with aversive conditions such as pain, heat, loud noise, foul odors, violations of personal space, and crowding and with unpleasant emotional states such as sadness, grief, and depression.

➤ **According to social learning theory, what causes aggressive behavior?**

According to social learning theory, people acquire aggressive responses by observing aggressive models in the family, the subculture, and the media and by having aggressive responses reinforced.

KEY TERMS

aggression (p. 408)
frustration-aggression hypothesis (p. 409)
scapegoating (p. 409)
personal space (p. 410)
crowding (p. 410)

Prejudice and Discrimination

➤ **What is the difference between prejudice and discrimination?**

Prejudice consists of (usually negative) attitudes toward others based on their gender, religion, race, or membership in a particular group. Discrimination consists of actions against others based on the same factors.

➤ **What are in-groups and out-groups?**

An in-group is a social group in which there is a strong sense of togetherness and from which others are excluded; an out-group consists of individuals or groups specifically identified by an in-group as not belonging.

➤ **How does prejudice develop, according to the social learning theory?**

According to this theory, prejudice is learned the same way other attitudes are–through modeling and reinforcement.

➤ **What are stereotypes?**

Stereotypes are widely shared beliefs about the characteristics of members of various social groups (racial, ethnic, or religious), including the assumption that the members of such groups are usually all alike.

KEY TERMS

prejudice (p. 411)
discrimination (p. 411)
realistic conflict theory (p. 411)
in-group (p. 411)
out-group (p. 411)
social cognition (p. 412)
stereotypes (p. 412)

Surf It !

Want to be sure you've absorbed the material in Chapter 14, "Social Psychology," before the big test? Visiting **www.ablongman.com/ woodmastering1e** can put a top grade within your reach. The site is loaded with free practice tests, flashcards, activities, and links to help you review your way to an A.

Answers to all the Study Guide questions are provided at the end of the book.

Section One: Chapter Review

1. Which of the following statements about first impressions is *false?*
   a. People usually pay closer attention to early information they receive about a person than to later information.
   b. Early information forms a framework through which later information is interpreted.
   c. First impressions often serve as self-fulfilling prophecies.
   d. The importance of first impressions is greatly overrated.

2. People tend to make _____ attributions to explain their own behavior and _____ attributions to explain the behavior of others.
   a. situational; situational
   b. situational; dispositional
   c. dispositional; situational
   d. dispositional; dispositional

3. Attributing Mike's poor grade to his lack of ability is a dispositional attribution. (true/false)

4. Match each term with a description.
   ____ (1) Brian sees Kelly at the library often and begins to like her.
   ____ (2) Lori assumes that because Michael is handsome, he must be popular and sociable.
   ____ (3) Kate and Kurt are going together and are both very attractive.
   a. matching hypothesis
   b. halo effect
   c. mere-exposure effect

5. Physical attractiveness is a very important factor in initial attraction. (true/false)

6. People are usually drawn to those who are more opposite than similar to themselves. (true/false)

7. Match the technique for gaining compliance with the appropriate example.
   ____ (1) Meghan agrees to sign a letter supporting an increase in taxes for road construction. Later she agrees to make 100 phone calls urging people to vote for the measure.
   ____ (2) Jude refuses a phone request for a $24 donation to send four needy children to the circus but does agree to give $6.
   ____ (3) Lexie agrees to babysit for her next-door neighbors' two girls and then is informed that their three nephews will be there, too.

   a. door-in-the-face technique
   b. low-ball technique
   c. foot-in-the-door technique

8. What percentage of subjects in the Asch study never conformed to the majority's unanimous incorrect response?
   a. 70%   **c.** 25%
   b. 33%   **d.** 5%

9. What percentage of the subjects in Milgram's original obedience experiment administered what they thought was the maximum 450-volt shock?
   a. 85%   **c.** 45%
   b. 65%   **d.** 25%

10. Which of the following statements regarding the effects of social facilitation (the presence of other people) is true?
   a. Performance improves on all tasks.
   b. Performance worsens on all tasks.
   c. Performance improves on easy tasks and worsens on difficult tasks.
   d. Performance improves on difficult tasks and worsens on easy tasks.

11. Social loafing is most likely to occur when
   a. individual output is monitored.
   b. individual output is evaluated.
   c. a task is challenging.
   d. individual output cannot be identified.

12. What occurs when members of a very cohesive group are more concerned with preserving group solidarity than with evaluating all possible alternatives in making a decision?
   a. groupthink   **c.** social facilitation
   b. group polarization **d.** social loafing

13. Which of the following is *not* one of the three components of an attitude?
   a. cognitive component
   b. emotional component
   c. physiological component
   d. behavioral component

14. All of the following are ways to reduce cognitive dissonance *except*
   a. changing an attitude.
   b. changing a behavior.
   c. explaining away the inconsistency.
   d. strengthening the attitude and behavior.

15. People who have made a great sacrifice to join a group usually decrease their liking for the group. (true/false)

16. Credibility relates most directly to the communicator's
    a. attractiveness.
    b. expertise and trustworthiness.
    c. likability.
    d. personality.

17. With a well-informed audience, two-sided messages are more persuasive than one-sided messages. (true/false)

18. High-fear appeals are more effective than low-fear appeals if they provide definite actions that people can take to avoid dreaded outcomes. (true/false)

19. The bystander effect is influenced by all of the following *except*
    a. the number of bystanders.
    b. the personalities of bystanders.
    c. whether the bystanders appear calm.
    d. whether the situation is ambiguous.

20. Altruism is one form of prosocial behavior. (true/false)

21. As the number of bystanders at an emergency increases, the probability that the victim will receive help decreases. (true/false)

22. In an ambiguous situation, a good way to determine if an emergency exists is to look at the reactions of other bystanders. (true/false)

23. Social psychologists generally believe that aggression stems from an aggressive instinct. (true/false)

24. Pain, extreme heat, loud noise, and foul odors have all been associated with an increase in aggressive responses. (true/false)

25. According to the frustration-aggression hypothesis, frustration _____ leads to aggression.
    a. always   c. rarely
    b. often   d. never

26. Which of the following statements is *not* true of personal space?
    a. It functions to protect privacy and regulate intimacy.
    b. How much personal space a person requires is affected by culture, race, gender, and personality.

    c. The size of a person's personal space is fixed.
    d. Invasions of personal space are usually perceived as unpleasant.

27. The social learning theory of aggression emphasizes all of the following *except* that
    a. aggressive responses are learned from the family, the subculture, and the media.
    b. aggressive acts are learned through modeling.
    c. most aggression results from frustration.
    d. when aggression responses are reinforced, they are more likely to continue.

28. Research tends to support the notion that a person can drain off aggressive energy by watching others behave aggressively in sports or on television. (true/false)

29. Research suggests that media violence is probably related to increased aggression. (true/false)

30. Match the example with the term.
    ____ (1) Jose was promoted because his firm needed one Hispanic manager.
    ____ (2) Darlene thinks that all White Americans are racists.
    ____ (3) Carlotta hired a woman to be her assistant because she doesn't like working with men.
    ____ (4) Bill doesn't like Jews.
    a. stereotypic thinking
    b. discrimination
    c. prejudice
    d. tokenism

31. Members of an in-group often like out-group members as individuals. (true/false)

32. Social learning theory asserts that prejudice develops and is maintained through
    a. competition.
    b. us-versus-them thinking.
    c. modeling and reinforcement.
    d. genetic inheritance.

33. African Americans no longer believe that racism is a major problem in U.S. society. (true/false)

Section Two: Match Terms with Definitions

_____ (1) effect of one major positive or negative trait

_____ (2) as more viewers gather at the scene of an emergency, a victim's chances of help are reduced

_____ (3) geographic closeness

_____ (4) the blocking of an impulse

_____ (5) attitudes and standards of a group

_____ (6) relatively stable evaluation of a person, object, situation, or issue

_____ (7) impact of passive spectators on performance

_____ (8) the tendency of individuals to go along with the group even if they disagree

_____ (9) widely shared beliefs about traits of members of certain groups

_____ (10) the fact that one's overall impression is influenced by a first impression

_____ (11) displacing aggression onto innocent people

_____ (12) making a large request in the hope of gaining compliance with a subsequent small request

_____ (13) the intentional infliction of harm on another

a. frustration

b. proximity

c. aggression

d. scapegoating

e. bystander effect

f. halo effect

g. door-in-the-face technique

h. social norms

i. attitude

j. groupthink

k. stereotypes

l. audience effect

m. primacy effect

Section Three: Fill in the Blank

1. A(n) _____ is a relatively stable evaluation of a person, object, situation, or issue.

2. Research reveals that our overall impression of another person is more influenced by the first information we have about the individual than by later information about the person. This tendency is called the _____ _____ .

3. Jaime explained his poor grade on his math test by saying that he is a right-brained person and, therefore, more the artistic type than the analytical type. He is making a _____ attribution.

4. We tend to use _____ factors to explain our own behavior and _____ factors to explain the behavior of others.

5. Sal tends to attribute his successes to internal factors and his failure to situational factors. This tendency is known as the _____ _____ _____ .

6. People tend to infer generally positive or negative traits in a person as a result of observing one major positive or negative trait. This tendency is known as the _____ effect.

7. A classic study in social psychology is Milgram's research on _____ . His experiment revealed that most participants were willing to follow orders and deliver the strongest possible shock to a confederate for giving wrong answers in a memory test.

8. Individual performance may be affected by the mere physical presence of others. This effect is known as _____ _____ .

9. Group polarization refers to the tendency of group members, following a discussion, to take a more _____ position on the issue at hand.

10. A(n) _____ is a widely shared belief about the characteristics of members of various social groups and includes the assumption that all members of a social group are alike.

11. As the number of bystanders at an emergency increases, the probability that anyone will help a victim decreases. This phenomenon is known as the _____ effect.

12. Theo suffered serious injury while attempting to save a child from being run over by a car. Theo's action is an example of _____ .

13. Most psychologists agree that _____ _____ can play a role in aggression.

14. The _____ hypothesis suggests that frustration can result in aggression.

15. _____ occurs when a person is the undeserving victim of someone else's displaced aggression, which is due to that person's frustration.

16. A(n) _____ is an inference about the cause of our own or another's behavior.

17. _____ is changing or adopting an attitude or behavior to be consistent with the norms of a group or the expectations of others.

18. The term _____ _____ refers to the ways people usually process social information.

Section Four: Comprehensive Practice Test

1. Dispositional attribution is to _____ as situational attribution is to _____ .
   a. external factors; internal factors
   b. others; self
   c. self; others
   d. internal factors; external factors

2. Crystal attributed Asher's poor oral presentation to his basic lack of motivation to be a good student and to be prepared for class. Assuming Crystal was wrong and Asher's poor performance was due to some other, external factor, Crystal was making an error called the self-serving bias. (true/false)

3. Crystal's own oral presentation was also poor. She explained that the students in the front row were goofing off and distracting her. Crystal was excusing her performance with the
   a. primary attribution error.
   b. fundamental self-bias error.
   c. self-serving bias.
   d. error of external factors.

4. The concept of proximity relates to
   a. attribution.   c. aggression.
   b. attraction.   d. prejudice.

5. In the past few decades people have become less influenced by physical attractiveness and more influenced by internal factors such as personality. (true/false)

6. Jesse's mother reminded him to check his tie and comb his hair prior to meeting the interviewer at his college admissions interview. Jesse's mother was probably concerned about the _____ effect.
   a. attenuation   c. Harvard
   b. Soloman   d. halo

7. The old adage "Birds of a feather flock together" summarizes the concept of _____, one of the factors that influence attraction.
   a. attribution   c. similarity
   b. social influence   d. proximity

8. Research reveals that low autonomic nervous system arousal levels seem to be related to aggressive behavior. (true/false)

9. Messsages about smoking are most effective if framed _____, while those about dietary change are best if framed _____ .
   a. positively, negatively
   b. negatively, positively

10. The terms *stereotype* and *prejudice* are actually different words for the same thing. (true/false)

11. A negative attitude toward a person based on gender, religion, race, or membership in a certain group is known as
    a. discrimination.   c. a stereotype.
    b. prejudice.   d. social dissonance.

12. Strategies such as changing a behavior, changing an attitude, explaining away an inconsistency, or minimizing the importance of an inconsistency are all used to reduce
    a. cognitive distortion bias.
    b. relative attribution frustration.
    c. cognitive dissonance.
    d. inconsistency anxiety.

13. _____ are the attitudes and standards of behavior expected of members of a particular group.
    a. Values   c. Social norms
    b. Social rules   d. Social postures

14. Those who hold a minority opinion have more influence on a majority group if
    a. the opinion is stated vaguely so its departure from the majority opinion is disguised.
    b. the opinion is clearly stated and well organized.
    c. the opinion is stated as a question.
    d. the opinion is stated with qualifications that complement the majority opinion.

15. One strategy to induce compliance to a request is known as the _____ technique. In this strategy, the person making the request secures a favorable response to a small request with the aim of making the person more likely to agree to a larger request later.
    a. door-in-the-face   c. foot-in-the-door
    b. low-ball   d. risky shift

16. A good example of the door-in-the-face technique is to ask $10,000 for your used car, hoping that the buyer, who is likely to refuse to pay that much, will then be willing to agree to pay $8,000, the price you wanted in the first place. (true/false)

17. Social loafing refers to
    a. the tendency to avoid social contact and interpersonal relationships.
    b. the tendency to exert less effort when working with others on a common task.
    c. the tendency to be less productive when working alone than with others.
    d. the tendency to see others' work as more externally motivated than one's own.

18. A common finding on audience effects is that when we are being watched, we tend to do better on easy tasks and on more difficult tasks at which we are more proficient. (true/false)

19. Which of the following is *not* listed as a component of an attitude?
   a. social component
   b. behavioral component
   c. cognitive component
   d. emotional component

Section Five: Critical Thinking

1. Prepare a convincing argument supporting each of these positions:
   a. The Milgram study should have been conducted because it provided vitally important information about the troubling human tendency to inflict pain and suffering on others in obedience to authority figures.
   b. Despite the value of the knowledge the Milgram study provided, it should never have been conducted because it subjected research participants to tremendous stress.

2. Prepare a convincing argument supporting each of these positions:
   a. Aggression results largely from biological factors (nature).
   b. Aggression is primarily learned (nurture).

3. Review the factors influencing impression formation and attraction discussed in this chapter. Prepare a dual list of behaviors indicating what you should and should not do if you wish to make a better impression on other people and to increase their liking for you.

APPENDIX: STATISTICAL METHODS

Statistics, a branch of mathematics, enables psychologists and other scientists to organize, describe, and draw conclusions about the quantitative results of their studies. We will explore the two basic types of statistics that psychologists use—descriptive statistics and inferential statistics.

Descriptive Statistics

Descriptive statistics are statistics used to organize, summarize, and describe data. Descriptive statistics include measures of central tendency, variability, and relationship.

Measures of Central Tendency

A **measure of central tendency** is a measure or score that describes the center, or middle, of a distribution of scores. The most widely used and most familiar measure of central tendency is the **mean,** the arithmetic average of a group of scores. The mean is computed by adding all the single scores and dividing the sum by the number of scores.

Carl sometimes studies and does well in his classes, but he occasionally procrastinates and fails a test. Table A.1 (on page 426) shows how Carl performed on the seven tests in his psychology class last semester. Carl computes his mean score by adding up all his test scores and dividing the sum by the number of tests. Carl's mean, or average, score is 80.

The mean is an important and widely used statistical measure of central tendency, but it can be misleading when a group of scores contains one or several extreme scores. Table A.2 (on page 426) lists the annual incomes of ten people in rank order. When an income of $1 million is averaged with several more modest incomes, the mean does not provide a true picture of the group. Therefore, when one or a few individuals score far above or below the middle range of a group, a different measure of central tendency should be used. The **median** is the middle score or value when a group of scores are arranged from highest to lowest. When there are an odd number of scores, the score in the middle is the median. When there are an even number of scores, the median is the average of the two middle scores. For the ten incomes arranged from highest to lowest in Table A.2, the median is $27,000, which is the average of the middle incomes, $28,000 and $26,000. The $27,000 median income is a truer reflection of the comparative income of the group than is the $124,700 mean.

Another measure of central tendency is the **mode.** The mode is easy to find because it is the score that occurs most frequently in a group of scores. The mode of the annual-income group in Table A.2 is $22,000.

Describing Data with Tables and Graphs

A researcher tested 100 students for recall of 20 new vocabulary words 24 hours after they had memorized the list. The researcher organized the scores in a **frequency distribution**—an arrangement showing the numbers of scores that fall within equal-sized class intervals. To organize the 100 test scores, the researcher decided to use intervals of 2 points each. Next, the researcher tallied the fre-

descriptive statistics
Statistics used to organize, summarize, and describe data.

measure of central tendency
A measure or score that describes the center, or middle, of a distribution of scores (example: mean, median, or mode).

mean
The arithmetic average of a group of scores; calculated by adding all the single scores and dividing the sum by the number of scores.

median
The middle score or value when a group of scores are arranged from highest to lowest.

mode
The score that occurs most frequently in a group of scores.

frequency distribution
An arrangement showing the numbers of scores that fall within equal-sized class intervals.

Table A.1	Carl's Psychology Test Scores
Test 1	98
Test 2	74
Test 3	86
Test 4	92
Test 5	56
Test 6	68
Test 7	86
Sum:	560
Mean: $560 \div 7 = 80$	

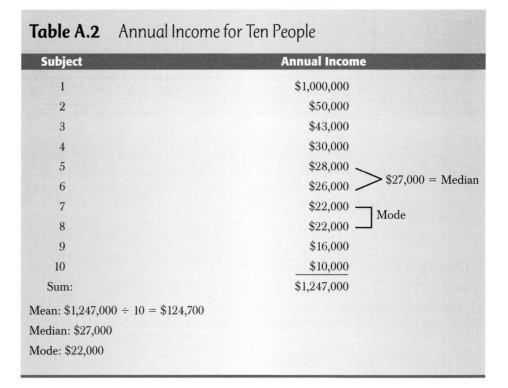

Table A.2 Annual Income for Ten People

Subject	Annual Income
1	$1,000,000
2	$50,000
3	$43,000
4	$30,000
5	$28,000
6	$26,000
7	$22,000
8	$22,000
9	$16,000
10	$10,000
Sum:	$1,247,000

$27,000 = Median

Mode

Mean: $1,247,000 ÷ 10 = $124,700

Median: $27,000

Mode: $22,000

histogram
A bar graph that depicts the number of scores within each class interval in a frequency distribution.

frequency polygon
A line graph that depicts the frequency, or number, of scores within each class interval in a frequency distribution.

variability
How much the scores in a distribution spread out, away from the mean.

range
The difference between the highest score and the lowest score in a distribution of scores.

quency (number of scores) within each 2-point interval. Table A.3 presents the resulting frequency distribution.

The researcher then made a **histogram,** a bar graph that depicts the number of scores within each class interval in the frequency distribution. The intervals are plotted along the horizontal axis, and the frequency of scores in each interval is plotted along the vertical axis. Figure A.1 shows the histogram for the 100 test scores.

Another common method of representing frequency data is the **frequency polygon.** As in a histogram, the class intervals are plotted along the horizontal axis and the frequencies are plotted along the vertical axis. However, in a frequency polygon,

Table A.3 Frequency Distribution of 100 Vocabulary Test Scores

Class Interval	Tally of Scores in Each Class Interval	Number of Scores in Each Class Interval (Frequency)
1–2	I	1
3–4	II	2
5–6	IIII I	6
7–8	IIII IIII IIII III	18
9–10	IIII IIII IIII IIII III	23
11–12	IIII IIII IIII IIII III	23
13–14	IIII IIII IIII II	17
15–16	IIII III	8
17–18	I	1
19–20	I	1

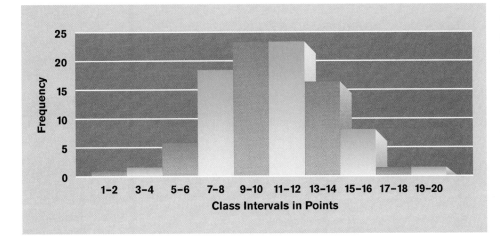

> **Figure A.1**

A Frequency Histogram

Vocabulary test scores from the frequency distribution in Table A.3 are plotted here in the form of a histogram. Class intervals of 2 points each appear on the horizontal axis. Frequencies of the scores in each class interval are plotted on the vertical axis.

standard deviation
A descriptive statistic reflecting the average amount that scores in a distribution deviate, or vary, from their mean.

normal curve
A symmetrical, bell-shaped frequency distribution that represents how scores are normally distributed in a population; most scores fall near the mean, and fewer and fewer scores occur in the extremes either above or below the mean.

> **Figure A.2**

A Frequency Polygon

Vocabulary test scores from the frequency distribution in Table A.3 are plotted here in the form of a frequency polygon. Class intervals of 2 points each appear on the horizontal axis. Frequencies of the scores in each class interval are plotted on the vertical axis.

each class interval is represented by a graph point that is placed at the middle (midpoint) of the class interval so that its vertical distance above the horizontal axis shows the frequency of that interval. Lines are drawn to connect the points, as shown in Figure A.2. The histogram and the frequency polygon are simply two different ways of presenting data.

Measures of Variability

In addition to a measure of central tendency, researchers also need a measure of the **variability** of a set of scores–how much the scores spread out, away from the mean. Both groups in Table A.4 (on page 428) have a mean and a median of 80. However, the scores in Group II cluster tightly around the mean, while the scores in Group I vary widely from the mean.

The simplest measure of variability is the **range**–the difference between the highest and lowest scores in a distribution of scores. Table A.4 reveals that Group I has a range of 47, indicating high variability, while Group II has a range of only 7, showing low variability. Unfortunately, the range reveals only the difference between the lowest score and the highest score; it tells nothing about the scores in between.

The **standard deviation** is a descriptive statistic reflecting the average amount that scores in a distribution deviate, or vary, from their mean. The larger the standard deviation, the greater the variability in a distribution of scores. Refer to Table A.4 and note the standard deviations for the two distributions of test scores. In Group I, the relatively large standard deviation of 18.1 reflects the wide variability in that distribution. By contrast, the small standard deviation of 2.14 in Group II indicates that the variability is low, and you can see that the scores cluster tightly around the mean.

The Normal Curve

Psychologists and other scientists often use descriptive statistics in connection with an important type of frequency distribution known as the **normal curve,** pictured in Figure A.3 (on page 428). If a large number of people are measured on any of a wide variety of traits (such as height or IQ score), the great majority of values will cluster in the middle, with fewer and fewer individuals measuring extremely low or high on these variables. Note that slightly over 68% of the scores in a normal distribution fall within 1 standard deviation of the mean (34.13% within 1 standard deviation above the mean, and 34.13% within 1 standard deviation below the mean). Almost 95.5% of the scores in a normal distribution lie

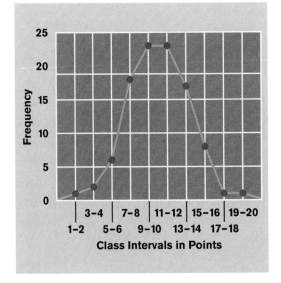

Table A.4 Comparison of Range and Standard Deviation for Two Small Groups of Scores Having Identical Means and Medians

Group I			Group II		
Test	**Score**		**Test**	**Score**	
1	99		1	83	
2	99		2	82	
3	98		3	81	
4	80	Median	4	80	Median
5	72		5	79	
6	60		6	79	
7	52		7	76	
Sum:	560		Sum:	560	

Mean: $560 \div 7 = 80$ Mean: $560 \div 7 = 80$

Median: 80   Median: 80

Range: $99 - 52 = 47$ Range: $83 - 76 = 7$

Standard deviation: 18.1   Standard deviation: 2.14

---

between 2 standard deviations above and below the mean. And the vast majority of scores in a normal distribution—99.72%—fall between 3 standard deviations above and below the mean.

Using the properties of the normal curve and knowing the mean and the standard deviation of a normal distribution, we can find where any score stands (how high or low) in relation to all the other scores in the distribution. For example, on the Wechsler intelligence scales, the mean IQ is 100 and the standard deviation is 15. Thus, 99.72% of the population has an IQ score within 3 standard deviations above and below the mean, ranging from an IQ of 55 to an IQ of 145.

➤ **Figure A.3**

The Normal Curve

The normal curve is a symmetrical, bell-shaped curve that represents how scores are normally distributed in a population. Slightly over 68% of the scores in a normal distribution fall within 1 standard deviation above and below the mean. Almost 95.5% of the scores lie between 2 standard deviations above and below the mean, and about 99.75% fall between 3 standard deviations above and below the mean.

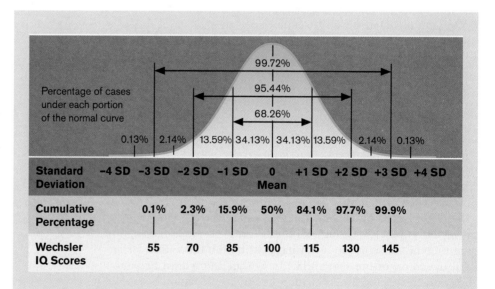

The Correlation Coefficient

A **correlation coefficient** is a number that indicates the degree and direction of relationship between two variables. Correlation coefficients can range from +1.00 (a perfect positive correlation) to .00 (no correlation) to −1.00 (a perfect negative correlation), as illustrated in Figure A.4. A **positive correlation** indicates that two variables vary in the same direction. An increase in one variable is associated with an increase in the other variable, or a decrease in one variable is associated with a decrease in the other. There is a positive correlation between the number of hours college students spend studying and their grades. The more hours they study, the higher their grades are likely to be. A **negative correlation** means that an increase in one variable is associated with a decrease in the other variable. There may be a negative correlation between the number of hours students spend watching television and studying. The more hours they spend watching TV, the fewer hours they may spend studying, and vice versa.

The sign (+ or −) in a correlation coefficient merely tells whether the two variables vary in the same or opposite directions. (If no sign appears, the correlation is assumed to be positive.) The number in a correlation coefficient indicates the relative strength of the relationship between the two variables–the higher the number, the stronger the relationship. For example, a correlation of −.70 is higher than a correlation of +.56; a correlation of −.85 is just as strong as one of +.85. A correlation of .00 indicates that no relationship exists between the variables. IQ and shoe size are examples of two variables that are not correlated.

Table A.5 (on page 430) shows the measurements of two variables–high school GPA and college GPA for 11 college students. Looking at the data, we can see that 6 of the 11 students had a higher GPA in high school, while 5 of the students had a higher GPA in college. A clearer picture of the actual relationship is shown by the *scatterplot* in Figure A.5 (on page 430). High school GPA (variable X) is plotted on the horizontal axis, and college GPA (variable Y) is plotted on the vertical axis.

One dot is plotted for each of the 11 students at the point where high school GPA, variable X, and college GPA, variable Y, intersect. For example, the first student is represented by a dot at the point where her high school GPA of 2.0 on the horizontal (x) axis and college GPA of 1.8 on the vertical (y) axis intersect. The scatterplot in Figure A.5 reveals a relatively high correlation between high school and college GPAs, because the dots cluster near the diagonal line. It also shows that the correlation is pos-

correlation coefficient
A numerical value indicating the strength and direction of relationship between two variables, which ranges from +1.00 (a perfect positive correlation) to −1.00 (a perfect negative correlation).

positive correlation
A relationship between two variables in which both vary in the same direction.

negative correlation
A relationship between two variables in which an increase in one variable is associated with a decrease in the other variable.

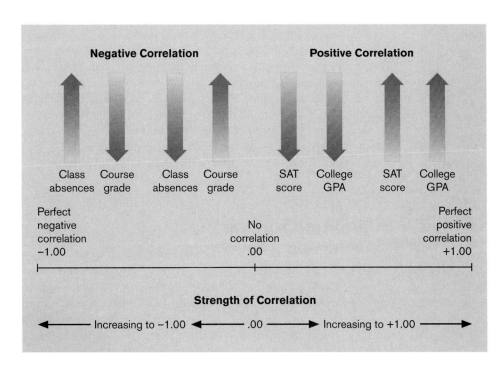

➤ **Figure A.4**

Understanding Correlation Coefficients

Correlation coefficients can range from −1.00 (a perfect negative correlation) through .00 (no correlation) to +1.00 (a perfect positive correlation). As the arrows indicate, a negative correlation exists when an increase in one variable is associated with a decrease in the other variable, and vice versa. A positive correlation exists when both variables tend to either increase or decrease together.

inferential statistics
Statistical procedures that allow researchers to make inferences about the characteristics of the larger population from observations and measurements of a sample and to derive estimates of how much confidence can be placed in those inferences.

population
The entire group of interest to researchers and to which they wish to generalize their findings; the group from which a sample is selected.

Table A.5 High School and College GPAs for 11 Students

Student	High School GPA (Variable X)	College GPA (Variable Y)
1	2.0	1.8
2	2.2	2.5
3	2.3	2.5
4	2.5	3.1
5	2.8	3.2
6	3.0	2.2
7	3.0	2.8
8	3.2	3.3
9	3.3	2.9
10	3.5	3.2
11	3.8	3.5

itive, because the dots run diagonally upward from left to right. The correlation coefficient for the high school and college GPAs of these 11 students is .71. If the correlation were perfect (1.00), all the dots would fall exactly on the diagonal line.

A scatterplot shows whether a correlation is low, moderate, or high and whether it is positive or negative. Scatterplots that run diagonally up from left to right reveal positive correlations. Scatterplots that run diagonally down from left to right indicate negative correlations. The closer the dots are to the diagonal line, the higher the correlation. The scatterplots in Figure A.6 depict a variety of correlations. It is important to remember that correlation does not demonstrate cause and effect. Even a perfect correlation (+1.00 or −1.00) does not mean that one variable causes or is caused by the other. Correlation shows only that two variables are related.

Not all relationships between variables are positive or negative. The relationships between some variables are said to be *curvilinear*. A curvilinear relationship exists when two variables correlate positively (or negatively) up to a certain point and then change direction. For example, there is a positive correlation between physical strength and age up to about 40 or 45 years of age. As age increases from childhood to middle age, so does the strength of handgrip pressure. But beyond middle adulthood, the relationship becomes negative, and increasing age is associated with decreasing handgrip strength. Figure A.6(d) shows a scatterplot of this curvilinear relationship.

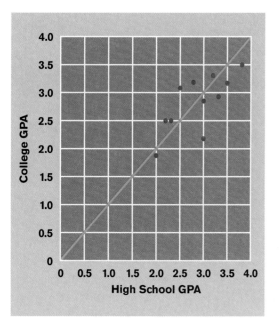

➤ Figure A.5

A Scatterplot

A scatterplot reveals a relatively high positive correlation between the high school and college GPAs of the 11 students listed in Table A.5. One dot is plotted for each of the 11 students at the point where high school GPA (plotted on the horizontal axis) and college GPA (plotted on the vertical axis) intersect.

Inferential Statistics

Inferential statistics allow researchers (1) to make inferences about the characteristics of the larger population from their observations and measurements of a sample and (2) to derive estimates of how much faith or confidence can be placed in those inferences. In statistical theory, a **population** is the entire group that is of interest to researchers—the group to which they wish to apply their findings.

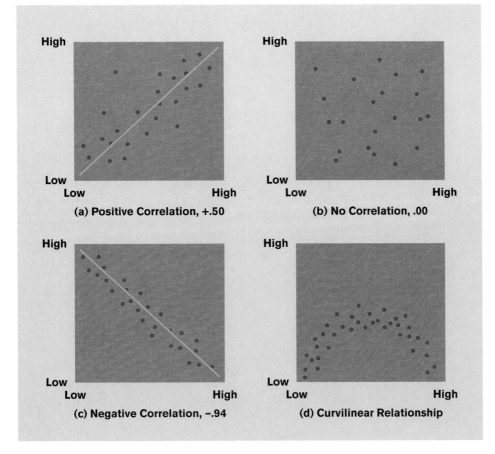

A Variety of Scatterplots
A scatterplot moving diagonally up from left to right, as in (a), indicates a positive correlation. A scatterplot moving diagonally down from left to right, as in (c), indicates a negative correlation. The more closely the dots cluster around a diagonal line, the higher the correlation. Scatterplot (b) indicates no correlation. Scatterplot (d) shows a curvilinear relationship that is positive up to a point and then becomes negative. Age and strength of handgrip have a curvilinear relationship: Handgrip increases in strength up to about age 40 and then decreases with continued aging.

For example, a population could be all the registered voters in the United States. Usually, researchers cannot directly measure and study the entire population of interest. Consequently, they make inferences about a population from a relatively small **sample** selected from that population. For researchers to draw conclusions about the larger population, the sample must be representative–that is, its characteristics must mirror those of the larger population. (See Chapter 1 for more information about representative samples.)

Statistical Significance

Suppose 200 students are randomly assigned either to an experimental group that will be taught psychology with innovative materials or to a control group that will receive traditional instruction. At the end of the semester, researchers find that the mean test scores of the experimental group are considerably higher than those of the control group. To conclude that the instructional methods caused the difference, the researchers must use **tests of statistical significance** to estimate how often the experimental results could have occurred by chance alone. The estimates derived from tests of statistical significance are stated as probabilities. A probability of .05 means that the experimental results would be expected to occur by chance no more than 5 times out of 100. The .05 level of significance is usually required as a minimum for researchers to conclude that their findings are statistically significant. Often the level of significance reached is even more impressive, such as the .01 level. The .01 level means that the probability is no more than 1 in 100 that the results occurred by chance.

The inferences researchers make are not absolute. They are based on probability, and there is always a possibility, however small, that experimental results could occur by chance. For this reason, replication of research studies is recommended.

sample
The portion of any population that is selected for study and from which generalizations are made about the entire population.

tests of statistical significance
Statistical tests that estimate the probability that a particular research result could have occurred by chance.

ANSWERS TO STUDY GUIDE QUESTIONS

Chapter 1 (page 28)

Section One: Chapter Review 1. scientific method
2. description, explanation, prediction, control 3. false
4. (1) d (2) a (3) b (4) c 5. false 6. true 7. (1) d (2) c
(3) a (4) b 8. c 9. d 10. true 11. false 12. b
13. positive 14. valid 15. true 16. b 17. c 18. d
19. true 20. false 21. (1) c (2) c (3) c (4) a (5) b (6) a & b
(7) a, b, & c 22. (1) c (2) a (3) d (4) e (5) b 23. (1) d
(2) a (3) f (4) e (5) b (6) c 24. (1) b (2) c (3) a (4) b (5) a
(6) c 25. (1) b (2) c (3) d (4) a (5) e (6) g (7) f

Section Two: Who Said This? 1. Skinner 2. Wundt
3. James 4. Watson 5. Maslow 6. Sumner
7. Calkins 8. Rogers 9. Wertheimer

Section Three: Fill In the Blank 1. theory
2. naturalistic observation 3. population; representative
sample 4. hypothesis 5. independent; dependent
6. sociocultural 7. predictions; cause; effect
8. structuralism 9. functionalism 10. psychoanalysis
11. cognitive 12. psychoanalytic 13. clinical

Section Four: Comprehensive Practice Test 1. b 2. b
3. d 4. c 5. c 6. b 7. a 8. d 9. c 10. a 11. c
12. false 13. false 14. true 15. false 16. true
17. true 18. false 19. false 20. false 21. true

Chapter 2 (page 58)

Section One: Chapter Review 1. a 2. c 3. d
4. action 5. b 6. d 7. b 8. b 9. hippocampus
10. (1) b (2) a (3) f (4) c (5) e (6) d (7) g 11. b 12. a
13. (1) d (2) c (3) a (4) b 14. (1) d (2) a (3) e (4) b (5) c
15. (1) a (2) b (3) a (4) a (5) b 16. d 17. c 18. (1) b
(2) c (3) a 19. b 20. a 21. c 22. c 23. b 24. c
25. a 26. (1) d (2) a (3) e (4) c (5) b

Section Two: Label the Brain 1. frontal lobe 2. motor
cortex 3. parietal lobe 4. occipital lobe 5. cerebellum
6. pons 7. medulla 8. corpus callosum 9. pituitary
gland

Section Three: Fill In the Blank 1. dendrite 2. neurotransmitters 3. limbic 4. primary visual cortex
5. parietal 6. frontal 7. left 8. axon 9. brain; spinal
cord 10. sympathetic 11. hypothalamus 12. action
potential 13. Broca's 14. hippocampus 15. temporal
16. cerebellum 17. peripheral 18. substantia nigra

Section Four: Comprehensive Practice Test 1. b 2. d
3. a 4. a 5. c 6. b 7. c 8. b 9. d 10. b 11. a
12. c 13. b 14. c 15. d 16. true 17. true

Chapter 3 (page 88)

Section One: Chapter Review 1. sensation 2. absolute
3. false 4. c 5. transduction 6. b 7. (1) d (2) c (3) b
(4) e (5) a 8. rods; cones 9. c 10. d 11. hertz; decibels 12. (1) b (2) a (3) c 13. d 14. c 15. c 16. olfaction 17. c 18. sweet, sour, salty, bitter, umami 19. taste
bud 20. false 21. kinesthetic 22. vestibular; inner ear
23. (1) c (2) a (3) b 24. binocular 25. (1) c (2) b (3) a
(4) d 26. c 27. top-down 28. c

Section Two: Multiple Choice 1. a 2. d 3. d 4. c
5. d 6. d 7. b 8. c 9. a 10. a 11. c 12. a
13. c 14. a 15. a 16. a 17. b 18. b 19. c 20. d
21. b 22. b 23. c

Section Three: Fill In the Blank 1. a 2. difference
3. psychophysics 4. transduction 5. sensory adaptation 6. cornea 7. opponent-process 8. frequency
9. umami 10. Gestalt 11. figure-ground 12. closure
13. binocular disparity

Section Four: Comprehensive Practice Test 1. c 2. a
3. d 4. c 5. b 6. d 7. a 8. c 9. a 10. c 11. c
12. b 13. d 14. a 15. d 16. b 17. true 18. d
19. true 20. c 21. false 22. a 23. c 24. d 25. c
26. b 27. a

Chapter 4 (page 114)

Section One: Chapter Review 1. a 2. suprachiasmatic
nucleus 3. d 4. false 5. (1) a (2) b (3) a (4) a (5) a
6. c 7. false 8. d 9. b 10. (1) d (2) b (3) a (4) c
11. restorative theory; circadian theory 12. c 13. false
14. b 15. false 16. c 17. true 18. (1) a (2) b (3) c
(4) d 19. b 20. true 21. false 22. c 23. a
24. sociocognitive; neodissociation; dissociated control
25. false 26. d 27. true 28. true 29. (1) b (2) a (3) d
(4) c 30. b 31. b 32. a 33. c 34. d 35. c

Section Two: Identify the Drug 1. c 2. d 3. f 4. b
5. e 6. a 7. g

Section Three: Fill In the Blank 1. consciousness
2. delta 3. REM rebound 4. REM 5. parasomnias
6. apnea 7. narcolepsy 8. mood; perception; thought
9. meditation 10. dependence 11. crash
12. dopamine 13. cocaine

Section Four: Comprehensive Practice Test 1. true
2. b 3. c 4. c 5. b 6. b 7. false 8. d 9. c
10. d 11. false 12. b 13. b 14. false 15. false
16. c 17. c 18. true

Chapter 5 (page 144)

Section One: Chapter Review 1. Ivan Pavlov 2. conditioned 3. extinction 4. existing conditioned stimulus
5. b 6. conditioned; unconditioned 7. a 8. false
9. c 10. true 11. true 12. b 13. c 14. b 15. d
16. negative 17. continuous; partial 18. d 19. a
20. false 21. a 22. false 23. true 24. true
25. learned helplessness 26. biofeedback 27. behavior
modification 28. insight 29. d 30. b 31. b
32. (1) b, d (2) a (3) c

Section Two: Identify the Concept 1. variable-ratio reinforcement 2. classical conditioning of emotions 3. negative reinforcement 4. generalization 5. positive reinforcement 6. extinction in operant conditioning 7. fixed-interval reinforcement 8. punishment 9. observational learning 10. secondary reinforcement 11. insight

Section Three: Fill In the Blank 1. stimuli; response; consequences 2. Learning 3. the sound of the truck 4. the food 5. salivation 6. neutral 7. generalization 8. discrimination 9. higher-order 10. conditioned; unconditioned 11. effect; Edward Thorndike 12. successive approximations 13. Negative; positive 14. discriminative 15. primary; secondary 16. continuous; partial 17. motivation 18. aggressive

Section Four: Comprehensive Practice Test 1. a 2. c 3. c 4. d 5. b 6. c 7. b 8. c 9. a 10. d 11. b 12. false 13. b 14. b 15. d 16. c 17. false

Chapter 6 (page 172)

Section One: Chapter Review 1. d 2. (1) b (2) c (3) a 3. (1) d (2) b (3) a (4) c 4. c 5. c 6. (1) a (2) c (3) b (4) a (5) C 7. c 8. d 9. a 10. false 11. a 12. c 13. true 14. false 15. b 16. true 17. true 18. episodic; semantic 19. a 20. true 21. d 22. a 23. (1) c (2) e (3) a (4) b (5) d 24. c 25. false 26. true 27. a 28. d

Section Two: Complete the Diagrams 1. large 2. visual, 1/10 second; auditory, 2 seconds 3. about seven items 4. less than 30 seconds 5. unlimited 6. from minutes to a lifetime 7. Declarative 8. Episodic 9. Motor 10. classically

Section Three: Fill In the Blank 1. encoding 2. rehearsal 3. working 4. long 5. semantic 6. recall 7. middle 8. state dependent 9. hippocampal region 10. potentiation 11. mnemonics 12. anterograde amnesia 13. proactive 14. repression 15. encoding 16. massed 17. overlearning

Section Four: Comprehensive Test 1. c 2. a 3. c 4. b 5. nondeclarative 6. a 7. d 8. b 9. false 10. true 11. false 12. d 13. a 14. c 15. c 16. true 17. false 18. a 19. b 20. true

Chapter 7 (page 209)

Section One: Chapter Review 1. c 2. b 3. d 4. additive strategy 5. Framing 6. a 7. b 8. c 9. false 10. false 11. (1) c (2) d (3) b (4) e (5) a 12. false 13. true 14. true 15. (1) b (2) c (3) a 16. a 17. b 18. b 19. b 20. false 21. true 22. (1) b (2) a (3) a (4) b (5) a 23. false 24. b 25. optimism 26. false 27. c

Section Two: Important Concepts and Psychologists 1. Rosch 2. Tversky 3. Newell and Simon 4. Whorf 5. Spearman 6. Sternberg 7. Terman 8. Wechsler 9. Galton 10. Goleman

Section Three: Fill In the Blank 1. cognition 2. Imagery 3. exemplar 4. additive 5. elimination by aspects 6. psycholinguistics 7. syntax 8. linguistic relativity 9. Howard Gardner 10. validity 11. neural processing speed 12. contextual 13. reliability 14. creativity

Section Four: Comprehensive Practice Test 1. b 2. b 3. prototype 4. false 5. a 6. d 7. a 8. d 9. a 10. false 11. true 12. true 13. c 14. d 15. a 16. b 17. false 18. b 19. true 20. true

Chapter 8 (page 250)

Section One: Chapter Review 1. b 2. (1) b (2) c (3) a 3. true 4. c 5. true 6. (1) c (2) a (3) b 7. a 8. b 9. c 10. true 11. (1) c (2) b (3) a (4) e (5) d 12. true 13. (1) c (2) b (3) a 14. false 15. b 16. false 17. c 18. false 19. d 20. true 21. c 22. later 23. c 24. a 25. d

Section Two: Important Psychologists and Concepts 1. cognitive development 2. psychosocial development 3. temperament 4. attachment 5. nativist view of language development 6. moral reasoning 7. death and dying 8. gender schema theory

Section Three: Fill In the Blank 1. schema 2. conventional 3. fifth 4. zygote 5. teratogens 6. maturation 7. avoidant 8. telegraphic speech 9. overregulation 10. Kohlberg 11. personal fable 12. Crystallized; fluid 13. Bargaining

Section Four: Comprehensive Practice Test 1. false 2. b 3. b 4. b 5. a 6. b 7. d 8. b 9. a 10. b 11. b 12. true 13. b 14. d 15. c 16. c 17. c 18. true 19. b 20. a 21. b 22. true 23. b

Chapter 9 (page 282)

Section One: Chapter Review 1. extrinsic 2. a 3. b 4. d 5. c 6. feeding; satiety 7. c 8. c 9. d 10. maintain 11. d 12. biological 13. c 14. anorexia nervosa; bulimia nervosa 15. a 16. false 17. c 18. true 19. true 20. b 21. true 22. b 23. false 24. true 25. false 26. c 27. a 28. b 29. c 30. d 31. c 32. b 33. true 34. false 35. a 36. c

Section Two: Important Psychologists and Concepts 1. drive-reduction theory 2. hierarchy of needs 3. need for achievement 4. event creates physical arousal, which is identified as an emotion 5. event creates physical arousal plus emotion 6. cognitive appraisal of a stimulus results in emotion 7. facial-feedback hypothesis

Section Three: Fill In the Blank 1. Motives 2. intrinsic 3. extrinsic 4. instinct 5. arousal 6. lateral; ventromedial 7. exercise 8. Anorexia; bulimia 9. social 10. James–Lange 11. Cannon–Bard 12. Schachter–Singer 13. basic 14. birth 15. excitement 16. testosterone 17. homeostasis 18. heterosexual; homosexual

Section Four: Comprehensive Practice Test 1. a 2. a 3. c 4. d 5. a 6. c 7. d 8. false 9. d 10. true 11. d 12. c 13. a 14. false 15. c 16. false 17. d 18. c 19. true

Chapter 10 (page 309)

Section One: Chapter Review 1. false 2. false 3. true 4. true 5. c 6. d 7. d 8. false 9. false 10. d 11. resistance 12. exhaustion 13. physiological; psychological 14. a 15. problem-focused; emotion-focused 16. true 17. before 18. c 19. b 20. a 21. c 22. a 23. c 24. true 25. d 26. false 27. a 28. b 29. Alcohol 30. d

Section Two: The Biopsychosocial Model of Health and Illness 1. genetics, relaxation, healthy lifestyle 2. lack of exercise, poor diet, disease and injury, toxic chemicals, pollution 3. stress management skills, giving and receiving love, optimism 4. depression, pessimism, worry, anxiety, poor coping skills, stress 5. social responsibility, social policy, social groups 6. loneliness, poverty, exploitation, violence

Section Three: Fill In the Blank 1. biomedical; biopsychosocial 2. health psychology 3. sympathetic nervous system 4. alarm 5. resistance 6. cognitive 7. proactive 8. AIDS 9. homosexual and bisexual males 10. hassles 11. psychoneuroimmunology 12. A 13. cognition 14. Primary 15. high blood pressure 16. stressor 17. approach–avoidance

Section Four: Comprehensive Practice Test 1. false 2. b 3. a 4. c 5. a 6. true 7. true 8. c 9. racism 10. true 11. c 12. false 13. a 14. true 15. true

Chapter 11 (page 335)

Section One: Chapter Review 1. true 2. unconscious 3. a 4. c 5. b 6. false 7. true 8. birth 9. d 10. b 11. Oedipus complex 12. c 13. collective 14. c 15. c 16. c 17. a 18. d 19. d 20. c 21. a 22. d 23. false 24. a 25. b 26. negligible 27. false 28. (1) a (2) c (3) d (4) b (5) e 29. d 30. c

Section Two: Complete the Table 1. Freud; Behavior arises mostly from unconscious conflict between pleasure-seeking id and moral-perfectionistic superego, with ego as mediator. 2. Bandura, Rotter; Behavior results from an interaction between internal cognitive factors and environmental factors. 3. Maslow, Rogers; Behavior springs from the person's motivation to become self-actualized or fully functioning and reflects the person's unique perception of reality and conscious choices. 4. Allport, Cattell, Eysenck; Behavior springs from personality traits that may be influenced by both heredity and environment.

Section Three: Fill In the Blank 1. id 2. ego 3. preconscious 4. oral, anal, phallic, genital 5. cardinal 6. surface; source 7. reciprocal determinism 8. collective unconscious 9. genes; environment 10. observation 11. Jung's 12. projective 13. Minnesota Multiphasic Personality Inventory 14. self-efficacy 15. source 16. archetype 17. collectivist; individualistic/collectivist

Section Four: Comprehensive Practice Test 1. c 2. c 3. b 4. false 5. b 6. c 7. a 8. a 9. b 10. d 11. b 12. c 13. false 14. false 15. c 16. d

Chapter 12 (page 362)

Section One: Chapter Review 1. false 2. a 3. (1) c (2) a (3) b (4) d 4. (1) a (2) d (3) b (4) c 5. d 6. (1) c (2) a (3) b (4) d 7. c 8. (1) b (2) c (3) a 9. false 10. b 11. false 12. true 13. false 14. (1) e (2) d (3) b (4) c (5) a (6) f 15. false 16. true 17. (1) d (2) b (3) e (4) c (5) a 18. Paraphilias 19. c 20. c

Section Two: Identify the Disorder 1. major depression 2. paranoid schizophrenia 3. bipolar disorder 4. agoraphobia 5. dissociative amnesia 6. borderline personality disorder 7. sexual dysfunction 8. obsessive-compulsive disorder

Section Three: Fill In the Blank 1. biological 2. schizophrenia 3. positive 4. delusion 5. negative 6. major depressive disorder 7. manic 8. somatoform 9. panic 10. involuntary thoughts; urge to perform a certain act 11. conversion 12. multiple personality 13. personality 14. sexual identity 15. Hallucinations 16. phobia 17. antisocial

Section Four: Comprehensive Practice Test 1. c 2. b 3. d 4. b 5. true 6. b 7. a 8. false 9. d 10. b 11. true 12. d 13. c 14. true 15. d 16. c 17. false 18. b 19. a

Chapter 13 (page 388)

Section One: Chapter Review 1. d 2. Gestalt 3. Person-centered 4. Psychodynamic 5. c 6. c 7. false 8. operant 9. b 10. d 11. (1) c (2) b (3) a (4) d 12. c 13. false 14. b 15. d 16. true 17. (1) c (2) b (3) a (4) c (5) c 18. b 19. d 20. a 21. false 22. false 23. b 24. (1) a (2) c (3) b (4) c 25. c 26. are

Section Two: Identify the Therapy 1. e 2. a 3. d 4. f 5. b 6. g 7. c

Section Three: Fill In the Blank 1. psychological; biological 2. transference 3. directive 4. interpersonal 5. family 6. self-help group 7. operant 8. behavior modification 9. cognitive 10. schizophrenia 11. depression 12. bipolar disorder 13. suicidal depression 14. clinical 15. free association 16. time out 17. lobotomy 18. psychoanalyst

Section Four: Comprehensive Practice Test 1. c 2. c 3. b 4. false 5. d 6. a 7. b 8. a 9. a 10. b 11. b 12. a 13. c 14. a 15. b 16. d 17. c 18. true 19. false 20. false

Chapter 14 (page 419)

Section One: Chapter Review 1. d 2. b 3. true 4. (1) c (2) b (3) a 5. true 6. false 7. (1) c (2) a (3) b 8. c 9. b 10. c 11. d 12. a 13. c 14. d 15. false 16. b 17. true 18. true 19. b 20. true 21. true 22. false 23. false 24. true 25. b 26. c 27. c 28. false 29. true 30. (1) d (2) a (3) b (4) c 31. false 32. c 33. false

Section Two: Glossary Matching 1. f 2. e 3. b 4. a 5. h 6. i 7. l 8. j 9. k 10. m 11. d 12. g 13. c

Section Three: Fill In the Blank 1. attitude 2. primacy effect 3. dispositional 4. situational; personality 5. self-serving bias 6. halo 7. obedience 8. social facilitation 9. extreme 10. stereotype 11. bystander 12. altruism 13. biological factors 14. frustration–aggression 15. Scapegoating 16. attribution 17. Conformity 18. social cognition

Section Four: Comprehensive Practice Test 1. d 2. false 3. c 4. b 5. false 6. d 7. c 8. true 9. b 10. false 11. b 12. c 13. c 14. b 15. c 16. true 17. b 18. true 19. a

REFERENCES

Note: Bracketed numbers following references indicate chapter(s) in which they are cited.

Abbot, N. C., Stead, L. F., White, A. R., Barnes, J., & Ernst, E. (2000). Hypnotherapy for smoking cessation. *Cochrane Database System Review, 2,* CD001008. [4]

Abraham, H., & Duffy, F. (2001). EEG coherence in post-LSD visual hallucinations. *Psychiatry Research: Neuroimaging, 107,* 151–163. [4]

Abramowitz, J. S. (1997). Effectiveness of psychological and pharmacological treatments for obsessive-compulsive disorder: A quantitative review. *Journal of Consulting and Clinical Psychology, 65,* 44–52. [13]

Abrams, D., Wetherell, M., Cochrane, S., Hogg, M. A., & Turner, J. C. (1990). Knowing what to think by knowing who you are: Self-categorization and the nature of norm formation, conformity and group polarization. *British Journal of Social Psychology, 29* (Pt. 2), 97–119. [14]

Abramson, P., & Herdt, G. (1990). The assessment of sexual practices relevant to the transmission of AIDS: A global perspective. *Journal of Sex Research, 27,* 215–232. [10]

Ackerman, M. D., & Carey, M. P. (1995). Psychology's role in the assessment of erectile dysfunction: Historical precedents, current knowledge, and methods. *Journal of Consulting and Clinical Psychology, 63,* 862–876. [12]

Adams, J. H., Graham, D. I., & Jennett, B. (2000). The neuropathology of the vegetative state after an acute brain insult. *Brain, 123,* 1327–1338. [2]

Ader, D. N., & Johnson, S. B. (1994). Sample description, reporting, and analysis of sex in psychological research: A look at APA and APA division journals in 1990. *American Psychologist, 49,* 216–218. [1]

Ader, R. (1985). CNS immune systems interactions: Conditioning phenomena. *Behavioral and Brain Sciences, 9,* 760–763. [5]

Ader, R. (2000). On the development of psychoneuroimmunology. *European Journal of Pharmacology, 405,* 167–176. [10]

Ader, R., & Cohen, N. (1982). Behaviorally conditioned immunosuppression and murine systemic Lupus erythematosus. *Science, 215,* 1534–1536. [5]

Ader, R., & Cohen, N. (1993). Psychoneuroimmunology: Conditioning and stress. *Annual Review of Psychology, 44,* 53–85. [5]

Adler, A. (1927). *Understanding human nature.* New York: Greenberg. [11]

Adler, A. (1956). In H. L. Ansbacher & R. R. Ansbacher (Eds.), *The individual psychology of Alfred Adler: A systematic presentation in selections from his writings.* New York: Harper & Row. [11]

Adler, J. (1997, Spring/Summer). It's a wise father who knows . . . . *Newsweek* [Special Edition], p. 73. [8]

Agras, W. S., Rossiter, E. M., Arnow, B., Telch, C. F., Raeburn, S. D., Bruce, B., & Koran, L. M. (1994). One-year follow-up of psychosocial and pharmacologic treatments for bulimia nervosa. *Journal of Clinical Psychiatry, 55,* 179–183. [9]

Agras, W. S., Walsh, T., Fairburn, C. G., Wilson, T., & Kraemer, H. C. (2000). A multicenter comparison of cognitive-behavioral therapy and interpersonal psychotherapy for bulimia nervosa. *Archives of General Psychiatry, 57,* 459–466. [13]

Ahmad, S. (1994, November). *Culturally sensitive caregiving for the Pakistani woman.* Lecture presented at the Medical College of Virginia Hospitals, Richmond, VA. [3]

Aiken, L. R. (1997). *Psychological testing and assessment* (9th ed.). Boston: Allyn & Bacon. [7]

Ainsworth, M. (2000). ABCs of "internet therapy." *Metanoia* [Online]. Retrieved from http://www.metanoia.org [13]

Ainsworth, M. D. S. (1973). The development of infant-mother attachment. In B. Caldwell & H. Ricciuti (Eds.), *Review of child development research* (Vol. 3). Chicago: University of Chicago Press. [8]

Ainsworth, M. D. S. (1979). Infant-mother attachment. *American Psychologist, 34,* 932–937. [8]

Ainsworth, M. D. S., Blehar, M. C., Walters, E., & Wall, S. (1978). *Patterns of attachment.* Hillsdale, NJ: Erlbaum. [8]

Al'absi, M., Hugdahl, K., & Lovallo, W. (2002). Adrenocortical stress responses and altered working memory performance. *Psychophysiology, 39,* 95–99. [6]

Albrecht, K. (1979). *Stress and the manager: Making it work for you.* Englewood Cliffs, NJ: Prentice-Hall. [10]

Alexander, G. E., Furey, M. L., Grady, C. L., Pietrini, P., Brady, D. R., Mentis, M. J., & Schapiro, M. B. (1997). Association of premorbid intellectual function with cerebral metabolism in Alzheimer's disease: Implications for the cognitive reserve hypothesis. *American Journal of Psychiatry, 154,* 165–172. [8]

Allen, B. P. (1997). *Personality theories: Development, growth, and diversity* (2nd ed.). Boston: Allyn & Bacon. [11]

Allen, K. W. (1996). Chronic nailbiting: A controlled comparison of competing response and mild aversion treatments. *Behaviour Research and Therapy, 34,* 269–272. [13]

Allison, T., Puce, A., & McCarthy, G. (2000). Social perception from visual cues: Role of the STS region. *Trends in Cognitive Sciences, 4,* 267–278. [14]

Allport, G. W. (1954). *The nature of prejudice.* Reading, MA: Addison-Wesley. [14]

Allport, G. W. (1961). *Pattern and growth in personality.* New York: Holt, Rinehart & Winston. [11]

Allport, G. W., & Odbert, J. S. (1936). Trait names: A psycho-lexical study. *Psychological Monographs, 47*(1, Whole No. 211), 1–171. [11]

Alpert, B., Field, T., Goldstein, S., & Perry, S. (1990). Aerobics enhances cardiovascular fitness and agility in preschoolers. *Health Psychology, 9,* 48–56. [10]

Alsaker, F. D. (1995). Timing of puberty and reactions to pubertal changes. In M. Rutter (Ed.), *Psychosocial disturbances in young people* (pp. 37–82). New York: Cambridge University Press. [8]

Amato, S. (1998). Human genetics and dysmorphy. In R. Behrman & R. Kliegman (Eds.), *Nelson essentials of pediatrics* (3rd ed., pp. 129–146). Philadelphia: W. B. Saunders. [8]

American Association of Retired Persons. (2002). *Evaluating health information on the Internet: How good are your sources?* [Online article]. Retrieved November 1, 2002, from http://www.aarp.org/confacts/health/wwwhealth.html. [10]

American Cancer Society. (2002). *Cancer facts & figures 2002.* [Online report]. Retrieved November 10, 2002, from http://www.cancer.org/downloads/STT/CancerFacts&Figures2002TM [12]

American Medical Association. (1994). Report of the Council on Scientific Affairs: Memories of childhood abuse. CSA Report 5-A-94. [6]

American Psychiatric Association. (1993a). Practice guideline for eating disorders. *American Journal of Psychiatry, 150,* 212–228. [9]

American Psychiatric Association. (1993c). *Statement approved by the Board of Trustees, December 12, 1993.* Washington, DC: Author. [6]

American Psychiatric Association. (1994). *Diagnostic and statistical manual of mental disorders* (4th ed.). Washington DC: Author. [4, 10, 11, 12, 15]

American Psychiatric Association. (1997). Practice guideline for the treatment of patients with Alzheimer's disease and other dementias of late life. *American Journal of Psychiatry, 154,* 1–39. [8]

American Psychiatric Association. (2000). *The diagnostic and statistical manual of mental disorders* (4th Ed.), Text revision. Washington, DC: Author. [12]

American Psychological Association. (1994). *Interim report of the APA Working Group on Investigation of Memories of Childhood Abuse.* Washington, DC: Author. [6]

American Psychological Association. (1995). Psychology: Scientific problem-solvers—Careers for the 21st century [Online brochure]. Retrieved March 7, 2002, from http://www.apa.org/students/brochure/outlook.html#bachelors [1]

American Psychological Association. (2000). Psychologists in the red [Online fact sheet]. Retrieved March 7, 2002, from http://www.apa.org/ppo/issues/ebsinthered.html [1]

American Psychological Association. (2002). Ethical principles of psychologists and code of conduct. *American Psychologist, 57,* 1060–1073. [1]

Anagnostaras, S. B., Josselyn, S. A., Frankland, P. W., & Silva, A. J. (2000). Computer-assisted behavioral assessment of Pavlovian fear conditioning in mice. *Learning & Memory, 7,* 48–57. [5]

Anand, B. K., & Brobeck, J. R. (1951). Hypothalamic control of food intake in rats and cats. *Yale Journal of Biological Medicine, 24,* 123–140. [9]

Andersen, B. L., & Cyranowski, J. M. (1995). Women's sexuality: Behaviors, responses, and individual differences. *Journal of Consulting and Clinical Psychology, 63,* 891–906. [9]

Anderson, C., & Bushman, B. (2001). Effects of violent video games on aggressive behavior, aggressive cognition, aggressive affect, physiological arousal, and prosocial behavior: A meta-analytic review of the scientific literature. *Psychological Science, 12,* 353–359. [5]

Anderson, C. A., & Anderson, K. B. (1996). Violent crime rate studies in philosophical context: A destructive testing approach to heat and southern culture of violence effects. *Journal of Personality and Social Psychology, 70,* 740–756. [14]

Anderson, C. A., & Dill, K. E. (2000). Video games and aggressive thoughts, feelings, and behavior in the laboratory and in life. *Journal of Personality & Social Psychology, 78,* 772–790. [14]

Anderson, S. M., Klatzky, R. L., & Murray, J. (1990). Traits and social stereotypes: Efficiency differences in social information processing. *Journal of Personality and Social Psychology, 59,* 192–201. [14]

Andreasen, N. C., Arndt, S., Alliger, R., Miller, D., & Flaum, M. (1995). Symptoms of schizophrenia: Methods, meanings, and mechanisms. *Archives of General Psychiatry, 52,* 341–351. [13]

Andreasen, N. C., Arndt, S., Swayze, V., II, Cizadlo, T., Flaum, M., O'Leary, D., Ehrhardt, J. C., & Yuh, W. T. C. (1994). Thalamic abnomalities in schizophrenia visualized through magnetic resonance image averaging. *Science, 266,* 294–298. [12]

Andreasen, N. C., & Black, D. W. (1991). *Introductory textbook of psychiatry.* Washington, DC: American Psychiatric Press. [4]

Anokhin, A., Vedeniapin, A., Sitevaag, E., Bauer, L., O'Connor, S., Kuperman, S., Porjesz, B., Reich, T., Begleiter, H., Polich, J., &

Rohrbaugh, J. (2000). The P300 brain potential is reduced in smokers. *Psychopharmacology, 149,* 409–413. [10]

Anstey, K., Stankov, L., & Lord, S. (1993). Primary aging, secondary aging, and intelligence. *Psychology and Aging, 8,* 562–570. [8]

Apgar, V., & Beck, J. (1982). A perfect baby. In H. E. Fitzgerald & T. H. Carr (Eds.), *Human Development 82/83* (pp. 66–70). Guilford, CT: Dushkin. [8]

Aram, D., & Levitt, I. (2002). Mother-child joint writing and storybook reading: Relations with literacy among low SES kindergarteners. *Merrill-Palmer Quarterly, 48,* 202–224. [8]

Archer, J. (1991). The influence of testosterone on human aggression. *British Journal of Social Psychology, 82*(Pt. 1), 1–28. [14]

Archer, J. (1996). Sex differences in social behavior: Are the social role and evolutionary explanations compatible? *American Psychologist, 51,* 909–917. [1]

Arehart-Treichel, J. (2002). Researchers explore link between animal cruelty, personality disorders. *Psychiatric News, 37,* 22. [12]

Aronson, E. (1976). Dissonance theory: Progress and problems. In E. P. Hollander & R. C. Hunt (Eds.), *Current perspectives in social psychology* (4th ed., pp. 316–328). New York: Oxford University Press. [14]

Aronson, E. (1988). *The social animal* (3rd ed.). San Francisco: W. H. Freeman. [14]

Aronson, E. (1990). Applying social psychology to desegregation and energy conservation. *Personality and Social Psychology Bulletin, 16,* 118–132. [14]

Aronson, E., & Mills, J. (1959). The effect of severity of initiation on liking for a group. *Journal of Abnormal and Social Psychology, 59,* 177–181. [14]

Aronson, E., Stephan, W., Sikes, J., Blaney, N., & Snapp, M. (1978). *Cooperation in the classroom,* Beverly Hills, CA: Sage. [14]

Asch, S. E. (1951). Effects of group pressure upon the modification and distortion of judgments. In H. Guetzkow (Ed.), *Groups, leadership, and men.* Pittsburgh, PA: Carnegie Press. [14]

Asch, S. E. (1955). Opinions and social pressure. *Scientific American, 193,* 31–35. [14]

Aspinwall, L. G., & Taylor, S. E. (1997). A stitch in time: Self-regulation and proactive coping. *Psychological Bulletin, 121,* 417–436. [10]

Atkinson, R. C., & Shiffrin, R. M. (1968). Human memory: A proposed system and its controlled processes. In K. W. Spence & J. T. Spence (Eds.), *The psychology of learning and motivation* (Vol. 2, pp. 89–195). New York: Academic. [6]

Atwood, J., & Donnelly, J. (2002). The children's war: Their reactions to devastating events. *Family Journal—Counseling & Therapy for Couples & Families, 10,* 11–18. [8]

Augestad, L. B. (2000). Prevalence and gender differences in eating attitudes and physical activity among Norwegians. *Eating and Weight Disorders: Studies on Anorexia, Bulimia, and Obesity, 5,* 62–72. [9]

Axelsson, A., & Jerson, T. (1985). Noisy toys: A possible source of sensorineural hearing loss. *Pediatrics, 76,* 574–578. [3]

Ayllon, T., & Azrin, N. H. (1965). The measurement and reinforcement of behavior of psychotics. *Journal of the Experimental Analysis of Behavior, 8,* 357–383. [5]

Ayllon, T., & Azrin, N. (1968). *The token economy: A motivational system for therapy and rehabilitation.* New York: Appleton-Century-Crofts. [5, 13]

Azar, B. (2000). A web of research. *Monitor on Psychology, 31* [Online version]. Retrieved March 13, 2002, from http://www.apa.org/monitor/ [1]

Azrin, N. H., & Holz, W. C. (1966). Punishment. In W. K. Honig (Ed.), *Operant behavior: Areas of research and application.* New York: Appleton-Century-Crofts. [5]

Bach, P., & Hayes, S. (2002). The use of acceptance and commitment therapy to prevent the rehospitalization of psychotic patients: A randomized controlled trial. *Journal of Consulting and Clinical Psychology, 70,* 1129–1139. [13]

Baddeley, A. (1990). *Human memory.* Boston: Allyn & Bacon. [6]

Baddeley, A. (1992). Working memory. *Science, 255,* 556–559. [6]

Baddeley, A. D. (1995). Working memory. In M. S. Gazzaniga (Ed.), *The cognitive neurosciences.* Cambridge, MA: MIT Press. [6]

Baer, L. (1996). Behavior theory: Endogenous serotonin therapy? *Journal of Clinical Psychiatry, 57*(6, Suppl.), 33–35. [13]

Baer, L., Rauch, S. L., Ballantine, T., Jr., Martuza, R., Cosgrove, R., Cassem, E., Giriunas, I., Manzo, P. A., Dimino, C., & Jenike, M. A. (1995). Cingulotomy for intractable obsessive-compulsive disorder. *Archives of General Psychiatry, 52,* 384–392. [13]

Bagby, R. M., Rogers, R., & Buis, T. (1994). Detecting malingered and defensive responding on the MMPI-2 in a forensic inpatient sample. *Journal of Personality Assessment, 62,* 191–203. [11]

Bahrick, H. P., Bahrick, P. O., & Wittlinger, R. P. (1975). Fifty years of memory for names and faces: A cross-sectional approach. *Journal of Experimental Psychology: General, 104,* 54–75. [6]

Bahrick, H. P., Hall, L. K., & Berger, S. A. (1996). Accuracy and distortion in memory for high school grades. *Psychological Science, 7,* 265–271. [6]

Bailey, J. M., & Benishay, D. S. (1993). Familial aggregation of female sexual orientation. *American Journal of Psychiatry, 150,* 272–277. [9]

Bailey, J. M., Nothnagel, J., & Wolfe, M. (1995). Retrospectively measured individual differences in childhood sex-typed behavior among gay men: Correspondence between self- and maternal reports. *Archives of Sexual Behavior, 24,* 613–622. [9]

Bailey, J. M., & Pillard, R. C. (1991). A genetic study of male sexual orientation. *Archives of General Psychiatry, 48,* 1089–1096. [9]

Bailey, J. M., & Pillard, R. C. (1994). The innateness of homosexuality. *Harvard Mental Health Letter, 10*(7), 4–6. [9]

Bailey, J. M., Pillard, R. C., Neale, M. C., & Agyei, Y. (1993). Heritable factors influence sexual orientation in women. *Archives of General Psychiatry, 50,* 217–223. [9]

Baldwin, J. D., & Baldwin, J. I. (1997). Gender differences in sexual interest. *Archives of Sexual Behavior, 26,* 181–210. [9]

Ball, S. G., Baer, L., & Otto, M. W. (1996). Symptom subtypes of obsessive-compulsive disorder in behavioral treatment studies: A quantitative review. *Behaviour Research and Therapy, 34,* 47–51. [12]

Ballenger, J. C., Pecknold, J., Rickels, K., & Sellers, E. M. (1993). Medication discontinuation in panic disorder. *Journal of Clinical Psychiatry, 54*(10, Suppl.), 15–21. [13]

Ballor, D. L., Tommerup, L. J., Thomas, D. P., Smith, D. B., & Keesey, R. E. (1990). Exercise training attenuates diet-induced reduction in metabolic rate. *Journal of Applied Physiology: Respiratory, Environmental, and Exercise Physiology, 68,* 2612–2617. [9]

Bandura, A. (1969). *Principles of behavior modification.* New York: Holt, Rinehart & Winston. [5]

Bandura, A. (1973). *Aggression: A social learning analysis.* Englewood Cliffs, NJ: Prentice-Hall. [14]

Bandura, A. (1976). On social learning and aggression. In E. P. Hollander & R. C. Hunt (Eds.), *Current perspectives in social psychology* (4th ed., pp. 116–128). New York: Oxford University Press. [14]

Bandura, A. (1977a). *Social learning theory.* Englewood Cliffs, NJ: Prentice-Hall. [5, 8, 11, 13]

Bandura, A. (1986). *Social functions of thought and action: A social-cognitive theory.* Englewood Cliffs, NJ: Prentice-Hall. [5, 11]

Bandura, A. (1989). Social cognitive theory. *Annals of Child Development, 6,* 1–60. [11]

Bandura, A. (1997a, March). Self-efficacy. *Harvard Mental Health Letter, 13*(9), 4–6. [11]

Bandura, A. (1997b). *Self-efficacy: The exercise of control.* New York: Freeman. [11]

Bandura, A., Adams, N. E., & Beyer, J. (1977). Cognitive processes mediating behavioral change. *Journal of Personality and Social Psychology, 35,* 125–139. [13]

Bandura, A., Jeffery, R. W., & Gajdos, E. (1975). Generalizing change through participant modeling with self-directed mastery. *Behaviour Research and Therapy, 13,* 141–152. [13]

Bandura, A., Ross, D., & Ross, S. A. (1961). Transmission of aggression through imitation of aggressive models. *Journal of Abnormal and Social Psychology, 63,* 575–582. [5]

Bandura, A., Ross, D., & Ross, S. A. (1963). Imitation of film-mediated aggressive models. *Journal of Abnormal and Social Psychology, 66,* 3–11. [5]

Bard, P. (1934). The neurohumoral basis of emotional reactions. In C. A. Murchison (Ed.), *Handbook of general experimental psychology.* Worcester, MA: Clark University Press. [9]

Barinaga, M. (1997). How jet-lag hormone does double duty in the brain. *Science, 277,* 480. [4]

Barlow, D. H. (1997). Cognitive-behavioral therapy for panic disorder: Current status. *Journal of Clinical Psychiatry, 58*(6, Suppl.), 32–36. [13]

Barron, F., & Harrington, D. M. (1981). Creativity, intelligence, and personality. *Annual Review of Psychology, 32,* 439–476. [7]

Barsh, G. S., Farooqi, I. S., & O'Rahilly, S. (2000). Genetics of body-weight regulation. *Nature, 404,* 644–651. [9]

Barsky, A. J. (1993, August). How does hypochondriasis differ from normal concerns about health? *Harvard Mental Health Letter, 10*(3), 8. [12]

Bartlett, A. (2002). Current perspectives on the goals of psychoanalysis. *Journal of the American Psychoanalytic Association, 50,* 629–638. [11]

Bartlett, F. C. (1932). *Remembering: A study in experimental and social psychology.* London: Cambridge University Press. [6]

Bartoshuk, L. M., & Beauchamp, G. K. (1994). Chemical senses. *Annual Review of Psychology, 45,* 419–449. [8]

Basic Behavioral Science Task Force of the National Advisory Mental Health Council. (1996). Basic behavioral science research for mental health: Perception, attention, learning, and memory. *American Psychologist, 51,* 133–142. [5]

Bass, E., & Davis, L. (1988). *The courage to heal.* New York: Harper & Row. [6]

Bassili, J. N. (1995). Response latency and the accessibility of voting intentions: What contributes to accessibility and how it affects vote choice. *Personality and Social Psychology Bulletin, 21,* 686–695. [14]

Bates, M., Labouvie, D., & Voelbel, G. (2002). Individual differences in latent neuropsychological abilities at addictions treatment entry. *Psychology of Addictive Behaviors, 16,* 35–46. [4]

Bateson, G. (1982). Totemic knowledge in New Guinea. In U. Neisser (Ed.), *Memory observed: Remembering in natural contexts.* San Francisco: W. H. Freeman. [6]

Batson, C. D., Batson, J. G., Griffitt, C. A., Barrientos, S., Brandt, J. R., Sprengelmeyer, P., & Bayly, M. J. (1989). Negative-state relief and the empathy-altruism hypothesis. *Journal of Personality and Social Psychology, 56,* 922–933. [14]

Baumgardner, A. H., Heppner, P. P., & Arkin, R. M. (1986). Role of causal attribution in personal problem solving. *Journal of Personality and Social Psychology, 50,* 636–643. [14]

Baumrind, D. (1967). Child care practices anteceding three patterns of preschool behavior. *Genetic Psychology Monographs, 75,* 43–88. [8]

Baumrind, D. (1971). Current patterns of parental authority. *Developmental Psychology Monographs, 4*(1, Pt. 2). [8]

Baumrind, D. (1980). New directions in socialization research. *American Psychologist, 35,* 639–652. [8]

Baumrind, D. (1991). The influence of parenting style on adolescent competence and substance use. *Journal of Early Adolescence, 11,* 56–95. [8]

Bavelier, D., Tomann, A., Hutton, C., Mitchell, T., Corina, D., Liu, G., & Neville, H. (2000). Visual attention to the periphery is enhanced in congenitally deaf individuals. *Journal of Neuroscience, 20,* 1–6. [3]

Bazan, S. (1998). Enhancing decision-making effectiveness in problem-solving teams. *Clinical Laboratory Management Review, 12,* 272–276. [14]

Bean, R., Perry, B., & Bedell, T. (2002). Developing culturally competent marriage and family therapists: Treatment guidelines for non–African American therapists working with African American families. *Journal of Marital & Family Therapy, 28,* 153–164. [13]

Beck, A. T. (1967). *Depression: Causes and treatment.* Philadelphia: University of Pennsylvania Press. [12]

Beck, A. T. (1976). *Cognitive therapy and the emotional disorders.* New York: New American Library. [13]

Beck, A. T. (1991). Cognitive therapy: A 30-year retrospective. *American Psychologist, 46,* 368–375. [12, 13]

Beck, A. T. (1993). Cognitive therapy: Past, present, and future. *Journal of Consulting and Clinical Psychology, 61,* 194–198. [13]

Bee, H., & Boyd, D. (2004). *The Developing Child.* Boston: Allyn & Bacon. [8]

Beirut, L., Dinwiddie, S., Begleiter, H., Crowe, R., Hesselbrock, V., Nurnberger, J., Porjesz, B., Schuckit, M., & Reich, T. (1998). Familial transmission of substance dependence: Alcohol, marijuana, cocaine, and habitual smoking: A report from the collaborative study on the genetics of alcoholism. *Archives of General Psychiatry, 55,* 982–988. [10]

Békésy, G. von (1957). The ear. *Scientific American, 197,* 66–78. [3]

Bekker, M. H. J. (1996). Agoraphobia and gender: A review. *Clinical Psychology Review, 16,* 129–146. [12]

Belcourt-Dittloff, A., & Stewart, J. (2000). Historical racism: Implications for Native Americans. *American Psychologist, 55,* 1164–1165. [10]

Bell, A. P., Weinberg, M. S., & Hammersmith, S. K. (1981). *Sexual preference: Its development in men and women.* Bloomington: Indiana University Press. [9]

Belsky, J., & Fearon, R. (2002). Infant-mother attachment security, contextual risk, and early development: A moderational analysis. *Development & Psychopathology, 14,* 293–310. [8]

Bem, S. L. (1981). Gender schema theory: A cognitive account of sex typing. *Psychological Review, 88,* 354–364. [8]

Bem, S. L. (1985). Androgyny and gender schema theory: A conceptual and empirical integration. In T. B. Sonderegger (Ed.), *Nebraska symposium on motivation: Psychology of gender* (Vol. 32, pp. 179–226). Lincoln: University of Nebraska Press. [8]

Benbow, C. P., & Stanley, J. C. (1980). Sex differences in mathematical ability: Fact or artifact? *Science, 210,* 1262–1264. [7]

Benbow, C. P., & Stanley, J. C. (1983). Sex differences in mathematical reasoning ability: More facts. *Science, 222,* 1029–1031. [7]

Benes, F. M. (2000). Emerging principles of altered neural circuitry in schizophrenia. *Brain Research Reviews, 31,* 251–269. [12]

Benjafield, J. G. (1996). *A history of psychology.* Boston: Allyn & Bacon. [1]

Benjamin, L., & Crouse, E. (2002). The American Psychological Association's response to *Brown v. Board of Education:* The case of Kenneth B. Clark. *American Psychologist, 57,* 38–50. [1]

Bennett, S. K. (1994). The American Indian: A psychological overview. In W. J. Lonner & R. Malpass (Eds.), *Psychology and culture* (pp. 35–39). Boston: Allyn & Bacon. [11]

Ben-Porath, Y. S., & Butcher, J. N. (1989). The comparability of MMPI and MMPI-2 scales and profiles. *Psychological Assessment: A Journal of Consulting and Clinical Psychology, 1,* 345–347. [11]

Benson, H. (1975). *The relaxation response.* New York: Avon. [4]

Benson, E. (2003). The unexpected benefits of basic science. *Monitor on Psychology, 34,* 36–37.

Berenbaum, S. A., Korman, K., & Leveroni, C. (1995). Early hormones and sex differences in cognitive abilities. *Learning and Individual Differences, 7,* 303–321. [7]

Berenbaum, S. A., & Snyder, E. (1995). Early hormonal influences on childhood sex-typed activity and playmate preferences: Implications for the development of sexual orientation. *Developmental Psychology, 31,* 31–42. [8, 9]

Berk, L. E. (1994). *Child development* (3rd ed.). Boston: Allyn & Bacon. [8]

Berkman, L. F., & Syme, S. L. (1979). Social networks, host resistance, and mortality: A nine-year followup study of Alameda County residents. *American Journal of Epidemiology, 109,* 184–204. [10]

Berkowitz, L. (1983). Aversively stimulated aggression: Some parallels and differences in research with animals and humans. *American Psychologist, 38,* 1135–1144. [14]

Berkowitz, L. (1988). Frustrations, appraisals, and aversively stimulated aggression. *Aggressive Behavior, 14,* 3–11. [14]

Berkowitz, L. (1990). On the formation and regulation of anger and aggression: A cognitive-neoassociationistic analysis. *American Psychologist, 45,* 494–503. [14]

Berlyne, D. E. (1960). *Conflict, arousal, and curiosity.* New York: McGraw-Hill. [9]

Bernal, M. E., & Castro, F. G. (1994). Are clinical psychologists prepared for service and research with ethnic minorities? Report of a decade of progress. *American Psychologist, 49,* 797–805. [13]

Bernardi, L., Sleight, P., Bandinelli, G., Cencetti, S., Fattorini, L., Wdowczyc-Szulc, J., & Lagi, A. (2001). Effect of rosary prayer and yoga mantras on autonomic cardiovascular rhythms: Comparative study. *BMJ: British Medical Journal, 323,* 1446–1449. [4]

Berndt, E. R., Koran, L. M., Finkelstein, S. N., Gelenberg, A. J., Kornstein, S. G., Miller, I. M., Thase, M. E., Trapp, G. A., & Keller, M. B. (2000). Lost human capital from early-onset chronic depression. *American Journal of Psychiatry, 157,* 940–947. [12]

Berndt, T. J. (1992). Friendship and friends' influence in adolescence. *Current Directions in Psychological Science, 1,* 156–159. [8]

Bernstein, I. L. (1985). Learned food aversions in the progression of cancer and its treatment. *Annals of the New York Academy of Sciences, 443,* 365–380. [5]

Bernstein, I. L., Webster, M. M., & Bernstein, I. D. (1982). Food aversions in children receiving chemotherapy for cancer. *Cancer, 50,* 2961–2963. [5]

Berquier, A., & Aston, R. (1992). Characteristics of the frequent nightmare sufferer. *Journal of Abnormal Psychology, 101,* 246–250. [4]

Berscheid, E., Dion, K., Walster, E., & Walster, G. W. (1971). Physical attractiveness and dating choice: A test of the matching hypothesis. *Journal of Experimental Social Psychology, 7,* 173–189. [14]

Besharat, M. (2001). Management strategies of sexual dysfunctions. *Journal of Contemporary Psychotherapy, 31,* 161–180. [12]

Beyenburg, S., Watzka, M., Clusmann, H., Blümcke, I., Bidlingmaier, F., Stoffel-Wagner, C. E. E., & Stoffel-Wagner, B. W. (2000). Androgen receptor mRNA expression in the human hippocampus. *Neuroscience Letters, 294,* 25–28. [8]

Beyrer, C. (2003). The HIV/AIDS vaccine research effort: An update. *The Hopkins HIV report* [January 2003 online edition]. Retrieved December 28, 2002, from http://hopkins-aids.edu/publications/report/jan03_3.html [10]

Bialystok, E. (1997). Effects of bilingualism and biliteracy on children's emerging concepts of print. *Developmental Psychology, 33,* 429–440. [7]

Bialystok, E., & Majumder, S. (1998). The relationship between bilingualism and the development of cognitive processes in problem solving. *Applied Psycholinguistics, 19,* 69–85. [7]

Bialystok, E., Shenfield, T., & Codd, J. (2000). Languages, scripts, and the environment: Factors in developing concepts of print. *Developmental Psychology, 36,* 66–76. [7]

Billiard, M., Pasquiré-Magnetto, V., Heckman, M., Carlander, B., Besset, A., Zachariev, Z., Eliaou, J. F., & Malafosse, A. (1994). Family studies in narcolepsy. *Sleep, 17,* S54–S59. [4]

Birren, J. E., & Fisher, L. M. (1995). Aging and speed of behavior: Possible consequences for psychological functioning. *Annual Review of Psychology, 46,* 329–353. [8]

Bishop, J., & Lane, R. C. (2000). Father absence and the attitude of entitlement. *Journal of Contemporary Psychotherapy, 30,* 105–117. [8, 9, 10]

Bisiach, E. (1996). Unilateral neglect and the structure of space representation. *Current Directions in Psychological Science, 5,* 62–65. [2]

Bjork, D. W. (1993). *B. F. Skinner: A life.* New York: Basic Books. [5]

Bjorklund, D. F., Cassel, W. S., Bjorklund, B. R., Brown, R. D., Park, C. L., Ernst, K., & Owen, F. A. (2000). Social demand characteristics in children's and adults' memory and suggestibility: The effect of different interviewers on free recall and recognition. *Applied Cognitive Psychology, 14,* 421–433. [6]

Blascovich, J., Wyer, N. A., Swart, L. A., & Kibler, J. L. (1997). Racism and racial categorization. *Journal of Personality and Social Psychology, 72,* 1364–1372. [14]

Blatt, S. J., Sanislow, C. A., III, Zuroff, D. C., & Pilkonis, P. A. (1996). Characteristics of effective therapists: Further analyses of data from the National Institute of Mental Health Treatment of Depression Collaborative Research Program. *Journal of Consulting and Clinical Psychology, 64,* 1276–1284. [13]

Bliese, P. D., & Castro, C. A. (2000). Role clarity, work overload and organizational support: Multilevel evidence of the importance of support. *Work & Stress, 14,* 65–73. [10]

Bliss, E. L., & Jeppsen, E. A. (1985). Prevalence of multiple personality among inpatients and outpatients. *American Journal of Psychiatry, 142,* 250–251. [12]

Bliss, T. V., & Lomo, T. (2000). Plasticity in a monosynaptic cortical pathway. *Journal of Physiology, 207,* 61. [6]

Bloom, B. S. (Ed.). (1985). *Developing talent in young people.* New York: Ballantine. [7]

Bloomer, C. M. (1976). *Principles of visual perception.* New York: Van Nostrand Reinhold. [3]

Blustein, D., Phillips, S., Jobin-Davis, K., & Finkelberg, S. (1997). A theory-building investigation of the school-to-work transition. *Counseling Psychology, 25,* 364–402. [8]

Blyth, D. A., Simmons, R. G., Bulcroft, R., Felt, D., VanCleave, E. F., & Bush, D. M. (1981). The effects of physical development on self-image and satisfaction with body-image for early adolescent males. In R. G. Simmons (Ed.), *Research in community and mental health* (Vol. 2). Greenwich, CT: JAI. [8]

Bochner, S. (1994). Cross-cultural differences in the self concept: A test of Hofstede's individualism/collectivism distinction. *Journal of Cross-Cultural Psychology, 25,* 273–283. [11]

Bogen, J. E., & Vogel, P. J. (1963). Treatment of generalized seizures by cerebral commissurotomy. *Surgical Forum, 14,* 431. [2]

Bohannon, J. N., III. (1988). Flashbulb memories for the Space Shuttle disaster: A tale of two theories. *Cognition, 29,* 179–196. [6]

Boivin, D. B., Czeisler, C. A., Dijk, D-J., Duffy, J. F., Folkard, S., Minors, D. S., Totterdell, P., & Waterhouse, J. M. (1997). Complex interaction of the sleep-wake cycle and circadian phase modulates mood in healthy subjects. *Archives of General Psychiatry, 54,* 145–152. [4]

Bonanno, G. A., Keltner, D., Holen, A., & Horowitz, M. J. (1995). When avoiding unpleasant emotions might not be such a bad thing: Verbal-autonomic response dissociation and midlife conjugal bereavement. *Journal of Personality and Social Psychology, 69,* 975–989. [8]

Bonnet, M. H., & Arand, D. L. (1995). We are chronically sleep deprived. *Sleep, 18,* 908–911 [4]

Bonson, K., Grant, S., Contoreggi, C., Links, J., Metcalfe, J., Weyl, H., Kurian, V., Ernst, M., & London, E. (2002). Neural systems and cue-induced cocaine craving. *Neurospsychopharmacology, 26,* 376–386. [4]

Borbely, A. A. (1984). Sleep regulation: Outline of a model and its implications for depression. In A. A. Borbely & J. L. Valatx (Eds.), *Sleep mechanisms.* Berlin: Springer-Verlag. [4]

Borbely, A. A., Achermann, P., Trachsel, L., & Tobler, I. (1989). Sleep initiation and initial sleep intensity: Interactions of homeostatic and circadian mechanisms. *Journal of Biological Rhythms, 4,* 149–160. [4]

Bornstein, R. F. (1989). Exposure and affect: Overview and meta-analysis of research, 1968–1987. *Psychological Bulletin, 106,* 265–289. [14]

Borrelli, B., Niaura, R., Keuthen, N. J., Goldstein, M. G., DePue, J. D., Murphy, C., & Abrams, D. B. (1996). Development of major depressive disorder during smoking-cessation treatment. Journal of *Clinical Psychiatry, 57,* 534–538. [10]

Bosse, R., Aldwin, C. M., Levenson, M. R., & Workman-Daniels, K. (1991). How stressful is retirement? *Journal of Gerontology, 46,* 9–14. [8]

Bouchard, T. J., Jr. (1994). Genes, environment, and personality. *Science, 264,* 1700–1701. [11]

Bouchard, T. J., Jr. (1997, September/October). Whenever the twain shall meet. *The Sciences, 37,* 52–57. [7]

Bouchard, T. J., Jr. (1998, May 13). Personal communication. [7]

Bouchard, T. J., Jr., Lykken, D. T., McGue, M., Segal, N. L., & Tellegen, A. (1990). Sources of human psychological differences: The Minnesota study of twins reared apart. *Science, 250,* 223–228. [7]

Bouchard, T. J., Jr., & McGue, M. (1981). Familial studies of intelligence: A review. *Science, 212,* 1055–1058. [7]

Bourassa, D., McManus, I., & Bryden, M. (1996). Handedness and eye-dominance: A meta-analysis of their relationship. *Laterality, 1,* 5–34. [2]

Bourassa, M., & Vaugeois, P. (2001). Effects of marijuana use on divergent thinking. *Creativity Research Journal, 13,* 411–416. [4]

Bowden, C., Lecrubier, Y., Bauer, M., Goodwin, G., Greil, W., Sachs, G., & von Knorring, L. (2000). Maintenance therapies for classic and other forms of bipolar disorder. *Journal of Affective Disorders, 59* (Suppl. 1), S57–S67. [13]

Bowen-Reid, T., & Harrell, J. (2002). Racist experiences and health outcomes: An examination of spirituality as a buffer. *Journal of Black Psychology, 28,* 18–36. [10]

Bower, G. H. (1973, October). How to . . . uh . . . remember! *Psychology Today,* pp. 63–70. [6]

Bowers, K. S. (1992). Imagination and dissociative control in hypnotic responding. *International Journal of Clinical and Experimental Hypnosis, 40,* 253–275. [4]

Bowers, K. S., & Farvolden, P. (1996). Revisiting a century-old Freudian slip-from suggestion disavowed to the truth repressed. *Psychological Bulletin, 119,* 355–380. [6]

Bowers, K. S., & Woody, E. Z. (1996). Hypnotic amnesia and the paradox of intentional forgetting. *Journal of Abnormal Psychology, 105,* 381–390. [4]

Brain imaging and psychiatry–Part I. (1997, January). *Harvard Mental Health Letter, 13*(7), 1–4. [2]

Brantner, J. P., & Doherty, M. A. (1983). A review of time out: A conceptual and methodological analysis. In S. Axelrod & J. Apsche (Eds.), *The effects of punishment on human behavior* (pp. 87–132). New York: Academic Press. [13]

Braun, A., Balkin, T., Wesensten, N., Gwadry, F., Carson, R., Varga, M., Baldwin, P., Belenky, G., & Herscovitch, P. (1998). Dissociated pattern of activity in visual cortices and their projections during human rapid eye movement sleep. *Science, 279,* 91–95. [4]

Braun, S. (1996). New experiments underscore warnings on maternal drinking. *Science, 273,* 738–739. [8]

Brawman-Mintzer, O., & Lydiard, R. B. (1996). Generalized anxiety disorder: Issues in epidemiology. *Journal of Clinical Psychiatry, 57*(7, Suppl.), 3–8. [12]

Brawman-Mintzer, O., & Lydiard, R. B. (1997). Biological basis of generalized anxiety disorder. *Journal of Clinical Psychiatry, 58*(3, Suppl.), 16–25. [12]

Bray, G. A. (1991). Weight homeostasis. *Annual Review of Medicine, 42,* 205–216. [9]

Bray, G. A., & Tartaglia, L. A. (2000). Medicinal strategies in the treatment of obesity. *Nature, 404,* 672–677. [9]

Breckler, S. J. (1984). Empirical validation of affect, behavior, and cognition as distinct attitude components. *Journal of Personality and Social Psychology, 47,* 1191–1205. [14]

Brennan, P. A., Raine, A., Schulsinger, F., Kirkegaard-Sorensen, L., Knop, J., Hutchings, B., Rosenberg, R., & Mednick, S. A. (1997). Psychophysiological protective factors for male subjects at high risk for criminal behavior. *American Journal of Psychiatry, 154,* 853–855. [14]

Brent, D., Oquendo, M., Birmaher, B., Greenhill, L., Kolko, D., Stanley, B., Zelazny, J., Brodsky, B., Bridge, J., Ellis, S., Salazar, J., & Mann, J. (2002). Familial pathways to early-onset suicide attempt. *Archives of General Psychiatry, 59,* 801. [12]

Brent, D. A., Bridge, J., Johnson, B. A., & Connolly, J. (1996). Suicidal behavior runs in families: A controlled family study of adolescent suicide victims. *Archives of General Psychiatry, 53,* 1145–1152. [12]

Breslau, N., Davis, G. C., Peterson, E. L., & Schultz, L. (1997). Psychiatric sequelae of posttraumatic stress disorder in women. *Archives of General Psychiatry, 54,* 81–87. [10]

Breslau, N., Kilbey, M. N., & Andreski, P. (1993). Nicotine dependence and major depression: New evidence from a prospective investigation. *Archives of General Psychiatry, 50,* 31–35. [10]

Broadbent, D. E. (1958). *Perception and communication.* New York: Pergamon Press. [6]

Brody, A., Saxena, S., Fairbanks, L., Alborzian, S., Demaree, H., Maidment, K., & Baxter, L. (2000). Personality changes in adult subjects with major depressive disorder or obsessive-compulsive disorder treated with paroxetine. *Journal of Clinical Psychiatry, 61,* 349–355. [11]

Brody, E. M., Johnson, P. T., & Fulcomer, M. C. (1984). What should adult children do for elderly parents? Opinions and preferences of three generations of women. *Journal of Gerontology, 39,* 736–746. [8]

Brody, E. M., Litvin, S. J., Hoffman, C., & Kleban, M. H. (1992). Differential effects of daughters' marital status on their parent care experiences. *The Gerontologist, 32,* 58–67. [8]

Brody, L. R. (1985). Gender differences in emotional development: A review of theories and research. *Journal of Personality, 53,* 102–149. [9]

Brody, N. (1992). *Intelligence* (2nd ed.). San Diego, CA: Academic. [7]

Brooks-Gunn, J., & Furstenberg, F. F. (1989). Adolescent sexual behavior. *American Psychologist, 44,* 249–257. [8]

Brotman, A. W. (1994). What works in the treatment of anorexia nervosa? *Harvard Mental Health Letter, 10*(7), 8. [9]

Broughton, W. A., & Broughton, R. J. (1994). Psychosocial impact of narcolepsy. *Sleep, 17,* S45–S49. [4]

Brown, A. (1996, Winter). Mood disorders in children and adolescents. *NARSAD Research Newsletter,* pp. 11–14. [12]

Brown, A. M. (1990). Development of visual sensitivity to light and color vision in human infants: A critical review. *Vision Research, 30,* 1159–1188. [8]

Brown, G. W., Harris, T. O., & Hepworth, C. (1994). Life events and endogenous depression: A puzzle reexamined. *Archives of General Psychiatry, 51,* 525–534. [12]

Brown, J. D., & Rogers, R. J. (1991). Self-serving attributions: The role of physiological arousal. *Personality and Social Psychology Bulletin, 17,* 501–506. [14]

Brown, J. L., & Pollitt, E. (1996). Malnutrition, poverty and intellectual development. *Scientific American, 274,* 38–43. [7]

Brown, R. (1973). *A first language: The early stages.* Cambridge, MA: Harvard University Press. [8]

Brown, R., Cazden, C., & Bellugi, U. (1968). The child's grammar from I to III. In J. P. Hill (Ed.), *Minnesota symposium on child psychology* (Vol. 2, pp. 28–73). Minneapolis: University of Minnesota Press. [8]

Brown, R., & Kulik, J. (1977). Flashbulb memories. *Cognition, 5,* 73–99. [6]

Brown, R., & McNeil, D. (1966). The "tip of the tongue" phenomenon. *Journal of Verbal Learning and Verbal Behavior, 5,* 325–337. [6]

Brown, W., O'Connell, A., & Fillit, H. (2002). New developments in pharmacotherapy for Alzheimer disease. *Drug Benefit Trends, 14,* 34–44. [8]

Brownlee, S., & Schrof, J. M. (1997, March 17). The quality of mercy. *U.S. News & World Report,* pp. 54–67. [3]

Buck, L. B. (1996). Information coding in the vertebrate olfactory system. *Annual Review of Neuroscience, 19,* 517–544. [3]

Buhusi, C., & Meck, W. (2002). Differential effects of methamphetamine and haloperidol on the control of an internal clock. *Behavioral Neuroscience, 116,* 291–297. [4]

Buller, D. B., Burgoon, M., Hall, J. R., Levine, N., Taylor, A. M., Beach, B. H., Melcher, C., Buller, M. K., Bowen, S. L., Hunsaker, F. G., & Bergen, A. (2000). Using language intensity to increase the success of a family intervention to protect children from ultraviolet radiation: Predictions from language expectancy theory. *Preventive Medicine, 30,* 103–113. [14]

Buonomano, D. V., & Merzenich, M. M. (1995). Temporal information transformed into a spatial code by a neural network with realistic properties. *Science, 267,* 1028–1030. [7]

Burchinal, M., Campbell, F., Bryant, D., Wasik, B., & Ramey, C. (1997). Early intervention and mediating processes in cognitive performance of children of low-income African American families. *Child Development, 68,* 935–954. [7]

Burt, D. B., Zembar, M. J., & Niederehe, G. (1995). Depression and memory impairment: A meta-analysis of the association, its pattern, and specificity. *Psychological Bulletin, 117,* 285–305. [6]

Busch, C. M., Zonderman, A. B., & Costa, P. T. (1994). Menopausal transition and psychological distress in a nationally representative sample: Is menopause associated with psychological distress? *Journal of Aging and Health, 6,* 209–228. [8]

Bushman, B. J. (1995). Moderating role of trait aggressiveness in the effects of violent media on aggression. *Journal of Personality and Social Psychology, 69,* 950–960. [14]

Bushman, B. J., & Cooper, H. M. (1990). Effects of alcohol on human aggression: An integrative research review. *Psychological Bulletin, 107,* 341–354. [14]

Busnel, M. C., Granier-Deferre, C., & Lecanuet, J. P. (1992). Fetal audition. *Annals of the New York Academy of Sciences, 662,* 118–134. [8]

Buss, D. M. (1984). Marital assortment for personality dispositions: Assessment with three different data sources. *Behavioral Genetics, 14,* 111–123. [14]

Buss, D. M. (1994). The strategies of human mating. *American Scientist, 82,* 238–249. [14]

Buss, D. M. (1999). *Evolutionary psychology: The new science of the mind.* Boston: Allyn & Bacon. [1, 9]

Buss, D. M. (2000a). *The dangerous passion: Why jealousy is as necessary as sex and love.* New York: Free Press. [1, 9]

Buss, D. M. (2000b). Desires in human mating. *Annals of the New York Academy of Sciences, 907,* 39–49. [1, 14]

Buss, D. M., Abbott, M., Angleitner, A., Asherian, A., Biaggio, A., Blanco-Villasenor, A., Bruchon-Schweitzer, M., et al. (1990). International preferences in selecting mates: A study of 37 cultures. *Journal of Cross-Cultural Psychology, 21,* 5–47. [14]

Buss, D. M., Larson, R., Westen, D., & Semmelroth, J. (1992). Sex differences in jealousy: Evolution, physiology, and psychology. *Psychological Science, 3,* 251–255. [1]

Buss, D., Shackelford, T., Kirkpatrick, L., & Larsen, R. (2001). A half century of mate preferences: The cultural evolution of values. *Journal of Marriage and the Family, 63,* 491–503. [1]

Bussey, K., & Bandura, A. (1999). Social cognitive theory of gender development and differentiation. *Psychological Review, 106,* 676–713. [8]

Butcher, J. N. (1992, October). International developments with the MMPI-2. *MMPI-2 News & Profiles, 3,* 4. [11]

Butcher, J. N., Dahlstrom, W. G., Graham, J. R., Tellegen, A., & Kaemmer, B. (1989). *Manual for the restandardized Minnesota Multiphasic Personality Inventory: MMPI-2. An administrative and interpretive guide.* Minneapolis: University of Minnesota Press. [11]

Butcher, J. N., & Graham, J. R. (1989). *Topics in MMPI-2 interpretation.* Minneapolis: Department of Psychology, University of Minnesota. [11]

Butcher, J. N., Graham, J. R., & Ben-Porath, Y. S. (1995). Methodological problems and issues in MMPI, MMPI-2, and MMPI-A research. *Psychological Assessment, 7,* 320–329. [11]

Butcher, J. N., & Rouse, S. V. (1996). Personality: Individual differences and clinical assessment. *Annual Review of Psychology, 47,* 89–111. [11]

Butler, R., & Lewis, M. (1982). *Aging and mental health* (3rd ed.). St. Louis: Mosby. [8]

Butterworth, G., Franco, F., McKenzie, B., Graupner, L., & Todd, B. (2002). Dynamic aspects of visual event perception and the production of pointing by human infants. *British Journal of Developmental Psychology, 20,* 1–24. [2]

Buunk, B. P., Angleitner, A., Oubaid, V., & Buss, D. M. (1996). Sex differences in jealousy in evolutionary and cultural perspective: Tests from the Netherlands, Germany and the United States. *Psychological Science, 7,* 359–363. [1]

Byne, W. (1993). Human sexual orientation: The biologic theories reappraised. *Archives of General Psychiatry, 50,* 228–239. [9]

Byne, W. (1994). The biological evidence challenged. *Scientific American, 270,* 50–55. [9]

Byne, W., & Parsons, B. (1993). Human sexual orientation: The biologic theories reappraised. *Archives of General Psychiatry, 50,* 228–239. [9]

Byne, W., & Parsons, B. (1994). Biology and human sexual orientation. *Harvard Mental Health Letter, 10*(8), 5–7. [9]

Cahill, L., & McGaugh, J. (1995). A novel demonstration of enhanced memory associated with emotional arousal. *Consciousness and Cognition, 4,* 410–421. [6]

Camp, D. S., Raymond, G. A., & Church, R. M. (1967). Temporal relationship between response and punishment. *Journal of Experimental Psychology, 74,* 114–123. [5]

Campbell, F. A., & Ramey, C. T. (1994). Effects of early intervention on intellectual and academic achievement: A follow-up study of children from low-income families. *Child development, 65,* 684–698. [7]

Campbell, F., Pungello, E., Miler-Johnson, S., Burchinal, M., & Ramey, C. (2001). The development of cognitive and academic abilities: Growth curves from an early childhood educational experiment. *Developmental Psychology, 37,* 231–242. [7]

Campbell, P., & Dhand, R. (2000). Obesity. *Nature, 404,* 631. [9]

Campbell, R., & Brody, E. M. (1985). Women's changing roles and help to the elderly: Attitudes of women in the United States and Japan. *The Gerontologist, 25,* 584–592. [8]

Campbell, S. S. (1995). Effects of timed bright-light exposure on shift-work adaptation in middle-aged subjects. *Sleep, 18,* 408–416. [4]

Cannon, T. D., Kaprio, J., Lönnqvist, J., Huttunen, M., & Koskenvuo, M. (1998). The genetic epidemiology of schizophrenia in a Finnish twin cohort: A population-based modeling study. *Archives of General Psychiatry, 55,* 67–74. [12]

Cannon, W. B. (1927). The James-Lange theory of emotions: A critical examination and an alternative theory. *American Journal of Psychology, 39,* 106–112. [9]

Cannon, W. B. (1929). *Bodily changes in pain, hunger, fear and rage* (2nd ed.). New York: Appleton. [2]

Cannon, W. B. (1935). Stresses and strains of homeostasis. *American Journal of Public Health, 189,* 1–14. [2]

Cardena, E. (2000). Hypnosis in the treatment of trauma: A promising, but not fully supported, efficacious intervention. *International Journal of Clinical Experimental Hypnosis, 48,* 225–238. [4]

Cardoso, S. H., de Mello, L. C., & Sabbatini, R. M. E. (2000). How nerve cells work. [On-line]. Retrieved from http://www.epub.org.br/cm/n09/fundamentos/transmissao/voo_i.htm [2]

Carlat, D. J., Camargo, C. A., Jr., & Herzog, D. B. (1997). Eating disorders in males: A report on 135 patients. *American Journal of Psychiatry, 154,* 1127–1132. [9]

Carlson, N. R. (1998). *Foundations of physiological psychology* (4th ed.). Boston: Allyn & Bacon. [4]

Carpenter, W. T., Jr. (1996). Maintenance therapy of persons with schizophrenia. *Journal of Clinical Psychiatry, 57*(9, Suppl.), 10–18. [13]

Carrier, J. (1980). Homosexual behavior in cross-cultural perspective. In J. Marmor (Ed.), *Homosexual behavior* (pp. 100–122). New York: Basic Books. [9]

Carroll, K. M., Rounsaville, B. J., Nich, C., Gordon, L. T., Wirtz, P. W., & Gawin, F. (1994). One-year follow-up of psychotherapy and pharmacotherapy for cocaine dependence: Delayed emergence of psychotherapy effects. *Archives of General Psychiatry, 51,* 989–997. [13]

Carson, R. C. (1989). Personality. *Annual Review of Psychology, 40,* 227–248. [11]

Carver, C. S., Pozo, C., Harris, S. D., Noriega, V., Scheier, M. F., Robinson, D. S., Ketcham, A. S., Moffat, F. L., Jr., & Clark, K. C. (1993). How coping mediates the effect of optimism on distress: A study of women with early stage breast cancer. *Journal of Personality and Social Psychology, 65,* 375–390. [10]

Carver, C. S., & Scheier, M. F. (1996). *Perspectives on personality* (3rd ed.). Boston: Allyn & Bacon. [11]

Casey, D. E. (1996). Side effect profiles of new antipsychotic agents. *Journal of Clinical Psychiatry, 57*(11, Suppl.), 40–45. [13]

Cash, T. F., & Derlega, V. J. (1978). The matching hypothesis: Physical attractiveness among same-sexed friends. *Personality and Social Psychology Bulletin, 4,* 240–243. [14]

Cash, T. F., & Janda, L. H. (1984, December). The eye of the beholder. *Psychology Today,* pp. 46–52. [14]

Caspi, A. (2000). The child is father of the man: Personality continuities from childhood to adulthood. *Journal of Personality & Social Psychology, 78,* 158–172. [11]

Caspi, A., Lynam, D., Moffitt, T. E., & Silva, P. A. (1993). Unraveling girls' delinquency: Biological, dispositional, and contextual contributions to adolescent misbehavior. *Developmental Psychology, 29,* 19–30. [8]

Caspi, A., & Silva, P. A. (1995). Temperamental qualities at age three predict personality traits in young adulthood: Longitudinal evidence from a birth cohort. *Child Development, 66,* 486–498. [8]

Cattell, R. B. (1950). *Personality: A systematic, theoretical, and factual study.* New York: McGraw-Hill. [11]

Cattell, R. B. (1993). *16PF® fifth edition profile sheet.* Champaign, IL: Institute for Personality and Ability Testing. [11]

Cattell, R. B., Eber, H. W., & Tatsuoka, M. M. (1977). *Handbook for the 16 personality factor questionnaire.* Champaign, IL: Institute of Personality and Ability Testing. [11]

Cattell, R. B., Saunders, D. R., & Stice, G. F. (1950). *The 16 personality factor questionnaire.* Champaign, IL: Institute of Personality and Ability Testing. [11]

Centers for Disease Control (CDC). (2000). *Some Facts about Chlamydia* [Online report]. Retrieved September 1, 2000, from http://www.cdc.gov [8]

Centers for Disease Control and Prevention. (2002). *HIV/AIDS Surveillance Report: Year-end Edition, 13,* 1–44. [10]

Chambless, D. L., & Goldstein, A. J. (1979). Behavioral psychotherapy. In R. J. Corsini (Ed.), *Current psychotherapies* (2nd ed., pp. 230–272). Itasca, IL: F. E. Peacock. [13]

Chao, R. (2001). Extending research on the consequences of parenting style for Chinese Americans and European Americans. *Child Development, 72,* 1832–1843. [8]

Chaplin, W. F., Philips, J. B., Brown, J. D., Clanton, N. R., & Stein, J. L. (2000). Handshaking, gender, personality, and first impressions. *Journal of Personality and Social Psychology, 19,* 110–117. [14]

Charness, N. (1989). Age and expertise: Responding to Talland's challenge. In L. W. Poon, D. C. Rubin, & B. A. Wilson (Eds.), *Everyday cognition in adulthood and old age.* New York: Cambridge University Press. [8]

Chase, M. H., & Morales, F. R. (1990). The atonia and myoclonia of active REM sleep. *Annual Review of Psychology, 41,* 557–584. [4]

Chen-Sea, M.-J. (2000). Validating the Draw-A-Man Test as a personal neglect test. *American Journal of Occupational Therapy, 54,* 391–397. [2]

Chincotta, D., & Underwood, G. (1997). Estimates, language of schooling and bilingual digit span. *European Journal of Cognitive Psychology, 9,* 325–348. [7]

Chira, S. (1992, February 12). Bias against girls is found rife in schools, with lasting damage. *The New York Times,* pp. A1, A23. [7]

Cho, K. (2001). Chronic "jet lag" produces temporal lobe atrophy and spatial cognitive deficits. *Nature Neuroscience, 4,* 567–568. [4]

Cho, K., Ennaceur, A., Cole, J., & Kook Suh, C. (2000). Chronic jet lag produces cognitive deficits. *Journal of Neuroscience, 20,* RC66. [4]

Chodoff, P. (1987). More on multiple personality disorder. *American Journal of Psychiatry, 144,* 124. [12]

Chollar, S. (1989). Conversation with the dolphins. *Psychology Today, 23,* 52–57. [7]

Chomsky, N. (1957). *Syntactic structures.* The Hague: Mouton. [8]

Chomsky, N. (1968). *Language and mind.* New York: Harcourt, Brace & World. [8]

Christensen, L. B. (1997). *Experimental methodology* (7th ed.). Boston: Allyn & Bacon. [1]

Christensen, L. B. (2001). *Experimental methodology* (8th ed.). Boston: Allyn & Bacon. [1]

Church, R. M. (1963). The varied effects of punishment on behavior. *Psychological Review, 70,* 369–402. [5]

Church, R. M. (1989). Theories of timing behavior. In S. P. Klein & R. Mowrer (Eds.), *Contemoprary learning theories: Instrumental conditioning theory and the impact of biological constraints on learning.* Hillsdale, NJ: Erlbaum. [5]

Cialdini, R. B., Cacioppo, J. T., Basset, R., & Miller, J. A. (1978). Low–ball procedure for producing compliance: Commitment then cost. *Journal of Personality and Social Psychology, 36,* 463–476. [14]

Cialdini, R. B., Vincent, J. E., Lewis, S. K., Catalan, J., Wheeler, D., & Darby, B. L. (1975). Reciprocal concessions procedure for inducing compliance: The door-in-the-face technique. *Journal of Personality and Social Psychology, 31,* 206–215. [14]

Clark, D. M., & Teasdale, J. D. (1982). Diurnal variation in clinical depression and accessibility of memories of positive and negative experiences. *Journal of Abnormal Psychology, 91,* 87–95. [6]

Clark, M. L., & Ayers, M. (1992). Friendship similarity during early adolescence: Gender and racial patterns. *Journal of Psychology, 126,* 393–405. [8]

Clarkson–Smith, L., & Hartley, A. A. (1990). Structural equation models of relationships between exercise and cognitive abilities. *Psychology and Aging, 5,* 437–446. [8]

Clay, R. (2002). Research on 9/11: What psychologists have learned so far. *APA Monitor on Psychology, 33,* 28–30. [10]

Clay, R., Daw, J., & Dittman, M. (2002). More research on America's response. *APA Monitor on Psychology, 33,* 31. [10]

Clayton, K. N. (1964). T-maze choice learning as a joint function of the reward magnitudes for the alternatives. *Journal of Comparative and Physiological Psychology, 58,* 333–338. [5]

Clayton, N. S. (1998). Memory and the hippocampus in food-storing birds: A comparative approach. *Neuropharmacology, 37,* 441–452. [6]

Cleckley, H. (1941). *The mask of sanity.* St. Louis: Mosby. [12]

Clément, K., Vaisse, C., Lahlou, N., Cabrol, S., Pelloux, V., Cassuto, D., Gourmelen, M., Dina, C., Chambaz, J., Lacorte, J-M., Basdevant, A., Bougnères, P., Lubouc, Y., Froguel, P., & Guy-Grand, B. (1998). A mutation in the human leptin receptor gene causes obesity and pituitary dysfunction. *Nature, 392,* 398–401. [9]

Cloitre, M., Koenen, K., Cohen, L., & Han, H. (2002). Skills training in affective and interpersonal regulation followed by exposure: A phase-based treatment for PTSD related to childhood abuse. *Journal of Consulting and Clinical Psychology, 70,* 1067–1074. [13]

Cloninger, C. R., Sigvardsson, S., Bohman, M., & von Knorring, A. L. (1982). Predispositions to petty criminality in Swedish adoptees, II. Cross-fostering analysis of gene-environment interaction. *Archives of General Psychiatry, 39,* 1242–1249. [14]

Cohen, L. L., & Shotland, R. L. (1996). Timing of first sexual intercourse in a relationship: Expectations, experiences, and perceptions of others. *Journal of Sex Research, 33,* 291–299. [9]

Cohen, S. (1988). Psychosocial models of the role of social support in the etiology of physical disease. *Health Psychology, 7,* 269–297. [10]

Cohen, S. (1996). Psychological stress, immunity, and upper respiratory infections. *Current Directions in Psychological Science, 5,* 86–89. [10]

Cohen, S., Doyle, W. J., Skoner, D. P., Rabin, B. S., & Gwaltney, J. M., Jr. (1997). Social ties and susceptibility to the common cold. *Journal of the American Medical Association, 277,* 1940–1944. [10]

Cohen, S., & Herbert, T. B. (1996). Health psychology: Psychological factors and physical disease from the perspective of human psychoneuroimmunology. *Annual Review of Psychology, 47,* 113–142. [10]

Cohen, S., & Williamson, G. M. (1991). Stress and infectious disease in humans. *Psychological Bulletin, 109,* 5–54. [10]

Colby, A., Kohlberg, L., Gibbs, J., & Lieberman, M. (1983). A longitudinal study of moral judgment. *Monographs of the Society for Research in Child Development, 48*(1–2, Serial No. 200). [8]

Cole, P. M. (1986). Children's spontaneous control of facial expression. *Child Development, 57,* 1309–1321. [9]

Cole, R., Smith, J., Alcala, Y., Elliott, J., & Kripke, D. (2002). Bright-light mask treatment of delayed sleep phase syndrome. *Journal of Biological Rhythms, 17,* 89–101. [4]

Coleman, C., King, B., Bolden-Watson, C., Book, M., Segraves, R., Richard, N., Ascher, J., Batey, S., Jamerson, B., & Metz, A. (2001). A placebo-controlled comparison of the effects on sexual functioning of bupropion sustained release and fluoxetine. *Clinical Therapeutics: The International Peer-Reviewed Journal of Drug Therapy, 23,* 1040–1058. [12]

Coles, M. E., & Heinberg, R. G. (2000). Patterns of anxious arousal during exposure to feared situations in individuals with social phobia. *Behaviour Research & Therapy, 38,* 405–424. [13]

Collaer, M. L., & Hines, M. (1995). Human behavioral sex differences: A role for gonadal hormones during early development. *Psychological Bulletin, 118,* 55–107. [8, 9]

Colombo, M., & Broadbent, N. (2000). Is the avian hippocampus a functional homologue of the mammalian hippocampus? *Neuroscience and Biobehavioral Reviews, 24,* 465–484. [6]

Colwell, J., & Payne, J. (2000). Negative correlates of computer game play in adolescents. *British Journal of Psychology, 91*(Pt. 3), 295–310. [14]

Conca, A., Swoboda, E., König, P., Koppi, S., Beraus, W., Künz, A., et al. (2000). Clinical impacts of single transcranial magnetic stimulation (sTMS) as an add-on therapy in severely depressed patients under SSRI treatment. *Human Psychopharmacology: Clinical and Experimental, 15,* 429–438. [13]

Condon, W. S., & Sander, L. W. (1974). Neonatal movement is synchronized with adult speech: Interactional participation and language acquisition. *Science, 183,* 99–101. [8]

Conrad, R. (1964). Acoustic confusions in immediate memory. *British Journal of Psychology, 55,* 75–84. [6]

Conroy, D., Poczwardowski, A., & Henschen, K. (2001). Evaluative criteria and consequences associated with failure and success for elite athletes and performing artists. *Journal of Applied Sport Psychology, 13,* 300–322. [9]

Conway, M. A., Cohen, G., & Stanhope, N. (1991). On the very long-term retention of knowledge acquired through formal education: Twelve years of cognitive psychology. *Journal of Experimental Psychology: General, 120,* 395–409. [6]

Consumer Reports. (1995, November) Mental health: Does therapy help? pp. 734–739. [13]

Cook, M., Mineka, S., Wolkenstein, B., & Laitsch, K. (1985). Observational conditioning of snake fear in unrelated rhesus monkeys. *Journal of Abnormal Psychology, 94,* 591–610. [5]

Coons, P. M. (1994). Confirmation of childhood abuse in child and adolescent cases of multiple personality disorder and dissociative disorder not otherwise specified. *Journal of Nervous and Mental Disease, 182,* 461–464. [12]

Coons, P. M., Bowman, E. S., Kluft, R. P., & Milstein, V. (1991). The cross-cultural occurrence of MPD: Additional cases from a recent survey. *Dissociation, 4,* 124–128. [12]

Cooper, L. A., & Shepard, R. N. (1984). Turning something over in the mind. *Scientific American, 251,* 106–114. [7]

Coplan, J. D., Papp, L. A., Pine, D., Marinez, J., Cooper, T. Rosenblum, L. A., Klein, D. F., & Gorman, J. M. (1997). Clinical improvement with fluoxetine therapy and noradrenergic function in patients with panic disorder. *Archives of General Psychiatry, 54,* 643–648. [13]

Cork, L. C., Clarkson, T. B., Jacoby, R. O., Gaertner, D. J., Leary, S. L., Linn, J. M., Pakes, S. P., Ringler, D. H., Strandberg, J. D., & Swindle, M. M. (1997). The costs of animal research: Origins and options. *Science, 276,* 758–759. [1]

Cornelius, M. D., Leech, S. L., Goldschmidt, L., & Day, N. L. (2000). Prenatal tobacco exposure: Is it a risk factor for early tobacco experimentation? *Nicotine & Tobacco Research, 2,* 45–52. [10]

Costa, P. T., Jr. (1996). Work and personality: Use of the NEO-PI-R in industrial/organisational psychology. *Applied Psychology: An International Review, 45,* 225–241. [11]

Costa, P. T., Jr., & McCrae, R. R. (1985). *The NEO Personality Inventory.* Odessa, FL: Psychological Assessment Resources. [11]

Costa, P. T., Jr., & McCrae, R. R. (1992). *NEO-PI-R: Revised NEO Personality Inventory (NEO-PI-R).* Odessa, FL: Psychological Assessment Resources. [11]

Costa, P. T., Jr., & McCrae, R. R. (1997). Stability and change in personality assessment: The Revised NEO Personality Inventory in the year 2000. *Journal of Personality Assessment, 68,* 8694. [11]

Costa E Silva, J. A., Chase, M., Sartorius, N., & Roth, T. (1996). Special report from a symposium held by the World Health Organization and the World Federation of Sleep Research Societies: An overview of insomnias and related disorders–recognition, epidemiology, and rational management. *Sleep, 19,* 412–416. [4]

Courage, M. L., & Adams, R. J. (1990). Visual acuity assessment from birth to three years using the acuity card procedures: Cross-sectional and longitudinal samples. *Optometry and Vision Science, 67,* 713–718. [8]

Courtney, S. M., Ungerleider, L. G., Keil, K., & Haxby, J. V. (1997). Transient and sustained activity in a distributed neural system for human working memory. *Nature, 386,* 608–611. [6]

Covey, E. (2000). Neural population coding and auditory temporal pattern analysis. *Physiology and Behavior, 69,* 211–220. [3]

Cowan, N. (1988). Evolving conceptions of memory storage, selective attention, and their mutual constraints within the human information-processing system. *Psychological Bulletin, 104,* 163–191. [6]

Coyle, J., & Draper, E. S. (1996). What is the significance of glutamate for mental health? *Harvard Mental Health Letter, 13*(6), 8. [2]

Craik, F. I. M., & Lockhart, R. S. (1972). Levels of processing: A framework for memory research. *Journal of Verbal Learning and Verbal Behavior, 11,* 671–684. [6]

Crimmins, E. M., & Ingegneri, D. G. (1990). Interaction and living arrangements of older parents and their children: Past trends, present determinants, future implications. *Research on Aging, 12,* 3–35. [8]

Crits-Christoph, P. (1992). The efficacy of brief dynamic psychotherapy: A meta-analysis. *American Journal of Psychiatry, 149,* 151–158. [13]

Crowther, J., Kichler, J., Shewood, N., & Kuhnert, M. (2002). The role of familial factors in bulimia nervosa. *Eating Disorders: The Journal of Treatment & Prevention, 10,* 141–151. [9]

Crystal, D. S., Chen, C., Fulligni, A. J., Stevenson, H. W., Hsu, C-C., Ko, H-J., Kitamura, S., & Kimura, S. (1994). Psychological maladjustment and academic achievement: A cross-cultural study of Japanese, Chinese, and American high school students. *Child Development, 65,* 738–753. [7]

Csikszentmihalyi, M. (1990). *Flow: The psychology of optimal experience.* Cambridge, England: Cambridge University Press. [9]

Cui, X-J., & Vaillant, G. E. (1996). Antecedents and consequences of negative life events in adulthood: A longitudinal study. *American Journal of Psychiatry, 153,* 21–26. [12]

Culbertson, F. M. (1997). Depression and gender: An international review. *American Psychologist, 52,* 25–31. [12]

Cunningham, M. R., Roberts, A. R., Barbee, A. P., Druen, P. B., & Wu, C-H. (1995). "Their ideas of beauty are, on the whole, the same as ours": Consistency and variability in the cross-cultural perception of female physical attractiveness. *Journal of Personality and Social Psychology, 68,* 261–279. [14]

Cupach, W. R., & Canary, D. J. (1995). Managing conflict and anger: Investigating the sex stereotype hypothesis. In P. J. Kalbfleisch & M. J. Cody (Eds.), *Gender, power, and communication in human relationships.* Hillsdale, NJ: Erlbaum. [9]

Curci, A., Luminet, O., Finkenauer, C., & Gisler, L. (2001). Flashbulb memories in social groups: A comparative test-retest study of the memory of French president Mitterrand's death in a French and a Belgian group. *Memory, 9,* 81–101. [6]

Cyranowski, J. M., Frand, E., Young, E., & Shear, M. K. (2000). Adolescent onset of the gender difference in lifetime rates of major depression. *Archives of General Psychiatry, 57,* 21–27. [12]

Dabbs, J. M., Jr., & Morris, R. (1990). Testosterone, social class, and antisocial behavior in a sample of 4,462 men. *Psychological Science, 1,* 209–211. [14]

Dahloef, P., Norlin-Bagge, E., Hedner, J., Ejnell, H., Hetta, J., & Haellstroem, T. (2002). Improvement in neuropsychological performance following surgical treatment for obstructive sleep apnea syndrome. *Acta Oto-Laryngologica, 122,* 86–91. [4]

Dale, N., & Kandel, E. R. (1990). Facilitatory and inhibitory transmitters modulate spontaneous transmitter release at cultured *Aplysia* sensorimotor synapses. *Journal of Physiology, 421,* 203–222. [6]

Daly, M., & Wilson, M. I. (1996). Violence against stepchildren. *Current Directions in Psychological Science, 5,* 77–81. [14]

Dallery, J., Silverman, K., Chutuape, M., Bigelow, G., & Stitzer, M. (2001). Voucher-based reinforcement of opiate plus cocaine abstinence in treatment-resistant methadone patients: Effects of reinforcer magnitude. *Experimental & Clinical Psychopharmacology, 9,* 317–325. [5]

Damasio, A. R. (1994). *Descartes' error: Emotion, reason, and the human brain.* New York: Lyons Press. [9]

Damasio, A. R. (1999). *The feeling of what happens: Body and emotion in the making of consciousness.* New York: Harcourt. [9]

Darley, J. M., & Latané, B. (1968a). Bystander intervention in emergencies: Diffusion of responsibility. *Journal of Personality and Social Psychology, 8,* 377–383. [14]

Darley, J. M., & Latané, B. (1968b, December). When will people help in a crisis? *Psychology Today,* pp. 54–57, 70–71. [14]

Darwin, C. (1965). *The expression of emotion in man and animals.* Chicago: University of Chicago Press. (Original work published 1872). [9]

Dasen, P. R. (1994). Culture and cognitive development from a Piagetian perspective. In W. J. Lonner & R. Malpass (Eds.), *Psychology and culture* (pp. 145–149). Boston: Allyn & Bacon. [8]

Dashiell, J. F. (1925). A quantitative demonstration of animal drive. *Journal of Comparative Psychology, 5,* 205–208. [9]

Davalos, D., Kisley, M., & Ross, R. (2002). Deficits in auditory and visual temporal perception in schizophrenia. *Cognitive Neuropsychiatry, 7,* 273–282. [12]

Davidson, J. R. T. (1997). Use of benzodiazepines in panic disorder. *Journal of Clinical Psychiatry, 58*(2, Suppl.), 26–28. [13]

Davis, S., Butcher, S. P., & Morris, R. G. M. (1992). The NMDA receptor antagonist D-2-amino-5-phosphonopentanoate (D-AP5) impairs spatial learning and LTP in vivo at intracerebral concentrations comparable to those that block LTP in vitro. *Journal of Neuroscience, 12,* 21–34. [6]

Davis, T. L. (1995). Gender differences in masking negative emotions: Ability or motivation? *Developmental Psychology, 31,* 660–667. [9]

Day, S., & Schneider, P. (2002). Psychotherapy using distance technology: A comparison of face-to-face, video, and audio treatment. *Journal of Counseling Psychology, 49,* 499–503. [13]

D'Azevedo, W. A. (1982). Tribal history in Liberia. In U. Neisser (Ed.), *Memory observed: Remembering in natural contexts.* San Francisco: W. H. Freeman. [6]

Deary, I. J., & Stough, C. (1996). Intelligence and inspection time: Achievements, prospects, and problems. *American Psychologist, 51,* 599–608. [7]

DeBortoli, M., Tifner, S., & Zanin, L. (2001). The effect of the human androsterone pheromone on mood in men. *Revista Intercontinental de Psicologia y Educacion, 3,* 23–28. [3]

DeCasper, A. J., & Spence, M. J. (1986). Prenatal maternal speech influences newborns' perception of speech sounds. *Infant Behavior and Development, 9,* 133–150. [8]

Deci, E. L., Koestner, R., & Ryan, R. M. (1999). A meta-analytic review of experiments examining the effects of extrinsic rewards on intrinsic motivation. *Psychological Bulletin, 125,* 627–668. [5]

Deese, J. (1959). On the prediction of occurrence of particular verbal intrusions in immediate recall. *Journal of Experimental Psychology, 58,* 17–22. [6]

Deinzer, R., Kleineidam, C., Stiller-Winkler, R., Idel, H., & Bachg, D. (2000). Prolonged reduction of salivary immunoglobulin (sIgA) after a major academic exam. *International Journal of Psychophysiology, 37,* 219–232. [10]

de Jong, P., & van der Leij, A. (2002). Effects of phonological abilities and linguistic comprehension on the development of reading. *Scientific Studies of Reading, 6,* 51–77. [8]

Delgado, J. M. R., & Anand, B. K. (1953). Increased food intake induced by electrical stimulation of the lateral hypothalamus. *American Journal of Physiology, 172,* 162–168. [9]

DeLongis, A., Folkman, S., & Lazarus, R. S. (1988). The impact of daily stress on health and mood: Psychological and social resources as mediators. *Journal of Personality and Social Psychology, 54,* 486–495. [10]

Deovell, L. Y., Bentin, S., & Soroker, N. (2000). Electrophysiological evidence for an early (pre-attentive) information processing deficit in patients with right hemisphere damage and unilateral neglect. *Brain, 123,* 353–365. [2]

De Raad, B., & Kokkonen, M. (2000). Traits and emotions: A review of their structure and management. *European Journal of Personality, 14,* 477–496. [11]

Devanand, D. P., Dwork, A. J., Hutchinson, M. S. E., Bolwig, T. G., & Sackeim, H. A. (1994). Does ECT alter brain structure? *American Journal of Psychiatry, 151,* 957–970. [13]

Devine, P. G. (1989). Stereotypes and prejudice: Their automatic and controlled components. *Journal of Personality and Social Psychology, 56,* 5–18. [14]

De Vos, S. (1990). Extended family living among older people in six Latin American countries. *Journal of Gerontology: Social Sciences, 45,* S87–94. [8]

deVries, H. A. (1986). *Fitness after 50.* New York: Scribner's. [8]

Dewsbury, D. A. (2000). Introduction: Snapshots of psychology circa 1900. *American Psychologist, 55,* 255–259. [1]

DeYoung, C., Peterson, J., & Higgins, D. (2002). Higher-order factors of the Big Five predict conformity: Are there neuroses of health? *Personality & Individual Differences, 33,* 533–552. [14]

Dickens, W., & Flynn, R. (2001). Heritability estimates versus large environmental effects: The IQ paradox resolved. *Psychological Review, 108,* 346–369. [7]

Diener, E., & Diener, C. (1996). Most people are happy. *Psychological Science, 7,* 181–185. [8]

DiLalla, L. F., & Gottesman, I. I. (1991). Biological and genetic contributors to violence–Widom's untold tale. *Psychological Bulletin, 109,* 125–129. [14]

Dindia, K., & Allen, M. (1992). Sex differences in self-disclosure: A meta-analysis. *Psychological Bulletin, 112,* 106–124. [9]

Dion, K., Berscheid, E., & Walster, E. (1972). What is beautiful is good. *Journal of Personality and Social Psychology, 24,* 285–290. [14]

Dipboye, R. L., Fromkin, H. L., & Wilback, K. (1975). Relative importance of applicant sex, attractiveness, and scholastic standing in evaluation of job applicant resumes. *Journal of Applied Psychology, 60,* 39–43. [14]

Dodge, K. A., Bates, J. E., & Pettit, G. S. (1990). Mechanisms in the cycle of violence. *Science, 250,* 1678–1683. [14]

Dodson, C. S., Koutstaal, W., & Schacter, D. L. (2000). Escape from illusion: Reducing false memories. *Trends in Cognitive Sciences, 4,* 391–397. [6]

Dogil, G., Ackerman, H., Grodd, W., Haider, H., Kamp, H., Mayer, J., Riecker, A., & Wildgruber, D. (2002). The speaking brain: A tutorial introduction to fMRI experiments in the production of speech, prosody, and syntax. *Journal of Neurolinguistics, 15,* 59–90. [7]

Dollard, J., Doob, L. W., Miller, N., Mowrer, O. H., & Sears, R. R. (1939). *Frustration and aggression.* New Haven: Yale University Press. [14]

Domino, G. (1984). California Psychological Inventory. In D. J. Keyser & R. C. Sweetland (Eds.), *Test Critiques* (Vol. 1, pp. 146–157). Kansas City: Test Corporation of America. [11]

Domjan, M, & Purdy, J. E. (1995). Animal research in psychology: More than meets the eye of the general psychology student. *American Psychologist, 50,* 496–503. [1]

Doob, L. W., & Sears, R. R. (1939). Factors determining substitute behavior and the overt expression of aggression. *Journal of Abnormal and Social Psychology, 34,* 293–313. [14]

Doyle, J. A., & Paludi, M. A. (1995). *Sex and gender* (3rd ed.). Madison, WI: Brown & Benchmark. [8]

Dreikurs, R. (1953). *Fundamentals of Adlerian psychology.* Chicago: Alfred Adler Institute. [11]

Drevets, W. C., Price, J. L., Simpson, J. R., Jr., Todd, R. D., Reich, T., Vannier, M., & Raichle, M. E. (1997). Subgenual prefrontal cortex abnormalities in mood disorders. *Nature, 386,* 824–827. [12]

Drummond, S. P. A., Brown, G. G., Gillin, J. C., Stricker, J. L., Wong, E. C., & Buxton, R. B. (2000). Altered brain response to verbal learning following sleep deprivation. *Nature, 403,* 655–657. [4]

Dryer, D. C., & Horowitz, L. M. (1997). When do opposites attract? Interpersonal complementarity versus similarity. *Journal of Personality and Social Psychology, 72,* 592–603. [14]

Duck, S. (1983). *Friends for life: The psychology of close relationships.* New York: St. Martin's Press. [8]

Dunkel-Schetter, C., Feinstein, L. G., Taylor, S. E., & Falke, R. L. (1992). Patterns of coping with cancer. *Health Psychology, 11,* 79–87. [10]

Dunn, J., Cutting, A., & Fisher, N. (2002). Old friends, new friends: Predictors of children's perspective on their friends at school. *Child Development, 73,* 621–635. [8]

Duyme, M. (1988). School success and social class: An adoption study. *Developmental Psychology, 24,* 203–209. [7]

Dywan, J., & Bowers, K. (1983). The use of hypnosis to enhance recall. *Science, 222,* 184–185. [4, 6]

Eagly, A. H., Ashmore, R. D., Makhijani, M. G., & Longo, L. C. (1991). What is beautiful is good . . . : A meta-analytic review of research on the physical attractiveness stereotype. *Psychological Bulletin, 110,* 109–128. [14]

Eagly, A. H., & Carli, L. (1981). Sex of researchers and sex-typed communications as determinants of sex differences in influence-ability: A meta-analysis of social influence studies. *Psychological Bulletin, 90,* 1–20. [14]

Eating disorders–part II. (1997, November). *Harvard Mental Health Letter,* 14(5), 1–5. [9]

Ebbinghaus, H. E. (1964). *Memory: A contribution to experimental psychology* (H. A. Ruger & C. E. Bussenius, Trans.). New York: Dover. (Original work published 1885). [6]

Eccles, J. S., & Jacobs, J. E. (1986). Social forces shape math attitudes and performance. *Signs, 11,* 367–389. [7]

Edwards, B., Atkinson, G., Waterhouse, J., Reilly, T., Godfrey, R., & Budgett, R. (2000). Use of melatonin in recovery from jet-lag following an eastward flight across 10 time-zones. *Ergonomics, 43,* 1501–1513. [4]

Edwards, K., & Smith, E. E. (1996). A disconfirmation bias in the evaluation of arguments. *Journal of Personality and Social Psychology, 71,* 5–24. [14]

Egeth, H. E. (1993). What do we not know about eyewitness identification? *American Psychologist, 48,* 577–580. [6]

Ehrhardt, A. A., Evers, K., & Money, J. (1968). Influence of androgen and some aspects of sexual dimorphic behavior in women with the late-treated adrenogenital syndrome. *Johns Hopkins Medical Journal, 123,* 115–122. [9]

Eichenbaum, H. (1997). Declarative memory: Insights from cognitive neurobiology. *Annual Review of Psychology, 48,* 547–572. [6]

Ekman, P. (1972). Universals and cultural differences in facial expression of emotion. In J. Cole (Ed.), *Nebraska symposium on motivation* (Vol. 19). Lincoln: University of Nebraska Press. [9]

Ekman, P. (1993). Facial expression and emotion. *American Psychologist, 48,* 384–392. [9]

Ekman, P., & Friesen, W. V. (1971). Constants across cultures in the face and emotion. *Journal of Personality and Social Psychology, 17,* 124–129. [9]

Ekman, P., & Friesen, W. V. (1975). *Unmasking the face: A guide to recognizing emotions from facial clues.* Englewood Cliffs, NJ: Prentice-Hall. [9]

Ekman, P., Levenson, R. W., & Friesen, W. V. (1983). Autonomic nervous system activity distinguishes among emotions. *Science, 221,* 1208–1210. [9]

Elal, G., Altug, A., Slade, P., & Tekcan, A. (2000). Factor structure of the Eating Attitudes Test (EAT) in a Turkish university sample. *Eating and Weight Disorders: Studies on Anorexia, Bulimia, and Obesity, 5,* 46–50. [9]

Elkin, I., Gibbons, R. D., Shea, M. T., Sotsky, S. M., Watkins, J. T., Pikonis, P. A., & Hedeker, D. (1995). Initial severity and differential treatment outcome in the National Institute of Mental Health Treatment of Depression Collaborative Research Program. *Journal of Consulting and Clinical Psychology, 63,* 841–847. [13]

Elkin, I., Shea, M. T., Watkins, J. T., et al. (1989). National Institute of Mental Health Treatment of Depression Collaborative Research Program: General effectiveness of treatments. *Archives of General Psychology, 46,* 971–982. [13]

Elkind, D. (1967). Egocentrism in adolescence. *Child Development, 38,* 1025–1034. [8]

Elkind, D. (1974). *Children and adolescents: Interpretive essays on Jean Piaget* (2nd ed.). New York: Oxford University Press. [8]

Ellason, J. W., & Ross, C. A. (1997). Two-year follow-up of inpatients with dissociative identity disorder. *American Journal of Psychiatry, 154,* 832–839. [12]

Elliot, A. J., & Devine, P. G. (1994). On the motivational nature of cognitive dissonance: Dissonance as psychological discomfort. *Journal of Personality and Social Psychology, 67,* 382–394. [14]

Ellis, A. (1961). *A guide to rational living.* Englewood Cliffs, NJ: Prentice-Hall. [13]

Ellis, A. (1977). The basic clinical theory of rational-emotive therapy. In A. Ellis & R. Grieger (Eds.), *Handbook of rational-emotive therapy* (pp. 3–33). New York: Springer. [13]

Ellis, A. (1993). Reflections on rational-emotive therapy. *Journal of Consulting and Clinical Psychology, 61,* 199–201. [13]

Ellis, R. (2001). A theoretical model of the role of the cerebellum in cognition, attention and consciousness. *Consciousness & Emotion, 2,* 300–309. [2]

Engel, G. L. (1977). The need for a new medical model: A challenge for biomedicine. *Science, 196,* 126–129. [10]

Engel, G. L. (1980). The clinical application of the biopsychosocial model. *American Journal of Psychiatry, 137,* 535–544. [10]

Engles, G. I., Garnefski, N., & Diekstra, R. F. W. (1993). Efficacy of rational-emotive therapy: A quantitative analysis. *Journal of Consulting and Clinical Psychology, 61,* 1083–1090. [13]

Epstein, J. (1983). Examining theories of adolescent friendships. In J. Epstein & N. Karweit (Eds.), *Friends in school.* New York: Academic Press. [8]

Epstein, J., Stern, E., & Silbersweig, D. (2001). Neuropsychiatry at the millennium: The potential for mind/brain integration through emerging interdisciplinary research strategies. *Clinical Neuroscience Research, 1,* 10–18. [13]

Erikson, E. H. (1980). *Identity and the life cycle.* New York: Norton. [8]

Erlenmeyer-Kimling, L., & Jarvik, L. F. (1963). Genetics and intelligence: A review. *Science, 142,* 1477–1479. [8]

Eron, L. D. (1987). The development of aggressive behavior from the perspective of a developing behaviorism. *American Psychologist, 42,* 435–442. [14]

Eronen, M., Hakola, P., & Tiihonen, J. (1996). Mental disorders and homicidal behavior in Finland. *Journal of Personality and Social Psychology, 53,* 497–501. [14]

Estes, W. K. (1994). *Classification and cognition.* New York: Oxford University Press. [7]

Etcoff, N., Ekman, P., Magee, J., & Frank, M. (2000). Lie detection and language comprehension. *Nature, 405,* 139. [2]

Evans, G. W., & Lepore, S. J. (1993). Household crowding and social support: A quasiexperimental analysis. *Journal of Personality and Social Psychology, 65,* 308–316. [14]

Evans, M. D., Hollon, S. D., DeRubeis, R. J., Piasecki, J. M., Grove, W. M., Garvey, M. J., & Tuason, V. B. (1992). Differential relapse following cognitive therapy and pharmacotherapy for depression. *Archives of General Psychiatry, 49,* 802–808. [13]

Everson, S. A., Goldberg, D. E., Kaplan, G. A., Cohen, R. D., Pukkala, E., Tuomilehto, J., & Salonen, J. T. (1996). Hopelessness and risk of mortality and incidence of myocardial infarction and cancer. *Psychosomatic Medicine, 58,* 113–121. [10]

Exner, J. E. (1993). *The Rorschach: A comprehensive system: Vol. 1. Basic foundations* (3rd ed.). New York: Wiley. [11]

Exton, M. S., von Auer, A. K., Buske-Kirschbaum, A., Stockhorst, U., Göbel, U., & Schedlowski, M. (2000). Pavlovian conditioning of immune function: Animal investigation and the challenge of human application. *Behavioural Brain Research, 110,* 129–141. [5]

Eysenbach, G., Powell, J., Kuss, O., & Sa, E. (2002). Empirical studies of health information for consumers on the World Wide Web: A systematic review. *JAMA: Journal of the American Medical Association, 287,* 2691–2700. [10]

Eysenck, H. J. (1990). Genetic and environmental contributions to individual differences: The three major dimensions of personality. *Journal of Personality, 58,* 245–261. [11]

Eysenck, H. J. (1994). The outcome problem in psychotherapy: What have we learned? *Behaviour Research and Therapy, 32,* 477–495. [13]

Fackelmann, K. (1997). Marijuana on trial: Is marijuana a dangerous drug or a valuable medicine? *Science News, 151,* 178–179, 183. [4]

Fagiolini, M., & Hensch, T. K. (2000). Inhibitory threshold for critical-period activation in primary visual cortex. *Nature, 404,* 183–186. [3]

Fagot, B. (1995). Observations of parent reactions to sex-stereotyped behavior: Age and sex effects. *Child Development, 62,* 617–628. [8]

Fairburn, C. G., Welch, S. L., Doll, H. A., Davies, B. A., & O'Connor, M. E. (1997). Risk factors for bulimia nervosa: A community-based case-control study. *Archives of General Psychiatry, 54,* 509–517. [9]

Falbo, T., & Polit, D. F. (1986). Quantitative review of the only child literature: Research evidence and theory development. *Psychological Bulletin, 100,* 176–189. [9]

Falloon, I. R. H. (1988). Expressed emotion: Current status. *Psychological Medicine, 18,* 269–274. [13]

Famighetti, R. (Ed.). (1997). *The world almanac and book of facts 1998.* Mahwah, NJ: World Almanac Books. [13]

Fang, C., & Myers, H. (2001). The effects of racial stressors and hostility on cardiovascular reactivity in African American and Caucasian men. *Health Psychology, 20,* 64–70. [10]

Fantz, R. L. (1961). The origin of form perception. *Scientific American, 204,* 66–72. [8]

Farah, M. J. (1995). The neural bases of mental imagery. In M. S. Gazzaniga (Ed.), *The cognitive neurosciences.* Cambridge, MA: MIT Press. [7]

Farde, L. (1996). The advantage of using positron emission tomography in drug research. *Trends in Neurosciences, 19,* 211–214. [2]

Farrer, L. A., & Cupples, A. (1994). Estimating the probability for major gene Alzheimer disease. *American Journal of Human Genetics, 54,* 374–383. [8]

Fauerbach, J., Lawrence, J., Haythornthwaite, J., & Richter, L. (2002). Coping with the stress of a painful medical procedure. *Behaviour Research & Therapy, 40,* 1003–1015. [11]

Faunce, G. (2002). Eating disorders and attentional bias: A review. *Eating Disorders: The Journal of Treatment & Prevention, 10,* 125–139. [9]

Fazio, R. H. (1989). On the power and functionality of attitudes: The role of attitude accessibility. In A. R. Pratkanis, S. J. Breckler, & A. G. Greenwald (Eds.), *Attitude structure and function* (pp. 153–179). Hillsdale, NJ: Erlbaum. [14]

Fazio, R. H., & Williams, C. J. (1986). Attitude accessibility as a moderator of the attitude perception and attitude-behavior relations: An investigation of the 1984 presidential election. *Journal of Personality and Social Psychology, 51,* 505–514. [14]

Federal Bureau of Investigation. (1999). United States crime rates 1960–1998 [On-line]. Retrieved from http://www.disastercenter.com/crime/uscrime.htm [14]

Fein, S., & Spencer, S. J. (1997). Prejudice as self-image maintenance: Affirming the self through derogating others. *Journal of Personality and Social Psychology, 73,* 31–44. [14]

Feingold, A. (1988). Matching for attractiveness in romantic partners and same-sex friends: A meta-analysis and theoretical critique. *Psychological Bulletin, 104,* 226–235. [14]

Fenton, W. S., & McGlashan, T. H. (1991). Natural history of schizophrenia subtypes: I. Longitudinal study of paranoid, hebephrenic, and undifferentiated schizophrenia. *Archives of General Psychiatry, 48,* 969–977. [12]

Fenton, W. S., & McGlashan, T. H. (1994). Antecedents, symptom progression, and long-term outcome of the deficit syndrome in schizophrenia. *American Journal of Psychiatry, 151,* 351–356. [12]

Fernald, A. (1993). Approval and disapproval: Infant responsiveness to vocal affect in familiar and unfamiliar languages. *Child Development, 64,* 637–656. [8]

Fernández-Dols, J.-M., & Ruiz-Belda, M.-A. (1995). Are smiles a sign of happiness? Gold medal winners at the Olympic games. *Journal of Personality and Social Psychology, 69,* 1113–1119. [9]

Festinger, L. (1957). *A theory of cognitive dissonance.* Evanston, IL: Row, Peterson. [14]

Fiatarone, M. A., Morley, J. E., Bloom, E. T., Benton, D., Makinodan, T., & Solomon, G. F. (1988). Endogenous opioids and the exercise-induced augmentation of natural killer cell activity. *Journal of Laboratory and Clinical Medicine, 112,* 544–552. [10]

Fiatarone, M. A., O'Neill, E. F., Ryan, N. D., Clements, K. M., Solares, G. R., Nelson, M. E., Roberts, S. B., Kehayias, J. J., Lipsitz, L. A., & Evans, W. J. (1994). Exercise training and nutritional supplementation for physical frailty in very elderly people. *New England Journal of Medicine, 330,* 1769–1775. [8]

Field, M., & Duka, T. (2002). Cues paired with a low dose of alcohol acquire conditioned incentive properties in social drinkers. *Psychopharmacology, 159,* 325–334. [5]

Field, T., Schanberg, S. M., Scfidi, F., Bauer, C. R., Vega-Lahr, N., Garcia, R., Nystrom, J., & Kuhn, C. (1986, May). Tactile/kinesthetic stimulation effects on preterm neonates. *Pediatrics, 77,* 654–658. [3]

Field, T. M., Cohen, D., Garcia, R., & Greenberg, R. (1984). Mother-stranger face discrimination by the newborn. *Infant Behavior and Development, 7,* 19–25. [8]

Finch, A. E., Lambert, M. J., & Brown, G. (2000). Attacking anxiety: A naturalistic study of a multimedia self-help program. *Journal of Clinical Psychology, 56,* 11–21. [13]

Finchilescu, G. (1988). Interracial contact in South Africa within the nursing context. *Journal of Applied Social Psychology, 18,* 1207–1221. [14]

Fink, B., & Penton-Voak, I. (2002). Evolutionary psychology of facial attractiveness. *Current Directions in Psychological Science, 11,* 154–158. [14]

Fiorito, G., & Scotto, P. (1992). Observational learning in *Octopus vulgaris. Science, 256,* 545–547. [5]

Fixx, J. F. (1978). *Solve It! A perplexing profusion of puzzles.* New York: Doubleday. [7]

Flavell, J. H. (1985). *Cognitive development.* Englewood, NJ: Prentice-Hall. [8]

Flavell, J. H. (1992). Cognitive development: Past, present, and future. *Developmental Psychology, 28,* 998–1005. [8]

Flavell, J. H. (1996). Piaget's legacy. *Psychological Science, 7,* 200–203. [8]

Fleck, D., Hendricks, W., DelBellow, M., & Strakowski, S. (2002). Differential prescription of maintenance antipsychotics to African American and White patients with new-onset bipolar disorder. *Journal of Clinical Psychiatry, 63,* 658–664. [13]

Fleming, J. D. (1974, July). Field report: The state of the apes. *Psychology Today,* pp. 31–46. [7]

Fletcher, J. M., Page, B., Francis, D. J., Copeland, K., Naus, M. J., Davis, C. M., Morris, R., Krauskopf, D., & Satz, P. (1996). Cognitive correlates of long-term cannabis use in Costa Rican men. *Archives of General Psychiatry, 53,* 1051–1057. [4]

Flood, J. F., Silver, A. J., & Morley, J. E. (1990). Do peptide-induced changes in feeding occur because of changes in motivation to eat? *Peptides, 11,* 265–270. [9]

Florian, V., Mikulincer, M., & Taubman, O. (1995). Does hardiness contribute to mental health during a stressful real-life situation? The roles of appraisal and coping. *Journal of Personality and Social Psychology, 68,* 687–695. [13]

Florio, V., Fossella, S., Maravita, A., Miniussi, C., & Marzi, C. (2002). Interhemispheric transfer and laterality effects in simple visual reaction time in schizophrenics. *Cognitive Neuropsychiatry, 7,* 97–111. [12]

Flynn, J. (1999). Searching for justice: The discovery of IQ gains over time. *American Psychologist, 54,* 5–20. [7]

Flynn, J. R. (1987). Race and IQ: Jensen's case refuted. In S. Modgil, & C. Modgil (Eds.), *Arthur Jensen: Consensus and controversy.* New York: Palmer Press. [7]

Foa, E. B. (1995). How do treatments for obsessive-compulsive disorder compare? *Harvard Mental Health Letter, 12*(1), 8. [13]

Foa, E. B., & Meadows, E. A. (1997). Psychosocial treatments for posttraumatic stress disorder: A critical review. *Annual Review of Psychology, 48,* 449–480. [10]

Fogel, J., Albert, S., Schnabel, F., Ditkoff, B., & Neugut, A. (2002). Internet use and social support in women with breast cancer. *Health Psychology, 21,* 398–404. [10]

Foley, D. J., Monjan, A. A., Brown, S. L., Simonsick, E. M., Wallace, R. B., & Blazer, D. G. (1995). Sleep complaints among elderly persons: An epidemiologic study of three communities. *Sleep, 18,* 425–432. [4]

Folkerts, H. (2000). Electroconvulsive therapy of depressive disorders. Ther. *Umsch, 57,* 290–294. [13]

Folkman, S. (1984). Personal control and stress and coping processes: A theoretical analysis. *Journal of Personality and Social Psychology, 46,* 839–852. [10]

Folkman, S., Chesney, M., Collette, L., Boccellari, A., & Cooke, M. (1996). Postbereavement depressive mood and its prebereavement predictors in HIV+ and HIV− gay men. *Journal of Personality and Social Psychology, 70,* 336–348. [8]

Folkman, S., & Lazarus, R. S. (1980). An analysis of coping in a middle-aged community sample. *Journal of Health and Social Behavior, 21,* 219–239. [10]

Ford, C. S., & Beach, F. A. (1951). *Patterns of sexual behavior.* New York: Harper & Row. [9]

Forgas, J. P., & Fiedler, K. (1996). Us and them: Mood effects on intergroup discrimination. *Journal of Personality and Social Psychology, 70,* 28–40. [14]

Foulkes, D. (1996). Sleep and dreams: Dream research: 1953–1993. *Sleep, 19,* 609–624. [4]

Fox, M. (2002). *Lucky Man: A Memoir.* New York: Hyperion Press. [10]

Fox, N. A., & Bell, M. A. (1990). Electrophysiological indices of frontal lobe development: Relations to cognitive and affective behavior in human infants over the first year of life. *Annals of the New York Academy of Sciences, 608,* 677–698. [8]

Frank, E., Anderson, B., Reynolds, C. F., III, Ritenour, A., & Kupfer, D. J. (1994). Life events and the research diagnostic criteria endogenous subtype. *Archives of General Psychiatry, 51,* 519–524. [12]

Frank, E., Kupfer, D. J., Wagner, E. F., McEachran, A. B., & Cornes, C. (1991). Efficacy of interpersonal psychotherapy as a maintenance treatment of recurrent depression: Contributing factors. *Archives of General Psychiatry, 48,* 1053–1059. [13]

Frankenburg, W. K., Dodds, J. B., Archer, P., et al. (1992). *Denver II Training Manual.* Denver: Denver Developmental Materials. [8]

Frantz, K., Hansson, K., Stouffer, D., & Parsons, L. (2002). 5-HT-sub-6 receptor antagonism potentiates the behavioral and neurochemical effects of amphetamine but not cocaine. *Neuropharmacology, 42,* 170–180. [4]

Franz, C. E., McClelland, D. C., & Weinberger, J. (1991). Childhood antecedents of conventional social accomplishment in midlife adults: A 36-year prospective study. *Journal of Personality and Social Psychology, 60,* 586–595. [8]

Fraser, A. M., Brockert, J. E., & Ward, R. H. (1995). Association of young maternal age with adverse reproductive outcomes. *New England Journal of Medicine, 332,* 1113–1117. [8]

Frazer, A. (1997). Antidepressants. *Journal of Clinical Psychiatry, 58*(6, Suppl.), 9–25. [13]

Frazer, N., Larkin, K., & Goodie, J. (2002). Do behavioral responses mediate or moderate the relation between cardiovascular reactivity to stress and parental history of hypertension. *Health Psychology, 21,* 244–253. [10]

Fredrikson, M., Annas, P., Fischer, H., & Wik, G. (1996). Gender and age differences in the prevalence of specific fears and phobias. *Behaviour Research and Therapy, 34,* 33–39. [12]

Freedman, J. L., & Fraser, S. C. (1966). Compliance without pressure: The foot-in-the-door technique. *Journal of Personality and Social Psychology, 4,* 195–202. [14]

Freud, A. (1958). *Adolescence: Psychoanalytic study of the child* (Vol. 13). New York: Academic Press. [8]

Freud, S. (1922). *Beyond the pleasure principle.* London: International Psychoanalytic Press. [6]

Freud, S. (1953a). The interpretation of dreams. In J. Strachey (Ed. and Trans.), *The standard edition of the complete psychological works of Sigmund Freud* (Vols. 4 and 5). London: Hogarth Press. (Original work published 1900). [4]

Freud, S. (1953b). Three essays on the theory of sexuality. In J. Strachey (Ed. and Trans.), *The standard edition of the complete psychological works of Sigmund Freud* (Vol. 7). London: Hogarth Press. (Original work published 1905). [11]

Freud, S. (1962). *Civilization and its discontents* (J. Strachey, Trans.). New York: W.W. Norton. (Original work published 1930). [11]

Freud, S. (1963a). *An autobiographical study* (J. Strachey, Trans.). New York: W.W. Norton. (Original work published 1925). [11]

Freud, S. (1963b). *A general introduction to psycho-analysis* (J. Riviere, Trans.). New York: Simon & Schuster. (Original work published 1920). [11]

Freud, S. (1965). *New introductory lectures on psychoanalysis* (J. Strachey, Trans.). New York: W. W. Norton. (Original work published 1933). [11]

Frey, K. P., & Eagly, A. H. (1993). Vividness can undermine the persuasiveness of messages. *Journal of Personality and Social Psychology, 65,* 32–44. [14]

Friedland, N., Keinan, G., & Regev, Y. (1992). Controlling the uncontrollable: Effects of stress on illusory perceptions of controllability. *Journal of Personality and Social Psychology, 63,* 923–931. [10]

Friedman, J. M. (1997). The alphabet of weight control. *Nature, 385,* 119–120. [9]

Friedman, J. M. (2000). Obesity in the new millennium. *Nature, 404,* 632–634. [9]

Friedman, M., & Rosenman, R. H. (1974). *Type A behavior and your heart.* New York: Fawcett. [10]

Friedman, M. I., Tordoff, M. G., & Ramirez, I. (1986). Integrated metabolic control of food intake. *Brain Research Bulletin, 17,* 855–859. [9]

Fry, A. F., & Hale, S. (1996). Processing speed, working memory, and fluid intelligence. *Psychological Science, 7,* 237–241. [7]

Fuligni, A. J., & Stevenson, H. W. (1995). Time use and mathematics achievement among American, Chinese, and Japanese high school students. *Child Development, 66,* 830–842. [7]

Fyer, A. J. (1993). Heritability of social anxiety: A brief review. *Journal of Clinical Psychiatry, 54*(12, Suppl.), 10–12. [12]

Gallagher, M., & Rapp, P. R. (1997). The use of animal models to study the effects of aging on cognition. *Annual Review of Psychology, 48,* 339–370. [8]

Gallistel, C. R., & Gibbon, J. (2000). Time, rate, and conditioning. *Psychological Review, 107,* 289–344. [5]

Gallup, G., Jr., & Hugick, L. (1990). Racial tolerance grows, progress on racial equality less evident. *Gallup Poll Monthly, No. 297,* 23–32. [14]

Galton, F. (1874). *English men of science: Their nature and nurture.* London: Macmillan. [7]

Ganellen, R. J. (1996). Comparing the diagnostic efficiency of the MMPI, MCMI-II, and Rorschach: A review. *Journal of Personality Assessment, 67,* 219–243. [11]

Garavan, H., Morgan, R. E., Levitsky, D. A., Hermer-Vasquez, L., & Strupp, B. J. (2000). Enduring effects of early lead exposure: Evidence for a specific deficit in associative ability. *Neurotoxicology and Teratology, 22,* 151–164. [7]

Garbarino, S., Beelke, M., Costa, G., Violani, C., Lucidi, F., & Ferrillo, F. (2002). Brain function and effects of shift work: Implications for clinical neuropharmacology. *Neuropsychobiology, 45,* 50–56. [4]

Garcia, J., & Koelling, A. (1966). Relation of cue to consequence in avoidance learning. *Psychonomic Science, 4,* 123–124. [5]

Gardner, H. (1983). *Frames of mind: The theory of multiple intelligence.* New York: Basic Books. [7]

Gardner, R. A., & Gardner, B. T. (1969). Teaching sign language to a chimpanzee. *Science, 165,* 664–672. [7]

Garland, A. F., & Zigler, E. (1993). Adolescent suicide prevention: Current research and social policy implications. *American Psychologist, 48,* 169–182. [12]

Garma, L., & Marchand, F. (1994). Non-pharmacological approaches to the treatment of narcolepsy. *Sleep, 17,* S97–S102. [4]

Garmon, L. C., Basinger, K. S., Gregg, V. R., & Gibbs, J. C. (1996). Gender differences in stage and expression of moral judgment. *Merrill-Palmer Quarterly, 42,* 418–437. [8]

Garrett, M., Garrett, J., & Brotherton, D. (2001). Inner circle/outer circle: A group technique based on Native American healing circles. *Journal for Specialists in Group Work, 26,* 17–30. [13]

Garry, M., & Loftus, E. R. (1994). Pseudomemories without hypnosis. *International Journal of Clinical and Experimental Hypnosis, 42,* 363–373. [6]

Gartner, J., & Whitaker-Azimitia, P. M. (1996). Developmental factors influencing aggression: Animal models and clinical correlates. *Annals of the New York Academy of Sciences, 794,* 113–120. [14]

Gastil, J. (1990). Generic pronouns and sexist language: The oxymoronic character of masculine generics. *Sex Roles, 23,* 629–643. [7]

Gates, A. I. (1917). Recitation as a factor in memorizing. *Archives of Psychology, 40.* [6]

Gawin, F. H. (1991). Cocaine addiction: Psychology and neurophysiology. *Science, 251,* 1580–1586. [4]

Gawronski, B., Alshut, E., Grafe, J., Nespethal, J., Ruhmland, A., & Schulz, L. (2002). Processes of judging known and unknown persons. *Zeitschrift fuer Sozialpsychologie, 33,* 25–34. [14]

Gazzaniga, M. S. (1983). Right hemisphere language following brain bisection: A 20-year perspective. *American Psychologist, 38,* 525–537. [2]

Ge, X., Brody, G., Conger, R., Simons, R., & Murry, V. (2002). Contextual amplification of pubertal transition effects on deviant peer affiliation and externalizing behavior among African American children. *Developmental Psychology, 38,* 42–54. [8]

Ge, X., Conger, R., & Elder, G. (2001). Pubertal transition, stressful life events, and the emergence of gender differences in adolescent depressive symptoms. *Developmental Psychology, 37,* 404–417. [8]

Geary, D. C. (1996). Sexual selection and sex differences in mathematical abilties. *Behavioral and Brain Sciences, 19,* 229–284. [7]

Geen, R. G. (1984). Human motivation: New perspectives on old problems. In A. M. Rogers & C. J. Scheier (Eds.), *The G. Stanley Hall lecture series* (Vol. 4). Washington, DC: American Psychological Association. [9]

Gehart, D., & Lyle, R. (2001). Client experience of gender in therapeutic relationships: An interpretive ethnography. *Family Process, 40,* 443–458. [13]

Geiselman, R. E., Schroppel, T., Tubridy, A., Konishi, T., & Rodriguez, V. (2000). Objectivity bias in eye witness performance. *Applied Cognitive Psychology, 14,* 323–332. [6]

Genesee, F. (1994). Bilingualism. In V. S. Ramachandran (Ed.), *Encyclopedia of human behavior* (Vol. 1, pp. 383–393). San Diego, CA: Academic. [7]

George, D., Umhau, J., Phillips, M., Emmela, D., Ragan, P., Shoaf, S., & Rawlings, R. (2001). Serotonin, testosterone, and alcohol in the etiology of domestic violence. *Psychiatry Research, 104,* 27–37. [1]

George, M. S., Ketter, T. A., & Post, R. M. (1993). SPECT and PET imaging in mood disorders. *Journal of Clinical Psychiatry, 54*(11, Suppl.), 6–13. [12]

Gerrits, M., Petromilli, P., Westenberg, H., Di Chiara, G., & van Ree, J. (2002). Decrease in basal dopamine levels in the nucleus accumbens shell during daily drug-seeking behavior in rats. *Brain Research, 924,* 141–150. [4]

Gerull, F., & Rappe, R. (2002). Mother knows best: The effects of maternal modelling on the acquisition of fear and avoidance behaviour in toddlers. *Behaviour Research & Therapy, 40,* 279–287. [5]

Gevins, A., Leong, H., Smith, M. E., Le, J., & Du, R. (1995). Mapping cognitive brain function with modern high-resolution electroencephalography. *Trends in Neurosciences, 18,* 429–436. [2]

Gibbons, A. (1991). Déjà vu all over again: Chimp-language wars. *Science, 251,* 1561–1562. [7]

Gibson, E., & Walk, R. D. (1960). The "visual cliff." *Scientific American, 202,* 64–71. [8]

Giedd, J. N., Rapoport, J. L., Garvey, M. A., Perlmutter, S., & Swedo, S. E. (2000). MRI assessment of children with obsessive-compulsive disorder or tics associated with streptococcal infection. *American Journal of Psychiatry, 157,* 2281–2283. [12]

Gilbert, D. T., & Malone, P. S. (1995). The correspondence bias. *Psychological Bulletin, 117,* 21–38. [14]

Gilligan, C. (1982). *In a different voice: Psychological theory and women's development.* Cambridge, MA: Harvard University Press. [8]

Ginsberg, G., & Bronstein, P. (1993). Family factors related to children's intrinsic/extrinsic motivational orientation and academic performance. *Child Development, 64,* 1461–1474. [9]

Ginty, D. D., Kornhauser, J. M., Thompson, M. A., Bading, H., Mayo, K. E., Takahashi, J. S., & Greenberg, M. E. (1993). Regulation of CREB phosphorylation in the suprachiasmatic nucleus by light and a circadian clock. *Science, 260,* 238–241. [2]

Ginzburg, K., Solomon, Z., & Bleich, A. (2002). Repressive coping style, acute stress disorder, and post-traumatic stress disorder after myocardial infarction. *Journal of the American Psychosomatic Society, 64,* 748–757. [10]

Glantz, L. A., & Lewis, D. A. (2000). Decreased dendritic spine density on prefrontal cortical pyramidal neurons in schizophrenia. *Archives of General Psychiatry, 57,* 65–73. [12]

Glass, D. C., & Singer, J. E. (1972). *Urban stress: Experiments in noise and social stressors.* New York: Academic Press. [10]

Glassman, A. H. (1993). What is the relationship between depression and cigarette smoking? *Harvard Mental Health Letter, 10(4),* 8. [10]

Glazer, W. M., Morgenstern, H., & Doucette, J. T. (1993). Predicting the long-term risk of tardive dyskinesia in outpatients maintained on neuroleptic medications. *Journal of Clinical Psychiatry, 54,* 133–139. [13]

Gleaves, D. J. (1996). The sociocognitive model of dissociative identity disorder: A reexamination of the evidence. *Psychological Bulletin, 120,* 42–59. [12]

Glover, J. A., & Corkill, A. J. (1987). Influence of paraphrased repetitions on the spacing effect. *Journal of Educational Psychology, 79,* 198–199. [6]

Gluck, M. A., & Myers, C. E. (1997). Psychobiological models of hippocampal function in learning and memory. *Annual Review of Psychology, 48,* 481–514. [2, 6]

Godden, D. R., & Baddeley, A. D. (1975). Context-dependent memory in two natural environments: On land and underwater. *British Journal of Psychology, 66,* 325–331. [6]

Goh, V. H., Tong, T. Y., & Lee, L. K. (2000). Sleep/wake cycle and circadian disturbances in shift work: Strategies for their management–a review. *Annals of the Academy of Medicine Singapore, 29,* 90–96. [4]

Gökcebay, N., Cooper, R., Williams, R. L., Hirshkowitz, M., & Moore, C. A. (1994). Function of sleep. In R. Cooper (Ed.), *Sleep.* New York: Chapman & Hall. [4]

Goldenberg, R. L., & Klerman, L. V. (1995). Adolescent pregnancy–another look. *New England Journal of Medicine, 332,* 1161–1162. [8]

Goleman, D. (1995). *Emotional intelligence.* New York: Bantam. [7]

Goleman, D., Kaufman, P., & Ray, M. (1992). *The creative spirit.* New York: Dutton. [7]

Gollan, T., & Silverberg, N. (2001). Tip-of-the-tongue states in Hebrew-English bilinguals. *Bilingualism: Language and Cognition, 4,* 63–83. [7]

Gonzalez, R., Ellsworth, P. C., & Pembroke, M. (1993). Response biases in lineups and showups. *Journal of Personality and Social Psychology, 64,* 525–537. [6]

Goodwin, G. M. (1996). How do antidepressants affect serotonin receptors? The role of serotonin receptors in the therapeutic and side effect profile of the SSRIs. *Journal of Clinical Psychiatry, 57*(4, Suppl.), 9–13. [13]

Goodwin, R., & Fitzgibbon, M. (2002). Social anxiety as a barrier to treatment for eating disorders. *International Journal of Eating Disorders, 32,* 103–106. [9]

Gordon, H. (2002). Early environmental stress and biological vulnerability to drug abuse. *Psychoneuroendocrinology, 27,* 115–126. [4]

Gottesmann, C. (2000). Hypothesis for the neurophysiology of dreaming. *Sleep Research Online, 3,* 1–4. [4]

Gottesman, I. I. (1991). *Schizophrenia genesis: The origins of madness.* New York: W. H. Freeman. [12]

Gottfried, A. E., Fleming, J. S., & Gottfried, A. W. (1994). Role of parental motivational practices in children's academic intrinsic motivation and achievement. *Journal of Educational Psychology, 86,* 104–113. [9]

Gottman, J. (with Silver, N.). (1994). *Why marriages succeed or fail and how you can make yours last.* New York: Simon & Schuster. [9]

Gough, H. (1987). *California Psychological Inventory: Administrator's Guide.* Palo Alto: Consulting Psychologists Press. [11]

Graham, S. (1992). "Most of the subjects were white and middle class": Trends in published research on African Americans in selected APA journals, 1970–1989. *American Psychologist, 47,* 629–639. [1]

Grant, B. F., & Dawson, D. A. (1998). Age at onset of alcohol use and its association with DSM-IV alcohol abuse and dependence: Results from the National Longitudinal Alcohol Epidemiologic Survey. *Journal of Substance Abuse, 9,* 103–110. [10]

Grant, B. F., Harford, T. C., Chou, P., Pickering, M. S., Dawson, D. A., Stinson, F. S., & Noble, J. (1991). Prevalence of DSM-III-R alcohol abuse and dependence: United States, 1988. *Alcohol Health & Research World, 15,* 91–96. [10]

Greden, J. F. (1994). Introduction Part III. New agents for the treatment of depression. *Journal of Clinical Psychiatry, 55*(2, Suppl.), 32–33. [2]

Green, B. L., Lindy, J. D., & Grace, M. C. (1985). Post-traumatic stress disorder: Toward DSM-IV. *Journal of Nervous and Mental Disorders, 173,* 406–411. [10]

Green, J., & Shellenberger, R. (1990). *The dynamics of health and wellness: A biopsychosocial approach.* Fort Worth: Holt, Rinehart & Winston. [10]

Green, J. P., & Lynn, S. J. (2000). Hypnosis and suggestion-based approaches to smoking cessation: An examination of the evidence. *International Journal of Clinical Experimental Hypnosis, 48,* 195–224. [4]

Green, J. T., & Woodruff-Pak, D. S. (2000). Eyeblink classical conditioning: Hippocampal formation is for neutral stimulus associations as cerebellum is for association-response. *Psychological Bulletin, 126,* 138–158. [5]

Green, L. R., Richardson, D. R., & Lago, T. (1996). How do friendship, indirect, and direct aggression relate? *Aggressive Behavior, 22,* 81–86. [14]

Gregory, R. J. (1996). *Psychological testing: History, principles, and applications* (2nd ed.). Boston: Allyn & Bacon. [11]

Greist, J. H. (1992). An integrated approach to treatment of obsessive compulsive disorder. *Journal of Clinical Psychiatry, 53*(4, Suppl.), 38–41. [13]

Greist, J. H. (1995). The diagnosis of social phobia. *Journal of Clinical Psychiatry, 56*(5, Suppl.), 5–12. [12]

Grogger, J., & Bronars, S. (1993). The socioeconomic consequences of teenage childbearing: Findings from a natural experiment. *Family Planning Perspectives, 25,* 156–161. [8]

Grogorenko, E. (2003). Intraindividual fluctuations in intellectual functioning: Selected links between nutrition and the mind. In R. Sternberg, J. Lautrey, & T. Lubart (Eds.), *Models of intelligence: International perspectives.* Washington, DC: American Psychological Association. [7]

Grogorenko, E., Jarvin, L., & Sternberg, R. (2002). School-based tests of the triarchic theory of intelligence: Three settings, three samples, three syllabi. *Contemporary Educational Psychology, 27,* 167–208. [7]

Gronfier, C., Luthringer, R., Follenius, M., Schaltenbrand, N., Macher, J. P., Muzet, A., & Brandenberger, G. (1996). A quantitative evaluation of the relationships between growth hormone secretion and delta wave electroencephalographic activity during normal sleep and after enrichment in delta waves. *Sleep, 19,* 817–824. [4]

Gross, J. (2002). Emotion regulation: Affective, cognitive, and social consequences. *Psychophysiology, 39,* 281–291. [9]

Grossman, H. J. (Ed.). (1983). *Manual on terminology and classification in mental retardation.* Washington, DC: American Association on Mental Deficiency. [7]

Grossman, T. (2002). Pre-homosexual childhoods: An empirical study of gender role conformity among homosexual men. *Zeitschrift fuer Sexualforschung, 15,* 98–119. [9]

Guilleminault, C. (1993). 1. Amphetamines and narcolepsy: Use of the Stanford database. *Sleep, 16,* 199–201. [4]

Gupta, D., & Vishwakarma, M. S. (1989). Toy weapons and firecrackers: A source of hearing loss. *Laryngoscope, 99,* 330–334. [3]

Gur, R. E., Cowell, P. E., Latshaw, A., Turetsky, B. I., Grossman, R. I., Arnold, S. E., Bilker, W. B., & Gur, R. C. (2000). Reduced dorsal and orbital prefrontal gray matter volumes in schizophrenia. *Archives of General Psychiatry, 57,* 761–768. [12]

Gurin, J. (1989, June). Leaner, not lighter. *Psychology Today,* pp. 32–36. [9]

Guthrie, R. V. (1998). *Even the rat was white* (2nd ed.). Boston: Allyn & Bacon. [1]

Haaga, D. A. F., Dyck, M. J., & Ernst, D. (1991). Empirical status of cognitive theory of depression. *Psychological Bulletin, 110,* 215–236. [12]

Habel, U., Kuehn, E., Salloum, J., Devos, H., & Schneider, F. (2002). Emotional processing in psychopathic personality. *Aggressive Behavior, 28,* 394–400. [12]

Haberlandt, D. (1997). *Cognitive psychology* (2nd ed.). Boston: Allyn & Bacon. [1, 7]

Hada, M., Porjesz, B., Chorlian, D., Begleiter, H., & Polich, J. (2001). Auditory P3a deficits in male subjects at high risk for alcoholism. *Biological Psychiatry, 49,* 726–738. [10]

Hager, W., Leichsenring, F., & Schiffler, A. (2000). When does a study of different therapies allow comparisons of their relative efficacy? *Psychother. Psychosom. Med. Psychol., 50,* 251–262. [13]

Halaas, J. L., Gajiwala, K. S., Maffei, M., Cohen, S. L., Chait, B. T., Rabinowitz, D., Lallone, R. L., Burley, S. K., & Friedman, J. M. (1995). Weight-reducing effects of the plasma protein encoded by the obese gene. *Science, 269,* 543–546. [9]

Halford, G. S. (1989). Reflections on 25 years of Piagetian cognitive developmental psychology, 1963–1988. *Human Development, 32,* 325–327. [8]

Hall, G. S. (1904). *Adolescence: Its psychology and its relations to physiology, anthropology, sex, crime, religion, and education* (Vol. 1). New York: Appleton-Century-Crofts. [8]

Halligan, P. W., & Marshall, J. C. (1994). Toward a principled explanation of unilateral neglect. *Cognitive Neuropsychology, 11,* 167–206. [2]

Halmi, K. A. (1996). Eating disorder research in the past decade. *Annals of the New York Academy of Sciences, 789,* 67–77. [9]

Halpern, D. F. (1992). *Sex differences in cognitive abilities* (2nd ed.). Hillside, NJ: Erlbaum. [7]

Hamer, D. H., Hu, S., Magnuson, V. L., Hu, N., & Pattatucci, A. M. L. (1993). A linkage between DNA markers on the X chromosome and male sexual orientation. *Science, 261,* 321–327. [9]

Hamilton, C. S., & Swedo, S. E. (2001). Autoimmune-mediated, childhood onset obsessive-compulsive disorder and tics: A review. *Clinical Neuroscience Research, 1,* 61–68. [12]

Hamilton, M. C. (1988). Using masculine generics: Does generic "he" increase male bias in the user's imagery? *Sex Roles, 19,* 785–789. [7]

Hanley, S., & Abell, S. (2002). Maslow and relatedness: Creating an interpersonal model of self-actualization. *Journal of Humanistic Psychology, 42,* 37–56. [11]

Hare, R. D. (1995, September). Psychopaths: New trends in research. *Harvard Mental Health Letter, 12*(3), 4–5. [12]

Hargadon, R., Bowers, K. S., & Woody, E. Z. (1995). Does counterpain imagery mediate hypnotic analgesia? *Journal of Abnormal Psychology, 104,* 508–516. [4]

Harkins, S. G., & Jackson, J. M. (1985). The role of evaluation in eliminating social loafing. *Personality and Social Psychology Bulletin, 11,* 456–465. [14]

Harkins, S. G., & Szymanski, K. (1989). Social loafing and group evaluation. *Journal of Personality and Social Psychology, 56,* 941–943. [14]

Harlow, H. F. (1950). Learning and satiation of response in intrinsically motivated complex puzzle performance by monkeys. *Journal of Comparative and Physiological Psychology, 43,* 289–294. [9]

Harlow, H. F., & Harlow, M. K. (1962). Social deprivation in monkeys. *Scientific American, 207,* 137–146. [8]

Harlow, J. M. (1848). Passage of an iron rod through the head. *Boston Medical and Surgical Journal, 39,* 389–393. [2]

Harlow, R. E., & Cantor, N. (1996). Still participating after all these years: A study of life task participation in later life. *Journal of Personality and Social Psychology, 71,* 1235–1249. [8]

Harris, J. A., Rushton, J. P., Hampson, E., & Jackson, D. N. (1996). Salivary testosterone and self-report aggressive and pro-social personality characteristics in men and women. *Aggressive Behavior, 22,* 321–331. [14]

Harris, L. J., & Blaiser, M. J. (1997). Effects of a mnemonic peg system on the recall of daily tasks. *Perceptual and Motor Skills, 84,* 721–722. [6]

Harrison, Y., & Horne, J. A. (2000). Sleep loss and temporal memory. *Journal of Experimental Psychology, 53,* 271–279. [4]

Hart, D., Hofmann, V., Edelstein, W., & Keller, M. (1997). The relation of childhood personality types to adolescent behavior and development: A longitudinal study of Icelandic children. *Developmental Psychology, 33,* 195–205. [8]

Hatashita-Wong, M., Smith, T., Silverstein, S., Hull, J., & Willson, D. (2002). Cognitive functioning and social problem-solving skills in schizophrenia. *Cognitive Neuropsychiatry, 7,* 81–95. [12]

Hay, D. F. (1994). Prosocial development. *Journal of Child Psychology and Psychiatry, 35,* 29–71. [14]

Hayley, W. E., Roth, D. L., Coleton, M. I., Ford, G. R., West, C. A. C., Collins, R. P., & Isobe, T. L. (1996). Appraisal, coping, and social support as mediators of well-being in Black and White family caregivers of patients with Alzheimer's disease. *Journal of Consulting and Clinical Psychology, 64,* 121–129. [8]

Hazlett-Stevens, H., Craske, M., Roy-Byrne, P., Sherbourne, C., Stein, M., & Bystritsky, A. (2002). Predictors of willingness to consider medication and psychosocial treatment for panic disorder in primary care patients. *General Hospital Psychology, 24,* 316–321. [13]

Hecht, S., Shlaer, S., & Pirenne, M. H. (1942). *Journal of General Physiology, 25,* 819. [3]

Hedges, L. B., & Nowell, A. (1995). Sex differences in mental test scores, variability, and numbers of high-scoring individuals. *Science, 269,* 41–45. [7]

Hedley, L. M., Hoffart, A., Dammen, T., Ekeberg, O., & Friis, S. (2000). The relationship between cognitions and panic attack intensity. *Acta Psychiatrica Scandinavica, 102,* 300–302. [12]

Heimen, J. (2002). Psychologic treatments for female sexual dysfunction: Are they effective and do we need them? *Archives of Sexual Behavior, 31,* 445–450. [12]

Held, R. (1993). What can rates of development tell us about underlying mechanisms? In C. E. Granrud (Ed.), *Visual perception and cognition in infancy* (pp. 75–89). Hillsdale, NJ: Erlbaum. [8]

Hendin, H., & Haas, A. P. (1991). Suicide and guilt as manifestations of PTSD in Vietnam combat veterans. *American Journal of Psychiatry, 148,* 586–591. [10]

Henkel, L. A., Franklin, N., & Johnson, M. K. (2000). Cross-modal source monitoring confusions between perceived and imagined events. *Journal of Experimental Psychology: Learning, Memory, and Cognition, 26,* 321–335. [6]

Henley, N. M. (1989). Molehill or mountain? What we know and don't know about sex bias in language. In M. Crawford & M. Gentry (Eds.), *Gender and thought: Psychological perspectives.* New York: Springer-Verlag. [7]

Henson, R., Shallice, T., Gorno-Tempini, M., & Dolan, R. (2002). Face repetition effects in implicit and explicit memory as measured by fMRI. *Cerebral Cortex, 12,* 178–186. [6]

Herbert, T. B., & Cohen, S. (1993). Depression and immunity: A meta-analytic review. *Psychological Bulletin, 113,* 472–486. [10]

Herkenham, M. (1992). Cannabinoid receptor localization in brain: Relationship to motor and reward systems. *Annals of the New York Academy of Sciences, 654,* 19–32. [4]

Herman, L. (1981). Cognitive characteristics of dolphins. In L. Herman (Ed.), *Cetacean behavior.* New York: Wiley. [7]

Hernandez, L., & Hoebel, B. G. (1989). Food intake and lateral hypothalamic self-stimulation covary after medial hypothalamic lesions or ventral midbrain 6-hydroxydopamine injections that cause obesity. *Behavioral Neuroscience, 103,* 412–422. [9]

Herness, S. (2000). Coding in taste receptor cells: The early years of intracellular recordings. *Physiology and Behavior, 69,* 17–27. [3]

Hershenson, M. (1989). *The moon illusion.* Hillsdale, NJ: Erlbaum. [3]

Hertzog, C. (1991). Aging, information processing speed, and intelligence. In K. W. Schaie & M. P. Lawton (Eds.), *Annual Review of Gerontology and Geriatrics* (Vol. 11, pp. 55–79). [8]

Hetherington, A. W., & Ranson, S. W. (1940). Hypothalamic lesions and adiposity in the rat. *Anatomical Record, 78,* 149–172. [9]

Higdon, H. (1975). *The crime of the century.* New York: Putnam. [11]

Higgins, A. (1995). Educating for justice and community: Lawrence Kohlberg's vision of moral education. In W. M. Kurtines & J. L. Gerwirtz (Eds.), *Moral development: An introduction* (pp. 49–81). Boston: Allyn & Bacon. [8]

Hilgard, E. R. (1986). *Divided consciousness: Multiple controls in human thought and action.* New York: Wiley. [4]

Hilgard, E. R. (1992). Dissociation and theories of hypnosis. In E. Fromm & M. R. Nash (Eds.), *Contemporary hypnosis research.* New York: Guilford. [4]

Hill, M., & Augoustinos, M. (2001). Stereotype change and prejudice reduction: Short- and long-term evaluation of a cross-cultural awareness programme. *Journal of Community & Applied Social Psychology, 11,* 243–262. [14]

Hillebrand, J. (2000). New perspectives on the manipulation of opiate urges and the assessment of cognitive effort associated with opiate urges. *Addictive Behaviors, 25,* 139–143. [4]

Hinton, G. E., Dayan, P., Frey, B. J., & Neal, R. M. (1995). The "wake-sleep" algorithm for unsupervised neural networks. *Science, 268,* 1158–1161. [7]

Hirsch, J. (1997). Some heat but not enough light. *Nature, 387,* 27–28. [9]

Hirschfeld, M. A. (1995). The impact of health care reform on social phobia. *Journal of Clinical Psychiatry, 56*(5, Suppl.), 13–17. [12]

Hobson, J. A. (1988). *The dreaming brain.* New York: Basic Books. [4]

Hobson, J. A. (1989). *Sleep.* New York: Scientific American Library. [4]

Hobson, J. A., & McCarley, R. W. (1977). The brain as a dream state generator: An activation-synthesis hypothesis of the dream process. *American Journal of Psychiatry, 134,* 1335–1348. [4]

Hodgins, S., Mednick, S. A., Brennan, P. A., Schulsinger, F., & Engberg, M. (1996). Mental disorder and crime: Evidence from a Danish birth cohort. *Journal of Personality and Social Psychology, 53,* 489–496. [14]

Hofstede, G. (1980). *Culture's consequences: International differences in work-related values.* Beverly Hills, CA: Sage. [11]

Hofstede, G. (1983). Dimensions of national cultures in fifty countries and three regions. In J. Deregowski, S. Dzuirawiec, and R. Annis (Eds.), *Explications in cross-cultural psychology.* Lisse: Swets and Zeitlinger. [11]

Holland, J. G., & Skinner, B. F. (1961). *The analysis of behavior.* New York: McGraw-Hill. [5]

Holloa, S., Thase, M., & Marches, J. (2002). Treatment and prevention of depression. *Psychological Science in the Public Interest, 3,* 39–77. [13]

Hollon, S., Thase, M., & Markowitz, J. (2002). Treatment and prevention of depression. *Psychological Science in the Public Interest, 3,* 39–77. [12]

Holloway, M. (1999, January). Flynn's effect. *Scientific American, 280,* 37–38. [7]

Holmes, T. H., & Masuda, M. (1974). Life change and illness susceptibility. In B. S. Dohrenwend & B. P. Dohrenwend (Eds.), *Stressful life events: Their nature and effects.* New York: Wiley. [10]

Holmes, T. H., & Rahe, R. H. (1967). The social readjustment rating scale. *Journal of Psychosomatic Research, 11,* 213–218. [10]

Hopkins, W., Dahl, J., & Pilcher, D. (2001). Genetic influence on the expression of hand preferences in chimpanzees (*Pan troglodytes*): Evidence in support of the right-shift theory and developmental instability. *Psychological Science, 12,* 299–303. [2]

Horgan, J. (1995, November). Gay genes, revisited. *Scientific American, 273,* 26. [9]

Horn, J. C., & Meer, J. (1987, May). The vintage years. *Psychology Today,* pp. 76–90. [8]

Horn, J. L. (1982). The theory of fluid and crystallized intelligence in relation to concepts of cognitive psychology and aging in adulthood. In F. I. M. Craik & S. Trehub (Eds.), *Aging and cognitive processes* (pp. 201–238). New York: Plenum Press. [8]

Horn, L. J., & Zahn, L. (2001). From bachelor's degree to work: Major field of study and employment outcomes of 1992–93 bachelor's degree recipients who did not enroll in graduate education by 1997 (NCES 2001–165). Retrieved March 7, 2002, from http://nces.ed.gov/pubs2001/quarterly/spring/q5_2.html [1]

Horne, J. (1992). Annotation: Sleep and its disorders in children. *Journal of Child Psychology and Psychiatry, 33,* 473–487. [4]

Horney, K. (1939). *New ways in psychoanalysis.* New York: W. W. Norton. [11]

Horney, K. (1937). *The neurotic personality of our time.* New York: W. W. Norton. [11]

Horney, K. (1945). *Our inner conflicts.* New York: W. W. Norton. [11]

Horney, K. (1950). *Neurosis and human growth.* New York: W. W. Norton. [11]

Horney, K. (1967). *Feminine psychology.* New York: W. W. Norton. [11]

Horwath, E., Lish, J. D., Johnson, J., Hornig, C. D., & Weissman, M. M. (1993). Agoraphobia without panic: Clinical reappraisal of an epidemiologic finding. *American Journal of Psychiatry, 150,* 1496–1501. [12]

Houlihan, D., Schwartz, C., Miltenberger, R., & Heuton, D. (1993). The rapid treatment of a young man's balloon (noise) phobia using in vivo flooding. *Journal of Behavior Therapy and Experimental Psychiatry, 24,* 233–240. [13]

Hovland, C. I., Lumsdaine, A. A., & Sheffield, F. D. (1949). *Experiments on mass communication.* Princeton, NJ: Princeton University Press. [14]

Howard, A. D., Feighner, S. D., Cully, D. F., Arena, J. P., Liberator, P. A., Rosenblum, C. I., et al. (1996). A receptor in pituitary and hypothalamus that functions in growth hormone release. *Science, 273,* 974–977. [2]

Howard, M. (2002). When does semantic similarity help episodic retrieval? *Journal of Memory & Language, 46,* 85–98. [6]

Hrushesky, W. J. M. (1994, July/August). Timing is everything. *The Sciences,* pp. 32–37. [4]

Hubel, D. H. (1963). The visual cortex of the brain. *Scientific American, 209,* 54–62. [3]

Hubel, D. H. (1995). *Eye, brain, and vision.* New York: Scientific American Library. [3]

Hubel, D. H., & Wiesel, T. N. (1959). Receptive fields of single neurons in the cat's striate cortex. *Journal of Physiology, 148,* 547–591. [3]

Hubel, D. H., & Wiesel, T. N. (1979). Brain mechanisms of vision. *Scientific American, 241,* 130–144. [3]

Hudson, J. I., Carter, W. P., & Pope, H. G., Jr. (1996). Antidepressant treatment of binge-eating disorder: Research findings and clinical guidelines. *Journal of Clinical Psychiatry, 57*(8, Suppl.), 73–79. [13]

Huesmann, L. R., & Moise, J. (1996, June). Media violence: A demonstrated public health threat to children. *Harvard Mental Health Letter, 12*(12), 5–7. [14]

Hughes, J. R. (1992). Tobacco withdrawal in self-quitters. *Journal of Consulting and Clinical Psychology, 60,* 689–697. [10]

Hull, C. L. (1943). *Principles of behavior.* New York: Appleton-Century-Crofts. [9]

Hultsch, D. F., & Dixon, R. A. (1990). Learning and memory in aging. In J. E. Birren & K. W. Schaie (Eds.), *Handbook of the psychology of aging* (3rd ed., pp. 359–374). San Diego: Academic Press. [8]

Hummer, R. A., Rogers, R. G., Nam, C. B., & Ellison, C. G. (1999). Religious involvement and U.S. adult mortality. *Demography, 36,* 273–285. [10]

Hunter, J. A., Reid, J. M., Stokell, N. M., & Platow, M. J. (2000). Social attribution, self-esteem, and social identity. *Current Research in Social Psychology, 5,* 97–125. [14]

Hurvich, L. M., & Jameson, D. (1957). An opponent-process theory of color vision. *Psychological Review, 64,* 384–404. [3]

Hyde, J. S., Fenema, E., & Lamon, S. J. (1990). Gender differences in mathematics performance: A meta-analysis. *Psychological Bulletin, 107,* 139–155. [7]

Hyde, J. S., & Linn, M. C. (1988). Gender differences in verbal ability: A meta-analysis. *Psychological Bulletin, 104,* 53–69. [7]

Hyman, I. E., Jr., Husband, T. H., & Billings, E. J. (1995). False memories of childhood. *Applied Cognitive Psychology, 9,* 181–197. [6]

Hyman, I. E., Jr., & Pentland, J. (1996). The role of mental imagery in the creation of false childhood memories. *Journal of Memory and Language, 35,* 101–117. [6]

Impicciatore, P., Pandolfini, C., Casella, N., & Bonati, M. (1997). Reliability of health information on the World Wide Web: Systematic survey of advice on managing fever in children at home. *British Medical Journal, 314,* 1875. [10]

Inglehart, R. (1990). *Culture shift in advanced industrial society.* Princeton, NJ: Princeton University Press. [8]

Inhelder, B. (1966). Cognitive development and its contribution to the diagnosis of some phenomena of mental deficiency. *Merrill-Palmer Quarterly, 12,* 299–319. [8]

Insel, T. R. (1990). Phenomenology of obsessive compulsive disorder. *Journal of Clinical Psychiatry, 51*(2, Suppl.), 4–8. [12]

International Food Information Council Foundation. (2000). *Does caffeine cause dependence?* [4]

Isenberg, D. J. (1986). Group polarization: A critical review and meta-analysis. *Journal of Personality and Social Psychology, 50,* 1141–1151. [14]

Ito, T. A., Miller, N., & Pollock, V. E. (1996). Alcohol and aggression: A meta-analysis on the moderating effects of inhibitory cues, triggering events, and self-focused attention. *Psychological Bulletin, 120,* 60–82. [14]

Izard, C. E. (1971). *The face of emotion.* New York: Appleton-Century-Crofts. [9]

Izard, C. E. (1977). *Human emotions.* New York: Plenum Press. [9]

Izard, C. E. (1990). Facial expressions and the regulation of emotions. *Journal of Personality and Social Psychology, 58,* 487–498. [9]

Izard, C. E. (1992). Basic emotions, relations among emotions, and emotion-cognition relations. *Psychological Review, 99,* 561–565. [9]

Izard, C. E. (1993). Four systems for emotion activation: Cognitive and noncognitive processes. *Psychological Review, 100,* 68–90. [9]

Jacklin, C. N. (1989). Female and male: Issues of gender. *American Psychologist, 44,* 127–133. [8]

Jackson, S. (2002). A study of teachers' perceptions of youth problems. *Journal of Youth Studies, 5,* 313–322. [14]

James, W. (1884). What is an emotion? *Mind, 9,* 188–205. [9]

James, W. (1890). *Principles of psychology.* New York: Holt. [1]

Jamieson, D. W., & Zanna, M. P. (1989). Need for structure in attitude formation and expression. In A. R. Pratkanis, S. J. Breckler, & A. G. Greenwald (Eds.), *Attitude structure and function* (pp. 383–406). Hillsdale, NJ: Erlbaum. [14]

Janis, I. L. (1982). *Groupthink: Psychological studies of policy decisions and fiascoes* (2nd ed.). Boston: Houghton Mifflin. [14]

Janssen, T., & Carton, J. (1999). The effects of locus of control and task difficulty on procrastination. *Journal of Genetic Psychology, 160,* 436–442. [11]

Jefferson, J. W. (1995). Social phobia: A pharmacologic treatment overview. *Journal of Clinical Psychiatry, 56*(5, Suppl.), 18–24. [13]

Jefferson, J. W. (1996). Social phobia: Everyone's disorder? *Journal of Clinical Psychiatry, 57*(6, Suppl.), 28–32. [12]

Jefferson, J. W. (1997). Antidepressants in panic disorder. *Journal of Clinical Psychiatry, 58*(2, Suppl.), 20–24. [13]

Jelicic, M., & Bonke, B. (2001). Memory impairments following chronic stress? A critical review. *European Journal of Psychiatry, 15,* 225–232. [6]

Jellinek, E. M. (1960). *The disease concept of alcoholism.* New Brunswick, NJ: Hillhouse Press. [10]

Jenike, M. A. (1990, April). Obsessive-compulsive disorder. *Harvard Medical School Health Letter, 12,* 4–8. [13]

Jenkins, J. H., & Karno, M. (1992). The meaning of expressed emotion: Theoretical issues raised by cross-cultural research. *American Journal of Psychiatry, 149,* 9–21. [13]

Jernigan, T. L., Butters, N., DiTraglia, G., Schafer, K., Smith, T., Irwin, M., Grant, I., Schuckit, M., & Cermak, L. S. (1991). Reduced cerebral grey matter observed in alcoholics using magnetic resonance imaging. *Alcoholism: Clinical and Experimental Research, 15,* 418–427. [10]

Jimerson, D. C., Wolfe, B. E., Metzger, E. D., Finkelstein, D. M., Cooper, T. B., & Levine, J. M. (1997). Decreased serotonin function in bulimia nervosa. *Archives of General Psychiatry, 54,* 529–534. [9]

Johnson, M. P., Duffy, J. F., Dijk, D-J., Ronda, J. M., Dyal, C. M., & Czeisler, C. A. (1992). Short-term memory, alertness and performance: A reappraisal of their relationship to body temperature. *Journal of Sleep Research, 1,* 24–29. [4]

Johnson, W. G., Tsoh, J. Y., & Varnado, P. J. (1996). Eating disorders: Efficacy of pharmacological and psychological interventions. *Clinical Psychology Review, 16,* 457–478. [9]

Johnston, L. E., O'Malley, P. M., & Bachman, J. G. (2001). *Monitoring the Future national results on adolescent drug use: Overview of key findings, 2000* (NIH Publication No. 01-4923). Rockville MD: National Institute on Drug Abuse. [1, 4]

Jonas, J. M., & Cohon, M. S. (1993). A comparison of the safety and efficacy of alprazolam versus other agents in the treatment of anxiety, panic, and depression: A review of the literature. *Journal of Clinical Psychiatry, 54*(10, Suppl.), 25–45. [13]

Jones, E. E. (1976). How do people perceive the causes of behavior? *American Scientist, 64,* 300–305. [14]

Jones, E. E. (1990). *Interpersonal perception.* New York: Freeman. [14]

Jones, E. E., & Nisbett, R. E. (1971). *The actor and the observer: Divergent perceptions of the causes of behavior.* New York: General Learning. [14]

Jones, M. C. (1924). A laboratory study of fear: The case of Peter. *Pedagogical Seminary, 31,* 308–315. [5]

Jorgensen, M., & Keiding, N. (1991). Estimation of spermarche from longitudinal spermaturia data. *Biometrics, 47,* 177–193. [8]

Judd, L. L., Akiskal, H. S., Zeller, P. J., Paulus, M., Leon, A. C., Maser, J. D., Endicott, J., Coryell, W., Kunovac, J. L., Mueller, T. I., Rice, J. P., & Keller, M. B. (2000). Psychosocial disability during the long-term course of unipolar major depressive disorder. *Archives of General Psychiatry, 57,* 375–380. [12]

Julien, R. M. (1995). *A primer of drug action* (7th ed.). New York: W.H. Freeman. [4, 8]

Jung, C. G. (1933). *Modern man in search of a soul.* New York: Harcourt Brace Jovanovich. [11]

Kagitcibasi, C. (1992). A critical appraisal of individualism-collectivism: Toward a new formulation. In U. Kim, H. C. Triandis, and G. Yoon (Eds.), *Individualism and collectivism: Theoretical and methodological issues.* Newbury Park, CA: Sage. [11]

Kahneman, D., & Tversky, A. (1984). Choices, values, and frames. *American Psychologist, 39,* 341–350. [7]

Kaladini, S., & McGuffin, P. (2003). The genetics of affective disorders: Present and future. In R. Plomin, J. DeFries, I. Craig, & P. McGuffin (Eds.), *Behavioral genetics in the postgenomic era* (pp. 481–502). Washington, DC: American Psychological Association. [12]

Kalichman, S., Benotsch, E., Weinhardt, L., Austin, J., Webster, L., & Chauncey, C. (2003). Health-related Internet use, coping, social support, and health indicators in people living with HIV/AIDS: Preliminary results from a community survey. *Health Psychology, 22,* 111–116. [10]

Kalish, H. I. (1981). *From behavioral science to behavior modification.* New York: McGraw-Hill. [5, 13]

Kaltiala-Heino, R., Rimpelae, M., Rissanen, A., & Rantanen, P. (2001). Early puberty and early sexual activity are associated with bulimic-type eating pathology in middle adolescence. *Journal of Adolescent Health, 28,* 346–352. [8]

Kampman, M., Keijsers, G., Hoogduin, C., & Hendriks, G. (2002). A randomized, double-blind, placebo-controlled study of the effects of adjunctive paroxetine in panic disorder patients unsuccessfully treated with cognitive-behavioral therapy alone. *Journal of Clinical Psychiatry, 63,* 772–777. [12]

Kane, J. M. (1996). Treatment-resistant schizophrenic patients. *Journal of Clinical Psychiatry, 57*(9, Suppl.), 35–40. [13]

Kanner, A. D., Coyne, J. C., Schaefer, C., & Lazarus, R. S. (1981). Comparison of two modes of stress measurement: Daily hassles and uplifts versus major life events. *Journal of Behavioral Medicine, 4,* 1–39. [10]

Kaplan, G. A., Wilson, T. W., Cohen, R. D., Kauhanen, J., Wu, M., & Salomen, J. T. (1994). Social functioning and overall mortality: Prospective evidence from the Kuopio Ischemic Heart Disease Risk Factor Study. *Epidemiology, 5,* 495–500. [10]

Karacan, I. (1988). Parasomnias. In R. L. Williams, I. Karacan, & C. A. Moore (Eds.), *Sleep disorders: Diagnosis and treatment* (pp. 131–144). New York: John Wiley. [4]

Karau, S. J., & Williams, K. D. (1993). Social loafing; a meta-analytic review and theoretical integration. *Journal of Personality and Social Psychology, 65,* 681–706. [14]

Karni, A., Tanne, D., Rubenstein, B. S., Askenasy, J. J. M., & Sagi, D. (1994). Dependence on REM sleep of overnight improvement of a perceptual skill. *Science, 265,* 679–682. [4]

Kastenbaum, R. (1992). *The psychology of death.* New York: Springer-Verlag. [8]

Katon, W. (1996). Panic disorder: Relationship to high medical utilization, unexplained physical symptoms, and medical costs. *Journal of Clinical Psychiatry, 57*(10, Suppl.), 11–18. [12]

Katz, E., Robles-Sotelo, E., Correia, C., Silverman, K., Stitzer, M., & Bigelow, G. (2002). The brief abstinence test: Effects of continued incentive availability on cocaine abstinence. *Experimental & Clinical Psychopharmacology, 10,* 10–17. [5]

Katz, G., Durst, R., & Knobler, H. (2001). Exogenous melatonin, jet lag, and psychosis: Preliminary case results. *Journal of Clinical Psychopharmacology, 21,* 349–351. [4]

Katz, G., Knobler, H., Laibel, Z., Strauss, Z., & Durst, R. (2002). Time zone change and major psychiatric morbidity: The results of a 6-year study in Jerusalem. *Comprehensive Psychiatry, 43,* 37–40. [4]

Kawachi, I., Colditz, G. A., Speizer, F. E., Manson, J. E., Stampfer, M. J., Willett, W. C., & Hennekens, C. H. (1997). A prospective study of passive smoking and coronary heart disease. *Circulation, 95,* 2374–2379. [10]

Kawanishi, Y., Tachikawa, H., & Suzuki, T. (2000). Pharmacogenomics and schizophrenia. *European Journal of Pharmacology, 410,* 227–241. [13]

Keating, C. R. (1994). World without words: Messages from face and body. In W. J. Lonner & R. Malpass (Eds.), *Psychology and culture* (pp. 175–182). Boston: Allyn & Bacon. [9]

Keefauver, S. P., & Guilleminault, C. (1994). Sleep terrors and sleepwalking. In M. Kryger, T. Roth, & W. C. Dement (Eds.), *Principles and practice of sleep medicine* (pp. 567–573). Philadelphia: W.B. Saunders. [4]

Keesey, R. E. (1988). The body-weight set point. What can you tell your patients? *Postgraduate Medicine, 83,* 114–118, 121–122, 127. [9]

Keitner, G. I., Ryan, C. E., Miller, I. W., & Norman, W. H. (1992). Recovery and major depression: Factors associated with twelve-month outcome. *American Journal of Psychiatry, 149,* 93–99. [12]

Kelner, K. L. (1997). Seeing the synapse. *Science, 276,* 547. [2]

Kendler, K. S., & Diehl, S. R. (1993). The genetics of schizophrenia: A current genetic-epidemiologic perspective. *Schizophrenia Bulletin, 19,* 261–285. [12]

Kendler, K. S., MacLean, C., Neale, M., Kessler, R., Heath, A., & Eaves, L. (1991). The genetic epidemiology of bulimia nervosa. *American Journal of Psychiatry, 148,* 1627–1637. [9]

Kendler, K. S., Neale, M. C., Kessler, R. C., Heath, A. C., & Eaves, L. J. (1992). The genetic epidemiology of phobias in women. *Archives of General Psychiatry, 49,* 273–281. [12]

Kendler, K. S., Neale, M. C., Kessler, R. C., Heath, A. C., & Eaves, L. J. (1993). The lifetime history of major depression in women: Reliability of diagnosis and heritability. *Archives of General Psychiatry, 50,* 863–870. [12]

Kendler, K. S., Neale, M. C., MacLean, C. J, Heath, A. C., Eaves, L. J., & Kessler, R. C. (1993). Smoking and major depression: A causal analysis. *Archives of General Psychiatry, 50,* 36–43. [10]

Kendler, K. S., Walters, E. E., Truett, K. R., Heath, A. C., Neale, M. C., Martin, N. G., & Eaves, L. J. (1994). Sources of individual differences in depressive symptoms: Analysis of two samples of twins and their families. *American Journal of Psychiatry, 151,* 1605–1614. [12]

Kenrick, D. T., & Gutierres, S. E. (1980). Contrast effects and judgments of physical attractiveness: When beauty becomes a social problem. *Journal of Personality and Social Psychology, 38,* 131–140. [9]

Kessler, R. C., McGonagle, K. A., Zhao, S., Nelson, C. B., Hughes, M., Eshleman, S., Wittchen, H-U., & Kendler, K. S. (1994). Lifetime and 12-month prevalence of DSM-III-R psychiatric disorders in the United States: Results from the National Comorbidity Survey. *American Journal of Psychiatry, 51,* 8–19. [12]

Kessler, R. C., Stein, M. B., & Berglund, P. (1998). Social phobia subtypes in the National Comorbidity Survey. *American Journal of Psychiatry, 155,* 613–619. [12]

Kiecolt-Glaser, J. K., Fisher, L. D., Ogrocki, P., Stout, J., Speicher, C. E., & Glaser, R. (1987). Marital quality, marital disruption, and immune function. *Psychosomatic Medicine, 49,* 13–34. [10]

Kiecolt-Glaser, J. K., Glaser, R., Gravenstein, S., Malarkey, W. B., & Sheridan, J. (1996). Chronic stress alters the immune response to influenza virus vaccine in older adults. *Proceedings of the National Academy of Science, 93,* 3043–3047. [10]

Kiecolt-Glaser, J., McGuire, L., Robles, T., & Glaser, R. (2002). Psychoneuroimmunology: Psychological influences on immune function and health. *Journal of Consulting and Clinical Psychology, 70,* 537–547. [10]

Kihlstrom, J. F. (1986). Strong inferences about hypnosis. *Behavioral and Brain Sciences, 9,* 474–475. [4]

Kihlstrom, J. F. (1995). The trauma-memory argument. *Consciousness and Cognition, 4,* 65–67. [6]

Kihlstrom, J. F., & Barnhardt, T. M. (1993). The self-regulation of memory: For better and for worse, with and without hypnosis. In D. M. Wegner & J. W. Pennebaker (Eds.), *Handbook of mental control.* Englewood Cliffs, NJ: Prentice Hall. [4]

Kilbride, J. E., & Kilbride, P. L. (1975). Sitting and smiling behavior of Baganda infants. *Journal of Cross-Cultural Psychology, 6,* 88–107. [8]

Kim, J. J., Mohamed, S., Andreasen, N. C., O'Leary, D. S., Watkins, L., Ponto, L. L. B., & Hichwa, R. D. (2000). Regional neural dysfunctions in chronic schizophrenia studied with positron emission tomography. *American Journal of Psychiatry, 157,* 542–548. [12]

Kim, K. H. S., Relkin, N. R., Lee, K-M., & Hirsch, J. (1997). Distinct cortical areas associated with native and second languages. *Nature, 388,* 171–174. [7]

Kimmel, H., Carroll, F., & Kuhar, M. (2003). Withdrawal from repeated cocaine alters dopamine transporter protein turnover in the rat striatum. *Journal of Pharmacology & Experimental Therapeutics, 304,* 15–21. [4]

Kimura, D. (1992). Sex differences in the brain. *Scientific American, 267,* 118–125. [7]

King, L. A., Walker, L. M., & Broyles, S. J. (1996). Creativity and the five-factor model. *Journal of Research on Personality, 30,* 189–203. [11]

Kinomura, S., Larsson, J., Gulyás, B., & Roland, P. E. (1996). Activation by attention of the human reticular formation and thalamic intralaminar nuclei. *Science, 271,* 512–515. [2]

Kinsey, A. C., Pomeroy, W. B., & Martin, C. E. (1948). *Sexual behavior in the human male.* Philadelphia: W. B. Saunders. [9]

Kinsey, A. C., Pomeroy, W. B., Martin, C. E., & Gebhard, P. H. (1953). *Sexual behavior in the human female.* Philadelphia: W. B. Saunders. [9]

Kirsch, I., & Lynn, S. J. (1995). The altered state of hypnosis: Changes in the theoretical landscape. *American Psychologist, 50,* 846–858. [4]

Kitayama, S., & Markus, H. R. (2000). The pursuit of happiness and the realization of sympathy: Cultural patterns of self, social relations, and well-being. In E. Diener & E. M. Suh (Eds.), *Subjective well-being across cultures.* Cambridge, MA: MIT Press. [11]

Kitayama, S., Markus, H. R., & Kurokawa, M. (2000). Culture, emotion, and well-being: Good feelings in Japan and the United States. *Cognition and Emotion, 14,* 93–124. [9]

Kite, M. E., Deaux, K., & Miele, M. (1991). Stereotypes of young and old: Does age outweigh gender? *Psychology and Aging, 6,* 19–27. [14]

Kiyatkin, E., & Wise, R. (2002). Brain and body hyperthermia associated with heroin self-administration in rats. *Journal of Neuroscience, 22,* 1072–1080. [4]

Klaczynski, P., Fauth, J., & Swanger, A. (1998). Adolescent identity: Rational vs. experiential processing, formal operations, and critical thinking beliefs. *Journal of Youth & Adolescence, 27,* 185–207. [8]

Klatzky, R. L. (1980). *Human memory: Structures and processes* (2nd ed.). New York: W. H. Freeman. [6]

Kleinman, A., & Cohen, A. (1997, March). Psychiatry's global challenge. *Scientific American, 276,* 86–89. [13]

Klerman, G. L., Weissman, M. N., Rounsaville, B. J., & Chevron, E. S. (1984). *Interpersonal therapy of depression.* New York: Academic Press. [13]

Kliegman, R. (1998). Fetal and neonatal medicine. In R. Behrman & R. Kliegman (Eds.), *Nelson essentials of pediatrics.* (3rd ed., pp. 167–225). Philadelphia: W. B. Saunders. [8]

Kluft, R. (1999). Dissociative disorders (Ch. 188). *Merck manual of diagnosis and therapy* (17th ed.) [Online version]. Retrieved January 7, 2003, from http://www.merck.com/puns/mmanual/section15/chapter188/188d.htm. [12]

Kluft, R. P. (1984). An introduction to multiple personality disorder. *Psychiatric Annals, 14,* 19–24. [12]

Kluft, R. P. (1993). Multiple personality disorder: A contemporary perspective. *Harvard Mental Health Letter, 10*(4), 5–7. [12]

Kobasa, S. (1979). Stressful life events, personality, and health: An inquiry into hardiness. *Journal of Personality and Social Psychology, 37,* 1–11. [10]

Kobasa, S. C., Maddi, S. R., & Kahn, S. (1982). Hardiness and health: A prospective study. *Journal of Personality and Social Psychology, 42,* 168–177. [10]

Kochanska, G. (1993). Toward a synthesis of parental socialization and child temperament in early development of conscience. *Child Development, 64,* 325–347. [14]

Kochavi, D., Davis, J., & Smith, G. (2001). Corticotropin-releasing factor decreases meal size by decreasing cluster number in Koletsky (LA/N) rats with and without a null mutation of the leptin receptor. *Physiology & Behavior, 74,* 645–651. [9]

Koehler, T, Tiede, G., & Thoens, M. (2002). Long and short-term forgetting of word associations: An experimental study of the Freudian concepts of resistance and repression. *Zeitschrift fuer klinische Psychologie, Psychiatrie und Psychotherapie, 50,* 328–333. [11]

Kohlberg, L. (1966). A cognitive-developmental analysis of children's sex-role concepts and attitudes. In E. E. Maccoby (Ed.), *The development of sex differences* (pp. 82–173). Stanford, CA: Stanford University Press. [8]

Kohlberg, L. (1968, September). The child as a moral philosopher. *Psychology Today,* pp. 24–30. [8]

Kohlberg, L. (1969). *Stages in the development of moral thought and action.* New York: Holt, Rinehart & Winston. [8]

Kohlberg, L. (1981). *Essays on moral development, Vol. 1. The philosophy of moral development.* New York: Harper & Row. [8]

Kohlberg, L. (1984). *Essays on moral development, Vol. 2. The psychology of moral development.* San Francisco: Harper & Row. [8]

Kohlberg, L. (1985). *The psychology of moral development.* San Francisco: Harper & Row. [8]

Kohlberg, L., & Gilligan, C. (1971). The adolescent as a philosopher: The discovery of the self in a postconventional world. *Daedalus, 100,* 1051–1086. [8]

Kohlberg, L., & Ullian, D. Z. (1974). In R. C. Friedman, R. M. Richart, & R. L. Vande Wiele (Eds.), *Sex differences in behavior* (pp. 209–222). New York: Wiley. [8]

Köhler, W. (1925). *The mentality of apes* (E. Winter, Trans.). New York: Harcourt Brace Jovanovich. [5]

Koltz, C. (1983, December). Scapegoating. *Psychology Today,* pp. 68–69. [14]

König, P., & Verschure, F. M. J. (2002). Neurons in action. *Science, 296,* 1817–1818. [7]

Kopp, C. P., & Kaler, S. R. (1989). Risk in infancy: Origins and implications. *American Psychologist, 44,* 224–230. [8]

Kosslyn, S. M., & Sussman, A. L. (1995). Roles of imagery in perception: Or, there is no such thing as immaculate perception. In M. S. Gazzaniga (Ed.), *The cognitive neurosciences.* Cambridge, MA: MIT Press. [7]

Kovacs, D., Mahon, J., & Palmer, R. (2002). Chewing and spitting out food among eating-disordered patients. *International Journal of Eating Disorders, 32,* 112–115. [9]

Kowatch, R., Suppes, T., Carmody, T., Bucci, J., Hume, J., Kromelis, M., Emslie, G., Weinberg, W., & Rush, A. (2000). Effect size of lithium, divalproex sodium, and carbamazepine in children and adolescents with bipolar disorder. *Journal of the American Academy of Child & Adolescent Psychiatry, 39,* 713–720. [13]

Kozak, M. J., Foa, E. B., & McCarthy, P. R. (1988). Obsessive-compulsive disorder. In C. G. Last & M. Herson (Eds.), *Handbook of anxiety disorders* (pp. 87–108). New York: Pergamon Press. [12]

Krantz, D. S., Grunberg, N. E., & Baum, A. (1985). Health psychology. *Annual Review of Psychology, 36,* 349–383. [10]

Kranzler, H. R., (1996). Evaluation and treatment of anxiety symptoms and disorders in alcoholics. Journal of Clinical Psychiatry, 57(6, Suppl.). [12]

Kraus, S. J. (1995). Attitudes and the prediction of behavior: A meta-analysis of the empirical literature. *Personality and Social Psychology Bulletin, 21,* 58–75. [14]

Krcmar, M., & Cooke, M. (2001). Children's moral reasoning and their perceptions of television violence. *Journal of Communication, 51,* 300–316. [5]

Kripke, D., Garfinkel, L., Wingard, D., Klauber, M., & Marler, M. (2002). Mortality associated with sleep duration. *Archives of General Psychiatry, 59,* 131–136. [4]

Kroll, N. E. A., Ogawa, K. H., & Nieters, J. E. (1988). Eyewitness memory and the importance of sequential information. *Bulletin of the Psychonomic Society, 26,* 395–398. [6]

Krueger, J. M., & Takahashi, S. (1997). Thermoregulation and sleep: Closely linked but separable. *Annals of the New York Academy of Sciences, 813,* 281–286. [4]

Krueger, W. C. F. (1929). The effect of overlearning on retention. *Journal of Experimental Psychology, 12,* 71–81. [6]

Kübler-Ross, Elisabeth. (1969). *On death and dying.* New York: Macmillan. [8]

Kucharska-Pietura, K., & Klimkowski, M. (2002). Perception of facial affect in chronic schizophrenia and right brain damage. *Acta Neurobiologiae Experimentalis, 62,* 33–43. [2]

Kuhn, D. (1984). Cognitive development. In M. H. Bernstein & M. E. Lamb (Eds.), *Developmental psychology.* Hillsdale, NJ: Erlbaum. [8]

Kuhn, D., Kohlberg, L., Langer, J., & Haan, N. (1977). The development of formal operations in logical and moral judgment. *Genetic Psychology Monographs, 95,* 97–188. [8]

Kuhn, D., & Lao, J. (1996). Effects of evidence on attitudes: Is polarization the norm? *Psychological Science, 7,* 115–120. [14]

Kumar, R., O'Malley, P., Johnston, L., Schulenberg, J., & Bachman, J. (2002). Effects of school-level norms on student substance abuse. *Prevention Science, 3,* 105–124. [14]

Kummervold, P., Gammon, D., Bergvik, S., Johnsen, J., Hasvold, T., & Rosenvinge, J. (2002). Social support in a wired world: Use of online mental health forums in Norway. *Nordic Journal of Psychiatry, 56,* 59–65. [10]

Kumpfer, K., Alvarado, R., Smith, P., & Ballamy, N. (2002). Cultural sensitivity and adaptation in family-based prevention interventions. *Prevention Science, 3,* 241–246. [13]

Kunda, Z., & Oleson, K. C. (1995). Maintaining stereotypes in the face of disconfirmation: Construction grounds for subtyping deviants. *Journal of Personality and Social Psychology, 68,* 565–579. [14]

Kunz, D., & Herrmann, W. M. (2000). Sleep-wake cycle, sleep-related disturbances, and sleep disorders: A chronobiological approach. *Comparative Psychology, 41*(2, Suppl. 1), 104–105. [4]

Kurup, R., & Kurup, P. (2002). Detection of endogenous lithium in neuropsychiatric disorders. *Human Psychopharmacology Clinical & Experimental, 17,* 29–33. [1, 2]

Lal, S. (2002). Giving children security: Mamie Phipps Clark and the racialization of child psychology. *American Psychologist, 57,* 20–28. [1]

Lam, L., & Kirby, S. (2002). Is emotional intelligence an advantage? An exploration of the impact of emotional and general intelligence on individual performance. *Journal of Social Psychology, 142,* 133–143. [7]

Lambe, E. K., Katzman, D. K., Mikulis, D. J., Kennedy, S. H., & Zipursky, R. B. (1997). Cerebral gray matter volume deficits after weight recovery from anorexia nervosa. *Archives of General Psychiatry, 54,* 537–542. [9]

Lamberg, L. (1996). Some schools agree to let sleeping teens lie. *Journal of the American Medical Association, 276,* 859. [4]

Lambert, G., Johansson, M., Agren, H., & Friberg, P. (2000). Reduced brain norepinephrine and dopamine release in treatment-refractory depressive illness. *Archives of General Psychiatry, 57,* 787–793. [12]

Lambert, W. E., Genesee, F., Holobow, N., & Chartrand, L. (1993). Bilingual education for majority English-speaking children. *European Journal of Psychology Education, 8,* 3–22. [7]

Lamborn, S. D., Mounts, N. S., Steinberg, L., & Dornbusch, S. M. (1991). Patterns of competence and adjustment among adolescents from authoritative, authoritarian, indulgent, and neglectful families. *Child Development, 62,* 1049–1065. [8]

Lamm, H. (1988). A review of our research on group polarization: Eleven experiments on the effects of group discussion on risk acceptance, probability estimation, and negotiation positions. *Psychological Reports, 62,* 807–813. [14]

Landis, C. A., Savage, M. V., Lentz, M. J., & Brengelmann, G. L. (1998). Sleep deprivation alters body temperature dynamics to mild cooling and heating, not sweating threshold, in women. *Sleep, 21,* 101–108. [4]

Landry, D. W. (1997, February). Immunotherapy for cocaine addiction. *Scientific American, 276,* 42–45. [4]

Lang, A., Craske, M., Brown, M., & Ghaneian, A. (2001). Fear-related state dependent memory. *Cognition & Emotion, 15,* 695–703. [6]

Lang, A. R., Goeckner, D. J., Adesso, V. J., & Marlatt, G. A. (1975). Effects of alcohol on aggression in male social drinkers. *Journal of Abnormal Psychology, 84,* 508–518. [1]

Lange, C. G., & James, W. (1922). *The emotions* (I. A. Haupt, Trans.). Baltimore: Williams and Wilkins. [9]

Langer, E. J., & Rodin, J. (1976). The effects of choice and enhanced personal responsibility for the aged: A field experiment in an institutional setting. *Journal of Personality and Social Psychology, 34,* 191–198. [10]

Langevin, B., Sukkar, F., Léger, P., Guez, A., & Robert, D. (1992). Sleep apnea syndromes (SAS) of specific etiology: Review and incidence from a sleep laboratory. *Sleep, 15,* S25–S32. [4]

Langlois, J. H., Kalakanis, L., Rubenstein, A. J., Larson, A., Hallam, M., & Smoot, M. (2000). Maxims or myths of beauty? A meta-analytic and theoretical review. *Psychological Bulletin, 126,* 390–423. [14]

Langlois, J. H., & Roggman, L. A. (1990). Attractive faces are only average. *Psychological Science, 1,* 115–121. [14]

Lara, M. E., Leader, J., & Klein, D. N. (1997). The association between social support and course of depression: Is it confounded with personality? *Journal of Abnormal Psychology, 106,* 478–482. [10]

Larson, R., & Verma, S. (1999). How children and adolescents spend time across the world: Work, play, and developmental opportunities. *Psychological Bulletin, 125,* 701–736. [7]

Latané, B., Williams, K., & Harkins, S. (1979). Many hands make light the work: The causes and consequences of social loafing. *Journal of Personality and Social Psychology, 37,* 822–832. [14]

Laumann, E. O., Gagnon, J. H., Michael, R. T., & Michaels, S. (1994). *The social organization of sexuality.* Chicago: University of Chicago Press. [9]

Laurent, J., Swerdik, M., & Ryburn, M. (1992). Review of validity research on the Stanford-Binet Intelligence Scale: Fourth Edition. *Psychological Assessment, 4,* 102–112. [7]

Lavie, P., Herer, P., Peled, R., Berger, I., Yoffe, N., Zomer, J., & Rubin, A-H. (1995). Mortality in sleep apnea patients: A multivariate analysis of risk factors. *Sleep, 18,* 149–157. [4]

Layton, L., Deeny, K., Tall, G., & Upton, G. (1996). Researching and promoting phonological awareness in the nursery class. *Journal of Research in Reading, 19,* 1–13. [8]

Lazarus, R. S. (1966). *Psychological stress and the coping process.* New York: McGraw-Hill. [10]

Lazarus, R. S. (1984). On the primacy of cognition. *American Psychologist, 39,* 124–129. [9]

Lazarus, R. S. (1991a). Cognition and motivation in emotion. *American Psychologist, 46,* 352–367. [9]

Lazarus, R. S. (1991b). Progress on a cognitive-motivational-relational theory of emotion. *American Psychologist, 46,* 819–834. [9]

Lazarus, R. S. (1995). Vexing research problems inherent in cognitive-mediational theories of emotion—and some solutions. *Psychological Inquiry, 6,* 183–187. [9]

Lazarus, R. S., & DeLongis, A. (1983). Psychological stress and coping in aging. *American Psychologist, 38,* 245–253. [10]

Lazarus, R. S., & Folkman, S. (1984). *Stress, appraisal, and coping.* New York: Springer. [10]

Lebow, J. L., & Gurman, A. S. (1995). Research assessing couple and family therapy. *Annual Review of Psychology, 46,* 27–57. [13]

Lecomte, T., & Lecomte, C. (2002). Toward uncovering robust principles of change inherent to cognitive-behavioral therapy for psychosis. *American Journal of Orthopsychiatry, 72,* 50–57. [13]

LeDoux, J. E. (1994). Emotion, memory, and the brain. *Scientific American, 270,* 50–57. [2]

LeDoux, J. E. (1996). *The emotional brain: The mysterious underpinnings of emotional life.* New York: Simon & Schuster. [9]

LeDoux, J. E. (2000). Emotion circuits in the brain. *Annual Review of Neuroscience, 23,* 155–184. [2, 9]

Lee, I., & Kesner, R. (2002). Differential contribution of NMDA receptors in hippocampal subregions to spatial working memory. *Nature Neuroscience, 5,* 162–168. [6]

Lehmann, H., Treit, D., & Parent, M. B. (2000). Amygdala lesions do not impair shock-probe avoidance retention performance. *Behavioral Neuroscience, 114,* 1107–1116. [5]

Leichtman, M. D., & Ceci, S. J. (1995). The effects of stereotypes and suggestions on preschoolers' reports. *Developmental Psychology, 31,* 568–578. [6]

Leitenberg, H., & Henning, K. (1995). Sexual fantasy. *Psychological Bulletin, 117,* 469–496. [4, 9]

Leland, J. (1997, Spring/Summer). The magnetic tube. *Newsweek* [Special Edition], pp. 89–90. [8]

Lenat, D. B. (1995, September). Artificial intelligence. *Scientific American, 273,* 80–82. [7]

Lenneberg, E. (1967). *Biological foundations of language.* New York: Wiley. [8]

Leon, M. (1992). The neurobiology of filial learning. *Annual Review of Psychology, 43,* 337–398. [8]

Lerman, D. C., & Iwata, B. A. (1996). Developing a technology for the use of operant extinction in clinical settings: An examination of basic and applied research. *Journal of Applied Behavior Analysis, 29,* 345–382. [13]

Lerman, D. C., Iwata, B. A., Shore, B. A., & Kahng, S. W. (1996). Responding maintained by intermittent reinforcement: Implications for the use of extinction with problem behavior in clinical settings. *Journal of Applied Behavior Analysis, 29,* 153–171. [5]

Lester, B. M., Hoffman, J., & Brazelton, T. B. (1985). The rhythmic structure of mother-infant interaction in term and preterm infants. *Child Development, 56,* 15–27. [8]

LeVay, S. (1991). A difference in hypothalamic structure between heterosexual and homosexual men. *Science, 253,* 1034–1037. [9]

LeVay, S., & Hamer, D. H. (1994). Evidence for a biological influence in male homosexuality. *Scientific American, 270,* 44–49. [9]

Levenson, R. W. (1992). Autonomic nervous system differences among emotions. *Psychological Science, 3,* 23–27. [9]

Levenson, R. W., Carstensen, L. L., & Gottman, J. M. (1993). Long-term marriage: Age, gender, and satisfaction. *Psychology and Aging, 8,* 301–313. [8]

Levenson, R. W., Ekman, P., & Friesen, W. (1990). Voluntary facial action generates emotion-specific autonomic nervous system activity. *Psychophysiology, 27,* 363–385. [9]

Levitt, E. E., & Duckworth, J. C. (1984). Minnesota Multiphasic Personality Inventory. In D. J. Keyser & R. C. Sweetland (Eds.), *Test critiques* (Vol. 1, pp. 466–472). Kansas City: Test Corporation of America. [11]

Levy-Shiff, R., Lerman, M., Har-Even, D., & Hod, M. (2002). Maternal adjustment and infant outcome in medically defined high-risk pregnancy. *Developmental Psychology, 38,* 93–103. [8]

Lewinsohn, P. M., & Rosenbaum, M. (1987). Recall of parental behavior by acute depressives, remitted depressives, and nondepressives. *Journal of Personality and Social Psychology, 52,* 611–619. [6]

Lewis, D. O., Pincus, J. H., Feldman, M., Jackson, L., & Bard, B. (1986). Psychiatric, neurological, and psychoeducational characteristics of 15 death row inmates in the United States. *American Journal of Psychiatry, 143,* 838–845. [14]

Lewis, M. (1995, January/February). Self-conscious emotions. *American Scientist, 83,* 68–78. [9]

Leyens, J-P., Yzerbyt, V., & Olivier, C. (1996). The role of applicability in the emergence of the overattribution bias. *Journal of Personality and Social Psychology, 70,* 219–229. [14]

Lidz, C., & Macrine, S. (2001). An alternative approach to the identification of gifted culturally and linguistically diverse learners: The contribution of dynamic assessment. *School Psychology International, 22,* 74–96. [7]

Lieblum, S. (2002). After sildenafil: Bridging the gap between pharmacologic treatment and satisfying sexual relationships. *Journal of Clinical Psychiatry, 63,* 17–22. [12]

Lijtmaer, R. (2001). Splitting and nostalgia in recent immigrants: Psychodynamic considerations. *Journal of the American Academy of Psychoanalysis, 29,* 427–438. [13]

Lim, V. (2002). The IT way of loafing on the job: Cyberloafing, neutralizing and organizational justice. *Journal of Organizational Behavior, 23,* 675–694. [14]

Lindenberger, U., Mayr, U., & Kliegl, R. (1993). Speed and intelligence in old age. *Psychology and Aging, 8,* 207–220. [8]

Linn, M. C., & Hyde, J. S. (1989). Gender, mathematics, and science. *Educational Researcher, 18,* 17–27. [7]

Linn, M. C., & Peterson, A. C. (1985). Emergence and characterization of sex differences in spatial ability: A meta-analysis. *Child Development, 56,* 1479–1498. [7]

Linn, R. L. (1982). Ability testing: Individual differences, prediction, and differential prediction. In A. K. Wigdor & W. R. Garner (Eds.), *Ability testing: Uses, consequences, and controversies* (Part II). Washington, DC: National Academy Press. [7]

Linszen, D. H., Dingemans, P. M., Nugter, M. A., Van der Does, J. W., Scholte, W. F., & Lenior, M. A. (1997). Patient attributes and expressed emotion as risk factors for psychotic relapse. *Schizophrenia Bulletin, 23,* 119–130. [13]

Linville, P. W., Fischer, G. W., & Salovey, P. (1989). Perceived distributions of the characteristics of in-group and out-group members: Empirical evidence and a computer simulation. *Journal of Personality and Social Psychology, 57,* 165–188. [14]

Lishman, W. A. (1990). Alcohol and the brain. *British Journal of Psychiatry, 156,* 635–644. [10]

Little, R. E., Anderson, K. W., Ervin, C. H., Worthington-Roberts, B., & Clarren, S. K. (1989). Maternal alcohol use during breast-feeding and infant mental and motor development at one year. *New England Journal of Medicine, 321,* 425–430. [8]

Loeber, R., & Hay, D. (1997). Key issues in the development of aggression and violence from childhood to early adulthood. *Annual Review of Psychology, 48,* 371–410. [14]

Loehlin, J. C. (1992). *The limits of family influence: Genes, experience, and behavior.* New York: Guilford. [11]

Loehlin, J. C., Horn, J. M., & Willerman, L. (1990). Heredity, environment, and personality change: Evidence from the Texas Adoption Project. *Journal of Personality, 58,* 221–243. [11]

Loehlin, J. C., Willerman, L., & Horn, J. M. (1987). Personality resemblance in adoptive families: A 10-year follow-up. *Journal of Personality and Social Psychology, 53,* 961–969. [11]

Loehlin, J. C., Willerman, L., & Horn, J. M. (1988). Human behavior genetics. *Annual Review of Psychology, 39,* 101–133. [11]

Loftus, E. F. (1979). *Eyewitness testimony.* Cambridge, MA: Harvard University Press. [6]

Loftus, E. F. (1984, February). Eyewitnesses: Essential but unreliable. *Psychology Today,* pp. 22–27. [6]

Loftus, E. F. (1993a). Psychologists in the eyewitness world. *American Psychologist, 48,* 550–552. [6]

Loftus, E. F. (1993b). The reality of repressed memories. *American Psychologist, 48,* 518–537. [6]

Loftus, E. F. (1997). Creating false memories. *Scientific American, 277,* 71–75. [6]

Loftus, E. F., & Hoffman, H. G. (1989). Misinformation and memory: The creation of new memories. *Journal of Experimental Psychology: General, 118,* 100–104. [6]

Loftus, E. F., & Loftus, G. R. (1980). On the permanence of stored information in the human brain. *American Psychologist, 35,* 409–420. [6]

Loftus, E. F., & Pickrell, J. (1995). The formation of false memories. *Psychiatric Annals, 25,* 720–725. [6]

London, E. D., Ernst, M., Grant, S., Bonson, K., & Weinstein, A. (2000). Orbitofrontal cortex and human drug abuse: Functional imaging. *Cerebral Cortex, 10,* 334–342. [5]

Long, D., & Baynes, K. (2002). Discourse representation in the two cerebral hemispheres. *Journal of Cognitive Neuroscience, 14,* 228–242. [2]

Long, G. M., & Crambert, R. F. (1990). The nature and basis of age-related changes in dynamic visual acuity. *Psychology and Aging, 5,* 138–143. [8]

Lopez, J. C. (2000). Shaky memories in indelible ink. *Nature Reviews Neuroscience, 1,* 6–7. [6]

Lott, B., & Saxon, S. (2002). The influence of ethnicity, social class and context on judgments about U.S. women. *Journal of Social Psychology, 142,* 481–499. [14]

Lotze, M., Montoya, P., Erb, M., Hulsmann, E., Flor, H., Klose, U., Birbaumer, N., & Grodd, W. (1999). Activation of cortical and cerebellar motor areas during executed and imagined hand movements: An fMRI study. *Journal of Cognitive Neuroscience, 11,* 491–501. [7]

Lubinsky, D., & Benbow, C. P. (1992). Gender differences in abilities and preferences among the gifted: Implications for the math science pipeline. *Current Directions in Psychological Science, 1,* 61–66. [7]

Lubman, D. I., Peters, L. A., Mogg, K., Bradley, B. P., & Deakin, J. F. (2000). Attentional bias for drug cues in opiate dependence. *Psychological Medicine, 30,* 169–175. [4]

Luchins, A. S. (1957). Experimental attempts to minimize the impact of first impressions. In C. I. Hovland (Ed.), *Yale studies in attitude and communication: Vol. 1. The order of presentation in persuasion* (pp. 62–75). New Haven, CT: Yale University Press. [14]

Luciano, M., Wright, M., Smith, G., Geffen, G., Geffen, L., & Martin, N. (2001). Genetic covariance among measures of information processing speed, working memory, and IQ. *Behavior Genetics, 31,* 581–592. [7]

Luciano, M., Wright, M., Smith, G., Geffen, G., Geffen, L., & Martin, N. (2003). Genetic covariance between processing speed and IQ. In R. Plomin, J. DeFries, I. Craig, & P. McGuffin (Eds.), *Behavioral genetics in the postgenomic era* (pp. 163–182). Washington, DC: American Psychological Association. [7]

Lucio, E., Reyes-Lagunes, I., & Scott, R. L. (1994). MMPI-2 for Mexico: Translation and adaptation. *Journal of Personality Assessment, 63,* 105–116. [11]

Lummis, M., & Stevenson, H. W. (1990). Gender differences in beliefs about achievement: A cross-cultural study. *Developmental Psychology, 26,* 254–263. [7]

Lustig, C., & Hasher, L. (2002). Working memory span: The effect of prior learning. *American Journal of Psychology, 115,* 89–101. [6]

Luu, P., Tucker, D., Derryberry, D., Reed, M., & Paulsen, C. (2003). Electrophysiological responses to errors and feedback in the process of action regulation. *Psychological Science, 14,* 47–53. [2]

Lydiard, R. B., Brawman-Mintzer, O., & Ballenger, J. C. (1996). Recent developments in the psychopharmacology of anxiety disorders. *Journal of Consulting and Clinical Psychology, 64,* 660–668. [13]

Lyketsos, C. G., Chen, L-S., & Anthony, J. C. (1999). Cognitive decline in adulthood: An 11.5-year follow-up of the Baltimore Epidemiologic Catchment Area Study. *American Journal of Psychiatry, 156,* 56–58. [8]

Lynn, S. J., Kirsch, I., Barabasz, A., Cardena, E., & Patterson, D. (2000). Hypnosis as an empirically supported clinical intervention: The state of the evidence and a look to the future. *International Journal of Clinical Experimental Hypnosis, 48,* 239–259. [4]

Lynn, S. J., & Nash, M. R. (1994). Truth in memory: Ramifications for psychotherapy and hypnotherapy. *American Journal of Clinical Hypnosis, 36,* 194–208. [4]

Lyvers, M. (2000). "Loss of control" in alcoholism and drug addiction: A neuroscientific interpretation. *Experimental and Clinical Psychopharmacology, 8,* 225–245. [4]

Lyvers, M. (2000). Cognition, emotion, and the alcohol–aggression relationship: Comment on Giancola. *Experimental Clinical Psychopharmacology, 8,* 612–617. [14]

Maccoby, E. E., & Martin, J. A. (1983). Socialization in the context of the family: Parent-child interaction. In P. H. Mussen (Ed.), *Handbook of child psychology* (4th ed., Vol. 4). New York: John Wiley. [8]

Macrae, C. N., Milne, A. B., & Bodenhausen, G. V. (1994). Stereotypes as energy-saving devices: A peek inside the cognitive toolbox. *Journal of Personality and Social Psychology, 66,* 37–47. [14]

Maguire, E. A., Gadian, D. G., Johnsrude, I. S., Good, C. D., Ashburner, J., Frackowiak, R. S. J., & Frith, C. D. (2000). Navigation-related structural change in the hippocampi of taxi drivers. *Proceedings of the National Academy of Science, 97,* 4398–4403. [6]

Maier, S. F., & Laudenslager, M. (1985, August). Stress and health: Exploring the links. *Psychology Today,* pp. 44–49. [10]

Main, M., & Solomon, J. (1990). Procedures for identifying infants as disorganized/disoriented during the Ainsworth Strange Situation. In M. Greenberg, D. Cicchetti, & M. Cummings (Eds.), *Attachment in the preschool years: Theory, research, and intervention* (pp. 121–160). Chicago: University of Chicago Press. [8]

Malkoff, S. B., Muldoon, M. F., Zeigler, Z. R., & Manuck, S. B. (1993). Blood platelet responsivity to acute mental stress. *Psychosomatic Medicine, 55,* 477–482. [10]

Manderscheid, R., & Henderson, M. (2001). *Mental health, United States, 2000* [Online version]. Rockville, MD: Center for Mental Health Services. Retrieved January 14, 2003, from http://www.mentalhealth.org/publications/allpubs/SMA01-3537/ [13]

Mandler, J. M. (1990). A new perspective on cognitive development in infancy. *American Scientist, 78*(3), 236–243. [8]

Manhal-Baugus, M. (2001). E-therapy: Practical, ethical, and legal issues. *CyberPsychology and Behavior, 4,* 551–563. [13]

Manly, T., Lewis, G., Robertson, I., Watson, P., & Datta, A. (2002). Coffee in the cornflakes: Time-of-day as a modulator of executive response control. *Neuropsychologia, 40,* 1–6. [4]

Manton, K. G., Siegler, I. C., & Woodbury, M. A. (1986). Patterns of intellectual development in later life. *Journal of Gerontology, 41,* 486–499. [8]

Manzardo, A., Stein, L., & Belluzi, J. (2002). Rats prefer cocaine over nicotine in a two-level self-administration choice test. *Brain Research, 924,* 10–19. [4]

Marcus, G. F. (1996). Why do children say "breaked"? *Current Directions in Psychological Science, 5,* 81–85. [8]

Marder, S. R. (1996). Clinical experience with risperidone. *Journal of Clinical Psychiatry, 57*(9, Suppl.), 57–61. [13]

Marín, G. (1994). The experience of being a Hispanic in the United States. In W. J. Lonner & R. Malpass (Eds.), *Psychology and culture* (pp. 23–27). Boston: Allyn & Bacon. [11]

Markovic, B. M., Dimitrijevic, M., & Jankovic, B. D. (1993). Immunomodulation by conditioning: Recent developments. *International Journal of Neuroscience, 71,* 231–249. [5]

Marks, I. (1987). The development of normal fear: A review. *Journal of Child Psychology and Psychiatry, 28,* 667–697. [8]

Marks, I. M. (1972). Flooding (implosion) and allied treatments. In W. S. Agras (Ed.), *Behavior modification.* New York: Little, Brown. [13]

Marshall, G. D., & Zimbardo, P. G. (1979). Affective consequences of inadequately explained physiological arousal. *Journal of Personality and Social Psychology, 37,* 970–988. [9]

Marshall, J. R. (1997). Alcohol and substance abuse in panic disorder. *Journal of Clinical Psychiatry, 58*(2, Suppl.), 46–49. [12]

Marshall, R. D., Schneier, F. R., Fallon, B. A., Feerick, J., & Liebowitz, M. R. (1994). Medication therapy for social phobia. *Journal of Clinical Psychiatry, 56*(6, Suppl.), 33–37. [13]

Marshall, W. L., & Segal, Z. (1988). Behavior therapy. In C. G. Last & M. Hersen (Eds.), *Handbook of anxiety disorders* (pp. 338–361). New York: Pergamon. [13]

Martikainen, P., & Valkonen, R. (1996). Mortality after the death of a spouse: Rates and causes of death in a large Finnish cohort. *American Journal of Public Health, 86,* 1087–1093. [8]

Martin, C. L., & Little, J. K. (1990). The relation of gender understanding to children's sex-typed preferences and gender stereotypes. *Child Development, 61,* 1427–1439. [8]

Martinez, C. (1986). Hispanics: Psychiatric issues. In C. B. Wilkinson (Ed.), *Ethnic psychiatry* (pp. 61–88). New York: Plenum. [13]

Martinez, J. L., Jr., & Derrick, B. E. (1996). Long-term potentiation and learning. *Annual Review of Psychology, 47,* 173–203. [6]

Martinez-Taboas, A. (1991). Multiple personality in Puerto Rico: Analysis of fifteen cases. *Dissociation, 4,* 189–192. [12]

Masataka, N. (1996). Perception of motherese in a signed language by 6-month-old deaf infants. *Developmental Psychology, 32,* 874–879. [8]

Masland, R. H. (1996). Unscrambling color vision. *Science, 271,* 616–617. [3]

Maslow, A. H. (1970). *Motivation and personality* (2nd ed.). New York: Harper & Row. [9]

Masters, W. H., & Johnson, V. E. (1966). *Human sexual response.* Boston: Little, Brown. [8, 9]

Masters, W. H., & Johnson, V. E. (1975). *The pleasure bond: A new look at sexuality and commitment.* Boston: Little, Brown. [9]

Matlin, M. W. (1989). *Cognition* (2nd ed.). New York: Holt, Rinehart & Winston. [6]

Matlin, M. W., & Foley, H. J. (1997). *Sensation and perception* (4th ed.). Boston: Allyn & Bacon. [3]

Matsunami, H., Montmayeur, J-P., & Buck, L. B. (2000). A family of candidate taste receptors in human and mouse. *Nature, 404,* 601–604. [3]

Matthews, K. A. (1992). Myths and realities of the menopause. *Psychosomatic Medicine, 54,* 1–9. [8]

Mayo Clinic. (1997, July). Coffee: What's the scoop on its health effects? *Mayo Clinic Health Letter.* [4]

Mazur, J. E. (1993). Predicting the strength of a conditioned reinforcer: Effects of delay and uncertainty. *Current Directions in Psychological Science, 2*(3), 70–74. [5]

McAdams, D. P. (1992). The five-factor model in personality: A critical appraisal. *Journal of Personality, 60,* 329–361. [11]

McAnulty, R. D., & Burnette, M. M. (2001). *Exploring human sexuality: Making healthy decisions* (pp. 144-150). Boston: Allyn & Bacon. [8]

McCann, U. D., Mertl, M., Eligulashvili, V., & Ricaurte, G. A. (1999). Cognitive performance in $(+/-)$ 3,4-methylenedioxymethamphetamine (MDMA, "ecstasy") users: A controlled study. *Psychopharmacology, 143,* 417–425. [4]

McCarthy, P. (1989, March). Ageless sex. *Psychology Today*, p. 62. [8]

McCartney, K., Harris, M. J., & Bernieri, F. (1990). Growing up and growing apart: A developmental meta-analysis of twin studies. *Psychological Bulletin, 107,* 226–237. [8]

McClearn, G. E., Johansson, B., Berg, S., Pedersen, N. L., Ahern, F., Petrill, S. A., & Plomin, R. (1997). Substantial genetic influence on cognitive abilities in twins 80 or more years old. *Science, 276,* 1560–1563. [7]

McClelland, D. C. (1958). Methods of measuring human motivation. In J. W. Atkinson (Ed.), *Motives in fantasy, action and society: A method of assessment and study.* Princeton, NJ: Van Nostrand. [9]

McClelland, D. C. (1961). *The achieving society.* Princeton, NJ: Van Nostrand. [9]

McClelland, D. C. (1985). *Human motivation.* New York: Cambridge University Press. [9]

McClelland, D. C., Atkinson, J. W., Clark, R. W., & Lowell, E. L. (1953). *The achievement motive.* New York: Appleton-Century-Crofts. [9]

McClelland, D. C., & Pilon, D. A. (1983). Sources of adult motives in patterns of parent behavior in early childhood. *Journal of Personality and Social Psychology, 44,* 564–574. [9]

McCormack, L., & Mellor, D. (2002). The role of personality in leadership: An application of the five-factor model in the Australian military. *Military Psychology, 14,* 179–197. [11]

McCormick, C. B., & Kennedy, J. H. (2000). Father-child separation, retrospective and current views of attachment relationship with father and self-esteem in late adolescence. *Psychological Reports, 86,* 827–834. [8]

McCrae, R. (1984). Situational determinants of coping responses: Loss, threat, and challenge. *Journal of Personality and Social Psychology, 46,* 919–928. [10]

McCrae, R. (2002). The maturation of personality psychology: Adult personality development and psychological well-being. *Journal of Research in Personality, 36,* 307–317. [11]

McCrae, R. R. (1993). Moderated analyses of longitudinal personality stability. *Journal of Personality and Social Psychology, 65,* 577–583. [11]

McCrae, R. R. (1996). Social consequences of experiential openness. *Psychological Bulletin, 120,* 323–337. [11]

McCrae, R. R., & Costa, P. T., Jr. (1987). Validation of the five-factor model of personality across instruments and observers. *Journal of Personality and Social Psychology, 52,* 81–90. [11]

McCrae, R. R., & Costa, P. T., Jr. (1990). *Personality in adulthood.* New York: Guilford. [11]

McCrae, R. R., Costa, P. T., Jr., Ostendorf, F., Angleitner, A., Hrebickova, M., Avia, S. J., Sanchez-Bernardos, M. L., Kusdil, M. E., Woodfield, R., Saunders, P. R., & Smith, P. B. (2000). Nature over nurture: Temperament, personality, and life span development. *Journal of Personality & Social Psychology, 78,* 173–186. [11]

McCue, J. M., Link, K. L., Eaton, S. S., & Freed, B. M. (2000). Exposure to cigarette tar inhibits ribonucleotide reductase and blocks lymphocyte proliferation. *Journal of Immunology, 165,* 6771–6775. [10]

McCullough, M. E., Hoyt, W. T., Larson, D. B., Koenig, H. G., & Thoresen, C. (2000). Religious involvement and mortality: A meta-analytic review. *Health Psychology, 19,* 211–222. [10]

McDonald, A. D., Armstrong, B. G., & Sloan, M. (1992). Cigarette, alcohol, and coffee consumption and prematurity. *American Journal of Public Health, 82,* 87–90. [8]

McDonald, C., & Murray, R. M. (2000). Early and late environmental risk factors for schizophrenia. *Brain Research Reviews, 31,* 130–137. [12]

McDonald, J. L. (1997). Language acquisition: The acquisition of linguistic structure in normal and special populations. *Annual Review of Psychology, 48,* 215–241. [7]

McDowell, C., & Acklin, M. W. (1996). Standardizing procedures for calculating Rorschach interrater reliability: Conceptual and empirical foundations. *Journal of Personality Assessment, 66,* 308–320. [11]

McElree, B., Jia, G., & Litvak, A. (2000). The time course of conceptual processing in three bilingual populations. *Journal of Memory & Language, 42,* 229–254. [7]

McGlashan, T. H., & Hoffman, R. E. (2000). Schizophrenia as a disorder of developmentally reduced synaptic connectivity. *Archives of General Psychiatry, 57,* 637–648. [12]

McGue, M., Bouchard, T. J., Jr., Iacono, W. G., & Lykken, D. T. (1993). Behavioral genetics of cognitive ability: A life-span perspective. In R. Plomin & G. E. McClearn (Eds.), *Nature, nurture and psychology* (pp. 59–76). Washington, DC: American Psychological Association. [8]

McGuinness, D. (1993). Gender differences in cognitive style: Implications for mathematics performance and achievement. In I. A. Penner, G. M. Batsche, H. M. Knoff, & D. L. Nelson (Eds.), *The challenge of mathematics and science education: Psychology's response.* Washington, DC: American Psychological Association. [9]

McGuire, W. J. (1985). Attitudes and attitude change. In G. Lindzey & E. Aronson (Ed.), *Handbook of social psychology* (Vol. 2, 3rd ed.). New York: Random House. [14]

McIntyre, C., Pal, S., Marriott, L., & Gold, P. (2002). Competition between memory systems: Acetylcholine release in the hippocampus correlates negatively with good performance on an amygdala-dependent task. *Journal of Neuroscience, 22,* 1171–1176. [2]

McKay, H., Glasgow, R., Feil, E., Boles, S., & Barrera, M. (2002). Internet-based diabetes self-management and support: Initial outcomes from the diabetes network project. *Rehabilitation Psychology, 47,* 31–48. [10]

McKellar, P. (1972). Imagery from the standpoint of introspection. In P. W. Sheehan (Ed.), *The function and nature of imagery* (pp. 36–63). New York: Academic Press. [7]

McKelvie, S. J. (1984). Relationship between set and functional fixedness: A replication. *Perceptual and Motor Skills, 58,* 996–998. [7]

McMellon, C., & Schiffman, L. (2002). Cybersenior empowerment: How some older individuals are taking control of their lives. *Journal of Applied Gerontology, 21,* 157–175. [10]

McNeil, T. F., Cantor-Graae, E., & Weinberger, D. R. (2000). Relationship of obstetric complications and differences in size of brain structures in monozygotic twin pairs discordant for schizophrenia. *American Journal of Psychiatry, 157,* 203–212. [12]

McReynolds, P. (1989). Diagnosis and clinical assessment: Current status and major issues. *Annual Review of Psychology, 40,* 83–108. [11]

Medina, J. H., Paladini, A. C., & Izquierdo, I. (1993). Naturally occurring benzodiazepines and benzodiazepine-like molecules in brain. *Behavioural Brain Research, 58,* 1–8. [13]

Mednick, S. A., Brennan, P., & Kandel, E. (1988). Predisposition to violence. *Aggressive Behavior, 14,* 25–33. [14]

Mednick, S. A., & Mednick, M. T. (1967). *Examiner's manual, Remote Associates Test.* Boston: Houghton-Mifflin. [7]

Meer, J. (1986, June). The age of reason. *Psychology Today,* pp. 60–64. [8]

Meeus, W., Dekovic, M., & Iedema, J. (1997). Unemployment and identity in adolescence: A social comparison perspective. *Career Development Quarterly, 45,* 369–380. [8]

Mellet, E., Tzourio-Mazoyer, N., Bricogne, S., Mazoyer, B., Dennis, M., & Kosslyn, S. M. (2000). Functional anatomy of high-resolution visual mental imagery. *Journal of Cognitive Neuroscience, 12,* 98–109. [7]

Meltzer, H. Y., Rabinowitz, J., Lee, M. A., Cola, P. A., Ranjan, R., Findling, R. L., & Thompson, P. A. (1997). Age at onset and gender of schizophrenic patients in relation to neuroleptic resistance. *American Journal of Psychiatry, 154,* 475–482. [13]

Melzack, R., & Wall, P. D. (1965). Pain mechanisms: A new theory. *Science, 150,* 971–979. [3]

Melzack, R., & Wall, P. D. (1983). *The challenge of pain.* New York: Basic Books. [3]

Merckelbach, H., Dekkers, T., Wessel, I., & Roefs, A. (2003). Dissociative symptoms and amnesia in Dutch concentration camp survivors. *Comprehensive Psychiatry, 44,* 65–69. [6]

Mertens, T. E., & Low-Beer, D. (1996). HIV and AIDS: Where is the epidemic going? *WHO Bulletin OMS, 74,* 121–128. [10]

Meyer, A. (1997, March/April). Patching up *testosterone. Psychology Today, 30,* 54–57, 66–70. [9]

Meyer, P. (1972). If Hitler asked you to electrocute a stranger, would you? In R. Greenbaum & H. A. Tilker (Eds.), *The challenge of psychology* (pp. 456–465). Englewood Cliffs, NJ: Prentice-Hall. [14]

Meyer-Bahlburg, H. F. L., Ehrhardt, A. A., Rosen, L. R., & Gruen, R. S. (1995). Prenatal estrogens and the development of homosexual orientation. *Developmental Psychology, 31,* 12–21. [9]

Michaels, J. W., Bloomel, J. M., Brocato, R. M., Linkous, R. A., & Rowe, J. S. (1982). Social facilitation and inhibition in a natural setting. *Replications in Social Psychology, 2,* 21–24. [14]

Middlebrooks, J. C., & Green, D. M. (1991). Sound localization by human listeners. *Annual Review of Psychology, 42,* 135–159. [3]

Miles, D. R., & Carey, G. (1997). Genetic and environmental architecture of human aggression. *Journal of Personality and Social Psychology, 72,* 207–217. [11, 14]

Miles, R. (1999). A homeostatic switch. *Nature, 397,* 215–216. [2]

Milgram, S. (1963). Behavioral study of obedience. *Journal of Abnormal and Social Psychology, 67,* 371–378. [14]

Milgram, S. (1965). Liberating effects of group pressure. *Journal of Personality and Social Psychology, 1,* 127–134. [14]

Miller, B., Norton, M., Curtis, T., Hill, E., Schvaneveldt, P., & Young, M. (1998). The timing of sexual intercourse among adolescents: Family, peer, and other antecedents: Erratum. *Youth & Society, 29,* 390. [8]

Miller, E. M. (2000). Homosexuality, birth order, and evolution: Toward an equilibrium reproductive economics of homosexuality. *Archives of Sexual Behavior, 29,* 11–34. [9]

Miller, G., Cohen, S., & Ritchey, A. (2002). Chronic psychological stress and the regulation of pro-inflammatory cytokines: A glucocorticoid-resistance model. *Health Psychology, 21,* 531–541. [10]

Miller, G. A. (1956). The magical number seven, plus or minus two: Some limits on our capacity for processing information. *Psychological Review, 63,* 81–97. [6]

Miller, J. G., Bersoff, D. M., & Harwood, R. L. (1990). Perceptions of social responsibilities in India and in the United States: Moral imperatives or personal decisions? *Journal of Personality and Social Psychology, 58,* 33–47. [14]

Miller, L. (1989, November). What biofeedback does (and doesn't) do. *Psychology Today,* pp. 22–23. [5]

Miller, N. E. (1941). The frustration-aggression hypothesis. *Psychological Review, 48,* 337–342. [14]

Miller, N. E. (1985, February). Rx: Biofeedback. *Psychology Today,* pp. 54–59. [5]

Miller, N. S., & Gold, M. S. (1994). LSD and Ecstasy: Pharmacology, phenomenology, and treatment. *Psychiatric Annals, 24,* 131–133. [4]

Miller, T. Q., Smith, T. W., Turner, C. W., Guijarro, M. L., & Hallet, A. J. (1996). A meta-analytic review of research on hostility and physical health. *Psychological Bulletin, 119,* 322–348. [10]

Miller, T. Q., Turner, C. W., Tindale, R. S., Posavac, E. J., & Dugoni, B. L. (1991). Reasons for the trend toward null findings in research on Type A behavior. *Psychological Bulletin, 110,* 469–485. [10]

Miller, W. C., Lindeman, A. K., Wallace, J., & Niederpruem, M. (1990). Diet composition, energy intake, and exercise in relation to body fat in men and women. *American Journal of Clinical Nutrition, 52,* 426–430. [9]

Millman, R. B., & Beeder, A. B. (1994). The new psychedelic culture: LSD, Ecstasy, "rave" parties and The Grateful Dead. *Psychiatric Annals, 24,* 148–150. [4]

Milner, B. (1970). Memory and the medial temporal regions of the brain. In K. H. Pribram & D. E. Broadbent (Eds.), *Biology of memory.* New York: Academic Press. [6]

Milner, B., Corkin, S., & Teuber, H. L. (1968). Further analysis of the hippocampal amnesic syndrome: 14-year follow-up study of H. M. *Neuropsychologia, 6,* 215–234. [6]

Milner, B. R. (1966). Amnesia following operation on the temporal lobes. In C. W. M. Whitty & O. L. Zangwill (Eds.), *Amnesia* (pp. 109–133). London: Butterworth. [6]

Milos, G., Spindler, A., Ruggiero, G., Klaghofer, R., & Schnyder, U. (2002). Comorbidity of obsessive-compulsive disorders and duration of eating disorders. *International Journal of Eating Disorders, 31,* 284–289. [9]

Mischel, W. (1966). A social-learning view of sex differences in behavior. In E. E. Maccoby (Ed.), *The development of sex differences* (pp. 56–81). Stanford, CA: Stanford University Press. [8]

Mischel, W. (1968). *Personality and assessment.* New York: Wiley. [11]

Mischel, W. (1973). Toward a cognitive social learning reconceptualization of personality. *Psychological Review, 80,* 252–283. [11]

Mischel, W. (1977). The interaction of person and situation. In D. Magnusson & N. S. Endler (Eds.), *Personality at the crossroads: Current issues in interactional psychology.* Hillsdale, NJ: Lawrence Erlbaum. [11]

Mishra, R. (1997). Cognition and cognitive development. In J. Berry, P. Dasen, & T. Saraswathi (Eds.), *Handbook of cross-cultural psychology* (Vol. 2, pp. 143–176). Boston: Allyn & Bacon. [8]

Mishra, R., & Singh, T. (1992). Memories of Asur children for locations and pairs of pictures. *Psychological Studies, 37,* 38–46. [6]

Mistry, J., & Rogoff, B. (1994). Remembering in cultural context. In W. J. Lonner & R. Malpass (Eds.), *Psychology and culture* (pp. 139–144). Boston: Allyn & Bacon. [6]

Mitler, M. M., Aldrich, M. S., Koob, G. F., & Zarcone, V. P. (1994). Narcolepsy and its treatment with stimulants. *Sleep, 17,* 352–371. [4]

Mitsis, E. M., Halperin, J. M., & Newcorn, J. H. (2000). Serotonin and aggression in children. *Current Psychiatry Reports, 2,* 95–101. [14]

Modestin, J. (1992). Multiple personality disorder in Switzerland. *American Journal of Psychiatry, 148,* 88–92. [12]

Moffitt, T. E., Caspi, A., Harkness, A. R., & Silva, P. A. (1993). The natural history of change in intellectual performance: Who changes? How much? Is it meaningful? *Journal of Child Psychology and Psychiatry, 34,* 455–506. [7]

Mohanty, A., & Perregaux, C. (1997). Language acquisition and bilingualism. In J. Berry, P. Dasen, & T. Saraswathi (Eds.), *Handbook of cross-cultural psychology. Vol. 2: Basic processes and human development.* Boston: Allyn & Bacon. [7]

Moldofsky, H., Gilbert, R., Lue, F. A., & MacLean, A. W. (1995). Sleep-related violence. *Sleep, 18,* 731–739. [4]

Money, J., & Schwartz, M. (1977). Dating, romantic and nonromantic friendships, and sexuality in 17 early-treated adrenogenital females, aged 16–25. In P. A. Lee et al. (Eds.), *Congenital adrenal hyperplasia.* Baltimore: University Park Press. [9]

Montejo, A., Llorca, G., Izquierdo, J., & Rico-Villademoros, F. (2001). Incidence of sexual dysfunction associated with antidepressant agents: A prospective multicenter study of 1022 outpatients. *Journal of Clinical Psychiatry, 62,* 10–21. [12]

Moore-Ede, M. (1993). *The twenty-four hour society.* Reading, MA: Addison-Wesley. [4]

Montgomery, G., Weltz, C., Seltz, M., & Bovbjerg, D. (2002). Brief presurgery hypnosis reduces distress and pain in excisional breast biopsy patients. *International Journal of Clinical & Experimental Hypnosis, 50,* 17–32. [4]

Montoya, A. G., Sorrentino, R., Lukas, S. E., & Price, B. H. (2002). Long-term neuropsychiatric consequences of "ecstasy" (MDMA): A review. *Harvard Review of Psychiatry 10(4),* 212–220. [4]

Moran, M. G., & Stoudemire, A. (1992). Sleep disorders in the medically ill patient. *Journal of Clinical Psychiatry, 53*(6, Suppl.), 29–36. [4]

Morgan, C. D., & Murray, H. A. (1935). A method for investigating fantasies: The Thematic Apperception Test. *Archives of Neurology and Psychiatry, 34,* 289–306. [11]

Morgan, C. D., & Murray, H. A. (1962). Thematic Apperception Test. 530–545. In H. A. Murray et al. (Eds.), *Explorations in personality: A clinical and experimental study of fifty men of college age.* New York: Science Editions. [11]

Morgan, C. L. (1996). Odors as cues for the recall of words unrelated to odor. *Perceptual and Motor Skills, 83,* 1227–1234. [6]

Morgan, M. J. (1999). Memory deficits associated with recreational use of ecstasy (MDMA). *Psychopharmacology, 141,* 30–36. [4]

Morgan, R., & Flora, D. (2002). Group psychotherapy with incarcerated offenders: A research synthesis. *Group Dynamics: Theory, Research, and Practice, 6,* 203–218. [13]

Morgan, R. E., Levitsky, D. A., & Strupp, B. J. (2000). Effects of chronic lead exposure on learning and reaction time in a visual discrimination task. *Neurotoxicology and Teratology, 22,* 337–345. [7]

Morin, C. M., & Wooten, V. (1996). Psychological and pharmacological approaches to treating insomnia: Critical issues in assessing their separate and combined effects. *Clinical Psychology Review, 16,* 521–542. [4]

Morofushi, M., Shinohara, K., Funabashi, T., & Kimnura, F. (2000). Positive relationship between menstrual synchrony and ability to smell 5alpha-androst-16-en-3alpha-ol. *Chemical Senses, 25,* 407–411. [3]

Morofushi, M., Shinohara, K., & Kimura, F. (2001). Menstrual and circadian variations in time perceptions in healthy women and women with premenstrual syndrome. *Neuroscience Research, 41,* 339–344. [4]

Morrison, A. M., & Von Glinow, M. S. (1990). Women and minorities in management. *American Psychologist, 45,* 200–208. [14]

Morrison, P., Allardyce, J., & McKane, J. (2002). Fear knot: Neurobiological disruption of long-term memory. *British Journal of Psychiatry, 180,* 195–197. [6]

Morrow, B. A., Roth, R. H., & Elsworth, J. D. (2000). TMT, a predator odor, elevates mesoprefrontal dopamine metabolic activity and disrupts short-term working memory in the rat. *Brain Research Bulletin, 52,* 519–523. [6]

Mościcki, E. K. (1995). Epidemiology of suicidal behavior. *Suicide and Life-Threatening Behavior, 25,* 22–31. [12]

Mourtazaev, M. S., Kemp, B., Zwinderman, A. H., & Kamphuisen, H. A. C. (1995). Age and gender affect different characteristics of slow waves in the sleep EEG. *Sleep, 18,* 557–564. [4]

Mui, A. C. (1992). Caregiver strain among black and white daughter caregivers: A role theory perspective. *The Gerontologist, 32,* 203–212. [8]

Mukerjee, M. (1997). Trends in animal research. *Scientific American, 276,* 86–93. [1]

Muller, L. (2002). Group counseling for African American males: When all you have are European American counselors. *Journal for Specialists in Group Work, 27,* 299–313. [13]

Mumtaz, S., & Humphreys, G. (2002). The effect of Urdu vocabulary size on the acquisition of single word reading in English. *Educational Psychology, 22,* 165–190. [8]

Munarriz, R., Talakoub, L., Flaherty, E., Gioia, M., Hoag, L., Kim, N., Traish, A., Goldstein, I., Guay, A., & Spark, R. (2002). Androgen replacement therapy with dehydroepiandrosterone for androgen insufficiency and female sexual dysfunction: Androgen and questionnaire results. *Journal of Sex & Marital Therapy, 28,* 165–173. [12]

Munroe, R. H., Shimmin, H. S., & Munroe, R. L. (1984). Gender role understanding and sex role preference in four cultures. *Developmental Psychology, 20,* 673–682. [8]

Murray, H. (1938). *Explorations in personality.* New York: Oxford University Press. [9, 11]

Murray, H. A. (1965). Uses of the Thematic Apperception Test. In B. I. Murstein (Ed.), *Handbook of projective techniques* (pp. 425–432). New York: Basic Books. [11]

Murray, K., & Abeles, N. (2002). Nicotine's effect on neural and cognitive functioning in an aging population. *Aging & Mental Health, 6,* 129–138. [8]

Myers, D. A. (1992). *The pursuit of happiness: Discovering the pathway to fulfillment, well-being, and enduring personal joy.* New York: Avon. [9]

Myers, D. G., & Bishop, G. D. (1970). Discussion effects on racial attitudes. *Science, 169,* 778–779. [14]

Myers, D. G., & Lamm, H. (1975). The polarizing effect of group discussion. *American Scientist, 63,* 297–303. [14]

Nader, K., Schafe, G. E., & Le Doux, J. E. (2000). Fear memories require protein synthesis in the amygdala for reconsolidation after retrieval. 722–726. [6]

Nadon, R., Hoyt, I. P., Register, P. A., & Kilstrom, J. F. (1991). Absorption and hypnotizability: Context effects reexamined. *Journal of Personality and Social Psychology, 60,* 144–153. [4]

Nash, J. M. (1997, March 24). Gift of love. *Time,* pp. 80–82. [8]

Nash, M., & Baker, E. (1984, February). Trance encounters: Susceptibility to hypnosis. *Psychology Today,* pp. 18, 72–73. [4]

Nathans, J. (1989). The genes for color vision. *Scientific American, 260,* 42–49. [3]

National Center for Health Statistics (NCHS). (2000, June 23. Gonorrhea–United States, 1998. *MMWR Weekly, 49,* 538–542. [10]

National Center for Health Statistics. (2000). *Health, United States, 2000 with adolescent health chartbook* [On-line]. Retrieved from http://www.cdc.gov/nchs/products/pubs/pubd/hus/huslistserv.htm [10]

National Center for Health Statistics. (2001a). Death rates for 358 selected causes, by 10-year age groups, race, and sex: United States, 1999-2000. *National Vital Statistics Report, Vol. 49,* No. 8 [Online version]. Retrieved November 10, 2002, from http://www.cdc.gov/nchs/data/dvs/VS00100.WTABLE12.pdf [12]

National Center for Health Statistics. (2001b). Deaths from Each Cause, by 5-Year Age Groups, Hispanic Origin, Race for Non-Hispanic Population, and Sex: United States, 1999-2000. *National Vital Statistics Report, Vol. 49,* No. 11 [Online version]. Retrieved November 10, 2002, from http://www.cdc.gov/nchs/fastats/pdf/nvsr49_11tb2.pdf [12]

National Center for Health Statistics. (2002a). Deaths, Percent of Total Deaths, and Death Rates for the 15 Leading Causes of Death in 5-year Age Groups, by Race and Sex: United States, 1999-2000. *National Vital Statistics Report, Vol. 50,* No. 16 [Online version]. Retrieved November 10, 2002, from http://www.cdc.gov/nchs/data/dvs/LCWK1_2000.pdf [12]

National Center for Health Statistics. (2002b). *Fast Stats A to Z: Mental Health* [Online fact sheet]. Retrieved November 9, 2002 from http://www.cdc.gov/nchs/fastats/mental.htm. [12]

National Institute of Mental Health (NIMH). (1999). Does this sound like you? [On-line]. Retrieved from http://www.nimh.nih.gov/soundlikeyou.htm [12]

National Institute of Mental Health. (1999c). The invisible disease–depression [On-line]. Retrieved from http://www.nimh.nih.gov/publicat/invisible.cfm [12]

National Institute of Mental Health. (2001). *The numbers count: Mental disorders in America.* Washington, DC: Author. NIMH Report No. 01-4584. [12]

National Institute on Aging. (2001). Progress report on Alzheimer's Disease: Taking the next steps. Silver Spring, MD: Alzheimer's Disease Education and Referral Center (ADEAR) of the National Institute on Aging. [8]

National Institute on Alcohol Abuse and Alcoholism (NIAAA). (2001). *Trends in alcohol-related fatal traffic crashes, United States, 1977–99.* (Surveillance report #56). Rockville MD: Author. [10]

National Research Council. (1993). *Losing generations: Adolescents in high risk settings.* Washington, DC: National Academy Press. [8]

National Safety Council. (1997). *Accident facts.* Chicago: Author. [10]

Needleman, H. L., Riess, J. A., Tobin, M. J., Biesecker, G. E., & Greenhouse, J. B. (1996). Bone lead levels and delinquent behavior. *Journal of the American Medical Association, 275,* 363–369. [14]

Neimark, E. D. (1981). Confounding with cognitive style factors: An artifact explanation for the apparent nonuniversal incidence of formal operations. In I. Sigel, D. Brodzinsky, & R. Golinkoff (Eds.), *New directions in Piagetian research and theory*. Hillsdale, NJ: Erlbaum. [8]

Neimark, J., Conway, C., & Doskoch, P. (1994, September/October). Back from the drink. *Psychology Today*, pp. 46–53. [10]

Neisser, U. (1967). *Cognitive psychology*. New York: Appleton-Century-Crofts. [6]

Neisser, U., Boodoo, G., Bouchard, T. J., Jr., Boykin, A. W., Brody, N., Ceci, S. J., Halpern, D. F., Loehlin, J. C., Perloff, R., Sternberg, R. J., & Urbina, S. (1996). Intelligence: Knowns and unknowns. *American Psychologist, 51,* 77–101. [7]

Neisser, U., & Harsch, N. (1992). Phantom flashbulbs: False recollections of hearing the news about Challenger. In E. Winograd & U. Neisser (Eds.), *Affect and accuracy in recall: Studies of "flashbulb" memories* (pp. 9–31). New York: Cambridge University Press. [6]

Neitz, J., Neitz, M., & Kainz, M. (1996). Visual pigment gene structure and the severity of color vision defects. *Science, 274,* 801–804. [3]

Nelson, J. C. (1997). Safety and tolerability of the new antidepressants. *Journal of Clinical Psychiatry, 58*(6, Suppl.), 26–31. [13]

Nestadt, G., Samuels, J., Riddle, M., Bienvenu, J., Liang, K., LaBuda, M., Walkup, J., Grados, M., & Hoehn-Saric, R. (2000). A family study of obsessive-compulsive disorder. *Archives of General Psychiatry, 57,* 358-363. [12]

Neugarten, B. L. (1968). The awareness of middle age. In B. Neugarten (Ed.), *Middle age and aging* (pp. 93–98). Chicago: University of Chicago Press. [8]

Newell, A., & Simon, H. A. (1972). *Human problem solving*. Englewood Cliffs, NJ: Prentice-Hall. [7]

Newberg, A., Alavi, A., Baime, M., Pourdehnad, M., Santanna, J., & d'Aquili, E. (2001). The measurement of regional cerebral blood flow during the complex cognitive task of meditation: A preliminary SPECT study. *Psychiatry Research: Neuroimaging, 106,* 113–122. [4]

Ng, S. H. (1990). Androcentric coding of man and his in memory by language users. *Journal of Experimental Social Psychology, 26,* 455–464. [7]

Nguyen, P. V., Abel, T., & Kandel, E. R. (1994). Requirement of a critical period of transcription for induction of a late phase of LTP. *Science, 265,* 1104–1107. [6]

Ni, W., Constable, R. T., Menci, W. E., Pugh, K. R., Fulbright, R. K., & Shaywitz, S. E. (2000). An event-related neuroimaging study distinguishing form and content in sentence processing. *Journal of Cognitive Neuroscience, 12,* 120–133. [7]

Nicholl, C. S., & Russell, R. M. (1990). Analysis of animal rights literature reveals the underlying motives of the movement: Ammunition for counter offensive by scientists. *Endocrinology, 127,* 985–989. [1]

Nickerson, R. S., & Adams, M. J. (1979). Long-term memory for a common object. *Cognitive Psychology, 11,* 287–307. [6]

Nicol, S. E., & Gottesman, I. I. (1983). Clues to the genetics and neurobiology of schizophrenia. *American Scientist, 71,* 398–404. [12]

Nisbett, R. E., & Wilson, T. D. (1977). The halo effect: Evidence for unconscious alteration of judgments. *Journal of Personality and Social Psychology, 35,* 250–256. [14]

Nogrady, H., McConkey, K. M., & Perry, C. (1985). Enhancing visual memory: Trying hypnosis, trying imagination, and trying again. *Journal of Abnormal Psychology, 94,* 195–204. [4]

Nordentoft, M., Lou, H. C., Hansen, D., Nim, J., Pryds, O., Rubin, P., & Hemmingsen, R. (1996). Intrauterine growth retardation and premature delivery: The influence of maternal smoking and psychosocial factors. *American Journal of Public Health, 86,* 347–354. [8]

Norris, F. H., & Kaniasty, K. (1996). Received and perceived social support in times of stress: A test of the social support deterioration deterrence model. *Journal of Personality and Social Psychology, 71,* 498–511. [10]

Norris, J. E., & Tindale, J. A. (1994). *Among generations: The cycle of adult relationships*. New York: Freeman. [8]

Novello, A. C. (1990). The Surgeon General's 1990 report on the health benefits of smoking cessation: Executive summary. *Morbidity and Mortality Weekly Report, 39* (No. RR–12). [10]

Nowak, M. A., & McMichael, A. J. (1995). How HIV defeats the immune system. *Scientific American, 273,* 58–65. [10]

Noyes, R., Jr., Burrows, G. D., Reich, J. H., Judd, F. K., Garvey, M. J., Norman, T. R., Cook, B. L., & Marriott, P. (1996). Diazepam versus alprazolam for the treatment of panic disorder. *Journal of Clinical Psychiatry, 57,* 344–355. [13]

Nutt, D. (2000). Treatment of depression and concomitant anxiety. European *Neuropsychopharmacology, 10* (Suppl. 4), S433–S437. [13]

O'Brien, C. P. (1996). Recent developments in the pharmacotherapy of substance abuse. *Journal of Consulting and Clinical Psychology, 64,* 677–686. [4]

O'Leary, K. D., & Smith, D. A. (1991). Marital interactions. *Annual Review of Psychology, 42,* 191–212. [14]

Oliver, J. E. (1993). Intergenerational transmission of child abuse: Rates, research, and clinical implications. *American Journal of Psychiatry, 150,* 1315–1324. [14]

Oliver, M. B., & Hyde, J. S. (1993). Gender differences in sexuality: A meta-analysis. *Psychological Bulletin, 114,* 29–51. [9]

Oller, D., Cobo-Lewis, A., & Eilers, R. (1998). Phonological translation in bilingual and monolingual children. *Applied Psycholinguistics, 19,* 259–278. [7]

O'Neil, H. (2000, September 28). A perfect witness. *St. Louis Post-Dispatch*, p. A8. [6]

Orman, M. (1996). *How to conquer public speaking fear* [Online report]. Retrieved January 7, 2003, from http://www.stress-cure.com/jobstress/speak.html [12]

Orne, M. (1983, December 12). Hypnosis "useful in medicine, dangerous in court." *U.S. News & World Report*, pp. 67–68. [4]

Öst, L-G., & Westling, B. E. (1995). Applied relaxation vs. cognitive behavior therapy in the treatment of panic disorder. *Behavior Research and Therapy, 33,* 145–158. [13]

Ostrom, T. M., Carpenter, S. L., Sedikides, C., & Li, F. (1993). Differential processing of in-group and out-group information. *Journal of Personality and Social Psychology, 64,* 21–34. [14]

Otto, M. W., Pollack, M. H., Sachs, G. S., Reiter, S. R., Meltzer-Brody, S., & Rosenbaum, J. F. (1993). Discontinuation of benzodiazepine treatment: Efficacy of cognitive-behavioral therapy for patients with panic disorder. *American Journal of Psychiatry, 150,* 1485–1490. [13]

Overmeier, J. B., & Seligman, M. E. P. (1967). Effects of inescapable shock upon subsequent escape and avoidance responding. *Journal of Comparative and Physiological Psychology, 67,* 28–33. [5]

Oyewumi, L. (1998). Jet lag and relapse of schizoaffective psychosis despite maintenance clozapine treatment. *British Journal of Psychiatry, 173,* 268. [4]

Padian, N. S. et al. (1991). Female-to-male transmission of human immunodeficiency virus. *Journal of the American Medical Association, 266,* 1664–1667. [10]

Paivio, S. C., & Greenberg, L. S. (1995). Resolving "unfinished business": Efficacy of experiential therapy using empty-chair dialogue. *Journal of Consulting and Clinical Psychology, 63,* 419–425. [13]

Palinscar, A. S., & Brown, A. L. (1984). Reciprocal teaching of comprehension-fostering and comprehension-monitoring activities. *Cognition and Instruction, 1,* 117–175. [14]

Pandolfini, C., & Bonati, M. (2002). Follow up on the quality of public oriented health information on the World Wide Web: Systematic re-evaluation. *British Medical Journal, 324,* 582–583. [10]

Pansu, P., & Gilibert, D. (2002). Effect of causal explanations on work-related judgments. *Applied Psychology: An International Review, 51,* 505–526. [14]

Papousek, I., & Schulter, G. (2002). Covariations of EEG asymmetries and emotional states indicate that activity at frontopolar locations is particularly affected by state factors. *Psychophysiology, 39,* 350–360. [9]

Paraherakis, A., Charney, D., & Gill, K. (2001). Neuropsychological functioning in substance-dependent patients. *Substance Use & Misuse, 36,* 257–271. [4]

Parke, R. D. (1977). Some effects of punishment on children's behavior—revisited. In E. M. Heterington, E. M. Ross, & R. D. Parke (Eds.), *Contemporary readings in child psychology.* New York: McGraw-Hill. [5]

Parkinson, W. L., & Weingarten, H. P. (1990). Dissociative analysis of ventromedial hypothalamic obesity syndrome. *American Journal of Physiology, 259,* 829–835. [9]

Parrott, A. C., Buchanan, T., Scholey, A. B., Heffernan, T., Ling, J., & Rodgers, J. (2002). Ecstasy/MDMA attributed problems reported by novice, moderate, and heavy recreational users. *Human Psychopharmacology 17(6),* 309–312. [4]

Partinen, M. (1994). Epidemiology of sleep disorders. In M. Kryger, T. Roth, & W. C. Dement (Eds.), *Principles and practice of sleep medicine* (pp. 437–453). Philadelphia: W.B. Saunders. [4]

Partinen, M., Hublin, C., Kaprio, J., Koskenvuo, M., & Guilleminault, C. (1994). Twin studies in narcolepsy. *Sleep, 17,* S13–S16. [4]

Parvizi, J., & Damasio, A. (2001). Consciousness and the brainstem. *Cognition, 79,* 135–159. [4]

Pastore, N. (1950). The role of arbitrariness in the frustration-aggression hypothesis. *Journal of Abnormal and Social Psychology, 47,* 728–731. [14]

Patricelli, G., Uy, J., Walsh, G., & Borgia, G. (2002). Male displays adjusted to female's response. *Nature, 415,* 279–280. [7]

Patterson, C. J. (1995). Sexual orientation and human development: An overview. *Developmental Psychology, 31,* 3–11. [9]

Patterson, J. (1998). Expressive vocabulary of bilingual toddlers: Preliminary findings. *Electronic Multicultural Journal of Communication Disorders, 1,* Retrieved April 11, 2001, from www.asha.ucf.edu/patterson.html [7]

Paul, T., Schroeter, K., Dahme, B., & Nutzinger, D. (2002). Self-injurious behavior in women with eating disorders. *American Journal of Psychiatry, 159,* 408–411. [9]

Paul, W. E. (1993). Infectious diseases and the immune system. *Scientific American, 269,* 90–99. [10]

Paulesu, E., McCrory, E., Fazio, L., Menoncello, N., Brunswick, N., Cappa, S. F., et al. (2000). A cultural effect on brain function. *Nature Neuroscience, 3,* 91–96. [7]

Paulus, P. B., Cox, V. C., & McCain, G. (1988). *Prison crowding: A psychological perspective.* New York: Springer-Verlag. [14]

Paunonen, S. V., Keinonen, M., Trzebinski, J., Forsterling, F., Grishenko-Roze, N., Kouznetsova, L., & Chan, D. W. (1996). The structure of personality in six cultures. *Journal of Cross-Cultural Psychology, 27,* 339–353. [11]

Pause, B. M., & Krauel, K. (2000). Chemosensory event-related potentials (CSERP) as a key to the psychology of odors. *International Journal of Psychophysiology, 36,* 105–122. [3]

Pavlov, I. P. (1960). *Conditioned reflexes: An investigation of the physiological activity of the cerebral cortex* (G. V. Anrep, Trans.). New York: Dover. (Original translation published 1927). [5]

Payami, H., Montee, K., & Kaye, J. (1994). Evidence for familial factors that protect against dementia and outweigh the effect of increasing age. *American Journal of Human Genetics, 54,* 650–657. [8]

Pedersen, D. M., & Wheeler, J. (1983). The Müller-Lyer illusion among Navajos. *Journal of Social Psychology, 121,* 3–6. [3]

Penfield, W. (1969). Consciousness, memory, and man's conditioned reflexes. In K. Pribram (Ed.), *On the biology of learning* (pp. 129–168). New York: Harcourt Brace Jovanovich. [6]

Penfield, W. (1975). *The mystery of the mind: A critical study of consciousness and the human brain.* Princeton, NJ: Princeton University Press. [6]

Pennisi, E. (1997). Tracing molecules that make the brain-body connection. *Science, 275,* 930–931. [10]

Pepperberg, I. M. (1991, Spring). Referential communication with an African grey parrot. *Harvard Graduate Society Newsletter,* 1–4. [7]

Pepperberg, I. M. (1994a). Numerical competence in an African gray parrot (Psittacus erithacus). *Journal of Comparative Psychology, 108,* 36–44. [7]

Pepperberg, I. M. (1994b). Vocal learning in grey parrots *(Psittacus erithacus)*: Effects of social interaction, reference, and context. *The Auk, 111,* 300–314 . [7]

Perls, F. S. (1969). *Gestalt therapy verbatim.* Lafayette, CA: Real People Press. [13]

Perls, T. T. (1995). The oldest old. *Scientific American, 272,* 70–75. [8]

Perrett, D. I., May, K. A., & Yoshikawa, S. (1994). Facial shape and judgements of female attractiveness. *Nature, 368,* 239–242. [14]

Perry, R., & Zeki, S. (2000). The neurology of saccades and covert shifts in spatial attention: An event-related fMRI study. *Brain, 123,* 2273–2288. [3]

Pert, C. B., Snowman, A. M., & Snyder, S. H. (1974). Localization of opiate receptor binding in presynaptic membranes of rat brain. *Brain Research, 70,* 184–188. [2]

Pesonen, A., Raeikkoenen, K., Keskivaara, P., & Keltikangas-Jaervinen, L. (2003). Difficult temperament in childhood and adulthood: Continuity from maternal perceptions to self-ratings over 17 years. *Personality & Individual Differences, 34,* 19–31. [11]

Peters, A., Leahu, D., Moss, M. B., & McNally, J. (1994). The effects of aging on area 46 of the frontal cortex of the rhesus monkey. *Cerebral Cortex, 6,* 621–635. [8]

Peterson, A. C. (1987, September). Those gangly years. *Psychology Today,* pp. 28–34. [8]

Peterson, I. (1993). Speech for export: Automating the translation of spoken words. *Science News, 144,* 254–255. [7]

Peterson, L. R., & Peterson, M. J. (1959). Short-term retention of individual verbal items. *Journal of Experimental Psychology, 58,* 193–198. [6]

Petri, H. L. (1996). *Motivation: Theory, research, and applications* (4th ed.). Pacific Grove, CA: Brooks/Cole. [9]

Petty, R. E., Wegener, D. T., & Fabrigar, L. R. (1997). Attitudes and attitude change. *Annual Review of Psychology, 48,* 609–647. [14]

Phillips, G. P., & Over, R. (1995). Differences between heterosexual, bisexual, and lesbian women in recalled childhood experiences. *Archives of Sexual Behavior, 24,* 1–20. [9]

Phillips, K., Fulker, D. W., Carey, G., & Nagoshi, C. T. (1988). Direct marital assortment for cognitive and personality variables. *Behavioral Genetics, 18,* 347–356. [14]

Phillips, S. T., & Ziller, R. C. (1997). Toward a theory and measure of the nature of nonprejudice. *Journal of Personality and Social Psychology, 72,* 420–434. [14]

Piaget, J. (1963). *Psychology of intelligence.* Patterson, NJ: Littlefield, Adams. [8]

Piaget, J. (1964). *Judgment and reasoning in the child.* Patterson, NJ: Littlefield, Adams. [8]

Piaget, J., & Inhelder, B. (1969). *The psychology of the child.* New York: Basic Books. [8]

Pich, E. M., Pagliusi, S. R., Tessari, M., Talabot–Ayer, D., van Huijsduijnen, R. H., & Chiamulera, C. (1997). Common neural substrates for the addictive properties of nicotine and cocaine. *Science, 275,* 83–86. [4]

Pietrzak, R., Laird, J., Stevens, D., & Thompson, N. (2002). Sex differences in human jealousy: A coordinated study of forced-choice, continuous rating scale, and physiological responses on the same subjects. *Evolution & Human Behavior, 23,* 83–94. [9]

Pigott, T. A. (1996). OCD: Where the serotonin selectivity story begins. *Journal of Clinical Psychiatry, 57(6,* Suppl.), 11–20. [12]

Pilcher, J. J., Lambert, B. J., & Huffcutt, A. I. (2000). Differential effects of permanent and rotating shifts on self-report sleep length: A meta-analytic review. *Sleep, 23,* 155–163. [4]

Pillow, D. R., Zautra, A. J., & Sandler, I. (1996). Major life events and minor stressors: Identifying mediational links in the stress process. *Journal of Personality and Social Psychology, 70,* 381–394. [10]

Pinel, J. P. L. (2000). *Biopsychology* (4th ed.). Boston: Allyn & Bacon. [2]

Pinker, S. (1994). *The language instinct: How the mind creates language.* New York: Morrow. [7]

Pittenger, D. J. (1993). The utility of the Myers-Briggs Type Indicator. *Review of Educational Research, 63,* 467–488. [11]

Pitz, G. F., & Sachs, N. J. (1984). Judgment and decision: Theory and application. *Annual Review of Psychology, 35,* 139–163. [7]

Plomin R. (2003). General cognitive ability. In R. Plomin, J. DeFries, I. Craig, & P. McGuffin (Eds.), *Behavioral genetics in the postgenomic era* (pp. 183–202). Washington, DC: American Psychological Association. [7]

Plomin, R., DeFries, J., Craig, I., & McGuffin, P. (2003). *Behavioral genetics in the postgenomic era.* Washington, DC: American Psychological Association. [12]

Plomin, R., DeFries, J. C., McClearn, G. E., & Rutter, M. (1997). *Behavioral genetics* (3rd ed.). New York: Freeman. [7]

Plomin, R., Owen, M. J., & McGuffin, P. (1994). The genetic basis of complex human behaviors. *Science, 264,* 1733–1739. [7]

Plomin, R., & Rende, R. (1991). Human behavioral genetics. *Annual Review of Psychology, 42,* 161–190. [7]

Plous, S. (1996). Attitudes toward the use of animals in psychological research and education: Results from a national survey of psychologists. *American Psychologist, 51,* 1167–1180. [1]

Plummer, D. L., & Slane S. (1996). Patterns of coping in racially stressful situations. *Journal of Black Psychology, 22,* 302–315. [10]

Pollack, R. H. (1970). Müller-Lyer illusion: Effect of age, lightness, contrast and hue. *Science, 179,* 93–94. [3]

Pontieri, F. C., Tanda, G., Orzi, F., & Di Chiara, G. (1996). Effects of nicotine on the nucleus accumbens and similarity to those of addictive drugs. *Nature, 382,* 255–257. [4]

Porjesz, B., Begleiter, H., Reich, T., Van Eerdewegh, P., Edenberg, H., Foroud, T., Goate, A., Litke, A., Chorlian, D., Stimus, A., Rice, J., Blangero, J., Almasy, L., Sorbell, J., Bauer, L., Kuperman, S., O'Connor, S., & Rohrbaugh, J. (1998). Amplitude of visual P3 event-related potential as a phenotypic marker for a predisposition to alcoholism: Preliminary results from the COGA project. *Alcoholism: Clinical & Experimental Research, 22,* 1317–1323. [10]

Porte, H. S., & Hobson, J. A. (1996). Physical motion in dreams: One measure of three theories. *Sleep, 105,* 3329–3335. [4]

Porter, F. L., Porges, S. W., & Marshall, R. E. (1988). Newborn pain cries and vagal tone: Parallel changes in response to circumcision. *Child Development, 59,* 495–505. [8]

Posada, G., Jacobs, A., Richmond, M., Carbonell, O., Alzate, G., Bustamante, M., & Quiceno, J. (2002). Maternal caregiving and infant security in two cultures. *Developmental Psychology, 38,* 67–78. [8]

Posner, M. I. (1996, September). Attention and psychopathology. *Harvard Mental Health Letter, 13*(3), 5–6. [2]

Postman, L., & Phillips, L. W. (1965). Short-term temporal changes in free recall. *Quarterly Journal of Experimental Psychology, 17,* 132–138. [6]

Power, F. C., Higgins, A., & Kohlberg, L. (1989). *Lawrence Kohlberg's approach to moral education.* New York: Columbia University Press. [8]

Power, K. G., Sharp, D. M., Swanson, V., & Simpson, R. J. (2000). Therapist contact in cognitive behaviour therapy for panic disorder and agoraphobia in primary care. *Clinical Psychology & Psychotherapy, 7,* 37–46. [13]

Powlishta, K. K. (1995). Intergroup processes in childhood: Social categorization and sex role development. *Developmental Psychology, 31,* 781–788. [8]

Pratkanis, A. R. (1989). The cognitive representation of attitudes. In A. R. Pratkanis, S. J. Breckler, & A. G. Greenwald (Eds.), *Attitude structure and function* (pp. 71–93). Hillsdale, NJ: Erlbaum. [14]

Premack, D. (1971). Language in chimpanzees. *Science, 172,* 808–822. [7]

Premack, D., & Premack, A. J. (1983). *The mind of an ape.* New York: Norton. [7]

Price, R., Choi, J., & Vinokur, A., (2002). Links in the chain of adversity following job loss: How financial strain and loss of personal control lead to depression, impaired functioning, and poor health. *Journal of Occupational Health Psychology, 7,* 302–312. [10]

Prien, R. F., & Kocsis, J. H. (1995). Long-term treatment of mood disorders. In F. E. Bloom & D. J. Kupfer (Eds.), *Psychopharmacology: The fourth generation of progress* (pp. 1067–1079). New York: Raven. [13]

Prigerson, H. G., Bierhals, A. J., Kasl, S. V., Reynolds, C. F., III, Shear, M. K., Day, N., Beery, L. C., Newsom, J. T., & Jacobs, S. (1997). Traumatic grief as a risk factor for mental and physical mortality. *American Journal of Psychiatry, 154,* 616–623. [10]

Prince, A. (1998). Infectious diseases. In B. Kliegman (Ed.), *Nelson essentials of pediatrics* (pp. 315-418). Philadelphia: W.B. Saunders. [10]

Prinz, P. N., Vitiello, M. V., Raskind, M. A., & Thorpy, M. J. (1990). Geriatrics: Sleep disorders and aging. *New England Journal of Medicine, 323,* 520–526. [4]

Provine, R. R. (1996, January/February). Laughter. *American Scientist, 84,* 38–45. [9]

Pryke, S., Lindsay, R. C. L., & Pozzulo, J. D. (2000). Sorting mug shots: Methodological issues. *Applied Cognitive Psychology, 14,* 81–96. [6]

Psychologists' pigeons score 90 pct. picking Picasso. (1995, May 7). *St. Louis Post-Dispatch,* p. 2A. [5]

Public Agenda Online. (2002). *The Issues: Race.* [Online report] Retrieved November 13, 2002, from http://www.public-agenda.com/issues/overview.dfm?issue_type=race [14]

Putnam, F. W. (1989). *Diagnosis and treatment of multiple personality disorder.* New York: Guilford Press. [12]

Putnam, F. W. (1992). Altered states: Peeling away the layers of a multiple personality. *The Sciences, 32,* 30–36. [12]

Putnam, F. W., & Loewenstein, R. J. (1993). Treatment of multiple personality disorder: A survey of current practices. *American Journal of Psychiatry, 150,* 1048–1052. [12]

Pulvermüller, F., Mohr, B., Schleichert, H., & Veit, R. (2000). Operant conditioning of left-hemispheric slow cortical potentials and its effect on word processing. *Biological Psychology, 53,* 177–215. [5]

Querido, J., Warner, T., & Eyberg, S. (2002). Parenting styles and child behavior in African American families of preschool children. *Journal of Clinical Child & Adolescent Psychology, 31,* 272–277. [8]

Quinn, T. The global HIV/AIDS pandemic 2002: A status report. *The Hopkins HIV report* [September 2002 online edition]. Retrieved December 28, 2002, from http://hopkins-aids.edu/publications/report/sept02_5.html [10]

Quiroga, T., Lemos-Britton, Z., Mostafapour, E., Abbott, R., & Berninger, V. (2002). Phonological awareness and beginning reading in Spanish-speaking ESL first graders: Research into practice. *Journal of School Psychology, 40,* 85–111. [8]

Rachman, S. (1997). The conditioning theory of fear acquisition: A critical examination. *Behavior Research and Therapy, 15,* 375–387. [12]

Rachman, S. J., & Wilson, G. T. (1980). *The effects of psychological therapy* (2nd ed.). New York: Pergamon. [13]

Ragozzino, M., Detrick, S., & Kesner, R. (2002). The effects of prelimbic and infralimbic lesions on working memory for visual objects in rats. *Neurobiology of Learning & Memory, 77,* 29–43. [6]

Rahe, R. J., Meyer, M., Smith, M., Kjaer, G., & Holmes, T. H. (1964). Social stress and illness onset. *Journal of Psychosomatic Research, 8,* 35–44. [10]

Raine, A. (1996). Autonomic nervous system factors underlying disinhibited, antisocial, and violent behavior: Biosocial perspectives and treatment implications. *Annals of the New York Academy of Sciences, 794,* 46–59. [14]

Ramey, C. (1993). A rejoinder to Spitz's critique of the Abecedarian experiment. *Intelligence, 17,* 25–30. [7]

Ramey, C., & Campbell, F. (1987). The Carolina Abecedarian project. An educational experiment concerning human malleability. In J. J. Gallagher & C. T. Ramey (Eds.), *The malleability of children* (pp. 127–140). Baltimore: Brookes. [7]

Ramsay, D. S., & Woods, S. C. (1997). Biological consequences of drug administration: Implications for acute and chronic tolerance. *Psychological Review, 104,* 170–193. [4]

Rao, S. C., Rainer, G., & Miller, E. K. (1997). Integration of what and where in the primate prefrontal cortex. *Science, 276,* 821–824. [6]

Rasmussen, S. A., & Eisen, J. L. (1990). Epidemiology of obsessive compulsive disorder. *Journal of Clinical Psychiatry, 51*(2, Suppl.), 10–13. [12]

Rasmussen, S. A., Eisen, J. L., & Pato, M. T. (1993). Current issues in the pharmacologic management of obsessive compulsive disorder. *Journal of Clinical Psychiatry, 54*(6, Suppl.), 4–9. [13]

Raz, A., Deouell, L., & Bentin, S. (2001). Is pre-attentive processing compromised by prolonged wakefulness? Effects of total sleep deprivation on the mismatch negativity. *Psychophysiology, 38,* 787–795. [4]

Reis, H. T., Wilson, I. M., Monestere, C., Bernstein, S., Clark, K., Seidl, E., Franco, M., Gioioso, E., Freeman, L., & Radoane, K. (1990). What is smiling is beautiful and good. *European Journal of Social Psychology, 20,* 259–267. [14]

Reite, M., Buysse, D., Reynolds, C., & Mendelson, W. (1995). The use of polysomnography in the evaluation of insomnia. *Sleep, 18,* 58–70. [4]

Reneman, L., Booig, J., Schmand, B., van den Brink, W., & Gunning, B. (2000). Memory disturbances in "Ecstasy" users are correlated with an altered brain serotonin neurotransmission. *Psychopharmacology, 148,* 322–324. [4]

Renzetti, C. M., & Curran, D. J. (1992). *Women, men, and society.* Boston: Allyn & Bacon. [14]

Rescorla, R. A. (1967). Pavlovian conditioning and its proper control procedures. *Psychological Review, 74,* 71–80. [5]

Rescorla, R. A. (1968). Probability of shock in the presence and absence of CS in fear conditioning. *Journal of Comparative and Physiological Psychology, 66,* 1–5. [5]

Rescorla, R. A. (1988). Pavlovian conditioning: It's not what you think it is. *American Psychologist, 43,* 151–160. [5]

Rescorla, R. A., & Wagner, A. R. (1972). A theory of Pavlovian conditioning: Variations in the effectiveness of reinforcement and nonreinforcement. In A. Black & W. F. Prokasy (Eds.), *Classical conditioning: II. Current research and theory.* New York: Appleton. [5]

Restak, R. (1988). *The mind.* Toronto: Bantam. [7]

Restak, R. (1993, September/October). Brain by design. *The Sciences,* pp. 27–33. [2]

Revensuo, A. (2000). The reinterpretation of dreams: An evolutionary hypothesis of the function of dreaming. *Behavioral & Brain Science, 23.* [4]

Reynolds, E. (2002). Benefits and risks of folic acid to the nervous system. *Journal of Neurology, 72,* 567–571. [8]

Rhéaume, J., & Ladouceur, R. (2000). Cognitive and behavioural treatments of checking behaviours: An examination of individual cognitive change. *Clinical Psychology & Psychotherapy, 7,* 118–127. [13]

Rhodes, N., & Wood, W. (1992). Self-esteem and intelligence affect influenceability: The mediating role of message reception. *Psychological Bulletin, 111,* 156–171. [14]

Rice, M. L., Huston, A. C., Truglio, R., & Wright, J. (1990). Words from "Sesame Street": Learning vocabulary while viewing. *Developmental Psychology, 26,* 421–428. [8]

Richter, W., Somorjai, R., Summers, R., Jarmasz, M., Ravi, S., Menon, J. S., et al. (2000). Motor area activity during mental rotation studied by time-resolved single-trial fMRI. *Journal of Cognitive Neuroscience, 12,* 310–320. [7]

Rickels, K., Schweizer, E., Weiss, S., & Zavodnick, S. (1993). Maintenance drug treatment for panic disorder II. Short- and long-term outcome after drug taper. *Archives of General Psychiatry, 50,* 61–68. [13]

Riedel, G. (1996). Function of metabotropic glutamate receptors in learning and memory. *Trends in Neurosciences, 19,* 219–224. [2, 6]

Roan, S. (2000, March 6). Cyber analysis. *L.A. Times.* [13]

Roberts, B. W., & DelVecchio, W. F. (2000). The rank-order consistency of personality traits from childhood to old age: A quantitative review of longitudinal studies. *Psychological Bulletin, 126,* 3–25. [11]

Roberts, P., & Moseley, B. (1996, May/June). Fathers' time. *Psychology Today, 29,* 48–55, 81. [8]

Robins, C. J., & Hayes, A. M. (1993). An appraisal of cognitive therapy. *Journal of Consulting and Clinical Psychology, 61,* 205–214. [13]

Robins, R. W., Gosling, S. D., & Craik, K. H. (1999). An empirical analysis of trends in psychology. *American Psychologist, 54,* 117–128. [1]

Robinson, D., Phillips, P., Budygin, E., Trafton, B., Garris, P., & Wightman, R. (2001). Sub-second changes in accumbal dopamine during sexual behavior in male rats. *Neuroreport: For Rapid Communication of Neuroscience Research, 12,* 2549–2552. [4]

Rodin, J., & Salovey, P. (1989). Health psychology. *Annual Review of Psychology, 40,* 533–579. [10]

Rodin, J., Wack, J., Ferrannini, E., & DeFronzo, R. A. (1985). Effect of insulin and glucose on feeding behavior. *Metabolism, 34,* 826–831. [9]

Roediger, H. L., III, & McDermott, K. B. (1995). Creating false memories: Remembering words not presented in lists. *Journal of Experimental Psychology: Learning, Memory, and Cognition, 21,* 803–814. [6]

Roesch, S. C., & Amirkhan, J. H. (1997). Boundary condition for self-serving attributions: Another look at the sports pages. *Journal of Applied Social Psychology, 27,* 245–261. [14]

Rogers, C. R. (1951). *Client-centered therapy: Its current practice, implications, and theory.* Boston: Houghton Mifflin. [13]

Rogolf, B., & Mistry, J. (1985). Memory development in cultural context. In M. Pressley & C. Brainerd (Eds.), *The cognitive side of memory development.* New York: Springer-Verlag. [6]

Romach, M., Busto, U., Somer, G., et al. (1995). Clinical aspects of chronic use of alprazolam and lorazepam. *American Journal of Psychiatry, 152,* 1161–1167. [13]

Roorda, A., & Williams, D. R. (1999). The arrangement of the three cone classes in the living human eye. *Nature, 397,* 520–521. [3]

Rosch, E. H. (1973). Natural categories. *Cognitive Psychology, 4,* 328–350. [7]

Rosch, E. H. (1978). Principles of categorization. In E. H. Rosch & B. Lloyd (Eds.), *Cognition and categorization.* Hillsdale, NJ: Erlbaum. [7]

Rosch, E. H. (1987). Linguistic relativity. *Et Cetera, 44,* 254–279. [7]

Rose, R. J., Koskenvuo, M., Kaprio, J., Sarna, S., & Langinvainio, H. (1988). Shared genes, shared experiences, and similarity of personality: Data from 14,288 adult Finnish co-twins. *Journal of Personality and Social Psychology, 54,* 161–171. [11]

Rosen, R. C. (1996). Erectile dysfunction: The medicalization of male sexuality. *Clinical Psychology Review, 16,* 497–519. [12]

Rosenbluth, R., Grossman, E. S., & Kaitz, M. (2000). Performance of early-blind and sighted children on olfactory tasks. *Perception, 29,* 101–110. [3]

Rosengren, A., Tibblin, G., & Wilhelmsen, L. (1991). Self-perceived psychological stress and incidence of coronary artery disease in middle-aged men. *American Journal of Cardiology, 68,* 1171–1175. [10]

Rosenvinge, J. H., Matinussen, M., & Ostensen, E. (2000). The comorbidity of eating disorders and personality disorders: A meta-analytic review of studies published between 1983 and 1998. *Eating and Weight Disorders: Studies on Anorexia, Bulimia, and Obesity, 5,* 52–61. [9]

Rosenzweig, M. R. (1961). Auditory localization. *Scientific American, 205,* 132–142. [3]

Ross, C. A., Anderson, G., Fleisher, W. P., & Norton, G. R. (1991). The frequency of multiple personality disorder among psychiatric inpatients. *American Journal of Psychiatry, 148,* 1717–1720. [12]

Ross, C. A., Norton, G. R., & Wozney, K. (1989). Multiple personality disorder: An analysis of 236 cases. *Canadian Journal of Psychiatry, 34,* 413–418. [12]

Ross, J., Baldessarini, R. J., & Tondo, L. (2000). Does lithium treatment still work? Evidence of stable responses over three decades. *Archives of General Psychiatry, 57,* 187–190. [13]

Rossow, I., & Amundsen, A. (1997). Alcohol abuse and mortality: a 40-year prospective study of Norwegian conscripts. *Social Science & Medicine, 44,* 261–267. [10]

Roth, T. (1996b). Social and economic consequences of sleep disorders. *Sleep, 19,* S46–S47. [4]

Rotton, J., & Cohn, E. G. (2000). Violence is a curvilinear function of temperature in Dallas: A replication. *Journal of Personality & Social Psychology, 78,* 1074–1082. [14]

Rotton, J., Frey, J., Barry, T., Milligan, M., & Fitzpatrick, M. (1979). The air pollution experience and physical aggression. *Journal of Applied Social Psychology, 9,* 397–412. [14]

Rowe, D. C. (1987). Resolving the person-situation debate: Invitation to an interdisciplinary dialogue. *American Psychologist, 42,* 218–227. [11]

Royall, D., Chiodo, L., Polk, M., & Jaramillo, C. (2002). Severe dysosmia is specifically associated with Alzheimer-like memory deficits in nondemented elderly retirees. *Neuroepidemiology, 21,* 68–73. [3]

Rozell, E., Pettijohn, C., & Parker, R. (2002). An empirical evaluation of emotional intelligence: The impact on management development. *Journal of Management Development, 21,* 272–289. [7]

Rubinstein, G. (2001). Sex-role reversal and clinical judgment of mental health. *Journal of Sex & Marital Therapy, 27,* 9–19. [13]

Ruby, N., Dark, J., Burns, D., Heller, H., & Zucker, I. (2002). The suprachiasmatic nucleus is essential for circadian body temperature rhythms in hibernating ground squirrels. *Journal of Neuroscience, 22,* 357–364. [4]

Rudman, L., Ashmore, R., & Gary, M. (2001). "Unlearning" automatic biases: The malleability of implicit prejudice and stereotypes. *Journal of Personality & Social Psychology, 81,* 856–868. [14]

Ruggero, M. A. (1992). Responses to sound of the basilar membrane of the mammalian cochlea. *Current Opinion in Neurobiology, 2,* 449–456. [3]

Ruggiero, K. M., & Taylor, D. M. (1997). Why minority group members perceive or do not perceive the discrimination that confronts them: The role of self-esteem and perceived control. *Journal of Personality and Social Psychology, 72,* 373–389. [14]

Rumbaugh, D. M. (1977). *Language learning by a chimpanzee: The Lana project.* New York: Academic Press. [7]

Rushton, J. P., Fulker, D. W., Neale, M. C., Nias, D. K. B., & Eysenck, H. J. (1986). Altruism and aggression: The heritability of individual differences. *Journal of Personality and Social Psychology, 50,* 1192–1198. [11]

Russell, J. A. (1995). Facial expressions of emotion: What lies beyond minimal universality? *Psychological Bulletin, 118,* 379–391. [9]

Sachs, G., Grossman, F., Ghaemi, S., Okamoto, A., & Bosden, C. (2002). Combination of a mood stabilizer with risperidone or haloperidol for treatment of acute mania: A double-blind, placebo-controlled comparison of efficacy and safety. *American Journal of Psychiatry, 159,* 1146–1154. [13]

Sackeim, H. A., Luber, B., Katzman, G. P., Moeller, J. R., Prudic, J., Devanand, D. P., & Nobler, M. S. (1996). The effects of electroconvulsive therapy on quantitative electroencephalograms. *Archives of General Psychiatry, 53,* 814–824. [13]

Sackeim, H. A., Prudic, J., Devanand, D. P., Nobler, M. S., Lisanby, S. H., Peyser, S., Fitzsimons, L., Moody, B. J., & Clark, J. (2000). A prospective, randomized, double-blind comparison of bilateral and right unilateral electroconvulsive therapy at different stimulus intensities. *Archives of General Psychiatry, 57,* 425–434. [13]

Saczynski, J., Willis, S., & Schaie, K. W. (2002). Strategy use in reasoning training with older adults. *Aging, Neuropsychology, & Cognition, 9,* 48–60. [8]

Salgado, J. F. (1997). The five factor model of personality and job performance in the European community. *Journal of Applied Psychology, 82,* 30–43. [11]

Salin-Pascual, R., Gerashchenko, D., Greco, M., Blanco-Centurion, C., & Shiromani, P. (2001). Hypothalamic regulation of sleep. *Neuropsychopharmacology, 25,* S21–S27. [2]

Salisch, M. (2001). Children's emotional development: Challenges in their relationships to parents, peers, and friends. *International Journal of Behavioural Development, 25,* 310–319. [9]

Salo, J., Niemelae, A., Joukamaa, M., & Koivukangas, J. (2002). Effect of brain tumour laterality on patients' perceived quality of life. *Journal of Neurology, Neurosurgery, & Psychiatry, 72,* 373–377. [2]

Salovey, P., & Mayer, J. D. (1990). Emotional intelligence. *Imagination, cognition, and personality, 9,* 185–211. [7]

Salovey, P., & Pizarro, D. (2003). The value of emotional intelligence. In R. Sternberg, J. Laufrey, & T. Lubart (Eds.), *Models of intelligence: International perspectives* (pp. 263–278). Washington, DC: American Psychological Association. [9]

Salthouse, T. A. (1996). The processing-speed theory of adult age differences in cognition. *Psychological Review, 103,* 403–428. [8]

Sanbonmatsu, D. M., & Fazio, R. H. (1990). The role of attitudes in memory-based decision making. *Journal of Personality and Social Psychology, 59,* 614–622. [14]

Sanes, J. N., & Donoghue, J. P. (2000). Plasticity and primary motor cortex. *Annual Review of Neuroscience, 23,* 393–415. [2]

Sanfilippo, M., Lafargue, T., Rusinek, H., Arena, L., Loneragan, C., Lautin, A., Feiner, D., Rotrosen, J., & Wolkin, A. (2000). Volumetric measure of the frontal and temporal lobe regions in schizophrenia. *Archives of General Psychiatry, 57,* 471–480. [12]

Sano, M., Ernesto, C., Thomas, R. G., Kauber, M. R., Schafer, K., Grundman, M., Woodbury, P., Growdon, J., Cotman, C. W., Pfeiffer, E., Schneider, L. S., & Thal, L. J. (1997). A controlled trial of selegiline, alpha-tocopherol, or both as treatment for Alzheimer's disease. *New England Journal of Medicine, 336,* 1216–1222. [8]

Santiago-Rivera, A., & Altarriba, J. (2002). The role of language in therapy with the Spanish-English bilingual client. *Professional Psychology: Research & Practice, 33,* 30–38. [13]

Şar, V., Yargic, L. I., & Tutkun, H. (1996). Structured interview data on 35 cases of dissociative identity disorder in Turkey. *American Journal of Psychiatry, 153,* 1329–1333. [12]

Sass, H., Soyha, M., Mann, K., & Zieglgänsberger, W. (1996). Relapse prevention by acamprosate: Results from a placebo-controlled study on alcohol dependence. *Archives of General Psychiatry, 53,* 673–680. [10]

Sateia, M. J., Doghramji, K., Hauri, P. J., & Morin, C. M. (2000). Evaluation of chronic insomnia. An American Academy of Sleep Medicine review. *Sleep, 23,* 243–308. [4]

Savage, M., & Holcomb, D. (1999). Adolescent female athletes' sexual risk-taking behaviors. *Journal of Youth and Adolescence, 28,* 583–594. [8]

Savage-Rumbaugh, E. S. (1986). *Ape language.* New York: Columbia University Press. [7]

Savage-Rumbaugh, E. S. (1990). Language acquisition in a nonhuman species: Implications for the innateness debate. *Developmental Psychology, 26,* 599–620. [7]

Savage-Rumbaugh, E. S. (1993). Language learnability in man, ape, and dolphin. In H. L. Roitblat, L. M. Herman, & P. E. Nachtigall (Eds.), *Language and communication: Comparative perspectives. Comparative cognition and neuroscience* (pp. 457–484). Hillsdale, NJ: Erlbaum. [7]

Savage-Rumbaugh, E. S., Sevcik, R. A., Brakke, K. E., & Rumbaugh, D. M. (1992). Symbols: Their communicative use, communication, and combination by bonobos (Pan paniscus). In L. P. Lipsitt & C. Rovee-Collier (Eds.). *Advances in infancy research* (Vol. 7, pp. 221–278). Norwood, NJ: Ablex. [7]

Scarr, S., & Weinberg, R. (1976). The influence of "family background" on intellectual attainment. *American Sociological Review, 43,* 674–692. [7]

Schachter, S., & Singer, J. E. (1962). Cognitive, social, and physiological determinants of emotional state. *Psychological Review, 69,* 379–399. [9]

Schaie, K. W. (1990). Late life potential and cohort differences in mental abilities. In M. Perlmutter (Ed.), *Late life potential* (pp. 43–61). Washington, DC: Gerontological Society. [8]

Schaie, K. W. (1993). Ageist language in psychological research. *American Psychologist, 48,* 49–51. [1]

Schaie, K. W. (1994). The course of adult intellectual development. *American Psychologist, 49,* 304–313. [8]

Schaie, K. W. (1995). *Intellectual development in adulthood: The Seattle Longitudinal Study.* New York: Cambridge University Press. [8]

Schaie, K. W., & Willis, S. L. (1996). *Adult development and aging* (4th ed.). New York: HarperCollins. [8]

Schenck, C. H., & Mahowald, M. W. (1995). A polysomnographically documented case of adult somnambulism with long-distance automobile driving and frequent nocturnal violence: Parasomnia with continuing danger as a noninsane automatism? *Sleep, 18,* 765–772. [4]

Schenck, C. H., & Mahowald, M. W. (2000). Parasomnias. Managing bizarre sleep-related behavior disorders. *Postgraduate Medicine, 107,* 145–156. [4]

Scherer, K. R., & Wallbott, H. G. (1994). Evidence for universality and cultural variation of differential emotion response patterning. *Journal of Personality and Social Psychology, 66,* 310–328. [9]

Scheuffgen, K., Happé, F., Anderson, M., & Frith, U. (2000). High "intelligence," low "IQ"? Speed of processing and measured IQ in children with autism. *Developmental Psychopathology, 12,* 183–190. [7]

Schiff, M., & Lewontin, R. (1986). *Education and class: The irrelevance of IQ genetic studies.* Oxford, England: Clarendon. [7]

Schlenger, W., Caddell, J., Ebert, L., Jordan, B., Rourke, K., Wilson, D., Thalji, L., Dennis, J., Fairbank, J., & Kulka, R. (2002). Psychological reactions to terrorist attacks: Findings from the National Study of Americans' Reactions to September 11. *JAMA: Journal of the American Medical Association, 288,* 581–588. [10]

Schofield, J. W., & Francis, W. D. (1982). An observational study of peer interaction in racially mixed "accelerated" classrooms. *Journal of Educational Psychology, 74,* 722–732. [8]

Scholl, T. O., Heidiger, M. L., & Belsky, D. H. (1996). Prenatal care and maternal health during adolescent pregnancy: A review and meta-analysis. *Journal of Adolescent Health, 15,* 444–456. [8]

Schou, M. (1997). Forty years of lithium treatment. *Archives of General Psychiatry, 54,* 9–13. [13]

Schreurs, B. G. (1989). Classical conditioning of model systems: A behavioral review. *Psychobiology, 17,* 145–155. [5]

Schuckit, M., Edenberg, H., Kalmijn, J., Flury, L., Smith, T., Reich, T., Beirut, L., Goate, A., & Foroud, T. (2001). A genome-wide search for genes that relate to a low level of response to alcohol. *Alcoholism: Clinical & Experimental Research, 25,* 323–329. [4]

Schuckit, M. A., Tipp, J. E., Bergman, M., Reich, W., Hesselbrock, V. M., & Smith, T. L. (1997). Comparison of induced and independent major depressive disorders in 2,945 alcoholics. *American Journal of Psychiatry, 154,* 948–957. [10]

Schulz, R., & Heckhausen, J. (1996). A life span model of successful aging. *American Psychologist, 51,* 702–714. [8]

Schwartz, G. E. (1982). Testing the biopsychosocial model: The ultimate challenge facing behavioral medicine? *Journal of Consulting and Clinical Psychology, 50,* 1040–1052. [10]

Scott, J. (1996). Cognitive therapy of affective disorders: a review. *Journal of Affective Disorders, 37,* 1–11. [13]

Scott, S. K., Young, A. W., Calder, A. J., Hellawell, D. J., Aggleton, J. P., & Johnson, M. (1997). Impaired auditory recognition of fear and anger following bilateral amygdala lesions. *Nature, 385,* 254–257. [2]

Seeman, M., & Seeman, A. Z. (1992). Life strains, alienation, and drinking behavior. *Alcoholism: Clinical and Experimental Research, 16,* 199–205. [10]

Seidman, S. (2002). Exploring the relationship between depression and erectile dysfunction in aging men. *Journal of Clinical Psychiatry, 63,* 5–12. [12]

Segall, M. H. (1994). A cross-cultural research contribution to unraveling the nativist/empiricist controversy. In J. Lonner & R. Malpass (Eds.), *Psychology and culture* (pp. 135–138). Boston: Allyn & Bacon. [3]

Segall, M. H., Campbell, D. T., & Herskovitz, M. J. (1966). *The influence of culture on visual perception.* Indianapolis: Bobbs-Merrill. [3]

Seligman, M. E. P. (1970). On the generality of the laws of learning. *Psychological Review, 77,* 406–418. [5]

Seligman, M. E. P. (1972). Phobias and preparedness. In M. E. P. Seligman & J. L. Hager (Eds.), *Biological boundaries of learning.* Englewood Cliffs, NJ: Prentice Hall. [5]

Seligman, M. E. P. (1975). *Helplessness: On depression, development and death.* San Francisco: Freeman. [5]

Seligman, M. E. P. (1990). *Learned optimism: How to change your mind and your life.* New York: Simon & Schuster. [10, 11]

Seligman, M. E. P. (1991). *Learned optimism.* New York: Knopf. [5]

Seligman, M. E. P. (1995). The effectiveness of psychotherapy: The Consumer Reports Study. *American Psychologist, 50,* 965–974. [13]

Seligman, M. E. P. (1996). Science as an ally of practice. *American Psychologist, 51,* 1072–1079. [13]

Selye, H. (1956). *The stress of life.* New York: McGraw-Hill. [10]

Sensky, T., Turkington, D., Kingdon, D., Scott, J. L., Scott, J., Siddle, R., O'Carroll, M., & Barnes, T. R. E. (2000). A randomized controlled trial of cognitive-behavioral therapy for persistent symptoms in schizophrenia resistant to medication. *Archives of General Psychiatry, 57,* 165–172. [13]

Serdula, M. K., Collins, M. E., Williamson, D. F., Anda, R. F., Pamuk, E. P., & Byers, T. E. (1993). Weight control practices of U.S. adolescents and adults. *Annals of Internal Medicine, 119,* 667–671. [9]

Serpell, R., & Hatano, G. (1997). Education, schooling, and literacy. In J. Berry, P. Dasen, & T. Saraswathi (Eds.), *Handbook of cross-cultural psychology* (Vol. 2, pp. 339–376). Boston: Allyn & Bacon. [8]

Shackelford, T., Buss, D., & Bennett, K. (2002). Forgiveness or breakup: Sex differences in responses to a partner's infidelity. *Cognition & Emotion, 16,* 299–307. [1]

Shaffer, D., Gould, M. S., Fisher, P., Trautman, P., Moreau, D., Kleinman, M., & Flory, M. (1996). Psychiatric diagnosis in child and adolescent suicide. *Archives of General Psychiatry, 53,* 339–348. [12]

Sharp, D., Cole, M., & Lave, C. (1979). Education and cognitive development: The evidence from experimental research. *Monographs of the Society for Research in Child Development, 44*(1–2, Serial No. 178). [8]

Shaw, J. I., & Steers, W. N. (2001). Gathering information to form an impression: Attribute categories and information valence. *Current Research in Social Psychology, 6,* 1–21. [14]

Shaw, J. S., III. (1996). Increases in eyewitness confidence resulting from postevent questioning. *Journal of Experimental Psychology: Applied, 2,* 126–146. [6]

Shears, J., Robinson, J., & Emde, R. (2002). Fathering relationships and their associations with juvenile delinquency. *Infant Mental Health Journal, 23,* 79–87. [8]

Sheehan, D. V. (1983). *The anxiety disease.* New York: Scribner's. [12]

Sheehan, D. V., & Raj, A. B. (1988). Monoamine oxidase inhibitors. In C. G. Last & M. Hersen (Eds.), *Handbook of anxiety disorders* (pp. 478–506). New York: Pergamon. [13]

Shepard, R. J. (1986). Exercise in coronary heart disease. *Sports Medicine, 3,* 26–49. [10]

Shepperd, J. (2001). The desire to help and behavior in social dilemmas: Exploring responses to catastrophes. *Group Dynamics, 5,* 304–314. [14]

Sher, A. E., Schechtman, K. B., & Piccirillo, J. F. (1996). The efficacy of surgical modifications of the upper airway in adults with obstructive sleep apnea syndrome. *Sleep, 19,* 156–177. [4]

Sherbourne, C. D., Wells, K. B., & Judd, L. L. (1996). Functioning and well-being of patients with panic disorder. *American Journal of Psychiatry, 153,* 213–218. [12]

Sherif, M. (1956). Experiments in group conflict. *Scientific American, 195,* 53–58. [14]

Sherif, M. (1958). Superordinate goals in the reduction of intergroup conflict. *American Journal of Sociology, 63,* 349–358. [14]

Sherif, M., & Sherif, C. W. (1967). The Robbers' Cave study. In J. F. Perez, R. C. Sprinthall, G. S. Grosser, & P. J. Anastasiou, *General psychology: Selected readings* (pp. 411–421). Princeton, NJ: D. Van Nostrand. [14]

Sherman, C. (1994, September/October). Kicking butts. *Psychology Today,* 41–45. [10]

Shimamura, A. P., Berry, J. M., Mangela, J. A., Rusting, C. L., & Jurica, P. J. (1995). Memory and cognitive abilities in university professors: Evidence for successful aging. *Psychological Science, 6,* 271–277. [8]

Shneidman, E. (1989). The Indian summer of life: A preliminary study of septuagenarians. *American Psychologist, 44,* 684–694. [7]

Shneidman, E. S. (1994). Clues to suicide, reconsidered. *Suicide and Life-Threatening Behavior, 24,* 395–397. [12]

Shoda, Y., Mischel, W., & Peake, P. K. (1990). Predicting adolescent cognitive and self-regulatory competencies from preschool delay of gratification. *Developmental Psychology, 26,* 978–986. [7]

Siegler, R. S. (1991). *Children's thinking* (2nd ed.). Englewood Cliffs, NJ: Prentice-Hall. [8]

Siegrist, J., Peter, R., Junge, A., Cremer, P., & Seidel, D. (1990). Low status control, high effort at work and ischemic heart disease: Prospective evidence from blue-collar men. *Social Science and Medicine, 31,* 1127–1134. [10]

Silva, C. E., & Kirsch, I. (1992). Interpretive sets, expectancy, fantasy proneness, and dissociation as predictors of hypnotic response. *Journal of Personality and Social Psychology, 63,* 847–856. [4]

Silver, R., Holman, E., McIntosh, D., Poulin, M., & Gil-Rivas, V. (2002). Nationalwide longitudinal study of psychological responses to September 11. *JAMA: Journal of the American Medical Association, 288,* 1235–1244. [10]

Simon, H. B. (1988, June). Running and rheumatism. *Harvard Medical School Health Letter, 13,* 2–4. [10]

Simons, J., & Carey, K. (2002). Risk and vulnerability for marijuana use problems: The role of affect dysregulation. *Psychology of Addictive Behaviors, 16,* 72–75. [4, 9]

Simpson, E. L. (1974). Moral development research. *Human Development, 17,* 81–106. [8]

Singer, M. I., Miller, D. B., Guo, S., Flannery, D. J., Frierson, T., & Slovak, K. (1999). Contributors to violent behavior among elementary and middle school children. *Pediatrics, 104*(Pt. 1), 878–884. [14]

Singh, B. (1991). Teaching methods for reducing prejudice and enhancing academic achievement for all children. *Educational Studies, 17,* 157–171. [14]

Singh, D. (1995). Female health, attractiveness, and desirability for relationships: Role of breast asymmetry and waist-hip ratio. *Ethology and Sociobiology, 16,* 445–481. [14]

Singh, S., & Darroch, J. (2000). Adolescent pregnancy and childbearing: Levels and trends in industrialized countries. *Family Planning Perspectives, 32,* 14–23. [8]

Sivacek, J., & Crano, W. D. (1982). Vested interest as a moderator of attitude-behavior consistency. *Journal of Personality and Social Psychology, 43,* 210–221. [14]

Skinner, B. F. (1953). *Science and human behavior.* New York: Macmillan. [5]

Skinner, B. F. (1957). *Verbal behavior.* New York: Appleton Century. [8]

Skrabalo, A. (2000). Negative symptoms in schizophrenia(s): The conceptual basis. *Harvard Brain, 7,* 7–10. [12]

Slaby, R. G., Roedell, W. C., Arezzo, D., & Hendrix, K. (1995). *Early violence prevention.* Washington, DC: National Association for the Education of Young Children. [8]

Slawinski, E. B., Hartel, D. M., & Kline, D. W. (1993). Self-reported hearing problems in daily life throughout adulthood. *Psychology and Aging, 8,* 552–561. [8]

Slobin, D. (1972, July). Children and language: They learn the same all around the world. *Psychology Today,* pp. 71–74, 82. [8]

Smith, M. L., Glass, G. V., & Miller, T. I. (1980). *The benefits of psychotherapy.* Baltimore: Johns Hopkins University Press. [13]

Smith, S. M. 91979). Remembering in and out of context. *Journal of Experimental Psychology: Human Learning and Memory, 5,* 460–471. [6]

Smith, T., & Ruiz, J. (2002). Psychosocial influences on the development and course of coronary heart disease: Current status and implications for research and practice. *Journal of Consulting and Clinical Psychology, 70,* 548–568. [10]

Smolar, A. (1999). Bridging the gap: Technical aspects of the analysis of an Asian immigrant. *Journal of Clinical Psychoanalysis, 8,* 567–594. [13]

Snarey, J. R. (1985). Cross-cultural universality of social-moral development: A critical review of Kohlbergian research. *Psychological Bulletin, 97,* 202–232. [8]

Snarey, J. R. (1995). In communitarian voice: The sociological expansion of Kohlbergian theory, research, and practice. In W. M. Kurtines & J. L. Gerwirtz (Eds.), *Moral development: An introduction* (pp. 109–134). Boston: Allyn & Bacon. [8]

Sobin, C., & Sackeim, H. A. (1997). Psychomotor symptoms of depression. *American Journal of Psychiatry, 154,* 4–17. [12]

Sokolov, E. N. (2000). Perception and the conditioning reflex: Vector encoding. *International Journal of Psychophysiology, 35,* 197–217. [3]

Soler, H., Vinayak, P., & Quadagno, D. (2000). Biosocial aspects of domestic violence. *Psychoneuroendocrinology, 25,* 721–739. [14]

Spangler, D. L., Simons, A. D., Monroe, S. M., & Thase, M. E. (1996). Gender differences in cognitive diathesis-stress domain match: Implications for differential pathways to depression. *Journal of Abnormal Psychology, 105,* 653–657. [12]

Spanos, N. P. (1986). Hypnotic behavior: A social-psychological interpretation of amnesia, analgesia, and "trance logic." *Behavioral and Brain Sciences, 9,* 499–502. [4]

Spanos, N. P. (1991). A sociocognitive approach to hypnosis. In S. J. Lynn & J. W. Rhue (Eds.), *Theories of hypnosis: Current models and perspectives* (pp. 324–361). New York: Guilford. [4]

Spanos, N. P. (1994). Multiple identity enactments and multiple personality disorder: A sociocognitive perspective. *Psychological Bulletin, 116,* 143–165. [4]

Spearman, C. (1927). *The abilities of man.* New York: Macmillan. [7]

Sperling, G. (1960). The information available in brief visual presentations. *Psychological Monographs: General and Applied, 74,* Whole No. 498, 1–29. [6]

Sperry, R. W. (1964). The great cerebral commissure. *Scientific American, 210*, 42–52. [2]

Spiers, H., Maguire, E., & Burgess, N. (2001). Hippocampal amnesia. *Neurocase, 7*, 357–382. [6]

Sporer, S. L., Penrod, S., Read, D., & Cutler, B. (1995). Choosing, confidence, and accuracy: A meta-analysis of the confidence-accuracy relation in eyewitness identification studies. *Psychological Bulletin, 118*, 315–327. [6]

Sprecher, S., & Hatfield, E. (1996). Premarital sexual standards among U.S. college students: Comparison with Russian and Japanese students. *Archives of Sexual Behavior, 25*, 261–288. [9]

Sprecher, S., & Regan, P. C. (1996). College virgins: How men and women perceive their sexual status. *Journal of Sex Research, 33*, 3–15. [9]

Squire, L. R. (1992). Memory and the hippocampus: A synthesis from findings with rats, monkeys, and humans. *Psychological Review, 99*, 195–231. [6]

Squire, L. R., Knowlton, B., & Musen, G. (1993). The structure and organization of memory. *Annual Review of Psychology, 44*, 453–495. [6]

Staal, W. G., Pol, H. E. H., Schnack, H. G., Hoogendoorn, M. L. C., Jellema, K., & Kahn, R. S. (2000). Structural brain abnormalities in patients with schizophrenia and their healthy siblings. *American Journal of Psychiatry, 157*, 416–421. [12]

Stafford, J., & Lynn, S. (2002). Cultural scripts, memories of childhood abuse, and multiple identities: A study of role-played enactments. *International Journal of Clinical & Experimental Hypnosis, 50*, 67–85. [6]

Stage, K. B., Glassman, A. H., & Covey, L. S. (1996). Depression after smoking cessation: Case reports. *Journal of Clinical Psychiatry, 57*, 467–469. [10]

Stanton, M. E. (2000). Multiple memory systems, development and conditioning. *Behavioural Brain Research, 110*, 25–37. [5]

Stattin, H., & Magnusson, D. (1990). *Pubertal maturation in female development*. Hillsdale, NJ: Erlbaum. [8]

Steblay, N. M. (1992). A meta-analytic review of the weapon focus effect. *Law and Human Behavior, 16*, 413–424. [6]

Steele, J., & Mayes, S. (1995). Handedness and directional asymmetry in the long bones of the human upper limb. *International Journal of Osteoarchaeology, 5*, 39–49. [2]

Steffens, A. B., Scheurink, A. J., & Luiten, P. G. (1988). Hypothalamic food intake regulating areas are involved in the homeostasis of blood glucose and plasma FFA levels. *Physiology and Behavior, 44*, 581–589. [9]

Steffensen, M., & Calker, L. (1982). Intercultural misunderstandings about health care: Recall of descriptions of illness and treatments. *Social Science and Medicine, 16*, 1949–1954. [6]

Stein, A. H., & Friedrich, L. K. (1975). Impact of television on children and youth. In E. M. Hetherington (Ed.), *Review of child development research* (Vol. 5, pp. 183–256). Chicago: University of Chicago Press. [8]

Stein, M. B., & Kean, Y. M. (2000). Disability and quality of life in social phobia: Epidemiologic findings. *American Journal of Psychiatry, 157*, 1606–1613. [12]

Stein, M. B., Walker, J. R., & Forde, D. R. (1996). Public-speaking fears in a community sample: Prevalence, impact on functioning, and diagnostic classification. *Archives of General Psychiatry, 53*, 169–174. [12]

Stein-Behrens, B., Mattson, M. P., Chang, I., Yeh, M., & Sapolsky, R. (1994). Stress exacerbates neuron loss and cytoskeletal pathology in the hippocampus. *Journal of Neuroscience, 14*, 5373–5380. [10]

Steinberg, L. (1990). Autonomy, conflict, and harmony in the family relationship. In S. S. Feldman & R. E. Glen (Eds.), *At the threshold: The developing adolescent*. Cambridge, MA: Harvard University Press. [8]

Steinberg, L., & Dornbusch, S. (1991). Negative correlates of part-time employment during adolescence: Replication and elaboration. *Developmental Psychology, 27*, 304–313. [8]

Steinberg, L., Elman, J. D., & Mounts, N. S. (1989). Authoritative parenting, psychosocial maturity, and academic success among adolescents. *Child Development, 60*, 1424–1436. [8]

Steinberg, L., Lamborn, S. D., Darling, N., Mounts, N. S., & Dornbusch, S. M. (1994). Over-time changes in adjustment and competence among adolescents from authoritative, authoritarian, indulgent, and neglectful families. *Child Development, 65*, 754–770. [8]

Steinman, L. (1993). Autoimmune disease. *Scientific American, 269*, 106–114. [10]

Steinmetz, J. E. (2000). Brain substrates of classical eyeblink conditioning: A highly localized but also distributed system. *Behavioural Brain Research, 110*, 13–24. [5]

Stemberger, R. T., Turner, S. M., Beidel, D. C., & Calhoun, K. S. (1995). Social phobia: An analysis of possible developmental factors. *Journal of Abnormal Psychology, 104*, 526–531. [12]

Sternberg, R., Castejon, J., Prieto, M., Hautamacki, J., & Grogorenko, E. (2001). Confirmatory factor analysis of the Sternberg Triarchic Abilities Test in three international samples: An empirical test of the triarchic theory of intelligence. *European Journal of Psychological Assessment, 17*, 1–16. [7]

Stephenson, M. T., & Witte, K. (1998). Fear, threat, and perceptions of efficiency from frightening skin cancer messages. *Public Health Review, 26*, 147–174. [14]

Steptoe, A. (2000). Stress, social support and cardiovascular activity over the working day. *International Journal of Psychophysiology, 37*, 299–308. [10]

Steriade, M. (1996). Arousal: Revisiting the reticular activating system. *Science, 272*, 225–226. [2]

Stern, W. (1914). *The psychological methods of testing intelligence*. Baltimore: Warwick and York. [7]

Sternberg, R. J. (1985a). *Beyond IQ: A triarchic theory of human intelligence*. New York: Cambridge University Press. [7]

Sternberg, R. J. (1986a). *Intelligence applied: Understanding and increasing your intellectual skills*. San Diego: Harcourt Brace Jovanovich. [7]

Sternberg, R. J. (1986b). A triangular theory of love. *Psychological Review, 93*, 119–135. [14]

Sternberg, R. J. (1987). Liking versus loving: A comparative evaluation of theories. *Psychological Bulletin, 102*, 331–345. [14]

Stevenson, H. W. (1992). Learning from Asian schools. *Scientific American, 267*, 70–76. [7]

Stevenson, H. W., Chen, C., & Lee, S. Y. (1993). Mathematics achievement of Chinese, Japanese, and American children: Ten years later. *Science, 259*, 53–58. [7]

Stevenson, H. W., Lee, S. Y., Chen, C., Stigler, J. W., Hsu, C. C., & Kitamura, S. (1990). Contexts of achievement. *Monographs of the Society for Research in Child Development, 55*(1–2, Serial No. 221). [7]

Stevenson, H. W., Lee, S. Y., & Stigler, J. W. (1986). Mathematics achievement of Chinese, Japanese, and American children. *Science, 231*, 693–699. [7]

Stewart, V. M. (1973). Tests of the "carpentered world" hypothesis by race and environment in America and Zambia. *International Journal of Psychology, 8*, 83–94. [3]

Strack, F., Martin, L. L., & Stepper, S. (1988). Inhibiting and facilitating conditions of facial expressions: A nonobtrusive test of the facial feedback hypothesis. *Journal of Personality and Social Psychology, 54*, 768–777. [9]

Strawbridge, W. J., Cohen, R. D., Shema, S. J., & Kaplan, G. A. (1997). Frequent attendance at religious services and mortality over 28 years. *American Journal of Public Health, 87*, 957–961. [10]

Styron, W. (1990). *Darkness visible: A memoir of madness*. New York: Vintage. [12]

Suarez, M. G. (1983). Implications of Spanish-English bilingualism in the TAT stories. Unpublished doctoral dissertation, University of Connecticut. [13]

Sullivan, A., Maerz, J., & Madison, D. (2002). Anti-predator response of red-backed salamanders (*Plethodon cinereus*) to chemical cues from garter snakes (*Thamnophis sirtalis*): Laboratory and field experiments. *Behavioral Ecology & Sociobiology, 51,* 227–233. [3]

Sullivan, E., Fama, R., Rosenbloom, M., & Pfefferbaum, A. (2002). A profile of neuropsychological deficits in alcoholic women. *Neuropsychology, 16,* 74–83. [10]

Sullivan, E. V. (1977). A study of Kohlberg's structural theory of moral development: A critique of liberal social science ideology. *Human Development, 20,* 352–376. [8]

Sullivan, M. J. L., Bishop, S. R., & Pivik, J. (1995). The pain catastrophizing scale: Development and validation. *Psychological Assessment, 7,* 524–532. [3]

Sung, K-T. (1992). Motivations for parent care: The case of filial children in Korea. *International Journal of Aging and Human Development, 34,* 109–124. [8]

Super, C. W. (1981). Behavioral development in infancy. In R. H. Munroe, R. L. Munroe, & B. B. Whiting (Eds.), *Handbook of cross-cultural human development* (pp. 181–269). Chicago: Garland. [8]

Sussman, S., & Dent, C. W. (2000). One-year prospective prediction of drug use from stress-related variables. *Substance Use & Misuse, 35,* 717–735. [4]

Swan, G., & Carmelli, D. (2002). Impaired olfaction predicts cognitive decline in nondemented older adults. *Neuroepidemiology, 21,* 58–67. [3]

Swanson, L. W. (1995). Mapping the human brain: past, present, and future. *Trends in Neurosciences, 18,* 471–474. [2]

Swanson, N. G. (2000). Working women and stress. *Journal of the American Medical Womens Association, 55,* 276–279. [10]

Sweatt, J. D., & Kandel, E. R. (1989). Persistent and transcriptionally dependent increase in protein phosphorylation in long-term facilitation of Aplysia sensory neurons. *Nature, 339,* 51–54. [6]

Sweller, J., & Levine, M. (1982). Effects of goal specificity on means-end analysis and learning. *Journal of Experimental Psychology: Learning, Memory, and Cognition, 8,* 463–474. [7]

Symons, C. S., & Johnson, B. T. (1997). The self-reference effect in memory: A meta-analysis. *Psychological Bulletin, 121,* 371–394. [6]

Takahashi, S., Matsuura, M., Tanabe, E., Yara, K., Nonaka, K., Fukura, Y., Kikuchi, M., & Kojima, T. (2000). Age at onset of schizophrenia: Gender differences and influence of temporal socioeconomic change. *Psychiatry and Clinical Neurosciences, 54,* 153–156. [12]

Takanishi, R. (1993). The opportunities of adolescence—research, interventions, and policy: Introduction to the special issue. *American Psychologist, 48,* 85–87. [8]

Tamminga, C. A. (1996, Winter). The new generation of antipsychotic drugs. *NARSAD Research Newsletter,* pp. 4–6. [13]

Tamminga, C. A., & Conley, R. R. (1997). The application of neuroimaging techniques to drug development. *Journal of Clinical Psychiatry, 58*(10, Suppl.), 3–6. [2]

Tanda, G., Pontieri, F. E., & Di Chiara, G. (1997). Cannabinoid and heroin activation of mesolimbic dopamine transmission by a common μ1 opioid receptor mechanism. *Science, 276,* 2048–2050. [4]

Tang, M-X., Jacobs, D., Stern, Y., Marder, K., Schofield, P., Gurland, B., Andrews, H., & Mayeux, R. (1996). Effect of oestrogen during menopause on risk and age at onset of Alzheimer's disease. *Lancet, 348,* 429–432. [8]

Tanner, J. (1990). *Fetus into man: Physical growth from conception to maturity.* Cambridge, MA: Harvard University Press. [8]

Tanner, J. M. (1990). *Fetus into man* (2nd ed.). Cambridge MA: Harvard University Press. [7]

Taylor, D. M., Helms Tillery, S. J., & Schwartz, A. B. (2002). Direct cortical control of 3D neuroprosthetic devices. *Science, 296,* 1829–1832. [7]

Taylor, E. (1996, July/August). Peace Timothy Leary. *Psychology Today, 29,* 56–59, 84. [4]

Taylor, S. E. (1991). *Health psychology* (2nd ed.). New York: McGraw-Hill. [10]

Taylor, S. E., & Repetti, R. L. (1997). Health psychology: What is an unhealthy environment and how does it get under the skin? *Annual Review of Psychology, 48,* 411–447. [10]

Tchanturia, K., Serpell, L., Troop, N., & Treasure, J. (2001). Perceptual illusions in eating disorders: Rigid and fluctuating styles. *Journal of Behavior Therapy & Experimental Psychiatry, 32,* 107–115. [9]

Tellegen, A., Lykken, D. T., Bouchard, T. J., Jr., Wilcox, K. J., Segal, N. L., & Rich, S. (1988). Personality similarity in twins reared apart and together. *Journal of Personality and Social Psychology, 54,* 1031–1039. [11]

Teng, E., Stefanacci, L., Squire, L. R., & Zola, S. M. (2000). Contrasting effects on discrimination learning after hippocampal lesions and conjoint hippocampal-caudate lesions in monkeys. *Journal of Neuroscience, 20,* 3853–3863. [6]

Tepper, B., & Ullrich, N. (2002). Influence of genetic taste sensitivity to 6-*n*-propylthiouracil (PROP), dietary restraint and disinhibition on body mass index in middle-aged women. *Physiology & Behavior, 75,* 305–312. [3]

Terman, L. M. (1925). *Genetic studies of genius, Vol. 1: Mental and physical traits of a thousand gifted children.* Stanford, CA: Stanford University Press. [7]

Terman, L. M., & Oden, M. H. (1947). *Genetic studies of genius, Vol. 4: The gifted child grows up.* Stanford, CA: Stanford University Press. [7]

Terrace, H. S. (1979, November). How Nim Chimpski changed my mind. *Psychology Today,* 65–76. [7]

Terrace, H. S. (1981). A report to an academy. *Annals of the New York Academy of Sciences, 364,* 115–129. [7]

Terrace, H. S. (1985). In the beginning was the "name." *American Psychologist, 40,* 1011–1028. [7]

Terrace, H. S. (1986). *Nim: A chimpanzee who learned sign language.* New York: Columbia University Press. [7]

Tew, J. D., Mulsant, B. H., Haskett, R. F., Prudic, J., Thase, M. E., Crowe, R. R., Dolata, D., Begley, A. E., Reynolds, C. F., III, & Sackeim, H. A. (1999). Acute efficacy of ECT in the treatment of major depression in the old-old. *American Journal of Psychiatry, 156,* 1865–1870. [13]

Tham, K., Borell, L., & Gustavsson, A. (2000). The discovery of disability: A phenomenological study of unilateral neglect. *American Journal of Occupational Therapy, 54,* 398–406. [2]

Thase, M. E., Frank, E., Mallinger, A. G., Hammer, T., & Kupfer, D. J. (1992). Treatment of imipramine-resistant recurrent depression, III: Efficacy of monoamine oxidise inhibitors. *Journal of Clinical Psychiatry, 53*(1, Suppl.), 5–11. [13]

Thase, M. E., & Kupfer, D. J. (1996). Recent developments in the pharmacotherapy of mood disorders. *Journal of Consulting and Clinical Psychology, 64,* 646–659. [13]

Thigpen, C. H., & Cleckley, H. M. (1984). On the incidence of multiple personality disorder. *International Journal of Clinical and Experimental Hypnosis, 32,* 63–66. [12]

Thomas, A., Chess, S., & Birch, H. G. (1970). The origin of personality. *Scientific American, 223,* 102–109. [8]

Thomas, J. L. (1992). *Adulthood and aging.* Boston: Allyn & Bacon. [8]

Thompson, R. F., Swain, R., Clark, R., & Shinkman, P. (2000). Intracerebellar conditioning—Brogden and Gantt revisited. *Behavioural Brain Research, 110,* 2–11. [5]

Thompson, S. C., Sobolew-Shubin, A., Galbraith, M. E., Schwankovsky, L., & Cruzen, D. (1993). Maintaining perceptions of control: Finding perceived control in low-control circumstances. *Journal of Personality and Social Psychology, 64,* 293–304. [10]

Thorn, A., & Gathercole, S. (1999). Language-specific knowledge and short-term memory in bilingual and non-bilingual children. *Quarterly Journal of Experimental Psychology: Human Experimental Psychology, 52A,* 303–324. [7]

Thorndike, E. (1898). Some experiments on animal intelligence. *Science, 7*(181), 818–824. [5]

Thorndike, E. L. (1970). *Animal intelligence: Experimental studies.* New York: Macmillan. (Original work published 1911). [5]

Thornhill, R., & Gangestad, G. W. (1994). Human fluctuating asymmetry and sexual behavior. *Psychological Science, 5,* 297–302. [14]

Thurstone, L. L. (1938). *Primary mental abilities.* Chicago: University of Chicago Press. [7]

Tidey, J., O'Neill, S., & Higgins, S. (2002). Contingent monetary reinforcement of smoking reductions, with and without transdermal nicotine, in outpatients with schizophrenia. *Experimental and Clinical Psychopharmacology, 10,* 241–247. [13]

Tiihonen, J., Isohanni, M., Räsänen, P., Koiranen, M., & Moring, J. (1997). Specific major mental disorders and criminality: A 26-year prospective study of the 1966 northern Finland birth cohort. *American Journal of Psychiatry, 154,* 840–845. [14]

Toastmasters International. (2003). *10 tips for successful public speaking* [Online document]. Retrieved January 7, 2003, from http://www.toastmasters.org/tips.asp [12]

Tolman, E. C. (1932). *Purposive behavior in animals and men.* New York: Appleton-Century-Crofts. [5]

Tolman, E. C., & Honzik, C. H. (1930). Introduction and removal of reward, and maze performance in rats. *University of California Publications in Psychology, 4,* 257–275. [5]

Tomkins, S. (1962). *Affect, imagery, and consciousness: The positive effects* (Vol. 1). New York: Springer. [9]

Tomkins, S. (1963). *Affect, imagery, and consciousness: The negative effects* (Vol. 2). New York: Springer. [9]

Tori, C., & Bilmes, M. (2002). Multiculturalism and psychoanalytic psychology: The validation of a defense mechanisms measure in an Asian population. *Psychoanalytic Psychology, 19,* 701–721. [11]

Torrey, E. (1992). *Freudian fraud: The malignant effect of Freud's theory on American thought and culture,* New York: Harper Collins. [11]

Toufexis, A. (1988, February 22). Older—but coming on strong. *Time,* pp. 76–79. [8]

Traverso, A., Ravera, G., Lagattolla, V., Testa, S., & Adami, G. F. (2000). Weight loss after dieting with behavioral modification for obesity: The predicting efficiency of some psychometric data. *Eating and Weight Disorders: Studies on Anorexia, Bulimia, and Obesity, 5,* 102–107. [9]

Travis, J. (1996). Brains in space. *Science News, 149,* 28–29. [2]

Trevitt, J., Carolson, B., Correa, M., Keene, A., Morales, M., & Salamone, J. (2002). Interactions between dopamine D1 receptors and gamma-aminobutyric acid mechanisms in substantia nigra pars reticulata of the rat: Neurochemical and behavioral studies. *Psychopharmacology, 159,* 229–237. [2]

Triandis, H. C. (1994). *Culture and social behavior.* New York: McGraw-Hill. [9]

Triandis, H. C., McCusker, C., Betancourt, H., Iwao, S., Leung, K., Salazar, J. M., Setiadi, B., Sinha, J. B. P., Touzard, H., & Zaleski, Z. (1993). An etic-emic analysis of individualism and collectivism. *Journal of Cross-Cultural Psychology, 24,* 366–383. [11]

Triplett, N. (1898). The dynamogenic factors in pacemaking and competition. *American Journal of Psychology, 9,* 507–533. [14]

Trivedi, M. J. (1996). Functional neuroanatomy of obsessive-compulsive disorder. *Journal of Clinical Psychiatry, 57*(8, Suppl.), 26–36. [13]

Tsai, S., Kuo, C., Chen, C., & Lee, H. (2002). Risk factors for completed suicide in bipolar disorder. *Journal of Clinical Psychiatry, 63,* 469–476. [12]

Tulving, E. (1974). Cue-dependent forgetting. *American Scientist, 62,* 74–82. [6]

Tulving, E. (2002). Episodic memory: From mind to brain. *Annual Review of Psychology, 53,* 1–25. [6]

Tulving, E., & Thompson, D. M. (1973). Encoding specificity and retrieval processes in episodic memory. *Psychological Review, 80,* 352–373. [6]

Tuncer, A. M., & Yalcin, S. S. (2000). Multimedia and children in Turkey. *Turkish Journal of Pediatrics, 41*(Suppl.), 27–34. [8]

Turner, J. C., Hogg, M. A., Oakes, P. J., Reicher, S. D., & Wetherell, M. S. (1987). *Rediscovering the social group: A self-categorization theory.* Oxford, England: Blackwell. [14]

Tversky, A. (1972). Elimination by aspects: A theory of choice. *Psychological Review, 79,* 281–299. [7]

Tweed, R., & Lehman, D. (2002). Learning considered within a cultural context: Confucian and Socratic approaches. *American Psychologist, 57,* 89–99. [1]

Two missing after 9/11 found [Online article]. *Daily Hampshire Gazette* (September 7, 2002). Retrieved November 8, 2002, from http://www.gazettenet.com [12]

Tzschentke, T. M. (2001). Pharmacology and behavioral pharmacology of mesocortical dopamine system. *Progress in Neurobiology, 63,* 241–320. [12]

Uchino, B. N., Cacioppo, J. T., & Kiecolt-Glaser, J. K. (1996). The relationship between social support and physiological processes: A review with emphasis on underlying mechanisms and implications for health. *Psychological Bulletin, 119,* 488–531. [10]

Underwood, B. J. (1957). Interference and forgetting. *Psychological Review, 64,* 49–60. [6]

U.S. Bureau of the Census. (1997). *Statistical abstract of the United States 1997* (117th ed.). Washington, DC: U.S. Government Printing Office. [8, 10, 11]

U.S. Bureau of the Census. (1999). *Statistical Abstracts of the United States 1999* (119th ed.). Washington DC: U.S. Government Printing Office. [12]

U.S. Bureau of the Census. (2000). Native resident population estimates of the United States by sex, race, and Hispanic origin. Population Estimates Program, Population Division [On-line]. Retrieved from http://www.census.gov/populationestimates/nation/nativity/nbtab003.txt [1]

U.S. Bureau of the Census. (2001). *Statistical abstract of the United States.* Washington, DC: U.S. Government Printing Office. [8, 12]

U.S. Department of Health and Human Services. (2000). Reducing tobacco use: *A report of the Surgeon General—executive summary.* Atlanta: Department of Health and Human Services, Centers for Disease Control and Prevention, National Center for Chronic Disease Prevention and Health Promotion, Office on Smoking and Health. [10]

U.S. Department of Justice. (1998). *Alcohol and crime: An analysis of national data on the prevalence of alcohol involvement in crime.* (NCJ-168632). Washington, DC: Author. [10]

Utsey, S., Chae, M., Brown, C., & Kelly, D. (2002). Effect of ethnic group membership on ethnic identity, race-related stress and quality of life. *Cultural Diversity & Ethnic Minority Psychology, 8,* 367–378. [10]

Valleroy, L. A., Harris, J. R., & Way, P. O. (1990). The impact of HIV infection on child survival in the developing world. *AIDS, 4,* 667–672. [10]

van Assema, P., Martens, M., Ruiter, A., & Brug, J. (2001). Framing of nutrition education messages in persuading consumers of the advantages of a healthy diet. *Journal of Human Nutrition & Dietetics, 14,* 435–442. [14]

Van Cauter, E. (2000). Slow-wave sleep and release of growth hormone. *Journal of the American Medical Association, 284,* 2717–2718. [4]

van den Hout, M., & Merckelbach, H. (1991). Classical conditioning: Still going strong. *Behavioural Psychotherapy, 19,* 59–79. [5]

Vander Meer, R., & Alonso, L. (2002). Queen primer pheromone affects conspecific fire ant (*Solenopsis invicta*) aggression. *Behavioral Ecology & Sociobiology, 51,* 122–130. [3]

Van der Zee, K., Thijs, M., & Schakel, L. (2002). The relationship of emotional intelligence with academic intelligence and the Big Five. *European Journal of Personality, 16,* 103–125. [7]

van Elst, L. T., Woermann, F. G., Lemieux, L., Thompson, P. J., & Trimble, M. R. (2000). Affective aggression in patients with temporal lobe epilepsy. *Brain, 123,* 234–243. [14]

van IJzendoorn, M. (1995). Adult attachment representations, parental responsiveness, and infant attachment: A meta-analysis on the predictive validity of the Adult Attachment Interview. *Psychological Bulletin, 117,* 387–403. [8]

Vargha-Khadem, F., Gadian, D. G., Watkins, D. E., Connelly, A., Van Paesschen, W., & Mishkin, M. (1997). Differential effects of early hippocampal pathology on episodic and semantic memory. *Science, 277,* 376–380. [2, 6]

Vasterling, J., Duke, L, Brailey, K., Constans, J., Allain, A., & Sutker, P. (2002). Attention, learning, and memory performances and intellectual resources in Vietnam veterans: PTSD and no disorder comparisons. *Neuropsychology, 16,* 5–14. [10]

Vazdarjanova, A. (2000). Does the basolateral amygdala store memories for emotional events? *Trends in Neurosciences, 23,* 345–346. [5]

Verhaeghen, P., Marcoen, A., & Goossens, L. (1993). Facts and fiction about memory aging: A quantitative integration of research findings. *Journal of Gerontology, 48,* 157–171. [8]

Vetulani, J., & Nalepa, I. (2000). Antidepressants: Past, present and future. *European Journal of Pharmacology, 405,* 351–363. [13]

Viemerö, V. (1996). Factors in childhood that predict later criminal behavior. *Aggressive Behavior, 22,* 87–97. [14]

Villani, S. (2001). Impact of media on children and adolescents: A 10-year review of the research. *Journal of the American Academy of child & Adolescent Psychiatry, 40,* 392–401. [5]

Vincent, M., & Pickering, M. R. (1988). Multiple personality disorder in childhood. *Canadian Journal of Psychiatry, 33,* 524–529. [12]

Vinokur, A., & Burnstein, E. (1978). Depolarization of attitudes in groups. *Journal of Personality and Social Psychology, 36,* 872–885. [14]

Visser, P. S., & Krosnick, J. A. (1998). Development of attitude strength over the life cycle: Surge and decline. *Journal of Personality & Social Psychology, 75,* 1389–1410. [14]

Vitousek, K., & Manke, F. (1994). Personality variables and disorders in anorexia nervosa and bulimia nervosa. *Journal of Abnormal Psychology, 103,* 137–147. [9]

Volis, C., Ashburn-Nardo, L., & Monteith, M. (2002). Evidence of prejudice-related conflict and associated affect beyond the college setting. *Group Processes & Intergroup Relations, 5,* 19–33. [14]

Volkow, N. D., & Fowler, J. S. (2000). Addiction, a disease of compulsion and drive: Involvement of the orbitofrontal cortex. *Cerebral Cortex, 10,* 318–325. [4, 5]

Volkow, N. D., Wang, G-J., Fowler, J. S., Hitzemann, R., Angrist, B., Gatley, S. J., et al. (1999). Association of methylphenidate-induced craving with changes in right straito-orbiotfrontal metabolism in cocaine abusers: Implications in addiction. *American Journal of Psychiatry, 156,* 19–26. [4]

Volkow, N. D., Wang, G-J., Fischman, M. W., Foltin, R. W., Fowler,, J. S., Abumrad, N. N., Vitkun, S., Logan, J., Gatley, S. J., Pappas, N., Hitsemann, R., & Shea, C. E. (1997a). Relationship between subjective effects of cocaine and dopamine transporter occupancy. *Nature, 386,* 827–830. [4]

Vollrath, M. (2000). Personality and hassles among university students: A three-year longitudinal study. *European Journal of Personality, 14,* 199–215. [11]

Von Dras, D. D., & Siegler, I. C. (1997). Stability in extraversion and aspects of social support at midlife. *Journal of Personality and Social Psychology, 72,* 233–241. [10]

Voyer, D., & Rodgers, M. (2002). Reliability of laterality effects in a dichotic listening task with nonverbal material. *Brain & Cognition, 48,* 602–606. [9]

Vuorenkoski, L., Kuure, O., Moilanen, I., & Peninkilampi, V. (2000). Bilingualism, school achievement, and mental wellbeing: A follow-up study of return migrant children. *Journal of Child Psychology & Psychiatry & Allied Disciplines, 41,* 261–266. [7]

Wadden, T. A. (1993). Treatment of obesity by moderate and severe caloric restriction: Results of clinical research trials. *Annals of Internal Medicine, 119,* 688–693. [9]

Wald, G. (1964). The receptors of human color vision. *Science, 145,* 1007–1017. [3]

Wald, G., Brown, P. K., & Smith, P. H. (1954). Iodopsin. *Journal of General Physiology, 38,* 623–681. [3]

Walker, D. (2000). Online therapy? Not yet. *CBS News.* New York: CBS. [13]

Walker, I., & Crogan, M. (1998). Academic performance, prejudice and the Jigsaw classroom: New pieces to the puzzle. *Journal of Community & Applied Social Psychology, 8,* 381–393. [14]

Walker, L. (1989). A longitudinal study of moral reasoning. *Child Development, 60,* 157–166. [8]

Walster, E., & Walster, G. W. (1969). The matching hypothesis. *Journal of Personality and Social Psychology, 6,* 248–253. [14]

Walters, C. C., & Grusec, J. E. (1977). *Punishment.* San Francisco: Freeman. [5]

Ward, C. (1994). Culture and altered states of consciousness. In W. J. Lonner & R. Malpass (Eds.), *Psychology and culture* (pp. 59–64). Boston: Allyn & Bacon. [4]

Wark, G. R., & Krebs, D. L. (1996). Gender and dilemma differences in real-life moral judgment. *Developmental Psychology, 32,* 220–230. [8]

Warshaw, M. G., & Keller, M. B. (1996). The relationship between fluoxetine use and suicidal behavior in 654 subjects with anxiety disorders. *Journal of Clinical Psychiatry, 57,* 158–166. [13]

Wasserman, E. A., & Miller, R. R. (1997). What's elementary about associative learning? *Annual Review of Psychology, 48,* 573–607. [5]

Waterman, A. (1985). Identity in the context of adolescent psychology. *New Directions for Child Development, 65,* 1014–1027. [8]

Watson, D. (2001). Dissociations of the night. *Journal of Abnormal Psychology, 110,* 526–535. [4]

Watson, D. (2002). Predicting psychiatric symptomatology with the Defense Style Questionnaire-40. *International Journal of Stress Management, 9,* 275–287. [11]

Watson, J. B. (1913). Psychology as the behaviorist views it. *Psychological Review, 20,* 158–177. [1, 5]

Watson, J. B., & Rayner, R. (1920). Conditioned emotional reactions. *Journal of Experimental Psychology, 3,* 1–14. [5]

Weaver, J. B., Masland, J. L., & Zillmann, D. (1984). Effect of erotica on young men's aesthetic perception of their female sexual partners. *Perceptual and Motor Skills, 58,* 929–930. [9]

Webb, W. (1995). The cost of sleep-related accidents: A reanalysis. *Sleep, 18,* 276–280. [4]

Webb, W. B. (1975). *Sleep: The gentle tyrant.* Englewood Cliffs, NJ: Prentice-Hall. [4]

Webb, W. B., & Campbell, S. S. (1983). Relationships in sleep characteristics of identical and fraternal twins. *Archives of General Psychiatry, 40,* 1093–1095. [4]

Weber, S. E. (1996). Cultural aspects of pain in childbearing women. *Journal of Obstetric, Gynecologic & Neonatal Nursing, 25,* 67–72. [3]

Weekes, J. R., Lynn, S. J., Green, J. P., & Brentar, J. T. (1992). Pseudomemory in hypnotized and task-motivated subjects. *Journal of Abnormal Psychology, 101,* 356–360. [4]

Weeks, D. L., & Anderson, L. P. (2000). The interaction of observational learning with overt practice: Effects on motor skill learning. *Acta Psychologia, 104,* 259–271. [5]

Weigman, O., & van Schie, E. G. (1998). Video game playing and its relations with aggressive and prosocial behaviour. *British Journal of Social Psychology, 37*(Pt. 3), 367–378. [14]

Weiner, I. B. (1996). Some observations on the validity of the Rorschach Inkblot Method. *Psychological Assessment, 8,* 206–213. [11]

Weiner, I. B. (1997). Current status of the Rorschach Inkblot Method. *Journal of Personality Assessment, 68,* 5–19. [10]

Weiss, J. M. (1972). Psychological factors in stress and disease. *Scientific American, 226,* 104–113. [10]

Weissman, M. M., Bland, R. C., Canino, G. J., Faravelli, C., Greenwald, S., Hwu, H-G., Joyce, P. R., Karam, E. G., Lee, C-K., Lellouch, J., Lepine, J-P., Newman, S. C., Rubio-Stepic, M., Wells, J. E., Wickramaratne, P. J., Wittchen, H-U., & Yeh, E-K. (1996). Cross-national epidemiology of major depression and bipolar disorder. *Journal of the American Medical Association, 276,* 293–299. [12]

Weissman, M. M., Bland, R. C., Canino, G. J., Faravelli, C., Greenwald, S., Hwu, H-G., et al. (1997). The cross national epidemiology of panic disorder. *Archives of General Psychiatry, 54,* 305–309. [12]

Weissman, M. M., Bland, R. C., Canino, G. J., Greenwald, S., Hwu, H-G., Lee, C. K., Newman, S. C., Oakley-Browne, M. A., Rubio-Stipec, M., Wickramaratne, P. J., Wittchen, H-U., & Yeh, E-K. (1994). The cross national epidemiology of obsessive compulsive disorder. *Journal of Clinical Psychiatry, 55*(3, Suppl.), 5–10. [12]

Wells, G. L. (1993). What do we know about eyewitness identification? *American Psychologist, 48,* 553–571. [6]

Wender, P. H., Kety, S. S., Rosenthal, D., et al. (1986). Psychiatric disorders in the biological and adoptive families of adoptive individuals with affective disorders. *Archives of General Psychiatry, 43,* 923–929. [12]

Wesensten, N., Balenky, G., Kautz, M., Thorne, D., Reichardt, R., & Balkin, T. (2002). Maintaining alertness and performance during sleep deprivation: Modafinil versus caffeine. *Psychopharmacology, 159,* 238–247. [4]

Westergaard, G., & Lussier, I. (1999). Left-handedness and longevity in primates. *International Journal of Neuroscience, 99,* 79–87. [2]

Wetherell, J., Gatz, M., & Craske, M. (2003). Treatment of generalized anxiety disorder in older adults. *Journal of Consulting and Clinical Psychology, 71,* 31–40.

Wetter, M. W., Baer, R. A., Berry, T. R., Robison, L. H., & Sumpter, J. (1993). MMPI-2 profiles of motivated fakers given specific symptom information: A comparison to matched patients. *Psychological Assessment, 5,* 317–323. [11]

Wheeler, M. A., Stuss, D. T., & Tulving, E. (1997). Toward a theory of episodic memory: The frontal lobes and autonoetic consciousness. *Psychological Bulletin, 121,* 331–354. [6]

Whisenhunt, B. L., Williamson, D. A., Netemeyer, R. G., & Womble, L. G. (2000). Reliability and validity of the Psychosocial Risk Factors Questionnaire (PRFQ). *Eating and Weight Disorders: Studies on Anorexia, Bulimia, and Obesity, 5,* 1–6. [9]

Whitam, F. L., Diamond, M., & Martin, J. (1993). Homosexual orientation in twins: A report on 61 pairs and three triplet sets. *Archives of Sexual Behavior, 22,* 187–296. [9]

White, D. P. (1989). Central sleep apnea. In M. H. Kryger, T. Roth, & W. C. Dement (Eds.), *Principles and practice of sleep medicine* (pp. 513–524). Philadelphia: W. B. Saunders. [4]

White, G. L., & Mullen, P. E. (1989). *Jealousy: Theory, research, and clinical strategies.* New York: Guilford. [9]

White, S. D., & DeBlassie, R. R. (1992). Adolescent sexual behavior. *Adolescence, 27,* 183–191. [8]

Whitehouse, D. (2000). Rats control robot arm with brain power alone [On-line]. Retrieved from http://www.robotbooks.com/robot-rats.htm [7]

Whitehurst, G. J., Fischel, J. E., Caulfield, M. B., DeBaryshe, B. D., & Valdez-Menchaca, M. C. (1989). Assessment and treatment of early expressive language delay. In P. R. Zelazo & R. Barr (Eds.), *Challenges to developmental paradigms: Implications for assessment and treatment* (pp. 113–135). Hillsdale, NJ: Erlbaum. [8]

Whorf, B. L. (1956). Science and linguistics. In J. B. Carroll (Ed.), *Language, thought, and reality: Selected writings of Benjamin Lee Whorf.* Cambridge, MA: MIT Press. [7]

Wickelgren, I. (1996). For the cortex, neuron loss may be less than thought. *Science, 273,* 48–50. [8]

Wicker, A. W. (1969). Attitudes versus action: The relationship of verbal and overt behavioral responses to attitude objects. *Journal of Social Issues, 25,* 41–78. [14]

Widiger, T. A., Frances, A., Spitzer, R. L., & Williams, J. B. W. (1988). The DSM-III-R personality disorders: An overview. *American Journal of Psychiatry, 145,* 786–795. [12]

Widom, C. S. (1989). Does violence beget violence? A critical examination of the literature. *Psychological Bulletin, 106,* 3–28. [5, 14]

Widom, C. S., & Maxfield, M. G. (1996). A prospective examination of risk for violence among abused and neglected children. *Annals of the New York Academy of Sciences, 794,* 224–237. [14]

Widom, C. S., & Morris, S. (1997). Accuracy of adult recollections of childhood victimization: Part 2. Childhood sexual abuse. *Psychological Bulletin, 9,* 34–46. [6]

Wiggins, J. S. (Ed.) (1996). *The five-factor model of personality: Theoretical perspectives.* New York: Guilford. [11]

Wilcox, D., & Hager, R. (1980). Toward realistic expectation for orgasmic response in women. *Journal of Sex Research, 16,* 162–179. [9]

Wilken, J. A., Smith, B. D., Tola, K., & Mann, M. (2000). Trait anxiety and prior exposure to non-stressful stimuli: Effects on psychophysiological arousal and anxiety. *International Journal of Psychophysiology, 37,* 233–242. [9]

Williams, J. (2003). Dementia and genetics. In R. Plomin, J. de Fries, I. Craig, & P. McGuffin (Eds.), *Behavioral genetics in the postgenomic era* (pp. 503–528). Washington, DC: APA. [8]

Williams, K., Harkins, S. G., & Latané, B. (1981). Identifiability as a deterrent to social loafing: Two cheering experiments. *Journal of Personality and Social Psychology, 40,* 303–311. [14]

Williams, R. (1993). *Anger kills.* New York: Times Books. [10]

Willoughby, T., Wood, E., McDermott, C., & McLaren, J. (2000). Enhancing learning through strategy instruction and group interaction: Is active generation of elaborations critical? *Applied Cognitive Psychology, 14,* 19–30. [6]

Wilson, F. R. (1998). *The hand: How its use shapes the brain, language, and human culture.* New York: Pantheon. [2]

Wilson, W., Mathew, R., Turkington, T., Hawk, T., Coleman, R. E., & Provenzale, J. (2000). Brain morphological changes and early marijuana use: A magnetic resonance and positron emission tomography study. *Journal of Addictive Diseases, 19,* 1–22. [4]

Winch, R. F. (1958). *Mate selection: A study of complementary needs.* New York: Harper & Row. [14]

Wink, P., & Helson, R. (1993). Personality change in women and their partners. *Journal of Personality and Social Psychology, 65,* 597–605. [8]

Winograd, E. (1988). Some observations on prospective remembering. In M. M. Gruneberg, P. E. Morris, & R. N. Sykes (Eds.), *Practical aspects of memory: Current research and issues: Vol. 1* (pp. 348–353). Chichester, England: John Wiley & Sons. [6]

Winokur, G., Coryell, W., Keller, M., Endicott, J., & Akiskal, H. S. (1993). A prospective follow-up of patients with bipolar and primary unipolar affective disorder. *Archives of General Psychiatry, 50,* 457–465. [12]

Wolfson, A., & Carskadon, M. (1998). Sleep schedules and daytime functioning in adolescents. *Child Development, 69,* 875–887. [4]

Wolpe, J. (1958). *Psychotherapy by reciprocal inhibition.* Stanford, CA: Stanford University Press. [13]

Wolpe, J. (1973). *The practice of behavior therapy* (2nd ed.). New York: Pergamon. [13]

Wood, J., Cowan, P., & Baker, B. (2002). Behavior problems and peer rejection in preschool boys and girls. *Journal of Genetic Psychology, 163,* 72–88. [8]

Wood, J. M., Nezworski, M. T., & Stejskal, W. J. (1996). The Comprehensive System for the Rorschach: A critical examination. *Psychological Science, 7,* 3–10. [11]

Wood, W., Lundgren, S., Ovellette, J. A., Busceme, S., & Blackstone, T. (1994). Minority influence: A meta-analytic review of social influence processes. *Psychological Bulletin, 115,* 323–345. [14]

Wood, W., Wong, F. Y., & Chachere, J. G. (1991). Effects of media violence on viewers' aggression in unconstrained social interaction. *Psychological Bulletin, 109,* 371–383. [5, 14]

Woods, S. C., & Gibbs, J. (1989). The regulation of food intake by peptides. *Annals of the New York Academy of Sciences, 575,* 236–243. [9]

Woodward, A. L., Markman, E. M., & Fitzsimmons, C. M. (1994). Rapid word learning in 13- and 18-month-olds. *Developmental Psychology, 30,* 553–566. [8]

Woody, E. Z., & Bowers, K. S. (1994). A frontal assault on dissociated control. In S. J. Lynn & J. W. Rhue (Eds.), *Dissociation: Clinical, theoretical and research perspectives* (pp. 52–79). New York: Guilford. [4]

Word, C. O., Zanna, M. P., & Cooper, J. (1974). The nonverbal mediation of self-fulfilling prophecies in interracial interaction. *Journal of Experimental Social Psychology, 10,* 109–120. [14]

Worrel, J. A., Marken, P. A., Beckman, S. E., & Ruehter, V. L. (2000). Atypical antipsychotic agents: A critical review. *American Journal of Health System Pharmacology, 57,* 238–255. [13]

Worthen, J., & Wood, V. (2001). Memory discrimination for self-performed and imagined acts: Bizarreness effects in false recognition. *Quarterly Journal of Experimental Psychology, 54A,* 49–67. [6]

Wright, J. C., & Mischel, W. (1987). A conditional approach to dispositional constructs: The local predictability of social behavior. *Journal of Personality and Social Psychology, 53,* 1159–1177. [11]

Wu, C., & Shaffer, D. R. (1987). Susceptibility to persuasive appeals as a function of source credibility and prior experience with the attitude object. *Journal of Personality and Social Psychology, 52,* 677–688. [14]

Yackinous, C., & Guinard, J. (2002). Relation between PROP (6-*n*-propylthiouracil) taster status, taste anatomy and dietary intake measures for young men and women. *Appetite, 38,* 201–209. [3]

Yanagita, T. (1973). An experimental framework for evaluation of dependence liability in various types of drugs in monkeys. *Bulletin of Narcotics, 25,* 57–64. [4]

Yang, C., & Spielman, A. (2001). The effect of a delayed weekend sleep pattern on sleep and morning functioning. *Psychology & Health, 16,* 715–725. [4]

Yapko, M. D. (1994). Suggestibility and repressed memories of abuse: A survey of psychotherapists' beliefs. *American Journal of Clinical Hypnosis, 36,* 163–171. [4]

Zajonc, R. B. (1980). Feeling and thinking: Preferences need no inferences. *American Psychologist, 35,* 151–175. [9]

Zajonc, R. B. (1984). On the primacy of affect. *American Psychologist, 39,* 117–123. [9]

Zajonc, R. B., & Sales, S. M. (1966). Social facilitation of dominant and subordinate responses. *Journal of Experimental Social Psychology, 2,* 160–168. [14]

Zald, D. H., & Pardo, J. V. (2000). Functional neuroimaging of the olfactory system in humans. *International Journal of Psychophysiology, 36,* 165–181. [3]

Zaragoza, M. S., & Mitchell, K. J. (1996). Repeated exposure to suggestion and the creation of false memories. *Psychological Science, 7,* 294–300. [6]

Zatorre, R., Belin, P., & Penhune, V. (2002). Structure and function of the auditory cortex: Music and speech. *Trends in Cognitive Sciences, 6,* 37–46. [2]

Zborowski, M. (1952). Cultural components in response to pain. *Journal of Social Issues, 8,* 16–30. [3]

Zhang, X., Cohen, H., Porjesz, B., & Begleiter, H. (2001). Mismatch negativity in subjects at high risk for alcoholism. *Alcoholism: Clinical & Experimental Research, 25,* 330–337. [10]

Zimbardo, P. G. (1972). Pathology of imprisonment. *Society, 9,* 4–8. [14]

Zisapel, N. (2001). Circadian rhythm sleep disorders: Pathophysiology and potential approaches to management. *CNS Drugs, 15,* 311–328. [4]

Zola, S. M., Squire, L. R., Teng, E., Stenfanacci, L., Buffalo, E. A., & Clark, R. E. (2000). Impaired recognition memory in monkeys after damage limited to the hippocampal region. *Journal of Neuroscience, 20,* 451–463. [6]

Zucker, A., Ostrove, J., & Stewart A. (2002). College-educated women's personality development in adulthood: Perceptions and age differences. *Psychology & Aging, 17,* 236–244. [8[

Zuger, B. (1990, August). Changing concepts of the etiology of male homosexuality. *Medical Aspects of Human Sexuality, 24,* 73–75. [9]

absolute threshold The minimum amount of sensory stimulation that can be detected 50% of the time.

accommodation In vision, the action of the lens in changing shape as it focuses objects on the retina, becoming more spherical for near objects and flatter for far objects. In learning, the process by which existing schemes are modified and new schemes are created to incorporate new objects, events, experiences, or information.

acetylcholine (ah-SEET-ul-KOH-leen) A neurotransmitter that plays a role in learning, memory, and rapid eye movement (REM) sleep and causes the skeletal muscle fibers to contract.

acquired immune deficiency syndrome (AIDS) A devastating and incurable illness that is caused by the human immunodeficiency virus (HIV) and progressively weakens the body's immune system, leaving the person vulnerable to opportunistic infections that usually cause death.

action potential The sudden reversal of the resting potential, which initiates the firing of a neuron.

actor-observer effect The tendency to attribute one's own behavior primarily to situational factors and the behavior of others primarily to internal or dispositional factors.

additive strategy A decision-making approach in which each alternative is rated on each important factor affecting the decision and then the alternative rated highest overall is chosen.

adolescence The developmental stage that begins at puberty and encompasses the period from the end of childhood to the beginning of adulthood.

adoption study method A method researchers use to study the relative effects of heredity and environment on behavior and ability in children adopted shortly after birth, by comparing them with their biological and adoptive parents.

adrenal glands (ah-DREE-nal) A pair of endocrine glands that release hormones that prepare the body for emergencies and stressful situations and also release the corticoids and small amounts of the sex hormones.

aerobic exercise (ah-RO-bik) Exercise that uses the large muscle groups in continuous, repetitive action and increases oxygen intake and breathing and heart rates.

afterimage The visual sensation that remains after a stimulus is withdrawn.

aggression The intentional infliction of physical or psychological harm on another.

agoraphobia (AG-or-uh-FO-bee-uh) An intense fear of being in a situation from which immediate escape is not possible or in which help is not immediately available in case of incapacitating anxiety.

alarm stage The first stage of the general adaptation syndrome, when there is emotional arousal and the defensive forces of the body are prepared to fight or flee.

algorithm A systematic, step-by-step procedure, such as a mathematical formula, that guarantees a solution to a problem of a certain type if applied appropriately and executed properly.

alpha wave The type of brain wave associated with deep relaxation.

altered state of consciousness A mental state other than ordinary waking consciousness, such as sleep, meditation, hypnosis, or a drug-induced state.

altruism Behavior aimed at helping another, requiring some self-sacrifice and not designed for personal gain.

Alzheimer's disease (ALZ-hye-merz) An incurable form of dementia characterized by progressive deterioration of intellect and personality, resulting from widespread degeneration of brain cells.

amnesia A partial or complete loss of memory resulting from brain trauma or psychological trauma.

amplitude Measured in decibels, the magnitude or intensity of a sound wave, determining the loudness of the sound.

amygdala (ah-MIG-da-la) A structure in the limbic system that plays an important role in emotion, particularly in response to aversive stimuli.

analogy heuristic A rule of thumb that applies a solution that solved a problem in the past to a current problem that shares many features with the past problem.

anorexia nervosa An eating disorder characterized by an overwhelming, irrational fear of being fat, compulsive dieting to the point of self-starvation, and excessive weight loss.

anterograde amnesia The inability to form long-term memories of events occurring after a brain injury or brain surgery (although memories formed before the trauma are usually intact).

antidepressants Drugs that are prescribed to treat depression and some anxiety disorders.

antipsychotic drugs Drugs used to control severe psychotic symptoms, such as the delusions and hallucinations of schizophrenics; also known as *neuroleptics* or *atypical neuroleptics*.

antisocial personality disorder A disorder marked by lack of feeling for others; selfish, aggressive, irresponsible behavior; and willingness to break the law, lie, cheat, or exploit others for personal gain.

anxiety disorders   Psychological disorders characterized by severe anxiety (e.g., panic disorder, phobias, general anxiety disorder, obsessive-compulsive disorder).

applied research   Research conducted to solve practical problems.

approach–approach conflict   A conflict arising from having to choose between desirable alternatives.

approach–avoidance conflict   A conflict arising when the same choice has both desirable and undesirable features.

aptitude test   A test designed to predict a person's achievement or performance at some future time.

archetype   (AR-kea-type) Existing in the collective unconscious, an inherited tendency to respond in particular ways to universal human situations.

arousal   A state of alertness and mental and physical activation.

arousal theory   A theory suggesting that the aim of motivation is to maintain an optimal level of arousal.

artificial intelligence   The programming of computer systems to simulate human thinking in solving problems and in making judgments and decisions.

assimilation   The process by which new objects, events, experiences, or information are incorporated into existing schemes.

association areas   Areas of the cerebral cortex that house memories and are involved in thought, perception, learning, and language.

attachment   The strong affectionate bond a child forms with the mother or primary caregiver.

attitude   A relatively stable evaluation of a person, object, situation, or issue.

attribution   An inference about the cause of one's own or another's behavior.

audience effects   The impact of passive spectators on performance.

audition   The sensation of hearing; the process of hearing.

authoritarian parents   Parents who make arbitrary rules, expect unquestioned obedience from their children, punish transgressions, and value obedience to authority.

authoritative parents   Parents who set high but realistic standards, reason with the child, enforce limits, and encourage open communication and independence.

availability heuristic   A cognitive rule of thumb that says that the probability of an event or the importance assigned to it is based on its availability in memory.

aversion therapy   A behavior therapy in which an aversive stimulus is paired with an undesirable behavior until the behavior becomes associated with pain and discomfort.

avoidance–avoidance conflict   A conflict arising from having to choose between undesirable alternatives.

axon   (AK-sahn) The slender, tail-like extension of a neuron, which transmits impulses to the dendrites or cell body of other neurons or to muscles or glands.

babbling   Vocalization of the basic speech sounds (phonemes), which begins between 4 and 6 months.

basic emotions   Emotions that are found in all cultures, that are reflected in the same facial expressions across cultures, and that emerge in children according to their biological timetable; fear, anger, disgust, surprise, joy or happiness, and sadness or distress are usually considered basic emotions.

basic research   Research conducted to advance knowledge rather than for its practical application.

behavior modification   The systematic application of the learning principles of operant or classical conditioning or observational learning to individuals or groups in order to eliminate undesirable behavior and/or encourage desirable behavior.

behavior therapy   A treatment approach employing the principles of operant conditioning, classical conditioning, and/or observational learning theory to eliminate inappropriate or maladaptive behaviors and replace them with more adaptive ones.

behavioral genetics   A field of research that investigates the relative effects of heredity and environment on behavior and ability.

behaviorism   The school of psychology founded by John B. Watson that views observable, measurable behavior as the appropriate subject matter for psychology and emphasizes the key role of environment as a determinant of behavior.

beta wave   (BAY-tuh) The type of brain wave associated with mental or physical activity.

binocular depth cues   Depth cues that depend on two eyes working together; they include convergence and binocular disparity.

biofeedback   The use of sensitive equipment to give people precise feedback about internal physiological processes so that they can learn, with practice, to control them.

biological therapy   A therapy (drug therapy, ECT, or psychosurgery) that is based on the assumption that most mental disorders have physical causes.

biomedical model   A perspective that focuses on illness rather than on health, explaining illness in terms of biological factors without regard to psychological and social factors.

biopsychosocial model   A perspective that focuses on health as well as illness and holds that both are determined by a combination of biological, psychological, and social factors.

bipolar disorder   A mood disorder in which manic episodes alternate with periods of depression, usually with relatively normal periods in between.

bottom-up processing   Information processing in which individual components or bits of data are combined until a complete perception is formed.

brainstem   The structure that begins at the point where the spinal cord enlarges as it enters the brain and that includes the medulla, the reticular formation, and the pons.

brightness   The dimension of visual sensation that is dependent on the intensity of light reflected from a surface and that corresponds to the amplitude of the light wave.

Broca's area   (BRO-kuz) The area in the left frontal lobe that controls the production of speech sounds.

bulimia nervosa   An eating disorder characterized by repeated and uncontrolled episodes of binge eating, usually followed by purging—that is, self-induced vomiting and/or the use of large quantities of laxatives and diuretics.

bystander effect The fact that as the number of bystanders at an emergency increases, the probability that the victim will receive help decreases, and help, if given, is likely to be delayed.

Cannon–Bard theory The theory that an emotion-provoking stimulus is transmitted simultaneously to the cortex, providing the feeling of an emotion, and the sympathetic nervous system, causing the physiological arousal.

case study An in-depth study of one or a few individuals that consists of information gathered through observation, interviews, and perhaps psychological testing.

catatonic schizophrenia (KAT-uh-TAHN-ik) A type of schizophrenia characterized by complete stillness or stupor and/or periods of great agitation and excitement; patients may assume unusual postures and remain in them for long periods.

cell body The part of a neuron that contains the nucleus and carries out the neuron's metabolic functions.

central nervous system (CNS) The brain and the spinal cord.

cerebellum (sehr-uh-BELL-um) The brain structure that executes smooth, skilled body movements and regulates muscle tone and posture.

cerebral cortex (seh-REE-brul KOR-tex) The gray, convoluted covering of the cerebral hemispheres that is responsible for higher mental processes such as language, memory, and thinking.

cerebral hemispheres (seh-REE-brul) The right and left halves of the cerebrum, covered by the cerebral cortex and connected by the corpus callosum.

cerebrum (seh-REE-brum) The largest structure of the human brain, consisting of the two cerebral hemispheres connected by the corpus callosum and covered by the cerebral cortex.

chromosomes Rod-shaped structures in the nuclei of body cells, which contain all the genes.

circadian rhythm (sur-KAY-dee-un) The regular fluctuation from high points to low points of certain bodily functions within each 24-hour period.

circadian theory The theory that sleep evolved to keep humans out of harm's way during the night and that sleepiness ebbs and flows according to a circadian rhythm.

classical conditioning A learning process through which one stimulus comes to predict the occurrence of another stimulus and to elicit a response similar to or related to the response evoked by that stimulus.

co-action effects The impact on performance of the presence of others engaged in the same task.

cochlea (KOK-lee-uh) The snail-shaped, fluid-filled chamber in the inner ear that contains the hair cells (the sound receptors).

cognition The mental processes that are involved in acquiring, storing, retrieving, and using information and that include sensation, perception, imagery, concept formation, reasoning, decision making, problem solving, and language.

cognitive dissonance (COG-nuh-tiv) The unpleasant state that can occur when people become aware of inconsistencies among their attitudes or among their attitudes and their behavior.

cognitive map A mental representation of a spatial arrangement such as a maze.

cognitive processes Mental processes such as thinking, knowing, problem solving, and remembering.

cognitive psychology The school of psychology that studies mental processes such as memory, problem solving, decision making, perception, language, and other forms of cognition; often uses the information-processing approach.

cognitive therapies Therapies that assume that maladaptive behavior can result from irrational thoughts, beliefs, and ideas, which the therapist tries to change.

cognitive therapy A therapy designed to change maladaptive behavior by changing the person's irrational thoughts, beliefs, and ideas.

collective unconscious In Jung's theory, the most inaccessible layer of the unconscious, which contains the universal experiences of humankind transmitted to each individual.

color blindness The inability to distinguish some or all colors, resulting from the absence of normal genes for the three color pigments.

compliance Acting in accordance with the wishes, suggestions, or direct requests of another person.

compulsion A persistent, irresistible, irrational urge to perform an act or ritual repeatedly.

concept A mental category used to represent a class or group of objects, people, organizations, events, situations, or relations that share common characteristics or attributes.

conditioned response (CR) A response that comes to be elicited by a conditioned stimulus as a result of its repeated pairing with an unconditioned stimulus.

conditioned stimulus (CS) A neutral stimulus that, after repeated pairing with an unconditioned stimulus, becomes associated with it and elicits a conditioned response.

conditions of worth Conditions on which the positive regard of others rests.

cones The receptor cells in the retina that enable humans to see color and fine detail in adequate light but that do not function in dim light.

confederate Someone who is posing as a participant in an experiment but is actually assisting the experimenter.

conformity Changing or adopting an attitude or behavior to be consistent with the social norms of a group or the expectations of other people.

confounding variables Any factors or conditions other than the independent variable that could cause observed changes in the dependent variable.

conscious (KON-chus) The thoughts, feelings, sensations, or memories of which a person is aware at any given moment.

consciousness An awareness of one's own perceptions, thoughts, feelings, sensations, and external environment.

conservation The concept that a given quantity of matter remains the same despite being rearranged or changed in appearance, as long as nothing is added or taken away.

consolidation A physiological change in the brain that must take place for encoded information to be stored in memory.

consolidation failure Any disruption in the consolidation process that prevents a permanent memory from forming.

continuous reinforcement Reinforcement that is administered after every desired or correct response; the most effective method of conditioning a new response.

control group In an experiment, a group that is similar to the experimental group and is exposed to the same experimental environment but is not exposed to the independent variable; used for purposes of comparison.

conventional level Kohlberg's second level of moral development, in which right and wrong are based on the internalized standards of others; "right" is whatever helps or is approved of by others, or whatever is consistent with the laws of society.

conversion disorder A somatoform disorder in which a person suffers a loss of motor or sensory functioning in some part of the body; the loss has no physical cause but solves some psychological problem.

coping Efforts, through action and thought, to deal with demands that are perceived as taxing or overwhelming.

cornea (KOR-nee-uh) The transparent covering on the front surface of the eyeball that bends light rays inward through the pupil.

corpus callosum (KOR-pus kah-LO-sum) The thick band of nerve fibers that connects the two cerebral hemispheres and makes possible the transfer of information and the synchronization of activity between them.

correlation coefficient A numerical value that indicates the strength and direction of the relationship between two variables; ranges from +1.00 (a perfect positive correlation) to −1.00 (a perfect negative correlation).

correlational method A research method used to establish the degree of relationship (correlation) between two characteristics, events, or behaviors.

creativity The ability to produce original, appropriate, and valuable ideas and/or solutions to problems.

critical period A period so important to development that a harmful environmental influence at that time can keep a bodily structure from developing normally or can impair later intellectual or social development.

critical thinking The process of objectively evaluating claims, propositions, or conclusions to determine whether they follow logically from the evidence presented.

crowding A subjective perception that there are too many people in a defined space.

crystallized intelligence Aspects of intelligence, including verbal ability and accumulated knowledge, that tend to increase over the life span.

CT (computerized tomography) scan A brain-scanning technique that uses a rotating X-ray tube and high-speed computer analysis to produce slice-by-slice, cross-sectional images of the brain (or other body part).

culturally sensitive psychotherapy An approach to therapy that considers cultural variables in the diagnosis and treatment of psychological disorders.

culture-fair intelligence test An intelligence test that uses questions that will not penalize those whose culture differs from the mainstream or dominant culture.

decay theory A theory of forgetting that holds that the neural trace, if not used, disappears with the passage of time.

decibel (DES-ih-bel) A unit of measurement of the intensity or loudness of sound based on the amplitude of the sound wave; abbreviated dB.

decision making The process of considering alternatives and choosing among them.

declarative memory The subsystem within long-term memory that stores facts, information, and personal life experiences; also called *explicit memory.*

defense mechanism An unconscious, irrational means used by the ego to defend against anxiety; involves self-deception and the distortion of reality.

delta wave The type of brain wave associated with slow-wave (deep) sleep (Stage 3 and Stage 4 sleep).

delusion A false belief, not generally shared by others in the culture, that cannot be changed despite strong evidence to the contrary.

delusions of grandeur False beliefs that one is a famous person or a person who has some great knowledge, ability, or authority.

delusions of persecution False beliefs that a person or group is trying in some way to harm one.

dendrites (DEN-drytes) The branchlike extensions of a neuron that receive impulses from other neurons.

dependent variable The variable that is measured at the end of an experiment and is presumed to vary as a result of manipulations of the independent variable.

depressants A category of drugs that decrease activity in the central nervous system, slow down bodily functions, and reduce sensitivity to outside stimulation; also called *downers.*

depth perception The ability to see in three dimensions and to estimate distance.

descriptive research methods Research methods that yield descriptions of behavior rather than causal explanations.

descriptive statistics Statistics used to organize, summarize, and describe data.

developmental psychology The study of how humans grow, develop, and change throughout the life span.

difference threshold The smallest increase or decrease in a physical stimulus required to produce a difference in sensation that is noticeable 50% of the time.

diffusion of responsibility The feeling among bystanders at an emergency that the responsibility for helping is shared by the group, so each person feels less compelled to act than if he or she alone bore the total responsibility.

directive therapy An approach in which the therapist takes an active role in determining the course of therapy sessions and provides answers and suggestions to the patient.

discrimination In classical conditioning, the learned ability to distinguish between similar stimuli so that the conditioned response occurs only with the original conditioned stimulus, not similar stimuli. In social psychology, behavior, usually negative, directed toward others based on their gender, religion, race, or membership in a particular group.

discriminative stimulus   A stimulus that signals whether a certain response or behavior is likely to be followed by reward or punishment.

disorganized schizophrenia   The most serious type of schizophrenia, marked by inappropriate affect, silliness, laughter, grotesque mannerisms, and bizarre behavior.

displacement   The phenomenon that occurs when short-term memory is holding its maximum amount of information and each new item entering short-term memory pushes out an existing item.

display rules   Cultural rules that dictate how emotions should be expressed, and when and where their expression is appropriate.

dispositional attribution   Attributing a behavior to some internal cause, such as a personal trait, motive, or attitude; an internal attribution.

dissociative amnesia   A dissociative disorder in which there is a loss of memory of limited periods in one's life or of one's entire identity.

dissociative disorders   Disorders in which, under stress, one loses the ability to integrate one's consciousness, identity, and memories of important personal events.

dissociative fugue   (FEWG) A dissociative disorder in which one has a complete loss of memory of one's entire identity, travels away from home, and may assume a new identity.

dissociative identity disorder (DID)   A dissociative disorder in which two or more distinct personalities occur in the same person, each taking over at different times.

dominant gene   The gene of any pair that is expressed in the individual.

door-in-the-face technique   A strategy in which someone makes a large, unreasonable request with the expectation that the person will refuse but will then be more likely to respond favorably to a smaller request at a later time.

dopamine   (DOE-pah-meen) A neurotransmitter that plays a role in learning, attention, and movement.

double-blind technique   An experimental procedure in which neither the participants nor the researchers know who is in the experimental and control groups until after the results have been gathered; used as a control for experimenter bias.

drive   A state of tension or arousal brought about by an underlying need, which motivates an organism to engage in behavior that will satisfy the need and reduce the tension.

drive-reduction theory   A theory of motivation suggesting that a need creates an unpleasant state of arousal or tension, that is, a drive, which impels the organism to engage in behavior that will satisfy the need and reduce the tension.

drug tolerance   A condition in which the user becomes progressively less affected by the drug so that larger and larger doses are necessary to achieve the same effect.

DSM-IV   The *Diagnostic and Statistical Manual of Mental Disorders, Fourth Edition,* a manual published by the American Psychiatric Association, which describes about 290 mental disorders and their symptoms.

ego   (EE-go) In Freudian theory, the rational, largely conscious system of personality, which operates according to the reality principle.

elaborative rehearsal   A technique used to encode information into long-term memory by considering its meaning and associating it with other information already stored in long-term memory.

electroconvulsive therapy (ECT)   A treatment in which an electric current is passed through the brain, causing a seizure; usually reserved for severely depressed patients who are either suicidal or unresponsive to other treatment.

electroencephalogram (EEG)   (ee-lek-tro-en-SEFF-uh-lo-gram) A record of brain-wave activity made by a machine called an electroencephalograph.

embryo   The developing human organism during the period (week 3 through week 8) when the major systems, organs, and structures of the body develop.

emotion   A feeling state involving physiological arousal, a cognitive appraisal of the situation arousing the state, and an outward expression of the state.

emotional intelligence   A type of intelligence that includes an awareness of and an ability to manage one's own emotions, the ability to motivate oneself, empathy, and the ability to handle relationships successfully.

emotion-focused coping   A response aimed at reducing the emotional impact of the stressor.

encoding   Transforming information into a form that can be stored in short-term or long-term memory.

encoding failure   A breakdown in the process by which information enters long-term memory, which results in an inability to recall the information.

endocrine system   (EN-duh-krin) A number of ductless glands located in various parts of the body that manufacture and secrete hormones into the bloodstream or lymph fluids, thus affecting cells in other parts of the body.

endorphins   (en-DOOR-fins) Chemicals produced naturally by the brain that reduce pain and positively affect mood.

epinephrine   (EP-ih-NEF-rin) A neurotransmitter that affects the metabolism of glucose and causes energy stored in muscles to be released during exercise.

episodic memory   (ep-ih-SOD-ik) The part of declarative memory that contains memories of personally experienced events.

evolutionary psychology   The school of psychology that studies how humans' genetically inherited tendencies and dispositions influence a wide range of behaviors.

exemplars   The individual instances, or examples, of a concept that are stored in memory from personal experience.

exhaustion stage   The final stage of the general adaptation syndrome, occurring if the organism fails in its efforts to resist the stressor.

experimental group   In an experiment, the group that is exposed to the independent variable, or the treatment.

experimental method   The research method in which researchers randomly assign participants to groups and control all conditions other than one or more independent variables, which are then manipulated to determine their effect on some behavioral measure—the dependent variable in the experiment.

experimenter bias   A phenomenon that occurs when the researcher's preconceived notions in some way influence the participants' behavior and/or the interpretation of experimental results.

exposure and response prevention   A behavior therapy that exposes patients with obsessive-compulsive disorder to stimuli generating increasing anxiety; patients must agree not to carry out their normal rituals for a specified period of time after exposure.

extinction   In classical conditioning, the weakening and often eventual disappearance of the conditioned response, caused by repeated presentation of the conditioned stimulus without the unconditioned stimulus. In operant conditioning, the weakening and often eventual disappearance of the conditioned response when reinforcement is withheld.

extrinsic motivation   The desire to perform an act to gain a reward or to avoid an undesirable consequence.

facial-feedback hypothesis   The idea that the muscular movements involved in certain facial expressions trigger the corresponding emotions (for example, smiling makes one feel happy).

family therapy   Therapy involving an entire family, based on the assumption that an individual's problem is caused and/or maintained in part by problems within the family unit.

feature detectors   Neurons in the brain that respond to specific features of a sensory stimulus (for example, to lines or angles).

fetal alcohol syndrome   A condition, caused by maternal alcohol intake during pregnancy, in which the baby is born mentally retarded, with a small head and facial, organ, and behavioral abnormalities.

fetus   The developing human organism during the period (week 9 until birth) when rapid growth and further development of the structures, organs, and systems of the body occur.

fight-or-flight response   A response to stress in which the sympathetic nervous system and the endocrine glands prepare the body to fight or flee.

five-factor theory   A trait theory that attempts to explain personality using the Big Five, broad dimensions that are composed of a constellation of personality traits.

fixation   Arrested development at a psychosexual stage occurring because of excessive gratification or frustration at that stage.

fixed-interval schedule   A schedule in which a reinforcer is given following the first correct response after a fixed period of time has elapsed.

fixed-ratio schedule   A schedule in which a reinforcer is given after a fixed number of correct responses.

flashbulb memory   An extremely vivid memory of the conditions surrounding one's first hearing the news of a surprising, shocking, or highly emotional event.

flooding   A behavioral therapy used to treat phobias, during which clients are exposed to the feared object or event (or asked to imagine it vividly) for an extended period until their anxiety decreases.

fluid intelligence   Aspects of intelligence involving abstract reasoning and mental flexibility, which peak in the early 20s and decline slowly as people age.

foot-in-the-door technique   A strategy designed to secure a favorable response to a small request at first, with the aim of making the person more likely to agree later to a larger request.

formal concept   A concept that is clearly defined by a set of rules, a formal definition, or a classification system; also known as an *artificial concept.*

fovea   (FO-vee-uh) A small area of the retina, 1/50 of an inch in diameter, that provides the clearest and sharpest vision because it has the largest concentration of cones.

framing   The way information is presented so as to emphasize either a potential gain or a potential loss as the outcome.

fraternal (dizygotic) twins   Twins, no more alike genetically than ordinary siblings, who develop after two eggs are released during ovulation and fertilized by two different sperm.

free association   A psychoanalytic technique used to explore the unconscious by having patients reveal whatever thoughts or images come to mind.

frequency   Measured in a unit called the hertz (Hz), the number of sound waves or cycles per second, determining the pitch of the sound.

frequency distribution   An arrangement showing the numbers of scores that fall within equal-sized class intervals.

frequency polygon   A line graph that depicts the frequency, or number, of scores within each class interval in a frequency distribution.

frontal lobes   The lobes of the brain that control voluntary body movements, speech production, and such functions as thinking, motivation, planning for the future, impulse control, and emotional responses.

frustration–aggression hypothesis   The hypothesis that frustration produces aggression.

functional MRI (fMRI)   A brain-imaging technique that reveals both brain structure and brain activity.

functionalism   An early school of psychology that was concerned with how mental processes help humans and animals adapt to their environments.

***g* factor**   Spearman's term for a general intellectual ability that underlies all mental operations to some degree.

gender roles   Cultural expectations about the behavior appropriate for each gender.

gender-sensitive therapy   An approach to therapy that takes into account the effects of gender on both the therapist's and the patient's behavior.

general adaptation syndrome (GAS)   The predictable sequence of reactions (alarm, resistance, and exhaustion stages) that organisms show in response to stressors.

generalization   In classical conditioning, the tendency to make a conditioned response to a stimulus similar to the original conditioned stimulus. In operant conditioning, the tendency to make a learned response to a stimulus that is similar to one which was originally reinforced.

generalized anxiety disorder An anxiety disorder in which people experience excessive anxiety or worry that they find difficult to control.

genes The segments of DNA that are located on the chromosomes and are the basic units for the transmission of all hereditary traits.

Gestalt (geh-SHTALT) A German word roughly meaning "form" or "pattern."

Gestalt psychology The school of psychology that emphasizes that individuals perceive objects and patterns as whole units and that the perceived whole is more than the sum of its parts.

Gestalt therapy A therapy that was originated by Fritz Perls and that emphasizes the importance of clients' fully experiencing, in the present moment, their feelings, thoughts, and actions and taking personal responsibility for their behavior.

group polarization The tendency of members of a group, after group discussion, to shift toward a more extreme position in whatever direction they were leaning initially–either more risky or more cautious.

groupthink The tendency for members of a very cohesive group to feel such pressure to maintain group solidarity and to reach agreement on an issue that they fail to weigh available evidence adequately or to consider objections and alternatives.

gustation The sensation of taste.

hair cells Sensory receptors for hearing, found in the cochlea.

hallucination A sensory perception in the absence of any external sensory stimulus; an imaginary sensation.

hallucinogens (hal-LU-sin-o-jenz) A category of drugs, sometimes called *psychedelics*, that alter perception and mood and can cause hallucinations.

halo effect The tendency to infer generally positive or negative traits in a person as a result of observing one major positive or negative trait.

hardiness A combination of three psychological qualities shared by people who can undergo high levels of stress yet remain healthy: a sense of control over one's life, commitment to one's personal goals, and a tendency to view change as a challenge rather than as a threat.

hassles Little stressors, which include the irritating demands and troubled relationships that can occur daily and, according to Lazarus, can cause more stress than do major life changes.

health psychology The field concerned with the psychological factors that contribute to health, illness, and recovery.

heritability An index of the degree to which a characteristic is estimated to be influenced by heredity.

heuristic (yur-RIS-tik) A rule of thumb that is derived from experience and used in decision making and problem solving, even though there is no guarantee of its accuracy or usefulness.

higher-order conditioning Conditioning that occurs when a neutral stimulus is paired with an existing conditioned stimulus, becomes associated with it, and gains the power to elicit the same conditioned response.

hippocampal region A part of the brain's limbic system, which includes the hippocampus itself (primarily involved in the formation of episodic memories) and its underlying cortical areas (involved in the formation of semantic memories).

hippocampus (hip-po-CAM-pus) A structure in the limbic system that plays a central role in the formation of long-term memories.

histogram A bar graph that depicts the number of scores within each class interval in a frequency distribution.

homeostasis The tendency of the body to maintain a balanced internal state with regard to oxygen level, body temperature, blood sugar, water balance, and so forth.

hormones Substances that are manufactured and released in one part of the body but affect other parts of the body.

hue The property of light commonly referred to as color (red, blue, green, etc.), determined primarily by the wavelength of light reflected from a surface.

human immunodeficiency virus (HIV) The virus that causes AIDS.

humanistic psychology The school of psychology that focuses on the uniqueness of human beings and their capacity for choice, growth, and psychological health.

humanistic therapies Therapies that assume that people have the ability and freedom to lead rational lives and make rational choices.

hypnosis A procedure through which one person, the hypnotist, uses the power of suggestion to induce changes in thoughts, feelings, sensations, perceptions, or behavior of another person, the subject.

hypochondriasis (HI-poh-kahn-DRY-uh-sis) A somatoform disorder in which persons are preoccupied with their health and convinced that they have some serious disorder even though there is no evidence of any medical problem.

hypothalamus (HY-po-THAL-uh-mus) A small but influential brain structure that controls the pituitary gland and regulates hunger, thirst, sexual behavior, body temperature, and a wide variety of emotional behaviors.

hypothesis A prediction about the relationship between two or more variables.

hypothetico-deductive thinking The ability to base logical reasoning on a hypothetical premise.

id (ihd) The unconscious system of the personality, which contains the life and death instincts and operates on the pleasure principle.

identical (monozygotic) twins Twins with exactly the same genes, who develop after one egg is fertilized by one sperm and then the zygote splits into two parts.

illusion A false perception of actual stimuli involving a misperception of size, shape, or the relationship of one element to another.

imagery The representation in the mind of a sensory experience–visual, auditory, gustatory, motor, olfactory, or tactile.

imaginary audience A belief of adolescents that they are or will be the focus of attention in social situations and that others will be as critical or approving as they are of themselves.

incentive An external stimulus that motivates behavior (examples: money, fame).

inclusion Educating mentally retarded students in regular rather than special schools by placing them in regular classes for part of the day or having special classrooms in regular schools; also called *mainstreaming.*

independent variable In an experiment, any factor or condition that the researcher manipulates in order to determine its effect on another condition or behavior known as the dependent variable.

individualism/collectivism dimension The term used to signify a culture's emphasis either on individuals or on group relationships.

inferential statistics Statistical procedures that allow researchers to make inferences about the characteristics of the larger population from observations and measurements of a sample and to derive estimates of how much confidence can be placed in those inferences.

information-processing theory An approach to the study of memory and problem solving that uses the computer as a model for human thinking.

in-group A social group in which there is a strong sense of togetherness and from which others are excluded.

inner ear The innermost portion of the ear, containing the cochlea, the vestibular sacs, and the semicircular canals.

insight The sudden realization of the relationship between elements in a problem situation, which makes the solution apparent.

insight therapy Any type of psychotherapy based on the notion that psychological well-being depends on self-understanding.

instinct theory The notion that human behavior is motivated by certain innate tendencies, or instincts, shared by all individuals.

intelligence An individual's ability to understand complex ideas, to adapt effectively to the environment, to learn from experience, to engage in various forms of reasoning, and to overcome obstacles through mental effort.

intelligence quotient (IQ) An index of intelligence, originally derived by dividing mental age by chronological age and then multiplying by 100, but now derived by comparing an individual's score with the scores of others of the same age.

interference Memory loss that occurs because information or associations stored either before or after a given memory hinder the ability to recall it.

interpersonal therapy (IPT) A brief psychotherapy designed to help depressed people better understand and cope with problems relating to their interpersonal relationships.

intrinsic motivation The desire to perform an act because it is satisfying or pleasurable in and of itself.

James–Lange theory The theory that emotional feelings result when an individual becomes aware of a physiological response to an emotion-provoking stimulus (for example, feeling fear because of trembling).

just noticeable difference (JND) The smallest change in sensation that a person is able to detect 50% of the time.

kinesthetic sense The sense providing information about relative position and movement of body parts.

laboratory observation A research method in which behavior is studied in a laboratory setting, where researchers can exert more control and take more precise measurements.

language A means of communicating thoughts and feelings, using a system of socially shared but arbitrary symbols (sounds, signs, or written symbols) arranged according to rules of grammar.

latent learning Learning that occurs without apparent reinforcement but that is not demonstrated until sufficient reinforcement is provided.

lateral hypothalamus (LH) The part of the hypothalamus that acts as a feeding center and, when activated, signals an animal to eat; when the LH is destroyed, the animal refuses to eat.

lateralization The specialization of one of the cerebral hemispheres to handle a particular function.

law of effect Thorndike's law of learning, which states that the connection between a stimulus and a response will be strengthened if the response is followed by a satisfying consequence and weakened if the response is followed by discomfort.

Lazarus theory The theory of emotion stating that an emotion-provoking stimulus triggers a cognitive appraisal, which is followed by the emotion and the physiological arousal.

learned helplessness The learned response of resigning oneself passively to aversive conditions, rather than taking action to escape or avoid them; learned through repeated exposure to inescapable or unavoidable aversive events.

learning A relatively permanent change in behavior, knowledge, capability, or attitude that is acquired through experience and cannot be attributed to illness, injury, or maturation.

left hemisphere The hemisphere that controls the right side of the body, coordinates complex movements, and, in 95% of right-handers and 62% of left-handers, controls the production of speech and written language.

lens The transparent structure behind the iris that changes shape as it focuses images on the retina.

levels-of-processing model A model of memory as a single system in which retention depends on how deeply information is processed.

limbic system A group of structures deep within the brain, including the amygdala and hippocampus, that are collectively involved in emotion, memory, and motivation.

linguistic relativity hypothesis The notion that the language a person speaks largely determines the nature of that person's thoughts.

lithium A drug used in bipolar disorder to control the symptoms in a manic episode and to even out the mood swings and reduce recurrence of future manic or depressive states.

locus of control A concept used to explain how people account for what happens in their lives—people with an internal locus of control see themselves as primarily in control of their behavior and its consequences; those with an external locus of control perceive what happens to be in the hands of fate, luck, or chance.

long-term memory The relatively permanent memory system with a virtually unlimited capacity.

long-term potentiation (LTP) A long-lasting increase in the efficiency of neural transmission at the synapses.

low-ball technique A strategy to gain compliance by making a very attractive initial offer to get a person to agree to an action and then making the terms less favorable.

low-birthweight baby A baby weighing less than 5.5 pounds.

lymphocytes The white blood cells, including B cells and T cells, that are key components of the immune system.

major depressive disorder A mood disorder marked by feelings of great sadness, despair, guilt, worthlessness, and hopelessness.

manic episode (MAN-ik) A period of extreme elation, euphoria, and hyperactivity, often accompanied by delusions of grandeur and by hostility if activity is blocked.

massed practice Learning in one long practice session, as opposed to spacing the learning in shorter practice sessions over an extended period.

matching hypothesis The notion that people tend to have spouses, lovers, or friends who are approximately equivalent in social assets such as physical attractiveness.

maturation Changes that occur according to one's genetically determined biological timetable of development.

mean The arithmetic average of a group of scores; calculated by adding all the single scores and dividing the sum by the number of scores.

means–end analysis A heuristic strategy in which the current position is compared with the desired goal and a series of steps are formulated and taken to close the gap between them.

measure of central tendency A measure or score that describes the center, or middle, of a distribution of scores (example: mean, median, or mode).

median The middle score or value when a group of scores are arranged from highest to lowest.

meditation In the concentrative form, a group of techniques that involve focusing attention on an object, a word, one's breathing, or one's body movement in order to block out all distractions, to enhance well-being, and to achieve an altered state of consciousness.

medulla (muh-DUL-uh) The part of the brainstem that controls heartbeat, blood pressure, breathing, coughing, and swallowing.

menarche (men-AR-kee) The onset of menstruation.

menopause The cessation of menstruation, occurring between ages 45 and 55 and signifying the end of reproductive capacity.

mental retardation Subnormal intelligence reflected by an IQ below 70 and by adaptive functioning severely deficient for one's age.

mental set The tendency to apply a familiar strategy to the solution of a problem without carefully considering the special requirements of that problem.

mere-exposure effect The tendency of people to develop a more positive evaluation of some person, object, or other stimulus with repeated exposure to it.

metabolic rate (meh-tuh-BALL-ik) The rate at which the body burns calories to produce energy.

microelectrode An electrical wire so fine that it can be inserted near or into a single neuron.

middle ear The portion of the ear containing the ossicles, which connect the eardrum to the oval window and amplify the sound vibrations as they travel to the inner ear.

mode The score that occurs most frequently in a group of scores.

model The individual who demonstrates a behavior or serves as an example in observational learning.

modeling Another name for observational learning.

monocular depth cues (mah-NOK-yu-ler) Depth cues that can be perceived by only one eye.

mood disorders Disorders characterized by extreme and unwarranted disturbances in feeling or mood.

morphemes The smallest units of meaning in a language.

motivated forgetting Forgetting through repression in order to protect oneself from a memory that is too painful, anxiety- or guilt-producing, or otherwise unpleasant.

motivation The process that initiates, directs, and sustains behavior to satisfy physiological or psychological needs or wants.

motives Needs or desires that energize and direct behavior toward a goal.

motor cortex The strip of tissue at the rear of the frontal lobes that controls voluntary body movement.

MRI (magnetic resonance imaging) A diagnostic scanning technique that produces high-resolution images of the structures of the brain.

myelin sheath (MY-uh-lin) The white fatty coating wrapped around some axons that acts as insulation and enables impulses to travel much faster than they do in unsheathed axons.

naive idealism A type of thought in which adolescents construct ideal solutions for problems.

naive subject A person who has agreed to participate in an experiment but is not aware that deception is being used to conceal its real purpose.

narcotics A class of depressant drugs derived from the opium poppy and producing pain-relieving and calming effects.

natural concept A concept acquired not from a definition but through everyday perceptions and experiences; also known as a *fuzzy concept.*

naturalistic observation A research method in which the researcher observes and records behavior in its natural setting, without attempting to influence or control it.

nature–nurture controversy The debate over whether intelligence and other traits are primarily the result of heredity or environment.

need for achievement (*n* Ach) The need to accomplish something difficult and to perform at a high standard of excellence.

negative correlation A relationship between two variables in which an increase in one variable is associated with a decrease in the other variable.

negative reinforcement The termination of an unpleasant condition after a response in order to increase the probability that the response will be repeated.

neonate A newborn infant up to 1 month old.

neural networks Computer systems that are intended to mimic the human brain.

neuron (NEW-ron) A specialized cell that conducts impulses through the nervous system and has three major parts: a cell body, dendrites, and an axon.

neuroscience A field that combines the work of psychologists, biologists, biochemists, medical researchers, and others in the study of the structure and function of the nervous system.

neurotransmitter (NEW-ro-TRANS-mit-er) A chemical that is released into the synaptic cleft from the axon terminal of a sending neuron, crosses the synapse, and binds to appropriate receptor sites on the dendrites or cell body of a receiving neuron, influencing that cell either to fire or not to fire.

nondeclarative memory The subsystem within long-term memory that consists of skills acquired through repetitive practice, habits, and simple classically conditioned responses; also called *implicit memory*.

nondirective therapy An approach in which the therapist acts to facilitate growth, giving understanding and support rather than proposing solutions, answering questions, or actively directing the course of therapy.

norepinephrine (nor-EP-ih-NEF-rin) A neurotransmitter affecting eating and sleep.

normal curve A symmetrical, bell-shaped frequency distribution that represents how scores are normally distributed in a population; most scores fall near the mean, and fewer and fewer scores occur in the extremes either above or below the mean.

norms Standards based on the range of test scores of a large group of people who are selected to provide the bases of comparison for those who take the test later.

NREM dreams Mental activity occurring during NREM sleep that is more thoughtlike in quality than REM dreams are.

NREM sleep Non–rapid eye movement sleep, consisting of the four sleep stages and characterized by slow, regular respiration and heart rate, an absence of rapid eye movements, and blood pressure and brain activity that are at a 24-hour low point.

object permanence The realization that objects continue to exist, even when they can no longer be perceived.

observational learning Learning by observing the behavior of others and the consequences of that behavior; learning by imitation.

obsession A persistent, recurring, involuntary thought, image, or impulse that invades consciousness and causes great distress.

obsessive-compulsive disorder (OCD) An anxiety disorder in which a person suffers from recurrent obsessions and/or compulsions.

occipital lobes (ahk-SIP-uh-tul) The lobes of the brain that contain the primary visual cortex, where vision registers, and association areas involved in the interpretation of visual information.

Oedipus complex (ED-uh-pus) Occurring in the phallic stage, a conflict in which the child is sexually attracted to the opposite-sex parent and feels hostility toward the same-sex parent.

olfaction (ol-FAK-shun) The sensation of smell; the process of smelling.

olfactory bulbs Two matchstick-sized structures above the nasal cavities, where smell sensations first register in the brain.

olfactory epithelium Two 1-square-inch patches of tissue, one at the top of each nasal cavity, which together contain about 10 million olfactory neurons, the receptors for smell.

operant conditioning A type of learning in which the consequences of behavior are manipulated in order to increase or decrease that behavior in the future.

outer ear The visible part of the ear, consisting of the pinna and the auditory canal.

out-group A social group specifically identified by an in-group as not belonging.

overextension The act of using a word, on the basis of some shared feature, to apply to a broader range of objects than is appropriate.

overlearning Practicing or studying material beyond the point where it can be repeated once without error.

overregularization The act of inappropriately applying the grammatical rules for forming plurals and past tenses to irregular nouns and verbs.

panic attack An attack of overwhelming anxiety, fear, or terror.

panic disorder An anxiety disorder in which a person experiences recurrent unpredictable attacks of overwhelming anxiety, fear, or terror.

paranoid schizophrenia (PAIR-uh-noid) A type of schizophrenia characterized by delusions of grandeur or persecution.

parasomnias Unusual behaviors that occur while a person is sleeping, such as sleepwalking and sleeptalking.

parasympathetic nervous system The division of the autonomic nervous system that is associated with relaxation and the conservation of energy and that brings the heightened bodily responses back to normal following an emergency.

parietal lobes (puh-RY-uh-tul) The lobes of the brain that contain the somatosensory cortex (where touch, pressure, temperature, and pain register) and other areas that are responsible for body awareness and spatial orientation.

partial reinforcement A pattern of reinforcement in which some portion, rather than 100%, of the correct responses are reinforced.

participant modeling A behavior therapy in which an appropriate response is modeled in graduated steps and the client attempts each step, encouraged and supported by the therapist.

perception   The process by which sensory information is actively organized and interpreted by the brain.

perceptual constancy   The tendency to perceive objects as maintaining stable properties, such as size, shape, brightness, and color, despite differences in distance, viewing angle, and lighting.

perceptual set   An expectation of what will be perceived, which can affect what actually is perceived.

period of the zygote   The approximately 2-week-long period between conception and the attachment of the zygote to the uterine wall.

peripheral nervous system (PNS)   (peh-RIF-er-ul) The nerves connecting the central nervous system to the rest of the body.

permissive parents   Parents who make few rules or demands and allow children to make their own decisions and control their own behavior.

personal fable   An exaggerated sense of personal uniqueness and indestructibility, which may be the basis for adolescent risk taking.

personal space   An area surrounding each individual, much like an invisible bubble, that is considered to belong to the person and is used to regulate the closeness of interactions with others.

personal unconscious   In Jung's theory, the layer of the unconscious containing all of the thoughts and experiences that are accessible to the conscious, as well as repressed memories and impulses.

personality   A person's characteristic patterns of behaving, thinking, and feeling.

personality disorder   A continuing, inflexible, maladaptive pattern of behaving and relating to others that causes great distress or impaired functioning and differs significantly from the patterns expected in the person's culture.

personality inventory   A paper-and-pencil test with questions about a person's thoughts, feelings, and behaviors, which is scored according to a standard procedure.

person-centered therapy   A nondirective humanistic therapy in which the therapist creates a warm, accepting climate, freeing clients to be themselves and releasing their natural tendency toward positive growth.

persuasion   A deliberate attempt to influence the attitudes and/or behavior of another.

PET (positron-emission tomography) scan   A brain-imaging technique that reveals activity in various parts of the brain based on the amounts of oxygen and glucose consumed.

pheromones   Chemicals excreted by humans and other animals that act as signals to and elicit certain patterns of behavior from members of the same species.

phobia   (FO-bee-ah) A persistent, irrational fear of an object, situation, or activity that the person feels compelled to avoid.

phonemes   The smallest units of sound in a spoken language.

physical drug dependence   A compulsive pattern of drug use in which the user develops a drug tolerance coupled with unpleasant withdrawal symptoms when the drug use is discontinued.

pituitary gland   The endocrine gland located in the brain and often called the "master gland," which releases hormones that control other endocrine glands as well as a growth hormone.

placebo   (pluh-SEE-bo) Some inert substance, such as a sugar pill or an injection of saline solution, given to the control group in an experiment to avoid the placebo effect.

placebo effect   The phenomenon that occurs when a person's response to a treatment in an experiment is due to expectations regarding the treatment rather than to the treatment itself.

plasticity   The brain's ability to recover from damage and adapt to new demands.

population   The entire group that is of interest to researchers and to which they wish to generalize their findings; the group from which a sample is selected.

positive correlation   A relationship between two variables in which both vary in the same direction.

positive reinforcement   A reward or pleasant consequence that follows a response and increases the probability that the response will be repeated.

postconventional level   Kohlberg's highest level of moral development, in which moral reasoning involves weighing moral alternatives; "right" is whatever furthers basic human rights.

posttraumatic stress disorder (PTSD)   A prolonged and severe stress reaction to a catastrophic event or to chronic intense stress.

pragmatics   The patterns of intonation and social roles associated with a language.

preconscious   The thoughts, feelings, and memories that a person is not consciously aware of at the moment but that may be brought to consciousness.

preconventional level   Kohlberg's lowest level of moral development, in which moral reasoning is based on the physical consequences of an act; "right" is whatever avoids punishment or gains a reward.

prejudice   Negative attitudes toward others based on their gender, religion, race, or membership in a particular group.

prenatal   Occurring between conception and birth.

presbyopia   (prez-bee-O-pee-uh) A condition, occurring in the mid- to late 40s, in which the lenses of the eyes no longer accommodate adequately for near vision, and reading glasses or bifocals are required for reading.

preterm infant   An infant born before the 37th week and weighing less than 5.5 pounds; a premature infant.

primacy effect   In memory, the tendency to recall the first items on a list more readily than the middle items. In social psychology, the tendency for an overall impression of another to be influenced more by the first information that is received about that person than by information that comes later.

primary appraisal   An evaluation of the meaning and significance of a potentially stressful event according to how it will affect one's well-being–whether it is perceived as irrelevant or as involving harm or loss, threat, or challenge.

primary auditory cortex   The part of the temporal lobes where hearing registers in the cerebral cortex.

primary drive   A state of tension or arousal arising from a biological need; one not based on learning.

primary mental abilities   According to Thurstone, seven relatively distinct capabilities that singly or in combination are involved in all intellectual activities.

primary reinforcer   A reinforcer that fulfills a basic physical need for survival and does not depend on learning.

primary visual cortex   The area at the rear of the occipital lobes where vision registers in the cerebral cortex.

proactive coping   Efforts or actions taken in advance of a potentially stressful situation to prevent its occurrence or to minimize its consequences.

problem solving   Thoughts and actions required to achieve a desired goal that is not readily attainable.

problem-focused coping   A response aimed at reducing, modifying, or eliminating a source of stress.

projective test   A personality test in which people respond to inkblots, drawings of ambiguous human situations, incomplete sentences, and the like by projecting their own inner thoughts, feelings, fears, or conflicts onto the test materials.

prosocial behavior   Behavior that benefits others, such as helping, cooperation, and sympathy.

prospective forgetting   Forgetting to carry out some action, such as mailing a letter.

prototype   An example that embodies the most common and typical features of a concept.

proximity   Geographic closeness; a major factor in attraction.

psychiatrist   A mental health professional who is a medical doctor.

psychoactive drug   A drug that alters normal mental functioning—mood, perception, or thought—and thus may be abused.

psychoanalysis   (SY-co-ah-NAL-ih-sis) Freud's term for both his theory of personality and his therapy for treating psychological disorders.

psychodynamic therapies   Therapies that attempt to uncover childhood experiences that explain a patient's current difficulties.

psycholinguistics   The study of how language is acquired, produced, and used and how the sounds and symbols of language are translated into meaning.

psychological disorders   Mental processes and/or behavior patterns that cause emotional distress and/or substantial impairment in functioning.

psychological drug dependence   A craving or irresistible urge for a drug's pleasurable effects.

psychological perspectives   General points of view used for explaining people's behavior and thinking, whether normal or abnormal.

psychologist   A mental health professional who possesses a doctoral degree in psychology.

psychology   The scientific study of behavior and mental processes.

psychoneuroimmunology   (sye-ko-NEW-ro-IM-you-NOLL-oh-gee) A field in which psychologists, biologists, and medical researchers study the effects of psychological factors on the immune system.

psychosexual stages   A series of stages through which the sexual instinct develops; for each stage, a part of the body becomes the center of new pleasures and conflicts.

psychosis   (sy-CO-sis) A psychological disorder marked by loss of contact with reality and a seriously impaired ability to function.

psychosocial stages   Erikson's eight developmental stages for the entire life span; each is defined by a conflict that must be resolved satisfactorily in order for healthy personality development to occur.

psychosurgery   Brain surgery to treat some severe, persistent, and debilitating psychological disorder or severe chronic pain.

psychotherapy   The treatment for psychological disorders that uses psychological rather than biological means and primarily involves conversations between patient and therapist.

puberty   A period of rapid physical growth and change that culminates in sexual maturity.

punishment   The removal of a pleasant stimulus or the application of an unpleasant stimulus, which tends to suppress a response.

random assignment   In an experiment, the assignment of participants to experimental and control groups by using a chance procedure, which guarantees that each has an equal probability of being placed in any of the groups; used as a control for selection bias.

range   The difference between the highest score and the lowest score in a distribution of scores.

rational-emotive therapy   A directive, confrontational therapy developed by Albert Ellis and designed to challenge and modify the irrational beliefs thought to cause personal distress.

realistic conflict theory   The notion that prejudices arise when social groups must compete for scarce resources and opportunities.

recall   A measure of retention that requires a person to remember material with few or no retrieval cues, as in an essay test.

recency effect   The tendency to recall the last items on a list more readily than those in the middle of the list.

receptors   Sites on the dendrite or cell body of a neuron that will interact only with specific neurotransmitters.

recessive gene   A gene that will not be expressed if paired with a dominant gene but will be expressed if paired with another recessive gene.

reciprocal determinism   Bandura's concept that behavior, cognitive factors, and environment all influence and are influenced by one another.

recognition   A measure of retention that requires a person to identify material as familiar, or as having been encountered before.

reconstruction   An account that is not an exact replica of a remembered event but has been pieced together from a few highlights, using information that may or may not be accurate.

reflexes Built-in responses to certain stimuli that neonates need to ensure survival in their new world.

rehearsal The act of purposely repeating information in order to maintain it in short-term memory or to transfer it to long-term memory.

reinforcement An event that follows a response and increases the strength of the response and/or the likelihood that it will be repeated.

reinforcer Anything that strengthens a response or increases the probability that it will occur.

relationship therapies Therapies that attempt to improve patients' interpersonal relationships or create relationships in order to provide them with support.

relearning method A way of measuring memory retention in terms of the percentage of time saved in relearning material compared with the time required to learn it originally; also called the *savings method*.

reliability The ability of a test to yield nearly the same score when the same people are tested and then retested on the same test or an alternative form of the test.

REM dreams A type of dream having a storylike quality and occuring almost continuously during each REM period; more vivid, visual, and emotional than NREM dreams.

REM rebound The increased amount of REM sleep that occurs after REM deprivation; often associated with unpleasant dreams or nightmares.

REM sleep Sleep characterized by rapid eye movements, paralysis of large muscles, fast and irregular heart rate and respiration rate, increased brain-wave activity, and vivid dreams.

representative sample A group of participants selected from a larger population in such a way that important subgroups are included in the sample in the same proportions as they are found in the larger population.

representativeness heuristic A thinking strategy based on how closely a new object or situation is judged to resemble or match an existing prototype of that object or situation.

repression Removing from one's consciousness disturbing, guilt-provoking, or otherwise unpleasant memories so that one is no longer aware that a painful event occurred.

resistance stage The second stage of the general adaptation syndrome, when there are intense physiological efforts to either resist or adapt to the stressor.

resting potential The membrane potential of a neuron at rest, about -70 millivolts.

restorative theory The theory that the function of sleep is to restore body and mind.

reticular formation A structure in the brainstem that plays a crucial role in arousal and attention and that screens sensory stimuli entering the brain.

retina The layer of tissue at the back of the eye that contains the rods and the cones and onto which the incoming image is projected by the lens.

retrieval The act of bringing to mind material that has been stored in memory.

retrieval cue Any stimulus or bit of information that aids in the retrieval of a particular memory from long-term memory.

retrograde amnesia (RET-ro-grade) A loss of memory affecting experiences that occurred shortly before a loss of consciousness.

reuptake The process by which neurotransmitter molecules are taken from the synaptic cleft back into the axon terminal for later use, thus terminating their excitatory or inhibitory effect on the receiving neuron.

reversibility The realization that any change in the shape, position, or order of matter can be reversed mentally.

right hemisphere The hemisphere that controls the left side of the body and that, in most people, is specialized for visual-spatial perception and for interpreting nonverbal behavior.

robotics The science of automating human and animal functions.

rods The light-sensitive receptors in the retina that allow humans to see in dim light.

sample A portion of any population that is selected for study and from which generalizations are made about the larger population.

saturation The degree to which light waves producing a color are of the same wavelength; the purity of a color.

scapegoating Displacing aggression onto minority groups or other innocent targets not responsible for the frustrating situation.

Schachter–Singer theory A two-stage theory of emotion stating that for an emotion to occur, there must be (1) physiological arousal and (2) a cognitive explanation for the arousal.

schedule of reinforcement A systematic program for administering reinforcements that has a predictable effect on behavior.

schemas The integrated frameworks of knowledge about people, objects, and events, which are stored in long-term memory and affect the encoding and recall of information.

scheme Piaget's term for a cognitive structure or concept used to identify and interpret information.

schizophrenia (SKIT-soh-FREE-nee-ah) A severe psychological disorder characterized by loss of contact with reality, hallucinations, delusions, inappropriate or flat affect, some disturbance in thinking, social withdrawal, and/or other bizarre behavior.

scientific method The orderly, systematic procedures researchers follow as they identify a research problem, design a study to investigate the problem, collect and analyze data, draw conclusions, and communicate their findings.

secondary appraisal An evaluation of one's coping resources prior to deciding how to deal with a stressful event.

secondary reinforcer A neutral stimulus that becomes reinforcing after repeated pairings with other reinforcers.

secondary sex characteristics Those physical characteristics that are not directly involved in reproduction but distinguish the mature male from the mature female.

selection bias The assignment of participants to experimental or control groups in such a way that systematic differences among the groups are present at the beginning of the experiment.

self-actualization Developing to one's fullest potential.

self-efficacy A person's belief in his or her ability to perform competently in whatever is attempted.

self-serving bias The tendency to attribute personal successes to dispositional causes and failures to situational causes.

semantic memory The part of declarative memory that holds general knowledge; a mental encyclopedia or dictionary.

semantics The meaning or the study of meaning derived from morphemes, words, and sentences.

semicircular canals Three fluid-filled tubular canals in the inner ear that provide information about rotating head movements.

senile dementia A state of mental deterioration caused by physical deterioration of the brain and characterized by impaired memory and intellect and by altered personality and behavior; also referred to as *senility*.

sensation The process through which the senses pick up visual, auditory, and other sensory stimuli and transmit them to the brain; sensory information that has registered in the brain but has not been interpreted.

sensory adaptation The process of becoming less sensitive to an unchanging sensory stimulus over time.

sensory memory The memory system that holds information coming in through the senses for a period ranging from a fraction of a second to several seconds.

sensory receptors Specialized cells in the sense organs that detect and respond to sensory stimuli–light, sound, odors, etc.–and transduce (convert) the stimuli into neural impulses.

separation anxiety The fear and distress shown by a toddler when the parent leaves, occurring from 8 to 24 months and reaching a peak between 12 and 18 months.

serial position effect The tendency to remember the beginning and ending items of a sequence or list better than the middle items.

serotonin (ser-oh-TOE-nin) A neurotransmitter that plays an important role in regulating mood, sleep, impulsivity, aggression, and appetite.

set point The weight the body normally maintains when one is trying neither to gain nor to lose weight; if weight falls below the normal level, appetite increases and metabolic rate decreases; if weight is gained, appetite decreases and metabolic rate increases to its original level.

sex chromosomes The 23rd pair of human chromosomes, which carry the genes that determine one's sex, primary and secondary sex characteristics, and other sex-linked traits.

sexual dysfunction A persistent or recurrent problem that causes marked distress and interpersonal difficulty and that may involve any or some combination of the following: sexual desire, sexual arousal, the pleasure associated with sex or orgasm.

sexual orientation The direction of one's sexual preference–toward members of the opposite sex (heterosexuality), toward one's own sex (homosexuality), or toward both sexes (bisexuality).

sexual response cycle The four phases–excitement, plateau, orgasm, and resolution–that make up the human sexual response in both males and females, according to Masters and Johnson.

shaping An operant conditioning technique that consists of gradually molding a desired behavior (response) by reinforcing responses that become progressively closer to it.

short-term memory The memory system that holds about seven (a range from five to nine) items for less than 30 seconds without rehearsal; also called *working memory* because it is the mental workspace for tasks being thought about at any given moment.

situational attribution Attributing a behavior to some external cause or factor operating in the situation; an external attribution.

Skinner box A soundproof chamber with a device for delivering food and either a bar for rats to press or a disk for pigeons to peck; used in operant conditioning experiments.

sleep cycle A period of sleep lasting about 90 minutes and including one or more stages of NREM sleep followed by REM sleep.

slow-wave sleep Stage 3 and Stage 4 sleep; deep sleep.

social cognition Mental processes that people use to notice, interpret, understand, remember, and apply information about the social world and that enable them to simplify, categorize, and order that world.

social facilitation Any positive or negative effect on performance due to the presence of others, either as an audience or as co-actors.

social loafing The tendency to put forth less effort when working with others on a common task than when working alone.

social motives Motives acquired through experience and interaction with others.

social norms The attitudes and standards of behavior expected of members of a particular group.

social phobia An irrational fear and avoidance of social situations in which one might embarrass or humiliate oneself by appearing clumsy, foolish, or incompetent.

social psychology The study of how the actual, imagined, or implied presence of others influences the thoughts, feelings, and behavior of individuals.

Social Readjustment Rating Scale (SRRS) Holmes and Rahe's stress scale, which ranks 43 life events from most to least stressful and assigns a point value to each.

social roles Socially defined behaviors considered appropriate for individuals occupying certain positions within a group.

social support Tangible support, information, advice, and/or emotional support provided in time of need by family, friends, and others; the feeling of being loved, valued, and cared for.

socialization The process of learning socially acceptable behaviors, attitudes, and values.

somatoform disorders (so-MAT-uh-form) Disorders in which physical symptoms are present but are due to psychological rather than physical causes.

somatosensory cortex (so-MAT-oh-SENS-or-ee) The strip of tissue at the front of the parietal lobes where touch, pressure, temperature, and pain register in the cerebral cortex.

specific phobia A marked fear of a specific object or situation; any phobia other than agoraphobia and social phobia.

spinal cord An extension of the brain, extending from the base of the brain through the entire spinal column, that transmits messages between the brain and the peripheral nervous system.

split-brain operation An operation, performed in severe cases of epilepsy, in which the corpus callosum is cut, separating the cerebral hemispheres and usually lessening the severity and frequency of grand mal seizures.

spontaneous recovery The reappearance of an extinguished response (in a weaker form) when an organism is exposed to the original conditioned stimulus after a rest period.

standard deviation A descriptive statistic reflecting the average amount that scores in a distribution deviate, or vary, from their mean.

standardization Establishing norms for comparing the scores of people who will take a test in the future; administering tests using a prescribed procedure.

state-dependent memory effect The tendency to recall information better if one is in the same psychological state (mood) as when the information was encoded.

stereotypes Widely shared beliefs about the characteristic traits, attitudes, and behaviors of members of various social groups (racial, ethnic, religious), including the assumption that the members of such groups are usually all alike.

stimulants A category of drugs that speed up activity in the central nervous system, suppress appetite, and cause a person to feel more awake, alert, and energetic; also called *uppers*.

stimulus (STIM-yu-lus) Any event or object in the environment to which an organism responds; plural is *stimuli*.

stimulus motives Motives that cause humans and other animals to increase stimulation and that appear to be unlearned (examples: curiosity and the need to explore, manipulate objects, and play).

storage The act of maintaining information in memory.

stranger anxiety A fear of strangers common in infants at about 6 months and increasing in intensity until about 12 months, and then declining in the second year.

stress The physiological and psychological response to a condition that threatens or challenges a person and requires some form of adaptation or adjustment.

stressor Any stimulus or event capable of producing physical or emotional stress.

structuralism The first formal school of psychology, aimed at analyzing the basic elements, or structure, of conscious mental experience through the use of introspection.

subjective night The time during a 24-hour period when body temperature is lowest and when the internal clock is telling a person to go to sleep.

successive approximations A series of gradual steps, each of which is more like the final desired response.

superego (sue-per-EE-go) The moral system of the personality, which consists of the conscience and the ego ideal.

survey A method in which researchers use interviews and/or questionnaires to gather information about the attitudes, beliefs, experiences, or behaviors of a group of people.

symbolic function The understanding that one thing–an object, a word, a drawing–can stand for another.

sympathetic nervous system The division of the autonomic nervous system that mobilizes the body's resources during stress, emergencies, or heavy exertion, preparing the body for action.

synapse (SIN-aps) The junction where the axon of a sending neuron communicates with a receiving neuron across the synaptic cleft.

syntax The aspect of grammar that specifies the rules for arranging and combining words to form phrases and sentences.

systematic desensitization A behavior therapy that is used to treat phobias and that involves training clients in deep muscle relaxation and then having them confront a graduated series of anxiety-producing situations (real or imagined) until they can remain relaxed while confronting even the most feared situation.

tactile Pertaining to the sense of touch.

taste aversion The dislike and/or avoidance of a particular food that has been associated with nausea or discomfort.

taste buds Structures composed of 60 to 100 sensory receptors for taste.

telegraphic speech Short sentences that follow a strict word order and contain only essential content words.

temperament A person's behavioral style or characteristic way of responding to the environment.

temporal lobes The lobes of the brain that contain the primary auditory cortex and association areas for interpreting auditory information.

teratogens Harmful agents in the prenatal environment, which can have a negative impact on prenatal development or even cause birth defects.

tests of statistical significance Statistical tests that estimate the probability that a particular research result could have occurred by chance.

thalamus (THAL-uh-mus) The structure, located above the brainstem, that acts as a relay station for information flowing into or out of the forebrain.

theory A general principle or set of principles proposed to explain how a number of separate facts are related.

timbre (TAM-burr) The distinctive quality of a sound that distinguishes it from other sounds of the same pitch and loudness.

time out A behavior modification technique used to decrease the frequency of undesirable behavior by withdrawing an individual from all reinforcement for a period of time.

token economy A behavior modification technique that motivates and reinforces socially acceptable behaviors with tokens that can be exchanged for desired items or privileges.

top-down processing Application of previous experience and conceptual knowledge to recognize the whole of a perception and thus easily identify the simpler elements of that whole.

traits Personal characteristics used to describe or explain personality.

transference An intense emotional reaction by a patient during psychoanalysis involving the display of feelings and attitudes toward the analyst that were present in a significant past relationship of the patient.

trial and error An approach to problem solving in which one solution after another is tried in no particular order until an answer is found.

triangular theory of love Sternberg's theory that three components—intimacy, passion, and decision/commitment—singly and in various combinations, produce seven different kinds of love.

triarchic theory of intelligence Sternberg's theory that there are three types of intelligence: componential (analytical), experiential (creative), and contextual (practical).

twin study method A method researchers use to study the relative effects of heredity and environment on a variety of characteristics by comparing pairs of identical and fraternal twins.

Type A behavior pattern A behavior pattern marked by a sense of time urgency, impatience, excessive competitiveness, hostility, and anger; considered a risk factor in coronary heart disease.

Type B behavior pattern A behavior pattern marked by a relaxed, easygoing approach to life; not associated with coronary heart disease.

unconditional positive regard Unqualified caring and nonjudgmental acceptance of another.

unconditioned response (UR) A response that is invariably elicited by the unconditioned stimulus without prior learning.

unconditioned stimulus (US) A stimulus that elicits a specific response without prior learning.

unconscious (un-KON-chus) For Freud, the primary motivating force of behavior, containing repressed memories, as well as instincts and wishes that have never been conscious.

underextension Restricting the use of a word to only a few, rather than to all, members of a class of objects.

undifferentiated schizophrenia A catchall category used when symptoms of schizophrenia do not fit into one of the other categories or conform to more than one of them.

uplifts The positive experiences in life, which can neutralize the effects of many of the hassles.

validity The ability of a test to measure what it is intended to measure.

variability How much the scores in a distribution spread out, away from the mean.

variable-interval schedule A schedule in which a reinforcer is given after the first correct response following a varying time of nonreinforcement based on an average time.

variable-ratio schedule A schedule in which a reinforcer is given after a varying number of nonreinforced responses based on an average ratio.

ventromedial hypothalamus (VMH) The part of the hypothalamus that acts as a satiety center and, when activated, signals an animal to stop eating; when the VMH is destroyed, the animal overeats, becoming obese.

vestibular sense (ves-TIB-yu-ler) Sense that provides information about the body's movement and orientation in space through sensory receptors in the semicircular canals and the vestibular sacs, which detect changes in the movement and orientation of the head.

visible spectrum The narrow band of electromagnetic waves, 380–760 nanometers in length, that are visible to the human eye.

visual cliff An apparatus used to test depth perception in infants and young animals.

Weber's law The law stating that the just noticeable difference (JND) for all the senses depends on a proportion or percentage of change in a stimulus rather than on a fixed amount of change.

Wernicke's area The language area in the left temporal lobe that is involved in comprehension of the spoken word and in formulation of coherent speech and written language.

withdrawal symptoms The physical and psychological symptoms (usually the opposite of those produced by the drug) that occur when a regularly used drug is discontinued and that terminate when the drug is taken again.

working backwards A heuristic strategy in which a person discovers the steps needed to solve a problem by defining the desired goal and working backwards to the current condition; also called *backward search*.

Yerkes–Dodson law The principle that performance on tasks is best when the arousal level is appropriate to the difficulty of the task—higher arousal for simple tasks, moderate arousal for tasks of moderate difficulty, and lower arousal for complex tasks.

Dale, N., 161
Dallery, J., 132
Daly, M., 410
Damasio, A., 96
Damasio, A. R., 274
Darley, J. M., 407
Darroch, J., 236
Darwin, C., 275
Dasen, P. R., 216
Dashiell, J. F., 258
Davalos, D., 345
Davidson, J. R. T., 379
Davis, L., 157
Davis, S., 162
Davis, T. L., 276
Dawson, D. A., 304
Day, S., 384
D'Azevedo, W. A., 158
de Jong, P., 232
De Raad, B., 322
De Vos, S., 243
Deary, I. J., 196
DeBlassie, R. R., 236
DeBortoli, M., 73
DeCasper, A. J., 227
Deci, E. L., 136
Deese, J., 156
Deinzer, R., 301
Delgado, J. M. R., 261
DeLongis, A., 288
DelVecchio, W. F., 325
Dent, C. W., 107
Deovell, L. Y., 46
Department of Behavior Biology, Walter
    Reed Army Institute of Research, 100
Derlega, V. J., 397
Derrick, B. E., 162
Devanand, D. P., 381
Devine, P. G., 405, 414
deVries, H. A., 240
Dewsbury, D. A., 18
DeYoung, C., 400
Dhand, R., 263
Dickens, W., 200
Diehl, S. R., 346
Diener, C., 235
Diener, E., 235
Diindia, K., 279
DiLalla, L. F., 408, 410
Dill, K. E., 411
Dion, K., 397
Dipboye, R. L., 397
Dixon, R. A., 241
Dodge, K. A., 410
Dodson, C. S., 156, 158
Dogil, G., 190
Doherty, M. A., 372
Dollard, J., 409
Domino, G., 330
Domjan, M., 16
Donnelly, J., 234
Donoghue, J. P., 44
Doob, L. W., 409
Dornbusch, S., 233
Doyle, J. A., 234
Draper, E. S., 38
Dreikurs, R., 319
Drevets, W. C., 349

Drummond, S. P. A., 100
Dryer, D. C., 397
Duck, S., 237
Duckworth, J. C., 330
Duffey, F., 109
Duka, T., 126
Dunkel-Schetter, C., 299
Dunn, J., 233
Duyme, M., 199
Dywan, J., 104

Eagly, A. H., 397, 400, 406
Ebbinghaus, H. E., 163, 166
Eccles, J. S., 201
Edwards, B., 97
Edwards, K., 406
Egeth, H. E., 156
Ehrhardt, A. A., 269
Eichenbaum, H., 42, 161
Eisen, J. L., 355
Ekman, P., 46, 272, 274, 275, 276, 277
Elal, G., 264
Elkin, I., 370, 378
Elkind, D., 237
Ellason, J. W., 356
Elliot, A. J., 405
Ellis, A., 375
Ellis, R., 41
Engel, G. L., 296
Engles, G. I., 375
Epstein, J., 237, 368
Erikson, E. H., 221
Erlenmeyer-Kimling, L., 198
Eron, L. D., 410
Eronen, M., 409
Estes, W. K., 179
Etcoff, N., 46
Evans, G. W., 410
Evans, M. D., 376
Everson, S. A., 302
Exner, J. E., 331
Exton, M. S., 126
Eysenbach, G., 306
Eysenck, H. J., 323, 382

Fackelmann, K., 109
Fagiolini, M., 68
Fagot, B., 234
Falbo, T., 271
Falloon, I. R. H., 370
Famighetti, R., 379
Fang, C., 294
Fantz, R. L., 226
Farah, M. J., 178
Farde, L., 49
Farrer, L. A., 242
Farvolden, P., 157
Fauerbach, J., 318
Faunce, G., 263
Fazio, R. H., 404, 405
Fearon, R., 229
Federal Bureau of Investigation, 408
Fein, S., 413
Feingold, A., 397
Fenton, W. S., 345, 346
Fernald, A., 232
Fernández-Dols, J.-M., 276
Festinger, L., 405

Fiatarone, M. A., 240, 306
Fiedler, K., 412
Field, M., 126
Field, T., 75
Field, T. M., 227
Finch, A. E., 371
Finchilescu, G., 415
Fink, B., 397
Fisher, L. M., 240
Fitzgibbon, M., 265
Fixx, J. F., 183
Flavell, J. H., 217
Fleck, D., 385
Fleming, J. D., 186
Fletcher, J. M., 109
Flood, J. F., 261
Flora, D., 371
Florian, V., 302
Florio, V., 346
Flynn, J., 200
Flynn, J. R., 200
Flynn, R., 200
Foa, E. B., 293, 373
Fogel, J., 306
Foley, D. J., 99
Foley, H. J., 72, 73
Folkerts, H., 380
Folkman, S., 245, 295, 296
Ford, C. S., 268
Forgas, J. P., 412
Foulkes, D., 100
Fowler, J. S., 111
Fox, M., 287
Fox, N. A., 229
Frackenburg, W. K., 228
Francis, W. D., 233
Frank, E., 349, 370
Frank, M., 46
Frantz, K., 108
Franz, C. E., 232
Fraser, A. M., 237
Fraser, S. C., 401
Frazer, A., 378
Frazer, N., 297
Fredrikson, M., 353
Freedman, J. L., 401
Freud, A., 235
Freud, S., 101, 165, 315, 316, 318
Frey, K. P., 406
Friedland, N., 291
Friedman, J. M., 262
Friedman, M., 298
Friedman, M. I., 261
Friedrich, L. K., 235
Friesen, W. V., 275
Fry, A. F., 196
Fuligni, A. J., 203
Furstenberg, F. F., 236
Fyer, A. J., 353

Gallagher, M., 239
Gallistel, C. R., 121
Gallup, G., Jr., 414
Galton, F., 197
Ganellen, R. J., 331
Gangestad, G. W., 396
Garavan, H., 195
Garbarino, S., 97

Hunter, J. A., 395
Hurvich, L. M., 68
Hyde, J. S., 201, 265
Hyman, I. E., Jr., 157

Impicciatore, P., 306
Ingegneri, D. G., 243
Inglehart, R., 242, 243
Inhelder, B., 214, 216
Insel, T. R., 354
International Food Information Council, 111
Isenberg, D. J., 403
Ito, T. A., 409
Iwata, B. A., 372
Izard, C. E., 274, 276, 277

Jacklin, C. N., 234
Jackson, J. M., 402
Jackson, S., 415
Jacobs, J. E., 201
James, W., 17, 271
Jamieson, D. W., 404
Jamison, D., 69
Janda, L. H., 397
Janis, I. L., 403
Janssen, T., 321
Jarvik, L. F., 198
Jefferson, J. W., 353, 354, 378
Jelicic, M., 162
Jellinek, E. M., 305
Jenike, M. A., 374
Jenkins, J. H., 370
Jeppsen, E. A., 356
Jernigan, T. L., 305
Jerson, T., 84
Jimerson, D. C., 264
Johnson, B. T., 152
Johnson, M. P., 96
Johnson, S. B., 15
Johnson, W. G., 263, 265
Johnson, V. E., 240, 266, 267, 268
Johnston, L. E., 8, 95, 106
Jonas, J. M., 379
Jones, E. E., 395
Jones, M. C., 124
Jorgensen, M. 235
Judd, L. L., 348
Julien, R. M., 109, 225
Jung, C. G., 318

Kagitcibasi, C., 327
Kahneman, D., 181
Kaler, S. R., 225
Kalichman, S., 306
Kalidini, S., 349
Kalish, H. I., 136, 373
Kaltiala-Heino, R., 235
Kampman, M., 354
Kandel, E. R., 161, 162
Kane, J. M., 377
Kaniasty, K., 303
Kanner, A. D., 288, 290
Kaplan, G. A., 302
Karacan, I., 102
Karau, S. J., 402
Karni, A., 98
Karno, M., 370

Kastenbaum, R., 244
Katon, W., 352
Katz, G., 96, 132
Kawachi, I., 304
Kawanishi, Y., 378
Kean, Y. M., 353
Keating, C. R., 276
Keefauver, S. P., 102
Keesey, R. E., 262
Keiding, N., 235
Keitner, G. I., 348
Keller, M. B., 378
Kelner, K. L., 34
Kendler, K. S., 264, 304, 346, 349, 352
Kennedy, J. H., 230
Kenrick, D. T., 268
Kesner, R., 161, 162
Kessler, R. C., 341, 342, 349, 351, 352, 353, 359
Kiecolt-Glaser, J., 301
Kiecolt-Glaser, J. K., 301
Kihlstrom, J. F., 104, 105, 155
Kilbride, J. E., 227
Kilbride, P. L., 227
Kim, J. J., 346
Kim, K. H. S., 189
Kimmel, H., 108
Kimura, D., 201
King, L. A., 324
Kinomura, S., 40
Kinsey, A. C., 265, 268
Kirby, S., 203
Kirsch, I., 104, 105
Kitayama, S., 276, 327
Kite, M. E., 413
Kiyatkin, E., 108
Klaczynski, P., 221
Klatzky, R. L., 151
Kleinman, A., 383
Klerman, G. L., 370
Klerman, L. V., 237
Kliegman, R., 225
Klimkowski, M., 46
Kluft, R., 356
Kluft, R. P., 356
Kobasa, S., 302
Kobasa, S. C., 302
Kochanska, G., 406
Kochavi, D., 262
Kocsis, J. H., 379
Koehler, T., 315
Koelling, A., 125
Kohlberg, L., 217, 219, 221, 234
Köhler, W., 137
Kokkonen, M., 322
Koltz, C., 409
König, P., 177
Kopp, C. P., 225
Kosslyn, S. M., 178
Kovacs, D., 264
Kowatch, R., 379
Kozak, M. J., 354
Krantz, D. S., 288
Kranzler, H. R., 352
Krauel, K., 73
Kraus, S. J., 405
Krebs, D. L., 220
Kripke, D., 99

Kroll, N. E. A., 156
Kromar, M., 141
Krosnick, J. A., 404
Krueger, J. M., 98
Krueger, W. C. F., 166, 167
Kübler-Ross, E., 244
Kucharska-Pietura, K., 46
Kuhn, D., 216, 219, 403
Kulik, J., 158
Kumar, R., 399
Kummervold, P., 306
Kumpfer, K., 383
Kunda, Z., 412
Kunz, D., 100
Kupfer, D. J., 378, 379
Kurup, P., 22, 38
Kurup, R., 22, 38

Ladouceur, R., 373
Lal, S., 18
Lam, L., 203
Lambe, E. K., 264
Lamberg, L., 103
Lambert, G., 349
Lambert, W. E., 189
Lamborn, S. D., 233, 237
Lamm, H., 403
Landis, C. A., 100
Landry, D. W., 107, 108
Lane, R. C., 230
Lang, A., 160
Lang, A. R., 9, 10
Lange, C. G., 271
Langer, E. J., 290
Langevin, B., 103
Langlois, J. H., 396
Lao, J., 403
Lara, M. E., 303
Larson, R., 203
Latané, B., 402, 407
Laudenslager, M., 301
Laumann, E. O., 265, 268
Laurent, J., 193
Lavie, P., 103
Layton, L., 232
Lazarus, R. S., 272, 273, 288, 295, 296
Lebow, J. L., 370
Lecomte, C., 377
Lecomte, T., 377
LeDoux, J. E., 41, 273, 274
Lee, I., 161, 162, 178
Lehman, D., 22
Lehmann, H., 127
Leichtman, M. D., 156
Leitenberg, H., 268
Leland, J., 235
Lenat, D. B., 184
Lenneberg, E., 231
Leon, M., 226
Lepore, S. J., 410
Lerman, D. C., 130, 372
Lester, B. M., 229
LeVay, S., 269
Levenson, R. W., 242, 272, 274
Levine, M., 182
Levitt, E. E., 329
Levitt, I., 232
Levy-Schiff, R., 224

Mourtazaev, M. S., 99
Mui, A. C., 243
Mukerjee, M., 16
Mullen, P. E., 279
Muller, L., 385
Mumtaz, S., 232
Munarriz, R., 358
Munroe, R. H., 234
Murray, H., 270, 331
Murray, H. A., 331
Murray, K., 242
Murray, R. M., 347
Myers, C. E., 42, 161
Myers, D. G., 278, 403
Myers, H., 294

Nader, K., 150, 165
Nadon, R., 104
Nalepa, I., 378, 381
Nash, J. M., 242
Nash, M., 104
Nash, M. R., 104
Nathans, J., 69
National Center for Health Statistics, 297, 298, 303, 341, 350, 351
National Institute of Mental Health, 341, 348, 349, 352
National Institute on Aging, 242
National Institute on Alcohol Abuse and Alcoholism, 305
National Research Council, 237
Neale, M. C., 304, 349
Needleman, H. L., 409
Neimark, E. D., 216
Neimark, J., 304, 305
Neisser, U., 155, 158, 190, 196, 197
Neitz, J., 70
Nelson, J. C., 378
Nestadt, G., 354
Neugarten, B. L., 239
Newberg, A., 104
Newell, A., 182
Ng, S. H., 188
Nguyen, P. V., 162
Ni, W., 190
Nicholl, C. S., 16
Nickerson, R. S., 164
Nicol, S. E., 347
Nisbett, R. E., 395, 397
Nogrady, H., 104
Nordentoft, M., 225
Norris, F. H., 303
Norris, J. E., 239
Novello, A. C., 304
Nowak, M. A., 300
Nowell, A., 201
Noyes, R., Jr., 379
Nutt, D., 378

O'Brien, C. P., 7, 107
Odbert, J. S., 322
Oden, M. H., 195
O'Leary, K. D., 397
Oleson, K. C., 412
Oliver, J. E., 410
Oliver, M. B., 265
Oller, D., 189
O'Neil, H., 149

Orman, M., 359
Orne, M., 105
Öst, L-G., 376
Ostrom, T. M., 412
Otto, M. W., 379
Over, R., 270
Overmeier, J. B., 136
Oyewumi, L., 96

Padian, N. S., 301
Paivio, S. C., 369
Palinscar, A. S., 403
Paludi, M. A., 234
Pandolfini, C., 306
Pansu, P., 395, 396
Papousek, I., 274
Paraherakis, A., 108
Pardo, J. V., 73
Parke, R. D., 134
Parkinson, W. L., 261
Parrott, A. C., 95
Parsons, B., 269
Partinen, M., 102, 103
Parvizi, J., 96
Pastore, N., 409
Patricelli, G., 184
Patterson, C. J., 270
Patterson, J., 189
Paul, T., 264
Paul, W. E., 299
Paulesu, E., 190
Paulus, P. B., 410
Paunonen, S. V., 324
Pause, B. M., 73
Pavlov, I. P., 121, 123
Payami, H., 242
Payne, J., 411
Pedersen, D. M., 84
Penfield, W., 155
Pennisi, E., 295
Pentland, J., 157
Penton-Voak, I., 397
Pepperberg, I. M., 187
Perls, F. S., 369
Perls, T. T., 240
Perregaux, C., 189
Perrett, D. I., 396
Perry, R., 68
Pert, C. B., 39
Pesonen, A., 325
Peters, A., 239
Peterson, A. C., 201, 235
Peterson, I., 184
Peterson, L. R., 152, 153
Peterson, M. J., 152, 153
Petri, H. L., 256
Petty, R. E., 404
Phillips, G. P., 270
Phillips, K., 397
Phillips, L. W., 159
Phillips, S. T., 412
Piaget, J., 214
Pich, E. M., 107
Pickering, M. R., 356
Pickrell, J., 157
Pietrzak, R., 279
Pigott, T. A., 355
Pilcher, J. J., 97

Pillard, R. C., 269
Pillow, D. R., 288
Pilon, D. A., 271
Pinel, J. P. L., 36
Pinker, S., 188
Pittenger, D. J., 330
Pitz, G. F., 180
Pizarro, D., 277
Plomin, R., 198, 199, 346
Plous, S. 16
Plummer, D. L., 293
Polit, D. ., 271
Pollack, K. H., 83
Pollitt, E., 200
Pontieri, F. C., 107
Porjesz, B., 305
Porte, H. S., 98
Porter, F. L., 226
Posada, G., 229
Posner, M. I., 46
Postman, L., 159
Power, F. C., 219
Power, K. G., 376
Powlishta, K. K., 234
Pratkanis, A. R., 404
Premack, A. J., 186
Premack, D., 186
Price, R., 292
Prien, R. F., 379
Prigerson, H. G., 302
Prince, A., 301
Prinz, P. N., 99
Provine, R. R., 275
Pryke, S., 156
Public Agenda Online, 414
Pulvermüller, F., 128
Purdy, J. E., 16
Putnam, F. W., 356

Querido, J., 233
Quinn, T., 300
Quiroga, T., 232

Rachman, S., 354
Rachman, S. J., 373
Ragozzino, M., 161
Rahe, R. H., 288
Rahe, R. J., 288
Raine, A., 409
Raj, A. B., 378
Ramey, C., 199, 200
Ramsay, D. S., 107
Ranson, S. W., 261
Rao, S. C., 152
Rapp, P. R., 239
Rappe, R., 139
Rasmussen, S. A., 355, 379
Rayner, R., 123
Raz, A., 100
Regan, P. C., 266
Reis, H. T., 396
Reite, M., 103
Rende, R., 199
Reneman, L., 111
Renzetti, C. M., 413
Repetti, R. L., 297
Rescorla, R. A., 124
Restak, R., 36, 188

Steriade, M., 40
Stern, W., 193
Sternberg, R., 192
Sternberg, R. J., 191, 206, 398, 399
Stevenson, H. W., 201, 202, 203
Stewart, J., 294
Stewart, V. M., 83
Stoudemire, A., 99
Stough, C., 196
Strack, F., 276, 277
Strawbridge, W. J., 302
Suarez, M. G., 384
Sullivan, A., 73
Sullivan, E., 305
Sullivan, E. V., 220
Sullivan, M. J. L., 76
Sung, K-T., 243
Super, C. W., 227
Sussman, A. L., 178
Sussman, S., 107
Swan, G., 73
Swanson, L. W., 34
Swanson, N. G., 292
Sweatt, J. D., 162
Swedo, S. E., 354
Sweller, J., 182
Syme, S. L., 303
Symons, C. S., 152
Szymanski, K., 402

Takahashi, S., 98, 347
Takanishi, R., 235
Tamminga, C. A., 50, 378
Tanda, G., 107
Tang, M-X., 242
Tanner, J. M., 200, 235
Tartaglia, L. A., 263
Taylor, D. M., 177, 413
Taylor, E., 109
Taylor, S. E., 296, 297
Tchanturia, K., 263
Teasdale, J. D., 160
Tellegen, A., 325
Teng, E., 154
Tepper, B., 74
Terman, L. M., 194, 195
Terrace, H. S., 186
Tew, J. D., 380
Tham, K., 46
Thase, M. E., 376, 378, 379
Thigpen, C. H., 356
Thomas, A., 227, 228
Thompson, D. M., 159
Thompson, R. F., 127
Thompson, S. C., 291
Thorn, A., 189
Thorndike, E., 127
Thorndike, E. L., 127
Thornhill, R., 396
Thurstone, L. L., 191
Tidey, J., 372
Tiihonen, J., 409
Tindale, J. A., 239
Toastmasters International, 359
Tolman, E. C., 137
Tomkins, S., 276
Tori, C., 318
Torrey, E., 313

Toufexis, A., 240
Traverso, A., 265
Travis, J., 50
Trevitt, J., 41
Triandis, H. C., 276, 326
Triplett, N., 401
Trivedi, M. J., 382
Tsai, S., 350
Tulving, E., 159, 161, 166
Tuncer, A. M., 235
Turner, J. C., 411
Tversky, A., 180, 181
Tweed, R., 22
Tzschentke, T. M., 346

Uchino, B. N., 302
Ullian, D. Z., 234
Ullrich, N., 74
Underwood, B. J., 164
Underwood, G., 189
U.S. Bureau of the Census, 15, 189, 239, 242, 243, 301, 327, 351
U.S. Department of Health and Human Services, 303, 304
U.S. Department of Justice, 305
Utsey, S., 294

Vaillant, G. E., 349
Valkonen, R., 243
van Assema, P., 406
Van Cauter, E., 97, 99
van den Hout, M., 126
van der Leij, A., 232
Van der Zee, K., 203
van Elst, L. T., 409
van IJzendoorn, M., 229
van Schie, E. G., 411
Vander Meer, R., 73
Vargha-Khadem, F., 42, 161
Vasterling, J., 293
Vaugeois, P., 109
Vazdarjanova, A., 127
Verhaeghen, P., 241
Verma, S., 203
Verschure, F. M. J., 177
Vetulani, J., 378, 381
Viermerö, V., 411
Villani, S., 140
Vincent, M., 356
Vinokur, A., 403
Vishwakarma, M. S., 84
Visser, P. S., 404
Vitousek, K., 264
Vogel, P. J., 47
Volis, C., 414
Volkow, N. D., 107, 111
Vollrath, M., 324
Von Dras, D. D., 303
Von Glinow, M. S., 413
Voyer, D., 274
Vuorenkoski, L., 189

Wadden, T. A., 263
Wagner, A. R., 124
Wald, G., 68
Walk, R. D., 227
Walker, D., 384
Walker, I., 415

Walker, L., 220
Wall, P. D., 76
Wallbott, H. G., 272, 275
Walster, E., 397
Walster, G. W., 397
Walters, C. C., 133
Walters, E. E., 349
Ward, C., 106
Wark, G. R., 220
Warshaw, M. G., 378
Wasserman, E. A., 121
Waterman, A., 221
Watson, D., 101, 315
Watson, J. B., 19, 123
Weaver, J. B., 268
Webb, W., 100
Webb, W. B., 99, 102
Weber, S. E., 76
Weekes, J. R., 104
Weeks, D. L., 139
Weigman, O., 411
Weinberg, M. S., 270
Weinberg, R., 199
Weiner, I. B., 331
Weingarten, H. P., 261
Weiss, J. M., 290
Weissman, M. M., 348, 352, 354
Wells, G. L., 156
Wender, P. H., 349
Wesensten, N., 97, 108
Westergaard, G., 53
Westling, B. E., 376
Wetter, M. W., 329
Wheeler, J., 84
Wheeler, M. A., 153
Whisenhunt, B. L., 264
Whitaker-Azimitia, P. M., 409
Whitam, F. L., 269
White, D. P., 103
White, G. L., 279
White, S. D., 236
Whitehouse, D., 177
Whitehurst, G. J., 231
Whorf, B. L., 188
Wickelgren, I., 239
Wicker, A. W., 404
Widiger, T. A., 358
Widom, C. S., 133, 158, 410
Wiesel, T. N., 68
Wiggins, J. S., 323
Wilcox, D., 267
Wilken, J. A., 271
Williams, C. J., 405
Williams, D. R., 68
Williams, J., 242
Williams, K., 402
Williams, K. D., 402
Williams, R., 298
Williamson, G. M., 301
Willis, S. L., 240
Willoughby, T., 153
Wilson, F. R., 53
Wilson, G. T., 373
Wilson, M. I., 410
Wilson, T. D., 397
Wilson, W., 109
Winch, R. F., 397
Wink, P., 239

Androsterone, 73
Anger, 244, 274
Animal Mind, The (Washburn), 18
Animals
    language in, 186–187
    research with, 16
Anisomycin, 165
Anorexia nervosa, 263–264
Antabuse, 375
Antagonists, 37
Anterograde amnesia, 161
Antibodies, 299, 301
Anticonvulsant drugs, 379
Antidepressant drugs, 348, 354, 355, 358, 376, **378**
Antigens, 299
Antipsychotic drugs, 377–378
Antisocial personality disorder, 357, **358–360**
Anvil (of ear), 71
Anxiety
    defense mechanisms and, 315, 316
    GABA and, 38
    memory and, 160
    separation, 229
    stranger, 229
Anxiety disorders, 351–355, 344. *See also specific types of disorders*
    treatment of, 378
APA. *See* American Psychological Association
Aphasia, 46
    Broca's 46
    Wernicke's, 46
Aplysia, 162
Apnea, sleep, 103
Applied research, 6
Approach-approach conflict, 290
Approach-avoidance conflict, 290
Aptitude tests, 194
Archetypes, 318
Aristotle, 16
Arousal, 258, 259
    low level, 409
    sexual, 267–268
Arousal theory, 258, 260
Artificial intelligence, 21, 184
Asch's study of conformity, 399, 400
Asian Americans
    authoritarian parenting by, 233
    parental expectations of, 202–203
    and suicide, 304
Assessment. *See also* Intelligence tests; Personality assessment; Personality inventories; Tests
    behavioral, 327–328
Assimilation, 214
Assisted suicides, 245
Association, free, 368
Association areas, 42, 45
Asthma, 244
Asur people, of India, 159
Atkinson-Shiffrin model of memory, 150, 151
Atmospheric perspective, 82
Attachment, 229–230
"Attacking Anxiety," 371
Attitude, 404–405
    sexual, 265–266

Attraction, 396–399
    factors influencing, 396
    physical attractiveness and, 396–397
    romantic, 397–398
Attractiveness, physical, 396–397
Attribution, 395–396
    dispositional, 395
    situational, 395
Atypical neuroleptics, 377–378
Audience, 406
Audience effects, 401
Audition, 71. *See also* Hearing
Auditory canal, 71
Auditory cortex, 46
Authoritarian parents, 232, 233, 237
Authoritative parents, 232, 237
Autoimmune disease, 299, 301
Automatic thoughts, 375
Autonomic nervous system, 51, 409
Autonomy versus shame and doubt, 221, 222
Availability heuristic, 180
Aversion, taste, 125
Aversion therapy, 374–375
Avoidance-avoidance conflict, 290
Avoidance learning, 135
Avoidant attachment, 229
Axon, 34, 35
Axon terminals, 34, 35

B cells, 299, 301
Babbling, 230
Back to the Future, 287
Backward search, 182
Barbiturates, 38, 108, 110
Bargaining, 244
Barney & Friends, 235
Bartlett, Frederick, 155, 158
Baseline, 137
Basic emotions, 274, 275
Basic research, 5
Basic trust versus basic mistrust, 221, 222
Basilar membrane, 71, 72
Bass, Ellen, 157
Beckham, Albert Sidney, 18
Behavior
    abnormal, 340–343
    operant conditioning and, 128–130
    prosocial, 406–408
    sexual, 265–266
Behavior modification, 136, 137, 140, 354, **371–372**
Behavior therapy, 371–375, 381
Behavioral assessment, 327–328
Behavioral genetics, 198
Behavioral perspective, 23
Behaviorism, 19
Bel, 70
Bell curve, 194
Bell, Alexander Graham, 70
Benzodiazepines, 379
Berger, Hans, 48
Beta wave, 48
Bias
    ageism and, 15–16
    experimenter, 11
    gender, 15, 219–220
    observer, 6–7

    overgeneralization, 15
    selection, 11
    self-serving, 395
Biased sample, 7
Big Five, 323–324, 326, 400
Bilingualism, 188–190
Binet, Alfred, 192, 193
Binet-Simon Intelligence Scale, 192
Binge eating, 264, 378
Binocular depth cues, 80
Binocular disparity, 80
Biofeedback, 136
Biological clock, 41
Biological motives, 256
Biological perspective, 23
    on mood disorders, 349
    on psychological disorders, 341, 343
Biological predispositions, in classical conditioning, 125
Biological psychology, 21-22
Biological therapy, 377–380, 381
Biomedical model, 296
Biopsychosocial model, 296, 297
Biopsychosocial perspective, 341, 343
Bipolar disorder, 349, 378, 379
    treatment for, 384
Birth order, 271
Bisexuality, 268
    bulimia and, 264
Blind spot, 67
Blood-injection-injury phobia, 353
"Bobo Doll" research, 139
Body weight, 262–263. *See also* Dieting; Eating disorders
Borderline personality disorder, 357
Boring, E. G., 82
Bottom-up processing, 85
Boyle, Robert, 70
Braille, 63
Brain
    alcohol and, 305
    cerebral hemispheres of, 42–48
    changes with aging of, 239–240
    emotion and, 273–274
    immune system and, 301
    information-processing theory and, 20
    language and, 190
    lateralization of, 45–47
    in mood disorders, 349
    neurotransmitters of, 38-39
    plasticity of, 44
    REM sleep and, 98
    reward circuit in, 108
    in schizophrenia, 345–346
    sleep deprivation and, 100
    structures of, 40–42
    techniques for study of, 48–50
    tumors of, 409
    visual information and, 67–68
Brain damage, 41, 161
    aggression and, 409
    electroconvulsive therapy and, 380–381
    memory and, 161
    mental retardation and, 195
    MDMA and, 95, 109, 111
Brain-imaging techniques, 49–50, 196. *See also individual techniques*
    antisocial personality disorder and, 360

dreaming and, 101
of human olfactory functioning, 73
imagery and, 178
meditation and, 104
neural processing speed and, 196
Brainstem, 40
Breast cancer, 306
Brief psychodynamic therapy, 368
Brightness, 68
Brightness constancy, 79
British Medical Association, 306
Broca's aphasia, 46
Broca's area, 43, **46,** 189, 190
Bulimia nervosa, 264–265, 376
Bush, George, 53
Buss, David, 21
Bystander effect, 407

Caffeine, 108, 110, 111, 225
California Psychological Inventory (CPI), 330
California Test of Mental Maturity, 194
Calkins, Mary Whiton, 18
Calories, 263
Cancer, 298–299, 306, 341
Cannon-Bard theory (of emotion), **272,** 273
Capriati, Jennifer, 139
Cardinal trait, 322–323
Careers, in adulthood, 238–239
Carrey, Jim, 348
Case study, 7, 14
Cat in the Hat, The, 227
Catatonic schizophrenia, 346
Cattell's Sixteen Personality Factor Questionnaire, 323
Cause-effect relationships, 6, 8, 13, 14
CCK, 261
Cell body, 34, 35
Central nervous system (CNS), 38, **39**–48, 227. *See also* Brain; Spinal cord
Central traits, 323
Cerebellum, 40–41, 43, 127, 178, 190
Cerebral cortex, 40, 42, 346
Cerebral hemispheres, 42–48
Cerebrum, 42, 43
Challenge, hardiness and, 302
Chapin, John, 177
Chat rooms, illness and, 306
Chemotherapy, classical conditioning and, 125
Chicken pox, 225
Child abuse
as predictor of substance abuse, 107
social learning theory of aggression and, 410
Child pornography, 357
Childbirth, pain during, 76
Childhood, 230–235
gender role development in, 233–234
homosexuality in adulthood and, 270
influence of television in, 234–235
language development in, 230–232
observational learning and, 139
psychosexual stages of, 317
sleep in, 99
socialization in, 232–233
stage theories of development in, 215, 218, 220, 221, 222

Childhood abuse, memories of, 158
Chimpanzees, 53, 138, 186–187
Cholecystokinin (CCK), 261
Chomsky, Noam, 186
Chromosomes, 223
sex, 223
X, 269
Chunking, 151, 152
Cingulotomy, 382
Cingulum, 380
Circadian rhythms, 96–97
Circadian theory, 100
Cirrhosis, 305
Clark, Kenneth, 18
Clark, Mamie Phipps, 18
Classical conditioning, 120–124
avoidance learning and, 135
biological predispositions in, 125
cognitive perspective on, 124–125
contemporary views of, 124–127
in everyday life, 125–127
of fear, 123, 124, 126
Pavlov and, 120–123
psychological drug dependence and, 107
of taste aversions, 125
therapies based on, 373
Watson and, 123–124
Claustrophobia, 353
Client-centered therapy, 20
Clinical psychologist, 24, 25, 383
Clinton, Bill, 53
Clomipramine, 378
Closure, Gestalt principle of, 78
Clozapine, 377, 378
CNS. *See* Central nervous system
Co-action effects, 401
Cobain, Kurt, 339
Cocaine, 108, 110, 244
addiction to, 376
during pregnancy, 225
REM sleep and, 98
schizophrenia and, 346
Cochlea, 71, 72
Codeine, 108
Cognition, 178
social, 412
Cognitive abilities, gender differences in, 201. *See also* Intelligence
Cognitive Abilities Test, 194
Cognitive-behavioral therapy, 376
Cognitive development, Piaget's theory of, 214–217, 218
Cognitive developmental theory, 234
Cognitive dissonance, 405
Cognitive learning, 137-141
Cognitive map, 138
Cognitive-neoassociationistic model, 410
Cognitive performance, sleep deprivation and, 100
Cognitive perspective, 23, 342, 343
on classical conditioning, 124–125
on mood disorders, 349
on stress, 295
Cognitive processes, 137
Cognitive psychology, 20–21
Cognitive therapies, 375–377
Cognitive therapy, 375–377, 381
Collective unconscious, 318

Color blindness, 69, **70**
Color vision, 18, 68–70
Commitment, 398, 399
hardiness and, 302
Companionate love, 399
Compliance, 400–401
Componential intelligence, 191
Compulsion, 354
Computerized tomography (CT) scan, 49
Concept, 178–179
formal, 178, 179
natural, 178–179
Concrete operations stage, 215, 218
Conditioned response (CR), 121
Conditioned stimulus (CS), 121
Conditions of worth, 322
Cones, 66, 67, 68, 69
Confederate, 394, 400
Confessions of Nat Turner, The (Styron), 339
Conflict
approach-approach, 290
approach-avoidance, 290
avoidance-avoidance, 290
Conformity, 399–400
Confounding variables, 11
Conscience, 315
Conscientiousness, 324
Conscious, 314
Consciousness, 96. *See also* Altered states of consciousness
Conservation, 215, 216
Conservation tasks, 217
Consolidation, 150
Consolidation failure, 164–165
Constancy, perceptual, 78–79
Consummate love, 399
Contact comfort, 229
Contextual intelligence, 192
Continuity, Gestalt principle of, 78
Continuous reinforcement, 130
Control
as goal of psychology, 5, 6
hardiness and, 302
stress and, 290–291
Control group, 10
Conventional level, 218, 220
Convergence, 80
Conversion disorder, 355, 356
Convolutions, 42
Coping, 295–296
emotion-focused, 295
proactive, 296
problem-focused, 295
Cornea, 66
Coronary heart disease, 297–298
Corpus callosum, 40, 42, 43, 47
Correlation coefficient, 12, 428–429
Correlational method, 12–13, 14
Cortisol, 162
Cotton, Ronald, 149
Counseling psychologist, 24, 383
Couple therapy, 370, 381
Courage to Heal, The (Bass and Davis), 157
CPI, 330
Crack, during pregnancy, 225
Cramming, 24
Creativity, 204–206

Critical periods, 225
Critical thinking, 6
Cross-cultural studies. *See also* Culture
  of academic achievement, 201–203
  of DID, 356
  of gender development, 234
  of Kohlberg's theory of moral develop-
    ment, 219, 220
  of OCD, 354
  of panic disorder, 352
  of physical attractiveness, 396–397
  of Piaget's stages of cognitive develop-
    ment, 216
  of social loafing, 402
Cross-dressing, 270
Crowding, 409, 410
Cruise, Tom, 53
Crystallized intelligence, 241
CT (computerized tomography) scan, 49
Culturally sensitive psychotherapy, 383
Culture. *See also* Cross-cultural studies
  abnormal behavior and, 340
  altered states of consciousness and,
    105–106
  bulimia and, 264
  care of elderly and, 243–245
  depression and, 348
  display rules and, 275–276
  emotional expressions across, 275–276
  handedness and, 53
  infant motor development and, 227
  influence on pain of, 76
  jealousy and, 22
  language and, 188–189
  mate selection and, 398
  memory and, 158–159
  perception of illusions and, 82, 83–84
  personality and, 326–327, 330
  punishment and, 134–135
  sexual behavior norms in, 267–268
  social responsibility norms and, 406–407
Culture-fair intelligence tests, 197
Cumulative recorder, 128
Curve of forgetting, 163
Curvilinear, 429

DA. See Dopamine
Dahmer, Jeffrey, 341
Dani people, of New Guinea, 188
Darkness Visible: A Memoir of Madness
  (Styron), 339
Darrow, Clarence, 313
Darwin, Charles, 17, 275
Davis, Laura, 157
Deaf mothers, 232
Death, 244–245. *See also* Suicide
  among alcoholics, 305
Debriefing, 14
Decay theory, 164
Deception, in research, 15, 394
Decibel (dB), 70
Decision making, 179–181
  additive strategy of, 179–180
  through elimination by aspects, 180
  framing and, 181
  heuristics and, 180–181
Declarative memory, 153, 154, 161
Deep Blue, 184

Defense mechanisms, 315, 316
Dehydroepiandrosterone (DHEA), 358
Delta wave, 49, 98–99, 380
Delusion, 344
Delusion of grandeur, 344, 346
Delusion of persecution, 345, 346
Dement, William, 103
Dementia
  loss of olfaction and, 73
  senile, 242
Dendrites, 34, 35
Denial, 316
  of dying, 244
Dependent variable, 9, 14
Depressants, 108, 110
Depression, 245, 339, 347–348, 379. *See also*
  Antidepressant drugs; Major depres-
  sive disorder
  alcohol and, 304–305
  culture and, 348
  in late adulthood, 243
  prevalence of, 348
  psychotic, 348
  sexual dysfunctions and, 358
  smoking and, 304
  as stage of dying, 244
  therapy for, 370, 376
Depth perception, 68, 80–81, 227
Derailment, 345
Description, as goal of psychology, 5
Descriptive research methods, 6–8, 14
Descriptive statistics, 424–429
Development
  gay and lesbian experiences in, 270
  heredity and, 223–224
  psychosexual stages of, 315–318
  stage theories of, 214–221
Developmental psychologists, 25
Developmental psychology, 214. *See also*
  specific stages and types of development
DHEA, 358
Diabetes, 54, 306
Diagnostic and Statistical Manual of Mental
  Disorders (Fourth Edition), 343, 356,
  357
DID, 356
Dieting, 263
Difference threshold, 65
Difficult children, 228
Diffusion of responsibility, 407
Directive therapy, 369
Discrimination, 123, 411–415
  in operant conditioning, 129
  in workplace, 413–414
Discriminative stimulus, 129
Disorganized/disoriented attachment, 230
Disorganized schizophrenia, 346
Displacement, 151, 316
Display rules, 275–276
Dispositional attribution, 395
Dissociative amnesia, 355
Dissociative disorder, 344, 355–356
Dissociative fugue, 356
Dissociative identity disorder (DID),
  356
Divalproex, 349, 379
Diversity education, 415
Dizygotic twins, 198, 224

DNA, 223. *See also* Chromosomes; Genes
Dolphins, 187
Domestic violence, 409
  alcohol and, 305
  as predictor of substance abuse, 107
Dominant gene, 223
Door-in-the-face technique, 401
Dopamine (DA), **38,** 101, 106, 108
  receptors for, 378
  in schizophrenia, 346
Double-blind technique, 11
Down syndrome, 195
Downers, 108
Dreams
  activation-synthesis hypothesis of, 102
  analysis of, 368
  interpretation of, 101–102
  latent content of, 101
  manifest content of, 101, 102
  NREM, 100
  REM, 100
Drive, 257
Drive-reduction theory, 257–258, 260
Drug(s)
  psychoactive, 106–111
  antidepressant, 348
  dependence on, 107–108
  early-maturing girls and, 236
  effects on neural transmission of, 37
  environmental cues for use of, 126
  during pregnancy, 245
Drug therapy, 377–379
Drug tolerance, 107
Drug treatment, for sexual dysfunctions,
  358
DSM-IV, **343,** 356, 357
Dynamic assessment, 197

Ear, 71–72
Eardrum, 71
Easy children, 228
Eating disorders, 263–265, 344
Ebbinghaus, Hermann, 163
Eclectic perspective, 24
Ecstasy (MDMA), 95, 109, 110, 111
Education
  diversity, 415
  formal, 216
  of professional psychologists, 25
Educational psychologists, 25
EEG. *See* Electroencephalogram
Effectiveness, of therapy, 382
Efferent neurons, 34
Egg cells, 223
Ego, 314, 315
Ego ideal, 315
Ego integrity versus despair, 221, 222
Egocentrism, 215
Einstein, Albert, 53, 206, 259
Ejaculation, 235
Elaborative rehearsal, 152
Electroconvulsive therapy (ECT),
  379–381
Electroencephalogram (EEG), 48–49
Electromagnetic spectrum, 66
Elimination by aspects, 180
E-mail counseling, 384
Embryo, 224

Genetics (cont.)
  response to alcohol and drugs and, 107
  sleep patterns and, 99
Genital stage, 317
Gestalt, 78, 79
Gestalt psychology, 20
Gestalt therapy, 369
Gifted students, 194–195
Glial cells, 34
Globalization, 4
Glucagon, 54
Glucocorticoids, 295
Glucose, 261
Glutamate, 38, 74
Goldberg, Whoopi, 53
Gonads, 54
Good boy–nice girl orientation, 218
Graduate Record Examination (GRE), 194
Gray matter, 42
GRE, 194
Gregory, R. L., 83
Grieving process, 244–245
Grossly disorganized behavior, 345
Group influence, 401–403
Group polarization, 403
Group therapy, 20, **370–371**
Groupthink, 403
Growth hormone, 97, 98
Gustation, 74

Hair cells, 72, 77
Hall, G. Stanley, 235
Hallucinations, 344
Hallucinogen persisting perception disorder
  (HPPD), 109
Hallucinogens, 109, 110
Halo effect, 328, 397
Hammer, 71
Handedness, 53
Happiness, 278
Hardiness, 302
Harlow's studies of attachment in infant
  monkeys, 229
Harmonics, 71
Hassles, 288, 290, 324
Hassles Scale, 288
Hathaway, Starke, 328
Head injuries, 44
Healing circles, 385
Health, 296–303
  exercise and, 305–306
  lifestyle and, 297, 298, 300, 303–306
Health care, access to, 294
Health psychology, 296–297
Hearing, 70–72
  in infancy, 226
  loss of, 84
  theories of, 72
Heart disease, 297–298
Helmholtz, Hermann von, 17, 68, 72
Helping. See Prosocial behavior
Hemingway, Ernest, 339
Hemispheric interference, 46
Heredity, 223–224. See also Chromosomes;
  Genes; Genetics; Heritability
Hering, Ewald, 68
Heritability, 198
  of aggression, 408

of alcoholism, 305
of body weight, 262
of intelligence, 197–199
of mood disorders, 349
of obsessive-compulsive disorder,
  354–355
of personality, 325
of phobias, 353–354
of schizophrenia, 346
of sexual orientation, 269
Heroin, 109, 244
  during pregnancy, 225
Hertz (Hz), 70
Heuristics, 180–181, 182
  analogy, 183
  availability, 180
  representativeness, 180
Hierarchy of needs, 20
High EE, 370
High in expressed emotion, 370
Higher-order conditioning, 122
Hindbrain, 40
Hippocampal region, 161
Hippocampus, 42, 126, 127, 154, 157, 161,
  162, 295, 346
Hispanic Americans, 18, 242, 243, 294
  collectivism and, 327
Histogram, 425
Historical racism, 293–294
Histrionic personality disorder, 357
HIV, 225, 299-301
Hoffman, Paul, 77
Holmes and Rahe's Social Readjustment
  Rating Scale, 288, 289
Homeostasis, 257, 258
Homosexuality, 268, 269
  bulimia and, 264
Hormones, 52–53. See also individual
  hormones
  gender role development and, 233
  memory and, 162
  sex, 54
  sexual response cycle and, 267
Hospice care, 244
Host personality, 356
Hostility, 298
Hot flashes, 238
HPPD, 109
Hue, 68
Human immunodeficiency virus (HIV),
  225, **299-**301
Humanistic perspective, 23
Humanistic psychology, 19–20,
  321–322
Humanistic therapies, 369
Hunger, 261–265
Hurvich, Leon, 68-69
Hyperopia, 66
Hypnosis, 104–105
  recovered memories and, 157
Hypochondriasis, 355
Hypothalamus, 40, **41,** 349
  lateral, 261
  sexual orientation and, 269
Hypothalamus, ventromedial, 261
Hypothesis, 8
Hypothetico-deductive thinking,
  215

Iatmul people, of New Guinea, 158
Id, 314, **315**
Identical twins, 99, 198, **224,** 262, 269,
  347
Identity crisis, 221
Identity formation, 221
Identity versus role confusion, 221, 222
Illicit drug, 106
Illness
  factors reducing, 302–303
  stress and, 301
Illusion, 82–83
Imagery, 178
Imaginary audience, 237
Imipramine, 378
Imitation, in language development, 231
Immune system, 299–301
  classical conditioning and, 126
  exercise and, 306
  stress and, 301–302
Implicit memory, 153
Impression formation, 394–395
Impulsivity, drug use and, 107
Inappropriate affect, 345, 346
Incentive, 256
Inclusion, 196
Independent variable, 9, 14
Individual psychology, 319
Individualism/collectivism dimension,
  326–327
Industrial/organizational psychologists, 25
Industry versus inferiority, 221, 222
Infancy, 226–230
  attachment and, 229–230
  babbling in, 230
  emotional expression in, 275
  intervention and IQ and, 199–200
  learning in, 227
  motor development in, 227, 228
  perceptual development in, 226–227
  psychosexual stage of, 317
  sleep in, 99
  stage theories of development in, 215,
    218, 221, 222
  temperament in, 227–229
Infants, preterm, 225
Infatuated love, 398, 399
Inferential statistics, 429–430
Infidelity, sexual, 21, 22
Information-processing theory, 20–21
In-group, 411
Initiative versus guilt, 221, 222
Inner ear, 71
Insanity, 340
Insight, 137
Insight therapy, 368–369
Insomnia, 103
Inspection-time task, 196
Instinct theory, 257, 260
Insulin, 54, 261
Intelligence, 190–192. See also Intelligence
  quotient; Intelligence tests
  artificial, 21, 184
  componential, 191
  contextual, 192
  crystallized, 241
  emotional, 203–204
  experiential, 192

Memory. *See also* Amnesia; Forgetting; Long-term memory; Sensory memory; Short-term memory
  Atkinson-Shiffrin model of, 150, 151
  bilingualism and, 189
  biology and, 161–162
  culture and, 158–159
  declarative, 153, 154, 161, 162
  distortion of, 156
  emotion and, 162
  environmental context and, 159–160
  episodic, 153, 154, 161
  explicit, 153
  eyewitness testimony and, 156–157
  false, 104
  flashbulb, 158
  hippocampus and, 42, 157
  hormones and, 162
  implicit, 153
  improving, 24, 166–169
  levels-of-processing model of, 153
  loss of. *See* Amnesia
  neuronal changes in, 161–162
  nondeclarative, 153, 154, 161
  in old age, 241
  processes in, 150
  as reconstruction, 155
  REM sleep and, 98
  repressed, 157-158
  retrieval in, 159–160
  semantic, 153, 154, 161
  state-dependent, 160
  tasks in, 154–155
  working, 152
Menarche, 235
Menopause, 238
Menstrual cycle, 54
Menstrual synchrony, 73
Mental age, 192
Mental Health Net, 384
Mental health professionals, 383
Mental retardation, 195
  fetal alcohol syndrome and, 225
Mental set, 183–184
Mentality of Apes, The (Köhler), 137
Mere-exposure effect, 396, 406
Metabolic rate, 262, 263
Metalinguistic skills, 189
Method of loci, as memory aid, 168
Michael J. Fox Foundation for Parkinson's Disease Research, 287
Michelangelo, 53
Microelectrode, 49
Midbrain, 40, 41
Middle ear, 71
Milgram, Stanley, 393, 394, 400
Minnesota Center for Twin and Adoption Research, 198
Minnesota Multiplastic Personality Inventory (MMPI), 328–330
Minnesota Twin Registry, 198
Minnesota twin study, 325, 326
Minor tranquilizers, 379
Minorities, in psychology, 18
Miscarriage, 225, 237, 244
Misinformation effect, 156
Mister Rogers' Neighborhood, 141, 235
MMPI, 328–330

MMPI-2, 328–330
MMPI-A, 330
Mnemonic devices, 168–169
Modafinil, 97
Mode, 424
Model, 139
Modeling, 138
  participant, 375
Monitoring the Future Survey, 95
Moniz, Egas, 382
Monoamine oxidase (MAO) inhibitors, 378
Monoamines, 38
Monocular depth cues, 80, 81
Monozygotic twins, 198, **224**
Mood disorders, 347–351, 344. *See also individual mood disorders*
Moral development, Kohlberg's theory of, 217–221
Moral reasoning, 217-221
Morphemes, 185
Morphine, 108
Motherese, 232
Motion parallax, 82
Motivated forgetting, 165
Motivation, 256
  arousal theory of, 258, 260
  drive-reduction theory and, 257–258, 260
  extrinsic, 256, 257
  instinct theory and, 257, 260
  intrinsic, 256, 257
  Maslow's hierarchy of needs as, 259–260
Motives, 256
  sexual, 265–268
  social, 270–271
  stimulus, 258
Motor cortex, 43, 44
Motor development, in infancy, 227, 228
Motor nerves, 51
Motor neurons, 34
Movement and Mental Imagery (Washburn), 18
Mozart, 206
MRI (magnetic resonance imaging), 49
Müller-Lyer illusion, 83, 84
Multifactorial traits, 224
Multiple sclerosis, 299
Muniz, Frankie, 24
Myelin, in aging, 239–240
Myelin sheath, 35, 36
Myers-Briggs Type Indicator (MBBTI), 330
Myopia, 66

n Ach, 270–271
Naïve idealism, 237
Naïve subject, 394
Narcissistic personality disorder, 357
Narcolepsy, 102-103
Narcotics, 108
Nardil, 378
National Assessment of Educational Progress, 201
National Comorbidity Survey, 342
National Institute of Drug Abuse, 95, 109
National Institute of Mental Health, 370
National Institutes of Health, 16
National Task Force on Women and Depression, 348
Native Americans, 244, 327
  and Müller-Lyer illusion, 84

and smoking, 303
and suicide, 350
and therapy, 385
Nativist position, 231
Natural concepts, 178–179
Naturalistic observation, 6–7, 14
Nature-nurture controversy, 197–199
  personality and, 325–327
Navigational skills, hippocampus and, 161
NE. *See* Norepinephrine
Nearsightedness, 66
Need for achievement, 270–271
Needs, hierarchy of, 259–260
Negative correlation, 428
Negative reinforcement, 130, 132, 135
NEO Personality Inventory (NEO-PI), 324
Neodissociation theory of hypnosis, 105
Neo-Freudians, 19, 318–320
Neonates, 226. *See also* Infancy
Nervous system, 38
  autonomic, 51, 409
  central, 38, **39**–48, 227
  parasympathetic, 51, **52,** 288
  peripheral, 38, 39, 50–52
  somatic, 51
  sympathetic, **51**–52
Neural networks, 184
Neural processing speed, intelligence and, 196
Neural transmission, effect of drugs on, 37
Neuroleptics, 377
Neuron, 34–36
  afferent, 34
  efferent, 34
  memory changes in, 161–162
  olfactory, 72–73
Neuropsychologists, 25
Neuroscience, 22
Neurotic personality, 319
Neuroticism, 323, 324
Neurotransmitter, 36–37
  dreams and, 101
  in mood disorders, 349
  variety of, 37–39
New York Longitudinal Study, 227
Nicotine, 108, 110
Nicotine patch, 304
Nightmares, 98, 102, 296
Nim Chimpsky, 186
Nodes of Ranvier, 35, 36
Noise, hearing loss and, 84
Nondeclarative memory, 153, 154, 161
Nondirective therapy, 369
Nonsense syllables, 163
Noradrenalin. *See* Norepinephrine
Norepinephrine (NE), **38,** 53, 54, 101, 162, 349, 378
Normal curve, 195, **426**–427
Norms, 193
NREM dreams, 100
NREM sleep, 97, 98
Nucleus accumbens, 106, 108
Nursery rhymes, 232
Nutrition, in pregnancy, 245

Obedience, Milgram study on, 393, 394, 400
Obesity, 262

Positive correlation, 428
Positive reinforcement, 130, 135
Positron-emission tomography. *See* PET
Postconventional level, 219, 220
Posttraumatic stress disorder (PTSD),
    292–293, 378
    hypnosis and, 105
Poverty
    attachment and, 229
    in late adulthood, 242
Pragmatics, 185–186
Preconscious, 314
Preconventional level, 218, 220
Prediction
    correlation and, 12–13
    as goal of psychology, 5
Prefrontal cortex, 100, 101, 152, 409
Pregnancy. *See also* Prenatal care; Prenatal
        development
    exercise in, 245
    nutrition in, 245
    smoking during, 245, 304
    substance use and abuse in, 225, 245
    teenage, 236–237
Prejudice, 411–415
Premarital sex, 265
Premature birth. *See* Preterm infants
Prenatal, 224
Prenatal care, 224, 245
Prenatal development
    negative influences on, 224–225
    stages of, 224, 225
Preoperational stage, 215, 218
Presbyopia, 68, 238
Pretend play, 215
Preterm infants, 225, 237, 244
Primacy effect, 159, 395
Primary appraisal, 295
Primary auditory cortex, 43, 45, 65
Primary drives, 261
Primary mental abilities, 191
Primary Mental Abilities Test, 191
Primary reinforcer, 130
Primary visual cortex, 43, 45, 65, 68, 101
Principles of Psychology (James), 17
Proactive coping, 296
Proactive interference, 164
Problem-focused coping, 295
Problem solving, 181–185
    approaches to, 181–183
    artificial intelligence and, 184
    creative, 204–206
    impediments to, 183–184
Progesterone, 54, 267
Project Talent Mathematics, 201
Projection, 316
Projective test, 330–332
Prosocial behavior, 406–408
Prospective forgetting, 166
Protein synthesis, memory consolidation
        and, 162, 165
Prototype, 179
Proximity, 396
    Gestalt principle of, 78
Prozac, 378, 382
Pseudomemories, 104
Psychedelics, 109
Psychiatric social worker, 383

Psychiatrist, 382, 383
Psychoactive drugs, 106–111
    effects and withdrawal symptoms of, 110
    types of, 108–111
Psychoanalysis, 19, 314–318, 342, 368, 380
Psychoanalyst, 383
Psychoanalytic perspective, 23
Psychodynamic perspective, 342, 343
Psychodynamic therapies, 368
Psychoeducation, 384
Psycholinguistics, 185
Psychological disorders, 340. *See also*
        specific disorders
    DSM-IV categories for, 344
    perspectives on, 341–343
    prevalence of, 341
Psychological drug dependence, 107
Psychological perspectives, 22–24
Psychological tests, 13, 14
Psychologist, 382
    types of, 24–25
Psychology, 4
    evolutionary, 21, 397
    feminine, 319
    founding of, 17
    goals of, 5–6
    history of, 16–18
    humanistic, 321–322
    individual, 319
    schools of thought in, 18–21
    social, 394
    women and minorities in, 18
Psychoneuroimmunology, 301
Psychosexual stages, 315–318
Psychosis, 343
Psychosocial stages, 221–222
Psychosurgery, 382
Psychotherapy, 368, 382
    for depression, 348
Psychotic depression, 348
Puberty, 235–236
Public speaking, fear of, 359
Punishment, 132–135
Pupil, 66
Purging, 264
Puzzle box, 127

Racial segregation, 18
Racial stereotyping, 414–415
Racism
    historical, 293–294
    perceptions of, 414–415
    stress and, 293–294
Ramey's infant intervention, 200
Random assignment, 11
Random sample, 7
Range, 426
Rapid eye movement. *See* REM
Rapid transcranial magnetic stimulation
        (rTMS), 381
Rating scales, 328
Ratio schedules, 131
Rational-emotive therapy, 375, 376
Rationalization, 316
Rave dances, 95
Rayner, Rosalie, 123
Reaction formation, 316
Realistic conflict theory, 411

Reality principle, 315
Recall, 154
    free, 154
    serial, 154
Received support, 303
Recency effect, 159
Receptors, 36
    dopamine, 378
    olfactory, 73
    sensory, 65
    serotonin, 378
Recessive gene, 223
Reciprocal determinism, 320
Reciprocal liking, 396
Reciprocity, 396
Recognition, 154
Reconstruction, 155
Reflexes, 226
Refractory period
    of neuron, 36
    in sexual response cycle, 267
Regional cerebral blood flow, 178
Regression, 316
Rehearsal, 152
    elaborative, 152
Reinforcement, 130–131
    continuous, 130
    negative, 130, 132, 135
    partial, 130
    positive, 130, 135
    schedules of, 131–132
Reinforcement contingency, 137
Reinforcer, 128
    primary, 130
    secondary, 130
Relationship therapies, 370–371
Relative size, 81
Relaxation response, 104
Relearning method, 154
Reliability, 13, 194
Religious faith, resistance to stress and ill-
        ness and, 302
REM dreams, 100
REM rebound, 98, 102
REM sleep, 98
Remembering. *See* Memory
Remote Associates Test, 204
Replicable, 5
Representative sample, 7, 8
Representativeness heuristic, 180–181
Repressed memories, 157–158
Repression, 165, 315, 316
Research
    correlational methods in, 12–13
    descriptive methods of, 6–8, 14
    ethics in, 13–15, 16
    experimental, 8–12, 14
    participant-related bias in, 15–16
    participants in, 13–16
    survey, 7–8
    use of animals in, 16
Resistance, 368
Resistance stage, 295
Resistant attachment, 230
Resolution phase, 267
Respondent conditioning. *See* Classical
        conditioning
Resting potential, 34, 36

Restorative theory (of sleep), **99**–100
Reticular activating system (RAS), 40
Reticular formation, 40, 41
Retina, 66
Retinal disparity, 80
Retirement, 242
Retrieval, 150, 159–160
Retrieval cues, 154, 160
Retroactive interference, 164
Retrograde amnesia, 165
Reuptake, 37
Reversibility, 215
Revised NEO Personality Inventory
   (NEO-PI-R), 324
Reward. *See* Positive reinforcement
Reward circuits, 108
Rheumatoid arthritis, 299
Rhodopsin, 66
Rhyme, as memory aid, 168
Right hemisphere, specialized functions
   of, **46**–47
Risperidone, 377, 378
Ritual trance, 105
Road rage, 6
Robber's Cave, 411–412, 414
Robotics, 184–185
Rods, 66, 67
Rogers, Carl, 19, 20, 322, 369
Rogoff, Barbara, 158
Romantic attraction, 397–398
Romantic love, 398, 399
Romantic relationships, 21
Roosevelt, Eleanor, 259
Rorschach, Hermann, 331
Rorschach Inkblot Method, 331
Rosen, Richard, 149
rTMS, 381
Rubella, 225

Sample, 7, 14, 430
   biased, 7
   random, 7
   representative, 7, 8
Sanchez, Jorge, 18
Sarah, 186
SAT, 13, 194, 201
Satiety center, 261
Saturation, 68
Savings method, 154
Savings score, 163
Scapegoating, 409
Scatterplot, 428, 429, 430
Schachter-Singer theory (of emotion),
   272, 273
Schedules of reinforcement, 131–132, 133
Schemas, 155
Scheme, 214
Schizophrenia, 38, 343–347, 409
   behavior therapies in, 372
   brain abnormalities in, 345–346
   causes of, 346–347
   dopamine activity and, 38
   dreams and, 101
   gender and, 347
   negative symptoms of, 345
   positive symptoms of, 344–345
   treatment for, 370, 377, 384
   types of, 346

Scholastic Assessment Test (SAT), 13, 194,
   201
School psychologist, 383
Schweitzer, Albert, 259
Scientific method, 5
Seattle Longitudinal Study, 238
Secondary appraisal, 295
Secondary reinforcer, 130
Secondary sex characteristics, 54, 235
Secondhand smoke, 304
Secure attachment, 229
Sedentary lifestyle, 297
Selection bias, 11
Selective serotonin reuptake inhibitors
   (SSRIs), 378
Self-actualization, 20, 259, **321**–322,
   369
Self-efficacy, 320
Self-fulfilling prophecy, 201
Self-help group, 371
Self-knowledge, 203
Self-motivation, 203
Self-serving bias, 395
Seligman, Martin, 332
Semantic memory, 153, 154, 161
Semantics, 185
Semicircular canals, 77
Senile dementia, 242
Sensation, 64–65. *See also* Senses
Sensation seekers, 257
Senses. *See also individual senses;* Pain;
   Sensation
   kinesthetic, 77
   skin, 75
   vestibular, 77
Sensorimotor stage, 215, 218
Sensory adaptation, 65
Sensory memory, 150, 151, 153
Sensory nerves, 51
Sensory neurons, 34
Sensory receptors, 65
Separation anxiety, 229
Serial position effect, 159
Serial recall, 154
Serotonin, 38, 101, 111, 264, 349, 355, 378,
   409
   MDMA and, 95
Seratonin receptors, 378
Sesame Street, 141, 235
Set point, 262
Set-point theory, 262
Sex
   extramarital, 265
   premarital, 265
Sex chromosomes, 223
Sex discrimination, 292
Sex hormones, 54
Sexual abuse, recovered memories of, 157
Sexual arousal, 267–268
Sexual attitudes, 265–266
Sexual Behavior in the Human Female (Kinsey),
   265
Sexual Behavior in the Human Male (Kinsey),
   265
Sexual behavior, surveys of, 265–266
Sexual disorders, 357–358
Sexual dysfunction, 357, 358
   SSRIs and, 378

Sexual fantasies, 268
Sexual harassment, 292
Sexual infidelity, 21, 22
Sexual masochism, 357
Sexual motives, 265–268
Sexual orientation, 268–270
Sexual response cycle, 266–267
   in late adulthood, 240–241
Sexual sadism, 357
Sexuality, adolescence and, 236
Sexually explicit films, 268
Shading, 82
Shadow, 82
Shape constancy, 79
Shaping, 128, 129
   in language development, 231
Shift work, 97
Shiritori, 232
Short-term memory, 109, **151,** 153, 161, 162
Sigler, Jamie-Lynn, 264
Sign language, 232
   animals and, 186–187
Sildenafil citrate, 358
Similarity
   attraction and, 397
   Gestalt principle of, 78
Simmons, Ruth, 213
Simon, Theodore, 192, 193
Simpatía, 327
Situational attribution, 395
Situational phobias, 353
16 PF, 323
Size constancy, 78
Skin senses, 75
Skinner, B. F., 19, 320
Skinner box, 128, 129
Sleep, 97–103. *See also* Dreams
   deprivation of, 100, 301
   disorders of, 102–103
   disturbances in, 102
   functions of, 99–100
   melatonin and, 96
   NREM, 97, 98
   REM, 98
   and studying, 24
   variations in, 99
Sleep apneas, 103
Sleep cycles, 41, 98–99
Sleep terrors, 102
Sleeptalking, 102
Sleepwalking, 102
Slow-to-warm-up children, 228
Slow-wave sleep, 99
Smell, 72–74
Smiling, 278
Smith, Will, 150
Smoking, 405
Smoking
   behavior modification and, 372
   cognitive dissonance and, 405
   health and, 303–304
   in pregnancy, 245
   prenatal development and, 225
Social adjustment, in late adulthood,
   242–243
Social cognition, 412
Social-cognitive learning, 138. *See also*
   Observational learning

Social desirability response, 8
Social development, in adulthood, 239
Social facilitation, 401–402
Social influence, 399–401
 compliance and, 400–401
 conformity and, 399–400
 obedience and, 400
Social learning theorists, 234
Social learning theory of aggression,
 410–411
Social loafing, 402
Social motives, 256, 270–271
Social norms, 399
Social Organization of Sexuality (Laumann
 and others), 265
Social perception, 394–396
 attribution as, 395–396
 impression formation as, 394–395
Social phobia, 353, 359
 treatment of, 378
Social psychologists, 25
Social psychology, 394
**Social Readjustment Rating Scale
 (SRRS), 288,** 289
Social responsibility norms, 406–407
Social roles, 403
Social support, 302–303
 Internet and, 306
Socialization, in childhood, **232**–233
Sociocognitive theory of hypnosis, 105
Sociocultural perspective, 22, 23
Somatic nervous system, 51
Somatoform disorders, 344, 355
Somatosensory cortex, 43, 44, 45, 75
Somnambulism, 102
Somniloquy, 102
Sophocles, 316
Sopranos, The, 264
Sound, 70–71
Source traits, 323
Spatial abilities, 201
Spears, Britney, 324
Specific phobia, 353
Sperm cells, 223
Spin City, 287
Spinal cord, 30–40
Split-brain operation, 47–48
Spontaneous recovery, 122, 123
SQUID (superconducting quantum inter-
 ference device), 50
SSRIs, 378
SSRS, 288, 289
Stage theories of development, 214-221
Standard deviation, 426
Standardization, 194
Standardized tests, 13
Stanford-Binet Intelligence Scale, 193
State-dependent memory effect, 160
Statistical significance, 430
Statistics
 descriptive, 424–429
 inferential, 429–430
Stelazine, 377
Stereotypes, 412
Stereotyping, 414, 415
Sternberg's theory of love, 398–399
Stillbirth, 237, 244
Stimulants, 108, 110

Stimulus, 120
 discriminative, 129
Stimulus motives, 258
Stirrup, of ear, 71
Storage, 150
Stranger anxiety, 229
Stream of consciousness, 17
Streisand, Barbra, 353
Stress, 288
 catastrophic events and, 292–293
 coping strategies for, 295–296
 coronary heart disease and, 298
 factors reducing, 302–303
 immune system and, 301–302
 major life, 349–350
 in pregnancy, 245
 racism and, 293–294
 responding to, 294–296
 sources of, 288–294
 theories of, 295
 in workplace, 291–292, 298
Stressors, 288
 control over, 290–291
Structuralism, 17
Structured interview, 328
Studying, techniques for, 24, 137
Styron, William, 339
Subjective night, 97
Sublimation, 316
Substance abuse, 106–107, 304–305
Substance dependence, 107
Substance-related disorders, 344
Substantia nigra, 40, 41
Successive approximations, 128, 129
Sudden infant death syndrome, 244
Suicide
 adolescent, 203
 assisted, 245
 in late adulthood, 243
 posttraumatic stress disorder and, 293
 race, gender and age and, 350–351
Sullivan, Anne, 63
Sumner, Francis Cecil, 18
Superconducting quantum interference de-
 vice (SQUID), 50
Superego, 314, 315
Support
 perceived, 303
 received, 303
 social, 302–303, 306
Suppression, 165
Suprachiasmatic nucleus (SCN), 96
Supreme Court, 18
Surface traits, 323
Surgery, hypnosis and, 105
Survey, 7–8, 14
Swazi people, of Africa, 158
Symbol board, 187
Symbolic function, 215
Sympathetic nervous system, 51–52
Synapse, 34
 memory formation and, 162
Synaptic clefts, 34, 35, 37
Synaptic vesicles, 36, 37
Syntax, 185, 190, 231
Systematic desensitization, 373, 374

T cells, 299, 301, 304

Tactile, 75
Tardive dyskinesia, 377, 378
Taste, 74–75
 in infancy, 226
Taste aversion, 125
Taste buds, 74, 75
TAT. *See* Thematic Apperception Test
Teenage pregnancy, 236–237
Teenagers. *See* Adolescence
Telegraphic speech, 231
Television
 aggression and, 139
 childhood influence of, 234–235
 classical conditioning and, 126, 127
 violence and, 140–141, 410–411
Temperament, 227–229
Temporal lobe epilepsy, 409
Temporal lobes, 43, 45, 100, 161
Teratogens, 225
Terman, Lewis M., 193
Terrorist attacks, 6
Test anxiety, 24
Testes, 54
Testosterone, 267
 aggression and, 409
 decline in, 238
Tests. *See also* Intelligence tests; Personality
 inventory; *individual tests*
 aptitude, 194
 paired-associates, 18
 projective, 330–332
 psychological, 13, 14
 reliability and validity of, 194
 requirement of, 194
 standardization of, 194
 standardized, 13
Tests of statistical significance, 430
Tetrahydrocannabinol, 109
Texture gradient, 82
Thalamus, 40, 41, 68, 73, 346
THC (tetrahydrocannabinol), 109
Thematic Apperception Test (TAT), 270,
 331-332, 383
Theory, 5
Theory of dissociated control, 105
Therapeutic alliance, 383
Therapists, 382, 383
Therapy
 aversion, 374–375
 based on classical conditioning, 373
 behavior, 371–375, 382
 biological, 377–380, 382
 client-centered, 20
 cognitive, 375–377, 382
 couple, 370, 382
 culturally sensitive, 383–385
 directive, 369
 drug, 377–379
 electroconvulsive, 379–380
 evaluation of, 382
 family, 370, 382
 gender-sensitive, 385
 Gestalt, 369
 group, 20, 370–371
 humanistic, 369
 insight, 368–369
 Internet, 384
 interpersonal, 370, 381

CREDITS

Photos

CHAPTER 1

p. 2: © Alexander Stewart/Getty Images/The Image Bank; **3:** © Richard Lord/The Image Works; **6:** © Ron Chapple; **9:** © ImageState-Pictor/PictureQuest; **13:** © George Gerd/Getty Images/Taxi; **15:** © David Stoecklein/CORBIS; **18:** © Barbara Alper/Stock Boston, LLC; **20:** Eyewire; **24:** AP/Wide World Photos

CHAPTER 2

p. 32: © B. Busco/Getty Images/The Image Bank; **35:** Reprinted with permission from Damasio H, Grabowski T, Frank R, Galaburda AM, Damasio AR: The return of Phineas Gage: Clues about the brain from a famous patient. *Science,* 264:1102–1105, © 1994. American Association for the Advancement of Science. Photo courtesy of H. Damasio, Human Neuroanatomy and Neuroimaging Laboratory, Department of Neurology, University of Iowa; **34:** © BioPhoto/Photo Researchers, Inc.; **44:** © Bernardo Bucci/CORBIS; **45:** © Richard Gross/CORBIS Stock Market; **49:** © Alexander Tsiaras/Photo Researchers, Inc.; **53:** AP/Wide World Photos

CHAPTER 3

p. 62: © Michael Schwartz/The Image Works; **63:** © Bettmann/CORBIS; **64:** © Philip Condit II/Getty Images/Stone; **69 (both):** © Robert Harbison; **74:** © Stewart Cohen/Getty Images/Stone; **81 (top left):** © Kent Meireis/The Image Works; **81 (top left middle):** © James Rendklev/Getty Images/The Image Bank; **81 (top right middle):** © Bernd Euler/plus 49/The Image Works; **81 (top right):** © Mike Yamashita/Woodfin Camp & Associates; **81 (bottom left):** © 2000 Craig Tuttle/CORBIS Stock Market; **81 (bottom middle):** © Randi Anglin/Syracuse Newspaper/The Image Works; **81 (bottom right):** © Pete Turner/Getty Images/The Image Bank; **83:** © Richard Lord Ente/The Image Works; **84:** AP/Wide World Photos

CHAPTER 4

p. 94: © Dick Luria/Getty Images/Taxi; **95:** AP/Wide World Photos; **97:** © Firefly Productions/CORBIS; **99:** © Russell D. Curtis/Photo Researchers, Inc.; **101:** © Dex Images/CORBIS; **103:** © Louis Psihoyos/Matrix International; **104:** © The Next Best Thing Photo: Ron Batzdorff/The Everett Collection; **105 (top):** © Francoise Sauze/Science Photo Library/Photo Researchers, Inc.; **105 (bottom):** © Peter Schommartz/Getty Images; **107:** © Ghislian & Marie David de Lossy/Getty Images/The Image Bank; **108:** © Lester Sloan/Woodfin Camp & Associates; **109:** © Francoise de Mulder/CORBIS; **111:** © ImageState-Pictor/PictureQuest

CHAPTER 5

p. 118: © Lawrence Migdale/Stock Boston, LLC; **119:** AP/Wide World Photos; **121:** © Bettmann/CORBIS; **125:** © Ed Kashi; **126:** Courtesy of the National Fluid Milk Processor Promotion Board; **127:** © Digital Vision/Getty Images; **129:** © Nina Leen/TimePix; **132:** © Javier Pierini/CORBIS; **135:** © Jeff Greenberg/The Image Works; **136:** © Will & Demi McIntyre/Photo Researchers, Inc.; **137:** © Michael Newman/PhotoEdit; **135 (all):** Courtesy of Dr. Albert Bandura, Stanford University; **141:** © Edouard Berne/Getty Images/Stone

CHAPTER 6

p. 148: © Dean Wong/CORBIS; **149:** AP/Wide World Photos; **151:** © Kent Wood/Photo Researchers, Inc.; **153:** AP/Wide World Photos; **155:** Royalty Free/CORBIS; **156:** © Grantpix/Photo Researchers, Inc.; **157:** © James Shaffer/PhotoEdit; **158:** AP/Wide World Photos; **159:** © M & E Bernheim/Woodfin Camp & Associates; **161:** © Darren Robb/Getty Images/Taxi; **162 (both):** adapted from Maguire et al., 2000

CHAPTER 7

p. 176: © Yellow Dog Productions/Getty Images/The Image Bank; **177:** © Nancy Richmond/The Image Works; **178:** AP/Wide World Photos; **179 (left):** © Jim Simncen/Getty Images/Stone; **179 (right):** © Art Wolfe/Getty Images/Stone; **180:** © Jeff Greenberg/PhotoEdit; **184 (top):** © Topham Picture Point/The Image Works; **184 (bottom):** © Barbara L. Johnson/Reuters/Getty Images; **187:** CNN/A&B Archives; **189:** © Bob Daemmrich/The Image Works; **192 (left):** © Bernard Wolf; **192 (middle):** © Rafael Macia/Photo Researchers, Inc.; **192 (right):** © B & C Alexander/Photo Researchers, Inc; **193:** Photosynthesis Archives; **198:** © Portfield/Chickering/Photo Researchers, Inc.; **202:** Peter Menzel/Material World

CHAPTER 8

p. 212: © George Shelley/CORBIS; **213:** AP/Wide World Photos; **224 (left):** © Francis Leroy/Science Photo Library/Photo Researchers, Inc.; **224 (middle & right):** Lennart Nilsson/Bonniers; **227:** © Mark Richards/PhotoEdit; **229:** © Martin Rogers/Stock Boston, LLC.; **230:** © Joe Canini/The Image Works; **232:** © Robert E Daemmrich Photography; **233:** © Will and Demi McIntyre/Photo Researchers, Inc.; **240:** ©Ron Dalquist/Getty Images/Stone; **241:** © David Young Wolff/PhotoEdit

CHAPTER 9

p. 254: © Sean Cayton/The Image Works; **255:** © Steven Hirsch/Corbis Sygma; **259:** © Don Mason/CORBIS; **264:** AP/Wide World Photos; **267:** © Tom & DeAnn McCarthy/CORBIS Stock Market; **269:** © Bob Daemmrich/Stock Boston, LLC.; **271:** AP/Wide World Photos; **275:** Reprinted by permission of the Human Interaction Laboratory/© Paul Ekman 1975; **276:** © David Young-Wolff/PhotoEdit; **278:** © PhotoDisc/Getty Images

CHAPTER 10

p. 286: © Jim Cummins/Getty Images/Taxi; **287:** © David McNew/Getty Images; **290:** © Natalie Fobes/CORBIS; **291:** © Spencer Grant/PhotoEdit; **292:** © Alvis Upitis/Getty Images/The Image Bank; **294:** © Michael Newman/PhotoEdit; **298:** © Davis Barber/PhotoEdit; **300:** AP/Wide World Photos; **303:** © Tony Freeman/PhotoEdit; **305:** © Robert Harbison

CHAPTER 11

p. 312: © Michael Schwarz/The Image Works; **313:** © Bettmann/CORBIS; **318 (top):** © Archive Photos/Getty Images; **318 (bottom):** © Bettmann/CORBIS; **319:** © Charles Gupton/Getty Images/Stone; **322:** © Bettmann/CORBIS; **324:** AP/Wide World Photos; **325:** © Ariel Skelley/CORBIS; **327 (top):** © Chris Arend/Getty Images/Stone; **327 (bottom):** © Jose L. Pelaez/CORBIS Stock Market

CHAPTER 12

p. 338: © Tony Freeman/PhotoEdit; **339:** AP/Wide World Photos; **340 (left):** © Robert Harbison; **340 (right):** © Dean Conger/CORBIS; **345:** From Clinical Brain Disorders Branch, National Institute of Mental Health; **346:** © Will Hart; **348:** © The Kobal Collection/Morgan Creek International/Farmer, J; **353:** AP/Wide World Photos; **354:** © Spencer Grant/PhotoEdit; **356:** © Rob Crandall/Stock Boston, LLC.; **359:** © Jose Pelaez/CORBIS Stock Market

CHAPTER 13

p. 366: © Mug Shots/CORBIS; **367:** © David W. Hamilton/Getty Images/The Image Bank; **367 (inset):** © Patrick J. LaCroix/Getty Images/The Image Bank; **368:** © Bettmann/CORBIS; **369:** © Michael Rougier/TimePix,

Inc.; **371:** © Bruce Ayers/Getty Images/Stone; **372:** © LWA-Dann Tardif/CORBIS; **373:** © Dennis MacDonald/PhotoEdit; **376:** © Leif Skoogfors/Woodfin Camp & Associates; **378:** © Paul S. Howell/Getty Images; **379:** © J. Wilson/Woodfin Camp & Associates; **384:** © Jose Pelaez/CORBIS Stock Market

CHAPTER 14

p. 392: © The Image Works; **393:** From the film *Obedience* copyright 1965 by Stanley Milgram and distributed by Penn State Media Sales; **395:** © C. Gatewood/The Image Works; **397 (top):** © J. Christopher Briscoe/Photo Researchers, Inc.; **397(bottom):** © Lon C. Diehl/PhotoEdit; **400:** William Vandevert/Scientific American; **403 (top):** © Mark Richards/PhotoEdit; **403 (bottom):** Philip G. Zimbardo, Inc.; **406:** AP/Wide World Photos; **407:** © Dan Miller/Woodfin Camp & Associates; **409:** © Paul Gish; **413:** © Gary A. Conner/PhotoEdit; **414:** © Ariel Skelley/CORBIS

Text and Art

Figure 6.3, p. 152: From "Short-term Retention of Individual Items" by L. R. Peterson & M. J. Peterson, *Journal of Experimental Psychology, 58,* 1959.

Try It! 6.3, p. 164: Drawing based on "Long-Term Memory for a Common Object" by R. S. Nickerson & M. J. Adams, *Cognitive Psychology, 11,* 1979, p. 297. Reprinted by permission of Acedemic Press and R. S. Nickerson.

Try It! 7.2, p. 183: From *Solve It! Perplexing Profusion of Puzzles* by James F. Fixx. Copyright © 1978 by James F. Fixx. Used by permission of Doubleday, a division of Bantam Doubleday Dell Publishing Group, Inc.

Figure 7.2, p. 183: Reprinted with permission from "Language in Chimpanzees?" by David Premack, *Science, 172,* 1971, pp. 808–822. Copyright 1971 by the American Association for the Advancement of Science.

Figure 7.9, p. 202: Illustration by Laurie Grace from "Learning from Asian Schools" by Harold W. Stevenson, *Scientific American,* December 1992, p. 73. Reprinted by permission of Laurie Grace.

Figure 8.1, p. 217: From *Child Development,* Third Edition, by Laura E. Berk. Copyright © 1994 by Allyn and Bacon. Reprinted by permission.

Figure 8.4, p. 228: Taken from part of *Denver II Training Manual* by W. K. Frankenburg, J. Dodds, P. Archer, et al., 1992. Published by Denver Developmental Materials, Inc., Denver CO. Reprinted by permission of W. K. Frankenburg.

Table 10.1, p. 290: From "Comparison of Two Modes of Stress Management: Daily Hassles and Uplifts versus

Major Life Events" by Allen D. Kanner, James C. Coyne, C. Schaefer, and R. S. Lazarus, *Journal of Behavioral Medicine, 4,* 1981, pp. 1–39. Reprinted by permission of the publisher and authors.

Figure 10.4, p. 276: From "Personal Control and Stress and Coping Process: A Theoretical Analysis" by Susan K. Folkman, *Journal of Personality and Social Psychology, 46,* 1984, pp. 839–852. Copyright 1984 by the American Psychological Association. Adapted by permission of the publisher and author.

Figure 10.5, p. 297: Figure from *The Dynamics of Health and Wellness: A Biopsychosocial Approach* by Judith Green and Robert D. Shellenberger, p. 21, copyright © 1991 by Holt, Rinehart and Winston, reproduced by permission of the publisher.

Try It! 11.2, p. 323: Adaptation from Cattell's *16PF® Fifth Edition Profile Sheet.* Copyright © 1993 by the Institute for Personality and Ability Testing, Inc., P.O. Box 1188 Champaign, IL U.S.A. 61824-1188. Used with permission.

Practice Tests

Answers can be found in the Student Solutions Manual.

1. Psychology is a science because of

    a. its reliance on common sense.
    b. the nature of the body of knowledge that comprises it.
    c. what psychologists investigate.
    d. the way in which psychologists acquire knowledge.

2. Dr. Barry was quite relieved when a lab in Alaska found that rats that had been exposed to uncontrollable electric shocks increased their alcohol consumption. He had found the same thing in a series of experiments he performed looking at the effects of stress on alcohol use. The Alaskan data demonstrate that

    a. Dr. Barry is probably an alcoholic.
    b. Dr. Barry's results are replicable.
    c. Dr. Barry's results are valid.
    d. Dr. Barry's hypothesis is correct.

3. All of the following are basic goals of psychological research *except*

    a. description   **c.** designation
    b. explanation   **d.** control

4. Which of the following is the best example of an applied research effort?

    a. an exploration of how smiling affects mood
    b. a determination of which of two medications is more effective in treating the primary symptoms of schizophrenia
    c. a description of the neuronal events that occur when new memories are formed
    d. a case study of a child deprived of normal exposure to language

5. All of the following are limitations of naturalistic observation as a research method *except*

    a. Cause-and-effect relationships cannot be determined.
    b. The potential for observer bias exists.
    c. Observations may have to be made for long periods in order to observe the desired behavior.
    d. The experimental setting is artificial.

6. A researcher is interested in how lighting affects mood. If an experiment were designed to test the effects of lighting on mood, the lighting would be the

    a. dependent variable.
    b. independent variable.
    c. hypothesis.
    d. theory.

7. In a study of the effect of amphetamine on running speed, it was found that all participants in the control group were on the track team. The composition of this control group introduces a

    a. confounding variable.
    b. dependent variable.
    c. representative sample.
    d. random sample.

8. There is a positive correlation between time spent studying and grades earned. Based on this observation, which of the following is *true*?

    a. If you spend more time studying, you will earn higher grades.
    b. If you earn high grades, you spend a lot of time studying.
    c. Those students who do not study do not earn good grades.
    d. Students who study more are more likely to earn high grades.

9. Correlational data

    a. allow predictions to be made.
    b. can be used to establish a cause-and-effect relationship.
    c. are more useful than experiment data.
    d. control for all forms of bias.

10. _____ is a research method employed by Wundt and Titchener that has been criticized for not being objective.

    a. Behaviorism
    b. Functionalism
    c. Introspection
    d. Structuralism

11. All of the following are neo-Freudians *except*

    a. Adler   **c.** Jung
    b. Horney   **d.** Titchener

12. Which school of psychology emphasizes the use of mental processes to learn and remember information?

    a. behaviorism
    b. cognitive psychology
    c. humanistic psychology
    d. structuralism

13. Which of the following is a question that a biological psychologist might seek to answer?

   a. How have changes in the environment over the last century altered the behavior of wild deer?

   b. What effect do early life experiences have on later life choices?

   c. Do seasonal fluctuations in hormones produce changes in behavior?

   d. Can memory aids facilitate learning?

14. Dr. Smith believed that depression is a consequence of faulty thinking. With which psychological perspective is Dr. Smith's view most consistent?

   a. biological

   b. cognitive

   c. humanistic

   d. Freudian

15. Which of the following is a barrier to critical thinking?

   a. independent thinking

   b. suspension of judgment

   c. objective evaluation of data

   d. relying on common sense

16. Watching children on a playground to collect data on sex differences in play behavior is an example of the use of which of the following research methods?

   a. case study

   b. correlation

   c. experiment

   d. naturalistic observation

17. "Increasing time spent studying will increase test scores." This prediction is an example of a(n)

   a. confounding variable.

   b. hypothesis.

   c. independent variable.

   d. theory.

18. The double-blind technique serves to control for

   a. experimenter bias.

   b. placebo effects.

   c. the expectancies of the subjects.

   d. all of the above.

19. Which of the following correlation coefficients indicates the strongest relationship?

   a. −0.5

   b. 0.0

   c. +0.1

   d. +0.3

20. What type of psychologist would be most likely to argue that men are unfaithful because such behavior increases their ability to pass on their genes?

   a. biological

   b. cognitive

   c. evolutionary

   d. psychoanalytic

21. An experiment is a descriptive research method.

   a. true

   b. false

22. Correlational data may be used to establish a cause-effect relationship.

   a. true

   b. false

23. Experimenter bias may be a source of confounding variables.

   a. true

   b. false

24. Correlation coefficients have values from .00 to +1.00.

   a. true

   b. false

25. A valid test measures what it is designed to measure.

   a. true

   b. false

26. Freud's establishment of a psychological laboratory marks the birth of psychology as a formal academic discipline.

   a. true

   b. false

27. Behaviorists view the environment as the primary determinant of behavior.

   a. true

   b. false

28. A random sample is obtained when all individuals in the population of interest have an equal likelihood of being selected.

   a. true

   b. false

29. According to the APA, it takes about 2 years beyond the bachelor's degree to complete a doctorate.

   a. true

   b. false

30. There are no ethical restrictions limiting the research conducted on animals.

   a. true

   b. false

31. What is the scientific method? Describe the procedures that are followed when the scientific method is employed.

32. Explain why an experiment usually includes both an experimental group and a control group.

33. Name and describe four major psychological perspectives. According to each perspective selected, what is the primary determinant of your behavior?

1. Psychology is defined as the scientific study of
   a. behavior and mental processes.
   b. human behavior.
   c. mental processes.
   d. how people think, learn, and remember.

2. A general principle that is used to explain a set of related facts is known as a(n)
   a. correlation.
   b. experiment.
   c. hypothesis.
   d. theory.

3. Which of the following is a basic goal of psychology that requires the proposal of testable theories?
   a. description
   b. explanation
   c. proposition
   d. control

4. A case study typically involves all of the following *except*
   a. interviews.
   b. experimental manipulation.
   c. psychological testing.
   d. observation.

5. Which research method is most likely to be employed when psychologists explore the attitudes of a group of people?
   a. naturalistic observation
   b. laboratory observation
   c. case study
   d. survey

6. A researcher is interested in how lighting affects test scores. If an experiment were designed to test the effects of lighting on test scores, the test scores would be the
   a. dependent variable.
   b. independent variable.
   c. hypothesis.
   d. theory.

7. Which of the following factors must be controlled for in an experiment?
   a. selection bias
   b. confounding variables
   c. the placebo effect
   d. all of the above

8. If your psychology exam contains math problems, you would probably complain that it is not
   a. reliable.
   b. valid.
   c. replicable.
   d. biased.

9. _____ is generally recognized as the "father of psychology."
   a. Freud
   b. Skinner
   c. Watson
   d. Wundt

10. William James is known for authoring a classic psychology textbook and was an advocate of
    a. behaviorism.
    b. functionalism.
    c. introspection.
    d. structuralism.

11. Which of the following believed that psychologists must study that which is observable and measurable?
    a. Freud
    b. Skinner
    c. Titchener
    d. Watson

12. Which school of psychology proposes that people are innately good?
    a. behaviorism
    b. humanistic psychology
    c. psychoanalysis
    d. structuralism

13. The belief that mental illnesses are the result of chemical imbalances is consistent with the _____ perspective.
    a. behavioral
    b. biological
    c. cognitive
    d. evolutionary

14. In the double-blind technique for conducting an experiment, who is "blind"?
    a. the participants
    b. the experimenter
    c. the participants and the experimenter
    d. half of the participants

15. Why can't all research questions be addressed with experiments?
    a. Experiments can only be conducted on humans.
    b. There may be no ethical way of using an experiment to answer some questions.
    c. Cause-and-effect relationships are often more readily revealed with correlational data.
    d. Controlling for confounding variables is often difficult.

16. Which research method would you be most likely to use to look at the relationship between education and salary?

    a. case study
    b. correlational method
    c. double-blind technique
    d. experimental method

17. A survey is an example of

    a. an experimental method.
    b. introspection.
    c. laboratory observation.
    d. a descriptive research method.

18. Client-centered therapy was introduced by

    a. Freud.
    b. Watson.
    c. Rogers.
    d. Wundt.

19. Because the population of pet animals consists of 30% dogs, 20% cats, and 50% birds, John selected a sample with the same proportions. John is trying to achieve a _____ sample.

    a. biased
    b. confounded
    c. random
    d. representative

20. An eclectic perspective

    a. uses a combination of approaches to explain behavior.
    b. employs only unbiased techniques.
    c. rejects psychoanalytical explanation.
    d. does all of the above.

21. Research into techniques designed to improve learning is an example of applied research.

    a. true
    b. false

22. A random sample is, by definition, one that mirrors the population of interest.

    a. true
    b. false

23. When participants' expectations alter their response to a treatment, experiment bias has occurred.

    a. true
    b. false

24. The closer the value of a correlation coefficient is to zero, the stronger the correlation.

    a. true
    b. false

25. Titchener was a student of Wundt's who brought Wundt's ideas to the United States.

    a. true
    b. false

26. Freud believed that much of any person's mental life was unconscious.

    a. true
    b. false

27. Behaviorism focuses on how evolution has enabled humans to adapt to their environments.

    a. true
    b. false

28. Observer bias is a potential confounding variable in laboratory observations.

    a. true
    b. false

29. Deception may be used in psychological research only when it is absolutely necessary.

    a. true
    b. false

30. Maslow was a neo-Freudian.

    a. true
    b. false

31. What is a theory? Explain the value and significance of theories.

32. What are the four basic goals of psychology? Name and explain each.

33. Differentiate between an experiment and a correlational study. What are the advantages of each?

CHAPTER 2: PRACTICE TEST 1

1. Phineas Gage experienced changes in his personality as a result of damage to his

    a. cerebellum.
    b. frontal lobe.
    c. medulla.
    d. occipital lobe.

2. A neuron at rest

    a. fires only twice every hour.
    b. has no electrical charge.
    c. carries a negative electrical charge.
    d. is described as being presynaptic.

3. Neurotransmitter release occurs when
    a. the nodes of Ranvier have been stimulated.
    b. myelin is present.
    c. synaptic vesicles are formed.
    d. an action potential arrives at an axon terminal.

4. A drug may increase the effectiveness of a neurotransmitter by
    a. interfering with reuptake.
    b. increasing reuptake.
    c. binding to and blocking receptors.
    d. inhibiting action potentials.

5. Which of the following neurotransmitters is involved in both Parkinson's disease and schizophrenia?
    a. acetylcholine
    b. dopamine
    c. epinephrine
    d. serotonin

6. Following a serious head trauma, John was drowsy and seemed unable to focus his attention. It is most likely that he suffered damage to his
    a. cerebellum.
    b. hypothalamus.
    c. medulla.
    d. reticular formation.

7. The hippocampus plays a central role in
    a. emotion.
    b. coordinating movement.
    c. memory.
    d. reflexive responses.

8. Which lobes contain the somatosensory cortex?
    a. frontal
    b. occipital
    c. parietal
    d. temporal

9. The processing of auditory information begins in the _____ lobe.
    a. temporal
    b. parietal
    c. occipital
    d. frontal

10. Sperry's studies of split-brain patients revealed that
    a. only the left hemisphere can produce alpha waves.
    b. most people can't see objects in their right visual field.
    c. severing the corpus callosum results in severe memory deficits.
    d. only the left hemisphere with its verbal abilities can state what it has seen.

11. When an action potential arrives at the _____, neurotransmitter molecules are released.
    a. nucleus
    b. axon terminal
    c. cell body
    d. dendrite

12. The electrical charge on a resting neuron is
    a. known as an action potential.
    b. about +50 mV.
    c. created by the distribution of ions.
    d. a consequence of the binding of neurotransmitters.

13. What type of brain-wave activity is seen when one is awake but in a state of deep relaxation?
    a. alpha wave
    b. beta wave
    c. delta wave
    d. gamma wave

14. Which of the following provides information about brain structure, but not brain function?
    a. EEG
    b. fMRI
    c. MRI
    d. PET

15. The unmyelinated areas of an axon
    a. are called nodes of Ranvier.
    b. give axons their characteristic white color.
    c. allow neurotransmitters to be released at any point along the axon.
    d. are a sign of mental illness.

16. When you move your arm or leg, the neurotransmitter that causes the muscle contraction is _____ and the part of the nervous system that releases this neurotransmitter is the _____ nervous system.
    a. acetylcholine; central
    b. acetylcholine; somatic
    c. dopamine; central
    d. dopamine; somatic

17. Which of the following is referred to as the "master gland"?
    a. hypothalamus
    b. hippocampus
    c. pituitary
    d. thyroid

18. After a neuron fires, there is a brief period during which another action potential cannot be generated. This is known as the
    a. "all or none" principle.
    b. lack of excitatory amino acid.
    c. refractory period.
    d. excess of negatively charged ions.

19. Neurotransmitters are
   a. found in vesicles in the synaptic cleft.
   b. released upon arrival of an action potential at an axon terminal.
   c. effective only when they act on receptors in the central nervous system.
   d. always bound to receptors.

20. Following a stroke, Mrs. Sanchez was not able to move her right hand. This deficit suggests that her stroke may have damaged her
   a. right temporal lobe.
   b. left temporal lobe.
   c. right frontal lobe.
   d. left frontal lobe.

21. Afferent neurons carry signals from the central nervous system to the glands and muscles.
   a. true
   b. false

22. When a neuron is sufficiently stimulated, an action potential occurs.
   a. true
   b. false

23. Any neurotransmitter can fit into any receptor.
   a. true
   b. false

24. Serotonin is a monoamine that is involved in regulating mood.
   a. true
   b. false

25. The medulla handles automatic functions and is part of the midbrain.
   a. true
   b. false

26. The limbic system is a series of brain structures involved in emotion.
   a. true
   b. false

27. The corpus callosum connects the left and right hemispheres of the brain.
   a. true
   b. false

28. Wernicke's area is involved in language production and is found in the frontal lobe.
   a. true
   b. false

29. A CT scan can be used to visualize brain tumors.
   a. true
   b. false

30. A rush of adrenalin could best be described as an effect of a sudden activation of the parasympathetic nervous system.
   a. true
   b. false

31. Explain the process of communication in the nervous system.

32. Name and describe the function of each of the four sets of lobes of the brain.

33. Why did Phineas Gage survive after a large rod penetrated his brain?

CHAPTER 2: PRACTICE TEST 2

1. Which of the following neurons are the most numerous?
   a. afferent neurons
   b. efferent neurons
   c. interneurons
   d. sensory neurons

2. Communication between two _____ occurs at a _____ .
   a. glial cells; dendrite
   b. glial cells; synapse
   c. neurons; dendrite
   d. neurons; synapse

3. An action potential
   a. crosses the synapse.
   b. travels down an axon.
   c. has a negative charge.
   d. occurs only in dendrites and glial cells.

4. Neurotransmitters
   a. are stored in synaptic vesicles.
   b. allow messages to travel from the cell body of a neuron to the axon terminal.
   c. usually accumulate in the cell body.
   d. operate according to the "all-or-none" principle.

5. A drug that mimics the effects of a neurotransmitter is a(n)
   a. action potential.
   b. agonist.
   c. antagonist.
   d. excitatory chemical.

6. Which of the following neurotransmitters causes muscles to contract?
   a. acetylcholine
   b. dopamine
   c. epinephrine
   d. serotonin

7. Damage to which of the following would be most likely to result in death?
   a. cerebellum
   b. hypothalamus
   c. brainstem
   d. reticular formation

8. Most sensory information must pass through the _____ before traveling on to higher brain centers.
   a. cerebral cortex
   b. hippocampus
   c. substantia nigra
   d. thalamus

9. The motor cortex is found in the
   a. frontal lobes.
   b. occipital lobes.
   c. parietal lobes.
   d. temporal lobes.

10. Which of the following is an amino acid that serves as an inhibitory neurotransmitter in the brain?
    a. acetylcholine
    b. dopamine
    c. GABA
    d. glutamate

11. Damage to an area in the _____ would be most likely to result in deficits in speech comprehension.
    a. frontal lobe
    b. occipital lobe
    c. parietal lobe
    d. temporal lobe

12. Severing the corpus callosum
    a. is lethal.
    b. results in severe language deficits.
    c. may be used as a treatment for epilepsy.
    d. caused the changes in personality observed in Phineas Gage.

13. Functional MRI (fMRI)
    a. provides information about both brain structure and function.
    b. is used to measure brain waves.
    c. requires the injection of radioactive substances.
    d. is the oldest technique for visualizing the living brain.

14. When you are excited or scared, the nervous system responds by preparing the body for action. The part of the nervous system that produces this response is the
    a. central nervous system.
    b. parasympathetic nervous system.
    c. somatic nervous system.
    d. sympathetic nervous system.

15. All of the following are endocrine glands *except* the
    a. amygdala.
    b. gonads.
    c. pancreas.
    d. thyroid.

16. The space between two neurons must be "bridged" in order for communication to occur. Communication between two neurons is made possible by
    a. glial cells.
    b. hormones.
    c. ions.
    d. neurotransmitters.

17. Which of the following is most directly involved in the coordination of movement?
    a. cerebellum
    b. frontal lobes
    c. occipital lobes
    d. medulla

18. A drug that acted by blocking neurotransmitter receptors is best described as a(n)
    a. agonist.
    b. amino acid.
    c. antagonist.
    d. reuptake inhibitor.

19. A memory of how an object feels against the skin would most likely be stored in the
    a. hippocampus.
    b. hypothalamus.
    c. limbic system.
    d. parietal lobes.

20. A(n) _____ is essentially a series of X rays of the brain.
    a. CT scan
    b. EEG
    c. MRI scan
    d. PET scan

21. A resting glial cell carries an electrical charge of about 70 millivolts.

   a. true
   b. false

22. The myelin sheath is a fatty coating that can be found wrapped around some axons.

   a. true
   b. false

23. When a neurotransmitter binds to a receptor, the effect is always excitatory.

   a. true
   b. false

24. The central nervous system consists of the brain and the spinal cord.

   a. true
   b. false

25. Simple sobriety tests are designed to test the function of the cerebellum.

   a. true
   b. false

26. Gray matter is gray because it is myelinated.

   a. true
   b. false

27. Experiences can create changes in the adult cerebral cortex.

   a. true
   b. false

28. Unilateral neglect is usually caused by damage to the left hemisphere.

   a. true
   b. false

29. An EEG can reveal what is happening in individual neurons.

   a. true
   b. false

30. The peripheral nervous system consists of two divisions, sympathetic and parasympathetic.

   a. true
   b. false

31. Explain why you don't run out of neurotransmitters.

32. What is the difference between neurotransmitters and hormones?

CHAPTER 3: PRACTICE TEST 1

1. Sensation is the

   a. process of making sense out of incoming information.
   b. final step in recognizing an unfamiliar object.
   c. process of receiving incoming sensory information.
   d. mechanism by which our expectations modify our experiences.

2. Sensation is to perception as _____ is to _____ .

   a. brain; eye
   b. eye; brain
   c. light; eye
   d. eye; light

3. Every time I ask my neighbor to turn down her stereo and she says she has, I can't tell. Which of the following explains why she needs to make a big change when she is playing her music very loudly in order for me to detect a difference?

   a. difference threshold
   b. sensory adaptation
   c. absolute threshold
   d. Weber's law

4. Which of the following explains why ill-fitting shoes make you uncomfortable at first, but then don't bother you at all?

   a. difference threshold
   b. sensory adaptation
   c. absolute threshold
   d. Weber's law

5. Age-related changes in the ability to see objects that are near to you is due to changes in the

   a. cornea.
   b. lens.
   c. pupil.
   d. retina.

6. Which of the following statements is *true*?

   a. Rods and cones are equally sensitive.
   b. Only rods provide detailed vision.
   c. There are five different types of cones, each maximally sensitive to light of a different wavelength.
   d. There are many more rods than cones.

7. In the middle ear, sound waves are
    a. amplified.
    b. collected.
    c. received.
    d. transduced.

8. Sound waves are transduced into neural signals in the
    a. pinna.
    b. outer ear.
    c. middle ear.
    d. inner ear.

9. Differences in olfactory sensitivity
    a. may be a means of identifying who is at risk for the development of dementia.
    b. are seen between the young and the old.
    c. provide an explanation for why only some women experience menstrual synchrony.
    d. All of the above are true.

10. Recent evidence suggests that there may be a fifth taste sensation. This taste sensation is called
    a. origami.
    b. umami.
    c. gustation.
    d. papillae.

11. At which lobes of the brain does tactile information first arrive?
    a. frontal
    b. temporal
    c. occipital
    d. parietal

12. According to the gate-control theory of pain,
    a. some people possess a "gate" that prevents pain messages from being delivered to the brain.
    b. a part of the spinal cord acts as a "gate" that must be closed in order for pain messages to be received by the brain.
    c. rubbing an injured body part can prevent pain messages from reaching the brain.
    d. there is a structure in the brain that acts as a "gate," preventing the most severe pain experiences from getting to the brain.

13. Culture has been shown to influence
    a. the magnitude of physiological responses to pain.
    b. what experiences are painful.
    c. how pain is expressed.
    d. the length of labor.

14. If you could not tell where your leg was, it is most likely that your
    a. brainstem is damaged.
    b. kinesthetic sense is not working properly.
    c. vestibular sense is impaired.
    d. tactile system is not functioning normally.

15. Individuals who are dressed alike may be perceived as belonging to a group. This is consistent with the Gestalt principle of
    a. figure-ground.
    b. similarity.
    c. proximity.
    d. continuity.

16. The size of an image on the retina and the size you perceive the actual object to be
    a. may be unrelated.
    b. are always correlated.
    c. do not change.
    d. explain size constancy.

17. All of the following are monocular depth perception cues *except*
    a. motion parallax.
    b. interposition.
    c. convergence.
    d. shading.

18. An illusion is
    a. a sensory experience with no basis in reality.
    b. a perception in the absence of a stimulus.
    c. an inherited false perception.
    d. a misperception.

19. Which of the following explains how we know that a stop sign says STOP even if some of the letters are hidden?
    a. top-down processing
    b. bottom-up processing
    c. sensory distortion
    d. perceptual constancy

20. According to the Gestalt psychologists, _____ does *not* account for the way in which we perceive the world.
    a. top-down processing
    b. bottom-up processing
    c. observer bias
    d. confirmation bias

21. Absolute threshold refers to the smallest amount of change that can be detected more than 50% of the time.
    a. true
    b. false

22. If you became blind today, your sense of smell would immediately be heightened.
    a. true
    b. false

23. According to Weber's law, if a 10% change is necessary for there to be a detectable difference when a stimulus is small, a 10% change will also be necessary when the stimulus is large.
    a. true
    b. false

24. Sensory adaptation interferes with the ability to shift one's attention to a significant change in the environment.

    a. true
    b. false

25. Light enters the eye through the pupil.

    a. true
    b. false

26. After leaving the eye, visual impulses travel directly to the occipital lobe of the brain.

    a. true
    b. false

27. The inner ear begins with the eardrum.

    a. true
    b. false

28. Olfaction is a chemical sense.

    a. true
    b. false

29. The receptor cells involved in gustation are continually replaced.

    a. true
    b. false

30. The skin is the largest organ of the body.

    a. true
    b. false

31. The receptor cells involved in olfaction are in the nose.

    a. true
    b. false

32. Explain the two theories of color vision. Why is more than one theory needed to explain the processes that underlie the perception of color?

33. What do place theory and frequency theory propose?

34. What are the Gestalt principles of perceptual organization?

CHAPTER 3: PRACTICE TEST 2

1. Perception is to sensation as _____ is to _____ .

    a. hearing; recognition
    b. recognition; hearing
    c. ear; brain
    d. brain; recognition

2. The minimum amount of sensory stimulation that can be detected 50% of the time is the

    a. just noticeable difference.
    b. sensory detector.
    c. difference threshold.
    d. absolute threshold.

3. Sensory adaptation occurs because

    a. receptors are not able to maintain a response for an extended period of time.
    b. information about an unchanging stimulus ceases to be sent to the brain.
    c. the brain no longer responds to a stimulus that is unchanging.
    d. sensory receptors only respond to change.

4. The outer surface of the eye is the

    a. cornea.
    b. lens.
    c. pupil.
    d. retina.

5. Which of the following statements is *true*?

    a. There is no such thing as a "blind spot."
    b. The blind spot is a region of the retina that is entirely cones.
    c. A blind spot exists at an area of the retina with no rods or cones.
    d. The blind spot is a region of the retina that is entirely rods.

6. Rods are to cones as _____ is to _____ .

    a. color; detail
    b. detail; color
    c. black and white; detail
    d. detail; black and white

7. Which of the following statements is *false*?

    a. There are many more rods than cones.
    b. Cones provide us with the ability to see color.
    c. There are three different types of cones, each maximally sensitive to light of a different wavelength.
    d. The fovea contains only rods.

8. The frequency of a sound wave determines the _____ we perceive.

    a. pitch
    b. timbre
    c. volume
    d. wavelength

9. Transduction of a sound wave
   a. occurs at the eardrum.
   b. follows amplification of the sound wave.
   c. happens in the middle ear.
   d. requires that the pinna be functional.

10. According to frequency theory,
    a. frequencies higher than 1,000 Hz can't be heard.
    b. timbre and frequency are the same thing.
    c. an incoming sound wave with a low frequency may cause hair cells to vibrate at the same frequency.
    d. an incoming sound wave at a high frequency may cause hair cells to vibrate at the same frequency.

11. The more sensory receptors you have in a given area on your body surface
    a. the less gustation you experience.
    b. the more pain that area will perceive.
    c. the greater the two-point threshold.
    d. the more sensitive that area will be.

12. All of the following are one of the three major types of chronic pain *except*
    a. low-back pain.
    b. neck pain.
    c. headache.
    d. arthritis.

13. Pain is of interest to psychologists because
    a. it is the source of many mental illnesses.
    b. so often pain is "all in the head."
    c. pain has both a physical and an emotional component.
    d. hypnosis and acupuncture are the two most effective ways of treating chronic pain.

14. The bending of hair cells is involved in
    a. kinesthesis.
    b. the vestibular sense.
    c. audition.
    d. the vestibular sense and audition.

15. The semicircular canals are necessary for
    a. normal audition.
    b. determining where your arm is.
    c. sensing the rotation of your head.
    d. pain perception.

16. We tend to perceive those things that are close together as belonging together. This is explained by the Gestalt principle of
    a. figure-ground.
    b. similarity.
    c. proximity.
    d. continuity.

17. According to the Gestalt principles of perceptual organization,
    a. sometimes a cigar is just a cigar.
    b. the size of an image on the retina never changes.
    c. color perception is determined by retinal processes.
    d. the whole is more than the sum of the parts.

18. Why are we able to perceive the world in three dimensions?
    a. We sense the world in three dimensions.
    b. The brain determines depth from cues provided by the eyes.
    c. Experience has taught us many monocular depth cues.
    d. We don't; it is rare for humans to be able to see three dimensions.

19. Illusions
    a. are the same thing as hallucinations.
    b. occur when binocular depth cues are not functioning effectively.
    c. are always inborn.
    d. are, to some extent, learned.

20. One binocular cue for depth perception involves
    a. how far the eyes have turned in or out to view an object.
    b. the difference in the arrival time of an image at each eye.
    c. how blurred images become when they are far away.
    d. the organization of multiple visual cues into an integrated whole.

21. Sensation is the process of interpreting incoming sensory information.
    a. true
    b. false

22. If a 10% change in volume is needed for a difference to be detected when the volume is low, a 10% change will be needed to produce a detectable change when the volume is high.
    a. true
    b. false

23. Accommodation is the process of modifying the amount of light that enters the eye.
    a. true
    b. false

24. The transduction of light occurs in the retina.
    a. true
    b. false

25. The trichromatic theory provides an explanation for why negative afterimages occur.

    a. true
    b. false

26. Place theory provides an explanation of how we perceive frequencies greater than 150 Hz.

    a. true
    b. false

27. Men are generally more sensitive to odors than women.

    a. true
    b. false

28. The Müller-Lyer illusion is universal.

    a. true
    b. false

29. The Gestalt principles are consistent with the concept of top-down processing.

    a. true
    b. false

30. Motion parallax is a binocular depth cue.

    a. true
    b. false

31. Color perception occurs in the retina.

    a. true
    b. false

32. Explain the progression of a sound wave from its arrival at the eardrum to its arrival in the brain.

33. Explain the use of binocular depth cues.

34. Distinguish between bottom-up and top-down processing.

CHAPTER 4: PRACTICE TEST 1

1. MDMA, or Ecstasy, has been shown to have destructive effects on _____ receptors.

    a. dopamine
    b. GABA
    c. norepinephrine
    d. serotonin

2. Circadian rhythms exist for

    a. appetite.
    b. learning efficiency.
    c. energy level.
    d. all of the above.

3. Jet lag

    a. occurs only when traveling from east to west.
    b. is an effective treatment for some mental disorders.
    c. may be treated with exposure to bright light.
    d. develops when cues to the time of day are not available.

4. NREM sleep is characterized by

    a. slow and regular respiration.
    b. intense brain activity.
    c. epinephrine release.
    d. vivid dreams.

5. The "lightest" sleep occurs during

    a. REM periods.
    b. Stage 1.
    c. Stage 2.
    d. Stage 4.

6. Which of the following statements is *true*?

    a. Sleeping six or fewer hours per night may be a health risk.
    b. Teenagers average 9 hours of sleep a night.
    c. The percentage of time spent in REM sleep changes from early adulthood to late adulthood.
    d. Sleep problems become less likely with age.

7. Which of the following was seen in a study of the effects of sleep deprivation on brain activity?

    a. Activity in all brain areas was depressed in those who were sleep deprived.
    b. The parietal lobes of the sleep deprived were highly active.
    c. The temporal lobes of the sleep deprived were highly active.
    d. Both the temporal and parietal lobes showed greatly reduced neuronal activity.

8. To which of the following neurotransmitters has the intense brain activity seen during REM sleep been attributed?

    a. epinephrine
    b. serotonin
    c. acetylcholine
    d. dopamine

9. The manifest content of a dream refers to

    a. the dream as it is remembered.
    b. the meaning behind the disguised story the dreamer experiences.
    c. the guilty desires that are expressed.
    d. the future life events predicted by many dreams.

10. What do sleepwalking and sleep terrors have in common?

   a. Both are seen only in children.
   b. Both are remembered in the morning.
   c. Neither is associated with anxiety.
   d. Both occur during Stage 4 sleep.

11. Which of the following causes excessive daytime sleepiness?

   a. sleep apnea
   b. somniloquy
   c. somnambulism
   d. parasomnia

12. Research on hypnotism has demonstrated that

   a. only 65% of people are hypnotizable.
   b. there is a correlation between the expectation of being hypnotizable and achieving a hypnotic state.
   c. any command will be followed by someone in a deep hypnotic state.
   d. hypnosis produces greater honesty than any truth serum.

13. A psychoactive drug is one that

   a. causes hallucinations.
   b. is addictive.
   c. has psychological effects.
   d. improves mood.

14. Job absenteeism due to alcohol intoxication is an indication of

   a. alcoholism.
   b. substance abuse.
   c. substance addiction.
   d. substance dependence.

15. When the brain has adapted to the presence of a drug

   a. substance abuse has developed.
   b. the user is psychologically dependent.
   c. less dopamine is released.
   d. tolerance has developed.

16. Alcohol

   a. is a stimulant.
   b. decreases activity in the central nervous system.
   c. and tranquilizers can be taken together safely.
   d. increases sensitivity to a variety of stimuli.

17. Hallucinogens are also known as

   a. depressants.
   b. narcotics.
   c. stimulants.
   d. psychedelics.

18. Caffeine

   a. has no harmful effects.
   b. does not produce psychological dependence.
   c. can lead to withdrawal symptoms such as headaches.
   d. is just as addicting as nicotine.

19. High doses of _____ can produce delusions and hallucinations.

   a. alcohol
   b. amphetamine
   c. caffeine
   d. nicotine

20. The reward pathways of the brain appear to use the neurotransmitter

   a. acetylcholine.
   b. dopamine.
   c. epinephrine.
   d. serotonin.

21. Meditation produces an altered state of consciousness.

   a. true
   b. false

22. Shift changes that require workers to stay up later are less detrimental than those that require a shift of sleep patterns in the opposite direction.

   a. true
   b. false

23. Melatonin levels rise just prior to waking.

   a. true
   b. false

24. During REM sleep, both the brain and the body are active.

   a. true
   b. false

25. Delta waves are seen during deep sleep.

   a. true
   b. false

26. The need to sleep after being awake and active for a long period of time is explained by the circadian theory of sleep.

   a. true
   b. false

27. Sleep deprivation leads to measurable changes in cognitive functioning.

   a. true
   b. false

28. Dreaming does not occur during NREM sleep.

   a. true
   b. false

29. Both dreaming and psychotic mental states are associated with high levels of the neurotransmitter dopamine.

   a. true
   b. false

30. According to the sociocognitive theory of hypnosis, a hypnotic state is the product of a split in consciousness.

   a. true
   b. false

31. Some drugs may be psychologically addicting and not physically addicting.

   a. true
   b. false

32. Describe the four NREM sleep stages.

33. Explain the function of sleep.

34. Discuss two different explanations of why we dream.

CHAPTER 4: PRACTICE TEST 2

1. Consciousness refers to

   a. all that we are aware of.
   b. our emotions.
   c. being awake.
   d. normal brain activity.

2. Daily rhythms are made possible by the

   a. hypothalamus.
   b. hippocampus.
   c. retina.
   d. suprachiasmatic nucleus.

3. Jet lag occurs because

   a. there is a disruption of circadian rhythms.
   b. crossing time zones puts great stress on the body.
   c. the SCN stops functioning.
   d. melatonin production is suspended.

4. The deepest sleep stage is

   a. NREM.
   b. REM.
   c. Stage 3.
   d. Stage 4.

5. During _____ sleep, there is intense brain activity and the large muscles of the body are paralyzed.

   a. NREM
   b. REM
   c. Stage 3
   d. Stage 4

6. Sleep stages 3 and 4 are also known as

   a. alpha sleep.
   b. beta sleep.
   c. REM sleep.
   d. slow-wave sleep.

7. According to the circadian theory of sleep

   a. humans should be nocturnal.
   b. it was once dangerous for humans to be active at night.
   c. predators are more active during the day.
   d. sleep is needed to recover from the exertions of the day.

8. Studies of brain activity and REM sleep

   a. find that few brain areas are active during REM sleep.
   b. demonstrate that there is no relationship between dreams and brain activity.
   c. reveal that the prefrontal cortex is quite active during REM sleep.
   d. show that brain areas associated with both emotions and vision are active during REM sleep.

9. Which of the following is an evolutionary psychology explanation for dreaming?

   a. Dreams allow us to express unfulfilled desires.
   b. Dreams provide us with a means of simulating and practicing life-threatening events that we might have to face.
   c. Dreams allow us to figure out what is really disturbing us, even when we can't admit it.
   d. Dreams are an outlet for aggressive impulses.

10. According to the activation-synthesis hypothesis

   a. only the manifest content of dreams has significance.
   b. the latent content of most dreams is readily interpreted.
   c. the activity of the brain should be consistent with the content of the dream experienced.
   d. dreams do not occur during NREM sleep.

11. Somnambulism

   a. occurs during REM sleep.
   b. is usually seen in Stage 2 sleep.
   c. does not occur in children.
   d. is more commonly referred to as sleepwalking.

12. Nightmares and night terrors

   a. occur during different stages of sleep.
   b. are both seen during REM sleep.
   c. are the same thing.
   d. predict mental illness.

13. Narcolepsy

    a. is caused by prenatal exposure to toxins.
    b. may be treated with depressants.
    c. is rarely seen in adults.
    d. can be treated with stimulants.

14. For which of the following has hypnosis been shown to be most effective?

    a. pain management
    b. weight loss
    c. schizophrenia
    d. nicotine addiction

15. Marijuana is best described as a

    a. depressant.
    b. hallucinogen.
    c. narcotic.
    d. stimulant.

16. All experiences that we get pleasure from increase the availability of _____ in the limbic system.

    a. dopamine
    b. GABA
    c. norepinephrine
    d. serotonin

17. All of the following are factors that contribute to the development of substance abuse *except*

    a. genetics.
    b. climate.
    c. personality.
    d. a history of child abuse.

18. Withdrawal symptoms

    a. mimic the effects of the drug.
    b. and side effects of a drug are usually similar.
    c. may contribute to continued drug use.
    d. are not seen when the use of depressants is discontinued.

19. Drug-related cues

    a. may cause craving for the drug.
    b. can become unconditioned stimuli.
    c. prevent drug tolerance.
    d. do not arouse unique responses in brains of addicts.

20. All of the following are stimulants *except*

    a. amphetamine.
    b. caffeine.
    c. cocaine.
    d. heroin.

21. The body's response to medication differs across the course of a day.

    a. true
    b. false

22. Working when your body is experiencing your subjective night puts you at risk for psychological and physiological problems.

    a. true
    b. false

23. Despite the belief that it is safe, Ecstasy has been found to destroy brain cells.

    a. true
    b. false

24. Melatonin release increases during REM sleep.

    a. true
    b. false

25. Dreaming occurs only during REM sleep.

    a. true
    b. false

26. REM sleep appears to be important for the consolidation of memories.

    a. true
    b. false

27. Delta waves are characteristic of Stage 2 sleep.

    a. true
    b. false

28. The optimal amount of sleep for all adults is $8\frac{1}{2}$ hours.

    a. true
    b. false

29. Individuals suffering from delusional mental illnesses do not dream.

    a. true
    b. false

30. According to the National Institute of Drug Abuse, marijuana shows promise as a treatment for certain medical conditions.

    a. true
    b. false

31. THC is the active ingredient in LSD.

    a. true
    b. false

32. Describe the sleep cycles that occur during a typical night of sleep.

33. Discuss the three theories of hypnosis.

34. Distinguish between substance abuse, physical drug dependence, and psychological drug dependence.

1. Presents have always made little Janie happy. After several of her birthday parties were hosted by clowns, Janie is clearly pleased whenever she sees a clown. If Janie's reaction were described as a product of classical conditioning, what would be the unconditioned response?

   a. happiness in response to presents
   b. happiness in response to clowns
   c. presents
   d. clowns

2. Which of the following is an example of learning?

   a. a loss of appetite after a dramatic event
   b. being irritable due to lack of sleep
   c. avoiding an ice patch that you previously slipped on
   d. developing the ability to walk as an infant

3. In order to extinguish a classically conditioned response,

   a. the unconditioned stimulus is presented without the conditioned stimulus.
   b. the conditioned stimulus is presented without the unconditioned stimulus.
   c. the length of time between the conditioned stimulus and the unconditioned stimulus is decreased.
   d. the length of time between the conditioned stimulus and the unconditioned stimulus is increased.

4. Watson's work with Little Albert demonstrated that

   a. all fears are learned.
   b. young boys are naturally fearful of many stimuli.
   c. conditioning can not be used to treat phobias.
   d. some fears may be learned responses.

5. If ringing a bell does not consistently signal that food is coming,

   a. extinction will occur.
   b. a conditioned response to the bell ringing will not be acquired.
   c. spontaneous recovery is less likely.
   d. discrimination is likely.

6. Which of the following did Pavlov believe to be the critical element in classical conditioning of a response?

   a. predictability
   b. preparedness
   c. reliability
   d. repeated pairing

7. After years of having her cat Lester run into the kitchen every time she used the electric can opener, Katy began to use a handheld opener to open his food. After a number of false alarms (when Katy was opening a can of soup for herself), Lester no longer came running whenever he heard the can opener. After many weeks of not reacting to the electric can opener, Lester once again runs into the kitchen upon hearing it. Which of the following best explains this?

   a. discrimination
   b. extinction
   c. generalization
   d. spontaneous recovery

8. All of the following brain structures appear to be important for some form of learning *except* the

   a. amygdala.
   b. cerebellum.
   c. hippocampus.
   d. hypothalamus.

9. Which of the following pairings is correct?

   a. Pavlov; law of effect
   b. Skinner; operant conditioning
   c. Thorndike; classical conditioning
   d. Bandura; latent learning

10. John drives a truck with a diesel engine. As a consequence, his dog has come to associate the sound of the diesel engine with John's arrival at home. In fact, Fido shows excitement whenever he hears a diesel truck. Which of the following does this demonstrate?

    a. discrimination
    b. extinction
    c. generalization
    d. spontaneous recovery

11. Extinction

    a. of a classically conditioned response occurs when reinforcement is no longer provided.
    b. does not occur when a behavior is acquired though operant conditioning.
    c. and spontaneous recovery are seen only when behaviors have been classically conditioned.
    d. occurs with both classical and operant conditioning.

12. The sight of a needle causes Jeremy to experience an intense craving for heroin. Which of the following best explains this?

    a. Jeremy enjoys the appearance of needles and finds them exciting.
    b. The needle has become associated with the effects of the drug.
    c. The needle is an unconditioned stimulus that produces an intense response.
    d. Jeremy's treatment has been ineffective.

13. Jenny gives her daughter candy to stop her from crying. In operant conditioning terms, which of the following is Jenny providing to her daughter?

    a. positive reinforcement
    b. negative reinforcement
    c. secondary reinforcement
    d. punishment

14. Pavlov has grown tired of seeing his dogs salivate whenever they hear a tone. The process for terminating this behavior is known as

   a. punishment.
   b. reinforcement.
   c. generalization.
   d. extinction.

15. I get one movie free after I rent five. This is an example of

   a. a fixed-ratio schedule.
   b. a variable-ratio schedule.
   c. a fixed-interval schedule.
   d. a variable-interval schedule.

16. Advertisements designed to influence men often use an attractive women as a(n)

   a. conditioned stimulus.
   b. unconditioned stimulus.
   c. signal for discrimination.
   d. cue for extinction.

17. Escape learning

   a. is not an effective way to acquire a response.
   b. and punishment are the same thing.
   c. involves both classical conditioning and operant conditioning.
   d. occurs when a behavior is negatively reinforced.

18. Latent learning

   a. is a form of operant conditioning in which reinforcement is provided on a variable-interval schedule.
   b. refers to learning that occurs but is not immediately demonstrated.
   c. is only possible in animals capable of verbal communication.
   d. and punishment both suppress the demonstration of learned behaviors.

19. We need not spend our lives making mistakes in order to learn many valuable lessons. Which of the following best explains why this is true?

   a. classical conditioning
   b. cognitive maps
   c. observational learning
   d. operant conditioning

20. Bandura's work demonstrated that

   a. children may learn to handle frustration with aggression.
   b. only children exposed to violence will be violent.
   c. juvenile delinquency is a consequence of failing to punish negative behaviors.
   d. punishment is never effective.

21. An unconditioned response is a natural reaction to a stimulus.

   a. true
   b. false

22. Being startled by a loud noise is an example of a conditioned response.

   a. true
   b. false

23. A conditioned stimulus is somewhat like a signal that indicates that an unconditioned stimulus is coming.

   a. true
   b. false

24. In Watson's work with Little Albert, the white rat was the conditioned stimulus.

   a. true
   b. false

25. Pavlov laid the groundwork for many of the behavioral therapies used today.

   a. true
   b. false

26. Rescorla demonstrated that repeated pairing of two stimuli is not the critical element in classical conditioning.

   a. true
   b. false

27. Immune responses can be classically conditioned.

   a. true
   b. false

28. The cerebellum is the storage site in the brain for emotional memories.

   a. true
   b. false

29. Pavlov was concerned about the role of cognitive factors in classical conditioning.

   a. true
   b. false

30. Money is a primary reinforcer.

   a. true
   b. false

31. If I am paid based on the amount of time that has passed, I am being paid on a fixed-interval schedule.

   a. true
   b. false

32. Explain how classical conditioning can be used in treating someone with a learned fear.

33. How do biological predispositions affect what can and can't be learned?

34. Discuss the factors that influence the learning of a response acquired through operant conditioning.

1. Learning is
   a. a permanent change in behavior produced by an early life event.
   b. acquired through interactions with the environment.
   c. a product of maturation.
   d. a consequence of temporary fluctuations in mood.

2. Just prior to her computer locking up, Hilda hears a dull clicking sound. After this frustrating situation happens a number of times (she hears a click and the computer locks up), Hilda finds that she is very upset when she hears the clicking sound. Hilda's response to the clicking could be described as a(n)
   a. conditioned stimulus.
   b. unconditioned stimulus.
   c. conditioned response.
   d. unconditioned response.

3. Pavlov has grown tired of seeing his dogs salivate whenever they hear a tone. The process for terminating this behavior involves
   a. presenting the conditioned stimulus without the conditioned response.
   b. presenting the unconditioned stimulus without the unconditioned response.
   c. presenting the conditioned stimulus without the unconditioned response.
   d. presenting the conditioned stimulus without the unconditioned stimulus.

4. After the pairing of a loud noise with a white rat, Little Albert exhibited fear in response to other white and furry things. Which of the following explains why this occurred?
   a. classical conditioning
   b. operant conditioning
   c. generalization
   d. extinction

5. After pairing sweetened water with an immune-suppressing drug, the sweetened water becomes a conditioned stimulus. What is the conditioned response?
   a. the immune-suppressing drug
   b. the sweetened water
   c. illness
   d. immune suppression

6. Edward Thorndike is credited with
   a. the law of effect.
   b. demonstrating the errors made by Pavlov.
   c. exploring the role of learning in establishing fear responses.
   d. discovering the principles of operant conditioning.

7. Which of the following best explains why rats are more likely to associate a taste with illness than with being shocked?
   a. biological predisposition
   b. conditioned fear
   c. innate taste aversion
   d. predictability

8. Jenny gives her daughter candy to stop her from crying. In operant conditioning terms, Jenny's behavior is likely to continue because it is
   a. positively reinforced.
   b. negatively reinforced.
   c. classically conditioned.
   d. negatively punished.

9. Primary reinforcers
   a. are things such as money and prizes that most people are happy to receive.
   b. become reinforcing through their association with satisfaction of basic needs.
   c. are only rewarding when they are an alternative to punishment.
   d. satisfy basic needs.

10. When teaching a dog a new trick, which of the following should be used to get the best results?
    a. continuous reinforcement
    b. a fixed-ratio schedule
    c. a variable-ratio schedule
    d. All of the above would be equally effective.

11. What benefit is there to partial reinforcement of a behavior?
    a. The behavior will be learned more quickly.
    b. Resistance to extinction will be greater.
    c. Spontaneous recovery will be less likely.
    d. Punishment will be ineffective.

12. If I reward myself with a 10-minute break after I have graded four papers, this is an example of a
    a. fixed-ratio schedule.
    b. variable-ratio schedule.
    c. fixed-interval schedule.
    d. variable-interval schedule.

13. When an oddly flavored ice cream is given before chemotherapy, it is hoped that the ice cream will serve as a(n)
    a. conditioned stimulus.
    b. counter-conditioning stimulus.
    c. pleasant distraction.
    d. unconditioned stimulus.

14. When Molly's parents stopped paying her to do her chores, she eventually stopped doing them. Which of the following best explains Molly's failure to continue doing her chores when reinforcement is no longer being provided?

   a. classical conditioning
   b. extinction
   c. punishment
   d. spontaneous recovery

15. Which of the following statements about research on violence and the media is correct?

   a. There is no justification for regulating the amount of TV violence children view.
   b. Watching a live person behave aggressively has a greater impact on behavior than viewing a film of the person's behavior.
   c. Only violent video games have been shown to be influential.
   d. Virtually all forms of media violence have been shown to have an effect on aggressive behavior.

16. Who conducted the "Bobo Doll" studies?

   a. Bandura
   b. Pavlov
   c. Skinner
   d. Tolman

17. According to research findings,

   a. observational learning is a uniquely human phenomenon.
   b. "monkey see, monkey do" is one way to describe a type of learning.
   c. the development of cognitive maps is a uniquely human ability.
   d. observing has minimal effects on human behavior.

18. All of the following are applications of operant conditioning except

   a. behavior modification.
   b. biofeedback.
   c. cognitive maps.
   d. token economies.

19. Students walk right past the library every day. It does not appear that they know where this important resource is. One Monday morning, a sign in the parking lot says "Free donuts in the library." Students swarm to the library, demonstrating that they have learned its location. This scenario could be said to demonstrate

   a. classical conditioning.
   b. insight.
   c. latent learning.
   d. operant conditioning.

20. Before Professor Jones asks a question, she always clears her throat. To avoid being called on, students will bury their noses in their books whenever Professor Jones clears her throat. This is an example of

   a. avoidance learning.
   b. classical conditioning.
   c. escape learning.
   d. punishment.

21. Technically, babies learn to walk and crawl.

   a. true
   b. false

22. Classical conditioning occurs most readily when the unconditioned stimulus is presented just before the conditioned stimulus.

   a. true
   b. false

23. Most Vietnam War veterans who used heroin in Vietnam continued to do so on returning to the United States.

   a. true
   b. false

24. Memories of conditioned fear responses are stored in the amygdala.

   a. true
   b. false

25. Rats appear to be biologically prepared to associate lights and noise with electric shock.

   a. true
   b. false

26. Generalization and discrimination are seen in both operant and classical conditioning.

   a. true
   b. false

27. The cerebellum plays a primary role in conditioned fear responses.

   a. true
   b. false

28. Skinner is known for his work with hungry cats and "puzzle boxes."

   a. true
   b. false

29. Environmental cues can serve as conditioned stimuli.

   a. true
   b. false

30. Negative reinforcement occurs when an undesirable behavior is rewarded.

   a. true
   b. false

31. Secondary reinforcers become reinforcing through learning.

    a. true
    b. false

32. Explain the phenomena of extinction and spontaneous recovery.

33. Discuss how the contemporary view of classical conditioning differs from that of Pavlov.

34. Explain the process of shaping, and describe how it might be used. What form of learning is this?

CHAPTER 6: PRACTICE TEST 1

1. Sometimes I can't seem to recall the name of someone whom I have known for some time, even though I had no problem with her or his name in the past. Which of my memory processes appears to be failing?

    a. amnesia
    b. encoding
    c. storage
    d. retrieval

2. The capacity (size) of short-term memory

    a. cannot be increased.
    b. is not limited.
    c. can be increased by organizing items to be remembered into larger units.
    d. can be increased through the use of elaborative consolidation.

3. Which type of memory task does answering a multiple-choice question involve?

    a. recall
    b. recognition
    c. rehearsal
    d. relearning

4. Memory is most like a(n)

    a. historical novel.
    b. black-and-white photograph.
    c. video recording without sound.
    d. essay based on incomplete notes.

5. Research on depression and memory has revealed that

    a. most depressed people show severe and permanent memory impairments.
    b. retrieval deficits underlie most depressive episodes.
    c. negative events are more readily recalled by those who are depressed.
    d. semantic memories are most severely affected by depression.

6. Ebbinghaus

    a. demonstrated the importance of encoding material for later recall.
    b. discovered that information retained for more than a few days was likely to still be remembered a month later.

    c. illustrated that short-term memory has a capacity of about 15 items.
    d. distinguished between episodic and semantic memory.

7. Which of the following memory systems holds information for as little as a fraction of a second?

    a. episodic
    b. semantic
    c. sensory
    d. short-term

8. Memories for where and when you learned something are part of _____ memory.

    a. episodic
    b. implicit
    c. nondeclarative
    d. semantic

9. Which of the following memory systems does *not* appear to be affected by removal of the hippocampal region?

    a. episodic memory
    b. explicit memory
    c. nondeclarative memory
    d. semantic memory

10. After being given a new locker combination, I can't seem to recall the old one anymore. This is best explained by

    a. anterograde amnesia.
    b. proactive interference.
    c. retrograde amnesia.
    d. retroactive interference.

11. Some memory researchers argue that early episodic memories may not be formed because of an immature

    a. cerebellum.
    b. cerebral cortex.
    c. hippocampus.
    d. hypothalamus.

12. The inability to recall the color of your mailbox is best explained by

    a. anterograde amnesia.
    b. decay theory.
    c. encoding failure.
    d. proactive interference.

13. Research has revealed that inhibiting protein synthesis in the brain

    a. prevents memory retrieval.
    b. may actually "erase" some memories.
    c. does not prevent LTP.
    d. facilitates memory consolidation.

14. "Flashbulb" memories are

    a. generally formed from semantic information.
    b. more likely to be forgotten than memories of insignificant events.
    c. usually not as accurate as we think they are.
    d. the most enduring and accurate type of episodic memories.

15. Prospective forgetting

    a. and memory suppression are the same thing.
    b. is always a form of motivated forgetting.
    c. may often be the result of encoding failure.
    d. can be the result of interference, consolidation failure, or motivated forgetting.

16. Which of the following is *not* a recommended studying practice?

    a. spaced practice
    b. massed practice
    c. overlearning
    d. recitation

17. After Jim's surgery, he was unable to form new long-term memories. Jim appears to be suffering from

    a. anterograde amnesia.
    b. retrograde amnesia.
    c. epilepsy.
    d. proactive interference.

18. Research on childhood memories has demonstrated that

    a. hypnosis is an effective technique for bringing early memories of trauma into consciousness.
    b. we have no memory for events that occurred before age 7.
    c. simply imagining experiences can lead to false memories.
    d. fictitious childhood memories can not be experimentally induced.

19. The "tip-of-the-tongue" phenomenon can best be explained as

    a. anterograde amnesia.
    b. retrograde amnesia.
    c. an encoding failure.
    d. a retrieval failure.

20. After being knocked unconscious in a football game, Bob could not remember the play that preceded his loss of consciousness. His is a case of

    a. anterograde amnesia.
    b. proactive interference.
    c. retrograde amnesia.
    d. retroactive interference.

21. Short-term memory holds more information than sensory memory does.

    a. true
    b. false

22. Schemas provide expectations about new experiences and aid in the storage of information.

    a. true
    b. false

23. Memory repression and memory suppression are the same thing.

    a. true
    b. false

24. According to research, overlearning should be avoided because it increases the likelihood of stress-related forgetting.

    a. true
    b. false

25. Recall of material appearing in the middle of a list is better than that of material at the beginning of a list.

    a. true
    b. false

26. The memory deficits exhibited by H.M. have been primarily attributed to his epilepsy.

    a. true
    b. false

27. Cortisol, a stress hormone, has been shown to facilitate remembering.

    a. true
    b. false

28. The amygdala plays a significant role in establishing emotional memories.

    a. true
    b. false

29. The more certain a witness is of his or her testimony, the more likely it is to be accurate.

    a. true
    b. false

30. The hippocampus appears to be important for remembering where things are.

    a. true
    b. false

31. Hypnosis and guided imagery are reliable techniques for uncovering repressed memories of trauma.

    a. true
    b. false

32. Explain what elaborative rehearsal is and how it facilitates learning.

33. What is long-term potentiation, and how is it related to learning?

34. Discuss the causes of forgetting.

CHAPTER 6: PRACTICE TEST 2

1. All information from the senses is held in _____ memory for a brief period of time.

   a. episodic
   b. semantic
   c. sensory
   d. short-term

2. Which of the following can be used to increase the length of time information remains in short-term memory?

   a. chunking
   b. encoding
   c. elaborative rehearsal
   d. rehearsal

3. Sometimes information is not forgotten, it has just never been processed into a form that can be stored in memory. The failure to attend to a stimulus in order to remember it is called a(n) _____ failure.

   a. consolidation
   b. encoding
   c. storage
   d. retrieval

4. Memories of how to do something are part of _____ memory.

   a. declarative
   b. episodic
   c. explicit
   d. nondeclarative

5. *Working memory* is another name for _____ memory.

   a. episodic
   b. semantic
   c. sensory
   d. short-term

6. H.M.'s amnesia is thought to be due primarily to

   a. abnormal neuronal activity resulting from his epilepsy.
   b. the removal of his hippocampus.
   c. nutritional deficits resulting from his alcoholism.
   d. the damage to various brain regions resulting from his drug abuse.

7. The other day I accidentally called my husband by an old boyfriend's name. Which of the following might I use to explain this blunder?

   a. anterograde amnesia
   b. decay theory
   c. encoding failure
   d. proactive interference

8. Overlearning

   a. is likely to improve test performance.
   b. increases the likelihood of stress-related forgetting.
   c. maximizes the amount of interference that will occur.
   d. prevents memory consolidation.

9. Errors in eyewitness testimony can be minimized by

   a. allowing the witness to see a photograph of a suspect before identifying the suspect in a lineup.
   b. using people in the lineup who look similar to the suspect.
   c. having the witness view all the participants in a lineup simultaneously.
   d. using only witnesses who differ in race from the suspect.

10. Which of the following is *not* a form of motivated forgetting?

   a. prospective forgetting
   b. repression
   c. retrograde amnesia
   d. suppression

11. In order for information contained in long-term memory to be used, it must be

   a. encoded.
   b. moved into sensory memory.
   c. retrieved.
   d. transduced.

12. Because of the serial position effect,

   a. we are most likely to forget the first few digits of a phone number.
   b. items in the middle of a shopping list are most likely to be forgotten.
   c. emotional events are less likely than nonemotional events to be encoded.
   d. information at the beginning of a list is less likely to be stored in long-term memory.

13. Through the use of rows of letters and different tones, Sperling showed

   a. how memories are consolidated.
   b. how to increase the capacity of long-term memory.

c. the length of short-term memory.
d. the size of sensory memory.

14. Information kept in short-term memory for more than 30 seconds usually has been

a. chunked.
b. consolidated.
c. rehearsed.
d. visually encoded.

15. The recency effect is most likely due to the fact that the information

a. is in long-term memory.
b. has been consolidated.
c. is associated with fewer retrieval cues.
d. is still in short-term memory.

16. Working memory

a. and short-term memory are the same.
b. and sensory memory are the same.
c. is an outdated term that reflects early misconceptions about the nature of long-term memory.
d. consists of five distinct components.

17. Information contained in long-term memory is most commonly stored in _____ form.

a. auditory
b. olfactory
c. verbal
d. visual

18. Long-term potentiation

a. has been demonstrated only in sea snails.
b. appears to be necessary for some forms of learning to occur.
c. is a temporary decrease in the strength of neuronal firing.
d. explains why emotion contributes to the strength of some memories.

19. Long-term memory

a. has a limited capacity.
b. does not hold information about manual skills.
c. has no known limits to its storage capacity.
d. holds all information permanently.

20. The memory of how to ride a bike is best described as a(n) _____ memory.

a. declarative
b. episodic
c. explicit
d. nondeclarative

21. Physiological changes are necessary for the storage of information in memory.

a. true
b. false

22. Sperling demonstrated that short-term memory has a capacity of about seven items.

a. true
b. false

23. Short-term memory holds information for a longer period of time than sensory memory does.

a. true
b. false

24. All information in short-term memory enters long-term memory.

a. true
b. false

25. Chunking can be used to increase the length of time information is in short-term memory.

a. true
b. false

26. According to the levels-of-processing model, the more deeply an item is processed, the more likely that it will be remembered over time.

a. true
b. false

27. Recall tasks are the most sensitive type of memory test.

a. true
b. false

28. Schemas may both aid and distort memory.

a. true
b. false

29. Research has consistently supported the notion that memory is generally quite accurate.

a. true
b. false

30. Retrograde amnesia is thought to be the result of an encoding failure.

a. true
b. false

31. The existence of the serial position effect contradicts what is commonly believed to be true about short-term and long-term memory.

a. true
b. false

32. Describe the main subsystems of long-term memory.

33. What are the three types of tasks used to measure memory? Provide an example of each.

34. What has research revealed about the relationship between context and memory? How could this knowledge be applied to everyday life?

1. _____ are acquired through experience.

   a. Artificial concepts
   b. Formal concepts
   c. Fundamental concepts
   d. Natural concepts

2. Which of the following is an example of a concept?

   a. cat
   b. Siamese
   c. Persian
   d. tabby

3. When Fido found that he could not get through the doorway with his stick held horizontally, he managed to pull it through vertically. Fido found a new approach to an old problem; that is, he

   a. developed a new concept.
   b. employed an algorithm.
   c. overcame mental set.
   d. relied on the representativeness heuristic.

4. Which of the following would be the most likely proto-type of the concept _vehicle_?

   a. an elevator
   b. a yacht
   c. a car
   d. a bicycle

5. Intonation and social rules are part of the _____ of language.

   a. phonics
   b. pragmatics
   c. semantics
   d. syntax

6. The news coverage of plane crashes often leads the public to believe that dying in a plane crash is more common than dying in a car crash. This misconception can be attributed to the use of

   a. the availability heuristic.
   b. elimination by aspects.
   c. framing.
   d. the representativeness heuristic.

7. According to the linguistic relativity hypothesis,

   a. Eskimos have many words for snow because they think about snow more than other peoples.
   b. thinking influences perceptions and, as a consequence, language.
   c. because most cultures have just one word for snow, they think about snow in a more limited way than the Eskimos do.
   d. if snow were more common throughout the world, there would be more words for it.

8. According to Spearman,

   a. contextual intelligence is necessary for success.
   b. there is just one general form of intelligence.
   c. experiential intelligence is one of the three forms of intelligence all humans possess.
   d. everyone has a high level of at least one form of intelligence.

9. Which of the following is _not_ a morpheme?

   a. _re-_
   b. _-ed_
   c. _-s_
   d. _-ive_

10. A child with a mental age of 5 and a chronological age of 10 has an IQ of

   a. 50.
   b. 100.
   c. 10.
   d. 500.

11. Terman's work with the gifted

   a. supported the notion that the mentally gifted are usually physically challenged.
   b. demonstrated the need to recognize at least eight different types of intelligence.
   c. found that those who are mentally gifted are likely to excel in many areas.
   d. showed that mental illness is more common among the gifted.

12. You've been told that one woman out of a group of 20 is a vegetarian. You assume that it is the woman who is wearing jeans and a t-shirt (the others are in dresses and suits). Which of the following did you employ in making this decision?

   a. the availability heuristic
   b. formal concepts
   c. framing
   d. the representativeness heuristic

13. Early interventions designed to enrich the environment of poor children

   a. rarely have an effect.
   b. have demonstrated that such efforts can have lasting effects.
   c. support the heritability of intelligence.
   d. demonstrate that nature cannot be altered by nurture.

14. A lengthy process that will eventually yield a correct solution is a(n)

   a. algorithm.
   b. artificial concept.
   c. heuristic.
   d. means-end analysis.

15. Which of the following statements about gender and cognitive abilities is *true*?

    a. There is greater variation in cognitive abilities among females than among males.

    b. Cognitive differences between the genders are average differences, not absolute differences.

    c. Parental influences are clearly the source of commonly observed gender differences in cognitive abilities.

    d. Male superiority in math has consistently been observed at all ages.

16. If a trait is highly heritable,

    a. it is completely attributable to genes.

    b. nature plays no role in the trait's persistence.

    c. the influence of genes on the trait is greater than the influence of the environment.

    d. environmental factors are more important to the trait than genetic influences.

17. The smallest units of sound in a spoken language are

    a. dipthongs.

    b. linguics.

    c. morphemes.

    d. phonemes.

18. Sternberg referred to creative intelligence as _____ intelligence.

    a. analytical

    b. componential

    c. contextual

    d. experiential

19. _____ tests are designed to predict future performance.

    a. Achievement

    b. Aptitude

    c. Assessment

    d. Approval

20. An intelligence test that is designed to give all those who take it an equal chance of success is a _____ test.

    a. culture-fair

    b. reliable

    c. standardized

    d. valid

21. Trial and error is an example of an algorithm.

    a. true

    b. false

22. Primate studies have demonstrated that other animal species can develop humanlike language capabilities.

    a. true

    b. false

23. There is only one phoneme for each letter used in the English language.

    a. true

    b. false

24. Research to date has revealed that only humans are capable of language.

    a. true

    b. false

25. All individuals with IQs less than 70 are classified as mentally retarded.

    a. true

    b. false

26. Bilingualism during childhood is associated with an improved ability to think about language.

    a. true

    b. false

27. The letter *a* is both a morpheme and a phoneme.

    a. true

    b. false

28. Cross-cultural studies suggest that observed differences in academic achievement across cultures are largely due to differences in parental attitudes about academic achievement.

    a. true

    b. false

29. *Syntax* refers to the meaning of language.

    a. true

    b. false

30. To have an IQ greater than 100, your mental age must be greater than your chronological age.

    a. true

    b. false

31. Neural networks are computer systems intended to mimic the functioning of the human brain.

    a. true

    b. false

32. What have attempts to teach language to nonhuman primates demonstrated?

33. Discuss the advantages and disadvantages of being bilingual.

34. What is intelligence?

1. An example that is considered most typical of a concept is a(n)

   a. algorithm.
   b. fuzzy concept.
   c. heuristic.
   d. prototype.

2. Although you may think of a tomato as a vegetable, it is actually a fruit. When you categorize a tomato as a fruit, you are using a(n)

   a. formal concept.
   b. fuzzy concept.
   c. natural concept.
   d. operational definition.

3. Componential intelligence can be described as

   a. street smarts.
   b. book smarts.
   c. creativity.
   d. common sense.

4. When you conclude that it's a duck because it walks and quacks like a duck, you are employing

   a. the availability heuristic.
   b. elimination by aspects.
   c. framing.
   d. the representativeness heuristic.

5. "The girl chased the car" and "the car was chased by the girl"

   a. are identical in syntax.
   b. differ semantically.
   c. violate several phonological rules.
   d. differ with respect to syntax but not semantics.

6. A good test must be reliable. A reliable test

   a. can be used to make predictions about future achievement.
   b. is constructed using norms.
   c. measures what it is designed to measure.
   d. yields comparable results each time it is administered to a given individual.

7. Hitting the toaster always seems to make it work. When you have problems with the blender, you try hitting it as well. Which of the following is this an example of?

   a. algorithm
   b. analogy heuristic
   c. means-end analysis
   d. trial and error

8. Dynamic assessment

   a. is the latest trend in aptitude testing.
   b. is the most effective way of minimizing errors in problem solving.
   c. provides a means to minimize cultural bias.
   d. is a technique used to differentiate gifted individuals from those who excel in just one domain.

9. The smallest unit of meaning in a language is a

   a. dicticon.
   b. morpheme.
   c. phoneme.
   d. suffix.

10. Emotional intelligence

    a. and IQ are highly correlated.
    b. is characterized by the ability to suppress emotions.
    c. has no impact on relationships.
    d. involves an awareness of and ability to manage emotions.

11. Which of the following can be a barrier to problem solving?

    a. algorithm
    b. analogy heuristic
    c. functional fixedness
    d. means-end analysis

12. If this test is a valid test,

    a. you will get the same score each time you take it.
    b. your performance on it will predict how well you will do on future tests on this topic.
    c. it will assess your understanding of Chapter 7.
    d. individuals from any culture have an equal likelihood of performing well on it.

13. Which of the following is *not* a criticism of studies of language in nonhuman primates?

    a. Symbols are not an appropriate substitute for words.
    b. Experimenter bias may play a role in some positive findings.
    c. Although chimps have been trained to use many symbols, the number learned is not sufficient to be viewed as a language.
    d. The behaviors of the chimps are more a product of operant conditioning than a consequence of language learning.

14. Which of the following statements about creativity and IQ is *true*?

    a. Individuals with IQs greater than 120 tend to be highly creative.
    b. There is no relationship between IQ and creativity.
    c. Since creativity is a form of intelligence, the relationship to IQ cannot be studied.
    d. Highly creative people tend to be above average in intelligence.

15. Computer systems
    a. have been designed that operate just like the human brain.
    b. cannot yet comprehend the meaning of changes in tone of voice.
    c. can consider context and exceptions when making decisions.
    d. are better than humans at recognizing a particular face.

16. When Jill finally figured out how to solve a problem, she exclaimed, "I never thought to do it that way!" Jill's statement suggests that _____ was a barrier to her problem solving.
    a. an algorithm
    b. functional fixedness
    c. means-end analysis
    d. mental set

17. Psychologists define *intelligence* as
    a. a single trait that enables one to solve problems.
    b. the ability to find novel solutions to complex problems.
    c. a fixed personality trait.
    d. none of the above.

18. Fraternal twins
    a. are not used in studies of heritability.
    b. are also called *monozygotic twins*.
    c. share no more genes than any other pair of siblings.
    d. are often more comparable than identical twins.

19. The SAT is a(n)
    a. achievement test.
    b. aptitude test.
    c. culture-fair test.
    d. intelligence test.

20. According to Gardner, all of the following are forms of intelligence *except*
    a. bodily-kinesthetic.
    b. emotional.
    c. spatial.
    d. interpersonal.

21. The belief that a coin toss is more likely to come up "heads" after many "tails" have been thrown can be blamed on the availability heuristic.
    a. true
    b. false

22. *Syntax* refers to the rules of word order.
    a. true
    b. false

23. According to the linguistic relativity hypothesis, the language you speak influences how you think about the world.
    a. true
    b. false

24. Unlike a heuristic, an algorithm guarantees that the correct solution will eventually be found.
    a. true
    b. false

25. Studies of the thinking of people who have many words for colors have supported the linguistic relativity hypothesis.
    a. true
    b. false

26. When an object is visualized, the areas of the brain involved with processing visual information show an increase in activity.
    a. true
    b. false

27. Morphemes are the smallest units of sound in a spoken language.
    a. true
    b. false

28. Exemplars are based on formal concepts.
    a. true
    b. false

29. The language learning of both chimps and humans is dependent on operant conditioning.
    a. true
    b. false

30. The English language has 26 phonemes.
    a. true
    b. false

31. Pragmatic rules determine how one should speak to authority figures.
    a. true
    b. false

32. Discuss two strategies that are used when making decisions.

33. Distinguish between functional fixedness and mental set. Provide an example for each.

34. What conclusions can be made about the heritability of intelligence?

1. All of the following proposed a stage theory of development *except*
   a. Ainsworth.
   b. Erikson.
   c. Kohlberg.
   d. Piaget.

2. In order to think in the abstract and hypothesize about the future,
   a. generativity must be attained.
   b. hypothetico-deductive thinking must occur.
   c. one must have had many years of formal schooling.
   d. postconventional reasoning is required.

3. Thirty-year-old James bases his behavior on rewards and punishments he will receive. If he can steal something and not get caught, he will do so. James's moral reasoning is at the _____ level.
   a. preoperational
   b. concrete operations
   c. preconventional
   d. conventional

4. An infant can be said to possess a scheme for nursing at her or his mother's breast. When the infant has to modify this scheme to nurse from a bottle, _____ occurs.
   a. accommodation
   b. assimilation
   c. maturation
   d. symbolic function

5. Which of the following does *not* provide evidence of language being biologically determined?
   a. the likelihood of babbling
   b. the occurrence of overextension
   c. the changes in language seen at about 8 months of age
   d. the content of cooing

6. Which of the following is *true* of Piaget's stages of development?
   a. All children pass through them at the same rate.
   b. The transition from one stage to another is sudden.
   c. Each stage is characterized by quantitatively different ways of reasoning.
   d. The environment affects the rate at which a child moves through the stages.

7. Which of the following is consistent with a social learning explanation for gender role development?
   a. Molly's mom smiles and tells her that her mudpies look delicious.
   b. Jimmy likes to play with dolls.
   c. Suzy's dad compliments her on how well she can throw a ball.
   d. James identifies with his dad when he realizes that being jealous of him is not going to get rid of him.

8. The recognition that a symbol can be used to represent an object develops during Piaget's _____ stage.
   a. concrete operations
   b. formal operations
   c. preoperational
   d. sensorimotor

9. Caffeine
   a. is a well-established teratogen.
   b. consumed during pregnancy is more dangerous than smoking and less dangerous than drinking alcohol.
   c. increases the likelihood of Down syndrome.
   d. should be consumed only in moderation during pregnancy.

10. Which of the following statements about puberty is true?
    a. Puberty begins with the onset of adolescence.
    b. Puberty is a concept that describes the transition from childhood to adulthood.
    c. During puberty, primary sex characteristics appear.
    d. During puberty, the reproductive organs mature.

11. Kohlberg has been criticized because
    a. he underestimated the abilities of young children.
    b. there may be gender differences in moral reasoning.
    c. few people attain full formal operational thinking.
    d. postconventional reasoning is too rare to study effectively.

12. _____ parents believe that children should be seen and not heard.
    a. Absent
    b. Authoritative
    c. Authoritarian
    d. Permissive

13. Seeing her father in a kilt, Sally exclaimed "Daddy is a girl! He's wearing a skirt." With this statement, Sally is exhibiting that she has not yet acquired the concept of
    a. gender identity.
    b. gender constancy.
    c. gender roles.
    d. gender stability.

14. According to Erikson, children develop a sense of pride in their accomplishments during the _____ stage.
    a. autonomy versus shame and doubt
    b. generativity versus stagnation

c. industry versus inferiority
d. initiative versus guilt

15. Crystallized intelligence
    a. does not develop until middle age.
    b. peaks in the early 20s.
    c. consists of abstract reasoning and mental flexibility.
    d. usually increases over the life span.

16. A _____ gene will always be expressed.
    a. dominant   c. polygenic
    b. multifactorial   d. recessive

17. Which of the following is *not* correlated with good cognitive functioning in the elderly?
    a. being a man
    b. a long marriage to an intelligent spouse
    c. education level
    d. a stimulating work environment

18. Temperament
    a. is genetically determined and unaffected by the environment.
    b. appears to be correlated with personality later in life.
    c. can rarely be detected within the first few weeks of life.
    d. can be reliably categorized in only 35% of infants.

19. A study of the terminally ill identified five stages that the dying pass through in coming to terms with death. The second of these stages is
    a. anger.
    b. bargaining.
    c. depression.
    d. denial.

20. Jill's decisions as to what is right and what is wrong are based on what is approved by others. Jill's moral reasoning seems to be at the _____ level.
    a. preconventional
    b. preoperational
    c. concrete operational
    d. conventional

21. Developmental psychologists only study child development.
    a. true
    b. false

22. A lack of intellectual pursuits has consistently been found to be a risk factor for Alzheimer's disease.
    a. true
    b. false

23. Japanese women report stronger feelings of obligation toward their elders than American women do.
    a. true
    b. false

24. Monozygotic twins are no more alike than any other siblings.
    a. true
    b. false

25. The order in which children pass through Piaget's stages varies.
    a. true
    b. false

26. All adolescents in developed countries demonstrate full formal operational thinking.
    a. true
    b. false

27. The end of Piaget's sensorimotor period is indicated by the development of object permanence.
    a. true
    b. false

28. Conservation is necessary for the development of the concept of reversibility.
    a. true
    b. false

29. For teens, attending religious services is negatively correlated with sexual experience.
    a. true
    b. false

30. White males over age 75 have the highest suicide rate of any group in the United States.
    a. true
    b. false

31. Research consistently demonstrates that maturing early has more positive consequences than negative consequences for both males and females.
    a. true
    b. false

32. Name and describe each of Erikson's stages. What is unique about his theory?

33. How has attachment been studied in humans and in nonhuman primates? What have these studies revealed about attachment?

34. Describe the three parenting styles. Which produces the best results?

1. The major accomplishment of Piaget's first stage is the
   a. development of symbolic function.
   b. ability to use language.
   c. recognition that objects not seen still exist.
   d. attainment of conservation.

2. Which of the following is *not* a criticism of Kohlberg's theory?
   a. His work is culturally biased.
   b. He did not see a relationship between moral development and cognitive development.
   c. Moral reasoning does not lead to moral behavior.
   d. His work exhibits a liberal bias.

3. A zygote has
   a. 23 chromosomes.
   b. 50,000 genes.
   c. 23 pairs of chromosomes.
   d. 46 pairs of chromosomes.

4. According to Piaget, we begin life with a limited number of _____ with which we organize the world.
   a. accommodations
   b. assimilations
   c. prototypes
   d. schemes

5. "Mama give cookie me" could be an example of
   a. babbling.
   b. overextension.
   c. telegraphic speech.
   d. underextension.

6. Which of Piaget's stages is characterized by the ability to use language and the absence of an understanding that breaking a cookie in half does not make more cookie?
   a. concrete operations
   b. formal operations
   c. preoperational
   d. sensorimotor

7. Early-maturing girls
   a. perform better academically.
   b. are less likely to develop eating disorders.
   c. are usually less self-conscious.
   d. have more unwanted pregnancies.

8. Of the following, who proposed a stage theory that included the whole life span?
   a. Erikson
   b. Freud
   c. Kohlberg
   d. Piaget

9. "I'll go to church every day if you let me live" would be characteristic of
   a. preoperational thought.
   b. the first stage in dealing with death.
   c. conventional morality.
   d. none of the above

10. Which of the following does *not* provide evidence for the role of the environment in cognitive development?
    a. Cultural differences have been observed in the achievement of certain abilities.
    b. Experience has an impact on the rate at which children pass through the various developmental stages.
    c. Formal schooling increases the likelihood of the development of hypothetico-deductive reasoning.
    d. Children throughout the world pass through the same cognitive stages in the same order.

11. Hospices are
    a. an inexpensive alternative to hospitals.
    b. agencies that aid in making death easier.
    c. centers where the dying meet to share their fears.
    d. modern birthing centers that employ technology to facilitate bonding.

12. Life satisfaction appears to be most strongly related to
    a. cognitive function.
    b. income.
    c. employment.
    d. health.

13. In order to establish an individual's level of moral reasoning, Kohlberg looked at
    a. what an individual would do in a given dilemma.
    b. why a particular decision would be made in dealing with a given dilemma.
    c. how an individual would respond emotionally to a moral dilemma.
    d. the cognitive abilities of the individual.

14. Which of the following is *not* a physical change typically associated with aging?
    a. becoming more nearsighted
    b. hearing loss
    c. a breakdown of myelin
    d. impaired night vision

15. Which of the following is *true*?
    a. Babies have near perfect vision at birth.
    b. Infants show a preference for their mother's face during the first few days of life.
    c. Despite a common belief, infant color vision is fully developed at birth.
    d. Like kittens, human infants are blind for several days or weeks.

16. Young adults who are determining whether to live their life alone or with a partner are in Erikson's _____ stage.

    a. identity versus role confusion
    b. initiative versus guilt
    c. intimacy versus isolation
    d. trust versus mistrust

17. When a teen complains that her mother just can't understand what she is feeling, she is exhibiting

    a. conventional morality.
    b. formal operational thought.
    c. fear of the imaginary audience.
    d. awareness of the personal fable.

18. During which prenatal period do the major organs of the body develop?

    a. period of the embryo
    b. fetal period
    c. teratogenic period
    d. period of the zygote

19. Which type of parenting appears to produce the best results in the United States?

    a. absent
    b. authoritative
    c. authoritarian
    d. permissive

20. Identical twins

    a. develop from two zygotes.
    b. are the same as fraternal twins.
    c. carry all the same genes.
    d. are frequently born when a woman uses fertility drugs.

21. All types of conservation develop simultaneously.

    a. true
    b. false

22. The effects of exposure to a particular teratogen are largely determined by the timing of the exposure.

    a. true
    b. false

23. Learning nursery rhymes may aid in the development of skills that facilitate reading.

    a. true
    b. false

24. Research finds that the majority of adolescents report that they are happy.

    a. true
    b. false

25. Gender stability has developed when a child internalizes a gender identity.

    a. true
    b. false

26. All babies, including those who are deaf, babble.

    a. true
    b. false

27. Newborns do not feel pain.

    a. true
    b. false

28. The environment affects the rate at which children pass through Piaget's stages.

    a. true
    b. false

29. Ainsworth demonstrated the importance of "contact comfort."

    a. true
    b. false

30. The visual cliff is used to study infant visual preferences.

    a. true
    b. false

31. There is no research to indicate that father–child relationships have a positive effect on development.

    a. true
    b. false

32. Distinguish between accommodation and assimilation.

33. Discuss the visual and auditory preferences of newborns. What are newborns able to do, and how can their preferences be studied?

34. What evidence is there to indicate a biological basis for language acquisition?

1. All of the following focus primarily on the satisfaction of physiological needs *except*
   a. arousal theory.
   b. drive-reduction theory.
   c. instinct theory.
   d. Maslow's hierarchy of needs.

2. Which of the following is *not* described as a subprocess of motivation?
   a. activation
   b. focus
   c. intensity
   d. persistence

3. Which of the following theories of emotion has the most difficulty in accounting for the role of the amygdala in fear responses?
   a. Cannon-Bard
   b. James-Lange
   c. Lazarus
   d. Maslow

4. Sondra studies in order to avoid earning a low grade. This behavior is an example of
   a. biological motivation.
   b. extrinsic motivation.
   c. implicit motivation.
   d. intrinsic motivation.

5. Which of the following is *not* a "basic emotion"?
   a. anger
   b. fear
   c. jealousy
   d. disgust

6. Which of the following is an example of a display rule?
   a. Americans express pleasure with a smile.
   b. The Japanese grimace when disgusted.
   c. Laughter first appears at about 4 months of age.
   d. Girls will smile when presented with a gift, even if they do not like it.

7. The notion that needs arise as some natural balance is disturbed is largely based on
   a. arousal theory.
   b. biological motives.
   c. homeostasis.
   d. instinct theory.

8. Studies of the role of facial expressions in emotion have found that
   a. the effects of facial expressions on physiological measures of emotion are unknown.
   b. making a happy face may produce a greater physiological measure of emotion than remembering a happy event.
   c. facial expressions affect mood only when a person is told directly to smile or frown.
   d. smiling is as likely to make you feel sad as it is to make you feel happy.

9. Social motives
   a. are found at the base of Maslow's hierarchy of needs.
   b. include the need for affiliation and the need for power.
   c. have a well-defined biological origin.
   d. reflect universal human needs for survival.

10. Primary drives
    a. are unlearned.
    b. develop through experience.
    c. do not generally determine behavior.
    d. arise when psychological needs have not been met.

11. On realizing that the shadow was a man with a gun, my heart began to race and at the same time I felt afraid. With which of the following theories of emotion is this scenario most consistent?
    a. Cannon-Bard
    b. James-Lange
    c. Lazarus
    d. Schachter-Singer

12. As I felt my heart race, I looked around for a reason why. As I stared into Jimmy's eyes, I realized that my heart was racing as a result of my love for him. With which of the following theories of emotion is this scenario most consistent?
    a. Cannon-Bard
    b. James-Lange
    c. Lazarus
    d. Schachter-Singer

13. All of the following may stimulate hunger *except*
    a. elevations in insulin.
    b. external cues, such as the sight of a tasty dessert.
    c. low levels of blood glucose.
    d. stimulation of the ventromedial hypothalamus.

14. A high need for achievement
    a. is commonly seen in middle children.
    b. is associated with the selection of achievable, yet challenging, goals.
    c. cannot be taught.
    d. may lead to a fear of taking chances.

15. Cultural differences are found in
    a. the strength of emotional expressions.
    b. what elicits emotional responses.
    c. how emotions are shared.
    d. all of the above

16. The need for achievement (*n* Ach)
    a. can be assessed with the Thematic Apperception Test (TAT).
    b. is a powerful primary drive.
    c. decreases as success increases.
    d. and birth order are unrelated.

17. Which of the following are *not* learned?
    a. display rules
    b. secondary reinforcers
    c. social motives
    d. stimulus motives

18. What role does leptin play in the regulation of body weight?
    a. It serves as a satiety signal and stimulates eating when blood sugar drops.
    b. It is produced by fat cells and may signal to the brain that energy expenditure needs to be increased when fat stores are high.
    c. Overproduction of it causes obesity by decreasing activity levels and energy usage.
    d. It affects immune function and causes weight loss when one is ill.

19. Which of the following best explains why some people enjoy reading while others are bored by it?
    a. arousal theory
    b. drive-reduction theory
    c. instinct theory
    d. Yerkes-Dodson law

20. On realizing that his insurance would not cover the damage to his car, John became angry and then his heart began to race. This sequence of events is consistent with the views of
    a. Cannon.
    b. Schachter.
    c. Lazarus.
    d. Maslow.

21. Motives that are a consequence of the norms of the society that one lives in are known as social motives.
    a. true
    b. false

22. The hormone cholecystokinin may serve as a "fullness" signal.
    a. true
    b. false

23. There appears to be a relationship between obsessive-compulsive disorder and eating disorders.
    a. true
    b. false

24. Research suggests that male homosexuality is about twice as common as female homosexuality.
    a. true
    b. false

25. Each of the basic emotions is associated with a distinctive physiological response pattern.
    a. true
    b. false

26. While anorexia nervosa is more common among women than among men in Western cultures, this is not the case in other societies.
    a. true
    b. false

27. There is some evidence to suggest that a gene on the Y chromosome may influence sexual orientation.
    a. true
    b. false

28. A loss of 10–15% of original body weight is necessary for a diagnosis of bulimia nervosa.
    a. true
    b. false

29. Individuals who are in control of their emotions are less likely to develop drug problems.
    a. true
    b. false

30. Stress always has a negative effect on task performance.
    a. true
    b. false

31. Fear of pregnancy is the most common reason cited for not having sex before marriage.
    a. true
    b. false

32. Discuss some of the factors that determine body weight. What can be said about the effectiveness of dieting?

33. Compare and contrast the James-Lange and Cannon-Bard theories of emotion.

34. Distinguish between intrinsic and extrinsic motivation, and provide examples of each.

1. Teachers usually say that they have chosen their profession because they enjoy it, not because of the money they will earn. In other words, they are _____ motivated.

   a. biologically
   b. socially
   c. extrinsically
   d. intrinsically

2. When I realized I was crying, I became quite sad. With which of the following theories of emotion is this scenario most consistent?

   a. Cannon-Bard
   b. James-Lange
   c. Lazarus
   d. Schachter-Singer

3. Curiosity is a(n)

   a. basic need.
   b. drive.
   c. incentive.
   d. stimulus motive.

4. Which of the following is the best example of intrinsic motivation?

   a. fishing to put food on the table
   b. cleaning your room to avoid punishment
   c. reading the text assigned for class
   d. singing in the shower

5. Which of the following statements about bulimia nervosa is *true*?

   a. Anorexics are unlikely to develop bulimia.
   b. Antidepressant drugs may help to reduce the frequency of binges.
   c. There is no evidence for a role of culture in this disorder.
   d. While anorexics are likely to exhibit signs of obsessive-compulsive disorder, such behaviors are rarely seen in bulimics.

6. According to Masters and Johnson, the final phase of the human sexual response cycle is

   a. the excitement phase.
   b. orgasm.
   c. the plateau phase.
   d. the resolution phase.

7. Sex differences are seen in all of the following *except*

   a. the incidence of homosexuality.
   b. the role of hormones in sexual interest.
   c. the likelihood of engaging in premarital sex.
   d. the incidence of bulimia nervosa.

8. Stimulation of the _____ has been shown to result in eating behavior.

   a. hunger center
   b. satiety center
   c. lateral hypothalamus
   d. ventromedial hypothalamus

9. Which of the following theories requires that the body's responses to fear, anger, and disgust differ?

   a. arousal theory
   b. James-Lange theory
   c. Lazarus theory
   d. Schachter-Singer theory

10. The work of Simon LeVay

   a. illustrated the role of the amygdala in fear responses.
   b. demonstrated that external factors influence eating behavior.
   c. suggested that there may be differences in the brain that relate to sexual orientation.
   d. led to further studies of the role of biological factors in motivation.

11. Anorexia nervosa

   a. only occurs in the United States.
   b. does not involve an altered perception of the self.
   c. is characterized by an excessive caloric restriction and a lack of interest in food.
   d. may lead to irreversible brain damage.

12. The fact that smiling may actually make you feel happier is most consistent with

   a. arousal theory.
   b. drive-reduction theory.
   c. the James-Lange theory.
   d. the Cannon-Bard theory.

13. Which of the following theories best explains why different people may be highly motivated by very different things?

   a. arousal theory
   b. drive-reduction theory
   c. Maslow's hierarchy of needs
   d. Yerkes-Dodson law

14. Which of the following was *not* a finding of the Kinsey report?

   a. The majority of men reported having had sexual intercourse before marriage.
   b. Men reported extramarital affairs more frequently than women did.
   c. African Americans were more likely to be unfaithful to their partners than White Americans were.
   d. Women were more likely to have had sex before marriage than they were to have had an extramarital affair.

15. I find that when tests are really simple, I do better on them if I feel somewhat concerned about my performance. Which of the following predicts that, under some circumstances, stress facilitates performance?

    a. arousal theory
    b. drive-reduction theory
    c. Schachter-Singer theory
    d. Yerkes-Dodson law

16. According to studies on animals, which of the following would be least likely to affect food intake?

    a. administration of cholecystokinin
    b. destruction of the amygdala
    c. removal of the pancreas
    d. stimulation of the lateral hypothalamus

17. Which of the following claims that performance varies with level of arousal?

    a. arousal theory
    b. drive-reduction theory
    c. instinct theory
    d. Yerkes-Dodson law

18. Basic emotions are

    a. affected in no way by environment.
    b. expressed the same way universally.
    c. found in all cultures.
    d. learned.

19. Which of the following is *not* consistent with Maslow's hierarchy of needs?

    a. Before looking for his friends, Jim first finds an umbrella to keep himself dry.
    b. Clara deprives herself of food in order to gain approval from her friends.
    c. After starting a career in which she can support herself, Jill starts to date.
    d. Self-actualization is not possible until basic biological needs have been met.

20. After falling, a child often looks toward the mother before reacting. Depending on how the mother responds, the child will respond to the situation by either crying or laughing. Which of the following would best explain this phenomenon?

    a. James-Lange theory
    b. arousal theory
    c. Schachter-Singer theory
    d. drive-reduction theory

21. Instinct theory is an accepted explanation for much of human behavior.

    a. true
    b. false

22. A motive is a need or desire that directs behavior toward a goal.

    a. true
    b. false

23. The administration of leptin might be one way to treat obesity.

    a. true
    b. false

24. Research on the role of the family environment in determining sexual orientation has demonstrated that homosexual men are likely to have overly involved mothers.

    a. true
    b. false

25. Perception of both happy and sad emotions is an important function of the amygdala.

    a. true
    b. false

26. The motivation of those who participate in "extreme" sports is adequately explained by arousal theory.

    a. true
    b. false

27. Testosterone is involved in both male and female sexual interest and responsiveness.

    a. true
    b. false

28. The main focus of treatment for anorexia is to get the patient to realize that she or he has a problem.

    a. true
    b. false

29. According to the facial feedback hypothesis, happiness can be experienced only when you are smiling.

    a. true
    b. false

30. Display rules dictate the extent to which you should express what you truly are feeling.

    a. true
    b. false

31. The development of facial expressions is influenced very little by the environment.

    a. true
    b. false

32. Name and describe the four theories of motivation.

33. What evidence exists, if any, to support a biological explanation for homosexuality?

34. Discuss the role of cognition in each of the four theories of emotion discussed in this chapter.

1. Posttraumatic stress disorder (PTSD)
   a. is seen in about 20% of the population.
   b. is usually seen only in men who have been involved in combat.
   c. may be experienced only by those who are directly affected by some trauma.
   d. is often associated with the development of other psychological problems.

2. Lazarus
   a. failed to consider the role of cognition in stress.
   b. found that welcome events may counteract the effects of negative experiences.
   c. believed that the death of a spouse was the most stressful life event for women.
   d. did not recognize that positive life events, such as getting married, may be stressful.

3. Which of the following groups reports the highest level of race-related stress?
   a. African Americans
   b. Asian Americans
   c. Native Americans
   d. Hispanic Americans

4. Having to choose between two types of ice cream that you like is an example of a(n)
   a. dietary challenge.
   b. approach–approach conflict.
   c. avoidance–avoidance conflict.
   d. approach–avoidance conflict.

5. Which of the following is an example of emotion-focused coping?
   a. Jane found a new owner for her destructive puppy.
   b. Jane worked hard at training the puppy to behave.
   c. Jane reasoned that the puppy would soon mature and stop eating her shoes.
   d. Jane no longer allowed the puppy in the house.

6. Health psychology
   a. is based on the biomedical model.
   b. focuses on how psychological factors influence health.
   c. does not recognize the role of modern medicine in maintaining health.
   d. employs only psychological means to achieve better health.

7. Determining whether or not you have the money to pay for repairs to your car is a part of
   a. the alarm response.
   b. an avoidance–avoidance conflict.
   c. a secondary appraisal.
   d. proactive coping.

8. The Type B behavior pattern
   a. has not been associated with any negative health consequences.
   b. may increase the risk of developing cancer.
   c. is commonly seen in alcoholics.
   d. can be more damaging than the Type A pattern, because the easygoing manner of the Type B personality often brings less success in life.

9. Alcohol
   a. does not damage the brain.
   b. may be involved in up to 75% of cases of domestic abuse.
   c. causes 65% of U.S. traffic accidents.
   d. consumption is a form of problem-focused coping.

10. According to Holmes and Rahe's view of stress,
    a. only unpleasant life events are stressful.
    b. men and women differ in how they respond to life's challenges.
    c. life events that produce the most change are the most stressful.
    d. divorce is only a moderate source of stress when children are not involved.

11. Which of the following is *not* a benefit of exercise?
    a. increased efficiency of the heart
    b. increased energy
    c. increased bone density
    d. increased LDL

12. Which element of the Type A personality has been found to be associated with coronary heart disease?
    a. competitiveness
    b. hostility
    c. impatience
    d. time urgency

13. Being forewarned of a major life change is most likely to
    a. increase the stress experienced.
    b. decrease the stress experienced.
    c. have a protective effect if the person has a means of coping.
    d. initiate a stress response before it is necessary.

14. According to Lazarus,
    a. stress has no effect on immune function.
    b. cognition plays no role in the stress response.
    c. only real instances of harm or loss cause stress.
    d. the level of stress experienced is largely determined by the perceived ability to cope.

15. Ignoring a stressor

    a. usually increases its impact.

    b. is a form of emotion-focused coping.

    c. results in an increase in glucocorticoid release.

    d. may increase the likelihood of experiencing anxiety-related symptoms.

16. According to Albrecht, all of the following are variables that must be in a person's comfort range in order to experience job satisfaction *except*

    a. workload.

    b. job status.

    c. mental challenge.

    d. pay.

17. Which of the following has been found to increase the risk of cancer?

    a. moderate alcohol consumption

    b. high activity levels

    c. homosexuality

    d. promiscuous sexual behavior

18. According to the text, the most frequent consequence of on-the-job stress is probably

    a. decreased effectiveness on the job.

    b. divorce and other problems at home.

    c. workplace violence.

    d. depression.

19. Which of the following is *not* a risk factor for becoming an alcoholic?

    a. being a woman

    b. beginning to drink at an early age

    c. experiencing depression

    d. having a family history of alcoholism

20. The process of primary appraisal involves

    a. determining whether or not a situation matters to you.

    b. evaluating your ability to cope with a challenge.

    c. considering your options for dealing with a crisis.

    d. activation of the sympathetic nervous system.

21. Deciding whether or not to sleep late and be late for work is an example of an avoidance–avoidance conflict.

    a. true

    b. false

22. According to the accepted definition of *stress*, it is incorrect to describe an exam as a stress.

    a. true

    b. false

23. It has been suggested that the high incidence of high blood pressure among African Americans is a consequence of historical racism.

    a. true

    b. false

24. Emotion-focused coping and primary appraisal are the same thing.

    a. true

    b. false

25. Brain-imaging techniques may one day be used to predict who is at risk for developing alcoholism.

    a. true

    b. false

26. Regular exposure to second-hand smoke has not been reliably linked to any health problems.

    a. true

    b. false

27. The cognitive impairment seen in many alcoholics is usually permanent.

    a. true

    b. false

28. Breaking up with a boyfriend who has been unfaithful is an example of emotion-focused coping.

    a. true

    b. false

29. According to Lazarus, a stressor does not cause stress unless it is perceived as threatening.

    a. true

    b. false

30. About 90% of ex-smokers quit without assistance.

    a. true

    b. false

31. PTSD is a common response to typical life stressors.

    a. true

    b. false

32. Discuss the roles of predictability and control in stress and health.

33. What is the general adaptation syndrome?

34. Discuss the lifestyle factors that put one at risk for coronary heart disease.

1. The most effective strategies for coping with cancer
   a. involve denial.
   b. employ only problem-focused coping.
   c. focus on the positive.
   d. increase the risk of secondary infections.

2. The most important lifestyle factor to change in order to decrease the likelihood of coronary heart disease is
   a. activity level.
   b. alcohol consumption.
   c. family history.
   d. high blood pressure.

3. A diagnosis of AIDS is made when
   a. HIV reaches a critical level in the body.
   b. HIV is detected in the blood.
   c. there is evidence of HIV-related damage to the immune system.
   d. the damage to the immune system due to HIV leads to opportunistic infections.

4. The Social Readjustment Rating Scale
   a. can be used to reliably predict the risk of illness.
   b. provides a way of measuring life stress.
   c. recognizes that there are individual differences in how people respond to life events.
   d. places too much emphasis on the role of the environment in dealing with challenges.

5. According to Albrecht, all of the following are variables that must be within a person's comfort zone to experience job satisfaction *except*
   a. level of human contact.
   b. environmental variables.
   c. frequency of breaks.
   d. accountability.

6. During secondary appraisal,
   a. resistance declines.
   b. proactive coping ceases to be effective.
   c. resources are evaluated.
   d. the significance of a potential stressor is determined.

7. AIDS progresses more quickly in all of the following *except*
   a. men.
   b. smokers.
   c. the very young.
   d. those over 50.

8. Which of the following is associated with an increased risk of heart disease?
   a. anger
   b. denial
   c. proactive temperament
   d. time urgency

9. Which of the following is a personal factor that reduces the impact of stress and illness?
   a. helpfulness
   b. hopelessness
   c. optimism
   d. pessimism

10. The Hassles Scale is clearly preferable to the Social Readjustment Rating Scale in that it
    a. acknowledges that both positive and negative events can be sources of stress.
    b. provides a way of measuring life stress.
    c. recognizes that there are individual differences in how people respond to life events.
    d. provides a more objective approach to the study of life stress.

11. Prolonged secretion of glucocorticoids
    a. is normal.
    b. enhances immune function.
    c. may damage the hippocampus.
    d. produces dangerous decreases in blood pressure.

12. The three qualities that are characteristics of psychological hardiness are
    a. commitment, optimism, and challenge.
    b. commitment, control, and challenge.
    c. commitment, control, and persistence.
    d. commitment, optimism, and persistence.

13. The general adaptation syndrome was proposed by
    a. Holmes and Rahe.
    b. Lazarus.
    c. Maslow.
    d. Selye.

14. Religious faith
    a. has been shown to have a direct effect on health.
    b. has been shown to be correlated with better health habits.
    c. is a form of problem-focused coping.
    d. is frequently accompanied by denial, and together they have a negative effect on health status.

15. Social support
    a. is rarely provided.
    b. may increase the likelihood of surviving a heart attack.
    c. tends to increase over time following a natural disaster.
    d. that is received is more important than perceived social support.

16. Which of the following statements about stress is *true*?

    a. Events that are stressful for women are usually perceived by men as simply hassles.

    b. All people find that the loss of a spouse is the most stressful life event.

    c. Only events that disrupt our lives are sources of stress.

    d. Uplifts may serve to cancel out the effects of hassles.

17. Of which of the following groups are members most likely to smoke?

    a. African American men

    b. Asian American men

    c. Hispanic American men

    d. Native American men

18. Having to choose between the lesser of two evils is an example of a(n)

    a. primary appraisal.

    b. secondary appraisal.

    c. avoidance–avoidance conflict.

    d. approach–avoidance conflict.

19. Psychological hardiness

    a. has been found to decrease the rate of progression of many forms of cancer.

    b. refers to factors that appear to protect one from developing AIDS.

    c. may protect high-level executives from stress.

    d. is a combination of problem-focused and emotion-focused coping.

20. In which stage of the general adaptation syndrome does illness become likely?

    a. activation

    b. alarm

    c. resistance

    d. exhaustion

21. While people vary in what they view as a hassle, those events that act as uplifts are universal.

    a. true

    b. false

22. There is no evidence to suggest that cognitive factors influence the level of stress people experience.

    a. true

    b. false

23. Proactive coping might consist of cleaning the house before a critical relative visits.

    a. true

    b. false

24. A stressor is something that causes stress.

    a. true

    b. false

25. Feeling that one has control of a situation is more important than actually controlling the situation.

    a. true

    b. false

26. The resistance stage of the general adaptation syndrome is characterized by a burst of energy that aids in dealing with the challenge at hand.

    a. true

    b. false

27. The strong sense of ethnic identity among African Americans protects them from experiencing racial stress.

    a. true

    b. false

28. Racial stress is experienced only in environments in which racism occurs.

    a. true

    b. false

29. Unemployment is usually more stressful than most high-stress jobs.

    a. true

    b. false

30. "Survivor guilt" is commonly seen in those with PTSD.

    a. true

    b. false

31. Research has demonstrated that having control over simple choices can lead to improvements in health.

    a. true

    b. false

32. Discuss the different types of coping. Provide examples of situations in which each type of coping is likely to be effective.

33. Discuss some of the evidence that supports the belief that psychological factors have an effect on health.

34. What role does cognition play in mediating the effects of stress?

1. After the teacher gave her a bad grade that she didn't feel she deserved, Jill went home and yelled at her brother. This is an example of
   a. denial.
   b. displacement.
   c. projection.
   d. repression.

2. Psychoanalysis refers to all of the following *except*
   a. a personality theory.
   b. a form of therapy that focuses on the unconscious.
   c. a theory proposed by Freud.
   d. a method for unlearning unhealthy behaviors.

3. Self-efficacy
   a. may make depression more likely.
   b. is an individual's perception of how likely he or she is to succeed.
   c. refers to how well one performs when given a challenge.
   d. is highly correlated with an external locus of control.

4. The collective unconscious
   a. contains archetypes.
   b. determines the ego ideal.
   c. reflects the views of the society in which one lives.
   d. was proposed by Adler.

5. Julie's therapist told her that she is anxious because she has been hiding her true self in order to earn her husband's approval. Her therapist's view is most consistent with the view of
   a. Horney.
   b. Freud.
   c. Maslow.
   d. Rogers.

6. If everything that you do reflects kindness, it could be said that for you kindness is a _____ trait.
   a. cardinal
   b. central
   c. source
   d. surface

7. The preconscious is most like
   a. implicit memory.
   b. long-term memory.
   c. sensory memory.
   d. short-term memory.

8. Twin studies of personality
   a. have consistently revealed the significance of the environment in determining personality.
   b. find that identical twins reared apart are more alike on many personality dimensions that those raised together.

   c. demonstrate that fraternal twins are no more alike than identical twins.
   d. reveal that as much as 50% of the variation in aggressiveness may be determined by genes.

9. Maslow
   a. was a neo-Freudian.
   b. introduced the term *inferiority complex*.
   c. believed that we are forever motivated to be the best that we can be.
   d. argued that people's goals in life are established by early interactions with their caregivers.

10. The Oedipal conflict
   a. has been scientifically demonstrated.
   b. is necessary for the development of a mature sexual identity.
   c. signals the end of the latency stage.
   d. occurs during the phallic stage.

11. Which personality system acts according to the reality principle?
   a. ego
   b. id
   c. superego
   d. ego ideal

12. Individualism
   a. is highly correlated with extroversion.
   b. is genetically determined.
   c. may be the most important factor in predicting worker productivity.
   d. is generally valued in the United States but is not characteristic of all cultural groups.

13. Which of the following is a neo-Freudian who focused on the conscious and the desire to achieve superiority?
   a. Adler
   b. Jung
   c. Horney
   d. Skinner

14. The major limitation of rating scales is that
   a. insignificant behaviors are overemphasized.
   b. the ratings may be subjective.
   c. they focus the rater's attention on specific behaviors.
   d. their standardized format allows for little variation in the ratings.

15. Be worried when your girlfriend accuses you of cheating, because she herself may be cheating and accusing you in an instance of
   a. denial.
   b. displacement.

c. projection.
d. sublimation.

16. The Rorschach Inkblot Method
    a. can be effectively used to screen job applicants for psychological disorders.
    b. is better than the MMPI at identifying neurotic disorders.
    c. might be used by a psychoanalyst.
    d. provides an objective means of evaluating personality traits.

17. A psychoanalyst might attribute Lorraine's drinking problem to
    a. fixation in the anal stage.
    b. fixation in the oral stage.
    c. incomplete development of the ego.
    d. incomplete development of the superego.

18. Freud believed that being sloppy and messy could result from an inadequate resolution of the challenges of the _____ stage.
    a. anal
    b. genital
    c. oral
    d. phallic

19. Which of the following countries has been described as having an individualistic culture?
    a. Australia
    b. Colombia
    c. Ecuador
    d. Venezuela

20. The most problematic element of behavioral approaches to personality assessment might be
    a. avoiding the influence of an observer on behavior.
    b. gathering enough information to make a meaningful assessment.
    c. the general lack of usefulness of such measures.
    d. the inability to evaluate internal forces.

21. There is no evidence to support the use of repression to avoid unwanted thoughts.
    a. true
    b. false

22. Freud's theories have been used to justify blaming parents for the crimes of their children.
    a. true
    b. false

23. Horney developed what came to be called *individual psychology.*
    a. true
    b. false

24. The ego is present at birth.
    a. true
    b. false

25. Freud's theory cannot be scientifically evaluated.
    a. true
    b. false

26. The tendency of people to believe in a god is an archetype.
    a. true
    b. false

27. Observable qualities of personality are referred to as *source traits.*
    a. true
    b. false

28. Freud believed the preconscious was the primary force guiding a person's behavior.
    a. true
    b. false

29. The United States was found to have the most extroverted culture in a study of 53 countries.
    a. true
    b. false

30. Reaction formation could be described as denial followed by an action consistent with that denial.
    a. true
    b. false

31. Peak experiences occur when psychosexual conflicts are successfully resolved.
    a. true
    b. false

32. Name and describe the three systems of personality proposed by Freud.

33. What is humanistic psychology, and how does it differ from psychoanalysis?

34. Explain the five-factor theory of personality.

1. Accepting someone no matter what he or she says or has done is a component of
    a. revealing the collective unconscious.
    b. person-centered therapy.
    c. poor parenting.
    d. psychoanalysis.

2. The id
    a. acts according to the reality principle.
    b. develops during the first year of life.
    c. is partially conscious.
    d. is the source of the libido.

3. In terms of the Big Five, an individual who is both outgoing and intellectually curious is described as
    a. extraverted and high on Neuroticism.
    b. extraverted and low on Neuroticism.
    c. extraverted and high on Openness to Experience.
    d. extraverted and low on Openness to Experience.

4. Trait theories
    a. are a type of learning theory.
    b. focus on the role of the unconscious.
    c. look at personal characteristics that are stable across situations.
    d. take a more optimistic view of human behavior than humanistic theories do.

5. Jane believes that how you think, the environment you live in, and your behavior all interact. Jane could be said to believe in
    a. free will.
    b. humanistic psychology.
    c. psychoanalysis.
    d. reciprocal determinism.

6. The Thematic Apperception Test
    a. asks the test taker to complete sentences.
    b. consists of ambiguous pictures.
    c. is a personality inventory.
    d. requires that test takers describe what they see in a series of inkblots.

7. Success in life is most likely if you
    a. are high in self-efficacy.
    b. have an external locus of control.
    c. believe in reciprocal determinism.
    d. use defense mechanisms effectively.

8. The MMPI-2
    a. cannot be used to detect abnormality.
    b. contains items designed to detect lies.
    c. reliably predicts behavior.
    d. is the most commonly used projective personality test.

9. The ego ideal
    a. is part of the ego.
    b. contains an understanding of what behaviors are rewarded.
    c. sets guidelines that limit the ego's flexibility.
    d. reflects society's view of what is right and wrong.

10. Which of the following is designed to reveal the unconscious?
    a. MBTI
    b. MMPI
    c. 16 PF
    d. TAT

11. Jan's hatred of dogs is so extreme she does not even admit it to herself. Interestingly, she chooses to volunteer at the local animal shelter. Which of Freud's defense mechanisms best explains Jan's choice?
    a. denial
    b. rationalization
    c. reaction formation
    d. repression

12. Who argued that psychological health requires overcoming irrational beliefs about perfection?
    a. Adler
    b. Freud
    c. Horney
    d. Jung

13. Strong identification with and attachment to the family is characteristic of
    a. collectivism.
    b. individualism.
    c. introversion.
    d. neuroticism.

14. Which of the following might the id say?
    a. You can't do that, you'll get punished.
    b. It's right to share.
    c. I want it now.
    d. Don't tell Mom.

15. Learning theories of personality
    a. cannot be tested.
    b. are able to account for most human behavior.
    c. are based solely on the principles of operant conditioning.
    d. have been criticized for not giving enough consideration to internal mental processes.

16. Adoption studies of personality
    a. provide evidence that the environment has little effect on personality.
    b. demonstrate that the environment has a significant effect on personality.

c. have been so problematic that conclusions are difficult to make.

d. find that the role of heredity in determining personality is consistently overemphasized.

17. An inadequate resolution of Freud's second psychosexual stage might result in

a. nail biting.

b. obesity.

c. flirtatiousness.

d. messiness.

18. Critics of trait theories

a. find that there is no consistency in personality traits.

b. argue that traits do not determine what a person will do, only what he or she is likely to do.

c. note that personality inventories have no predictive ability.

d. claim that personality is not something that can be measured in any meaningful way.

19. Jung's personal unconscious is

a. present at birth.

b. a product of the environment.

c. conceptually identical to Freud's ego.

d. the equivalent of Freud's ego ideal.

20. The 16 PF is designed to reveal

a. cardinal traits.

b. central traits.

c. source traits.

d. surface traits.

21. Repressed memories are stored in the preconscious.

a. true

b. false

22. The NEO Personality Inventory is used to measure the Big Five.

a. true

b. false

23. *Psychoanalysis* refers to the personality theory proposed by Freud.

a. true

b. false

24. According to Freud, the sex instinct is present at birth.

a. true

b. false

25. One element of personality is how someone thinks.

a. true

b. false

26. A trait theory views personality as inherited and unchangeable.

a. true

b. false

27. The id's pursuit of pleasure may be in conflict with the ego's pursuit of moral perfection.

a. true

b. false

28. Individuals with an internal locus of control believe that much is determined by fate.

a. true

b. false

29. According to Freud, denial is the most frequently used defense mechanism.

a. true

b. false

30. Adler is credited with introducing the term *inferiority complex*.

a. true

b. false

31. The superego imposes reality on the ego.

a. true

b. false

32. According to psychoanalytic theory, what are the different levels of consciousness, and how do they influence behavior?

33. What are defense mechanisms, and what purpose do they serve?

34. Distinguish between projective and objective methods for personality assessment, providing examples of each.

CHAPTER 12: PRACTICE TEST 1

1. Mental disorders

a. affect 50% of the population at any point in time.

b. occur only in adulthood.

c. affect almost a quarter of the adult population.

d. are less common than cancer.

2. Which of the following is *not* a major risk factor for suicide?

a. major depressive disorder

b. schizophrenia

c. specific phobia

d. substance abuse

3. Those with undifferentiated schizophrenia
   a. do not conform to the criteria for any of the schizophrenia types.
   b. cannot be treated.
   c. commonly alternate between stillness and agitation.
   d. usually exhibit many types of delusions.

4. Which situational phobia is treated most frequently by therapists?
   a. fear of heights
   b. fear of dogs
   c. fear of the natural elements
   d. fear of injury

5. Dr. Jones believes that abnormal behavior results from chemical imbalances in the brain that result from eating too much junk food. Dr. Jones takes a _____ view of mental illness.
   a. biological
   b. biopsychosocial
   c. cognitive
   d. psychodynamic

6. Individuals with obsessive-compulsive disorder
   a. do not find their behavior disturbing, even though others are likely to.
   b. engage in the compulsive behavior because they are compelled to.
   c. enjoy the compulsive behavior.
   d. use their compulsive behavior to ward off danger.

7. With which disorders are delusions of grandeur sometimes seen?
   a. depression and bipolar disorder
   b. depression and schizophrenia
   c. schizophrenia and bipolar disorder
   d. schizophrenia and agoraphobia

8. A behavior therapist would be most likely to
   a. recommend psychoanalysis.
   b. assist in replacing unhealthy behaviors with healthy ones.
   c. prescribe medications.
   d. focus on childhood as the source of adulthood problems.

9. After witnessing an automobile accident, June was blind for several weeks. June would most likely be diagnosed as having
   a. PTSD.
   b. schizophrenia.
   c. conversion disorder.
   d. specific phobia.

10. Individuals with paranoid schizophrenia
    a. experience only negative symptoms.
    b. have increased neural activity in the frontal lobes.

    c. hear voices.
    d. may be convinced that they are someone else.

11. An individual with dissociative amnesia
    a. is likely to remember those close to him or her.
    b. remembers how to carry out routine tasks.
    c. forgets who he or she is and is likely to adopt a new identity.
    d. exhibits multiple personalities.

12. A therapist who has adopted the _____ _____ might attribute a person's current psychological difficulties to problems in toilet training.
    a. biopsychosocial view
    b. cognitive perspective
    c. learning perspective
    d. psychodynamic perspective

13. Phobics
    a. believe that their fears are rational.
    b. rarely avoid the feared object.
    c. have usually experienced panic attacks.
    d. have an intense fear of situations from which they cannot escape.

14. Dissociative fugue is characterized by all of the following except
    a. adoption of a new and different identity during the fugue state.
    b. complete recall of the event that caused the fugue state.
    c. traveling away from home.
    d. rapid recovery.

15. Which of the following is a negative symptom of schizophrenia?
    a. dancing in an odd manner
    b. hearing voices
    c. inappropriate affect
    d. slowed movements

16. A compulsion becomes a psychological problem when
    a. the person experiences it more than once a day.
    b. it occurs in the absence of an obsession.
    c. the person believes that it is rational.
    d. it becomes very time-consuming.

17. "You are always unhappy because you expect too much from people." With which of the following perspectives is this statement most consistent?
    a. biopsychosocial view
    b. cognitive perspective
    c. learning perspective
    d. psychodynamic perspective

18. Which of the following statements is *true*?
    a. There is no evidence for a role of genes in the development of agoraphobia.
    b. Agoraphobia and panic disorder are clearly not related.
    c. Learning approaches to the treatment of agoraphobia are clearly ineffective.
    d. Antidepressant drugs may be used in the treatment of agoraphobia.

19. Which of the following is a psychomotor disturbance that might be seen in a depressed person?
    a. altered appetite
    b. fidgeting
    c. hallucinations
    d. loss of ability to experience pleasure

20. Social phobia
    a. is a specific phobia.
    b. is the most common mood disorder.
    c. may be more debilitating than agoraphobia.
    d. often consists of the fear of public speaking.

21. According to the learning perspective, psychological disorders result from learning inappropriate behaviors or not learning appropriate ones.
    a. true
    b. false

22. Women are more likely than men to commit suicide.
    a. true
    b. false

23. There is evidence to suggest that drug use can increase the risk of developing schizophrenia.
    a. true
    b. false

24. Agoraphobia is a situational phobia.
    a. true
    b. false

25. Over 75% of those who do not have social phobia report an extreme fear of speaking in public.
    a. true
    b. false

26. Disorganized schizophrenia tends to begin earlier in life than the other types.
    a. true
    b. false

27. Mental illness is more common than cancer.
    a. true
    b. false

28. The rate of recurrence is higher for bipolar disorder than it is for major depressive disorder.
    a. true
    b. false

29. Smelling something that is not there is an example of a hallucination.
    a. true
    b. false

30. *Insanity* is a legal term.
    a. true
    b. false

31. Most individuals diagnosed with major depressive disorder will be free of symptoms a year later.
    a. true
    b. false

32. Discuss the dimensions that must be looked at when considering whether or not a behavior is abnormal.

33. What are some factors that increase the likelihood of being diagnosed with a major depressive disorder?

34. Compare and contrast the somatoform disorders.

CHAPTER 12: PRACTICE TEST 2

1. Major depressive disorder
    a. has the same prevalence rate as bipolar disorder in all cultures.
    b. does not develop before age 15.
    c. is the number one cause of disability throughout the world.
    d. rarely reoccurs.

2. An individual diagnosed with dissociative identity disorder
    a. may complain of "lost time."
    b. is typically aware of all of his or her personalities.
    c. usually has two hosts and three alters.
    d. is usually a man.

3. All of the following are questions that should be asked when determining whether or not behavior is abnormal *except*:

   a. Is the behavior accepted within the person's own culture?
   b. Does the behavior upset others?
   c. Is the behavior maladaptive?
   d. Is the person a danger to anyone?

4. The most frequently occurring category of specific phobia is

   a. animal phobia.
   b. fear of the natural environment.
   c. injury phobia.
   d. situational phobia.

5. The individual with antisocial personality disorder

   a. appears to have no conscience.
   b. does not like parties.
   c. may feel great love and compassion for a chosen few.
   d. rarely engages in illegal behavior.

6. Which of the following types of schizophrenia is most likely to improve?

   a. catatonic
   b. differentiated
   c. disorganized
   d. paranoid

7. Drug treatments for sexual dysfunction

   a. can involve administering hormones.
   b. have been effective only for treating men.
   c. must accompany couples therapy.
   d. are usually designed to treat depression and other disorders that are the source of the dysfunction.

8. A similar emotional response to the words *chair* and *rape* is most likely to be seen in individuals with

   a. OCD.
   b. antisocial personality.
   c. hypochondriasis.
   d. sexual dysfunction.

9. Which of the following is *not* a characteristic of major depressive disorder?

   a. increased appetite
   b. decreased appetite
   c. increased energy
   d. decreased energy

10. An individual who always expects that the worst will happen and is always concerned about the future is most likely to be diagnosed with

    a. agoraphobia.
    b. generalized anxiety disorder.
    c. paranoid schizophrenia.
    d. specific phobia.

11. In contrast to those with hypochondriasis, individuals with conversion disorder

    a. believe that minor bodily symptoms are signs of more serious diseases.
    b. do not have a psychological disorder.
    c. have bodily symptoms that are of a psychological origin.
    d. are more likely to be faking.

12. Which of the following views of abnormal behavior is most likely to favor treatment that includes both drug therapy and talk therapy?

    a. biological perspective
    b. biopsychosocial perspective
    c. learning perspective
    d. psychodynamic perspective

13. There are some who believe that _____ is extremely rare or nonexistent.

    a. DID
    b. OCD
    c. antisocial personality disorder
    d. hypochondriasis

14. Those suffering from agoraphobia

    a. are usually men.
    b. believe that their fears are rational.
    c. fear panicking in public.
    d. rarely seek help.

15. Antidepressant drugs have been shown to be useful in the treatment of all of the following *except*

    a. agoraphobia.
    b. depression.
    c. OCD.
    d. schizophrenia.

16. Treatment that is consistent with the cognitive perspective

    a. employs learning principles to change behavior.
    b. focuses on changing thinking.
    c. involves the use of medication to restore the chemical balance of the mind.
    d. tries to uncover unconscious conflicts.

17. Which of the following is an example of compulsive behavior?

    a. avoiding places where panic attacks have occurred
    b. fearing closed places
    c. worrying about contamination
    d. counting to 3 after every bite

18. In the United States, which of the following groups has the lowest suicide rate?

    a. African Americans
    b. Asian Americans
    c. Hispanic Americans
    d. Native Americans

19. Which of the following is *not* a negative symptom of schizophrenia?
    a. a distorted sense of time
    b. low levels of neural activity
    c. social withdrawal
    d. flat affect

20. Which of the following is characteristic of individuals with panic disorder?
    a. delusions and hallucinations
    b. overwhelming anxiety about numerous things in their lives
    c. increased risk for substance abuse
    d. insomnia

21. There is no evidence of a biological basis for generalized anxiety disorder.
    a. true
    b. false

22. There is at least a 50% chance that you will experience a mental disorder at some point in your life.
    a. true
    b. false

23. Hearing voices is the most common delusion among schizophrenics.
    a. true
    b. false

24. Women are more likely than men to attempt suicide.
    a. true
    b. false

25. Most clinicians develop their own criteria for diagnosing psychological disorders.
    a. true
    b. false

26. According to the cognitive perspective, unresolved conflicts are a common source of psychological problems.
    a. true
    b. false

27. *Insanity* is a term used by mental health professionals.
    a. true
    b. false

28. About half of those who experience one depressive episode will have another.
    a. true
    b. false

29. Schizophrenics who experience only hallucinations and delusions have the worst outcomes.
    a. true
    b. false

30. The patient with disorganized schizophrenia may exhibit both positive and negative symptoms.
    a. true
    b. false

31. Individuals with bipolar disorder typically cycle between depressed and manic states with no periods of normalcy as long as they go untreated.
    a. true
    b. false

32. Distinguish between the positive and negative symptoms of schizophrenia.

33. Discuss the evidence to support the role of biological factors in mood disorders.

34. What characterizes each of the dissociative disorders, and what is believed to cause them?

CHAPTER 13: PRACTICE TEST 1

1. Gestalt therapy is a _____ therapy.
    a. behavior
    b. cognitive
    c. directive
    d. relationship

2. Interpersonal therapy (IPT)
    a. may be the most effective behavioral approach to the treatment of depression.
    b. has a high dropout rate.
    c. is not an effective therapy for treating depression.
    d. is a relatively brief form of therapy.

3. In what kind of therapy does the therapist take a very active role in determining the course of the therapy session?
    a. directive
    b. humanistic
    c. insight
    d. person-centered

4. Which of the following is *not* a form of insight therapy?
    a. brief psychodynamic therapy
    b. humanistic therapy
    c. interpersonal therapy
    d. person-centered therapy

5. Dina has been diagnosed with major depression. She has sought the assistance of a behavior therapist. The goal of her therapy is likely to be to

   a. determine what thought processes are causing the problem.

   b. explore how her early childhood experiences influence her current behavior.

   c. explore her current relationships.

   d. change the problematic behaviors that accompany her depression.

6. Family therapy

   a. focuses on getting the other family members to accept the mentally ill person.

   b. may be the best treatment for dealing with teen substance abuse.

   c. has no effect on the relapse rates of patients with schizophrenia.

   d. is only effective when used along with medication.

7. Which of the following is *not* a behavior modification technique?

   a. systematic desensitization

   b. time-out

   c. token economies

   d. transference

8. Which of the following is *not* an advantage of group therapy?

   a. It is less expensive.

   b. There is a sense of belonging.

   c. It is usually briefer than other forms of therapy.

   d. Learning from others may leave the participants feeling less alone.

9. Therapies based on classical conditioning

   a. are generally ineffective.

   b. can be used to treat phobias.

   c. are most commonly used to treat depression.

   d. include token economies and time-out.

10. What type of therapy is person-centered therapy?

   a. behavior

   b. biological

   c. cognitive

   d. insight

11. Which of the following is a treatment for obsessive-compulsive disorder?

   a. aversion therapy

   b. exposure and response prevention

   c. flooding

   d. systematic desensitization

12. One form of treatment for alcoholism involves the use of a drug that makes the alcoholic ill when she or he is

exposed to alcohol. What type of therapy is this an example of?

   a. behavior

   b. biological

   c. cognitive

   d. insight

13. In Ellis's ABC theory, the B stands for

   a. behavior.

   b. bidirectional.

   c. belief.

   d. better.

14. What does cognitive therapy focus on?

   a. achieving self-actualization

   b. changing thinking

   c. changing behavior

   d. remembering the past

15. A fatal blood defect may develop with the use of

   a. clozapine.

   b. Thorazine.

   c. Paxil.

   d. Prozac.

16. Which of the following is an advantage of atypical neuroleptics instead of typical neuroleptics?

   a. Atypical neuroleptics are more effective at treating the positive symptoms of schizophrenia.

   b. There are no side effects associated with atypical neuroleptics.

   c. Abuse of atypical neuroleptics is less likely.

   d. Atypical neuroleptics treat both the positive and negative symptoms of schizophrenia.

17. Which of the following work by blocking the reuptake of norepinephrine and serotonin?

   a. benzodiazepines

   b. monoamine oxidase inhibitors

   c. neuroleptics

   d. tricyclics

18. What disorder might divalproex, an anticonvulsant, be used to treat?

   a. anxiety

   b. bipolar disorder

   c. dissociative identity disorder

   d. schizophrenia

19. Which of the following would be used to treat both the depressed and manic phases of bipolar disorder?

   a. chlorpromazine

   b. fluoxetine

   c. lithium

   d. none of the above

20. For what disorder can ECT be an effective treatment?

    a. anxiety

    b. bipolar disorder

    c. generalized anxiety disorder

    d. major depression

21. Today's psychotherapies differ little from the therapies developed in Freud's time.

    a. true

    b. false

22. There are four different types of therapies used to treat emotional disorders.

    a. true

    b. false

23. Group therapy is an ineffective approach to treating depression.

    a. true

    b. false

24. The "empty chair" technique may be used in Gestalt therapy.

    a. true

    b. false

25. One part of interpersonal therapy may be the creation of new relationships to aid in dealing with psychological problems.

    a. true

    b. false

26. Neuroleptics work by increasing the activity of the neurotransmitter serotonin.

    a. true

    b. false

27. Behavior therapists view problematic behaviors as symptoms of some underlying disorder.

    a. true

    b. false

28. Exposure and response prevention is an effective cognitive approach to treating phobias.

    a. true

    b. false

29. Behavior modification techniques can be used to break bad habits.

    a. true

    b. false

30. Atypical neuroleptics are effective in treating both the depressed and manic phases of bipolar disorder.

    a. true

    b. false

31. SSRIs can cause permanent sexual dysfunction.

    a. true

    b. false

32. What is behavior modification?

33. What approach would a cognitive therapist take to treating a psychological disorder?

34. Discuss the biological approaches to the treatment of schizophrenia.

CHAPTER 13: PRACTICE TEST 2

1. Which of the following has been shown to be very effective in treating depression?

    a. group therapy

    b. interpersonal therapy

    c. biological treatment with neuroleptics

    d. systematic desensitization

2. Which type of therapy assumes that psychological well-being is dependent on achieving self-understanding?

    a. behavior therapy

    b. biological therapy

    c. cognitive therapies

    d. insight therapies

3. Which of the following is a typical goal of family therapy?

    a. determining the proper treatment for the mentally ill family member

    b. eliminating automatic thoughts

    c. improving communication patterns

    d. increasing the level of expressed emotion

4. Jillian's therapist asks her to imagine a snake while she practices the muscle relaxation techniques she has just learned. Which of the following forms of therapy is Jillian receiving?

    a. cognitive therapy

    b. flooding

c. interpersonal therapy

d. systematic desensitization

5. Which of the following is *not* characteristic of person-centered therapy?

    a. therapist playing the role of expert

    b. nondirective

    c. therapist providing unconditional positive regard

    d. direction of the therapy controlled by the client

6. Pairing something unpleasant with an undesirable behavior is the process involved in

    a. aversion therapy.

    b. flooding.

    c. systematic sensitization.

    d. tardive dyskinesia.

7. According to Ellis,

    a. emotional reactions are direct consequences of events.

    b. one's beliefs determine how one reacts to an event.

    c. the consequences of an action are more important than the action itself.

    d. adaptive behaviors must be learned.

8. Rational-emotive therapy is

    a. always brief.

    b. based on the principles of classical conditioning.

    c. directive.

    d. person-centered.

9. Which of the following produce tardive dyskinesia if used for a long period?

    a. drugs that increase the activity of the neurotransmitter dopamine

    b. drugs that inhibit the activity of the neurotransmitter dopamine

    c. drugs that increase the activity of the neurotransmitter GABA

    d. drugs that inhibit the activity of the neurotransmitter GABA

10. Behavior therapies view mental illness as

    a. the product of learning.

    b. an inability to reach self-actualization.

    c. the result of flawed thinking.

    d. a lack of insight.

11. Which of the following is an atypical neuroleptic?

    a. clozapine

    b. Thorazine

    c. Paxil

    d. Prozac

12. Which of the following is commonly treated with a naturally occurring salt?

    a. anxiety

    b. bipolar disorder

c. dissociative identity disorder

d. schizophrenia

13. Which of the following are *not* antidepressants?

    a. benzodiazepines

    b. monoamine oxidase inhibitors

    c. selective serotonin reuptake inhibitors

    d. tricyclics

14. Monoamine oxidase inhibitors have been found to be effective in treating all of the following *except*

    a. depression.

    b. panic disorder.

    c. schizophrenia.

    d. social phobia.

15. Which type of drugs produce intense withdrawal symptoms when a patient stops taking them?

    a. anticonvulsants

    b. antidepressants

    c. minor tranquilizers

    d. neuroleptics

16. Which of the following is *not* a benzodiazepine?

    a. divalproex

    b. Librium

    c. Valium

    d. Xanax

17. Under which circumstance is ECT used to treat major depression?

    a. when the patient is very old

    b. when the patient is very young

    c. when the patient is not able to tolerate the side effects of the SSRIs

    d. when the patient is suicidal

18. What do antipsychotics, antidepressants, and lithium have in common?

    a. Termination of their use produces an intense withdrawal syndrome.

    b. All produce dependence and are likely to be abused.

    c. They treat symptoms.

    d. They cure the disorders for which they are used.

19. Which of the following is a form of psychosurgery still used today?

    a. cingulotomy

    b. ECT

    c. EEG

    d. lobotomy

20. Culturally sensitive psychotherapy is important because

    a. it ensures that the proper medication will be prescribed.

    b. cultural factors need to be considered when choosing a therapeutic intervention.

c. the development of a therapeutic alliance is not possible if the client and therapist have different backgrounds.

d. cultural insensitivity is the underlying cause of most mood disorders.

21. Rogers developed interpersonal therapy.

  a. true

  b. false

22. Time-out is a behavioral modification technique that involves isolation from reinforcers when an undesirable behavior occurs.

  a. true

  b. false

23. A hostile and critical home environment increases the likelihood of relapse for a patient with schizophrenia.

  a. true

  b. false

24. Flooding has been found to be ineffective in the treatment of most phobias.

  a. true

  b. false

25. Alcoholics Anonymous is a self-help group.

  a. true

  b. false

26. One goal of Gestalt therapy is to become more self-accepting.

  a. true

  b. false

27. Interpersonal therapy is a form of relationship therapy.

  a. true

  b. false

28. Systematic desensitization is quicker and more effective than flooding for the treatment of most phobias.

  a. true

  b. false

29. Family therapy can be helpful in the treatment of schizophrenia.

  a. true

  b. false

30. Participant modeling may be used to treat phobias.

  a. true

  b. false

31. Self-help groups usually do not involve a therapist.

  a. true

  b. false

32. What is interpersonal therapy?

33. Describe the treatment approaches commonly used in behavior therapy.

34. What are the three types of drugs used to treat depression, and how do they work?

CHAPTER 14: PRACTICE TEST 1

1. Why would it be impossible to conduct Milgram's study today?

  a. It would not be possible to find willing volunteers.

  b. Deception is not legal.

  c. The likelihood of conformity is slim in today's society.

  d. It would be viewed as unethical.

2. Which of the following explains why first impressions are so important?

  a. cognitive dissonance

  b. foot-in-the-door effect

  c. primacy effect

  d. self-serving bias

3. The tendency to blame the victim of a crime for the occurrence of the crime is an example of a(n)

  a. actor-observer effect.

  b. dispositional attribution.

  c. primacy effect.

  d. situational attribution.

4. Which of the following is consistent with the actor-observer effect?

  a. Jill said that she ate the cake because she can't resist sweets.

  b. Claire said that Jill ate the cake because it was her birthday.

  c. Margie said that John ate the cake because he's a pig.

  d. Ginger said that she ate the cake because she has no self-control.

5. Whenever John loses, he claims that he has bad luck, but he attributes his successes to his great skill. John's behavior demonstrates

    a. cognitive dissonance.
    b. the actor-observer effect.
    c. prosocial behavior.
    d. a self-serving bias.

6. We tend to like those who are geographically near us. This physical nearness that influences attraction is known as

    a. the bystander effect.
    b. the mere-exposure effect.
    c. proximity.
    d. reciprocity.

7. The tendency to assume that physically attractive people have other positive qualities is known as the

    a. domino effect.
    b. halo effect.
    c. foot-in-the-door technique.
    d. mere-exposure effect.

8. According to Sternberg, infatuated love, "love at first sight," consists of

    a. passion and commitment.
    b. passion and intimacy.
    c. intimacy and commitment.
    d. none of the above

9. Sternberg's romantic love does not include

    a. commitment.
    b. intimacy.
    c. passion.
    d. persuasion.

10. The work of Solomon Asch demonstrated

    a. how willing most people are to violate social norms.
    b. the power of roles.
    c. that cognitive dissonance motivates most people to alter their attitudes.
    d. that most people will provide an incorrect answer when a majority of those present support that answer.

11. Which of the following is an example of the door-in-the-face technique?

    a. After Lisa refused to marry him, Bob asked her out on a date.
    b. Before asking her to go out on a date with him, Bob asked Lisa to lend him a quarter.
    c. After Lisa agreed to go for coffee with him, Bob gave her a rose.
    d. After Lisa agreed to go out with him, Bob told her that they would be going to his cousin's wedding.

12. The term *social facilitation* refers to

    a. the improvement in performance due to the presence of others.
    b. audience effects.
    c. any effect of the presence of others on performance.
    d. the ease with which tasks are accomplished when there is a coordinated group effort.

13. Under which of the following circumstances is social loafing most likely to occur?

    a. when performance is randomly evaluated
    b. when a task is difficult
    c. when a task is easy
    d. when there is no recognition of individual effort

14. In which of the following countries is social loafing most common?

    a. China
    b. India
    c. United States
    d. None of the above—there is no cross-cultural variation in social loafing.

15. After three friends discussed Karla's rudeness, they decided that her behavior could no longer be tolerated. Jill found that her anger at Karla was much greater after she and the others shared their experiences. Which of the following best explains the change in Jill's feelings about Karla?

    a. group polarization
    b. groupthink
    c. social facilitation
    d. social norms

16. Which of the following provides an explanation for the bystander effect?

    a. social loafing
    b. social norms
    c. social roles
    d. diffusion of responsibility

17. Which of the following statements about biology and aggression is *true*?

    a. There is no evidence of a genetic basis for aggression.
    b. Men are more physically aggressive than women.
    c. Most women are just as aggressive as most men.
    d. A high arousal level of the autonomic nervous system is correlated with aggressive tendencies.

18. According to the frustration-aggression hypothesis,

    a. frustration produces aggression.
    b. aggression leads to frustration.
    c. scapegoating is an effective way of handling aggression.
    d. scapegoating is an effective way of handling frustration.

19. The realistic conflict theory

   a. proposes that stereotypes are learned.

   b. views discrimination as a product of evolution.

   c. argues that hatred is necessary for society to function in a balanced manner.

   d. suggests that there is a positive correlation between prejudice and competition.

20. What is the difference between prejudice and discrimination?

   a. There is no difference.

   b. Prejudice is always negative.

   c. Prejudice refers to attitudes and discrimination to actions.

   d. Discrimination refers to attitudes and prejudice to actions.

21. A confederate is a naïve subject.

   a. true

   b. false

22. Research has demonstrated that a firm handshake makes a good first impression.

   a. true

   b. false

23. The mere-exposure effect explains why things we initially find unappealing may grow on us with repeated exposure over time.

   a. true

   b. false

24. Research suggests that the key to physical attractiveness is symmetry.

   a. true

   b. false

25. There is no support for the matching hypothesis.

   a. true

   b. false

26. Male and female preferences in mate selection are consistent with what evolutionary psychologists predict.

   a. true

   b. false

27. Obedience is adopting a behavior or attitude in order to be consistent with social norms.

   a. true

   b. false

28. In studies of both obedience and conformity, the presence of an ally alters behavior.

   a. true

   b. false

29. One way to increase the likelihood of being given a raise is to ask first for a bigger raise than you expect to get.

   a. true

   b. false

30. Social loafing is the tendency to expend less effort on a task when no one is looking.

   a. true

   b. false

31. Zimbardo's study demonstrated the power of social roles.

   a. true

   b. false

32. What is the actor-observer effect?

33. What is persuasion, and what factors should be considered when designing a persuasive message?

34. What are stereotypes?

CHAPTER 14: PRACTICE TEST 2

1. _____ is the process used to obtain social information about others.

   a. Cognitive dissonance

   b. Social cognition

   c. Social facilitation

   d. Social perception

2. When I drive recklessly, I say that I do so because I'm in a hurry. When someone else cuts me off, I conclude that they are rude. These different attributions provide an example of

   a. cognitive dissonance.

   b. the actor-observer effect.

   c. prosocial behavior.

   d. a self-serving bias.

3. According to the actor-observer effect, we are more likely to make _____ attributions for own behavior and _____ attributions for the behavior of others.

   a. internal; internal

   b. external; external

c. internal; external
d. external; internal

4. The self-serving bias is the tendency to make _____ attributions when explaining our successes and _____ attributions for our failures.

a. internal; internal
b. external; external
c. internal; external
d. external; internal

5. When her house was first painted, Kala hated the color. Eventually she came to like the color. Kala's change in feelings can be attributed to

a. a self-serving bias.
b. a situational attribution.
c. proximity.
d. the mere-exposure effect.

6. Which of the following explains why a used car salesman has an advantage if he is good-looking?

a. domino effect
b. halo effect
c. foot-in-the-door technique
d. mere-exposure effect

7. According to the matching hypothesis,

a. people want to be with someone who makes up for the qualities they lack.
b. attractive and intelligent people seek others who are not attractive, but of equal intelligence.
c. beautiful women seek out men of wealth and status.
d. couples mismatched in attractiveness are less likely to stay together.

8. According to Sternberg, which type of love consists of intimacy, commitment, and passion?

a. companionate
b. consummate
c. fatuous
d. romantic

9. Which of the following is true?

a. Maximum conformity occurs with a majority consisting of two people.
b. Maximum conformity occurs with a majority consisting of three people.
c. The more people in the majority, the greater the likelihood of compliance.
d. Having an ally does not affect the likelihood of conformity.

10. People who are _____ on emotional stability, Agreeableness, and Conscientiousness are _____ likely to conform.

a. low; more
b. high; less

c. high; more
d. None of the above; there is no relationship between personality variables and conformity.

11. Which of the following is an example of the foot-in-the-door technique?

a. After Lisa refused to marry him, Bob asked her out on a date.
b. Before asking her to go out on a date with him, Bob asked Lisa to lend him a quarter.
c. After Lisa agreed to go for coffee with him, Bob gave her a rose.
d. After Lisa agreed to go out with him, Bob told her they would be going to his cousin's wedding.

12. Which of the following best accounts for the influence of peer pressure?

a. conformity
b. group polarization
c. groupthink
d. obedience

13. _____ are socially defined behaviors that determine how one should behave when in a particular position.

a. Social expectations
b. Social mores
c. Social norms
d. Social roles

14. Which of the following is *not* a component of an attitude?

a. behavior
b. thoughts
c. emotions
d. structure

15. Which attitudes are most resistant to change?

a. those formed during times of stress
b. those based on one's own experiences
c. those passed down from generation to generation
d. those that violate social norms

16. Research suggests that attitudes predict behavior

a. most of the time.
b. 90% of the time.
c. only 10% of the time.
d. only when there is nothing else to guide behavior.

17. Dissonance is created by

a. conformity.
b. conflict.
c. bias.
d. stereotypes.

18. Which of the following is *not* a factor that makes the source of a message more persuasive?

a. attractiveness
b. credibility
c. likability
d. similarity

19. A one-sided message is most effective if
   a. the audience is intelligent.
   b. the audience is not intelligent.
   c. the message is complex.
   d. the message is simple.

20. Which of the following refers to self-sacrificing behavior that is done to benefit another and is not done for any personal gain?
   a. altruism
   b. empathy
   c. bystander facilitation
   d. prosocial behavior

21. In Milgram's study, the learner was a confederate.
   a. true
   b. false

22. First impressions are not affected by mood.
   a. true
   b. false

23. The preference for physically attractive people is first seen at about 16 months of age.
   a. true
   b. false

24. There is great similarity across cultures in the features that are perceived as attractive.
   a. true
   b. false

25. Some conformity is necessary for a society to be functional.
   a. true
   b. false

26. Asch demonstrated that there is no such thing as peer pressure.
   a. true
   b. false

27. Women are more likely to conform than men.
   a. true
   b. false

28. The tactic of getting someone to agree to some small request before asking them to agree to a larger request is known as the foot-in-the-door technique.
   a. true
   b. false

29. Social facilitation refers only to situations in which individual performance is improved by the physical presence of others.
   a. true
   b. false

30. Group polarization is the tendency of a group of like-minded individuals to take a more extreme position in the direction the group was leaning to begin with.
   a. true
   b. false

31. Suppression of dissenting views is an effective means of preventing groupthink.
   a. true
   b. false

32. What is social perception? Explain why first impressions are important.

33. Describe Sternberg's triangular theory of love.

34. What is an attitude? Under what circumstances is an attitude most likely to alter behavior?